FITZROY DEARBORN INTERNATIONAL DIRECTORY OF VENTURE CAPITAL FUNDS

1998–99

FITZROY DEARBORN INTERNATIONAL DIRECTORY OF VENTURE CAPITAL FUNDS

1998–99

Editors
JENNIFER SCHELLINGER
PATRICK HEENAN
MONIQUE LAMONTAGNE

FITZROY DEARBORN PUBLISHERS

CHICAGO • LONDON

For information, write to:

FITZROY DEARBORN PUBLISHERS
70 East Walton Street
Chicago, Illinois 60611
U.S.A.

or

FITZROY DEARBORN PUBLISHERS
11 Rathbone Place
London W1P 1DE
England

ISBN 1-884964-87-7

CONTENTS

HOW TO USE THE DIRECTORY

The 1998–99 Edition of the *Fitzroy Dearborn International Directory of Venture Capital Funds* is organized as earlier editions.

Readers looking for information will find funds within one of five sections; all entries are in alphabetical order within each of these sections:

Sections A–D include funds in the United States and Canada and are organized as: *Section A*—General Companies, companies that have interests in a variety of businesses; *Section B*—High Technology/Medical Funds; *Section C*—Minority and Socially-Useful Funds; *Section D*—Strategic Partners. **Section E** includes Venture Capital Funds outside the United States and Canada.

There are four indexes: an alphabetical listing of companies in the *Directory;* an index of all fund executives and their company affiliation; a geographic index, listing funds by country (and by state within the United States); and a category index, listing funds according to their investment preferences. Readers not looking for a specific fund, executive or location should first consult the Category Index, to establish which funds make investments in the area of their particular interest.

INTRODUCTION TO VENTURE CAPITAL

1. VCs, ANGELS, AND OTHER SMALL BUSINESS INVESTORS

> "Whatever you do early on in the life of your company should be oriented toward raising money for product development. . . . Money is the lifeblood of any company."
>
> —*Tom Weldon, entrepreneur*

The fight for money can be a desperate one, especially for a company struggling daily to stay in business. A company's early development often has more to do with establishing a product and creating a presence in the market than with turning a profit. Yet the inescapable fact is that fledgling businesses need cash, usually more than they can bring in as a result of their own operations. There is a pool of cash waiting to be tapped by these entrepreneurs: the venture capital market.

However simple the term *venture capital,* it fails to convey the kind and amount of cash waiting to be invested in young businesses. In a formal sense, venture capital refers to the venture capital funds, often called VCs, which try to reap high yields from fairly risky investments in small, growing, and potentially-lucrative business ventures. The deep pockets and business experience of fund managers can help guide entrepreneurs through their company's growing pains, the often turbulent and uncertain times during which expansion and its problems can evolve at breakneck speeds. In return for their capital and expertise, VCs expect a payoff for a job well done—a return on their investment commensurate to the risk assumed, and maybe more.

Yet although venture capital funds, such as Kleiner, Perkins, Caufield and Byers and Hambrecht and Quist, control large sums of venture capital, they make up only a part of the money pool, albeit a sizable one. Increasingly, individual investors—often called "angels" by those they choose to bless with funds—incubators, and small business investment companies are becoming important sources for entrepreneurs in need of financing.

A key question for any entrepreneur in need of financing is thus, "What is the best place for me to get money?" Savvy entrepreneurs make a comprehensive study of their options, because the simple answer—going to a venture capitalist—isn't always the best one. These entrepreneurs know that they have to establish a plan for obtaining capital, take their time, and sustain themselves long enough to pursue the best sources available to them. To secure financing, they must have a solid picture of both the venture capital market and their own business. Only then can they identify a suitable match and pursue it.

Starting with the private venture capital funds, this introduction examines sources of financing available to entrepreneurs in the United States and elsewhere: these sources include individuals, business incubators, small business investment companies, corporate venture capitalists, and commercial and investment banks. In one way, these sources are all the same: they have money to give. The differences have to do with the strings attached to that cash, strings that should give savvy entrepreneurs an indication of the investor's goals.

Following this review, the introduction examines the ways in which entrepreneurs ought to target and attract the money they need to sustain their businesses and make them grow. It also provides information on venture capital funds in Europe, Asia, and the Pacific Rim for entrepreneurs outside the United States with a similar goal: finding the financing they need to sustain and develop a new business venture.

THE VENTURE CAPITALISTS

A single title—VCs—belies the fact that venture capital companies can be quite diverse. Although some handle small sums of money, the average venture capital firm has funds ranging into the hundreds of millions of dollars. How they handle that money depends to a great extent on the firm's philosophy.

The generic venture capital firm is actually quite small given the amount of money it handles. On average, a firm may have eight to ten general partners who monitor investments and act, in effect, like money managers. Venture capital firms basically treat their business strategy like a cycle. They raise money to start a venture capital fund, invest the money, and "cash out" when the investment has matured.

The start of the cycle is much like fundraising. The venture capitalists solicit investments to start venture capital funds, then decide where this capital can best be invested. General partners normally invest in their own venture capital funds, but the most substantial amounts come from the limited partners—wealthy individuals, pension funds, corporations, endowments, banks—all of whom are looking for a better return on their money than they can earn with conventional investments. The funds created with their investments tend to last between seven and ten years, during which time the general partners take an active role in managing the fund's capital.

At a minimum, limited partners in the United States typically expect a 30 percent return on their investment. Rate of return is thus the venture capitalist's prime concern, and the way that venture capital companies have dealt with family businesses illustrates that point. They have tended to stay away from funding family businesses because, according to VC wisdom, such businesses rarely employ operating methods designed to achieve the highest rate of return. Bob Goldstein, a general partner with Berger, Goldstein and Company, has said, "If all the new generation needs is a capital infusion to fund a parent's retirement, I'd be very reluctant to bring a venture capitalist into the picture. If the next generation's need for capital includes plans for substantial growth, that's another story." In fact, American venture capital firms surpassed that 30 percent target in recent years, earning an average return of 47.4 and 42.1 percent in 1995 and 1996 respectively.

Despite this success, critics sometimes decry venture capitalists for (to paraphrase George Santayana) doubling their efforts while losing sight of their goal: to build businesses and industries. There's method in that myopia however: venture capital fund general partners collect not only on the profits they produce, but also on management fees of two to three percent of the fund's size. The result has been more megafunds—over $200 million—from which venture capitalists can collect a very healthy fee. And larger funds tend to steer money away from start-up businesses. The venture capitalist with a $100 million fund tries to invest at least $5 million at a time—more than many early stage companies need or warrant.

Venture capital firms tend to cluster around pockets of industries. For example, Silicon Valley in California has developed a booming venture capital infrastructure surrounding the area's high-tech industry. The result: most firms dole out investments to start-ups and growing small businesses in the immediate area. The American East Coast also has a concentration of venture capital firms, particularly in New York and Boston, that invest in companies in the same geographic area. That's only natural. Venture capital firms tend to pop up and invest wherever industries are either emerging or in place.

Recently, Seattle has become a hotbed of technology start-ups, as talented and aggressive Microsoft employees, often called "Baby Bills" after Microsoft chairman Bill Gates, cast out on their own. Sensing the opportunity, venture capitalists have followed. As one industry observer noted, "I've never seen venture capital funds sprout up faster than in Seattle in the past six months."

Despite Seattle's surge, California still reigns as the home of American venture capital. Of the geographic regions receiving the most venture capital in the second quarter of 1997, Silicon Valley led the United States with 32.5 percent of all dollars invested. New England, flush with industries spawned by research from such universities as Massachusetts Institute of Technology, accounted for the second biggest share with 10 percent. Does that leave the entrepreneur in southern Illinois or the innovator in Alaska out of luck? Not at all. Venture capitalists may typically invest close to home, but they will always make the exception for a good investment.

Venture capitalists also typically narrow their investments to specific fields. John Doerr, a general partner with Kleiner, Perkins, Caufield and Byers, refers to his firm's specialties as "bugs and drugs and bits and bytes," or biotechnology, pharmaceuticals, computer hardware, and software. Behind this philosophy lies very sound reasoning. Because venture capitalists spend so much time with entrepreneurs to ensure success, they must understand the businesses in which they're involved. Doerr, with a bachelor's and master's degree in engineering and sales experience with Intel, is expert in computer hardware and software—

Venture Capital Investments by Region, Second Quarter 1997

Source: Price Waterhouse.

Number of Companies Receiving Venture Capital, Second Quarter 1997

Region	Number of Companies
Silicon Valley	190
New England	91
Southeast	62
Midwest	48
New York Metro	45
Philadelphia Metro	36
LA/Orange County	34
Texas	33
DC/Metroplex	30
Northwest	29
San Diego	20

Source: Price Waterhouse.

also the focus of his investments. He leaves biotechnology and pharmaceutical to the other general partners.

In the second quarter of 1997 two industries claimed the bulk of venture capital investments: communications and software/information. This has been the trend since the early to mid-1990s, as Internet-driven businesses increasingly attract the attention of venture capitalists. These two

Venture Capital Investments by Industry, Second Quarter 1997

Industry	Investment Amount	% of Total
Biotechnology	150,121,000	4.7%
Business Services	125,828,000	4.0%
Communications	702,408,000	22.1%
Computers & Peripherals	195,121,000	6.1%
Consumer	173,285,000	5.4%
Distribution/Retailing	165,060,000	5.2%
Electronics & Instrumentation	63,213,000	2.0%
Environmental	23,848,000	0.7%
Healthcare	265,078,000	8.3%
Industrial	123,723,500	3.9%
Medical Instruments	165,186,000	5.2%
Miscellaneous	50,000	0.0%
Pharmaceuticals	97,327,000	3.1%
Semiconductors/Equipment	19,850,000	0.6%
Software & Information	910,618,000	28.6%
Total	$3,180,716,500	100.0%

Source: Price Waterhouse.

industry groups attracted roughly half of all invested venture capital during the second quarter of 1997. No other kind of business pulled in more than 10 percent, with the healthcare industry drawing 8.3 percent, computers and peripherals 6.1 percent, and biotechnology, consumer, medical instruments, and distribution/retailing around 5 percent.

American venture capital firms invested more than $10 billion in 1996, $2.3 billion in the first quarter of 1997, and $3.18 billion in the second quarter of 1997. Flush with money, they constantly look to the next investment. Yet the seeming bottomlessness of their coffers does not mean that there's plenty of money for everyone. The $10 billion that venture capital firms invested in 1996 is small compared to the $60 billion that emerging high-growth companies in the United States actually needed. Venture capitalists are extremely particular about their investments, and entrepreneurs ought to understand how they would fare with this kind of financier. Fortunately, entrepreneurs have other outlets to which they can turn.

Our discussion has dealt primarily with private venture capital firms. There are public venture capital firms as well. Their dealings are much the same as private firms except for one crucial point: being publicly-held companies, they must disclose most of their financial records. Also, unlike private venture capitalists, who typically manage funds that run a cycle from beginning to end, public firms maintain the fund as an ongoing concern. Public firms must also worry about upholding their stock price, a concern that private venture capitalists avoid.

EXPERT VIEWS

Brian Dovey, President, National Venture Capital Association

Brian H. Dovey is president of the National Venture Capital Association (NVCA) in Alexandria, Virginia, and general partner of Domain Associates, a Princeton, New Jersey venture capital firm. The NVCA represents almost 200 venture capital firms that account for almost 80 percent of all professional venture capital financing in the United States. It works actively to foster a broader understanding of the importance of venture capital to the American economy and to stimulate the flow of equity capital to emerging growth and developing companies. As an active participant in the venture capital industry and president of the industry's leading professional organization, Mr. Dovey offers a unique perspective on recent developments in venture capital.

The past couple of years have been an especially strong period for the VC industry, leading to some concern that this growth might shrink evaluation time. Is the current period different from past boom-and-bust cycles in the industry?

There certainly has been an increase in venture capital funding in recent years. But the current uptrend is different from those the industry has seen in the past. First, there's more desire on the part of venture capital firms to invest in established firms, as opposed to raw start-ups. So while the total dollar amount of venture capital financing has been higher, there has not been an exuberance to fund new firms. Instead, the investment is going into more established companies. That lowers risk.

Another important characteristic of the recent trend has been the information technology explosion, which has fueled the strong growth in venture capital funding. The Internet has affected the way so many companies do business. These changes have created opportunities that weren't nearly as numerous in the past, even during strong periods of VC funding. So while venture capital funding has grown dramatically, I don't think the evaluation process has been harmed by the strong growth this time around. You'll still see some bad investments, but not because evaluations have been shortchanged.

Venture capital firms have become increasingly specialized. Is this trend likely to continue?

Definitely. I think the idea of one person handling information technology, retail, and healthcare, for example, is going away. There are firms that concentrate on one industry, which is one type of specialization. But even firms that handle multiple industries are likely to have specialization within the firm. It's rare that you see the same partners in information technology and healthcare, for example. Instead, those partners will likely head up completely different groups. That specialization has become increasingly necessary. You have to know the industry—its competitive aspects, the drivers of success.

Is in-depth industry knowledge more important in the process of evaluating deals, or in providing management advice after the financing?

Both. In evaluations it's important to be familiar with other VC deals that might have been concluded in the industry. Then a venture capitalist must ask if a product is going to work, if it's a proprietary product, if the market is likely to choose the product over a competing product, and so on. Without proper industry knowledge, these questions can't be addressed adequately and evaluating whether to fund a venture becomes difficult.

Subsequent to the deal, the entrepreneur—who has some ability to select venture capital firms—is going to want a value-added investor, someone with connections to a Microsoft or the right drug company to help the start-up company fulfill its mission. The entrepreneur wants more than just the investment skill set. So whereas VCs need to develop the expertise to select the right companies to fund, the entrepreneur wants to select a VC that has specific expertise in the appropriate area.

Do emerging growth companies have more hurdles in obtaining funding when their concept or product is dramatically different from what's on the market?

It's important for the entrepreneur to seek VC firms that are knowledgeable in his or her industry, because a lack of understanding of the technology or industry does reduce the chance of investment. If you come in with a new concept in an unrelated industry, it's going to be an uphill fight. That doesn't mean there's no chance of getting funding for a revolutionary technology or concept, but the likelihood increases if it's in an industry the VC is familiar with and, ideally, has been through the process with a similar start-up. That's important to the start-up and to the VC.

How difficult is it for an entrepreneur who has an undeveloped idea to obtain VC financing?

VCs are accustomed to early-stage, partially-shaped ideas. We take a high risk and look for a high reward. We help the entrepreneur shape that idea and develop it, even partial ideas with problems to work out. The strength of the idea is the important thing. We also see our job as helping a company learn. If there's an entrepreneur who has a new idea for providing a service, and we are familiar with analogous companies that may have received funding, then our experience as VCs can help that entrepreneur. In the process, we lower our risk. It works well for both sides.

How important is the IPO market to your firm? Is it more important for later stage financing, or are you always watching it, regardless of the financing stage?

Our business is dependent to some extent on there being a good IPO market. It doesn't have to be crazy, however, and it's not something I worry about every day or month. But if the market was to shut down for three or four years, that would be a problem. At Domain, we're probably in a seven- or eight-year cycle from when we start a company to when we distribute it. And we don't distribute it as soon as the IPO is out. We hold on for another two or three years. The IPO is frequently more of a financing event than a liquidating event. It's a way for the company to finance itself over a specified time. But that doesn't mean it's a healthy, robust, liquid stock that we are ready to sell. There's usually a lot more work to be done with the company.

Does the trend of the broad stock market have some effect on the amount of funds available for venture capital investing?

VC investing has more to do with raising money from limited partners than with the stock market. As major pension plans, university endowments, and other investors put more money into venture capital, their investment rates are determined more by the returns they've got from venture capital investments in the past than by overall stock market trends. By and large, VC investors make asset allocation decisions and stick with them, independent of stock market returns.

You said that the information technology industry has played a big part in fueling the growth in venture capital in recent years. What other industries do you see showing growth in new venture formation in the coming years?

The more you see significant structural changes in an industry, the more opportunity there is, particularly for venture firms. It's the key driver in spotting future growth areas in venture capital. Start-up firms are often on the forefront when an industry is undergoing significant changes. When an industry is stable, larger firms may have a competitive advantage, but start-ups can often exploit major industry changes better than larger, more entrenched companies. One area where I see those changes occurring today is in the healthcare industry. I think the whole healthcare industry is likely to show growth in new idea formation. I would also expect growth in biotechnology in coming years and continued growth in segments of the information technology area.

THE REST OF THE MONEY POOL

Friends and Family

Sometimes the easiest choice is best one. Friends and family are often a valuable resource. They may not have millions like a venture capitalist, but millions are not always needed; in fact, the seed money needed to start a business is usually much less than that needed in later stages. In 1996, the average seed amount raised for business start-ups in the United States was $25,000.

Money is an expensive commodity. Yet friends and family are an informal source; their main concern is typically in getting the business off the ground, not in making a substantial return on their investment. And whereas a venture capitalist will seek ownership and may take a leading role in the business, close relations making a smaller investment tend to be less proprietary.

Angels

Angels—well-heeled individuals who invest their own capital in start-up and growing small businesses—are quickly becoming a major venture capital force. They take their name from the fact that they are quite often an entrepreneur's savior, at least to a certain extent.

Venture capital firms, for the reasons we've mentioned, have steadily moved away from financing early stage businesses. Angels have stepped in to fill that void, providing seed and early stage capital for many young businesses. In a sense, angels have taken a role much like that assumed by venture capital firms of the 1980s—willing to handle a bit more risk and ready to help steer the ship. The underlying motive behind their investments is still profit, but angels also have a desire to build strong businesses. Many angels actually accumulated their wealth as a result of their own successful start-ups or other start-ups in which they have previously invested, and they hope to pass on their knowledge and expertise to new entrepreneurs.

In effect, angels are a cross between the family investor and venture capital firms. They are more willing to take the risk during a company's early phase, yet they also bring to their investments a business acumen that friends and family might not possess.

The successful start-ups of the 1980s have spawned numerous angels ready to jump back into the action. A survey from the Center for Venture Research found that in 1996 250,000 angels invested in new businesses in the United States. As a group, angels, typically investing in chunks of $300,000 to $500,000, accounted for more than $10 billion in small business investment—matching the combined investment of American venture capital firms.

The growing number of angels has even led to the formation of angel networks. Some angels have started associations, similar to investment clubs, where prospectuses on new businesses are circulated to see if there is any interest among the angels involved. Given technology's rapid advancement, and the role it played in the creation of so many angels, it makes sense that angels are now also using the Internet as a

Angel Investors vs. Venture Capital Funds, 1996

Angel Investors, 1996

Number of angel investors	250,000
Number of investments annually	30,000–40,000
Annual investment	$10 billion–$20 billion
Average equity share	20% (ranges from 10%–40%)
Average investment size	$300,000–$500,000
Largest investment	$1 million
Length of investment	5–10 years
Average return on investment	25%–40%
Percentage of funds invested in start-ups	90%–100%
Hottest target industry	technology (internet technology, new technology, technology applications)

Venture Capital Funds, 1996

Number of venture funds	300–400
Number of investments annually	1,000
Annual investment	more than $10 billion
Average equity share in start-ups	41%
Average investment size	$3 million–$7 million
Length of investment	3–7 years (5 is most typical)
Largest investment	$110 million
Average return on investment	28%–40%
Percentage of funds invested in start-ups	10%
Hottest target industries	communications, healthcare

Sources: Center for Venture Research; National Venture Capital Association; VentureOne Corporation.

means to find new investments. The Internet has allowed angels to spread their wings: certain sites are devoted to listing start-ups in need of an angel's investment.

Small Business Investment Companies

Small business investment companies (SBICs) are privately owned and managed funds licensed by the United States Small Business Association (SBA). Federal support allows SBICs to secure government loans, enabling them to leverage each dollar raised privately into four dollars. The government's hope is that these institutions will make a concerted effort to aid the small businesses who need it most.

An interesting characteristic of SBICs is their investing strategy. Most venture capital firms finance companies in exchange for a share of equity. SBICs can take this standard path, but they must be concerned about servicing their own debt. An equity investment may not involve returns for anywhere from three to ten years, depending on the financing, and tying up capital that long may not be possible for an SBIC. Instead, SBICs commonly make loans to small businesses with an option to buy stock. Collecting interest on outstanding loans allows SBICs to service their own debt.

SBICs are also restricted by SBA guidelines. For instance, SBICs cannot invest in companies with a base net worth of over $ million. The venture must also have a net after tax profit, for the two prior years, of $2 million or less. Entrepreneurs should check with the SBA for the latest guidelines.

Corporate Venture Capital Funds

Major corporations have also reaped some venture capital investment benefits. Past the point of needing venture capital themselves, some established companies have actually established their own funds; they are much like private venture capital firms. Yet though corporations run their venture capital funds like the private funds, they pursue different objectives.

The most common goal is to keep abreast of technology. The maturation process often removes a company from the cutting-edge technology that created its success in the first place. By establishing venture capital funds, and making investments in new companies that are pursuing goals similar to its own, a company can retain that edge and keep up on new developments.

Indeed, a corporation's motives are typically strategic—driven by the need to learn about new technologies and gain increased expertise. Many corporations view their venture capital fund as an extension of their research and development. If the venture goes well, the young business becomes an acquisition target that can be merged with the company.

Entrepreneurs get more than money in this kind of deal. They frequently benefit from the parent's marketing and manufacturing expertise, as well as help in running a business. They can thus dedicate their attention to the company without concerns about establishing an outlet for the product or an advertising strategy. The parent company may also provide some more mundane, but necessary, resources such as office space, phones, and secretarial support—all of which can do a great deal toward reducing the start-up's overhead.

But this relationship can be far from ideal. A change in management might also change the parent company's direction, leaving the fledgling company floating midstream. Or a vision unshared by management and the entrepreneur could mean less entrepreneurial control over the venture. And then there's culture clash—the entrepreneurial process in the corporate setting. The new business's creative, explosive environment may, at times, be at odds with a buttoned-down corporate culture.

Incubators

Sometimes a business just needs a chance to start moving in the right direction. Incubators can provide the atmosphere to nurture the entrepreneurial spirit. Both private incubators and those sponsored by universities can help supply entrepreneurs with the business basics, and then some. Incubators, however, are far from a pipe-dream factory. Like any other venture capitalist, incubators screen applicants before allowing them in. Entrepreneurs still need a sound business plan, a marketable idea, and the potential for growth.

There are more that 550 incubators operated by universities and local economic development agencies. From office space to furniture to secretarial support, incubators attempt to give entrepreneurs the tools they need to take their venture to a new level—a self-sufficient one. Aside from business needs, the incubators, a home to many entrepreneurs at once, breed a creative and innovative environment.

For example, Jay Price and Andy MacKay launched AMX International, a software installation and training company that they built into an $8 million company, with the help of the Idaho Innovation Center. Price says that being part of an incubator cut down overhead costs and allowed the pair to concentrate on sales without worrying about cash flow. For $250 a month they got the support and office space that allowed them to move forward at their own pace.

Incubators can also provide the means for helping the entrepreneur attract additional financing once a company outgrows the incubator. Because being admitted to an incubator in the first place indicates a company's potential, other investors hoping to invest in promising businesses are also attracted to the company. Dinah Adkins, executive director of the National Business Incubation Association, says: "The fact that a business has been accepted into an incubator offers due diligence value to potential investors."

Bill Gross has taken the incubator idea to a new level, developing a private incubator called idealab! As the name suggests, idealab! is essentially an idea factory, where Gross's most creative thoughts, along with the ideas of others who work there, are given the chance to grow and thrive. A hatched idea brings together a development team that starts the development cycle. First, market research is done and a prototype is created. A CEO is then put in place, and a staff is hired as needed. All along, the prototype is refined and prepared to enter the marketplace as the market research effort continues. The hope is that, from there, the business will "go live" and continue to grow.

Since Gross opened his doors, idealab! has turned out 19 Internet-related start-ups, most of them based in Pasadena, California. Some of his ideas include:

- Answers.com—a Web site that, for a fee, will answer any question (e.g., what is the Ivory Coast's most abundant natural resource?) within 24 hours
- CitySearch—a site that provides Internet guides to local communities
- Entertainnet—a news broadcaster via your screen saver, with current topics focusing on the entertainment industry
- Smart Games—a library of nonviolent, intellectually challenging games

Gross has gone so far as to lure venture capital, not to fund his newly hatched ideas, but idealab! itself.

THE REST OF THE REST

There are many other venture capital sources available to entrepreneurs. SBICs and friends and family excluded, most of the venture capital investors discussed here deal primarily in equity financing—investing their money for an ownership stake in the venture. But certain outlets do provide new businesses with loans. Start-up commercial banks, which are on a similar path with other entrepreneurs, increasingly make loans to small business concerns.

Entrepreneurs can also find venture capital from investment banks. Although they usually deal with the initial public offering when a company decides to sell its stock publicly, investment banks will sometimes give businesses a needed cash infusion. And though profit motivates them just as it does other investors, investment bankers see venture capital as a means of building their clientele. A successful venture capital investment produces a company that may need the investment bank's services later down the line.

Some entrepreneurs, especially those in search of seed capital, tap informal sources such as credit cards and savings accounts, equity loans or mortgages. Such loans can often prove less costly than other forms of venture capital. They don't involve a share of ownership; the only price to be paid is interest.

THE START-UP CYCLE

To effectively solicit any sort of venture capital, entrepreneurs must understand their options. Entrepreneurs must decide what kind of money they want and how much they need. Some companies in the earliest development stages probably shouldn't consider certain financing sources, like venture capital funds, because this capital is so costly. As Alan Walton of Oxford Bioscience Partners notes, "Venture capital is expensive, so if entrepreneurs can find capital elsewhere, they are better off." If an entrepreneur decides what kind of funding he or she needs, he will know how to proceed.

But entrepreneurs must also know their own business—and not just its product or service. Many entrepreneurs focus on an idea's creation and implementation and let business details take care of themselves. But when looking for venture capital, the entrepreneur must make business details a prime concern. One crucial detail is in knowing just how mature a company really is.

The start-up phase should be considered a sequence of events. Companies generally navigate a path that starts with the seed capital stage and ends with an initial public offering. If the entrepreneur can pinpoint his company's progress in this sequence, he can help narrow the venture capital search even more, since certain investors stay away from, or gravitate toward, companies in certain stages of development. There's this caveat too: financing may be needed at each stage and going to, say, a venture capitalist for each stage quickly dilutes ownership.

EXPERT VIEWS

Paul Reynolds, Professor in Entrepreneurial Studies, Babson College

Dr. Paul Reynolds is the Paul T. Babson Professor in Entrepreneurial Studies at Babson College in Wellesley, Massachusetts. He received the Coleman Foundation Award for the best general topic paper at the 1994 Babson College Kauffman Entrepreneurship Research Conference. Dr. Reynolds is coordinator of the Entrepreneurial Research Consortium (ERC), a collection of 30 universities and research units around the world that are sponsoring studies of business start-ups and the entrepreneurial process. Here he shares his views on the entrepreneurial environment in the United States.

There seems to be some degree of variation in new venture formation among different regions in the United States. What are the key drivers of this?

The major factor that sparks business start-ups is growth in opportunity. If you have an area of strong population growth, there's going to be more opportunity, and you will see new businesses being created. That's why you see higher rates of company births in urban areas than in rural areas. Areas that have stable economies have lower rates of new company formation relative to areas where the economic structure is changing.

Most people start businesses between the age of 25 and 40. That's the age range where people have accumulated some level of experience, have access to resources, and have the energy to make it work. So you won't see a lot of start-ups in communities with a relative dearth of people in that age group.

How important, then, are inputs, such as access to capital and a qualified workforce, to new venture formation?

The first concerns are having a service or product that meets consumers' needs and knowing what the competition is doing. The evidence that's been collected suggests that input factors are clearly secondary, within some limits. The variation of financing available across urban areas in the United States, for example, is pretty trivial, as is the variation in tax rates. Now there are certainly situations where being able to locate competent employees or managerial talent are concerns, but those factors are secondary to knowing the market and being comfortable that you can sell something.

Too many people make the mistake of thinking that product and service markets are stable, in which case the only way to enter the market as a new firm is to undercut people on the basis of price. But if you understand that there is a constant churning and shifting in services and products, then creating new products and services and new ways of delivering them are paramount, and the inputs are secondary.

Once a firm has reached a more mature stage, those secondary factors would seem to carry more importance. What are some of the secondary factors that make certain regions hotbeds for growing companies?

Successful regions will typically have an infrastructure developed for a particular industry sector. There are geographical clusters of industries where you will find a network of people who have the training--suppliers, people with the skills to reach customers, and people who are financial specialists. It's not just software and multimedia, which receive so much attention. These clusters develop with certain types of manufacturing as well. There are different pockets of expertise all over the country. When there are a large number of small firms in a particular region, you see higher birth rates of businesses, because you'll have churning--people splitting off to develop their own firms. That encourages the development of regional hotbeds in a particular industry.

For example, there's a place on the Mississippi River on the Wisconsin-Minnesota border where about six or seven firms have been created that specialize in the composite fiber industry. The first of these firms was started by an individual who became an expert. At some point, one of his executives started a firm across the street. That pattern continued until there were the number of firms there are today. Now the local community college offers courses to train people in just this kind of manufacturing technology. All of the salespeople in that industry, as well as people who need the composites for their own processes, know about this area. You do not typically hear about places like this, but there are examples all over the country.

This whole trend is facilitated by the increased reliability, greater speed, and reduced costs of both communication and transportation. The big trend in the economy is that there are more small, highly-specialized, high-quality, low-cost businesses all over the country. And the whole system is more interdependent.

When a region becomes a hotbed for a particular industry, does it take a long time for an exchange of ideas to develop?

It's difficult to develop trust among people in the same industry. There have been efforts by consultants to promote networks in certain small manufacturing industries, for example. These consultants are trying to bring companies together to coordinate activity so they can collectively develop regional expertise. The problem is setting up a mechanism to get these people to trust each other. If I'm a small manufacturer, for example, why should I talk about a new technique I developed that might have allowed me to cut costs 5 percent? If I share those ideas, I might find that the other companies I was sharing them with are soon following the same strategy, and I'll lose customers. So institutionalizing the trust relationship is difficult to do. It's a social process that takes a long time to develop. The only place these trusting relationships exist with some regularity is in Europe, and that's because there are communities there that have had expertise in a particular area for centuries.

Do you see a tough transition for companies growing from small, internally-financed shops to the next stage, at which point they may have to go to a bank or an angel for money?

Most companies that are going to grow have prepared for that growth from the beginning. They will have assembled a team early on with different specializations. The most interesting thing about growth companies is the greater number of problems they must deal with relative to stable companies. There are simply many more complications, such as financing, providing sufficient space, finding employees, training, and keeping focus. But most people on a high-growth path expect these problems and are prepared for them.

This is where the incubator setting can have an impact. In a very unusual industry, a new firm's management team might have to travel across the country to find someone who knows the industry. But if that company is in a region that is an industry hotbed, it's much easier to find the people with different areas of expertise locally.

How important a role does venture capital play for firms entering the high-growth stage?

Many very high-growth firms don't have venture capital. There's a certain control tradeoff when a company obtains venture capital, and many companies started by individuals who have strong reputations in their industry can raise money within the industry. They don't have to go to a VC. Some start-up companies are unwilling to wait for a VC to do the due diligence and come up to speed on a new technology or new market. The venture capital industry has become more specialized to alleviate some of that problem. But the other trend is that most VC firms don't fund as many new firms. Instead, they work with businesses that have been in place for several years. That's where other sources of capital enter the picture. Some businesses can grow pretty well using internal earnings. It depends on how fast these companies grow.

It seems as though the angel network has become more organized. Have you seen that?

There is a big issue as to just what is going on with the angel network. If you look at the total amount of money invested in start-ups on an annual basis, and subtract from that the amount supplied by venture capital, SBA loans, and bank loans, you're left with a substantial amount of investment coming from other sources. Most people are assuming that may be coming from a network of wealthy individuals placing private funds in their region. But in a national study we're conducting at the ERC, we've discovered that there are a number of small, personal placements from family, friends, and neighbors. The amounts are small on an individual level, maybe between $5,000 and $10,000 on average. But our preliminary estimates are that 1 to 2 percent of households in the United States may participate in this type of funding. That becomes a pretty impressive amount. Still, it's hard to find the high-net-worth individuals. This is one of the real mysteries of how businesses get started. Where does the money comes from? The answer to that question, when all of the data is in, might surprise some people.

Is there any conclusive data about the success of government-sponsored incubators?

I'm not against the idea of incubators, but there is no evidence yet that shows companies do better in that setting. And the overall number of start-up companies in these incubators is relatively small relative to the total number of start-ups. There are other programs that might have a greater impact, however, including loan packages and marketing programs. Many of these programs are handled outside the government sector, but they're all designed to help start-ups. The problems are that they have had difficulty finding the people who are starting businesses and that the start-ups frequently don't know about these programs. More systematic promotion of these programs would help.

The government doesn't have good enough information on new firm formation to make decisions. Consequently, there is little understanding of how pervasive entrepreneurship is in the United States today. It plays a much more important role in our economy than most people realize.

Seed Stage

A new company's seed stage may involve nothing more than an idea ripe for development. The capital sought at this stage essentially will be used to determine the idea's viability: can it be realized? is there a market? will it have any competition? A small capital investment, from $15,000 to $200,000, is typically enough for this kind of implementation.

Private venture capital firms, and other large concerns, generally do not seed new businesses for several reasons. So early an investment is considered extremely risky. The venture hasn't even started to move forward yet, and any investment could be lost quickly. Seed money provides the greatest return on investment, but the new company may need ten years or more to generate that return. Finally, the money needed to seed a new business is often too small to interest private venture capital firms. They manage funds that can be at least $100 million in size, and they often prefer to make investments in $5 million increments—$25,000 is just too small. Venture capital firms would argue that it takes as much of their time and manpower to manage a $25,000 investment as a $5 million investment.

Thank heaven for angels, who often step in to finance smaller concerns. Angels are much more likely than venture fund managers to finance seed-stage businesses more readily and to nurture them through the entire start-up process. This is also a period in which friends and family may be the best option of all.

Start-Up Capital

After one year, when the business has formulated some kind of business plan and put together some kind of management team, the need for start-up financing might arise. Where seed capital gets the business moving,

Seed Capital, 1996

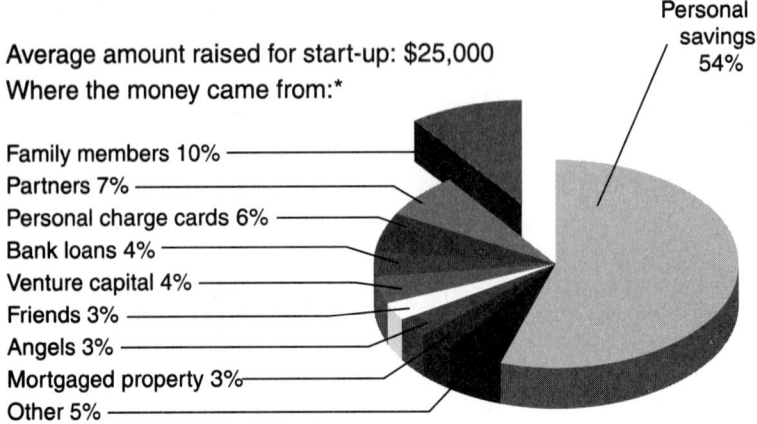

Average amount raised for start-up: $25,000
Where the money came from:*

Family members 10%
Partners 7%
Personal charge cards 6%
Bank loans 4%
Venture capital 4%
Friends 3%
Angels 3%
Mortgaged property 3%
Other 5%

Personal savings 54%

*Numbers do not add up to 100 because of rounding.

Source: Inc. 500 Almanac.

start-up capital is used to refine certain business aspects, like the product offering or marketing strategy. Again, this may not be the point to bring in venture capitalists, primarily because of the comparatively small amount of funding the enterprise is likely to need. An angel or loan from a bank are probably the best possibilities.

First and Second Stage Development

It's time for the product to come to market, or to start the full-force sales process. That's when first and second stage financing usually becomes necessary. By this phase the company's product or service should have gained sufficient acceptance that expansion seems promising. The problem is that expansion takes money, and venture capital, more specifically first and second stage financing, helps. An inflow of money helps develop the manufacturing and sales capabilities to allow the company to get a product or service to a larger marketplace. This might also be the time at which the company begins to acquire property, be it a plant or office space or equipment.

Mezzanine Financing

You can see the wheels moving. The business could now expand quite quickly, yet its success does not automatically translate into positive cash flow. Newly-started companies face this "cash burn" problem: fully matured expenses cannot be matched by sales levels still in their infancy.

Investment during this stage is called mezzanine, or expansion, financing, one of the more popular investments for private venture capital firms. Also called bridge financing, these investments are deemed less risky because at this point the business has developed roots; its established presence has made it a fairly safe investment. The amount of money invested may be more than that in earlier stages, but the firm is

Venture Capital Investments, Start-up vs. Later Stage

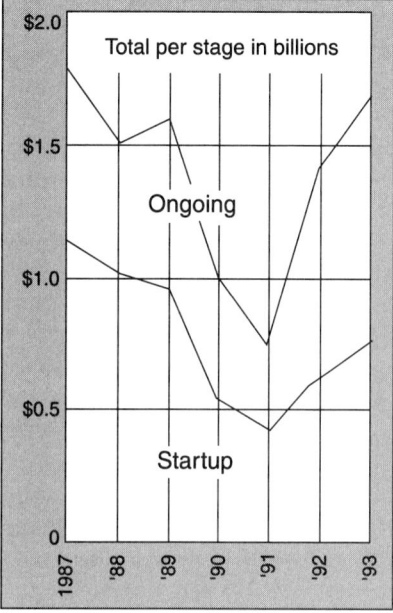

Source: Fortune.

closer to going public, and venture capital firms can reclaim their investment more quickly.

The IPO

A business comes of age when it is ready for its initial public offering (IPO). The IPO is seen as the finish line for most investors because their equity can now be sold to the public—they have a chance to cash out. From seed to IPO, ownership is little more than a figurative stake in a privately-held company. That is, it is a rather illiquid holding. The public stock sale, however, opens the door for getting back the investment and realizing a return on that investment.

Recent stock market trends would lead casual observers to imagine that once a company gets to the IPO stage, all is golden. But that's not necessarily true. IPOs that fail to make a splash rarely make news, even though they're quite common. Some companies rush to the initial public offering, often at investors' urgings, only to discover that they're not ready. Although the IPO is considered the finish line, the race shouldn't be one in which speed supplants preparedness.

The more companies that go public prematurely, the harder it will be for other start-ups to raise money. Venture capitalists watch the IPO market carefully and use it to determine the market's feeling toward new companies. Thus, the initial public offering has an impact on more than just the one company whose stock is up for sale. Any firm's "coming out" can have implications for start-ups in search of venture capital.

The IPO Market, 1984-95

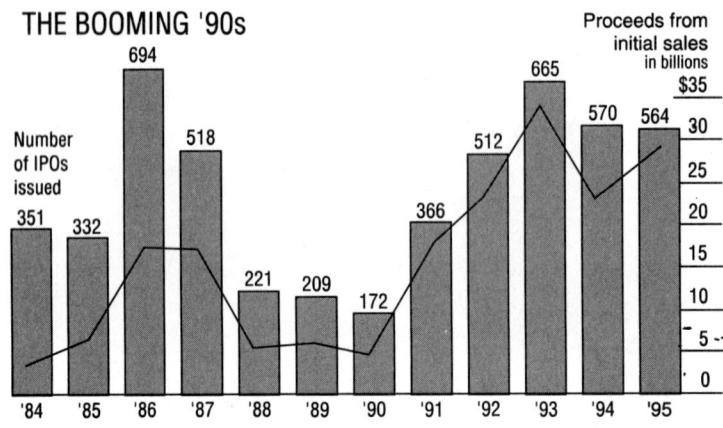

Source: Securities Data.

2. TARGETING—AND GETTING—THE MONEY

"We see 2000 business plans, of which we might visit 300, seriously consider and conduct due diligence on 50, and invest in 8 to 12."

—*John Martinson, managing partner, Edison Venture Fund*

"A venture capitalist's most important commodity is time. A partner in a big fund who serves on 10 company boards is not going to have the time. . . . If Steve Jobs walked into a megafund today, he would have no chance of getting financed."

—*Jack C. Carsten, former Intel senior vice president, current angel*

Such attitudes suggest a grim picture for entrepreneurs, but there is money out there. Entrepreneurs can choose between a multitude of ways to get financing, but some prove better than others for a given situation. At the outset, each entrepreneur must decide whether to be a sharpshooter or a buckshot artist. The sharpshooter narrows the field considerably, aiming for the sources that will provide for the best means for acquiring capital. Shooting buckshot requires less time—since you simply send out business plans to as many sources as possible—but your solicitations may fall on deaf ears. You might not even get the 2 percent reply you hope for. After all, raising venture capital is not a direct mail campaign. For the new entrepreneur, then, perhaps best plan is to learn about the venture capital market through directed research, not blind solicitations.

Taking Aim

Getting started, especially from a position of limited knowledge, can be the most difficult obstacle to overcome. Yet you can find a sketch of the venture capital marketplace through surveys done by several different market observers. Price Waterhouse (*www.pw.com/vc*), Coopers and Lybrand (*www.us.coopers.com/industry/vcwww01.html*), and the National Venture Capital Association (*www.nvca.org*) all release quarterly and yearly statistics pertaining to venture capital investments. These surveys provide entrepreneurs with a wealth of information, breaking down investments by geographic region, industry, venture capital company, and investment size. Directories such as this one can help as well, giving you some idea of who should be on your list of possible sources and who should be discarded.

Once you have identified firms where there might be a mutual interest—you're interested in their money and they're interested in your business—it's possible to dig a little further. Most venture capital firms put out some sort of fact sheet about their company, much like the entries in this international directory. The data may be a little generic, like average investment and types of industry in which the firm invests. But they should also include some information on the partners and their areas of concentration. This information will provide a contact name should you find a firm you want to pursue.

19

EXPERT VIEWS

Kirk D. Walden, National Director, Price Waterhouse U.S. Venture Capital Survey

Kirk D. Walden is national director of the Price Waterhouse U.S. Venture Capital Survey, conducted under the sponsorship of the Global Technology Industry Group. Each quarter, Price Waterhouse collects detailed information from U.S.-based venture capital firms on investments made in all companies in all industries nationwide. Since its launch in 1994, the survey has become a staple for venture capitalists, the financial community, policy makers, entrepreneurs, and the media in the United States and around the world.

Which industries are attracting venture capital in the U.S. today, and which are likely to do so in coming years?

From a broad perspective, technology businesses are the major recipients of venture capital today. And that has been the case historically. Some notable success stories in the technology area, Lotus and Compaq, for example, were started with venture capital. Over the past two or three years, the amount of venture capital going to technology companies relative to others has been more significant than ever. To give some perspective, U.S. venture capital investment was $9.5 billion in 1996, up from $7.5 billion in 1995. Out of that $2 billion increase, $1.8 billion went into technology companies. That trend has continued into 1997.

Part of the reason for this is that technology companies lend themselves to venture funding very well. They require a relatively small amount of money to get to a proof-of-concept stage, and then there are very clear milestones along the way that track the progress of the company or product. Other industries can require much more up-front investment. Retailers, for example, require investment for bricks and mortar and leases— big commitments—before anything happens. This helps to explain why software is the strongest segment. Money also goes into biotechnology, semiconductors, and computers and peripherals, but the strongest area is software. The category that receives a significant portion of venture capital investment is the communications sector, which tends to move in tandem with software. These two segments made up almost half of all venture capital investments in the first half of 1997.

How much of the growth in the technology sector can be attributed to Internet-related technology?

Internet companies are frequently grouped in either the software or communications categories, though some businesses fall outside. Taken as a separate category, however, the Internet certainly has grown and continues to grow. Price Waterhouse's quarterly venture capital surveys, for example, show increases in venture capital for Internet-related companies in every quarter since the first quarter of 1995. And that doesn't show signs of abating.

There are signs that start-up Internet companies may not be in as good a position to receive venture capital as those in the next stage of development. So while the number of Internet-related companies receiving funding continues to rise, the number of start-ups as a percentage of the total is decreasing. Still, the dollar amount of venture capital investment going to Internet-related companies should continue to grow.

Does the same pattern hold for venture capital overall—that VC firms are less likely to fund companies in the start-up stage than they are companies in later stages of development?

There has been a gap in funding start-ups, but that has for the most part been filled by angel investors. A company that needs $500,000 to $1 million may find that it's easier to receive funding from an angel investor than from a VC. If you think of the different sources of investment, it begins with internal financing, which might include credit cards or second mortgages; then friends and families; then angels; and then venture capital. I think angels will continue to take a more important role in the very early seed stages, especially in the technology segment, which requires less investment than manufacturing companies do.

There are two dynamics at work with the pattern of VCs funding more developed companies. The first is that VCs are not passive investors. They take an active role in the company. It goes beyond giving a company money and setting milestones. It has reached the point where a company will talk to several VC firms and select which one they want based on what expertise the VC firm has and how the firm can help with things like recruiting, supplier relationships, and maybe even customers. Given these expectations and the commitment required, the investment has to be large enough to be worthwhile for the venture capitalist. Span of control also becomes an issue as the number of investments a firm makes grows. If a VC firm funds too many companies, it will face the risk that it isn't contributing as much as it would like to. If this pattern continues, then investments eventually cease to be traditional venture capital and instead become purely financial investments.

Another factor to consider is that very often companies that need those smaller amounts of money prefer to look to other sources. Much of it depends on what type of company is receiving funding. Do they want to grow into a $100 million company in four or five years? If so, they will likely require funding that is significant enough to spark the interest of VC firms. If, on the other hand, a company is not seeking rapid growth and only requires a relatively small amount of money to get started, they will probably look to other sources for funding.

Are there significant differences as to which U.S. regions are receiving venture capital investment relative to a few years ago?

There is one significant difference that should be encouraging for firms seeking funding. About five years ago, a significant portion of venture capital money went into two regions: Silicon Valley and New England, partly because that is where the VCs were located. That's not as important any more, however. Silicon Valley is still at the top of the list in terms of companies being funded, and New England is still strong, just as it was five or six years ago. But beyond that, venture capital investment is pretty widely distributed. In a recent quarter, 11 regions of the United States each received more than $100 million invested in 20 or more companies. Each of these regions has its own set of specialization. Communications companies, for example, have received the lion's share of venture capital investment in Texas in recent quarters. Biotechnology companies, on the other hand, have received a notable portion of the investment in the San Diego area. The central message in this is that geocentricity is not as important as it once was. Good ideas can find funding, regardless of location. Of course, it still is easier for a VC to be able to walk across the street to visit the company it's funded, but it's not as critical as it might have been before.

What effect has specialization had on the venture capital industry?

So much of the growth this time around is coming from the technology sector, which itself has become more specialized. As the technology industry has become more specialized, so has the venture capital industry to some extent. As a VC partner, you have to know what you are looking at well enough to determine the efficacy of an investment. The industry, the market, the competition, the technology itself—all affect the valuation. That specialization helps to create some checks and balances because partners who know an industry well can see through companies that might not be ready or add value very quickly to companies that are.

What are the major differences between the current growth phase in the U.S. venture capital industry and those of the past?

Two factors argue that the high level of venture capital investment is not likely to slow down or bust anytime soon. The first is the growing importance of technology in everyday life. The convergence of technology and communications affects so many industries in so many different ways and not just in the United States, but in the rest of the world too. And that brings us to the second factor. U.S. companies are the acknowledged leaders in technology, which gives them incredible access to the global market. An idea that might be an average success in another category has the potential to be a worldwide success in the technology category. So the venture capital industry is less threatened today by a slowdown in the economy, or in the IPO market, than it might have been years ago.

The fact sheet might also include other important contacts, such as the fund's auditors and attorneys or even a list of companies in which it has invested. Use these contacts to the fullest; find out as much about them as you can. Your research can only enhance your chances to finance your business. If possible, arrange to meet as many of the contacts as you can: these meetings can be more than informational; they can lead to introductions. Think of this effort as also building your own network of contacts that can help you in your pursuit.

Meeting with the people involved in a venture capital firm's present or past investments not only gives you insight into the venture capital firm, but it may make you an ally of some entrepreneurs as well. Their businesses have traveled the same road you wish to travel, and they may be repositories for venture capital information that will provide you with invaluable guidance in your own search. And if things progress for your new business and you truly have a good relationship with the other entrepreneurs, they can make the introduction to venture capitalists—a much better method than "cold-calling" your way into a VC's office.

John Doerr, general partner of Kleiner, Perkins, Caufield and Byers, confirms the value of this strategy. A normal year might bring 3,000 business plans to his office; his company invests in 20 to 25 of them. Yet Doerr cannot recall a single investment in an *unsolicited* business plan. Obviously, those entrepreneurs in whom Doerr's company invests are those who came with an introduction. Relationships are very valuable in the world of venture capital.

After your research, you should be able to identify some venture capital firms who might be interested in your start-up venture. The two most important things to consider are *niche* and *stage*.

Say you have designed the prototype for a fast-running computer chip, but you have no means of production, and a capital infusion is the best way to get the process in gear. You make a list of likely venture capital firms. It consists of five names, one of which specializes in biotechnology, three in computers, and one in retail. You have some connection at each firm. Not that you write off the venture capital firms interested in retail and biotechnology, but you drop them to the bottom of the list (venture capitalists will sometimes cross industry or geographic boundaries if the idea and potential for profit are great—but specialization helps them and you).

Then comes the issue of financing stage. With nothing more than a prototype design, you are in need of some seed capital—an investment that many venture capital firms avoid. Looking over your list, you note that two of the three firms that specialize in technology make 15 to 20 percent of their investment at the seed stage, while the third stays away from all seedlings. Such information should be enough to tell you which of the three firms to contact first. (If, indeed, you opt for a private venture capital firm at this stage: remember that you may have better, cheaper options.)

THE VCs' DREAM VENTURE

A technological breakthrough is every entrepreneur's dream. The venture capitalist dreams of high return on investment, ranging anywhere from 30 to 100 percent. The question is, do these dreams coincide? Quite often they do, but not always. Venture capitalists know all too well that the latest, greatest innovation does not always make for the best investment. John Doerr, sold on the idea of a pen-operated computer, poured millions into a start-up that died a quick, brutal death. Even the best venture capitalists get carried away by visions of cutting-edge technology. But they quickly learn an expensive lesson: that there's more to a successful company than a "cool" product. "I often say that training a good venture capitalist is like crashing a few F-16s," Doerr says of the business's risky nature. "It costs about $30 million, straight down the drain."

Doerr also says, very tellingly, "What there is in our business is plenty of plans, plenty of entrepreneurs, and plenty of money. What there's a shortage of is great teams." Ann Winblad, general partner of Hummer Winblad, similarly notes, "Money is everywhere. The real challenge is intellectual capital. How good are the people you're doing business with, and can they engineer change?" The message is clear. VCs may dream of great products, but only in the hands of great people.

It's the People

Entrepreneurs don't always realize this particular truth. They invest their time developing a product and then slave over what they consider a fantastic business plan to win over investors. Yet, in reality, the new business's management team is often the first thing that venture capitalists examine.

Steve Arnold, a venture capitalist with Polaris Venture Partners and a former Microsoft executive says, "You're investing in technology and markets, but ultimately you're investing in people." Though it is in the service of a product or idea, a business really is moved forward by people—people of talent. Nothing scares a venture capitalist more than an entrepreneur with little or no experience of running a business or managing people. Quite often the innovator is an idea person with few business skills and even less desire to be an administrator.

Then there are the entrepreneur's colleagues. When reading through a business plan—more often scanned than thoroughly read—venture capitalists always note who's running the show. It helps immeasurably when the firm's management has a proven track record. It really doesn't matter whether the company is in biotechnology, computer hardware, or Internet applications: these businesses are driven by people. Never underestimate this factor in seeking funding. Georges Doriot, considered the founder of modern venture capital, counseled venture capitalists, "Always consider investing in a grade A man with a grade B idea. Never invest in grade B man with a grade A idea."

Technology

Not to scare away fledgling restaurateurs or retailers, but they might not be the best candidates to receive venture capital. These days technology start-ups seem to be the darlings of venture capitalists; they draw the largest portion of investment year after year. In the first quarter of 1997, technology companies received 62 percent of all investments. The attraction has to do with past and potential industry growth. Brian Dovey, president of the National Venture Capital Association, says, "There continues to be a healthy appetite for cutting-edge technologies which have the promise to offer healthy financial returns."

The personal computer boom that began in 1981 had, by 1990, caused that industry to grow from virtually nothing to a $100 billion juggernaut—what John Doerr calls the largest legal accumulation of wealth in history. And he should know. During that time, Doerr played a major role financing such start-ups as Compaq Computer, Lotus Development Corporation, and Sun Microsystems. Indeed, venture capital not only built businesses, it raised an entire industry. And when venture capitalists look at possible investments, that kind of potential is now constantly on their minds: how quickly will this investment grow and what kind of impact will it have? Doerr himself, and many others, now think they have a firm grip on a future growth industry—the Internet, an industry that, after all, developed directly from the personal computer.

Some of the biggest Internet winners so far include Amazon.com, Netscape Communications, and Yahoo! But there promise to be many more attempts to break into this rapidly growing industry, a fact borne out by the most recent venture capital statistics. In the last year alone, Internet start-ups, the number of which were already on the rise, experienced a sixfold increase. And from January 1995 to March 1997, the number of new Internet companies being funded increased more than 15 times. That is not to say that they will all survive, but this level of investment is a clear indication that the venture market sees great potential there.

Aside from high-tech fields based on the computer, other industries that have experienced considerable growth are also being rewarded. Healthcare start-ups, for example, attracted $1.2 billion in 1996, double the amount invested in 1995. And biotechnology start-ups, which certainly have a high-tech component, pull their share of venture capital as well.

What Is It? and Will It Sell?

They could be the two questions venture capitalists most frequently ask entrepreneurs. In essence, the venture capitalist wants to know if the product is worth a sizable investment and whether or not the market will open its arms to welcome that product. So which products attract the most venture capitalists by having the most market potential? Well, that's for you to decide.

It is well known that high technology—cutting-edge computer hardware, software, and Internet services—cause venture capitalists to salivate. But just because such products are high tech doesn't mean that they will inevitably be successful. Entrepreneurs are better served if they work on advances that use existing technology to move information better, faster, and more cheaply. Jackie MacDonald, general partner with Sippl MacDonald Ventures, says, "Entrepreneurs don't have to think revolution, just evolution."

Intuit is a case in point. The company developed a software program to handle personal finances, such as paying bills and maintaining a balanced checkbook—not a novel idea considering that there are some 30 other programs on the market that do the same things. But the competition's products were complex and laborious, often taking longer than paying bills by hand. Intuit's software, Quicken, cut that time in half and became a market leader simply by being better than its competition.

When Tom Weldon, an entrepreneur in the medical device industry, started Novoste, he knew just how important that philosophy was. Since his industry was regulated by the United States Food and Drug Administration (FDA), he knew that new products, especially innovative ones, could get stuck waiting for FDA approval. Therefore, any reliance on new products could seriously damage a company's cash flow. So Weldon decided on a two-pronged approach, focusing on both innovative and derivative products at the same time.

In fact, a company can sustain itself and live quite well off less than revolutionary products. The problem with once-in-a-lifetime innovations is that they come along just once in a lifetime.

THE ENTREPRENEURIAL VISION

Tom Weldon's strategy gave the venture capitalists a couple of things on which to chew. He focused on the products that he could successfully bring to market—the sign of a business's viability. But he also demonstrated entrepreneurial vision, a no-nonsense approach that didn't pin hopes on overly optimistic innovation. His grind-it-out philosophy, which aimed to keep his company in the black, was certain to attract potential venture capital investors.

The public tends to focus on high-flying, young entrepreneurs who have devised some head-spinning technology that will change the world. Unfortunately, prospective entrepreneurs often use such people as models for themselves and, by extension, their business plans. The reality is that venture capitalists want entrepreneurs who have a firm grasp of their particular business and of the risks involved, because developing a start-up is not quick and it is not easy. Jackie MacDonald, of Sippl MacDonald Ventures, says "All ventures are risky, and I want someone who acknowledges that."

Acknowledging the risk involved is just one sign that entrepreneurs know what they're doing. But they also need to have a firm grasp of the business's prospects: they often need to walk a fine line between being optimistic and being unrealistic. In the attempt to reign in an overly optimistic prognostication, entrepreneurs must avoid understating the possible payoff such a venture offers—a fine line indeed.

HOW FAR IN THE JOURNEY

Another factor venture capitalists consider is the new firm's stage of development. There are a few reasons for this concern. One has to do with investment duration. A venture capital investment can last anywhere from three to ten or more years, with the determining factor being how far along the new business is in its development. Later stage investments tend to have a quicker turnaround, meaning the venture capitalist can cash out more quickly and start building a new investment fund. This criticism has dogged venture capitalists, that they put a fund together only to invest and divest quickly to start a newer, bigger fund, one that will reap even greater management fees, that they concern themselves more with making money than with building businesses and industries.

But many venture capitalists dispute this criticism. It is true that a fund's size hinders some investment opportunities, as James J. Bochnowski, a partner of Delphi Ventures, explains: "With a $150 million to $200 million fund, you can no longer invest efficiently at a $1 million clip; you have to invest at least $5 million a clip." But Alan Patricof puts little credence in the critics' claims. "If the opportunity is big," the chairman of Patricof and Company Ventures says, "we'll start off small." And that flexibility is common with most venture capitalists. The industry standard, however, is to invest somewhere around Bochnowski's $5 million. These ongoing enterprises represent less risk and quite possibly less maintenance. Yet just as venture capitalists come in all shapes and sizes, so do their investments. And although the $5 million infusion is the standard for quite a few investment firms, it hardly defines the entire group. Many venture capitalists are still drawn to early stage companies that, despite their increased risk, offer the potential for increased profits. In fact, the venture capital industry is experiencing a generational change of sorts, with younger investors bringing their firms back to start-ups. In Boston, for example, two partners from the old-line firm of Burr Egan Deleage split off to start Polaris Venture Partners, a firm focused on early stage businesses.

And don't forget angels, the early stage entrepreneur's savior. They often jump at the chance to invest and help guide early stage ventures. Unlike venture capital funds, they invest substantially less and are well positioned to provide financing in the seed and early stages.

THE IPO FINISH LINE

Whether venture capitalists invest at the seed stage or provide mezzanine financing, the finish line remains constant: the initial public offering. Selling stock to the public finally gives investors the chance to value and gain a return on their equity.

Thus, the strength of the IPO market and the IPO success rate, as indicators of venture capital success, can have a major effect on how many companies receive funding. For example, early 1997 saw a decline in IPO numbers compared to the record pace set in 1995 and 1996, though the IPO market is still strong and still provokes investors to pour money into young enterprises. A continued slowdown or failed attempts to bring companies public could, however, negatively affect the number of enterprises that will receive financing.

Just as important as the number of deals is the success IPOs have when they enter the marketplace. Frequently, the news media offer headline coverage of IPO success stories such as those of Netscape Communications, Pixar, and more recently @Home—companies the stock price of which might rise anywhere from 50 to 100 percent or more on the opening day of trading. But those same markets are littered with companies that fared poorly, like Smith Micro Software: its stock price jumped from $12 to $14.50 on the opening day only to fall to $7.25 months later.

"Initial public offerings are the fuel that entrepreneurs' job engines run on," says Dan Case, chairman of Hambrecht and Quist. The pressure for a successful IPO is great. If failures increase, wary investors will stay away from the venture capital market.

Keen IPO observers note that companies' track records distinguish the winners from the losers. That is, the winners tend to have solid revenue streams or links to solid and credible partners. Too often, companies that lack these accomplishments push hard to get to the IPO stage only to fizzle out, to their shareholders' extreme ire.

THE PROACTIVE ENTREPRENEUR

If entrepreneurs err in one place, it might be in their focus on preparing the indestructible business plan—the assumption being that potential investors give this document the most serious consideration. Yet the truth is, venture capitalists investigate many more factors than just the business plan and often give these other factors greater weight. Brook Byers, of Kleiner Perkins, says, "The valuation process is not numbers crunching. It's really based more on experience. If you can't do the math in your head, it's probably not a venture deal." And big numbers are impressive only if they can be backed up with realistic expectations and expert management.

Help Yourself

The search process is a two-way street. As an entrepreneur, you need not passively sit back while venture capitalists investigate your business. If you know what's important to VCs, you can actively work to make your firm look more attractive. This effort can—and should be—more than just a beauty treatment. Aligning your business according to a venture capitalist's strictures might not land a capital investment every time, but it should certainly enhance your chances and also improve your enterprise's makeup. That is, venture capitalists look for particular ingredients precisely because they are the components that create successful companies. Even if your attempt at financing falls through, your company should still benefit from these adjustments.

Make the Match

It may sound repetitive, but it's too important to forget: make sure the venture capitalist you contact is likely to have some interest in your business—a potential interest you can glean from a database search or from company fact sheets like those in this directory. Gordon Baty, a partner with Zero Stage Capital, says, "Of every 100 [business] plans we get, 90 of them are completely irrelevant." This failure to connect stems from entrepreneurs' blindly sending out business plans. A little digging would uncover a firm's investment criteria, such as industry and geographic preferences, the stage of development in which they normally invest, and the amount of capital typically invested.

Just because venture capital firms are particular doesn't mean there isn't money out there for entrepreneurs. The onus is on entrepreneurs to locate their best chances and to make appropriate contacts.

Find Friends in High Places

Entrepreneurs must be willing to play any trump card they hold, and mutual friends or affiliations help. John Doerr isn't alone when he says that his company almost never invests in a company that sends him an unsolicited business plan. Networking is important in the world of venture capital.

If these relationships don't already exist, create them. Entrepreneurs should make an attempt to get to know a venture capitalist's previous investment targets, if only to get some information on the venture capitalist. This relationship, however, could lead to an direct introduction to the money source.

Accountants and lawyers are also important. Preparing a business plan, or simply preparing the business, might demand an accountant's or lawyer's services. You can help your own cause by using accountants and lawyers who have known ties to a venture capitalist. Such contacts ease the introduction process.

Such relationships work in the other direction too. Say you have already received a venture capital investment. That may open the doors to normally high-priced lawyers, accountants, or even real estate dealers. "Venture" accountants and "venture" lawyers may virtually donate their services to start-ups in the hope that, when these enterprises expand, they will retain the larger entity as a client.

Breaking Through Without the Breakthrough

Too many entrepreneurs focus on "breakthrough" products to the point that they lose sight of what makes a business viable—secure, profitable niches. Venture capitalists, however, realize the importance of these market niches, and they flock to companies that can service them.

Like Tom Weldon, entrepreneurs shouldn't forsake market innovations, but they must realize that companies should not rely on them. In fact, one of the biggest stumbling blocks when trying to obtain venture capital is that the venture capitalist perceives a lack of potential growth. A company that pins all its hopes on the marvels of a single product is rarely an adequate venture capital target. The entrepreneur must show that the business has more to offer.

The Management Team

Knowing the value that investors put on the management team should signal to entrepreneurs that they must be proactive in creating an impressive team. Novoste was Weldon's second attempt at a start-up, the first already having resulted in a successful business. When building his management team for this second enterprise, Weldon picked many of the players from his first company—a clear sign to venture capitalists not only that the company was comprised of people who knew what they needed to do, but also that the management team formed a cohesive unit that worked well together.

A new entrepreneur often names friends and family to key positions, many of whom don't have the skills to propel the company forward. Instead, entrepreneurs must start searching at once for the people they need to make the company successful and attractive to investors. Nothing is more impressive to venture capitalists than an entrepreneur who demonstrates business acuity—the drive to succeed and the know-how to make it happen.

Establishing Credibility

Many young businesses find it difficult to make a name for themselves. With a new product, the entrepreneur, particularly if he or she is in search of venture capital, must find ways to catapult his or her businesses to a credible stage. Establishing links with other credible sources helps.

One such example is EntreMed, a biotech firm that established itself as credible through its affiliations and joint ventures. Its first step was to sign an agreement with Judah Folkman, a prominent scientist who has done pioneering work in cancer-related research. This association lent so much credibility to EntreMed that in turn it was able to arrange a $76 million joint partnership with pharmaceutical giant Bristol-Myers Squibb.

It's true that creating such prominent associations is difficult for most start-ups, yet they can take smaller steps to achieve the same goal. Tom Weldon, also involved in the medical field, sought technical advisers. Weldon contacted a leading cardiologist and showed him one of the firm's early products, an innovative catheter. Weldon says, "I wanted to establish a personal relationship with him." And he did. Impressed, the cardiologist agreed to sign on as a scientific adviser to the company and provided a network of additional medical contacts.

Weldon also used trade journals and publications to publicize his company to both customers and investors. He considered it a step toward gaining a wider audience and building the firm's credibility.

Due Diligence

Contact has been made, and a venture capitalist firm starts to check out you and your business from a distance. The VCs like what they see and decide to move in for a closer examination. This process is called due diligence: the venture capitalist investigates the entrepreneur and the business's management team to see if they are suitable for investment.

The entire due diligence period make take anywhere from four to six weeks, on average, or even longer. Before the process begins, the entrepreneur ought to be fairly certain that he wants to do business with this particular venture capitalist. If the entrepreneur has doubts, he should seriously consider them before due diligence begins and both parties waste valuable time. The entrepreneur should also be fairly satisfied with the terms of a potential deal, which the venture capitalist will probably sketch out before the investigation begins. Finally, the timetable for the entire process should be understood so that both parties are comfortable with the agreed-upon schedule.

The Initial Meeting

The first step in due diligence is a meeting between the venture capitalist and the entrepreneur—sometimes the whole management team. This meeting is an attempt to cover the basics, and the entrepreneur should bring with him his business plan and any relevant background information. Discussion will most definitely cover the business's prospects—the specific market it should capture, how it will achieve its goals—and the entrepreneur must demonstrate a firm grasp of all the company's activities.

If the meeting feels a bit like an interview, that's because it is. The venture capitalist may also ask some personal questions to get a feel for the entrepreneur, to see if some level of trust can be established. Venture capitalists want to establish whether or not they feel confident doing business with the entrepreneur.

On-site Tour

Phase two can range from a basic question-and-answer session to a more elaborate interrogation of the entrepreneur about his business. Initial questions may address the product's uniqueness as judged against its competitors in the marketplace. The venture capitalist will also be interested in the manufacturing process and the delivery system—the company's actual ability to fill the product's defined market niche. Other questions regarding the company's financial stability or culture will be asked as well, and the entrepreneur should have the answers prepared beforehand. Since many of these questions are standard—and can therefore be anticipated—the entrepreneur should take some time to come up with solid, thoughtful answers.

Beyond the standard questions, the venture capitalist tries to analyze the entrepreneur. Does he or she have the experience to make a success of the new venture? Will he or she take the initiative to guide the firm in tough times? Is there a willingness on the entrepreneur's part to work hard and put in countless, and possibly thankless, hours while working toward the firm's success? The venture capitalist tacitly addresses these issues with each question and may try to do a little digging on the side. Most often, investors are interested in knowing the entrepreneur's educational background. If the entrepreneurs academic degree is in a subject related to the venture, then his or her academic performance sheds a light on the entrepreneur's competence. Venture capitalists want the best and brightest. And they may want to know about the entrepreneur's extracurricular activities—they too can suggest leadership or initiative.

The whole process may seem laborious, but when venture capitalists invest millions in a venture they want to feel that they have made a good choice from the outset. In addition to educational accomplishments, they'll examine other aspects of an entrepreneur's past, such as work experience. The venture capitalist will ask himself whether the entrepreneur's work experience has anything to do with the product or service of the new business. It doesn't hurt to have a successful track record building companies either.

Keep in mind that few entrepreneurs meet every criteria that venture capitalists devise. This process isn't a purely objective test from which an entrepreneur earns a grade that, in black and white, indicates whether an investment will be made. What these criteria do is to give the investor a means for judging an entrepreneur's skills and integrity. Above all else, venture capitalists want to know that they can trust the person in whom they are investing. That's why it's important to be candid about any issues that may seem troubling to the venture capitalist. Any misrepresentations or errors in information provided to the venture capitalists may be sufficient to lose their trust, the most vital ingredient in the venture capital relationship.

Holding the Reigns

Much of the investor's decision hinges on the entrepreneur. Innovators and experienced managers aren't necessarily mutually exclusive groups, but finding a person who is both can prove difficult. That's why venture capitalists are so thorough. They usually know when they meet an innovator. But whether this same person can successfully manage a business is another question entirely. In judging an entrepreneur, venture capitalists usually look for certain characteristics.

Motivational speeches, instead of inventions, may become the force driving the business. Investors want a leader running a company, someone who will take responsibility not only for the investor's capital, but also for the business's future and the employees' fate. A great leader can set a vision and make the company realize that vision. And an entrepreneur who can convey this authority to a venture capitalist will find that his or her company is one step closer to financing.

But leading a company is not done in isolation, and venture capitalists look for entrepreneurs who know the competition as well as their own business. How well does the entrepreneur know the market? How does he or she see the future of the industry? Where does this business fit in the big picture? These are questions venture capitalists ask, to which they hope to receive positive and convincing answers.

Meeting the Employees

One of the best ways that a venture capitalist can get a feel for a firm's "culture" is by meeting with employees in an impromptu question-and-answer session. Although the entrepreneur shouldn't make anything looked staged, a good leader will tell employees what to expect and what's expected of them.

What an investor hopes to achieve from such meetings is a sense of whether employees are happy with their jobs and the company and whether they get along with their employer. Venture capitalists look for honest answers from the employees. If the answers are positive, the venture capitalist will grow more confident in the business.

Meeting the Management Team

Given the importance placed on the management team, the venture capitalist's meeting with that team is crucial in the due diligence process. New entrepreneurs frequently name friends and family to management positions even if they're not prepared for them. Yet their inability to handle management tasks becomes magnified as the job grows with the business. These problems should be addressed before the meeting, both with the venture capitalist and management.

The entrepreneur must paint an accurate picture for the venture capitalist, noting whether certain officers may not be able to handle management responsibilities down the line. Two benefits come from this kind of honesty. The venture capitalist is in fact usually reassured—the entrepreneur has a handle on the business and can determine what is in the firm's best interest. Also, if the investor uncovers a soft spot in management, that problem can be solved before it gets out of hand.

With the management team in place for the meeting, the entrepreneur should take a seat in the background or maybe even sit out the meeting entirely. The venture capitalist has garnered the information he needs from the entrepreneur. Now it's time for management to demonstrate their knowledge and skills. Sometimes venture capitalists will decide to meet with management as a group and individually as well. They want to see how well the group works together, but they're also interested in how cohesive the group remains when apart.

The Outside Investigation

After meeting with a company, venture capitalists may do their own research to compare data. The primary thing they want to know: is the business viable? To answer that question, they'll ask everyone—other venture capitalist contacts, industry experts, consultants, and specialists. They are certain to ask whether the product or service is truly unique and whether it has a niche in the marketplace. Venture capitalists might also seek information from suppliers about the entrepreneur's company and product. They'll even go to the entrepreneur's competition—sometimes the most realistic evaluator of the entrepreneur's business.

What VCs Bring to the Table

Venture capitalists have deep pockets and are looking to spend. But money is money. Why go to a venture capitalist when plenty of other financing options exist? Especially given the high price venture capitalists charge for their money, there has to be a better choice. Isn't there?

No hard and fast rules here, but venture capital has certain perks that rarely accompany a bank loan or an investment from a family member. As Robert Duboc, president of Silicon Video, said on receiving $15 million from venture capitalists, "They've been essential in helping us attract the right management and giving us the credibility we need. And they will be critical in helping us get ready for the IPO."

Consider Intuit, the software company that created the better check balancer. The business grew at such speed that the founders, Scott Cook and Tom Proulx, came to a crossroads. An entrepreneurial management style no longer fit with the complex nature of the fast-growing company. They needed to make changes. The question was how.

The cheap answer was to hire consultants to help guide the company. More expensive, and the choice taken, was to bring in venture capitalists. Interestingly, the last thing Intuit needed was money. They needed management brains—talent prepared to be around for the long haul. "We were looking for parents, not night school teachers," said Cook when comparing venture capitalists to consultants. He knew that the venture capitalists' knowledge of handling a growing business came with a venture capital investment. "You get a lot of attention from people when you have a few million bucks of theirs," says Cook. Once they signed on with the venture capitalist, Intuit knew they had the know-how to move to the next level.

James Clark tells a similar story. He started Silicon Graphics with the help of venture capitalists, which cost him dearly. By the time the company was up and running, Clark retained only 1 percent ownership of the firm and eventually left embittered. Ever the entrepreneur, Clark rebounded with a new firm, one into which he plowed $3 million of his own. Yet despite having enough money to finance the rest, he turned to the venture capitalists again, who helped propel his new company, Netscape Communications, to meteoric heights.

Another value venture capitalists add is their talent network—a source from which Clark and Netscape got a talented CEO. Their friendly venture capitalist, the omnipresent John Doerr, has developed quite a skilled talent pool. Marc Andreeson of Netscape believes that is Doerr's greatest asset. He says, "[Silicon] Valley is full of money right now, and John [Doerr]'s is no better than anyone else's. There's smart money, dumb money, corporate money, Japanese money, pension fund money. If you have a decent idea, getting money isn't that hard." He says Doerr's success is very much tied to his ability to attract superstar engineers and executives.

And Doerr agrees, to an extent. Referring to himself as a "glorified recruiter," Doerr focuses on finding technical talent and management talent because they are today's scarce resources—not money, not ideas, but talent.

3. VENTURE CAPITAL IN EUROPE, ASIA, AND THE PACIFIC RIM

The United States has long been the acknowledged global leader in venture capital. But recent years have seen the American market maturing, with many countries that once lagged the United States catching up. The United Kingdom, for example, as the most mature of the non-U.S. venture capital markets, is overtaking the United States in early stage and development capital as a percent of gross domestic product (GDP). U.S. GDP penetration, according to figures produced by the British Venture Capital Association (BVCA), stood at 0.803 percent for 1995, compared to a slightly higher 0.812 percent in the U.K.

Meanwhile, parts of Asia and eastern Europe, particularly China and Russia, represent new investment frontiers with the potential for vast industry growth. During 1996, venture capital funds under management in Asia (China, Hong Kong, Japan, Korea, and Singapore) stood at $45.98 billion, and this figure is expected to grow to roughly $52 billion by the end of 1997.

Yet though some countries have experienced conditions favorable to a rapid expansion of the venture capital industry, these conditions are not universal, resulting in a considerable divergence of growth rates and maturity across the different national venture capital industries. What follows will address the diversity of venture capital industries that exist within Europe, Asia, and the Pacific Rim and provide some background on the types and performance of venture capital funds used outside of the United States.

Venture capital funds outside the United States typically are in one of three common categories: independent funds, captive funds, and semi-captive funds. Independent funds are firms, funds, or investment trusts (publicly listed or private) that have raised their capital from more than one source, usually institutional. Captive funds are managed on behalf of a parent institution by specialist venture capital organizations while remaining wholly-owned subsidiaries or divisions of the parent. Semi-captive funds invest on behalf of a parent in addition to managing independently-raised funds representing more than 5 percent of total managed funds.

Venture capital associations in continental Europe and the U.K. have only recently started tracking the performance of venture capital funds. In the U.K. in 1995, according to the British Venture Capital Association, overall returns to investors from independent venture capital funds rose. The pooled internal rate of return (IRR) to December 31, 1995, was an annualized 13 percent, up from 12.1 percent in 1994. In 1995 alone, these venture capital funds returned £0.8 billion to investors, representing a quarter of the original capital paid into the funds during the previous 15 years. Large management buyout funds, which have the shortest investment cycles, have to date produced the highest returns, with a pooled IRR of 23.8 percent in 1995, up from 23.1 percent in 1994.

The European Venture Capital Association produced its first ever pan-European performance study of private equity and venture capital for the years 1980 to 1990 at the end of 1996. The study focuses on independent funds, that is, those funds open to outside investors. During 1990, the pooled IRR for a cross-sample of 18 funds committing a total of ECU 1.13 billion[1] was 15.2 percent, far surpassing the returns of other asset classes during 1990. The sample size of funds, however, was very restricted. Looking at nine European private equity funds for 1990, the IRR was 20.2 percent. That compares to a 5.9 percent return on the Cazenove Rosenberg index for smaller quoted European companies, a 2.9 percent return for the ECU bond index, and a 6.4 percent return for bonds and all quoted companies tracked by Datastream.

WESTERN EUROPE

The venture capital industry in Europe has evolved constantly in recent years, and there is still considerable room for growth. The amount invested by European venture capital funds in 1995 rose 2 percent to ECU 5.5 billion, while the actual number of investments fell 13 percent to 4,995. The size of the average investment grew. Buyout investments, accounting for 46 percent of the total amount invested throughout Europe, totaled ECU 2.6 billion. Investment in the technology sector stands out as a particularly rapid growth area, totaling ECU 1.3 billion in 1995—24 percent of the total amount invested in European private equity—and showing a 54 percent growth rate in that year.

In recent years, 4.4 billion to 6.7 billion ECU of funds have been raised for investment by the European venture capital industry as a whole. The U.K. is the biggest fundraiser in Europe, raising between ECU 1.8 billion and ECU 3.8 billion in new funds each year. The second biggest fundraiser is France, at approximately 1 billion ECU per annum, followed by Germany, Italy, and the Netherlands.

Continental Europe has recently experienced major corporate and industrial reorganization, offering new investment opportunities—a very important condition for venture capital industry growth. Industries throughout continental Europe, which have long been burdened by overcapacity and reliance on government subsidies, are beginning to follow in the footsteps of the U.K., which underwent its major corporate and industrial restructuring in the 1980s. Several recent major privatizations, such as Germany's $13 billion privatization of Deutsche Telekom in early 1997, are evidence of this reorganization.

New life is also being breathed into the venture capital industry throughout Europe as start-up companies and spinoffs benefit from institutional innovations such as the pan-European Easdaq market, the Alternative

---

1. ECU = European Currency Unit, a notional value into which all European currencies can be converted for ease of figure comparison. At February 1997, the ECU was listed as 1 ECU to US$1.13.

Investment Market (AIM) in London, the Nouveau Marché in Paris, and the soon-to-be launched Neuer Market in Frankfurt.

Such opportunities in Europe are prompting a number of investment firms in the United States to expand or open offices across the Atlantic. San Francisco-based Robertson, Stephens and Company and Hambrect and Quist have opened or expanded offices in London and Paris during 1997, while other firms such as Montgomery Securities are on their way. They have already played key roles in developing the American high-tech industry and are hoping to do the same again in Europe's less advanced frontier. The coming of the Americans, of course, means more competition for European firms. But it would not be the first time. In previous years, American investment banking giants such as Lehman Brothers, Merrill Lynch, and Morgan Stanley have managed numerous European government-sponsored asset sales.

Also, although there has been protracted debate about the imminent deadline for European Monetary Union (EMU), many investors remain unclear as to what impact a single European currency will actually have on the venture capital industry. There is growing doubt that the 1999 deadline for currency convergence will be met. Even so, many believe it will be business as usual if and when the change occurs. Many European venture capital funds are limited partnerships, and investments are often locked up for three to six years. During that time, currency fluctuations can have a negative or a positive impact on those investments. A single currency would, it is hoped, reduce risk incurred through foreign exchange volatility.

The path to meet the rigorous economic criteria spelled out in the Maastricht Treaty, which among its various stipulations requires that countries meet a 3 percent target for public-sector deficits as a percentage of GDP, could, however, have negative consequences for the investment industry as a whole. Key countries such as Germany and France are already struggling to meet the targets. Policy moves aimed at meeting the Maastrict criteria could result in weaker economic growth, damaging both demand for and supply of investment funds—and consequently damaging the venture capital industry's growth potential.

United Kingdom

Venture capital in the United Kingdom has rapidly evolved over recent years from its nascent days during the late 1970s. In 1995, £2.5 billion was invested in 1,163 companies by the British Venture Capital Association's (BVCA) 200 members, compared with just £20 million in 1979. Of this £2.5 billion, £2.1 billion was invested in the U.K., of which 88 percent went into new companies. In just ten years, between 1984 and 1994, the U.K. venture capital industry has invested more than £14 billion in more than 14,000 companies.

These figures do not include funds raised by a growing sector of the U.K. market, known as "business angel" capital. This kind of capital goes directly to new and growing unquoted businesses from wealthy private individuals. Business angels usually provide finance in return for an equity stake in the private business, but they may also provide other long-term finance alongside or instead of equity. Investors registered with business angel networks tracked by the BVCA invested £22 million in 1995 alone.

In Britain, heated activity in management buyouts (MBOs) and management buy-ins (MBIs) has increased competition among venture capital providers. Last year, MBO and MBI activity reached the highest-ever volume in the U.K.: 619 deals worth £7,547 billion came to market, topping the previous high in 1989 of 600 deals worth £7,497 billion. MBOs and MBIs have been steadily rising over the past three years as large companies restructure their balance sheets and dispose of non-core assets. Competition has forced venture capital firms to diversify, with many seizing upon opportunities that have appeared with the resurgence of activity in smaller start-ups and early stage investments, particularly in the high-technology and biotechnology industries.

Start-up and early stage investments, particularly in technology, have traditionally been unattractive investments because of the additional risk involved. New capital commitments have tended to be small, making companies struggle harder for financial viability. More recently, however, the money being invested in start-ups has increased from earlier levels of £250,000 to £500,000 to much higher figures of £4 million to £6 million, putting start-up companies on a more stable footing within their industries.

In the U.K., pension fund investment in venture capital has until very recently played a bigger role than elsewhere in Europe. The venture capital industry is more mature in Britain, and pension funds have a longer tradition of unquoted equity investment. Over the period 1987 to 1994, about 23 percent of money raised by independent venture capital funds came from U.K. pension funds and another 16 percent from overseas, mainly U.S., pension funds.

The biggest single venture capital company in the U.K. is the mammoth investment trust 3i., which is listed on the London Stock Exchange and has a market capitalization of £3 billion. The company invests in small- and medium-sized companies, a sector that has grown as larger companies continue to downsize. 3i. believes there are 3.5 million businesses in the U.K., compared with fewer than 2,000 U.K. companies listed on the stock market, and invests in some 3,200 businesses, with 3,000 of those based in the U.K.

France

The French venture capital market is fairly mature, the second largest after that of the U.K. France has two principal venture capital vehicles: the Fonds Commun de Placement Risques (FCPRs) and the Société de Capital Risque (SCRs). Under certain circumstances, SCRs and FCPRs are exempt from tax, and shareholders are taxed only on distributed profits. In recent years, there has been a trend toward fund specialization as well as consolidation of smaller funds. Although the French banks remain the primary players in the industry, operating through subsidiaries or external funds, there is also a considerable amount of new venture capital raised from sources outside France, according to the European

Venture Capital Association. Overall, the legal and fiscal environment remains friendly toward the venture capital industry.

Germany

The German venture capital industry is dominated by captive and semi-captive venture capital funds, which are linked primarily with the banking and insurance industries. These funds have been set up as open-end funds and therefore have little difficulty raising money.

During the years 1983 to 1992, Germany's venture capital market experienced an annual growth rate of 22 percent. Until 1993, Germany was one of Europe's wealthiest countries, but during the 1993 recession the venture capital market underwent a phase of consolidation. Although the economy is still struggling, with unemployment at a postwar record of 12.2 percent in February 1997, the market has continued to grow and still shows promise for further expansion. Much of that promise, as with the rest of continental Europe, will hinge on the success of changes brought about from the sweeping corporate and industrial restructuring process.

The Bundesbank, Germany's central bank, has been calling for equity finance to play a greater role in the restructuring process, as in the past, when the big banks helped fuel the country's economic wealth by lending heavily to industry. The Bundesbank has said in public reports that corporate restructuring can be speeded up through increased use of share issues rather than bank finance and recommends a greater focus on share issues to help companies be more competitive on an international scale. This attitude may force the government to respond to the demands from the public and many institutions for efficiency improvements in the legal and tax framework for venture capital and for small and medium-sized companies.

Italy

Italy's venture capital market, the third largest in Europe in terms of new funds raised, has developed rapidly in recent years. The profile of players has been changing, with the public sector taking on a more active role in unquoted companies and in helping to start small and medium-sized enterprises. The amount invested in seed and start-up investments continues to increase, accounting for more than half of all investments made by Italian venture capital companies in the mid-1990s.

Institutional innovation in the form of the Italian Stockmarket for Medium and Small Companies has also assisted Italy's medium and small-sized companies, which have tended to be a fairly small market for venture capital funds in the past. The launch of this exchange is expected to offer a range of new opportunities for venture capitalists.

The Netherlands

The venture capital market in the Netherlands, the fourth largest in terms of new funds raised in Europe, is fairly mature. Independent firms continue to dominate the Dutch venture capital market, holding a market share of over 60 percent of all investments. Captive funds have a market share of one third, while the market share of public sector funds continues to fall, to little more than 5 percent at the end of 1995.

At present, the government is considering an experimental program for special techno-starter funds. To encourage investment among individuals, the government has introduced a fiscal stimulus for private investors. In 1993, the Dutch government launched a new fund intended to facilitate bigger investments in larger industrial firms. Since its inception, however, it has shown little activity. Meanwhile, companies have been offered a new source of exit routes, as in 1994 the main stock exchange incorporated a second-tier market called the Parallelmarkt.

EASTERN EUROPE

Eastern Europe is well into its seventh year of market-oriented reform and its fourth year of economic recovery. Gross domestic product in eastern Europe and the Baltics grew again in 1996, although the European Bank for Reconstruction and Development (EBRD) believes that pace slowed in 1996 to 4 percent growth, compared to the 5 percent growth seen in 1995. This is partly because western Europe's demand for the region's exports has slackened as many parts of the European Community cope with economic stagnation—particularly Germany, which was the main export destination for the central European transition economies.

Nonetheless, foreign direct investment (FDI) to the former Soviet Union bloc has been increasing dramatically, serving as an important means of bolstering the region's economic infrastructure. Figures from the United Nations Economic Commission for Europe show that FDI during 1995 rose by 60 percent to $45.7 billion, compared to $28.7 billion 12 months earlier. Hungary still accounts for 30 percent of the region's FDI stock, while Poland is now the second-ranking host country for foreign investment, with 17 percent of the regional stock, followed by Russia and the Czech Republic with 13 percent and 12 percent, respectively.

The London-based EBRD remains one of the biggest overall investors in this region. Founded in 1991 with the purpose of promoting transition towards open market-oriented economies and for promoting private and entrepreneurial initiative in central and eastern Europe and the countries of the former Soviet Union, the EBRD has provided $300 million to 30 different private equity funds for venture capital. The EBRD invests in a range of funds, which in turn focus on companies in early stage development, those with an established track record but in need of capital and management support to sustain their growth, or those that are newly privatized and in need of financial restructuring. Individual investments for entrepreneurs are typically below $200,000. For second-stage equity funds, initial investments range from $100,000 to $500,000.

The infrastructure inherited from the Communist regimes by the countries of eastern Europe has undergone vast restructuring in the past several years. Communism paid scant attention to consumer demand. Economies were burdened by excessive specialization and a drive for economic integration across countries of the region for political reasons. This attitude meant there was limited concern for economic costs. This was so virtually across the board, even in major industries such as telecommunications and the railways. For those companies that cannot immediately attract equity capital, the EBRD has developed Early Stage Equity Investment Funds. The program, among other things, is meant to help speed the privatization or post-privatization process of a large number of enterprises.

Russia was the first of the Commonwealth of Independent States (CIS) countries to liberalize prices and trade. Since 1994, the markets in a number of CIS countries, including Armenia, Georgia, Kazakstan, Ukraine, and Uzbekistan, have been liberalized. Azerbaijan, Belarus, Tajikistan, and Turkmenistan are still in the early stages of market-oriented reform.

Political reform—moving from one-party states to multiple-party democracies—has been one of the driving forces behind the gradual restoration of foreign investor confidence, important examples of which were the presidential elections in Russia and in Poland in 1996. Overall, however, the risks for foreign investors remain high. Although these economies continue to pursue reform, the financial markets are still far from stable. Stock markets remain highly volatile, and inflation is still high. The Czech Republic, for example, may have experienced 4 percent economic growth in 1996, but the country has a current account deficit that is expected to have grown to about 6 percent of GDP in 1996. The government is attempting to keep inflation down by controlling the local currency, but wages are rising rapidly, and the government has been slow to tighten fiscal policy.

There have been further, more visible instabilities. During 1995, there were a large number of bank failures in countries such as the Czech Republic, Krygystan, Latvia, Lithuania, and Russia. In response, the EBRD is hoping to soothe foreign investor confidence by encouraging investment that will make company management more accountable for performance.

Russian Federation

Russia represents a huge and growing market that international investors see as one of the next big frontiers in the world of emerging markets. At present, despite a huge demand for private equity, there is little money available for small and medium-size businesses. Investors have been hampered by share registration and ownership concerns as well as by corporate governance issues. There are, however, efforts underway to launch a Russian Venture Capital Association in Moscow. The association, which is still in the early planning stages, would include a range of international investors. There are already venture capital associations established in Poland, Hungary, the Czech Republic, Slovakia, and Slovenia.

If the venture capital industry does establish itself, the expected growth industries would be food processing, construction, and consumer products. The Moscow stock market, meanwhile, has risen rapidly since the last few months of 1996. Stocks jumped 60 percent in value during the first two months of 1997, after surging 156 percent in 1996. Market capitalization has practically doubled to $50 billion from late 1996 as the market attracts a greater range of investors, including U.S. mutual funds. Seven of the world's top 10 performing funds during 1996 were Russian equity funds, according to the fund-tracking firm Micropal Ltd. There are, however, underlying concerns about the market's inherent volatility as well as problems over transparency, as Russian companies are not required to disclose their full ownership structure. It can also be difficult to determine the true performance of a company because of limitations in the system's auditing procedures.

Meanwhile, there are a number of funds being set up to invest in existing medium-size businesses, typically companies that have up to 3,000 to 4,000 employees. Altogether approximately 40 local and international funds currently invest in Russian business. Typically, these funds link up with a sponsor like the EBRD, and in return for a capital infusion, the sponsor receives an equity stake of between 29 percent and 49 percent in a given company.

The development of a venture capital culture will take time, although investors say there are plenty of Russian companies with healthy assets on their balance sheets. These assets are often under-utilized because many smaller companies have a shortage of capital. There is thus a great need for venture capital and an opportunity for high investment returns, but only if the economy begins to gather greater momentum. The Russian economy is at present hounded by corruption, a troublesome legal infrastructure, and a fundamental lack of growth. Since the EBRD was founded in 1991, the Russian economy has shown negative growth. In 1992, the country's GDP growth was -14.4 percent, and although this contraction has slowed, the economy has yet to produce a positive rate of growth in GDP.

In addition to the effects of a poor growth environment, investor uncertainty prevails, as the Russian government has not yet lost its penchant for draconian economic measures. In February 1997, the Communist-dominated lower house of the Russian Parliament gave preliminary approval to a plan to ban foreign investment in sectors including telecommunications and electric utilities and to limit foreign investor involvement in such areas as financial services, printing, media, and advertising. Such proposals from the lower house are not uncommon, although few such measures ever see the light of day. Even so, they show that Russian authorities have been slow to change their old style of thinking.

Poland

Poland has been Europe's fastest growing major economy, experiencing growth rates of 5.2 percent in the mid-1990s. Poland also has eastern Europe's most highly-developed venture capital industry. Venture capital specialists, who currently provide funds for sectors such as manufacturing, construction, and technology, have found it easier to operate in Poland than elsewhere in eastern Europe partly because this country is further along in its privatization program.

In 1989 Poland launched a series of comprehensive market-oriented reforms. Later, after the election of a left-of-center coalition government in September 1993, the government started a program called "Strategy for Poland." A new privatization law was passed in July 1995 that reinforces the trend toward commercialization and aims to transfer authority for initiating privatization away from the Minister of Privatization to other government ministries. The existing telecommunications network, meanwhile, is seen as the next big growth opportunity in the country and is currently the most profitable area of business.

Over time, as the economy has developed, venture capitalists have become better understood and accepted in Poland—as shorter-term investors who will eventually look for an exit. Foreign direct investment has also been an important aspect of Poland's economic turnaround. During the first nine months of 1995, there was a total foreign investment of $1.6 billion, which was 23 percent higher than for all of 1994. Poland's largest investor was the United States, which has to date invested $1.815 billion and has committed a further $1.618 billion. Foreign investment is often channeled indirectly through local funds or regional funds set up abroad.

The size of the private sector has slowly grown in recent years, with the number of registered private companies reaching 2.2 million at the end of September 1995, up from 1.9 million at the end of 1993. Most small retail, wholesale, and construction enterprises (about 20,000) have already been privatized, and the "fast track" privatization program of small and medium-sized enterprises through public tender has already been accomplished. The increase in size of the private sector is an important source of demand for venture capital funds and as such provides a good growth environment for the Polish venture capital industry.

Hungary

In Hungary the venture capital industry is still in its infancy. The country is only just emerging from a tough austerity program launched to combat high inflation and high government spending. The country has also been slower to implement a privatization program than Poland, although this is now accelerating: the number of privatizations and management buyouts is now increasing, which in turn is sparking the need for venture capital, particularly in the food and service sectors.

The Budapest bourse is one of eastern Europe's better-performing stock markets. Even so, the Budapest exchange is still dominated by just 44 listed stocks, which in all are worth $5 billion. Six stocks make up 66 percent of that value, so liquidity, as elsewhere on eastern European bourses, is limited. Foreign investors, who have played an important role in the country's evolving privatization process, are allowed to buy shares in Hungarian firms up to 100 percent majority participation. All foreign investments in the country are fully protected and guaranteed, which may give overseas venture capital firms an advantage over domestic ones and hence hamper the growth of a domestic venture capital industry.

ASIA AND THE PACIFIC RIM

The Pacific Rim is a highly-diversified economic zone; investment climates vary from country to country. In the 1970s, the first wave of venture capital funds appeared in Asia, followed by a bigger wave in the mid-1980s, when investors moved into the booming technology market. Taiwan, Singapore, and Malaysia were particularly aggressive in this area. Today the range of investment opportunities in Asia is considerable, particularly in China.

The Pacific Rim is characterized by extremes of market ideology, economic environment, and development experience. Malaysia, Thailand, and the Philippines are young, growing markets that, like South Korea, are making huge advances in economic growth under regimes largely hostile to private allocation of venture capital.

Japan accounts by far for the largest pool of venture capital funds in Asia, primarily because it is the most developed economy in the region. According to the Hong Kong-based *Asian Venture Capital Journal*, the average deal size has been increasing from a traditional $1-2 million to $50-60 million. The actual size of individual funds is also growing. Currently, fund sizes can average between $300 million to $500 million. On the other hand, much of the venture capital in Japan's funds has not been pure equity. The bulk of Japan's venture capital funding has been through debt. More recently, some of the debt comprising Japan's funds has been written off or not renewed, meaning that the pool of available funds in Japan fell by $3 billion to $33 billion during 1996. Growth in Japan's venture capital industry has also slackened—and is expected to remain slow for some time yet—due to serious structural problems in the country's economy.

Many of Asia's economies are introducing changes that will gradually smooth the way for investors, including venture capital specialists. Many countries, for instance, are developing a mutual fund industry, while foreign institutions are pouring billions of dollars into Asia. Asian pension funds are being developed by their respective governments and are very active in the public markets. Also, many Asian governments are promoting technological development and technology transfer. At the same time, billions of dollars are being poured into Asian private equity.

Only a small portion of these investments, however, actually have access to the public markets, and there are many private companies waiting to go public. Asia lacks the small-cap exit routes available elsewhere in the world, such as Nasdaq in the United States. Many Asian governments are recognizing the need to develop their respective stock markets for a variety of reasons, including encouraging the numerous smaller Asian companies that list on overseas markets like Nasdaq to remain at home. Singapore has already introduced a small-cap stock exchange and is now allowing pension funds to invest in the public stock market, while Malaysia is in the planning stages for its own exchange. In Taiwan and Japan, meanwhile, existing over-the-counter stock markets remain fairly volatile for smaller listings. Vietnam has no stock exchange at all and is not expected to develop a stock market in the foreseeable future.

The transitions underway in Asia are not just economic in nature. As the respective governments coach their economies into development, they must also encourage the growth of an entrepreneurial culture, as traditionally Asian business culture has been dominated by a system oriented around the group rather than the individual, discouraging small-scale start-up activity.

Hong Kong

Hong Kong is considered China's gateway to the rest of the world, and its stock market capitalization of $360 billion absorbs China's many times over. It also has a sizable venture capital industry. According to the *Asia Pacific Private Equity Bulletin*, Hong Kong's funds under management in 1996 were $4.7 billion.

There is a sense of unease about what China will do now that it has regained sovereignty over Hong Kong and asserted its "one country, two systems" policy. That uncertainty had been fueled by political disputes between Britain and China over Beijing's plans to amend civil liberties laws and replace the territory's legislature, but many think it unlikely that Beijing will reverse Hong Kong's economic progress. This confidence was evident following the death of Deng Xiaoping, China's 92-year-old leader, in February 1997. Well before his death, there had been widespread fears that the event would unleash a bruising wave of losses on Hong Kong and Chinese financial markets, yet this did not happen. Instead, the markets took the news in their stride, indicating that there is an underlying belief that Deng's political successors will not interfere with Hong Kong's economic prosperity or derail China's transition toward a more open-market economy.

Foreign investors accessing China tend to do so by setting up funds in Hong Kong. Hong Kong taxes have historically been lower than in other regions, and the regulatory environment has created a fairly favorable environment. Indeed, much of the foreign investment funds raised in Hong Kong for direct investment and venture capital do not stay in the country's borders. Hong Kong is home to numerous regional funds that invest in other countries such as China and India.

There has been mounting pressure in Hong Kong's real estate-dominated market to support the territory's manufacturing sector, which now accounts for only 10 percent of GDP, compared with 24 percent in the late 1970s. Investment growth is also expected to shift from the public sector to the private sector as work is completed on the city's new airport, one of the world's largest infrastructure projects.

China

The Chinese venture capital industry is still in its infancy, and much of the venture capital raised for the region still comes through the "back door" of Hong Kong. British Invisibles, the cross-sector organization that promotes invisible exports, has been pressing China for greater foreign access to its markets since 1980, but the uncertainty of Chinese law has tended to discourage foreign participation, despite the fact that the desire to get involved is very much alive.

As China's economy has accelerated over the past decade, the pool of private wealth has grown. The country has also made some progress in taming its recent tendency toward runaway inflation. During 1996, the country's retail price inflation dipped below 7 percent, less than half the rate for the previous year. As the government moves slowly toward a market economy, the scope for expansion seems vast. The question is really one of time. It is far from clear how long it will be before China fully commits to an open market. Meanwhile, many companies are still owned by central government, towns, and communes.

There are also other limitations. Despite China's vast size, its stock market is still little more than a minnow, with a market capitalization of just $4 billion. The lack of liquidity has been another reason major foreign investors have stayed away. Leading U.S. pension funds such as California Public Employees' Retirement System (Calpers) have been notably reticent due to the lack of liquidity and transparency in China's financial markets. Calpers, the largest public pension fund in the United States, has committed $100 million in principle to direct investments in Chinese companies, but only $1 million has yet been invested. Calpers and eight other U.S. pension funds have committed $14.8 billion in Asia and placed $1.38 billion in Hong Kong and Taiwan investments, but, again, invested only $330 million in China. Such reservations could frustrate China's ambitions to build Shanghai into an Asian financial capital in the next century.

Japan

In recent years, Japan's economy has experienced a number of traumatic setbacks. It is only now starting to recover from a stock market crash triggered after the market peaked in 1989. The economy has also suffered from a long decline in its currency and the collapse of its property market. Ten years ago, however, Japan was one of the world's most formidable competitors in the international corporate arena. Japan's banks were one of the world's foremost lenders in the tide of spinoffs and mergers and acquisitions that transformed corporate America. Now, many of Japan's largest banks have experienced crippling debt levels, and a wave of consolidation is expected in this sector.

Indeed, the country's entire financial sector is facing a major reorganization. A supervisory agency "independent" of the finance ministry is being planned by the Japanese government to police the financial sector as the country prepares for a "big bang" financial deregulation. The financial reform measures, the biggest of such changes in 50 years, are aimed at reviving Japan's Tokyo markets and developing them to the size and sophistication of those of New York. Deregulation will include lifting a ban on holding companies, a ban which has long been seen as being a competitive handicap. The Japanese government will also scrap foreign exchange controls and give greater autonomy to the Bank of Japan.

Australia

The venture capital industry in Australia is at an interesting juncture. The country's economy depends increasingly on the proliferation of smaller companies, yet the larger, more established companies listed on Australia's stock exchange are experiencing a slump. The younger companies need capital that is not as yet readily available, indicating a mismatch between structural changes within the economy and the traditional markets of the financial sector. In contrast, New Zealand faces no such problem, as the economy is dominated by farming, raw material production, oil and gas, fishing, and forestry—industries that traditionally have little need to raise high-cost capital with venture capitalists.

There have been several attempts to boost the provision of venture capital in Australia. In the 1970s and 1980s, a number of small companies in high technology, raw materials, and oil tried to raise money on the back of a buoyant stock market, but many listed before they were sufficiently mature and disappeared practically overnight. During the 1980s, the government also introduced a special program offering tax advantages for new companies, but these programs ultimately foundered.

Still, the venture capital industry is beginning to recover in Australia: during 1995 the country raised $607Aus million in new funds (roughly US$772 million). That is almost double the $320Aus million raised in 1994 and a vast jump from the $57Aus million raised in 1990, according to the *Asian Venture Capital Journal*. In all, for 1995, the country had $2.3Aus billion under management.

The continued evolution of the venture capital industry could prove critical for Australia in the next few years as the economy experiences restructuring. The economy is being driven by unlisted companies, rather than by those that trade on the country's stock exchange, as sectors such as domestic manufacturing, large retail, and transport have all been struggling under import competition, a lack of tariff protection, and limited pricing power due to low inflation. Most of the country's new employment is created not in these industries, which are suffering the effects of overcapacity as in continental Europe, but in emerging companies in the service sector, many of which still need capital to diversify and develop their businesses. Many smaller high-tech players, for instance, are still one-product companies that run the risk of losing out to more diversified competitors in that fast-developing industry.

THE DIRECTORY

A

General
Companies

ABERLYN CAPITAL MANAGEMENT COMPANY, INC.

1000 Winter Street
Waltham, MA 02154

Telephone: 617-895-1144
Fax: 617-895-1645

Other Office Locations
18 Winter Place
Matawan, NJ 07747
Phone 908-583-5108, Fax 908-583-8499

Mission: Actively seeking new investments

Fund Size: not available
Founded: 1992
Average Investment: not available
Minimum Investment: $500,000

Investment Criteria: Second-stage

Industry Group Preference: Genetic Engineering, Medical/Health Related

Portfolio Companies: not available

Officers, Executives and Principals

Lawrence Hoffman, Chairman (Matawan)
Douglas R. Brian, President (Waltham)

ACCEL PARTNERS
One Embarcadero Center
San Francisco, CA 94111

Telephone: 415-989-5656
Fax: 415-989-5554

Other Office Locations
One Palmer Square
Princeton, NJ 08542
Phone 609-683-4500, Fax 609-683-0384

Mission: not available

Fund Size: $350 million
Founded: 1983
Average Investment: $500,000
Minimum Investment: Less than $100,000

Investment Criteria: Seed, Research and Development, Startup, First-stage, Second-stage, Mezzanine, Leveraged Buyout, Special Situations, Control-block Purchases

Industry Group Preference: Biotechnology, Communications, Computer Related, Electronic Components and Instrumentation, Genetic Engineering, High Technology, IndustrialProducts and Equipment, Medical/Health, Software

Portfolio Companies: American Surgical Technology, Medical Care International,Sportsmedicine Systems, U.S. Behaviorial Health, Liposome Co., Alldata, Linkware, MediaShare, Power Up Software, Synopsys, Veritas, XA Systems, Bridge Communications, Faralon Computing, Netlink, Ungermann-Bass, VitalinkCommunications, VMX, PictureTel

Officers, Executives and Principals

James W. Breyer, General Partner (San Francisco)
Education: BS, Computer Science and Economics, Stanford; MBA, Harvard University
Background: Managment Consultant, McKinsey & Co.; Product Management and Marketing, Apple Computer, Hewlett Packard
Directorships: Academic Systems, Jostens Learning, Macromedia, MediaShare, PageMart, Power Up Software, Spectrum

Luke B. Evnin, General Partner (San Francisco)

Paul H. Klingenstein, General Partner (San Francisco)
Education: AB, Harvard; MBA, Stanford
Background: EM Warburg, Pincus and Co., Biotechnology Experience
Directorships: EP Technologies, Isis Pharmaceuticals, Glyomed, Paidos Healthcare, Oncogenetics, U.S. Behavioral Health, Viagene

Arthur C. Patterson, General Partner (San Francisco)
Education: AB/MBA, Harvard University

Background: Adler and Co.; Vice President, Citicorp Venture Capital; Equity Committee, Citicorp's Investment Management Group
Directorships: PageMart, Raxco, The Santa Cruz Operation, Synercom, Trinzic, Unify, Veritas, Walker Interactive Systems

James P. Swartz, General Partner (Princeton)
Education: Engineering Sciences and Applied Physics, Harvard University; MS, Industrial Administration, Carnegie Mellon University
Background: Founding General Partner, Adler and Co.; Vice President, Citicorp Venture Capital; Vice President, Laird Inc.

James R. Flach, Venture Partner (San Francisco)

George Hara, Venture Partner (San Francisco)

Eugene D. Hill, Venture Partner (San Francisco)

THE ACQUISITION SEARCH CORPORATION

1150 Lake Hearn Drive
Suite 200
Atlanta, GA 30342

Telephone: 404-250-3250
Fax: 404-250-3212

Mission: Actively seeking new investments

Fund Size: not available
Founded: 1992
Average Investment: not available
Minimum Investment: $500,000

Investment Criteria: First-stage, Second-stage, Mezzanine, Leveraged Buyout, Special Situations, Control-block Purchases

Industry Group Preference: Communications, Computer Related, Consumer, Distribution, Electronic Components and Instrumentation, Energy/Natural Resources, Genetic Engineering, Industrial Products and Equipment, Medical/Health Related

Portfolio Companies: not available

Officers, Executives and Principals

Roger B. Orloff, President

ADLER AND COMPANY

c/o Venad Management, Inc.
239 South County Road
Palm Beach, FL 33480

Telephone: 561-659-2001
Fax: 561-659-7995

Other Office Locations
c/o Eurolink, Inc.
690 Market Street, Suite 702
San Francisco, CA 94104
Phone 415-398-6352, Fax 415-398-6355

c/o Venad Administrative Services, Inc.
100 First Stamford Place, Third Floor
Stamford, CT 06902
Phone 203-359-9595, Fax 203-359-0880

Mission: Reducing investment activity

Fund Size: not available
Founded: 1965
Average Investment: not available
Minimum Investment: $500,000

Investment Criteria: Second-stage, Mezzanine

Industry Group Preference: Communications, Computer Related, Consumer, Distribution, Electronic Components and Instrumentation, Energy/Natural Resources, Genetic Engineering, Industrial Products and Equipment, Medical/Health Related

Portfolio Companies: not available

Officers, Executives and Principals

Frederick R. Adler, President (Palm Beach)
Jay S. Nickse, Treasurer and Chief Financial Officer (Stamford)
Philip Chapman, Venture Manager (Stamford)
Jacques Vallee, Venture Manager (San Francisco)

ADS CAPITAL CORPORATION

1302 Osage Avenue
Santa Fe, NM 87505-3328

Telephone: 505-983-1769
Fax: 505-983-2887

Mission: not available

Fund Size: $1 million
Founded: not available
Average Investment: $50,000
Minimum Investment: not available

Investment Criteria: Seed to Startup

Industry Group Preference: Communications, Computer Related, Educational, Information Services, Medical/Health, Software

Portfolio Companies: American I-Beam, Better Education, Conquest Labs, InfoUSA, Mekanika, Sports Express, Life Resuscitation Technologies, Blue Star Technologies, Sucrose Ester Engineering Corporation

Officers, Executives and Principals

A. David Silver, Chairman
Education: BA/MBA, University of Chicago
Background: Corporate Finance, Kuhn, Loeb and Co., Chase Manhattan Bank
Directorships: Jeffery Norton Publishers, Better Education; Founder, I Have A Dream Foundation, Santa Fe

Benjamin A. Thom
Education: BA, Economics, Middlebury College
Background: Assistant Trader, Gruntal and Company
Directorships: Sports Express

Gregor D. Gordon
Education: BA, Economics, University of Utah
Background: Options Trader, Scott Andrews Group

Shasheen P. Shah
Education: BA, Philosophy, Colgate University
Background: Marketing, Jintech Inc.

ADVANCED MATERIALS PARTNERS INC.

45 Pine Street
New Canaan, CT 06840

Telephone: 203-966-6415
Fax: 203-966-8448
E-mail: AMPWKB@aol.com

Mission: Through its affiliate, Advanced Materials Investments, Inc., Advanced Materials Partners, Inc. Invests in and assists growing private companies whose products, competitive advantage and growth are based on new materials, chemical, and processing technologies. Lead or co-lead active investor bringing substantial business and corporate development expertise as member of the board.

Fund Size: not available
Founded: 1987
Average Investment: $1 - $2 million
Minimum Investment: $500,000

Investment Criteria: Seed to Acquisitions

Geographic Preference: United States, Canada, Europe

Industry Group Preference: Consumer, Commercial and Industrial Products, Manufacturing/Processing, Materials and Chemicals

Portfolio Companies: not available

Officers, Executives and Principals

Warner K. Babcock, Managing Director
Education: MBA, Emory University; BA, Chemistry, University of North Carolina
Background: Founder, advanced materials companies; Inventor with four U.S. patents
Directorships: Number of advanced materials companies

Stanley Roboff, Senior Director
Education: BS, Engineering, MIT
Background: Head of Uranium and Beryllium Branches for the Manhattan Project; Director, Special Materials Division, U.S. Atomic Energy Commission
Directorships: Several advanced material companies

Charles G. Pieroth, Director, Corporate Technology Assets
Education: MS, BS, Webb Institute; Licensed professional engineer
Background: Director, Technology Resource Management; Director, Technology Development; Director, Corporate Licensing, Northrop Grumman Corporation
Directorships: Advanced materials engineering centre

William W. Davison, Ph.D., Director, Technology Assessment
Education: Ph.D., MS, Ceramic Engineering, University of Illinois; BS, Ceramic Engineering, Ohio State University
Background: 12+ years experience in the advanced materials industry

ADVANCED TECHNOLOGY VENTURES

281 Winter Street
Suite 350
Waltham, MA 02154

Telephone: 617-290-0707
Fax: 617-684-0045

Other Office Locations
2884 Sand Hill Road, Suite 100
Menlo Park, CA 94025
Phone 415-321-8601, Fax 415-321-0934

Mission: Actively seeking new investments

Fund Size: $85 million
Founded: 1980
Average Investment: $1 million
Minimum Investment: $250,000

Investment Criteria: Startup, First-stage, Second-stage

Industry Group Preference: Biotechnology, Communications, Computer Related, Electronic Components
and Instrumentation, Energy/Natural Resources, Genetic Engineering, Industrial Products and Equipment,
Medical/Health Related, Software

Portfolio Companies: not available

Officers, Executives and Principals

Albert E. Paladino, Managing Partner (Waltham)
Education: BS/MS, Alfred University; PhD, MIT
Background: Deputy Director, Office of Energy Programs, U.S. Dept. of Commerce; Assistant Director, Tele-
phone Operations Technology Center, GTE Labs
Directorships: Advanced Energy Dynamics, Theta-J Corporation, Laser Science, MilliTech, Mosaic Systems

Pieter J. Schiller, Managing Partner (Waltham)

Jos C. Henkens, General Partner (Menlo Park)

Robert F. Sproull, Special Partner (Waltham)
Education: AB, Harvard; PhD, Stanford
Background: Associate Professor, Carnegie Mellon University; Research Staff, Xerox Corporation
Ivan E. Sutherland, Special Partner (Menlo Park)

William R. Sutherland, Special Partner (Menlo Park)

ALAN I. GOLDMAN AND ASSOCIATES

497 Ridgewood Avenue
Glen Ridge, NJ 07028-1821

Telephone: 201-509-8356
Fax: 201-509-8856

Mission: not available

Fund Size: not available
Founded: 1990
Average Investment: not available
Minimum Investment: $250,000

Investment Criteria: Second-stage, Mezzanine, Leveraged Buyout, Special Situations, Control-block Purchases

Geographic Preference: North America

Industry Group Preference: Communications, Computer Related, Consumer, Distribution, Electronic Components and Instrumentation, Energy/Natural Resources, Genetic Engineering, Industrial Products and Equipment, Medical/Health Related

Portfolio Companies: not available

Officers, Executives and Principals

Alan I. Goldman, Principal
Jerome Shiloff, Principal

ALIMANSKY CAPITAL GROUP, INC.

605 Madison Avenue
Suite 300
New York, NY 10022-1901

Telephone: 212-832-7300
Fax: 212-832-7338

Mission: Actively seeking new investments

Fund Size: not available
Founded: 1980
Average Investment: not available
Minimum Investment: $1 million

Investment Criteria: First-stage, Second-stage, Mezzanine, Leveraged Buyout, Special Situations

Industry Group Preference: Communications, Computer Related, Consumer, Distribution, Electronic Components and Instrumentation, Energy/NaturalResources, Genetic Engineering, Industrial Products and Equipment, Medical/Health Related

Portfolio Companies: not available

Officers, Executives and Principals

Burt Alimansky, Managing Director
Donald B. Blitzer, Associate Director
David Glickstein, Associate Director
Merlin D. Schulze, Associate Director
M. John Sterba, Associate Director
Stephen J. Swain, Associate Director

ALLIANCE BUSINESS INVESTMENT COMPANY

320 South Boston Avenue
Suite 1000
Tulsa, OK 74103

Telephone: 918-584-3581
Fax: 918-582-3403

Mission: not available

Fund Size: $13 million
Founded: not available
Average Investment: $1 million
Minimum Investment: not available

Investment Criteria: First Stage to Mezzanine

Industry Group Preference: Communications, Consumer Related, Diversified, Energy/Natural Resources, Environmental Protection, Food Services, Industrial Products, Information Services, Manufacturing/Processing, Medical/Health, Publishing, Transportation, Wholesaling/Distribution

Portfolio Companies: not available

Officers, Executives and Principals

Barry M. Davis, President
Education: BBA, Corporate Finance, University of Oklahoma
Directorships: Numar Corporation, Coleman Natural Products

ALLIANCE FINANCIAL OF HOUSTON

401 Studewood
Suite 200
Houston, TX 77007

Telephone: 713-868-8595
Fax: 713-869-4462

Mission: Actively seeking new investments

Fund Size: not available
Founded: 1993
Average Investment: not available
Minimum Investment: Less than $100,000

Investment Criteria: First-stage, Second-stage, Mezzanine, Leveraged Buyout, Special Situations, Turn-arounds

Industry Group Preference: Diversified

Portfolio Companies: not available

Officers, Executives and Principals

Attilio F. Galli, President and Chief Executive Officer
William M. Berry, Jr., Executive Vice President
Glyne Worrell, Vice President
Thu Hang J. Dao, Assistant Vice President

ALLIED CAPITAL

1666 K Street Northwest, 9th Floor
Washington, DC 20006

Telephone: 202-331-1112
Fax: 202-659-2053

Mission: Committed to investing in strong, growing companies by providing growth financing, buyout and acquisition capital, and financing for recapitalization.

Fund Size: $750 million
Founded: 1958
Average Investment: $2 million
Minimum Investment: $1 million

Investment Criteria: Second-stage to Leveraged Buyout

Geographic Preference: United States, OPIC-designated emerging countries

Industry Group Preference: Diversified

Portfolio Companies: not available

Officers, Executives and Principals

David Gladstone, Chairman
Education: BA, Government and Economics, University of Virginia; MA, Computer Science and Government, American University; MBA, Harvard
Background: Management Consultant, Price Waterhouse; Internal Consultant, IT&T
Directorships: NASDAQ, George Washington University, Riggs National Corporation

G. Cabell Williams, President
Education: BS, Rollins College
Directorships: Environmental Enterprises Fund

ALPHA CAPITAL PARTNERS

300 W. Monument Avenue
Suite 102
Dayton, OH 45402

Telephone: 513-222-2006

Other Office Locations
Three First National Plaza, Suite 1400
Chicago, IL 60602

Mission: not available

Fund Size: $35 million
Founded: 1984
Average Investment: $1.5 - $2.5 million
Minimum Investment: $500,000

Investment Criteria: First-stage to Leveraged Buyout

Geographic Preference: Midwestern United States

Industry Group Preference: Diversified

Portfolio Companies: Red Arrow Products, Sutton Tool, CarCare Enterprises, Valley Industries, Somatogen, Entek Scientific Corporation, Glenmark Shockley Communications, NorthWord Press, Merge Technology, Granitech, Cirrus Diagnostics, Sizzling Partners, Vista Restaurants, Pet Care Plus, Inc.

Officers, Executives and Principals

Andrew H. Kalnow, President
Education: BA, Lawrence University; MBA, Babson College

Orval Cook, Senior Vice President
Education: BME, Cornell; MBA, Harvard
Background: RFE Partners, Michigan Capital and Service

William J. Oberholtzer, Vice President
Education: BA, Kalamazoo College; MBA, University of Chicago

ALPHA PARTNERS

545 Middlefield Road
Suite 170
Menlo Park, CA 94025

Telephone: 415-617-9500
Fax: 415-617-9510

Mission: Reducing investment activity

Fund Size: not available
Founded: 1982
Average Investment: not available
Minimum Investment: Less than $100,000

Investment Criteria: Seed, Start-up

Industry Group Preference: Communications, Computer Related, Electronic Components and Instrumentation, Genetic Engineering, Medical/Health Related

Portfolio Companies: not available

Officers, Executives and Principals

Wallace F. Davis, General Partner
Paul C. Ely, Jr., General Partner
Glenn E. Penisten, General Partner
Samuel Urcis, General Partner

ALPINE TECHNOLOGY VENTURES

20300 Stevens Creek Boulevard
Suite 495
Cupertino, CA 95014

Telephone: 408-725-1810
Fax: 408-725-1207
E-mail: cath@alpineventures.com

Mission: Actively seeking new investments

Fund Size: $72 million
Founded: 1995
Average Investment: $1 - $2 million
Minimum Investment: $500,000

Investment Criteria: Seed, Startup, First-stage, Second-stage

Geographic Preference: California, preferably Silicon Valley-based

Industry Group Preference: Communications, Hardware, High Technology, Networks, Semiconductors, Software

Portfolio Companies: not available

Officers, Executives and Principals

Chuck K. Chan, General Partner
David Lane, General Partner

ALTAIR VENTURES, INC.

7550 France Avenue South
Minneapolis, MN 55435

Telephone: 612-896-1127
Fax: 612-896-4909

Mission: Actively seeking new investments

Fund Size: not available
Founded: 1984
Average Investment: not available
Minimum Investment: $250,000

Investment Criteria: Leveraged Buyout

Industry Group Preference: not available

Portfolio Companies: not available

Officers, Executives and Principals

Philip L. Hendershott, Chairman

AMERICAN ACQUISITION PARTNERS

175 South Street
Morristown, NJ 07960

Telephone: 201-267-7800
Fax: 201-267-7695

Mission: not available

Fund Size: not available
Founded: 1987
Average Investment: not available
Minimum Investment: $1 million

Investment Criteria: Leveraged Buyout, Management Buyout

Industry Group Preference: Chemicals, Communications, Consumer, Distribution, Electronic Components and Instrumentation, Industrial Products and Equipment, Manufacturing, Medical/Health Related

Portfolio Companies: not available

Officers, Executives and Principals

Ted Bustany, Managing Partner
Education: MBA, PhD, Chemical Engineering

Colin J. Draper, Managing Partner

AMERICAN COMMUNICATION

P.O. Box 9178
Greenville, SC 29604

Telephone: 803-421-0015
Fax: 803-370-0025

Mission: Actively seeking new investments

Fund Size: not available
Founded: 1988
Average Investment: not available
Minimum Investment: $100,000

Investment Criteria: Seed, Research and Development, Startup, First-stage, Second-stage, Mezzanine, Leveraged Buyout, Special Situations

Industry Group Preference: Communications, Computer Related, Consumer, Distribution, Electronic Components and Instrumentation, Energy/Natural Resources, Genetic Engineering, Industrial Products and Equipment, Medical/Health Related

Portfolio Companies: not available

Officers, Executives and Principals

Alan Burdick, President
Don Cozart, Vice President

AMERICAN RESEARCH AND DEVELOPMENT

45 Milk Street
Boston, MA 02109-5173

Telephone: 617-423-7500
Fax: 617-423-9655

Mission: not available

Fund Size: $90 million
Founded: not available
Average Investment: $500,000
Minimum Investment: not available

Investment Criteria: Seed to Second Stage

Industry Group Preference: Communications, Computer Related, Electronics, Energy/Natural Resources, High Technology, Industrial Products, Medical/Health

Portfolio Companies: Adra Systems, Advanced Technology Materials, American Superconductor, Anchor Systems Group, Aquidneck Power Limited Partnership, Cadre Technologies, Ceramics Process Systems, CERJAC, Earth's Best, Eidetic, Envoy Systems, Faradaics, Logos, North Atlantic Venture Fund, Raycom Systems

Officers, Executives and Principals

Francis J. Huges, Jr., General Partner
Education: SB/MS, Electrical Engineering, MIT; MBA, Harvard
Background: Boston Consulting Group; Designer of weather satellite control systems, RCA's Astro-Electronics Division

Harold L. Finelt, General Partner
Education: BS, Mechanical Engineering, Tufts; MBA, Finance, Babson College
Background: Robot and machine vision systems, Automatrix, Avco Systems, Irex Medical Instruments

Paul L. Rosenbaum, General Partner
Education: BSEE, Cornell; MBA, Harvard Business
Background: President and Chief Executive Officer, Xyplex; President and Chief Executive Officer, Proteon; President, Scitex America; Vice President International Operations, Codex Corporation

AMERICAN STRATEGIC INVESTMENTS, L.P.

P.O. Box 81891
Chicago, IL 60681

Telephone:
Fax:

Other Office Locations
233 East Wacker Drive, Suite 2411
Chicago, IL 60601
Phone 312-819-0524, Fax 312-540-9653

Mission: Actively seeking new investments

Fund Size: not available
Founded: 1976
Average Investment: not available
Minimum Investment: $100,000

Investment Criteria: Second-stage, Mezzanine, Leveraged Buyout, Special Situations, Control-block Purchases, Management Buyouts, Privatizations

Industry Group Preference: Communications, Computer Related, Consumer, Energy/Natural Resources, Industrial Products and Equipment, Medical/Health Related

Portfolio Companies: not available

Officers, Executives and Principals

Dennis McCarthy, Managing Director (Beverly Hills)
John Taylor, Managing Director (Beverly Hills)
Randolph C. Read, President (Beverly Hills and Chicago)
Steven Fox, Vice President (Beverly Hills)
Brian McCarthy, Vice President (Chicago)
Timothy Smith, Associate (Chicago)

AMERIMARK CAPITAL GROUP

1111 West Mockingbird
Suite 1111
Dallas, TX 75247

Telephone: 214-638-7878
Fax: 214-638-7612

Mission: Actively seeking new investments

Fund Size: not available
Founded: 1989
Average Investment: not available
Minimum Investment: $500,000

Investment Criteria: Second-stage, Mezzanine, Leveraged Buyout

Industry Group Preference: Communications, Consumer, Distribution, Industrial Products and Equipment

Portfolio Companies: not available

Officers, Executives and Principals

Charles R. Martin, Principal
Nicholas A. Wolpert

AMERITECH DEVELOPMENT CORPORATION

30 South Wacker Drive
37th Floor
Chicago, IL 60606

Telephone: 312-750-5083
Fax: 312-609-0244

Mission: not available

Fund Size: not available
Founded: 1983
Average Investment: not available
Minimum Investment: $500,000

Investment Criteria: Startup, First-stage, Second-stage

Industry Group Preference: Applications Software, Communications, Multi-media

Portfolio Companies: not available

Officers, Executives and Principals

Charles E. Ross, Director
Greg Smitherman, Director
Darrell Williams, Director

AMT VENTURE PARTNERS, LTD.

8204 Elmbrook
Suite 101
Dallas, TX 75247

Telephone: 214-905-9757
Fax: 214-905-9761

Other Office Locations
10929 Wickshire Way
North Bethesda, MD 20852
Phone 301-468-4838, Fax 301-468-6256

Mission: Actively seeking new investments

Fund Size: $18 million
Founded: 1989
Average Investment: not available
Minimum Investment: $500,000

Investment Criteria: First-stage, Second-stage

Industry Group Preference: Energy/Natural Resources, High Technology, Industrial Products and Equipment, Manufacturing/Processing

Portfolio Companies: Advanced Chemical Systems, AMT Capital, Automated Dynamics Corporation, Burnswick Technologies, Inc., Buehner Corporation, Infometrix, Inc., Katrina, Inc., Minco, Nanophase Technologies, Oxford Molecular Ltd., Quest Technology, Surface Technology Inc., Toranga Technologies, TPL, Ultra Optec

Officers, Executives and Principals

Peter N. Walmsley, General Partner (North Bethesda)
Education: PhD, Chemical Engineering, Manchester University, England
Background: Various positions at Dupont

Tom H. Delimitros, General Partner
Education: BS/MS, Ceramic Engineering, University of Washington; MBA, Harvard
Background: Chief Executive Officer, Magna Corporation; President, Perolin, Inc.
Directorships: EnClean Inc., Plains Resources, Inc.

Walter Cunningham, Partner
Stuart Schube, Partner

ANDERSON AND WELLS DBA SUNDANCE VENTURE PARTNERS, L.P.

One Arizona Center
Suite 750
Phoenix, AZ 85004

Telephone: 602-252-1450
Fax: 602-252-1450

Other Office Locations
10600 North De Anza Boulevard, Suite 215
Cupertino, CA 95014
Phone 408-257-8100, Fax 408-257-8111

Mission: Making few, if any, investments

Fund Size: not available
Founded: 1989
Average Investment: not available
Minimum Investment: $250,000

Investment Criteria: Second-stage, Mezzanine, Leveraged Buyout, Special Situations

Industry Group Preference: not available

Portfolio Companies: not available

Officers, Executives and Principals

Larry Wells, General Partner and Chairman (Cupertino)
Gregory S. Anderson, General Partner and President (Phoenix)
Brian N. Burns, General Partner and Vice President (Phoenix)

ANTARES CAPITAL CORPORATION

P.O. Box 410730
Melbourne, FL 32941-0730

Telephone: 407-777-4884
Fax: 407-444-5884

Mission: Actively seeking new investments

Fund Size: not available
Founded: 1993
Average Investment: $1 million
Minimum Investment: $250,000

Investment Criteria: First-stage, Second-stage, Mezzanine, Management Buyout

Geographic Preference: Southeastern United States and Texas

Industry Group Preference: Communications, Computer Related, Consumer, Electronic Components and
   Instrumentation, Industrial Products and Equipment, Information Services, Internet Content and Applications,
   Medical/Health Related, Retail, Software, Telecommunications

Portfolio Companies: not available

Officers, Executives and Principals

Randall E. Poliner
Education: BS, Electrical Engineering, Georgia Tech; MS, Electrical Engineering, Carnegie-Mellon; MBA,
   Harvard

ANTHEM CAPITAL, L.P.

16 Calvert Street
Baltimore, MD 21202

Telephone: 410-625-1510
Fax: 410-828-6084

Mission: Actively seeking new investments

Fund Size: not available
Founded: 1983
Average Investment: not available
Minimum Investment: $250,000

Investment Criteria: Startup, First-stage, Second-stage, Leveraged Buyout

Industry Group Preference: Communications, Computer Related, Distribution, Electronic Components and Instrumentation, Energy/Natural Resources, Industrial Products and Equipment

Portfolio Companies: not available

Officers, Executives and Principals

John C. Weiss III, Managing General Partner
William M. Gust, Managing General Partner
C. Edward Spiva, Chief Financial Officer

APEX INVESTMENT PARTNERS

233 South Wacker Drive
Suite 9500
Chicago, IL 60606

Telephone: 312-258-0320
Fax: 312-258-0592
E-mail: apex@apexvc.com

Mission: not available

Fund Size: $120 million
Founded: 1987
Average Investment: $500,000
Minimum Investment: not available

Investment Criteria: Startup to Leveraged Buyout

Geographic Preference: United States

Industry Group Preference: Consumer Products, Environmental/Industrial Productivity, Information Technology, Software, Specialty Retail, Telecommunications

Portfolio Companies: not available

Officers, Executives and Principals

James A. Johnson, Managing Partner
Education: MBA, Northwestern University
Background: Chief Financial Officer, Beatrice Foods

George Middlemans, Partner
Education: BA, Political Science/History, Pennsylvania State University; MA, Political Science, University of Pittsburg; MBA, Harvard; CPA
Background: Vice President, Citicorp Venture Capital

Frederick W. W. Bolander, Partner
Education: BA, MS, Electrical Engineering, University of Michigan; MBA, Harvard
Background: Marketing Manager, AT&T

ARCH VENTURE PARTNERS

20 North Wacker Drive, Suite 1849
Chicago, IL 60606

Telephone: 312-704-5830
Fax: 312-704-6841

Other Office Locations
9700 South Cass Ave., Building #200
Argonne, IL 60439
Phone 708-252-5962, Fax 708-252-2876

Mission: not available

Fund Size: $40 million
Founded: not available
Average Investment: $500,000 - $1 million
Minimum Investment: not available

Industry Group Preference: Biotechnology, High Technology, Industrial Products, Medical/Health, Publishing, Software

Portfolio Companies: Illinois Superconductor Corporation, NiOptics, Qmax, Eichrom Industries, Nanophase Technologies, Inc., Everyday Learning Corporation, Gen Vec, Aviron, AndreBio

Officers, Executives and Principals

Keith L. Crandell, Managing Director
Education: BS, Chemistry and Math, St. Lawrence University; MS, Chemistry, University of Texas, Arlington; MBA, University of Chicago
Background: President, Eichrom Industries; Marketing, Hercules, Inc.
Directorships: Eichrom Industries, Qmax and Engineering Animation

Robert T. Nelsen, Managing Director
Education: BS, Biology and Economics; MBA, University of Chicago
Directorships: Everday Learning Corporation, AndroBio Corporation, and Optein, Inc.

Steven Lazarus, Managing Director
Education: BA, honors, Dartmouth College; MBA, high distinction, Harvard; Baker Scholar
Background: Associate Dean, University of Chicago's Graduate School of Business; Senior Vice President, Baxter International; DeputyAssistant Secretary of Commerce, U.S. Government
Directorships: Amgen Corporation, Thousand Oaks, California; Primark Corporation, McLean, Virginia; Highland Park Hospital, Northwestern University, Chicago

ARETE VENTURES

6110 Executive Boulevard, Suite 1040
Rockville, MD 20852

Telephone: 301-881-2555
Fax: 301-770-2877

Mission: not available

Fund Size: $95 million
Founded: 1985
Average Investment: $1 million
Minimum Investment: $250,000

Investment Criteria: Startup to Leveraged Buyout

Industry Group Preference: Communications, Computer Related, Electric and Gas Utility Related, Electronics, Energy/Natural Resources, Industrial Products

Portfolio Companies: not available

Officers, Executives and Principals

Robert W. Shaw, President
Education: BS, BEP, Cornell University; PhD, Applied Physics, Stanford University; MPA, American University
Background: Senior Vice President, Booz, Allen and Hamilton, Bell Laboratories, Cavendish Laboratories (U.K.)
Directorships: Chairman, Evergreen Solar Corporation; Chairman, Superconductivity, Inc. Nanophase Technologies Corporation

George W. Levert, Vice President
Education: BSEE, Louisiana Tech; MSIM, Georgia Tech
Background: Oglethorpe Power Corporation; Consultant, Arthur Anderson and Co.; Officer,Civil Engineer Corps, U.S. Navy
Directorships: Metricom, Inc., Methane Treatment Technologies, Inc., Basic Measuring Instruments, Wave Air Corporation, Todd Combustion Inc.

Jake D. Tarr, Jr., Vice President
Education: BA, Roanoke College; MBA, Harvard Business School
Background: Goldman, Sachs and Co., Bank of New York
Directorships: Mycotech, Inc.

William T. Heflin, Vice President
Education: MS, BS, Mechanical Engineering, University of Illinois; MSM, MIT, Sloan School of Management
Background: Research Investment Advisors, Marcam Corporation, IBM

Todd D. Klein, Associate
Education: BBA, University of Texas; MBA, Harvard Business
Background: Vice President, Chemical Banking Corporation, Barr, Beatty, Devlin and Co., Salomon Brothers

THE ARGENTUM GROUP

The Chrysler Building
405 Lexington Avenue
New York, NY 10174

Telephone: 212-949-6262
Fax: 212-949-8294
E-mail: walterbar@argentumgroup.com

Mission: Actively seeking new investments

Fund Size: $20 million
Founded: 1988
Average Investment: $4 million
Minimum Investment: $1 million

Investment Criteria: Second-stage, Mezzanine, Leveraged Buyout, Special Situations

Geographic Preference: United States

Industry Group Preference: Business-to-Business, Environmental, Healthcare, Information Services, Infrastructure, Software, Specialty Chemicals and Materials, Specialty Distribution, Technology, Telecommunications

Portfolio Companies: Community Corrections Corporation, Eastern Environmental Services, Inc., Tri-Tek Information Systems, Inc. VPNet, Inc., Dynamic Healthcare Technologies, Inc., NuCo2, Inc., Omnipoint Corporation

Officers, Executives and Principals

Walter H. Barandiaran, Managing Director
Daniel Raynor, Managing Director
Benjamin Fishman, Vice President
Leslee Cowen, Associate
Jennifer Duong, Analyst

ARK CAPITAL MANAGEMENT

150 North Wacker Drive, Suite 2650
Chicago, IL 60606-1609

Telephone: 312-541-0330
Fax: 312-541-0335

Mission: Ark is a private equity investment advisor focusing on investment opportunities in middle market companies seeking growth capital ranging from $1 million to $3.5 million. In addition, Ark emphasizes investments in minority-owned businesses fitting its investment criteria.

Fund Size: $24 million
Founded: 1991
Average Investment: not available
Minimum Investment: $1 million

Investment Criteria: Later-stage, Growth, Growth Acquisition

Geographic Preference: United States

Industry Group Preference: Food Services, High Technology,Industrial, Manufacturing, Medical/Health

Portfolio Companies: not available

Officers, Executives and Principals

Michael Y. Granger, Principal
Education: MBA, Amos Tuck School, Dartmouth
Background: Investment Manager, Xerox Venture Capital; Principal, CIGNA Venture Capital

Xcylur R. Stoakley, Principal
Education: MBA, BSEE
Background: Manager of Venture Capital Investments, Ameritech Corporation

ARTESIAN CAPITAL

1700 Foshay Tower
821 Marquette Avenue South
Minneapolis, MN 55402

Telephone: 612-334-5600
Fax: 612-334-5601
E-mail: artesian@aol.com

Mission: Actively seeking new investments

Fund Size: $2.5 million
Founded: 1989
Average Investment: $200,000
Minimum Investment: Less than $100,000

Investment Criteria: Seed, Research and Development, Startup

Geographic Preference: Upper Midwestern United States

Industry Group Preference: Communications, Environmental Services, Genetic Engineering, Industrial Products and Equipment, Medical/Health Related

Portfolio Companies: Satellite Network Systems, Recyclights, Inc., Integ, Inc.

Officers, Executives and Principals

Frank B. Bennett, President
Education: BS, University of Oregon
Background: Vice President Corporate Finance, Piper, Jaffray and Hopwood; Vice President, Mayfield Corporation

ARTHUR P. GOULD AND COMPANY

One Wilshire Drive
Lake Success, NY 11020

Telephone: 516-773-3000
Fax: 516-773-3289

Mission: Actively seeking new investments

Fund Size: not available
Founded: 1968
Average Investment: not available
Minimum Investment: No minimum

Investment Criteria: Seed, Research and Development, Startup, First-stage, Second-stage, Mezzanine, Leveraged Buyout

Industry Group Preference: Communications, Computer Related, Consumer, Distribution, Electronic Components and Instrumentation, Energy/Natural Resources, Genetic Engineering, Industrial Products and Equipment, Medical/Health Related

Portfolio Companies: not available

Officers, Executives and Principals

Arthur P. Gould, President
Andrew G. Gould, Vice President
Julia Cooper, Treasurer

ASIA PACIFIC FUNDING GROUP INTERNATIONAL

49 West 12th Street
Executive Suite 3-D
New York, NY 10011

Telephone: 212-691-9895

Mission: Actively seeking new investments

Fund Size: not available
Founded: 1986
Average Investment: not available
Minimum Investment: not available

Investment Criteria: Seed, Start-up, First-stage, Second-stage, Mezzanine, Leveraged Buyout, Special Situations, Joint Ventures, Licensing, Mergers and Acquisitions

Geographic Preference: Asia and Pacific Rim including Australia, China, Japan, South Korea, Malaysia, Myanmar, India, Indonesia, Pakistan, Philippines, Laos, Thailand, Singapore, Taiwan, Sri Lanka, Vietnam

Industry Group Preference: Communications, Computer Related, Consumer, Food, Distribution, Electronics and Instrumentation, Energy/Natural Resources, Entertainment, Industrial Products and Equipment, Medical Health Related, Minerals and Mining, Oil and Gas, Real Estate, Recreation, Recycling

Portfolio Companies: Asia/Pacific Resources, Asia/Pacific Realty Group

Officers, Executives and Principals

Allan E. Skora, President, Managing General Partner
Kolay Tun, Senior Partner, Asia Pacific Region

ASPEN VENTURE PARTNERS, L.P.

3343 Peachtree Road, N.E.
East Tower, Suite 1140
Atlanta, GA 30326

Telephone: 404-399-1660
Fax: 404-399-1664

Mission: Actively seeking new investments

Fund Size: not available
Founded: 1984
Average Investment: not available
Minimum Investment: $3 million

Investment Criteria: Leveraged Buyout

Industry Group Preference: Distribution, Industrial Products and Equipment, Medical/Health Related

Portfolio Companies: not available

Officers, Executives and Principals

Richard L. Cravey, Managing Director
William S. Green, Managing Director
Edwin A. Wahlen, Jr., Managing Director
William A. Davis, Managing Director
Garrison M. Kitchen, Managing Director
Bart A. McLean, Managing Director

ASSET MANAGEMENT ASSOCIATES, INC.

2275 East Bayshore Road, Suite 150
Palo Alto, CA 94303

Telephone: 415-494-7400
Fax: 415-856-1826
E-mail: postmaster@assetman.com

Mission: To provide venture capital to seed and early-stage companies developing technology from the information, biological or physical sciences

Fund Size: $250.4 million
Founded: 1965
Average Investment: $3 million
Minimum Investment: $1 million

Investment Criteria: Seed to First Stage

Geographic Preference: West Coast of the United States, New England

Industry Group Preference: Biotechnology, Communications, Computer Related, Electronics, Industrial Products, Medical/Health

Portfolio Companies: Amgen, Tandem Computers, Remedy Corporation, Pharmacyclics

Officers, Executives and Principals

Craig C. Taylor, General Partner
Franklin P. Johnson, General Partner
John F. Shoch, General Partner
W. Ferrell Sanders, General Partner
Douglas E. Kelly, M.D., General Partner
Tony D. Bona, Chief Financial Officer

AT&T VENTURES

11 Eagle Rock Avenue
Suite 130
East Hanover, NJ 07936

Telephone: 973-221-3893
Fax: 973-428-8213

Other Office Locations
3000 Sand Hill Road
Building Four, Suite 235
Menlo Park, CA 94025
Phone 415-233-0617, Fax 415-854-4923

Mission: Actively seeking new investments

Fund Size: not available
Founded: 1991
Average Investment: not available
Minimum Investment: $500,000

Investment Criteria: Seed, Startup, First-stage, Second-stage, Mezzanine

Industry Group Preference: Communications, Computer Related, Consumer, Distribution, Electronic Components and Instrumentation, Medical/Health Related

Portfolio Companies: not available

Officers, Executives and Principals

R. Bradford Burnham, Director (East Hanover)
William H. Elliott, Managing General Partner (East Hanover)
Neal M. Douglas, General Partner (Menlo Park)
Dominick B. Turiano, Chief Financial Officer (East Hanover)

ATLANTIC CAPITAL

164 Cushing Highway
Cohasset, MA 02025

Telephone: 617-383-9449
Fax: 617-383-6040

Mission: Actively seeking new investments

Fund Size: not available
Founded: 1986
Average Investment: not available
Minimum Investment: Less than $100,000

Investment Criteria: Startup, First-stage

Industry Group Preference: Communications, Computer Related, Consumer, Distribution, Electronic Components and Instrumentation, Medical/Health Related

Portfolio Companies: Creative Finials and Lamp Parts

Officers, Executives and Principals

Fraser J. Cameron, President
Education: Boston University School of Management
Background: Stock Broker, E.F. Hutton, Merrill Lynch, Atlantic Capital

ATLANTIC COASTAL VENTURES, L.P.

1001 Connecticut Avenue, Northwest
Suite 622
Washington, DC 20036-2506

Telephone: 202-293-1166
Fax: 202-293-1181

Other Office Locations
1200 High Ridge Road, 2nd Floor
Stamford, CT 06905-1202
Phone 203-968-9753, Fax 203-968-8133

Mission: Actively seeking new investments

Fund Size: not available
Founded: 1984
Average Investment: $500,000 - $1 million
Minimum Investment: $500,000

Investment Criteria: Mezzanine, Leveraged Buyout, Special Situations

Industry Group Preference: Communications, Computer Related, Distribution

Portfolio Companies: not available

Officers, Executives and Principals

Walter L. Threadgill, General Partner
Don Greene, General Partner

ATLANTIC MEDICAL CAPITAL, L.P.

126 West 56th Street
Suite 1605
New York, NY 10019

Telephone: 212-878-1400

Other Office Locations
26, Dawson Place
London W2 4TJ
England
Phone: 171-776-1500

Mission: Actively seeking new investments

Fund Size: $77 million
Founded: 1993
Average Investment: not available
Minimum Investment: $3 million

Investment Criteria: Second-stage, Leveraged Buyout, Special Situations, Control-block Purchases

Geographic Preference: United States, United Kingdom, Europe

Industry Group Preference: Medical/Health Related

Portfolio Companies: not available

Officers, Executives and Principals

Dr. Michael J. Sinclair, Partner (London)
H. Tomkins O'Connor, Partner
J. Andrew Cowherd, Partner

AUSTIN VENTURES

114 W. 7th Street
Suite 1300
Austin, TX 78701

Telephone: 512-479-0055
Fax: 512-476-3952
E-mail: moreinfo@ausven.com

Mission: To work in partnership with talented entrepreneurs to help build some of America's successful growth companies

Fund Size: $273 million
Founded: 1979
Average Investment: $1 - $7 million
Minimum Investment: $1 million

Investment Criteria: All stages

Geographic Preference: Texas and Southwest United States

Industry Group Preference: Computer, Data Communications, Environmental, Healthcare, Semiconductors, Software, Specialty Retail, Telecommunications

Portfolio Companies: Benchmarq, Tivoli, VTEL, SynOptics, TechWorks, DAZEL, CompUSA, IntelliQuest, The Q, Petstuff, Matrix, CareLine, Classic Cable, PCSD, DialPage, Monitronics

Officers, Executives and Principals

Joseph C. Aragona, General Partner
Education: BA, cum laude, Harvard; MBA, Harvard Business School
Background: Merchant Banking Division, Bank of Boston; Corporate Lending Officer, Chemical Bank
Directorships: Technology Works, Pervasive Software, AnswerSoft, Human Code, Deja News, Reliant Data Systems

Kenneth P. DeAngelis, General Partner
Education: BA, cum laude, Harvard; MBA, Wharton School of Finance at University of Pennsylvania
Background: Merchant Banking Division Vice President, Bank of Boston
Directorships: Sports and Fitness Clubs, Lil' Things, Torch Health, Dominion Automotive

Jeffery C. Garvey, General Partner
Education: BA, honors, St. Lawrence University
Background: Senior Vice President, National and Specialized Lending Division, Provident National Bank; Lending Positions, Pittsburgh National Bank
Directorships: Celpage, PCS Development, Outdoor East, Kirtland Capital Partners, Classic Communications

John D. Thornton, General Partner
Education: BA, summa cum laude, Trinity University; MBA, Stanford Graduate School of Business
Background: McKinsey and Company
Directorships: Wireless Telecom, Metasolv, DAZEL, GardenEscape, Vignette

Blaine F. Wesner, General Partner
Education: BA, highest honors, University of Oklahoma; MBA, Harvard Business School
Background: Goldman Sachs and Company; Co-founder, Wesner Publications
Directorships: ClassiFACTS, Monitronics, Huxtable's, Summit Global

William P. Wood, Special Limited Partner
Education: BA, magna cum laude, Phi Beta Kappa, Brown University; MBA, Harvard Business School
Background: McKinsey and Co.; Marketing Manager, Procter and Gamble
Directorships: Rodeer, SMART Technologies, Matrix Service, IntelliQuest

AVERY BUSINESS DEVELOPMENT SERVICES

2506 St. Michel Court
Ponte Vedra, FL 32082

Telephone: 904-285-6033

Mission: Actively seeking new investments

Fund Size: not available
Founded: 1981
Average Investment: not available
Minimum Investment: $100,000

Investment Criteria: Seed, Research and Development, Startup, First-stage, Leveraged Buyout, Special Situations

Industry Group Preference: Communications, Computer Related, Consumer, Distribution, Energy/Natural Resources, Genetic Engineering, Industrial Products and Equipment, Medical/Health Related

Portfolio Companies: not available

Officers, Executives and Principals

Henry Avery, President
Education: SB, MIT
Directorships: Former Director, Macrochem Corporation

AXA CAPITAL CORPORATION

14 Wall Street
26th Floor
New York, NY 10005

Telephone: 212-421-7870
Fax: 212-410-4489

Mission: Actively seeking new investments

Fund Size: not available
Founded: 1992
Average Investment: not available
Minimum Investment: $100,000

Investment Criteria: Seed, Startup

Industry Group Preference: Communications, Computer Related, Genetic Engineering, Industrial Products and Equipment, Medical/Health Related

Portfolio Companies: not available

Officers, Executives and Principals

Ludmil Pandef, President

AZCA, INC.

100 Marine Parkway
Suite 305
Redwood City, CA 94065

Telephone: 415-598-9900
Fax: 415-598-9554

Other Office Locations
Kasumigaseki Bldg. 35F
3-2-5 Kasumigaseki
Chiyoda-ku, Tokyo 100
Japan
Phone 81-3-5512-7776, Fax 81-3-5512-7778

Mission: AZCA is a professional firm providing management consulting and merchant banking services to emerging high technology companies. The firm also evaluates and analyzes venture projects and arranges private placements.

Fund Size: not available
Founded: 1985
Average Investment: not available
Minimum Investment: not available

Investment Criteria: First-stage, Second-stage, Mezzanine

Industry Group Preference: Biotechnology, Electronic Components and Instrumentation, Energy/Natural Resources, Environmental, Information Technology, Life Science, Telecommunications

Portfolio Companies: not available

Officers, Executives and Principals

Masazumi Ishii, Managing Director
Shohei Kaneko, Principal
Tadashi Tanimoto, Engagement Manager

BACCHARIS CAPITAL, INC.

2420 Sand Hill Road
Suite 100
Menlo Park, CA 94025

Telephone: 415-342-8146
Fax: 415-854-3025

Mission: Actively seeking new investments

Fund Size: not available
Founded: 1990
Average Investment: not available
Minimum Investment: $500,000

Investment Criteria: Startup, First-stage, Second-stage, Mezzanine, Leveraged Buyout, Special Situations, Control-block Purchases, Recapitalizations, Turnarounds

Industry Group Preference: Communications, Consumer, Distribution, Energy/Natural Resources, Industrial Products and Equipment

Portfolio Companies: not available

Officers, Executives and Principals

Stephen P. Monticelli, Managing Director
Mary Bechmann, Managing Director

BACHOW AND ASSOCIATES, INC.

Three Bala Plaza East
Suite 502
Bala Cynwyd, PA 19004

Telephone: 610-660-4900
Fax: 610-660-4930
E-mail: info@bachow.com

Mission: Actively seeking new investments

Fund Size: not available
Founded: 1985
Average Investment: $8 - $12 million
Minimum Investment: $5 million

Investment Criteria: Second-stage, Leveraged Buyout, Special Situations, Control-block Purchases

Geographic Preference: United States - Northeast, Southeast, East Coast, Midwest, Gulf States, Middle Atlantic

Industry Group Preference: Communications, Computer Related, Electronic Components and Instrumentation, Energy/Natural Resources, Genetic Engineering, Industrial Products and Equipment

Portfolio Companies: Acme Paging, Anadigics, Bachtel Cellular, CARE Systems Incorporated, Coastal Communications, Cottonwood Communications, Discovery Schools, Genus, Innova, Paradigm Geophysical, Ltd., Tennessee Partners, L.P., Vista

Officers, Executives and Principals

Paul S. Bachow, Senior Managing Director
Steve Fisher, Managing Director
Frank H. Novaczek, Managing Director
Salvatore A. Grasso, Managing Director
Brian Flynn, Managing Director
Jay Seid, In-house Council
Samuel Schwartz, Vice President
Noah Walley, Vice President

BAILEY AND COMPANY, INC.

594 Spadina Avenue
Toronto, Ontario M5S 2H4
Canada

Telephone: 416-921-6930
Fax: 416-925-4670

Mission: Actively seeking new investments

Fund Size: not available
Founded: 1987
Average Investment: not available
Minimum Investment: $100,000

Investment Criteria: Research and Development, First-stage, Mezzanine, Special Situations, Mergers and Acquisitions

Industry Group Preference: Communications, Electronic Components and Instrumentation, Genetic Engineering, Industrial Products and Equipment, Medical/Health Related

Portfolio Companies: not available

Officers, Executives and Principals

W. Bruce C. Bailey, Senior Vice President

BAIRD CAPITAL PARTNERS

777 East Wisconsin Avenue
Milwaukee, WI 53202

Telephone: 414-765-3500
Fax: 414-298-7490

Other Office Locations
227 West Monroe Street
Suite 2100
Chicago, IL 60606
Phone 312-609-4701, Fax 312-609-4707

Mission: Actively seeking new investments

Fund Size: $75 million
Founded: 1991
Average Investment: $3 - $6 million
Minimum Investment: $2 million

Investment Criteria: Later-stage Growth Equity, Leveraged Buyouts

Geographic Preference: Midwestern United States and Florida

Industry Group Preference: Diversified

Portfolio Companies: not available

Officers, Executives and Principals

Sam Guren
David P. Pelisek
Shanti Mittra

BANC ONE CAPITAL PARTNERS CORPORATION

150 East Gay Street
24th Floor
Columbus, OH 43215

Telephone: 614-217-5100
Fax: 614-224-7675

Other Office Locations
300 Crescent Ct., Suite 1600
Dallas, TX 75201

Mission: not available

Fund Size: $160 million
Founded: 1976
Average Investment: $4 million
Minimum Investment: not available

Investment Criteria: Second Stage to Leveraged Buyout

Industry Group Preference: Communications, Educational, Industrial Products, Manufacturing/Processing, Medical/Health, Service Industries, Transportation

Portfolio Companies: not available

Officers, Executives and Principals

James H. Wolfe, Senior Vice President
Will K. Bixby, Senior Vice President
William P. Leahy, Managing Director
Suzanne B. Kriscunas, Managing Director

BANC ONE VENTURE CORPORATION

111 East Wisconsin Avenue
Milwaukee, WI 53202

Telephone: 414-765-2274

Mission: Actively seeking new investments/acquisitions.

Fund Size: not available
Founded: 1983
Average Investment: $2.5 million
Minimum Investment: $1 million, $10 million maximum

Investment Criteria: Later-stage, Leveraged Buyout, Management Buyout, Recapitalizations, Industry Consolidation

Geographic Preference: United States

Industry Group Preference: Consumer, Distribution, Education Related, Food/Beverage Manufacturing, Industrial Products and Equipment, Mail-Order Retailing, Metal Fabrication, Plastics Manufacturing, Polyethylene Bags/Film, Process Control Devices, Publishing, Railway Equipment, Waste Management Equipment

Portfolio Companies: not available

Officers, Executives and Principals

H. Wayne Foreman, President
Robert L. Cook, Jr., Vice President
Daniel J. Jagla, Vice President
Steven D. Peterson, Investment Officer
Ellie Berg, Marketing Officer

BANCBOSTON CAPITAL / BANCBOSTON VENTURES

100 Federal Street
Boston, MA 02110

Telephone: 617-434-2509
Fax: 617-434-1153

Other Office Locations
39, Victoria Street
London W1H 0ED
England
Phone 171-499-3333, Fax 171-222-5649

Jardine House
1, Connaught Place - Suite 801
Hong Kong
Phone 2-526-4361, Fax 2-845-9222

Mission: $200 million invested in 1995

Fund Size: $750 million
Founded: 1950
Average Investment: $3 - $7 million
Minimum Investment: $1 million

Investment Criteria: First stage to Leveraged Buyout

Industry Group Preference: Biotechnology, Computer Related, Consumer Related, High Technology, Media and Communications Technology, Medical/Health, Service Companies, Software

Portfolio Companies: Arcturus Pharmaceutical Corporation, Community Distributors, Ecoscience, Education Systems, Fitech, The Icing, IDEXX, Imaginarium, KB Alloys, Mathsoft, Mutual Risk Management, Novalis, Pacific Linen, Paul Capital Partners, Radio One, Roll Systems, Sedona, Serologicals, SunDisk

Officers, Executives and Principals

Craig Deery, Managing Director
Directorships: United TransNet, Jordans

Marcia T. Bates, Managing Director
Directorships: Serologicals

Peter Roberts, Director

BANCORP HAWAII, SBIC

130 Merchant Street
P.O. Box 2900
Honolulu, HI 96846

Telephone: 808-537-8286
Fax: 808-521-7602

Mission: To improve the profitability of its parent, Bancorp Hawaii, Inc., by generating substantial long-term capital appreciation through investments in emerging growth companies, leveraged acquisitions and other opportunities that demonstrate high growth potential. These objectives are pursued in a manner consistent with its parent's corporate mission

Fund Size: $2 million
Founded: 1984
Average Investment: $350,000
Minimum Investment: not available

Investment Criteria: Second-stage to Leveraged Buyout

Geographic Preference: Hawaii

Industry Group Preference: Diversified

Portfolio Companies: not available

Officers, Executives and Principals

Robert W. Paris, Chairman/President
Michael S. F. Chun, Vice President/Manager

BANEXI CORPORATION

3000 Sand Hill Road
Building Two, Suite 205
Menlo Park, CA 94025

Telephone: 415-854-3010
Fax: 415-854-3015
E-mail: EricVenture@msn.com

Other Office Locations
12, rue Chauchat
75009 Paris
France
Phone 33-1-4014-6413, Fax 33-1-4014-9119

Mission: Actively seeking new investments. Help build companies that develop a long-term sustainable competitive advantage and dominate their market segments on a global basis

Fund Size: $750 million, $150 million under management
Founded: 1972
Average Investment: $1.5 million
Minimum Investment: $250,000

Investment Criteria: First-stage, Second-stage, Mezzanine, Leveraged Buyout

Geographic Preference: United States, Europe

Industry Group Preference: Communications, Computer Related, Consumer, Distribution, Electronic Components and Instrumentation, Genetic Engineering, Industrial Products and Equipment, Services

Portfolio Companies: Applied Digital Access, CBT Group PLC, Broderbund Software, Insignia Solutions, CompUSA, Opta Food Ingredients, SportsLine USA, Efficient Market Services, Lil' Things, Store of Knowledge, Exponential, Ilog

Officers, Executives and Principals

Eric F. DiBenedetto, Managing Director (Menlo Park)
Education: MBA, Finance and Economics; BA, Math and Physics
Background: Managing Partner, Transatlantic Venture Partners; Investment Manager, The Atlantic Fund; Pargesa/Lambert Brussels; Bankers Trust
Directorships: Efficient Market Services

BANGERT DAWES READE DAVIS AND THOM

1140 Taylor Street
San Francisco, CA 94108

Telephone: 415-441-6161
Fax: 415-775-0744

Other Office Locations
One Madison Avenue
New York, NY 10010
Phone 212-689-7404

Mission: Actively seeking new investments

Fund Size: not available
Founded: 1975
Average Investment: not available
Minimum Investment: $500,000

Investment Criteria: Mezzanine, Leveraged Buyout, Special Situations

Industry Group Preference: Communications, Computer Related, Consumer, Distribution, Electronic Components and Instrumentation, Genetic Engineering, Industrial Products and Equipment, Medical/Health Related

Portfolio Companies: not available

Officers, Executives and Principals

Dexter Dawes, Chairman (San Francisco)
K. Deane Reade, President (New York)
Lambert Thom, Vice President (San Francisco)

BANK ONE EQUITY INVESTORS, INC.

451 Florida Street
P.O. Box 1511
Baton Rouge, LA 70821-1511

Telephone: 504-332-4421
Fax: 504-332-7929
E-mail: tadamek@b1equity.com

Mission: Actively seeking new investments

Fund Size: $80 million
Founded: 1974
Average Investment: $3 million
Minimum Investment: $1 million

Investment Criteria: Startup to Leveraged Buyout

Geographic Preference: Gulf South, Midwestern United States

Industry Group Preference: Diversified

Portfolio Companies: Seasafe, PetroComm, GS Theatres, Reel Entertainment, Thomas Pipe and Steel, Cardio-vascular Ventures, Central Pharmacy Services, Buckner Rental Service

Officers, Executives and Principals

Thomas J. Adamek, President
Shelley G. Whittington, Vice President
W. Stephen Keller, Investment Officer

BANKERS CAPITAL CORPORATION

3100 Gillham Road
Kansas City, MO 64109

Telephone: 816-531-1600
Fax: 816-531-1334

Mission: Actively seeking new investments

Fund Size: not available
Founded: 1975
Average Investment: not available
Minimum Investment: $100,000

Investment Criteria: Leveraged Buyout

Industry Group Preference: not available

Portfolio Companies: not available

Officers, Executives and Principals

Raymond E. Glasnapp, President
Lee Glasnapp, Vice President

BANKERS TRUST CAPITAL CORPORATION

BD Plaza
130 Liberty St.
New York, NY 10017

Telephone: 212-250-8083
Fax: 212-250-7651

Other Office Locations
300 South Grand Avenue
Los Angeles, CA 90071
Phone 213-620-8204, Fax 213-620-8106

Mission: Actively seeking new investments

Fund Size: $200 million
Founded: 1972
Average Investment: $5 million
Minimum Investment: $4 million

Investment Criteria: Second-stage, Mezzanine, Leveraged Buyout

Industry Group Preference: Communications, Computer Related, Consumer, Distribution, Electronic Components and Instrumentation, Energy/Natural Resources, Medical/Health Related

Portfolio Companies: not available

Officers, Executives and Principals

George Doomany, Managing Director
Adrienne Halper, Managing Director
Martin Jelenko, Managing Director (Los Angeles)
Robert Marakovits, Managing Director
James Zielinski, Managing Director
Chip Roellig, Vice President (Los Angeles)

BASTION CAPITAL CORPORATION

1999 Avenue of the Stars
Suite 2960
Los Angeles, CA 90067

Telephone: 310-788-5700
Fax: 310-277-7582

Mission: Actively seeking new investments

Fund Size: $125 million
Founded: 1994
Average Investment: $17 million
Minimum Investment: $5 million

Investment Criteria: Leveraged Buyout, Special Situations, Control-block Purchases

Industry Group Preference: Communications, Consumer, Distribution, Service

Portfolio Companies: Telemundo Group, Renaissance Cosmetics, Nextwave Telecommunications

Officers, Executives and Principals

Guillermo Bron, Managing Director
Daniel D. Villanueva, Managing Director
Thomas Clerkin, Managing Director
James Villanueva, Vice President
Severin S. White, Associate

THE BATAVIA GROUP, LTD.

38 East 57th Street
New York, NY 10022

Telephone: 212-308-1100
Fax: 212-308--1565

Mission: Actively seeking new investments

Fund Size: not available
Founded: not available
Average Investment: not available
Minimum Investment: $1 million

Investment Criteria: Research and Development, Control-block Purchases, Buyout and Acquisition

Industry Group Preference: None

Portfolio Companies: not available

Officers, Executives and Principals

Joep M.J. de Koning
Sam Arastek

BATTELLE VENTURE PARTNERS (aka SCIENTIFIC ADVANCES, INC.)

601 West Fifth Avenue
Columbus, OH 43201

Telephone: 614-424-7005
Fax: 614-424-4874

Mission: Actively seeking new investments

Fund Size: not available
Founded: 1981
Average Investment: not available
Minimum Investment: $250,000

Investment Criteria: Startup, First-stage, Second-stage

Industry Group Preference: Energy/Natural Resources, Industrial Products and Equipment

Portfolio Companies: not available

Officers, Executives and Principals

Paul F. Purcell, President

BATTERSON VENTURE PARTNERS

303 West Madison Street
Suite 1110
Chicago, IL 60606-3309

Telephone: 312-269-0300
Fax: 312-269-0021

Mission: Early-stage technology investments

Fund Size: not available
Founded: 1996
Average Investment: $1 - $3 million
Minimum Investment: $500,000

Investment Criteria: Equity investments in enterprises with potential to become very large companies

Geographic Preference: United States

Industry Group Preference: Biotechnology, Communications, Computer Related, High Technology, Materials, Medical/Health Related

Portfolio Companies: Nanophase Technologies, Cybersource Corporation, Paladin Holdings, Inc.

Officers, Executives and Principals

Leonard A. Batterson, Chairman and Chief Executive Officer
Peter Fuss, Executive Vice President - Technology
Sona Wang, General Partner

BAXTER ASSOCIATES, INC.

P.O. Box 1333
Stamford, CT 06904

Telephone: 203-323-3143

Mission: Actively seeking new investments

Fund Size: not available
Founded: 1981
Average Investment: not available
Minimum Investment: $100,000

Investment Criteria: Seed, Research and Development, Startup, First-stage, Leveraged Buyout, Special Situations

Industry Group Preference: Communications, Computer Related, Consumer, Distribution, Energy/Natural Resources, Genetic Engineering, Industrial Products and Equipment, Medical/Health Related

Portfolio Companies: not available

Officers, Executives and Principals

Carroll A. Greathouse, President

BAY PARTNERS

10600 North De Anza Boulevard
Cupertino, CA 95014-2031

Telephone: 408-725-2444
Fax: 408-446-4502

Mission: not available

Fund Size: not available
Founded: 1976
Average Investment: not available
Minimum Investment: $500,000

Investment Criteria: First-stage, Second-stage

Industry Group Preference: Communications, Computer Related, Genetic Engineering, Industrial Products
and Equipment

Portfolio Companies: not available

Officers, Executives and Principals

John E. Bosch, General Partner
Neal Dempsey, General Partner
John Freidenrich, General Partner

BAY STREET CORPORATION

205 Worth Avenue
P.O. Box 2137
Palm Beach, FL 33480

Telephone: 407-832-2155
Fax: 407-832-2435

Mission: Actively seeking new investments

Fund Size: not available
Founded: 1960
Average Investment: not available
Minimum Investment: $1 million

Investment Criteria: Leveraged Buyout, Control-block Purchases; furnishing liquidity to shareholders
  through minority investments

Industry Group Preference: Communications, Consumer, Distribution, Industrial Products and Equipment

Portfolio Companies: not available

Officers, Executives and Principals

George B. Kilborne, President

BCE VENTURES, INC.

1000, rue de la Gauchetière Ouest, Suite 3700
Montreal, Quebec H3B 4Y7
Canada

Telephone: 514-397-7171
Fax: 514-397-7392

Other Office Locations
181 Bay Street
Suite 4700
PO Box 794
Toronto, Ontario M5J 2T3
Canada
Phone 416-364-4101, Fax 416-364-7610

160 Elgin Street
Suite 1450
Ottawa, Ontario K1G 3J4
Canada
Phone 613-781-3072, Fax 613-781-5854

Mission: Actively seeking new investments in small to medium sized businesses founded on proprietary tele-communications technology with an investment focus on hardware and software products

Fund Size: Approximately $25 million
Founded: 1993
Average Investment: Approximately $3 to $5 million
Minimum Investment: Approximately $700,000

Investment Criteria: Post-Product Development; will consider some start-ups on a case by case basis

Geographic Preference: Canada, United States

Industry Group Preference: Telecommunications

Portfolio Companies: Pairgain Technologies, Inc., Plaintree Systems, Inc., Secure Computing Corporation, Faneuil ISG, Inc., Switchview, Inc., E/O Networks, SSiG Holdings, Inc., Medialight, Inc., The Bulldog Group, Inc., New Edge Technologies, Inc., VMI Technologies, Inc.

Officers, Executives and Principals

Peter S. Crombie, President and Chief Executive Officer (Montreal)
Robert Forbes, Vice President (Toronto)
Brian Kouri, Assistant Vice President and Treasurer (Montreal)
David McCarthy, Director, Ottawa Operations (Ottawa)
Gus Papageorgiou, Investment Manager (Montreal)
Jim Orlando, Investment Manager (Ottawa)

BCI ADVISORS, INC.
Glenpointe Centre West
Teaneck, NJ 07666

Telephone: 201-836-3900
Fax: 201-836-6368

Mission: Actively seeking new investments

Fund Size: $175 million
Founded: 1982
Average Investment: $7 million
Minimum Investment: $4 million

Investment Criteria: Expansion/Growth Capital

Geographic Preference: United States

Industry Group Preference: Communications, Consumer, Distribution, Electronic Components and Instrumentation, Entertainment, Environmental, Industrial Products and Equipment, Manufacturing, Media, Medical/Health Related

Portfolio Companies: not available

Officers, Executives and Principals

Donald P. Remey, Managing Director
Hoyt J. Goodrich, Managing Director
J. Barton Goodwin, Managing Director
Theodore T. Horton, Managing Director
Stephen J. Eley, Principal
Matthew E. Gormly III, Principal
Peter O. Wilde, Associate

BEACON PARTNERS, INC.

Six Landmark Square
Fourth Floor
Stamford, CT 06901-2792

Telephone: 203-359-5776
Fax: 203-359-5876

Mission: Actively seeking new investments

Fund Size: not available
Founded: 1976
Average Investment: not available
Minimum Investment: Less than $100,000

Investment Criteria: First-stage, Second-stage, Mezzanine, Leveraged Buyout, Turnarounds

Industry Group Preference: Communications, Computer Related, Consumer, Distribution, Electronic Components and Instrumentation, Energy/Natural Resources, Genetic Engineering, Industrial Products and Equipment, Medical/Health Related

Portfolio Companies: not available

Officers, Executives and Principals

Lawrence Gorfinkle, Managing Director
Leonard Vignola, Managing Director

BEHRMAN CAPITAL

126 East 56th Street
New York, NY 10022

Telephone: 212-980-6500
Fax: 212-980-7024

Mission: Actively seeking new investments

Fund Size: not available
Founded: 1992
Average Investment: not available
Minimum Investment: $2 million

Investment Criteria: Second-stage, Leveraged Buyout

Industry Group Preference: Communications, Computer Related, Electronic Components and Instrumentation, Genetic Engineering, Medical/Health Related

Portfolio Companies: not available

Officers, Executives and Principals

Darryl G. Behrman, Managing Partner
Grant G. Behrman, Managing Partner
David S. Andryc, Vice President
Mark P. Visser, Analyst

THE BENEFIT CAPITAL COMPANIES INC.

P.O. Box 542
Logandale, NV 89021

Telephone: 702-398-3222
Fax: 702-398-3700

Other Office Locations
19800 MacArthur Boulevard
Suite 1180
Irvine, CA 92612
Phone 714-833-3767, Fax 714-752-7569

Mission: Reducing investment activity

Fund Size: not available
Founded: 1984
Average Investment: not available
Minimum Investment: $500,000

Investment Criteria: Mezzanine, Leveraged Buyout, Management Buyout, ESOP Leveraged Buyouts, including those involving multiple investors

Industry Group Preference: Communications, Computer Related, Consumer, Distribution, Energy/Natural Resources, Industrial Products and Equipment, Medical/Health Related

Portfolio Companies: not available

Officers, Executives and Principals

Robert W. Smiley, Jr., Chairman and Chief Executive Officer (Logandale)
Edward M. Bixler, President (Irvine)
Kenneth Winslow, President (Dallas)
R. Alan Prosswimmer, Managing Director (Logandale)
Peter A. Wuebel, Managing Director (Logandale)

BERENSON MINELLA VENTURES

667 Madison Avenue
22nd Floor
New York, NY 10021

Telephone: 212-935-7676
Fax: 212-935-1499

Mission: Actively seeking to assist management in building companies around technologies or ideas

Fund Size: not available
Founded: not available
Average Investment: not available
Minimum Investment: $250,000

Investment Criteria: Seed, Research and Development, Startup, First-stage, Special Situations

Industry Group Preference: Communications, Computer Related, Consumer, Distribution, Electronic Components and Instrumentation, Energy/Natural Resources, Genetic Engineering, Industrial Products and Equipment, Medical/Health Related

Portfolio Companies: not available

Officers, Executives and Principals

Gregg Feinstein, Partner

BERKELEY INTERNATIONAL CAPITAL CORPORATION

650 California Street
Suite 2800
San Francisco, CA 94108-2609

Telephone: 415-249-0450
Fax: 415-392-3929

Mission: Actively seeking new investments

Fund Size: not available
Founded: 1977
Average Investment: not available
Minimum Investment: $1 million

Investment Criteria: Mezzanine, Leveraged Buyout, Special Situations

Industry Group Preference: Communications, Computer Related, Consumer, Distribution, Electronic Components and Instrumentation, Industrial Products and Equipment, Medical/Health Related

Portfolio Companies: not available

Officers, Executives and Principals

Michael J. Mayer, President

BERKSHIRE PARTNERS, LLC

One Boston Place
Boston, MA 02108-4401

Telephone: 617-227-0050
Fax: 617-227-6105

Mission: Private equity investment firm which both acquires and makes equity investments in growing companies

Fund Size: $750 million under management
Founded: 1986
Average Investment: $15 - $30 million
Minimum Investment: $7 million

Investment Criteria: Leveraged Buyout, Special Situations, Industry Consolidations, Privatizations, Recapitalizations, Minority Investments, Specialty Retail, Transportation

Industry Group Preference: Consumer, Distribution, Electronic Components and Instrumentation, Industrial Products and Equipment, Medical/Health Related

Portfolio Companies: not available

Officers, Executives and Principals

Bradley M. Bloom, Managing Director
Jane Brock-Wilson, Managing Director
Kevin T. Callaghan, Managing Director
J. Christopher Clifford, Managing Director
Russell L. Epker, Managing Director
Garth H. Greimann, Managing Director
Richard K. Lubin, Managing Director
Carl Ferenbach, Managing Director

BESSEMER VENTURE PARTNERS

83 Walnut Street
Wellesley Hills, MA 02181

Telephone: 617-237-6050
Fax: 617-235-7068

Other Office Locations
3000 Sand Hill Road
Building 3, Suite 225
Menlo Park, CA 94025
Phone 415-854-2200, Fax 415-854-7415

1025 Old Country Road, Suite 205
Westbury, NY 11590
Phone 516-997-2300, Fax 516-997-2371

Mission: not available

Fund Size: $300 million
Founded: not available
Average Investment: $750,000
Minimum Investment: not available

Investment Criteria: Seed to Leveraged Buyout

Industry Group Preference: Biotechnology, Communications, Computer Related, Consumer Related, Electronics, Financial Services, High Technology, Medical/Health, Retailing, Service Industries

Portfolio Companies: not available

Officers, Executives and Principals

Robert H. Buescher (Westbury)
William T. Burgin (Wellesley Hills)
Christopher F.O. Gabrieli (Wellesley Hills)
G. Felda Hardymon (Wellesley Hills)
David J. Cowan (Menlo Park)
Michael I. Barach (Wellesley Hills)
Robi L. Soni (Wellesley Hills)
Gautam A. Prakash (Wellesley Hills)
Bruce K. Graham (Menlo Park)

BLOOM AND COMPANY

110 Broad Street
Third Floor
Boston, MA 02110

Telephone: 617-542-1129
Fax: 617-423-2158

Mission: Actively seeking new investments

Fund Size: not available
Founded: 1983
Average Investment: not available
Minimum Investment: $1 million

Investment Criteria: Seed, Startup, First-stage, Second-stage, Mezzanine, Leveraged Buyout, Special Situations, Control-block Purchases, Expansion Capital

Industry Group Preference: not available

Portfolio Companies: not available

Officers, Executives and Principals

Jack S. Bloom, President
Jo Ann Jorge, Vice President
Jonathan Larson, Vice President
Diane Hassan, Controller

BLUE CHIP VENTURE COMPANY

2000 PNC Center
201 East Fifth Street
Cincinnati, OH 45202

Telephone: 513-723-2300
Fax: 513-723-2306

Mission: Actively seeking new investments

Fund Size: $60 million
Founded: 1992
Average Investment: $500,000 - $1 million
Minimum Investment: $500,000

Investment Criteria: First-stage, Second-stage, Leveraged Buyout, Special Situations

Geographic Preference: Midwestern United States

Industry Group Preference: Communications, Computer Related, Consumer, Energy/Natural Resources, Industrial Products and Equipment, Medical/Health Related

Portfolio Companies: not available

Officers, Executives and Principals

Z. David Patterson, General Partner
John H. Wyant, General Partner
Samuel E. Lynch, Manager
John T. Hogan, Manager
Todd G. Gardner, Analyst

BLUE RIDGE INVESTORS, LTD.

300 North Greene Street
Suite 2100
Greensboro, NC 27401

Telephone: 910-370-0576
Fax: 910-274-4984

Other Office Locations
380 Knollwood Street, Suite 410
Winston-Salem, NC 27103
Phone 910-721-1800, Fax 910-748-1208

Mission: Actively seeking new investments

Fund Size: $20 million
Founded: 1994
Average Investment: $2 million
Minimum Investment: $1 million

Investment Criteria: Second-stage, Mezzanine, Leveraged Buyout, Special Situations, Recapitalizations

Geographic Preference: Southeastern United States

Industry Group Preference: Communications, Computer Related, Consumer, Distribution, Electronic Components and Instrumentation, Industrial Products and Equipment, Medical/Health Related

Portfolio Companies: The Computer Group, Inc.

Officers, Executives and Principals

Edward K. Crawford, Chairman (Winston-Salem)
F. James Becher, Jr., President (Greensboro)
Edward C. McCarthy, Executive Vice President (Greensboro)
Russell R. Myers, Treasurer (Greensboro)
Richard T. Maclean (Greensboro)

BORANCO MANAGEMENT, L.L.C.

1528 Hillside Drive
Ft. Collins, CO 80524-1969

Telephone: 970-221-2297
Fax: 970-221-4787

Mission: To invest in, then mentor, profitable small businesses, particularly those involved in agribusiness

Fund Size: not available
Founded: 1994
Average Investment: $20,000
Minimum Investment: Less than $100,000

Investment Criteria: Second-stage

Geographic Preference: Colorado, Wyoming

Industry Group Preference: Agriculture, Genetic Engineering, Livestock

Portfolio Companies: ABS Global, Inc., Alta Genetics

Officers, Executives and Principals

John K. Rankin, Member/Manager
Education: BS, Illinois State University
Background: Animal Genetics, Agribusiness

Barbara A. Rankin, Certified Financial Planner, **Member/Manager**
Background: Certified Financial Planner

THE BOSTON AGENT
278 Wethersfield Street
Rowley, MA 01969

Telephone: 508-948-2777
Fax: 508-948-2779

Mission: Actively seeking new investments

Fund Size: not available
Founded: 1987
Average Investment: not available
Minimum Investment: $500,000

Investment Criteria: Startup, First-stage, Second-stage, Mezzanine, Special Situations, Control-block Purchases, Acquisitions

Industry Group Preference: Communications, Computer Related, Electronic Components and Instrumentation, Energy/Natural Resources, Genetic Engineering, Industrial Products and Equipment, Medical/Health Related

Portfolio Companies: not available

Officers, Executives and Principals

J.P. Luc Beaubien, President

BOSTON CAPITAL VENTURES

Old City Hall, 45 School Street
Boston, MA 02108

Telephone: 617-227-6550
Fax: 617-227-3847
E-mail: info@bvc.com

Mission: Boston Capital Ventures (BVC) is a private venture capital firm which invests in early stage companies in the healthcare and life sciences, information technology, and telecommunications industries

Fund Size: $150 million
Founded: 1982
Average Investment: $1 - $5 million
Minimum Investment: $500,000

Investment Criteria: Early-stage equity investment in private companies to supply capital for growth and expansion

Industry Group Preference: Healthcare, Information Technology, Life Sciences, Telecommunications

Portfolio Companies: Advertising Communications International American, Auto Funding Corporation, Brooks Fiber Properties, Child Health Systems, Continuity Marketing Corporation, ConXus Communications, The Cornerstone Group, Exa Corporation, GRASP Information Corporation, Healthcare First, ILEX Oncology, Intellon Corporation, MedSpan, Olympus Healthcare Group, Ominia, Revelation Technologies, SCC Communications, Sensitech, Teletrac, UniSite, Vertex Technologies, World Net Access

Officers, Executives and Principals

A. Dana Callow, Jr., General Partner
Education: BA, Tufts University; MBA, Amos Tuck School of Business, Dartmouth
Background: Management Consultant, Braxton Associated, Inc.; Tymshare; McDonnell Douglas Corporation

H.J. von der Goltz, General Partner
Education: BS, MIT; PMD Program, Harvard Business School
Background: Otto Wolff A.G. and Trinkaus Bank in Germany; Chief Executive Officer of major industrial businesses including a telecommunications company

Robert S. Sherman, Partner

Martin J. Hernon, Partner

Suresh Shanmugham, Principal

Robert W. Jevon, Principal

Frank P. Pinto, Principal

Christian Dubiel, Associate

BOSTON ENERGY TECHNOLOGY GROUP

800 Boylston Street
Boston, MA 02199

Telephone: 617-424-3698
Fax: 617-424-2266

Mission: Making few, if any, new investments

Fund Size: not available
Founded: 1993
Average Investment: not available
Minimum Investment: $500,000

Investment Criteria: Second-stage

Industry Group Preference: Communications, Energy/Natural Resources

Portfolio Companies: not available

Officers, Executives and Principals

Rick Zimbone, Senior Vice President
Philippe Frangules, Vice President

BOSTON FINANCIAL AND EQUITY CORPORATION

20 Overland Street
P.O. Box 71, Kenmore Station
Boston, MA 02215

Telephone: 617-267-2900
Fax: 617-267-2370

Mission: Actively seeking new investments

Fund Size: not available
Founded: 1968
Average Investment: not available
Minimum Investment: $100,000

Investment Criteria: Seed, Research and Development, Startup, First-stage, Second-stage, Mezzanine, Leveraged Buyout, Special Situations

Industry Group Preference: Communications, Computer Related, Consumer, Distribution, Electronic Components and Instrumentation, Genetic Engineering, Industrial Products and Equipment, Medical/Health Related

Portfolio Companies: not available

Officers, Executives and Principals

Adolf F. Monosson, President
James L. Beauregard, Senior Vice President
Deborah J. Monosson, Vice President

BOSTON VENTURES MANAGEMENT, INC.

21 Custom House Street
10th Floor
Boston, MA 02110

Telephone: 617-737-3700
Fax: 617-737-3709

Mission: Actively seeking new investments

Fund Size: not available
Founded: 1983
Average Investment: not available
Minimum Investment: $15 million

Investment Criteria: Second-stage, Leveraged Buyout, Special Situations, Control-block Purchases

Industry Group Preference: Communications, Consumer, Distribution

Portfolio Companies: not available

Officers, Executives and Principals

Richard C. Wallace, Director and President
Sherri L. Dettenrieder, Chief Financial Officer and Treasurer
Anthony J. Bolland, Director
Roy F. Coppedge III, Director
Martha H.W. Crowninshield, Director
Barbara M. Ginader, Director
William F. Thompson, Director
James M. Wilson, Director

BRAD PEERY CAPITAL

145 Chapel Drive
Mill Valley, CA 94941

Telephone: 415-389-0625
Fax: 415-389-1336

Mission: Actively seeking new investments

Fund Size: not available
Founded: 1991
Average Investment: not available
Minimum Investment: $100,000

Investment Criteria: Second-stage, Mezzanine

Industry Group Preference: Communications

Portfolio Companies: not available

Officers, Executives and Principals

Brad Peery, Chairman
Karen Landry, Marketing Director

BRADFORD VENTURES, LTD.

1212 Avenue of the Americas
Suite 1802
New York, NY 10036

Telephone: 212-221-4620
Fax: 212-764-3467

Mission: Actively seeking new investments

Fund Size: not available
Founded: 1974
Average Investment: not available
Minimum Investment: not available

Investment Criteria: Leveraged Buyout, Control-block Purchases

Industry Group Preference: Distribution, Industrial Products and Equipment

Portfolio Companies: not available

Officers, Executives and Principals

Barbara M. Henagan, Senior Managing Director
Robert J. Simon, Senior Managing Director

BRENNER SECURITIES CORPORATION

Two World Trade Center
38th Floor
New York, NY 10048

Telephone: 212-839-7300
Fax: 212-839-7339

Mission: not available

Fund Size: not available
Founded: 1990
Average Investment: not available
Minimum Investment: $5 million

Investment Criteria: Mezzanine, Leveraged Buyout, Special Situations

Industry Group Preference: Communications, Medical/Health Related

Portfolio Companies: not available

Officers, Executives and Principals

David B. Boris, Senior Managing Director
Jonathan A. Intrater, Managing Director
Gerald Koerner, Managing Director
Chesley Maddox-Dorsey, Senior Vice President
Grant E. Harshbarger, Vice President
Eric Meltzer, Vice President
Robert M. Salisbury, Vice President
Inder S. Sodhi, Vice President

BRINSON PARTNERS, INC.

209 South LaSalle Street
Chicago, IL 60604-1295

Telephone: 312-220-7100
Fax: 312-220-7110

Mission: Brinson Partners, Inc. is one of the major global institutional money management firms, managing approximately $58 billion in assets for institutional investors. The Private Markets Group of Brinson Partners, Inc. has been making investments since 1972 and currently manages $2.6 billion. Brinson Partners, Inc. is actively involved in making investments in all areas of the private markets industry including partnership investing, secondary interests, direct investing and distribution management.

Fund Size: $2.6 billion
Founded: 1972
Average Investment: $1- $30 million
Minimum Investment: $1 million

Investment Criteria: Early-stage, Growth Equity Financings, Management Buyouts, Restructurings

Industry Group Preference: Diversified

Portfolio Companies: not available

Officers, Executives and Principals

A. Bart Holaday, Managing Partner
Education: BS, Air Force Academy; BA/MA, Oxford University (Rhodes Scholar); JD, George Washington Law School
Background: Managing Partner, Private Markets Group; Vice President and Principal, Inno Ven Venture Capital Founder; President, Tenax Oil and Gas
Directorships: National Venture Capital Association

Thomas D. Berman, Partner
Education: SB/SM, MIT
Background: General Partner, Fairfield Venture Partners; Booz, Allen and Hamilton and Hewlett Packard

Robert D. Blank, Partner
Education: BA, Miami University; MM, Northwestern
Background: Wind Point Partners; Manager, State Funded Early Stage Venture Capital Fund; First National Bank of Chicago

Tim E. Bliamptis, Partner
Education: SB, SM, MIT; MBA, The Wharton School
Background: Manager, venture capital portfolios for endowment and pension funds; Consultant, technology companies; Designer, electronic systems

T. Bondurant French, Partner
Education: BA/MM, Northwestern University; CFA, Institute of Chartered Financial Analysts
Background: Guest lecturer, business schools, Wall Street firms
Directorships: Industry associations

Terry Gould, Partner
Education: BA, Dartmouth; MBA, Stanford University
Background: Management Consultant with firms in Boston and San Francisco; Founder, Manager, two entrepreneurial companies

Sarah B. Jacobs, Partner
Education: BS, University of Illinois; MBA, University of Chicago
Background: Financial Administrative Team, Private Markets Group; Site Selector for real estate developer; Sales Associate, real estate investment banking firm

Glen A. Kleczka, Partner
Education: BS, Marquette University; MS, University of Wisconsin Graduate School of Business; CFA, Institute of Chartered Financial Analysts
Background: CNA Financial

Marc E. Sacks, Partner
Education: BA, Queens College; MBA, Cornell University
Background: Program Manager, Private Investments, IBM Pension Fund

David S. Timson, Partner
Education: BS/MS, University of Illinois
Background: Vice President Finance and Administration, Microelectronic Packaging; Director, Venture Management and Analysis; Greyhound

Katherine M. Todd, Partner
Education: AD, Smith College, magna cum laude; JD, Harvard University, cum laude
Background: Partner, Testa, Hurwitz and Thibeault

Marianne L. Woodward, Partner
Education: BS, Washington University; MBA, University of Chicago; CFA, Institute of Chartered Financial Analysts
Background: First Scholar Management Training Program, First Chicago Corporation Manager, Mark Twain Brokerage Services, Mark Twain Bancshares

Thomas D. Berman, Partner
Education: SB/SM, MIT
Background: General Partner, Fairfield Venture Partners; Booz, Allen and Hamilton and Hewlett Packard

BRISTOL INVESTMENT TRUST

842A Beacon Street
Boston, MA 02215-3199

Telephone: 617-566-5212
Fax: 617-267-0932

Mission: Making few, if any, new investments

Fund Size: not available
Founded: 1966
Average Investment: not available
Minimum Investment: Less than $100,000

Investment Criteria: First-stage, Second-stage, Mezzanine

Industry Group Preference: Consumer, Distribution, Medical/Health Related

Portfolio Companies: not available

Officers, Executives and Principals

Bernard G. Berkman, Trustee
Stephen V. O'Donnell, Jr., Trust Officer

BROADMARK CAPITAL CORPORATION

3030 U.S. Bank Centre
1420 Fifth Avenue
Seattle, WA 98101-2333

Telephone: 206-623-1200
Fax: 206-623-2213

Other Office Locations
20, avenue Kleber
75116 Paris
France
Phone 33-1-4500-6001, Fax 33-1-4500-8282

Mission: Actively seeking new investments

Fund Size: not available
Founded: 1986
Average Investment: not available
Minimum Investment: $1 million

Investment Criteria: First-stage, Second-stage, Mezzanine, Leveraged Buyout

Industry Group Preference: Communications, Computer Related, Consumer, Distribution, Electronic Components and Instrumentation, Energy/Natural Resources, Genetic Engineering, Industrial Products and Equipment, Medical/Health Related

Portfolio Companies: not available

Officers, Executives and Principals

Daniel Lebard, Chairman (Paris)
Joseph L. Schocken, President (Seattle)
Reed A. Corry, Executive Vice President (Seattle)
Christophe Bernand, Vice President (Paris)
Francois Lacombe, Vice President (Paris)
Timothy C. Dunton, Senior Associate (Seattle)
David Powell, Senior Associate (Seattle)
Lina Ismail, Senior Analyst (Paris)

BRUCE F. GLASPELL AND ASSOCIATES

10400 Academy Road, Northeast
Suite 313
Albuquerque, NM 87111

Telephone: 505-293-9590
Fax: 505-293-9590

Mission: Actively seeking new investments

Fund Size: not available
Founded: 1974
Average Investment: not available
Minimum Investment: Less than $100,000

Investment Criteria: Seed, Research and Development, Startup, First-stage, Second-stage, Leveraged Buyout, Special Situations

Industry Group Preference: Communications, Computer Related, Consumer, Distribution, Electronic Components and Instrumentation, Energy/Natural Resources, Genetic Engineering, Industrial Products and Equipment, Medical/Health Related

Portfolio Companies: not available

Officers, Executives and Principals

Bruce F. Glaspell, General Partner

BUFFALO CAPITAL CORPORATION

Mount Morris Road
Box 278
Geneseo, NY 14454

Telephone: 716-243-4310
Fax: 716-243-1864

Other Office Locations
Buffalo Capital (Canada) Limited
One Toronto Street, Suite 810
Toronto, Ontario M5C 2V7
Canada
Phone 416-868-0773, Fax 416-868-6700

Mission: Actively seeking new investments and require significant influence with management. Normally on lead or sale, outside investor and active on the Board.

Fund Size: $40 million
Founded: 1969
Average Investment: $1 million
Minimum Investment: $500,000

Investment Criteria: Second-stage, Mezzanine, Leveraged Buyout

Geographic Preference: Northwestern and Northeastern United States, Canada

Industry Group Preference: Computer Related, Consumer, Distribution, Energy/Natural Resources, Industrial Products and Equipment, Media Communications, Medical/Health Related

Portfolio Companies: Motion Works Group, Ltd., HTE, Inc.

Officers, Executives and Principals

John H. Hickman III, Chairman
Education: Yale Law School
Background: Former Chairman and Chief Executive Officer, Nevada National Bank, Lockwood International, Seilon, Inc., PSC, Inc.

John H. Hickman IV, Vice President

Scott C. Mitchell, Vice President

BURR, EGAN, DELEAGE AND COMPANY

One Post Office Square, Suite 3800
Boston, MA 02109-2183

Telephone: 617-482-8020
Fax: 617-482-1944

Other Office Locations
One Embarcadero Center, Suite 4050
San Francisco, CA 94111-3729
Phone 415-362-4022, Fax 415-362-6178

Mission: not available

Fund Size: $600 million
Founded: not available
Average Investment: $1 - $5 million
Minimum Investment: not available

Investment Criteria: Startup to Expansion

Industry Group Preference: Biotechnology, Broadcast/Cable/Radio, Communications, Computer Related, Diversified, Electronics, High Technology, Information Services, Medical/Health, Software, Wholesaling/Distribution

Portfolio Companies: Tandon, Hologic, Genentech, Cephalon, Continental Cablevision, Merisel, Silicon Valley Group, Tandem, Federal Express, Chiron Corporation, Versaflex

Officers, Executives and Principals

Craig L. Burr, Founder
Education: BA, cum laude in Economics; MBA, Harvard
Background: Partner, TA Associates
Directorships: New England Venture Capital

Jean Deleage, Founder (San Francisco)
Education: PhD, Economics, Sorbonne; MS, Electrical Engineering, Ecole Superieure d'Electricite
Background: Director, Western Association of Venture Capitalists
Directorships: Tandon Corporation, Chiron Corporation, Versaflex Delivery Systems, SyQuest Technology, Stratagene Cloning Systems, Abaxis

William P. Egan, Founder
Education: BA, Fairfield University; MBA, Wharton
Background: Partner, TA Associates; Manager Venture Capital, Bank of New England
Directorships: National Venture Captial Association

Jonathan A. Flint, Partner
Education: JD, University of Virginia Law School; BA, high honors, Hobart College
Background: Associate, Testa, Hurwitz and Thibeault; Impeachment Inquiry Staff, U.S. House Judiciary Committee, Watergate

Timothy Dibble, Partner
Education: BA, Economics, Wesleyan University
Background: Officer, First National Bank of Boston

Guy Paul Nohra, Partner (San Francisco)
Education: MBA, University of Chicago; BA, Stanford University
Background: Product Manager of Medical Products, Security Pacific Trading Corporation; Assistant to the
President of Boles and Co.

John A. Hawkins, Partner (San Francisco)
Education: BA, English literature; MBA, Harvard
Background: Alex, Brown and Sons, Inc.; Securities Analyst, Woodmann Kirkpatrick and Gilbreath

CABLE AND HOWSE VENTURES

777 108th Avenue, N.E.
Suite 2300
Bellevue, WA 98004-5118

Telephone: 206-646-3040
Fax: 206-646-3041

Mission: not available

Fund Size: $160 million
Founded: 1977
Average Investment: $1 million
Minimum Investment: Less than $100,000

Investment Criteria: Seed, Startup, First-stage, Second-stage, Special Situations

Industry Group Preference: Biotechnology, Communications, Computer Related, Consumer, Electronic Components and Instrumentation, Energy/Natural Resources, Genetic Engineering, High Technology, Industrial Products and Equipment, Medical/Health Related, Software

Portfolio Companies: not available

Officers, Executives and Principals

Thomas J. Cable, General Partner
Elwood D. Howse, Jr., General Partner
Wayne C. Wager, General Partner

CALGARY ENTERPRISES, INC.

Four Park Avenue
Suite 12G
New York, NY 10016-5310

Telephone: 212-683-0119
Fax: 212-683-3119
E-mail: 74663.3472@compuserve.com

Mission: Provide financial advisory, investment banking (private placement of debt and equity with strategic and/or financial institutional capital sources) and management consulting services to a client

Fund Size: not available
Founded: 1988
Average Investment: not available
Minimum Investment: $5 million

Investment Criteria: Second-stage, Mezzanine, Leveraged Buyout, Special Situations, Private Placement of Debt/Equity, Start-ups

Industry Group Preference: not available

Portfolio Companies: not available

Officers, Executives and Principals

Steven Insalaco, President

CAMPBELL VENTURES

375 Forest Avenue
Palo Alto, CA 94301

Telephone: 415-853-0766
Fax: 415-853-0205

Mission: Actively seeking new investments

Fund Size: not available
Founded: 1978
Average Investment: not available
Minimum Investment: Less than $100,000

Investment Criteria: Seed, Startup, First-stage

Industry Group Preference: Communications, Computer Related, Genetic Engineering

Portfolio Companies: not available

Officers, Executives and Principals

Dean Campbell

CANAAN PARTNERS

105 Rowayton Avenue
Rowayton, CT 06853

Telephone: 203-855-0400
Fax: 203-854-9117

Other Office Locations
2884 Sand Hill Road, Suite 115
Menlo Park, CA 94025
Phone 415-854-8092, Fax 415-854-8127

Mission: not available

Fund Size: $400 million
Founded: 1987
Average Investment: $1 - $3 million
Minimum Investment: $500,000

Investment Criteria: Seed to Leveraged Buyout

Industry Group Preference: Biotechnology, Communications, Environmental Protection, Financial Services, Industrial Products, Insurance, Medical/Health, Retailing, Software

Portfolio Companies: Advance ParadigM, CapMAC Holdings, Concord Communications, GenVec, Integrated Packaging and Assembly Corporation, International Network Services, Inc., Suiza Foods Corporation, Sync Research, Visigenic Software

Officers, Executives and Principals

Harry T. Rein, Managing General Partner
Education: Emory University and Oglethore College; MBA, Darden School at University of Virginia
Background: President and Chief Executive Officer, GE Ventures; Management, Polaroid Corporation; Vice President, Transaction Systems; Director of Corporate Planning, Gulf

Gregory Kopchinsky, General Partner
Education: MBA, JD, Columbia; MS, Engineering, Kharkov Polytechnik Institute, USSR
Background: Vice President, JP Morgan; Attorney, Davis Pold and Wardell

Robert J. Migliorino, General Partner
Education: BS, Business Administration, Drexel University
Background: Vice President, Treasurer, GE Venture Capital

Stephen L. Green, General Partner
Education: Amherst College
Background: GE Venture Capital

Eric A. Young, General Partner (Menlo Park)
Education: BS, Mechanical Engineering, Cornell; MS, Management in Finance, Northwestern
Background: GE Venture Capital

Deepak Kamra, General Partner (Menlo Park)
Education: MBA, Harvard University; Bachelor of Commerce, Carleton University
Background: Aspect Telecommunications, ROLM Corporation

CANADIAN CORPORATION FUNDING, LTD.
70 University Avenue, Suite 1450
Toronto, Ontario M5J 2M4
Canada

Telephone: 416-977-1450
Fax: 416-977-6764

Other Office Locations
1010 Sherbrooke Street West, Suite 2210
Montreal, Quebec H3A 2R7
Canada
Phone 514-287-9884, Fax 514-287-9030

Mission: Actively seeking new investments

Fund Size: not available
Founded: 1979
Average Investment: not available
Minimum Investment: $1 million

Investment Criteria: Mezzanine

Industry Group Preference: Communications, Consumer, Distribution, Electronic Components and Instrumentation, Energy/Natural Resources, Industrial Products and Equipment, Medical/Health Related

Portfolio Companies: not available

Officers, Executives and Principals

Paul J. Lowenstein, Chairman and Chief Executive Officer (Montreal)
Richard D. Kinlough, Executive Vice President (Toronto)

CANADIAN VENTURE FOUNDERS CORPORATION

114 Lakeshore Road East
Oakville, Ontario L6J 6N2
Canada

Telephone: 905-842-9770
Fax: 905-842-9774

Mission: Actively seeking new investments

Fund Size: not available
Founded: 1989
Average Investment: not available
Minimum Investment: $100,000

Investment Criteria: Seed, Startup, First-stage, Second-stage, Mezzanine

Industry Group Preference: not available

Portfolio Companies: not available

Officers, Executives and Principals

Malcolm Gissing, President
Jeffrey Dreben, Vice President
Robert B. Nally, Vice President

CAPFORM PARTNERS

2390 El Camino Real
Palo Alto, CA 94306

Telephone: 415-854-1119
Fax: 415-854-1757

Mission: Actively seeking new investments

Fund Size: not available
Founded: 1980
Average Investment: not available
Minimum Investment: $100,000

Investment Criteria: Startup, First-stage

Industry Group Preference: Communications, Computer Related, Distribution, Electronic Components and Instrumentation, Energy/Natural Resources, Industrial Products and Equipment

Portfolio Companies: not available

Officers, Executives and Principals

William J. Dobbin, General Partner
Carol H. Lefcourt, General Partner
Robert G. Teal, General Partner

CAPITAL CITIES CAPITAL, INC.

77 West 66th Street
New York, NY 10023

Telephone: 212-456-7224
Fax: 212-456-3928

Other Office Locations
Financial Advisor: William Sword and Co.
34 Chambers Street
Princeton, NJ, 08542
Phone 609-924-6710, Fax 609-924-3890

Mission: Actively seeking new investments

Fund Size: not available
Founded: 1993
Average Investment: not available
Minimum Investment: $3 million

Investment Criteria: All stages; prefer Mid and Later Stages

Industry Group Preference: Consumer

Portfolio Companies: not available

Officers, Executives and Principals

William Sword, Jr., Managing Director (Princeton)
George Cain, President
Joanna Lei, Vice President/Director
Victor Lee, Director
Ann-Marie McGowan, Director
William Schmidt, Vice President (Princeton)

CAPITAL DIMENSIONS VENTURE FUND, INC.

Two Appletree Square
Suite 335
Minneapolis, MN 55425-1637

Telephone: 612-854-3007
Fax: 612-854-6657

Mission: Reducing investment activity

Fund Size: $21 million
Founded: 1987
Average Investment: $500,000
Minimum Investment: $250,000

Investment Criteria: First-stage, Second-stage, Mezzanine, Leveraged Buyout

Industry Group Preference: Communications, Computer Related, Energy/Natural Resources, Industrial Products and Equipment

Portfolio Companies: not available

Officers, Executives and Principals

Dean R. Pickerell, President
Thomas F. Hunt, Jr., Vice President
Brenda L. Leonard, Investment Manager

CAPITAL EXPRESS, L.L.C.

205 Chubb Avenue
Lyndhurst, NJ 07071

Telephone: 201-507-8998 ext. 1300
Fax: 201-507-0833

Mission: Actively seeking new investments

Fund Size: not available
Founded: 1994
Average Investment: $500,000
Minimum Investment: $250,000

Investment Criteria: Startup, First-stage, Second-stage

Geographic Preference: New York Metropolitan area, Florida, East Coast

Industry Group Preference: Direct Marketing, Housewares, Juvenile Products, Sports Related

Portfolio Companies: Forman Interactive Corporation, 1-800-BIRTHDAY, Money Hunt Properties, Mirrotek International

Officers, Executives and Principals

Niles Cohen, Managing Member
Teddy Struhl, Member
Warren Struhl, Member
Miles Spencer, Member

CAPITAL INVESTMENT CORPORATION

351 South Sherman, #101
Richardson, TX 75081

Telephone: 214-238-1195
Fax: 214-238-1181

Mission: Actively seeking new equity investments in early stage companies with proven technical products

Fund Size: not available
Founded: 1987
Average Investment: $750,000
Minimum Investment: $300,000

Investment Criteria: Early-Stage, Turnarounds

Geographic Preference: Southwestern United States, particularly North Texas

Industry Group Preference: Electronics, Manufacturing/Processing

Portfolio Companies: Active Control, Innovative Air Systems

Officers, Executives and Principals

Mitch Wescott, Managing Partner
Education: MBA, University of Rochester
Background: Executive positions with building products manufacturer, metals distributor, and international
  bank

THE CAPITAL NETWORK

3925 West Braker Lane
Austin, TX 78759

Telephone: 512-305-0826
Fax: 512-305-0836

Mission: Actively seeking new investments

Fund Size: $50 million
Founded: 1991
Average Investment: $750,000
Minimum Investment: $100,000

Investment Criteria: Seed, Research and Development, Startup, First-stage, Second-stage, Mezzanine, Leveraged Buyout, Special Situations

Geographic Preference: United States, Canada, Central and South America

Industry Group Preference: Distribution, Diversified, High Technology, Medical Health, Specialty Manufacturing

Portfolio Companies: not available

Officers, Executives and Principals

David H. Gerhardt, Director

CAPITAL RESOURCE PARTNERS

85 Merrimac Street
Suite 200
Boston, MA 02114

Telephone: 617-723-9000
Fax: 617-723-9819

Mission: Actively seeking new investments

Fund Size: not available
Founded: 1987
Average Investment: not available
Minimum Investment: $5 million

Investment Criteria: Second-stage, Mezzanine, Leveraged Buyout, Special Situations

Industry Group Preference: Communications, Computer Related, Consumer, Distribution, Electronic Components and Instrumentation, Energy/Natural Resources, Genetic Engineering, Industrial Products and Equipment, Medical/Health Related

Portfolio Companies: not available

Officers, Executives and Principals

Robert C. Ammerman, Managing Partner
Fred C. Danforth, Managing Partner
Alexander S. McGrath, Partner
Cheryl L. Walsh, Partner and Chief Financial Officer
Stephen M. Jenks, Partner
Christopher J. Carter, Investment Manager

CAPITAL SERVICES AND RESOURCES, INC.

5159 Wheelis Drive
Suite 106
Memphis, TN 38117

Telephone: 901-761-2156
Fax: 901-767-0060

Mission: Actively seeking new investments

Fund Size: not available
Founded: 1977
Average Investment: $100,000 to $5 million
Minimum Investment: $100,000

Investment Criteria: Second-stage, Leveraged Buyout, Special Situations, Capital Equipment Leasing

Industry Group Preference: Agriculture, Communications, Computer Related, Construction Equipment, Distribution, Electronic Components and Instrumentation, Energy/Natural Resources, Hotels, Industrial Equipment, Medical/Health Equipment, Municipal Capital Equipments, Restaurant (franchised) Equipment

Portfolio Companies: not available

Officers, Executives and Principals

A.P. Bancroft, Associate
S.L. Bancroft, Associate
P.F. Freund, Associate
J.B. Hays, Associate

CAPITAL SOUTHWEST CORPORATION

12900 Preston Road, Suite 700
Dallas, TX 75230

Telephone: 972-233-8242
Fax: 972-233-7362

Mission: To achieve capital appreciation through long-term investments in businesses believed to have favorable growth potential

Fund Size: $300 million
Founded: 1961
Average Investment: $2 million
Minimum Investment: $1 million

Investment Criteria: First-stage to Leveraged Buyout

Geographic Preference: Domestic United States

Industry Group Preference: High Technology, Manufacturing/Processing, Medical/Health, Retailing, Service Industries, Specialty Chemicals

Portfolio Companies: Alamo Group, Balco, All Components, American Homestar, Amfibe, Cherokee Communications, Data Race, Dennis Tool, Dymetrol, Encore Wire, Lil' Things, Mail-Well, Mylan Lass, PTS Holdings, Palm Harbor Homes, Petsmart, The Rectorseal Corporation, SDI Holding, Skylawn, Tecnol, Texas Petrochemical, Texas Shredder, Whitmore Manufacturing

Officers, Executives and Principals

William R. Thomas, President and Chairman of the Board
Education: MBA, with distinction, Harvard; BS, Chemical Engineering, Texas A&M
Background: Past Chairman, NASBIC; Governor-at-Large, National Associate of Securities Dealers; Past Chairman, National Associate of Securities Dealers Corporate Advisory Board

J. Bruce Duty, Senior Vice President
Education: BBA, honors, University of Texas; CPA
Background: Consultant, Alford, Meroney and Co.

Patrick F. Hammner, Vice President
Education: MBA, honors, University of Texas; BS, cum laude, Mechanical Engineering, Southern Methodist University
Background: Engineer, Otis Engineering Corporation

Tim Smith, Vice President/Secretary-Treasurer
Education: MBA, Harvard; BBA, magna cum laude, Accounting, Baylor University; CPA
Background: KPMG Peat Marwick

Scott Coller, Vice President
Education: MBA, honors, University of Texas; BS, magna cum laude, Aerospace Engineering, Texas A&M
Background: Engineer, Northrop Corporation

THE CAPITAL STRATEGY MANAGEMENT COMPANY

233 South Wacker Drive
P.O. Box 06334
Chicago, IL 60606-0344

Telephone: 312-444-1170

Mission: Actively seeking new investments, primarily early-stage

Fund Size: not available
Founded: 1982
Average Investment: $100,000 - $5 million
Minimum Investment: $100,000

Investment Criteria: Seed, Startup, First-stage, Second-stage, Leveraged Buyout, Control-block Purchases

Geographic Preference: Midwestern United States

Industry Group Preference: Communications, Computer Related, Consumer, Distribution, Electronic Components and Instrumentation, Energy/Natural Resources, Industrial Products and Equipment

Portfolio Companies: not available

Officers, Executives and Principals

Eric E. von Bauer, President and Chief Executive Officer

CAPITAL TECHNOLOGIES, INC.

1340 Centre Street
Newton Center, MA 02159

Telephone: 617-969-2690
Fax: 617-969-5147

Mission: Actively seeking new investments

Fund Size: not available
Founded: 1980
Average Investment: not available
Minimum Investment: Less than $100,000

Investment Criteria: Seed

Industry Group Preference: Computer Related, Industrial Products and Equipment

Portfolio Companies: not available

Officers, Executives and Principals

Edward Fredkin, Chairman
Joyce Fredkin, President
George A. Chamberlain III

CARDINAL VENTURES, L.L.C.

8910 Purdue Road
Suite 690
Indianapolis, IN 46268

Telephone: 317-228-5070
Fax: 317-228-5080

Mission: Actively seeking new investments

Fund Size: not available
Founded: 1993
Average Investment: not available
Minimum Investment: $250,000

Investment Criteria: Leveraged Buyouts with management

Industry Group Preference: Communications, Consumer, Distribution, Industrial Products and Equipment

Portfolio Companies: not available

Officers, Executives and Principals

John F. Ackerman, Principal
James L. Smeltzer, Principal
Douglas P. Conner, Principal

CARIAD CAPITAL, INC.

One Turks Head Place
Suite 1550
Providence, RI 02903-2215

Telephone: 401-751-8111
Fax: 401-751-8222
E-mail: ravandenberg@worldnet.att.net

Mission: Actively seeking new investments in private companies, small subsidiaries and/or divisions being divested by larger firms with annual revenues ranging from $10 million to $75 million and with annual pre-tax profits from $1 million to $10 million

Fund Size: not available
Founded: 1992
Average Investment: not available
Minimum Investment: $2 million

Investment Criteria: Leveraged Buyout, Control-block Purchases

Geographic Preference: Continental United States preferably east of the Rocky Mountains

Industry Group Preference: Industrial Products and Equipment

Portfolio Companies: Comsec Narragansett Security, Inc., Cushcraft Corporation, Kachina Semiconductor Services, Inc., Monaco Coach Company

Officers, Executives and Principals

Roger A. Vandenberg, President and Founder
Education: BS, Engineering, West Point Academy; MBA, Dartmouth College
Background: Seventeen years of experience in acquiring and investing in manufacturing and service businesses

Geraldine McNulty, Vice President
Education: BA, Economics, Brandeis University; MBA, Babson College
Background: CPA

Mary A. Ferreira, Controller
Education: BS, Accounting, Bryant College

CARILLON CAPITAL, INC.

Suite 1480, Kettering Tower
Dayton, OH 45423-1480

Telephone: 937-228-7920
Fax: 937-496-4055

Mission: Actively seeking new investments

Fund Size: not available
Founded: 1992
Average Investment: $750,000
Minimum Investment: $250,000

Investment Criteria: Second-stage, Mezzanine, Leveraged Buyout, Special Situations, Control-block Purchases

Industry Group Preference: Communications, Computer Related, Consumer, Distribution, Electronic Components and Instrumentation, Energy/Natural Resources, Industrial Products and Equipment, Medical/Health Related

Portfolio Companies: The Ultra-Met Company, Crysteco, Inc., MiracleCorp of Australia, GE SemiTechnologies, Inc.

Officers, Executives and Principals

C. Ronald McSwiney, Managing Director
William M. Sherk, Jr., Managing Director

CARL MARKS AND COMPANY, INC.

135 East 57th Street
New York, NY 10022

Telephone: 212-909-8428
Fax: 212-980-2630

Mission: Actively seeking new investments

Fund Size: not available
Founded: 1925
Average Investment: not available
Minimum Investment: $100,000

Investment Criteria: Startup, First-stage, Second-stage, Leveraged Buyout, Special Situations

Industry Group Preference: Communications, Computer Related, Consumer, Distribution, Electronic Components and Instrumentation, Energy/Natural Resources, Industrial Products and Equipment, Medical/Health Related

Portfolio Companies: not available

Officers, Executives and Principals

Howard Davidoff, Vice President
Robert Davidoff, Vice President

CARNEGIE VENTURE RESOURCES, INC.

301 North Harrison Street
Suite 157
Princeton, NJ 08540

Telephone: 609-921-0178
Fax: 609-921-0178

Mission: Actively seeking new investments

Fund Size: not available
Founded: 1983
Average Investment: not available
Minimum Investment: $100,000

Investment Criteria: Seed, Startup, First-stage, Second-stage, Leveraged Buyout

Industry Group Preference: Computer Related, Consumer, Distribution, Electronic Components and Instrumentation, Genetic Engineering, Industrial Products and Equipment, Medical/Health Related

Portfolio Companies: not available

Officers, Executives and Principals

James F. Mrazek, President
Dr. Neil Bodick, Director
R. Douglas Hulse, Director

CAROLINAS CAPITAL INVESTMENT CORPORATION

6337 Morrison Boulevard
Charlotte, NC 28211

Telephone: 704-362-8222
Fax: 704-362-8227

Mission: Actively seeking new investments

Fund Size: not available
Founded: 1988
Average Investment: $500,000
Minimum Investment: $100,000

Investment Criteria: First-stage, Second-stage, Mezzanine, Leveraged Buyout

Geographic Preference: North and South Carolina

Industry Group Preference: not available

Portfolio Companies: not available

Officers, Executives and Principals

Edward S. Goode, President

CASCADIA PACIFIC MANAGEMENT, LLC

4370 NE Halsey Street
Suite 233
Portland, OR 97213

Telephone: 503-282-2885
Fax: 503-282-2976
E-mail: tedbern@earthlink.net

Other Office Locations
Seed Management
#450-1122 Mainland Street
Vancouver, BC
Canada V6B 5L1
Phone 604-683-3685, Fax 604-689-4198

Mission: not available

Fund Size: $30 million, including $10 million Canadian
Founded: 1994
Average Investment: $300,000 - $500,000
Minimum Investment: not applicable

Investment Criteria: Seed to Start-up

Geographic Preference: British Columbia, Oregon

Industry Group Preference: Biotechnology, Computer Related, Electronics, Energy/Natural Resources, Environmental Protection, High Technology, Industrial Products, Information Services, Manufacturing/Processing, Medical/Health, Software

Portfolio Companies: TCC Communications, Biozyme, Hyperactive New Media, Westport Engineering, Ncompass Labs, UWI Unisoft Wares, Dehydration Research, GMW Speakertape, Cabana RV, Full Sail Ales Oregon Dehydration, International Bioclinical, Virtual Corporation, Radisys Corporation, ELD Manufacturing, FEI Company, Antivirals, Ralin Medical, Pacific Basin Shelter Company, 3C Semiconductor, Cascade Oncogenics PrintPaks, Sapient Health Network, Templex Technology

Officers, Executives and Principals

John Beaulieu, President
Education: BA, MA, University of Santa Clara
Background: Marketing and Financing, Ford Motor Co.; General Management Consulting, Arthur Young and Co.; Vice President, American Standard; Senior Vice President, American Bank Stationary; President, Steelcraft Corporation

Wayne Embree
Education: BA, Natural Sciences, MA, Urban and Regional Planning, University of Oregon
Background: Oregon Legislative Assembly; Consultant Marketing and Finance, Arizona Governors Office; Manager of Space Systems and Communication Operations, US Air Force

Doug Moore, Chief Financial Officer
Education: BA, Mathematics, Willamette University; MA, Industrial Administration, Carnegie-Mellon University
Background: Boise Cascade, Evans Products, Dow Chemical

THE CASTLE GROUP, LTD.

375 Park Avenue
Suite 1501
New York, NY 10152

Telephone: 212-832-4330
Fax: 212-832-4389

Mission: Actively seeking new investments

Fund Size: not available
Founded: 1990
Average Investment: not available
Minimum Investment: $500,000

Investment Criteria: Seed, Research and Development, Startup, First-stage, Second-stage, Control-block Purchases

Industry Group Preference: Computer Related, Genetic Engineering, Medical/Health Related

Portfolio Companies: not available

Officers, Executives and Principals

Lindsay A. Rosenwald, Chairman
William A. Ryan, Jr., Director, Technical Assessment
John Prendergast, Director, Operations
John Landow, Vice President
A. Joseph Rudick, Vice President

THE CATALYST GROUP, INC.

The Catalyst Fund, Ltd.
Three Riverway
Suite 770
Houston, TX 77056

Telephone: 713-623-8133
Fax: 713-623-0473

Mission: The Catalyst Fund, Ltd. is actively pursuing new mezzanine/subordinate termloan investments with an emphasis on manufacutring, service and wholesale distribution businesses

Fund Size: $20 million
Founded: 1991
Average Investment: $1 million
Minimum Investment: $500,000

Investment Criteria: Mezzanine, Acquisition Capital

Geographic Preference: United States

Industry Group Preference: Energy Services and Equipment, Manufacturing, Service, Wholesale/Distribution

Portfolio Companies: Lone Star Overnight, LP, ACR Group, Inc., Flintlock, Ltd., Deck the Walls, Inc., SpectraCell Labs, Inc., AGM Memorial, Inc., Summit Moulding and Frame, Inc.

Officers, Executives and Principals

Rick Herrman, Partner
Ron Nixon, Partner
Steve Gillioz, Vice President
Brandon Jacob, Marketing Director

THE CATALYST GROUP, INC.

Catalyst Capital Partners I and II
Three Riverway
Suite 770
Houston, TX 77056

Telephone: 713-623-8133
Fax: 713-623-0473

Mission: Catalyst Capital Partners I and II have been formed to make majority equity stakes in select companies. Catalyst Capital Partners I has made five investments and is fully invested. Catalyst Capital Partners II is actively pursuing new controlling equity investments with an emphasis on namufacturing, service and wholesale/distribution.

Fund Size: not available
Founded: 1990 (Catalyst Capital Partners I); 1996 (Catalyst Capital Partners II)
Average Investment: $2.5 million
Minimum Investment: $1 million

Investment Criteria: Controlling Equity Investments

Geographic Preference: United States

Industry Group Preference: Energy Services and Equipment, Manufacturing, Service, Wholesale/Distribution

Portfolio Companies: Manifold Valve Service, Inc., Compressor Dynamics, Inc., Elliott Valve and Repair, Ltd., Aluma-Craft Corporation, Inc.

Officers, Executives and Principals

Rick Herrman, Partner
Ron Nixon, Partner
Steve Gillioz, Vice President
Brandon Jacob, Marketing Director

CBM VENTURES, INC.
101 Federal Street
Suite 1900
Boston, MA 02110

Telephone: 617-342-7053
Fax: 617-342-7262

Mission: Actively seeking new investments

Fund Size: not available
Founded: 1993
Average Investment: not available
Minimum Investment: $100,000

Investment Criteria: Seed, Startup, First-stage

Industry Group Preference: Energy/Natural Resources, Industrial Products and Equipment

Portfolio Companies: not available

Officers, Executives and Principals

Charles M. Hutchins, Treasurer

THE CENTENNIAL FUNDS

1428 Fifteenth Street
Denver, CO 80202

Telephone: 303-405-7500
Fax: 303-405-7575
E-mail: inquire@Centennial.com

Other Office Locations
1330 Post Oak, Suite 1525
Houston, TX 77056
Phone 713-627-9200, Fax 713-627-9292, E-mail dhull@wynd.net

Mission: Centennial is seeking investments in service and technology companies in the electronic communications industry

Fund Size: $385 million
Founded: 1981
Average Investment: $12 million
Minimum Investment: $500,000 (seed): $5 million (early-stage)

Investment Criteria: Seed, Start-up, Early-stage, Late-stage

Industry Group Preference: Communications, Electronics

Portfolio Companies: Brooks Fiber Properties, Inc., Castle Tower Holdings Corp, HighGround Systems, Inc., Preferred Networks, Inc., Intercel, Inc., World-Net Access, Inc. Pluto Technologies, Inc.

Officers, Executives and Principals

Adam Goldman, General Partner
Education: MBA, Kellogg Graduate School of Management at Northwestern University

Steven C. Halstedt, General Partner
Education: MBA, Amos Tuck School of Business Administration at Dartmouth College

Donald H. Parsons, Jr., General Partner
Education: MBA, University of Michigan Business School

Jeffrey H. Schutz, General Partner
Education: BA, Economics, Middlebury College; MBA, University of Virginia

G. Jackson Tankersley, Jr., General Partner
Education: MBA, Amos Tuck School of Business Administration at Dartmouth College

David C. Hull, Jr., General Partner
Education: BS, Chemical Engineering; MBA, University of Texas at Austin; CPA

CENTER FOR BUSINESS INNOVATION

4747 Troost Avenue
Kansas City, MO 64110

Telephone: 816-561-8567
Fax: 816-756-1530

Mission: not available

Fund Size: not available
Founded: not available
Average Investment: $25,000
Minimum Investment: not available

Investment Criteria: Startups to $1 million sales

Geographic Preference: Kansas City Area

Industry Group Preference: Diversified

Portfolio Companies: Millennium, Comprose

Officers, Executives and Principals

Robert J. Sherwood, President
Education: BS, MS Engineering, University of Kansas; MBA, California State
Background: Founder of three startups that are now public

CENTER FOR NEW VENTURE ALLIANCE
CSUH School of Business
Hayward, CA 94542-3070

Telephone: 510-538-5200

Mission: Reducing investment activity

Fund Size: not available
Founded: 1985
Average Investment: not available
Minimum Investment: No minimum

Investment Criteria: Seed, Research and Development, Startup, Special Situations

Industry Group Preference: Communications, Computer Related, Consumer, Distribution, Electronic Components and Instrumentation, Energy/Natural Resources, Genetic Engineering, Industrial Products and Equipment, Medical/Health Related

Portfolio Companies: not available

Officers, Executives and Principals

Dr. Ric Singson, Co-Director
Dr. Norman Smothers, Co-Director
Larry Udell, Co-Director

CEO ADVISORS

1061 Maitland Center Commons
Suite 209
Maitland, FL 32751

Telephone: 407-660-9327

Mission: Reducing investment activity. Currently acting more as an advisor (business and financial) for early-stage companies. Look at business from a realistic potential "investor" viewpoint. Participate in business strategies for company development.

Fund Size: not available
Founded: 1989
Average Investment: $250,000+
Minimum Investment: not available

Investment Criteria: Seed, Research and Development, Startup, First-stage

Industry Group Preference: Communications, Computer Related, Consumer, Electronic Components and Instrumentation, Genetic Engineering, Industrial Products and Equipment, Medical/Health Related

Portfolio Companies: not available

Officers, Executives and Principals

G. Arthur Herbert, Principal
Education: BS, Engineering, US Naval Academy; MBA, Harvard
Background: 20 years Managing General Partner of three venture capital partnerships (Electro Science), 13 years various executive line and staff positions at Radiation, Inc. (Now Harris)
Directorships: Techne Corporation, Autonomous Technologies Corporation, Seavin Corporation, Vitacare, Inc.

CEO VENTURE FUND

4516 Henry Street
Pittsburgh, PA 15213

Telephone: 412-687-3451
Fax: 412-687-2791

Other Office Locations
1950 Old Gallows Road, Suite 440
Vienna, VA 22182
Phone 703-847-8823, Fax 703-506-8817

Mission: Formed by successful entrepreneurs and business development specialists to be a lead investor in the Mid-Atlantic region. The funds are a series of partnerships totaling $45 million designed to provide equity capital of $500,000 to $3 million. The CEO Venture Fund invests in early and later stage companies and has also completed a number of small management buyouts. A distinguishing feature of the CEO Venture Fund is the expertise the Partners provide to portfolio companies as they prepare for the opportunitites and challenges of growth.

Fund Size: $45 million
Founded: 1985
Average Investment: $2 million
Minimum Investment: $500,000

Investment Criteria: First-stage, Second-stage, Leveraged Buyout, Start-up

Industry Group Preference: Communications, Electronic Components and Instrumentation, Factory and Office Automation, Health Care Products and Services, Industrial Products, Information and Business Services, Software, Voice and Data Communications Software

Portfolio Companies: Adaptive Technology, American Computer and Electronics Corporation, BTG, Biological Detection Systems, Compucare, CME Conference Video, Databook, Daxus, Document Services, Montronix, Suprex

Officers, Executives and Principals

James Colker, Managing Partner (Pittsburgh)
Education: BS, Physics, University of Pittsburgh

William R. Newlin, Managing Partner (Pittsburgh)
Education: Princeton University; University of Pittsburgh School of Law

Glen F. Chatfield, General Partner (Pittsburgh)
Education: BS, Engineering Science, Pennsylvania State University

Gary P. Golding, General Partner (Vienna)
Education: Boston College; MA, University of Pittsburgh

Gene Yost, General Partner (Pittsburgh)
Education: BA, Washington and Jefferson College

Gary G. Glausser, Chief Financial Officer (Pittsburgh)
Education: BS, John Carroll University; MBA, University of Pittsburgh; CPA

CERULEAN FUND/WGC ENTERPRISES, INC.

1701 East Lake Avenue, Suite 170
Glenview, IL 60025

Telephone: 708-657-8002
Fax: 708-657-8168

Mission: not available

Fund Size: $50 million
Founded: not available
Average Investment: $2 million
Minimum Investment: not available

Investment Criteria:

Geographic Preference: Midwestern United States

Industry Group Preference: Computer Related, Consumer Related, Industrial Products, Manufacturing/Processing, Medical/Health, Retailing, Service Industries, Software, Toys

Portfolio Companies: Spectrix, Questar, Napersoft, Global Communicators, Dynasty Technologies, Success Magazine, Safety Diagnostics, Honsa Ergonomics, Scientific Nutrition Development, Bantum Lithotripter

Officers, Executives and Principals

Phil Roth
Brian Dettmann
Walter G. Cornett, III

CHANEN, PAINTER AND COMPANY, LTD.

701 Fifth Avenue
Suite 7450
Seattle, WA 98104

Telephone: 206-386-5656
Fax: 206-386-5376

Mission: not available

Fund Size: not available
Founded: 1988
Average Investment: not available
Minimum Investment: $1 million

Investment Criteria: First-stage, Second-stage, Mezzanine, Leveraged Buyout, Special Situations, International Technology Licensing

Industry Group Preference: not available

Portfolio Companies: not available

Officers, Executives and Principals

Gordon L. Chanen, Principal
J. Scott Painter, Principal
Stephen Campbell, Principal
John R. Miller, Principal
G. Robert Lewis, Associate
John Easterbrooks, Investment Analyst

CHARLES RIVER VENTURES

1000 Winter Street
Suite 3300
Waltham, MA 02154

Telephone: 617-487-7060
Fax: 617-487-7065

Mission: To invest in early-stage, high potential companies with the objective of building rigorous, high-growth businesses, which produce substantial capital gains

Fund Size: $280 million
Founded: 1970
Average Investment: $2 million
Minimum Investment: $1 million

Investment Criteria: First to Second-stage; market size $250 million; equity position greater than 10 percent

Industry Group Preference: Communications, Software

Portfolio Companies: Parametric, Sybase, Chipcom, Cascade Communications, ON Technology, Agile Networks

Officers, Executives and Principals

Donald W. Feddersen, General Partner
Education: BA, Purdue University; MBA, University of Chicago
Background: President and Chief Executive Officer, Applicon; Software Specialty

Stephen E. Coit, General Partner
Education: BA, MBA, Harvard

Michael J. Zak, General Partner
Education: BA, Cornell; MBA Harvard
Background: Communication Specialty

Richard M. Burnes, Jr., General Partner
Education: BA, Harvard; MBA, Boston University
Background: Founder, Charles River Ventures

Ted R. Dintersmith, General Partner
Education: BA, William and Mary College; Ph.D., Stanford University
Background: General Manager, Analog Devices

CHARTER VENTURE CAPITAL

525 University Avenue, Suite 1500
Palo Alto, CA 94302

Telephone: 415-325-6953
Fax: 415-325-4762
E-mail: lundberg@CCapital.com

Mission: not available

Fund Size: not available
Founded: 1982
Average Investment: $1 million
Minimum Investment: $100,000

Investment Criteria: Seed to Leveraged Buyout, Large Market or Proprietary Technology

Industry Group Preference: High Technology, Medical/Health

Portfolio Companies: Metricom, Univax Biologics, EP Technologies

Officers, Executives and Principals

A. Barr Dolan, Partner
Education: BA, Cornell University; MBA, Stanford University

Johnson Cha, Partner
Education: BS, Carnegie Mellon; MBA, Stanford University

Dave Lundberg, Associate
Education: BS, MBA, Stanford University

CHARTER VENTURE GROUP, INC.

2600 Citadel Plaza Drive
Suite 600
Houston, TX 77008

Telephone: 713-863-0704

Mission: Actively seeking new investments

Fund Size: not available
Founded: 1981
Average Investment: not available
Minimum Investment: Less than $100,000

Investment Criteria: First-stage, Second-stage, Mezzanine, Leveraged Buyout, Special Situations

Industry Group Preference: Communications, Consumer, Distribution, Energy/Natural Resources, Industrial Products and Equipment, Medical/Health Related

Portfolio Companies: not available

Officers, Executives and Principals

Winston Davis, President
Mike Roy, Vice President, Counsel
Jonathan Finger, Vice President, Investments

CHASE CAPITAL PARTNERS

380 Madison Avenue
12th Floor
New York, NY 10017

Telephone: 212-622-3100
Fax: 212-622-3101

Other Office Locations
840 Apollo Street, Suite 223
El Segundo, CA 90245
Phone 310-335-1955, Fax 310-335-1965

125 London Wall
London EC2Y 5AJ
England
Phone 44-171-777-3365, Fax 44-171-777-4731

150 Beach Road
#31-00-Gateway West
Singapore 189720
Singapore
Phone 65-290-1651 Fax 65-290-1337

Mission: Actively seeking new investments

Fund Size: $40 billion
Founded: 1984
Average Investment: not available
Minimum Investment: $2 million

Investment Criteria: Startup, First-stage, Second-stage, Mezzanine, Leveraged Buyout, Special Situations

Geographic Preference: Domestic, International

Industry Group Preference: Apparel, Automotive, Chemicals, Consumer, Direct Mail, Energy, Health Care, Information Services, Insurance and Financial Services, Media and Telecommunications, Power, Restaurants, Retail

Portfolio Companies: not available

Officers, Executives and Principals

Jeffrey C. Walker, Managing Partner
Mitchell J. Blutt, M.D. Executive Partner
Arnold L. Chavkin, Partner
David L. Ferguson, Partner (El Segundo)
Shahan Soghikian, Partner (London)
Yu-Seng Ting, Partner (Singapore)
H. Scott McKinley, Managing Director (Singapore)

CHATHAM VENTURE CORPORATION

420 Bedford Street
Lexington, MA 02173

Telephone: 617-863-0970
Fax: 617-862-6836

Mission: Making few, if any, new investments

Fund Size: not available
Founded: 1982
Average Investment: not available
Minimum Investment: $500,000

Investment Criteria: Mezzanine, Special Situations

Industry Group Preference: Communications, Computer Related, Electronic Components and Instrumentation, Industrial Products and Equipment

Portfolio Companies: not available

Officers, Executives and Principals

David F. Millet, Partner

CHEMICALS AND MATERIALS ENTERPRISE ASSOCIATES

250 Montgomery Street
11th Floor
San Francisco, CA 94104

Telephone: 415-352-1520
Fax: 415-352-1524

Other Office Locations
One Cleveland Center
1375 East Ninth Street, Suite 2700
Cleveland, OH 44114
Phone 216-861-4800, Fax 216-621-4543

Mission: Actively seeking new investments

Fund Size: $41 million
Founded: 1989
Average Investment: $1 million
Minimum Investment: Less than $100,000

Investment Criteria: Seed, Startup, First-stage, Second-stage

Industry Group Preference: Biotechnology, Distribution, Electronic Components and Instrumentation, Energy/Natural Resources, Genetic Engineering, High Technology, Industrial Products and Equipment, Medical/Health Related

Portfolio Companies: Aerotrans, Candescent Technologies, Conceptus, Endocardial Therapeutics, Flextronics, Fluid Propulsion Technologies, Metcal, Nanodyne, Physiometrix, Targeted, Genetics, Vitesse, Semiconductor, ZC Optics

Officers, Executives and Principals

Thomas R. Baruch, General Partner (San Francisco)
Donald L. Murfin, General Partner (Cleveland)

CHERRY TREE INVESTMENTS, INC.

3800 West 80th Street, #1400
Minneapolis, MN 55431

Telephone: 612-893-9012
Fax: 612-893-9036
E-mail: Cherrytree@msn.com

Mission: not available

Fund Size: $87 million
Founded: 1982
Average Investment: $1 million
Minimum Investment: not available

Investment Criteria: Seed to Second-stage

Geographic Preference: Midwestern United States

Industry Group Preference: Consumer, Diversified, Educational, Information Services, Multi-Unit Businesses

Portfolio Companies: Arbor Health Care, Ringer Corporation, Fourth Shift, TRO Learning, Computer Petroleum Corporation, FSI International, Aurum Software, Transport America, Insignia Systems, Harmony Brook, Pet Food Warehouse

Officers, Executives and Principals

Gordon F. Stofer, Partner
Education: BA, Cornell University; MBA, Harvard Business School

Tony Christianson, Partner
Education: BA, St. Johns University; MBA, Harvard Business School

Daniel Albright, Associate
Education: BA, University of St. Thomas; MBA, University of Minnesota

CHURCHILL CAPITAL, INC.

ESOP Group
2400 and 3100 Metropolitan Centre
333 South Seventh Street
Minneapolis, MN 55402

Telephone: 612-673-6633
Fax: 612-673-6630
E-mail: info@churchillnet.com

Mission: Actively seeking new investments

Fund Size: $188 million
Founded: 1987
Average Investment: $6 million
Minimum Investment: $2 million

Investment Criteria: Mezzanine, Leveraged Buyout, Management Buyouts, Recapitalizations, Refinancings, Asset Purchases, Growth Capital, Capital Expenditures, ESOP's

Industry Group Preference: Business-to-business Service and Products, Communications, Consumer, Distribution, Electronic Components and Instrumentation, General Manufacturing, Industrial Products and Equipment, Medical/Health Related, Service Industries

Portfolio Companies: not available

Officers, Executives and Principals

John J. Fauth, Chairman and Director
Education: BS, Georgetown University
Background: Co-Founder, Churchill Capital, Inc.; Founder, The Churchill Companies; Vice President and Senior Credit Officer, Citicorp (USA), Inc.

Michael J. Hahn, President and Chief Executive Officer
Education: BS, Boston College; MBA, University of Chicago
Background: Co-founded Churchill Capital in 1987; Vice President, Regional Executive, and Senior Credit Officer, Citicorp North America, Inc.

Joseph G. Kohler, Secretary and General Counsel
Education: BA, Ohio University; MBA, University of Cincinnati; JD, Drake University; CPA
Background: Counsel and former Partner, Lindquist and Vennum; Tax Attorney, Shell Oil Company, Arthur Andersen and Company

Kevin C. Dooley, Senior Vice President and Legal Counsel
Education: BA, St. Lawrence; JD, Syracuse University
Background: Partner, Business and Finance Group, Rider, Bennett, Egan and Arundel

Barry S. Lindquist, Senior Vice President, Investment, Underwriting and Administration
Education: BS, University of Wisconsin; MBA, University of Michigan
Background: Vice President, Area Manager and Senior Credit Officer, Citicorp Private Bank

Mark Kaplan, Senior Vice President, Quantitative Strategies
Education: BA, Harvard College; MA, University of St. Thomas
Background: Senior Vice President, Public Finance Department, Norwest Investment Services; Vice President, Dain Bosworth Inc.

Robin L. Howe, Principal
Education: BA, Brown University
Background: Vice President and Senior Transactor, Heller Financial; Investment Associate, CF Capital Corporation

Robert L. Davis, Principal
Education: BA, MME, Rice University; MBA, JD, Stanford University
Background: Managing Partner, Fabyanski, Svoboda, Westra, Davis and Hart; Practiced law for 22 years in New York, London and Minneapolis

David J. Wakefield, Principal
Education: BS, San Diego State University
Background: Vice President and Investment Committee member, Pacific Corporate Group

Jeffrey A. Mudge, Senior Analyst
Education: BBA, University of Texas, MBA, University of Minnesota
Background: Commercial Banking Officer, First Bank System

Thomas A. Kreimer, Controller
Education: BA, University of St. Thomas; CPA
Background: Senior Accountant, Charles Bailly and Co.

Debra D. Gardner, Assistant Controller
Education: BA, University of Northern Iowa; CPA
Background: Staff Accountant, Price Waterhouse, LLP

CHURCHILL CAPITAL, INC.

Subordinated Debt Group
2400 and 3100 Metropolitan Centre
333 South Seventh Street
Minneapolis, MN 55402

Telephone: 612-673-6633
Fax: 612-673-6630
E-mail: info@churchillnet.com

Mission: Actively seeking new investments

Fund Size: $250 million
Founded: 1987
Average Investment: $6 million
Minimum Investment: $2 million

Investment Criteria: Mezzanine, Leveraged Buyout, Management Buyouts, Recapitalizations, Refinancings, Asset Purchases, Growth Capital, Capital Expenditures

Industry Group Preference: Business-to-business Service and Products, Communications, Consumer, Distribution, Electronic Components and Instrumentation, General Manufacturing, Industrial Products and Equipment, Medical/Health Related, Service Industries

Portfolio Companies: not available

Officers, Executives and Principals

John J. Fauth, Chairman and Director
Education: BS, Georgetown University
Background: Co-Founder, Churchill Capital, Inc.; Founder, The Churchill Companies; Vice President and Senior Credit Officer, Citicorp (USA), Inc.

Michael J. Hahn, President and Chief Executive Officer
Education: BS, Boston College; MBA, University of Chicago
Background: Co-founded Churchill Capital in 1987; Vice President, Regional Executive, and Senior Credit Officer, Citicorp North America, Inc.

Joseph G. Kohler, Secretary and General Counsel
Education: BA, Ohio University; MBA, University of Cincinnati; JD, Drake University; CPA
Background: Counsel and former Partner, Lindquist and Vennum; Tax Attorney, Shell Oil Company, Arthur Andersen and Company

Kevin C. Dooley, Senior Vice President and Legal Counsel
Education: BA, St. Lawrence; JD, Syracuse University
Background: Partner, Business and Finance Group, Rider, Bennett, Egan and Arundel

Barry S. Lindquist, Senior Vice President, Investment, Underwriting and Administration
Education: BS, University of Wisconsin; MBA, University of Michigan
Background: Vice President, Area Manager and Senior Credit Officer, Citicorp Private Bank

Mark Kaplan, Senior Vice President, Quantitative Strategies
Education: BA, Harvard College; MA, University of St. Thomas
Background: Senior Vice President, Public Finance Department, Norwest Investment Services; Vice President, Dain Bosworth Inc.

Michael D. McHugh, Principal
Education: BS, University of Nebraska
Background: Vice President, First Bank National Association; Commercial Banking Officer, Norwest Bank

Sandra A. Mayasich, Principal
Education: BS, University of Minnesota; CPA
Background: Senior Asset Manager, Northstar Resource Group; Staff Accountant, Touche, Ross and Co.

Michael J. Hall, Principal
Education: BA, Columbia College; BS, Columbia School of Engineering and Applied Science; MBA, New York University Stern School of Business
Background: Vice President, Heller Financial, Wells Fargo Bank, and Security Pacific Bank

Thomas M. Gray, Analyst
Education: BS, New York University
Background: Corporate Financial Analyst, Piper Jaffrey, Inc.

Thomas A. Kreimer, Controller
Education: BA, University of St. Thomas; CPA
Background: Senior Accountant, Charles Bailly and Co.

Debra D. Gardner, Assistant Controller
Education: BA, University of Northern Iowa; CPA
Background: Staff Accountant, Price Waterhouse, LLP

CIBC WOOD GUNDY CAPITAL

425 Lexington Avenue
New York, NY 10017

Telephone: 212-856-3736
Fax: 212-697-1544

Other Office Locations
161 Bay Street, Sixth Floor
Toronto, Ontario M5J 2S8
Canada
Phone 416-594-8022, Fax 416-594-8037

Mission: Actively seeking new investments

Fund Size: $200 million
Founded: 1989
Average Investment: $8 million
Minimum Investment: $2 million

Investment Criteria: Second-stage, Mezzanine, Leveraged Buyout, Special Situations

Industry Group Preference: Communications, Computer Related, Consumer, Distribution, Electronic Components and Instrumentation, Energy/Natural Resources, Genetic Engineering, Industrial Products and Equipment, Medical/Health Related

Portfolio Companies: not available

Officers, Executives and Principals

David Kassie (Toronto)
Jill Denham (Toronto)
John B. Breen (Toronto)
Richard Brekka (New York)
Geoff Browne (Toronto)
Ken Kilgour (Toronto)
Barry Stewart (New York)
Alan Wearing (Toronto)

CID EQUITY PARTNERS

2850 One American Square
Box 82074
Indianapolis, IN 46282

Telephone: 317-269-2350
Fax: 317-269-2355

Other Office Locations
Two Nationwide Plaza, Suite 805
Columbus, OH 43215
Phone 614-222-8185, Fax 614-222-8190

Mission: Actively seeking new investments in high-growth companies

Fund Size: $216 million
Founded: 1981
Average Investment: $3 million
Minimum Investment: $1 million

Investment Criteria: Startup, First-stage, Second-stage, Management Buyout, Special Situations

Geographic Preference: Midwestern United States

Industry Group Preference: Communications, Computer Related, Consumer, Distribution, Electronic Components and Instrumentation, Engineering Services, Environmental Products and Services, Financial Services, Industrial Products and Equipment, Information Technology, Medical/Health Related, Transportation

Portfolio Companies: Contour Hardening, Inc., Core Source, Inc., Propane Continental, Inc., Enzymol International, Inc., Cold Jet, Inc., Welcare International, Inc., Bohdan Automation, Inc., Trans2 Corporation, Compression, Inc., DMAC, Inc., Long Term Care Physicians Corporation, Safety and Rescue Systems, Inc., Salesoft, Inc., Varis Corporation, Imageware Corporation, Open Port Technology, Inc., Receivables Funding Corporation, TelServe, Inc., Alta Analytics, Inc., Megan Health, Inc., Auxein Corporation

Officers, Executives and Principals

John T. Hackett, Managing General Partner (Indianapolis)
John C. Aplin, General Partner (Indianapolis)
Robert A. Compton, General Partner (Indianapolis)
Kevin E. Sheehan, General Partner (Indianapolis)
William S. Oesterle, General Partner (Columbus)
Jennifer H. Page, Senior Associate (Indianapolis)

CILCORP VENTURES, INC.

300 Hamilton Square
Suite 300
Peoria, IL 61602

Telephone: 309-675-8836
Fax: 309-675-8800

Mission: Reducing investment activity

Fund Size: not available
Founded: 1985
Average Investment: not available
Minimum Investment: $250,000

Investment Criteria: Startup, First-stage, Second-stage

Industry Group Preference: Energy/Natural Resources, Genetic Engineering, Industrial Products and Equipment

Portfolio Companies: not available

Officers, Executives and Principals

R.J. Sprowls, President

CIRCLE VENTURES, INC.

26 North Arsenal Avenue
Indianapolis, IN 46201

Telephone: 317-636-7242
Fax: 317-469-4550

Mission: Actively seeking new investments

Fund Size: not available
Founded: 1983
Average Investment: not available
Minimum Investment: Less than $100,000

Investment Criteria: Second-stage, Mezzanine, Leveraged Buyout, Special Situations

Industry Group Preference: not available

Portfolio Companies: not available

Officers, Executives and Principals

Carrie Walkup, President
Susan Meyer, Treasurer
Theresia Paauwe, Secretary
William Konyha, Assistant Secretary

THE CIT GROUP/EQUITY INVESTMENTS
THE CIT GROUP/VENTURE CAPITAL, INC.
650 CIT Drive
Livingston, NJ 07039

Telephone: 201-740-5181
Fax: 201-740-5555
E-mail: www.citgroup.com

Other Office Locations
1211 Avenue of the Americas
New York, NY 10036
Phone 212-536-1905, Fax 212-536-1912
E-mail: www.citgroup.com

Mission: Will function as deal originator and sponsor or investor in deals created by others; actively seeking new investments

Fund Size: $100 million
Founded: 1990
Average Investment: $3.5 million
Minimum Investment: $1 million

Investment Criteria: Second-stage, Mezzanine, Leveraged Buyout, Growth Capital

Geographic Preference: United States

Industry Group Preference: Aviation and Aerospace, Apparel and Textiles, Automotive Parts, Chemicals, Entertainment and Leisure, Food Products, Healthcare, Information Processing, Medical Products, Packaging, Paper, Plastics, Precision Manufacturing, Printing, Specialty Retailing, Telecommunications, Transportation

Portfolio Companies: Columbia Holding Corporation, Lionheart Industries, Interlab Holdings, Mail-Well, The Lofland Company, Berry Plastics Corporation, Rex-Rosenlew International, Store of Knowledge, Magic Cinemas, Sterling Chemicals, Texas Petrochemicals, DuPont Imaging, Ventana Medical Systems, Genvec, Trophix Pharmaceuticals, Mitotix, Focal, Recombinant Biocatalysis, Spectrascan, Micro Therapeutics

Officers, Executives and Principals

Paul J. Laud, President (Livingston)
Colby W. Collier, Managing Director (Livingston)
Bruce Schackman, Managing Director (Livingston)
Kevin P. Falvey, Vice President (Livingston)
Christopher L. Weiler, Vice President (Livingston)
Janice C. Beckmen, Investment Officer (Livingston)

THE CIT GROUP/VENTURE CAPITAL, INC.

650 CIT Drive
Livingston, NJ 07039-5795

Telephone: 201-740-5181
Fax: 201-740-5555

Mission: not available

Fund Size: $50 million
Founded: not available
Average Investment: $2 million
Minimum Investment: not available

Investment Criteria: Second-stage to Leveraged Buyout

Industry Group Preference: Aerospace, Biotechnology, Communications, Consumer Related, Environmental Protection, Food Services, Information Services, Manufacturing/Processing, Medical/Health, Publishing, Service Industries, Transportation

Portfolio Companies: Optical Sensors, Iomed, Timothy's Coffees of the World, The Lofland Company

Officers, Executives and Principals

Paul J. Laud, President
Colby Collier, Vice President
Kevin Falvey, Vice President
Christopher Weiler, Investment Officer

CITICORP VENTURE CAPITAL, LTD.

399 Park Avenue
14th Floor
New York, NY 10043

Telephone: 212-559-1127
Fax: 212-888-2940

Mission: Actively seeking new investments

Fund Size: not available
Founded: 1968
Average Investment: not available
Minimum Investment: $1 million

Investment Criteria: Second-stage, Leveraged Buyout, Special Situations

Industry Group Preference: Communications, Computer Related, Consumer, Distribution, Electronic Components and Instrumentation, Energy/Natural Resources, Genetic Engineering, Industrial Products and Equipment, Medical/Health Related

Portfolio Companies: not available

Officers, Executives and Principals

William T. Comfort, Chairman
Peter G. Gerry, President
Byron Knief, Senior Vice President
James L. Luikart, Vice President
Thomas F. McWilliams, Vice President
Kilin To, Vice President
Noelle Cournoyer, Assistant Vice President
Joseph Silvestri, Assistant Vice President

CLAFLIN CAPITAL MANAGEMENT, INC.

77 Franklin Street
Boston, MA 02110

Telephone: 617-426-6505
Fax: 617-482-0016

Other Office Locations
Ukraine Fund
20 Pushkinskaya Street, Apartment #26
Kiev 252004
Ukraine
Phone 38004-228-6216

Mission: Actively seeking new investments

Fund Size: $57 million
Founded: 1978
Average Investment: $500,000
Minimum Investment: Less than $100,000

Investment Criteria: Seed, Startup, First-stage

Industry Group Preference: Communications, Computer Related, Consumer, Distribution, Electronic Components and Instrumentation, Industrial Products and Equipment, Medical/Health Related

Portfolio Companies: not available

Officers, Executives and Principals

Thomas M. Claflin II, General Partner
Lloyd C. Dahmen, General Partner
John O. Flender, General Partner
Joseph Stavenhagen, General Partner
Frederick Keming Zhang, General Partner
Walter M. Bird III, General Partner
Rolf S. Stutz, General Partner

CLAIRVEST GROUP, INC.

22 St. Clair Avenue East, Suite 1700
Toronto, Ontario M4T 2S3
Canada

Telephone: 416-925-9270
Fax: 416-925-5753

Mission: To assist managed companies in an entrepreneurial fashion to accelerate their development

Fund Size: $150 million
Founded: 1987
Average Investment: $10 - 20 million
Minimum Investment: $5 million

Investment Criteria: Leveraged Buyout, Special Situations, Control-block Purchases, Turnaround, Growth
Companies (not venture capital)

Geographic Preference: Canada

Industry Group Preference: Communications, Distribution, Financial Services, Food, Industrial Products and
Equipment, Manufacturing, Medical/Health Related, Retailing

Portfolio Companies: National Rubber, Tempo (Industrial Diamonds), Continental Pharma, Premdor, Western
Co-Axial Cable, Trentway-Wagner Buses, Sparkling Spring Water, Marks Work Wearhouse, Signature Security Group, Datamark, Sportscope, Consoltex Group

Officers, Executives and Principals

Joseph L. Rotman, President, Chief Executive Officer and Managing Director
Philip Goodeve, Managing Director
Jeff Parr, Managing Director
Kenneth B. Rotman, Managing Director
Graham Rosenberg, Vice President
Rob Crocker, Director, Finance

CLARION CAPITAL CORPORATION

1801 East 9th Street, Suite 510
Cleveland, OH 44114

Telephone: 216-687-1096
Fax: 216-694-3545

Mission: not available

Fund Size: $25 million
Founded: not available
Average Investment: $500,000
Minimum Investment: not available

Investment Criteria: First-stage to Leveraged Buyout

Industry Group Preference: Biotechnology, Communications, Computer Related, Electronics, Energy/Natural Resources, Environmental Protection

Portfolio Companies: not available

Officers, Executives and Principals

Morton Cohen, Chairman/President
Education: MBA, Wharton
Background: Chief Executive Officer, Childers Products Co. and Tera California; Governor, Montreal Stock Exchange; Board of Governors of NASBIC
Directorships: Chairman, Monitek Technologies; Director, Rapitech Systems, Small's Oilfield Services, American Natural Energy Corporation, Zemex Corporation

CMNY CAPITAL, L.P.
135 East 57th Street
New York, NY 10022

Telephone: 212-909-8400
Fax: 212-980-2630

Mission: not available

Fund Size: $75 million
Founded: not available
Average Investment: $500,000
Minimum Investment: not available

Investment Criteria: none

Industry Group Preference: Diversified

Portfolio Companies: not available

Officers, Executives and Principals

Robert Davidoff, General Partner
Education: BBA, City College of New York
Directorships: Instanet, Delta Data Systems, Audio/Video Affiliates, Hubco Exploration, Transmagnetics, Milgray Electronics

Howard Davidoff, Partner

CMNY CAPITAL II, L.P.

135 East 57th Street
New York, NY 10022

Telephone: 212-909-8428
Fax: 212-980-2630

Mission: Actively seeking new investments

Fund Size: not available
Founded: 1989
Average Investment: not available
Minimum Investment: $250,000

Investment Criteria: First-stage, Mezzanine, Leveraged Buyout

Industry Group Preference: Communications, Computer Related, Consumer, Distribution, Electronic Components and Instrumentation, Energy/Natural Resources, Industrial Products and Equipment, Medical/Health Related

Portfolio Companies: not available

Officers, Executives and Principals

Robert Davidoff, General Partner
Howard Davidoff, Partner

CODE, HENNESSY AND SIMMONS, LP
CODE, HENNESSY AND SIMMONS II, LP

10 South Wacker Drive
Suite 3175
Chicago, IL 60606

Telephone: 312-876-1840
Fax: 312-876-3854

Mission: Actively seeking new investments

Fund Size: $82.5 million (CHS, LP); $155 million (CHS II)
Founded: 1989; 1994
Average Investment: not available
Minimum Investment: $5 million

Investment Criteria: Leveraged Buyout

Industry Group Preference: Consumer, Industrial Products and Equipment

Portfolio Companies: not available

Officers, Executives and Principals

Andrew W. Code, Principal
Daniel J. Hennessy, Principal
Brian P. Simmons, Principal
Thomas J. Formolo, Managing Director
Peter M. Gotsch, Managing Director
Jon S. Vesely, Managing Director

COGNIZANT ENTERPRISES

200 Nyala Farms Road
Westport, CT 06880

Telephone: 203-222-4595
Fax: 203-222-4592

Other Office Locations
One Canal Park
Cambridge, MA 02141
Phone 617-374-5543, Fax 617-374-5585

Mission: Actively seeking new investments in the information technology and services markets. We have a strong track record of providing assistance to portfolio management teams in areas such as strategic planning, developing key partnering relationships and IPO preparation and execution.

Fund Size: $60 million (Information Partners); $80 million (Information Associates)
Founded: 1989
Average Investment: $3 million
Minimum Investment: $500,000

Investment Criteria: Early-stage to Leveraged Buyout

Geographic Preference: not applicable

Industry Group Preference: Information Services, Information Technology

Portfolio Companies: (Information Partners): Aspect Development, Course Technology, Dataware Technologies, EduServ Technologies, Environmental Data Resources, Florists Transworld Delivery, Gartner Group, Inc., Jostens Learning Corporation, Market Metrics, Inc., MAXM Systems Corporation, MediQual Systems Inc., Oacis Healthcare Systems, One Source Information Services, Risk Management Solutions, SR Research, Inc., T.R.A.D.E. Inc., Strategic Mapping, Inc., Stream International, Inc., TSI International, Inc., The WEFA Group, Inc. (Information Associates): DAOU Systems, Inc., Nets, Inc., Internet Profiles Corporation, Online Interactive, Inc., Firefly Network, Evolving Systems, Inc., Internet Securities, Inc., Pegasus Systems, Silicon Valley Internet Partners, Vality Technology, Inc.

Officers, Executives and Principals

Dennis G. Sisco, President
Venetia Kontogouris, Senior Vice President, Venture Development
Peter Meekin, Vice President, Venture Development
Cynthia Cronk-Brockhoff, Associate, Venture Development

COHEN AND COMPANY, LLC

800 Third Avenue
New York, NY 10022

Telephone: 212-317-2250
Fax: 212-317-2255
E-mail: nlcohen@aol.com

Other Office Locations
1100 Franklin Avenue
Garden City, NY 11530

Mission: Cohen and Company, LLC was formed to provide growth, acquisition and special situations capital for companies with valuations between $5 million and $100 million. We expect that many of our transactions will come from generational situations and divisional managers who want to acquire their divisions and then expand. Furthermore, we believe that our prior experience makes an ideal partner for turnarounds and recapitalizations. We will also consider, in addition to control positions, minority positions and/or mezzanine capital investments.

Fund Size: not available
Founded: 1994
Average Investment: not available
Minimum Investment: $500,000

Investment Criteria: Second-stage, Mezzanine, Leveraged Buyout, Special Situations, Control-block Purchases, Recapitalizations, Turnarounds

Geographic Preference: International

Industry Group Preference: not available

Portfolio Companies: not available

Officers, Executives and Principals

Neil L. Cohen, President
Charles T. Collins, Associate

COLEMAN VENTURE GROUP

5909 Northern Boulevard
P.O. Box 244
East Norwich, NY 11732

Telephone: 516-626-3642
Fax: 516-626-9722

Mission: Actively seeking new investments

Fund Size: not available
Founded: 1965
Average Investment: $250,000
Minimum Investment: Less than $100,000

Investment Criteria: Seed, Startup, First-stage, Special Situations

Industry Group Preference: Electronic Components and Instrumentation, Energy/Natural Resources, Industrial Products and Equipment

Portfolio Companies: not available

Officers, Executives and Principals

Gregory S. Coleman, President
Roger V. Coleman, Vice President

COLORADO VENTURE MANAGEMENT

4845 Pearl East Circle, Suite 300
Boulder, CO 80303

Telephone: 303-440-4055
Fax: 303-440-4636

Mission: To invest risk capital in start-up to early stage, technology-based businesses.

Fund Size: $12.5 million
Founded: 1979
Average Investment: $200,000
Minimum Investment: $25,000

Investment Criteria: Seed to First-stage

Geographic Preference: Rocky Mountains

Industry Group Preference: Biotechnology, Communications, Computer Related, Diversified, Energy/Natural Resources, High Technology, Information Services

Portfolio Companies: not available

Officers, Executives and Principals

R.D. Bloomer, Managing General Partner
Ed Wetherbee, General Partner
William E. Coleman, General Partner

COMMTECH INTERNATIONAL

535 Middlefield Road
Suite 200
Menlo Park, CA 94025

Telephone: 415-328-0190

Mission: Making few, if any, new investments

Fund Size: not available
Founded: 1983
Average Investment: not available
Minimum Investment: $100,000

Investment Criteria: Seed, Startup, Research and Development

Geographic Preference: California

Industry Group Preference: Communications, Computer Related, Distribution, Electronic Components and Instrumentation, Internet Related, Medical/Health Related

Portfolio Companies: Acuprint, Inc., Amati Communications Corporation, Colorep, Inc., Franz, Inc., Micro-bionics, Inc., Scriptel Holding Corporation

Officers, Executives and Principals

Dr. Gerald Marxman, President
Frank Kocsis, Vice President
Raymond Paynter, Associate

COMMUNICATIONS EQUITY ASSOCIATES, INC.

101 East Kennedy Boulevard
Suite 3300
Tampa, FL 33602

Telephone: 813-226-8844
Fax: 813-225-1513
E-mail: http://www.commequ.com

Other Office Locations

375 Park Avenue, Suite 3808
New York, NY 10152
Phone 212-319-1968, Fax 212-319-4293

1235 Westlakes Drive, Suite 245
Berwyn, PA 19312
Phone 610-251-0650, Fax 610-251-9180

33 Cavendish Square
London W1M 0BQ
Phone 44-171-290-5000, Fax 44-171-290-5025

9 Raffles Plaza
Singapore 048619
Phone 65-533-2002, Fax 65-532-2002

Level 1/175 MacQuarie Street
Sydney, NSW 2000
Australia
Phone 61-2-9367-3000, Fax 61-2-9367-3111

Mission: Actively seeking new investments

Fund Size: $214 million
Founded: 1973
Average Investment: not available
Minimum Investment: $1 million

Investment Criteria: First-stage, Second-stage, Mezzanine, Leveraged Buyout, Special Situations

Geographic Preference: Global

Industry Group Preference: Communications, Entertainment, Media

Portfolio Companies: not available

Officers, Executives and Principals

J. Patrick Michaels, Jr., Chairman (Tampa)
Harold D. Ewen, Vice Chairman (Tampa)
David A. Burns, Chief Operating Officer (Tampa)
H. Gene Gawthrop, Director (Tampa)

COMPASS TECHNOLOGY PARTNERS

1550 El Camino Real
Suite 275
Menlo Park, CA 94025

Telephone: 415-322-7595
Fax: 415-366-7597

Other Office Locations
128 East 31st Street
New York, NY 10016-6848
Phone 212-685-2763, Fax 212-689-5301

Mission: Actively seeking new investments

Fund Size: not available
Founded: 1988
Average Investment: not available
Minimum Investment: No minimum

Investment Criteria: Mezzanine, Leveraged Buyout, Special Situations

Industry Group Preference: Communications, Computer Related, Consumer, Distribution, Electronic Components and Instrumentation, Genetic Engineering, Industrial Products and Equipment, Medical/Health Related

Portfolio Companies: not available

Officers, Executives and Principals

David G. Arscott, General Partner (Atherton)
Leon H. Dulberger, General Partner (New York)

CONNING AND COMPANY

City-Place II
185 Asylum Street
Hartford, CT 06103

Telephone: 203-527-1131
Fax: 203-520-1299

Mission: Actively seeking new investments

Fund Size: not available
Founded: 1985
Average Investment: not available
Minimum Investment: Over $1 million

Investment Criteria: Startup, First-stage, Second-stage, Mezzanine, Leveraged Buyout, Special Situations

Portfolio Companies: not available

Officers, Executives and Principals

M.W. Slayton, Chairman, President and Chief Executive Officer
Joseph D. Sargent, Vice Chairman
Stephan L. Christiansen, Senior Vice President
John B. Clinton, Senior Vice President
Gordon G. Pratt, Senior Vice President
Steven F. Piaker, Vice President
Gerard Vecchio, Vice President
James T. Bagley, Assistant Vice President and Chief Financial Officer

CONSUMER VENTURE PARTNERS

3 Pickwick Plaza
Greenwich, CT 06830

Telephone: 203-629-8800

Mission: CVP invests exclusively in consumer products and services. Specifically, CVP looks for opportunities in specialty retail, direct response, niche product, and restaurant companies

Fund Size: $85 million
Founded: 1986
Average Investment: $2.5 million
Minimum Investment: $1 million

Investment Criteria: Early expansion, $500,000 sales

Industry Group Preference: Consumer Related, Financial Services, Restaurants, Retailing, Service Industries

Portfolio Companies: Gymboree Corporation, Pacific Sunwear of California, Natural Wonders, Inc., Sportstown, Petstuff

Officers, Executives and Principals

Christopher P. Kirchen, General Partner
Pearson C. Cummin III, General Partner
David Yarnell, Vice President

CONTINENTAL ILLINOIS VENTURE CORPORATION

231 South LaSalle Street
Chicago, IL 60697

Telephone: 312-828-8021
Fax: 312-987-6763

Mission: Actively seeking new investments

Fund Size: not available
Founded: 1970
Average Investment: not available
Minimum Investment: $5 million

Investment Criteria: Leveraged Buyout, Special Situations, Control-block Purchases

Industry Group Preference: not available

Portfolio Companies: not available

Officers, Executives and Principals

Christopher J. Perry, President
Daniel G. Helle, Managing Partner
Marcus D. Wedner, Managing Partner
William B. Franklin, Chief Financial Officer

CONTINENTAL S.B.I.C.

P.O. Box 3723
Arlington, VA 22203

Telephone: 703-527-5200
Fax: 703-527-3700

Mission: Actively seeking new investments

Fund Size: not available
Founded: 1989
Average Investment: not available
Minimum Investment: $100,000

Investment Criteria: Second-stage, Mezzanine, Leveraged Buyout, Special Situations

Geographic Preference: East Coast

Industry Group Preference: Computer Related, Consumer, Distribution, Electronic Components and Instrumentation, Energy/Natural Resources, Industrial Products and Equipment

Portfolio Companies: not available

Officers, Executives and Principals

Arthur L. Walters, President
Mark W. Walters, Vice President
Thomas Goodfellow, Treasurer

COPLEY VENTURE PARTNERS

600 Atlantic Avenue, 13th Floor
Boston, MA 02210-2214

Telephone: 617-722-6030
Fax: 617-523-7739

Mission: Not seeking new investments; current investments fully funded

Fund Size: $60 million
Founded: not available
Average Investment: $1 million
Minimum Investment: not available

Investment Criteria: Startup to Second-stage

Industry Group Preference: Biotechnology, Communications, Computer Related, Consumer Related, Educational, Electronics, Food Services, Industrial Products, Medical/Health, Publishing, Retailing, Software

Portfolio Companies: not available

Officers, Executives and Principals

David J. Ryan, General Partner
Julius Jensen III, General Partner
Matthias Plum, Jr., General Partner
Henry F. Sears, Associate

CORAL GROUP, INC.

60 South Sixth Street
Suite 3510
Minneapolis, MN 55402

Telephone: 612-335-8666
Fax: 612-335-8668

Other Office Locations
3000 Sand Hill Road
Building Three, Suite 210
Menlo Park, CA 94025
Phone 415-854-5226, Fax 415-854-7415

Mission: Actively seeking new investments

Fund Size: $227 million
Founded: 1983
Average Investment: $3 million - $ 5 million
Minimum Investment: $100,000

Investment Criteria: Seed, Research and Development, Startup, First-stage, Second-stage, Mezzanine

Industry Group Preference: Communications, Computer Related, Electronic Components and Instrumentation, Genetic Engineering, Information Services and Technology, Medical/Health Related, Software, Wireless Communication

Portfolio Companies: not available

Officers, Executives and Principals

Yuval Almog, Managing Partner (Minneapolis)
Peter H. McNerney, General Partner (Minneapolis)
Linda L. Watchmaker, Chief Financial Officer (Minneapolis)
Karen Boezi, General Venture Partner (Menlo Park)
William Baumel, Senior Associate (Minneapolis
Mark C. Headrick, Associate (Minneapolis)

CORESTATES ENTERPRISE FUND

1345 Chestnut Street
Philadelphia, PA 19146

Telephone: 215-973-6519
Fax: 215-973-6900

Mission: not available

Fund Size: $35 million
Founded: not available
Average Investment: $2 million
Minimum Investment: not available

Investment Criteria: $1 million to $10 million sales, First to Later-stage

Geographic Preference: Pennsylvania

Industry Group Preference: Broadcast/Cable/Radio, Environmental Services, Financial Services, Medical/ Health

Portfolio Companies: Home Health Corporation of America, Osiris Holding Corporation, CPF Funding Corporation, Coast Manufacturing, Urban Outfitters

Officers, Executives and Principals

Michael F. Donoghue, Managing Director
Education: BSFS, International Economics, Georgetown; MBA, University of Virginia
Background: Vice President, Communications Media Group, Philadelphia National Bank; Research Analyst, Energy and Environmental Analysis, U.S. Deptartment of Energy

Maureen P. Quinn, Assistant Vice President
Education: BS, Pennsylvania State University; MBA, Drexel University
Background: Merrill Lynch Pierce Fenner and Smith; Project lease and Financing Group, Merrill Lynch Capital Markets

CORINTHIAN CAPITAL CORPORATION

10255 West Higgins Road
Suite 220
Rosemont, IL 60018

Telephone: 708-827-0800
Fax: 708-827-0815

Mission: Actively seeking new investments

Fund Size: not available
Founded: 1989
Average Investment: not available
Minimum Investment: $500,000

Investment Criteria: Second-stage, Mezzanine, Leveraged Buyout, Special Situations

Industry Group Preference: Communications, Computer Related, Industrial Products and Equipment, Medical/Health Related

Portfolio Companies: Premier One, Inc.

Officers, Executives and Principals

William R. Cross, President
Education: BA Yale. MBA Harvard.
Background: Corning, Inc., Patricof and Co.
Directorships: Premier One, Inc. (Minneapolis).

CORNERSTONE MANAGEMENT

325 Distel Circle
Suite 100
Los Altos, CA 94022

Telephone: 415-988-9203
Fax: 415-988-9202

Mission: Actively seeking new investments

Fund Size: $60 million
Founded: 1984
Average Investment: $3 million
Minimum Investment: $1 million

Investment Criteria: Second-stage, Special Situations

Geographic Preference: West Coast

Industry Group Preference: Communications, Computer Related

Portfolio Companies: not available

Officers, Executives and Principals

J. Michael Gullard, Partner
Education: BA, MBA, Stanford University

Thomas R. Rice, Partner
Education: BS, Ph.D., Stanford University; MS, MIT

Douglas G. DeVivo, Partner
Education: BS, Rensselaer Polytechnic; Ph.D., Northeastern University; MBA, University of California at Berkeley

CORPORATE GROWTH ASSISTANCE, LTD.

19 York Ridge Road
North York, Ontario M2P 1R8
Canada

Telephone: 416-222-7772
Fax: 416-222-6091

Other Office Locations
Boden's Ride, Swinley Forest
South Ascot, Berkshire SL5 9LE
England
Phone 44-1344-20738, Fax 44-1334-25130

Mission: Actively seeking new investments

Fund Size: not available
Founded: 1967
Average Investment: $1 million
Minimum Investment: $500,000

Investment Criteria: Third-stage, Mezzanine, Leveraged Buyout

Geographic Preference: Toronto and surrounding area

Industry Group Preference: Communications, Computer Related, Consumer, Distribution, Electronic Components and Instrumentation, Energy/Natural Resources, Industrial Products and Equipment, Medical/Health Related

Portfolio Companies: not available

Officers, Executives and Principals

Dan Hill, Partner (South Ascot)
Millard S. Roth, President (North York)

CORPORATE VENTURE PARTNERS, L.P.

171 East State Street
Suite 261
Ithaca, NY 14850

Telephone: 607-277-8024
Fax: 607-277-8027
E-mail: CVP@cvpventures.com

Mission: Reducing investment activity

Fund Size: $26 million
Founded: 1988
Average Investment: $1.5 million
Minimum Investment: $250,000

Investment Criteria: First-stage

Industry Group Preference: Communications, Computer Related, Consumer, Electronic Components and Instrumentation, Genetic Engineering, Industrial Products and Equipment, Medical/Health Related

Portfolio Companies: Spectrum Holobyte, Inc., Inference Corporation, Career Horizons, Inc., Yes! Entertainment Corporation, Software Developers Co., Secure Computing Corporation, Tessera, Inc., Databook Inc., Spectra, Inc.

Officers, Executives and Principals

David Constine, General Partner
Education: BME, Cornell; MBA, Harvard
Background: General Partner, Venturtech Associates; Chief Financial Officer, Director, Shareholder, Point 4 Data Corporation; Officer, Investment Manager, Donald Lufkin and Jenrette

Stephen M. Puricelli, General Partner
Education: BS, MBA, Rensselaer Polytechnic Institute
Background: Investment Officer, Norstar Venture Capital; Financial Analyst, Norstar Bancorp

THE CRESTVIEW FINANCIAL GROUP

431 Post Road East
Suite One
Westport, CT 06880-4403

Telephone: 203-222-0333
Fax: 203-222-0000

Mission: Actively seeking new investments

Fund Size: not available
Founded: 1969
Average Investment: not available
Minimum Investment: $100,000

Investment Criteria: Seed, Research and Development, First-stage, Second-stage, Mezzanine, Exit Strategies

Industry Group Preference: Communications, Computer Related, Consumer, Distribution, Electronic Components and Instrumentation, Energy/Natural Resources, Genetic Engineering, Industrial Products and Equipment, Medical/Health Related

Portfolio Companies: not available

Officers, Executives and Principals

Norman M. Marland, President
Robert J. Ready, Vice President

CROSSPOINT VENTURE PARTNERS

One First Street
Suite 2
Los Altos, CA 94022

Telephone: 415-948-8300
Fax: 415-948-6172
E-mail: partners@crosspointvc.com

Other Office Locations
18552 MacArthur Boulevard, Suite 400
Irvine, CA 92612
Phone 714-852-1611, Fax 714-852-9804, E-mail partners@crosspointvc.com

Mission: not available

Fund Size: $300 million
Founded: 1970
Average Investment: $500,000 - $6 million
Minimum Investment: not available

Investment Criteria: Seed, Start-up

Geographic Preference: Western United States

Industry Group Preference: Communications, Financial Services, Healthcare, Medical Devices, Networking

Portfolio Companies: 280 Inc., Brocade Communications Systems, Inc., Corn21, Inc., Diamond Lane Communications, DIVA Communications, Inc., Efficient Networks, Inc., eT Communications, Inc. Fabrik Communications, Inc. inquiry.com, Jetstream Communications, Juniper Networks, Inc., PairGain Technologies, Inc. PowerWave, Procure Soft, Softwire Corporation, StarRidge Networks, Inc., Toll Free Cellular, US Web Corporation, XYLAN Corporation, Aspen Peripherals, Expersoft, Integrated Partners, Inc., Microfield Graphics, Inc., Motion Analysis Corporation, Portrait Display Labs ReportSmith, Inc., Sagent Technology, Serius Software, STAC, Inc., Alexon Corporation, Anergen, Inc., Anesta Corporation, Cornerstone Physicians Corporation, Employee Care Corporation, Global Vision, Informed Access Systems, Infusion Systems Corporation, Integrated Neurosciences Consortium, Irori, Paradigm Health Corporation, Paradigm Biosciences, Inc. Sonus Pharmaceutical, TheraTx, Inc., Vitaphore Corporation, Arithmos, Inc., Athens, Inc., Accredited Home Lenders, Anytime Access, Automotive Assistance Group, National IPF Company, Onyx Acceptance Corporation, Hello Direct, Inc., INMAC Corporation, The Office Club, Inc.

Officers, Executives and Principals

John Mumford, Managing General Partner
Education: BS, Arizona State University; MBA, Stanford
Background: Founder, Crosspoint Corporation; Management Consultant, Peat Marwick Mitchell and Co.;
  IBM; Director National Venture Capital Association
Directorships: Office Depot, Hello Direct

Rich Shapero, General Partner
Education: BS, University of California Berkeley
Background: Management Positions at SUN, Shiva, AST, TOPS
Directorships: PowerWave

Seth Neiman, General Partner
Education: BA and Graduate Studies, Ohio State University
Background: Vice President and Founder, Coactive Computing; Management Positions at SUN, TOPS, Dahl-
  gren Control Systems and Maxitron Corporation

Don Milder, General Partner (Irvine)
Education: BA, Union College; MBA, Harvard
Background: President, TRIMED Corporation, Infusion Systems; Business Development and Marketing,
  Dynatech and Eastman Kodak
Directorships: TheraTx, Sonus Pharmaceutical

Robert A. Hoff, General Partner (Irvine)
Education: BA, Bucknell University; MBA Harvard
Background: President, Marwit Capital Corporation; President of the Southern Pacific Regional Association of
  SBIC's, General Electric
Directorships: PairGain Technologies, Onyx Acceptance

Barbara Lubash, Venture Partner
Education: BS, Tufts University; SM, Harvard
Background: President, Pacific Review Services; Senior Vice President, Private Healthcare Systems, Manage-
  ment Positions at Hewlett Packard Company and Harvard Community Health Plan

CROWN ADVISORS

67 East Park Place
Morristown, NJ 07960

Fax: 212-619-5073

Mission: not available

Fund Size: $300 million
Founded: not available
Average Investment: $500,000 - $1.5 million
Minimum Investment: not available

Investment Criteria: First-stage to Second-stage

Industry Group Preference: Diversified

Portfolio Companies: Lotus, Compaq, Medahts, Intuit

Officers, Executives and Principals

Chester Sivda, General Partner
David F. Bellet, General Partner
Jeff Hamren, General Partner
Margaret McNamara, General Partner

CRUTTENDEN AND COMPANY, INC.

18301 Von Karman
Suite 100
Irvine, CA 92612

Telephone: 714-757-5700
Fax: 714-852-9603
E-mail: http://www.crut.com

Other Office Locations
809 Presido, Suite B
Santa Barbara, CA 93101
Phone 805-966-5205, Fax 805-966-9302

600 California Street, 14th Floor
San Francisco, CA 94104
Phone 415-782-5000, Fax 415-982-1965

1050 17th Street, Suite 1900
Denver, CO 80265
Phone 303-595-3377, Fax 303-595-0599

11150 Santa Monica Boulevard, Suite 230
Los Angeles, CA 90025
Phone 310-235-2195, Fax 310-235-2199

520 Pike Street, Suite 1010
Seattle, WA 98101
Phone 206-587-0733, Fax 206-667-9028

Mission: Actively seeking new investments

Fund Size: not available
Founded: 1981
Average Investment: not available
Minimum Investment: $2 million

Investment Criteria: Second-stage, Mezzanine, Leveraged Buyout, Special Situations, Control-block Purchases, Public Offerings, Private Placements

Industry Group Preference: Communications, Computer Related, Consumer, Distribution, Electronic Components and Instrumentation, Energy/Natural Resources, Genetic Engineering, Industrial Products and Equipment, Medical/Health Related

Portfolio Companies: not available

Officers, Executives and Principals

Walter Cruttenden III, Chairman and Chief Executive Officer (Irvine)
Byron C. Roth, President (Irvine)
Ed Hall, Chief Financial Officer (Irvine)
David Walters, Managing Director (Irvine)
Jeffrey Logsdon, Director of Research (Irvine)

CURETON AND COMPANY, INC.

1100 Louisiana
Suite 3250
Houston, TX 77002

Telephone: 713-658-9806
Fax: 713-658-0476

Mission: Actively seeking new investments

Fund Size: not available
Founded: 1974
Average Investment: not available
Minimum Investment: $1 million

Investment Criteria: First-stage, Second-stage, Leveraged Buyout, Special Situations

Geographic Preference: Texas, Louisana, Oklahoma

Industry Group Preference: Communications, Computer Related, Consumer, Distribution, Electronic Components and Instrumentation, Energy/Natural Resources, Environmental, Industrial Products and Equipment, Manufacturing, Oil Field Services

Portfolio Companies: not available

Officers, Executives and Principals

Stewart Cureton, Jr., President
Robert B. Antonoff, Executive Vice President

CW GROUP, INC.

1041 Third Avenue
Second Floor
New York, NY 10021

Telephone: 212-308-5266
Fax: 212-644-0354

Mission: Actively seeking new investments

Fund Size: $110 million
Founded: 1982
Average Investment: $1 million
Minimum Investment: Less than $100,000

Investment Criteria: Seed, Research and Development, Startup, First-stage, Second-stage, Mezzanine, Leveraged Buyout, Special Situations, Control-block Purchases

Industry Group Preference: Biotechnology, Genetic Engineering, Medical/Health Related

Portfolio Companies: not available

Officers, Executives and Principals

Walter Channing, Jr., Managing General Partner
Education: AB, MBA, Harvard
Background: Founder, Channing, Weinberg and Co.; President, Merrimack Laboratories
Directorships: Quantam Medical Systems, Sterivet Laboratories, Gabrielli Medical Information Systems

Barry Weinberg, Managing General Partner
Education: BS, Engineering, MIT; MBA, New York University
Background: Founder, Channing, Weinberg and Co.; Chairman and Chief Executive Officer, General Computer Systems
Directorships: Biomatrix, Diamont Delectro-Tech, Micro-Sonics, Gambro

Charles M. Hartman, Managing General Partner
Education: BS, Notre Dame; MBA, University of Chicago
Background: Director, Acquisition and Licensing, Johnson and Johnson
Directorships: Queue Systems, Photec Diagnostics, Business Research Corporation, Nutritional Management, Computers in Medicine, Membrox

Scott M. Ciccone, Vice President

Eric S. Schlesinger, Vice President

D. H. BLAIR INVESTMENT BANKING CORPORATION

44 Wall Street
New York, NY 10005

Telephone: 212-495-5000
Fax: 212-269-1438

Mission: Actively seeking new investments

Fund Size: not available
Founded: 1904
Average Investment: not available
Minimum Investment: $100,000

Investment Criteria: Research and Development, Startup, First-stage, Leveraged Buyout

Industry Group Preference: Communications, Computer Related, Consumer, Distribution, Electronic Components and Insturmentation, Energy/Natural Resources, Genetic Engineering, Industrial Products and Equipment, Medical/Health Related

Portfolio Companies: not available

Officers, Executives and Principals

J. Morton Davis, Chairman and Chief Executive Officer
Howard Phillips, Director, Corporate Finance
Martin A. Bell, General Counsel and Senior Vice President
Jonathan Turkel, Associate General Counsel and Vice President
Patricia Riley, Assistant General Counsel and Vice President
Leonard A. Katz, Vice President
Andrew H. Plevin, Vice President
Guy Spier, Vice President

THE DAKOTA GROUP

P.O. Box 1025
Menlo Park, CA 94025

Telephone: 415-519-5222
Fax: 415-851-4899

Other Office Locations
10209 Chastain Drive, N.E.
Atlanta, GA 30343
Phone 404-851-0100, Fax 404-851-0100

Mission: Actively seeking new investments

Fund Size: not available
Founded: 1990
Average Investment: not available
Minimum Investment: $100,000

Investment Criteria: Seed, Startup, First-stage, Second-stage, Special Situations

Industry Group Preference: Communications, Computer Related, Distribution, Industrial Products and Equipment

Portfolio Companies: not available

Officers, Executives and Principals

Stephen A. Meyer, General Partner (Menlo Park)
Tom Fisher, General Partner (Atlanta)

DARLING VENTURES, LTD.

95 Cyons Plain Road
Weston, CT 06883

Telephone: 203-227-2132
Fax: 203-227-2082

Mission: not available

Fund Size: $10 million
Founded: not available
Average Investment: $2 million
Minimum Investment: not available

Investment Criteria: Profitable, First-stage to Leveraged Buyout

Industry Group Preference: Broadcast/Cable/Radio, Communications, Consumer Related

Portfolio Companies: Marine Optical Inc.

Officers, Executives and Principals

Thomas C. Darling, Director
Background: Director, Barclays Capital Corporation; Vice President, Citicorp Venture Capital; Vice President, Wertheim and Co.; Associate, Becker Communications

DAVIS GROUP

P.O. Box 69953
Los Angeles, CA 90069

Telephone: 213-848-8612
Fax: 213-848-8613

Mission: Actively seeking new investments

Fund Size: not available
Founded: 1969
Average Investment: not available
Minimum Investment: Less than $100,000

Investment Criteria: Startup, First-stage, Leveraged Buyout, Special Situations

Industry Group Preference: Communications, Computer Related, Consumer, Distribution, Energy/Natural Resources, Genetic Engineering, Industrial Products and Equipment, Medical/Health Related

Portfolio Companies: not available

Officers, Executives and Principals

Roger W. Davis, Chairman
Edward C. Herbert, Partner
M.L.D. Thompson, Partner

DAVIDSON CAPITAL PARTNERS

2601 South Bayshore Drive
Suite 1147
Miami, FL 33133

Telephone: 305-250-4681

Mission: Actively seeking new investments

Fund Size: not available
Founded: 1991
Average Investment: not available
Minimum Investment: $2 million

Investment Criteria: Second-stage, Mezzanine, Leveraged Buyout

Geographic Preference: Southwest

Industry Group Preference: Communications, Computer Related, Consumer, Distribution, Electronic Components and Instrumentation, Industrial Products and Equipment, Medical/Health Related, Retailing

Portfolio Companies: not available

Officers, Executives and Principals

James W. Davidson, President
Education: BA, Vanderbilt; MBA, Wharton
Background: Investment Banking, Goldman Sachs and Co.
Directorships: DataNet Corporation, The Florida Venture Forum, former Director of American Savings of Florida

DAVIS VENTURE PARTNERS, L.P.

320 South Boston
Suite 1000
Tulsa, OK 74103-3703

Telephone: 918-584-7272
Fax: 918-582-3403

Other Office Locations
2121 San Jacinto, Suite 975
Dallas, TX 75201
Phone 214-954-1822, Fax 214-969-0256

12 Greenway Plaza, Suite 600
Houston, TX 77046
Phone 713-993-0440, Fax 713-621-2297

Mission: Actively seeking new investments

Fund Size: $4.5 million
Founded: 1985
Average Investment: $2.5 million
Minimum Investment: $1 million

Investment Criteria: First-stage, Second-stage, Mezzanine, Leveraged Buyout

Geographic Preference: Southwest and Southcentral United States

Industry Group Preference: Computer Related, Consumer, Distribution, Electronic Components and Instrumentation, Energy/Natural Resources, Industrial Products and Equipment, Medical/Health Related

Portfolio Companies: not available

Officers, Executives and Principals

Barry M. Davis, Managing General Partner (Tulsa)
Michael A. Stone, General Partner (Dallas)
Philip A. Tuttle, General Partner (Houston)
Elmer C. Wilkening, General Partner (Tulsa)

DE VRIES AND COMPANY, INC.

800 West 47th Street
Kansas City, MO 64112

Telephone: 816-756-0055
Fax: 816-756-0061

Mission: Actively seeking new investments

Fund Size: not available
Founded: 1984
Average Investment: not available
Minimum Investment: $500,000

Investment Criteria: Second-stage, Mezzanine, Leveraged Buyout, Later-stage Expansion

Industry Group Preference: Communications, Computer Related, Consumer, Distribution, Electronic Components and Instrumentation, Energy/Natural Resources, Genetic Engineering, Industrial Products and Equipment, Medical/Health Related

Portfolio Companies: not available

Officers, Executives and Principals

Mark E. Scott, Vice President
Rose Marie Femk, Senior Associate
Robert J. De Vries

DEALMAKER CAPITAL CORPORATION

1408 Lark Drive
P.O. Box 15245
Evansville, IN 47716-0245

Fax: 812-477-6499

Mission: Actively seeking new investments

Fund Size: not available
Founded: 1985
Average Investment: $1 million
Minimum Investment: $250,000

Investment Criteria: Seed, Research and Development, Startup, First-stage, Second-stage, Special Situations

Geographic Preference: Global

Industry Group Preference: Consumer, Distribution, Energy/Natural Resources, Industrial Products and
  Equipment

Portfolio Companies: not available

Officers, Executives and Principals

Chuck Frary, Chairman
Lori Frary, Analyst
Robert Soaper, Analyst
Janet Koonce, Analyst
Peter Cooper, Analyst
Terese Larres, Research

DEMUTH, FOLGER AND WETHERILL

Glenpointe Centre East
300 Frank W. Burr Blvd.
Teaneck, NJ 07666

Telephone: 201-836-6000
Fax: 201-836-5666

Mission: Actively seeking new investments in high-growth market-niche companies

Fund Size: $80 million
Founded: 1983
Average Investment: $3 to $8 million
Minimum Investment: $1 million

Investment Criteria: Second-stage, Special Situations, Control-block Purchases, Management Buyout

Geographic Preference: United States

Industry Group Preference: Business Services, Communications, Distribution, Medical/Health Related, Specialty Manufacturing

Portfolio Companies: Advanced Performance Technology, American Pathology Resources, General Rental, Great Lakes Health Plan, Hamilton Funeral Services, Pediatric Services of America, Spectrascan Health Services, Tuttle's Nurseries

Officers, Executives and Principals

Donald F. DeMuth, General Partner
Education: BA, BSEE, Rutgers; MBA, Harvard
Background: Founding General Partner
Directorships: Advanced Performance Technology, Tuttle's Nurseries

Thomas W. Folger, General Partner
Education: BS, MS, MIT; MBA, Harvard
Background: Founding General Partner
Directorships: IEC Electronics, Micrion

David C. Wetherill, General Partner
Education: BA, Princeton; Wharton
Background: Healthcare Industry, twenty years; DFW, eight years
Directorships: Learning Services, Spectrascan Health Services, Great Lakes Health Plan

Lisa Roumell
Education: BA, MBA, Harvard
Background: First Century Partners, ten years; DFW, two years
Directorships: Hamilton Funeral Services, General Rental, Tuttle's Nurseries

DEUCALION VENTURE PARTNERS

19501 Brooklime
Sonoma, CA 95476

Telephone: 707-938-4974
Fax: 707-938-8921

Mission: High return venture capital investments

Fund Size: $5 million
Founded: 1987
Average Investment: $500,000
Minimum Investment: $100,000

Investment Criteria: Seed to Second-stage

Geographic Preference: San Francisco Bay Area

Industry Group Preference: Database Publishing, Financial Services, Medical/Health Related, Software

Portfolio Companies: Biosource, Applied Imaging, Pherin, Erox, Datis, Lease Partners

Officers, Executives and Principals

Stephen L. Pease

DEVELOPMENT CORPORATION OF AUSTIN

1600 Eighth Avenue, N.W.
Austin, MN 55912

Telephone: 507-433-0346
Fax: 507-433-0361
E-mail: DCA@RTC.TEC.US.MN

Mission: Local economic betterment

Fund Size: $1.5 million
Founded: 1986
Average Investment: $50,000
Minimum Investment: $10,000

Investment Criteria: Seed, Startup, First-stage

Geographic Preference: Austin, Minnesota and Mower County, Minnesota

Industry Group Preference: Communications, Computer Related, Consumer, Distribution, Electronic Components and Instrumentation, Energy/Natural Resources, Genetic Engineering, Industrial Products and Equipment, Medical/Health Related

Portfolio Companies: not available

Officers, Executives and Principals

George G. Brophy, President and Chief Executive Officer

DILLON READ VENTURE CAPITAL

555 California Street, Suite 4950
San Francisco, CA 94104

Telephone: 415-296-7900
Fax: 415-296-8956

Other Office Locations
535 Madison Avenue, 8th Floor
New York, NY 10022
Phone 212-906-7000, Fax 212-308-5107

260 Franklin Street
Boston, MA 02110
Phone 617-439-6217

Mission: not available

Fund Size: 4 funds: $180 million
Founded: 1982
Average Investment: $2 - $5 million
Minimum Investment: not available

Investment Criteria: not available

Industry Group Preference: Biotechnology/Healthcare, Energy Services, Environmental, Financial Services, Retailing

Portfolio Companies: Alpha Beta Technologies, SunDisk, Centaur Pharmaceutical, Learning Smith, UroCar, Willbros Group, InterEnergy

Officers, Executives and Principals

Craig A.T. Jones, Investment Officer
Education: BA, California State University; Magna cum laude, Harvard Law School
Background: Advent International; Investment Manager, The Centennial Funds; Management Consultant, Bain and Co.
Directorships: Alteon, Alpha Beta Technology, AutoImmune, CytoDiagnostics, LaJolla Pharmaceutical, Penederm, Virus Research Institute; Chairman, Arcturus

Dr. Graham K. Crooke, Investment Manager
Education: MD, University of Western Australia; MBA, Stanford
Background: Booz, Allen and Hamilton; Intensive Care, Hematology, Nephrology, Transplant Medicine, Emergency Medicine

Lawrence A. Bettino, Investment Manager
Education: BSEE, RPI; MBA, Harvard
Background: Loglo Design Engineer, IBM
Directorships: Emcore Corporation and Power Integrations

Peter A. Leidel, Investment Manager

Education: BBA, University of Wisconsin; MBA, Wharton

Background: Management, Mobile Corporation; KPMO Peat Marwick. U.S. Patent and Trademark Office; CPA

Directorships: Meenan Oil, Fintube, Willbros, Cornell-Cox Group, Atlantic Little Neck Clam Farms

Robert A. Young, Investment Manager

Education: BS, Chemistry, University of Delaware; PhD, Physical Chemistry, MIT

Background: President, IBM Instruments; 18 years with IBM Corporation, management, sales, marketing

DOANE RAYMOND CHARTERED ACCOUNTANTS

421 Bay Street, Fifth Floor
Sault Ste. Marie, Ontario P6A 6N2
Canada

Telephone: 705-945-9700
Fax: 705-945-9705

Other Office Locations
200 Bay Street
North Tower, Suite 1000
Toronto, Ontario M5J 2P9
Canada
Phone 416-863-1234, Fax 416-360-4949

200 Barrington Street
Halifax, Nova Scotia B3J 2P8
Canada
Phone 902-421-1734, Fax 902-421-1677

1066 West Hastings Street
Vancouver, Bristish Columbia V6E 3X1
Canada
Phone 604-687-2711, Fax 604-685-6569

Mission: Actively seeking new investments

Fund Size: not available
Founded: 1920
Average Investment: not available
Minimum Investment: $100,000

Investment Criteria: Second-stage, Leveraged Buyout

Industry Group Preference: Computer Related, Consumer, Distribution, Electronic Components and Instrumentation, Energy/Natural Resources, Industrial Products and Equipment

Portfolio Companies: not available

Officers, Executives and Principals

B.C. Magill, CA, Partner (Sault Ste. Marie)
R.L. McNeil, CA, Partner (Sault Ste. Marie)

DOMAIN ASSOCIATES

One Palmer Square
Princeton, NJ 08542

Telephone: 609-683-5656
Fax: 609-683-9789

Other Office Locations
650 Town Center Drive, Suite 810
Costa Mesa, CA 92626
Phone 714-434-6227, Fax 714-754-6802

Mission: Actively seeking new investments

Fund Size: $200 million
Founded: 1985
Average Investment: $1 million
Minimum Investment: $500,000 (except seed financing)

Investment Criteria: Seed, First-stage, Second-stage

Industry Group Preference: Electronic Components and Instrumentation, Genetic Engineering, Industrial Products and Equipment, Medical/Health Related

Portfolio Companies: not available

Officers, Executives and Principals

James C. Blair, General Partner (Princeton)
Education: BSE, Princeton University; MSE, PhD, University of Pennsylvania
Background: Involved in the creation of over thirty life science ventures; F.S. Smither; White, Weld and Co.; Engineering Manager, RCA Corporation
Directorships: Managing Director, Rothschild

Brian H. Dovey, General Partner (Princeton)
Education: BA, Colgate University; MBA, Harvard
Background: President, Rorer; President, Survival Technology; Management Positions, Howmedica, Howmet Corporation and New York Telephone
Directorships: British Bio-technology, Creative BioMolecules, ReSound Corporation, National Venture Capital Association

Richard S. Schneider, General Partner (Costa Mesa)
Education: BS, University of California, Berkeley; PhD, University of Wisconsin; Post Doctorate, MIT; Stanford Graduate School of Business Executive Program
Background: Vice President, 3i Ventures Corporation; President, Gensia Pharmaceuticals; President, Biomedical Consulting Associates; Associate, Healthcare

Jesse Treu, General Partner (Princeton)

Kathleen K. Schoemaker, Administrative General Partner (Princeton)

DOMINION VENTURES, INC.
44 Montgomery Street
Suite 4200
San Francisco, CA 94104

Telephone: 415-362-4890
Fax: 415-394-9245

Other Office Locations
60 State Street
21st Floor
Boston, MA 02109
Phone 619-367-8575, Fax 619-367-0323

3000 Sand Hill Road
Building Two, Suite 205
Menlo Park, CA 94025
Phone 415-854-5932, Fax 415-854-1957

Mission: not available

Fund Size: $100 million (Dominion Fund IV)
Founded: 1985
Average Investment: $500,000 - $8 million
Minimum Investment: $250,000

Investment Criteria: Venture Leasing, Mezzanine/Subordinated Debt, Equity

Geographic Preference: United States

Industry Group Preference: Diversified (excluding Real Estate, Entertainment, Oil and Gas)

Portfolio Companies: Actimed Labs, Inc., Advanced Access, Avid Therapeutics, Capstone Turbine Corporation, Ciena, Cohesive Technologies, Coral Systems, Microcide Pharmaceuticals, Myriad Genetics, National Dispatch Center, Nextstar, Park Lane Group, Single Chip Systems, T.E.N., Tivoli Systems, Trophix Pharmaceuticals, Vesicare, VIDAmed, Inc., Xylan Corporation

Officers, Executives and Principals

Geoffrey T. Woolley, Managing General Partner and Founder
Education: BS, Finance, Brigham Young University; MBA, University of Utah
Background: Director of Acquisitions, Equitec Financial Group, Inc.

Michael K. Lee, Managing General Partner and Founder
Education: BA, MBA, Brigham Young University
Background: Director of Operations at Equitec Financial Group, Inc.

Kendall J. Cooper, Partner, Chief Financial Officer
Education: BA, Economics, Brigham Young University; MBA, University of California Los Angeles; CPA
Background: Director of Due Diligence and Documentation, Equitec Financial Group, Inc.; Emerging Business Specialist, Deloitte, Haskins and Sells

Randolph Werner, Partner
Education: BA, Economics, Ithaca College; MA, Economics, The College of William and Mary; Ph.D., Economic History, University of Virginia
Background: Vice President of Boston Financial and Equity Corporation

Brian Smith, Partner
Education: BA, Brigham Young University; MBA, University of Indiana
Background: Associate, CID Ventures

DOUGERY AND WILDER

155 Bovet Road
Suite 350
San Mateo, CA 94402

Telephone: 415-358-8701
Fax: 415-358-8706

Mission: Actively seeking new investments

Fund Size: $130 million
Founded: 1981
Average Investment: $250,000 - $3 million
Minimum Investment: $250,000

Investment Criteria: Seed, Startup, First-stage, Second-stage, Leveraged Buyout

Industry Group Preference: Communications, Computer Related, Electronic Components and Instrumentation, Genetic Engineering, Industrial Products and Equipment, Medical/Health Related

Portfolio Companies: ABTOX, Ace Software Corporation, Alantec, Associates Optical, Celtrix Pharmaceuticals, Compression Labs, Cornerstone Imaging, Cymed, EnDys Environmental Products, File Net, In Focus Systems, Intevac, Microgenics, Neurex, Novell, Republic Telecom Systems Corporation, Telecom Services Group, Unify Corporation, Vanguard Automation

Officers, Executives and Principals

Henry L.B. Wilder, Partner
Education: BS, Physics, U.S. Naval Academy; MBA Stanford University
Background: Citicorp Venture Capital; Finnigan Instruments; Engineering Line Manager, U.S. Navy
Directorships: ABTOX, Associated Optical, Cymed, Ensys Environmental, VIA Medical

John R. Dougery, Partner
Education: AB, Mathematics, University of California, Berkeley; MBA, Stanford University
Background: Vice President and General Manager, Western Region of Citicorp Venture Capital; Founding Management Team, Ciablo Systems; CPA, Price Waterhouse

DOWNER AND COMPANY

211 Congress Street
Boston, MA 02110

Telephone: 617-482-6200
Fax: 617-482-6201

Other Office Locations
370 rue St. Honore
75001 Paris
France
Phone 33-1-42-61-47-47, Fax 33-1-42-61-48-48

Mission: Actively seeking new investments

Fund Size: not available
Founded: 1975
Average Investment: not available
Minimum Investment: $250,000

Investment Criteria: Startup, First-stage, Second-stage, Mezzanine

Industry Group Preference: Computer Related, Consumer, Distribution, Electronic Components and Instrumentation, Industrial Products and Equipment, Medical/Health Related

Portfolio Companies: not available

Officers, Executives and Principals

Charles W. Downer (Boston)
Thomas C. Munnell (Paris)
Robert H. Reilly (Boston)
Ashley E. Rountree (Paris)

DRAPER FISHER ASSOCIATES

400 Seaport Court, #250
Redwood City, CA 94063

Telephone: 415-599-9000
Fax: 415-599-9726
E-mail: sj@Drapervc.com

Mission: not available

Fund Size: $200 million
Founded: 1985
Average Investment: $500,000 -$3 million
Minimum Investment: $100,000

Investment Criteria: Seed to First-stage

Geographic Preference: West Coast

Industry Group Preference: Information Technology

Portfolio Companies: Aspect Telecommunications, Cypress Research, Upside Publishing, Digidesign, Parametric Technologies, Banyan Systems, Combinet, Medior, Software Quality Automation, Cybermedia, Four II, Hot Mail, PowerAgent

Officers, Executives and Principals

John H. Fisher, Managing Director
Education: BA, magna cum laude, MBA, Harvard
Background: Alex, Brown and Sons; Associate, ABS Ventures; Associate, Capital Markets Group, Bank America
Directorships: Abacus Concepts, Differential Corrections, Sonnet Financial, QuestLink Systems Inc., Claremont Systems, DataMind

Timothy C. Draper, Managing Director
Education: BS, Electrical Engineering, Stanford University; MBA, Harvard
Background: Marketing Engineer, Hewlett Packard; Assistant to the President, Apollo Computer; Alex, Brown and Sons
Directorships: Cypress Research, PLX Technology, Upside Publishing, I-Cube Inc., Photonic Power, Virtual Computer, Four II

Lawrence Kubal, Managing Director
Education: Cum laude, with distinction, departmental honors, Duke University; MBA, Stanford
Background: Founder, Labrador Associates; Senior Associate, Booz, Allen and Hamilton; Executive Vice President, Avalance; Product Manager, Market Research
Directorships: GTI, Vividus, Differential Corrections

Stephen T. Jurvetson, Managing Director
Education: BS, Electrical Engineering, Stanford University; MS, Electrical and Industrial Engineering, Stanford University; MBA, Stanford University
Background: Hewlett-Packard, Bain and Company, Apple Computer, Next Computer
Directorships: Release, Interwoven, Fastparts HotMail, iTV

DRESDNER KLEINWORTH BENSON

75 Wall Street
New York, NY 10005

Telephone: 212-351-5500
Fax: 212-429-3139

Mission: Actively seeking new investments

Fund Size: not available
Founded: 1989
Average Investment: not available
Minimum Investment: $3 million

Investment Criteria: Second-stage, Mezzanine, Leveraged Buyout, Special Situations

Industry Group Preference: Communications, Computer Related, Consumer, Distribution, Electronic Components and Instrumentation, Energy/Natural Resources, Industrial Products and Equipment, Medical/Health Related

Portfolio Companies: not available

Officers, Executives and Principals

Christopher Wright, Managing Partner
Mike Khougaz, Partner
Bob Wickey, Partner

DRESNER CAPITAL RESOURCES, INC.

29 South LaSalle Street
Suite 310
Chicago, IL 60603

Telephone: 312-726-3600
Fax: 312-726-7448

Mission: Actively seeking new investments

Fund Size: not available
Founded: 1992
Average Investment: not available
Minimum Investment: $250,000

Investment Criteria: Second-stage, Mezzanine, Leveraged Buyout

Industry Group Preference: Communications, Computer Related, Consumer, Distribution, Electronic Components and Instrumentation, Industrial Products and Equipment, Medical/Health Related

Portfolio Companies: not available

Officers, Executives and Principals

Steven M. Dresner, President
John C. Riddle, Vice President
Alan Bernstein, Vice President

DRUG ROYALTY CORPORATION, INC.
Eight King Street East, Suite 202
Toronto, Ontario M5C 1B5
Canada

Telephone: 416-863-1865
Fax: 416-863-5161

Mission: Actively seeking new investments

Fund Size: not available
Founded: 1993
Average Investment: not available
Minimum Investment: $100,000

Investment Criteria: Research and Development, Special Situations, Royalties

Industry Group Preference: Genetic Engineering, Medical/Health Related

Portfolio Companies: not available

Officers, Executives and Principals

Jim Webster, Vice President, Finance and Business Development
Dr. John McCulloch, Scientific Advisor

DRYSDALE ENTERPRISES

177 Bovet Road, Suite 600
San Mateo, CA 94402

Telephone: 415-341-6336
Fax: 415-341-1329

Mission: not available

Fund Size: $30 million
Founded: not available
Average Investment: $1 million
Minimum Investment: not available

Investment Criteria: Seed to Later-stage

Industry Group Preference: Communications, Financial Services, Food Services

Portfolio Companies: International Wireless Communications, Radiphone, Moblecom, SkyCable, Philippine Wireless, Pelican Agri Products, Pepsi Philippines, Windmill Holdings.

Officers, Executives and Principals

George M. Drysdale, President
Education: BS, Engineering, Harvey Mudd College; MBA, JD, Stanford
Background: General Partner, Hambrecht and Quist Venture Partners; Managing General Partner, Westar Capital

DSV PARTNERS

221 Nassau Street
Princeton, NJ 08542

Telephone: 609-924-6420
Fax: 609-683-0174

Other Office Locations
620 Newport Center Drive, Suite 990
Newport Beach, CA 92660
Phone 714-759-5657, Fax 714-760-6947

Mission: Actively seeking new investments

Fund Size: $100 million
Founded: 1968
Average Investment: not available
Minimum Investment: $1 million

Investment Criteria: Seed, Startup, First-stage, Second-stage, Leveraged Buyout

Industry Group Preference: Biotechnology, Communications, Computer Related, Distribution, Electronic Components and Instrumentation, Energy/Natural Resources, Environmental Protection, High Technology, Industrial Products, Information Services, Medical/Health Related, Software

Portfolio Companies: not available

Officers, Executives and Principals

John K. Clarke, Partner (Princeton)
Education: BA, Economics and Biology, MBA, Wharton
Background: General Electric

Morton Collins, Partner (Princeton)
Education: BS, Chemical Engineering, University of Delaware; MA, PhD, Chemical Engineering, Princeton University
Background: Founder of Data Science Ventures
Directorships: National Venture Capital Association

James J. Miller, Partner (Princeton)
Education: BS, Engineering and Applied Science, Yale University; MBA, Wharton School
Background: Texas Instruments

James R. Bergman, Partner (Princeton)
Education: BS, Engineering, MBA, University of California Los Angeles
Directorships: National Venture Capital Association

Kevin G. Connors, Partner (Newport Beach)

Robert S. Hillas, Partner (Newport Beach)
Education: BA, Mathematics, Dartmouth; MBA, Stanford University
Background: General Partner, E.M. Warburg, Pincus and Co.

EASTECH MANAGEMENT COMPANY, INC.

45 Milk Street
Boston, MA 02110

Telephone: 617-423-1096
Fax: 617-423-9655

Mission: Making few, if any, new investments

Fund Size: not available
Founded: 1981
Average Investment: not available
Minimum Investment: $250,000

Investment Criteria: Seed, Startup, First-stage, Second-stage, Leveraged Buyout

Industry Group Preference: Communications, Computer Related, Electronic Components and Instrumentation, Industrial Products and Equipment

Portfolio Companies: not available

Officers, Executives and Principals

Fontaine K. Richardson, General Partner
G. Bickley Stevens II, General Partner
Michael H. Shanahan, Partner

EDELSON TECHNOLOGY PARTNERS

Whiteweld Centre
300 Tice Boulevard
Woodcliff Lake, NJ 07675

Telephone: 201-930-9898
Fax: 201-930-8899

Mission: Stategic fund for multinational coporations

Fund Size: $102 million
Founded: 1984
Average Investment: $1 million
Minimum Investment: $250,000

Investment Criteria: Seed, Startup, First-stage, Second-stage, Mezzanine, Leveraged Buyout

Industry Group Preference: Communications, Computer Related, Electronic Components and Instrumentation, Genetic Engineering, Industrial Products and Equipment

Portfolio Companies: not available

Officers, Executives and Principals

Harry Edelson, Managing Partner (Woodcliff Lake)
Jack Fox, Partner (Woodcliff Lake)

EDGE CAPITAL CORPORATION

70 Mews Lane
South Orange, NJ 07079

Telephone: 201-762-3343
Fax: 201-761-8476

Other Office Locations
11310 South Orange Blossom Trail, Suite 212
Orlando, FL 32837

Mission: Actively seeking new investments

Fund Size: not available
Founded: 1990
Average Investment: not available
Minimum Investment: $100,000

Investment Criteria: Seed, Startup, First-stage, Second-stage, Mezzanine, Leveraged Buyout, Special Situations, Bridge Financing for Initial Public Offerings

Industry Group Preference: Communications, Computer Related, Consumer, Distribution, Electronic Components and Instrumentation, Energy/Natural Resources, Genetic Engineering, Industrial Products and Equipment, Medical/Health Related

Portfolio Companies: not available

Officers, Executives and Principals

John F. Yeomans, Jr., Managing Director (South Orange and Orlando)
Pat E. Romo, Analyst (South Orange)

EGL HOLDINGS, INC.

6600 Peachtree-Dunwoody Road
300 Embassy Row, Suite 630
Atlanta, GA 30328

Telephone: 770-399-5633
Fax: 770-393-4825

Mission: Actively seeking new investments

Fund Size: $40 million
Founded: 1988
Average Investment: not available
Minimum Investment: $1 million

Investment Criteria: Mezzanine, Leveraged Buyout, Development Capital

Industry Group Preference: Communications, Computer Related, Consumer, Distribution, Electronic Components and Instrumentation, Industrial Products and Equipment, Medical/Health Related

Portfolio Companies: Zarina, Artcraft, InfoMed, SoftKey International, Checkmate

Officers, Executives and Principals

John H. Dunn, Jr., Managing Director
Education: AB Psychology, Princeton University; MBA University of South Carolina
Background: Leveraged Acquistions, Merger, Acquisitions and Divestiture, Debt and Equity Placements, Citibank, CIT Financial, Citicorp Investment Bank, Bankers Trust

David O. Ellis, Managing Partner
Education: BS Chemistry, St. Andrews; Senior Executive Program, MIT; PhD, Biophysics
Background: Executive Management, Transactions, Venture Capital, Software Sciences, B.H. Blackwell, Investors in Industry

Richard V. Lawry, Partner
Background: Executive Management (UK and USA), Transactions, Strategic Planning and Corporate Development, Executive UK Chartered Accountant, Glynwed Inc., Glynwed International plc, Greenalls Group plc

Salvatore A. Massaro, Partner
Education: BS, BA, Georgetown University; MBA, Harvard University
Background: Venture Capital, Transactions, Corporate Financial Management, Financial Consulting, Prudential Bache Venture Capital, Telesphere International, Price Waterhouse

Murali Anantharaman, Vice President
Education: MBA, Harvard University; MS, Operations Research, Case Western Reserve; BA, English, Madras University
Background: Manufacturing Management, Management Strategy Consulting, Transactions, Buyout Venture Capital Investing, GE, CSP International

William B. Knopka, Vice President
Education: BS, Chemistry, Canisius College; MS, PhD, Organic Chemistry, Seton Hall University
Background: Executive Management, Company Startups, Transactions, Interchem Development Co., Goodyear, American Cyanamid, FMC Corporation, The Performance Management Group

William J. Lassiter, Vice President

ELECTRA INC.

70 East 55th Street
New York, NY 10022

Telephone: 212-319-0081
Fax: 212-319-3069

Mission: not available

Fund Size: $200 million
Founded: not available
Average Investment: $3 - $15 million
Minimum Investment: not available

Investment Criteria: Second-stage Management Buyout

Industry Group Preference: Food Services, Industrial Products, Manufacturing/Processing, Medical/Health

Portfolio Companies: Tensar, Ralcom Office Communications, Act III, Danskin, U.S. Long Distance Corporation, Atlantic Coast Airlines, Sportstown, O-Cedar Holdings, Careline, Yes Entertainment.

Officers, Executives and Principals

Mr. Peter A. Carnwath, Managing Director
John L. Pouschine, Senior Vice President
Diane M. Smith, Vice President

THE ELMHURST GROUP

One Bigelow Square
Suite 630
Pittsburgh, PA 15291

Telephone: 412-281-8731
Fax: 412-281-9463

Mission: Actively seeking new investments

Fund Size: not available
Founded: 1974
Average Investment: not available
Minimum Investment: $500,000

Investment Criteria: Leveraged Buyout, Special Situations, Control-block Purchases

Industry Group Preference: Communications, Consumer, Distribution, Medical/Health Related

Portfolio Companies: not available

Officers, Executives and Principals

Dan Altman, President
William E. Hunt, Vice President

EMERALD VENTURE GROUP

15373 Innovation Drive
Suite 100
San Diego, CA 92128

Telephone: 619-451-1001
Fax: 619-451-1003

Mission: Actively seeking new investments

Fund Size: not available
Founded: 1987
Average Investment: not available
Minimum Investment: More than $100,000

Investment Criteria: Seed, Research and Development, Startup, First-stage, Second-stage, Mezzanine, Leveraged Buyout

Industry Group Preference: Diversified

Portfolio Companies: not available

Officers, Executives and Principals

Gerry Simoni, President
Cherie Simoni, Vice President
Joyce Belkonen, Senior Business Consultant
Jim Peterson, Senior Business Consultant
Michelle Pruett, Senior Business Analyst
Barbara Connaughay, Business Analyst

ENDEAVOR CAPITAL MANAGEMENT

830 Post Road East
Westport, CT 06880

Telephone: 203-341-7788
Fax: 203-341-7799

Other Office Locations
1880 Pacific Avenue, Suite 703
San Francisco, CA 94109
Phone 415-441-8966, Fax 415-441-4264

1540 Packard
Ann Arbor, MI 48104
Phone 313-996-3032, Fax 313-996-0886

Mission: Actively seeking new investments

Fund Size: not available
Founded: 1992
Average Investment: not available
Minimum Investment: $250,000

Investment Criteria: First-stage, Second-stage, Leveraged Buyout, Special Situations

Industry Group Preference: Communications, Computer Related, Consumer, Distribution, Electronic Components and Instrumentation, Industrial Products and Equipment, Medical/Health Services, Software

Portfolio Companies: not available

Officers, Executives and Principals

Anthony F. Buffa, Managing General Partner
Nancy E. Haar, General Partner
Steven J. Carnevale, General Partner (San Francisco)
Ronald R. Reed, General Partner (Ann Arbor)
Thomas B. Pennell, Associate

ENTERPRISE DEVELOPMENT FUND

425 North Main Street
Ann Arbor, MI 48104

Telephone: 313-663-3213
Fax: 313-663-7358

Mission: Actively seeking new investments

Fund Size: not available
Founded: 1987
Average Investment: not available
Minimum Investment: Less than $100,000

Investment Criteria: Seed, Startup, First-stage

Industry Group Preference: Communications, Computer Related, Electronic Components and Instrumentation, Genetic Engineering, Industrial Products and Equipment, Medical/Health Related

Portfolio Companies: not available

Officers, Executives and Principals

Mary L. Campbell, Partner
Hayden H. Harris, Partner
Thomas S. Porter, Partner

ENTERPRISE INVESTORS

375 Park Avenue
Suite 1902
New York, NY 10152

Telephone: 212-339-8330
Fax: 212-339-8359

Other Office Locations
ul. Nowy Swiat 6/12
00-400 Warsaw
Poland
Phone 48-2-625-1921, Fax 48-2-625-7933

Mission: Actively seeking new investments

Fund Size: not available
Founded: 1990
Average Investment: not available
Minimum Investment: $500,000

Investment Criteria: First-stage, Second-stage, Leveraged Buyout, Privatizations

Industry Group Preference: Communications, Computer Related, Consumer, Distribution, Electronic Components and Instrumentation, Energy/Natural Resources, Industrial Products and Equipment, Medical/Health Related

Portfolio Companies: not available

Officers, Executives and Principals

Robert G. Faris, President and Chief Executive Officer
Barbara J. Lundberg, Executive Vice President (Warsaw)
Tuomo Matakka, Senior Vice President (Warsaw)
Jacek Siwicki, Senior Vice President (Warsaw)
Robert J. Manz, Vice President (Warsaw)
Heather Potters, Vice President (Warsaw)
Dariusz Pronczuk, Vice President (Warsaw)
Michal Rusiecki, Vice President (Warsaw)

ENTERPRISE PARTNERS

5000 Birch Street
Suite 6200
Newport Beach, CA 92660

Telephone: 714-833-3650
Fax: 714-833-3652

Other Office Locations
7979 Ivanhoe Avenue, Suite 550
La Jolla, CA 92037
Phone 619-454-8833

12011 San Vincente Boulevard, Suite 330
Los Angeles, CA 90049
Phone 310-476-3000

Mission: Actively seeking new investments

Fund Size: $200 million
Founded: 1985
Average Investment: $2 million
Minimum Investment: No minimum

Investment Criteria: Seed, Research and Development, Startup, First-stage, Second-stage, Mezzanine, Leveraged Buyout

Industry Group Preference: Biotechnology, Communications, Computer Related, Consumer, Distribution, Electronic Components and Instrumentation, Genetic Engineering, Industrial Products and Equipment, Medical/Health Related

Portfolio Companies: Homedco, TOKOS, On Assignment, Ligand, Regency Health.

Officers, Executives and Principals

James H. Berglund, General Partner (La Jolla)

James P. Gauer, General Partner (Los Angeles)

Charles D. Martin, General Partner (Newport Beach)
Background: General Partner, Westar Capital

Andrew E. Senyei, General Partner (Newport Beach)
Background: Founder, President, Molecular Biosystems; Chief Executive Officer, Adeza Biomedical, Inc.; Assistant Professor, Departments of Obstetrics, Gynecology and Pediatrics
Directorships: Molecular Biosystems, Ligand Pharmaceuticals, Regency Health Services, Genetrix, Paidos Healthcare, Sonus Pharmaceuticals, Adeza

Jack W. Reich, Senior Vice President (La Jolla)

ENTERPRISE VENTURE CAPITAL CORPORATION OF PENNSYLVANIA

111 Market Street
Johnstown, PA 15901

Telephone: 814-535-7597
Fax: 814-535-8677

Mission: Actively seeking new investments

Fund Size: not available
Founded: 1984
Average Investment: not available
Minimum Investment: Less than $100,000

Investment Criteria: Startup, First-stage, Leveraged Buyout

Industry Group Preference: Communications, Computer Related, Consumer, Distribution, Electronic Components and Instrumentation, Energy/Natural Resources, Genetic Engineering, Industrial Products and Equipment, Medical/Health Related

Portfolio Companies: not available

Officers, Executives and Principals

Elmer Laslo, President
Bill Blasco, Portfolio Manager

EQUITAC

2000 Glen Echo Road
Suite 101
Nashville, TN 37215-8838

Telephone: 615-383-8673
Fax: 615-383-8693

Mission: Actively seeking new investments

Fund Size: not available
Founded: 1992
Average Investment: not available
Minimum Investment: $250,000

Investment Criteria: Second-stage, Mezzanine, Leveraged Buyout

Industry Group Preference: Communications, Computer Related, Consumer, Distribution, Electronic Components and Instrumentation, Industrial Products and Equipment, Medical/Health Related

Portfolio Companies: not available

Officers, Executives and Principals

Damon W. Byrd, President
Jeffrey R. Gould, Director, Investments
W. Mark Gill, Director
W. Alexander Steele, Corporate Secretary

EQUITY SOUTH ADVISORS, L.L.C.

3399 Peachtree Road Northeast
1790 Lenox Building
Atlanta, GA 30326

Telephone: 404-237-6222
Fax: 404-261-1578

Mission: Equity South pursues acquisitions or substantial equity investments in businesses with revenues from $5 million to $75 million and who have growth potential from internal efforts or through acquisitions

Fund Size: $42 million
Founded: 1987
Average Investment: $2 million - $5 million
Minimum Investment: $1 million

Investment Criteria: Later-stage to Leveraged Buyout, Control Positions

Geographic Preference: Southeastern, Southwestern, Mid-Atlantic United States

Industry Group Preference: Diversified

Portfolio Companies: CCS Technology Group Inc., Visibility, Inc., Sports and Recreation, Inc., Furniture Holdings Corporation

Officers, Executives and Principals

Douglas L. Diamond, Managing Director
Education: BS, University of Virginia
Background: CPA, Arthur Anderson and Co.; Director, Grubb and Williams, Ltd.
Directorships: Visibility, Inc., Furniture Holdings Corporation

John Y. Williams, Managing Director
Education: BS, Georgia Institute of Technology; MBA, Harvard
Directorships: Tech Data Corporation, Furniture Holdings Corporation

Stephen B. Grubb, Managing Director
Education: BA, The Citadel; JD, University of South Carolina; MBA, Emory University
Background: President, Stephen B. Grubb and Co.; Executive Vice President, Roe, Martin and Neiman Inc.; Managing Director, Grubb and Williams Ltd.; Chief Executive Officer, Paysys International, Inc.
Directorships: Paysys International, Inc., Visibility, Inc.

H. Ross Arnold III

Michael H. Dunn

EQUUS CAPITAL CORPORATION

2929 Allen Parkway
25th Floor
Houston, TX 77019

Telephone: 713-529-0900
Fax: 713-529-9545

Mission: Actively seeking new investments

Fund Size: not available
Founded: 1983
Average Investment: not available
Minimum Investment: $1 million

Investment Criteria: Mezzanine, Leveraged Buyout, Special Situations

Industry Group Preference: Consumer, Distribution, Energy/Natural Resources, Industrial Products and Equipment, Medical/Health Related

Portfolio Companies: not available

Officers, Executives and Principals

Sam P. Douglass, Chairman
Nolan Lehmann, President
Lisa R. Darrough, Vice President
Gary L. Forbes, Vice President
Randall B. Hale, Vice President

ESQUIRE CAPITAL CORPORATION

69 Veterans Highway
Commack, NY 11725

Telephone: 516-462-6946
Fax: 516-864-8152

Mission: Actively seeking new investments

Fund Size: not available
Founded: 1988
Average Investment: not available
Minimum Investment: Less than $100,000

Investment Criteria: Prefer role as deal originator but will also invest in deals created by others

Industry Group Preference: not available

Portfolio Companies: not available

Officers, Executives and Principals

C.C. Chou, President
F. Eliassen, Investment Manager

ESSEX-WOODLANDS HEALTH VENTURES, L.P.

2170 Buckthorne Place, Suite 170
The Woodlands, TX 77380

Telephone: 713-367-9999
Fax: 713-298-1295

Other Office Locations
190 South LaSalle Street
Suite 2800
Chicago, IL 60603
Phone 312-444-6040, Fax 312-444-6034

Mission: Only after attaining a thorough understanding of the selected market segment will the principals of Essex-Woodlands Health Ventures, L.P. pursue potential investment candidates. Essex-Woodlands will generally assume the role of lead investor in structuring and syndicating a financing and will take a proactive approach to managing their investments and actively participate in the creation, development and growth of each new enterprise.

Fund Size: $50 million
Founded: 1994
Average Investment: $2 million
Minimum Investment: $1 million

Investment Criteria: Seed to Second-stage

Geographic Preference: Central corridor of the United States

Industry Group Preference: Biomedical, Medical/Health

Portfolio Companies: Active Services Corporation, American Holistic Centers, DigiTrace Care Services, Inc., Healthcare Resource Management, Inc., Health Systems Technology, Inc., Hepatix, Inc., MIST, Inc., Protocol Work Systems, Inc., Ring Medical Inc., Sedona Healthcare Group, Inc., Targeted Genetics Corporation, Zonagen, Inc.

Officers, Executives and Principals

James L. Currie, General Partner (Chicago)
Education: BA, Pennsylvania State University
Background: President and Principal Stockholder, Central Scientific, Inc.
Directorships: DigiTrace Care Services, Protocol Work Systems, Zonagen, Inc.

Marc S. Sandroff, General Partner (Chicago)
Education: BA, Washington University; MBA, University of Chicago
Background: Participated in venture capital process of Allstate Insurance Company; direct operating responsibilities as a general partner and/or management principal of several rehabilitation and long term care facilities
Directorships: Active Service Corporation, American Holistic Centers, Health Systems Technology, Protocol Work Systems, Sedona Healthcare

Martin P. Sutter, General Partner (Woodlands)
Education: BS, Louisiana State University; MBA, University of Houston
Background: President, Woodlands Venture Capital Co.; various operations, marketing and finance positions in the health care industry
Directorships: Hepatix, Targeted Genetics Corporation, Ring Medical, Zonagen, Inc.

EUCLID PARTNERS CORPORATION

50 Rockefeller Plaza
Suite 1022
New York, NY 10020

Telephone: 212-489-1770
Fax: 212-757-1686
E-mail: graham@euclidpartners.com

Mission: Actively seeking new investments

Fund Size: not available
Founded: 1970
Average Investment: $1 million
Minimum Investment: $500,000

Investment Criteria: Startup, First-stage, Second-stage, Control-block Purchases

Industry Group Preference: Communications, Computer Related, Genetic Engineering, Medical/Health Related

Portfolio Companies: Biosite Diagnostics, Gigatronics, Grasp Information Corporation, Individual, Inc., Multex Systems, Netegrity, Power Center Systems, Symphony Pharmaceuticals, Sys-Tech Solutions, Therion Biologics, Wang, Zynaxis Corporation

Officers, Executives and Principals

A. Bliss McCrum, Jr., Partner
Education: Princeton University; MBA, Wharton
Background: Senior Officer, Director and executive committee member, Dominick and Dominick
Directorships: Grasp Information Corporation, Power Center Systems

Milton J. Pappas, Partner
Education: Case Western Reserve University; Cleveland Marshall Law School; CFA
Background: Vice President Drexel Harriman Ripley, Cleveland Trust Company, Merrill, Turben and Company, Inc., First of Michigan Corporation
Directorships: Multex Systems, Netegrity, New York Venture Forum, Inc., Sys-Tech Solutions

Stephen K. Reidy, Partner
Education: Middlebury College; MBA, Columbia University; MA, International Affairs, Columbia University
Background: Metropolitan Life, U.S. Information Agency (USSR and West Germany)
Directorships: Biosite Diagnostics, Power Center Systems, Symphony Pharmaceuticals, Zynaxis

Graham D.S. Anderson, Partner
Education: Yale College, University of Glasgow; Yale Law School
Background: Susman Godfrey, LLP, Salzinger and Company Management Consultants

EXPONENTIAL BUSINESS DEVELOPMENT COMPANY

216 Walton Street
Syracuse, NY 13202-1227

Telephone: 315-474-4500
Fax: 315-474-4682

Mission: Actively seeking new investments

Fund Size: not available
Founded: 1993
Average Investment: not available
Minimum Investment: Less than $100,000

Investment Criteria: Startup, First-stage

Industry Group Preference: not available

Portfolio Companies: not available

Officers, Executives and Principals

Paul M. Solomon, Partner
Michael D. Marvin, Partner
Robert L. Godgart, Partner
J. Jeffrey Solomon, Partner

FAIRFAX PARTNERS / THE VENTURE FUND OF WASHINGTON

8000 Towers Crescent Drive
Suite 940
Vienna, VA 22182

Telephone: 703-847-9486
Fax: 703-847-0911
E-mail: fairfaxpartners.com

Mission: While national in scope, Fairfax Partners II will become recognized as the premier venture capital firm, the venture fund of choice for co-investment, in the Washington D.C., metropolitan and surrounding areas. As a balanced fund, Fairfax Partners II will provide early-stage capital to incubate new businesses, as well as comprehensive growth capital for later-stage companies. Fairfax Partners II will draw on the experience of its managing directors and advisory board to identify and manage opportunities and risks by combining the best current venture capital knowledge and empirical methodologies. Fairfax Partners II will be a fair investor to its portfolio companies while striving to provide superior returns to its partners and other stakeholders.

Fund Size: $15 million
Founded: 1989
Average Investment: $10 million
Minimum Investment: $1 million

Investment Criteria: Seed to Mezzanine

Geographic Preference: Southern Mid-Atlantic United States

Industry Group Preference: Communications, Healthcare, Software

Portfolio Companies: APACHE Medical Systems, Indigo Medical, Collagenex Pharmaceuticals, Industrial Flexible Materials, DentalCare Partners, OvaMed-BEI Medical, VasoMedex, Vista Restaurants, IIemaColl Products

Officers, Executives and Principals

Stephen W. Ritterbush, PhD, Managing Director
Education: MA, PhD, International Economics, Tufts and Harvard; MS, Geophysics; BS, Engineering, BA, Political Science
Background: Officer and Director, ICF International, Inc.; President, Arthur D. Little, Far East; Joint Venture Partner, Advent International

Raymond List, Managing Director
Education: MBA, Harvard; BS, MS, Engineering

Bruce K. Gouldey, PhD, Managing Director
Education: PhD, Operations Research and Finance, University of Pittsburgh; ScB, Applied Mathematics, Brown University

Andrew D. Klingenstein, Managing Director
Education: JD, University of Virginia; BA, Yale

FANWOOD AND COMPANY

609 West 114th Street
Suite 22
New York, NY 10025

Telephone: not available

Mission: Actively seeking new investments

Fund Size: not available
Founded: 1990
Average Investment: not available
Minimum Investment: $500,000

Investment Criteria: First-stage, Second-stage, Mezzanine, Leveraged Buyout

Industry Group Preference: Communications, Computer Related, Consumer

Portfolio Companies: not available

Officers, Executives and Principals

Edward Weissberg, Managing Partner
Claudia Stone, Associate

FARM BUREAU LIFE INSURANCE COMPANY

5400 University Avenue
West Des Moines, IA 50266

Telephone: 515-225-5500

Mission: Actively seeking new investments

Fund Size: not available
Founded: 1984
Average Investment: not available
Minimum Investment: $500,000

Investment Criteria: First-stage, Second-stage, Mezzanine, Leveraged Buyout, Special Situations

Industry Group Preference: Communications, Computer Related, Consumer, Distribution, Electronic Components and Instrumentation, Energy/Natural Resources, Genetic Engineering, Industrial Products and Equipment, Medical/Health Related

Portfolio Companies: not available

Officers, Executives and Principals

Jeffrey R. Tollefson, Vice President, Alternative Investments
Richard Warming

FARRELL CAPITAL CORPORATION

Two Greenwich Plaza
Greenwich, CT 06830

Telephone: 203-861-2236
Fax: 203-861-2240

Mission: not available

Fund Size: not available
Founded: not available
Average Investment: not available
Minimum Investment: not available

Investment Criteria: not available

Industry Group Preference: not available

Portfolio Companies: not available

Officers, Executives and Principals

William L. Farrell, President
James J. McCarvill, Jr.

FCP INVESTORS

100 North Tampa Street
Suite 2410
Tampa, FL 33602

Telephone: 813-222-8000
Fax: 813-222-8001

Mission: Actively seeking new investments. Acquires profitable private companies with historical pre-tax profits of at least $1.5 million, working in partnership with operating managers. FCP does not provide venture capital for emerging businesses.

Fund Size: $200 million
Founded: 1988
Average Investment: not available
Minimum Investment: $2 million

Investment Criteria: Leveraged Buyout, Recapitalizations

Geographic Preference: Continental United States

Industry Group Preference: Consumer, Industrial Products, Niche Manufacturing, Value-added Distribution

Portfolio Companies: Standard Tool, Classic Rope, Perfecto, Manan Medical, Atlantic Coast Fire Protection, Aquarium Systems, PTN Publishing, Booda Products, Aspen Pet Products, Prodelin Corporation, Consumer Product Enterprises, Katzenberg Brothers, Rutland Plastic Technologies, Adva-Lite, Niemand Industries, Thompson Paint and Body Supply, Lorvic Corporation, CCP

Officers, Executives and Principals

John F. Kirtley, Partner
P. Jeffrey Leck, Partner
Glenn Oken, Partner
Peter Franz, Partner
Jay Jester, Vice President
Felix Wong, Partner
David Malizia, Vice President
Krista Pegnetter, Vice President

FEDERAL BUSINESS DEVELOPMENT BANK

800, square Victoria, Bureau 4600
Tour de la Place-Victoria, C.P. 335
Montreal, Quebec H4Z 1L4
Canada

Telephone: 514-283-1896
Fax: 514-283-7675

Other Office Locations
777 Bay Street, 29th Floor
Toronto, Ontario M5G 2C8
Canada
Phone 416-973-0034, Fax 416-973-5529

601 West Hastings Street, Suite 700
Vancouver, British Columbia V6B 5G9
Canada
Phone 604-666-7815, Fax 604-666-7650

Mission: Actively seeking new investments

Fund Size: not available
Founded: 1975
Average Investment: not available
Minimum Investment: $250,000

Investment Criteria: Startup, First-stage, Second-stage, Mezzanine, Leveraged Buyout, Turnaround, Management Buyout

Industry Group Preference: Communications, Computer Related, Consumer, Distribution, Electronic Components and Instrumentation, Energy/Natural Resources, Genetic Engineering, Industrial Products and Equipment, Medical/Health Related

Portfolio Companies: not available

Officers, Executives and Principals

Peter R. Forton, Vice President (Montreal)
David Bennett, Assistant Vice President (Vancouver)
G. Rick Cornwall, Assistant Vice President (Ottawa)
Tony Charnish, Investment Manager (Vancouver)
Brian Elder, Investment Manager (Vancouver)
Robert Inglese, Investment Manager (Montreal)
Karl Reckziegal, Investment Manager (Toronto)
Roger Wilson, Investment Manager (Toronto)

FHL CAPITAL CORPORATION

600 20th Street North
Suite 350
Birmingham, AL 35203

Telephone: 205-328-3098
Fax: 205-323-0001

Mission: Primarily interested in acquiring control positions in profitable companies

Fund Size: not available
Founded: 1984
Average Investment: not available
Minimum Investment: $1 million

Investment Criteria: Mezzanine, Leveraged Buyout, Special Situations

Geographic Preference: Southeastern United States

Industry Group Preference: Distribution, Manufacturing, Service

Portfolio Companies: not available

Officers, Executives and Principals

Edwin W. Finch III, President
Kevin Keck, Vice President
T. Morris Hackney, Principal

FIDELITY CAPITAL

82 Devonshire Street - R25C
Boston, MA 02109

Telephone: 617-563-9160
Fax: 617-476-5015

Mission: Actively seeking new investments

Fund Size: not available
Founded: 1971
Average Investment: $1.5 million
Minimum Investment: $500,000

Investment Criteria: First-stage, Second-stage, Leveraged Buyout, Special Situations

Industry Group Preference: Communications, Computer Related, Consumer, Distribution, Electronic Components and Instrumentation, Genetic Engineering, Industrial Products and Equipment, Medical/Health Related

Portfolio Companies: not available

Officers, Executives and Principals

John J. Remondi, Managing Director
James C. Curvey, President
Timothy Hillon, Senior Vice President
Neal Yanofsky, Vice President
Warren Morrison, Vice President
Anne Cooke, Analyst
Peter Mann, Associate
Stephen Kramer, Associate

FINANCIAL CAPITAL RESOURCES, INC.

5151 San Jose Street
Tampa, FL 33629

Telephone: 813-281-5486

Mission: Actively seeking new investments

Fund Size: not available
Founded: 1989
Average Investment: not available
Minimum Investment: $1 million

Investment Criteria: Leveraged Buyout, Structuring, Mergers and Acquisitions

Geographic Preference: United States

Industry Group Preference: Metal Products, Mortgage Banking Companies/Banks

Portfolio Companies: not available

Officers, Executives and Principals

Hilary Whitley, Principal

FINANCIAL RESOURCES CORPORATION

6501 Broadway Extension
Suite 300
Oklahoma City, OK 73116

Telephone: 405-840-0049
Fax: 405-842-0795

Mission: We are a venture capital investment banking and business consulting firm for growth oriented companies whose mission is to assist clients through the capital formation process.

Fund Size: not available
Founded: 1989
Average Investment: not available
Minimum Investment: Less than $100,000

Investment Criteria: Startup, First-stage, Second-stage, Mezzanine, Special Situations

Geographic Preference: Southwest

Industry Group Preference: Communications, Computer Related, Consumer, Distribution, Energy/Natural Resources, Genetic Engineering, High Technology, Industrial Products and Equipment, Manufacturing, Medical/Health Related, Retail

Portfolio Companies: not available

Officers, Executives and Principals

Jim Ratchford, President

FIRST ANALYSIS CORPORATION

233 South Wacker Drive, Suite 9600
Chicago, IL 60606

Telephone: 312-258-1400
Fax: 312-258-0334

Mission: not available

Fund Size: $200 million
Founded: not available
Average Investment: $1 million
Minimum Investment: not available

Investment Criteria: First-stage, Second-stage

Industry Group Preference: Communications, Computer Related, Electronics, Energy/Natural Resources, Environmental Protection, Financial Services, High Technology, Information Services, Insurance, Manufacturing/Processing, Service Industries, Software

Portfolio Companies: not available

Officers, Executives and Principals

Bret Maxwell, Managing Director of Private Equity
Education: BS, Industrial Engineering, MBA, Northwestern
Background: Consulting, Arthur Andersen and Co.

Brian Hand, Managing Director
Education: BS, MS, Electrical Engineering, Rensselaer Polytechnic Institute; MBA, Northwestern
Background: Development, advanced manufacturing robots, IBM

F. Oliver Nicklin, President
Education: BS, Chemical Engineering, University of Texas; MBA, Harvard
Background: Founder, First Analysis; Chief Operating Officer, William Blair and Co.; Strategic Planning, Amoco and Exxon Corporation

Allan Cohen, Executive Vice President
Education: BS, Chemistry, State University New York, Buffalo; MBA, University of Chicago; PhD, Physical Chemistry, Northwestern
Background: Kemper Securities, Valspar, Sherwin-Williams Co., and Champion International

Steve Bouck, Vice President
Education: BS, MS, Aeronautical Engineering, Rensselaer Polytechnic Institute; MBA, Finance, Wharton
Background: Marketing, Hewlett Packard; Engineer, Dresser Industries and Jet Propulsion Laboratory

FIRST CAPITAL GROUP OF TEXAS II

750 East Mulberry
Suite 350
San Antonio, TX 78212

Telephone: 210-736-4233
Fax: 210-736-5449

Other Office Locations
7200 North Mopac, #450
Austin, TX 78731
Phone 512-346-4263, Fax 512-346-0195

Mission: not available

Fund Size: $31.1 million
Founded: 1984
Average Investment: $1 million
Minimum Investment: $500,000

Investment Criteria: Second-stage to Leveraged Buyout

Geographic Preference: Texas

Industry Group Preference: Diversified

Portfolio Companies: not available

Officers, Executives and Principals

Jeffrey P. Blanchard, Investment Manager
Background: Investment Manager, Victoria Capital Corporation

Ward Greenwood, Investment Manager (Austin)
Background: Founder, Nueces Ventures

FIRST CENTURY PARTNERS

One Partner Square
Suite 425
Princeton, NJ 08452

Telephone: 609-683-8848
Fax: 609-683-8123

Mission: not available

Fund Size: $100 million
Founded: not available
Average Investment: $2.5 million
Minimum Investment: not available

Investment Criteria: Start-up to Later-stage

Industry Group Preference: Consumer Related, Manufacturing/Processing, Medical/Health, Retailing, Wholesaling/Distribution

Portfolio Companies: HASCO Holdings Corporation, Border Foods, Inc., Floral Plant Growers, LLC, Frame-n-Lens Optical, Inc.

Officers, Executives and Principals

Michael Myers, General Partner
Education: MBA, Harvard University; JD, George Washington University; BS, University of Illinois
Background: Co-Founder, First Century; J.H. Whitney and Company Venture Capital Firm; Lawyer, General Electric
Directorships: Office Depot, Inc., Vista, Inc., Wynstar, Inc.

FIRST CHARTER PARTNERS, INC.

405 Park Avenue
New York, NY 10022

Telephone: 212-644-9700
Fax: 212-644-9700

Mission: Actively seeking new investments

Fund Size: not available
Founded: 1993
Average Investment: not available
Minimum Investment: $500,000

Investment Criteria: Second-stage, Leveraged Buyout, Special Situations

Industry Group Preference: Consumer, Distribution, Industrial Products and Equipment, Medical/Health Related

Portfolio Companies: not available

Officers, Executives and Principals

Miles Stuchin, Chairman and Chief Exeutive Officer
Eric Gilchrest, President

FIRST FIDELITY PRIVATE CAPITAL

550 Broad Street
NJ 1558
Newark, NJ 07102

Telephone: 201-565-6101
Fax: 201-565-6281

Mission: Actively looking for new investments in companies with sales less than $50 million.

Fund Size: not available
Founded: 1987
Average Investment: $1 million
Minimum Investment: $500,000

Investment Criteria: Mezzanine, Leveraged Buyout, All Stages, Growth Capital

Geographic Preference: Eastern Seaboard: Norther Virginia to Connecticut

Industry Group Preference: Communications, Consumer, Distribution, Healthcare, Industrial Products and Equipment, Manufacturing, Technology, Transportation, Wholesale Trade

Portfolio Companies: not available

Officers, Executives and Principals

Stephen M. Lane, President and Secretary
Keith Vallacchi, Treasurer

FIRST NEW ENGLAND CAPITAL, L.P.

100 Pearl Street
Hartford, CT 06103

Telephone: 860-293-3333
Fax: 860-293-3338

Mission: Actively seeking new investments

Fund Size: not available
Founded: 1988
Average Investment: not available
Minimum Investment: $400,000

Investment Criteria: Second-stage, Mezzanine, Leveraged Buyout

Industry Group Preference: Consumer, Distribution, Energy/Natural Resources, Industrial Products and
  Equipment

Portfolio Companies: not available

Officers, Executives and Principals

Richard C. Klaffky, President
John L. Ritter, Executive Vice President

FIRST PRINCETON CAPITAL

1 Garret Mountain Plaza, 9th Floor
West Paterson, NJ 07424

Telephone: 201-278-8111
Fax: 201-278-4290

Mission: Actively seeking new investments

Fund Size: $5 million
Founded: 1981
Average Investment: $500,000
Minimum Investment: $250,000

Investment Criteria: Second-stage, Loan and Equity

Geographic Preference: Northeastern, Mid-Atlantic United States

Industry Group Preference: Consumer Related, Information Services, Manufacturing/Processing, Publishing

Portfolio Companies: not available

Officers, Executives and Principals

Michael Lytell, President
Education: BA, Johns Hopkins University
Background: Founder, Norcrown Bank of Roseland, NJ.; President, Lytell Associates, Inc.; Vice President,
  Russ Bern, Berrie and Company, Inc.

FIRST SECURITY BUSINESS INVESTMENT CORPORATION

15 East 100 South Street
Suite 100
Salt Lake City, UT 84111

Telephone: 801-246-5737
Fax: 801-246-5740

Mission: Actively seeking new investments

Fund Size: not available
Founded: 1993
Average Investment: not available
Minimum Investment: $250,000

Investment Criteria: Second-stage, Mezzanine, Leveraged Buyout

Industry Group Preference: Communications, Computer Related, Distribution, Industrial Products and Equipment, Medical/Health Related

Portfolio Companies: not available

Officers, Executives and Principals

Mark Howell, President
Sam Jeppson, Executive Vice President
Butch Alder, Vice President and Manager

FIRST SOURCE CAPITAL CORPORATION

100 North Michigan Street
P.O. Box 1602
South Bend, IN 46634

Telephone: 219-235-2180
Fax: 219-235-2719

Mission: Actively seeking new investments

Fund Size: not available
Founded: 1983
Average Investment: not available
Minimum Investment: $200,000

Investment Criteria: Second-stage, Mezzanine, Leveraged buyout, Specia lsituations

Industry Group Preference: Communications, Computer Related, Consumer,Distribution, Electronic Components and Instrumentation, Energy/NaturalResources, Genetic Engineering, Industrial Products and Equipment,Medical/Health Related

Portfolio Companies: not available

Officers, Executives and Principals

Christopher J. Murphy III, President
Eugene L. Cavanaugh, Vice President

FIRST UNION CAPITAL PARTNERS

One First Union Center
Fifth Floor
Charlotte, NC 28288-0732

Telephone: 704-374-4806
Fax: 704-374-6711

Mission: Actively seeking new investments

Fund Size: not available
Founded: 1988
Average Investment: not available
Minimum Investment: $1 million

Investment Criteria: First-stage, Second-stage, Mezzanine, Leveraged Buyout, Special Situations, Control-block Purchases

Industry Group Preference: Communications, Consumer, Distribution, Industrial Products and Equipment, Medical/Health Related

Portfolio Companies: not available

Officers, Executives and Principals

W. Barnes Hauptfuher, Managing Partner
Ted A. Gardner, Partner
Scott B. Perper, Partner
Kevin J. Roche, Partner
James C. Cook, Partner
David B. Carson, Vice President
Michael Egues, Vice President
Frederick W. Eubank II, Vice President

FIRST WALL STREET SBIC, L.P.

26 Broadway, Suite 1320
New York, NY 10004

Telephone: 212-742-3770
Fax: 212-742-3776

Mission: not available

Fund Size: $12 million
Founded: 1989
Average Investment: $600,000
Minimum Investment: $300,000

Investment Criteria: Second-stage

Geographic Preference: Northeastern United States

Industry Group Preference: Diversified

Portfolio Companies: not available

Officers, Executives and Principals

Alan Farkas, President
Education: BS, Economics, University of Pennsylvania; LLM, New York University; LLB, Brooklyn Law
  School
Background: Attorney, CPA, Main Hurdman; President, Franklin Corporation

Paul Pollock, Vice President
Education: BA, Accounting, Bernard M. Baruch College
Background: CPA, Coopers and Lybrand

FJC GROWTH CAPITAL CORPORATION

200 West Court Square
Suite 340
Huntsville, AL 35801

Telephone: 205-922-2918
Fax: 205-922-2909

Mission: Actively seeking new investments

Fund Size: $1 million
Founded: 1989
Average Investment: $250,000 - $500,000
Minimum Investment: $100,000

Investment Criteria: Second-stage

Industry Group Preference: Consumer Related, Manufacturing/Processing, Real Estate/Construction, Wholesaling/Distribution

Portfolio Companies: not available

Officers, Executives and Principals

Francisco L. Collazo, President
William B. Noojin, Vice President and General Manager

FLEET EQUITY PARTNERS

50 Kennedy Plaza
Providence, RI 02903

Telephone: 401-278-6770
Fax: 401-278-6387

Mission: Actively seeking new investments

Fund Size: not available
Founded: 1982
Average Investment: not available
Minimum Investment: $5 million

Investment Criteria: Leveraged Buyout, Special Situations, Management Buyouts

Industry Group Preference: Communications, Consumer, Distribution, Industrial Products and Equipment, Medical/Health Related

Portfolio Companies: not available

Officers, Executives and Principals

Donald E. Bates, Partner
Habib Y. Gorgi, Partner
Michael A. Gorman, Partner
Thadeus J. Mocarski, Partner
Rory B. Smith, Partner
Robert M. Van Degna, Partner

FLORIDA CAPITAL VENTURES, LTD.

880 Riverside Plaza
100 West Kennedy Boulevard
Tampa, FL 33602

Telephone: 813-229-2294
Fax: 813-229-2028

Mission: Actively seeking new investments

Fund Size: not available
Founded: 1989
Average Investment: not available
Minimum Investment: $250,000

Investment Criteria: First-stage, Second-stage, Mezzanine, Leveraged Buyout, Special Situations

Industry Group Preference: Communications, Computer Related, Consumer, Distribution, Electronic Components and Instrumentation, Energy/Natural Resources, Genetic Engineering, Industrial Products and Equipment, Medical/Health Related

Portfolio Companies: not available

Officers, Executives and Principals

Warren L. Miller, President
Michael M. Macinnes, Vice President

FONDS DE SOLIDARITÉ DES TRAVAILLEURS DU QUEBEC

8717, rue Berri
Montreal, Quebec H2M 2T9
Canada

Telephone: 514-383-8383
Fax: 514-383-2502

Mission: Actively seeking new investments

Fund Size: not available
Founded: 1983
Average Investment: not available
Minimum Investment: $250,000

Investment Criteria: Startup, First-stage, Second-stage, Leveraged Buyout

Industry Group Preference: Communications, Computer Related, Consumer, Distribution, Electronic Components and Instrumentation, Energy/Natural Resources, Genetic Engineering, Industrial Products and Equipment, Medical/Health Related

Portfolio Companies: not available

Officers, Executives and Principals

Claude Blanchet, President
Denis Dionne, Executive Vice President
Pierre Laflamme, Executive Vice President
Jean Martin, Executive Vice President
Richard Bourget, Vice President
Luc Charron, Vice President
Roger Giraldeau, Vice President
Helen Levesque, Vice President

THE FOOD FUND, L. P.

5720 Smetana Drive
Suite 300
Minnetonka, MN 55343

Telephone: 612-939-3950
Fax: 612-939-8106

Mission: Actively seeking new investments

Fund Size: $10 million
Founded: 1990
Average Investment: $500,000
Minimum Investment: $100,000

Investment Criteria: Startup, First-stage, Second-stage, Leveraged Buyout, Special Situations

Geographic Preference: United States

Industry Group Preference: Consumer, Distribution, Industrial Products and Equipment

Portfolio Companies: Aquahealth, Inc., American Specialty Confections, Inc., Award Baking International, Daily Bread Company, Inc., Hoffman Aseptic Packaging, Keurig, Inc., Moline Technology, Inc., Mrs. Clark's Foods, Inc., Orval Kent Foods Company, Packaged Ice, Inc., Pappy's Foods Company, Stars Beverage Company, Uncle B's Bakery, Inc.

Officers, Executives and Principals

John Trucano, Managing General Partner
Richard Coonrad, General Partner
Jenny Skinner, Associate

FORESTER VENTURES

160 Robin Road
Hillsborough, CA 94010

Telephone: 415-342-8828
Fax: 415-342-7968

Mission: not available

Fund Size: $10 million
Founded: not available
Average Investment: $500,000
Minimum Investment: not available

Investment Criteria: First-stage to Leveraged Buyout

Geographic Preference: West Coast

Industry Group Preference: Communications, Computer Related, Electronics, Industrial Products

Portfolio Companies: not available

Officers, Executives and Principals

Patrick Forester, President

FORREST BINKLEY AND BROWN

800 Newport Center Drive
Suite 725
Newport Beach, CA 92660

Telephone: 714-729-3222
Fax: 714-729-3226

Mission: Actively seeking new investments

Fund Size: not available
Founded: 1993
Average Investment: not available
Minimum Investment: $2 - $6 million

Investment Criteria: Second-stage, Leveraged Buyout, Special Situations

Industry Group Preference: Communications, Computer Related, Consumer, Genetic Engineering, Medical/ Health Related

Portfolio Companies: not available

Officers, Executives and Principals

Greg Forrest, Partner
Nick Binkley, Partner
Jeff Brown, Partner
Stephen G. Stewart, Principal
Doug Walter, Associate

FORWARD VENTURES

10975 Torreyana Road
Suite 230
San Diego, CA 92121

Telephone: 619-677-6077
Fax: 619-452-8799

Mission: Actively seeking new investments

Fund Size: not available
Founded: 1990
Average Investment: not available
Minimum Investment: $100,000

Investment Criteria: Seed, Research and Development, Startup, First-stage

Industry Group Preference: Genetic Engineering, Medical/Health Related

Portfolio Companies: not available

Officers, Executives and Principals

Standish M. Fleming, General Partner
Dr. Ivor Royston, General Partner

FOUNDERS EQUITY, INC.

200 Madison Avenue
Second Floor
New York, NY 10016

Telephone: 212-953-0100
Fax: 212-953-0626

Mission: Actively seeking new investments

Fund Size: not available
Founded: 1969
Average Investment: not available
Minimum Investment: $1 million

Investment Criteria: Leveraged Buyout, Special Situations, Turnarounds

Industry Group Preference: Communications, Computer Related, Consumer, Distribution, Industrial Products and Equipment, Medical/Health Related

Portfolio Companies: not available

Officers, Executives and Principals

Warren H. Haber, Chairman and Chief Exeutive Officer
John L. Teeger, President

FOWLER, ANTHONY AND COMPANY

20 Walnut Street
Wellesley, MA 02181

Telephone: 617-237-4201
Fax: 617-237-7718

Mission: Actively seeking new investments. Current emphasis on buyouts, both private and subsidiaries/divisions of public companies. Any size.

Fund Size: not available
Founded: 1976
Average Investment: not available
Minimum Investment: $100,000

Investment Criteria: Seed, Startup, First-stage, Second-stage, Mezzanine, Leveraged Buyout, Special Situations, Control-block Purchases

Industry Group Preference: Communications, Computer Related, Consumer, Distribution, Electronic Components and Instrumentation, Food, Industrial Products and Equipment, Medical/Health Related, Medical Instrumentation, Technical Services

Portfolio Companies: not available

Officers, Executives and Principals

John A. Quagliaroli, President

FOX AND COMPANY, INC.

423 Ballytore Circle
Wynnewood, PA 19096

Telephone: 610-642-6953

Mission: Actively seeking new investments

Fund Size: not available
Founded: 1984
Average Investment: not available
Minimum Investment: Less than $100,000

Investment Criteria: Startup, First-stage, Second-stage, Leveraged Buyout

Industry Group Preference: Communications, Computer Related, Distribution, Electronic Components and Instrumentation, Energy/Natural Resources, Genetic Engineering, Industrial Products and Equipment, Medical/Health Related

Portfolio Companies: not available

Officers, Executives and Principals

Larry Fox, President

FRAZIER AND COMPANY

601 Union Street
Suite 2110
Seattle, WA 98101

Telephone: 206-621-7200
Fax: 206-621-1848

Mission: Actively seeking new investments

Fund Size: not available
Founded: 1991
Average Investment: not available
Minimum Investment: $2 million

Investment Criteria: Mezzanine

Industry Group Preference: Genetic Engineering, Medical/Health Related

Portfolio Companies: not available

Officers, Executives and Principals

Alan Frazier, Managing Partner
Bob Kupor, General Partner
Fred Silverstein, General Partner
Jon Gilbert, Vice President
Nader Naini, Associate
Bridget Rauvola, Marketing Associate

THE FREMONT GROUP

50 Fremont Street
Suite 3700
San Francisco, CA 94105

Telephone: 415-768-4258
Fax: 415-284-8191

Mission: Actively seeking new investments

Fund Size: not available
Founded: 1980
Average Investment: not available
Minimum Investment: $25 million

Investment Criteria: Special Situations, Recapitalizations, Corporate Acquisitions, Later-stage Ventures, Management Buyouts

Industry Group Preference: Communications, Computer Related, Consumer, Distribution, Energy/Natural Resources, Industrial Products and Equipment, Medical/Health Related

Portfolio Companies: not available

Officers, Executives and Principals

Robert Jaunich II, Managing Director
Gil Lamphere, Managing Director
James A. Bondoux, Managing Principal
James T. Farrell, Principal
Thomas D. Willardson, Principal
Kevin J. Kendrick, Associate

FRONTENAC COMPANY

135 South LaSalle Street
Suite 3800
Chicago, IL 60603

Telephone: 312-368-0044
Fax: 312-368-9520

Mission: not available

Fund Size: $300 million
Founded: not available
Average Investment: $500,000 - $40 million
Minimum Investment: not available

Investment Criteria: Startup to Leveraged Buyout

Geographic Preference: Midwestern United States

Industry Group Preference: Biotechnology, Consumer Related, High Technology, Manufacturing/Processing, Medical/Health, Retailing, Service Industries

Portfolio Companies: American Healthcorp, GalenPharma, GenDerm, Pediatric Nursing Specialists of America, Phycor, Anatel Instruments, Plindrome, Platinum, Chalk-Line, Contemporary Books, U.S. Playing Card Company, DeVry, Eastern Lobby Shops, Bradley Printing Co.

Officers, Executives and Principals

Martin J. Koldyke, Founder
Education: Purdue University; United States Army, Counter-Intelligence Corps
Background: Vice President, Dean Witter and Co.; Founder, The Foundation for Excellence in Teaching; Trustee, Northwestern

James E. Cowie, General Partner
Education: Colby College; MBA, Stanford
Background: Merrill Lynch Capital Markets; U.S. Senate, SBA Legislative Affairs
Directorships: Steris Corporation, Platinum Technology, Persoft, Anatel Instrument Corporation, Palindrome Corporation

Joan S. Fortune, General Partner
Education: Catholic University; MS, Organic Chemistry, University of Wisconsin; MBA, University of Chicago
Background: Management Consultant, Hayes/Hill, G.D. Searle and Co., American Hospital Supply Corporation

Laura P. Pearl, General Partner
Education: BS, Accounting, summa cum laude, University of Illinois; MBA, University of Chicago
Background: Ernst and Whinney; CPA, CMA
Directorships: Homex Corporation

Rodney L. Goldstein, General Partner
Education: Honors, Princeton; MBA, Wharton
Background: Booz, Allen and Hamilton, Salomon Brothers
Directorships: Consolidated Stores Corporation, Contemporary Books, DeVry, Eastern Lobby Shops, Levy
  Restaurants L.P., Marks

Roger S. McEniry, General Partner
Education: Honors, Williams; MBA, University of Michigan
Background: Citicorp
Directorships: ChalkLine, Home Fashions, Prestolite Electric, The U.S. Playing Card Co.

FRONTLINE CAPITAL, INC.

3475 Lenox Road
Suite 400
Atlanta, GA 30326

Telephone: 404-240-7280
Fax: 404-240-7281

Mission: Actively seeking new investments

Fund Size: not available
Founded: 1994
Average Investment: not available
Minimum Investment: $500,000

Investment Criteria: not available

Industry Group Preference: Communications, Consumer, Distribution, Electronic Components and Instrumentation, Energy/Natural Resources, Industrial Products and Equipment, Medical/Health Related

Portfolio Companies: not available

Officers, Executives and Principals

David A. Weil, Chairman and Chief Exeutive Officer
Joe B. Wolfe, President and Chief Executive Officer

FROST CAPITAL PARTNERS, INC.

44 Montgomery Street
22nd Floor
San Francisco, CA 94114

Telephone: 415-274-2400
Fax: 415-274-2444

Other Office Locations
26 Remington Street
London, NI 8DH
U.K.

Mission: The leading merger, acquisition, and financial advisory firm serving developers and publishers in the entertainment and education software industry.

Fund Size: not available
Founded: 1986
Average Investment: not available
Minimum Investment: $1 million

Investment Criteria: Second-stage, Mezzanine, Bridge Lending

Industry Group Preference: Computer Related, Entertainment and Educational Software

Portfolio Companies: not available

Officers, Executives and Principals

Ian Berman, Managing Director
Dean Frost, Managing Director
Hamish Stewart, Managing Director (London)
Ron Heller, Director
Brian Feldman, Director

FRY CONSULTANTS, INC.

2100 Powers Ferry Road
Suite 125
Atlanta, GA 30339

Telephone: 770-266-8888
Fax: 770-266-8899

Other Office Locations
2720 River Road, Suite 200
Des Plaines, IL 60018
Phone 708-296-1225, Fax 708-296-1226

5145 Chillicothe Road
Cleveland, OH 44022
Phone 216-338-3336, Fax 216-338-3999

Zang Mansion
709 Clarkson Street
Denver, CO 80218
Phone 303-837-0872, Fax 303-863-1737

680 Fifth Avenue, 11th Floor
New York, NY 10019
Phone 212-664-8875, Fax 212-664-8872

1401 Weatherstone Drive
Paoli, PA 19301
Phone 215-296-2498

World Trade Center, Suite 289
San Francisco, CA 94111
Phone 415-288-0700, Fax 415-391-0202

50 Wingold Avenue, L
North York, Ontario M6B 1P7
Canada
Phone 416-781-4658, Fax 416-781-4577

73 Princedale Road
London W11 4NS
England
Phone 441-71-221-5680, Fax 441-71-229-4713

Sandport House
17 Coburg Street
Leith, Edinburgh, EH6 6ET
Scotland
Phone 44-31-553-1415, Fax 44-31-553-1322

27 Campbell Street, Helensburgh
Dunbartonshire G84 8YG
Glasgow, Scotland
Phone 44436-671371, Fax 44436-671371

Ground Level, 357 Military Road
Cremorne Junction NSW 2090
Sydney, Australia
Phone 612-9953-8066, Fax 612-9909-3378

17-1-901, Masago 3-chome
Mihama-ku, Chiba City
Chiba Prefecture 261
Tokyo, Japan
Phone 8143-279-0354, Fax 8143-278-3965

Wienfeldstrasse 24
D-65187 Wiesbaden
Germany
Phone 49-611-86979, Fax 49-611-86926

Mission: Actively seeking new investments and providing consulting services

Fund Size: not available
Founded: 1942
Average Investment: not available
Minimum Investment: $100,000

Investment Criteria: Seed, Research and Development, Startup, First-stage, Second-stage, Mezzanine, Leveraged Buyout, Special Situations, Control-block Purchases

Geographic Preference: United States

Industry Group Preference: Communications, Computer Related, Consumer, Distribution, Electronic Components and Instrumentation, Energy/Natural Resources, Genetic Engineering, Industrial Products and Equipment, Medical/Health Related

Portfolio Companies: not available

Officers, Executives and Principals

Ian MacFarlane, Chairman (Atlanta)
Garland G. Fritts, President (Atlanta)
D. Jack Hensler, Managing Principal (Atlanta)
L. Lyne Smith, Managing Principal (Atlanta)
Adnan W. Kubba, Managing Principal (Des Plaines)
James S. Stotter, Managing Principal (Cleveland)
Mark H. Towery, Managing Director (Atlanta)
Gary Barker, Consulting Principal (Atlanta)
Adnan W. Kubba, Managing Principal (Chicago)
David R. Tennant, Managing Principal (Denver)
Fiona M. Thorp, Managing Principal (Glasgow)

Mark Pavan, Managing Principal (London)
W. Lynden Gillis, Managing Principal (New York)
Dr. John Haldi, Managing Principal (New York)
Frederick D. Brown, Counsel (Philadelphia)
Nicholas A. Maczkov, Managing Principal (San Francisco)
Michael J. Walker, Managing Principal (Sydney)
Mitsuo Morinaga, Managing Principal (Tokyo)
Jon Arnold, Managing Principal (Toronto)
Dr. Ing Bruno Hake, Managing Principal (Wiesbaden)

G.A. HERRERA AND COMPANY

5847 San Felipe
Suite 2370
Houston, TX 77057

Telephone: 713-268-4073
Fax: 713-784-3360

Other Office Locations
8301 Gancy Drive, Suite 100
Austin, TX 78750
Phone 512-794-0958, Fax 512-794-0959

Mission: Actively seeking new investments

Fund Size: not available
Founded: 1992
Average Investment: not available
Minimum Investment: $500,000

Investment Criteria: Second-stage, Mezzanine, Leveraged Buyout

Industry Group Preference: Communications, Computer Related, Consumer, Distribution, Energy/Natural Resources, Industrial Products and Equipment, Medical/Health Related

Portfolio Companies: not available

Officers, Executives and Principals

Gilbert A. Herrera, Principal (Houston)
Gregory K. Lewis, Principal (Austin)

THE GARON FINANCIAL GROUP

751 Laurel Avenue
Suite 121
San Carlos, CA 94070

Telephone: 415-654-0164
Fax: 415-654-0165

Mission: Actively seeking new investments

Fund Size: not available
Founded: 1994
Average Investment: not available
Minimum Investment: Less than $100,000

Investment Criteria: Seed, Research and Development, Startup, First-stage, Second-stage, Special Situations

Industry Group Preference: Communications, Computer Related, Consumer, Distribution, Electronic Components and Instrumentation, Energy/Natural Resources, Genetic Engineering, Industrial Products and Equipment, Medical/Health Related

Portfolio Companies: not available

Officers, Executives and Principals

Jeffrey L. Garon, Principal
George Beck, Principal
Mark Caires, Associate

GCC INVESTMENTS, INC.

27 Boylston Street
Chestnut Hill, MA 02167

Telephone: 617-278-5600
Fax: 617-278-5458

Mission: Actively seeking new investments

Fund Size: not available
Founded: 1993
Average Investment: $10 - $20 million
Minimum Investment: $5 million

Investment Criteria: Second-stage, Mezzanine, Special Situations, Control-block Purchases

Industry Group Preference: Communications, Consumer, Distribution

Portfolio Companies: Vision Express Group, U.K. Ltd, YoungWorld Stores Group, KabelMedia, Crescent Communications

Officers, Executives and Principals

John G. Berylson, President
Education: BA, Brown University; MA, New York University; MBA, Harvard

Michael A. Greeley, Senior Vice President
Education: BA, Williams College; MBA, Harvard

Robert A. Morse, Associate
Education: BSE, Princeton University

Noreen M'Quade, Office Manager
Education: BS, Boston University

GCI

30875 Crosspoint Circle
Suite 100
Waukesha, WI 53186

Telephone: 414-798-5080
Fax: 414-798-5087

Mission: Actively seeking new investments

Fund Size: not available
Founded: 1990
Average Investment: not available
Minimum Investment: $250,000

Investment Criteria: First-stage, Second-stage, Leveraged Buyout

Geographic Preference: United States

Industry Group Preference: Chemicals, Data Compression, Plastics Manufacturing

Portfolio Companies: not available

Officers, Executives and Principals

William Schleicher, President

GE CAPITAL EQUITY GROUP

260 Long Ridge Road
Stamford, CT 06927

Telephone: 203-357-3100
Fax: 203-357-3945

Mission: Actively seeking new investments

Fund Size: not available
Founded: not available
Average Investment: not available
Minimum Investment: $3 million

Investment Criteria: Mezzanine, Leveraged Buyout, Special Situations

Industry Group Preference: not available

Portfolio Companies: not available

Officers, Executives and Principals

Robert T. Thompson, Managing Director
John T. Carleton, Senior Vice President
Patrick J. McNeela, Senior Vice President
Robert J. Shanfield, Senior Vice President
George L. Hashbarger, Vice President
Frederic E. Wakeman III, Associate

GENESEE FUNDING, INC.

70 Linden Oaks
Third Floor
Rochester, NY 14625

Telephone: 716-383-5550
Fax: 716-383-5305

Mission: Actively seeking new investments

Fund Size: not available
Founded: 1986
Average Investment: not available
Minimum Investment: $100,000

Investment Criteria: Second-stage, Mezzanine, Leveraged Buyout

Industry Group Preference: Communications, Computer Related, Consumer, Distribution, Electronic Components and Instrumentation, Industrial Products and Equipment, Medical/Health Related

Portfolio Companies: not available

Officers, Executives and Principals

Stuart Marsh, President

GENESIS DIRECT, INC.

One Bridge Plaza
Suite 680
Fort Lee, NJ 07024

Telephone: 201-947-8181 ext. 236
Fax: 201-947-8626
E-mail: DSRose@msn.com

Mission: To become a dominant direct-response marketing company generating sales in excess of $1 billion within five years

Fund Size: $37 million
Founded: 1995
Average Investment: not available
Minimum Investment: not available

Investment Criteria: Sales greater than $1 million with a profit margin above 50 percent, as well as an upward sales trend with excellent growth prospects and a market potential of greater than $20 million

Geographic Preference: International

Industry Group Preference: Consumer, Business-to Business Markets, Institutional Markets

Portfolio Companies: not available

Officers, Executives and Principals

Douglas S. Rose, Vice President, Corporate Development
Education: BA, Political and Economic Philosophy, University of Vermont
Background: Founding Managing Director, Grendel Capital Company; Vice President, Niederhoffer and Niederhoffer, Inc.; Acquisition Analyst, Manhattan Venture Company; Coordinator of Business Development, Intermarket International Inc.

THE GENESIS FUND, LTD.

520 Post Oak Boulevard
Suite 130
Houston, TX 77027

Telephone: 713-622-9595

Mission: Reducing investment activity

Fund Size: not available
Founded: 1986
Average Investment: not available
Minimum Investment: $250,000

Investment Criteria: Seed, First-stage, Second-stage, Mezzanine, Leveraged Buyout

Industry Group Preference: Computer Related, Electronic Components and Instrumentation, Energy/Natural Resources, Genetic Engineering, Industrial Products and Equipment, Medical/Health Related

Portfolio Companies: not available

Officers, Executives and Principals

Walter Cunningham, Partner
Stuart Schube, Partner

GENESIS SEED FUND, LTD.

Two Penn Center Plaza, Suite 410
Philadelphia, PA 19102

Telephone: 215-988-0010
Fax: 215-568-0029

Mission: not available

Fund Size: $9 million
Founded: not available
Average Investment: $350,000
Minimum Investment: not available

Investment Criteria: Seed to Second-stage

Geographic Preference: East Coast

Industry Group Preference: Biotechnology, Broadcast/Cable/Radio, Computer Related, Electronics, High Technology, Industrial Products, Medical/Health, Publishing, Transportation

Portfolio Companies: not available

Officers, Executives and Principals

Michael A. Cuneo, Partner
Education: BES, Johns Hopkins University; MSME, Northwestern University; MBA, Wharton
Background: Vice President, Rotan Mosle Inc.; Vice President, Curtin and Co.

Steve N. Economou, Vice President

GENSTAR INVESTMENT CORPORATION

Metro Tower
950 Tower Lane, Suite 1170
Foster City, CA 94404

Telephone: 415-286-2350
Fax: 415-286-2383

Mission: Actively seeking new investments

Fund Size: not available
Founded: 1987
Average Investment: not available
Minimum Investment: Equity investment: $5 million

Investment Criteria: Leveraged Buyout

Industry Group Preference: Basic Manufacturing, Basic Services

Portfolio Companies: Wolverine Tube Inc., Gentek Building Products Inc., Seaspan International, Prestulite Electric Inc.

Officers, Executives and Principals

Ross J. Turner, Chairman
Angus A. MacNaughton, President
Richard D. Paterson, Executive Vice President
John A. (Jack) West, Executive Vice President
Mark E. Bandeen, Senior Vice President
Daniel J. Boverman, Vice President
Jean-Pierre Cante, Vice President

GEOCAPITAL PARTNERS

One Bridge Plaza
Fort Lee, NJ 07024

Telephone: 201-461-9292
Fax: 201-346-9191
E-mail: investments@geocapital.com

Mission: not available

Fund Size: $200 million
Founded: 1984
Average Investment: $4 million
Minimum Investment: $1.5 million

Investment Criteria: Startup to Leveraged Buyout

Industry Group Preference: Communications, Computer Related, High Technology, Information Services, Service Industries

Portfolio Companies: Axon Networks, MemberWorks, Catalina Marketing, Expert Software, Logic Works, Netcom Online Comm., Relay Technology, SPSS, D-Vision Systems, PhotoDisc, National Bankcard Association

Officers, Executives and Principals

Lawrence W. Lepard, Partner
Education: BA Economics, Colgate University; MBA, Harvard
Background: Investment Analyst and Officer, Continental Illinois Venture Corporation; Financial Analyst, Smith Barney, Harris Upham and Co.; Partner, Summit Partners
Directorships: Netcom On-Line Communications Milky Way Networks

Richard A. Vines, Partner
Education: MBA, Georgia State University; BS, Business Administration, University of Nebraska; CPA
Background: Deloitte, Haskins and Sells; Director of Marketing, Comshare; Director of Valuation Services, Broadview Associates; US Air Force

Stephen J. Clearman, Partner
Education: MS, Columbia University; JD, Harvard Law School
Background: Partner, Adler and Co.
Directorships: Expert Software, World Access, Seamed Corporation

Mark N. Diker, Principal
Education: BA, Government, Harvard College; MBA, Harvard, Baker Scholar
Background: Vice President, Bankers Trust Company (Tokyo office)

GESTION CAPIDEM, INC.

1595, boulevard Wilfrid-Hamel, Edifice B
Quebec City, Quebec G1N 3Y7
Canada

Telephone: 418-681-1910
Fax: 418-527-1967

Other Office Locations
165, Taschereau, Bureau 201
St.-Joseph de Beauce, Quebec G0S 2V0
Canada
Phone 418-397-4676

Mission: Actively seeking new investments

Fund Size: not available
Founded: 1988
Average Investment: not available
Minimum Investment: Less than $100,000

Investment Criteria: Startup, First-stage, Second-stage, Leveraged Buyout

Industry Group Preference: Communications, Computer Related, Distribution, Electronic Components and
   Instrumentation, Genetic Engineering, Industrial Products and Equipment, Medical/Health Related

Portfolio Companies: not available

Officers, Executives and Principals

Pierre Tardif, President
Serge Olivier, Regional Director (St.-Joseph de Beauce)
André Nadeau, Managing Director (Quebec City)
Gilles Desharnais, Project Manager (Quebec City)

GIDEON HIXON VENTURES

821 Marquette Avenue
Suite 1900
Minneapolis, MN 55402

Telephone: 612-904-2314
Fax: 612-204-0912

Mission: The Gideon Hixon fund provides financing and other assistance to promising, emerging growth companies.

Fund Size: $12 million
Founded: 1989
Average Investment: $750,000
Minimum Investment: $100,000

Investment Criteria: Startup, First-stage

Industry Group Preference: Information Services, Medical, Software

Portfolio Companies: Differential Corrections, Inc., Coda Music Technology, Sensitech, B-Tree Verification Systems, Health Management Alliance

Officers, Executives and Principals

Benson K. Whitney, Managing General Partner
Education: BA, Vassar College; JD, University of Minnesota

GLYNN VENTURES

3000 Sand Hill Road
Building Four, Suite 235
Menlo Park, CA 94025

Telephone: 415-854-2215
Fax: 415-854-8083

Mission: not available

Fund Size: $25 million
Founded: 1983
Average Investment: $500,000
Minimum Investment: $250,000

Investment Criteria: Startup, First-stage, Second-stage, Mezzanine, Leveraged Buyout

Industry Group Preference: Communications, Computer Related, Consumer, Electronic Components and Instrumentation, Genetic Engineering, Industrial Products and Equipment, Medical/Health Related

Portfolio Companies: not available

Officers, Executives and Principals

John W. Glynn, Jr., General Partner
Education: BS, Notre Dame; JD, University of Virginia; MBA, Stanford
Background: General Partner, Lamoreaux, Glynn Associates; Special Partner, New Enterprise Associates
Directorships: Molecular Design, The Learning Company

Steve Rosston

Daryl Messinger

GOLDER, THOMA, CRESSEY, RAUNER, INC.

6100 Sears Tower
Chicago, IL 60606-6402

Telephone: 312-382-2200
Fax: 312-382-2201
E-mail: info@gtcr.com

Mission: Actively seeking new investments

Fund Size: $1.2 billion
Founded: 1980
Average Investment: $15 million
Minimum Investment: $5 million

Investment Criteria: Leveraged Buyout, Special Situations, Industry Consolidations

Geographic Preference: United States

Industry Group Preference: Business Services, Communications, Distribution, Financial Services, Healthcare

Portfolio Companies: American Habilitation Services, American Medserve Corporation, Cable Design Technologies Inc., Cherrydale Farms, Inc., The Coinmach Corporation, Corestaff, Inc., Dickson Media, Inc., Ero Industries, Esquire Communications, Ltd., Excalibur Tubular Corporation, Global Imaging Systems, Inc., International Computer Graphics, Inc., ITI Marketing Services, Inc. Keystone Group Holdings, Lason Systems, Inc. MS Financial Inc., National Equipment Services, Inc., Polymer Group, Inc., Principal Hospital Company, PTN Holding Corporation, Risk Management Alternatives, Shahdill, Inc., Ullo International, Inc., U.S. Aggregates, Inc., U.S. Security Associates, Inc.

Officers, Executives and Principals

Carl D. Thoma, Principal
Education: BS, Oklahoma State University; MBA, Stanford University
Background: Acting Head, Equity Group at First Chicago Investment Corporation; President, National Venture Capital Association
Directorships: Ero Industries, Inc., Global Imaging Systems, Inc., MS Financial, Inc., National Equipment Services, Paging Network, Inc., PTN Holding Corporation, U.S. Security Associates

Bryan C. Cressey, Principal
Education: BS, University of Washington; JD, cum laude, Harvard University; MBA, Harvard University
Background: Senior Investment Manager, First Chicago's Venture Group; Member, Illinois and Washington Bar Associations
Directorships: American Habilitation, Inc., American Medserve Corporation, Cable Design Technologies

Bruce V. Rauner, Principal
Education: BA, Dartmouth College; MBA, Harvard University
Background: Strategic Consultant, Bain and Company
Directorships: Cherrydale Farms, Inc., Coinmach Laundry Corporation, Corestaff, Inc., Ero Industries, Inc., Lason Systems, Inc., Polymer Group, Inc., U.S. Aggregates, Inc.

David A. Donnini, Principal
Education: BA, Yale University; MBA, Stanford University
Background: Strategic Consultant, Bain and Company
Directorships: Cherrydale Farms, Inc., Coinmach Laundry Corporation, Keystone Group Holdings, Polymer Group, Inc., U.S. Aggregates, Inc.

Lee M. Mitchell, Principal
Education: BA, Wesleyan University; JD, University of Chicago
Background: President and Chief Executive Officer of major privately-owned company with interests in publishing, communications, paper manufacturing and commercial real estate
Directorships: American Medserve Corporation, Ero Industries, Inc. Dickson Media, Inc., ITI Marketing, Paging Network, Inc. U.S. Security Associates, Inc.

Donald J. Edwards, Principal
Education: BS, University of Illinois; MBA, Harvard University
Background: Associate, Mergers and Acquisitions, Lazard Freres and Company
Directorships: Corestaff, Inc.

Joseph P. Nolan, Principal
Education: BS University of Illinois; MBA, University of Chicago
Background: Vice President, Corporation Finance Group, Dean Witter Reynolds, Inc.
Directorships: Esquire Communications, Ltd., Lason Systems, Inc., Principal Hospital Company, Ullo International, Inc.

James P. Tenbroek, Associate
Education: BA, Dartmouth College; MEE Cornell: MBA, Harvard University
Background: Engineering Manager, Imaging Systems Division, Hewlett-Packard Company
Directorships: ITI Marketing, Inc. U.S. Security Associates, Inc.

William C. Kessinger, Associate
Education: MSIE, Stanford University; BSIE, Stanford University; MBA, Harvard University
Background: Associate, Prudential Asset Management (Asia); Principal, Parthenon Group
Directorships: Cable Design Technologies, Global Imaging Systems, Inc., National Equipment Services

Philip A. Canfield, Associate
Education: BBA, University of Texas; MBA, University of Chicago
Background: Corporate Finance Group, Kidder, Peabody and Company
Directorships: MS Financial

Vincent H. Hemmer, Associate
Education: BS, University of Pennsylvania; MBA, Harvard University
Background: Consultant, The Monitor Company

Timothy P. McAdam, Associate
Education: BA, Dartmouth College; MBA, Stanford University
Background: Associate, TA Associates; Investment Banking Analyst, Merrill Lynch and Company

Mark Slavonia, Associate
Education: BA, Princeton University; MBA, Stanford University
Background: Senior Associate, Barents Group of KPMG

GORFINKLE ASSOCIATES, INC.

Six Landmark Square
Fourth Floor
Stamford, CT 06901-2792

Fax: 203-359-5876

Mission: Actively seeking new investments

Fund Size: not available
Founded: 1988
Average Investment: not available
Minimum Investment: $250,000

Investment Criteria: Second-stage, Mezzanine, Leveraged Buyout

Industry Group Preference: Communications, Consumer, Distribution, Energy/Natural Resources, Genetic Engineering, Industrial Products and Equipment, Medical/Health Related

Portfolio Companies: not available

Officers, Executives and Principals

Lawrence Gorfinkle, Partner

GRAYSON AND ASSOCIATES

Republic Plaza
370 17th Street, 52nd Floor
Denver, CO 80202

Telephone: 303-592-2203
Fax: 303-592-1510

Mission: Actively seeking new investments

Fund Size: not available
Founded: 1986
Average Investment: not available
Minimum Investment: $500,000

Investment Criteria: First-stage, Second-stage, Mezzanine, Leveraged Buyout

Industry Group Preference: Distribution, Genetic Engineering, Medical/Health Related

Portfolio Companies: not available

Officers, Executives and Principals

Gerald Grayson, President
Donald C. Freeman, Jr., Partner

GREATER DETROIT BIDCO, INC.

645 Griswold, Suite 2146
Detroit, MI 48226

Telephone: 313-962-4326
Fax: 313-962-0134

Mission: not available

Fund Size: $7 million
Founded: not available
Average Investment: $450,000
Minimum Investment: not available

Investment Criteria: Second-stage

Geographic Preference: Michigan

Industry Group Preference: Communications, Manufacturing/Processing

Portfolio Companies: not available

Officers, Executives and Principals

Dione Alexander-Johnson Frazier, President

GREATER PHILADELPHIA VENTURE CAPITAL CORPORATION

351 East Conestoga Road
Wayne, PA 19087

Telephone: 610-688-6829
Fax: 610-254-8958

Mission: not available

Fund Size: not available
Founded: 1971
Average Investment: not available
Minimum Investment: Less than $100,000

Investment Criteria: First-stage, Second-stage, Mezzanine, Leveraged Buyout, Special Situations

Industry Group Preference: Communications, Computer Related, Consumer, Distribution, Medical/Health Related

Portfolio Companies: not available

Officers, Executives and Principals

Fred Choate, Chairman and Manager
Michael Haskins, Secretary
Morton Bransburg, Assistant Secretary

GREEN MOUNTAIN CAPITAL, L.P.

RD1, Box 1503
Waterbury, VT 05676

Telephone: 802-244-8981
Fax: 802-244-8990

Mission: Actively seeking new investments

Fund Size: not available
Founded: 1993
Average Investment: not available
Minimum Investment: $100,000

Investment Criteria: Second-stage, Mezzanine

Industry Group Preference: not available

Portfolio Companies: not available

Officers, Executives and Principals

Wayne Granquist, Chairman
Michael Sweatman, President
Charles Kireker, Vice President
Zoe Erdman, Assistant General Manager

GRENDEL CAPITAL COMPANY

529 Fifth Avenue
New York, NY 10017

Telephone: 212-427-4453

Mission: Actively seeking new investments

Fund Size: not available
Founded: 1993
Average Investment: not available
Minimum Investment: $500,000

Investment Criteria: Second-stage, Mezzanine, Leveraged Buyout, Special Situations, Control-block Purchases, Turnarounds

Industry Group Preference: Communications, Consumer, Distribution, Industrial Products and Equipment, Medical/Health Related

Portfolio Companies: not available

Officers, Executives and Principals

Douglas S. Rose, Managing Director

GREYLOCK MANAGEMENT CORPORATION

One Federal Street
26th Floor
Boston, MA 02110

Telephone: 617-423-5525
Fax: 617-482-0059

Other Office Locations
399 Park Avenue, 28th Floor
New York, NY 10022
Phone 212-688-8868, Fax 212-207-1019

755 Page Mill Road, Suite B-140
Palo Alto, CA 94304
Phone 415-493-5525, Fax 415-493-5575

Mission: not available

Fund Size: $200 million
Founded: not available
Average Investment: $1 million
Minimum Investment: not available

Investment Criteria: Startup to Leveraged Buyout

Industry Group Preference: Biotechnology, Broadcast/Cable/Radio, Communications, Computer Related, Diversified, Electronics, Energy/Natural Resources, High Technology, Industrial Products, Medical/Health, Publishing, Retailing

Portfolio Companies: not available

Officers, Executives and Principals

Donald K. Miller, Chairman (New York)

David N. Strohm, Partner

Charles P. Waite, Partner
Education: BA, Kenyon; MBA, Harvard
Background: Cardiovascular Specialist, Cobe Laboratories; General Partner, Hambrecht and Quist Venture
  Partners
Directorships: VISIC, EAN

Daniel S. Gregory, Partner

Henry F. McCance, Partner

Robert P. Henderson, Partner

William W. Helman, Partner

Michael D. Dolbec, Associate

GRIEVE, HORNER, BROWN AND ASCULAI

Eight King Street East, Suite 1300
Toronto, Ontario M5C 1B5
Canada

Telephone: 416-362-7668
Fax: 416-366-6330

Mission: Actively seeking new investments

Fund Size: not available
Founded: 1976
Average Investment: not available
Minimum Investment: $100,000

Investment Criteria: Startup, First-stage, Second-stage

Industry Group Preference: Communications, Computer Related, Consumer, Distribution, Energy/Natural Resources, Genetic Engineering, Medical/Health Related

Portfolio Companies: not available

Officers, Executives and Principals

Anthony Brown
Ralph Horner

GROTECH CAPITAL GROUP

9690 Deereco Road, Suite 800
Timonium, MD 21093

Telephone: 410-560-2000
Fax: 410-560-1910

Mission: To assist the management teams of our partner companies to actualize their vision by investing Grotech's capital supported by our experience, coaching, creativity and contacts

Fund Size: $212 million
Founded: 1984
Average Investment: not available
Minimum Investment: not available

Investment Criteria: First-stage to Leveraged Buyout

Geographic Preference: Mid-Atlantic United States

Industry Group Preference: Broadcast/Cable/Radio, Communications, Computer Related, Consumer Related, Diversified, Educational, Electronics, Food Services, High Technology, Industrial Products, Publishing, Software, Transportation

Portfolio Companies: Cowan Systems, Lloyd's Food Products, Master Power, Piatl Holdings, Transmodal Corporation, Trifoods International, Central Florida Satellite, Ensys Environmental Products, Secure Computing Corporation, Zynaxis, Inc., A&W Restaurants Inc., Actimed Laboratories, Brighams, Inc., Dentalco, Inc., Digex, Enterprise Network Applications, Forensic Technologies, Network Construction Services, Phoenix Services Quality Software Products, Thunderbird Technologies, U.S. Design, U.S. Vision, Inc., American Auto Funding Corporation, Entek Corporation, Nassau Broadcasting Partners, Palm Environmental Funding Corporation, Regency Homes, Pussers Restaurants, Epic Therapeutics, Inc.

Officers, Executives and Principals

Frank A. Adams, President and Chief Executive Officer
Hugh A. Woltzen, Managing Director
Dennis J. Shaughnessy, Managing Director
Stuart D. Frankel, Managing Director
J. Roger Sullivan, Jr., Special Partner

GRUBSTEIN HOLDINGS, LTD.
1940 Westwood Boulevard
Suite 208
Los Angeles, CA 90025

Telephone: 310-575-8720

Mission: not available

Fund Size: not available
Founded: 1987
Average Investment: not available
Minimum Investment: $1 million

Investment Criteria: Second-stage, Mezzanine, Leveraged Buyout

Industry Group Preference: Communications, Computer Related, Consumer, Distribution, Energy/Natural
  Resources, Genetic Engineering, Industrial Products and Equipment, Medical/Health Related

Portfolio Companies: not available

Officers, Executives and Principals

Peter S. H. Grubstein, Principal
Douglas R. Shooker, Principal

GRYPHON VENTURES, L.P.

222 Berkeley Street
Suite 1600
Boston, MA 02116

Telephone: 617-267-9191
Fax: 617-267-4293
E-mail: all@gryphoninc.com

Mission: Actively seeking new investments

Fund Size: $56 million
Founded: 1986
Average Investment: $2 million
Minimum Investment: $1 million

Investment Criteria: Startup, First-stage, Second-stage

Geographic Preference: United States

Industry Group Preference: Communications, Energy/Natural Resources, Fuel Additives, Genetic Engineering, Industrial Products and Equipment, Lubricant Additives, Medical/Health Related, Refinery Chemicals

Portfolio Companies: Energy Biosystems, IGEN, Optex Communications Corporation, Geltech, Hyperion Catalysis International, Inc., Scotgen BioPharmaceuticals, Quantex Corporation

Officers, Executives and Principals

William F. Aikman, Managing General Partner
Education: Brown University; University of Pennsylvania; Harvard University
Background: President, Gryphon Management Company, Inc.; President and Chief Executive Officer, Massachusetts Technology Development Corporation
Directorships: Massachusetts Certified Development Corporation, Geltech, Optex

Edward B. Lurier, General Partner
Background: Vice Chairman, Damon Corporation; Senior Vice President, all of Damon product companies; Board of Trustees, Dana Farber Cancer Center
Directorships: Energy Biosystems, Hyperion, IGEN, Optex, Scotgen Biopharmaceuticals

Andrew J. Atkinson, Vice President, Investment Analysis
Education: Harvard University, honors
Background: Market Strategist and Planner, Dun and Bradstreet Software; Founding Member and Senior Marketing Research Analyst, McCormack and Dodge Corporation; Research and Analysis Group, Management Consultant on shareholder value issues
Directorships: Optex

HALPERN, DENNY AND COMPANY

500 Boylston Street
Boston, MA 02116

Telephone: 617-536-6602
Fax: 617-536-8535

Mission: Actively seeking new investments

Fund Size: not available
Founded: 1991
Average Investment: not available
Minimum Investment: $1 million

Investment Criteria: First-stage, Second-stage, Leveraged Buyout, Control-block Purchases

Geographic Preference: not available

Industry Group Preference: Communications, Consumer, Distribution, Manufacturing, Retail

Portfolio Companies: LearningSmith, Big Party, Lids, Hollywood Digital, Boston Common Press

Officers, Executives and Principals

John D. Halpern, Partner
Education: Yale University, magna cum laude, Phi Beta Kappa; MBA, Harvard
Background: Founder, Vice-Chairman and Director of North American client development and strategy, **Bain and Company**

George P. Denny III, Partner
Education: Harvard College; MBA, Harvard; Baker Scholar
Background: Director, Brown Brothers Harriman; Head of San Francisco and Tokyo offices, **Managing Director, Bain Holdings**

William J. LaPoint, Partner
Education: MIT, honors; MBA, Harvard
Background: Project Manager, Bain and Company

David P. Malm, Partner
Education: Brown University, magna cum laude; MBA, Harvard
Background: Morgan Stanley and Co., Investment Banking Group; Bain and Company's consulting and leverage buyout/venture capital practices

HAMBRECHT AND QUIST GROUP

One Bush Street
San Francisco, CA 94104

Telephone: 415-576-3300
Fax: 415-576-3624

Other Office Locations
230 Park Avenue, 21st Floor
New York, NY 10169
Phone 212-207-1400, Fax 212-207-1521

50 Rowes Wharf, 4th Floor
Boston, MA 02110
Phone 617-574-0500, Fax 617-574-0547

4365 Executive Drive, Suite 1540
San Diego, CA 92121
Phone 619-546-8181

The Registry
Royal Mint Court
London EC3 N 4EY
Phone 44-171-481-0175, Fax 44-171-481-3183

3 rue Amelie
Paris, France 75007
Phone 33-1-45-50-7607, Fax 33-1-45-50-7564

H&Q Taiwan Co. Ltd.
32F-1, International Trade Building
333 Keelung Road, Sec. 1
Taipei, 10548 Taiwan R.O.C.
Phone 8862-722-9805, Fax 8862-722-2106

PCI Bank Tower II 22/F
Makati Avenue, corner HV de la Costa St., 22nd Floor
Makati, Metro Manila
Philippines
Phone 63-2-819-5776, Fax 63-2-815-9217

Sathorn City Tower
Suite 1207, 12th Floor
175 South Sathorn Road Sathorn District
Bangkok 10120
Thailand
Phone 662-679-6312, Fax 662-679-6316

1606 Asia Pacific Finance Tower
Citibank Plaza
3 Garden Road

Central Hong Kong
Phone 852-2868-4780, Fax 852-2810-4883

79 Anson Road #11-03
Singapore 079906
Phone 65-221-8144, Fax 65-222-0729

8F, Tekko Building
1-8-2 Marunouchi, Chiyoda-ku
Tokyo 100
Phone 81-3-3284-9882, Fax 81-3-3212-0628

No. 84 - G & 84 - 1
Jalan 1/76 D, Desa Pandan
55100 Kuala Lumpur, Malaysia
Phone 60-3-982-8288, Fax 60-3-982-6289

Plaza Bapindo Menara II
24th Floor, Unit 11
Jl. Jend. Sudirman Kav. 54-55
Jakarta 12190 Indonesia
Phone 62-21-526-6483, Fax 62-21-526-6487

Mission: Actively seeking new investments

Fund Size: not available
Founded: 1968
Average Investment: not available
Minimum Investment: $500,000

Investment Criteria: Research and Development, Startup, First-stage, Mezzanine, Leveraged Buyout, Special Situations, Control-block Purchases

Industry Group Preference: Communications, Computer Related, Consumer, Distribution, Electronic Components and Instrumentation, Energy/Natural Resources, Genetic Engineering, Industrial Products and Equipment, Medical/Health Related

Portfolio Companies: not available

Officers, Executives and Principals

William R. Hambrecht, Co-Chief Executive Officer (San Francisco)
Nancy E. Pfund, Principal (San Francisco)
Standish O'Grady, Principal (San Francisco)
Bama B. Rucker, Principal (San Francisco)
Ben Wegbreit, Principal (San Francisco)
Jackie Berterretche, Chief Financial Officer (San Francisco)
Sam Kingsland, Associate (San Francisco)
Jim Robinson, Associate (San Francisco)

HAMBRO INTERNATIONAL EQUITY PARTNERS

650 Madison Avenue
New York, NY 10022

Telephone: 212-223-7400
Fax: 212-223-0305

Other Office Locations
404 Wyman Street
Suite 365
Waltham, MA 02154
Phone 617-523-7767, Fax 617-290-0999

Mission: not available

Fund Size: $150 million
Founded: not available
Average Investment: not available
Minimum Investment: not available

Investment Criteria: Seed to Recapitalizations

Industry Group Preference: Computer Related, Consumer Related, Electronics, Retailing, Software

Portfolio Companies: American Waste Services, Corporate Software, Komag, Meca Ventures, PCA International, Solectron, Staples, Telematics, Pacific Linen, Pet Smart, United Weight Control Corporation, Veeco Instruments Acquisition Corporation

Officers, Executives and Principals

Edwin A. Goodman, Managing Partner
Education: Yale University; MBA, Columbia
Background: Alan Patricof Associates; Chairman, Venture Leasing Conference
Directorships: Pacific Linen, J. Peterman, Simpson and Fisher Companies, Inc., Staples Inc. and Watch Hill
  Retail Group

Alexander R. Hambro, General Partner

Arthur C. Spinner, General Partner
Education: BS Honors, International Economics, Claremont Men's College; MBA, Harvard
Background: Loeb Rhoades and Company
Directorships: Edsun Labs., Komag, Rasna, Republic Telcom Systems, Telematics International, Transition
  Technology, Tylan General Corporation

Charles L. Dimmler, General Partner
Education: University of California at Davis; Advanced Management Program, Harvard
Background: Officer, U.S. Marine Corps; Richardson Merrell, Inc.; American Can Company
Directorships: Innovir Laboratories, Telcor Opthalmi Pharmaceuticals

Richard A. D'Amore, General Partner (Waltham)
Education: Summa cum laude, Northeastern University; MBA, Harvard; Baker Scholar

Background: Arthur Young and Company, Bain and Company
Directorships: Avatar Tech, Corporate Software, Data Ease International, European Software Publishing, IDE
  Corporation, Keyfile Corporation, MathSoft, Meca Ventures

William J. Geary, General Partner (Waltham)
Education: BS, Accounting and Finance, magna cum laude, Boston College
Background: Arthur Andersen and Co.; Vice President Finance and Administration, MathSoft; Vice President
  Finance, UST Merchant Bancorp
Directorships: QuadTech

Frances N. Janis, General Partner
Education: BS, Marketing and Economics, cum laude, State University New York, Albany; MBA,cum laude,
  Management Intern Program, Northeastern
Background: Worldwide Headquarters of the Continental Group working with the controller in the area of SEC
  compliance
Directorships: Growing Healthy, IVF Australia, Smart Names, and United Weight Control Corporation

HAMILTON ROBINSON AND COMPANY, INC.

One Rockefeller Plaza
Suite 1410
New York, NY 10020

Telephone: 212-332-1220
Fax: 212-332-1225

Mission: Actively seeking new investments

Fund Size: not available
Founded: 1984
Average Investment: not available
Minimum Investment: $5 million

Investment Criteria: Leveraged Buyout, Later-stage Expansion

Industry Group Preference: Consumer, Distribution, Energy/Natural Resources, Industrial Products and Equipment, Medical/Health Related

Portfolio Companies: AGCO Corporation, DZ Industries, Inc.

Officers, Executives and Principals

Hamilton Robinson, Jr., Managing Director
Education: Princeton; Harvard Law
Directorships: AGCO, DZ Industries

Scott I. Oakford, Managing Director
Education: Claremont

James T. Cullen, Jr., Director

Debra K. Salkin, Chief Financial Officer

HANIFEN IMHOFF CAPITAL PARTNERS LLP

1125 17th Street
Suite 1520
Denver, CO 80202

Telephone: 303-291-5209
Fax: 303-291-5237

Mission: Actively seeking new investments

Fund Size: $60 million
Founded: 1994
Average Investment: $2.1 million
Minimum Investment: $1 million

Investment Criteria: Mezzanine, Later-stage

Geographic Preference: United States, with emphasis on Rocky Mountain region

Industry Group Preference: Manufacturing, Service and Distribution

Portfolio Companies: CPS Systems, Bright Start, Inc., Tripac International, Inc, RBM Precision Metal Products, Inc., Fitzpatrick Electrical Supply Company, National Metalwares, L.P., Warterfied Holdings, New Tech Tool Corporation, Atlas Environmental, Inc. Language Management International, Associated Bodywork and Massage Professionals, Inc., Sight and Sound Distribution, Inc., BMK, Inc., Microwave Components Enterprises, Inc.

Officers, Executives and Principals

Edward C. Brown, Managing Partner
Education: Yale University; MBA, Finance, with distinction, Cornell University; US Navy Lieutenant
Background: Vice President and Director, Lincoln National Investment Management Co., FBS Capital, FBS
  Merchant Bank, Dain Bosworth, Toro Company, Arthur Anderson

Paul A. Lyons, Jr., Principal
Education: BS, Business Administration, Georgetown University; United States Marine Corps
Background: Consultant/Manager, Kirkpatrick Pettis, Mitsubishi Trust, Irving Trust Company

Stephen N. Sangalis, Investment Manager
Education: MBA, Indiana University; BSBA, University of Colorado
Background: Rice Capital Corporation, US Treasury Department, Denver

HARBOUR FINANCIAL COMPANY

200 Lowder Brook Drive
Suite 2400
Westwood, MA 02090

Telephone: 617-461-0460
Fax: 617-461-0467

Mission: Actively seeking new investments

Fund Size: not available
Founded: 1980
Average Investment: not available
Minimum Investment: $500,000

Investment Criteria: Startup, First-stage, Second-stage, Mezzanine, Leveraged Buyout, Special Situations

Industry Group Preference: Communications, Computer Related, Distribution, Electronic Components and Instrumentation, Energy/Natural Resources, Genetic Engineering, Industrial Products and Equipment, Medical/Health Related

Portfolio Companies: not available

Officers, Executives and Principals

John R. Schwanbeck, President

HART VENTURES

P.O. Box 26363
Austin, TX 78755

Telephone: 512-349-2291
Fax: 512-349-2291

Mission: Actively seeking new investments

Fund Size: $25 million
Founded: 1996
Average Investment: $1 million
Minimum Investment: $100,000

Investment Criteria: Seed, Research and Development, Startup, First-stage, Second-stage, Mezzanine, Leveraged Buyout, Special Situations

Geographic Preference: United States and International

Industry Group Preference: Distribution, Diversified, High Technology, Medical Health, Specialty Manufacturing

Portfolio Companies: not available

Officers, Executives and Principals

David H. Gerhardt

HARVEST PARTNERS, INC.

767 Third Avenue
7th Floor
New York, NY 10017

Telephone: 212-838-7776
Fax: 212-593-0734

Mission: Actively seeking new investments

Fund Size: not available
Founded: 1976
Average Investment: not available
Minimum Investment: $1 million

Investment Criteria: Mezzanine, Leveraged Buyout

Industry Group Preference: Consumer, Distribution, Industrial Products and Equipment, Medical/Health Related

Portfolio Companies: not available

Officers, Executives and Principals

Harvey P. Mallement, Managing Partner
Harvey J. Wertheim, Managing Partner
William J. Kane, General Partner
Ira D. Kleinman, General Partner
Frank H. Low, Senior Vice President
Jack Prizzi, Special Limited Partner

HEALTH CAPITAL GROUP

16940 Edgewater Lane
Huntington Beach, CA 92649

Telephone: 714-377-1136
Fax: 714-377-1138

Mission: Actively seeking new investments

Fund Size: not available
Founded: 1986
Average Investment: not available
Minimum Investment: $250,000

Investment Criteria: Startup, First-stage, Second-stage, Mezzanine, Leveraged Buyout

Industry Group Preference: Communications, Computer Related, Consumer, Distribution, Electronic Components and Instrumentation, Energy/Natural Resources, Genetic Engineering, Industrial Products and Equipment, Medical/Health Related

Portfolio Companies: not available

Officers, Executives and Principals

Denis Kollar, M.D., President

HEALTHCARE VENTURES I, II, III AND IV, L.P.

379 Thornall Street
Edison, NJ 08837

Telephone: 908-906-4600
Fax: 908-906-1450

Other Office Locations
One Kendall Square, Building 300
Cambridge, MA 02139
Phone 617-252-4343

Mission: Actively seeking new investments

Fund Size: not available
Founded: 1986
Average Investment: not available
Minimum Investment: $500,000

Investment Criteria: Seed, Research and Development, Startup, First-stage, Second-stage

Geographic Preference: United States

Industry Group Preference: Genetic Engineering, Medical/Health Related

Portfolio Companies: not available

Officers, Executives and Principals

Wallace H. Steinberg, Chairman
John W. Littlechild, Vice Chairman
Ronald Shiftan, Vice Chairman
Harold R. Werner, Vice Chairman
William W. Crouse, Vice Chairman
James H. Cavanaugh, PhD., President

HEARTLAND CAPITAL FUND, LTD.

11930 Arbor Street
Suite 201
Omaha, NE 68144

Telephone: 402-333-8840
Fax: 402-333-8944
E-mail: HrtlndCptl@aol.com

Mission: Actively seeking new investments

Fund Size: $11 million
Founded: 1992
Average Investment: $1 million
Minimum Investment: $500,000

Investment Criteria: Seed, Startup, First-stage, Second-stage, Mezzanine

Geographic Preference: Central United States

Industry Group Preference: Communications, Computer Related, Consumer, Distribution, Electronic Components and Instrumentation, Energy/Natural Resources, Genetic Engineering, Industrial Products and Equipment, Information Technology, Medical/Health Related

Portfolio Companies: not available

Officers, Executives and Principals

Bradley K. Edwards, General Partner
Patrick A. Rivelli, General Partner
John G. Gustafson, Associate

HELIX INVESTMENTS, LTD.

70 York Street, Suite 1700
Toronto, Ontario M5J 1S9
Canada

Telephone: 416-367-1290
Fax: 416-367-3614

Other Office Locations
470 San Antonio Road, Suite 100
Mountain View, CA 94040
Phone 415-917-7311, Fax 415-917-7314

Mission: Actively seeking new investments

Fund Size: not available
Founded: 1968
Average Investment: not available
Minimum Investment: $100,000

Investment Criteria: Seed, Startup, First-stage, Leveraged Buyout

Industry Group Preference: Communications, Computer Related, Consumer, Distribution, Electronic Components and Instrumentation, Energy/Natural Resources, Genetic Engineering, Industrial Products and Equipment, Medical/Health Related

Portfolio Companies: not available

Officers, Executives and Principals

Donald C. Webster, President (Toronto)
Keith Lue, Vice President (Toronto)
Matt Ocko, Vice President (Mountain View)
Jim Wooder, Vice President (Toronto)
Richard Black, Vice President (Toronto)
May Anis, Secretary and Treasurer (Toronto)

HELLER EQUITY CAPITAL

500 West Monroe Street
Chicago, IL 60661

Telephone: 312-441-7200
Fax: 312-441-7378

Mission: not available

Fund Size: not available
Founded: not available
Average Investment: $3 - $10 million
Minimum Investment: not available

Investment Criteria: Second Stage to Leveraged Buyout

Industry Group Preference: Computer Related, Diversified, Manufacturing/Processing, Medical/Health, Publishing, Service Industries

Portfolio Companies: D.S. Brown Company, Caronia Corporation, Clamshell Building, DBL Labs, Dunn Tire, Employer's Security Company, Expressions, Indian Head Industries, MedQuist, Merx, Preferred Pipe Products, Tom's Foods, Vendell Heathcare, The Wilson Center

Officers, Executives and Principals

John M. Goense, Managing Director
Education: BS, Accounting and Business, Aquinas College; MBA, University of Chicago
Background: Kidder, Peabody and Co., Commerical Banking

John H. Underwood, Principal
Education: BBA, MBA, University of Wisconsin
Background: Leveraged Capital Division, Citicorp; First National Bank of Chicago

Mark A. Bounds, Principal
Education: BA, University of Iowa; MBA, University of Chicago

Ned Jenssen, Principal
Education: BA, Yale; MM, Northwestern University
Background: Dean Witter Reynolds, Inc.

HELLMAN AND FRIEDMAN

One Maritime Plaza
Twelfth Floor
San Francisco, CA 94111

Telephone: 415-788-5111
Fax: 415-788-0176

Mission: Actively seeking new investments

Fund Size: not available
Founded: not available
Average Investment: not available
Minimum Investment: $50 million

Investment Criteria: Second-stage, Mezzanine, Leveraged Buyout, Special Situations

Industry Group Preference: not available

Portfolio Companies: not available

Officers, Executives and Principals

F. Warren Hellman
Tully M. Friedman
John Pasquesi
Mitch Cohen

HENRY AND COMPANY

4370 La Jolla Village Drive
Suite 400
San Diego, CA 92122-1251

Telephone: 619-453-1655
Fax: 619-546-3030

Mission: Making few, if any, new investments

Fund Size: not available
Founded: 1983
Average Investment: not available
Minimum Investment: $500,000

Investment Criteria: First-stage, Second-stage

Industry Group Preference: Medical/Health Related

Portfolio Companies: not available

Officers, Executives and Principals

Albert J. Henry, Chairman
June M. Knaudt, Vice President

HERBERT YOUNG SECURITIES, INC.

98 Cuttermill Road
Great Neck, NY 11021

Telephone: 516-487-8300
Fax: 516-487-8319

Mission: Actively seeking new investments

Fund Size: not available
Founded: 1959
Average Investment: not available
Minimum Investment: $100,000

Investment Criteria: First-stage, Second-stage, Mezzanine, Leveraged Buyout, Special Situations

Industry Group Preference: Communications, Computer Related, Consumer, Distribution, Electronic Components and Instrumentation, Energy/Natural Resources, Industrial Products and Equipment, Medical/Health Related, Pharmaceuticals

Portfolio Companies: not available

Officers, Executives and Principals

Herbert D. Levine, President
Melvin Norman, Vice President
Jonathan A. Salerno, Vice President

HERITAGE VENTURE PARTNERS II, L.P.

135 North Pennsylvania Street
Suite 2380
Indianapolis, IN 46204

Telephone: 317-635-5696
Fax: 317-635-5699

Mission: Seeking radio stations in university markets

Fund Size: not available
Founded: 1981
Average Investment: not available
Minimum Investment: $250,000

Investment Criteria: Second-stage, Leveraged Buyout, Special Situations

Industry Group Preference: Communications

Portfolio Companies: not available

Officers, Executives and Principals

Arthur A. Angotti, Chairman and President
Julia M. Rogers, Treasurer

HFT CORPORATION

140 Sylvan Avenue
Englewood Cliffs, NJ 07632

Telephone: 201-585-9097
Fax: 201-585-5082

Mission: Actively seeking new investments

Fund Size: not available
Founded: 1989
Average Investment: not available
Minimum Investment: No minimum

Investment Criteria: No preference

Industry Group Preference: not available

Portfolio Companies: not available

Officers, Executives and Principals

Andra Patko, President
Ivan Grosz, Managing Director, Investment Banking
Robert Halasz, Managing Director, Trade
Lynn Kelly, Managing Director, Finance

HICKORY VENTURE GROUP

200 West Courtside Square, Suite 100
Huntsville, AL 35801

Telephone: 205-539-1931
Fax: 205-539-5130

Mission: not available

Fund Size: $60 million
Founded: not available
Average Investment: $1 million
Minimum Investment: not available

Investment Criteria: Second-stage to Leveraged Buyout

Geographic Preference: East of the Rocky Mountains

Industry Group Preference: Diversified

Portfolio Companies: Advanced Aluminum Products, Curaflex Health Services, Delphi, The Forgotten Woman, Jackson Business Form, MedExpress/National Laboratory Center, Microdynamics, Mobile Technology, Montgomery Tank Lines, Perceptron, Premiere Cinemas, Romanoff International Value Merchants

Officers, Executives and Principals

J. Thomas Noojin, President
Background: Founder, Hickory Group; President, Invesat Capital Corporation; General Manager, Alabama Capital; Chairman NASBIC

HIGHLAND CAPITAL PARTNERS

Two International Place
Boston, MA 02110

Telephone: 617-531-1500
Fax: 617-531-1550

Mission: Actively seeking new investments

Fund Size: not available
Founded: 1988
Average Investment: not available
Minimum Investment: $500,000

Investment Criteria: Seed, Research and Development, Startup, First-stage, Second-stage, Mezzanine, Special Situations

Industry Group Preference: Communications, Computer Related, Electronic Components and Instrumentation, Genetic Engineering, Medical/Health Related

Portfolio Companies: not available

Officers, Executives and Principals

Robert F. Higgins, Managing General Partner
Paul A. Maeder, Managing General Partner
David J. Duval, Chief Financial Officer
James McLean, General Partner
Wyc Grousbeck, General Partner
Burt Hurlock, General Partner
Daniel Nova, General Partner
Kendall Backstrand, Analyst

HINSLEY VENTURE CAPITAL, INC.

4101 Bob White
Richmond, TX 77469

Telephone: 281-342-8600
Fax: 281-342-9997

Mission: Actively seeking new investments

Fund Size: not available
Founded: 1985
Average Investment: not available
Minimum Investment: $100,000

Investment Criteria: First-stage, Second-stage

Geographic Preference: Texas

Industry Group Preference: Consumer, Distribution, Genetic Engineering, Industrial Products and Equipment

Portfolio Companies: not available

Officers, Executives and Principals

George Hinsley, Chief Executive Officer
Ray Hinsley

HMS GROUP

One First Street, Suite 6
Los Altos, CA 94022

Telephone: 415-917-0390
Fax: 415-917-0394

Mission: The founders of HMS have years of experience in investing in and helping to build successful companies in the information industry, and industry relationships to make material contributions to early-stage companies in which they have invested.

Fund Size: $19 million
Founded: 1982
Average Investment: $1.5 million
Minimum Investment: $500,000

Investment Criteria: Seed, Startup, First-stage

Industry Group Preference: Computer Related, Electronics, High Technology, Software

Portfolio Companies: not available

Officers, Executives and Principals

Frank R. Atkinson, General Partner
Education: AB, Stanford; MBA, University of California at Los Angeles
Background: Continental Capital Corporation; Triad Venture Captial Corporation; Consultant, Thompson Clive and Partners;
Directorships: President and founder of the Western Association of Venture Capitalists

R.G. Grey, General Partner
Education: BS, MBA, University of California at Los Angeles; JD, University of San Francisco
Background: Founded Vidar Corporation Telecommunications Consulting firm (Transwitch) and Vanguard Venture Capital

Michael C. Hone, General Partner
Education: BS, JD, University of California
Background: Workout Expert; Faculty, University of San Francisco; Continental Capital Corporation; Founded first HMS Venture Capital Fund

HOAK COMMUNICATIONS PARTNERS, L.P.

One Galleria Tower
Suite 1050
13355 Noel Road
Dallas, TX 75240

Telephone: 972-960-4848
Fax: 972-960-4899
E-mail: jmhoak@ix.netcom.com

Other Office Locations
551 Fifth Avenue, Suite 3700
New York, NY 10017
Phone 212-557-0867, Fax 212-557-0876

Mission: Focused on making lead, privately negotiated equity and equity-related investments; actively seeking new investment opportunities with companies who possess a proven management team with the ability to build and manage a large enterprise and whose operations are profitable on an operating cash flow basis or a roll-up strategy in an industry with a proven business model. In addition, we are interested in companies with value-added products or services with limited risk of technological obsolescence and which have sustainable barriers to entry. Finally, the company must have medium-term potential to reach an enterprise value of $200 million, preferably with public market opportunity in the medium-term.

Fund Size: $130 million
Founded: 1996
Average Investment: $20 - $25 million
Minimum Investment: $10 million

Investment Criteria: Buyouts, Recapitalizations, Growth Financing

Geographic Preference: United States

Industry Group Preference: Advertising and Promotion, Cable Television, Communications, Entertainment, Information Services, Media Services and Equipment, Print Media/Publishing, Radio and Television Broadcasting, Telecommunications Services and Equipment

Portfolio Companies: None

Officers, Executives and Principals

James M. Hoak, Jr., Principal (Dallas)
Thomas L. Harrison, Principal (Dallas)
Frederick B. Pickering, Jr., Principal (New York)
George B. Moore, Vice President (New York)
Robert A. Sussman, Vice President (Dallas)
J. Hale Hoak, Analyst (Dallas)

HOLDING CAPITAL GROUP, INC.

685 Fifth Avenue
14th Floor
New York, NY 10022

Telephone: 212-486-6670
Fax: 212-486-0843

Other Office Locations
4018 Wingren Drive
Irving, TX 75062
Phone 212-486-6670, Fax 212-486-0843

1301 Fifth Avenue, Suite 3410
Seattle, WA 98101

Mission: Actively seeking new investments

Fund Size: not available
Founded: 1975
Average Investment: not available
Minimum Investment: $100,000

Investment Criteria: Leveraged Buyout

Industry Group Preference: not available

Portfolio Companies: not available

Officers, Executives and Principals

James W. Donaghy, President (New York)
Timothy F. Healy, Vice President (New York)

HOOK PARTNERS

13760 Noel Road
Suite 705
Dallas, TX 75240

Telephone: 214-991-5457
Fax: 214-991-5458

Mission: Actively seeking new investments

Fund Size: $25 million
Founded: 1978
Average Investment: $100,000 - $250,000
Minimum Investment: $100,000

Investment Criteria: Seed, Startup

Industry Group Preference: Communications, Computer Related, Consumer, Distribution, Electronic Components and Instrumentation, Medical/Health Related

Portfolio Companies: Vitesse Semiconductor, Harmonic Lightwaves, Power Integrations, NetSolve, Clarify, Adaptive Solutions, TriQuint Semiconductors, Genta, IC Works, Wireless Access, MAXM Systems, VidaMed

Officers, Executives and Principals

David J. Hook, Partner

John B. Hook, Partner

Albert A. Augustus
Background: In venture capital since 1968

HORIZON CAPITAL PARTNERS, L.P.

225 East Mason Street
Sixth Floor
Milwaukee, WI 53202

Telephone: 414-271-2200
Fax: 414-271-4016

Mission: Actively seeking new investments

Fund Size: not available
Founded: 1990
Average Investment: not available
Minimum Investment: $1 million

Investment Criteria: Mezzanine,Leveraged Buyout

Industry Group Preference: Consumer, Distribution, Electronic Components and Instrumentation, Industrial Products and Equipment

Portfolio Companies: Gelber Industries, Inc., Surface Systems, Inc., Orval Kent Food Co., Xymex Technologies, Inc.

Officers, Executives and Principals

Robert M. Feerick, Partner
Education: Phi Beta Kappa,Georgetown University; MBA, University of Chicago
Background: Chairman, The Corporate Development Group; General Partner, Frontenac Company

Paul A. Stewart, Partner
Education: Mechanical Engineering, State University of New York at Buffalo; MBA, summa cum laude, Texas A&M University
Background: Vice President in venture capital subsidiary of NCNB Texas, formerly RepublicBank

Paul W. Sweeney, Partner
Education: Finance, Georgetown University
Background: The Corporate Development Group

HORN VENTURE PARTNERS
20300 Stevens Creek Boulevard, #330
Cupertino, CA 95014

Telephone: 408-725-0774
Fax: 408-725-0327

Mission: Actively seeking new investments

Fund Size: $95 million
Founded: 1982
Average Investment: $1 million
Minimum Investment: $500,000

Investment Criteria: Expansion to Later-stage

Industry Group Preference: Consumer, Education Related, Restaurants, Retailing, Software

Portfolio Companies: Buffets Inc., Cardiff Software, CardioLogic Systems, Inc., Cardiopulmonary Corporation, Famiglia Toscana, Inc., Individual, Inc., IXYS Corporation, Keravision, Inc., Oclassen Pharmaceuticals, Ribozyme Pharmaceuticals, Roadhouse Grill, Inc., Roasters Corporation, Sonoma Valley Bagel Company, Timothy's Coffees of the World

Officers, Executives and Principals

Dr. Christian F. Horn, President and Managing Partner
Education: MS, Physical Chemistry, Technical University, Dresden, Germany; Ph.D., Polymer Chemistry, Technical University Aachen, Germany
Background: Founder, Horn Ventures; Executive Positions, W.R. Grace and Company, Hoechst AG, Davy Powergas, Ltd., Union Carbide; 47 US patents

Robert E. Pedigo, Vice President and General Partner
Education: MBA, George Washington University; BA, University of California at Berkeley
Background: Vice President, W.R. Grace and Company; Vice President, Finance, Chemed Corporation; President, one of Chemed specialty chemical startups; Commander, U.S. Navy

HOUSTON VENTURE PARTNERS

401 Louisiana Street
Eighth Floor
Houston, TX 77002

Telephone: 713-222-8600
Fax: 713-222-8932

Mission: Actively seeking new investments

Fund Size: not available
Founded: 1986
Average Investment: not available
Minimum Investment: $250,000

Investment Criteria: Startup, First-stage, Second-stage, Mezzanine, Leveraged Buyout

Industry Group Preference: Computer Related, Electronic Components and Instrumentation, Energy/Natural Resources, Genetic Engineering, Industrial Products and Equipment, Medical/Health Related

Portfolio Companies: not available

Officers, Executives and Principals

Harvard H. Hill, Jr., Managing Partner
Roger A. Ramsey, General Partner
Glenda Overbeck, Associate

HOWARD, LAWSON AND COMPANY

Two Penn Center Plaza
Suite 410
Philadelphia, PA 19102

Telephone: 215-988-0010
Fax: 215-568-0029

Mission: Actively seeking new investments

Fund Size: not available
Founded: 1972
Average Investment: not available
Minimum Investment: $500,000

Investment Criteria: Second-stage, Mezzanine, Leveraged Buyout

Industry Group Preference: Computer Related, Consumer, Distribution, Electronic Components and Instrumentation, Energy/Natural Resources, Industrial Products and Equipment, Medical/Health Related

Portfolio Companies: not available

Officers, Executives and Principals

Michael A. Cuneo, Partner
Steve N. Economou, Vice President

HUMANA VENTURE CAPITAL

500 West Main Street
Louisville, KY 40202

Telephone: 502-580-1663
Fax: 502-580-1690

Mission: Actively seeking new investments

Fund Size: not available
Founded: 1961
Average Investment: not available
Minimum Investment: $500,000

Investment Criteria: First-stage, Second-stage, Mezzanine, Leveraged Buyout

Industry Group Preference: Medical/Health Related

Portfolio Companies: not available

Officers, Executives and Principals

W. Roger Drury, Senior Vice President, Finance
Judith B. Farmer, Director, Equity Investment

IAI VENTURE CAPITAL GROUP

P.O. Box 357
3700 First Bank Place
Minneapolis, MN 55440

Telephone: 612-376-2825
Fax: 612-376-2616

Mission: not available

Fund Size: $150 million
Founded: not available
Average Investment: $1 million
Minimum Investment: not available

Investment Criteria: Seed to Second-stage

Industry Group Preference: Biotechnology, Broadcast/Cable/Radio, Communications, Computer Related, Consumer Related, Electronics, Energy/Natural Resources, High Technology, Industrial Products, Medical/ Health, Publishing, Software, Transportation

Portfolio Companies: not available

Officers, Executives and Principals

Yuval Almog, Managing Partner
David Koehler, Partner
Noel P. Rahn, Partner
Peter H. McNerney, Partner
Steven G. Rothmeier, Partner

IDANTA PARTNERS LTD.

4660 LaJolla Village Drive, Suite 850
San Diego, CA 92122

Telephone: 619-452-9690
Fax: 619-452-2013

Mission: not available

Fund Size: $500 million
Founded: 1971
Average Investment: $1 million
Minimum Investment: $500,000

Investment Criteria: Seed to Leveraged Buyout

Geographic Preference: United States

Industry Group Preference: Diversified

Portfolio Companies: not available

Officers, Executives and Principals

David J. Dunn, Founder (1971) and Managing Partner
Education: BS, Naval Academy; MBA, Harvard University
Background: Partner, J.H. Whitney and Co.
Directorships: Iomega Corporation, Visionary Design Systems, Munchkin, Inc., Hyper Parallel, Inc.

Dev Purkayastha, General Partner (with Idanta since 1978)
Education: BA, honors, Ganhati University; MBA, Harvard
Background: Auditor, Price Waterhouse
Directorships: Munchkin, Inc., Silverman's, Cosmederm Technologies, Savantage, Inc.

Perscilla Faily, General Partner (with Idanta since 1993)
Background: Bain and Company, Boston
Directorships: Savantage, Inc.

Jonathan Huberman, Associate

Anne Crossway, Associate

IEG VENTURE MANAGEMENT, INC.
70 West Madison Street
Chicago, IL 60602

Telephone: 312-993-7500
Fax: 312-454-0369

Mission: not available

Fund Size: not available
Founded: 1983
Average Investment: not available
Minimum Investment: $100,000

Investment Criteria: Seed, Startup, First-stage, Second-stage

Industry Group Preference: Communications, Computer Related, Distribution, Electronic Components and Instrumentation, Energy/Natural Resources, Industrial Products and Equipment, Medical/Health Related

Portfolio Companies: not available

Officers, Executives and Principals

Francis I. Blair, President
Marian M. Zamlynski, Operations Manager and Vice President

IMPEX VENTURE MANAGEMENT COMPANY

Executive Park Tower
P.O. Box 3527
Albany, NY 12203-0527

Telephone: 518-458-1908
Fax: 518-458-1908

Mission: Actively seeking new investments

Fund Size: not available
Founded: 1980
Average Investment: $1 million
Minimum Investment: Less than $100,000

Investment Criteria: Startup, First-stage, Second-stage, Mezzanine, Leveraged Buyout, Special Situations

Industry Group Preference: Communications, Computer Related, Consumer, Distribution, Electronic Components and Instrumentation, Energy/Natural Resources, Genetic Engineering, Industrial Products and Equipment, Medical/Health Related

Portfolio Companies: not available

Officers, Executives and Principals

Jay C. Banker, Managing General Partner
Michael J. Banker, General Partner

INCO VENTURE CAPITAL MANAGEMENT

145 King Street West
Suite 1500
Toronto, Ontario M5H 4B7
Canada

Telephone: 416-361-7680

Mission: not available

Fund Size: $40 million
Founded: 1974
Average Investment: $500,000 - $1 million
Minimum Investment: $250,000

Investment Criteria: Second-stage, Mezzanine, Leveraged Buyout, Special Situations

Industry Group Preference: Biotechnology, Communications, Computer Related, Consumer, Distribution, Electronic Components and Instrumentation, Energy/Natural Resources, Genetic Engineering, Medical/Health Related

Portfolio Companies: Immunogen, Hauston Biotechnology, Liant Software, Tartan, Xenova, Datamedia, ViraChem, TVSM Holdings, Nimbus Medical

Officers, Executives and Principals

Stuart Feiner, President

INCORPORATED INVESTORS

P.O. Box 1336
Crystal Bay, NV 89402-1336

Telephone: 702-832-9798
Fax: 702-832-9031

Other Office Locations
28, rue de Syren
L-5870 Alzingen
Luxembourg
Phone 352-366-444, Fax 352-366-441

Mission: Actively seeking new investments

Fund Size: $100 million
Founded: 1991
Average Investment: $1.5 million
Minimum Investment: $750,000

Investment Criteria: First-stage, Second-stage, Special Situations, Management Buyouts

Geographic Preference: United States, Germany, Brazil, Argentina

Industry Group Preference: Commercial Software Development, Communications, Computer Related, Electronic Components and Instrumentation, Electronic Displays, HDTV, Industrial Products and Equipment, Lasers, Telecommunications Networks

Portfolio Companies: not available

Officers, Executives and Principals

Jeffrey A. Barry, Managing Director (Crystal Bay)
Michael A. Cassin, Senior Advisor (Crystal Bay)
Ralf G. Bahr (Crystal Bay)
Bernard C.G. Perier, Directeur General (Luxembourg)

INNOCAL, L.P.

600 Anton Boulevard
Suite 1270
Costa Mesa, CA 92626

Telephone: 714-850-6784
Fax: 714-850-6798

Other Office Locations
Park 80 West
Plaza One
Saddle Brook, NJ 07663
Phone 201-845-4900, Fax 201-845-3388

Mission: Actively seeking new investments

Fund Size: $75 million
Founded: 1993
Average Investment: not available
Minimum Investment: $500,000

Investment Criteria: Startup, First-stage, Second-stage, Mezzanine, Leveraged Buyout, Special Situations, Control-block Purchases

Industry Group Preference: Communications, Computer Related, Consumer, Electronic Components and Instrumentation, Energy/Natural Resources, Genetic Engineering, Industrial Products and Equipment, Medical/Health Related, Multimedia, Software

Portfolio Companies: not available

Officers, Executives and Principals

James E. Houlihan III, General Partner (Costa Mesa)
H.D. Lambert, General Partner (Costa Mesa)
Gerald A. Lodge, General Partner (Saddle Brook)
Raun J. Rasmussen, General Partner (Saddle Brook)
Russell J. Robelen, General Partner (Costa Mesa)
Eric S. Harrison, Associate (Costa Mesa)

INNOVATION ONTARIO CORPORATION

56 Wellesley Street West
Toronto, Ontario M7A 2E7
Canada

Telephone: 416-326-1025
Fax: 416-326-1109

Mission: Actively seeking new investments

Fund Size: not available
Founded: 1986
Average Investment: not available
Minimum Investment: $100,000

Investment Criteria: Startup, First-stage, Second-stage

Industry Group Preference: Communications, Computer Related, Electronic Components and Instrumentation, Energy/Natural Resources, Genetic Engineering, Industrial Products and Equipment, Medical/Health Related

Portfolio Companies: not available

Officers, Executives and Principals

Charles Lum, Acting Director
Bob Roy, Senior Manager

INNOVEST GROUP, INC.

1600 Market Street
Suite 2601
Philadelphia, PA 19103

Telephone: 215-564-3960
Fax: 215-569-3272

Mission: Actively seeking new investments

Fund Size: not available
Founded: 1971
Average Investment: not available
Minimum Investment: $250,000

Investment Criteria: Startup, First-stage, Second-stage, Mezzanine, Leveraged Buyout, Special Situations

Industry Group Preference: Communications, Computer Related, Consumer, Distribution, Electronic Components and Instrumentation, Energy/Natural Resources, Industrial Products and Equipment, Medical/Health Related

Portfolio Companies: not available

Officers, Executives and Principals

Richard E. Woosnam, President
Barbara S. Demchick, Controller

INROADS CAPITAL PARTNERS

1603 Orrington Avenue
Suite 2050
Evanston, IL 60201

Telephone: 847-864-2000
Fax: 847-864-9692

Mission: not available

Fund Size: not available
Founded: 1993
Average Investment: not available
Minimum Investment: not available

Investment Criteria: Second-stage, Leveraged Buyout

Industry Group Preference: Consumer, Medical/Health Related

Portfolio Companies: not available

Officers, Executives and Principals

Margaret Fisher, General Partner
Jerrold Carrington, General Partner
Sona Wang, General Partner

INSURANCE VENTURE PARTNERS, INC.

31 Brookside Drive, Suite 211
Greenwich, CT 06830

Telephone: 203-861-0030
Fax: 203-861-2745

Mission: not available

Fund Size: not available
Founded: 1984
Average Investment: not available
Minimum Investment: Less than $100,000

Investment Criteria: First-stage, Second-stage, Leveraged Buyout

Industry Group Preference: Insurance

Portfolio Companies: not available

Officers, Executives and Principals

Bernard M. Brown, Principal
Philip W. Ness, Jr.

INTEGRATED CONSORTIUM, INC.

50 Ridgecrest Road
Kentfield, CA 94904

Telephone: 415-925-0386
Fax: 415-461-2726

Mission: Actively seeking new investments

Fund Size: not available
Founded: not available
Average Investment: not available
Minimum Investment: $100,000

Investment Criteria: First-stage, Second-stage, Mezzanine, Leveraged Buyout

Industry Group Preference: Consumer

Portfolio Companies: not available

Officers, Executives and Principals

Terry McGovern, President

INTEREQUITY CAPITAL CORPORATION

220 Fifth Avenue
New York, NY 10001

Telephone: 212-779-2022
Fax: 212-779-2103

Mission: Provide long-term capital for growing companies in the United States

Fund Size: not available
Founded: 1990
Average Investment: $500,000 - $2 million
Minimum Investment: $250,000

Investment Criteria: Startup to Leveraged Buyout

Geographic Preference: United States

Industry Group Preference: Diversified

Portfolio Companies: not available

Officers, Executives and Principals

Abraham Goldstein, Secretary, Managing Director
Education: Ph.D., University of Toronto; MBA, University of Chicago
Background: Vice President, Acquisition Finance Group, Canadian Imperial Bank of Commerce; Senior Manager, Mergers and Acquisitions, Canadian Imperial Investment Bank; Member, Mergers and Acquisitions Group, Illinois National Bank

Irwin Schlass, President, Managing Director
Education: BA, City University of New York; MA, University of Denver
Background: Divisional Head of Sales and Marketing, GTE/US Sprint; President, I.S. Enterprises and Harval Development Corporation

Frank Brenner, Managing Director
Education: BA, Lehigh; JD, Harvard
Background: Director, New York County Lawyers Association; Assistant District Attorney and Judge of the Criminal Court of New York; Founder, Skirpan Lighting Control Corporation

Monte Engler, Managing Director
Education: BA, New York University; Cornell University Law School
Background: Founder, Cellular Systems, Inc.; Parnter, Javits, Hinckley, Rabin and Engler

Ken Leon, Director
Education: MBA, Accounting and Finance, New York University
Background: Senior Vice President, Chicago Corporation; Senior Vice President, Lehman Brothers; Managing Director, Bear Stearns and Company; Vice President, LF Rothschild; Vice President, Chemical Bank; Senior Accountant, Touche Ross and Company

John Radziwill, Managing Director
Education: Oxford University
Background: President, Radix Organization and Radix Group International; Member, English and Welsh bar associations

Stephen Raphael, Executive Vice President, Managing Director
Education: Economics, Hofstra University
Background: Senior Managing Director, Board of Directors, Bear Stearns and Co., Hayden Stone

George Sarner, Managing Director
Education: BA, Dartmouth College
Background: Senior Managing Director, Bear Stearns and Co.; Vice President and Treasurer, G.C. Haas and Company

Jack P. Schleifer, Treasurer, Managing Director
Education: BBA, Baruch College of the City University of New York
Background: Schleifer Realty Company; CPA

Mike Weinblatt, Managing Director
Education: BS, Management, Syracuse University
Background: President, Weinblatt Communication; President, NBC Entertainment, NBC Enterprises; President, Multimedia Entertainment, Showtime Entertainment

Eugene Wong, Managing Director
Education: BA, Physics, Cornell University; MBA, Finance, Columbia University
Background: Managing Director, AmerAsia Partners; Founding Managing Partner, The International Harvest Group; Managing Director, High Yield Securities Department, Prudential Securities; Senior Vice President, High Yield Department, Drexel Burnham Lambert

INTERNATIONAL DEVELOPMENT PARTNERS, LTD.

330 Madison Avenue
Suite 1100
New York, NY 10017

Telephone: 212-297-3314
Fax: 212-972-6569

Mission: Actively seeking new investments

Fund Size: not available
Founded: 1988
Average Investment: not available
Minimum Investment: $500,000

Investment Criteria: First-stage, Second-stage, Special Situations

Industry Group Preference: Communications, Computer Related, Electronic Components and Instrumentation, Energy/Natural Resources, Genetic Engineering, Medical/Health Related

Portfolio Companies: not available

Officers, Executives and Principals

Roy Dickerson, Managing Director
Paul Siegel, Managing Director

INTERNATIONAL MERCHANT BANCORP, LTD.

112 Arlene Drive
Walnut Creek, CA 94595

Telephone: 510-930-0982
Fax: 510-938-2783

Other Office Locations
23 Cielo Vista Drive
Monterey, CA 93940

Mission: Making few, if any, new investments

Fund Size: not available
Founded: 1985
Average Investment: $10 million
Minimum Investment: $1 million

Investment Criteria: not available

Industry Group Preference: Communications, Computer Related, Consumer, Distribution, Electronic Components and Instrumentation, Genetic Engineering, Industrial Products and Eqiupment, Medical/Health Related

Portfolio Companies: not available

Officers, Executives and Principals

Ryan Kelly, Chairman (Monterey)
Stevan Cloudtree, President (Walnut Creek)

INTERWEST PARTNERS

3000 Sand Hill Road
Building #3, Suite 255
Menlo Park, CA 94025-7112

Telephone: 415-854-8585
Fax: 415-854-4706

Other Office Locations
13455 Noel Road
Suite 1670
Dallas, TX 75240
Phone 214-392-7279, Fax 214-490-6348

Mission: Actively seeking new investments

Fund Size: $615 million
Founded: 1979
Average Investment: $5 million
Minimum Investment: $1 million

Investment Criteria: Seed to Recapitalizations

Geographic Preference: United States

Industry Group Preference: Biotechnology, High Technology, Medical/Health, Retailing, Service Industries

Portfolio Companies: Xilinx, Office Depot, Cor Therapeutics, Ventritex, Cyrix, Gadzooks, Corporate Express

Officers, Executives and Principals

Wallace R. Hawley, Founding Partner
Education: BA, Stanford University; MBA, Harvard
Background: President, SHV North America Holding Corporation; Project Manager, McKinsey and Co., Inc.

W. Scott Hedrick, Founding Partner
Education: BA, University of Southern California, Santa Barbara; MBA, University of Southern California
Background: Partner SHV's Venture Capital Subsidiary, American-Euro Interfund. Bank of America's venture
  capital subsidiary
Directorships: Office Depot, NVCA

Robert R. Momsen, Partner
Education: BS, MBA, Stanford University
Background: Chief Financial Officer, Life Instruments Corporation of Denver, Colorado; Operations Manage-
  ment, Vail Associates
Directorships: Ventritex, Cor Therapeutics, Arthrocare, Integ, Urologix, Innovasive Devices

Philip T. Gianos, Partner
Education: BS, MS, Electrical Engineering, Stanford University; MBA, Harvard
Background: Engineering Positions, IBM; two U.S. patents and one European patent
Directorships: Xilinx, Inc., WAVC

Harvey B. Cash, Partner
Education: BS, Electrical Engineering, Texas A&M; MBA, Western Michigan University
Background: Marketing Engineer, Texas Instruments; Founder, Mostek Semiconductor
Directorships: AMX Corporation, Benchmarq Microelectronics, Cyrix Corporation, Heritage Media, ProNet

Alan W. Crites, Partner
Education: BA, Michigan State University; MBA, Harvard University
Background: General Electric Company, GE Medical Systems Division, GE Information Services, GE Computer Service
Directorships: Gadzooks, Inc., Oacis Healthcare

Arnold L. Oronsky, Partner
Education: BS, New York University's University College; Ph.D., Columbia University's College of Physicians and Surgeons
Background: Vice President, Discovery Research, Lederle Lab Division, American Cyanamid; Assistant Professor, Harvard Medical School

John E. Zeisler, Partner
Education: BS, Communications, Boston University
Background: Senior Vice President of Marketing, Netcom Online Communications; Chief Executive Officer, Pensoft Corporation; Co-Founder, Vice President of Marketing, Claris Corporation
Directorships: Infoseek Corporation

W. Stephen Holmes, Administrative Partner and Chief Financial Officer
Education: BS, Lehigh University; MBA, Harvard
Background: Chief Financial Officer, Specialty Brands

INVESTAMERICA INVESTMENT ADVISORS, INC.

101 Second Street Southeast, Suite 800
Cedar Rapids, IA 52401

Telephone: 319-363-8249
Fax: 319-363-9683

Mission: not available

Fund Size: $30 million
Founded: 1985
Average Investment: $500,000 - $1 million
Minimum Investment: not available

Investment Criteria: First-stage to Acquisitions

Industry Group Preference: High Technology, Manufacturing/Processing, Retailing, Service Industries

Portfolio Companies: not available

Officers, Executives and Principals

David R. Schroder, President
Education: BSFS, Georgetown University; MBA, University of Wisconsin
Background: President and Director, MorAmerica Capital Corporation; Vice President, Kentucky Highlands
  Investment Corporation

Robert A. Comey, Executive Vice President
Education: AB, Economics, Brown University; MBA, Fordham University
Background: Vice President, Director, MorAmerica Capital Corporation; Vice President RIHT Capital Corpo-
  ration; President Tower Ventures

Kevin F. Mullane, Vice President
Education: BSBA, MBA, Rockhurst College
Background: Vice President, MorAmerica Capital Corporation

Steven J. Massey, Vice President
Education: BS, University of Pennsylvania
Background: Vice President, MorAmerica Capital Corporation

INVESTAMERICA VENTURE GROUP, INC.

911 Main Street, Suite 2724
Commerce Tower
Kansas City, MO 64105

Telephone: 816-842-0114
Fax: 816-471-7339

Mission: not available

Fund Size: $50 million
Founded: not available
Average Investment: $500,000
Minimum Investment: not available

Investment Criteria: First-stage to Acquisitions

Industry Group Preference: High Technology, Manufacturing/Processing, Retailing, Service Industries

Portfolio Companies: not available

Officers, Executives and Principals

Kevin F. Mullane, Vice President
Education: BSBA, MBA, Rockhurst College
Background: Vice President, MorAmerica Capital Corporation

INVESTISSEMENT DESJARDINS

2 Complexe Desjardins, C.P. 760
Montreal, Quebec H5B 1B8
Canada

Telephone: 514-281-7131
Fax: 514-281-7808

Mission: Actively seeking new investments

Fund Size: not available
Founded: not available
Average Investment: not available
Minimum Investment: $250,000

Investment Criteria: Second-stage, Mezzanine, Leveraged Buyout, Control-block Purchases

Industry Group Preference: Communications, Computer Related, Consumer, Distribution, Electronic Components and Instrumentation, Energy/Natural Resources, Genetic Engineering, Industrial Products and Equipment, Medical/Health Related

Portfolio Companies: not available

Officers, Executives and Principals

Pierre Brunet, Senior Vice President, Investment

INVESTMENT SECURITIES OF COLORADO, INC.

4605 Denice Drive
Englewood, CO 80111

Telephone: 303-796-9192

Mission: Making few, if any, new investments

Fund Size: not available
Founded: 1970
Average Investment: not available
Minimum Investment: Less than $100,000

Investment Criteria: Seed, Startup

Industry Group Preference: Industrial Products and Equipment, Medical/Health Related

Portfolio Companies: not available

Officers, Executives and Principals

Vern D. Kornelsen, President

IOWA SEED CAPITAL CORPORATION

200 East Grand Avenue
Suite 330
Des Moines, IA 50309

Telephone: 515-242-4860
Fax: 515-242-4722

Mission: IOWA: State-sponsored fund to help launch technology-based, growth-oriented companies.

Fund Size: cumulative $12 million
Founded: 1983
Average Investment: $250,000
Minimum Investment: not available

Investment Criteria: Seed to Startup

Geographic Preference: Iowa

Industry Group Preference: Diversified

Portfolio Companies: not available

Officers, Executives and Principals

Gregg Barcus, President
George Lipper, Investment Manager
Mark Tubbs, Investment Manager

IPS INDUSTRIAL PROMOTION SERVICES, LTD.

60 Columbia Way, Suite 720
Markham, Ontario L3R 0C9
Canada

Telephone: 905-475-9400
Fax: 905-475-5003

Mission: Actively seeking new investments

Fund Size: not available
Founded: 1977
Average Investment: not available
Minimum Investment: $250,000

Investment Criteria: Second-stage, Leveraged Buyout, Special Situations, Control-block Purchases

Industry Group Preference: Communications, Computer Related, Consumer, Distribution, Electronic Components and Instrumentation, Energy/Natural Resources, Genetic Engineering, Industrial Products and Equipment, Medical/Health Related

Portfolio Companies: not available

Officers, Executives and Principals

Mohamed Ismail, Chairman
Nizar Alibhai, President
Shamsh Dhala, Vice President
Afzal Sovani, Executive Officer

J.B. POINDEXTER AND COMPANY, INC.
1100 Louisiana
Suite 5400
Houston, TX 77002

Telephone: 713-655-9800
Fax: 713-951-9038

Mission: not available

Fund Size: not available
Founded: 1980
Average Investment: not available
Minimum Investment: $5 million

Investment Criteria: Leveraged Buyout

Industry Group Preference: Distribution, Electronic Components and Instrumentation, Industrial Products
  and Equipment

Portfolio Companies: not available

Officers, Executives and Principals

Keith Stubbs, Manager, Business Development

J.E. MANN AND COMPANY

10 Old Road Lane
Mt. Kisco, NY 10549

Telephone: 914-241-0297
Fax: 914-241-0726
E-mail: jem58@Columbia.edu

Mission: Reducing investment activity

Fund Size: not available
Founded: 1983
Average Investment: not available
Minimum Investment: $100,000

Investment Criteria: First-stage

Industry Group Preference: Communications, Computer Related, Distribution, Electronic Components and Instrumentation, Industrial Products and Equipment, Specialty Chemical

Portfolio Companies: Cyberchrome, Inc., CyberResearch, Inc., National Chemistry, Inc., General Clutch Corporation, Magtype Co., New Hampshire Business Development Corporation, New England Retail Express, Inc., Crestbury, Ltd.

Officers, Executives and Principals

James Mann, Founder (1983) and President
Education: AB, Rutgers University; JD, Rutgers; LLM, Harvard
Background: Co-founder Crestbury LTD in 1974
Directorships: Natural Chemistry, Inc., CyberChrome, Inc., New Hampshire Business Development Corporation

J.E. SCHNEIDER AND ASSOCIATES, INC.

400 East 58th Street
New York, NY 10022

Telephone: 212-750-8192
Fax: 212-750-8326
E-mail: JES-nyc@worldnet.att.net

Mission: Consulting firm specializing in the development of business plans

Fund Size: not available
Founded: 1988
Average Investment: not available
Minimum Investment: not available

Investment Criteria: Seed, Research and Development, Startup, First-stage, Second-stage, Mezzanine, Leveraged Buyout, Special Situations

Geographic Preference: United States, Canada

Industry Group Preference: Communications, Computer Related, Consumer, Distribution, Electronic Components and Instrumentation, Energy/Natural Resources, Genetic Engineering, Industrial Products and Equipment, Medical/Health Related

Portfolio Companies: not available

Officers, Executives and Principals

Judith E. Schneider, President

J.E.L. AND ASSOCIATES

Nine Cot Hill Road
Bedford, MA 01730

Telephone: 617-275-8420
Fax: 617-275-1638

Mission: Actively seeking new investments

Fund Size: not available
Founded: 1981
Average Investment: not available
Minimum Investment: $250,000

Investment Criteria: First-stage, Second-stage, Mezzanine, Leveraged Buyout

Industry Group Preference: Communications, Computer Related, Consumer, Distribution, Electronic Components and Instrumentation, Energy/Natural Resources, Genetic Engineering, Industrial Products and Equipment, Medical/Health Related

Portfolio Companies: not available

Officers, Executives and Principals

Joseph E. Levangie, Chief Executive Officer
Cynthia M. Barker, Senior Associate
Steven Georgiev, Special Advisor

J.G. FOGG AND COMPANY, INC.

400 Post Avenue
Westbury, NY 11590

Telephone: 516-333-0218
Fax: 516-333-2724

Mission: Actively seeking new investments

Fund Size: not available
Founded: 1993
Average Investment: not available
Minimum Investment: $500,000

Investment Criteria: Second-stage, Mezzanine, Leveraged Buyout, Special Situations

Industry Group Preference: Diversified

Portfolio Companies: not available

Officers, Executives and Principals

Joseph G. Fogg III, Chairman and Chief Executive Officer
E. Gayle McGuigan, Jr., Managing Director
Hartley R. Rogers, President
Deborah C. Verma, Treasurer
Harry A. Shaw, Associate

J.H. WHITNEY & COMPANY

177 Broad Street
Stamford, CT 06901

Telephone: 203-973-1400
Fax: 203-973-1422
E-mail: jhwhitney.com

Other Office Locations
630 Fifth Avenue
Suite 3200
New York, NY 10111
Phone 212-332-2400, Fax 212-332-2422

Mission: Actively seeking new investments

Fund Size: $600 million
Founded: 1946
Average Investment: $8 million
Minimum Investment: not available

Investment Criteria: Early-stage to Leveraged Buyout

Industry Group Preference: Diversified

Portfolio Companies: not available

Officers, Executives and Principals

Michael C. Brooks, Managing Partner (Stamford)
Peter M. Castleman, Managing Partner (Stamford)
James H. Fordyce, General Partner (Stamford)
Jeffrey R. Jay, General Partner (Stamford)
William Laverack, Jr., General Partner (Stamford)
Ray E. Newtsa, III, General Partner (Stamford)
Daniel J. O'Brien, General Partner and Chief Financial Officer (Stamford)
Benno C. Schmidt, General Partner (New York)
Michael. P. Stone, General Partner (Stamford)

J. P. MORGAN CAPITAL CORPORATION

60 Wall Street
14th Floor
New York, NY 10260

Telephone: 212-648-9000
Fax: 212-648-5032

Other Office Locations
101 California Street, 38th Floor
San Francisco, CA
Phone 415-954-4735

60 Victoria Embankment
London EC4Y OJP
England
Phone 44-71-325-4835, Fax 44-71-325-8258

Edinburgh Tower
15 Queen's Road, 23rd Floor
Central Hong Kong
Phone 852-841-1168

Mission: Actively seeking new investments

Fund Size: not available
Founded: 1985
Average Investment: not available
Minimum Investment: $10 million

Investment Criteria: Second-stage, Special Situations

Industry Group Preference: Communications, Computer Related, Consumer, Distribution, Electronic Components and Instrumentation, Energy/Natural Resources, Genetic Engineering, Industrial Products and Equipment, Medical/Health Related

Portfolio Companies: not available

Officers, Executives and Principals

David M. Cromwell, President and Managing Director (New York)
Seth Cunningham, Managing Director (New York)
Brian T. Murphy, Managing Director (London)
Thomas M. Snell, Managing Director (New York)
Leigh Anderson, Vice President (New York)
Willa Berghuis, Vice President (New York)
Charles Ewald, Vice President (New York)
Peter Gleason, Vice President (New York)

JAFCO AMERICA VENTURES, INC.

555 California Street
Suite 4380
San Francisco, CA 94104

Telephone: 415-788-0706
Fax: 415-788-0709

Other Office Locations
Two World Financial Center
Building B, 17th Floor
New York, NY 10281
Phone 212-667-9001, Fax 212-667-1004

Mission: Actively seeking new investments

Fund Size: not available
Founded: 1984
Average Investment: not available
Minimum Investment: $500,000

Investment Criteria: First-stage, Second-stage, Mezzanine

Industry Group Preference: Communications, Computer Related, Electronic Components and Instrumentation, Genetic Engineering, Industrial Products and Equipment, Medical/Health Related

Portfolio Companies: not available

Officers, Executives and Principals

Katsuhiko Saito, President (San Francisco)
Bill Shelander, General Manager (San Francisco)
Hisashi Washiyama, General Manager (New York)
Charles W. Keough (New York)
Shin Koga (San Francisco)
Michael Colby Orsak (San Francisco)
James Wei (San Francisco)
Satoshi Yamaguchi (New York)

JAMES A. MATZDORFF AND COMPANY

9903 Santa Monica Boulevard
Suite 374
Beverly Hills, CA 90212

Telephone: 310-854-4634
E-mail: roadking@deltanet.com

Other Office Locations
Available upon request

Mission: Actively seeking new investments. Arrange corporate financing, restructuring of troubled debt, recapitalization financing, leveraged acquisition financing, financing searches.

Fund Size: $100 million
Founded: 1977
Average Investment: $2+ million
Minimum Investment: $1 million

Investment Criteria: Second-stage, Mezzanine, Leveraged Buyout, Special Situations

Geographic Preference: United States

Industry Group Preference: Diversified

Portfolio Companies: Available upon request

Officers, Executives and Principals

James A. Matzdorff, Founder (1977) and Managing Director
Education: BS, Finance, University of Southern California; MBA ,Finance, Loyola University
Background: Bank of America, Corporate Finance Department
Directorships: Republican National Committee Member

JAMES B. KOBAK AND COMPANY

2701 Summer Street
Suite 200
Stamford, CT 06905

Telephone: 203-363-2221
Fax: 203-363-2218

Mission: not available

Fund Size: not available
Founded: 1971
Average Investment: not available
Minimum Investment: Other

Investment Criteria: not available

Industry Group Preference: not available

Portfolio Companies: not available

Officers, Executives and Principals

James B. Kobak

JEFFERSON CAPITAL FUND, LTD.

Financial Center, Suite 1625
P.O. Box 370928
Birmingham, AL 35237

Telephone: 205-324-7709
Fax: 205-252-6812

Mission: Actively seeking new investments

Fund Size: not available
Founded: 1991
Average Investment: not available
Minimum Investment: $250,000

Investment Criteria: Leveraged Buyout, Special Situations, Control-block Purchases

Industry Group Preference: Communications, Consumer, Distribution, Industrial Products and Equipment, Medical/Health Related

Portfolio Companies: not available

Officers, Executives and Principals

Lana E. Sellers, Managing Director

JOHNSEN SECURITIES

224 East 49th Street
New York, NY 10017

Telephone: 212-486-2846
Fax: 212-758-2374

Mission: not available

Fund Size: $15 million
Founded: not available
Average Investment: $1 million
Minimum Investment: not available

Investment Criteria: First-stage to Leveraged Buyout

Industry Group Preference: Biotechnology, Manufacturing/Processing, Medical/Health, Wholesaling/Distribution

Portfolio Companies: Windsoft, Taylor Medical, Buffalo Medical, ARx.

Officers, Executives and Principals

B. Scott Asen, President
Education: Harvard College
Background: Manager, Pioneer Ventures; Investor, Advanced Technology Labs; (acquired by Squibb) and in Paradyne (acquired by AT&T)

Gordon T. Boyd, Partner
Education: BS, MA, University of Washington; Post Graduate Economics, University of Chicago
Background: Chairman, Marshall Products; Financial Management, Weyerhaeuser Co.; President, Weyerhaeuser
Directorships: Worldwide Container

Michael S. Bisulca, Partner
Education: Wilkes-Barre College
Background: Founder and President, Marshall Products, Inc.; Chairman, Buffalo Medical Specialties; President, Omron Healthcare, Inc.

Walter C. Johnsen, Partner
Education: BS, MS, Cornell University; MBA, Columbia University
Background: Chief Financial Officer, Marshall Products; Venture Capital and Leveraged Buyout, Smith Barney, Harris Upham; General Partner, Smith Barney's First Century

JOHNSON AND JOHNSON DEVELOPMENT CORPORATION

One Johnson and Johnson Plaza
New Brunswick, NJ 08933

Telephone: 908-524-3218
Fax: 908-247-5309

Mission: Actively seeking new investments

Fund Size: not available
Founded: 1973
Average Investment: not available
Minimum Investment: No preference

Investment Criteria: Seed, Startup, First-stage, Second-stage

Industry Group Preference: Consumer, Electronic Components and Instrumentation, Genetic Engineering, Medical/Health Related

Portfolio Companies: not available

Officers, Executives and Principals

James R. Utaski, President
S. Lambard, Vice President
T.P. Oei, Vice President
B. Vale, Vice President
S.L.R. Hamilton, Associate Director

THE JORDAN, EDMISTON GROUP, INC.

885 Third Avenue
New York, NY 10022

Telephone: 212-754-0710
Fax: 212-754-0337

Mission: Actively seeking new investments

Fund Size: not available
Founded: 1987
Average Investment: not available
Minimum Investment: $1 million

Investment Criteria: Second-stage, Mezzanine, Leveraged Buyout, Special Situations

Industry Group Preference: Consumer, Trade

Portfolio Companies: not available

Officers, Executives and Principals

Wilma Jordan, Co-Chairman
Mark Edmiston, Co-Chairman
James Zielinski, Managing Director
Bill Hitzig, Associate Managing Director
Mary Taylor, Associate
Eric Dobi, Associate
Jeffrey Mettel, Associate

JOSEPHBERG GROSZ AND COMPANY, INC.

810 Seventh Avenue
27th Floor
New York, NY 10019

Telephone: 212-974-9926
Fax: 212-397-5832

Mission: Actively seeking new investments

Fund Size: not available
Founded: 1986
Average Investment: not available
Minimum Investment: $500,000

Investment Criteria: Seed, Research and Development, Startup, First-stage, Second-stage, Mezzanine, Leveraged Buyout

Industry Group Preference: Communications, Computer Related, Consumer, Distribution, Electronic Components and Instrumentation, Energy/Natural Resources, Genetic Engineering, Industrial Products and Equipment, Medical/Health Related

Portfolio Companies: not available

Officers, Executives and Principals

Richard Josephberg, Chairman
Daniel Amzallag, Head, European Operations

KAHALA INVESTMENTS, INC.

8214 Westchester Drive
Suite 715
Dallas, TX 75225

Telephone: 214-987-0077
Fax: 214-987-2332

Mission: Actively seeking new investments

Fund Size: not available
Founded: 1978
Average Investment: not available
Minimum Investment: $100,000

Investment Criteria: Mezzanine, Leveraged Buyout, Special Situations, Control-block Purchases, Management Buyouts

Industry Group Preference: Communications, Consumer, Distribution, Energy/Natural Resources, Industrial Products and Equipment

Portfolio Companies: not available

Officers, Executives and Principals

Lee R. Slaughter, Jr., President
Nancy E. Craig, Associate
Debby J. Slaughter, Associate

KANSAS CITY EQUITY PARTNERS

233 West 47th Street
Kansas City, MO 64112

Telephone: 816-960-1771
Fax: 816-960-1777
E-mail: ngarren@kcep.com

Mission: not available

Fund Size: $30 million
Founded: not available
Average Investment: $1 million
Minimum Investment: not available

Investment Criteria: Multiple Exit Options

Geographic Preference: Kansas City area

Industry Group Preference: Diversified

Portfolio Companies: not available

Officers, Executives and Principals

Paul Henson, President
Education: BS, MS, Electrical Engineering, University of Nebraska
Background: President, Chairman and Chief Executive Officer, Sprint Corporation
Directorships: Armco, Duke Power Co., Hallmark Cards, Kansas City, Southern Industries, Sprint Corporation

Bill Reisler, Vice President
Education: BS, Economics, University of Illinois; MBA Entrepreneurship, University of Southern California
Background: Hallmark, Sprint and entrepreneurial new product development; President and Executive Director, Center for Business Innovation

Jack Le Claire, Vice President
Education: BS, Aeronautical Engineering, University of Kansas
Background: Corporate Vice President, Trans World Airlines; Managing Director, Center for Business Innovation, Kansas City

KANSAS VENTURE CAPITAL, INC.

6700 Antioch Plaza
Suite 460
Overland Park, KS 66204

Telephone: 913-262-7117
Fax: 913-262-3509

Mission: Actively seeking new investments

Fund Size: not available
Founded: 1977
Average Investment: not available
Minimum Investment: $250,000

Investment Criteria: First-stage, Second-stage, Mezzanine, Leveraged Buyout

Industry Group Preference: Communications, Computer Related, Distribution, Electronic Components and Instrumentation, Genetic Engineering, Industrial Products and Equipment, Medical/Health Related

Portfolio Companies: not available

Officers, Executives and Principals

Rex E. Wiggins, President
Thomas C. Blackburn, Vice President
Marshall D. Parker, Vice President

KBL HEALTHCARE, INC.

645 Madison Avenue
14th Floor
New York, NY 10022

Telephone: 212-319-5555
Fax: 212-319-5591

Mission: Actively seeking new investments

Fund Size: not available
Founded: 1991
Average Investment: not available
Minimum Investment: $100,000

Investment Criteria: Seed, Research and Development, Startup, First-stage, Second-stage, Mezzanine, Leveraged Buyout, Special Situations

Industry Group Preference: Genetic Engineering, Medical/Health Related

Portfolio Companies: not available

Officers, Executives and Principals

Marlene R. Krauss, M.D., Chairman and Chief Executive Officer
Zachary C. Berk, Chief Operating Officer and Managing Director
Jordan S. Davis, Managing Director
Robert L. Reisley, Managing Director
Gary L. Wilhelm, Associate

KEARSARGE VENTURES

41 Brook Street
Manchester, NH 03104

Telephone: 603-625-1466
Fax: 603-625-2383

Mission: not available

Fund Size: $11 million
Founded: not available
Average Investment: $500,000
Minimum Investment: not available

Investment Criteria:

Geographic Preference: New Hampshire

Industry Group Preference: Diversified

Portfolio Companies: not available

Officers, Executives and Principals

Alan Voulgaris, General Partner
Peter Danforth, General Partner

KESTREL VENTURE MANAGEMENT

31 Milk Street
Boston, MA 02109

Telephone: 617-451-6722
Fax: 617-451-3322

Mission: To earn above average venture returns for Limited Partners by providing capital and exceptional support to small, growing companies

Fund Size: $50+ million
Founded: 1975
Average Investment: $500,000
Minimum Investment: $150,000

Investment Criteria: Seed to Leveraged Buyouts

Geographic Preference: Northeastern United States

Industry Group Preference: Diversified

Portfolio Companies: Animated Images, Atlantic Bancorp, AT/Comm, Boston Restaurant Associates, Cambridge Applied Systems, Chatham Village Foods, Colonial Mills, DataCube, Falcon Detection Technologies, Helio Optics, Holometrix, Keyfile, Littlepoint, MDI Instruments, Multilink, New England Water Heater, Optical Sensors, Pendulum Design, PixelVision, Progressive Technologies, Sensitech, Separation Technologies, Stedt Hydraulic Crane, Tech Pak, Transfusion Technologies, USDATA, Voicetek, W.F. Wood

Officers, Executives and Principals

Nuri A.E.Z. Wissa, General Partner
Edward J. Stewart III, General Partner
R. Gregg Stone, General Partner

KEY EQUITY CAPITAL CORPORATION

127 Public Square
Sixth Floor
Cleveland, OH 44114

Telephone: 216-689-5776
Fax: 216-689-3204

Other Office Locations
700 Fifth Avenue, 48th Floor
Seattle, WA 98110
Phone 206-684-6480, Fax 206-689-5450

Mission: Actively seeking new investments

Fund Size: $125 million
Founded: 1960
Average Investment: $5 - $7 million
Minimum Investment: $3 million

Investment Criteria: Leveraged Buyout, Growth Equity, Turnarounds / Special Situations

Geographic Preference: United States

Industry Group Preference: Aerospace, Defense, Diversified, Electronic Equipment and Components, Energy/Natural Resources, Environmental Protection, Food Services/Products, Materials and Chemicals, Medical/Health Related, Wholesaling/Distribution

Portfolio Companies: not available

Officers, Executives and Principals

David P. Given, Manager, Senior Investment Officer
John F. Kirby, Vice President, Senior Investment Officer
Stephen R. Haynes, Vice President, Senior Investment Officer
Robert S. Wainio, Vice President, Senior Investment Officer (Seattle)
James P. Marra, Jr., Vice President
Sean P. Ward, Vice President
Tracy L. Williams, Assistant Vice President

KEYSTONE MINORITY CAPITAL FUND, L.P.

5907 Penn Avenue
Suite 212
Pittsburgh, PA 15206

Telephone: 412-363-3325
Fax: 412-363-3626

Mission: Actively seeking new investments

Fund Size: not available
Founded: 1994
Average Investment: not available
Minimum Investment: $100,000

Investment Criteria: Startup, First-stage, Second-stage, Mezzanine, Leveraged Buyout; minority-owned businesses only

Industry Group Preference: Communications, Computer Related, Consumer, Distribution, Electronic Components and Instrumentation, Energy/Natural Resources, Genetic Engineering, Industrial Products and Equipment, Medical/Health Related

Portfolio Companies: not available

Officers, Executives and Principals

Earl F. Hord, Managing General Partner
I.N. Rendall Harper, General Partner
Mark Vernallis, General Partner
Milton A. Washington, General Partner
Gregory W. Ramsey

KEYSTONE VENTURE CAPITAL MANAGEMENT COMPANY

1601 Market Street
Suite 2500
Philadelphia, PA 19103

Telephone: 215-241-1200
Fax: 215-241-1211

Mission: Actively seeking new investments

Fund Size: not available
Founded: 1983
Average Investment: not available
Minimum Investment: $500,000

Investment Criteria: First-stage, Second-stage, Mezzanine, Leveraged Buyout

Industry Group Preference: Communications, Computer Related, Consumer, Distribution, Electronic Components and Instrumentation, Energy/Natural Resources, Genetic Engineering, Industrial Products and Equipment, Medical/Health Related

Portfolio Companies: not available

Officers, Executives and Principals

Kerry Dale, General Partner
Peter E. Liget, General Partner
G. Kenneth Macrae, General Partner
Shanti Kandaswamy, Associate

KINGSBURY ASSOCIATES

3655 Nobel Drive
Suite 490
San Diego, CA 92122

Telephone: 619-677-0600
Fax: 619-677-0800

Mission: Private venture capital firm investing own capital in start-up, early and medium stage ventures

Fund Size: not available
Founded: 1993
Average Investment: not available
Minimum Investment: $250,000; pref. $500,000 - $1 million

Investment Criteria: Startup, First-stage, Second-stage

Geographic Preference: West Coast, California

Industry Group Preference: Biotechnology, Distribution, Genetic Engineering, Industrial Products and Equipment, Medical/Health Related

Portfolio Companies: Amylin, Biosite Diagnostics, Chromagen, CORE, Cytel, Digirad, EDiX, Exos, Grey-Stone, Health Data Sciences, J&J, Novatrix, Prograft, Pyxis, Raytel, Sequana, Transkaryotic Therapies, Inc.

Officers, Executives and Principals

Timothy J. Wollaeger
Education: BA, Economics, Yale; US Navy Officer 1966-1969; MBA, Stanford University
Background: Individual General Partner, Kingsbury; General Manager, Baxter Travenol Laboratories (now Baxter International) Travenol Mexico
Directorships: Amylin Pharmaceuticals, Biosite Diagnostics, Chromagen, Digirad, EDiX, Exos, Novatrix, Pyxis, Raytel

KINSHIP PARTNERS

400 Skokie Boulevard
Suite 265
Northbrook, IL 60062

Telephone: 847-291-1466
Fax: 847-291-1890

Other Office Locations
1900 West Garvey Avenue South
Suite 200
West Covina, CA 91790
Phone 818-962-3562, Fax 818-962-0758

Mission: not available

Fund Size: $20 million
Founded: not available
Average Investment: $500,000
Minimum Investment: not available

Investment Criteria:

Geographic Preference: Southern California, Midwestern United States

Industry Group Preference: Biotechnology, Communications, Computer Related, Consumer Related, High Technology, Medical/Health, Software

Portfolio Companies: Applied Digital Access, Calling Communications, Endgate Technology, NiOptics, Oculon, PCs Compleat, PetCare Superstore, Shaman Pharmaceuticals

Officers, Executives and Principals

Michael I. Block, Managing Director
Education: BS, Accounting, University of Chicago; MS, Taxation, JD, DePaul University
Background: Financial, tax and legal positions, FMC Corporation, Gould Inc., and Shell Oil Co.; Director of Corporate Development, GD Searle

Edward F. Tuck, Managing Director
Education: BS, Electrical Engineering, Missouri School of Mines and Metallurgy
Background: Engineering and Manufacturer, LenKurt (General Telephone and Electronics); Founder, Kebby Microwave; Vice President and Technical Director, ITT

Evangeline H. Rocha, Vice President
Education: AB, Ancient Near Eastern Studies, Brown University
Background: Systems Engineer, IBM

KITTY HAWK CAPITAL

2700 Cottsgate Road
Suite 202
Charlotte, NC 28211

Telephone: 704-362-3909
Fax: 704-362-2774

Mission: A private venture capital firm investing its own capital in rapidly growing private companies located in the Southeastern United States

Fund Size: $50 million
Founded: 1980
Average Investment: $2 million
Minimum Investment: $500,000

Investment Criteria: Seed to Leveraged Buyout

Geographic Preference: Southeastern United States

Industry Group Preference: Diversified

Portfolio Companies: not available

Officers, Executives and Principals

Walter H. Wilkinson, General Partner
Education: BS, North Carolina State University; MBA, Harvard Business School
Background: Associate, North Carolina-based venture capital firm; Founder, Kitty Hawk Capital
Directorships: Chairman of the Board of Governors, National Association of Small Business Investment Companies; Board of Directors, Council for Entrepreneurial Development; Officer, several venture-backed companies

W. Chris Hegele, General Partner
Education: BS, University of North Carolina; MBA, University of North Carolina, Chapel Hill
Background: Arthur Andersen and Co.
Directorships: Numerous venture-backed companies, Board of Metrolina Entrepreneurial Council

Steve Buchanan, General Partner
Education: BS, Finance, Virginia Polytechnic Institute and State University
Background: 20 years general business management experience with over 13 years in the venture capital industry; Allsop Venture Partners; FBS Venture Capital Company

KOBE STEEL USA

1735 Technology Drive
Suite 820
San Jose, CA 95110

Telephone: 408-436-9714
Fax: 408-436-0548

Mission: Making few, if any, new investments

Fund Size: not available
Founded: 1991
Average Investment: not available
Minimum Investment: $500,000

Investment Criteria: First-stage, Second-stage

Industry Group Preference: Electronic Components and Instrumentation

Portfolio Companies: not available

Officers, Executives and Principals

Y. Suguta

KYOCERA INTERNATIONAL, INC.

Corporate Development
8611 Balboa Avenue
San Diego, CA 92123

Telephone: 619-576-2600
Fax: 619-569-9412

Other Office Locations
5-22 Kitainoue-cho
Higashino, Yamashino-ku
Kyoto 607
Japan

Mission: Making few, if any, new investments

Fund Size: not available
Founded: 1979
Average Investment: not available
Minimum Investment: $100,000

Investment Criteria: Second-stage

Industry Group Preference: Communications, Computer Related, Consumer, Distribution, Electronic Components and Instrumentation

Portfolio Companies: not available

Officers, Executives and Principals

Dennis Q. Murphy, Vice President (San Diego)
Arthur N. Nishioka, Assistant General Manager (San Diego)
Tsuyoshi Mano, Manager (Kyoto)

THE LAGACY FUNDS, INC.

1400 34th Street, Northwest
Washington, DC 20007

Telephone: 202-659-1100
Fax: 202-342-7474

Other Office Locations
P.O. Box 30091
Jackson, WY 83001
Phone 307-733-8080

Mission: Actively seeking new investments

Fund Size: not available
Founded: 1989
Average Investment: not available
Minimum Investment: $500,000

Investment Criteria: Mezzanine, Leveraged Buyout, Special Situations, Control-block Purchases, Family Businesses

Industry Group Preference: Communications, Computer Related, Consumer, Distribution, Energy/Natural Resources, Industrial Products and Equipment, Medical/Health Related

Portfolio Companies: not available

Officers, Executives and Principals

Jonathan J. Ledecky, President (Washington)

LAMBDA FUND MANAGEMENT

380 Lexington Avenue
54th Floor
New York, NY 10168

Telephone: 212-682-3454
Fax: 212-682-9231

Mission: not available

Fund Size: $40 million
Founded: not available
Average Investment: $1.5 million
Minimum Investment: not available

Investment Criteria: First-stage to Later-stages

Industry Group Preference: Diversified

Portfolio Companies: not available

Officers, Executives and Principals

Anthony Lamport, General Partner
Education: BA, MBA, Harvard
Directorships: Alinabal, Powertec, Great Southwest Industries, Votan

Richard Dumler, General Partner
Education: BA, Georgetown University; MBA, University of Michigan
Background: Partner, Bessemer Venture Partners; Investment Manager, Bessemer Securities; Private Placement
  Department, Allstate Insurance

LASALLE CAPITAL GROUP, INC.
70 West Madison Street
Suite 5710
Chicago, IL 60602

Telephone: 312-236-7041
Fax: 312-236-0720

Mission: Actively seeking new investments

Fund Size: not available
Founded: 1992
Average Investment: not available
Minimum Investment: $250,000

Investment Criteria: Leveraged Buyout, Special Situations, Turnaround

Industry Group Preference: Consumer, Distribution, Industrial Products and Equipment

Portfolio Companies: Continental Scale Corporation, Bearing Belt and Chain, Inc., Harris and Mallow, Inc., SealRite Windows, Inc., SNE Enterprises Limited Partnership, Belmor Manufacturing Limited Partnership, Wm. E. Wright Limited Partnership, Deflects-Shield Corporation, Copperfield Chimney Supply, Inc., Golf-Mark Limited Partnership, Goode Furniture Companies

Officers, Executives and Principals

Charles S. Meyer, Chairman
Education: BA, Political Economy, Colorado College
Background: Vice President, W.T. Grimm and Co.; Manager with family-owned distribution company
Directorships: Harris and Mallow, Bearing Belt and Chain, Copperfield Chimney Supply, Precision Products, Deflect-Shield, Elm Packaging, Outlook Windows

William V. Glastris, Jr., Principal
Education: BA, Economics, Northwestern University; MM, Northwestern University
Background: Golder, Thoma and Cressey
Directorships: Copperfield Chimney Supply, Deflects-Shield, Elm Packaging, GolfMark

Rocco J. Martino, Principal
Education: BBA, Finance, University of Notre Dame; MBA, Loyola University of Chicago; CPA
Background: Partner, Price Waterhouse
Directorships: Wm. E. Wright, Precision Products Group, Classics International Entertainment

Anthony R. Pesavento
Education: BS, Finance, University of Illinois; MBA, University of Chicago
Background: Principal, Carl Street Partners; Associate, Benedetto, Gartland and Greene, Inc.; Associate, J.P. Morgan and Co., General Electric
Directorships: Cherry Tree Toys, Precision Products Group

LAWRENCE FINANCIAL GROUP

701 Teakwood
P.O. Box 491773
Los Angeles, CA 90049

Telephone: 310-471-4060
Fax: 310-472-3155

Mission: Actively seeking new investments

Fund Size: $80 million
Founded: 1989
Average Investment: $1 million
Minimum Investment: $100,000

Investment Criteria: Second-stage

Industry Group Preference: Communications, Computer Related, Consumer, Distribution, Electronic Components and Instrumentation, Genetic Engineering, Industrial Products and Equipment, Medical/Health Related

Portfolio Companies: Ancor Finance, Austin Financial, Saturn Funding

Officers, Executives and Principals

Larry Hurwitz, Chief Executive Officer
Education: MBA, Harvard
Background: New York Stock Exchange Broker/Dealer
Directorships: Harvard Alumni Association

L. D. CARNEY AND ASSOCIATES, INC.

155 North Market Street
Suite 100
Wichita, KS 67202

Telephone: 316-264-5056
Fax: 316-265-8079

Mission: Making few, if any, new investments

Fund Size: not available
Founded: 1991
Average Investment: not available
Minimum Investment: $100,000

Investment Criteria: Second-stage, Mezzanine, Leveraged Buyout, Special Situations

Industry Group Preference: Distribution, Industrial Products and Equipment, Medical/Health Related

Portfolio Companies: not available

Officers, Executives and Principals

Larry Carney, President

LEASING TECHNOLOGIES INTERNATIONAL, INC.

Soundview Plaza
1266 Main Street
Stamford, CT 06902

Telephone: 203-967-4300
Fax: 203-323-2394

Other Office Locations
10 Liberty Square
Boston, MA, 02109
Phone 617-426-4116, Fax 617-482-6475

Two Clearfield Road
P.O. Box 447
Admore, PA 19003-0447
Phone 610-446-4479, Fax 610-446-3771

51 Argue 110 Blvd., #1
San Francisco, CA 94118
Phone 415-387-1802

2737 Union Street
San Francisco, CA 94123
Phone 415-922-0192, Fax 415-922-0193

Mission: To support the growth and development of early-stage venture-capital-backed companies by providing equipment lease lines (primarily for high technology equipment) and other financial services.

Fund Size: $30 million
Founded: 1983
Average Investment: $400,000
Minimum Investment: $100,000

Investment Criteria: Seed, Startup, First-stage, Second-stage, Mezzanine, Leveraged Buyout

Industry Group Preference: Communications, Computer Related, Consumer, Distribution, Electronic Components and Instrumentation, Genetic Engineering, Industrial Products and Equipment, Medical/Health Related

Portfolio Companies: Confidential

Officers, Executives and Principals

F. Jared Sprole, President and Chief Executive Officer (Stamford)
Education: BA, Yale University
Background: Founder, President, Chief Executive Officer, LTI Ventures Leasing Corporation; Chief Financial Officer, Intech Capital Corporation; Vice President, Bank of Boston
Directorships: LTI Ventures Leasing, Leasing Technologies International, Inc., The Knapp Fund

William I. MacDonald, Senior Vice President (Boston)
Education: BA, Tufts University; Advanced Management School, Harvard University
Background: Senior Vice President, Bank of Boston; Thirty-one years managing NYC Lending Corresponding
  Banking and Banking Services Division

Arnold J.Hoegler, Vice President and Controller (Stamford)
Education: BA, St. John's University; CPA
Background: Founder, LTI Ventures Leasing; Seven years as leasing and financial services manager at KPMG
  Peat Marwick

George A. Parker, Vice President (Stamford)
Education: BA, Wake Forest; MBA, University of North Carolina
Background: Vice President, Finance of DPF Computer Leasing; Second Vice President, Continental Illinois
  Bank; Founder, LTI Ventures Leasing
Directorships: LTI Ventures Leasing, Leasing Technologies International, Inc., Atlantic Computer Funding Cor-
  poration

Robert Simon, Vice President, Technical (Stamford)
Education: BA, City College of New York; MA, Columbia University
Background: Founder, Vice President and Controller, LTI Ventures Leasing; Forty years (beginning with Sperry
  Univac in the 1950s) computer experience

Geoffrey W. Smith, Vice President (Boston)

Keth A. Brinks, Regional Manager (Admore)

THE LEK/ALCAR CONSULTING GROUP, L.P.

12100 Wilshire Boulevard
Suite 1700
Los Angeles, CA 90025

Telephone: 310-442-6500
Fax: 310-207-4210

Other Office Locations
101 Federal Street
Boston, MA 02110
Phone 617-951-9500, Fax 617-951-9392

5215 Old Orchard Road
Suite 600
Skokie, IL 60077-1035

Mission: Making few, if any, new investments

Fund Size: not available
Founded: 1983
Average Investment: not available
Minimum Investment: Less than $100,000

Investment Criteria: Seed, Research and Development, Startup, First-stage

Industry Group Preference: Communications, Computer Related, Consumer, Distribution, Electronic Components and Instrumentation, Energy/Natural Resources, Genetic Engineering, Industrial Products and Eqiupment, Medical/Health Related

Portfolio Companies: not available

Officers, Executives and Principals

Scott Sclecter, Partner (Los Angeles)
Dan Schechter, Vice President (Los Angeles)
Marc Kozin, Vice President (Boston)
Stuart Jackson, Vice President (Skokie)

LEONARD MAUTNER ASSOCIATES

1434 Sixth Street
Suite 10
Santa Monica, CA 90401

Telephone: 310-393-9788

Mission: Reducing investment activity

Fund Size: not available
Founded: 1969
Average Investment: not available
Minimum Investment: $100,000

Investment Criteria: Seed, Startup, First-stage, Special Situations

Industry Group Preference: Communications, Computer Related, Electronic Components and Instrumentation, Industrial Products and Equipment, Medical/Health Related

Portfolio Companies: not available

Officers, Executives and Principals

Leonard Mautner, President
Milton Rosenberg, Associate
Myron Kayton

LEPERCQ CAPITAL MANAGEMENT

1675 Broadway
New York, NY 10019

Telephone: 212-698-0795
Fax: 212-262-0144

Mission: not available

Fund Size: $32 million
Founded: not available
Average Investment: $4.3 million
Minimum Investment: not available

Investment Criteria: Strong Management

Industry Group Preference: Broadcast/Cable/Radio, Communications, Educational, Medical/Health

Portfolio Companies: Children's Discovery Centers of America Inc., Sunrise Preschools Inc., New Century
  Education Corporation, Wescom Broadcasting Group, MNI Group Inc.

Officers, Executives and Principals

Michael J. Connelly, President
Education: BA, Michigan State; JD, Columbia University
Background: Executive Vice President, Foster Management Co.; Partner, Casey Lane and Mittendorf

James I. Griffin, Vice President
Education: BA, Dartmouth University; MBA, Columbia University
Background: Vice-President, E.A. Pollite and Co.

Richard A. Glaser, Vice President
Education: BA, Haverford College; MA, Columbia University
Background: Associate, Merrill Lynch

LEVMARK CAPITAL CORPORATION

175 Memorial Highway
Suite 2-7
New Rochelle, NY 10801

Telephone: 914-654-9410
Fax: 914-654-9425

Other Office Locations
2801 Buford Highway, Northeast
Suite T25
Atlanta, GA 30329
Phone 404-636-9680, Fax 404-636-9698

Mission: Actively seeking new investments

Fund Size: not available
Founded: 1990
Average Investment: not available
Minimum Investment: $1 million

Investment Criteria: Second-stage, Leveraged Buyout, Special Situations

Industry Group Preference: Communications, Consumer, Medical/Health Related, PCS

Portfolio Companies: not available

Officers, Executives and Principals

Leon Wright, Chairman (New Rochelle)
Emma Fluker, Director (Atlanta)
Richard Venegar, Director (Atlanta)
Christina Dunbar, Director (New Rochelle)

LF INTERNATIONAL, INC.

360 Post Street
Suite 705
San Francisco, CA 94108

Telephone: 415-399-0110
Fax: 415-399-9222

Other Office Locations
Lifung Tower, China Hong Kong City
33 Canton Road
Kowloon
Hong Kong
Phone 852-3-736-1111, 852-2-736-1111

Lifung Tower, Eighth Floor
No. 1, Nanking East Road Sec. 4
Taipei
Taiwan
Phone 886-2-712-4523, Fax 886-2-715-3830

12/F - 15/F, Song Am Building
84, Nonhyun-Dong Kangnam-ku
Seoul, Korea
Phone 82-2-3441-6500, Fax 82-2-3443-8999

#13-01104 Comcentre 1 Tower Block
31 Exeter Road
Singapore 239732
Phone 65-738-1887, Fax 65-738-6739

LF Europe, NV
Dreuscamps 12
7822 Meslin L'eveque
Belgium
Phone 32-68-250230, Fax 32-68-552602

Mission: Actively seeking new investments. Core business is to help entrepreneurial companies achieve success by providing equity capital, Asian sourcing expertise, and operational support during their critical growth stage.

Fund Size: not available
Founded: 1982
Average Investment: $1 million
Minimum Investment: $250,000

Investment Criteria: First-stage, Second-stage, Special Situations

Geographic Preference: United States

Industry Group Preference: Consumer, Distribution

Portfolio Companies: Lewis Galoob Toys, Cyrk Inc., Wilke Rodriguez, Body FX, Santana, Ltd., Winco Fireworks, The Millwork Trading Company, Ltd.

Officers, Executives and Principals

Michael Hsieh, Partner (San Francisco)
Victor Fung, Partner (Hong Kong)
William Fung, Partner (Hong Kong)
Harrison Chang, Investment Manager (San Francisco)

LIBERTY BIDCO INVESTMENT CORPORATION

30833 Northwestern Highway
Suite 211
Farmington Hills, MI 48334

Telephone: 810-626-6070
Fax: 810-626-6072

Mission: Actively seeking new investments

Fund Size: not available
Founded: 1988
Average Investment: not available
Minimum Investment: $250,000

Investment Criteria: Second-stage, Mezzanine, Leveraged Buyout, Special Situations

Industry Group Preference: Communications, Computer Related, Consumer, Distribution, Electronic Components and Instrumentation, Industrial Products and Equipment, Medical/Health Related

Portfolio Companies: not available

Officers, Executives and Principals

Pearl Holforty, President
M.J. Hilker, Vice President

LIBERTY ENVIRONMENTAL PARTNERS

220 Montgomery Street
Penthouse 10
San Francisco, CA 94104

Telephone: 415-834-1600
Fax: 415-834-1603

Mission: Actively seeking new investments

Fund Size: not available
Founded: 1993
Average Investment: not available
Minimum Investment: $100,000

Investment Criteria: Startup, First-stage, Second-stage

Industry Group Preference: Consumer, Distribution, Energy/Natural Resources, Industrial Products and Equipment

Portfolio Companies: not available

Officers, Executives and Principals

Tim Woodward, Principal
Donald Hichens, General Partner

LINC CAPITAL PARTNERS, INC.

303 East Wacker Drive
Suite 1000
Chicago, IL 60601

Telephone: 312-946-1000
Fax: 312-938-4290

Mission: Actively seeking new investments

Fund Size: not available
Founded: 1987
Average Investment: $1.2 million
Minimum Investment: $500,000

Investment Criteria: First-stage, Second-stage, Mezzanine, Leveraged Buyout

Geographic Preference: United States

Industry Group Preference: Communications, Hardware, Information Technology, Medical/Health Related, Software

Portfolio Companies: not available

Officers, Executives and Principals

Martin Zimmerman, Chairman
Robert Laing, President
Marc Chabot, Vice President
Mark Zimmerman, Vice President
James LaFeber, Assistant Vice President

LITTLE INVESTMENT COMPANY

33 Broad Street
10th Floor
Boston, MA 02109

Telephone: 617-742-2790
Fax: 617-723-7107

Mission: Actively seeking new investments

Fund Size: not available
Founded: 1992
Average Investment: not available
Minimum Investment: $100,000

Investment Criteria: Leveraged Buyout, Special Situations, Control-block Purchases

Industry Group Preference: Communications, Distribution, Industrial Products and Equipment

Portfolio Companies: not available

Officers, Executives and Principals

Arthur D. Little, Principal

LIVINGSTON CAPITAL, LTD.

191 University Boulevard
Suite 302
Denver, CO 80206

Telephone: 303-329-3033
Fax: 303-329-3226

Other Office Locations
745 Sherman Street
Suite 200
Denver, CO 80203
Phone 303-866-9850

Mission: Actively seeking new investments

Fund Size: not available
Founded: 1988
Average Investment: not available
Minimum Investment: Less than $100,000

Investment Criteria: Startup, First-stage, Second-stage, Leveraged Buyout, Special Situations

Industry Group Preference: Diversified

Portfolio Companies: not available

Officers, Executives and Principals

Gregory Pusey, President

LM CAPITAL CORPORATION

515 North Flagler Drive
Suite 1704
West Palm Beach, FL 33401

Telephone: 561-833-9700
Fax: 561-833-4745

Mission: Actively seeking new investments

Fund Size: not available
Founded: 1988
Average Investment: not available
Minimum Investment: $1 million

Investment Criteria: Leveraged Buyout

Industry Group Preference: Consumer, Distribution, Industrial Products and Equipment, Medical/Health
  Related

Portfolio Companies: not available

Officers, Executives and Principals

Leslie M. Corely, President
Ricardo Corley, Vice President
Armand Batocadi, Vice President

LOEB PARTNERS CORPORATION

61 Broadway
Suite 2450
New York, NY 10006

Telephone: 212-483-7000
Fax: 212-425-7090

Mission: Actively seeking new investments

Fund Size: not available
Founded: 1931
Average Investment: varies widely
Minimum Investment: Less than $100,000

Investment Criteria: Seed, Research and Development, Startup, First-stage, Second-stage, Leveraged Buyout, Special Situations

Industry Group Preference: Communications, Computer Related, Consumer, Distribution, Electronic Components and Instrumentation, Energy/Natural Resources, Genetic Engineering, Industrial Products and Equipment, Medical/Health Related

Portfolio Companies: not available

Officers, Executives and Principals

Thomas L. Kempner, Chairman
Warren D. Bagatelle, Managing Director
Frederick H. Fruitman, Managing Director
Norman N. Mintz, Managing Director
Michael R. Stanfield, Managing Director
Harvey L. Tepner, Managing Director

THE LONGCHAMP GROUP, INC.

730 Fifth Avenue
New York, NY 10019

Telephone: 212-397-8800
Fax: 212-397-8975

Mission: Making few, if any, new investments

Fund Size: not available
Founded: 1982
Average Investment: not available
Minimum Investment: $500,000

Investment Criteria: Second-stage, Mezzanine, Special Situations

Industry Group Preference: Consumer, Distribution

Portfolio Companies: not available

Officers, Executives and Principals

Jean Karoubi, President

LOWE FINANCIAL GROUP, INC.

67 Wall Street
Suite 2411
New York, NY 10005

Telephone: 212-323-7970

Mission: Actively seeking new investments

Fund Size: not available
Founded: 1974
Average Investment: not available
Minimum Investment: $500,000

Investment Criteria: Seed, Startup, First-stage, Second-stage, Special Situations

Industry Group Preference: Communications, Computer Related, Consumer, Distribution, Electronic Components and Instrumentation, Energy/Natural Resources, Industrial Products and Equipment, Medical/Health Related

Portfolio Companies: not available

Officers, Executives and Principals

C.L. Lowe, President

LOYALHANNA VENTURE FUND

P.O. Box 81927
Pittsburgh, PA 15217

Telephone: 412-687-9027
Fax: 412-681-0960

Other Office Locations
P.O. Box 36
Ligonier, PA 15658
Phone 412-928-1440, Fax 412-238-6508

Mission: Making few, if any, new investments

Fund Size: not available
Founded: 1984
Average Investment: not available
Minimum Investment: $250,000

Investment Criteria: First-stage, Second-stage, Mezzanine, Leveraged Buyout

Industry Group Preference: Diversified

Portfolio Companies: not available

Officers, Executives and Principals

James H. Knowles, Jr., General Partner (Pittsburgh and Ligonier)

LRF INVESTMENTS, INC.

Venture Management Consultants
60 Wells Avenue
Newton, MA 02159

Telephone: 617-928-9888
Fax: 617-964-5318

Mission: Making few, if any, new investments

Fund Size: not available
Founded: 1987
Average Investment: not available
Minimum Investment: $250,000

Investment Criteria: Second-stage, Mezzanine, Leveraged Buyout, Special Situations

Industry Group Preference: Computer Related, Consumer, Distribution, Electronic Components and Instrumentation, Energy/Natural Resources, Genetic Engineering, Industrial Products and Equipment, Medical/Health Related

Portfolio Companies: not available

Officers, Executives and Principals

Richard L. Tuck, Partner

LUBAR AND COMPANY

777 East Wisconsin Avenue, Suite 3380
Milwaukee, WI 53202

Telephone: 414-291-9000
Fax: 414-291-9061

Mission: not available

Fund Size: $100 million
Founded: not available
Average Investment: $500,000 - $10 million
Minimum Investment: not available

Investment Criteria: Second-stage to Leveraged Buyout

Industry Group Preference: Diversified

Officers, Executives and Principals

David J. Lubar, President

LUBRIZOL CORPORATION

Corporate Planning and Investment Division
29400 Lakeland Boulevard
Wickliffe, OH 44092

Telephone: 216-943-4200
Fax: 216-943-9093

Mission: To invest in specialty chimical and related equipment

Fund Size: not available
Founded: 1979
Average Investment: not available
Minimum Investment: $500,000

Investment Criteria: Seed, Startup, First-stage, Second-stage, Special Situations

Industry Group Preference: Industrial Products and Equipment

Portfolio Companies: not available

Officers, Executives and Principals

Gregory D. Taylor, Treasurer
David Brisky, Human Resources
C.W. Purcell, Secretary

M AND I VENTURES

770 North Water Street
Milwaukee, WI 53202

Telephone: 800-342-2265
Fax: 414-765-7850

Mission: not available

Fund Size: $75 million
Founded: not available
Average Investment: $1 million
Minimum Investment: not available

Investment Criteria: Startup to Leveraged Buyout

Industry Group Preference: Electronics, Industrial Products, Information Services, Medical/Health

Portfolio Companies: CNR Health, Converter Concepts, Eder Industries, Encore Paper, Florence Eiseman, Gray Soft, Great Lakes Packaging, Jordan Controls, Kelch, Kisco Water Treatment, Merx, Milwaukee Brush Manufacturing, Shade Information, Specialty Coffee Holdings, Superconductivity, Tekra Corporation, U.S. Music Corporation, Wisconsin Porcelain

Officers, Executives and Principals

Thomas G. Smith, Vice President
William G. Krugler, Vice President
Gregory J. Myers, Vice President

M AND F ASSOCIATES, L.P.

45 Rockefeller Plaza
Suite 601
New York, NY 10111

Telephone: 212-332-2929
Fax: 212-332-2920

Mission: Actively seeking new investments

Fund Size: not available
Founded: 1988
Average Investment: not available
Minimum Investment: $1.25 million

Investment Criteria: Leveraged Buyout

Industry Group Preference: Communications, Computer Related, Consumer, Distribution, Electronic Components and Instrumentation, Energy/Natural Resources, Industrial Products and Equipment, Medical/Health Related

Portfolio Companies: not available

Officers, Executives and Principals

John J. Murphy, Jr., Managing Partner
Thomas Keane, Partner
Janet Daly, Partner

MADISON DEARBORN PARTNERS

Three First National Plaza, Suite 1330
Chicago, IL 60602

Telephone: 312-732-5400
Fax: 312-732-4098

Mission: not available

Fund Size: $550 million
Founded: not available
Average Investment: $10 - $50 million
Minimum Investment: not available

Investment Criteria: First-stage to Leveraged Buyout

Industry Group Preference: Broadcast/Cable/Radio, Communications, Consumer Related, Energy/Natural Resources, Industrial Products, Manufacturing/Processing, Medical/Health, Retailing, Service Industries

Portfolio Companies: Acme General, Air and Water Technologies, Airnet Services, Bayou Steel, Bizmart, Buckeye Florida, Dan River, Falcon First Communications, Georgia Marble, Hannover Healthcare, Prime Cable of Alaska, Sports Authority, Tyco Toys, View Master Ideal

Officers, Executives and Principals

John A. Canning, Jr.
Education: AB, Dennison University; JD, Duke University
Background: Executive Vice President, The First National Bank of Chicago; President, First Chicago Venture Capital
Directorships: Bayou Steel, The Interlake Corporation, Northwestern Memorial Corporation, Tyco Toys

Kent P. Dauten
Education: BA, Dartmouth College; MBA, Harvard
Background: Senior Vice President, First Chicago Venture Capital; Management Consultant, Booz, Allen and Hamilton
Directorships: Health Management Associates, Genesis Health Ventures and Southern Food Groups

Paul R. Wood
Education: BS, University of Illinois; MBA, Columbia
Background: First Chicago Venture Capital, Continental Illinois Bank
Directorships: Calumet Holdings, Duo-Tang, Inc., Rail Holdings

Samuel M. Mencoff
Education: AB, Brown; MBA, Harvard
Background: First Chicago Venture Capital, Industrial National Bank
Directorships: Buckeye Cellulose Corporation, Georgia Marble Holding, Golden Oak Mining, Huntway Partners

William J. Hunckler III
Education: BS, Miami University; MM, Northwestern University
Background: First Chicago Venture Capital
Directorships: County Seat Holdings, Western Industries

MAGNOLIA VENTURE CAPITAL CORPORATION

P.O. Box 2749
Jackson, MS 39207

Telephone: 601-352-5201
Fax: 601-355-1804

Mission: Actively seeking new investments

Fund Size: not available
Founded: 1994
Average Investment: not available
Minimum Investment: $250,000

Investment Criteria: Seed, Research and Development, Startup, First-stage, Second-stage

Industry Group Preference: Communications, Computer Related, Consumer, Distribution, Electronic Components and Instrumentation, Energy/Natural Resources, Genetic Engineering, Industrial Products and Equipment, Medical/Health Related

Portfolio Companies: not available

Officers, Executives and Principals

Steve D. Caldwell, Chairman and Chief Executive Officer
Edward I.H. Bennett, Jr., President

MANAGEMENT RESOURCE PARTNERS

181 Second Avenue
Suite 542
San Mateo, CA 94401

Telephone: 415-401-5850
Fax: 415-401-6750

Mission: Actively seeking new investments

Fund Size: not available
Founded: 1981
Average Investment: not available
Minimum Investment: $250,000

Investment Criteria: Leveraged Buyout, Turnaround Buyout

Industry Group Preference: Computer Related, Consumer, Distribution, Electronic Components and Instrumentation, Industrial Products and Equipment, Medical/Health Related

Portfolio Companies: not available

Officers, Executives and Principals

Michael Ramelot, General Partner
John Roberts, General Partner

MANCHESTER HUMPHREYS, INC.

101 Dyer Street
Suite 300
Providence, RI 02903

Telephone: 401-454-0400
Fax: 401-454-0403

Mission: Actively seeking new investment

Fund Size: not available
Founded: 1992
Average Investment: not available
Minimum Investment: $500,000

Investment Criteria: Leveraged Buyout, Expansion Financings

Industry Group Preference: Electronic Components and Instrumentation, Industrial Products and Equipment, Medical/Health Related

Portfolio Companies: not available

Officers, Executives and Principals

Ernest D. Humphreys, Chairman
Robert D. Manchester, President

MANHATTAN VENTURE COMPANY, INC.

340 East 57th Street
New York, NY 10022

Telephone: 212-688-4445
Fax: 212-486-3138

Mission: Manhattan Venture Company is an investment banking firm specializing in arranging mergers, acquisitions and divestitures

Fund Size: not available
Founded: 1968
Average Investment: not available
Minimum Investment: $5 million

Investment Criteria: Startup, First-stage, Second-stage, Mezzanine, Leveraged Buyout

Industry Group Preference: Communications, Computer Related, Consumer, Distribution, Electronic Components and Instrumentation, Industrial Products and Equipment, Medical/Health Related

Portfolio Companies: not available

Officers, Executives and Principals

Maurice Pfursich, President

MARATHON VENTURE PARTNERS

388 Market Street
Suite 900
San Francisco, CA 94111

Telephone: 415-989-1915

Mission: not available

Fund Size: not available
Founded: 1987
Average Investment: not available
Minimum Investment: $100,000

Investment Criteria: Seed, Startup, First-stage, Second-stage, Leveraged Buyout

Industry Group Preference: Communications, Computer Related, Electronic Components and Instrumentation, Genetic Engineering

Portfolio Companies: not available

Officers, Executives and Principals

Thomas J. Bonomo, General Partner

MARKETCORP VENTURE ASSOCIATES, L.P. (MCV)

285 Riverside Avenue
Westport, CT 06880

Telephone: 203-226-2413
Fax: 203-222-6456

Mission: Reducing investment activity

Fund Size: not available
Founded: 1984
Average Investment: not available
Minimum Investment: $250,000

Investment Criteria: First-stage, Second-stage, Mezzanine, Leveraged Buyout

Industry Group Preference: Computer Related, Consumer, Distribution

Portfolio Companies: not available

Officers, Executives and Principals

E. Bulkeley Griswold, General Partner
Stepehen T. Rossetter, General Partner

MARLBOROUGH CAPITAL ADVISORS

399 Boylston Street
Boston, MA 02116

Telephone: 617-578-1722
Fax: 617-421-9631

Mission: Actively seeking new investments

Fund Size: not available
Founded: 1987
Average Investment: $4.5 million
Minimum Investment: $3 million

Investment Criteria: Mezzanine, Leveraged Buyout, Recapitalizations

Geographic Preference: United States

Industry Group Preference: Communications, Consumer, Distribution, Industrial Products and Equipment, Medical/Health Related

Portfolio Companies: not available

Officers, Executives and Principals

Margaret L. Lanoix, General Partner
Gayle M. Slattery, General Partner
Timothy J. Durkin, Partner

MARLEAU, LEMIRE, INC.

One Place Ville-Marie, Suite 3601
Montreal, Quebec H3B 3P2
Canada

Telephone: 514-877-3800
Fax: 514-875-6415

Other Office Locations
150 King Street West
Suite 2400, Box 62
Toronto, Ontario M5H 1J9
Canada
Phone 416-595-5500, Fax 416-595-1487

999 West Hastings Street, Suite 500
Vancouver, British Columbia V6C 2W2
Canada
Phone 604-668-7900, Fax 604-668-7965

793 Washington Street, Suite One
Brookline, MA 02146-2121

Mission: Actively seeking new investments

Fund Size: not available
Founded: 1989
Average Investment: not available
Minimum Investment: $500,000

Investment Criteria: Second-stage, Mezzanine, Leveraged Buyout, Special Situations

Industry Group Preference: Communications, Computer Related, Consumer, Distribution, Electronic Components and Instrumentation, Energy/Natural Resources, Industrial Products and Equipment, Medical/Health Related

Portfolio Companies: not available

Officers, Executives and Principals

Pierre Martin, Vice President, Corporate Finance (Montreal)
Richard Whittall, Vice President, Corporate Finance (Vancouver)
Don McDonald, Associate, Corporate Finance (Toronto)

MARWIT CAPITAL, LLC

180 Newport Center Drive
Suite #200
Newport Beach, CA 92660

Telephone: 714-640-6234
Fax: 714-720-8077

Mission: Marwit Capital is primarily a long-term subordinated debt investor, particularly mezzanine and later-stage. Primary focus is on established companies with a three to five year history of stable cash flow.

Fund Size: $30 million
Founded: 1962
Average Investment: $500,000 - $1 million
Minimum Investment: $250,000

Investment Criteria: Mezzanine, Later-stage

Geographic Preference: United States

Industry Group Preference: Basic Manufacturing, Distribution, Service Sector, Software, Telecommunications

Portfolio Companies: not available

Officers, Executives and Principals

Matthew L. Witte, President, Chief Executive Officer
Chris L. Britt, Principal
Jeffrey P. Schaffer, Vice President

MASSACHUSETTS TECHNOLOGY DEVELOPMENT CORPORATION (MTDC)

148 State Street
Boston, MA 02109

Telephone: 617-723-4920
Fax: 617-723-5983

Mission: Actively seeking new investments

Fund Size: $22.5 million
Founded: 1978
Average Investment: $250,000
Minimum Investment: Less than $100,000

Investment Criteria: Seed, Startup, First-stage, Second-stage

Geographic Preference: Massachusetts only

Industry Group Preference: Communications, Computer Related, Electronic Components and Instrumentation, Energy/Natural Resources, Genetic Engineering, Industrial Products and Equipment, Medical/Health Related

Portfolio Companies: Amcard Systems, College Counsel, GammaGraphX, IMC Systems Group, Invantage, Milestone Systems, Mission Critical Technologies, Veda Design, VenturCom, Augment Systems, PixelVision Technology, Reflection Technology, Vibrint, VST Technology, Cambridge Applied Systems, IVS, MicroE, Triple I Corporation, Tytronics, Endogen, Harvard Medical Corporation, AT/Comm, Concord Communications, Fotec, MultiLink, Voicetek Corporation, Fiber Spar and Tube Company, SelecTech, Sensitech, Specific Surface Corporation, Millitech Corporation

Officers, Executives and Principals

John F. Hodgman, President
Education: BA, magna cum laude, Boston College; University of Virginia Law School

Robert J. Crowley, Executive Vice President
Education: BA, Fairfield University; MBA, Boston College Graduate School of Management

Robert J. Creeden, Vice President
Education: BA, College of the Holy Cross; MBA, Suffolk University

Kathleen F. Birmingham, Associate
Education: BS, University of Notre Dame; MBA, cum laude, Olin Graduate School of Business at Babson College

Mark C.M. Grader, Associate
Education: BA, Tufts University; MA, Fletcher School of Law and Diplomacy at Tufts University; MBA, Harvard Business School

William J. Wilcoxson, Associate
Education: BA, cum laude, St. Lawrence University; MBA, Kellogg Graduate School of Management at Northwestern University

MASSEY BURCH INVESTMENT GROUP

310 25th Avenue North, Suite 103
Nashville, TN 37203

Telephone: 615-329-9448
Fax: 615-329-9237

Mission: not available

Fund Size: $170 million
Founded: not available
Average Investment: $1 million
Minimum Investment: not available

Investment Criteria: Seed to Leveraged Buyout

Geographic Preference: Southeastern, Southwestern United States

Industry Group Preference: Biotechnology, Communications, Computer Related, Consumer Related, Educational, Electronics, Environmental Protection, High Technology, Medical/Health

Portfolio Companies: not available

Officers, Executives and Principals

Donald M. Johnston, President and Chief Operating Officer
Education: BA, Vanderbilt University; MBA, Southern Methodist University
Background: President, InterFirst Bank's Venture Capital and Corporate Finance Group; Executive, First Dallas, Ltd.(London)

Lucious E. Burch III, Chief Executive Officer
Education: BA, University of North Carolina
Background: Commercial Banker, Morgan Guaranty Trust Co. in New York

Frank B. Sheffield, Jr., Vice President and Principal
Education: BA, University of Virginia
Background: Portfolio Management

MATERIA MANAGEMENT ASSOCIATES, L.P.
3435 Carillon Point
Kirkland, WA 98033

Telephone: 206-822-4100
Fax: 206-827-4086
E-mail: MateriaVentures@MSN.com

Mission: Actively seeking new investments in early-stage companies commercializing applications of advanced materials technologies

Fund Size: $18 million capital under management
Founded: 1986
Average Investment: $500,000 - $1 million
Minimum Investment: $250,000

Investment Criteria: Startup, First-stage, Second-stage, Mezzanine

Geographic Preference: United States

Industry Group Preference: Advanced Materials Technology, Industrial Products and Equipment

Portfolio Companies: not available

Officers, Executives and Principals

Clare E. Nordquist, General Partner
Education: BS, Ceramic Engineering, University of Washington; MBA, University of Denver
Background: Prior to Materia, Mr. Nordquist was engaged in a private consulting business focusing on the ceramics industry. 1960-1981 Coors Porcelain Company. Spearheaded ceramic substrates development project. Chairmain of the Board, Group Vice President, Vice President of Marketing and Sales and Plant Manager.
Directorships: Several portfolio company boards, Voix Corporation, Washington Technology Center

MATRIX CAPITAL

The Decotah Building
370 Selby Avenue, Suite 318
St. Paul, MN 55102

Telephone: 612-298-8849
Fax: 612-298-0602

Mission: Actively seeking new investments

Fund Size: not available
Founded: 1992
Average Investment: not available
Minimum Investment: $250,000

Investment Criteria: Research and Development, Startup, First-stage, Second-stage

Industry Group Preference: Electronic Components and Instrumentation, Energy/Natural Resources, Genetic Engineering, Industrial Products and Equipment, Medical/Health Related

Portfolio Companies: not available

Officers, Executives and Principals

George J. Economy
Dennis P. Ferrill

MATRIX CAPITAL MARKETS GROUP, INC.

11 South 12th Street
P.O. Box 1816
Richmond, VA 23218

Telephone: 804-780-0060
Fax: 804-780-0158

Other Office Locations
212 South Tryon Street, Suite 1200
Charlotte, NC 28281
Phone 704-335-0500, Fax 704-335-0098

4400 Silas Creek Parkway
Suite 200
Winston-Salem, NC 27104
Phone 910-768-6608, Fax 910-768-7666

Mission: Actively seeking new investments

Fund Size: not available
Founded: 1988
Average Investment: not available
Minimum Investment: $1 million

Investment Criteria: Second-stage, Mezzanine, Growth Capital

Industry Group Preference: Consumer, Electronic Components and Instrumentation, Manufacturing Concerns, Medical/Health Related

Portfolio Companies: not available

Officers, Executives and Principals

W. John Fedora, Managing Director (Winston-Salem)
Jeffrey G. Moore, President (Richmond)
J. David Carroll, Vice President (Richmond)
William H. Weirich, Principal (Richmond)

MATRIX PARTNERS

1000 Winter Street
Suite 4500
Boston, MA 02154

Telephone: 617-890-2244
Fax: 617-890-2288

Other Office Locations
2500 Sand Hill Road
Suite 113
Menlo Park, CA 94025
Phone 415-854-3131, Fax 415-854-3296

Mission: Actively seeking new investments

Fund Size: $195 million
Founded: 1982
Average Investment: $1 million
Minimum Investment: $500,000

Investment Criteria: Startup, First-stage, Second-stage, Mezzanine, Leveraged Buyout

Industry Group Preference: Communications, Computer Related, Electronic Components and Instrumentation, Genetic Engineering, Medical/Health Related

Portfolio Companies: not available

Officers, Executives and Principals

Timothy A. Barrows, General Partner (Boston)
Paul J. Ferri, General Partner (Boston)
Frederick K. Fluegel, General Partner (Menlo Park)
W. Michael Humphreys, General Partner (Boston)
Andrew Marcuvitz, General Partner (Boston)
Joseph D. Rizzi, General Partner (Menlo Park)
Andrew W. Verhalen, General Partner (Menlo Park)
John C. Boyle, General Partner (Menlo Park)

MATRIX VENTURE FUNDS, INC.

839 North Jefferson Street
Suite 201
Milwaukee, WI 53202

Telephone: 414-220-9483
Fax: 414-228-0070

Mission: Actively seeking investment banking assignments, valuations and mergers and acquisitions work

Fund Size: not available
Founded: 1983
Average Investment: not available
Minimum Investment: $250,000

Investment Criteria: Startup, First-stage, Second-stage, Leveraged Buyout

Geographic Preference: Midwestern United States

Industry Group Preference: Computer Related, Distribution, Electronic Components and Instrumentation, Industrial Products and Equipment, Medical/Health Related

Portfolio Companies: not available

Officers, Executives and Principals

Lawrence J. Kujawski, President
Jonathan V. Goodman, Secretary

MAYFAIR CAPITAL PARTNERS, INC.

158 Mt. Olivet Avenue
Newark, NJ 07114

Telephone: 201-242-6655
Fax: 201-621-2816

Other Office Locations
Energy and Technology Investment Consultants, SA
45, quai Wilson
Ch-1201 Geneva
Switzerland
Phone 41-22-732-2527, Fax 41-22-732-2673

Penick Technologies/Penick Corporation
158 Mount Olivet Avenue
Newark, NJ 07114
Phone 201-621-2802, Fax 201-621-2816

Mission: Actively seeking new investments

Fund Size: not available
Founded: 1980
Average Investment: not available
Minimum Investment: $100,000

Investment Criteria: Mezzanine, Leveraged Buyout, Special Situations

Industry Group Preference: Consumer, Distribution, Electronic Components and Instrumentation, Energy/
 Natural Resources, Genetic Engineering, Industrial Products and Equipment, Medical/Health Related

Portfolio Companies: not available

Officers, Executives and Principals

Aris P. Christoudoulou, PhD, President (Newark)
Bruno Lepinoy, Affiliate (Geneva)

MAYFIELD FUND

2800 Sand Hill Road, Suite 250
Menlo Park, CA 94025

Telephone: 415-854-5560
Fax: 415-854-5712
E-mail: info@mayfield.com

Mission: not available

Fund Size: $700 million
Founded: 1969
Average Investment: $3 million
Minimum Investment: not available

Investment Criteria: Seed to Second-stage

Industry Group Preference: Biotechnology, Communications, Computer Related, Electronics, Environmental Protection, Medical/Health, Service Industries

Portfolio Companies: not available

Officers, Executives and Principals

A. Grant Heidrich III, General Partner
Education: BA, Human Biology, Stanford; MBA, Columbia University
Background: Vice President, Wood River Capital

F. Gibson "Gib" Myers, Jr., General Partner
Education: BS, Engineering, Dartmouth; MBA, Stanford
Background: Marketing Manager, Hewlett-Packard

Michael J. Levinthal, General Partner
Education: BS, MS, Engineering, MBA, Stanford
Background: Partner, New Enterprise Associates

William D. Unger, General Partner
Education: BA, University of Illinois
Background: Founded Positek, executive search firm

Wendell G. Van Auken, General Partner

Kevin A. Fong, General Partner

Yogen K. Dalal, General Partner

Russell C. Hirsch, General Partner, Ph.D., M.D.

Wendy Sawyer Hitton, General Partner

MBA VENTURE GROUP

1004 Olde Towne Road
Suite 102
Irving, TX 75061

Telephone: 972-790-6699
Fax: 972-790-6699

Mission: Actively seeking new investments

Fund Size: not available
Founded: 1990
Average Investment: not available
Minimum Investment: $250,000

Investment Criteria: Seed, Research and Development, Startup, First-stage, Mezzanine, Leveraged Buyout

Industry Group Preference: Communications, Computer Related, Consumer, Distribution, Electronic Components and Instrumentation, Energy/Natural Resources, Genetic Engineering, Industrial Products and Equipment, Medical/Health Related

Portfolio Companies: not available

Officers, Executives and Principals

John L. Mason, President
J.A. Breck, Vice President

MBW MANAGEMENT, INC.

365 South Street
2nd Floor
Morristown, NJ 07960

Telephone: 201-285-5533
Fax: 201-285-5108

Other Office Locations
350 Second Street
Suite Seven
Los Altos, CA 94022
Phone 415-941-2392, Fax 415-941-2865

2929 Plymouth Road
Suite 210
Ann Arbor, MI 48105
Phone 313-747-9401, Fax 313-747-9704

Mission: Making few, if any, new investments

Fund Size: not available
Founded: 1984
Average Investment: not available
Minimum Investment: $250,000

Investment Criteria: Startup, First-stage, Second-stage, Mezzanine, Leveraged Buyout, Special Situations

Industry Group Preference: Communications, Computer Related, Consumer, Distribution, Electronic Components and Instrumentation, Genetic Engineering, Industrial Products and Equipment, Medical/Health Related

Portfolio Companies: not available

Officers, Executives and Principals

Philip E. McCarthy, Managing Director (Morristown)
James R. Weersing, Managing Director (Los Altos)
Ian R.N. Bund, Managing Director (Ann Arbor)
Lawrence A. Brown, Consultant (Los Altos)

McCOWN De LEEUW AND COMPANY

3000 Sand Hill Road
Building Three, Suite 290
Menlo Park, CA 94025-7111

Telephone: 415-854-6000
Fax: 415-854-0853

Other Office Locations
101 East 52nd Street, 31st Floor
New York, NY 10022
Phone 212-355-5500, Fax 212-355-6283

Mission: Actively seeking new investments

Fund Size: not available
Founded: 1983
Average Investment: not available
Minimum Investment: $5 million

Investment Criteria: Leveraged Buyout, Special Situations, Recapitalizations

Industry Group Preference: Consumer, Distribution, Energy/Natural Resources, Industrial Products and Equipment, Medical/Health Related

Portfolio Companies: not available

Officers, Executives and Principals

George E. McCown, Managing Partner (Menlo Park)
Education: BS, Mechanical Engineering, Stanford; MBA, Harvard University
Background: 30 years general management and investment experience; Senior Vice President, Boise Cascade Corporation; President, Boise Cascade Home and Land Corporation, American Research and Development Corporation
Directorships: BMC West Corporation, Graphic Arts Center, Inc., Systems Control, Inc., Thrifty Foods, Inc., Vans, Inc.

David E. De Leeuw, Managing Partner (New York)
Education: BA, History, Lafayette College; MBA, Columbia University
Background: 25 years investment banking and corporate finance, Citibank, W.R. Grace and Co.
Directorships: Nimbus CD International, Inc., DEC International, Inc., DIMAC Corporation, Tiara Motorcoach Co., Papa Gino's, Inc., Vans, Inc., Victoria Mortgage Co., Specialty Paperboard, Inc.

Charles Ayres, Partner (New York)
Education: BA, Economics, Duke University; MBA, Amos Tuck School, Dartmouth College
Background: Founded HMA Investments, Inc.; Lazard Freres and Co., Kidder Peabody and Co.
Directorships: Nimbus CD International, Inc., Tiara Motorcoach Company, Papa Ginos, Inc.

Robert B. Hellman, Partner (Menlo Park)
Education: BA, Economics, Stanford University; MS, Economics, London School of Economics; MBA, Harvard University

Background: Mergers and Acquisitions Department of Farley Industries; Consultant, Bain and Co.
Directorships: Graphic Arts Center, BMC West, Vans, Inc., DIMAC Corporation, Nimbus CD International, Inc.

David E. King, Partner (New York)

Steven A. Zuckerman, Partner (Menlo Park)

Tyler T. Zachem, Principal

Phil B. Collins, Principal

McKEE AND COMPANY

3003 North Central Avenue
Suite 100
Phoenix, AZ 85012

Telephone: 602-954-0333
Fax: 602-266-5774

Mission: Actively seeking new investments

Fund Size: not available
Founded: 1987
Average Investment: not available
Minimum Investment: $1 million

Investment Criteria: Second-stage, Mezzanine, Leveraged Buyout

Industry Group Preference: Communications, Consumer, Distribution, Electronic Components and Instrumentation, Energy/Natural Resources, Genetic Engineering, Industrial Products and Equipment, Medical/Health Related

Portfolio Companies: not available

Officers, Executives and Principals

William B. McKee, Chairman
Gary J. Sherman, President
Jan Charles Koontz, Senior Vice President, Investment Banking
Mark Jazwin, Analyst

MDS HEALTH VENTURES CAPITAL CORPORATION

100 International Boulevard
Etobicoke, Ontario M9W 6J6

Telephone: 416-675-7661
Fax: 416-213-4232

Mission: Actively seeking new investments

Fund Size: $400 million
Founded: 1995
Average Investment: $1.5 million
Minimum Investment: $1 million

Investment Criteria: Seed, Startup, First-stage, Second-stage, Mezzanine

Industry Group Preference: Genetic Engineering, Medical/Health Related

Portfolio Companies: Canadian Medical Discoveries Fund Inc. The Health Care and Biotechnology Venture Fund, MDS Health Ventures Inc., B.C. Life Sciences, L.P., Neuroscience Partners, L.P.

Officers, Executives and Principals

Edward K. Rygiel, President
Richard L. Lockie, Senior Vice President
Michael J. Callaghan, Senior Vice President
Frank Gleeson, Senior Vice President
Keith J. Dorrington, Senior Vice President
Denis Ho, Vice President
Joe Elliott, Vice President
John Connolly, Vice President
R. Paul Gilmor, Vice President
Brian Baker, Director, Finance and Administration
Nitin Kaushal, Senior Investment Manager
Riaz Bandali, Investment Analyst
Michael Cross, Associate Investment Manager

MDS VENTURES PACIFIC, INC.

555 West 8th Avenue
Suite 305
Vancouver, British Columbia V5Z 1C6
Canada

Telephone: 604-872-8464
Fax: 604-872-2977

Mission: Actively seeking new investments

Fund Size: $22 million
Founded: 1994
Average Investment: $1 million
Minimum Investment: $100,000

Investment Criteria: Seed, Research and Development, Startup, First-stage, Second-stage

Geographic Preference: North America, particularly Northwest

Industry Group Preference: Medical/Health Related

Portfolio Companies: AnorMed, Inc., Darwin Molecular Corporation, Micrologix Biotech Corporation, Neuromotion, Inc., Prolinx, Inc., Stressgen Biotechnologies Corporation, Terragen Diversity, Inc., U.V. Systems Technology, Inc.

Officers, Executives and Principals

David Scott, President
Bob Rieder, Vice President

MDT ADVISORS, INC.

125 Cambridge Park Drive
Cambridge, MA 02140

Telephone: 617-234-2200
Fax: 617-234-2210

Mission: not available

Fund Size: $556 million
Founded: not available
Average Investment: $1 million
Minimum Investment: not available

Investment Criteria: First-stage to Leveraged Buyout

Industry Group Preference: Diversified

Portfolio Companies: not available

Officers, Executives and Principals

Schorr Berman, President and Chief Executive Officer
Jay V. Senerchia, Principal
Lawrence Kernan, Principal
Michael E.A. O'Malley, Principal

MED TECH VENTURES

201 Tabor Road
Morris Plains, NJ 07950

Telephone: 201-540-6212
Fax: 201-540-2119

Mission: Actively seeking new investments

Fund Size: $20 million
Founded: 1983
Average Investment: $500,000 - $1 million
Minimum Investment: $250,000

Investment Criteria: Seed to Initial Public Offering; human therapeutic focus; revenues not required

Industry Group Preference: Biotechnology, Genetic Engineering, Medical/Health

Portfolio Companies: not available

Officers, Executives and Principals

Fred G. Weiss, President
Education: BA, University of Pennsylvannia; MBA, University of Chicago
Background: Vice President, Planning, Investment and Development, Warner-Lambert Co.; Vice President, Treasurer, Warner Lambert Co.

Marilyn Hartig, PhD, Vice President

Wendell Wierenga, PhD, Vice President

MEDCORP DEVELOPMENT FUND

464 High Drive
Laguna Beach, CA 92651

Telephone: 714-497-3443
Fax: 714-640-2407

Mission: Making few, if any, new investments

Fund Size: not available
Founded: 1987
Average Investment: not available
Minimum Investment: $250,000

Investment Criteria: Seed, Research and Development, Startup, First-stage, Second-stage

Industry Group Preference: Genetic Engineering, Medical/Health Related

Portfolio Companies: not available

Officers, Executives and Principals

J.D. Glass, Managing Director

MEDIA VENTURE PARTNERS

111 San Pablo Avenue
San Francisco, CA 94127-1535

Telephone: 415-661-3818
Fax: 415-661-2542
E-mail: 7007.6324@compuserve.com

Mission: Actively seeking new investments

Fund Size: not available
Founded: 1994
Average Investment: not available
Minimum Investment: Less than $100,000

Investment Criteria: Seed, Startup, First-stage, Second-stage, Leveraged Buyout, Special Situations, Control-block Purchases

Industry Group Preference: Communications, Computer Related

Portfolio Companies: not available

Officers, Executives and Principals

James H. Gardner, Managing General Partner

MEDIA/COMMUNICATIONS PARTNERS

75 State Street
Suite 2500
Boston, MA 02109

Telephone: 617-345-7200
Fax: 617-345-7201

Mission: Actively seeking new investments

Fund Size: not available
Founded: 1976
Average Investment: not available
Minimum Investment: $5 million

Investment Criteria: Creation of new companies to make a number of sequential acquisitions

Industry Group Preference: Communications

Portfolio Companies: not available

Officers, Executives and Principals

David D. Croll, Managing General Partner
Richard H. Churchill, Jr., General Partner
Stephen F. Gormley, General Partner
James F. Wade, General Partner
Christopher S. Gaffney, General Partner
John G. Hayes, General Partner
Peter H.O. Claudy, Vice President
Mark Evans, Associate

MEDICAL INNOVATION PARTNERS

9900 Bren Road East, Suite 421
Minnetonka, MN 55343

Telephone: 612-931-0154
Fax: 612-931-0003

Mission: not available

Fund Size: $61 million
Founded: not available
Average Investment: $50,000 - $1.5 million
Minimum Investment: not available

Investment Criteria:

Geographic Preference: Minnesota, Upper Midwestern United States

Industry Group Preference: Medical/Health

Portfolio Companies: not available

Officers, Executives and Principals

Timothy I. Maudlin, Partner
Education: BA, St. Olaf College; MA, Management, Northwestern University
Background: Financial Planner, Arthur Andersen and Co., G.D. Searle and Co.

Mark B. Knudson, PhD, Partner
Education: PhD, Physiology and Pharmacology, Faculty Member, Washington School of Medicine

Robert S. Nickoloff, Partner
Education: BA, Wesleyan University; JD, University of Michigan
Background: Corporate Lawyer, 30 years
Directorships: Board of Governors, University of Minnesota Hospital and Clinic; Director, Green Tree Acceptance, Inc., Minnesota

MEDICAL VENTURE HOLDINGS, INC.

World Financial Center
200 Liberty Street
New York, NY 10281

Telephone: 212-667-6045
Fax: 212-667-6047

Mission: Reducing investment activity

Fund Size: $50 million
Founded: 1986
Average Investment: not available
Minimum Investment: $25 million

Investment Criteria: Seed, Startup, First-stage, Second-stage, Mezzanine

Industry Group Preference: Genetic Engineering, Medical/Health Related

Portfolio Companies: Cortex, HBO and Company, O'Classen, Somatogen, Uro Cor, Xenova, Corvita, Gliatech, Hepatix, Integra Med, Kera Vision, La Jolla, Synaptic, Targeted Genetics, Immune Response

Officers, Executives and Principals

Philippe Sommer, Managing Director

MEDMAX VENTURES, L.L.C.

800 Cottage Grove Road
Suite 212
Bloomfield, CT 06002

Telephone: 860-286-2960
Fax: 860-286-9960

Other Office Locations
City Gate, North Building
Ben-Gurion Street
46785 Herzlia
Israel
Phone 972-9-95-1990, Fax 972-9-951-1992

Mission: Actively seeking new investments. To invest in high-tech medically-related Israeli companies, or US companies with a significant Israeli Research and Development component

Fund Size: not available
Founded: 1991
Average Investment: $1.1 million
Minimum Investment: $500,000

Investment Criteria: Seed, Research and Development, Startup, First-stage, Second-stage

Geographic Preference: United States, Israel

Industry Group Preference: Distribution, Genetic Engineering, Medical/Health Related

Portfolio Companies: ESC, Ltd., Haifa, Israel Intelligene, Ltd., Jerusalem TransScan Research and Development, Ltd., Applied Spectral Imaging, Ltd., Migdal Haemek, NeuroMod, Inc.

Officers, Executives and Principals

Halley S. Faust, M.D., Managing Director (Bloomfield)
Education: MD, Jefferson Medical College; MPH, University of Michigan
Background: Significant experience in most business areas of the health care industry
Directorships: ESC, Intelligene, TransScan, Kelson, NeuroMod

Noam Karstaedt, Vice President (Herzlin)
Education: MBA, Stanford University
Background: Consulting and operating experience in start-up and established companies internationally
Directorships: Applied Spectral Imaging, Intelligene, NeuroMod

MEDTECH INTERNATIONAL, INC.

1742 Carriageway
Sugarland, TX 77478

Telephone: 713-980-8474
Fax: 713-980-6343

Mission: Actively seeking new investments

Fund Size: not available
Founded: 1991
Average Investment: not available
Minimum Investment: $100,000

Investment Criteria: Seed, Research and Development, Startup, First-stage, Second-stage, Mezzanine, Leveraged Buyout, Special Situations

Industry Group Preference: Communications, Computer Related, Consumer, Distribution, Electronic Components and Instrumentation, Energy/Natural Resources, Genetic Engineering, Industrial Products and Equipment, Medical/Health Related

Portfolio Companies: not available

Officers, Executives and Principals

Dave Banker, President and Managing Partner
Bill Banker, Partner

MEIER MITCHELL AND COMPANY

Four Orinda Way
Suite 200B
Orinda, CA 94563

Telephone: 510-254-9520
Fax: 510-254-9528

Mission: To provide equipment financing to venture-capital-backed start-ups

Fund Size: Over $80 million
Founded: 1984
Average Investment: not available
Minimum Investment: $500,000

Investment Criteria: Seed, Research and Development, Startup, First-stage, Second-stage, Mezzanine

Industry Group Preference: Biotechnology/Life Sciences, Communications, Computers, Electronic Components and Instrumentation

Portfolio Companies: Actel, Microlinear, Information Storage Devices, Power Integrations, Broadband Technologies, Arris Pharmaceuticals, Neurogen, Nexstar, Viagene

Officers, Executives and Principals

Lee F. Meier, Managing Director
James V. Mitchell, Managing Director
Patricia W. Leicher, Managing Director

THE MELBOURNE GROUP, INC.

1900 South Harbor City Boulevard
Suite 227
Melbourne, FL 32901

Telephone: 407-726-6484

Mission: Actively seeking new investments in order to evaluate and analyze venture projects and arrange private placements

Fund Size: not available
Founded: 1985
Average Investment: $1 million - $5 million
Minimum Investment: $500,000

Investment Criteria: Second-stage

Geographic Preference: United States

Industry Group Preference: Communications, Electronic Components and Instrumentation, Energy/Natural Resources, Genetic Engineering, Industrial Products and Equipment, Medical/Health Related

Portfolio Companies: not available

Officers, Executives and Principals

Stephen Baur, President

MENLO VENTURES

3000 Sand Hill Road, Building #4, Suite 100
Menlo Park, CA 94025

Telephone: 415-854-8540
Fax: 415-854-7059
E-mail: dubose@menlo.ventures.com

Mission: To provide long-term capital and management support to early-stage and emerging growth companies

Fund Size: $710 million
Founded: 1976
Average Investment: $4 million
Minimum Investment: $1 million

Investment Criteria: Seed to Later-stage

Geographic Preference: United States

Industry Group Preference: Biotechnology, Communications, Computer Related, Healthcare Services, Medical Devices, Software

Portfolio Companies: Ascend Communications, Asyst Technologies, Gilead Sciences, UUNet Technologies, InfoSeek, Evolutionary Technologies, HNC Software, Matrix Pharmaceutical, Clarify, Red Brick, EndoVascular Technologies

Officers, Executives and Principals

H. Dubose Montgomery, General Partner
Education: BS, MS, Electrical Engineering, BS, Management Science, MIT; MBA, Harvard
Background: Research, Bell Laboratories

Thomas H. Bredt, General Partner
Education: BS, Science Engineering, University of Michigan; MEE, Electrical Engineering, New York University; Ph.D., Computer Science, Stanford
Background: Senior Vice President and Director, Information Systems Group, Dataquest Inc. Hewlett Packard, Bell Laboratories; Electrical Engineering Faculty, Stanford

Douglas C. Carlisle, General Partner
Education: BS, Electrical Engineering, University of California at Berkeley; JD, MBA, Stanford
Background: Design Engineer, ROLM Corporation

John W. Jarve, General Partner
Education: BS, MS, Electrical Engineering, MIT; MBA, Stanford University
Background: Charles Stark Draper Laboratory at Harvard Medical School, Booz, Allen and Hamilton, Intel Corporation

Michael D. Laufer, M.D., General Partner
Education: BS, Bioengineering, University of Colorado; MD, Stanford University School of Medicine
Background: Medical Director, Emergency Medicine, University of California at San Francisco, Mount Zion Medical Center; Faculty, University of California at San Francisco and Stanford University

Sonja L. Hoel, General Partner
Education: BS, Commerce, University of Virginia; MBA, Harvard University Graduate School of Business
Background: Associate, Edison Venture Fund; Business Development, Symantec Corporation; Investment Analyst, TA Associates

MENTOR CAPITAL PARTNERS, LTD.

P.O. Box 560
Yardley, PA 19067

Telephone: 215-736-8882
Fax: 215-736-8882

Mission: Actively seeking new investments

Fund Size: $12.5 million
Founded: 1994
Average Investment: $500,000 - $750,000
Minimum Investment: $100,000

Investment Criteria: Second-stage, Mezzanine, Leveraged Buyout, Special Situations

Geographic Preference: Mid-Atlantic United States: Pennsylvania, New Jersey, Delaware, Maryland

Industry Group Preference: Communications, Computer Related, Consumer, Distribution, Electronic Components and Instrumentation, Energy/Natural Resources, Industrial Products and Equipment, Medical/Health Related

Portfolio Companies: not available

Officers, Executives and Principals

Edward F. Sager, Jr., President
Education: BSME, Lafayette College; MBA, New York University
Background: 25 years venture capital experience, First Pennsylvania Bank, Sprout Group of Donaldson Lufkin and Jenrette

George P. Stasen, Vice President
Education: BS, MBA, Drexel University
Background: Investment Portfolio Manager; Vice President, President of various companies

MERIDIAN VENTURE PARTNERS

259 Radnor-Chester Road
Radnor, PA 19087-5128

Telephone: 610-254-2999
Fax: 610-254-2996
E-mail: MVPART@lx.netcom.com

Mission: not available

Fund Size: $25 million
Founded: not available
Average Investment: $1 million
Minimum Investment: not available

Geographic Preference: Mid-Atlantic United States

Industry Group Preference: Broadcast/Cable/Radio, Computer Related, Environmental Protection, Financial Services, Medical/Health, Retailing, Software

Portfolio Companies: Nationwide Remittance Centers, Comprehensive Addiction Programs, Vermont Microsystems, Verbex Voice Systems, Soft-Switch, Legal Communication, LoneStar Broadcasting Corporation, Omega Health Systems, Philadelphia Financial Group, The Fairways Group, Mothers Work, Homecare USA

Officers, Executives and Principals

Raymond R. Rafferty, Jr., General Partner
Education: BA, JD, Villanova
Background: Founder, Chairman and Chief Executive Officer, Delaware Valley Venture Group; helped organize Century IV Partners and The Penn Venture
Directorships: Nationwide Remittance Centers, Philadelphia Financial Group, American Guardian Life Assurance Co., Comprehensive

Robert E. Brown, General Partner
Education: Princeton University; JD, MBA, University of Pennsylvania
Background: Delaware Valley Venture Group; Advisory Board, Penn Venture Fund; Consultant, Arthur Andersen

Bernard B. Markey, General Partner
Education: BA, Villa Nova University; J.L. Kellogg Graduate School at Northwestern University
Background: Analyst, U.S. Golf Management, Inc.; Marketing, IBM and Mentor Computer Systems
Directorships: Verbex Voice Systems, HomeCare U.S.A., HTE, Inc., Lonestar Broadcasting

Joseph A. Hawk, Associate
Education: BA, Haverford College
Background: First Fidelity Bank

MESBIC VENTURES HOLDING COMPANY

North Central Plaza One, Suite 710
12655 North Central Expressway
Dallas, TX 75243

Telephone: 972-991-1597
Fax: 972-991-1647
E-mail: mesbic@gan.net

Mission: To provide long-term venture capital to well-managed growing businesses owned and managed by mostly African-American and Hispanic-American company builders

Fund Size: $46 million
Founded: 1970
Average Investment: $500,000
Minimum Investment: $500,000

Investment Criteria: Second-stage, Mezzanine, Buyouts

Geographic Preference: Primarily Southwestern United States, must have at least 51% of revenues within the United States

Industry Group Preference: Aerospace, Automobile, Broadcast, Communications, Contract Manufacturing, Electronics, Engineering Services, Food Manufacturers, Proprietary Products, Specialty Industries

Portfolio Companies: El Dorado Communications, Inc., F.A.C.E. Inc., H-R Industries, Inc. McDonald Technologies International, Inc., Radio One, Inc., Simeus Holdings, Inc.

Officers, Executives and Principals

Donald Lawhorne, President
Education: BBA, MBA
Background: College Teacher, Manufacturing Supervisor, 14 years venture capital experience

Thomas Gerron, Executive Vice President and Chief Financial Officer
Education: BBA
Background: Controller, Management Consulting Firm; 16 years venture capital experience; CPA

Divakar R. Kamath, Executive Vice President
Education: BSME, MS, MBA
Background: Senior Executive, Acquisition Fund; 18 years venture capital experience

Oscar Trevino, Jr., Senior Vice President
Education: BBA, MBA, JD
Background: Consumer and asset-based lending experience, five years venture capital experience

Linda Roach, Senior Vice President
Education: BA, MBA
Background: College Teacher, Corporate Lender, one year venture capital experience

MESIROW PRIVATE EQUITY

350 North Clark Street
Chicago, IL 60610-4796

Telephone: 312-595-6099
Fax: 312-595-6211

Mission: not available

Fund Size: $155 million
Founded: not available
Average Investment: $1 million
Minimum Investment: not available

Investment Criteria: Expansion to Leveraged Buyout

Industry Group Preference: Manufacturing/Processing, Retailing, Service Industries, Wholesaling/Distribution

Portfolio Companies: New West, H and C Holdings, Zentec, Purity, Applicance Control Technology, Azteca Foods, Bell Sports, The Chuckles, U.S. Robotics, Copperfield Chimney Supply, SunMedia, STH, OTI, Red Arrow Products Co.

Officers, Executives and Principals

Daniel P. Howell, Managing Director
Education: BA, Government, Lawrence University; MBA, University of Wisconsin
Background: Investment Officer, MorAmerica Capital Corporation; Vice President, M and I Ventures Corporation
Directorships: AUS, Red Arrow Products Co.

Thomas E. Galuhn, Managing Director
Education: BS, Finance, Notre Dame; MBA, University of Chicago
Background: General Partner, Longworth Ventures; Assistant Vice President, Institutional Venture Capital, First National Bank of Chicago

William P. Sutter Jr., Managing Director and Executive Vice President
Education: BA, Yale University; MBA, Stanford University
Background: Corporate Finance, Smith Barney Harris Upham and Co.
Directorships: Now Products

Mary Kay Hanevold, Investment Analyst

Michael S. Smith, Investment Analyst

METAPOINT PARTNERS

Three Centennial Drive
Peabody, MA 01960

Telephone: 508-531-4444
Fax: 508-531-6662
E-mail: mail@metapoint.com

Mission: Actively seeking new investments

Fund Size: $21 million
Founded: 1988
Average Investment: $2.4 million
Minimum Investment: $1.5 million

Investment Criteria: Leveraged Buyout

Geographic Preference: North America, preferably eastern and central time zones

Industry Group Preference: Industrial Products and Equipment

Portfolio Companies: Universal Protective Packaging, Inc., Marathon Power Technologies Company, Wood Structures, Inc., ATI Global, Inc., NPC, Inc.

Officers, Executives and Principals

E. Paul Casey, Chairman
Keith C. Shaughnessy, President
Stuart I. Mathews, Senior Vice President
Luke McInnis, Vice President

METROPOLITAN CAPITAL CORPORATION

7110 Rainwater Place
Lorton, VA 22079

Telephone: 703-550-8530
Fax: 703-339-0296

Mission: Reducing investment activity

Fund Size: not available
Founded: 1970
Average Investment: not available
Minimum Investment: $100,000

Investment Criteria: Second-stage, Mezzanine

Industry Group Preference: Diversified

Portfolio Companies: not available

Officers, Executives and Principals

J.B. Toomey, President
K.A. Idle, Secretary and Administrator

MIDDLEFIELD CAPITAL FUND

One First Canadian Place, 58th Floor, P.O. Box 192
Toronto, Ontario M5X 1A6
Canada

Telephone: 416-362-8602
Fax: 416-362-7925

Other Office Locations
199 Bishopsgate
London EC2M 3T4
England
Phone 44-171-814-6644, Fax 44-171-600-5050

Mission: Actively seeking new investments

Fund Size: not available
Founded: 1985
Average Investment: not available
Minimum Investment: $3 million

Investment Criteria: Second-stage, Mezzanine, Leveraged Buyout

Geographic Preference: North America, Europe

Industry Group Preference: Communications, Distribution, Electronic Components and Instrumentation, Energy/Natural Resources, Industrial Products and Equipment, Medical/Health Related

Portfolio Companies: not available

Officers, Executives and Principals

Garth Jestley, President and Chief Executive Officer (Toronto)
Sylvia Stinson, Vice President (Toronto)
M.J. Brasseur, Director (Toronto)
P.A. Braaten, Director (London)

MIDDLEWEST VENTURES

201 North Illinois Street
Suite 2240
Indianapolis, IN 46204

Telephone: 317-237-2323
Fax: 317-237-2325

Other Office Locations
2229 Central Park Avenue
Evanston, IL 60201

Mission: To generate high rates of returns for limited partners by investing in early-stage companies in the Midwestern region of the United States

Fund Size: $32 million
Founded: 1985
Average Investment: $1.5 million
Minimum Investment: $500,000

Investment Criteria: Seed, Startup, Early-stage

Geographic Preference: Middle third of United States

Industry Group Preference: Biotechnology, Communications, Computer Related, Electronics, Environmental Protection, Medical/Health, Software

Portfolio Companies: IMPATH, Bioanalytical Systems, First Merchants Acceptance Corporation, Express Shipping Centers

Officers, Executives and Principals

Charles L. Rees, General Partner
Background: Director, Venture Capital Division, Allstate Insurance Company

Thomas A. Hiatt, General Partner
Background: Eli Lilly and Company; Founder, biotechnology company; Director, Fifth Third Bank of Indiana
Directorships: The Fifth Third Bank of Indiana

Marcy H. Shockey, General Partner (Evanston)
Background: Allstate Insurance Company; Leasing, International Banking, Lending, Venture Capital, First Chicago Corporation
Directorships: First Merchants Acceptance Corporation, IMPATH, Inc., LNS Group, Wes-Tech, Inc.

MIDMARK CAPITAL, L.P.

466 Southern Boulevard
Chatham, NJ 07928

Telephone: 201-822-2999
Fax: 201-822-8911

Mission: Actively seeking new investments

Fund Size: not available
Founded: 1989
Average Investment: not available
Minimum Investment: $500,000

Investment Criteria: Leveraged Buyout, Special Situations, Control-block Purchases

Industry Group Preference: Communications, Computer Related, Consumer, Distribution, Electronic Components and Instrumentation, Industrial Products and Equipment, Medical/Health Related

Portfolio Companies: not available

Officers, Executives and Principals

Wayne L. Clevenger, Managing Director
Denis Newman, Managing Director
Joseph R. Robinson, Managing Director

MIDWOOD SECURITIES, INC.

One Battery Park Plaza
26th Floor
New York, NY 10004

Telephone: 212-742-9600
Fax: 212-742-9614

Mission: Actively seeking new investments

Fund Size: not available
Founded: 1988
Average Investment: not available
Minimum Investment: $1 million

Investment Criteria: First-stage, Second-stage, Mezzanine, Leveraged Buyout, Control-block Purchases, Special Public Equity Situations

Industry Group Preference: Communications, Computer Related, Consumer, Distribution, Genetic Engineering, Industrial Products and Equipment, Medical/Health Related

Portfolio Companies: not available

Officers, Executives and Principals

Terry L. March, President and Chief Executive Officer
Park Benjamin, Managing Director
Robert L. Gilbert, Managing Director

MILLER/ZELL VENTURE GROUP

4715 Frederick Drive, Southwest
Atlanta, GA 30336

Telephone: 404-691-7400
Fax: 404-699-2189

Mission: Actively seeking new investments

Fund Size: not available
Founded: 1987
Average Investment: not available
Minimum Investment: $250,000

Investment Criteria: Leveraged Buyout, Special Situations

Industry Group Preference: Consumer

Portfolio Companies: not available

Officers, Executives and Principals

Harmon B. Miller, Chairman
Gary Meyers, Chief Financial Officer and Vice-President

MILLICORP

c/o Millipore Corporation
80 Ashby Road
Bedford, MA 01730

Telephone: 617-533-2209
Fax: 617-533-3162

Mission: not available

Fund Size: not available
Founded: 1985
Average Investment: not available
Minimum Investment: $100,000

Investment Criteria: Startup, First-stage, Second-stage

Industry Group Preference: Diversified

Portfolio Companies: not available

Officers, Executives and Principals

Geoffrey Nunes
Education: AB, LLB
Background: Corporate Law, Mergers and Acquisitions

MIRALTA CAPITAL, INC.
475 Dumont Avenue, Suite 300
Dorval, Quebec H9S 5W2
Canada

Telephone: 514-631-2682

Other Office Locations
250 Bloor Street East, Suite 301
Toronto, Ontario M4W 1E6
Canada
Phone 416-925-4274

Mission: Actively seeking new investments

Fund Size: $75 million
Founded: 1992
Average Investment: $5 million
Minimum Investment: $1 million

Investment Criteria: First-stage, Second-stage, Leveraged Buyout

Industry Group Preference: Communications, Computer Related, Consumer, Electronic Components and Instrumentation, Genetic Engineering, Industrial Products and Equipment, Medical/Health Related

Portfolio Companies: not available

Officers, Executives and Principals

Ronald M. Meade, Chairman
Eric E. Baker, President
Robert Mee, Vice President
Christopher J. Winn, Vice President, Finance

MITCHELL HUTCHINS INSTITUTIONAL INVESTORS

c/o PaineWebber
1285 Avenue of the Americas
15th Floor
New York, NY 10019

Telephone: 212-713-3448
Fax: 212-247-4876

Mission: Actively seeking new investments

Fund Size: not available
Founded: 1980
Average Investment: not available
Minimum Investment: $500,000

Investment Criteria: First-stage, Second-stage, Mezzanine, Leveraged Buyout, Control-block Purchases, Financial Restructurings

Industry Group Preference: Communications, Computer Related, Consumer, Distribution, Electronic Components and Instrumentation, Energy/Natural Resources, Genetic Engineering, Industrial Products and Equipment, Medical/Health Related

Portfolio Companies: not available

Officers, Executives and Principals

Howard W. Geiger, Senior Vice President
Donald P. Spencer, Senior Vice President
Drew J. Guff, Senior Vice President
Jason Huemer, Vice President
Mark Tincher, Managing Director

MK GLOBAL VENTURES

2417 East Bayshore Road, Suite 520
Palo Alto, CA 94303

Telephone: 415-424-0151
Fax: 415-494-2753

Mission: not available

Fund Size: $100 million
Founded: 1987
Average Investment: $2 million
Minimum Investment: not available

Investment Criteria: Startup to Later-stage

Geographic Preference: California, East Coast of United States

Industry Group Preference: Communications, Computer Related, High Technology, Information Services, Software

Portfolio Companies: Proxim, Hypermedia Communications, Spinergy, Semitest, Cross Access, Stratege, Lanquest, NetFrame, Orvox, Action Tech, Asante, General Winevess

Officers, Executives and Principals

Michael D. Kaufman, Managing General Partner
Education: MS, BSME, Polytechnic University of New York
Background: Oak Investment Partners, Xerox

Austin Grose, Chief Financial Officer
Education: MBA, Thunderbird
Background: Arthur Andersen and Co.

Greg Lahann, General Partner
Education: BS, San Jose State
Background: Price Waterhouse

Rigdon Currie, Partner
Education: BS, Georgia Institute of Technology; MBA, Harvard
Background: Xerox

Susan Kaufman, Partner
Education: MA, New York University
Background: Vice President, Save Warmblod and Associates

MONSANTO VENTURE CAPITAL III, INC.

3481 Rider Trail South
St. Louis, MO 63045

Telephone: 314-344-9351
Fax: 314-344-9333

Mission: Actively seeking new investments

Fund Size: not available
Founded: 1988
Average Investment: not available
Minimum Investment: $500,000

Investment Criteria: Startup, First-stage, Second-stage, Mezzanine, Leveraged Buyout, Special Situations

Industry Group Preference: Energy/Natural Resources, Industrial Products and Equipment, Medical/Health Related

Portfolio Companies: not available

Officers, Executives and Principals

Charles R. Eggert, Vice President

MONTGOMERIE, HUCK AND COMPANY

146 Bluenose Drive, P.O. Box 538
Lunenburg, Nova Scotia B0J 2C0
Canada

Telephone: 902-634-7125
Fax: 902-634-7130
E-mail: huck@tallships.istar.ca

Mission: Consultants to growing companies contemplating ventrue fund solicitations in the areas of growth financing, buyout, and acquisition financing.

Fund Size: not available
Founded: 1989
Average Investment: $1 million
Minimum Investment: $500,000

Investment Criteria: First-stage, Second-stage, Mezzanine, Leveraged Buyout, Acquisitions

Geographic Preference: Northeastern United States, Canada

Industry Group Preference: Computer Related, Industrial Products and Equipment

Portfolio Companies: not available

Officers, Executives and Principals

Christopher C. Huck, Managing Director
Laurie J. Fisher, Vice President

MONTGOMERY MEDICAL VENTURES

600 Montgomery Street
San Francisco, CA 94111

Telephone: 415-627-2451
Fax: 415-627-2054

Mission: Making few, if any, new investments

Fund Size: $136 million
Founded: 1984
Average Investment: $500,000
Minimum Investment: not available

Investment Criteria: Seed to First-stage

Industry Group Preference: Biotechnology, Medical/Health

Portfolio Companies: not available

Officers, Executives and Principals

Dr. Stephen J. Sogin, General Partner
Jack Olshansky, General Partner
Stephen Weiss, General Partner
Leslie Huang, Chief Financial Officer
Alan Kittner, Limted Partner
Peter Yorke, Limited Partner

MOORE AND ASSOCIATES

7137 Woodridge Avenue
Oklahoma City, OK 73132

Telephone: 405-842-1010
Fax: 405-842-9981

Mission: Actively seeking new investments

Fund Size: not available
Founded: 1987
Average Investment: not available
Minimum Investment: $500,000

Investment Criteria: Startup, First-stage, Second-stage, Mezzanine, Leveraged Buyout

Industry Group Preference: Communications, Computer Related, Consumer, Distribution, Electronic Components and Instrumentation, Energy/Natural Resources, Genetic Engineering, Industrial Products and Equipment, Medical/Health Related

Portfolio Companies: not available

Officers, Executives and Principals

Guerry L. Moore, Managing Director
C.R. Moore, Analyst

MORGAN KEEGAN MERCHANT BANKING FUND II, L.P.

50 Front Street
20th Floor
Memphis, TN 38103

Telephone: 901-524-4100

Mission: Actively seeking new investments

Fund Size: not available
Founded: not available
Average Investment: not available
Minimum Investment: $500,000

Investment Criteria: Mezzanine

Industry Group Preference: Communications, Computer Related, Consumer, Distribution, Energy/Natural
Resources, Industrial Products and Equipment, Medical/Health Related

Portfolio Companies: not available

Officers, Executives and Principals

Mitch Reese, Managing Director
Brian Hanfenest, Associate

MORGAN STANLEY VENTURE PARTNERS

1221 Avenue of the Americas
33rd Floor
New York, NY 10020

Telephone: 212-762-7900
Fax: 212-762-7951

Other Office Locations
3000 Sand Hill Road
Building Four, Suite 250
Menlo Park, CA 94025
Phone 415-233-2600

Mission: Actively seeking new investments

Fund Size: not available
Founded: 1981
Average Investment: not available
Minimum Investment: $2 million

Investment Criteria: Second-stage, Mezzanine, Leveraged Buyout

Industry Group Preference: Communications, Computer Related, Consumer, Distribution, Electronic Components and Instrumentation, Genetic Engineering, Medical/Health Related

Portfolio Companies: not available

Officers, Executives and Principals

Guy L. de Chazal, General Partner (New York)
Robert J. Loarie, General Partner (Menlo Park)
Andrew Cooper, Vice President (New York)
Scott S. Halsted, Vice President (Menlo Park)
M. Fazle Husain, Associate (New York)
Richard A. Schultz, Associate (New York)
James Norrod, Principal (New York)
Debra Abramovitz, Principal (New York)

MORGENTHALER VENTURES

700 National City Bank Building
Cleveland, OH 44114

Telephone: 216-621-3070
Fax: 216-621-2817

Other Office Locations
2730 Sand Hill Road, #280
Menlo Park, CA 94025
Phone 415-233-7600, Fax 415-233-7606

Mission: not available

Fund Size: $275 million
Founded: 1968
Average Investment: $3 - $5 million
Minimum Investment: $500,000

Investment Criteria: Startup to Leveraged Buyouts, Special Situations

Geographic Preference: United States

Industry Group Preference: Biotechnology, Communications, Hardware, Healthcare Services and Devices, Industrial Products, Information Technology, Software

Portfolio Companies: American Paper, Chrysalis, Censtor, Cytel, ProAir Services, Endgate, Gliatech, NeTpower, Applied Intelligent Systems, Premisys Communications, Perclose, Quick Logic, Ribozyme, Sequana, Vivo Software, Wastequip, Hypres, Inverness Castings Group, ReGenisys, Vical, Centennial Security Holdings, Informix, Medtronic, CardioThoracic Systems, Intrinsa, Molecular Applications Group

Officers, Executives and Principals

David T. Morgenthaler, Managing Partner
Education: BS, MS, Mechanical Engineering, MIT
Background: President and Chairman, National Venture Capital Association; President, Foseco
Directorships: Ribozyme

John D. Lutsi, General Partner
Education: BS, Youngstown State University; MBA, Loyola College
Background: Senior Vice President, Private Investments, Pitcairn Financial Management Group; Vice President Finance, Raymark Corporation, Carborundum Company
Directorships: American Paper, ProAir

Robert C. Bellas, Jr., General Partner
Education: BS, Engineering, U.S. Naval Academy; MBA, Stanford
Background: General Manager, Electronics Products Division of Gulf Oil; Marketing and Management, Acurex Corporation, EMI Therapy Systems
Directorships: Vical, CardioThoracic Systems, Molecular Applications Group

Robert D. Pavey, General Partner
Education: BS, Physics, William and Mary; MS, Metallurgical Engineering, Columbia; MBA, Harvard
Background: President, National Venture Capital Association; Management, Foseco
Directorships: AISI, Chrysalis, Endgate, Gliatech, Intrinsa

Gary J. Morgenthaler, General Partner
Education: BA, Harvard
Background: Founder, Chief Executive Officer, Ingres Corporation; McKinsey and Co.; Tymshare, Inc.; Stanford University
Directorships: Premisys, NeTpower, Molecular Applications Group

Paul S. Brentlinger, Partner
Education: BA, MBA, University of Michigan
Background: Senior Vice President, Corporate Finance, Vice President Corporate Development, Harris Corporation
Directorships: Hypres, Wastequip, Centennial Security Holdings, Inverness Castings Group

Peter G. Taft, Principal
Education: MBA, Harvard University, BA, Amherst College
Background: Corporate Finance Department, McDonald and Company Securities, Inc.
Directorships: American Paper Group, ProAir

G. Gary Shaffer, Partner
Education: BA, Engineering sciences, Dartmouth College; MBA, Stanford
Background: Consultant, Arthur D. Little, Inc.; Marketing Manager, Spectraphysics

Theodore A. Laufik, Chief Financial Officer and Partner
Education: BBA, MBA, Cleveland State University; CPA
Background: CPA and Chief Financial Officer of a real estate development firm; Touche Ross and Company

MOUNTAIN VENTURES, INC.

P.O. Box 1738
London, KY 40743

Telephone: 606-864-5175
Fax: 606-864-5194

Mission: not available

Fund Size: $2 million
Founded: not available
Average Investment: $250,000
Minimum Investment: not available

Investment Criteria: Five to seven years of profitable business

Geographic Preference: Eastern Kentucky

Industry Group Preference: Manufacturing/Processing

Portfolio Companies: not available

Officers, Executives and Principals

L. Ray Moncreif, President and Chief Executive Officer
Education: BS, Accounting, Louisiana Tech University
Background: Chief Executive Officer, Outdoor Venture Corporation; President, Medical Management Corporation; Chief Executive Officer, T.Q. Inc., Sunshine Valley Farms Inc.
Directorships: Outdoor Venture, T.Q. Inc., Manufacturers Services Corporation, Databeam, Sunshine Valley Farms

Elmer Parlier, Vice President, Investments
Education: CPA; BS, Accounting
Background: Chief Financial Officer, Outdoor Venture Corporation
Directorships: Casecrasi Corporation, Cumberland Gap Provision Co.

MST PARTNERS

841 Broadway
Suite 504
New York, NY 10003

Telephone: 212-674-1900
Fax: 212-674-6821

Mission: Actively seeking new investments

Fund Size: not available
Founded: 1989
Average Investment: not available
Minimum Investment: $2 million

Investment Criteria: Leveraged Buyout, Special Situations

Industry Group Preference: Distribution, Electronic Components and Instrumentation, Industrial Products and Equipment, Medical/Health Related

Portfolio Companies: not available

Officers, Executives and Principals

J. Andrew McWethy, Partner
Barry A. Solomon, Partner
Stephan A. Tuttle, Partner

MULTIMEDIA BROADCAST INVESTMENT CORPORATION

1001 Connecticut Avenue, Northwest
Suite 622
Washington, DC 20036-2506

Telephone: 202-293-1166
Fax: 202-293-1181

Mission: Actively seeking new investments

Fund Size: not available
Founded: 1979
Average Investment: not available
Minimum Investment: $100,000

Investment Criteria: Mezzanine, Leveraged Buyout, Special Situations

Geographic Preference: United States

Industry Group Preference: Communications, Computer Related, Distribution

Portfolio Companies: not available

Officers, Executives and Principals

Walter L. Threadgill, President and Chief Executive Officer

MVP VENTURES

45 Milk Street
9th Floor
Boston, MA 02109

Telephone: 617-457-5200
Fax: 617-482-5931

Mission: Actively seeking new investments

Fund Size: $120 million
Founded: 1988
Average Investment: $2 million
Minimum Investment: $500,000

Investment Criteria: Startup, First-stage, Second-stage, Mezzanine, Foreign Market Entry

Industry Group Preference: Communications, Computer Related, Consumer, Electronic Components and Instrumentation, Energy/Natural Resources, Genetic Engineering, Industrial Products and Equipment, Medical/Health Related

Portfolio Companies: not available

Officers, Executives and Principals

John G. Turner, Managing General Partner
Jonathan J. Fleming, General Partner
Michael F. Schiavo, General Partner
Peter A. Schober, General Partner

N. L. DAILEY ASSOCIATES

596 Lake Drive
Suite 702
Guilford, CT 06437

Telephone: 203-457-0090
Fax: 203-457-1755

Mission: To help a team and its leader do new business design and development

Fund Size: not available
Founded: 1986
Average Investment: not available
Minimum Investment: not available

Investment Criteria: Seed, Research and Development, Startup, First-stage, Second-stage

Industry Group Preference: Computer Related, Electronic Components and Instrumentation, Industrial Products and Equipment, Medical/Health Related

Portfolio Companies: not available

Officers, Executives and Principals

Nils L. Dailey, Principal

NAGELVOORT AND COMPANY, INC.

450 Park Avenue
New York, NY 10022-2605

Telephone: 212-308-4400
Fax: 212-308-3939

Mission: Actively seeking new investments

Fund Size: not available
Founded: 1985
Average Investment: $5 million
Minimum Investment: $1 million

Investment Criteria: Leveraged Buyout

Geographic Preference: United States based assets

Industry Group Preference: Consumer, Distribution, Industrial Products and Equipment, Metals Recycling

Portfolio Companies: not available

Officers, Executives and Principals

Terry L. Nagelvoort, Managing Director
Mark A. Nagelvoort, Principal

NASSAU CAPITAL, INC.

22 Chambers Street
Second Floor
Princeton, NJ 08542

Telephone: 609-924-3555
Fax: 609-924-8887

Mission: Actively seeking new investments

Fund Size: not available
Founded: 1994
Average Investment: not available
Minimum Investment: $3 million

Investment Criteria: Second-stage, Mezzanine, Leveraged Buyout, Special Situations

Industry Group Preference: Communications, Computer Related, Consumer, Energy/Natural Resources

Portfolio Companies: not available

Officers, Executives and Principals

Randall A. Hack, President
Robert L. Honstein, Vice President
Loren Busby, Associate

NATIONAL CITY CAPITAL

1965 East Sixth Street
Cleveland, OH 44114

Telephone: 216-575-2491
Fax: 216-575-9965

Mission: not available

Fund Size: $150 million
Founded: 1979
Average Investment: $3.5 million
Minimum Investment: $1 million

Investment Criteria: First-stage to Leveraged Buyout, No Start-ups

Geographic Preference: Midwestern United States

Industry Group Preference: Diversified

Portfolio Companies: not available

Officers, Executives and Principals

William H. Schecter, President and Chairman
Carl E. Baldassarre, Managing Director
Richard J. Martinko, Managing Director
Todd S. McCuaig, Vice President
O. Adam Kimberly, Associate
Christopher P. Dowd, Associate

NATIONAL CORPORATE FINANCE, INC.

2082 Southeast Bristol
Suite 203
Newport Beach, CA 92660

Telephone: 714-756-2006

Mission: Actively seeking new investments

Fund Size: Ample
Founded: 1983
Average Investment: doubles and triples
Minimum Investment: $500,000

Investment Criteria: Leveraged Buyout, Special Situations, Control-block Purchases, Debt Financing, Consolidating Acquisitions, Estate Planning

Industry Group Preference: Communications, Consumer, Distribution, Electronic Components and Instrumentation, Energy/Natural Resources, Industrial Products and Equipment, Medical/Health Related

Portfolio Companies: not available

Officers, Executives and Principals

Steven R. Rabago, President

NATIONAL INVESTMENT MANAGEMENT, INC.

2601 Airport Drive
Suite 210
Torrance, CA 90505

Telephone: 310-791-2622
Fax: 310-791-2619

Mission: Actively seeking new investments

Fund Size: not available
Founded: not available
Average Investment: not available
Minimum Investment: $1 million

Investment Criteria: Leveraged Buyout

Industry Group Preference: Consumer, Distribution, Industrial Products and Equipment, Medical/Health Related

Portfolio Companies: not available

Officers, Executives and Principals

Richard D. Robins, President

NATIONSBANK LEVERAGED CAPITAL GROUP

901 Main Street
66th Floor
Dallas, TX 75202-2911

Telephone: 214-508-0900
Fax: 214-508-0604

Other Office Locations
100 North Tryon Street, 10th Floor
Charlotte, NC 28255
Phone 704-386-8063, Fax 704-386-6432

Mission: Actively seeking new investments

Fund Size: not available
Founded: 1961
Average Investment: not available
Minimum Investment: $1 million

Investment Criteria: Second-stage, Mezzanine, Leveraged Buyout, Special Situations, Expansion, Management Buyouts, Recapitalizations

Industry Group Preference: Communications, Computer Related, Consumer, Distribution, Electronic Components and Instrumentation, Energy/Natural Resources, Genetic Engineering, Industrial Products and Equipment, Medical/Health Related

Portfolio Companies: not available

Officers, Executives and Principals

Chet Walker, Jr., President (Charlotte)
Mike Elliott, Senior Vice President (Charlotte)
Travis Hain, Senior Vice President (Charlotte)
Ann Hayes, Senior Vice President (Charlotte)
Doug Williamson, Senior Vice President (Dallas)
Walker Poole, Senior Vice President (Charlotte)
Trey Sheridan, Senior Vice President (Charlotte)
Scott Colvert, Vice President

NATIVE VENTURE CAPITAL COMPANY, LTD.

10408 124th Street, Suite 505
Edmonton, Alberta T5N 1R5
Canada

Telephone: 403-488-7101
Fax: 403-488-3023

Mission: Actively seeking new investments

Fund Size: not available
Founded: 1981
Average Investment: not available
Minimum Investment: $100,000

Investment Criteria: Seed, Startup, First-stage, Second-stage, Leveraged Buyout

Industry Group Preference: Diversified

Portfolio Companies: not available

Officers, Executives and Principals

Milt Pahl, President and Chief Executive Officer

NATURAL VENTURE PARTNERS, INC.

250 Central Avenue
Needham, MA 02194

Telephone: 617-491-4747
Fax: 617-444-8115

Other Office Locations
1377 Linden Drive
Boulder, CO 80304
Phone 303-449-7047, Fax 303-440-0955

Mission: Actively seeking new investments

Fund Size: not available
Founded: 1993
Average Investment: not available
Minimum Investment: $200,000

Investment Criteria: First-stage, Second-stage, Leveraged Buyout

Industry Group Preference: Consumer, Distribution

Portfolio Companies: not available

Officers, Executives and Principals

Anthony J. Harnett, Chairman (Needham)
Barnet M. Feinblum, President (Boulder)
Vincent V. Fantegrossi, Executive Vice President (Needham)

NATWEST USA CAPITAL CORPORATION

175 Water Street, 25th Floor
New York, NY 10038

Telephone: 212-602-1200
Fax: 212-602-2149

Mission: not available

Fund Size: $20 million
Founded: not available
Average Investment: $1 million
Minimum Investment: not available

Investment Criteria: Second-stage to Buyouts

Industry Group Preference: Broadcast/Cable/Radio, Consumer Related, Electronics, Environmental Protection, Food Services, Industrial Products

Portfolio Companies: not available

Officers, Executives and Principals

Orville G. Aarons, General Manager
David W. Todhunter, Vice President
Phillip Krall, Vice President

NAZEM AND COMPANY

645 Madison Avenue, 12th Floor
New York, NY 10022

Telephone: 212-644-6433
Fax: 212-371-2150

Other Office Locations
3000 Sand Hill Road
Building #2, Suite 205
Menlo Park, CA 94025
Phone 415-854-3110, Fax 415-854-3015

Mission: not available

Fund Size: $150 million
Founded: not available
Average Investment: $1 million
Minimum Investment: not available

Investment Criteria: Seed to Leveraged Buyout

Industry Group Preference: Biotechnology, Communications, Computer Related, Electronics, Environmental Protection, High Technology, Medical/Health, Service Industries

Portfolio Companies: Apollo Computer, Applied Immune Sciences, Cirrus Logic, Genesis Health Ventures, Liposome Technology, Media Vision, Medical Care America, Oxford Health Plans, Republic Health Spectranetics, Ungermann-Bass, Universal Health

Officers, Executives and Principals

Fred F. Nazem, Managing Partner
Education: BS, Biochemistry, Ohio State University; MS, Physical Chemistry, University of Cincinnati; MBA, Columbia
Background: Founder and Manager, Collier Enterprises and Nazem and Lieber; Founder and Chief Executive Officer, GeoCapital Corporation Investment Management

Paul C. Dali, General Partner
Education: BS, University of California
Background: General Partner, 3i Ventures; President and Chief Executive Officer, Regis McKenna; General Manager, Personal Computer Systems Division, Apple Computer

NEEDHAM AND COMPANY, INC.

445 Park Avenue
New York, NY 10022

Telephone: 212-371-8300
Fax: 212-751-1450

Other Office Locations
One Post Office Square
Suite 3710
Boston, MA 02109
Phone 617-457-0900, Fax 617-457-0920

3000 Sand Hill Road
Building Four, Suite 150
Menlo Park, CA 94025
Phone 415-854-9111, Fax 415-854-9853

Mission: Actively seeking new investments. Private equity capital for the expansion of private and smaller public growth companies; liquidity for longer-term shareholders in private and smaller public growth companies; strategic acquisitions and management-led buyouts of growth companies.

Fund Size: $60 million
Founded: 1992
Average Investment: $1.5 million
Minimum Investment: none

Investment Criteria: Mezzanine, Leveraged Buyout, Special Situations

Industry Group Preference: Computer Related, Consumer, Information Systems, Medical Deices, Physician Practice Management, Semiconductors, Specialty retail, Technology, Telecommunications

Portfolio Companies: AITech International, Array Microsystems, Inc., Capital Health Partners, L.P., Cardima, Inc., Carrier Access Corporation, Corsair Communications, Inc., Cutter and Buck, Inc., DAOU Systems, Inc., Digital Arts and Sciences Corporation, Digital Generation Systems, Inc., FED Corp, Galileo Technology, Inc. Integrated Micro Solutions, Inc., Interventional Technologies, Inc., JT Storage, Inc., Lecroy Corporation, Lids Corporation, marketplace Information Systems, Inc., PACE Health Management Systems, Inc., Patient Info-systems, Inc., Pediatric Ventures, Inc., Rise Technology Company, Inc., SeaMED Corporation, Silicon Magic Corporation, Silicon Valley Research, Sourcecom Corporation, Transcell Systems, Inc., U.S. Vision, Inc., Vision Software Tools, WaferScale Integration, Inc. Zydacron, Inc.

Officers, Executives and Principals

George A. Needham, General Partner (New York)
Education: Bucknell University, Stanford Graduate School of Business
Background: Founder, Chairman and Chief Executive Officer, Needham and Company; Managing Director, The First Boston Corporation

John C. Michaelson, Managing General Partner (New York)
Education: Oxford University, Harvard Business School
Background: Associate, The First Boston Corporation

John J. Prior, Jr., Managing Director (New York)
Education: Harvard College, Harvard Business School
Background: Managing Director, Lehman Brothers

Margaret S.C. Johns, Vice President (Boston)
Education: Columbia University School of Engineering and Applied Science, Stanford University, Harvard
  Business School
Background: Member, Technical Staff, Sandia National Laboratories

Jack J. Iacovone, Associate (New York)
Education: Pace University
Background: Certified Public Accountant, KPMG Peat Marwick

Glen W. Albanese, Portfolio Administrator (New York)
Education: Pace University
Background: Certified Public Accountant, PaineWebber Group, Inc.

NEIGHBORHOOD ECONOMIC DEVELOPMENT CORPORATION

1660 L Street Northwest, Suite 308
Washington, DC 20036

Telephone: 202-775-8815
Fax: 202-223-0544

Mission: not available

Fund Size: $10 million
Founded: not available
Average Investment: $250,000
Minimum Investment: not available

Investment Criteria: Positive Cashflow, Net Worth, Tangible Collateral

Geographic Preference: Washington, D.C.

Industry Group Preference: Diversified

Portfolio Companies: not available

Officers, Executives and Principals

Loyd M. Arrington, Jr., President
Education: BA, Economics and Business Administration; MBA, Finance and Business Policy, Stanford University
Background: Chief, Capital Development, U.S. Deptartment of Commerce, Minority Business Development Agency

NELSON CAPITAL CORPORATION

3401 West End Avenue
Suite 300
Nashville, TN 37203

Telephone: 615-292-8787
Fax: 615-385-3150

Mission: Actively seeking new investments

Fund Size: not available
Founded: 1984
Average Investment: not available
Minimum Investment: $500,000

Investment Criteria: First-stage, Second-stage, Mezzanine, Leveraged Buyout

Industry Group Preference: Consumer, Distribution, Industrial Products and Equipment, Medical/Health Related

Portfolio Companies: not available

Officers, Executives and Principals

Edward G. Nelson, President
David M. Wilds, Vice President
John K. Harrington, Vice President
Mary Etta Skeen, Treasurer

NEPA VENTURE FUNDS

125 Goodman Drive
Bethlehem, PA 18015

Telephone: 610-865-6550
Fax: 610-865-6427

Mission: Actively seeking new investments

Fund Size: not available
Founded: 1984
Average Investment: not available
Minimum Investment: $250,000

Investment Criteria: Seed, Research and Development, Startup, First-stage, Second-stage, Leveraged Buyout

Industry Group Preference: Communications, Computer Related, Consumer, Distribution, Electronic Components and Instrumentation, Energy/Natural Resources, Genetic Engineering, Industrial Products and Equipment, Medical/Health Related

Portfolio Companies: not available

Officers, Executives and Principals

Frederick J. Beste III
Glen R. Bressner
Marc F. Benson

NEST VENTURE PARTNERS

3590 North First Street
Suite 200
San Jose, CA 95134

Telephone: 415-493-0921
Fax: 415-857-0900

Mission: Actively seeking new investments

Fund Size: not available
Founded: 1983
Average Investment: not available
Minimum Investment: Less than $100,000

Investment Criteria: Seed, Startup, First-stage, Leveraged Buyout

Industry Group Preference: Communications, Computer Related, Consumer, Distribution, Electronic Components and Instrumentation, Energy/Natural Resources, Genetic Engineering, Industrial Products and Equipment, Medical/Health Related

Portfolio Companies: not available

Officers, Executives and Principals

Gary W. Almond, General Partner
Joe D. Diulie, General Partner

NEW BUSINESS CAPITAL FUND, LTD.

5805 Torreon, Northeast
Albuquerque, NM 87109

Telephone: 505-822-8445

Mission: Making few, if any, new investments

Fund Size: not available
Founded: 1987
Average Investment: not available
Minimum Investment: Less than $100,000

Investment Criteria: Seed, Startup, First-stage

Industry Group Preference: Communications, Computer Related, Consumer, Distribution, Electronic Components and Instrumentation, Energy/Natural Resources, Genetic Engineering, Industrial Products and Equipment, Medical/Health Related

Portfolio Companies: not available

Officers, Executives and Principals

Paul N. Vosburgh, President
Robert H. Rea, Vice President
Jane Vosburgh

NEW ENGLAND PARTNERS

One Boston Place
Suite 2100
Boston, MA 02108

Telephone: 617-624-8400
Fax: 617-624-8999

Mission: Actively seeking new investments

Fund Size: $25 million (New England Growth Fund I), $75 million (New England Growth Fund II)
Founded: 1992
Average Investment: $2 - $6 million
Minimum Investment: $1 million

Investment Criteria: Mezzanine, Leveraged Buyout

Geographic Preference: East Coast of the United States

Industry Group Preference: Consumer, Distribution, Electronic Components and Instrumentation, Industrial Products and Equipment, Medical/Health Related

Portfolio Companies: not available

Officers, Executives and Principals

Robert J. Hanks, Principal
Edwin Snape, Principal
John F. Rousseau, Jr.

NEW ENTERPRISE ASSOCIATES

1119 St. Paul Street
Baltimore, MD 21202

Telephone: 410-244-0115
Fax: 410-752-7721

Other Office Locations
2490 Sand Hill Road, #4-235
Menlo Park, CA 94025
Phone 415-854-9499, Fax 415-854-9397

Mission: Invest in and help grow innovative companies developing products/services of genuine value and with real profit potential

Fund Size: $1 billion
Founded: 1977
Average Investment: $1 - $6 million
Minimum Investment: $100,000

Investment Criteria: Seed, Early-stage through Mezzanine

Industry Group Preference: Biotechnology, Communications, Computer Related, Electronics, Healthcare Services, High Technology, Information Services and Products, Medical and Life Sciences, Software

Portfolio Companies: Acoustic Imaging, AMERICAID, AMISYS, Ascend, Autoimmune, AUNET, Be, Cardima, CardioThoracic, Cybermedia, GelTex, HealthSouth, Integrated Health, MedPartners, MedicaLogic, Neopath, Opta, Progress Software, QuickLogic, Sherpa, Silicon Graphics, Trilogy Development, Tripod, UUNET, Vitesse, Zymark

Officers, Executives and Principals

Peter Barris, General Partner
Education: MBA, Dartmouth; BSEE, Northwestern University
Background: President and Chief Executive Officer, LEGENT; Senior Vice President and General Manager, UCCEL; Vice President and General Manager, GE Information Services
Directorships: AMISYS, AUNET, Evolutionary Technologies, NetStart, PathNet, Tripod

Nancy L. Dorman, Administrative General Partner
Education: MBA, Loyola College; BA, Political Science, University of Maryland
Background: Domestic Policy Staff of the White House (Carter Administration)

Arthur J. Marks, General Partner
Education: MBA, Harvard Business School; BS, University of Michigan
Background: President, Software Products Operation, GE Information Services; General Manager, X-Ray Products Department, GE Medical Systems
Directorships: AMISYS, Biztravel.com, Business Matters, ESSENCE, Netrix, Object Design, Platinum Software, Progress Software, Trilogy Development, Windata

John M. Nehra, General Partner
Education: BA, University of Michigan
Background: Managing Director, Alex Brown and Sons, Inc.

Directorships: American Day Behavioral Health Systems, Bridge Medical, EndoMatrix, ExploraMed, Health Cost Controls, Iotek, Network Management Services, Optical Sensors, Summit Medical, Transfusion Technology, Vivra

Charles W. Newhall III, General Partner
Education: MBA, Harvard Business School; BA, University of Pennsylvania
Background: Vice President, T. Rowe Price and Associates
Directorships: AMERICAID, American Day Behavioral Health Systems, Arcon, CSTI, ElderHealth, HealthSouth, Integrated Health, MedPartners, Opta, Sensors for Science and Medicine

Nora Zietz, Partner
Education: MBA, Southern Methodist University; MS, North Texas State University; BA, Columbia
Background: Technology Analyst, Eppler, Guerin and Turner
Directorships: Tripod

Stewart Alsop, Partner (Menlo Park)
Education: BS, Occidental College
Background: Executive Vice President, InfoWorld Publishing Company; Founder, Industry Publishing Company
Directorships: Portole Communications

Ronald H. Kase, General Partner (Menlo Park)
Education: MBA, University of Chicago; BS, Purdue University
Background: Berkley International, Eastman Kodak Company, Advanced Micro Devices
Directorships: Endocardial Solutions, EndoMatrix, ExploraMed/TransVascular, MedicaLogic, Pacific Dental Benefits, Presidio Systems, Primary Health

C. Richard Kramlich, General Partner (Menlo Park)
Education: MBA, Harvard University; BS, Northwestern University
Background: General Partner, Arthur Rock and Associates; Executive Vice President, Gardner and Preston Moss
Directorships: Ascend Communications, Com21, Graphix Zone, InfoGear, Juniper, Lumisys, Macromedia, NeoPath, Netsolve, Sherpa, Silicon Graphics, SyQuest, Verticom, Visual EDGE, Voysys

Thomas C. McConnell, General Partner (Menlo Park)
Education: MBA, Stanford University School of Business; BA, Dartmouth University
Background: Apple Computer Corporation, The Boston Consulting Group
Directorships: Applied Imaging, Bridge Medical, CardioThoracic Systems, Conceptus, EndoTex, Innovasive Devices, Sequana Therapeutics, Single Chip Systems

Peter T. Morris, General Partner (Menlo Park)
Education: MBA, Stanford University School of Business; BSEE, Stanford University
Background: General Manager, Telebit Corporation
Directorships: Advanced Telecommunications Modules, AUNET, Berkeley Networking, CyberMedia, Gadzoox, Packeteer

Mark W. Perry, General Partner (Menlo Park)
Education: MBA, Harvard Business School; BA, Amherst College
Background: Vice Chairman/Executive Vice President/Chief Executive Officer, Silicon Graphics; Executive Vice President/Chief Operating Officer, Sonoma Vineyards; Partner, Arthur Young and Company
Directorships: Arbor Software, AVIRNEX Communications, Be, BigBook, Cogit, Exabyte Corporation, Warp Speed

NEW VENTURE CAPITAL CORPORATION OF MARYLAND

11214 Whisperwood Lane
Rockville, MD 20852-2003

Telephone: 301-897-2003
Fax: 301-897-2005

Mission: Making few, if any, new investments

Fund Size: not available
Founded: 1981
Average Investment: not available
Minimum Investment: Less than $100,000

Investment Criteria: Seed, Startup, First-stage

Industry Group Preference: Communications, Computer Related, Consumer, Energy/Natural Resources, Industrial Products and Equipment, Medical/Health Related

Portfolio Companies: not available

Officers, Executives and Principals

Lewis A. Rivlin, Chairman and Chief Executive Officer
Dianne M. Farrington, Vice-President and Corporate Secretary

NEW VENTURE RESOURCES

5875 Lehman Drive
Suite 201C
Colorado Springs, CO 80918

Telephone: 719-598-9272

Mission: Actively seeking new investments

Fund Size: not available
Founded: not available
Average Investment: not available
Minimum Investment: Less than $100,000

Investment Criteria: Seed, Startup

Industry Group Preference: Computer Related, Distribution, Electronic Components and Instrumentation, Genetic Engineering, Industrial Products and Equipment, Medical/Health Related

Portfolio Companies: not available

Officers, Executives and Principals

Richard L. Petritz, Principal
Jeffrey M. Cooper, Principal

NEWBURY VENTURES

505 Sansome Street
15th Floor
San Francisco, CA 94111

Telephone: 415-296-7408
Fax: 415-788-0647

Other Office Locations
Oxton Israel Capital, Ltd
50 Dizengoff Street
Top Tower, 23rd Floor
Tel Aviv 64332
Israel
Phone 972-3-531-3333, Fax 972-3-531-3322

Mission: Actively seeking new investments

Fund Size: not available
Founded: 1992
Average Investment: not available
Minimum Investment: $250,000

Investment Criteria: Startup, First-stage, Second-stage, Mezzanine, Leveraged Buyout

Industry Group Preference: Communications, Computer Related, Electronic Components and Instrumentation, Energy/Natural Resources, Genetic Engineering, Industrial Products and Equipment, Medical/Health Related

Portfolio Companies: not available

Officers, Executives and Principals

Bruce J. Bauer, General Partner (San Francisco)
Michael W. Loughry, General Partner (San Francisco)
Jay B. Morrison, General Partner (San Francisco)
Ygal I. Ozechov, General Partner (San Francisco)
Erel Margalit, Partner (Tel Aviv)

NEWBURY, PIRET AND COMPANY, INC.

One Boston Place
26th Floor
Boston, MA 02108

Telephone: 617-367-7300
Fax: 617-367-7301

Mission: We are an investment banking firm that raises capital in the form of equity, subordinated debt, corporate partnerships, and technology transfer

Fund Size: not available
Founded: 1981
Average Investment: not available
Minimum Investment: $3 million

Investment Criteria: Mezzanine, Leveraged Buyout, Special Situations

Industry Group Preference: Biotechnology, Communications, Computer Related, Drugs, Electronic Components and Instrumentation, Energy/Natural Resources, Environmental, Genetics, Life Sciences, Medical/Health Related, Pharmaceutical, Waste Management

Portfolio Companies: not available

Officers, Executives and Principals

Hugh Taylor, Managing Director

Mr. William J. Kridel, Jr., Director

Marguerite A. Piret, President
Education: AB, Radcliffe College, Harvard University; MBA, Harvard
Background: President and Founder, Newbury, Piret and Co.; Managing Director, Kridel Securities Corporation; Commercial Loan Officer, Fleet Bank
Directorships: Biosafe, Inc.

John F. O'Brien, Managing Director

Laura Montgomery, Vice President

Dr. John Piret, Director of Research

NIPPON ENTERPRISE DEVELOPMENT CORPORATION

540 Cowper Street
Suite 200
Palo Alto, CA 94301

Telephone: 415-854-8760
Fax: 415-462-9379

Other Office Locations
H.Q. JBP Oval 3F
52-2 5-chome Jingumae
Shibuya-ku, Tokyo 150
Japan
Phone 81-3-3797-9559, Fax 81-3-3797-9589

Mission: Actively seeking new investments

Fund Size: not available
Founded: 1989
Average Investment: not available
Minimum Investment: $250,000

Investment Criteria: First-stage, Second-stage, Mezzanine

Industry Group Preference: Communications, Computer Related, Distribution, Electronic Components and Instrumentation, Genetic Engineering, Medical/Health Related

Portfolio Companies: not available

Officers, Executives and Principals

Jun Hosoya
Akira Minakuchi
Tyee Harpster

NOBLE VENTURES INTERNATIONAL, INC.

1693 Noble Drive
Atlanta, GA 30306

Telephone: 404-364-2345
Fax: 404-892-5743

Mission: Actively seeking new investments

Fund Size: not available
Founded: 1989
Average Investment: not available
Minimum Investment: $250,000

Investment Criteria: First-stage, Second-stage, Mezzanine, Leveraged Buyout

Industry Group Preference: Communications, Computer Related, Distribution, Energy/Natural Resources, Industrial Products and Equipment, Medical/Health Related

Portfolio Companies: not available

Officers, Executives and Principals

John J. Huntz, Managing Partner

NORO-MOSELEY PARTNERS

9 North Parkway Square
4200 Northside Parkway Northwest
Atlanta, GA 30327

Telephone: 404-233-1966
Fax: 404-239-9280

Mission: not available

Fund Size: $100 million
Founded: 1983
Average Investment: $1 million
Minimum Investment: not available

Investment Criteria: Startup to Leveraged Buyout

Geographic Preference: Southeastern United States

Industry Group Preference: Diversified

Portfolio Companies: not available

Officers, Executives and Principals

Charles D. Moseley Jr., General Partner
Education: BS, Industrial Engineering, MBA, Harvard
Background: Senior Vice President and Director, Robinson-Humphrey Co., Inc., acquired by American
  Express; Director, Corporate Finance Deptartment, American Express

Jack R. Kelly, Jr., General Partner
Education: BS, Physics, Georgia State; Program for Management Development, Harvard Business School
Background: Executive Vice President, Chief Executive Officer and Director, Scientific-Atlanta

Russell R. French, General Partner
Education: BA, Emory University; JD, University of Virginia
Background: Lawyer, King and Spalding, clients included: Coca-Cola Co., Georgia Pacific, Tun Trust, Bell-
  South and Emory University

Charles A. Johnson, General Partner
Education: BA, Duke University
Backgound: Co-Founder, Chief Exeuctive Officer, Sales Technologies, Inc.; Management Consultant, McKin-
  sey and Company; Sales/Marketing, Procter and Gamble

NORTH AMERICA INVESTMENT CORPORATION

Mercantile Plaza
Suite 813
Hato Rey, Puerto Rico 00919

Telephone: 787-754-6177
Fax: 787-754-6181

Mission: Actively seeking new investments

Fund Size: not available
Founded: not available
Average Investment: not available
Minimum Investment: $100,000

Investment Criteria: Second-stage

Industry Group Preference: Consumer, Distribution, Medical/Health Related

Portfolio Companies: not available

Officers, Executives and Principals

Rita V. de Fajardo
Zoe Blasini
Zulma Vilella de Lopez
Fiori Vilella
Carlos Lopez
Manuel A. Moreda

NORTH AMERICAN BUSINESS DEVELOPMENT COMPANIES, L.L.C.

135 South LaSalle Street
Suite 4000
Chicago, IL 60603

Telephone: 312-332-4950
Fax: 312-332-1540

Other Office Locations
312 S.E. 17th Street, Suite 300
Fort Lauderdale, FL 33316
Phone 954-463-0681, Fax 954-527-0904

Mission: Manager of North American Funds, equity-capital partnerships that specialize in acquiring or purchasing controlling interests in profitable small businesses ($5 - $35 million in annual revenues) with significant untapped growth potential. Limited partner investors in the Funds are a small, select group of major institutional investors. Actively seeking new investments.

Fund Size: $115 million
Founded: 1989
Average Investment: $5 - $10 million
Minimum Investment: $2 million

Investment Criteria: Buyouts

Geographic Preference: Preferably Midwestern or Southeastern United States

Industry Group Preference: Diversified

Portfolio Companies: ACR Electronics, Minnesota Educational Computing Corporation, Gateway Healthcare Corporation, AMTEC Precision Products, Inc., J&B Foods Corporation

Officers, Executives and Principals

Charles L. Palmer, President (Fort Lauderdale)
Robert L. Underwood, Executive Vice President (Chicago)
R. David Bergonia, Executive Vice President (Chicago)
Patrick A. McGivney, Vice President (Chicago)
Craig Dougherty, Principal (Chicago)

NORTH AMERICAN CAPITAL CORPORATION

510 Broad Hollow Road
Suite 205
Melville, NY 11747

Telephone: 516-752-9600
Fax: 516-752-9618

Mission: Actively seeking new investments

Fund Size: not available
Founded: 1976
Average Investment: not available
Minimum Investment: $1 million

Investment Criteria: Second-stage, Mezzanine, Leveraged Buyout

Industry Group Preference: Diversified

Portfolio Companies: not available

Officers, Executives and Principals

Stanley P. Roth, Chairman
William G. Davis, Managing Director
Don W. Fleischauer, Chief Financial Officer
Kipp Gosewehr, Executive Vice President
Ira L. Weinberg, Executive Vice President
Steven W. Roth, Senior Vice President

NORTH ATLANTIC CAPITAL CORPORATION

70 Center Street
Portland, ME 04101

Telephone: 207-772-4470
Fax: 207-772-3257
E-mail: info@northatlanticcapital.com

Other Office Locations
76 St. Paul Street, Suite 600
Burlington, VT 05401
Phone 802-658-7820, Fax 802-658-5757

Mission: Actively seeking new investments

Fund Size: $65 million
Founded: 1986
Average Investment: $1.5 million
Minimum Investment: $500,000

Investment Criteria: First-stage, Second-stage, Mezzanine, Leveraged Buyout

Geographic Preference: Northern New England area of the United States

Industry Group Preference: Communications, Computer Related, Consumer, Distribution, Electronic Components and Instrumentation, Energy/Natural Resources, Genetic Engineering, Industrial Products and Equipment, Medical Health Related

Portfolio Companies: not available

Officers, Executives and Principals

David M. Coit, President (Portland)
G. Clyton Kyle, Vice President (Portland)
Gregory B. Peters, Vice President (Burlington)
Albert W. Coffrin III, Vice President (Portland)

NORTH BRIDGE VENTURE PARTNERS

404 Wyman Street
Suite 365
Waltham, MA 02154

Telephone: 617-290-0004
Fax: 617-290-0999

Mission: Actively seeking new investments

Fund Size: not available
Founded: 1994
Average Investment: not available
Minimum Investment: No minimum

Investment Criteria: Seed, Research and Development, Startup, First-stage

Industry Group Preference: Communications, Computer Related, Distribution, Electronic Components and Instrumentation, Genetic Engineering, Medical/Health Related

Portfolio Companies: not available

Officers, Executives and Principals

Edward Anderson, General Partner
Richard D'Amore, General Partner
Robert Walkingshaw, General Partner
William Geary, General Partner

THE NORTH CAROLINA ENTERPRISE FUND

3600 Glenwood Avenue, Suite 107
Raleigh, NC 27612

Telephone: 919-781-2691
Fax: 919-783-9195

Mission: Private, for-profit fund soliciting quality venture capital investment opportunities

Fund Size: $23 million
Founded: 1989
Average Investment: $1 million
Minimum Investment: $500,000

Investment Criteria: Startup to Leveraged Buyout

Geographic Preference: North Carolina

Industry Group Preference: Biotechnology, Communications, Computer Related, Consumer Related, Electronics, Environmental Protection, Financial Services, Industrial Products, Insurance, Manufacturing/Processing, Medical/Health, Software, Transportation, Wholesaling/Distribution

Portfolio Companies: BroadBand Technologies, Inc., Concept Fabrics, Inc., Encelle, Inc., EnSys Environmental Products, Inc., Genesis North Carolina, Inc., Global Software, Inc., Investment Mortgage Corporation, Microcosm Technologies, Inc., PCX Corporation, RF Micro Devices, Inc., Rostra Precision Controls, Inc., SELEE Corporation, Southern Assisted Living, Inc., Sphinx Pharmaceuticals

Officers, Executives and Principals

Charles T. Closson, Chief Executive Officer and President
Joseph A. Veil, Vice President, Investments
Nancy P. Owens, Vice President and Chief Financial Officer

NORTH RIVERSIDE VENTURE GROUP

50 Technology Park/Atlanta
Norcross, GA 30092

Telephone: 404-446-5556
Fax: 404-446-8627

Mission: Making few, if any, new investments

Fund Size: not available
Founded: 1984
Average Investment: not available
Minimum Investment: $250,000

Investment Criteria: Second-stage, Mezzanine, Leveraged Buyout, Special Situations

Industry Group Preference: Consumer, Distribution

Portfolio Companies: not available

Officers, Executives and Principals

Thomas R. Barry, President
Pelham Wilder III, Vice President
Kimberly B. Casey, Controller

NORTH TEXAS MESBIC, INC.

12770 Coit Road
Suite 240
Dallas, TX 75251-1316

Telephone: 972-991-8060
Fax: 972-991-8061

Mission: Actively seeking new investments

Fund Size: not available
Founded: 1991
Average Investment: not available
Minimum Investment: Less than $100,000

Investment Criteria: Second-stage, Mezzanine

Industry Group Preference: Diversified

Portfolio Companies: not available

Officers, Executives and Principals

Allan M. Lee, President

NORTHEAST VENTURES

One State Street
Suite 1720
Hartford, CT 06103

Telephone: 860-547-1414
Fax: 860-246-8755

Mission: Actively seeking new investments

Fund Size: not available
Founded: 1989
Average Investment: not available
Minimum Investment: Over $1 million

Investment Criteria: Secondaries of Direct Investment Portfolios

Industry Group Preference: Communications, Computer Related, Electronic Components and Instrumentation, Energy/Natural Resources, Genetic Engineering, Industrial Products and Equipment, Medical/Health Related

Portfolio Companies: not available

Officers, Executives and Principals

Edgar O. Cheney, Jr., Partner
W. Bryan Satterlee, Partner

NORTHEAST VENTURES CORPORATION

802 Alworth Building
Duluth, MN 55802

Telephone: 218-722-9915
Fax: 218-722-9871
E-mail: ventures@skypoint.com

Mission: Northeast Ventures is a venture capital firm focusing its investment activity primarily in the seven counties of northeastern Minnesota. Northeast Ventures invests in both new and expanding businesses, and will consider investments in a wide range of industries. The amount and terms of its investments are based on the specific needs of the business, though all investments will include some equity component, and typical initial investments tend to range from $150,000 to $350,000. For larger financing requirements, Northeast Ventures will assemble both additional investors, as well as appropriate sources of debt, for a complete financial package.

Fund Size: $8,700,000
Founded: 1990
Average Investment: $250,000 - $400,000
Minimum Investment: none

Investment Criteria: Start-up, Expansion, Buyout, Restructing

Geographic Preference: Northeastern Minnesota

Industry Group Preference: Communications, Electronic Components and Instrumentation, Industrial Products and Equipment, Medical/Health Related

Portfolio Companies: not available

Officers, Executives and Principals

Nick Smith, Chairman and Chief Executive Officer
Greg Sandbulte, President and Chief Operating Officer
Tom Van Hale, Vice President

NORTHLAND CAPITAL VENTURE PARTNERSHIP

613 Missabe Building
227 West First Street
Duluth, MN 55802

Telephone: 218-772-0545
Fax: 218-722-7241

Mission: Actively seeking new investments

Fund Size: not available
Founded: 1967
Average Investment: not available
Minimum Investment: Less than $100,000

Investment Criteria: First-stage, Second-stage, Leveraged Buyout, Special Situations

Industry Group Preference: Computer Related, Consumer, Distribution, Medical/Health Related

Portfolio Companies: not available

Officers, Executives and Principals

George G. Barnum, Jr., President
John C. Andresen, Vice President
Elizabeth J. Barnum, Vice President
Max C. Rheinberger, Jr., Vice President

NORTHWEST OHIO VENTURE FUND

300 Madison Avenue, Suite 1525
Toledo, OH 43604

Telephone: 419-244-9112
Fax: 419-244-9554

Mission: Actively seeking new investments

Fund Size: $15 million
Founded: 1992
Average Investment: $500,000
Minimum Investment: $150,000

Investment Criteria: Seed to Buyouts

Geographic Preference: Ohio, Michigan

Industry Group Preference: Diversified

Portfolio Companies: Aastrom Bioscience, Inc., Auxein Corporation, Cold Jet, Inc., Entek IRD International, Health Care Solutions, Inc., Highway Safety Vision Corporation, Pico Systems, Inc., Receivables Funding Corporation, Vertical Merchandising Systems, Inc.

Officers, Executives and Principals

Barry P. Walsh, Managing Partner
Education: Bowling Green State University
Background: Over 20 years of venture capital experience; President, Harbor Capital Advisors and Harbor Fund; Senior Associate, Regional Financial Enterprises; Partner, Arthur Young (Ernst and Young)
Directorships: President and board member of several start-up companies

Curtis D. Crocker, Investment Manager
Education: BS, Olivet Nazarene University; MBA, Indiana University
Background: Associate, CID Venture Partners

Betty J. Csehi, Treasurer
Education: Bowling Green State University
Background: Senior Vice President and Director of Operations, Harbor Capital Advisors; Treasurer, Harbor Fund

NORTHWOOD VENTURES

485 Underhill Boulevard, Suite 205
Syosset, NY 11791

Telephone: 516-364-5544
Fax: 516-364-0879

Mission: Private equity investments in venture capital and management buyouts

Fund Size: not available
Founded: 1983
Average Investment: $1- $3 million
Minimum Investment: $500,000

Investment Criteria: First-stage, Second-stage, Third-stage, Mezzanine, Leveraged Buyouts

Geographic Preference: United States

Industry Group Preference: Communications, Consumer, Financial Institutions, Manufacturing/Processing, Retailing

Portfolio Companies: not available

Officers, Executives and Principals

Peter G. Schiff, General Partner
Education: BA, Lake Forest University; MBA, University of Chicago

Henry T. Wilson, Managing Director
Education: BA, MBA, University of Virginia

NORWEST VENTURE CAPITAL

2800 Piper Jaffray Tower
222 South 9th Street
Minneapolis, MN 55402-3388

Telephone: 612-667-1650
Fax: 612-667-1660

Other Office Locations
40 William Street, Suite 305
Wellesley, MA 02181
Phone 617-237-5870, Fax 617-237-6270

245 Lytton Avenue, Suite 250
Palo Alto, CA 94301
Phone 415-321-8000, Fax 415-321-8010

Mission: not available

Fund Size: $500 million
Founded: not available
Average Investment: $500,000 - $5 million
Minimum Investment: not available

Investment Criteria: Seed to Acquisition

Industry Group Preference: Biotechnology, Communications, Computer Related, Consumer Related, Electronics, Environmental Protection, Industrial Products, Information Services, Medical Health, Retailing, Service Industries, Software

Portfolio Companies: Actel Corporation, Concord Computing, Cray Research Inc., Datakey, McData Corporation, National Computer System Inc., Performance Semiconductor Corporation, System Industries Inc., Teradata Corporation, Zycad , AVIA Group International, Bright Horizons, Famous Restaurants Inc., Gymboree Corporation

Officers, Executives and Principals

Robert F. Zicarelli, Managing General Partner
Education: BS, MBA, Northwestern University
Background: Allstate Insurance Corporation
Directorships: Cadtel Systems, Performance Semiconductor Corporation, Spartanics, Inc., VEE Corporation

Daniel J. Haggerty, Managing General Partner
Education: University of St. Thomas
Background: Prudential Life Insurance Company of America
Directorships: Management Graphics, Network Systems Corporation

John E. Lindahl, General Partner
Education: University of Minnesota, Business and Economics degrees
Background: Norwest Bank
Directorships: Advance Machine Co., Gelco Pay Network, Norwesco, Inc.

John L. Thomson, General Partner
Education: BA, MBA, University of South Dakota
Background: Norwest Bank
Directorships: Automotive Industries Holding, Bostrom Seating, Jefferson Partners, MSP Communications, National Psychiatric Centers

Stephen R. Sefton, General Partner
Education: University of Notre Dame
Background: Norwest Bank Minneapolis
Directorships: Advanced Machine Co., Numatics Inc.

John P. Whaley, General Partner
Education: University of Minnesota; MBA, University of St. Thomas
Background: Norwest Corporation
Directorships: Lifestories, Linkscorp, Worain Glass and Electricity

Ernest C. Parizeau, General Partner
Education: AB, Engineering Science, MBA, Dartmouth College
Background: Texas Instruments and Data General Corporation
Directorships: The Coffee Connection, Recra Environmental, Ringer Corporation, Bright Horizons Children's Center

George J. Still, Jr., General Partner
Education: BS, with high distinction, Pennsylvania State University; MBA, Dartmouth College
Background: General Partner, Centennial Funds, Ernst and Young
Directorships: General Surgical Innovations, Masada Security, Norian Corporation, Northwest Mataile Television, Northwest Pipe and Casing Co.

Mark R. Littell, President

Robert E. LaBlanc, Director
Background: President, Robert E. LaBlanc Associates, a private investment banking firm; Vice Chairman, Continental Telecom, Inc.

Alfred Saffer, PhD, Director
Background: Vice Chairman, Halcon International Inc.; President and Chief Financial Oficer, Oxirane Corporation

Mark B. Anderson, Director
Education: BA, Economics, MBA, Finance and Accounting, University of Rochester
Background: Senior Vice President, European American Bank (EAB); Manager, EAB's New York Division.

Promod Haque, Investment Manager
Education: PhD, Electrical Engineering, MBA, Northwestern University
Background: Siemens, Thorn-EMI, Emergent Corporation, Dimensional Medicine Inc.
Directorships: Force Software, Information Advantage, Nonvolatile Electronics, Optical Sensors, Ruster Graphics, Show Case Corporation

Hazel Matthews-Forte, Controller-Secretary
Background: Administrative Officer, EAB Venture Corporation

Erik Togerson, Associate

NOVACAP INVESTMENTS, INC.

375 Roland Therrien Boulevard, Suite 210
Longueuil, Quebec J4H 4A6
Canada

Telephone: 514-651-5000
Fax: 514-651-7585
E-mail: novacap@generation.net

Other Office Locations
6525 Northwest Drive
Mississauga, Ontario L4V IK3
Canada
Phone 905-405-8767, Fax 905-629-4364
Contact Gordon Macfie

Mission: Actively seeking new investments

Fund Size: not available
Founded: 1981
Average Investment: not available
Minimum Investment: $1 million

Investment Criteria: Startup, First-stage, Second-stage, Mezzanine, Leveraged Buyout

Geographic Preference: Eastern Canada, Northeastern United States

Industry Group Preference: Communications, Computer Related, Consumer, Distribution, Electronic Components and Instrumentation, Energy/Natural Resources, Genetic Engineering, Industrial Products and Equipment, Medical/Health Related

Portfolio Companies: Imapro Corporation, RCR International Inc., Cascade Technologies Inc., Cable-Axion Digitel Inc., MAC Closures Inc., ABL Canada Inc., Medi-Man Rehabilitation Products Inc., Bertec Medical Inc., CE Cabinets Ltd.

Officers, Executives and Principals

Marc Beauchamp, President
Education: MBA
Directorships: MAC Closures

Jean-Pierre Chartrand, Vice President

Jacques Foisy, Vice President

NOVELTEK CAPITAL CORPORATION

521 Fifth Avenue
Suite 1700
New York, NY 10175

Telephone: 212-286-1963

Mission: Actively seeking new investments

Fund Size: not available
Founded: 1983
Average Investment: not available
Minimum Investment: $1 million

Investment Criteria: First-stage, Second-stage, Mezzanine, Special Situations, Control-block Purchases, Fast IPO Track

Geographic Preference: United States

Industry Group Preference: Communications, Computer Related, Consumer, Distribution, Electronic Components and Instrumentation, Energy/Natural Resources, Genetic Engineering, Industrial Products and Equipment, Medical/Health Related

Portfolio Companies: not available

Officers, Executives and Principals

Gabor (Gabe) Baumann, President

THE NTC GROUP

Three Pickwick Plaza
Greenwich, CT 06830

Telephone: 203-862-2804
Fax: 203-622-6250

Mission: Actively seeking new investments

Fund Size: not available
Founded: 1985
Average Investment: not available
Minimum Investment: $500,000

Investment Criteria: Seed, First-stage, Leveraged Buyout, Control-block Purchases

Industry Group Preference: Computer Related, Distribution, Electronic Components and Instrumentation, Industrial Products and Equipment

Portfolio Companies: not available

Officers, Executives and Principals

Thomas C. Foley, President
Jean-Pierre L. Conte, Vice President
Donald Fawcett, Associate

NTH POWER TECHNOLOGIES

50 California Street
15th Floor
San Francisco, CA 94111

Telephone: 415-433-6755
Fax: 415-433-2213
E-mail: NthMg@aol.com or NthNF@aol.com

Mission: Actively seeking new investments

Fund Size: $60 million
Founded: 1993
Average Investment: $1 - $2.5 million
Minimum Investment: $250,000

Investment Criteria: Startup, First-stage, Second-stage, Mezzanine

Industry Group Preference: Communications, Consumer Energy Products, Energy/Natural Resources, Industrial Products and Equipment

Portfolio Companies: Confidential

Officers, Executives and Principals

Nancy C. Floyd, Principal
Maurice E.P. Gunderson, Principal

NU CAPITAL ACCESS GROUP, LTD.

7677 Oakport Street
Suite 105
Oakland, CA 94621

Telephone: 510-635-7345
Fax: 510-635-7068

Mission: Actively seeking new investments

Fund Size: not available
Founded: 1993
Average Investment: not available
Minimum Investment: $250,000

Investment Criteria: Second-stage, Mezzanine, Leveraged Buyout, Special Situations

Industry Group Preference: Diversified

Portfolio Companies: not available

Officers, Executives and Principals

Rodney M. White, Managing Partner
Wil P. Stevens, Jr., Managing Partner

OAK INVESTMENT PARTNERS

4550 Northwest Center
90 South 7th Street
Minneapolis, MN 55402

Telephone: 612-339-9322
Fax: 612-337-8017

Other Office Locations
One Gorham Island
Westport, CT 06880

525 University Avenue, Suite 1300
Palo Alto, CA 94301

Mission: not available

Fund Size: $700 million
Founded: 1978
Average Investment: not available
Minimum Investment: $1 million

Investment Criteria: Startup to Leveraged Buyout

Industry Group Preference: Healthcare, Information Technology, Retail

Portfolio Companies: Filene's Basement, Office Depot, PETsMART, Whole Foods, Alkermes, Inc., Applied Immune Sciences, AVECOR, Cephalon, Genzyme Corporation, HBO and Co., Intelligent Surgical Lasers, Osteotech, Salutar, Actel Corporation, Bachman Information Systems, Compaq, Digital Sound Corporation, Easel Corporation, Megatest Corporation, Micom Systems, Seagate, Stratus, Sybase, Wellfleet

Officers, Executives and Principals

Edward F. Glassmeyer, Co-Founder (Westport)
Education: Princeton; MBA, Dartmouth
Background: Managing General Partner, Sprout Capital Group

Gerald R. Gallagher, General Partner
Education: BA, Princeton University; MBA, University of Chicago
Background: Vice Chairman, Dayton Hudson; Retail Industry Research Analyst, Donaldson, Lufkin and Jenrette

Fredric W. Harman, General Partner (Palo Alto)
Education: BS, MS, Electrical Engineering, Stanford; MBA, Harvard
Background: General Partner, Morgan Stanley's Venture Capital Group; Business Development, Huges Communications

Ann Huntress Lamont, General Partner (Westport)
Education: BA, Stanford University
Background: Research Associate, Hambrecht and Quist

Cathy Agee, Vice President
Education: BA, MBA, University of Minnesota
Background: Corporate Director of Planning and Analysis, Dayton Hudson

Bandel L. Carano (Palo Alto)
Education: BS, MS, Electrical Engineering, Stanford University
Background: Advisor, Morgan Stanley
Directorships: Stanford Engineering Venture Fund

Ginger M. More (Westport)
Education: Mathematics, University of Bridgeport
Background: Wright Investor's Service

OLYMPIC VENTURE PARTNERS

2420 Carillon Point
Kirkland, WA 98033

Telephone: 206-889-9192
E-mail: info@ovp.com

Other Office Locations
340 Oswego Pointe Drive
Suite 204
Lake Oswego, OR 97034
Phone 503-697-8766

Mission: Actively seeking new investments

Fund Size: not available
Founded: 1982
Average Investment: not available
Minimum Investment: $100,000

Investment Criteria: Seed, Startup, First-stage, Second-stage

Geographic Preference: Western third of North America

Industry Group Preference: Biotechnology, Communications, Computer Related, Electronic Components and Instrumentation, Energy/Natural Resources, Genetic Engineering, Medical/Health Related

Portfolio Companies: not available

Officers, Executives and Principals

George H. Clute, General Partner (Kirkland)
Gerard H. Langeler, General Partner (Lake Oswego)
Charles P. Waite, Jr., General Partner (Kirkland)
Bill Funcannon, Administrative Partner (Kirkland)

OLYMPUS PARTNERS

Metro Center: One Station Place
Stamford, CT 06902

Telephone: 203-353-5900
Fax: 203-353-5910

Mission: To build a diversified portfolio of growth companies, acquisitions and restructurings

Fund Size: $375 million
Founded: 1989
Average Investment: $15 million
Minimum Investment: $5 million

Investment Criteria: Growth Capital to Leveraged Buyouts and Turnarounds

Geographic Preference: United States

Industry Group Preference: Diversified

Portfolio Companies: Master Protection, LDI Corporation, American Residential Mortgage Corporation, Phar-Mor Inc., Auspex Systems, Champion Healthcare, Card Establishment Services, Sfuzzi, National Auto/ Truckstops, Newtex Communications, Garden Botanika, Walsh International, Truckstops of America, New Vision Television, Supra Corporation, Hvide Marine, Nebraska Book Company, Sterling Chemicals, FrontierVision, Pizza Express, Country Bank

Officers, Executives and Principals

Robert S. Morris, Managing Partner
Education: AB, Hamilton College; MBA, Amos Tuck School
Background: Senior Vice President, General Electric Investment Corporation; Management, GE, Manufacturing and Financial Service

Louis J. Mischionti, Partner
Education: BA, Yale University
Background: Managing Director, First Boston
Directorships: Hvide Marine, Nebraska Book Company, Truckstops of America

James A. Conroy, Vice President and Limited Partner
Education: BA, University of Virginia; MBA, Amos Tuck School
Background: Bain and Company; Associate, Private Finance, Goldman Sachs
Directorships: American Residential Mortgage Corporation, FrontierVision, Paracelsus

OMNIMED CORPORATION

4545 Post Oak Place
Suite 223
Houston, TX 77027

Telephone: 713-524-7373
Fax: 713-524-0987

Other Office Locations
5430 LBJ Freeway, Suite 1500
Dallas, TX 75240
Phone 972-661-2024, Fax 972-701-0530

Mission: Actively seeking new investments

Fund Size: not available
Founded: 1986
Average Investment: not available
Minimum Investment: $250,000

Investment Criteria: Startup, First-stage, Second-stage

Industry Group Preference: Medical/Health Related

Portfolio Companies: not available

Officers, Executives and Principals

Gary B. Wood, PhD, Chief Executive Officer (Dallas)
Ralph Weaver, Senior Vice President and Chief Financial Officer (Houston)

ONE LIBERTY VENTURES

One Liberty Square
Boston, MA 02109

Telephone: 617-423-1765
Fax: 617-338-4362

Mission: Actively seeking new investments

Fund Size: not available
Founded: 1982
Average Investment: not available
Minimum Investment: Less than $100,000

Investment Criteria: Seed, Startup, First-stage, Second-stage, Mezzanine

Industry Group Preference: Communications, Computer Related, Electronic Components and Instrumentation, Energy/Natural Resources, Genetic Engineering, Industrial Products and Equipment, Medical/Health Related

Portfolio Companies: not available

Officers, Executives and Principals

Daniel J. Holland, General Partner
Edwin M. Kanie, Jr., General Partner
Joseph T. McCullen, Jr., General Partner
Stephen J. Ricci, General Partner
Duncan C. McCallum, Senior Associate

ONEX CORPORATION

161 Bay Street, P.O. Box 700
Toronto, Ontario M5J 2S1
Canada

Telephone: 416-362-7711
Fax: 416-362-5765

Other Office Locations
712 Fifth Avenue
New York, NY 10019
Phone 212-582-2211, Fax 212-582-0909

Mission: Actively seeking new investments

Fund Size: not available
Founded: 1984
Average Investment: not available
Minimum Investment: not available

Investment Criteria: Leveraged Buyout, Control-block Purchases

Industry Group Preference: not available

Portfolio Companies: not available

Officers, Executives and Principals

Gerald W. Schwartz, President and Chief Executive Officer (Toronto)
Ewout Heerskink, Vice President (Toronto)
Mark L. Hilson, Vice President (Toronto)
Anthony R. Melman, Vice President (Toronto)
Timothy C. Collins, Senior Managing Director (New York)
Eric J. Rosen, Managing Director (New York)
Donald W. Lewtas, Director, Finance (Toronto)

ONONDAGA VENTURE CAPITAL FUND, INC.
714 State Tower Building
Syracuse, NY 13202

Telephone: 315-478-0157
Fax: 315-478-0158

Mission: Actively seeking new investments

Fund Size: $2.5 million
Founded: 1985
Average Investment: $150,000
Minimum Investment: $100,000

Investment Criteria: Second-stage, Mezzanine, Leveraged Buyout

Geographic Preference: Northeastern United States, Middle Atlantic States

Industry Group Preference: Computer Related, Consumer, Distribution, Electronic Components and Instrumentation, Energy/Natural Resources, Genetic Engineering, Industrial Products and Equipment, Medical/Health Related

Portfolio Companies: Aether Works, BioWorks, Frigo Design, Healthway Products, Opto Generic Devices

Officers, Executives and Principals

Russell King, Chairman
Irving W. Schwartz, President
Edward S. Green, Treasurer

ONSET VENTURES

2490 Sand Hill Road
Menlo Park, CA 94025-6940

Telephone: 415-327-5470
Fax: 415-327-5488

Other Office Locations
8911 Capital of Texas Highway
Austin, TX 78759
Phone 512-349-2255, Fax 512-349-2258

Mission: Actively seeking new investments

Fund Size: $100 million
Founded: 1984
Average Investment: $500,000 - $3 million
Minimum Investment: not available

Investment Criteria: Seed and Early-stage

Industry Group Preference: Information and Medical Technology

Portfolio Companies: Diversified

Officers, Executives and Principals

Robert F. Kuhling, Jr., Partner
Education: MBA, Harvard; BA, Economics, Hamilton College
Background: Director of Design Automation Marketing, Sun Microsystems; Vice President and Manager, Electronics Design Automation Business, GE - Calma

Terry L. Opdendyk, Partner
Education: BS, Michigan State University, Honors College; MS, Computer Science, Stanford University
Background: General Partner, Founder, Onset Venture Partnership; President, Visicorp; Executive, Intel; Manager, Hewlett Packard

Thomas E. Winter, Partner
Education: MS, Industrial Management, BS, Aeronautical Engineering, Georgia Institute of Technology

ONTARIO LIMITED

P.O. Box 23110
Sault Ste. Marie, Ontario P6A 6W6
Canada

Telephone: 705-253-0744
Fax: 705-253-0744

Mission: To obtain investments in projects at primary or second-stage financing to invest and/or to source funding for equity and/or long-term financing

Fund Size: $500 million
Founded: 1983
Average Investment: not available
Minimum Investment: $500,000

Investment Criteria: Second-stage

Geographic Preference: United States, Canada, Asia

Industry Group Preference: Computer Related, Consumer, Industrial Products, Real Estate

Portfolio Companies: not available

Officers, Executives and Principals

D.B. Stinson, President and Chief Executive Officer

OPPORTUNITY CAPITAL

2201 Walnut Avenue
Suite 210
Fremont, CA 94538

Telephone: 510-795-7000
Fax: 510-494-5439

Mission: Actively seeking new investments

Fund Size: $36 million
Founded: 1970
Average Investment: $1 million
Minimum Investment: $500,000

Investment Criteria: Second-stage, Mezzanine, Leveraged Buyout

Geographic Preference: West Coast of the United States

Industry Group Preference: Communications, Electronic Components and Instrumentation, Industrial Products and Equipment, Medical/Health Related

Portfolio Companies: not available

Officers, Executives and Principals

J. Peter Thompson, Managing Partner
Lewis E. Byrd, Partner

THE O'RENICK COMPANIES, INC.

10200 Holmes Road
Kansas City, MO 64131

Telephone: 816-942-5000

Mission: Actively seeking new investments

Fund Size: not available
Founded: 1978
Average Investment: not available
Minimum Investment: $100,000

Investment Criteria: Second-stage, Special Situations

Industry Group Preference: Distribution, Electronic Components and Instrumentation, Energy/Natural Resources, Industrial Products and Equipment

Portfolio Companies: not available

Officers, Executives and Principals

Albert C. Lundstrom, Principal

ORIEN VENTURES

315 Post Road West
Westport, CT 06880

Telephone: 203-454-0802
Fax: 203-454-0210

Mission: not available

Fund Size: $78 million
Founded: not available
Average Investment: $1 million
Minimum Investment: not available

Investment Criteria: Startup to Mezzanine

Industry Group Preference: Biotechnology, Communications, Computer Related, Consumer Related, Electronics, Energy/Natural Resources, Industrial Products, Medical/Health

Portfolio Companies: not available

Officers, Executives and Principals

George R. Kalan, Managing General Partner

ORION PARTNERS, L.P.

100 Federal Street
29th Floor
Boston, MA 02110-1819

Telephone: 617-338-1900
Fax: 617-338-1995

Mission: Actively seeking new equity investments in traditional buyouts and growth buyouts, as well as recapitalizations

Fund Size: $51 million
Founded: 1993
Average Investment: $5 - $10 million
Minimum Investment: $3 million

Investment Criteria: Leveraged Buyout, Management Buyout, Recapitalizations

Geographic Preference: United States

Industry Group Preference: Diversified

Portfolio Companies: Allied Foods, Marson Corporation, Uniform Printing and Supply, Inframetrics

Officers, Executives and Principals

Steven A. Kandarian, Managing Director
Robert J. Byrne, Director

OSCCO VENTURES

One First Street
Suite 15
Los Altos, CA 94022

Telephone: 415-917-0800
Fax: 415-917-0801

Mission: Actively seeking new investments

Fund Size: not available
Founded: 1962
Average Investment: not available
Minimum Investment: $100,000

Investment Criteria: Seed, Startup, First-stage, Second-stage

Industry Group Preference: Communications, Computer Related, Distribution, Electronic Components and Instrumentation, Energy/Natural Resources, Genetic Engineering, Industrial Products and Equipment, Medical/Health Related

Portfolio Companies: not available

Officers, Executives and Principals

Stephen E. Halprin, General Partner
F. Ward Paine, General Partner
Jonathan C. Baer, General Partner

OSCCO VENTURES, III

One First Street
Los Altos, CA 94022

Telephone: 415-917-0800
Fax: 415-917-0801

Mission: not available

Fund Size: $18.5 million
Founded: not available
Average Investment: $500,000
Minimum Investment: not available

Investment Criteria: Seed to First-stage

Geographic Preference: California, Western United States

Industry Group Preference: Diversified

Portfolio Companies: not available

Officers, Executives and Principals

F. Ward Paine, General Partner
Education: BSME, Princeton University
Background: 31 years in venture capital at Oscco

Stephen E. Halprin, General Partner
Education: BS, Industrial Management, MIT
Background: 25 years venture capital, Oscco

Jonathan C. Baer, Partner
Education: BS, Engineering, BA, Biology, Tufts University; MBA, Dartmouth

OXFORD FINANCIAL SERVICES CORPORATION

8180 Greensboro Drive
Suite 1000
McLean, VA 22102

Telephone: 703-790-0050
Fax: 703-790-3379

Other Office Locations
1055 Torrey Pines Road
Suite 205
La Jolla, CA 92037
Phone 619-551-0505, Fax 619-551-0789

Mission: Actively seeking new investments

Fund Size: not available
Founded: 1987
Average Investment: not available
Minimum Investment: $500,000

Investment Criteria: First-stage, Second-stage, Mezzanine

Industry Group Preference: Communications, Computer Related, Distribution, Electronic Components and Instrumentation, Energy/Natural Resources, Genetic Engineering, Industrial Products and Equipment, Medical/Health Related

Portfolio Companies: not available

Officers, Executives and Principals

J. Alden Philbrick IV, President
Stephen W. Smith, Executive Vice President (La Jolla)
James K. Barber, Regional Vice President
James H. Janssen, Regional Vice President (La Jolla)
Robert C. Vorder Bruegge, Regional Vice President
Linda S. Hearn, Vice President

OXFORD VENTURE CORPORATION

315 Post Road West
Westport, CT 06880

Telephone: 203-341-3300
Fax: 203-341-3309

Other Office Locations
45 Milk Street, 9th Floor
Boston, MA 02109
Phone 617-457-5250, Fax 617-482-5931

650 Town Center Drive, Suite 810
Costa Mesa, CA 92626
Phone 714-754-5719, Fax 714-754-6802

Mission: Making few, if any, new investments

Fund Size: not available
Founded: 1981
Average Investment: not available
Minimum Investment: $500,000

Investment Criteria: Startup, First-stage, Second-stage, Mezzanine, Leveraged Buyout

Industry Group Preference: Communications, Computer Related, Distribution, Electronic Components and Instrumentation, Genetic Engineering, Industrial Products and Equipment, Medical/Health Related

Portfolio Companies: not available

Officers, Executives and Principals

Stevan A. Birnbaum, General Partner
William R. Lonergan, General Partner
Kenneth W. Rind, General Partner
Cornelius T. Ryan, General Partner
Alan G. Walton, General Partner

PACIFIC HORIZON VENTURES

1001 Fourth Avenue Plaza,
Suite 4105
Seattle, WA 98154

Telephone: 206-682-1181
Fax: 206-682-8077

Mission: Actively seeking new investments

Fund Size: not available
Founded: 1991
Average Investment: not available
Minimum Investment: $250,000

Investment Criteria: First and Second-stage

Industry Group Preference: Communications, Medical/Health Related

Portfolio Companies: not available

Officers, Executives and Principals

Donald J. Elmer, Managing Director
Education: University of Pennsylvania
Background: Finance and General Management
Directorships: Creative Multimedia Corporation

PACIFIC MEZZANINE INVESTORS

610 Newport Center Drive
Suite 1100
Newport Beach, CA 92660

Telephone: 714-721-9944
Fax: 714-721-5446

Mission: Actively seeking new investments

Fund Size: not available
Founded: 1990
Average Investment: not available
Minimum Investment: $5 million

Investment Criteria: Mezzanine, Leveraged Buyout, Recapitalizations

Industry Group Preference: Consumer, Distribution, Industrial Products and Equipment, Medical/Health Related

Portfolio Companies: not available

Officers, Executives and Principals

Robert Bartholomew, President
Mitchell S. Vance, Principal
Schuyler G. Lance, Principal
Denise I. Chiang, Associate
James S. Shivlet, Associate
Tim Fay, Associate

PACIFIC NORTHWEST PARTNERS SBIC, L.P.

City Centre
500-108th Avenue, Northeast, Suite 800
Bellevue, WA 98004

Telephone: 206-646-7357
Fax: 206-646-7356

Mission: not available

Fund Size: $33 million
Founded: 1994
Average Investment: $1 million
Minimum Investment: $500,000

Investment Criteria: Seed, Startup, First-stage, Second-stage, Leveraged Buyout, Special Situations

Geographic Preference: Pacific Northwest of the United States

Industry Group Preference: Communications, Computer Related, Consumer, Electronic Components and Instrumentation

Portfolio Companies: not available

Officers, Executives and Principals

Theodore M. Wight, General Partner
Louis R. Kertesz, General Partner

PALM BEACH CAPITAL CORPORATION

7107 South Yale Avenue
Suite 233
Tulsa, OK 74136-6348

Telephone: 918-492-5956
Fax: 918-493-7313

Other Office Locations
3401 West Airport Freeway
Suite 106117
Irving, TX 75062
Phone 214-570-5003, Fax 214-570-5133

5701 Free Ferry Road
Suite 11
Fort Smith, AR 72903
Phone 501-452-6757, Fax 501-484-7728

Mission: Actively seeking new investments. Looking for outstanding entrepreneurs.

Fund Size: $3.4 million
Founded: 1990
Average Investment: $55,000
Minimum Investment: Less than $100,000

Investment Criteria: Seed

Industry Group Preference: Food Services, Manufacturing, Marketing Companies, Medical Research, Mining, Publishing, Retail Sales

Portfolio Companies: not available

Officers, Executives and Principals

John W. Townshend, President
Education: BBA, Stetson University
Background: Accounting, Tax Practice, Management Consulting, Registered Representative

PALMER PARTNERS, L.P.

300 Unicorn Park Drive
Woburn, MA 01801

Telephone: 617-933-5445
Fax: 617-933-0698

Mission: To back strong leaders in the fields of their choice

Fund Size: $52 million
Founded: 1972
Average Investment: $500,000
Minimum Investment: not available

Investment Criteria: Seed to Expansion

Geographic Preference: United States, International

Industry Group Preference: Diversified

Portfolio Companies: Advanced Circuit Technology, Arch Communications Group, Inc., Gensym Corporation, PETsMART, Inc., Advanced Visual Systems, Inc., CONXUS Communications, Inc., Dowden Publishing Company, Inc., I.D.E. Corporation, i-Logix, Inc., Overland Data, Inc., Triangle Software International, Inc.

Officers, Executives and Principals

William H. Congleton, Chairman
Education: BS, Chemical Engineering, Princeton University; MBA, Harvard
Background: Standard Oil; Senior Vice President, American Research and Development Corporation

John A. Shane, President
Education: AB, Economics, Princeton University; MBA, Harvard
Background: USN; Senior Vice President, American Research and Development Corporation

Alison J. Seavey, Treasurer
Education: BA, Beaver College; M.Ed, Boston University

PALMETTO SEED CAPITAL CORPORATION

P.O. Box 17526
Greenville, SC 29606

Telephone: 864-232-6198
Fax: 864-271-8374

Mission: Actively seeking new investments

Fund Size: not available
Founded: 1989
Average Investment: not available
Minimum Investment: $250,000

Investment Criteria: Seed, Startup, First-stage

Geographic Preference: South Carolina

Industry Group Preference: Communications, Computer Related, Consumer, Distribution, Electronic Components and Instrumentation, Energy/Natural Resources, Genetic Engineering, Industrial Products and Equipment, Medical/Health Related

Portfolio Companies: BPM Technology, Inc., Cardiovascular Diagnostics, Inc.

Officers, Executives and Principals

Jack Sterling, President
Capers A. Easterby, Vice President
J. Phillip Falls, Investment Officer

PALMS AND COMPANY, INC.

Palms Harbor Lights Building #103
515 Lake Street, Suite 103
Kirkland, WA 98033

Telephone: 206-828-6774
Fax: 206-827-5528
E-mail: palbank@eskimo.com / russia@aa.net

Other Office Locations
Sovintereco-MGIMO
Vernadsky Prospect 76
Moscow 117451
Russia
Phone 7-095-956-0341

Zelenograd K-460
Korpus 1126 rv.659
Moscow 103460
Russia
Phone 7-095-530-6692

Argakain Per. 1
St. Petersburg 191023
Russia
Phone 7-812-279-6516, Fax 7-812-521-4213

Vasilovsky St. 21, Apt. 18
Konokova
Tver Region 171280
Russia
Phone 7-08242-31099

Ulitsa Sverdlova 3
Box 263
Novosibirsk 630093
Russia
Phone 7-3832-237496, Fax 7-3832-238691

Aleutskaya Street 45a, Fifth Floor
Vladivostok 690009
Russia
Phone 7-4232-266967, Fax 7-4232-254738

21-a Gagarin Street, Apt. 75
Magadan 685027
Russia
Phone 7-41322-53680, Fax 7-41322-23028

Pr. Asddirova 46/2 Kv.66
Karaganda 470055

Kazakhstan
Phone 7-3212-580773, Fax 7-3212-580774

Nationalnaya Hotel, Suite 313
3 Lipskaya Ulitsa
Kiev 25201
Ukraine
Phone 7-044-2947652

Mission: To provide asynchronous 'just-in-time' distance education in monetary policy, finance, corporate finance; to provide skills in market economy management and syndication of capital for conversion of defense industries; reorganization of banks.

Fund Size: not available
Founded: 1934
Average Investment: $5 million
Minimum Investment: $1 million

Investment Criteria: Publicly-owned strong Western operating company as co-investor, or will syndicate capital for privately-owned Western company or Russian company

Geographic Preference: Westen United States, Russia

Industry Group Preference: Aircraft, Auto Manufacturing, Banks, Commodities and Natural Resource Processing, Defense Plant Conversion, Electronics, Export-Oriented Manufacturers, Food Products Packaging and Manufacturing, Fur Pelt Farms-Ranches, Internet Satellite Communication Systems, Metals Products, Oil and Gas, Urea Manufacturing

Portfolio Companies: not available

Officers, Executives and Principals

Dr. Viktor Savransky, Director (Moscow)
Dr. Peter J. Palms IV, President (Kirkland)
Anke van de Waal, Vice President (Kirkland)
Tate Ulsaker (Moscow)
Mikhail Rybakov (Moscow)
A. Yershov (St. Petersburg)
D. Baburov (St. Petersburg)
Irina Budrina (Vladivostok)

PANTHEON VENTURES, INC.

50 California Street
Suite 906
San Francisco, CA 94111

Telephone: 415-291-3100
Fax: 415-291-3132

Mission: not available

Fund Size: not available
Founded: not available
Average Investment: not available
Minimum Investment: not available

Investment Criteria: Mezzanine, Leveraged Buyout, Secondary Interests

Industry Group Preference: Diversified

Portfolio Companies: not available

Officers, Executives and Principals

David B. Braman, President
J. Jay Pierrepont, Vice President
Ian G. Deas, Chief Financial Officer

PAPPAJOHN CAPITAL RESOURCES

2116 Financial Center
Des Moines, IA 50309

Telephone: 515-244-5746
Fax: 515-244-2346

Mission: Actively seeking new investments

Fund Size: not available
Founded: 1969
Average Investment: not available
Minimum Investment: Less than $100,000

Investment Criteria: Seed, Startup, First-stage, Second-stage, Mezzanine, Leveraged Buyout

Industry Group Preference: Computer Related, Genetic Engineering, Medical/Health Related

Portfolio Companies: not available

Officers, Executives and Principals

John Pappajohn, President
Mathew Kinley, Chief Financial Officer

PARAGON VENTURE PARTNERS

3000 Sand Hill Road
Building One, Suite 275
Menlo Park, CA 94025

Telephone: 415-854-8000
Fax: 415-854-7260

Mission: Making few, if any, new investments

Fund Size: $30 million
Founded: 1984
Average Investment: $1.5 million
Minimum Investment: $250,000

Investment Criteria: Seed, Startup, First-stage, Second-stage, Mezzanine, Special Situations

Industry Group Preference: Communications, Computer Related, Electronic Components and Instrumentation, Medical/Health Related

Portfolio Companies: not available

Officers, Executives and Principals

Robert F. Kibble, General Partner
John S. Lewis, General Partner

PARIBAS PRINCIPAL, INC.

787 Seventh Avenue
New York, NY 10019-6016

Telephone: 212-841-2000
Fax: 212-841-3558

Mission: Actively seeking new investments. Paribas made seven equity investments in 1994

Fund Size: $50+ million committed
Founded: 1989
Average Investment: $2.5 million
Minimum Investment: $1.5 million, $10 million maximum

Investment Criteria: Leveraged Buyout, Special Situations, Control-block Purchases

Industry Group Preference: Business Services, Communications, Consumer, Distribution, Industrial Products and Equipment, Medical/Health Related

Portfolio Companies:

Officers, Executives and Principals

Miles Steven Alexander, President
Education: BA, MBA,University of North Carolina at Chapel Hill
Background: Managing Director in charge of Banque Paribas' North American Merchant Banking
Directorships: The Reilly Corporation, Alabama Outdoor Advertising LLC, Paribas Principal Inc.

Jeffrey J. Youle, Vice President and Secretary
Education: BA, Albion College; MBA, University of Michigan
Background: Eastern Regional Head of Merchant Banking at Banque Paribas
Directorships: Paribas Principal Inc.

PARSON CAPITAL CORPORATION

255 West Wacker Drive
Suite 1010
Chicago, IL 60606

Telephone: 312-541-4666
Fax: 312-541-4665

Mission: Actively seeking new investments

Fund Size: not available
Founded: 1990
Average Investment: not available
Minimum Investment: $1 million

Investment Criteria: Second-stage, Leveraged Buyout, Control-block Purchases

Industry Group Preference: Communications, Computer Related, Consumer, Distribution, Industrial Products and Equipment

Portfolio Companies: not available

Officers, Executives and Principals

John Jeffrey Louis III, Chairman
Samuel P. Chapman, President

PARTECH INTERNATIONAL

50 California Street, Suite 3200
San Francisco, CA 94111

Telephone: 415-788-2929
Fax: 415-788-6763

Mission: not available

Fund Size: $225 million
Founded: not available
Average Investment: $1 million
Minimum Investment: not available

Investment Criteria: Seed to Leveraged Buyout

Industry Group Preference: Biotechnology, Communications, Computer Related, Consumer Related, Diversified, Electronics, Environmental Protection, Industrial Products, Medical/Health

Portfolio Companies: not available

Officers, Executives and Principals

Thomas G. McKinley, Partner
Vincent Worms, Partner
Roland Van der Meer, Partner

PATRICOF AND COMPANY VENTURES, INC.

445 Park Avenue
New York, NY 10022

Telephone: 212-753-6300
Fax: 212-319-6155

Other Office Locations
2100 Geng Road, Suite 150
Palo Alto, CA 94303
Phone 415-494-9944, Fax 415-494-6751

100 Matson Ford Road, Building Five
Suite 470
Radnor, PA 19087
Phone 610-687-3030, Fax 610-687-8520

Mission: not available

Fund Size: $1.5 billion
Founded: not available
Average Investment: $3.5 million
Minimum Investment: not available

Investment Criteria: Startup to Leveraged Buyout

Industry Group Preference: Diversified

Portfolio Companies: Agouron Pharmaceuticals, Inc., Apple Computer, Inc., Bayou Steel Corporation, Business Insurance Corporation, Cellular Communications, Centocor, Creative BioModules, Cygnus Reserach Corporation, Data Scope Corporation, IST Associates, Inc., Office Depot, Protection One Inc., R.E. Harrington, Inc., Sunglass Hut Corporation, Total Pharmaceutical

Officers, Executives and Principals

Alan J. Patricof, Chairman
Background: Schroder, Naess and Thomas, Lambert and Co.; Vice President of Central National Corporation, Assistant to the Chairman of the Board, Northwest Indiana

John C. Baker, Senior Vice President
Background: Vice President of Marketing, GFI/Knoll International; Research Econometrician, Data Resources

Patricia M. Cloherty, Senior Vice President
Background: Deputy Administrator of the U.S. SBA; Formed Tessler and Cloherty, Inc.; Partner, Fifty Third Street Ventures, L.P.

Wilmer R. Bottoms, PhD, Senior Vice President (Palo Alto)
Background: Founder, President, Chairman, Varian Associates; Semiconductor Equipment Group; Princeton University, Electrical Engineering Faculty

Robert M. Chefitz, Vice President
Background: Senior Associate, Golder, Thoma and Cressey Co.

Janet G. Effland, Vice President (Palo Alto)
Background: Managing Director, CIN Investment Co. President of Logisticon, Inc. Vice President Qume Corporation Courier Terminal Systems, subsidiaries of ITT Corporation

George M. Jenkins, Vice President (Radnor)
Background: Division Head, Midlantic Bank

Kenneth P. Lawler, Senior Associate (Palo Alto)
Background: Principal, Bekley International Capital Corporation

Rebecca Byam, Senior Associate
Background: Assistant Director of the Special Investment Portfolio at the Ford Foundation

David A. Landau, Associate
Background: Brand Management, Procter and Gamble; Strategy Consultant, Monitor Company

Gregory M. Case, Associate (Radnor)
Background: Associate, Investments Orange Nassau

PAUL CAPITAL PARTNERS

10600 North De Anza Boulevard
Suite 250
Cupertino, CA 95014

Telephone: 408-973-1056
Fax: 408-973-8904

Mission: Actively seeking new investments

Fund Size: not available
Founded: 1991
Average Investment: not available
Minimum Investment: $250,000

Investment Criteria: Secondary Private Equity Market

Industry Group Preference: Diversified

Portfolio Companies: not available

Officers, Executives and Principals

Philip S. Paul, President
David Park, Partner
Jackie Brown, Controller
Bryon Sheets, Associate
Edward R. Hobart, Associate

PAULI AND COMPANY, INC.

7733 Forsyth Boulevard
Suite 2000
St. Louis, MO 63105

Telephone: 314-862-7575
Fax: 314-862-0544

Mission: Actively seeking new investments

Fund Size: not available
Founded: 1989
Average Investment: not available
Minimum Investment: $1 million

Investment Criteria: Second-stage, Mezzanine, Leveraged Buyout, Special Situations, Control-block Purchases, Initial Public Offerings

Industry Group Preference: Communications, Computer Related, Consumer, Distribution, Industrial Products and Equipment, Medical/Health Related

Portfolio Companies: not available

Officers, Executives and Principals

Chris H. Pauli, President
Michael P. Dimon, Senior Vice President, Investment Banking
Jean-Marie A. Pauli, Senior Vice President

PECKS MANAGEMENT PARTNERS, LTD.

One Rockefeller Plaza
New York, NY 10020

Telephone: 212-332-1333
Fax: 212-332-1334

Mission: Actively seeking new investments

Fund Size: not available
Founded: 1990
Average Investment: not available
Minimum Investment: $3 million

Investment Criteria: Mezzanine, Special Situations

Industry Group Preference: Diversified

Portfolio Companies: not available

Officers, Executives and Principals

Arthur W. Berry, Managing Director
Robert J. Cresci, Managing Director
Elaine E. Healy, Vice President
Karen S. Larson, Trader

PEGASUS VENTURES

One International Place
23rd Floor
Boston, MA 02110

Telephone: 617-946-1000
Fax: 617-946-1600

Mission: Actively seeking new investments

Fund Size: not available
Founded: not available
Average Investment: not available
Minimum Investment: $500,000

Investment Criteria: Startup, First-stage, Second-stage, Mezzanine, Leveraged Buyout

Industry Group Preference: Communications, Computer Related, Consumer, Distribution, Electronic Components and Instrumentation, Energy/Natural Resources, Genetic Engineering, Industrial Products and Equipment, Medical/Health Related

Portfolio Companies: not available

Officers, Executives and Principals

Charles A. Caffarella, Jr., Managing Partner
James W. Caffarella, Partner

PELL, RUDMAN AND COMPANY, INC.

100 Federal Street
37th Floor
Boston, MA 02110

Telephone: 617-357-9600
Fax: 617-357-9601

Mission: Making few, if any, new investments

Fund Size: not available
Founded: 1980
Average Investment: not available
Minimum Investment: $250,000

Investment Criteria: Startup, First-stage, Second-stage

Industry Group Preference: Communications, Computer Related, Consumer, Distribution, Electronic Components and Instrumentation, Industrial Products and Equipment, Medical/Health Related

Portfolio Companies: not available

Officers, Executives and Principals

Edward I. Rudman
David T. Riddiford
R. Gregg Stone

PENFUND PARTNERS, INC.

145 King Street West, Suite 1920
Toronto, Ontario M5H IJ8
Canada

Telephone: 416-865-0707
Fax: 416-364-6912

Other Office Locations
770 Sherbrooke Street West, Suite 1215
Montreal, Quebec H3A 1G1
Canada
Phone 514-499-9670, Fax 514-499-9673

Mission: Actively seeking new investments

Fund Size: not available
Founded: 1988
Average Investment: $2 - $3 million
Minimum Investment: $1 million

Investment Criteria: Second-stage, Mezzanine, Leveraged Buyout

Geographic Preference: Canada

Industry Group Preference: Communications, Computer Related, Consumer, Industrial Products and Equipment, Medical/Health Related

Portfolio Companies: not available

Officers, Executives and Principals

H. Rorison, President (Toronto)
G. McGrath, Vice President of Finance and Corporate Secretary (Toronto)

PENMAN ASSET MANAGEMENT, L.P.

333 West Wacker Drive
Suite 700
Chicago, IL 60606

Telephone: 312-444-2763
Fax: 312-750-4676
E-mail: lmanson@penmanpartners.com

Mission: Actively seeking new investments

Fund Size: $88 million
Founded: 1992
Average Investment: $3 - $10 million
Minimum Investment: $3 million

Investment Criteria: Leveraged Buyout

Geographic Preference: United States

Industry Group Preference: Consumer, Distribution

Portfolio Companies: Triad Holdings, LSC Acquisition, Fivestar Holdings, America's Favorite Chicken

Officers, Executives and Principals

Kelvin J. Pennington, Managing General Partner
Lawrence C. Manson, Jr., General Partner
Mark D. Schindel, Vice President
Gordon J. O'Brien, Associate

PENNSYLVANIA GROWTH FUND

Lhormer Real Estate
5850 Ellsworth Avenue, Suite 303
Pittsburgh, PA 15232

Telephone: 412-661-1000

Mission: Actively seeking new investments

Fund Size: not available
Founded: 1992
Average Investment: not available
Minimum Investment: $250,000

Investment Criteria: Second-stage, Mezzanine, Special Situations

Industry Group Preference: Computer Related, Consumer, Distribution, Electronic Components and Instrumentation, Industrial Products and Equipment, Medical/Health Related

Portfolio Companies: not available

Officers, Executives and Principals

Barry Lhormer, Partner
Hal Mendlowitz, Partner

PERMAL CAPITAL MANAGEMENT

900 Third Avenue
New York, NY 10022

Telephone: 212-418-6508
Fax: 212-418-6510

Mission: Actively seeking new investments

Fund Size: not available
Founded: 1964
Average Investment: not available
Minimum Investment: $500,000

Investment Criteria: Second-stage, Mezzanine, Leveraged Buyout, Special Situations, Control-block Purchases

Industry Group Preference: Communications, Computer Related, Consumer, Distribution, Electronic Components and Instrumentation, Genetic Engineering, Industrial Products and Equipment, Medical/Health Related

Portfolio Companies: not available

Officers, Executives and Principals

Jean R. Perrette, Chairman
Thomas M. DeLitto, President and Director
C. Redington Barrett III, Vice President and Director
Isaac R. Sovede, Director

PETERSON-SPENCER-FANSLER COMPANY

821 Marquette Avenue
Suite 1900
Minneapolis, MN 55402-2921

Telephone: 612-904-2305
Fax: 612-204-0913

Mission: Actively seeking new investments

Fund Size: not available
Founded: 1991
Average Investment: $300,000 - $400,000
Minimum Investment: Less than $100,000

Investment Criteria: Seed, Research and Development, Startup, First-stage, Second-stage

Geographic Preference: Upper Midwest area of the United States

Industry Group Preference: Medical Devices, Healthcare Services

Portfolio Companies: not available

Officers, Executives and Principals

Edson W. Spencer, Jr.

PFINGSTEN PARTNERS, L.P.

520 Lake Cook Road
Suite 375
Deerfield, IL 60015

Telephone: 847-374-9140
Fax: 847-374-9150

Mission: To provide equity capital to acquire and grow Midwest-based middle market companies in partnership with management

Fund Size: $26.3 million
Founded: 1989
Average Investment: $5 to $15 million
Minimum Investment: $5 million

Investment Criteria: Later-stage Growth Companies, Management Buyouts, Leveraged Buyouts

Geographic Preference: Midwestern United States

Industry Group Preference: Automotive Components, Consumer Products, Educational Products and Supplies, Distribution, Food Manufacturing and Processing, Metals, Packaging and Container Products, Plastics, Publishing, Specialty Chemicals

Portfolio Companies: Hallcrest, Inc., American Academic Suppliers, Inc., HUEBCORE Communications, Inc., Park Foods, L.P., Bargain Products, L.P.

Officers, Executives and Principals

Thomas S. Bagley, Managing General Partner
Richard W. Manning, General Partner
John H. Underwood, General Partner
John P. McNulty, Associate
Mary McClure, Associate

PHILADELPHIA VENTURES, INC.

The Bellevue
200 South Broad Street
Philadelphia, PA 19102

Telephone: 215-732-4445
Fax: 215-732-4644

Mission: Actively seeking new investments

Fund Size: not available
Founded: 1983
Average Investment: not available
Minimum Investment: $500,000

Investment Criteria: Startup, First-stage, Second-stage, Mezzanine, Leveraged Buyout

Industry Group Preference: Communications, Computer Related, Consumer, Distribution, Electronic Components and Instrumentation, Energy/Natural Resources, Genetic Engineering, Industrial Products and Equipment, Medical/Health Related

Portfolio Companies: not available

Officers, Executives and Principals

Walter M. Aikman, Managing Director
Charles A. Burton, Managing Director
Thomas R. Morse, Managing Director
Maria A. Hahn, Chief Financial Officer
Eric I. Aguiar, M.D., Vice President
Karen A. Griffith, Vice President

PHILLIPS-SMITH SPECIALTY RETAIL GROUP

5080 Spectrum Drive
Suite 700 West
Dallas, TX 75248

Telephone: 972-387-0725
Fax: 972-458-2560

Other Office Locations
102 South Tejon Street
Suite 1100
Colorado Springs, CO 80903
Phone 719-578-3301, Fax 719-578-8869

7 Locust Lane
Bronxville, NY 10708
Phone 914-961-0407, Fax 914-961-6169

Mission: Actively seeking new investments and committed to investing in strong, growing companies by providing growth financing, acquisition capital and financing for recapitalization.

Fund Size: $140 million
Founded: 1986
Average Investment: $1 - $5 million
Minimum Investment: $1 million

Investment Criteria: Seed to Initial Public Offering

Geographic Preference: United States

Industry Group Preference: Consumer Related, Restaurants, Retailing

Portfolio Companies: Buyer's Resource, Silverman's Factory Jewelers, Pacific Linen, Ulta 3, Gadzooks, Lil' Things, Best Friends Pet Care, Bikes, USA, Canyon Cafes, Hot Topic, Juice Club, Sneaker Stadium, Teach and Play Smart, Todo Wraps, We're Entertainment, Sutton Place Gourmet, GardenEscape, The Custom Foot and Golf America Stores

Officers, Executives and Principals

Donald J. Phillips, Founder and Managing General Partner
Education: MBA, Harvard Business School
Background: President, Chief Executive Officer, Pearle Health Services
Directorships: Silverman's Factory Jewelers, Ulta 3, Teach and Play Smart, GardenEscape

Cece Smith, Founder and Managing General Partner
Education: Magna cum laude, University of Michigan; CPA
Background: Executive Vice President, Finance and Administration, Pearle Health Services; Executive Vice President of S&A Restaurants
Directorships: Silverman's Factory Jewelers, Lil' Things, Hot Topics

G. Michael Machens, General Partner
Education: University of Illinois; CPA
Background: Chief Financial Officer, Blockbuster Entertainment; Chief Financial Officer, Compco Computer Centers; Controller, Pearle Health Services
Directorships: Buyer's Resource, Gadzooks, Teach and Play Smart, Canyon Cafes, Sneaker Stadium, Bikes USA, Golf America Stores

James T. Rothe, Principal (Colorado Springs)
Education: Ph.D., Marketing and Finance, University of Wisconsin
Background: Senior Vice President, Pearle Health Services; Marketing and Merchandising, Pearle Vision Centers
Directorships: Buyer's Resource, Todo Wraps

Craig Foley, Principal
Education: Kenyon College
Background: Founding Investor, Member of the Board of Directors, Chancellor Capital Management
Directorships: Juice Club, Todo Wraps, We're Entertainment

James A. Flynn, Principal
Education: BS, United States Naval Academy; MBA, Harvard Business School
Background: President and Chief Operating Officer, Popeyes and Church's Fried Chicken; Executive Vice President, Brown's Shoe
Directorships: Best Friends Pet Care, Sutton Place Gourmet, The Custom Foot

PHOENIX GROWTH CAPITAL CORPORATION

2401 Kerner Boulevard
San Rafael, CA 94901

Telephone: 415-485-4569
Fax: 415-485-4655
E-mail: normnelson@aol.com

Other Office Locations
641 East Morningside Drive
Atlanta, GA 30324
Phone 404-872-2406, Fax 404-876-1729
E-mail: rondemer@aol.com

3000 Sand Hill Road
Building 1, Suite 160
Menlo Park, CA 94024
Phone 415-854-8404, Fax 415-854-5732
E-mail: tkmphoenix@aol.com

Mission: Venture leasing and loans

Fund Size: $150 million
Founded: 1985
Average Investment: $1 million
Minimum Investment: $200,000

Investment Criteria: Venture Leasing, First-stage to Leveraged Buyout

Geographic Preference: United States

Industry Group Preference: Biotechnology, Communications, Computer Related, Electronics, Environmental Protection, Manufacturing/Processing, Medical/Health, Service Industries, Software

Portfolio Companies: Auravision, Biocircuits, C-Cube Microsystems, Digital Generation Systems, Inc., Lynx, Sunward Technologies, Terrapin Technologies, Inc.

Officers, Executives and Principals

Norm Nelson, Senior Vice President
Education: BS, Economics, Purdue University; MBA, San Francisco State
Background: Manager, West Coast office, Continental Bank Leasing

Ron Demer, Vice President (Atlanta)
Education: BA, Mechanical Engineering, Cornell; MBA, Harvard
Background: Vice President of major cable system operation; Director, captive leasing company for Raytheon; Vice President, Bankers Leasing, Keydata; Sales, IBM

Tom Morrison, Vice President (Menlo Park)
Education: BA, Yale University; MBA, Harvard Business School
Background: Entrepreneur, Founder of three companies; Fortune 500 Division President

Michael Hicks, New England Regional Manager (Canton)
Education: Boston University
Background: Equity, Lease Marketing, Boston Financial

PHOENIX HOME LIFE MUTUAL INSURANCE COMPANY

One American Row
P.O. Box 5056
Hartford, CT 06102-5056

Telephone: 860-403-5000

Mission: Actively seeking new investments

Fund Size: not available
Founded: not available
Average Investment: not available
Minimum Investment: $5 million

Investment Criteria: Seed, Research and Development, Startup, First-stage, Second-stage, Mezzanine, Leveraged Buyout, Special Situations, Control-block Purchases

Industry Group Preference: Diversified

Portfolio Companies: not available

Officers, Executives and Principals

Sandra Becker, Managing Director

THE PHOENIX PARTNERS

1000 Second Avenue, Suite 3600
Seattle, WA 98104

Telephone: 206-624-8968
Fax: 206-624-1907
E-mail: djohnsto@interserv.com

Mission: not available

Fund Size: $135 million
Founded: not available
Average Investment: $2 million
Minimum Investment: not available

Investment Criteria: Seed to Leveraged Buyout

Industry Group Preference: Biotechnology, CD Rom, Communications, Computer Related, Electronics, High Technology, Industrial Products Interactive Entertainment, Medical/Health, Multimedia, Software

Portfolio Companies: not available

Officers, Executives and Principals

Stuart C. Johnston, Managing General Partner
David B. Johnston, General Partner

PIEDMONT VENTURE PARTNERS, L.P.

227 West Trade Street
Suite 2325
Charlotte, NC 28202

Telephone: 704-333-2325
Fax: 704-333-0060
E-mail: compuserve73251.2021.com

Mission: Actively seeking new investments. Piedmont's goal is to achieve a high rate of long-term capital appreciation for its investors by providing the financing necessary to fuel North Carolina's next generation of entrepreneurial development.

Fund Size: not available
Founded: 1996
Average Investment: not available
Minimum Investment: $250,000

Investment Criteria: Seed, Startup, First-stage, Expansion

Geographic Preference: North Carolina

Industry Group Preference: Diversified

Portfolio Companies: not available

Officers, Executives and Principals

Stacy E. Anderson, Managing Principal
Education: BA, Duke University
Background: Vice President, Smith Barney, Harris Upham and Co.; Assistant Research Analyst, Dean Witter

Pamela K. Clement, Managing Principal
Education: BA, Cornell University
Background: President, Chief Operating Officer and Director, Sovereign Advisers, Inc.; President and Director, Prime Asset Management Corporation

William W. Neal, Managing Principal
Education: AB, Duke University
Background: President, Chief Executive Officer and Chairman, Broadway and Seymour; General Partner, Welsh Carson Anderson and Stowe; Group President, Automatic Data Processing; Vice President, Litton's Sweda Division

PIERCE INVESTMENT BANKING

2200 Clarendon Boulevard
Suite 1410
Arlington, VA 22201

Telephone: 703-516-7000
Fax: 703-516-7005

Mission: Actively seeking new investments. Specialize in emerging market financing and joint ventures in Latin America.

Fund Size: not available
Founded: 1986
Average Investment: not available
Minimum Investment: $500,000

Investment Criteria: Second-stage, Mezzanine, Private Placement, Joint Venture

Industry Group Preference: Convergent Technologies, Environment, Power, Telecommunications Broadcasting, Water

Portfolio Companies: not available

Officers, Executives and Principals

John P. Clark, Managing Director
William Graham, Managing Director
David Gregg III, Managing Director
Richard Holwill, Managing Director

PIONEER CAPITAL CORPORATION

60 State Street
Boston, MA 02109

Telephone: 617-422-4751
Fax: 617-742-7315

Mission: Actively seeking new investments

Fund Size: not available
Founded: 1980
Average Investment: not available
Minimum Investment: $250,000

Investment Criteria: Seed, Startup, First-stage, Second-stage, Mezzanine, Leveraged Buyout

Industry Group Preference: Communications, Computer Related, Consumer, Distribution, Electronic Components and Instrumentation, Genetic Engineering, Industrial Products and Equipment, Medical/Health Related

Portfolio Companies: not available

Officers, Executives and Principals

C.W. Dick, Partner
Christopher W. Lynch, Partner
Leigh E. Michl, Partner
Frank M. Polestra, Partner

PIPER JAFFRAY VENTURES, INC.

Piper Jaffray Technology Fund
222 South Ninth Street
Minneapolis, MN 55402

Telephone: 612-342-6447
Fax: 612-342-1036

Mission: Actively seeking new investments

Fund Size: $10 million
Founded: 1996
Average Investment: $500,000
Minimum Investment: $350,000

Investment Criteria: First-stage, Second-stage, Mezzanine

Geographic Preference: United States

Industry Group Preference: Technology

Portfolio Companies: not available

Officers, Executives and Principals

Gary Blauer, Managing Director

PIPER JAFFRAY VENTURES, INC.

Piper Jaffray Healthcare Fund I
Piper Jaffray Healthcare Fund II
222 South Ninth Street
Minneapolis, MN 55402

Telephone: 612-342-6345
Fax: 612-342-1036

Mission: Actively seeking new investments

Fund Size: $27 million (I) and $55 million (II)
Founded: 1992 and 1996
Average Investment: $1 - $3 million
Minimum Investment: $1 million

Investment Criteria: First-stage, Second-stage, Mezzanine

Geographic Preference: United States

Industry Group Preference: Medical/Health Related

Portfolio Companies: not available

Officers, Executives and Principals

Buzz Benson, Managing Director
Mike Seversen, Vice President

PITTSBURGH SEED FUND PARTNERS

2000 Technology Drive
Suite 150
Pittsburgh, PA 15219

Telephone: 412-687-4300
Fax: 412-687-4433

Mission: Making few, if any, new investments

Fund Size: not available
Founded: 1985
Average Investment: not available
Minimum Investment: $100,000

Investment Criteria: Seed, Startup, First-stage

Industry Group Preference: Communications, Computer Related, Consumer, Distribution, Electronic Components and Instrumentation, Energy/Natural Resources, Industrial Products and Equipment, Medical/Health Related

Portfolio Companies: not available

Officers, Executives and Principals

John R. Thorne, Founder and Chairman
Thomas N. Canfield, President
L. Frank Demmler, Vice President
J. Stuart Lovejoy

THE PITTSFORD GROUP, INC.

Eight Lodge Pole Road
Pittsford, NY 14534

Telephone and Fax: 716-223-3523

Mission: Actively seeking new investments

Fund Size: $30 million
Founded: 1975
Average Investment: $1.5 million
Minimum Investment: $100,000

Investment Criteria: Startup, First-stage, Second-stage

Geographic Preference: Northeastern United States, Ontario

Industry Group Preference: Computer Related, Industrial Products and Equipment

Portfolio Companies: not available

Officers, Executives and Principals

Logan M. Cheek III, Managing Principal

PK VENTURES, INC.
5802 Hartford Street
Tampa, FL 33619

Telephone: 813-287-0600
Fax: 813-287-0117

Mission: Actively seeking new investments

Fund Size: not available
Founded: 1986
Average Investment: not available
Minimum Investment: Equity of $1 million

Investment Criteria: Leveraged Buyout, Management Leveraged Buyouts

Industry Group Preference: Diversified

Portfolio Companies: not available

Officers, Executives and Principals

Robert L. Rose, President

THE PLATINUM GROUP, INC.

350 Fifth Avenue
Suite 7113
New York, NY 10118

Telephone: 201-944-8111
Fax: 201-944-5995

Mission: Actively seeking new investments

Fund Size: not available
Founded: 1990
Average Investment: not available
Minimum Investment: $100,000

Investment Criteria: Startup, First-stage, Second-stage, Leveraged Buyout

Industry Group Preference: Communications, Computer Related, Consumer, Distribution, Electronic Components and Instrumentation, Energy/Natural Resources, Genetic Engineering, Industrial Products and Equipment, Medical/Health Related

Portfolio Companies: not available

Officers, Executives and Principals

Harold P. Mintz, Managing Director
Leon Zemel, Financial Analyst

PLATINUM VENTURE PARTNERS

1815 South Meyers Road
Oakbrook Terrace, IL 60181

Telephone: 630-620-5000
Fax: 630-691-0710
E-mail: santer@platinum.com

Mission: All money raised from chief executive officers and entrepreneurs. These same investors help find, research and select investments. We don't feel like venture capitalists—we are successful entrepreneurs who are helping other entrepreneurs.

Fund Size: $55 million
Founded: 1992
Average Investment: $1.25 million
Minimum Investment: $500,000

Investment Criteria: First-stage, Second-stage

Industry Group Preference: Computer Related, Consumer, Entertainment Related, Medical/Health Related, Retail

Portfolio Companies: Campbell Software, Inc., Dynasty Technologies, House of Blues, Intouch Group, Spectrum Holobyte, Tomtec Imaging Systems, Nurse On Call, D-Vision Systems, BC Equity Funding LLC, Progressive Bagel Concepts, BlueRhino Corporation, Platinum Entertainment, IL Fornaio Corporation

Officers, Executives and Principals

Andrew Filipowski, Chief Executive Officer and President
Background: Founder, Chief Executive Officer, Chairman and President of Platinum Technology; Founder, President, Chief Executive Officer, DBMS, Inc., A.B. Dick, Motorola, Time, Inc.
Directorships: Marquette Venture Partners, Frontenac, Napersoft, Inc., Chicago High-Tech Associates, ITAA, Modagrafics, Inc., Intouch Group, Inc, American Oil and Gas Corporation

Steven Devick, Chief Operating Officer
Background: Chief Executive Officer, Platinum Entertainment; Devick Enterprises, Inc., Continental Capital Corporation, Platinum Development

Paul Humenansky, Chief Technical Officer
Background: Founder, Chief Operating Officer, Platinum Technology; Product Manager, DBMS, Inc.; Vice President, FMR Inc.

Michael Cullinane, Chief Financial Officer
Background: Senior Vice President, Chief Financial Officer, Platinum Technology; Chief Financial Officer and Vice President, DBMS, Inc.

Michael Santer, Vice President
Education: BS, Management Information Systems, University of Dayton; MBA, Northwestern
Background: Computer Science, MIS, recorded music, interactive software

PNC EQUITY MANAGEMENT CORPORATION

One PNC Plaza
Fifth Avenue and Wood Street, 19th Floor
Pittsburgh, PA 15222

Telephone: 412-762-7035
Fax: 412-762-6233

Mission: Actively seeking new investments

Fund Size: $100 million
Founded: 1990
Average Investment: $2 million
Minimum Investment: $1 million

Investment Criteria: Second-stage, Mezzanine, Leveraged Buyout, Special Situations

Industry Group Preference: Communications, Computer Related, Consumer, Distribution, Electronic Components and Instrumentation, Energy/Natural Resources, Genetic Engineering, Industrial Products and Equipment, Medical/Health Related

Portfolio Companies: not available

Officers, Executives and Principals

Gary J. Zentner, President
David McL. Hillman, Executive Vice President
David J. Blair, Senior Vice President and Principal
Peter V. Del Presto, Senior Vice President and Principal
Paul A. Giusti, Senior Vice President and Principal
Jack C. Glover, Vice President
Preston G. Walsh, Vice President
Deana B. Pittman, Director, Finance
Thomas H. O'Brien, Jr., Assistant Vice President

POINT VENTURE PARTNERS

600 Grant Street, 2970 USX Tower
Pittsburgh, PA 15219

Telephone: 412-261-1966
Fax: 412-261-1718

Mission: not available

Fund Size: $20 million
Founded: 1989
Average Investment: $1 million
Minimum Investment: $500,000

Investment Criteria: Startup to Mezzanine

Geographic Preference: Pittsburgh and surrounding area within 500 miles

Industry Group Preference: Biotechnology, Communications, Computer Related, Consumer Related, Electronics, Environmental Protection, Food Services, Medical/Health, Service Industries

Portfolio Companies: not available

Officers, Executives and Principals

Derek F. Minno, General Partner
Don J. Casturo, General Partner
Kent L. Engelmeier, General Partner

POLARIS VENTURE PARTNERS

Bay Colony Corporate Center
1000 Winter Street
Suite 3350
Waltham, MA 02154

Telephone: 617-290-0770
Fax: 617-290-0880
E-mail: partners@polarisventures.com

Other Office Locations
10900 N.E. 4th Street
Suite 2300
Bellevue, WA 98004
Phone 206-990-1527, Fax 206-990-1524

Mission: Actively seeking new investments in early-stage information technology and healthcare companies

Fund Size: $85 million
Founded: 1995
Average Investment: $1.5 - $3 million
Minimum Investment: $500,000

Investment Criteria: Seed, Start-up, First-stage, Second-stage

Geographic Preference: International

Industry Group Preference: Diagnostics, Information Technology, Healthcare, Internet Products and Services, Medical Devices, Medical Services, Software

Portfolio Companies: Accordant Health Services, Inc., Accusphere, Inc., AlphaBlox Corporation, Allaire Corporation, Classified Project, Inc., CyberSafe Corporation, deCODE genetics, Inc., SolidWorks Corporation

Officers, Executives and Principals

Terrance McGuire, General Partner
Education: MBA, Harvard Business School; MS, Engineering, Thayer School of Engineering, Dartmouth College; BS, Hobart College
Background: General Partner, Burr, Egan, Deleage and Company, Beta Partners; Associate, Golder, Thoma and Cressey; Consultant, Management Technologies
Directorships: Accordant Health Services, Accusphere, Inc., Ascent Pediatrics, Inc., Cubist Pharmaceuticals, Inc., deCODE, genetics, Inc., Inspire Pharmaceuticals, Inc., Integ Incorporated, Gingiss

Jonhthan Flint, General Partner
Education: JD, University of Virginia Law School; BA, high honors, Hobart College
Background: General Partner, Burr, Egan, Deleage and Company; Associate, Testa, Hurwitz and Thibeault
Directorships: AlphaBlox Corporation, Allaire Corporation, Berkeley Systems, Inc., Centra Software, Inc., SolidWorks Corporation

Stephen D. Arnold, General Partner
Education: Ph.D., Developmental Psychology; MA, Comparative Psychology; BA, Psychology, with honors

Background: Special Advisor, Information Technology Group, Burr, Egan, Deleage and Company; Vice President, Broadband Media Applications, Advanced Technology Division, Microsoft Corporation; President and Chief Operating Officer, Continuum Productions Corporation; Vice President, New Media Group, LucasArts Entertainment Company; Vice President and General Manager, Lucasfilm Games and Lucasfilm Learning, Lucasfilm, Ltd.
Directorships: CyberSafe Corporation, George Lucas Educational Foundation, Classified Project, Inc.

Brian Chee, Associate
Education: MBA, The Amos Tuck School, Dartmouth College; BS, Economics and Engineering, The United States Military Academy, West Point
Background: Sales and Marketing, Baxter Healthcare; Captain, United States Army Corps

POMONA CAPITAL

780 Third Avenue
New York, NY 10017

Telephone: 212-593-3639
Fax: 212-593-3987
E-mail: pomona@dti.net

Mission: Actively seeking new investments in efficient, predominantly private markets

Fund Size: $225+ million
Founded: 1994
Average Investment: not available
Minimum Investment: $1 million

Investment Criteria: Secondary interests in Venture Capital, Leveraged Buyout Funds, Private Investments in Public Companies, Restricted Stock in Public Companies, Special Situations, Undervalued Private Companies

Geographic Preference: Global

Industry Group Preference: Communications, Computer Related, Consumer, Healthcare Sciences and Services, Information Services, Media, Medical/Health Related

Portfolio Companies: not available

Officers, Executives and Principals

Michael D. Granoff, Chief Executive Officer
Frances J. Janis, Executive Vice President
Stephen M. Futrell, Vice President-Finance

PRIME CAPITAL MANAGEMENT COMPANY, INC.

1177 Summer Street
Stamford, CT 06905

Telephone: 203-964-0642
Fax: 203-964-0862

Mission: not available

Fund Size: $14 million
Founded: 1981
Average Investment: $600,000
Minimum Investment: $300,000

Investment Criteria: First to Second-stage

Industry Group Preference: Biotechnology, Computer Related, Electronics, Energy/Natural Resources, Industrial Products, Medical/Health

Portfolio Companies: not available

Officers, Executives and Principals

Dean E. Fenton, President
Education: AB, Harvard; MBA, Columbia
Background: General Partner, Sprout Capital Groups; Venture Capital Finance Director, Arthur D. Little, Inc.; Investment Associate, Boston Capital, Inc.
Directorships: Block Industries, Lifecodes Inc., Miscellaneous Software, Cognex

Theodore E. Elliot, Jr.
Education: AB, MBA, Harvard; LLB, New York University
Background: General Partner, General Electric Venture Capital
Directorships: Inpot-Outpot Corporation, Natural Interstate, Technology and Innovation Funds

PRIMUS VENTURE PARTNERS

1375 East Ninth Street
One Cleveland Center, Suite 2700
Cleveland, OH 44114

Telephone: 216-621-2185
Fax: 216-621-4543

Mission: not available

Fund Size: $100 million
Founded: not available
Average Investment: $1 - $5 million
Minimum Investment: not available

Investment Criteria: Proprietary or Unique, Startup to Acquisition

Geographic Preference: Midwestern United States

Industry Group Preference: Diversified

Portfolio Companies: Action Auto Rental Inc, Amerestate, American Steel and Wire Corporation, ARTS Technology, Astro Metallurgical, Bioanalytical Systems, The Brulin Corp, DeVry, Inc., Digital Analysis, Dirctel, Financial Security Systems, Gilatech, HDR Power Systems, HUEBCORE Communications, Inverness Development Corporation

Officers, Executives and Principals

James T. Bartlett, Managing Director
Education: BA, History, Amherst College; MBA, Harvard
Background: Chief Operating Officer, Acme-Cleveland Corporation, McKinsey and Co.; Member of SBA
Directorships: American Steel and Wire Corporation, Keithley Instruments, Kirtland Capital, LCI International, OttoSensors, Tweeds, Wast Quip

Loyal W. Wilson, Managing Director
Education: BA, Economics, University of North Carolina; MBA, Indiana University
Background: Senior Investment Manager, First Chicago Corporation
Directorships: Astro Metallurgical, DeVry, Directel, HDR Power Systems, Merit West, STERIS Corporation

Kevin J. McGinty, Managing Director
Education: BA, Economics, Ohio Wesleyan University; MBA, Cleveland State University
Background: Executive Vice President, Society National Bank; Senior Vice President Society Corporation, Manager, Bond Department, International Banking Division, Multinational
Directorships: Amerestate, Financial Security Services, Ohio Business, Machines, Ohio Sound and Music, Tri City Radio

William C. Mulligan, Managing Director
Education: BA, Economics, Dennison University; MBA, University of Chicago
Background: McKinsey and Company Inc., Deere and Company, The First National Bank of Chicago
Directorships: Bioanalytical Systems, The Brulin Corporation, HUEBCORE Communications, Isolab, National Medical Diagnostics, Underground

Jonathan E. Dick, Managing Director

PRINCETON AMERICAN FINANCIAL SERVICES CORPORATION

2222 East Camelback Road
Suite 200
Phoenix, AZ 85016

Telephone: 602-954-2600
Fax: 602-954-2633

Mission: Actively seeking new investments

Fund Size: not available
Founded: 1983
Average Investment: not available
Minimum Investment: $250,000

Investment Criteria: First-stage, Second-stage, Mezzanine, Leveraged Buyout, Special Situations

Industry Group Preference: Communications, Computer Related, Consumer, Distribution, Electronic Components and Instrumentation, Energy/Natural Resources, Industrial Products and Equipment, Medical/Health Related

Portfolio Companies: not available

Officers, Executives and Principals

Dale E. Eyman, Jr., President
Winston P. McKellar, Senior Vice President
Gordon Clark, Vice President
David S. Smith, Vice President
William C. Taylor, Vice President

PRIVATE CAPITAL CORPORATION

100 Brookwood Place
Suite 410
Birmingham, AL 35209

Telephone: 205-879-2722
Fax: 205-879-5121

Mission: not available

Fund Size: not available
Founded: not available
Average Investment: $750,000
Minimum Investment: not available

Investment Criteria: Startup to Leveraged Buyout

Geographic Preference: Southeastern United States

Industry Group Preference: Broadcast/Cable/Radio, Communications, Computer Related, Consumer Related, Electronics, Financial Services, Food Services, Insurance, Medical/Health

Portfolio Companies: not available

Officers, Executives and Principals

William W. Featheringill, President
Education: BE, Vanderbilt; MBA, JD, Columbia
Directorships: Seako, Industrial Supplies.

William P. Acker III, Vice President
Education: AB, Vanderbilt University; Postgraduate work, Finance, University of Alabama
Directorships: Metretek, Seako

PRIVATE EQUITY INVESTORS, INC.

115 East 62nd Street
New York, NY 10021

Telephone: 212-750-2933
Fax: 212-750-2685

Mission: Actively seeking new investments

Fund Size: not available
Founded: not available
Average Investment: not available
Minimum Investment: not available

Investment Criteria: Second-stage, Mezzanine, Leveraged Buyout, Special Situations, Secondary Purchases of Limited Partnerships, Portfolios of Direct Investments

Industry Group Preference: Diversified

Portfolio Companies: not available

Officers, Executives and Principals: not available

THE PRODUCTIVITY FUND I AND II
The Sears Tower, Suite 9500
Chicago, IL 60606

Telephone: 312-258-1400
Fax: 312-258-0334

Mission: not available

Fund Size: $40 million
Founded: not available
Average Investment: $500,000
Minimum Investment: not available

Investment Criteria: First to Second-stage

Industry Group Preference: Communications, Computer Related, Consumer Related, Electronics, Energy/ Natural Resources, Environmental Protection, Industrial Products, Medical/Health, Service Industries, Wholesaling/Distribution

Portfolio Companies: not available

Officers, Executives and Principals

Bret Maxwell, Managing Director
Education: BS, Industrial Engineering, MBA, Northwestern
Background: Arthur Andersen and Co., General Electric Co.

Oliver Nicklin, President
Education: BS, Chemical Engineering, University of Texas; MBA, Harvard
Background: President and Founder, First Analysis; William Blair and Co.

PROSPECT STREET INVESTMENT MANAGEMENT COMPANY, INC.

250 Park Avenue
17th Floor
New York, NY 10177

Telephone: 212-490-0480
Fax: 212-490-1566

Other Office Locations
Exchange Place, 37th Floor
Boston, MA 02100
Phone 617-742-3800, Fax 617-742-9455

Mission: Actively seeking new investments

Fund Size: $600 million
Founded: 1988
Average Investment: $4 million
Minimum Investment: $1 million

Investment Criteria: Second-stage, Special Situations, Control-block Purchases, Growth Companies, Equity

Industry Group Preference: All except Gaming, Tobacco, Liquor, Guns

Portfolio Companies: Robotics, Contaminated Soil Remediation, Natural Charcoal, Electronic Fixed Income Trading System, Specialty Medical Needles, Crafts Retailing, Specialty Media Production, Multi-media Entertainment

Officers, Executives and Principals

Joseph G. Cote, Co-President (New York)
Richard E. Omohundro, Jr., Co-President (Boston)
John F. Barry, Vice President (New York)
Ronald D. Celmer, Vice President (New York)
John A. Frabotta, Vice President (Boston)
Preston I. Carnes, Jr., Vice President (New York)
Kevin F. Littlejohn, Vice President (Boston)

THE PROVCO GROUP

Two Radnor Station
290 King of Prussia Road, Suite 314
Radnor, PA 19087

Telephone: 610-964-1642
Fax: 610-964-1647

Mission: Actively seeking new investments

Fund Size: not available
Founded: not available
Average Investment: not available
Minimum Investment: $100,000

Investment Criteria: First-stage, Second-stage

Industry Group Preference: Communications, Computer Related, Consumer, Distribution, Electronic Components and Instrumentation, Genetic Engineering, Medical/Health Related

Portfolio Companies: not available

Officers, Executives and Principals

Richard E. Caruso, PhD, President
Jerry N. Holtz, Vice President

PROVIDENCE EQUITY PARTNERS, INC.

50 Kennedy Plaza
Ninth Floor
Providence, RI 02903

Telephone: 401-751-1700
Fax: 401-751-1790

Mission: Actively seeking new investments

Fund Size: $365 million
Founded: 1991
Average Investment: $25 million
Minimum Investment: $10 million

Investment Criteria: Mezzanine, Leveraged Buyout, Second-stage, Control-block Purchases

Industry Group Preference: Communications

Portfolio Companies: not available

Officers, Executives and Principals

Jonathan M. Nelson, President
Glenn M. Creamer, Managing Director
Paul J. Salem, Managing Director
Raymond M. Mathieu, Chief Financial Officer
Mark A. Pelson, Vice President
Mark J. Masiello, Vice President

PRUDENTIAL EQUITY INVESTORS, INC.

717 Fifth Avenue
Suite 1100
New York, NY 10022

Telephone: 212-753-0901
Fax: 212-826-6798

Mission: Actively seeking new investments

Fund Size: $1 billion
Founded: 1982
Average Investment: $5 - $25 million
Minimum Investment: $5 million

Investment Criteria: Special Situations, Later-stage Equity, Leveraged Buyout

Industry Group Preference: Communications, Computer Related, Consumer, Distribution, Electronic Components and Instrumentation, Genetic Engineering, Industrial Products and Equipment, Medical/Health Related

Portfolio Companies: Card Establishment Services, The WinterBrook Beverage Group, Auspex Systems, Taco Cabana, Sunglass Hut, Total Pharmaceutical Care, Damark, Meadaphis, VMG, Office Mart, Health Management Associates, Amsco International, Picture Tel, Coventry Corporation, Lechters

Officers, Executives and Principals

Robert A. Knox, President
Education: BA, MBA, Boston University
Background: The Prudential, leveraged transactions
Directorships: Bridge Information Systems, Health Management Associates, Lechters

Dana J. O'Brien, Vice President
Education: BA, Hobart College; MBA, Wharton School at University of Pennsylvania
Directorships: Comdata, U.I. Video Holding

John A. Downer, Vice President
Education: BA, MBA, JD, Harvard University
Background: T. Rowe Price Associates, Harvard Management Corporation
Directorships: Medaphis, VMG Holdings

Mark Rossi, Vice President
Education: BA, Saint Vincent College; MBA, Northwestern University
Directorships: Conner Peripherals, Food for Health, Georgetown Leather Design

Martha L. Robinson, Vice President
Education: BA, Connecticut College; MBA, Columbia University
Directorships: Rebound, Total Pharmaceutical Care

Paul O. Hirschbiel, Vice President
Education: BA, MBA, University of North Carolina at Chapel Hill
Directorships: Dell Computer, Rebound, VMG Holdings

Paul S. Herndeen, Vice President
Education: BS, Boston College; MBA, University of Virginia
Background: Corporate Finance, Oppenheim and Co., Continental Bank
Directorships: Food for Health and Wehran Enviro Tech

William J. Nimmo, Vice President
Education: BA, MBA, Dartmouth College
Background: Mergers and Acquisitions, Corporate Finance, Capital Markets, J.P. Morgan
Directorships: Damark International, Georgetown Leather Design

QUAESTUS MANAGEMENT CORPORATION

330 East Kilbourn Avenue
Milwaukee, WI 53202

Telephone: 414-283-4500
Fax: 414-283-4505

Mission: Actively seeking new investments

Fund Size: not available
Founded: 1989
Average Investment: not available
Minimum Investment: $500,000

Investment Criteria: Second-stage, Mezzanine, Leveraged Buyout

Industry Group Preference: Communications, Computer Related, Medical/Health Related

Portfolio Companies: not available

Officers, Executives and Principals

Richard W. Weening, Chairman and President
Terrence J. Leahy, Vice President
Robert J. Wait, Research Director and Investment Associate
Barbara J. Kiely Miller, Administrative Associate
Singari Srivathsa, Investment Analysis

QUANTAM CAPITAL PARTNERS

4400 Northeast 25th Avenue
Fort Lauderdale, FL 33308

Telephone: 305-776-1133
Fax: 305-938-9406

Mission: not available

Fund Size: $9 million
Founded: not available
Average Investment: $350,000
Minimum Investment: not available

Investment Criteria: Second-stage to Leveraged Buyout

Industry Group Preference: Biotechnology, Broadcast/Cable/Radio, Communications, Computer Related, Educational, Electronics, Energy/Natural Resources, High Technology, Industrial Products, Medical/Health, Publishing, Software, Transportation

Portfolio Companies: not available

Officers, Executives and Principals

Elaine E. Healy, General Partner
James F. Healy, General Partner
Michael E. Chaney, General Partner

QUEST VENTURES

126 South Park Street
San Francisco, CA 94107

Telephone: 415-546-7118
Fax: 415-394-9291

Mission: not available

Fund Size: $30 million
Founded: not available
Average Investment: $500,000
Minimum Investment: not available

Investment Criteria: Seed to First-stage

Geographic Preference: Western United States

Industry Group Preference: Biotechnology, Communications, Computer Related, Consumer Related, Electronics, Energy/Natural Resources, Industrial Products, Medical/Health

Portfolio Companies: not available

Officers, Executives and Principals

William A. Boeger III, General Partner
Lucien Ruby, General Partner

QUINCY PARTNERS
P.O. Box 154
Glen Head, NY 11545

Telephone: 516-759-1752
Fax: 516-759-1754

Mission: Actively seeking new investments

Fund Size: not available
Founded: 1970
Average Investment: not available
Minimum Investment: $1 million

Investment Criteria: Leveraged Buyout, Special Situations

Industry Group Preference: Diversified

Portfolio Companies: not available

Officers, Executives and Principals

Donald J. Sutherland, President

R AND D FUNDING CORPORATION

440 Mission Court, Suite 250
Fremont, CA 94539

Telephone: 510-656-1855
Fax: 510-656-1949

Mission: not available

Fund Size: $250 million
Founded: not available
Average Investment: $5 million
Minimum Investment: not available

Investment Criteria: Research and Development to Mezzanine

Industry Group Preference: Biotechnology, Communications, Computer Related, Consumer Related, Electronics, Energy/Natural Resources, Industrial Products, Medical/Health

Portfolio Companies: not available

Officers, Executives and Principals

Richard E. Moser, President
Lawrence W. Bill, Vice President
Michael S. Hasley, Vice President

R. C. BERNER AND COMPANY

4312 Lakewoode Drive
Delray Beach, FL 33445-9003

Telephone: 561-498-2244
Fax: 561-498-2244

Mission: Making few, if any, new investments

Fund Size: not available
Founded: 1966
Average Investment: not available
Minimum Investment: not available

Investment Criteria: Second-stage, Mezzanine, Leveraged Buyout, Special Situations, Intermediary Only

Industry Group Preference: Communications, Computer Related, Consumer, Distribution, Electronic Components and Instrumentation, Energy/Natural Resources, Genetic Engineering, Industrial Products and Equipment, Medical/Health Related

Portfolio Companies: not available

Officers, Executives and Principals

Robert C. Berner, President
H.S. Berner, Treasurer

RADNOR VENTURE PARTNERS, L.P.

800 The Safeguard Building
435 Devon Park Drive
Wayne, PA 19087

Telephone: 610-975-9770
Fax: 610-975-9330

Mission: Making few, if any, new investments

Fund Size: not available
Founded: 1988
Average Investment: not available
Minimum Investment: $500,000

Investment Criteria: First-stage, Second-stage, Mezzanine

Industry Group Preference: Communications, Computer Related, Electronic Components and Instrumentation, Genetic Engineering, Industrial Products and Equipment, Medical/Health Related

Portfolio Companies: not available

Officers, Executives and Principals

Robert E. Keith, Jr., President
Ira M. Lubert, Managing Director
Mark J. DeNino, Managing Director
Christopher Moller, PhD, Managing Director
James Ratigan, Chief Financial Officer
Tami Fratis, Vice President
Stephen L. Amsterdam, Senior Associate

RAF VENTURES LP

165 Township Line Road
Suite 2100
Jenkintown, PA 19046

Telephone: 215-572-0738
Fax: 215-576-1640

Mission: Actively seeking new investments

Fund Size: not available
Founded: 1979
Average Investment: not available
Minimum Investment: $500,000

Investment Criteria: Seed, Startup, First-stage

Industry Group Preference: Consumer, Electronic Components and Instrumentation, Industrial Products and Equipment, Medical/Health Related

Portfolio Companies: not available

Officers, Executives and Principals

Robert A. Fox, Chief Executive Officer and Principal

RAND CAPITAL CORPORATION

2200 Rand Building
Buffalo, NY 14203

Telephone: 716-853-0802
Fax: 716-854-8480

Mission: not available

Fund Size: $12 million
Founded: not available
Average Investment: $350,000
Minimum Investment: not available

Investment Criteria: First-stage to Acquisition

Geographic Preference: Northeastern United States

Industry Group Preference: Diversified

Portfolio Companies: Auto Radiator Sales, Inc., Bison Data Corporation, Bydatel Corporation, Chem Pub LP, GFK, International Imaging Materials, Local Area Telecommunications, Measurement Specialties, Niagra Technology, Primages, Sheridan Infant Products, Software Performance Group, Three Sixty Corporation, Trader's Magazine, Trade Winds Fan Co.

Officers, Executives and Principals

Reginald B. Newman II, Chairman
Allen F. Grum, President

RBC VENTURES, INC.

2627 East 21st Street
Tulsa, OK 74114

Telephone: 918-744-5607
Fax: 918-743-8530
E-mail: rbcinc@ionet.net

Mission: Actively seeking new investments

Fund Size: not available
Founded: 1989
Average Investment: not available
Minimum Investment: $1 million

Investment Criteria: Second-stage, Mezzanine, Leveraged Buyout, Special Situations, Control-block Purchases

Geographic Preference: Oklahoma

Industry Group Preference: Diversified

Portfolio Companies: not available

Officers, Executives and Principals

Roger B. Collins, President
Anthony D. Allen, Chief Financial Officer

REALTY FUNDING GROUP INTERNATIONAL

49 West 12th Street
Executive Suite 3D
New York, NY 10011

Telephone: 212-691-9895

Mission: Actively seeking new investments

Fund Size: not available
Founded: 1989
Average Investment: not available
Minimum Investment: not available

Investment Criteria: Start-up, Construction Funding, Senior Debt, Special Situations, Acquisition Finance

Geographic Preference: International

Industry Group Preference: Real Estate

Portfolio Companies: not available

Officers, Executives and Principals

Allan E. Skora, President
Richard Quattlebaum, Senior Partner (North America)

RECOVERY EQUITY INVESTORS, L.P.

901 Mariners Island Boulevard
Suite 465
San Mateo, CA 94404

Telephone: 415-578-9752
Fax: 415-578-9842

Mission: Actively seeking new investments

Fund Size: $208 million
Founded: 1990
Average Investment: $10 million
Minimum Investment: $1 million

Investment Criteria: Special Situations, Turnarounds

Geographic Preference: United States

Industry Group Preference: Communications, Consumer, Distribution, Electronic Components and Instrumentation, Energy/Natural Resources, Industrial Products and Equipment, Medical/Health Related

Portfolio Companies: not available

Officers, Executives and Principals

Jeffrey A. Lipkin, General Partner
Joseph Finn-Egan, General Partner
Geof Bland, Associate

REDWOOD CAPITAL CORPORATION

P.O. Box 387
Brisbane, CA 94005

Telephone: 415-468-8200
Fax: 415-468-8202

Mission: Actively seeking new investments

Fund Size: not available
Founded: 1981
Average Investment: not available
Minimum Investment: $100,000

Investment Criteria: Seed, Startup, First-stage, Second-stage, Mezzanine, Leveraged Buyout

Industry Group Preference: Consumer

Portfolio Companies: not available

Officers, Executives and Principals

Krist Jake, President

REGULUS INTERNATIONAL CAPITAL COMPANY, INC.

140 Greenwich Avenue
Greenwich, CT 06830

Telephone: 203-625-9700
Fax: 203-625-9706

Mission: not available

Fund Size: not available
Founded: not available
Average Investment: $750,000
Minimum Investment: not available

Investment Criteria: Seed to Second-stage

Industry Group Preference: Biotechnology, Medical/Health, Oil and Gas, Packaging, Paper, Printing, Publishing

Portfolio Companies: not available

Officers, Executives and Principals

Clara Spalter, Partner
Education: BSC, California Tech; MBA, Stanford

Lee Miller, Partner
Education: BA, MBA, Stanford

REPRISE CAPITAL CORPORATION

400 Post Avenue
Westbury, NY 11590

Telephone: 516-338-2700
Fax: 516-338-2808

Other Office Locations
6345 Balboa Boulevard
Encino, CA 91316
Phone 818-776-2420, Fax 818-776-2434

Mission: Actively seeking new investments

Fund Size: not available
Founded: 1985
Average Investment: not available
Minimum Investment: $1 million

Investment Criteria: Turnarounds

Industry Group Preference: Consumer, Distribution, Electronic Components and Instrumentation, Industrial Products and Equipment

Portfolio Companies: not available

Officers, Executives and Principals

Stanley Tulchin, Chairman (Westbury)
Directorships: P.C.A. International Tapps Corporation

Norman Tulchin, Executive Vice President (Encino)

Jeffrey R. Tulchin, Vice President (Westbury)

RESOURCECAN, LTD.

Baine Johnston Centre, P.O. Box 5367
St. John's, Newfoundland A1C 5W2
Canada

Telephone: 709-576-1287
Fax: 709-576-1273

Mission: Actively seeking new investments

Fund Size: not available
Founded: 1981
Average Investment: not available
Minimum Investment: $250,000

Investment Criteria: Second-stage, Mezzanine, Leveraged Buyout

Industry Group Preference: Communications, Distribution, Electronic Components and Instrumentation, Energy/Natural Resources, Industrial Products and Equipment

Portfolio Companies: not available

Officers, Executives and Principals

Chris Collingwood, Chairman
Robert Crosbie, President
Rex Anthony, Treasurer

RFE INVESTMENT PARTNERS

36 Grove Street
New Canaan, CT 06840

Telephone: 203-966-2800
Fax: 203-966-3109

Mission: Actively seeking new investments

Fund Size: not available
Founded: 1979
Average Investment: not available
Minimum Investment: $5 million

Investment Criteria: Second-stage, Mezzanine, Leveraged Buyout, Special Situations

Industry Group Preference: Communications, Consumer, Distribution, Industrial Products and Equipment, Medical/Health Related

Portfolio Companies: not available

Officers, Executives and Principals

A. Dean Davis, General Partner
Michael J. Foster, General Partner
Howard C. Landis, General Partner
James A. Parsons, General Partner
Robert M. Williams, General Partner
Andrew J. Wagner, General Partner

RICE CAPITAL

5847 San Felipe
Suite 4350
Houston, TX 77057

Telephone: 713-783-7770
Fax: 713-783-9750

Mission: Actively seeking new investments

Fund Size: not available
Founded: 1989
Average Investment: not available
Minimum Investment: not available

Investment Criteria: Mezzanine

Industry Group Preference: Diversified

Portfolio Companies: not available

Officers, Executives and Principals

Don K. Rice, Managing Partner
Jeffrey P. Sangalis, Partner
Jeffrey A. Toole, Partner
James P. Wilson, Partner

RICHARD JAFFE AND COMPANY, INC.

7318 Royal Circle
Dallas, TX 75230

Telephone: 214-739-0800
Fax: 214-265-1999

Mission: Actively seeking new investments

Fund Size: not available
Founded: 1962
Average Investment: not available
Minimum Investment: Less than $100,000

Investment Criteria: Startup, First-stage, Leveraged Buyout, Special Situations

Industry Group Preference: Communications, Computer Related, Consumer, Distribution, Industrial Products and Equipment

Portfolio Companies: not available

Officers, Executives and Principals

Richard R. Jaffe, President

RICHLAND VENTURES

3100 West End Avenue
Suite 400
Nashville, TN 37203

Telephone: 615-383-8030
Fax: 615-269-0463

Mission: Actively seeking new investments

Fund Size: not available
Founded: 1994
Average Investment: not available
Minimum Investment: $1 million

Investment Criteria: Second-stage

Industry Group Preference: Communications, Consumer, Medical/Health Related

Portfolio Companies: not available

Officers, Executives and Principals

Jack Tyrrell, Partner
W. Patrick Ortale, Partner
Michael W. Blackburn, Associate

RIORDAN, LEWIS AND HADEN

300 South Grand Avenue, 29th Floor
Los Angeles, CA 90071

Telephone: 213-229-8500
Fax: 213-229-8597

Mission: not available

Fund Size: $75 million
Founded: not available
Average Investment: $4 million
Minimum Investment: not available

Investment Criteria: Startup to Leveraged Buyout

Geographic Preference: West Coast of the United States

Industry Group Preference: Biotechnology, Communications, Computer Related, Consumer Related, Electronics, Medical/Health

Portfolio Companies: not available

Officers, Executives and Principals

J. Christopher Lewis, General Partner
Patrick C. Haden, General Partner
Richard J. Riordan, General Partner

RIVER CAPITAL

Two Midtown Plaza
1360 Peachtree Street, Suite 1430
Atlanta, GA 30309

Telephone: 404-873-2166
Fax: 404-873-2158

Mission: Actively seeking new investments

Fund Size: not available
Founded: 1983
Average Investment: not available
Minimum Investment: $1 million

Investment Criteria: Mezzanine, Leveraged Buyout

Industry Group Preference: Consumer Products, Distribution, Light Manufacturing, Media

Portfolio Companies: not available

Officers, Executives and Principals

Jerry D. Withington, Principal
Education: BA, Economics, University of Kentucky; MA, Economics, Western Kentucky; MBA, University of
  Louisville
Background: Chief Operating Officer, Mitchell Steel; Senior Manager, Fuqua Industries, Teledyne
Directorships: Serv-O-Matic, Inc., Hometown Communications, Piedmont Holdings, Decor Gravure

F.W. Hulse IV, Managing Principal
Education: BA, Economics, University of Virginia; MBA, Harvard
Background: Chief Executive Officer, Hangar One, Inc.
Directorships: American Beechcraft, Decor Gravure, American Consumer Products

M. Andy Mason, Principal
Education: BS, Accounting, Auburn University; MBA, Emory University
Background: Managing Director, Duff and Phelps, Capital Markets; Vice President, Trivest, Inc.; Vice Presi-
  dent, GE Capital

Peter A. Williams, Vice President
Education: BA, Economics, Ripon College; MBA, Emory University
Background: Investment Manager, Confederation Life; Senior Investment Analyst, Metropolitan Life

RIVER CITIES CAPITAL FUND

221 East Fourth Street
Suite 2250
Cincinnati, OH 45202-4147

Telephone: 513-621-9700
Fax: 513-579-8939

Mission: Actively seeking new investments

Fund Size: $45 million
Founded: 1994
Average Investment: $1.2 million
Minimum Investment: $500,000

Investment Criteria: Startup, First-stage, Second-stage, Leveraged Buyout

Geographic Preference: Ohio, Kentucky, Indiana

Industry Group Preference: Diversified

Portfolio Companies: not available

Officers, Executives and Principals

R. Glen Mayfield
Edwin T. (Ted) Robinson
J. Eric Lenning
Joseph C. Von Lehman, Jr.
Murray R. Wilson

ROANOKE CAPITAL, LTD.

1111 Third Avenue, Suite 2220
Seattle, WA 98101

Telephone: 206-628-0606
Fax: 206-628-0479

Mission: not available

Fund Size: $30 million
Founded: not available
Average Investment: $1 million
Minimum Investment: not available

Investment Criteria: First-stage to Leveraged Buyout

Geographic Preference: Pacific Northwest region of the United States

Industry Group Preference: Diversified

Portfolio Companies: not available

Officers, Executives and Principals

Frances M. Conley, Founder
Education: BA, Emmanuel College; MBA, Harvard
Background: Senior Vice President, Rainier National Bank; Equities Analyst, Keystone Custodian Funds

Gerald R. Conley, Principal
Education: BS, University of California at Berkeley; MF, Yale; MBA, Harvard
Background: Manager, Hardwoods Division, Weyerhaeuser Co.; International Consultant, Arthur D. Little;
  U.S. Peace Corps, Brazil

ROBERTSON STEPHENS AND COMPANY, L.P.

555 California Street
Suite 2600
San Francisco, CA 94104

Telephone: 415-781-9700
Fax: 415-989-8575

Other Office Locations
One International Place, 23rd Floor
Boston, MA 02110
Phone 617-330-8690, Fax 617-330-8752

450 Park Avenue, 15th Floor
New York, NY 10022
Phone 212-319-8900

Harizomon Horikiri Building, Second Floor
1-7-3 Hirakawa-cho
Chiyoda-ku, Tokyo 102
Japan
Phone 81-3-5210-3341, Fax 81-3-5210-3345

Mission: Actively seeking new investments

Fund Size: not available
Founded: 1978
Average Investment: not available
Minimum Investment: No rigid minimum

Investment Criteria: Seed, Startup, First-stage, Second-stage, Mezzanine, Leveraged Buyout

Industry Group Preference: Computer Related, Consumer, Electronic Components and Instrumentation, Energy/Natural Resources, Genetic Engineering, Industrial Products and Equipment, Medical/Health Related

Portfolio Companies: not available

Officers, Executives and Principals

Paul H. Stephens, Chief Investment Officer (San Francisco)
G. Randy Hecht, Chief Operating Officer (San Francisco)
Molly C. Barger, Managing Director (San Francisco)
M. Kathleen Behrens, Managing Director (San Francisco)
David L. Goldsmith, Managing Director (San Francisco)
John M. Grillos, Managing Director (San Francisco)
Charles A. Hamilton, Managing Director (San Francisco)
Sy F. Kaufman, Managing Director (San Francisco)

ROGERS INVESTMENT CORPORATION

2800 Sand Hill Road
Suite 120
Menlo Park, CA 94025

Telephone: 415-854-2767
Fax: 415-854-2276

Mission: not available

Fund Size: not available
Founded: 1986
Average Investment: not available
Minimum Investment: $100,000

Investment Criteria: First-stage, Second-stage, Leveraged Buyout

Industry Group Preference: Communications, Computer Related, Industrial Products and Equipment

Portfolio Companies: not available

Officers, Executives and Principals

Roy L. Rogers, General Partner
Beatrice Pezino, Associate

ROSENFELD AND COMPANY

1211 Southwest Sixth Avenue
Portland, OR 97204

Telephone: 503-228-3255
Fax: 503-228-4529

Mission: Actively seeking new investments

Fund Size: not available
Founded: 1977
Average Investment: not available
Minimum Investment: $250,000

Investment Criteria: Second-stage, Mezzanine, Leveraged Buyout, Special Situations

Industry Group Preference: Consumer, Distribution, Electronic Components and Instrumentation, Energy/ Natural Resources, Genetic Engineering, Industrial Products and Equipment, Medical/Health Related

Portfolio Companies: not available

Officers, Executives and Principals

William W. Rosenfeld, Jr., Managing Partner

THE ROSER PARTNERSHIP, LTD.

1105 Spruce Street
Boulder, CO 80302

Telephone: 303-443-6436
Fax: 303-443-1885

Mission: Actively seeking new investments

Fund Size: not available
Founded: 1987
Average Investment: not available
Minimum Investment: Less than $100,000

Investment Criteria: Startup, First-stage, Second-stage

Industry Group Preference: Diversified

Portfolio Companies: not available

Officers, Executives and Principals

Christopher W. Roser, Partner
James L.D. Roser, Partner
Phillip Dignan, Jr., Partner

ROSEWOOD CAPITAL

1 Maritime Plaza, Suite 1330
San Francisco, CA 94111-3503

Telephone: 415-362-5526
Fax: 415-362-1192
E-mail: Howard_Rosenberg@msn.com

Mission: Actively seeking new investments

Fund Size: $80 million
Founded: 1985
Average Investment: $7 million
Minimum Investment: $3 million

Investment Criteria: Second-stage to Leveraged Buyout

Geographic Preference: Western half of United States

Industry Group Preference: Consumer Related, Financial Services, Food Services, Retail, Wholesaling/Distribution

Portfolio Companies: Noah's Bagels, Rubio's Restaurants, Sutton Place Gourmet, Napa Valley Kitchens, Rainbow Light, Gateway Learning Corporation, Juice Club

Officers, Executives and Principals

Chip Adams, Founder
Education: BA, Princeton; Stanford Business School
Background: Partner, Smith Barney Ventures; Founder, Fanueil Investments; Management Consultant, Bain and Co.

Kyle Anderson, General Partner
Education: BA, Princeton; Columbia Business School
Background: Vice President, First Boston Corporation

Doug Valenti, Partner
Education: BA, Georgia Tech; Stanford Business School
Background: McKinsey and Company, US Navy, Procter and Gamble

Howard Rosenberg, Associate
Education: BA, University of Pennsylvania; BS, Wharton School of Business

ROTHSCHILD VENTURES, INC.

1251 Avenue of the Americas
51st Floor
New York, NY 10020

Telephone: 212-403-3500
Fax: 212-403-3501

Mission: Actively seeking new investments

Fund Size: not available
Founded: 1949
Average Investment: not available
Minimum Investment: $500,000

Investment Criteria: Seed, Research and Development, Startup, First-stage, Second-stage, Mezzanine, Leveraged Buyout

Industry Group Preference: Communications, Computer Related, Consumer, Distribution, Electronic Components and Instrumentation, Energy/Natural Resources, Genetic Engineering, Industrial Products and Equipment, Medical/Health Related

Portfolio Companies: not available

Officers, Executives and Principals

Jess L. Belser, Managing General Partner
Scott T. Jones, Senior Vice President
James J. O'Neill, Senior Vice President
Sherri A. Croasdale, Assistant Vice President
Vincent Lopez, Assistant Vice President

ROYAL BANK CAPITAL CORPORATION

200 Bay Street, North Tower, 16th Floor
Toronto, Ontario M5J 2J5
Canada

Telephone: 416-974-5088
Fax: 416-974-8411

Other Office Locations
One Place Ville Marie
Ninth Floor, East Wing
Montreal, Quebec H3C 3A9
Canada
Phone 514-874-5081, Fax 514-874-2294

666 Burrard Street
Suite 1170-Park Place
Vancouver, British Columbia V6C 2X8
Canada
Phone 604-665-0460, Fax 604-665-8699

Mission: Actively seeking new investments

Fund Size: not available
Founded: 1969
Average Investment: not available
Minimum Investment: $1 million

Investment Criteria: Second-stage, Mezzanine, Leveraged Buyout

Industry Group Preference: Communications, Computer Related, Consumer, Distribution, Electronic Components and Instrumentation, Energy/Natural Resources, Genetic Engineering, Industrial Products and Equipment, Medical/Health Related

Portfolio Companies: not available

Officers, Executives and Principals

J. Sayegh, President (Toronto)
B.G. Laver, Vice President (Toronto)
Z. Sam Ruttonsha, Vice President (Toronto)
J.C. Arpin, Vice President (Montreal)
D.J. Elliott, Vice President (Vancouver)
P. LaForest, Managing Director, Small Business Venture Funds
S. Selby, Investment Manager (Toronto)
F.M. MacDonald, Investment Manager (Vancouver)
Peter P. Von Schilling, Investment Manager (Toronto)
P. Adamek, Investment Manager, Small Business Funds
J. Patterson, Investment Manager, Small Business Funds

ROYALTY CAPITAL FUND, L.P. I
ROYALTY CAPITAL MANAGEMENT, INC.
Five Downing Road
Lexington, MA 02173-6918

Telephone: 617-861-8490

Other Office Locations
12 Brady Loop
Andover, MA 01810-3224
Phone 508-474-9112

Mission: Actively seeking new investments where a royalty against gross revenue can return original capital within 18 months

Fund Size: not available
Founded: 1994
Average Investment: $200,000
Minimum Investment: Less than $100,000

Investment Criteria: Seed, Startup, First-stage, Second-stage, Special Situations—any stage in which revenue can be used to provide a royalty stream

Geographic Preference: Northeastern United States

Industry Group Preference: Communications, Computer Related, Consumer, Electronic Components and Instrumentation, Energy/Natural Resources, Genetic Engineering, Industrial Products and Equipment, Medical/Health Related

Portfolio Companies: not available

Officers, Executives and Principals

Arthur L. Fox, President (Lexington)
Education: BSEE, University of Maryland; MSEE, Massachusetts Institute of Technology
Background: Hewlett Packard Co., Westinghouse Corporation; Co-founder, Octek, Inc., Lexidata Corporation, Medicel, Inc.

John E. Trombly, Executive Vice President (Andover)
Education: BSEE, University of Lowell
Background: Hewlett Packard Company, Arthur D. Little, Inc., Co-founder, Octek, Inc.

ROYNAT, INC.

40 King Street West
26th Floor
Toronto, Ontario M5H 1H1
Canada

Telephone: 416-933-2730
Fax: 416-933-2783

Other Office Locations

1800 McGill College, Suite 1200
Montreal, Quebec H8A 3J6
Canada
Phone 514-987-4941, Fax 514-987-4908

400 Third Avenue, Suite 4500
Calgary, Alberta T2P 4H2
Canada
Phone 403-269-7755, Fax 403-269-7701

Purdy's Wharf Tower I
1959 Upper Water Street
Halifax, Nova Scotia B3J 3N2
Canada
Phone 902-429-3500, Fax 902-423-5607

Mission: Actively seeking new investments in growth companies, buyouts and acquisitions

Fund Size: $50 million
Founded: 1962
Average Investment: $1 million
Minimum Investment: $250,000

Investment Criteria: Second-stage, Mezzanine, Leveraged Buyout

Geographic Preference: Canada

Industry Group Preference: Communications, Computer Related, Consumer, Distribution, Electronic Components and Instrumentation, Industrial Products and Equipment, Manufacturing, Medical/Health Related

Portfolio Companies: not available

Officers, Executives and Principals

Earl Lande, Senior Vice President (Toronto)
James Webster, Director of Equity Investments (Toronto)
Bob Roy, Director of Equity Investments (Toronto)
Gustave Potuin, Regional Vice President (Montreal)
Jim Joseph, Regional Vice President (Calgary)
Douglas Stewart (Halifax)

RUDDICK INVESTMENT COMPANY

2000 Two First Union Center
Charlotte, NC 28282

Telephone: 704-372-5404
Fax: 704-372-6409

Mission: not available

Fund Size: $14 million
Founded: not available
Average Investment: $750,000
Minimum Investment: not available

Investment Criteria: First-stage to Mezzanine

Geographic Preference: Southeastern United States

Industry Group Preference: Diversified

Portfolio Companies: not available

Officers, Executives and Principals

Alan T. Dickson, President
Richard N. Brigden, Vice President

RUTLEDGE AND COMPANY, INC.

One Greenwich Office Park
51 Weaver
Greenwich, CT 06831-5156

Telephone: 203-869-8866
Fax: 203-869-7978

Mission: Actively seeking new investments

Fund Size: not available
Founded: 1991
Average Investment: not available
Minimum Investment: $2 million

Investment Criteria: Mezzanine, Leveraged Buyout, Control-block Purchases

Industry Group Preference: Communications, Consumer, Distribution, Industrial Products and Equipment

Portfolio Companies: not available

Officers, Executives and Principals

John Rutledge
Jerry St. Dennis

RYE VENTURE PARTNERS

189 Milton Road
Rye, NY 10580

Telephone: 914-921-4379
Fax: 914-921-4378

Mission: Actively seeking new investments

Fund Size: not available
Founded: 1993
Average Investment: not available
Minimum Investment: Less than $100,000

Investment Criteria: Seed

Industry Group Preference: Computer Related

Portfolio Companies: not available

Officers, Executives and Principals

Robert Clyatt, Director

S. R. ONE, LTD.

565 East Swedesford Road
Suite 315
Wayne, PA 19087

Telephone: 610-293-3400
Fax: 610-254-2940

Mission: not available

Fund Size: $100 million
Founded: not available
Average Investment: $1 million
Minimum Investment: not available

Investment Criteria: Seed to Leveraged Buyout

Industry Group Preference: Biotechnology, Medical/Health

Portfolio Companies: ActiMed Laboratories, Affinity Biotech, British Biotech., Cephalon, Cruachem Holdings, Genset, Gliatech, IDEC, Inhale Therapeutic Systems, International Canine Genetics, LaJolla Pharmaceuticals, NPS Pharmaceuticals, Quidel, Ribi ImmunoChem

Officers, Executives and Principals

Peter A. Sears, President
Brenda D. Gavin, DVM, Vice President
Doug Reed, MD, Vice President
John M. Gill, Vice President
Barbara J. Dalton, PhD, Investment Manager

SACHAR CAPITAL

545 Madison Avenue
10th Floor
New York, NY 10022

Telephone: 212-593-5317
Fax: 212-593-5316

Mission: Actively seeking new investments

Fund Size: not available
Founded: 1991
Average Investment: not available
Minimum Investment: $100,000

Investment Criteria: Seed, Research and Development, Startup, First-stage, Second-stage

Industry Group Preference: Communications, Computer Related, Medical/Health Related

Portfolio Companies: not available

Officers, Executives and Principals

Laura B. Sachar, President

SAE VENTURES

11 Forest Street
New Canaan, CT 06840

Telephone: 203-972-3100
Fax: 203-966-4197

Mission: Actively seeking new investments

Fund Size: not available
Founded: 1993
Average Investment: not available
Minimum Investment: $500,000

Investment Criteria: Research and Development, Startup, First-stage, Second-stage, Mezzanine, Leveraged
Buyout, Special Situations, Control-block Purchases

Industry Group Preference: Distribution, Genetic Engineering, Medical/Health Related

Portfolio Companies: not available

Officers, Executives and Principals

Frank A. Dinucci, Managing Director
Richard I. Steinhart, Managing Director
Andrew M. Ziolkowski, Managing Director

SAGE MANAGEMENT GROUP

2311 Webster Street
San Francisco, CA 94115

Telephone: 415-346-4036
Fax: 415-346-4310

Mission: The Sage Management Group is a corporate development firm whose clients are emerging technology intensive companies interested in business relationships with institutional investors and corporate partners. We work with critical mass technology intensive companies seeking additional growth through internal development and acquisition. We have client relationships with established companies interested in innovative companies within our business network. For innovative, emerging and critical mass companies, client projects are financing corporate partnering, including sale of business and merger acquisition. For established company clients projects are venture capital investment, acquisition and product and technology transfer. The Sage Management Group provides strategic partnering and investment services in the United States for Sumitomo Corporation.

Fund Size: not available
Founded: 1989
Average Investment: $500,000+
Minimum Investment: $500,000

Investment Criteria: First-stage, Second-stage, Mezzanine, Leveraged Buyout, Special Situations

Geographic Preference: United States, with focus on North Carolina

Industry Group Preference: Communications, Computer Related, Consumer, Electronic Components and Instrumentation, Energy/Natural Resources, Genetic Engineering, Industrial Products and Equipment, Medical/Health Related

Portfolio Companies: not available

Officers, Executives and Principals

Charles A. Bauer, Managing Principal
David G. Arscott

SAND HILL VENTURE GROUP

10393 Noel Avenue
Cupertino, CA 95014-1229

Telephone: 408-253-9294

Mission: not available

Fund Size: not available
Founded: 1983
Average Investment: not available
Minimum Investment: $100,000

Investment Criteria: Seed, Startup

Industry Group Preference: Computer Related

Portfolio Companies: not available

Officers, Executives and Principals

Stuart Evans, Partner
D. McCrea Graham II, Partner

THE SANDHURST VENTURE FUND, L.P.

351 East Conestoga Road
Wayne, PA 19087

Telephone: 610-254-8900
Fax: 610-254-8958

Mission: Actively seeking new investments

Fund Size: $8 million
Founded: 1987
Average Investment: $250,000 - several million
Minimum Investment: $500,000

Investment Criteria: Second-stage

Geographic Preference: Mid-Atlantic United States

Industry Group Preference: Consumer, Industrial Products and Equipment, Medical/Health Related

Portfolio Companies: not available

Officers, Executives and Principals

Richard J. DePiano, Managing Partner
Education: BS, Accounting, Drexel University
Background: Director of Tax Operations
Directorships: Director, Lafrance Corporation, Surgical Laser Technology, Managed Health Care Services, Shields Business Machines

Fred G. Choate
Education: JD, University of North Carolina
Background: Vice President of Investment for Penfund; President, Penfund's U.S. Operations; Manager, Greater Philadelphia Venutre Capital Corporation, SBIC

SANDTON FINANCIAL GROUP

21550 Oxnard Street
Suite 300
Woodland Hills, CA 91367

Telephone: 818-702-9283

Mission: Actively seeking new investments

Fund Size: not available
Founded: 1979
Average Investment: not available
Minimum Investment: $100,000

Investment Criteria: Seed, Research and Development, Startup, First-stage, Second-stage, Special Situations, Case-by-case Basis

Industry Group Preference: Diversified

Portfolio Companies: not available

Officers, Executives and Principals

Lawrence J. Gaiber, President

SAUGATUCK ASSOCIATES

One Canterbury Green
Stamford, CT 06901

Telephone: 203-348-6669
Fax: 203-324-6995

Mission: not available

Fund Size: $165 million
Founded: not available
Average Investment: $3 million
Minimum Investment: not available

Investment Criteria: Startup to Leveraged Buyout

Industry Group Preference: Diversified

Portfolio Companies: Atlantic Cellular Company, California Fish Growers, Dollar Dry Dock Bank, First Sun Capital Corporation, GDC International, Internatinal Marine Industries, MedRehab, Morgan Products, Phy-Cor, Pinnacle Care, Sentinel

Officers, Executives and Principals

Frank J. Hawlery, Founder
Education: BS, Physics, Phi Beta Kappa, University of North Carolina; MBA, Harvard
Background: General Partner, Foster Management Co.; Executive Vice President, Laidlaw-Coggeshall Inc., Lazard Freres, Eaton and Howard, Inc.
Directorships: Morgan Products, Sentinel Group and MedRehab

Owen Stevenson Crihfield, Managing Director
Education: BA, Comparative Government, Pomona College; MBA, with distinction, Harvard
Background: Vice President, Merrill Lynch Capital Markets, Emerging Growth Companies Group; Senior Analyst, Transamerica Computer Corporation
Directorships: First Sun Capital Corporation, Sentinel Group

Richard P. Campbell, Jr., Managing Director
Education: University of Pennsylvania; MBA, Wharton
Background: Executive Vice President and Chief Financial Officer, Paine Webber Group; PepsiCo.; Special Assistant to Henry Kissinger
Directorships: Atlantic Cellular Company, L.P.

John Dionne, Managing Director

SBCA/A. G. BARTHOLOMEW AND ASSOCIATES

4255 Knollgate Road
P.O. Box 231074
Montgomery, AL 36123

Telephone: 334-284-3640

Mission: Actively seeking new investments

Fund Size: not available
Founded: 1990
Average Investment: not available
Minimum Investment: Less than $100,000

Investment Criteria: Startup, First-stage, Second-stage, Special Situations

Industry Group Preference: Communications, Computer Related, Consumer, Distribution, Electronic Components and Instrumentation, Industrial Products and Equipment, Medical/Health Related

Portfolio Companies: not available

Officers, Executives and Principals

A.G. Bartholomew, President
Richard Bowden, Associate

SCHOONER CAPITAL INTERNATIONAL, L.P.

745 Atlantic Avenue
Boston, MA 02111

Telephone: 617-357-9031
Fax: 617-357-5545

Other Office Locations

Plac Powstancow Warszawy 1
Pokoj 256
00-950 Warsaw
Poland
Phone 48-22-269142, Fax 48-22-269136

Mission: Actively seeking new investments

Fund Size: not available
Founded: 1994
Average Investment: not available
Minimum Investment: $250,000

Investment Criteria: Startup, First-stage, Second-stage, Special Situations, Control-block Purchases

Industry Group Preference: Communications, Consumer Products, Energy/Natural Resources, Financial Services, Food and Beverage, Industrial Products and Equipment, Medical/Health Related

Portfolio Companies: Nzat Brzeg Edible Oils Company (Brzeg, Poland), Oborniki Furniture Co. (Oborniki, Poland), Molocuny Combinai (Krasnodar, Russia)

Officers, Executives and Principals

Vincent J. Ryan, Managing Director (Boston)
Education: BA, Boston University
Background: Chairman, Iron Mountain Group, White Eagle Industries, Schooner Poland; Founder, National Hydro and Arch Mobile Communications

Burton D. Sheppard, Managing Director (Boston)
Education: BA, Johns Hopkins University; Doctorate of Philosophy, Oxford University; JD, Boston College
Background: Corporate Attorney, Sullivan and Worcester; Partner, Kirk Sheppard and Company; Counsel to Chairman of Democratic National Committee; Assistant Professor, Wellesley College

SCHRODER VENTURES

787 Seventh Avenue
New York, NY 10019

Telephone: 212-841-3880
Fax: 212-582-1405

Mission: not available

Fund Size: $1.7 billion
Founded: not available
Average Investment: $100,000 - $3 million
Minimum Investment: not available

Investment Criteria: Seed to Leveraged Buyout

Industry Group Preference: Biotechnology, Communications, Computer Related, Consumer Related, Electronics, Entertainment, High Technology, Medical/Health, Publishing, Service Industries, Software

Portfolio Companies: Alexion Pharmaceuticals, Cambridge Bio Tech, Cell Therapeutics, CV Therapeutics, Gene Medicine, Genetic Systems Corporation, ICOS Corporation, Incyte Pharmaceuticals, LaJolla Pharmaceutical Co., MicroProbe, Neurcrine, Neurogen, Celgene, DNA Plant Technology, Envirogen, Mycogen

Officers, Executives and Principals

Jeffrey J. Collinson, Managing Partner
Education: Yale University; MBA, Harvard
Background: Corporate Development and Finance, Baxter International
Directorships: Incyte Pharmaceuticals, Envirogen, Neurogen

Barbara A. Piette, Partner
Education: BS, summa cum laude, Boston College; MBA, honors, Harvard; Registered Nurse
Background: Charles River Ventures, Wellmark Healthcare Services, MCI Communications, Yankee Group, McLean Hospital

Susan Wilner, Partner
Education: PhD, Public Health, Harvard University, Executive Program
Background: Director, Market Research and Investor Relations, Genetech; Teacher, University of California San Francisco Medical School
Directorships: Advanced Surgical Inc., Clinical Partners, Inc.

Timothy F. Howe, Partner
Education: BA, MBA, Columbia University
Background: Mergers and Aquisitions, Schroder Investment Banking Division; Analyst, Financial Control, J. Henry Schroder Bank and Trust Co.

SCIENTIFIC ADVANCES

601 West Fifth Avenue
Columbus, OH 43201-3195

Telephone: 614-424-7005
Fax: 614-424-4874

Mission: not available

Fund Size: $25 million
Founded: not available
Average Investment: $750,000
Minimum Investment: not available

Investment Criteria: Startup to Second Stage

Industry Group Preference: Biotechnology, Computer Related, Energy/Natural Resources, High Technology

Portfolio Companies: not available

Officers, Executives and Principals

Paul F. Purcell, President

SEED COMPANY PARTNERS

15301 Dallas Parkway
Suite 840
Dallas, TX 75248

Telephone: 972-458-5505
Fax: 972-458-5515

Mission: Actively seeking new investments

Fund Size: not available
Founded: 1992
Average Investment: not available
Minimum Investment: $500,000

Investment Criteria: Seed, Startup, First-stage

Industry Group Preference: Communications, Computer Related, Distribution, Electronic Components and Instrumentation, Industrial Products and Equipment

Portfolio Companies: not available

Officers, Executives and Principals

Lawrence Goldstein, General Partner
Allen Fleener, General Partner
Daniel B. Stuart, Consulting

SENTINEL CAPITAL PARTNERS

245 Park Avenue
41st Floor
New York, NY 10167

Telephone: 212-490-5945
Fax: 212-682-0082

Mission: Long-term capital appreciation

Fund Size: $75 million
Founded: 1995
Average Investment: $7.5 million
Minimum Investment: $5 million

Investment Criteria: Management Buyouts, Recapitalizations, Restructurings, Growth Capital

Geographic Preference: United States

Industry Group Preference: Consumer Related, Manufacturing/Processing, Retailing, Wholesaling/Distribution

Portfolio Companies: HASCO Holdings Corporation, Border Foods, Inc., Floral Plant Growers, LLC, Frame-n-Lens Optical, Inc.

Officers, Executives and Principals

David S. Lobel, Managing Partner
Education: MBA, MS, Stanford University; BS, honors, University of the Witwatersrand
Background: Managing Director, Smith Barney; General Partner, First Century Partners
Directorships: Frame-N-Lens Optical, Inc., HASCO Holdings Corporation, Border Foods, Inc. Floral Plant Growers, LLC

John F. McCormack, Partner
Education: CPA, BS, Accounting, Boston College
Background: Vice President, First Century Partners; Coopers and Lybrand

SG WARBURG

277 Park Avenue
New York, NY 10172

Telephone: 212-459-7000
Fax: 212-224-7251

Other Office Locations
31 Milk Street
Boston, MA, 02109
Phone 617-451-0490, Fax 617-451-7517

SG Warburg Options, Inc.
311 Wacker Drive, Suite 350
Chicago, IL 60606
Phone 312-554-3000, Fax 312-554-3033

Mission: not available

Fund Size: not available
Founded: 1971
Average Investment: not available
Minimum Investment: not available

Investment Criteria: not available

Industry Group Preference: Diversified

Portfolio Companies: not available

Officers, Executives and Principals

Simon Canning, Chief Executive Officer (New York)

SHAD RUN INVESTMENTS, INC.

P.O. Box 470730
San Francisco, CA 94147

Telephone: 415-885-6400
Fax: 415-929-6286

Mission: Actively seeking new investments

Fund Size: $10 million
Founded: 1992
Average Investment: $1 - $1.5 million
Minimum Investment: $500,000

Investment Criteria: Second-stage

Geographic Preference: United States

Industry Group Preference: Communications, Consumer, Medical/Health Related

Portfolio Companies: Jungle Jim's Playlands, Inc., Caribou Coffee Company, Widmer Brothers Brewing Company, Unisite, Inc.

Officers, Executives and Principals

Sara M. Hendrickson, President

SHALOR VENTURES

65 East India Row, Suite 16F
Boston, MA 02110

Telephone: 617-367-1077
Fax: 617-292-0407

Mission: Seeking new investments

Fund Size: not available
Founded: not available
Average Investment: $2 million
Minimum Investment: $500,000

Investment Criteria: No Start-ups

Geographic Preference: East Coast of the United States

Industry Group Preference: Consumer Related, Retailing

Portfolio Companies: not available

Officers, Executives and Principals

Arnold Siegel, President

THE SHANSBY GROUP

250 Montgomery Street
San Francisco, CA 94104

Telephone: 415-398-2500
Fax: 415-421-5120

Mission: Actively seeking new investments

Fund Size: not available
Founded: 1987
Average Investment: not available
Minimum Investment: $2 million

Investment Criteria: Leveraged Buyout, Turnarounds

Industry Group Preference: Consumer, Distribution

Portfolio Companies: not available

Officers, Executives and Principals

J. Gary Shansby, General Partner
Charles H. Esserman, General Partner

SHARED VENTURES, INC.

6550 York Avenue South
Edina, MN 55435

Telephone: 612-925-3411

Mission: Making few, if any, new investments

Fund Size: not available
Founded: 1981
Average Investment: not available
Minimum Investment: Less than $100,000

Investment Criteria: Startup, First-stage, Second-stage, Mezzanine

Industry Group Preference: Consumer, Distribution, Energy/Natural Resources, Industrial Products and Equipment, Medical/Health Related

Portfolio Companies: not available

Officers, Executives and Principals

Howard Weiner, President
Fred Weiner, Vice President

SHAW VENTURE PARTNERS

400 Southwest Sixth Avenue
Suite 1100
Portland, OR 97204-1636

Telephone: 503-228-4884
Fax: 503-227-2471

Mission: not available

Fund Size: $30 million
Founded: not available
Average Investment: $1 million
Minimum Investment: not available

Investment Criteria: Seed to Leveraged Buyout

Geographic Preference: Western United States

Industry Group Preference: Computer Related, Consumer Related, Electronics, High Technology, Medical/ Health, Retailing, Software

Portfolio Companies: not available

Officers, Executives and Principals

Ralph R. Shaw, General Partner
Reza Moazzami, Associate
William Newman, Associate

THE SHELTON COMPANIES, INC.

3600 One First Union Center
301 South College Street
Charlotte, NC 28202

Telephone: 704-348-2200
Fax: 704-348-2260

Mission: Actively seeking new investment

Fund Size: $50 million
Founded: 1991
Average Investment: $3 million - $5 million
Minimum Investment: $1 million

Investment Criteria: Second-stage, Leveraged Buyout, Control-block Purchases

Industry Group Preference: Consumer, Distribution, Industrial Products and Equipment

Portfolio Companies: not available

Officers, Executives and Principals

Charles M. Shelton, Principal
R. Edwin, Principal

SIERRA VENTURES

3000 Sand Hill Road, Building #4
Suite 210
Menlo Park, CA 94025

Telephone: 415-854-1000
Fax: 415-854-5593

Mission: not available

Fund Size: $165 million
Founded: not available
Average Investment: $1 million
Minimum Investment: not available

Investment Criteria: Seed to Second-stage

Industry Group Preference: Broadcast/Cable/Radio, Communciations, Computer Related, Consumer Related, Electronics, Financial Services, High Technology, Information Services, Medical/Health, Service Industries, Software

Portfolio Companies: Advanced Technology Materials, Advantage Product Technology, Analog Design Tools, Automated Compliance Systems, Automation Partners, Bayard Open Systems, CardioRhythm, Centrex Telemanagement, Cholestech, Clinical Partners, Datacopy, Digitran, Dynamic Broadcasting Network, Environmental Testing and Certification

Officers, Executives and Principals

Jeffrey M. Drazan, General Partner
Education: BSE, Management, Princeton; MBA, New York University
Background: AT&T, Long Lines, Information Systems, Bell Laboratories
Directorships: Centex, Digitran, StrataCom, Temporary Professional Support, Dynamic Broadcasting Network, Bayard Open Systems

Peter C. Wendell, General Partner
Education: BA, magna cum laude, Princeton; MBA, with distinction, Harvard
Background: Branch Manager, Data Processing Division, IBM; McKinsey and Co.; Faculty, Stanford University
Directorships: Environmental Testing and Certification Corporation, Centex Telemanagement, Datacopy, Laserscope, Teradata

Petri Vainio, General Partner
Education: MBA, Stanford University; MD, PhD, Biochemistry, highest academic honors, University of Helsinki
Background: KSV Chemicals, LEK Partnership
Directorships: CardioRhythm, Cholestech, Clinical Partners, RiboGene

SIGMA CAPITAL CORPORATION

40 Southeast Fifth Street
Suite 500
Boca Raton, FL 33432

Telephone: 407-368-9783

Mission: Actively seeking new investments

Fund Size: not available
Founded: 1988
Average Investment: not available
Minimum Investment: $100,000

Investment Criteria: Second-stage

Geographic Preference: Southeast Florida

Industry Group Preference: Communications, Consumer, Genetic Engineering, Industrial Products and Equipment, Medical/Health Related

Portfolio Companies: not available

Officers, Executives and Principals

Alvin S. Schwartz, President
Education: BBA, City College of New York
Directorships: Twelve profit corporations, two non-profit corporations

SIGMA PARTNERS

2884 Sand Hill Road
Suite 121
Menlo Park, CA 94025

Telephone: 415-854-1300
Fax: 415-854-1323

Other Office Locations
20 Custom House Street, Suite 830
Boston, MA 02110
Phone 617-330-7872, Fax 617-330-7975

Mission: Actively seeking new investments

Fund Size: not available
Founded: 1984
Average Investment: not available
Minimum Investment: $1 million

Investment Criteria: Seed, Startup, First-stage, Second-stage, Mezzanine, Leveraged Buyout, Special Situations, Control-block Purchases

Industry Group Preference: Communications, Computer Related, Electronic Components and Instrumentation, Industrial Products and Equipment, Medical/Health Related

Portfolio Companies: not available

Officers, Executives and Principals

Lawrence G. Finch, Partner (Menlo Park)
Clifford L. Haas, Partner (Menlo Park)
Gardner C. Hendrie, Partner (Boston)
J. Burgess Jamieson, Partner (Menlo Park)
C. Bradford Jeffries, Partner (Menlo Park)
Wade Woodson, Partner (Menlo Park)
Robert E. Davoli, Partner

SIGNAL CAPITAL CORPORATION

55 Ferncroft Road
Danvers, MA 01923

Telephone: 508-777-3866
Fax: 508-750-1301

Other Office Locations
One Sansome Street, Suite 2100
San Francisco, CA 94104
Phone 415-956-1400, Fax 415-956-1459

Mission: Actively seeking new investments

Fund Size: not available
Founded: not available
Average Investment: not available
Minimum Investment: $500,000

Investment Criteria: Startup, First-stage, Second-stage, Mezzanine, Leveraged Buyout, Special Situations

Industry Group Preference: Communications, Computer Related, Consumer, Distribution, Electronic Components and Instrumentation, Industrial Products and Equipment, Medical/Health Related

Portfolio Companies: not available

Officers, Executives and Principals

Eben S. Moulton, Managing Partner (Danvers)
Walter H. Leonard, Partner (Danvers)
Paul G. Giovancchini, Partner (Danvers)
Thomas W. Gorman, Partner (Danvers)
Gregory A. Hulecki, Partner (Danvers)
Jeffrey Holland, Partner (San Francisco)
Christopher Betts, Partner (San Francisco)

SILICON VALLEY BANK

3003 Tasman Drive
Santa Clara, CA 95054

Telephone: 408-654-7400
Fax: 408-727-8720

Other Office Locations
9150 Wilshire Boulevard, Suite 201
Beverly Hills, CA 90212
Phone 310-786-8640, Fax 310-786-8657

40 William Street, Suite 350
Wellesley, MA 02181
Phone 617-431-9901, Fax 617-431-9906

1731 Embarcadero, Suite 220
Palo Alto, CA 94303
Phone 415-812-0832, Fax 415-812-0640

18872 MacArthur Boulevard, Suite 100
Irvine, CA 92612
Phone 714-252-1300, Fax 714-252-0925

One Central Plaza, Suite 701
11300 Rockville Pike
Rockville, MD 20852
Phone 301-984-4977, Fax 301-984-6282

3000 Sand Hill Road, Suite 150
Building 4
Menlo Park, CA 94025
Phone 415-233-6600, Fax 415-233-6611

4430 Arapahoe Avenue, Suite 225
Boulder, CO 80303
Phone 303-938-0483, Fax 303-938-0486

32 Alcalde Road
Santa Fe, NM 87505
Phone 505-466-4346, Fax 505-466-4420

9442 Capital of Texas Highway North
Arboretum Plaza One, Suite 100-A
Austin, TX 78759
Phone 512-338-4240, Fax 512-338-4266

11000 S.W. Stratus, Suite 170
Beaverton, OR 97008
Phone 503-526-1123, Fax 503-526-0818

915 118th Avenue, SE, Suite 250
Bellevue, WA 98005
Phone 206-688-1368, Fax 206-646-8100

2 Palo Alto Square, Suite 110
Palo Alto, CA 94306
Phone 415-812-0682, Fax 415-493-5859

5414 Oberlin Drive, Suite 230
San Diego, CA 92121
Phone 619-657-9650, Fax 619-535-1611

899 Adams Street, Suite G-2
St. Helena, CA 94574
Phone 707-967-4826, Fax 707-967-4827

Mission: Actively seeking new investments as a limited partner in venture capital funds

Fund Size: not available
Founded: 1983
Average Investment: $200,000
Minimum Investment: $50,000

Investment Criteria: Startup, First-round

Geographic Preference: United States

Industry Group Preference: Communications, Computer Related, Life Sciences, Semiconductor, Software

Portfolio Companies: not available

Officers, Executives and Principals

John C. Dean, President and Chief Executive Officer, Corporate Headquarters
Harry W. Kellogg, Jr., Executive Vice President, Strategic Marketing Group, Corporate Headquarters

SIRROM CAPITAL

500 Church Street
Suite 200
Nashville, TN 37219-2320

Telephone: 615-256-0701
Fax: 615-726-1208

Mission: Actively seeking new investments

Fund Size: not available
Founded: 1992
Average Investment: not available
Minimum Investment: $500,000

Investment Criteria: Mezzanine

Industry Group Preference: Diversified

Portfolio Companies: not available

Officers, Executives and Principals

George M. Miller II, President
Carl Stratton, Chief Financial Officer
John C. Harrison, Vice President
Kathy Harris, Vice President

SOMMERSET CAPITAL CORPORATION

5025 Arapaho Road
Suite 417
Dallas, TX 75248

Telephone: 214-789-2940
Fax: 214-489-2942

Mission: Actively seeking new investments—makes five to six new investments per year

Fund Size: $83.7 million under management
Founded: 1988
Average Investment: $3 million - $8 million
Minimum Investment: $500,000

Investment Criteria: First-stage, Second-stage, Mezzanine, Leveraged Buyout

Industry Group Preference: Communications, Computer Related, Consumer, Distribution, Electronic Components and Instrumentation, Genetic Engineering, Industrial Products and Equipment, Medical/Health Related

Portfolio Companies: not available

Officers, Executives and Principals

Alan S. Hart, President and Partner
Education: LLB, BA, University of Toronto, Canada
Background: 15 years Senior Vice President, Winchester Capital Corporation
Directorships: Winchester Properties Corporation, Balnoral Properties Corporation

Don Carmichael, Vice President and Partner
Education: BA, University of British Columbia, Vancouver, Canada
Background: 20 years Senior Vice President, Winchester Capital Corporation
Directorships: Winchester Properties Corporation, Balnoral Properties Corporation

David Donovan, Vice President and Partner
Education: BA, MBA, University of Toronto, Canada
Background: 12 years Vice President, Winchester Capital Corporation
Directorships: Caledonian Capital Corporation

Brian D. Gibbs, Vice President and Partner
Education: BA, UBC, Vancouver, Canada
Background: 18 years Winchester Properties Corporation
Directorships: Winchester Properties Corporation, Balnoral Properties Corporation, Wellsgrey Properties Corporation

Terry Nelsen, Vice President and Partner
Education: BA, MBA, University of Minnesota
Background: 12 years Chartersquare Financial Corporation
Directorships: Wellsgrey Properties Corporation, Chartersquare Financial Corporation

Paul Gooden, Partner
Education: BA, LLB, University of Texas
Background: 10 years Chartersquare Financial Corporation, Senior Vice President, Administration

Donald R. Johnson, Partner
Education: BA, Northwestern
Background: Vice President, Horizon Financial Corporation, six years

Frank P. Smith, Partner

SORRENTO ASSOCIATES, INC.

4370 La Jolla Village Drive
Suite 1040
San Diego, CA 92122

Telephone: 619-452-3100
Fax: 619-452-7607

Mission: Actively seeking new investments

Fund Size: $102 million
Founded: 1985
Average Investment: $1 - $3 million
Minimum Investment: $500,000

Investment Criteria: Startup, First-stage, Second-stage, Mezzanine, Leveraged Buyout, Special Situations, Control-block Purchases

Geographic Preference: San Diego, California

Industry Group Preference: Communications, Computer Related, Consumer, Distribution, Electronic Components and Instrumentation, Genetic Engineering, Industrial Products and Equipment, Medical/Health Related

Portfolio Companies: not available

Officers, Executives and Principals

Robert M. Jaffe, President
Vincent J. Burgess, Vice President
Stewart D. Easterby, Associate

SOURCE CAPITAL CORPORATION

1700 One American Place
301 Main Street
Baton Rouge, LA 70825

Telephone: 504-383-1508
Fax: 504-383-1513
E-mail: request@sourcecap.com

Other Office Locations
2450 Severn Avenue, Suite 528
Metairie, LA 70001
Phone 504-833-1509, Fax 504-833-1548

Mission: Actively seeking new investments

Fund Size: not available
Founded: 1988
Average Investment: not available
Minimum Investment: $250,000

Investment Criteria: Seed, Startup, First-stage, Second-stage, Mezzanine

Geographic Preference: Southeastern United States

Industry Group Preference: Communications, Consumer, Distribution, Electronic Components and Instrumentation, Energy/Natural Resources, Genetic Engineering, Industrial Products and Equipment, Medical/Health Related

Portfolio Companies: not available

Officers, Executives and Principals

Kevin H. Couhig, President and Chief Executive Officer
Greg Naquin, Executive Vice President
Carol Perrin, Vice President
Mike Anderson, Vice President, Finance
Aaron Misenich, Corporate Services Officer (Metairie)

SOUTH ATLANTIC VENTURE FUND

614 West Bay Street, Suite 200
Tampa, FL 33606-2704

Telephone: 813-253-2500
Fax: 813-253-2360

Mission: not available

Fund Size: $58 million
Founded: not available
Average Investment: $2 million
Minimum Investment: not available

Investment Criteria: Startup to Leveraged Buyout

Industry Group Preference: Broadcast/Cable/Radio, Communications, Computer Related, Consumer Related, Electronics, Energy/Natural Resources, Financial Services, Food Services, High Technology, Industrial Products, Information Services, Insurance, Manufacturing/Processing, Medical/Health

Portfolio Companies: not available

Officers, Executives and Principals

Donald W. Burton, General Partner
Sandra P. Barber, General Partner
W. Scott Miller, General Partner

SOUTHERN CALIFORNIA VENTURES

406 Amapola Avenue
Suite 205
Torrance, CA 90501

Telephone: 310-787-4381
Fax: 310-787-4382

Other Office Locations
15303 Ventura Boulevard
Suite 1040
Sherman Oaks, CA 91403
Phone 818-502-2295, Fax 818-501-4190

Two Park Plaza
SW 750
Irvine, CA 92714
Phone 714-251-2785, Fax 714-251-2781

Mission: Making few, if any, new investments

Fund Size: not available
Founded: 1983
Average Investment: not available
Minimum Investment: Less than $100,000

Investment Criteria: Seed, Startup, First-stage

Industry Group Preference: Communications, Computer Related, Distribution, Electronic Components and Instrumentation, Industrial Products and Equipment, Medical/Health Related

Portfolio Companies: not available

Officers, Executives and Principals

B. Allen Lay, General Partner (Torrance)
Jay Raskin, General Partner (Sherman Oaks)
Pieter Halter, General Partner (Irvine)

SOUTHPORT PARTNERS

2425 Post Road
Southport, CT 06490

Telephone: 203-255-1231
Fax: 203-255-1178

Mission: Southport Partners is a technology investment banking firm, specializing in mergers and acquisitions, as well as raising equity capital from institutional sources with over $2 billion of transactions completed over the last ten years.

Fund Size: not available
Founded: 1986
Average Investment: not available
Minimum Investment: $5 million

Investment Criteria: Second-stage, Mezzanine, Leveraged Buyout

Geographic Preference: United States, Europe, Asia

Industry Group Preference: Communications, Computer Services, Entertainment, Internet-Related Products and Services, Networking, Software

Portfolio Companies: not available

Officers, Executives and Principals

Dale McIvor, General Partner
Katherine Watts, General Partner
J. Jeffery Nixon, General Partner

SOUTHWEST ENTERPRISE ASSOCIATES, L.P.

14457 Gillis Road
Dallas, TX 75244

Telephone: 214-450-3894

Other Office Locations
NEA Partners Southwest
235 Montgomery Street, Suite 1205
San Francisco, CA 94104
Phone 415-956-1579

1119 St. Paul Street
Baltimore, MD 21202
Phone 410-244-0115

Mission: Making few, if any, new investments

Fund Size: not available
Founded: 1983
Average Investment: not available
Minimum Investment: $250,000

Investment Criteria: Seed, Startup, First-stage

Industry Group Preference: Communications, Computer Related, Electronic Components and Instrumentation, Genetic Engineering, Industrial Products and Equipment, Medical/Health Related

Portfolio Companies: not available

Officers, Executives and Principals

C. Vincent Prothro, Managing General Partner (Dallas)
C. Richard Kramlich, General Partner (San Francisco)
Frank A. Bonsal, Jr., General Partner (Baltimore)
H. Leland Murphy, Associate (Dallas)

SOUTHWEST VENTURE GROUP

10878 Westheimer
Suite 178
Houston, TX 77042

Telephone: 713-827-8947
Fax: 713-461-1470

Mission: Actively seeking new investments

Fund Size: not available
Founded: 1970
Average Investment: $1 million
Minimum Investment: $500,000

Investment Criteria: Seed, Research and Development, Startup, First-stage, Second-stage, Mezzanine, Leveraged Buyout, Special Situations, Control-block Purchases, Shell Mergers

Industry Group Preference: Genetic Engineering, Medical/Health Related

Portfolio Companies: not available

Officers, Executives and Principals

David M. Klausmeyer, Partner
Education: BSS, Georgetown University
Background: Certified Public Accountant, Merger and Acquisition Specialist, Investment Banker
Directorships: Enterprise Technologies, S I Diamond, Life Stream Diagnostics, Nanodynamics, Inc, Imaging Products Inc., Pharmaceutical Labs, Inc.

William McLeod, Partner
Education: BS, University of Aberdeen; MBA, Harvard University
Background: Management, Mining, International Trade

David R. Strawn, Partner
Education: LLB, Arizona State University

SOUTHWEST VENTURE PARTNERS/HIXVEN PARTNERS

16414 San Pedro
Suite 345
San Antonio, TX 78332

Telephone: 210-402-1200
Fax: 210-402-1221

Mission: Reducing investment activity

Fund Size: not available
Founded: 1975/1983
Average Investment: not available
Minimum Investment: $100,000

Investment Criteria: Startup, First-stage, Second-stage, Leveraged Buyout

Industry Group Preference: Communications, Computer Related, Consumer, Distribution, Energy/Natural Resources, Genetic Engineering, Industrial Products and Equipment, Medical/Health Related

Portfolio Companies: not available

Officers, Executives and Principals

Michael Bell, President

SOVEREIGN FINANCIAL SERVICES

455 Sherman Street
Suite 520
Denver, CO 80203

Telephone: 303-722-1595
Fax: 303-722-1639

Mission: Private equity management and consulting

Fund Size: $100 million
Founded: 1987
Average Investment: not available
Minimum Investment: not available

Investment Criteria: not available

Industry Group Preference: not available

Portfolio Companies: not available

Officers, Executives and Principals

Katherine A. Cattanach, Ph.D., Managing Principal
Background: CPA

Gail C. Sweeney, Managing Principal
Education: MBA
Background: CPA

Mary Frances Kelley, Managing Principal
Education: CPA

Darien Gould, Analyst

SPECTRA ENTERPRISE ASSOCIATES

P.O. Box 7688
Thousand Oaks, CA 91359-7688

Telephone: 818-865-0213
Fax: 818-865-1309

Other Office Locations
1119 St. Paul Street
Baltimore, MD 21202
Phone 410-244-0115

Mission: not available

Fund Size: not available
Founded: 1986
Average Investment: not available
Minimum Investment: $250,000

Investment Criteria: Seed, Startup, First-stage, Second-stage

Industry Group Preference: Communications, Computer Related, Disk Drives, Defense Conversion, Electronic Components and Instrumentation, Industrial Products and Equipment, Semiconductor, Software

Portfolio Companies: not available

Officers, Executives and Principals

James A. Cole, General Partner (Thousand Oaks)
Directorships: Vitesse Semiconductor Corporation, Spectrian Corporation, Giga-Tronics, Inc.

Curran W. (Cub) Harvey, General Partner (Baltimore)

SPECTRUM EQUITY INVESTORS, L.P.

125 High Street
26th Floor
Boston, MA 02110

Telephone: 617-464-4600
Fax: 617-464-4601

Other Office Locations
245 Lytton Avenue, Suite 175
Palo Alto, CA 94301
Phone 415-464-4600, Fax 415-464-4601

Mission: Provide equity capital to companies in the communications, information, media, entertainment and interactive industries

Fund Size: $300 million
Founded: 1994
Average Investment: $1 - $50 million
Minimum Investment: $1 million

Investment Criteria: Seed, Startup, First-stage, Second-stage, Mezzanine, Leveraged Buyout, Special Situations

Industry Group Preference: Communications, Entertainment, Information, Interactive, Media

Portfolio Companies: PriCellular Corporation, Galaxy Telecom, L.P., Nassau Broadcasting, TSR Paging, PathNet, Inc. Washington PCS Group, Apex Site Management, Milliwave, L.P., Tut Systems

Officers, Executives and Principals

William P. Collatos, Managing General Partner (Boston)
Education: Harvard
Background: TA Associates

Brion B. Applegate, Managing General Partner (Palo Alto)
Education: Colgate University. Harvard Business School
Background: Burr, Egan Deleage

Kevin R. Maroni, General Partner (Boston)
Education: University of Michigan; Harvard Business School
Background: Manager of Finance and Development, Time Warner Telecommunications

Robert A. Nicholson, Associate (Boston)
Education: Williams College, Harvard Business School
Background: Bain and Company

Fred Wang, Associate (Palo Alto)
Education: Stanford University, Harvard Business School
Background: Mindscape; Vice President of Business Development, Boston Consulting Group

Matthew N. Mochary, Associate (Palo Alto)
Education: Yale University, Kellogg Graduate School of Management

SPEIRS CONSULTANTS, INC.

365 Stanstead
Montreal, Quebec H3R 1X5
Canada

Telephone: 514-342-3858
Fax: 514-342-1977

Mission: Actively seeking new investments

Fund Size: not available
Founded: 1991
Average Investment: not available
Minimum Investment: $250,000

Investment Criteria: not available

Geographic Preference: Central Canada, Northeastern United States

Industry Group Preference: Diversified

Portfolio Companies: not available

Officers, Executives and Principals

Derek Speirs, President
Education: Bachelor of Commerce, MBA, McGill University; Chartered Accountant
Background: Senior Vice President Finance and Development, Domtar Inc.; Vice President Finance, Consoltex

SPENCER TRASK SECURITIES

535 Madison Avenue
New York, NY 10022

Telephone: 212-355-5565

Mission: Actively seeking new investments

Fund Size: not available
Founded: 1991
Average Investment: not available
Minimum Investment: $1 million

Investment Criteria: Startup, First-stage, Management Buyout, Special Situations

Industry Group Preference: Communications, Computer Related, Consumer, Electronic Components and Instrumentation, Fiber Optics, Genetic Engineering, Industrial Products and Equipment, Internet-Related, Medical/Health Related

Portfolio Companies: Ciena, Myriad Genetics, Chad Therapeutics, University Online, Faroudja Labs

Officers, Executives and Principals

Kevin B. Kimberlin, Chairman
William P. Dioguardi, President
Laura M. McNamara, Manager, Investment Banking Group

SPOKANE CAPITAL MANAGEMENT CORPORATION

221 North Wall Street
Suite 628
Spokane, WA 99201

Telephone: 509-747-0728
Fax: 509-747-0758

Mission: Actively seeking new investments

Fund Size: not available
Founded: 1988
Average Investment: not available
Minimum Investment: $100,000

Investment Criteria: Second-stage

Industry Group Preference: Communications, Computer Related, Consumer, Distribution, Electronic Components and Instrumenataion, Genetic Engineering, Industrial Products and Equipment

Portfolio Companies: not available

Officers, Executives and Principals

David A. Clack, Chairman
Thomas C. Simpson, Managing Director
Jean J. Balek-Miner, Vice President

SPONSORED CONSULTING SERVICES

8929 Wilshire Boulevard
Suite 214
Beverly Hills, CA 90211

Telephone: 310-208-1234
Fax: 310-657-4486

Mission: Informally known as Dick Israel and Partners. Works throughout the U.S. in the completion of mergers and acquisitions, leveraged buyouts, recapitalizations, the arranging of venture capital investments and strategic planning to facilitate internal growth

Fund Size: not available
Founded: 1974
Average Investment: not available
Minimum Investment: $500,000

Investment Criteria: First-stage, Second-stage, Mezzanine, Leveraged Buyout, Special Situations

Industry Group Preference: Communications, Consumer, Distribution, Industrial Products and Equipment, Medical/Health Related

Portfolio Companies: not available

Officers, Executives and Principals

Dick Israel, President
Milton Freedman, Partner
Miles Killoch, Partner
Alan Weissman, Partner

SPROUT GROUP

277 Park Avenue
21st Floor
New York, NY 10172

Telephone: 212-892-3600
Fax: 212-892-3444

Other Office Locations
3000 Sand Hill Road
Building Four, Suite 270
Menlo Park, CA 94025
Phone 415-854-1550, Fax 415-854-8779

Mission: Actively seeking new investments

Fund Size: $1 billion
Founded: 1969
Average Investment: $2 - $5 million
Minimum Investment: $500,000

Investment Criteria: Seed, Startup, First-stage, Second-stage, Mezzanine, Leveraged Buyout, Special Situations

Geographic Preference: United States, Latin America, Canada

Industry Group Preference: Communications, Computer Related, Consumer, Distribution, Education, Electronic Components and Instrumentation, Genetic Engineering, Healthcare Services, Medical Devices, Retail

Portfolio Companies: Acorn Health Care, Amcomp, American Holistic Centers, Aptix, Aradigm, AtheroGenics, Attachmate, Avalon Ventures III, Biocircuits, Biometric Imaging, Brightware, CDR Therapeutics, The Cerplex Group, CIBUS Pharmaceuticals, Cardiovascular Ventures, Ceramica Zanon, Clarus Medical Systems, CombiChem, CommVault, Compex Services, Comprehensive Addiction Programs, Connective Therapeutics, Consumer Health Services, Corporate Express, Diatide, Dick's Clothing and Sporting Goods, Digitech Industries, The Edison Project, Educational Medical, Elder Health, Endocardial Solutions, Exogen, FemRx, First Physician Care, GMS Dental, Hall Kinion and Associates, Heidi's, Heritage Health Systems, HNC Software, Horizon Cellular, IVAC Holdings, Instrumentation Metrics, IntraBiotics, Loehmann's, Lynx Therapeutics, Mallory Holding, MedE America, Memberworks, Mycotech, Nanogen, Nebco Evans, Onyx Pharmaceuticals, OraVax, Orquest, Paracelsus Healthcare, Paradyne Corporation, Party Stores Holdings, Phase Metrics, Platinum Software, Prizm Pharmaceuticals, Quickturn Design Systems, Quintus, Sequana Therapeutics, Sunrise Assisted Living, Syanptics, Terranomics Ventures, Total Physician Services, Transcend Therapeutics, Urosurge, VascA, Visix Software, West Marine

Officers, Executives and Principals

Richard E. Kroon, Managing Partner (New York)
Education: BA, Yale University; MBA, Harvard Business School
Background: Donaldson, Lufkin and Jenrette, United States Department of Defense
Directorships: Educational Medical, Loehmann's, Amcorp

Patrick J. Boroian, General Partner (New York)
Education: BS, Miami University; MBA, DePaul University
Background: Odyssey Partners, Francorp

Robert E. Curry, General Partner (Menlo Park)
Education: BS, University of Illinois; MS, PhD, Purdue University
Background: Merrill Lynch Research and Development Management, Merrill Lynch Venture Capital , Becton-
  Dickson, BioRad Laboratories
Directorships: Biocircuits, Biometric Imaging, Clarus Medical Systems, Connective Therapeutics, Diatide,
  Instrumentation Metrics, Nanogen, Neocrin, Photon, Urosurge

Robert Finzi, General Partner (Menlo Park)
Education: BS, MS, Lehigh University; MBA, Harvard Business School
Background: Merrill Lynch Venture Capital, Menlo Ventures, Arthur Anderson Consulting Division
Directorships: The Cerplex Group, Compex Services, The Edison Project, GMS Dental, Phase Metrics, Plati-
  num Software

Keith B. Geeslin, General Partner (Menlo Park)
Education: BS, MS, Stanford University; MA, Oxford University
Background: Tymnet, United States Senate Commerce Committee
Directorships: Aptix, CommVault Systems, Compex Services, Paradyne Corporation, Quintus, Synaptics

Janet A. Hickey, General Partner (New York)
Education: Mount Holyoke College, University of St. Andrews
Background: General Electric, Eastman Dillon, Union Securities and Company
Directorships: Corporate Express, The Edison Project, Loehmann's, Party Stores Holdings

Kathleen D. LaPorte, General Partner (Menlo Park)
Education: BS, Yale University; MBA, Stanford University
Background: Asset Management Company, The First Boston Corporation
Directorships: CIBUS Pharmaceuticals, IntraBiotics Pharmaceuticals, FemRx, GMS Dental, Hall Kinion and
  Associates, Lynx Therapeutics, Onyx Pharmaceuticals, Sequana Therapeutics

Scott F. Meadow, General Partner (New York)
Education: BA, Harvard College, Harvard Business School
Background: William Blair and Company, Booz, Allen and Hamilton, Frontenac Company
Directorships: Heritage Health Systems, Sunrise Assisted Living

Arthur S. Zuckerman, Administrative General Partner (New York)
Education: BA, University of Pennsylvania; MBA, Columbia University
Background: Oxford Partners, Shearson/Lehman Brothers, Lehman Brothers Kuhn Loeb, Strategic Information
Directorships: Acorn Consulting

SRK MANAGEMENT COMPANY

126 East 56th Street
New York, NY 10022

Telephone: 212-371-0900
Fax: 212-371-1549

Mission: Prefer to fund and work with early-stage companies to create a meaningful entity in its market

Fund Size: not available
Founded: 1981
Average Investment: not available
Minimum Investment: $100,000

Investment Criteria: Seed, Startup, First-stage, Second-stage

Industry Group Preference: Communications, Computer Related, Distribution, Genetic Engineering, Industrial Products and Equipment, Medical/Health Related

Portfolio Companies: not available

Officers, Executives and Principals

Sidney R. Knafel, Managing Partner
Michael S. Willner

SSM CORPORATION

845 Crossover Lane
Suite 140
Memphis, TN 38117

Telephone: 901-767-1131
Fax: 901-767-1135

Other Office Locations
10528 Glass Mountain Trail
Austin, TX 78750
Phone 512-258-9429, Fax 512-258-9433

Mission: Actively seeking new investments

Fund Size: not available
Founded: 1973
Average Investment: not available
Minimum Investment: $1 million

Investment Criteria: Second-stage, Mezzanine, Leveraged Buyout, Special Situations, Control-block Purchases

Industry Group Preference: not available

Portfolio Companies: not available

Officers, Executives and Principals

C. Barham Ray, Chairman (Memphis)
Eric L. Jones, Partner (Austin)
James D. Witherington, Jr., President (Memphis)
William F. Harrison, Vice President (Memphis)
Ashley M. Mayfield, Vice President (Memphis)
R. Wilson Orr III, Vice President (Memphis)

ST. PAUL VENTURE CAPITAL

8500 Normandale Lake Boulevard
Suite 1940
Bloomington, MN 55437

Telephone: 612-830-7474
Fax: 612-830-7475

Mission: Actively seeking new investments

Fund Size: not available
Founded: 1988
Average Investment: $2 - $5 million
Minimum Investment: $1 million

Investment Criteria: Seed to Acquisition

Industry Group Preference: Computer Related, Consumer Products, High Technology, Information Services, Manufacturing/Processing, Medical/Health, Retailing, Service Industries

Portfolio Companies: Netlink, Tricord Systems, Broadband Technologies, Ascent Logic, Uniquest, Spine-Tech, Aristacom, Biotel, Sylvan Learning Systems, Auto Parts Club, Coffee Connection, P.M.T., Cardiometics, Select Comfort, Aetrium, Morris Air

Officers, Executives and Principals

Patrick A. Hopf, General Managing Partner
Education: BS, Business, University of Minnesota; MBA, University of Virginia
Background: Vice President, T. Rowe Price Associates; Founder, Family Entertainment Centers Inc.

Brian D. Jacobs, General Partner
Education: BS, MS, Mechanical Engineering, Massachusetts Institute of Technology; MBA, Stanford University
Background: Senior Associate, Security Pacific Venture Capital Group; Raychem Corporation; RCA; Polaroid; Westinghouse

Everett V. Cox, General Partner
Education: BS, MS, Mechanical Engineering, Stanford University; MBA, University of Southern California
Background: Senior Vice President/Chief Analyst, Security Pacific Venture Capital Group; Technical positions at McDonnell Douglas Corporation

Fredric R. Boswell, General Partner
Education: BS, MS, PhD, Electrical Engineering, Case Western Reserve University; MBA, Harvard
Background: President, ADC Telecommunications; President and Chief Executive Officer, E.F. Johnson Company
Directorships: Director, Telecommunications Industry Association, Minnesota High Technology Council

Nancy S. Olson, General Partner
Education: BA, Bacteriology, University of California at Berkeley; MBA, Wharton School of Business
Background: Managing Director, Dakin Securities; Founder Rx Capital; General Partner, Sequoia Capital

Jim Simons, General Partner

Michael Gorman, General Partner

Katherine Carney, Chief Financial Officer

Barb Shronts, Director of Partnership and Administration

STAMFORD FINANCIAL

Stamford Financial Building
Stamford, NY 12167

Telephone: 607-652-3311
Fax: 607-652-6301

Other Office Locations
86-19 88th Avenue
Woodhaven, NY 11421
Phone 718-847-6878, Fax 718-847-6994

Mission: Actively seeking new investments

Fund Size: not available
Founded: 1975
Average Investment: $5 - 10 million
Minimum Investment: $500,000

Investment Criteria: Second-stage

Industry Group Preference: Communications, Computer Related, Consumer, Distribution, Electronic Components and Instrumentation, Genetic Engineering, Medical/Health Related, Movie Industry

Portfolio Companies: High Tech Semiconductor, Inc., Northwestern Telecom, Inc., For Gentlemen Only, Inc., German Television, Inc., Delta Capital, Inc., Alliance Capital, Inc.

Officers, Executives and Principals

George C. Bergleitner III, Chairman of the Board
Education: JD, St. John's College
Background: Stock Broker

George C. Bergleitner, Jr., President (Stamford)
Education: MBA
Background: Accounting, Stock Broker
Directorships: Member Board of Directors of more than 30 public and private corporations

Murray Corn, Vice President (Woodhaven)
Education: Brooklyn College, Bio-Chemist Pharmacologist
Background: Vice President, Husson Vitamins
Directorships: Bio-Chem, Inc., Vital Signs, Inc.

Michael Reed, Vice President (Stamford)
Education: Hartwick College
Background: Stock Broker
Directorships: Caseys, Inc., Electronic Filing Centers, Papillon Danville International Licensing Corporation

Alexander C. Bross, Vice President and Treasurer
Education: MBE, Germany
Background: Money Market Manager, Stock Broker
Directorships: Member, Board of Directors of five public and private corporations

Richard B. Spinney, Secretary (Stamford)
Education: JD
Background: Attorney at Law
Directorships: National Bank of Stamford

William Bunchuck, Vice President, Public Relations (Stamford)
Education: BA
Background: CBS
Directorships: Christmas Feeling Fund

Steve Herring, Senior Consultant

STATE STREET BANK AND TRUST COMPANY

3414 Peachtree Road, NE
Suite 1010
Atlanta, GA 30326

Telephone: 404-364-9500
Fax: 404-261-4469

Mission: Actively seeking situation where standard bank financing falls short and sub debt is too expensive, which are often cash flow deals

Fund Size: not available
Founded: 1792
Average Investment: $10 million
Minimum Investment: $2 million

Investment Criteria: Leveraged Buyout, Special Situations

Geographic Preference: United States and Hong Kong banks

Industry Group Preference: Communications, Computer Related, Distribution, Industrial Products and Equipment, Manufacturing, Medical/Health Related, Service

Portfolio Companies: not available

Officers, Executives and Principals

Kent Mitchell, Vice President

STEPHENSON MERCHANT BANKING, INC.
100 Garfield Street
Denver, CO 80206

Telephone: 303-355-6000
Fax: 303-329-9107

Mission: Actively seeking new investments

Fund Size: not available
Founded: 1969
Average Investment: not available
Minimum Investment: $100,000

Investment Criteria: Leveraged Buyout, Special Situations, Control-block Purchases

Industry Group Preference: Computer Related, Consumer, Distribution, Industrial Products and Equipment

Portfolio Companies: not available

Officers, Executives and Principals

A. Emmet Stephenson, Jr., Senior Partner
Preston Sumner, Director

STERLING COMMERCIAL CAPITAL, INC.

175 Great Neck Road
Great Neck, NY 11021

Telephone: 516-482-7374
Fax: 516-487-0781

Mission: Actively seeking new investments

Fund Size: not available
Founded: 1988
Average Investment: $500,000 - $1 million
Minimum Investment: $250,000

Investment Criteria: Later-stage

Geographic Preference: Northeastern United States

Industry Group Preference: Consumer, Distribution, Manufacturing, Service

Portfolio Companies: not available

Officers, Executives and Principals

Harvey Granat, President
Harvey Rosenblatt, Executive Vice President
Philip H. Wachtler, Vice President

STERLING GRACE CAPITAL MANAGEMENT, L.P.

55 Brookville Road
P.O. Box 163
Glen Head, NY 11545

Telephone: 516-686-2200
Fax: 516-625-1685

Other Office Locations
515 Madison Avenue
Suite 2000
New York, NY 10022

Mission: Actively seeking new investments

Fund Size: not available
Founded: 1983
Average Investment: not available
Minimum Investment: $250,000

Investment Criteria: First-stage, Second-stage, Mezzanine, Leveraged Buyout, Special Situations, Control-block Purchases

Industry Group Preference: Communications, Computer Related, Consumer, Electronic Components and Instrumentation, Energy/Natural Resources, Genetic Engineering, Industrial Products and Equipment, Medical/Health Related

Portfolio Companies: not available

Officers, Executives and Principals

Oliver R. Grace, Jr., Chairman (New York)
John S. Grace, President (Glen Head)
Alec Rutherford, Analyst (Glen Head)
Davis P. Stowell, Analyst (Glen Head)

STERLING VENTURES, LTD.

276 Post Road West
Westport, CT 06880

Telephone: 203-226-8711
Fax: 203-454-5780

Mission: Actively seeking new investments

Fund Size: not available
Founded: 1991
Average Investment: not available
Minimum Investment: $3 million

Investment Criteria: Leveraged Buyout, Special Situations, Control-block Purchases, Recapitalizations

Industry Group Preference: not available

Portfolio Companies: American Buidings Company, David Thermal Technologies, Inc., Shape Technology Inc., Euro Outlet Malls, L.P.

Officers, Executives and Principals

Douglas Newhouse, Partner
Education: BA, Cornell University; MBA, University of Chicago
Background: President, Middex Capital Corporation; Senior Vice President, Lehman Brothers; Matuschka Group; Mitchell Hutchins, Inc.

William Selden, Partner
Education: BA, Dartmouth College; MBA, Columbia University
Background: Managing Director, Lehman Brothers; Executive Vice President, E.F. Hutton Inc.; Vice President, Eastdil Realty Inc.; Chief Financial Officer, Sunbelt Communications, Inc.; Vice President, Bankers Trust Company

M. William Macey, Partner

THE STILL RIVER FUND

100 Federal Street
29th Floor
Boston, MA 02110

Telephone: 617-348-2327
Fax: 617-348-2371

Mission: Actively seeking new investments

Fund Size: $28 million
Founded: 1994
Average Investment: $750, 000
Minimum Investment: $250,000

Investment Criteria: First-stage, Second-stage

Geographic Preference: Northeastern United States, particularly the Connecticut River Valley

Industry Group Preference: Communications, Computer Related, Consumer, Distribution, Electronic Components and Instrumentation, Industrial Products and Equipment, Medical/Health Related

Portfolio Companies: Business Technology, Inc., Continuity Marketing, Inc., Lids, Inc.

Officers, Executives and Principals

James A. Saalfield, Managing Partner
Joseph J. Tischler, General Partner

STOLBERG PARTNERS

445 Park Avenue
19th Floor
New York, NY 10022

Telephone: 212-826-1110
Fax: 212-826-0371

Mission: Actively seeking new investments

Fund Size: $70 million
Founded: 1993
Average Investment: $4 - $6 million
Minimum Investment: $1 million

Investment Criteria: Leveraged Buyout, Special Situations, Control-block Purchases

Industry Group Preference: Communications, Computer Related, Consumer, Distribution, Electronic Components and Instrumentation, Energy/Natural Resources, Industrial Products and Equipment, Medical/Health Related

Portfolio Companies: not available

Officers, Executives and Principals

E. Theodore Stolberg, Partner
Matthew M. Meehan, Partner
Walter P. Scano, Partner

STONEBRIDGE PARTNERS

Westchester Financial Center
50 Main Street
White Plains, NY 10606

Telephone: 914-682-2285
Fax: 914-682-0834

Other Office Locations
P.O. Box 512
Washington, PA 15301
Phone 412-223-0707

Mission: Actively seeking new investments

Fund Size: not available
Founded: 1986
Average Investment: not available
Minimum Investment: not available

Investment Criteria: Leveraged Buyout

Industry Group Preference: Industrial Products and Equipment, Medical/Health Related

Portfolio Companies: not available

Officers, Executives and Principals

Michael S. Bruno, Jr., General Partner (White Plains)
Harrison Wilson, General Partner (White Plains)
David Zackuson, General Partner (White Plains)
Dan Dye, General Partner (Washington, PA)

STRATEGIC ADVISORY GROUP, INC.
253 Main Street
P.O. Box 773
Sag Harbor, NY 11963

Telephone: 516-725-7746
Fax: 516-725-7739

Other Office Locations
94 Mohegan Drive
West Hartford, CT, 06117
Phone 203-523-4257, Fax 203-523-4530

Mission: not available

Fund Size: not available
Founded: 1992
Average Investment: not available
Minimum Investment: $500,000

Investment Criteria: First-stage, Second-stage, Mezzanine, Leveraged Buyout

Industry Group Preference: Communications, Computer Related, Consumer, Distribution, Electronic Components and Instrumentation, Energy/Natural Resources, Industrial Products and Equipment, Medical/Health Related

Portfolio Companies: not available

Officers, Executives and Principals

Pierce W. Hance, Managing Director (New York)
Carol W. Hance, Managing Director (New York)

STRATEGIC INVESTMENTS AND HOLDINGS, INC.

Cyclorama Building
369 Franklin Street
Buffalo, NY 14202

Telephone: 716-857-6000
Fax: 716-857-6490

Mission: A holding company seeking to acquire and develop successful companies in partnership with operating management.

Fund Size: Deal size: $10 - $100 million
Founded: 1983
Average Investment: not available
Minimum Investment: $500,000

Investment Criteria: Leveraged Buyout, Recapitalizations

Geographic Preference: Continental United States

Industry Group Preference: Food Processing, Manufacturing, Office Products, Paper

Portfolio Companies: General Manufactured Housing, Inc., Quality Foods Company, Microporous Products, LP, Technicarbon, Hampton Print Works, Inc.

Officers, Executives and Principals

Gary M. Brost, President
Education: BA, Allegheny College; MBA, State University of New York, Buffalo
Background: Numerous management positions at a major bank

Alan R. Abt, Executive Vice President
Education: BA, Political Science, St. Lawrence University
Background: Ten years international and domestic commercial lending

David M. Zebro, Executive Vice President
Education: BA, Political Science, State University of New York, Plattsburgh; MBA, Corporate Finance, State University of New York, Buffalo
Background: Senior management in finance and planning with several Fortune 500 companies

John F. Dunbar, Senior Vice President
Education: BS, MBA, State University of New York, Buffalo
Background: Five years operations management and project engineering functions

William L. Joyce, Senior Vice President
Education: Wharton; MBA, Harvard
Background: Ten years in a broad range of industrial operation positions, sales, marketing, finance, general management

Dennis Martin, Senior Vice President
Education: BS, Economics, MBA, Finance, Canisius College
Background: 13 years of commercial lending experience

STRATFORD CAPITAL PARTNERS, L.P.

200 Crescent Court
Suite 1650
Dallas, TX 75201

Telephone: 214-740-7377
Fax: 214-740-7340

Mission: Actively seeking new investments

Fund Size: not available
Founded: 1993
Average Investment: not available
Minimum Investment: $1 million

Investment Criteria: Mezzanine, Leveraged Buyout, Special Situations

Industry Group Preference: Consumer, Distribution, Industrial Products and Equipment

Portfolio Companies: not available

Officers, Executives and Principals

Michael D. Brown, Managing Partner
John G. Farmer, Managing Partner

SUMMIT CAPITAL ASSOCIATES, INC.

745 Fifth Avenue
Suite 900
New York, NY 10151

Telephone: 212-308-4155
Fax: 212-750-1850; 212-223-7363

Mission: Actively seeking new investments

Fund Size: not available
Founded: 1987
Average Investment: $1.5 million
Minimum Investment: $500,000

Investment Criteria: First-stage, Second-stage, Mezzanine, Leveraged Buyout

Industry Group Preference: Diversified

Portfolio Companies: not available

Officers, Executives and Principals

Richard Messina, Managing Director

SUMMIT CAPITAL GROUP
38 Sylvan Road
Madison, CT 06443

Telephone: 203-245-6870
Fax: 203-245-6865

Mission: Actively seeking new investments

Fund Size: not available
Founded: 1987
Average Investment: not available
Minimum Investment: $100,000

Investment Criteria: Mezzanine, Leveraged Buyout, Special Situations, Small Management Buyouts, Corporate Leveraged Financing

Industry Group Preference: Low Technology Manufacturing, Metal Fabrication, Plastics, Textiles

Portfolio Companies: not available

Officers, Executives and Principals

Lawrence J. Katz, Managing Partner
Rockwell D. Marsh, Managing Partner

SUN VALLEY VENTURES

2301 East Del Amo Boulevard
Carson, CA 90220

Telephone: 310-638-1370
Fax: 310-763-9503

Other Office Locations
160 Second Street
Ketchum, ID 83340
Phone 208-726-5005, Fax 208-726-5094

Mission: Actively seeking new investments

Fund Size: not available
Founded: 1993
Average Investment: not available
Minimum Investment: $100,000

Investment Criteria: Second-stage, Mezzanine, Leveraged Buyout, Special Situations, Control-block Purchases, Management Buyouts

Industry Group Preference: Computer Related, Consumer, Distribution, Electronic Components and Instrumentation, Industrial Products and Equipment, Medical/Health Related

Portfolio Companies: not available

Officers, Executives and Principals

Gerald W. Chamales, General Partner (Carson and Ketchum)
Daniel G. Styles, General Partner (Carson)
John V. Tunney, General Partner (Carson and Ketchum)
Joseph A. Kouba, Advisor
Christine V. McNamara, Advisor
Rick Rickertsen, Advisor

SUNDANCE VENTURE PARTNERS, L.P.

10600 North De Anza Boulevard
Suite 215
Cupertino, CA 95014

Telephone: 408-257-8100

Other Office Locations
400 East Van Buren
Suite 650
Phoenix, AZ 85004
Phone 602-252-3441, Fax 602-252-1450

Mission: Actively seeking new investments

Fund Size: not available
Founded: 1989
Average Investment: not available
Minimum Investment: $100,000

Investment Criteria: First-stage, Second-stage, Mezzanine, Leveraged Buyout, Special Situations, Subordinated Debt with Warrants

Industry Group Preference: Diversified

Portfolio Companies: not available

Officers, Executives and Principals

Gregory S. Anderson, General Partner (Phoenix)
Larry J. Wells, General Partner (Cupertino)
Brian Burns, Administrative Partner (Phoenix)

SWEENEY & COMPANY, INC.

P.O. Box 567
Southport, CT 06490

Telephone: 203-255-0220

Mission: To assure maximum valuation at cashout by gearing the going concern to achieve optimum reliable future profit growth as a result of recognition and management of those particular factors and practices crucial to its success.

Fund Size: not available
Founded: 1975
Average Investment: not available
Minimum Investment: $100,000

Investment Criteria: Seed, Research and Development, Startup, First-stage, Second-stage, Mezzanine, Leveraged Buyout, Joint Ventures, Product Licensing

Geographic Preference: Northeastern United States

Industry Group Preference: Communications, Computer Related, Consumer, Distribution, Electronic Instrumentation, Entertainment, Industrial Products and Equipment, Medical/Health Related

Portfolio Companies: not available

Officers, Executives and Principals

Brian M. Sweeney, President
Background: McKinsey, Citicorp/Citibank, Colgate-Palmolive

TA ASSOCIATES

125 High Street
Suite 2500
Boston, MA 02110

Other Office Locations
435 Tasso Street
Palo Alto, CA 94301
Phone 415-328-1210, Fax 415-326-4933

4516 Henry Street
Pittsburgh, PA 15213
Phone 412-441-4949, Fax 412-441-5784

Mission: not available

Fund Size: $700 million
Founded: not available
Average Investment: $2 - $25 million
Minimum Investment: not available

Investment Criteria: Seed to Initial Public Offering

Industry Group Preference: Computer Related, Financial Services, High Technology, Information Services, Medical/Health, Service Industries, Software

Portfolio Companies: AIM Management Group, Keystone Group, MidCoast Mortgage, Mutual Risk Management, Federal Express, Softsel Computer Products, Anasazi, Bridge Information Systems, I.P. Sharp Associates, Eastern Mountain Sports, Jenny Craig, Nu-Med, Copley Pharmaceuticals, Sunrise Medical, Broad Street Communications, Continental Cablevision

Officers, Executives and Principals

Kevin Landry, Managing Director and Chief Executive Officer

Jeffery T. Chambers, Senior General Partner (Palo Alto)
Education: BA, Economics, cum laude, Harvard College; MBA, Stanford
Background: Meredith Associates
Directorships: Anasazi, Colorado Memory Systems, Jenny Craig, Payment Services Co., Technology Solutions Co.

Jacqueline C. Morby, Senior General Partner (Pittsburgh)
Education: BA, Psychology, Stanford University; MS, Management, Simmons Graduate School of Management
Background: Administration and Marketing, Hughes Aircraft and Athena Scientific
Directorships: Invest Support Systems, Ontrack Computer Systems, QStar Technology, Raxco, Software 2000, New England Venture Capital

Michael C. Child, General Partner (Palo Alto)
Education: BS, Electrical Engineering, University of California at Davis; MBS, Stanford

Background: Product Manager, Rolm; Strategic Planning Consultant, Boston Consulting Group; Production Engineer, Hewlett Packard

Directorships: Artisoft, State of the Art, AST Research, Cadence Design Systems, Network General, Novellus Systems

Kurt R. Jaggers, Vice President (Palo Alto)

Education: BS, MS, Phi Beta Kappa, Electrical Engineering, Stanford University; MBA, Stanford

Background: Director, Carrier Marketing; Network Equipment Technician, Engineering Manager, Business Computer Corporation, Rolm Corporation

Directorships: Tident Micro Systems and Microtest

TAPPAN ZEE CAPITAL CORPORATION

201 Lower Notch Road
P.O. Box 416
Little Falls, NJ 07424

Telephone: 201-256-8280
Fax: 201-256-2841

Mission: Actively seeking new investments

Fund Size: not available
Founded: 1962
Average Investment: not available
Minimum Investment: $250,000

Investment Criteria: Leveraged Buyout, Debt or Debt with Equity Secured

Industry Group Preference: Diversified

Portfolio Companies: not available

Officers, Executives and Principals

Jeffrey Birnberg, President
Robert T. Laino, Treasurer

TAYLOR AND TURNER

PO Box 1512
Selnoma, CA 95476

Telephone: 707-939-1240
Fax: 707-939-1222

Mission: Reducing investment activity

Fund Size: not available
Founded: 1982
Average Investment: not available
Minimum Investment: Less than $100,000

Investment Criteria: Seed, Startup, First-stage, Special Situations, Control-block Purchases

Industry Group Preference: Communications, Computer Related, Electronic Components and Instrumentation, Energy/Natural Resources, Genetic Engineering, Industrial Products and Equipment, Medical/Health Related

Portfolio Companies: not available

Officers, Executives and Principals

William H. Taylor II, General Partner
Marshall C. Turner, Jr., General Partner

TDH

c/o Private Equity Management Company
919 Conestoga Road, Building 1, Suite 301
Rosemont, PA 19010

Telephone: 610-526-9970
Fax: 610-526-9971
E-mail: swhtdh@ix.netcom.com

Other Office Locations
Marketing Office:
4800 Montgomery Lane, Suite 875
Bethesda, MD 20814

Mission: To strike a fair balance between the risks inherent in investments and their potential—all within the context of prudent business practices. Through its expertise in structuring non-traditional financing arrangements and as a leader or originator of deals, TDH is able to uniquely craft its investments to benefit the portfolio company's specific needs and to ensure fair and realistic equity terms and conditions.

Fund Size: $50 million
Founded: 1978
Average Investment: $1.5 million
Minimum Investment: $800,000

Investment Criteria: First-stage to Leveraged Buyout

Geographic Preference: East Coast of the United States

Industry Group Preference: Broadcast/Cable/Radio, Communications, Computer Related, Consumer Related, Electronics, Environmental Protection, Industrial Products, Manufacturing/Processing, Medical/Health, Publishing, Retailing, Service Industries, Wholesaling/Distribution

Portfolio Companies: ESPN, Staples, Inc., Intelligent Electronics, Inc., Airges, Inc.

Officers, Executives and Principals

J.B. Doherty, Managing General Partner
Education: BSE, U.S. Naval Academy; MBA, Stanford University
Background: Founder, President Private Equity Management Co.; General Partner, K.S. Sweet Associates; Corporate Finance Blyth Eastman and Dillon, AT&T, Raychem Corporation
Directorships: Chairman of the Board of Lone Star Broadcasting, O-Cedar/Vining Household Products Co., Apollo Metals, Ltd.

James M. Buck III
Education: AB, Princeton University
Background: Founder, Vice President, Private Equity Management Co.; K.S. Sweet Associates; J.P. Morgan, Inc.
Directorships: Secretary and Assistant Treasurer of Lone Star Broadcasting, Inc.

Stephen W. Harris
Education: AB, Duke University; MBA, Wharton; CPA

Background: Founder, Vice President Private Equity Management Co.; General Partner, K.S. Sweet Associates; Sun Co.
Directorships: Lone Star Broadcasting, Inc., Apollo Metals, Ltd.

Thomas M. Balderston
Education: MA, Williams College; MBA, UCLA
Background: Founder, Vice President, Private Equity Management Co.; General Partner, K.S. Sweet Associates; Bank of Boston

TECH VENTURES, INC.

2060 Route 250, Suite 310
Penfield, NY 14526

Telephone: 716-377-7900
Fax: 716-377-7904
E-mail: Cherintec@aol.com

Other Office Locations
1325 Millersport Highway
Williamsville, NY 14221
Phone 716-633-4833, Fax 716-634-6122, E-mail szustak@aol.com

Mission: Actively seeking new investments

Fund Size: variable
Founded: 1985
Average Investment: $100,000
Minimum Investment: Less than $100,000; $500,000 maximum

Investment Criteria: Start-up, First-stage, Second-stage

Geographic Preference: Upstate New York

Industry Group Preference: Communications, Composites, Computer Related, Consumer, Distribution, Electronic Components and Instrumentation, Energy/Natural Resources, Genetic Engineering, Imaging, Industrial Products and Equipment, Manufacturing, Medical/Health Related, Optics, Software

Portfolio Companies: Ameritherm Inc., Ormec Systems, LaserMax, Pharmaceutical Discovery Corporation, Bydatel Corporation, Ironics Inc., Four Rivers Software, Opkor, Automated Dynamics

Officers, Executives and Principals

Paul Cherin, President (Penfield)
Education: BS, Chemistry, Brooklyn College; Ph.D., Chemical Physics, Polytechnical Institute of New York
Background: Technology
Directorships: Ameritherm Inc., Bydatel Corporation

William Szustak, Chief Financial Officer (Williamsville)
Education: BS, Accounting, Philosophy, Canisius College; MBA, Finance, University of Pittsburgh

Paul Grant, Vice President (Penfield)
Education: BS, Industrial Engineering, Georgia Institute of Technology; MBA, Drexel University
Background: Finance

Paul Pineo, Secretary (Penfield)
Education: BA, Cubly College; JD, Georgetown University; LLM, George Washington University
Background: Law

John Volpel, Director of Investment Evaluation (Penfield)
Education: BS, Mechanical Engineering, Michigan Tech; MS, Industrial Administration, Carnegie Mellon
Background: Manufacturing

TECHNOLOGY INVESTMENTS

P.O. Box 704
Los Altos, CA 94023

Telephone: 415-948-1561
Fax: 415-948-3003

Mission: not available

Fund Size: not available
Founded: 1990
Average Investment: not available
Minimum Investment: Less than $100,000

Investment Criteria: Seed, Startup, First-stage

Industry Group Preference: Communications, Computer Related, Electronic Components and Instrumentation, Energy/Natural Resources, Medical/Health Related

Portfolio Companies: not available

Officers, Executives and Principals

Jack C. Carsten

TECHNOLOGY PARTNERS

1550 Tiburon Boulevard, Suite A
Belvedere, CA 94920

Telephone: 415-435-1935
Fax: 415-435-5921

Mission: not available

Fund Size: $50 billion
Founded: not available
Average Investment: $100,000 - $4 million
Minimum Investment: not available

Investment Criteria: Seed to Second-stage

Industry Group Preference: Biotechnology, Communications, Computer Related, Information Services, Medical/Health

Portfolio Companies: Crystal Dynamics, Spectrum HoloByte, 3DO, Video Stream, PixelCraft, Qualix, Trident Systems, View Star, American Mobile Satellite Corporation, Domestic Automation, Calpte Biomedical, Cell Pathways, Cemax, Cholestech, Iris Medical Instruments, Medwave, Unisruge

Officers, Executives and Principals

Roger J. Quy, PhD, General Partner
Background: Hewlett-Packard Corporation, Oxford Instrument Group

William Hart, General Partner
Background: Cresap, McCormick and Paget, Inc., IBM Corporation

J.E. (Ted) Ardell, Special Partner
Background: Impell Corporation, Bechtel Corporation

Ira M. Ehrenpreis, Associate

TECHNOLOGY VENTURES CORPORATION

One Technology Center
115 University Boulevard, Southeast
Albuquerque, NM 87106

Telephone: 505-246-2882
Fax: 505-246-2891

Mission: To facilitate the commercialization of technology from the national laboratories, primarily Sandia, and the research universities in the region. A primary focus of Technology Venture Corporation (TVC) is attracting risk investment money, and it assists technology-based companies by facilitating technology transfer and coordinating management and business assistance.

Fund Size: not available
Founded: 1993
Average Investment: not available
Minimum Investment: Less than $100,000

Investment Criteria: Seed, Startup, First-stage, Second-stage; TVC does not invest, but serves as a link between equity investment sources and businesses seeking capital

Industry Group Preference: Diversified

Portfolio Companies: not available

Officers, Executives and Principals

Sherman McCorkle, President

TEK VENTURES, INC.

16C River Road
Nutley, NJ 07110

Telephone: not available

Mission: Actively seeking new investments

Fund Size: not available
Founded: 1992
Average Investment: not available
Minimum Investment: $500,000

Investment Criteria: Seed, Research and Development, Startup

Industry Group Preference: Communications, Computer Related, Consumer, Distribution

Portfolio Companies: not available

Officers, Executives and Principals

Peter Young, Managing Director
Gordon Lifeson, Associate

TESSLER AND CLOHERTY, INC.

155 Main Street
Cold Spring, NY 10516

Telephone: 914-265-4244
Fax: 914-265-4158

Other Office Locations
4521 PGA Boulevard, Suite 330
Palm Beach Gardens, FL 33418

Mission: Actively seeking new investments

Fund Size: not available
Founded: 1980
Average Investment: not available
Minimum Investment: $250,000

Investment Criteria: First-stage, Second-stage, Leveraged Buyout, Special Situations

Industry Group Preference: Energy/Natural Resources

Portfolio Companies: not available

Officers, Executives and Principals

Daniel Tessler
Anne Saunders, Manager (Cold Spring)

TEXAS GROWTH FUND

TGF Management Corporation
100 Congress Avenue, Suite 980
Austin, TX 78701

Telephone: 512-322-3100
Fax: 512-322-3101

Mission: not available

Fund Size: $127 million
Founded: 1992
Average Investment: $3 - $5 million
Minimum Investment: $2 million

Investment Criteria: Second-stage to Leveraged Buyout; revenues over $15 million

Geographic Preference: Texas

Industry Group Preference: Diversified

Portfolio Companies: Classic Communications, Independent Gas Holdings, Cable Healthcare Corporation, Sterling Foods, Silverado Food, Technology Works, Adminstaff, Inc, Coastal Towing, I-C Manufacturing, Inc., Garden Ridge Corporation, Total Safety, Inc., Q Clubs, Inc., Lil' Things, Inc. Argotyche, LP, Sovereign Business Forms, American Rockwool

Officers, Executives and Principals

James J. Kozlowski
Education: BA, MBA, Harvard
Background: Fortis Private Capital, Merrill Lynch, Tenneco

Stephen M. Soileau
Education: BA, Rice; MA, International Management, American Graduate School of International Management
Background: Creekwood Capital, Houston Industries

THACHER FINANCIAL GROUP, INC.

4401 El Camino Real
Suite F
Atascadero, CA 93422

Telephone: 805-466-5116
Fax: 805-466-3548
E-mail: npg@fix.net

Mission: Actively seeking new investments in the propane distribution industry

Fund Size: not available
Founded: 1985
Average Investment: not available
Minimum Investment: $50,000

Investment Criteria: Startup, Special Situations

Geographic Preference: Western United States

Industry Group Preference: Propane Distribution

Portfolio Companies: not available

Officers, Executives and Principals

William W. Thacher, President
Lynn D. Thacher, Secretary and Treasurer

THIRD MILLENNIUM VENTURE CAPITAL, LTD.

P.O. Box 1123
Los Altos, CA 94023

Telephone: 415-941-0336

Mission: Actively seeking new investments

Fund Size: not available
Founded: 1987
Average Investment: not available
Minimum Investment: Less than $100,000

Investment Criteria: Seed, Research and Development, Startup, First-stage, Second-stage

Industry Group Preference: Computer Related, Industrial Products and Equipment

Portfolio Companies: not available

Officers, Executives and Principals

Dr. John R. Koza, President
Dr. Martin A. Keane, Vice President

THOMPSON CLIVE, INC.

3000 Sand Hill Road
Building One, Suite 185
Menlo Park, CA 94025-7102

Telephone: 415-854-0314
Fax: 415-854-0670
E-mail: vc@internet.net

Other Office Locations
24 Old Bond Street
London W1X3DA
England
Phone 44-171-491-4809, Fax 44-171-493-9172

55, rue la Boetie
75008 Paris
France
Phone 33-1-4413-3606, Fax 33-1-4413-3746

Mission: Actively seeking new investments

Fund Size: $1 - $3 million
Founded: 1977
Average Investment: $1 - $5 million
Minimum Investment: $500,000

Investment Criteria: Startup, First-stage, Second-stage, Mezzanine, Leveraged Buyout, Special Situations

Industry Group Preference: Biotechnology, Communications, Computer Related, Distribution, Electronic Components and Instrumentation, Energy/Natural Resources, Genetic Engineering, High Technology, Industrial Products and Equipment, Medical/Health Related, Software

Portfolio Companies: not available

Officers, Executives and Principals

Peter Ziebelman, Managing Director (Menlo Park)
Education: BSC, Computer Science, Psychology Honors, Yale University; MS, Management, Stanford University; Sloan Fellow
Background: Marketing and Sales, Semiconductor Group of Texas Instruments, Ryan McFarland Corporation

Richard Thompson, Principal (London)

Colin Clive, Principal (London)

Michael Elias, Principal (Menlo Park and Paris)
Education: BA, honors, Biological Anthropology, Harvard University; MS, Neurobiology, Cambridge University; Marshall Scholarship
Background: Founding Member, Neuroscience Limited

Greg Ennis, Principal (Menlo Park)
Education: AB, Economics, Political Science, Stanford; MBA, University of California, Los Angeles
Background: Citibank Frankfurt, Germany

Robert E. Patterson, Principal (Menlo Park)

THORNER BIOVENTURES

P.O. 830
Larkspur, CA 94977

Telephone: 415-925-9304
Fax: 415-461-5855

Mission: Actively seeking new investments

Fund Size: not available
Founded: 1982
Average Investment: $200,000
Minimum Investment: $100,000

Investment Criteria: Seed, Startup, First-stage, Second-stage, Special Situations

Geographic Preference: California

Industry Group Preference: Computer Related, Consumer, Electronic Components and Instrumentation, Genetic Engineering, Industrial Products and Equipment, Medical/Health Related

Portfolio Companies: CyberMedia, E*Trade Group, Canji, R2 Technology, Mitokor, Quantum Magnetics

Officers, Executives and Principals

Tom Thorner, Managing General Partner
Oscar Winnipeg Fuddy, Special Partner

THREE ARCH PARTNERS

2800 Sand Hill Road
Suite 270
Menlo Park, CA 94025

Telephone: 415-854-5550
Fax: 415-854-9880

Mission: Focused on helping form new companies in the field of healthcare

Fund Size: $27 million
Founded: 1994
Average Investment: $1 million
Minimum Investment: $100,000

Investment Criteria: Seed, Startup, First-stage

Geographic Preference: West Coast of the United States

Industry Group Preference: Medical/Health Related

Portfolio Companies: Biopsys Medical, CardioThoracic Systems, General Surgical Innovations, Intesiva Healthcare, LocalMed, Odyssey Healthcare, Perclose, Prolifix

Officers, Executives and Principals

Thomas J. Fogarty, General Partner
Wilfred E. Jaeger, General Partner
Mark A. Wan, General Partner
Barclay Nicholson, Controller

THREE CITIES RESEARCH, INC.

135 East 57th Street
New York, NY 10022

Telephone: 212-838-9660
Fax: 212-980-1142

Other Office Locations
TCR Europe S.A.
229, boulevard Saint-Germain
75007 Paris
France
Phone 33-1-4705-7154, Fax 33-1-4705-7173

Mission: Actively seeking new investments

Fund Size: $245 million
Founded: 1972
Average Investment: not available
Minimum Investment: $5 million

Investment Criteria: Mezzanine, Leveraged Buyout, Difficult Transaction

Geographic Preference: United States

Industry Group Preference: Consumer, Distribution, Industrial Products and Equipment

Portfolio Companies: not available

Officers, Executives and Principals

Vivan de Mesquita (Paris)
J. William Uhrig (New York)
Willem F.P. de Vogel (New York)
H. Whitney Wagner (New York)
Thomas G. Weld (New York)
Karen Kochevar (New York)
Jon Skein (New York)

TRANSCAP ASSOCIATES

1845 Oak Street
Northfield, IL 60093

Telephone: 847-501-2500
Fax: 847-501-2656

Other Office Locations
11 Penn Plaza, 5th Floor
New York, NY 10001
Phone 212-946-2888, Fax 212-946-2889

300 North Lake Avenue, Suite 205
Pasadena, CA 91101
Phone 818-578-1500, Fax 818-578-3413

Mission: Committed to remaining the premier provider of purchase order and trade finance for growing, middle-market companies

Fund Size: $30 million
Founded: 1991
Average Investment: $500,000 - $3 million
Minimum Investment: no transaction minimum

Investment Criteria: First-stage, Second-stage, Third-stage, Bridge, Acquisition/Buyout

Geographic Preference: United States based companies

Industry Group Preference: Accessories/Apparel, Automotive Parts, Computers, Electronics, Furniture, Giftware, Housewares, Licensed Products, Medical Supplies, Non-Precious Metals, Novelties/Promotional Products, Printing, Sporting Goods, Textiles, Toys and Games, Video Products

Portfolio Companies: not available

Officers, Executives and Principals

Ira J. Edelson, President
Education: BSC, DePaul University
Background: CPA, Senior Partner, Deloitte and Touche; Senior Fiscal Policy Advisor, Mayor of Chicago; Instructor, Northwestern University Graduate School of Management; Member, Commercial Finance Association, American Institute of Certified Public Accountants and Illinois CPA Society

Michael Sear, Executive Vice President
Education: BSBA, Washington University; MBA, Harvard
Background: CPA, CMA, CFP; Manager of various investment partnerships; Chief Financial Officer of a rural cellular telephone company; Vice President, Acquisitions and Redevelopment for Midwest real estate firm; Member, Commercial Finance Association, American Institute of Certified Public Accountants, Illinois CPA Society and Institute of Certified Financial Planners

Michael R. Epton, Executive Vice President
Education: BS, JD, Northwestern University
Background: Office of the State's Attorney of Cook County; Partner in private firm specializing in litigation and pre-trial negotiation; Member, Commercial Finance Society

TRIAD INVESTORS CORPORATION

300 East Joppa Road
Suite 1111
Baltimore, MD 21286

Telephone: 410-828-6497
Fax: 410-337-7312

Mission: Actively seeking new investments

Fund Size: $25 million
Founded: 1989
Average Investment: $700,000
Minimum Investment: $100,000

Investment Criteria: Seed, Research and Development, Startup, First-stage

Geographic Preference: Mid-Atlantic United States

Industry Group Preference: Communications, Computer Related, Consumer, Electronic Components and Instrumentation, Energy/Natural Resources, Genetic Engineering, Industrial Products and Equipment, Medical/Health Related

Portfolio Companies: not available

Officers, Executives and Principals

Barbara Plantholt Melera, President
Jeffrey A. Davison, Vice President
Patricia S. McCarthy, Vice President

TRIAD VENTURES, LTD.

4600 Post Oak Place, Suite 100
Houston, TX 77027

Telephone: 713-627-9111
Fax: 713-627-9119

Other Office Locations
8911 Capital of Texas Highway
Suite 3320
Austin, TX 78759
Phone 512-343-8087, Fax 512-342-1993

Mission: not available

Fund Size: not available
Founded: not available
Average Investment: $1 million
Minimum Investment: not available

Investment Criteria: not available

Geographic Preference: Texas

Industry Group Preference: Diversified

Portfolio Companies: not available

Officers, Executives and Principals

Lloyd M. Bentsen, General Partner
Mary Bass, General Partner

TRIDENT CAPITAL, INC.

2480 Sand Hill Road
Suite 100
Menlo Park, CA 94025

Telephone: 415-233-4300
Fax: 415-233-4333

Other Office Locations
190 South LaSalle Street, Suite 2760
Chicago, IL 60603
Phone 312-630-5500, Fax 312-630-5501

11100 Santa Monica Boulevard, Suite 2020
Los Angeles, CA 90025
Phone 310-444-3840, Fax 310-444-3848

1001 Pennsylvania Avenue, N.W.
Washington, DC 20004
Phone 202-347-2626, Fax 202-347-1818

Mission: Actively seeking new investments

Fund Size: $120 million
Founded: 1993
Average Investment: $5 million
Minimum Investment: $1 million

Investment Criteria: Early-stage, First-stage, Second-stage, Mezzanine, Leveraged Buyout

Industry Group Preference: Information and Business Services

Portfolio Companies: Anasazi, Inc., AnyRiver Entertainment, Inc., The Compucare Company, CSG Systems International, Inc., Daou Systems, Inc., Digital Evolution Inc., Essense Systems, Inc., Evolving Systems, Inc., Firefly Network, Inc., GeoSystems Global Corporation, Internet Profiles Corporation, Internet Securities, Inc., Medicode Inc., Nets, Inc., OnLine Interactive, Inc., Pegasus Systems, Inc., Platinum Software Corporation, Production Group International Inc., Research Holdings, Ltd. Silicon Valley Internet Partners, The St. John Companies, TransGlobal Systems, Inc., Unison Software Inc., Vality Technology, Inc.

Officers, Executives and Principals

Donald R. Dixon, Partner (Menlo Park)
Stephen M. Hall, Partner (Menlo Park)
Robert C. McCormack, Partner (Chicago)
John H. Moragne, Partner (Menlo Park)
Rockwell A. Schnabel, Partner (Los Angeles)
Edward J. Mathias, Special Limited Partner (Washington)

TRILWOOD INVESTMENTS, LTD.

161 Bay Street, P.O. Box 523, Suite 4320
Toronto, Ontario M5J 2S1
Canada

Telephone: 416-869-3945
Fax: 416-869-1778

Mission: Actively seeking new investments

Fund Size: not available
Founded: 1989
Average Investment: not available
Minimum Investment: $3 million

Investment Criteria: Leveraged Buyout, Later-stage Financing

Industry Group Preference: not available

Portfolio Companies: not available

Officers, Executives and Principals

John C. Puddington, President
Douglas W. Moore, Vice President

TRINITY VENTURES

155 Bovet Road, Suite 660
San Mateo, CA 94402

Telephone: 415-358-9700
Fax: 415-358-9785

Mission: not available

Fund Size: $120 million
Founded: not available
Average Investment: $1 million
Minimum Investment: not available

Investment Criteria: Startup to Leveraged Buyout

Industry Group Preference: Biotechnology, Communications, Computer Related, Consumer Related, High Technology, Information Services, Medical/Health, Service Industries, Software

Portfolio Companies: Alldata, Answer Computer, Softdesk, Beyond, Digital Research, Digitalk, Forte, Lucid, Crescendo Communications, Wall Data, Conner Peripherals, IKOS Systems, Software Developers, Garden Fresh Restaurant, KidSource, Medical Self Care, PetStuff, Smith Sports Optics, Starbucks, Sweet Factory

Officers, Executives and Principals

James G. Shennan, Jr., General Partner
Education: Princeton University; MBA, Stanford
Background: Procter and Gamble; Chief Executive Officer, S&O Consultants
Directorships: The Office Place, Souplantation, Smith Sports Optics, Starbucks, Smog Busters

Noel J. Fenton, General Partner
Education: Cornell University; Stanford Business School
Background: Chief Executive Officer, Acurex and Covalent Systems
Directorships: Alldata, Answer Computer, Digital Research, Vertex Design Systems

Larry Orr, Senior Associate
Education: Harvard College; MBA, Stanford
Background: Mergers and Acqusitions, Niederhoffer, Cross and Zeckhauser; Turnarounds, Bain and Co.; Marketing, Hewlett-Packard's Information Networks Group

Terry Gould, Associate
Education: Dartmouth College; MBA, Stanford
Background: Boston Consulting Group; Chief Executive Officer, Innovative Leisure

TRIUNE CAPITAL

1888 Century Park East
Suite 1900
Los Angeles, CA 90067

Telephone: 310-284-6800
Fax: 310-284-3290

Mission: Actively seeking new investments

Fund Size: not available
Founded: 1981
Average Investment: not available
Minimum Investment: $1 million

Investment Criteria: First-stage, Second-stage, Mezzanine, Special Situations, Control-block Purchases

Geographic Preference: West Coast of the United States

Industry Group Preference: Communications, Computer Related, Consumer, Distribution, Electronic Components and Instrumentation, Genetic Engineering, Medical/Health Related

Portfolio Companies: not available

Officers, Executives and Principals

Bradley McManus, Principal

TSG VENTURES, INC.

177 Broad Street
12th Floor
Stamford, CT 06901

Telephone: 203-406-1500
Fax: 203-406-1590

Mission: Actively seeking new investments

Fund Size: not available
Founded: 1971
Average Investment: 1.5 million
Minimum Investment: $250,000

Investment Criteria: Second-stage, Leveraged Buyout

Industry Group Preference: Communications, Computer Related, Consumer, Distribution, Industrial Products and Equipment, Medical/Health Related

Portfolio Companies: not available

Officers, Executives and Principals

Duane E. Hill, President and Chief Executive Officer
Darryl B. Thompson, Senior Vice President
Cleveland A. Christopher, Vice President
Lawrence C. Morse, PhD, Vice President

TUCKER CAPITAL CORPORATION

One Palmer Square
Suite 315
Princeton, NJ 08542

Telephone: 609-924-5710

Mission: Actively seeking new investments

Fund Size: not available
Founded: 1982
Average Investment: not available
Minimum Investment: $1 million

Investment Criteria: Second-stage, Mezzanine, Leveraged Buyout, Special Situations

Industry Group Preference: Consumer, Distribution, Energy/Natural Resources, Industrial Products and Equipment, Medical/Health Related

Portfolio Companies: not available

Officers, Executives and Principals

David A. Baxendale, Managing Director
Craig L. Battle, President
Kemp P. Battle, Vice President

TVM TECHNO VENTURE MANAGEMENT

101 Arch Street
Suite 1950
Boston, MA 02110

Telephone: 617-345-9320
Fax: 617-345-9377

Other Office Locations
650 Town Center Drive, Suite 1350
Costa Mesa, CA 92626
Phone 714-545-6400, Fax 714-545-0106

Denninger-str 15
81679 Munich
Germany
Phone 49-89-99-8920, Fax 49-89-99-89-9255

Mission: Actively seeking new investments

Fund Size: not available
Founded: 1983
Average Investment: not available
Minimum Investment: $250,000

Investment Criteria: Startup, First-stage, Second-stage, Mezzanine, Foreign Market Entry

Industry Group Preference: Communications, Computer Related, Distribution, Electronic Components and Instrumentation, Energy/Natural Resources, Genetic Engineering, Industrial Products and Equipment, Medical/Health Related

Portfolio Companies: not available

Officers, Executives and Principals

Waldemar Jantz, Managing Partner (Munich)
Randall R. Lunn, Managing Partner (Boston and Costa Mesa)
John J. DiBello, Chief Financial Officer, Partner (Boston)
Friedrich Bornikoel, Partner (Munich)
Peter Kaleschke, Partner (Munich)
Patricia W. Dane, Controller (Boston)
Dr. Helmut Schuhsler, Partner (Munich)
Bernd Seivel, Controller, Partner (Munich)

U. S. MEDICAL RESOURCES CORPORATION

188 Lafayette Circle
Cincinnati, OH 45220-1105

Telephone: 512-281-3900
Fax: 512-281-3994

Mission: Actively seeking new investments in medical devices where they can market the products in the states of the former Soviet Union. They will handle all regulatory business in the former Soviet Union.

Fund Size: not available
Founded: 1988
Average Investment: not available
Minimum Investment: Less than $100,000

Investment Criteria: Startup, First-stage, Second-stage, Mezzanine, Leveraged Buyout, Special Situations

Geographic Preference: Within 25 miles of Cincinnati, Ohio

Industry Group Preference: Medical Devices or Supplies, Medical/Health Related

Portfolio Companies: not available

Officers, Executives and Principals

James E. Bowman, Jr., President
Education: MBA, University of North Carolina
Background: General Management and Export of New and Remanufactured Diagnostic Imaging Equipment

U. S. VENTURE PARTNERS

2180 Sand Hill Road, Suite 300
Menlo Park, CA 94025

Telephone: 415-854-9090
Fax: 415-854-3018

Other Office Locations
777 108th Avenue Northeast, Suite 2460
Bellevue, WA 98004
Phone 206-646-7620, Fax 206-646-3448

Mission: not available

Fund Size: $325 million
Founded: not available
Average Investment: $1 million
Minimum Investment: not available

Investment Criteria: Seed to Second-stage

Industry Group Preference: Biotechnology, Computer Related, Electronics, High Technology, Medical/
  Health, Retailing, Software

Portfolio Companies: Audrey Jones, Avia Group, Deja, Eyeonics, Fresh Choice, Garden Botanika, Gymboree,
  Applied Digital Access, Chronology, ElseWare, Genus, IC Works, Rasna, Redwood Design, Sun Microsystems, CareLink, Cell Genesys, Genta, Penderm, Advanced Cardiovascular Systems

Officers, Executives and Principals

Irwin Federman, General Partner
Education: BS, Economics, Brooklyn College; CPA; PhD, Engineering Science, Santa Clara University
Background: Concord Partners; President and Chief Executive Officer, Monolithic Memories; Chairman, Semi-
  conductor Industry Association
Directorships: Advanced Micro Devices, Western Digital Corporation, Komag, National Venture Capital Asso-
  ciation

Nancy E. Glaser, General Partner
Education: BA, Marshall University; MBA, Stanford
Background: Managing Director, Lord and Taylor, R.H. Macy's Inc.; Buyer, The Gap

Philip M. Young, General Partner
Education: BME, Cornell; MS, Engineering Physics, George Washington University; MBA, Harvard; Baker
  Scholar
Background: Concord Partners; President, Chief Executive Officer, Oximetrix; Abbott Critical Care
Directorships: Xoma, The Immune Response

Philip S. Schlein, General Partner
Education: BS, Economics, University of Pennsylvania
Background: Retail, R.H. Macy
Directorships: Apple Computer, Ross Stores, ReSound, Oxford Fine Clothing, R.H. Macy

Steven M. Krausz, General Partner
Education: BS, Electrical Engineering, MBA, Stanford University; Arjayu Miller Scholar
Background: Daisy Systems; Marketing Management, Direct Inc.; NASA Ames Research Center
Directorships: Verity, Inc.

William K. Bowes, Jr., General Partner
Education: BA, Economics, Stanford; MBA, Harvard
Background: Founder, U.S. Venture Partners; Senior Vice President and Director, Blyth and Co.
Directorships: Amgen, Applied Biosystems, Glycomed, XOMA

Dale J. Vogel, General Partner (Bellevue)
Education: BS, San Jose State University; MBA, Harvard
Background: General Partner, Northwest Venture Capital; President, K2 Corporation; President, JanSport; Management, Wickes; Chief Operating Officer, Aldila
Directorships: Gymboree, Garden Botanika, Chronology, Eyeonics

ULIN AND HOLLAND, INC.

176 Federal Street
Boston, MA 02110

Telephone: 617-261-6360
Fax: 617-261-6442

Mission: Actively seeking new investments

Fund Size: not available
Founded: 1992
Average Investment: not available
Minimum Investment: $5 million

Investment Criteria: Second-stage, Mezzanine

Industry Group Preference: Consumer, Distribution, Medical/Health Related

Portfolio Companies: not available

Officers, Executives and Principals

Peter A. Ulin, Managing Director
Nicholas Holland, Managing Director
Timothy Tully, Partner

UNC VENTURES

711 Atlantic Avenue
Boston, MA 02111

Telephone: 617-482-7070
Fax: 617-482-9720

Mission: not available

Fund Size: $30 million
Founded: not available
Average Investment: $100,000 - $2 million
Minimum Investment: not available

Investment Criteria: Startup to Acquisition

Industry Group Preference: Communications, Electronics, High Technology, Information Services, Medical/ Health

Portfolio Companies: Accent Hair Salons Inc., Biogrowth, Cirrus Logic, Cybernetics Systems International Corporation, Granite Broadcasting, Infolink, Ruggles Bedford Associates Inc., Suncoast Communications, The Westpark Limited Partnerships, U.S. Radio L.P., WDG-III San Francisco Medical Center., L.P., WDG Ventures, Ltd., Xinix, Inc.

Officers, Executives and Principals

Edward Dugger III, Managing Partner
Education: AB, cum laude, Harvard College; MA, Public Affairs and Urban Planning, Princeton University
Background: Irwin Management
Directorships: United Way of Massachusetts Bay, Greater Boston YMCA, Museum of Fine Arts Council, Museum of the National Center

Veronica Zizza, Treasurer

UNCO VENTURES, LTD.

520 Post Oak Boulevard
Suite 130
Houston, TX 77027

Telephone: 713-622-9067
Fax: 713-622-9007

Mission: not available

Fund Size: not available
Founded: 1988
Average Investment: not available
Minimum Investment: $250,000

Investment Criteria: Second-stage, Mezzanine

Industry Group Preference: Communications, Computer Related, Electronic Components and Instrumentation, Energy/Natural Resources, Medical/Health Related

Portfolio Companies: not available

Officers, Executives and Principals

Walter Cunningham, General Partner
Stuart Schube, General Partner

UNION STREET CAPITAL CORPORATION

P.O. Box 219
Mercer Island, WA 98040

Telephone: 206-343-7284
Fax: 206-623-9247

Mission: Actively seeking new investments

Fund Size: not available
Founded: 1983
Average Investment: not available
Minimum Investment: Less than $100,000

Investment Criteria: Second-stage, Leveraged Buyout

Industry Group Preference: Communications, Computer Related, Consumer, Distribution, Electronic Components and Instrumentation, Energy/Natural Resources, Industrial Products and Equipment, Medical/Health Related

Portfolio Companies: not available

Officers, Executives and Principals

Stanton J. Barnes, Partner

UNION VENTURE CORPORATION

445 South Figueroa Street
Los Angeles, CA 90071

Telephone: 213-236-4092
Fax: 213-688-0101

Mission: Reducing investment activity

Fund Size: not available
Founded: 1967
Average Investment: not available
Minimum Investment: $250,000

Investment Criteria: Second-stage, Mezzanine, Leveraged Buyout, Special Situations

Industry Group Preference: Communications, Consumer, Energy/Natural Resources

Portfolio Companies: not available

Officers, Executives and Principals

Robert Dawson, Officer

UNIROCK MANAGEMENT CORPORATION

1228 15th Street
Suite 201
Denver, CO 80202

Telephone: 303-623-4500
Fax: 303-623-9006

Mission: Actively seeking new investments

Fund Size: not available
Founded: 1988
Average Investment: not available
Minimum Investment: $250,000

Investment Criteria: Second-stage, Mezzanine, Leveraged Buyout

Geographic Preference: Colorado

Industry Group Preference: Diversified

Portfolio Companies: not available

Officers, Executives and Principals

Franklin S. Wimer, President and Principal
Education: BE, Chemical Engineering, Yale University; LLB, JD, Seton Hall University
Background: Advisor, United Banks of Colorado; Consultant, Resource Technology Associates, Ladd Petroleum; Owner, President and Chief Executive Officer, HOP, Inc.; Director, Part-Owner, Trindex Oil and Gas; Senior Vice President, Barber Oil Corporation; Chairman, American House Doctor; Vice President and Principal, Stemp and Company; President, Candlelight House, Inc.; Technical Sales and Marketing, Union Carbide Corporation

Scott H. Maierhofer, Vice President and Principal
Education: BA, Labor Relations, Pennsylvania State University; MBA, University of Denver
Background: Acting Chief Financial Officer, Vista Restaurants; Investment Officer, Merchant Banking Group, United Bank of Denver; Financial Analyst, United Bank of Denver, American Television and Communications Corporation, Gary-Williams Oil Producer

Lisa N. Johnson, Vice President and Principal
Education: BBA, Economics and Finance, Baylor University
Background: Vice President, Norwest Business Credit, Inc.; Vice President, Corporate Banking Division, United Bank of Denver

John M. Hereford, Associate
Education: BA, History, Amherst College; MBA, Harvard Business School
Background: New Services Division, TeleCommunications, Inc.; Overseas Private Investment Corporation

UST PRIVATE EQUITY INVESTORS FUND

114 West 47th Street
New York, NY 10036

Telephone: 212-852-3949
Fax: 212-852-3975

Mission: Actively seeking new investments

Fund Size: not available
Founded: not available
Average Investment: not available
Minimum Investment: $1 million

Investment Criteria: Second-stage, Mezzanine, Leveraged Buyout

Industry Group Preference: Communications, Computer Related, Consumer, Distribution, Electronic Components and Instrumentation, Energy/Natural Resources, Genetic Engineering, Industrial Products and Equipment, Medical/Health Related

Portfolio Companies: not available

Officers, Executives and Principals

David Fann, President

VALLEY CAPITAL CORPORATION

100 Martin Luther King Boulevard
Suite 212, Krystal Building
Chattanooga, TN 37402

Telephone: 423-265-1557
Fax: 423-265-1588

Mission: Actively seeking new investments

Fund Size: $2 million
Founded: 1982
Average Investment: $25,000 - $300,00
Minimum Investment: Less than $100,000

Investment Criteria: First-stage to Later-stage

Geographic Preference: Tennessee

Industry Group Preference: Communications, Computer Related, Consumer, Distribution, Electronic Components and Instrumentation, Energy/Natural Resources, Industrial Products and Equipment, Medical/Health Related

Portfolio Companies: not available

Officers, Executives and Principals

Lamar J. Partridge, President
Faye Robinson, Administrative Assistant

VALLEY MANAGEMENT, INC.

100 West Martin Luther King Boulevard
Suite 210, Krystal Building
Chattanooga, TN 37402

Telephone: 423-265-0774
Fax: 423-265-1588

Mission: Actively seeking new investments

Fund Size: $15 million
Founded: 1993
Average Investment: $500,000
Minimum Investment: $100,000

Investment Criteria: First-stage to Later-stage

Geographic Preference: Tennessee, Georgia, Alabama, Mississippi, Kentucky, North Carolina

Industry Group Preference: Communications, Consumer, Distribution, Electronic Components and Instrumentation, Industrial Products and Equipment, Medical/Health Related

Portfolio Companies: not available

Officers, Executives and Principals

Langston J. Walker, President

VALLEY VENTURES, L.P.

6155 North Scottsdale Road
Suite 100
Scottsdale, AZ 85250-5412

Telephone: 602-661-6600
Fax: 602-661-6262

Mission: Fund raising and seeking equity investments focused in life sciences

Fund Size: not available
Founded: 1984
Average Investment: not available
Minimum Investment: $500,000

Investment Criteria: Second-stage, Mezzanine, Leveraged Buyout

Geographic Preference: Southwestern United States

Industry Group Preference: Communications, Electronic Components and Instrumentation, Industrial Products and Equipment, Medical/Health Related

Portfolio Companies: not available

Officers, Executives and Principals

John M. Holliman III, General Partner
Terence E. Wraters, General Partner

VECTOR FUND MANAGEMENT, L.P.

1751 Lake Cook Road
Suite 350
Deerfield, IL 60015

Telephone: 847-940-1970
Fax: 847-374-3899

Mission: Actively seeking new investments in healthcare and life science industries

Fund Size: $51.1 million
Founded: 1994
Average Investment: $2 - $3 million
Minimum Investment: $1 million

Investment Criteria: Mezzanine, Special Situations, Private Placements in Public Companies

Industry Group Preference: Biotechnology, Diagnostics, Healthcare Services, Life Sciences, Medical Devices, Pharmaceuticals

Portfolio Companies: Cambridge Antibody Technology, Cell Therapeutics, HealthTech Services, IBAH, Life-Cell, Magainin Pharmaceuticals, Martek Biosciences, Maternicare, Matrix Pharmaceuticals, Pharmacopeia

Officers, Executives and Principals

Sandra Panem, Ph.D., President
Education: Ph.D., Microbiology, SB, Biochemistry, University of Chicago
Background: 25 years life science industry, money management, scientific research and biomedical policy; Vice President, Oppenheimer Global Biotech Fund; Salomon Brothers; Alfred Sloan Foundation
Directorships: HealthTech Services, IBAH, Martek Biosciences, Synaptic Pharmaceuticals

K. Flynn McDonald, Vice President
Education: MBA, Harvard Business School, JD, University of Virginia; BA, Human Biology, Stanford University
Background: 12 years technology management and venture capital experience; Vice President, Technology Funding; Vice President, Raychem Ventures and Controller/Director of Business Development, Technology Sector, Raychem Corporation; Allied Corporation; International Law and Business Development
Directorships: LifeCell, Maternicare

D. Theodore Berghorst, Partner
Education: BBA, University of Michigan; MBA, Northwestern
Background: Chairman, Chief Executive Officer and Founder, Vector Securities International; Managing Director, Co-Head of Life Sciences, Kidder Peabody and Co.; Citibank

Peter F. Drake, Ph.D., Partner
Education: BA, Biology, Bowdoin College; Ph.D., Neurobiology, Biochemistry, Bryn Mawr University
Background: Executive Vice President, Founder, Vector Securities International; Vice President, Kidder Peabody and Co.; Institutional Investor, "All-Star Team"; Senior Research Associate, Department of Genetics and Anatomy, Case Western University

James L. Foght, Ph.D., Partner
Education: BS, University of Akron; Ph.D., Organic Chemistry, University of Illinois
Background: President and Founder, Vector Securities International; Senior Vice President and Co-Head of Life Sciences/Medical Products Group, Kidder Peabody and Company; Research Scientist, Managing Director, DuPont UK; Head of Pharmaceuticals for Europe, Africa and Middle East, Director of Worldwide Technology Evaluation and Acquisitions-Biomedical Products, EI du Pont de Nemours and Company
Directorships: Cambridge Antibody Technology

VEGA CAPITAL CORPORATION

80 Business Park Drive
Armonk, NY 10504

Telephone: 914-273-1025
Fax: 914-273-1028

Mission: not available

Fund Size: $10 million
Founded: 1968
Average Investment: $500,000
Minimum Investment: $100,000

Investment Criteria: Second-stage to Recapitalizations

Industry Group Preference: Diversified

Portfolio Companies: not available

Officers, Executives and Principals

Ronald Linden, President and Director
Education: University of Maryland; Syracuse University; State University New York, Binghamton
Background: Public Accounting and Health Care Finance; President, NERASBIC
Directorships: Vacuum Industries, Walicin Shoe Company

VENCA MANAGEMENT

2293 Washington Street
Suite Two
San Francisco, CA 94115

Telephone: 415-885-2100
Fax: 415-885-1410

Other Office Locations
7-14-11-104 Minami Aoyama
Minato-ku, Tokyo 108
Japan
Phone 81-3-3486-1807, Fax 81-3-3486-1068

Mission: not available

Fund Size: not available
Founded: 1983
Average Investment: not available
Minimum Investment: $250,000

Investment Criteria: Startup, First-stage, Second-stage

Industry Group Preference: Genetic Engineering, Medical/Health Related

Portfolio Companies: not available

Officers, Executives and Principals

Carolynn Gandolfo, General Partner (San Francisco)
Koichi Itoh, General Partner (Tokyo)

VENCAP, INC.

10180-101st Street, Suite 1980
Edmonton, Alberta T5J 3S4
Canada

Telephone: 403-420-1171
Fax: 403-429-2451

Mission: Actively seeking new investments

Fund Size: $100 million
Founded: 1983
Average Investment: $5 - $10 million
Minimum Investment: $5 million

Investment Criteria: Second-stage, Mezzanine, Leveraged Buyout

Geographic Preference: Western Canada, Pacific Northwest, Rocky Mountain Corridor of United States

Industry Group Preference: Communications, Computer Related, Consumer, Distribution, Electronic Components and Instrumentation, Industrial Products and Equipment

Portfolio Companies: Forzani Group, Mark's Work Wearhouse, Pacific Linen, The Churchill Corporation, Nascor, Inc., BIOSYS, Applied Microsystems, Crystalline Materials, Medwave, Biomira, Camelot Superabsorbents, Ltd., Coinstar, Inc., The ESYS Corporation, Fletcher's Fine Foods, Highwood Resources, Nextwave Design Automation, PRIZM, Railink Investments, Redwood Microsystems, Sangstat, Taro Industries, Thermatrix, Thixotech

Officers, Executives and Principals

Ian Morris, Vice President and Chief Financial Officer
Bill McKenzie, Vice President
David Stitt, Vice President
Frank Stack, Vice President

VENCON MANAGEMENT, INC.

301 West 53rd Street
Suite 10F
New York, NY 10019

Telephone: 212-581-8787
Fax: 212-397-4126

Mission: Actively seeking new investments

Fund Size: not available
Founded: 1972
Average Investment: not available
Minimum Investment: $250,000

Investment Criteria: Seed, Startup, First-stage, Second-stage, Leveraged Buyout, Special Situations

Industry Group Preference: Communications, Electronic Components and Instrumentation, Energy/Natural Resources, Genetic Engineering, Industrial Products and Equipment, Medical/Health Related

Portfolio Companies: not available

Officers, Executives and Principals

Irvin Barash, President
H. Herman Zand, Treasurer
Julie Lamb, Research Analyst
Katia Richard, Research Assistant
Diana Torres, Research Assistant

VENROCK ASSOCIATES

30 Rockefeller Plaza
Suite 5508
New York, NY 10112

Telephone: 212-649-5600
Fax: 212-649-5788

Other Office Locations
755 Page Mill Road
Suite A230
Palo Alto, CA 94304
Phone 415-493-5577, Fax 415-493-6443

Mission: Actively seeking new investments

Fund Size: not available
Founded: 1969
Average Investment: not available
Minimum Investment: $500,000

Investment Criteria: Seed, Research and Development, Startup, First-stage, Second-stage

Industry Group Preference: Communications, Computer Related, Distribution, Electronic Components and Instrumentation, Energy/Natural Resources, Genetic Engineering, Industrial Products and Equipment, Medical/Health Related

Portfolio Companies: not available

Officers, Executives and Principals

Peter O. Crisp, General Partner (New York)
Anthony B. Evnin, General Partner (New York)
David R. Hathaway, General Partner (New York)
Patrick F. Latterell, General Partner (Palo Alto)
Ted H. McCourtney, General Partner (New York)
Kimberley A. Rummelsburg, General Partner (New York)
Anthony Sun, General Partner (Palo Alto)
Ray A. Rothrock, General Partner (New York)
Terence J. Garnett, Venture Partner (Palo Alto)
Jason E. Green, Associate (New York)
Nicholas G. Galakatos, Associate (New York)

VENTANA FINANCIAL RESOURCES, INC.

249 Market Square
Lake Forest, IL 60045

Telephone: 847-234-3434

Mission: Actively seeking new investments

Fund Size: not available
Founded: 1984
Average Investment: not available
Minimum Investment: $100,000

Investment Criteria: Seed, Research and Development, Startup, First-stage, Second-stage, Mezzanine, Leveraged Buyout

Industry Group Preference: Communications, Computer Related, Consumer, Distribution, Electronic Components and Instrumentation, Energy/Natural Resources, Genetic Engineering, Industrial Products and Equipment, Medical/Health Related

Portfolio Companies: not available

Officers, Executives and Principals

Albert J. Montano, Chairman

VENTANA MANAGEMENT

18881 Von Karman Avenue
Suite 350
Irvine, CA 92715

Telephone: 714-476-2204
Fax: 714-752-0223

Other Office Locations
8880 Rio San Diego Drive
Rio Vista Towers, Suite 500
San Diego, CA 92108
Phone 619-291-2757, Fax 619-295-0189

Mission: not available

Fund Size: $140 million
Founded: not available
Average Investment: $500,000
Minimum Investment: not available

Investment Criteria: Seed to Bridge

Industry Group Preference: Biotechnology, Communications, Computer Related, Consumer Related, Electronics, Energy/Natural Resources, High Technology, Industrial Products, Medical/Health, Publishing, Software, Transportation

Portfolio Companies: Advanced Tissue Sciences, Air Methods, Auto Parts Club, Corvas International, Cymer Laser, Darox, Fuisz Tech., Intelligent Surgical Lasers, La Jolla Pharmaceuticals, McGaw, National Medical Waste, PDG Environmental, Somatix Therapy, Telios Pharmaceuticals, Unifet UnisSyn Technologies, BTX, Coral Biomedical

Officers, Executives and Principals

Thomas O. Gephart, Managing Partner
Tom Gephart, Vice President
Dan L. Dearen, Senior Associate (San Diego)
Scott Burri, Senior Associate (San Diego)
Sebastian Alexanderson, Associate (San Diego)

VENTEX MANAGEMENT, INC.

1001 Fannin Street
Suite 1095
Houston, TX 77002

Telephone: 713-659-7870
Fax: 713-659-7855

Mission: Actively seeking new investments

Fund Size: not available
Founded: 1978
Average Investment: not available
Minimum Investment: $1 million

Investment Criteria: Second-stage, Mezzanine, Leveraged Buyout, Special Situations

Industry Group Preference: Communications, Computer Related, Consumer, Distribution, Electronic Components and Instrumentation, Energy/Natural Resources, Genetic Engineering, Industrial Products and Equipment, Medical/Health Related

Portfolio Companies: not available

Officers, Executives and Principals

Richard S. Smith, President
David M. Miller, Vice President
Annette Lestoquoy, Assistant Vice President

VENTEX PARTNERS

1001 Fannin Street
Suite 1095
Houston, TX 77002

Telephone: 713-659-7860
Fax: 713-659-7855

Mission: not available

Fund Size: not available
Founded: not available
Average Investment: $1 - $5 million
Minimum Investment: not available

Investment Criteria: Startup to Leveraged Buyout

Geographic Preference: Texas, Sunbelt region of the United States

Industry Group Preference: Communications, Manufacturing/Processing, Medical/Health, Retailing, Transportation, Wholesaling/Distribution

Portfolio Companies: not available

Officers, Executives and Principals

David M. Miller
Richard S. Smith

VENTURA AMERICA

8230 Leesburg Pike
Suite 710
Vienna, VA 22182

Telephone: 703-442-4500
Fax: 703-442-4500

Mission: Reducing investment activity

Fund Size: not available
Founded: 1984
Average Investment: not available
Minimum Investment: Less than $100,000

Investment Criteria: Seed, Startup, First-stage

Industry Group Preference: Communications, Computer Related, Consumer, Distribution, Electronic Components and Instrumentation, Industrial Products and Equipment

Portfolio Companies: not available

Officers, Executives and Principals

James R. Ball, General Partner
Daniel E. Moore, General Partner

VENTURA CAPITAL MANAGEMENT CORPORATION

P.O. Box 372626
Satellite Beach, FL 32937

Telephone: 407-777-1969

Mission: Actively seeking new investments

Fund Size: not available
Founded: 1974
Average Investment: not available
Minimum Investment: Less than $100,000

Investment Criteria: First-stage, Second-stage, Leveraged Buyout

Industry Group Preference: Communications, Computer Related, Consumer, Distribution, Electronic Components and Instrumentation, Energy/Natural Resources, Genetic Engineering, Industrial Products and Equipment, Medical/Health Related

Portfolio Companies: not available

Officers, Executives and Principals

Dr. Robert A. Adams, President

VENTURE ASSOCIATES, LTD.

4950 East Evans Street
Suite 105
Denver, CO 80222-5209

Telephone: 303-758-8710
Fax: 303-758-8747
E-mail: jarkebauer@venturea.com

Other Office Locations
4811 Trailwood Way
Springfield, MO 65804
Phone 417-882-9218

Mission: Actively seeking new investments

Fund Size: not available
Founded: 1982
Average Investment: not available
Minimum Investment: $100,000 (private placements)

Investment Criteria: Seed, Startup, First-stage, Second-stage, Special Situations

Industry Group Preference: Communications, Computer Related, Consumer, Distribution, Electronic Components and Instrumentation, Energy/Natural Resources, Genetic Engineering, Industrial Products and Equipment, Medical/Health Related

Portfolio Companies: not available

Officers, Executives and Principals

James B. Arkebauer, President (Denver)
Peter A. Thompson, Vice President
Stephen D. Replin, Associate
R. Kent Wooldridge (Springfield)

VENTURE CAPITAL FUND OF NEW ENGLAND

160 Federal Street, 23rd Floor
Boston, MA 02110

Telephone: 617-439-4646
Fax: 617-439-4652

Mission: not available

Fund Size: $80 million
Founded: 1981
Average Investment: $1 million
Minimum Investment: $500,000

Investment Criteria: Startup to Second-stage

Geographic Preference: Northeastern United States

Industry Group Preference: Biotechnology, Broadcast/Cable/Radio, Communications, Computer Related, Electronics, High Technology, Industrial Products, Information Services, Medical/Health, Software

Portfolio Companies: Progress Software, Cytogen, Groundwater Technology, Concord Computing, Individual, Protocare, Mentor Clinical Care, Credence Systems, Spectrian, Steinbrecher, Thermatrix, Western Wireless, Ultracision, U.S. Data, Loudoun Telecommunications, Transcend Therapeutics

Officers, Executives and Principals

Harry J. Healer, General Partner
Education: BSBA, Babson College
Background: Vice President, First Capital Corporation of Boston; Vice President, First Venture Capital Corporation
Directorships: Concord Computing Corporation, Cytogen, Groundwater Technology, Thermatrix, Extraction Systems, Optimax Systems, Progress Software, Preception Technology

Kevin J. Dougherty, General Partner
Education: BA, Williams College
Background: Vice President, Bank of Boston; Vice President, Massachusetts Capital Resource Company
Directorships: Keytek Instruments, Pathway Design, Mentor Clinical Care Prestocare, Commonwealth Care, Occupational Health and Rehabilitation, Individual, Sierra Research and Technology, High Road

Richard A. Farrell, General Partner
Education: BSBA, MBA, Boston University
Background: President, First Capital Corporation of Boston; President, First Venture Capital Corporation
Directorships: Allied Devices Corporation, Auburn International, Cadec Systems, Cape-Island, Dowden Communications

William C. Mills, General Partner
Education: BA, Chemistry, Princeton; MS, Chemistry, MIT; MM, Management, MIT
Background: Partner, Paine Webber Venture Management
Directorships: Cytogen, Spectrian, Ultracision, Transcend Therapeutics, Omnirel

VENTURE CAPITAL FUND, INC.

Banco Popular Building
Tetuan Street #206, Suite 701
San Juan, Puerto Rico 00902

Telephone: 809-725-5285
Fax: 809-721-1735

Mission: Actively seeking new investments

Fund Size: $12 million
Founded: 1989
Average Investment: $500,000
Minimum Investment: $250,000

Investment Criteria: Seed, Startup, First-stage, Second-stage, Mezzanine

Geographic Preference: Southeastern United States, Puerto Rico, Caribbean

Industry Group Preference: Communications, Computer Related, Consumer, Distribution, Electronic Components and Instrumentation, Energy/Natural Resources, Genetic Engineering, Industrial Products and Equipment, Medical/Health Related

Portfolio Companies: not available

Officers, Executives and Principals

Zoilo Medez, Partner
Education: BS, MS, Industrial Engineering, Rensselaer Polytechnic Institute
Background: Financial Consulting, Banking

Cyril L. Meduna, President
Education: BS, MBA
Directorships: Various, including portfolio companies

VENTURE FIRST ASSOCIATES
1901 South Harbor City Boulevard
Suite 501
Melbourne, FL 32901

Telephone: 407-952-7750
Fax: 407-952-5787

Other Office Locations
4811 Thornwood Drive
Acworth, GA 30102
Phone 770-928-3733

500 Old Greensboro Road
Chapel Hill, NC 27516
Phone 919-929-1065

Mission: not available

Fund Size: $75 million
Founded: not available
Average Investment: $500,000 - $3 million
Minimum Investment: not available

Investment Criteria: Seed to Second-stage

Geographic Preference: Southeastern United States

Industry Group Preference: Aeronautics, Data Processing, Environmental, Glass Ceramics and Silica, Graphic Arts, Horticulture, Medical/Health, Minerals, Satellites, Telecommunications

Portfolio Companies: Geltech, Inc., TransGlobal Services, Inc., Thunderbird Technologies, Inc., MCHI, Inc., Ivex Corporation, Med Images Corporation, Minco, Inc., Strategic Diagnostics, Inc., Sun River Corporation, AirNet Communications, Inc., MedAcoustics, Inc., ImageLinks, Inc., Flash Comm, Inc.

Officers, Executives and Principals

S. Douglass Mullins, General Partner
Education: BS, Systems Engineering, Georgia Tech; MBA, Harvard
Background: Chief of Naval Operations, Ford Motor Co.; Executive Vice President, Ronson Corporation; Vice President, Mead Corporation

Andrew W. Grubbs, General Partner
Education: BS, Mechanical Engineering, North Carolina State University; MBA, Darden University of Virginia
Background: Design Engineer and Venture Manager, General Electric Corporation; General Partner, Emerging Growth Partners

VENTURE FOUNDERS CORPORATION

29 Domino Drive
Concord, MA 01742

Telephone: 508-287-4950
Fax: 508-287-0568

Other Office Locations
Kidlington Business Center
Four Lakesmere Close
Kidlington, Oxfordshire OX5 1L6
England
Phone 44-865-370510, Fax 44-865-370520

Excelsiorlaan 21/4
B-1930 Zaventem
Belgium
Phone 32-2-725-1440, Fax 32-2-725-1609

Canadian Venture Founders Corporation
75 Navy Street
Oakville, Ontario L6J 1Z3
Canada
Phone 905-842-9770, Fax 905-842-9774

Mission: Reducing investment activity

Fund Size: not available
Founded: 1973
Average Investment: not available
Minimum Investment: Less than $100,000

Investment Criteria: Seed, Research and Development, Startup, First-stage

Industry Group Preference: Communications, Computer Related, Electronic Components and Instrumentation, Energy/Natural Resources, Genetic Engineering, Medical/Health Related

Portfolio Companies: not available

Officers, Executives and Principals

Alexander L.M. Dingee, Jr., Chairman and General Partner (Lexington)
Edward H. Getchell, President and General Partner (Lexington)
Joseph M. Frye, Jr., General Partner and Director (Kidlington)
David T. Riddiford, General Partner (Lexington)

VENTURE FUNDING GROUP INTERNATIONAL

49 West 12th Street
Executive Suite
New York, NY 10011

Telephone: 212-691-9895

Mission: Actively seeking new investments

Fund Size: not available
Founded: 1976
Average Investment: not available
Minimum Investment: Less than $100,000

Investment Criteria: Seed, Research and Development, Startup, First-stage, Second-stage, Mezzanine, Leveraged Buyout, Special Situations, Joint Ventures, Acquisitions and Mergers

Geographic Preference: North America, United Kingdom, Europe, Asia and Pacific Rim, Africa, Middle East, Latin and South America, Russia

Industry Group Preference: Communications, Computer Related, Consumer, Distribution, Electronic Components and Instrumentation, Energy/Natural Resources, Genetic Engineering, Industrial Products and Equipment, Medical/Health Related, Oil and Gas, Real Estate, Recycling, Theme Parks

Portfolio Companies: not available

Officers, Executives and Principals

Allan E. Skora, President

VENTURE FUNDING, LTD.

321 Fisher Building
Detroit, MI 48202

Telephone: 313-871-3606
Fax: 313-873-4935

Mission: Making few, if any, new investments

Fund Size: not available
Founded: 1983
Average Investment: not available
Minimum Investment: $250,000

Investment Criteria: Seed, Research and Development, Startup, Leveraged Buyout, Special Situations

Industry Group Preference: Communications, Consumer, Genetic Engineering, Medical/Health Related

Portfolio Companies: not available

Officers, Executives and Principals

E.I. Schuster, Chairman
M. Schuster, Vice President

VENTURE GROWTH ASSOCIATES

1550 El Camino Real
Suite 275
Menlo Park, CA 94025

Telephone: 415-323-8100
Fax: 415-854-3254

Mission: Actively seeking new investments

Fund Size: not available
Founded: 1982
Average Investment: not available
Minimum Investment: $1 million

Investment Criteria: First-stage, Second-stage, Mezzanine, Leveraged Buyout

Industry Group Preference: Communications, Computer Related, Consumer, Distribution, Electronic Components and Instrumentation, Energy/Natural Resources, Genetic Engineering, Industrial Products and Equipment, Medical/Health Related

Portfolio Companies: not available

Officers, Executives and Principals

James R. Berdell, Managing Partner
William H. Welling, Managing Partner
Sally Bishop, Research Associate

VENTURE INVESTMENT MANAGEMENT COMPANY, LLC

33 Broad Street
Boston, MA 02109

Telephone: 617-227-1300
Fax: 617-227-2336

Mission: Actively seeking new investments

Fund Size: Approximately $10 million per year
Founded: 1982
Average Investment: $1 million
Minimum Investment: $250,000

Investment Criteria: Seed, Startup, First-stage

Geographic Preference: Northeastern, Mid-Atlantic United States

Industry Group Preference: Communications, Computer Related, Electronic Components and Instrumentation, Energy, Life Sciences

Portfolio Companies: Agency Management Technologies, Apex Medical, Inc., Corporation for Laser Optics, Evergreen Solar, Inc., FaxNet Corporation, Focus Enhancements, Infonautics Corporation, Monitoring Technologies Corporation

Officers, Executives and Principals

Robert C. Roeper, Managing Director
John C. Evans, Partner
U. Haskell Crocker, Partner
Valle R. Nelsen, Partner
Mark I. Robinson, Partner
William C. Osborn, Partner

VENTURE INVESTORS OF WISCONSIN

565 Science Drive, Suite A
Madison, WI 53711

Telephone: 608-233-3070
Fax: 608-238-5120
E-mail: viw@macc.wisc.edu

Other Office Locations
924 East Juneau Avenue
Suite 617
Milwaukee, WI 53202
Phone 414-298-3070, Fax 414-272-4327

Mission: not available

Fund Size: $8 million
Founded: 1982
Average Investment: $250,000
Minimum Investment: not available

Investment Criteria: Seed to Second-stage

Geographic Preference: Wisconsin

Industry Group Preference: Diversified

Portfolio Companies: not available

Officers, Executives and Principals

Roger H. Ganser, President
Education: BED, University of Wisconsin, Whitewater; MPA, University of New York
Background: President, Madison Development Corporation; Vice President, Madison Capital Corporation; Vice
  President, Sail Co.; Director, Department of Development

John Neis, Vice President
Education: BS, University of Utah; MS, University of Wisconsin

VENTURES WEST MANAGEMENT, INC.

Suite 280-1285
West Pender Street
Vancouver, British Columbia V6E 4BI
Canada

Telephone: 604-688-9495
Fax: 604-687-2145
E-mail: dberkowitz@ventureswest.com

Other Office Locations
880-410 22nd Street East
Saskatoon, Saskatchewan S7K 5T6
Canada
Phone 306-653-8887, Fax 306-653-8886

1002-181 University Avenue
Toronto, Ontario M5H 3M7
Phone 416-861-0700, Fax 416-861-0866

Mission: Actively seeking new investments

Fund Size: $300+ million
Founded: 1973
Average Investment: not available
Minimum Investment: $500,000

Investment Criteria: Startup, First-stage, Second-stage

Geographic Preference: Canada

Industry Group Preference: Communications, Computer Related, Distribution, Electronic Components and Instrumentation, Energy/Natural Resources, Genetic Engineering, Industrial Products and Equipment, Medical/Health Related

Portfolio Companies: not available

Officers, Executives and Principals

Michael J. Brown, President (Vancouver)
Robin J. Louis, Executive Vice President and Chief Operating Officer (Vancouver)
J. Derek Douglas, Vice President (Vancouver)
Howard L. Riback, Vice President, Finance (Vancouver)
Sam Znaimer, Vice President (Vancouver)
Mark H. Leonard, Vice President (Toronto)
Terry Grieve, Vice President (Saskatoon)
Barry Geleiere, Vice President (Toronto)
Ted Anderson, Vice President (Toronto)
Nancy Harrison, Vice President (Vancouver)
David A. Berkowitz, Associate (Vancouver)
John Bruce, Associate (Vancouver)

THE VERMONT VENTURE CAPITAL FUND, L.P.

76 St. Paul Street
Suite 600
Burlington, VT 05401

Telephone: 802-658-7840
Fax: 802-658-5757

Other Office Locations
70 Center Street
Portland, ME 04101
Phone 207-772-4470, Fax 207-772-3257

Mission: Actively seeking new investments

Fund Size: not available
Founded: 1988
Average Investment: not available
Minimum Investment: $100,000

Investment Criteria: Startup, First-stage, Second-stage, Mezzanine, Leveraged Buyout

Industry Group Preference: Communications, Computer Related, Consumer, Distribution, Electronic Components and Instrumentation, Energy/Natural Resources, Genetic Engineering, Industrial Products and Equipment, Medical/Health Related

Portfolio Companies: not available

Officers, Executives and Principals

Gregory B. Peters, Managing Partner (Burlington)
David M. Coit, Partner (Portland)

VERTEX MANAGEMENT (II) PTE, LTD./VERTEX MANAGEMENT, INC.

Three Lagoon Drive
Suite 220
Redwood City, CA 94065

Telephone: 415-591-0947
Fax: 415-591-5926

Other Office Locations
77 Science Drive, #02-15
Cintech III
Singapore Science Park
Singapore 0511
Phone 65-870-0613, Fax 65-777-1878

Mission: Actively seeking new investments

Fund Size: not available
Founded: 1988
Average Investment: not available
Minimum Investment: $500,000

Investment Criteria: Second-stage, Mezzanine, Near Profit, Profitable

Industry Group Preference: Communications, Computer Related, Consumer, Distribution, Electronic Components and Instrumentation, Industrial Products and Equipment

Portfolio Companies: not available

Officers, Executives and Principals

Mr. Lee Kheng Nam, General Manager (Singapore)
Mrs. Koh Soo Boon, Deputy General Manager and Vice President (Singapore)
Charles C. Wu, Vice President (Redwood City)
*Jonathan Chee, Assi*stant Vice President (Redwood City)
Nellie Lim, Assistant Vice President (Redwood City)
Dr. Christina Lim, Assistant General Manager
Mr. Chua Joo Hock, Senior Manager (Singapore)

VIRGINIA CAPITAL, L.P.

9 South 12th Street
Suite 400
Richmond, VA 23219

Telephone: 804-648-4802
Fax: 804-648-4809
E-mail: vacapital@aol.com

Mission: not available

Fund Size: $14 million
Founded: 1991
Average Investment: $500,000
Minimum Investment: $250,000

Investment Criteria: Second-stage to Acquisition

Geographic Preference: Virginia

Industry Group Preference: no preference, but will not consider real estate or finance

Portfolio Companies: not available

Officers, Executives and Principals

Patrick K. Donnelly, President
Robert P. Louthan, Vice President

VISTA GROUP

36 Grove Street
New Canaan, CT 06840

Telephone: 203-972-3400
Fax: 203-966-0844

Mission: not available

Fund Size: $340 million
Founded: not available
Average Investment: $500,000 - $5 million
Minimum Investment: not available

Investment Criteria: Startup to Leveraged Buyout

Industry Group Preference: Educational, Environmental Protection, Food Services, Information Services, Manufacturing/Processing, Medical/Health, Service Industries

Portfolio Companies: Artificial Intelligence Corporation, Bachman Information Systems, Inc., EASEL Corporation, Crop Genetics International, Plant Genetics, United AgriSeeds, Concord Communications, Concord Data Systems, Equinox Systems, Genesis Electronics, BioGrowth, Cyberonics, Cyclex, Gillead Sciences, Innovative Surgical Products, Valid Logic Systems

Officers, Executives and Principals

Edwin Snape, Managing General Partner
Education: PhD, Metallurgy, University of Leeds, England
Background: Founder, Liposome Company

Gerald B. Bay, Managing General Partner
Education: BSSE, Purdue; MBA, Xavier University
Background: Twenty years of investing experience; President of a communications company; Co-founder of a corporate venture capital company

John F. Tomlin, General Partner
Education: BA, Vanderbilt; MBA, University of Chicago
Background: Continental Illinois Venture Corporation; Vice President, small electronics distributor

Robert P. "Skip" Cummins, General Partner
Education: BA, Dartmouth; MBA, University of Illinois
Background: Continental Illinois Venture Corporation

VITALE HOLDINGS, INC.

6337 Morrison Boulevard
Charlotte, NC 28211

Telephone: 704-362-8225
Fax: 704-362-8221

Mission: Actively seeking new investments

Fund Size: not available
Founded: 1985
Average Investment: not available
Minimum Investment: $250,000

Investment Criteria: Mezzanine, Leveraged Buyout

Industry Group Preference: Communications, Consumer, Distribution, Energy/Natural Resources

Portfolio Companies: not available

Officers, Executives and Principals

Jody B. Vitale, Partner
Joseph Vitale, Partner
Laurence Levine, Director

VK VENTURES

600 California Street
Suite 1700
San Francisco, CA 94111

Telephone: 415-391-5600
Fax: 415-397-2744

Other Office Locations
11661 San Vicente Boulevard
Suite 709
Los Angeles, CA 90049
Phone 310-820-2970, Fax 310-820-5032

Mission: Making few, if any, new investments

Fund Size: not available
Founded: 1978
Average Investment: not available
Minimum Investment: $100,000

Investment Criteria: Second-stage, Mezzanine, Leveraged Buyout

Industry Group Preference: Communications, Computer Related, Consumer, Distribution, Electronic Components and Instrumentation, Genetic Engineering, Medical/Health Related

Portfolio Companies: not available

Officers, Executives and Principals

F. Van Kasper, General Partner (San Francisco)
Bruce P. Emmelth, General Partner (Los Angeles)
David H. Horwich, Vice President (Los Angeles)

V S AND A COMMUNICATIONS PARTNERS, L.P.

350 Park Avenue
New York, NY 10022

Telephone: 212-935-4990
Fax: 212-935-0877

Mission: Actively seeking new investments

Fund Size: not available
Founded: 1987
Average Investment: not available
Minimum Investment: $5 million

Investment Criteria: Leveraged Buyout, Special Situations

Industry Group Preference: Communications

Portfolio Companies: not available

Officers, Executives and Principals

Jeffrey T. Stevenson, President and General Partner
S. Gerard Benford, Executive Vice President and General Partner
John J. Veronis, General Partner
John S. Suhler, General Partner

WACHTEL AND COMPANY, INC.
1101 14th Street, Northwest
Washington, DC 20005-5680

Telephone: 202-898-1144

Mission: Actively seeking new investments

Fund Size: not available
Founded: 1961
Average Investment: not available
Minimum Investment: Less than $100,000

Investment Criteria: Startup, First-stage, Second-stage

Industry Group Preference: Communications, Computer Related, Consumer, Distribution, Electronic Components and Instrumentation, Energy/Natural Resources, Industrial Products and Equipment, Medical/Health Related

Portfolio Companies: not available

Officers, Executives and Principals

Sidney B. Wachtel
Wendie L. Wachtel
Bonnie K. Wachtel
Irma S. Wachtel

WAKEFIELD GROUP

1110 East Morehead Street
P.O. Box 36329
Charlotte, NC 28236

Telephone: 704-372-0355
Fax: 704-372-8216

Mission: Actively seeking new investments

Fund Size: not available
Founded: 1988
Average Investment: not available
Minimum Investment: $500,000

Investment Criteria: First-stage, Second-stage, Mezzanine, Leveraged Buyout

Industry Group Preference: not available

Portfolio Companies: not available

Officers, Executives and Principals

Thomas C. Nelson
Anna Spangler Nelson
Michael Elliott

WALDEN GROUP OF VENTURE CAPITAL

750 Battery Street, 7th Floor
San Francisco, CA 94111

Telephone: 415-391-7225
Fax: 415-391-7262

Mission: not available

Fund Size: $150 million
Founded: not available
Average Investment: $1 million
Minimum Investment: not available

Investment Criteria: Seed to Leveraged Buyout

Geographic Preference: West Coast of the United States

Industry Group Preference: Computer Related, Environmental Protection, Medical/Health, Retailing

Portfolio Companies: not available

Officers, Executives and Principals

Arthur S. Berliner, General Partner

George S. Sarlo, General Partner
Education: BS, University of Arizona; MBA, Harvard
Background: President, Ashfield and Co.; Vice President, William D. Witter
Directorships: Rugged Digital Systems, Elantec, Mass Merchandising

WALNUT CAPITAL CORPORATION

Two North LaSalle Street
Suite 2200
Chicago, IL 60602

Telephone: not available

Other Office Locations
8000 Towers Crescent Drive
Suite 1070
Vienna, VA 22182
Phone 703-448-3771, Fax 703-448-7751

Mission: Actively seeking new investments

Fund Size: not available
Founded: 1983
Average Investment: not available
Minimum Investment: $100,000

Investment Criteria: Startup, First-stage, Second-stage, Mezzanine, Leveraged Buyout

Industry Group Preference: Communications, Computer Related, Consumer, Distribution, Electronic Components and Instrumentation, Energy/Natural Resources, Genetic Engineering, Industrial Products and Equipment, Medical/Health Related

Portfolio Companies: not available

Officers, Executives and Principals

Burton W. Kanter, President
Michael Faber, Vice President (Vienna)

WARBURG, PINCUS VENTURES

466 Lexington Avenue
New York, NY 10017-3147

Telephone: 212-878-0600
Fax: 212-878-9351

Mission: not available

Fund Size: $4 billion
Founded: not available
Average Investment: $10 million
Minimum Investment: not available

Investment Criteria: Seed to Second-stage

Industry Group Preference: Diversified

Portfolio Companies: not available

Officers, Executives and Principals

Lionel Pincus, Chairman
Education: BA, University of Pennsylvania; MBA, Columbia
Directorships: Orion Pictures, Western Pacific Industries, SFN Companies, Mattel

John J. Vegelstein, Vice Chairman
Education: Harvard College
Directorships: Orion Pictures, Mattel, DeVry, SFN Companies

Harold Brown, Senior Managing Director

Rodman Moorhead III, Senior Managing Director
Education: BA, MBA, Harvard
Directorships: Symbion, Centrafarm, Synergen, Vestar Research Medical Review

Errol M. Cook, Managing Director

Christopher W. Brody, Managing Director
Education: BA, MBA, Harvard
Directorships: Gartner Group, Ortel, Shaughnessey Holdings, Hypress

Howard Newman, Managing Director

Sidney Lapidus, Managing Director
Education: AB, Princeton University; LLB, Columbia
Directorships: Allied Supermarkets, Banner Industries, Dallas Media Investors, Ingersoll Publications, Mead
  Trucking

WARNER CAPITAL GROUP, INC.

28025 Dorthy Road
Suite 203
Agoura Hills, CA 91301

Telephone: 818-879-2279
Fax: 818-879-2272

Mission: Actively seeking new investments

Fund Size: not available
Founded: 1992
Average Investment: not available
Minimum Investment: $500,000

Investment Criteria: Seed, Research and development, Startup, First-stage, Second-stage, Mezzanine, Leveraged Buyout, Special Situations

Industry Group Preference: Communications, Computer Related, Consumer, Distribution, Electronic Components and Instrumentation, Energy/Natural Resources, Genetic Engineering, Industrial Products and Equipment, Medical/Health Related

Portfolio Companies: not available

Officers, Executives and Principals

Thomas S. Shubert, President

WEDBUSH CAPITAL PARTNERS

1000 Wilshire Boulevard
Suite 900
Los Angeles, CA 90017

Telephone: 213-688-4545
Fax: 213-688-6642

Mission: Reducing investment activity

Fund Size: not available
Founded: 1987
Average Investment: not available
Minimum Investment: $500,000

Investment Criteria: Second-stage, Leveraged Buyout, Recapitalizations

Industry Group Preference: Diversified

Portfolio Companies: not available

Officers, Executives and Principals

Barton I. Guerwitz, Managing General Partner
Peter H. Griffith, Limited Partner

WEISS, PECK AND GREER VENTURE PARTNERS

555 California Street, Suite 3130
San Francisco, CA 94104

Telephone: 415-622-6864
Fax: 415-989-5108
E-mail: WPGVP.com

Mission: To serve as lead investors in early and expansion stage information technology and healthcare companies managed by entrepreneurs possessing the vision, energy and integrity to build large, sustainable enterprises

Fund Size: $400 million
Founded: 1971
Average Investment: $2 million
Minimum Investment: $500,000

Investment Criteria: Seed to Mezzanine

Geographic Preference: United States

Industry Group Preference: Biotechnology, Communications, Electronics, Medical Devices, Medical Services, Semiconductors, Software

Portfolio Companies: not available

Officers, Executives and Principals

Philip Greer, Managing General Partner
Education: AB, Princeton; MBA, Harvard

Gill Logan, Managing General Partner
Education: BS, MBA, University of Southern California

Annette Bianchi, General Partner
Education: BSE, MSE, University of Pennsylvania; MBA, Wharton

Ellen Feeney, General Partner
Education: BS, Duke University; MS, University of California at Davis

Christopher Schaepe, General Partner
Education: BS, MS, MIT; MBA, Stanford University

Philip Black, General Partner
Education: AB, Stanford University

Dr. Paul Low, Senior Advisor
Education: BSEE, MS, University of Vermont; Ph.D., Stanford University

Peter Nieh, Associate
Education: BSEE, AB, MBA, Stanford University

WELLMAX, INC.

6905 Telegraph Road
Suite 330
Bloomfield Hills, MI 48301

Telephone: 810-646-3554
Fax: 810-646-6220

Mission: Actively seeking new investments

Fund Size: not available
Founded: 1976
Average Investment: not available
Minimum Investment: Less than $100,000

Investment Criteria: First-stage, Second-stage, Leveraged Buyout, Special Situations

Geographic Preference: Midwestern, Southeastern United States

Industry Group Preference: Consumer, Distribution, Electronic Components and Instrumentation, Genetic Engineering, Industrial Products and Equipment, Manufacturing, Medical/Health Related

Portfolio Companies: not available

Officers, Executives and Principals

Jack E. Maxwell, President
Education: BS, Mechanical Engineering, Case Institute of Technology; MBA, Harvard
Background: Independent Consultant, Vice President, American Motors; Vice President, Booz, Allen, and Hamilton; Chairman, Ingersoll Products, Wheel Horse Products, Mercury Plastics Windsor Products

WELSH, CARSON, ANDERSON AND STOWE

320 Park Avenue
25th Floor
New York, NY 10022

Telephone: 212-893-9500
Fax: 212-893-9575

Mission: Actively seeking new investments

Fund Size: not available
Founded: not available
Average Investment: not available
Minimum Investment: not available

Investment Criteria: First-stage, Second-stage, Leveraged Buyout, Special Situations

Industry Group Preference: Diversified

Portfolio Companies: not available

Officers, Executives and Principals

Patrick J. Welsh, General Partner
Russell L. Carson, General Partner
Bruce K. Anderson, General Partner
Richard H. Stowe, General Partner
Anthony J. de Nicola, General Partner
James B. Hoover, General Partner
Thomas E. McInerney, General Partner
Robert A. Minicucci, General Partner
Laura Vanburen, General Partner
Paul Queally, General Partner

WEST CENTRAL CAPITAL CORPORATION

440 Northlake Center
Suite 206
Dallas, TX 75238

Telephone: 214-348-3969

Mission: not available

Fund Size: not available
Founded: 1964
Average Investment: not available
Minimum Investment: not available

Investment Criteria: Second-stage

Industry Group Preference: Communications, Consumer, Distribution, Industrial Products and Equipment, Medical/Health Related

Portfolio Companies: not available

Officers, Executives and Principals

Howard W. Jacob, President
Barbara C. Evans, Vice President

WESTAR CAPITAL

950 South Coast Drive
Suite 165
Costa Mesa, CA 92626

Telephone: 714-434-5160
Fax: 714-434-5166

Other Office Locations
777 Campus Commons Drive
Suite 200
Sacramento, CA 95825
Phone 916-565-7660, Fax 916-485-1050

Mission: Actively seeking new investments

Fund Size: not available
Founded: 1987
Average Investment: not available
Minimum Investment: $3 million

Investment Criteria: Leveraged Buyout, Special Situations, Control-block Purchases

Industry Group Preference: Communications, Computer Related, Consumer, Distribution, Electronic Components and Instrumentation, Energy/Natural Resources, Industrial Products and Equipment, Medical/Health Related

Portfolio Companies: not available

Officers, Executives and Principals

Dale T. Jabour, Director, Finance (Costa Mesa)
John W. Clark, General Partner

WESTERLY PARTNERS

620 Newport Center Drive
11th Floor
Newport Beach, CA 92660

Telephone: 714-955-2000
Fax: 714-955-1812

Other Office Locations
1716 Cottonwood Point
Fort Collins, CO 80524
Phone 303-484-8196, Fax 303-484-1160

67 Wall Street, Suite 2411
New York, NY 10005
Phone 212-323-8226

Mission: Actively seeking new investments

Fund Size: not available
Founded: 1978
Average Investment: not available
Minimum Investment: $500,000

Investment Criteria: Second-stage, Leveraged Buyout, Special Situations

Industry Group Preference: Communications, Computer Related, Consumer, Distribution, Electronic Components and Instrumentation, Energy/Natural Resources, Genetic Engineering, Industrial Products and Equipment, Medical/Health Related

Portfolio Companies: Eagleson Industries, Chrysalis International, Dynamic Science International

Officers, Executives and Principals

Russell R. Diehl, Managing Director (Newport Beach)
Education: BA, Lake Forest College; MS, American University
Background: Investment Banking, Union Bank, Bank of New York

Collis R. Woodward, Managing Director (Fort Collins)
Education: BSEE, University of California, Los Angeles
Background: Accounting, Ernst and Young

Lee Broad, Managing Director (Newport Beach)
Education: BA, RPI; MBA, Columbia University
Background: Management Consulting, A.T. Kierney

Paul G.Hines, Managing Director (New York)
Education: BA, MBA, Harvard University
Background: E.F. Hutton and Co., W.E. Simon (WESRAY) Merchant Banking

WESTERN TECHNOLOGY INVESTMENT

2010 North First Street
Suite 310
San Jose, CA 95131

Telephone: 408-436-8577

Mission: Actively seeking new investments

Fund Size: not available
Founded: 1980
Average Investment: not available
Minimum Investment: $250,000

Investment Criteria: Seed, Research and Development, Startup, First-stage, Second-stage, Mezzanine, Leveraged Buyout, Special Situations

Industry Group Preference: Diversified

Portfolio Companies: not available

Officers, Executives and Principals

Ronald W. Swenson, President
Salvador O. Guiterrez, Vice President

WESTFINANCE CORPORATION

3201 New Mexico Avenue, Northwest
Suite 350
Washington, DC 20016

Telephone: 202-895-1390
Fax: 202-966-8141

Mission: Actively seeking new investments

Fund Size: not available
Founded: 1981
Average Investment: not available
Minimum Investment: $250,000

Investment Criteria: Seed, Startup, First-stage, Second-stage

Geographic Preference: Mid-Atlantic United States

Industry Group Preference: Communications, Computer Related, Consumer, Distribution, Electronic Components and Instrumentation, Energy/Natural Resources, Genetic Engineering, Industrial Products and Equipment, Medical/Health Related

Portfolio Companies: not available

Officers, Executives and Principals

C. Stevens Avery II, President
Education: U.S. Military Academy (West Point); Harvard Business School
Background: Finance
Directorships: Numerous

WESTFORD TECHNOLOGY VENTURES, L.P.

17 Academy Street
Newark, NJ 07102

Telephone: 201-624-2131
Fax: 201-624-2008

Mission: not available

Fund Size: not available
Founded: 1987
Average Investment: not available
Minimum Investment: $250,000

Investment Criteria: Startup, First-stage, Second-stage

Industry Group Preference: Communications, Computer Related, Distribution, Electronic Components and Instrumentation, Industrial Products and Equipment

Portfolio Companies: not available

Officers, Executives and Principals

Jeffrey T. Hamilton, General Partner
Susan J. Trammell, Associate

WESTON PRESIDIO CAPITAL

One Federal Street
21st Floor
Boston, MA 02110

Telephone: 617-988-2500
Fax: 617-988-2515

Other Office Locations
343 Sansome Street
Suite 1210
San Francisco, CA 94104-1316
Phone 415-398-0770, Fax 415-398-0990

Mission: Actively seeking new investments

Fund Size: not available
Founded: 1991
Average Investment: not available
Minimum Investment: $1.5 million

Investment Criteria: Private Equity

Industry Group Preference: Communications, Computer Related, Consumer, Distribution, Electronic Components and Instrumentation, Energy/Natural Resources, Genetic Engineering, Industrial Products and Equipment, Medical/Health Related

Portfolio Companies: not available

Officers, Executives and Principals

Michael F. Cronin, Managing Partner (Boston)
Michael P. Lazarus, Managing Partner (San Francisco)
James B. McElwee, General Partner (San Francisco)
Carlo A. von Schroeter, General Partner (Boston)
Philip W. Halperin, Principal (San Francisco)
Thomas A. Patterson (San Francisco)
Kevin M. Hayes (Boston)
Dianne M. Hillyard (Boston)
Jenifer Rice, Administration

WGC ENTERPRISES

1701 East Lake Avenue
Suite 170
Glenview, IL 60025

Telephone: 847-657-8002
Fax: 847-657-8168

Mission: Provides consulting, financial advice, placement and merger/acquisition help for small to medium size companies. Acts as vehicle for acquisition of middle market companies for private investment groups.

Fund Size: $20 million
Founded: 1987
Average Investment: $2 million
Minimum Investment: $500,000

Investment Criteria: Seed to Later-stages

Geographic Preference: Northwest Chicago and surrounding area within 150 miles

Industry Group Preference: Computers, Electronics, Medical/Health Related, Systems Integration, Toys

Portfolio Companies: Questar, Spectirx, Napersoft, Honsa Ergonomic Tools, Econometrics, DEH Printed Circuits, Inc.

Officers, Executives and Principals

Walter G. Cornett III, President
Education: BS, Georgia Tech; MBA, Harvard
Background: Founder, seven companies; Founder and Manager of five funds, including two State of Illinois funds; Founder, Investor, Board Member or Consultant for over 100 early-stage companies

Brian J. Dettmann, Principal
Education: BA, Iowa State; MBA, Dartmouth Tech
Background: Chief Executive Officer, DEH Printed Circuits, Inc.; Corporate Finance, Solomon Brothers, CPA/ Financial Consultant, Arthur Andersen

Oak Stevens, Vice President
Education: Purdue University; Kellogg School at Northwestern University
Background: Manager, Marketing, Sales and Customer Service for several computer companies

George Roe, Managing Director, General Counsel
Education: BA, Marquette University; AAS, Universidad Interamericana in Mexico; JD, DePaul University
Background: Instructor on legal aspects of bankruptcy for business managers and CPA's; Lawyer, Commercial Transactions, Bankruptcy and Federal Taxation

Louie Y. Liu, Vice President
Education: BS, Material Science, Tsinghua University; MS, Mechanical Engineering, MS, Nuclear Engineering, Ohio State University; MBA, University of Chicago
Background: AT&T Bell Labs; Intuit; Westinghouse Electric

THE WHARTON GROUP, INC.

Three Piedmont Center
Suite 400
Atlanta, GA 30305

Telephone: 404-231-1365
Fax: 404-231-1390

Mission: Actively seeking new investments

Fund Size: not available
Founded: 1986
Average Investment: not available
Minimum Investment: $1 million

Investment Criteria: Startup, First-stage, Second-stage, Mezzanine, Special Situations

Industry Group Preference: Computer Related, Consumer, Distribution, Industrial Products and Equipment

Portfolio Companies: not available

Officers, Executives and Principals

John R. Perlman, Managing Director
Lester H. Gallant, Managing Director

WILLIAM A. M. BURDEN AND COMPANY

10 East 53rd Street
32nd Floor
New York, NY 10022

Telephone: 212-872-1133
Fax: 212-872-1198

Mission: Actively seeking new investments

Fund Size: not available
Founded: 1949
Average Investment: not available
Minimum Investment: $500,000

Investment Criteria: Mezzanine, Leveraged Buyout, Special Situations, Control-block Purchases

Industry Group Preference: Communications, Consumer, Distribution, Electronic Components and Instrumentation, Energy/Natural Resources, Industrial Products and Equipment, Medical/Health Related

Portfolio Companies: not available

Officers, Executives and Principals

Jeffrey A. Weber, President and Chief Executive Officer

WILLIAM BLAIR CAPITAL PARTNERS

222 West Adams Street
Suite 3300
Chicago, IL 60606

Telephone: 312-236-1600
Fax: 312-368-9418

Mission: not available

Fund Size: $135 million
Founded: not available
Average Investment: $2 million
Minimum Investment: not available

Investment Criteria: First-stage to Leveraged Buyout

Industry Group Preference: Broadcast/Cable/Radio, Communications, Consumer Related, High Technology, Medical/Health, Retailing

Portfolio Companies: Bright Horizons Children's Centers, Links Corporation, UI Video Holding, American Healthcorp, Champion Healthcare, HealthSound Rehabilitation Corporation, Remcor Products, Technetics, Alaska Cable, The Sports Authority, Staples, Supermac Technologies, Cornerstone Technologies

Officers, Executives and Principals

Ellen Carnahan, Partner
Education: BA, Accounting, University of Notre Dame; MBA, Statistics, University of Chicago
Background: Vice President Marketing and Planning, SPSS Inc.; Manager, Financial Planning and Analysis, Trailer Train Co.; Senior Auditor, Price Waterhouse
Directorships: Desktop Data Inc., Cornerstone Technologies

Gregg S. Newmark, Partner
Education: BS, Engineering, Princeton; JD, MBA, Harvard
Background: Management Consultant, Bain and Co.; Consultant in microcomputer software publishing industry
Directorships: CareCare Enterprises, Bright Horizons Children's Centers, UI Video Holdings, Technetics, Links Corporation

Samuel B. Guren, Partner
Education: BA, History, University of Wisconsin; MBA, Finance and Accounting, Wharton Graduate School
Background: Continental Illinois National Bank
Directorships: Amherst Associates, Stanford Corporation, Marks Brothers Jewelers, Prime Cable of Alaska

WILLIAM E. SIMON AND SONS, INC.

310 South Street
P.O. Box 1913
Morristown, NJ 07962-1913

Telephone: 201-898-0290
Fax: 201-993-0925

Other Office Locations
1090 Wilshire Boulevard, Suite 1750
Los Angeles, CA 90024
Phone 310-914-2410, Fax 310-575-3174

2402A Great Eagle Centre
23 Harbour Road
Wanchai
Hong Kong
Phone 852-511-1668, Fax 852-588-1328

Mission: Actively seeking new investments

Fund Size: not available
Founded: 1988
Average Investment: not available
Minimum Investment: $3 million

Investment Criteria: Second-stage, Mezzanine

Industry Group Preference: Communications, Consumer, Distribution, Energy/Natural Resources, Industrial Products and Equipment

Portfolio Companies: not available

Officers, Executives and Principals

William E. Simon, Senior, Chairman
J. Peter Simon, Executive Director
Mark J. Butler, Chief Financial Officer
Jan Greer, Managing Director
Stephanie T. Mott, Vice President
Andrew H. Richards, Vice President
Conor T. Mullet, Associate

WINDHAM CAPITAL ADVISORY SERVICES

5065 Westheimer
Suite 726
Houston, TX 77056

Telephone: 713-622-1866
Fax: 713-993-9678

Mission: Provide corporate finance advisory and investment banking services to middle market companies

Fund Size: not applicable
Founded: 1987
Average Investment: not available
Minimum Investment: $1 million

Investment Criteria: Second-stage, Mezzanine, Leveraged Buyout, Control-block Purchases

Geographic Preference: Southwestern United States

Industry Group Preference: Consumer, Distribution, Electronic Components and Instrumentation, Energy/ Natural Resources, Industrial Products and Equipment, Medical/Health Related

Portfolio Companies: None. Advisory and intermediary only.

Officers, Executives and Principals

James M. Windham, Jr., President

WINDPOINT PARTNERS

676 North Michigan Avenue
Suite 3300
Chicago, IL 60611

Telephone: 312-649-4000
Fax: 312-649-9644

Mission: not available

Fund Size: $126 million
Founded: not available
Average Investment: $500,000 - $9 million
Minimum Investment: not available

Investment Criteria: Seed to Leveraged Buyout

Industry Group Preference: Broadcast/Cable/Radio, Communications, Manufacturing/Processing, Medical/ Health, Service Industries

Portfolio Companies: Aastrom Bioscience, Inc., Alloyd Co., Alternative Resources Corporation, Biosys, CAD Information Systems, Centigram Corporation, Cerulean Fund, Cirrus Diagnostic, Clinicom, Cor Therapeutics, Coventry, Effective Management Systems, Genderm, Global Technology Systems, Irwin Magnetic Systems, McCarthy Holding Co., Medina Broadcast Group

Officers, Executives and Principals

Arthur DelVesco, General Partner
Education: Henry Rutgers Scholar, Rutgers University; MBA, Harvard
Background: Senior Investment Manager, First Chicago Equity Group
Directorships: Alloyd Co., CliniCom, McCarthy Holding Co., Multi Market Communications

James E. Forrest, General Partner
Education: BSEE, magna cum laude, Michigan State University; MBA, Harvard
Background: Vice President Strategic Planning, Gould Instrument Group; Product Manager to President of the Recording Systems Division
Directorships: Alloyd, CAD Information Systems, Morton Metalcraft, Power Trends, and Wozniak Industries

Robert L. Cummings, General Partner
Education: BSME, RPI; MBA, Harvard
Background: General Partner, Robertson, Colman and Stephens
Directorships: Alternative Resources Corporation, Cerulean Fund, Global Technology Systems Inc., Professional Veterinary Hospitals of America

S. Curtis Johnston III, General Partner
Education: BA, Cornell University; MM, Northwestern University
Background: Entrepreneur; General Manager, Mexico, S.C. Johnson and Son, Inc.

Todd G. Smith, Chief Financial Officer
Education: Illinois State University
Background: KPMG Peat Marwick, Audit Manager

Christopher Joseph, Investment Manager
Education: BA, Miami University; MBA, University of Chicago
Background: Merchant Banking Associate, First National Bank of Chicago; Associate, First Chicago's Venture Capital Unit
Directorships: Alloyd, Alternative Resources Corporation, Morton Metalcraft

WINGATE PARTNERS, INC.

750 North St. Paul
Suite 11200
Dallas, TX 75201

Telephone: 214-720-1313
Fax: 214-871-8799

Other Office Locations
950 Echo Lane
Suite 335
Houston, TX 77024
Phone 713-973-7722, Fax 713-973-8237

Mission: Actively seeking new investments

Fund Size: not available
Founded: 1987
Average Investment: not available
Minimum Investment: not available

Investment Criteria: Leveraged Buyout, Control-block Purchases

Industry Group Preference: Consumer, Distribution, Electronic Components and Instrumentation, Energy/
Natural Resources, Industrial Products and Equipment, Medical/Health Related

Portfolio Companies: not available

Officers, Executives and Principals

Frederick B. Hegi, Jr., General Partner (Dallas)
James A. Johnson, General Partner (Dallas)
Jay I. Applebaum, Vice President (Dallas)
Robert E. Taylor, Jr., Vice President (Dallas)
Douglass A. Smith, General Partner
Michael Decker, General Partner

WINTHROP VENTURES

74 Trinity Place
New York, NY 10006

Telephone: 212-422-0100

Mission: Actively seeking new investments

Fund Size: not available
Founded: 1972
Average Investment: not available
Minimum Investment: $500,000

Investment Criteria: Startup, First-stage, Second-stage, Buyout, Acquisition

Industry Group Preference: Communications, Computer Related, Consumer, Distribution, Electronic Components and Instrumentation, Energy/Natural Resources, Genetic Engineering, Industrial Products and Equipment, Medical/Health Related

Portfolio Companies: not available

Officers, Executives and Principals

Cyrus Brown
Carol Brown
Henry Trimble

WITECH CORPORATION

1000 Northwater
Suite 1805
Milwaukee, WI 53202

Telephone: 414-347-1550
Fax: 414-221-4990

Mission: not available

Fund Size: $40 million
Founded: not available
Average Investment: $500,000 - $2 million
Minimum Investment: not available

Investment Criteria: Seed to Leveraged Buyout

Geographic Preference: Wisconsin, Michigan

Industry Group Preference: Diversified

Portfolio Companies: not available

Officers, Executives and Principals

J. Stephen Anderson, Vice President
Background: Vice President, Corporate Finance Department, Robert W. Baird and Co.; Treasurer, Joseph Schlitz Brewing Co.; Mellon National Bank

WOODHOUSE PARTNERS

345 East 93rd Street
Suite 30C
New York, NY 10128

Telephone: 212-831-2431

Mission: Actively seeking new investments

Fund Size: not available
Founded: 1983
Average Investment: not available
Minimum Investment: Less than $100,000

Investment Criteria: Seed, Startup, First-stage, Leveraged Buyout, Special Situations

Industry Group Preference: Computer Related, Consumer, Distribution, Electronic Components and Instrumentation, Genetic Engineering, Medical/Health Related

Portfolio Companies: not available

Officers, Executives and Principals

Macaulay Woodhouse, Partner
Johan Bork, Partner

WOODSIDE FUND

4133 Mohr Avenue, Suite H
Pleasanton, CA 94566

Telephone: 510-462-0326
Fax: 510-462-4398

Mission: not available

Fund Size: $30 million
Founded: not available
Average Investment: $750,000
Minimum Investment: not available

Investment Criteria: Seed to Second-stage

Geographic Preference: West Coast of the United States

Industry Group Preference: Biotechnology, Computer Related, Electronics, Energy/Natural Resources, Industrial Products, Medical/Health, Software

Portfolio Companies: not available

Officers, Executives and Principals

V. Frank Mendicino, General Partner

WORKING VENTURES CANADIAN FUND, INC.

250 Bloor Street East, Suite 1600
Toronto, Ontario M4W 1E6
Canada

Telephone: 416-934-7777
Fax: 416-929-2421
E-mail: general@WorkingVentures.ca

Other Office Locations
830-410 22nd Street East
Saskatoon, Saskatchewan
Canada S7K 5T6
Phone 306-242-1023, Fax 306-242-9959

133 Prince William Street
Saint John, New Brunswick
Canada E2L 2B5
Phone 506-652-5704, Fax 506-652-5706

148 York Street, Suite 202
London, Ontario
Canada N6A 1A9
Phone 519-645-2120, Fax 519-645-3051

9 Antares Drive
Nepean, Ontario
Canada K2E 7V5
Phone 613-225-4775, Phone 613-225-4508

Purdy's Wharf, Tower 1
1959 Upper Water Street, Suite 407
Halifax, Nova Scotia
Canada B3J 3N2
Phone 902-492-2292, Fax 902-492-1101

Mission: Actively seeking new investments

Fund Size: $860 million
Founded: 1989
Average Investment: $3 million
Minimum Investment: $500,000

Investment Criteria: First-stage, Second-stage, Mezzanine, Leveraged Buyout, Special Situations

Geographic Preference: Canada only

Industry Group Preference: Communications, Computer Related, Consumer, Distribution, Electronic Components and Instrumentation, Energy/Natural Resources, Genetic Engineering, Industrial Products and Equipment, Medical/Health Related

Portfolio Companies: Pantheon Inc., Lava Systems, Inc., Trillium Valley Fish Farms, Ltd., Toi Kinnoir, Inc., LMS Labor Management Systems, Ltd., Accelerix Inc., Simba Technologies, Inc., Combined Media, Inc., Westwood and Best Corporation, Tempkraft Canada, Inc., Indigo Manufacturing, Inc., News Theatre, Inc., Delphi Solutions, Inc., AllCanada Express Ltd., Vascular Therapeutics Canada, Inc., Atlantic Video Lottery, Inc., Cleanol Services, Inc., Promis Systems Corporation Ltd., NovAtel Wireless Technologies, Ltd., SimEx Inc., General Wellbeing, Jones Packaging, Inc., Genesis Microchip, Inc., Claude Resources, inc., PEI Capital, Inc., PrimeNet Communications, Inc., Gest-Accor Group, The KW Optical Group, applied Analytics Corporation, Obex Technologies, Inc., Cadsoft Corporation, Research In Motion Ltd., Coreco, Inc., DiscoverWare, Inc., Digital Processing Systems, Inc., Resolution Pharmaceutical's Inc., Synsorb Biotech, Inc., MPACT Immedia Corporation, Algoods, Inc., Dalsa Corporation, Scintrex Ltd., Antel Optronics, Inc., Dipix Technologies, Inc. Gavel and Gown Software, Inc., Upper Canada Brewing Company, Ltd., Morphometrix Technologies, Inc., EGO Resources, Ltd., Develcon Electronics, Ltd., Yogen Fruz World-Wide, Inc., Camelot Superabsorbents, Ltd., Secure Computing Canada, Inc., Newgen Restaurant Services, Inc. Iona Appliances, Inc., LanSer Wireless, Inc., Norstar Entertainment, Inc. M&I Door Systems, Ltd., Raymond Steel, Ltd., International Wallcoverings, Ltd., Teklogix International, Inc., Recreation Services International, Inc., Perle Systems, Ltd., Hegyi GeoTechnologies International, Inc., Helitactics Ltd., ISTAR internet.inc, Certicorn Corporation, Karo (Toronto) Inc., Lower Lakes Towing, Ltd., PageMart Canada Holding Corporation, Humboldt Flour Mills, Inc., Fulcrum Technologies, Inc., GlycoDesign Inc., Star Data Systems, Inc., Trimark Athletic Supplies, Inc., Automatic Cutting, Inc., Hamilton Douglas Industries, Ltd., Virtek Vision International, Inc., Cary Peripherals, Inc. Life Imaging Systems, Inc., Marsh Engineering, CF Hospitality, Inc., Beamscope Canada Inc., MDC Communications Corporation, ObjectArts, Inc., Trentway-Wagar, Inc., Inverpower Controls, Ltd.

Officers, Executives and Principals

Ron Begg, President
Jim Hall, Senior Vice President, Investments
Bill Danis, Vice President, Investments
Jim Whitaker, Vice President, Investments
Don Morrison, Portfolio Manager
David Rogers, Portfolio Manager
Valerie Scott, Senior Investment Manager
Paul Cataford, Senior Investment Manager
Elizabeth Seger, Senior Investment Manager
Scott Clark, Senior Investment Manager
Robert Wilson, Senior Investment Manager
Brad Munro, Senior Investment Manager (Saskatchewan)
Adam Adamou, Investment Manager
Bruce Wylie, Investment Manager
Andrew Abouchar, Investment Manager
Tim Patterson, Investment Manager
Marc Lipton, Investment Manager
Leela Akerboom, Investment Manager
Valerie Millen, Investment Manager (New Brunswick)
Richard Jankura, Investment Manager (London)
Bonnie Wright, Investment Manager (Nepean)
Stephen Lund, Investment Manager (Nova Scotia)

WORLDWIDE FINANCIAL SERVICES

22966 Via Aimiento
Mission Viejo, CA 92691

Telephone: 714-597-1833
Fax: 714-597-1833

Mission: Actively seeking new investments

Fund Size: not available
Founded: 1983
Average Investment: not available
Minimum Investment: $250,000

Investment Criteria: Startup, First-stage, Second-stage, Mezzanine, Leveraged Buyout, Special Situations

Industry Group Preference: Communications, Computer Related, Consumer, Distribution, Electronic Components and Instrumentation, Energy/Natural Resources, Genetic Engineering, Industrial Products and Equipment, Medical/Health Related

Portfolio Companies: not available

Officers, Executives and Principals

John H. Breon, Principal

XEROX TECHNOLOGY VENTURES

101 Continental Boulevard
El Segundo, CA 90245

Telephone: not available

Mission: Making few, if any, new investments

Fund Size: not available
Founded: 1989
Average Investment: not available
Minimum Investment: No minimum

Investment Criteria: Second-stage

Industry Group Preference: Communications

Portfolio Companies: not available

Officers, Executives and Principals

Robert V. Adams, President and Chief Executive Officer
Robert H. Curtin, Vice President
Jeffrey C. Tung, Vice President
Michael N. Salzman, Director, Finance and Administration

ZAHREN FINANCIAL CORPORATION

40 Tower Lane
Avon, CT 06001

Telephone: 860-678-7537
Fax: 860-677-4036

Mission: Actively seeking new investments

Fund Size: not available
Founded: 1984
Average Investment: not available
Minimum Investment: $250,000

Investment Criteria: First-stage, Second-stage, Mezzanine, Leveraged Buyout

Industry Group Preference: Energy/Natural Resources, Industrial Products and Equipment

Portfolio Companies: not available

Officers, Executives and Principals

Bernard J. Zahren, President
Martin F. Laughlin, Executive Vice President

ZS FUND L.P.

120 West 45th Street
Suite 2600
New York, NY 10036

Telephone: 212-398-6200
Fax: 212-398-1808

Mission: Actively seeking new investments

Fund Size: $135 million
Founded: 1985
Average Investment: $5 - $30 million
Minimum Investment: $5 million

Investment Criteria: Leveraged Buyout, Family Recapitalizations

Geographic Preference: North America

Industry Group Preference: Communications, Computer Related, Consumer, Distribution, Electronic Components and Instrumentation, Industrial Products and Equipment, Manufacturing, Medical/Health Related, Wholesaling

Portfolio Companies: Corral West Ranchwear, Inc., Dairy Fresh, Inc., Market Facts, Inc., Mazel Stores, Inc., Kaye Group, Inc., Von Hoffman Corporation, Gentry Shops, Inc., Frankel Shops, Inc.

Officers, Executives and Principals

Ned L. Sherwood, Managing Partner
Henrik Falktoft, Partner
Robert Horne, Partner
Jeffery Oyster, Partner
Douglas Brown, Partner

B

High Technology/Medical Funds

ABS VENTURES, L.P.

One South Street
Suite 2150
Baltimore, MD 21202

Telephone: 410-895-3895
Fax: 410-895-3899

Other Office Locations
404 Wyman Street
Suite 365
Waltham, MA 02154
Phone 617-890-3103

Mission: not available

Fund Size: $128 million
Founded: not available
Average Investment: $500,000
Minimum Investment: not available

Investment Criteria: Startup to Mezzanine

Industry Group Preference: Computer Related, Electronics, Energy/Natural Resources, High Technology, Industrial Products, Medical/Health

Portfolio Companies: not available

Officers, Executives and Principals

Bruns H. Grayson, Managing Partner
Education: BA, Harvard; MA, Oxford University; JD, University of Virginia
Background: Associate, Adler and Co.; Consultant, McKinsey and Co.
Directorships: Crop Genetics, International Laser Machines, Scarborough Systems, Software Corporation of America, Sensormedics, Anadigics, Systems Center, Genra Group

Edward T. Anderson, Managing Partner (Waltham)
Education: BA, University of Pennsylvania; MBA, Harvard

ACCEL PARTNERS

One Embarcadero Center
San Francisco, CA 94111

Telephone: 415-989-5656
Fax: 415-989-5554

Other Office Locations

One Palmer Square
Princeton, NJ 08542
Phone 609-683-4500, Fax 609-683-0384

Mission: not available

Fund Size: $350 million
Founded: 1983
Average Investment: $500,000
Minimum Investment: Less than $100,000

Investment Criteria: Seed, Research and Development, Startup, First-stage, Second-stage, Mezzanine, Leveraged Buyout, Special Situations, Control-block Purchases

Industry Group Preference: Biotechnology, Communications, Computer Related, Electronic Components and Instrumentation, Genetic Engineering, High Technology, Industrial Products and Equipment, Medical/Health, Software

Portfolio Companies: American Surgical Technology, Medical Care International, Sportsmedicine Systems, U.S. Behaviorial Health, Liposome Co., Alldata, Linkware, MediaShare, Power Up Software, Synopsys, Veritas, XA Systems, Bridge Communications, Faralon Computing, Netlink, Ungermann-Bass, Vitalink Communications, VMX, PictureTel

Officers, Executives and Principals

James W. Breyer, General Partner (San Francisco)
Education: BS, Computer Science and Economics, Stanford; MBA, Harvard University
Background: Managment Consultant, McKinsey and Co.; Product Management and Marketing, Apple Computer and Hewlett Packard
Directorships: Academic Systems, Jostens Learning, Macromedia, MediaShare, PageMart, Power Up Software, Spectrum

Luke B. Evnin, General Partner (San Francisco)

Paul H. Klingenstein, General Partner (San Francisco)
Education: AB, Harvard; MBA, Stanford
Background: EM Warburg, Pincus and Co., biotechnology experience
Directorships: EP Technologies, Isis Pharmaceuticals, Glyomed, Paidos Healthcare, Oncogenetics, U.S. Behavioral Health, Viagene

Arthur C. Patterson, General Partner (San Francisco)
Education: AB, MBA, Harvard University

Background: Adler and Co.; Vice President, Citicorp Venture Capital; Equity Committee, Citicorp's Investment Management Group; International Monetary

Directorships: PageMart, Raxco, The Santa Cruz Operation, Synercom, Trinzic, Unify, Veritas, Walker Interactive Systems

James P. Swartz, General Partner (Princeton)

Education: Engineering Sciences and Applied Physics, Harvard University; MS, Industrial Administration, Carnegie Mellon University

Background: Founder, Accel Partners; Founding General Partner, Adler and Co.; Vice President, Citicorp Venture Capital; Vice President, Laird Inc.

James R. Flach, Venture Partner (San Francisco)

George Hara, Venture Partner (San Francisco)

Eugene D. Hill, Venture Partner (San Francisco)

ADVANCED TECHNOLOGY VENTURES

281 Winter Street
Suite 350
Waltham, MA 02154

Telephone: 617-290-0707
Fax: 617-290-684-0045

Other Office Locations
2884 Sand Hill Road, Suite 100
Menlo Park, CA 94025
Phone 415-321-8601, Fax 415-321-0934

Mission: Actively seeking new investments

Fund Size: $85 million
Founded: 1980
Average Investment: $1 million
Minimum Investment: $250,000

Investment Criteria: Startup, First-stage, Second-stage

Industry Group Preference: Biotechnology, Communications, Computer Related, Electronic Components and Instrumentation, Energy/Natural Resources, Genetic Engineering, Industrial Products and Equipment, Medical/Health Related, Software

Portfolio Companies: not available

Officers, Executives and Principals

Albert E. Paladino, Managing Partner (Waltham)
Education: BS, MS, Alfred University; PhD, MIT
Background: Deputy Director, Office of Energy Programs, U.S. Department of Commerce; Assistant Director, Telephone Operations Technology Center, GTE Labs
Directorships: Advanced Energy Dynamics, Theta-J Corporation, Laser Science, MilliTech, Mosaic Systems

Pieter J. Schiller, Managing Partner (Waltham)

Jos C. Henkens, General Partner (Menlo Park)

Robert F. Sproull, Special Partner (Waltham)
Education: AB, Harvard; PhD, Stanford
Background: Associate Professor, Carnegie Mellon University; Research Staff, Xerox Corporation

Ivan E. Sutherland, Special Partner (Menlo Park)

William R. Sutherland, Special Partner (Menlo Park)

ALAFI CAPITAL

P.O. Box 7338
Berkeley, CA 94707

Telephone: 510-653-7425
Fax: 510-653-6231

Mission: not available

Fund Size: $60 million
Founded: not available
Average Investment: $500,000
Minimum Investment: not available

Investment Criteria: Seed to Second-stage

Industry Group Preference: Biotechnology, Electronics, Medical/Health

Portfolio Companies: not available

Officers, Executives and Principals

Chris Alafi, Partner
Moshe Alafi, General Partner

ALLSOP VENTURE PARTNERS

2750 First Avenue, Northeast
Cedar Rapids, IA 52402

Telephone: 319-363-8971
Fax: 319-363-9519

Other Office Locations
7400 College Boulevard, Suite 302
Overland Park, KS 66210
Phone 913-338-0820, Fax 913-338-1019

55 West Port Plaza, Suite 575
St. Louis, MO 63146
Phone 314-434-1688, Fax 314-434-6560

Mission: not available

Fund Size: $105 million
Founded: not available
Average Investment: $1 million
Minimum Investment: not available

Investment Criteria: First-stage to Leveraged Buyout

Industry Group Preference: Communications, Computer Related, Consumer Related, Electronics, High Technology, Industrial Products, Medical/Health, Transportation

Portfolio Companies: ABW, Advanced Aluminum, ALC Commun., Autographix, Capital Group, Cardiovascular Devices, Centigram Corporation, CNS, DW Freight, Gator Industries, Industrial Data Terminals, Medical Care International, My Alarm, PayCom Systems, PetCare Plus, ProNet, Steris, Taylor, Wroght Washer Manufacturing

Officers, Executives and Principals

Paul D. Rhines, General Partner
Education: BA, Accounting, University of Northern Iowa
Background: Auditor, U.S. Federal Government; Wilson Sporting Goods; Executive Vice President, MorAmerica
Directorships: Board of Governors, NASBIC

Robert W. Allsop, General Partner
Background: President, MorAmerica Capital Corporation; Past President, NASBIC

Larry C. Maddox, General Partner (Overland)
Education: MBA, University of Iowa; BS, Industrial Engineering, Texas Tech
Background: Regional Vice President, MorAmerica Capital Corporation

Robert L. Kuk, General Partner (St. Louis)
Education: BA, History, University of North Dakota; MBA, Northern Illinois University
Background: Regional Vice President, MorAmerica Capital

Michael J. Meyer, Principal (Overland)
Education: CPA, BA, Luther College
Background: Vice President Corporate Operations and Finance, Gascard Club; Vice President, Consumer Growth Capital; Senior Vice President, Gill Capital

Bart A. McLean, Principal (St. Louis)
Education: BS, Economics, Business Administration, Phi Beta Kappa, University of Delaware; MBA, Indiana University
Background: Commercial Lending Officer, Energency Banking Group of Republic Bank; Republic Venture Group

ALPINE TECHNOLOGY VENTURES

20300 Stevens Creek Boulevard
Suite 495
Cupertino, CA 95014

Telephone: 408-725-1810
Fax: 408-725-1207
E-mail: cath@alpineventures.com

Mission: Actively seeking new investments

Fund Size: $72 million
Founded: 1995
Average Investment: $1 - $2 million
Minimum Investment: $500,000

Investment Criteria: Seed, Startup, First-stage, Second-stage

Geographic Preference: California, preferably Silicon Valley-based

Industry Group Preference: Communications, Hardware, High Technology, Networks, Semiconductors, Software

Portfolio Companies: not available

Officers, Executives and Principals

Chuck K. Chan, General Partner
David Lane, General Partner

AMPERSAND VENTURES

55 William Street, Suite 240
Wellesley, MA 02181

Telephone: 617-239-0700
Fax: 617-239-0824

Mission: Ampersand Ventures is committed to generating superior returns for its investors by building on its leadership position in the specialty materials and chemicals sector of the private equity marketplace

Fund Size: $100 million
Founded: 1988
Average Investment: $5 - $10 million
Minimum Investment: $3 million

Investment Criteria: All stages

Geographic Preference: United States

Industry Group Preference: Biotechnology, Communications, Computer Related, Electronics, Energy/Natural Resources, High Technology, Industrial Products, Medical/Health

Portfolio Companies: Adflex Solutions, Smartflex Systems, Daniel Products, Huntington, V.I. Technologies, Tomah Products, OraVax, Soane BioSciences, Novel Experimental Technology, Kroy Industries

Officers, Executives and Principals

Robert A. Charpie, Chairman
Richard A. Charpie, Managing General Partner
Charles D. Yie, General Partner
Stuart A. Auerbach, General Partner
Peter D. Parker, General Partner
Eric W. Linsley, Partner
Paul C. Zigman, Partner
David V. Ragone, Special Partner
David J. Parker, Principal

APPLIED TECHNOLOGY
One Cranberry Hill
Lexington, MA 02173

Telephone: 617-862-8622
Fax: 617-862-8367
E-mail: ellie-mccormack@apptec.com

Other Office Locations
1001 West Avenue, Suite B
Austin, TX 78701
Phone 512-479-8622, Fax 512-474-5126, E-mail 75720.3146@compuserve.com

1010 El Camino Real, Suite 300
Menlo Park, CA 94025
Phone 415-326-8622, Fax 415-326-8163, E-mail eflath@ix.netcom.com

Mission: To manage venture capital programs with investments focused on early-stage companies developing enabling information technologies and content

Fund Size: $84 million
Founded: 1983
Average Investment: $550,000 - $2 million
Minimum Investment: not available

Investment Criteria: Early Stage

Geographic Preference: United States

Industry Group Preference: High Technology, Information Services, Publishing, Software

Portfolio Companies: Adaptive Logic, Inc., Business Matters, Inc., Component Software Corporation, ContentWare, CoStar Corporation, Cybersmith, Dialect, DigiCash, B.V., Digital F/X, Inc., Farcast, Fluent, Inc., FutureTense, Inc., Headbone Interactive, Human Code, Inc., I-Space, Information Storage Devices, Internet Securities, Kub Systems, Logistic Solutions, Inc., Magnascreen Corporation, Maker Communications, MoneyStar, Net Contents, NetPhone, Inc., NetScheme Corporation, Network Sound and Light, NewCode Technology, Inc., Pervasive Software, Inc., Privacy, ProLinx Labs Corporation, Reflection Technology, Inc., Replica Corporation, Vertigo Development Group, Vista Information Solutions XTRA On-Line Corporation

Officers, Executives and Principals

David Boucher, Managing General Partner
Background: Vice President, Kurzweil Computer Products; Chief Executive Officer Interleaf
Directorships: Interleaf, Reflection Technology, Viewlogic, Wang Laboratories, XTRA On-Line, MoneyStar, Human Code, Btrieve

Frederick Bamber, Managing General Partner
Background: Founder, Applied Technology. Vice President, DRI
Directorships: Information Storage Devices, Interleaf, NetScheme, I-Space, NetPhone, New Code, Connected, FutureTense

Thomas Grant, Managing General Partner
Background: Vice President, DRI.; Senior Management, Softbridge Microsystems
Directorships: Vertigo, Headbone, DigiCash, Cybersmith, Net Contents, Enternet Securities

Nicholas Negroponte, Special General Partner
Background: Founding Director, MIT's Media Laboratory
Directorships: AMP, Magnascreen, Reflection Technology, Wired, Motorola

Gene Flath, Special General Partner
Background: Fairchild Semiconductor; Founder, Intel
Directorships: ProLinx, ISD

ARTHUR ROCK AND COMPANY

One Maritime Plaza, Suite 1220
San Francisco, CA 94111

Telephone: 415-981-3921
Fax: 415-981-3924

Mission: not available

Fund Size: not available
Founded: not available
Average Investment: $1 million
Minimum Investment: not available

Investment Criteria: Seed to Leveraged Buyout

Industry Group Preference: Communications, Computer Related, Electronics, Medical/Health

Portfolio Companies: not available

Officers, Executives and Principals

Arthur Rock, Principal
Katherine Styles, Associate

ASPEN VENTURES

One Post Office Square
Suite 3320
Boston, MA 02109

Telephone: 617-426-2151
Fax: 617-426-2181

Mission: not available

Fund Size: $140 million
Founded: not available
Average Investment: $1 million
Minimum Investment: not available

Investment Criteria: Seed to Mezzanine

Industry Group Preference: Biotechnology, Communications, Computer Related, Electronics, Environmental Protection, High Technology, Information Services, Medical/Health, Software

Portfolio Companies: not available

Officers, Executives and Principals

Allan Ferguson, Partner
Michael Du Cros, Partner
Nicholas Papantonis, Partner
Connor Seabrook, Associate

ATLAS VENTURE

222 Berkeley Street
Suite 1950
Boston, MA 02116

Telephone: 617-859-9290
Fax: 617-859-9292
E-mail: boston@atlasventure.com

Other Office Locations
Naarderpoort 1
1411 MA Naarden
The Netherlands
Phone 31-35-695-4800, Fax 31-35-695-4888, E-mail amsterdam@atlasventure.nl

Steinstrasse 70
D-81667 Munich
Germany
Phone 49-89-4587-45-0, Fax 49-89-4587-45-45, E-mail munich@atlasventure.de

32 bis, boulevard Haussman
75009 Paris
France
Phone 33-1-45-23-4120, Fax 33-1-45-23-4121, E-mail paris@atlasventure.fr

Mission: Atlas Venture is a partnership of international venture capitalists formed to finance high technology
businesses seeking success in the global economy

Fund Size: $325 million
Founded: 1980
Average Investment: $3 million
Minimum Investment: $500,000

Investment Criteria: Seed, Start-up, Early-stage, Later-stage

Geographic Preference: Northeast, West Coast United States, Western Europe

Industry Group Preference: Information Technology, Life Sciences

Portfolio Companies: Adcon Telemetry GmbH, Aethos Communications, Ltd., Allo Cine SA, Applied Language Technologies, Inc., ArQule, Inc., Ascent Pediatrics, Inc., Beyond, Inc., BinTec Computersysteme
GmbH, Biovector Therapeutics SA, Business Objects SA, Cardima, Inc., Cerulean Technology, Inc., Chipcom
Corporation, Core Technologies, Ltd., Cosmos Bay SA, CytoMed, Inc., DALiM GmbH, Danionics A/S, Data-
logix International, Inc., DataMind Corporation, deCODE genetics, Inc., Diagonal SA, Diatide, Inc., Eisen-
harz Holding BV, Epic Multimedia Group Plc, Epoch Systems, Inc., European Software Publishing, Ltd.,
Exelixis Pharmaceuticals, Inc., FASTech Integration, Inc., Firefly Network, Inc., Floreal Environmental
Europe BV, FutureTense, Inc., Genias Software GmbH, GenPharm International, Inc., GeoTel Communications Corporation, Hexagen Plc, Ilog SA, Inoteb SA, International Medical Products Group BV, Internet
Health LLC, IntroGene BV, Klotz GmbH, Laboratories Effik SA, MediSpectra, Inc., Mesacon GmbH, Microcide Pharmaceuticals, Inc., Micromet GmbH, Micronas Semiconductor Holding AG, Mikron GmbH, MorphoSys GmbH, Network Integrity, Inc., Neurochem, Inc., NitroMed, Inc., OnDisplay, Inc., Oxford

GlycoSciences Plc, PCs Compleat, Inc., Peptide Therapeutics Group, Plc, Pharming BV, POET Holdings, Inc., Power Integrations, Inc., Prolifix Ltd., Prolin Automation BV, Quadrant Healthcare Plc, SEZ Holding AG, Sattler-Huning Datentechnik GmbH, Scriptgen Pharmaceuticals, Inc., Software Ley GmbH, SolidWorks Corporation, Spark Holding NV, Spea Software AG, Therexsys Ltd., TomTec Imaging Systems, Inc., Transfusion Technologies Corporation, TranSwitch Corporation, TransScan Research and Development Company, Ltd., Trophix Pharmaceuticals, Inc., Unicate BV, Uniface International BV, Vermeer Technologies, Inc., Versant Object Technology Corporation, Viewlogic Systems, Inc., Watermark Software, Inc. WaveLight Laser Technologie GmbH

Officers, Executives and Principals

Philippe Claude, General Partner (Paris)
Allan R. Ferguson, General Partner (Boston)
Barry J. Fidelman, General Partner (Boston)
Jean-Francois Formela, General Partner (Boston)
Rolf Gunther, General Partner (Munich)
Michiel de Haan, General Partner (Amsterdam)
Gerard Montanus, General Partner (Amsterdam)
Werner Schauerte, General Partner (Munich)
Christopher Spray, General Partner (Boston)
Axel Bichara, Partner (Boston)
Hans Bosman, Partner, Chief Financial Officer, Europe (Amsterdam)
Michael J.F. Du Cros, Partner (Boston)
Jeanne Larkin Henry, Partner, Chief Financial Officer, United States (Boston)
Ingo Johannsen, Partner (Munich)
Rob Zegelaar, Partner (Amsterdam)

AVALON VENTURES

1020 Prospect Street, Suite 405
La Jolla, CA 92037

Telephone: 619-454-3803
Fax: 619-454-5329

Mission: not available

Fund Size: not available
Founded: not available
Average Investment: $750,000
Minimum Investment: not available

Investment Criteria: Seed, Startup

Industry Group Preference: Biotechnology, Computer Related, Electronics, Industrial Products, Medical/ Health

Portfolio Companies: not available

Officers, Executives and Principals

Kevin J. Kinsella, Managing General Partner
Dean A. Hovey, General Partner
John T. Hendrick, General Partner
Lawrence A. Bock, General Partner
Kevin C. Gorman, Associate

BATTERY VENTURES

20 William Street
Suite 200
Wellesley, MA 02181

Telephone: 617-237-1001
Fax: 617-237-7788
E-mail: rick@battery.com

Mission: Information technology, 6-8 investments/year

Fund Size: $85 million, $42 million
Founded: 1994, 1988
Average Investment: $3.5 million
Minimum Investment: $2 million including follow-ons

Investment Criteria: Seed to Leveraged Buyout; $1 million in revenues

Industry Group Preference: Communications, Information Services, Software

Portfolio Companies: Amber Wave Systems, Inc., Banyan Systems, Inc., Brooktrout Technology, Inc., Concord Communications, Inc., Concord Data Systems, Inc., Digitran Corporation, Fore Systems, Inc., InfoSeek Corporation, Instream Corporation, Meridian Data, Inc., Network Equipment Technologies, Inc., Systems Center, Inc., Xircom, Inc., All City Communications, Inc., AMSC, Dial Page, Inc. General Wireless, Inc., NEXTEL Communications, Inc., PCS Development Corporation, Phoenix Wireless, Inc., PowerFone, Inc., Aurum Software, Inc., AnswerSoft, Inc., Cullinet, HNC, Inc., Keyfile Corporation, Legent Corporation, Marcam Corporation, Mentor Graphics Corporation, Phoenix Technologies, Ltd., ProCD, Inc., Peerless Systems Corporation, Unify Corporation, Viewlogic Systems, Inc., In Focus Systems, Inc., Stratasys, Inc., Universal Electronics, Inc., Open Port Technology, Inc., Packet Engines, Performance Telecom, Inc., Radnet Ltd., UniSite, Inc., Export Software International, J. Frank Consulting, Inc., PictureWorks Technology, Inc., Xact Labs, Inc. VDONet Corporation, Ltd.

Officers, Executives and Principals

Oliver D. Curme, General Partner
Education: BA, Brown University; MBA, Harvard
Background: Officer, First National Bank of Boston, High Tech Division

Richard D. Frisbie, General Partner
Education: BA, JD, Harvard
Background: Vice President and Partner, Urban National Corporation
Directorships: New England Venture Capital Association, National Venture Capital Association

Robert G. Barrett, General Partner
Education: Harvard College; MBA, Harvard
Background: New England Regional Manager, First Chicago

Thomas J. Crotty, Partner
Education: Notre Dame; MBA, Wharton
Background: Abacus Ventures

Howard Anderson, General Partner
Education: BA, University of Pennsylvania; MBA, Harvard
Background: President and Founder, Yankee Group

Todd A. Dagres, General Partner
Education: BS, Trinity College; MBA, Boston University
Background: Principal and Senior Technology Analyst, Montgomery Security

James Currier, Associate
Education: BA, Princeton
Background: GTE, Star TV

Jonathan Roosevelt, Associate
Education: BA, Harvard

Peter Hartigan, Associate
Education: BA, Duke University

Morgan Jones, Associate
Education: BS, Harvard; MS, Stanford

Ravi Mohan, Associate
Education: BS, Cornell; MBA, University of Michigan

BAXTER INTERNATIONAL

One Baxter Parkway
Deerfield, IL 60015

Telephone: 847-948-2000
Fax: 847-948-2025

Mission: not available

Fund Size: not available
Founded: not available
Average Investment: not available
Minimum Investment: not available

Investment Criteria: Seed to Leveraged Buyout

Industry Group Preference: Biotechnology, Medical/Health

Portfolio Companies: not available

Officers, Executives and Principals

David Jones, Vice President
Education: AB, Dartmouth; MBA, JD, University of Southern California
Background: Vice President, Union Venture Corporation; Partner, InterVen Management
Directorships: Gigabit Logic, Sensor Medics Corporation

Al Reid, Manager

Sandra Cartie, Director

BRANTLEY VENTURE PARTNERS

20600 Chagrin Boulevard, Suite 1150
Cleveland, OH 44122

Telephone: 216-283-4800
Fax: 216-283-5324

Mission: To achieve maximum return on investment by building profitable companies from the early stages to $50 to 100 million in revenue.

Fund Size: $100 million
Founded: 1987
Average Investment: $750,000
Minimum Investment: not available

Investment Criteria: Early Stage, Growth Buildups; companies with potential to reach $50 million in revenues

Industry Group Preference: Biotechnology, Computer Related, Electronics, Environmental Protection, Health Care Services, High Technology, Industrial Products, Information, Software

Portfolio Companies: Collaborative Clinical Research, Continental, Recycling, DeCrane Aircraft Holdings, Financial Integration, Gliatech, Health Care Solutions, Macronex, Medirisk, Momentum Software, Vectra Banking, Ohmicron, Pediatric Services of America, RF Micro Devices, SysteMed, TBN, Transmodal, Inc.

Officers, Executives and Principals

Robert P. Pinkas, Founding Partner
Education: BA, AB, AM, Harvard University; JD, University of Pennsylvania
Background: Management Consultant, McKinsey and Co.; Attorney, Simpson Thatcher and Bartlett
Directorships: Continental Recycling, Macronex, Medirisk, Ohmicron, Pediatric Services of America, TBN, Transmodal

Raymond J. Rund, Partner
Education: BS, Engineering, Yale; MSEE, Carnegie Mellon; MBA, Harvard
Background: Engineering, Manufacturing and Marketing, Westinghouse Labs, Intel, Kerthley Instruments, McKinsey and Co.
Directorships: DeCrane AircraftHoldings, Financial Integration, Momentum Software, RF Micro Devices, Automated Systems and Products, Inc.

Timothy G. Biro, Partner
Education: MBA, Finance, Marketing and Strategic Planning, Wharton; MS, Microbiology, Pennsylvania State University; BA, Pharmacy, Temple
Background: Superintendent of Pharmaceutical Manufacturer, Merck
Directorships: Collaborative Clinical Research, Health Care Solutions, Transmodal Corporation, Anti-ox, Edison Biotech. Center

Michael J. Finn, Partner
Education: BS, MS, Michigan State University
Background: Vice President, Sears Divestment Co.; Department Director, Michigan Department of Treasury
Directorships: Thomas Group

BRENTWOOD VENTURE CAPITAL

11150 Santa Monica Boulevard, Suite 1200
Los Angeles, CA 90025

Telephone: 310-477-7678
Fax: 310-312-1868

Other Office Locations
1920 Main Street, Ste. 820
Irvine, CA 92714
Phone 714-251-1010, Fax 714-251-1011

3000 Sand Hill Road, Building 1, Suite 260
Menlo Park, CA 94025

Mission: not available

Fund Size: $500 million
Founded: 1972
Average Investment: $ 3 million
Minimum Investment: $1 million

Investment Criteria: Seed to Mezzanine

Industry Group Preference: Biotechnology, Electronics, Information Technology, Medical/Health

Portfolio Companies: ISOCOR, Continuus Software, Documentum, Object Design, The Dodge Group, CommQuest, CommVision, Diva, Polycom, Xylan, Arithmos, Aastrom, Depotech, Aradigm, Biopsys, Imagyn, Perclose, WebTV Networks

Officers, Executives and Principals

David W. Chonette, General Partner (Irvine)
G. Bradford Jones, General Partner
Ross A. Jaffe, MD, General Partner (Menlo Park)
John L. Walecka, General Partner (Menlo Park)
Jeffrey D. Brody, General Partner (Menlo Park)

CABLE AND HOWSE VENTURES

777 108th Avenue, Northeast
Suite 2300
Bellevue, WA 98004-5118

Telephone: 206-646-3040
Fax: 206-646-3041

Mission: not available

Fund Size: $160 million
Founded: 1977
Average Investment: $1 million
Minimum Investment: Less than $100,000

Investment Criteria: Seed, Startup, First-stage, Second-stage, Special Situations

Industry Group Preference: Biotechnology, Communications, Computer Related, Consumer, Electronic Components and Instrumentation, Energy/Natural Resources, Genetic Engineering, High Technology, Industrial Products and Equipment, Medical/Health Related, Software

Portfolio Companies: not available

Officers, Executives and Principals

Thomas J. Cable, General Partner
Elwood D. Howse, Jr., General Partner
Wayne C. Wager, General Partner

CAPITAL FOR BUSINESS, INC.

11 South Meramec, Suite 1430
St. Louis, MO 63105

Telephone: 314-746-7427
Fax: 314-746-8739

Other Office Locations
1000 Walnut Street, 18th Floor
Kansas City, MO 64106
Phone 816-234-2357

Mission: Specializes in management buyouts, acquisitions and mergers, and expansions of privately-held companies or subordinated debt with common stock warrants

Fund Size: $47 million
Founded: 1959
Average Investment: $1 million
Minimum Investment: $500,000

Investment Criteria: Second-stage to Buyouts

Industry Group Preference: Aerospace, Broadcast/Cable/Radio, Communications, Computer Related, Defense, Electronics, Energy/Natural Resources, High Technology, Industrial Products, Manufacturing/Processing, Software

Portfolio Companies: Abrasive Engineering and Technology, Affiliated Metals, American Medical Claims, Central Fiber Corporation, Citation Computer Systems, Hutchinson Foundry Products, Marketmakers International, Mesa Industries, Microdynamics, Performance Controls, Peterson Machine Tool, Petroleum Recycling, TLG Electronics, United States Filter, Wondermaid

Officers, Executives and Principals

James F. O'Donnell, Chairman
Education: BA, Psychology, University of Minnesota; MBA, University of Chicago; CPA
Background: Commerce Bancshares

Bart S. Bergman, President
Education: BSBA, Illinois State University
Background: Commerce Bancshares

Stephen B. Broun, Senior Vice President
Education: BSBA, St. Louis University; MBA, Washington University
Background: Senior Associate of a major St. Louis brokerage firm

Hollis A. Huels, Investment Officer
Education: CPA; BS, Drake University
Background: Senior Financial Analyst, Heller International; Auditor, Deloitte and Touche

Matthew H. Barry, Investment Officer
Education: BSBA, MBA, St. Louis University
Background: Financial Analyst, Kenamare Capital Corporation

CAPITAL HEALTH VENTURE PARTNERS

20 North Wacker Drive
Suite 2200
Chicago, IL 60606

Telephone: 312-781-1910
Fax: 312-427-1247

Other Office Locations
2084 South Milwaukee Street
Denver, CO 80210
Phone 303-692-8600, Fax 303-692-9656

Mission: not available

Fund Size: $40 million
Founded: not available
Average Investment: $750,000
Minimum Investment: not available

Investment Criteria: Startup to Leveraged Buyout

Geographic Preference: Northeastern, Midwestern, Rocky Mountains regions of the United States

Industry Group Preference: Biotechnology, Medical/Health

Portfolio Companies: not available

Officers, Executives and Principals

Dan J. Mitchell, Partner
Education: BS, Finance, University of Illinois; MBA, University of California at Berkeley
Background: Limited Market Advisor, First National Bank of Chicago
Directorships: Softyme

Frederick R. Blume, Partner

Kinney L. Johnson, Partner

CATALYST VENTURES

1119 St. Paul Street
Baltimore, MD 21202

Telephone: 410-244-0123
Fax: 410-752-7721

Mission: not available

Fund Size: $15 million
Founded: not available
Average Investment: $500,000
Minimum Investment: not available

Investment Criteria: not available

Geographic Preference: Mid-Atlantic United States

Industry Group Preference: Biotechnology, Communications, Computer Related, Electronics, High Technology, Industrial Products, Medical/Health

Portfolio Companies: not available

Officers, Executives and Principals

John M. Nehra, Managing General Partner

CHEMICALS AND MATERIALS ENTERPRISE ASSOCIATES

235 Montgomery Street
Suite 1025
San Francisco, CA 94104

Telephone: 415-352-1520
Fax: 415-352-1524

Other Office Locations
One Cleveland Center
1375 East Ninth Street, Suite 2700
Cleveland, OH 44114
Phone 216-861-4800, Fax 216-621-4543

Mission: Actively seeking new investments

Fund Size: $41 million
Founded: 1989
Average Investment: $1 million
Minimum Investment: Less than $100,000

Investment Criteria: Seed, Startup, First-stage, Second-stage

Industry Group Preference: Biotechnology, Distribution, Electronic Components and Instrumentation, Energy/Natural Resources, Genetic Engineering, High Technology, Industrial Products and Equipment, Medical/Health Related

Portfolio Companies: Aerotrans, Candescent Technologies, Conceptus, Endocardial Therapeutics, Flextronics, Fluid Propulsion Technologies, Metcal, Nanodyne, Physiometrix, Targeted Genetics, Vitesse Semiconductor, ZC Optics

Officers, Executives and Principals

Thomas R. Baruch, General Partner (San Francisco)
Donald L. Murfin, General Partner (Cleveland)

COMDISCO VENTURE GROUP

770 Tamalpais Drive, #300
Corte Madera, CA 94925

Telephone: 415-924-6400
Fax: 415-924-6458

Mission: not available

Fund Size: not available
Founded: not available
Average Investment: $250,000 - $3 million
Minimum Investment: not available

Investment Criteria: Venture Leasing

Industry Group Preference: Biotechnology, Communications, Computer Related, Medical/Health

Portfolio Companies: Arbor Software Corporation, Cyrix Edify NetLabs, Amylin Corporation, Telios Pharmaceuticals, Medtronic/CardioRhythm, Magellan Systems

Officers, Executives and Principals

Peggy Parker, Regional Port Manager

COMDISCO VENTURES

3000 Sand Hill Road
Building 1, Suite 155
Menlo Park, CA 94025

Telephone: 415-854-9484
Fax: 415-854-4026

Mission: Growth capital

Fund Size: $500 million
Founded: 1987
Average Investment: $2 - $3 million
Minimum Investment: $200,000

Investment Criteria: Venture Leasing, Mezzanine Debt and Equity

Geographic Preference: United States

Industry Group Preference: Biotechnology, Communications, Computer Related, Internet Related, Medical Health, Software

Portfolio Companies: Arbor Software, Cyrix, Edify, Amylin, Aradigm, Aspect Development, Cascade Communications, Documentum, Forte Software, Heartstream, Human Genome Sciences Microcide Pharmaceuticals, Neurex, Oacis Healthcare, Pharmacyclics, Red Brick, S3, Sybase, Vantitive, Visio, WorldTalk

Officers, Executives and Principals

Kevin J. McQuillan
James P. Labe

COMMONWEALTH BIOVENTURES

One Innovation Drive
Worcester, MA 01600

Telephone: 508-797-0500

Mission: not available

Fund Size: $20 million
Founded: not available
Average Investment: $500,000
Minimum Investment: not available

Investment Criteria: Seed

Geographic Preference: Massachusetts

Industry Group Preference: Biotechnology, Environmental Protection, Medical/Health

Portfolio Companies: not available

Officers, Executives and Principals

Robert G. Foster, President and Chief Executive Officer
Gustav A. Christensen, Executive Vice President
Gloria W. Doubleday, Vice President

COMMUNITY TECHNOLOGY FUND

881 Commonwealth Avenue
Boston, MA 02100

Telephone: 617-353-4550
Fax: 617-353-6141

Mission: not available

Fund Size: $50 million
Founded: not available
Average Investment: $500,000
Minimum Investment: not available

Investment Criteria: Seed to First-stage

Industry Group Preference: Communications, Computer Related, Electronics, Energy/Natural Resources, High Technology, Industrial Products, Medical Health, Software

Portfolio Companies: not available

Officers, Executives and Principals

John E. Bagaley, Jr., Managing Director
Education: BA, PhD, Philosophy, Yale University; JD, University of Texas
Background: General Counsel, Lower Colorado River Authority. Houston First Financial Group, Texas Commerce Bancshares
Directorships: American Medical Communications, American Surgical Technology, Brite-Line Industry, Cellcor Therapies, ClearFlow, Equine Technology, Fairchild Medical Systems

William J. Golden, Director
Education: BS, Mechanical Engineering, Notre Dame; MBA, Harvard; DFA
Background: Senior Management, Arthur D. Little, Inc.,Zero Stage Capital, First Stage Capital; Senior Management, Trammel Crow
Directorships: Cynosure, Lab Connections, MDI Instruments, Men's Health Centers, ZerRes

CONNECTICUT SEED VENTURES

200 Fischer Drive
Avon, CT 06001

Telephone: 203-677-0183

Mission: not available

Fund Size: $11 million
Founded: not available
Average Investment: $1 million
Minimum Investment: not available

Investment Criteria: Seed to Second-stage

Geographic Preference: Connecticut

Industry Group Preference: Biotechnology, High Technology, Medical/Health

Portfolio Companies: Targetech, Advanced Technology Materials, Transcoitch, Cardiopulmonary Devices, Mergent International

Officers, Executives and Principals

Samuel F. McKay, Managing General Partner
Education: Degrees in physics and finance
Background: Founding Partner, Ventech Partners; Manager, Connecticut General's Venture Capital Program and Special Equity Fund

CORNERSTONE MANAGEMENT

325 Distel Circle
Suite 100
Los Altos, CA 94022

Telephone: 415-988-9203
Fax: 415-988-9202

Mission: Actively seeking new investments

Fund Size: $60 million
Founded: 1984
Average Investment: $3 million
Minimum Investment: $1 million

Investment Criteria: Second-stage, Special Situations

Geographic Preference: West Coast of the United States

Industry Group Preference: Communications, Computer Related

Portfolio Companies: not available

Officers, Executives and Principals

J. Michael Gullard, Partner
Education: BA, MBA, Stanford University

Thomas R. Rice, Partner
Education: BS, Ph.D., Stanford University; MS, MIT

Douglas G. DeVivo, Partner
Education: BS, Rensselaer Polytechnic; Ph.D., Northeastern University; MBA, University of California at Berkeley

CORONADO VENTURE FUNDS

P.O. Box 65420
Tucson, AZ 85728-5420

Telephone: 602-577-3764
Fax: 602-299-8491

Mission: not available

Fund Size: $5 million
Founded: not available
Average Investment: $500,000
Minimum Investment: not available

Investment Criteria: Seed to Second-stage

Industry Group Preference: Biotechnology, Communications, Computer Related, Electronics, High Technology, Medical/Health

Portfolio Companies: Ventana Medical Systems, Inc. Crystal Semiconductor, Corporation, Acoustic Imaging Technologies, MetaLink Corporation

Officers, Executives and Principals

James M. Strickland, Managing General Partner

CORPORATE VENTURE PARTNERS, L.P.

171 East State Street
Suite 261
Ithaca, NY 14850

Telephone: 607-277-8024
Fax: 607-277-8027

Mission: Reducing investment activity

Fund Size: $26.232 million
Founded: 1988
Average Investment: $1.5 million
Minimum Investment: $250,000

Investment Criteria: First-stage

Industry Group Preference: Communications, Computer Related, Consumer, Electronic Components and Instrumentation, Genetic Engineering, Industrial Products and Equipment, Medical/Health Related

Portfolio Companies: Spectrum Holobyte, Inc., Inference Corporation, Career Horizons, Inc., Yes! Entertainment Corporation, Software Developers Co., Secure Computing Corporation, Tessera, Inc., Databook Inc., Spectra, Inc.

Officers, Executives and Principals

David Constine, General Partner
Education: BME, Cornell; MBA, Harvard
Background: General Partner, Venturtech Associates; Chief Financial Officer, Director, Shareholder, Point 4 Data Corporation; Officer, Investment Management Business; Donald Lufkin

Stephen M. Puricelli, General Partner
Education: BS, MBA, Rensselaer Polytechnic Institute
Background: Investment Officer, Norstar Venture Capital; Financial Analyst, Norstar Bancorp

CROSS TECHNOLOGIES

6475 Upper York Road
P.O. Box 200
Solebury, PA 18963

Telephone: 630-323-1211
Fax: 630-323-1221

Mission: not available

Fund Size: $2 million
Founded: 1989
Average Investment: $200,000
Minimum Investment: not available

Investment Criteria: Startup to Second-stage

Geographic Preference: Midwest, Mid-Atlantic United States

Industry Group Preference: Advanced Materials, Electronics

Portfolio Companies: not available

Officers, Executives and Principals

Robert W. Cross, General Manager

CULLINANE AND DONNELLY VENTURE

265 Church Street
New Haven, CT 06510

Telephone: 203-772-1440
Fax: 203-527-7844

Mission: not available

Fund Size: $53 million
Founded: not available
Average Investment: $1 million
Minimum Investment: not available

Investment Criteria: Startup to Second-stage

Geographic Preference: Northeastern United States

Industry Group Preference: Communications, Computer Related, Electronics, Environmental Protection, Insurance, Medical/Health

Portfolio Companies: not available

Officers, Executives and Principals

John R. Cullinane, General Partner
James F. Donnelly, General Partner

CW GROUP, INC.

1041 Third Avenue
Second Floor
New York, NY 10021

Telephone: 212-308-5266
Fax: 212-644-0354

Mission: Actively seeking new investments

Fund Size: $110 million
Founded: 1982
Average Investment: $1 million
Minimum Investment: Less than $100,000

Investment Criteria: Seed, Research and Development, Startup, First-stage, Second-stage, Mezzanine, Leveraged Buyout, Special Situations, Control-block Purchases

Industry Group Preference: Biotechnology, Genetic Engineering, Medical/Health Related

Portfolio Companies: not available

Officers, Executives and Principals

Walter Channing, Jr., Managing General Partner
Education: AB, MBA, Harvard
Background: Founder, Channing, Weinberg and Co.; President, Merrimack Laboratories
Directorships: Quantam Medical Systems, Sterivet Laboratories, Gabrielli Medical Information Systems

Barry Weinberg, Managing General Partner
Education: BS, Engineering, MIT; MBA, New York University
Background: Founder, Channing, Weinberg and Co.; Chief Executive Officer, General Computer Systems
Directorships: Biomatrix, Diamont Delectro-Tech, Micro-Sonics, Gambro

Charles M. Hartman, Managing General Partner
Education: BS, Notre Dame; MBA, University of Chicago
Background: Director, Acquisition and Licensing, Johnson and Johnson
Directorships: Queue Systems, Photec Diagnostics, Business Research Corporation, Nutritional Management, Computers in Medicine, Membrox

Scott M. Ciccone, Vice-President

Eric S. Schlesinger, Vice-President

DELPHI BIOVENTURES, L.P.

3000 Sand Hill Road
Building 1, Suite 135
Menlo Park, CA 94025

Telephone: 415-854-9650
Fax: 415-854-2961

Mission: not available

Fund Size: $88 million
Founded: not available
Average Investment: $1 million
Minimum Investment: not available

Investment Criteria: Seed to Second-stage

Geographic Preference: West Coast, Rocky Mountains region of the United States

Industry Group Preference: Biotechnology, Medical/Health

Portfolio Companies: not available

Officers, Executives and Principals

Costa G. Sevastopoulos, General Partner
David L. Douglass, General Partner
James J. Bochnowski, General Partner

DOMAIN ASSOCIATES

One Palmer Square
Princeton, NJ 08542

Telephone: 609-683-5656
Fax: 609-683-9789

Other Office Locations
650 Town Center Drive, Suite 810
Costa Mesa, CA 92626
Phone 714-434-6227, Fax 714-754-6802

Mission: Actively seeking new investments

Fund Size: $200 million
Founded: 1985
Average Investment: $1 million
Minimum Investment: $500,000 (except seed financing)

Investment Criteria: Seed, First-stage, Second-stage

Industry Group Preference: Electronic Components and Instrumentation, Genetic Engineering, Industrial
  Products and Equipment, Medical/Health Related

Portfolio Companies: not available

Officers, Executives and Principals

James C. Blair, General Partner (Princeton)
Education: BSE, Princeton University; MSE, PhD, University of Pennsylvania
Background: Involved in the creation of over thirty life-science ventures; F.S. Smither; White, Weld and Co.;
  Engineering Manager, RCA Corporation
Directorships: Managing Director, Rothschild

Brian H. Dovey, General Partner (Princeton)
Education: BA, Colgate University; MBA, Harvard
Background: President, Rorer; President, Survival Technology; Management Positions, Howmedica, Howmet
  Corporation, New York Telephone
Directorships: British Bio-technology, Creative BioMolecules, ReSound Corporation, National Venture Capital
  Association

Richard S. Schneider, General Partner (Costa Mesa)
Education: BS, University of California at Berkeley; PhD, University of Wisconsin; Post Doctorate, MIT; Stanford Graduate School of Business Executive Program
Background: Vice President, 3i Ventures Corporation; President, Gensia Pharmaceuticals; President, Biomedical Consulting Associates; Associate, Healthcare

Jesse Treu, General Partner (Princeton)

Kathleen K. Schoemaker, Administrative General Partner (Princeton)

DOUGERY AND WILDER

155 Bovet Road
Suite 350
San Mateo, CA 94402

Telephone: 415-358-8701
Fax: 415-358-8706

Mission: Actively seeking new investments

Fund Size: $130 million
Founded: 1981
Average Investment: $250,000 - $3 million
Minimum Investment: $250,000

Investment Criteria: Seed, Startup, First-stage, Second-stage, Leveraged Buyout

Industry Group Preference: Communications, Computer Related, Electronic Components and Instrumentation, Genetic Engineering, Industrial Products and Equipment, Medical/Health Related

Portfolio Companies: ABTOX, Ace Software Corporation, Alantec Associates Optical, Celtrix Pharmaceuticals, Compression Labs, Cornerstone Imaging, Cymed, EnDys Environmental Products, File Net, In Focus Systems, Intevac, Microgenics, Neurex, Novell, Republic Telecom Systems Corporation, Telecom Services Group, Unify Corporation, Vanguard Automation

Officers, Executives and Principals

Henry L.B. Wilder, Partner
Education: BS, Physics, U.S. Naval Academy; MBA, Stanford University
Background: Citicorp Venture Capital; Finnigan Instruments; Engineering Line Manager, U.S. Navy
Directorships: ABTOX, Associated Optical, Cymed, Ensys Environmental, VIA Medical

John R. Dougery, Partner
Education: AB, Mathematics, University of California at Berkeley; MBA, Stanford University
Background: Vice President and General Manager, Western Region of Citicorp Venture Capital; Founding Management Team, Ciablo Systems; CPA, Price Waterhouse

DSC VENTURES
20111 Stevens Creek Boulevard, Suite 130
Cupertino, CA 95014

Telephone: 408-252-3800
Fax: 408-252-0757

Mission: not available

Fund Size: $50 million
Founded: not available
Average Investment: $1 million
Minimum Investment: not available

Investment Criteria: First-stage to Bridge

Geographic Preference: Northeastern, Southwestern United States, California

Industry Group Preference: Communications, Computer Related, Electronics, High Technology, Information Services, Software

Portfolio Companies: not available

Officers, Executives and Principals

Dan Tomkins, Managing General Partner
David R. Bleile, General Partner

DSV PARTNERS

221 Nassau Street
Princeton, NJ 08542

Telephone: 609-924-6420
Fax: 609-683-0174

Other Office Locations
620 Newport Center Drive, Suite 990
Newport Beach, CA 92660
Phone 714-759-5657, Fax 714-760-6947

Mission: Actively seeking new investments

Fund Size: $100 million
Founded: 1968
Average Investment: not available
Minimum Investment: $1 million

Investment Criteria: Seed, Startup, First-stage, Second-stage, Leveraged Buyout

Industry Group Preference: Biotechnology, Communications, Computer Related, Distribution, Electronic Components and Instrumentation, Energy/Natural Resources, Environmental Protection, High Technology, Industrial Products, Information Services, Medical/Health Related, Software

Portfolio Companies: not available

Officers, Executives and Principals

John K. Clarke, Partner (Princeton)
Education: BA, Economics, Biology; MBA, Wharton
Background: General Electric

Morton Collins, Partner (Princeton)
Education: BS, Chemical Engineering, University of Delaware; MA, PhD, Chemical Engineering, Princeton University
Background: Founder of Data Science Ventures
Directorships: National Venture Capital Association

James J. Miller, Partner (Princeton)
Education: BS, Engineering and Applied Science, Yale University; MBA, Wharton School
Background: Texas Instruments

James R. Bergman, Partner (Princeton)
Education: BS, Engineering; MBA, University of California at Los Angeles
Directorships: National Venture Capital Association

Kevin G. Connors, Partner (Newport Beach)

Robert S. Hillas, Partner (Newport Beach)
Education: BA, Mathematics, Dartmouth; MBA, Stanford University
Background: General Partner, E.M. Warburg, Pincus and Co.

E G AND G VENTURE PARTNERS

100 Conifer Hill Drive, Suite 303
Danvers, MA 01923

Telephone: 508-777-7182
Fax: 508-777-9840

Other Office Locations
700 East El Camino Real, Suite 270
Mountain View, CA 94040
Phone 415-967-2822, Fax 415-967-2616

Mission: not available

Fund Size: $50 million
Founded: not available
Average Investment: $750,000
Minimum Investment: not available

Investment Criteria: Startup to Middle-stages

Geographic Preference: California, New England region of the United States

Industry Group Preference: Biotechnology, Communications, Computer Related, Electronics, High Technology, Medical/Health, Software

Portfolio Companies: Agilis Corporation, Biosys, CareLink Corporation, Chromatic Technology, Codon, Datawatch, Dynaco, Falco Data Products, Gamma Microwave, Landec Labs, LaserData, Magni Systems, Matrix Pharmaceuticals, Natural Language, Proconics, RasterOps, Resumix, SiScan Systems, Steinbrecher, Vasocor, VLSI Packaging Materials

Officers, Executives and Principals

John A. Blaeser, General Partner
Education: BS, Electrical Engineering, Northwestern University
Background: Executive Vice President, Gould, Inc.; President and General Manager, Programmable Control Division; Vice President Marketing, Sales and Marketing Positions, GE

Andres A. Buser, General Partner (Mountain View)
Education: Graduate degree in electronics, Swiss Federal Institute of Technology, Zurich
Background: Chief Executive Officer, PPS Manufacturing; General Manager, Applied Electrochemistry; Vice President, Director of Sales and Marketing, EG&G Reticon

C. Gerald Diamond (Mountain View)
Education: BS, Industrial Management, MIT
Background: Senior Manager, Intel; President, Intel International; Vice President, Corporate Business Development, VisiCorp; International Business Consultant

EL DORADO VENTURES

20300 Stevens Creek Boulevard, Suite 395
Cupertino, CA 95014

Telephone: 408-725-2474
Fax: 408-252-2762

Mission: not available

Fund Size: $100 million
Founded: 1986
Average Investment: $200,000 - $1 million
Minimum Investment: not available

Investment Criteria: Seed to First-stage

Industry Group Preference: Communications, Computer Related, Electronics, High Technology, Information Services, Medical/Health, Software

Portfolio Companies: Access Health Marketing, Inc., Accom, Applied Genetics, Gold Disk, Report Smith, Novellus Systems, Optical Specialties, Paradigm Technology, Quorum Software, Security Control Systems, Vantage Analysis

Officers, Executives and Principals

Gary W. Kalbach, Founding General Partner
Education: BS, Business Administration, University of California at Berkeley; MBA, San Jose State University
Background: General Partner, West Coast, Sprout Group

Shanda Bahles, General Partner
Education: BSEE, with distinction, MBA, Stanford University
Background: Engineering, Marketing and Management positions at Infotek, Millennium Systems, Magnuson Computer Systems, Fortune Systems

Thomas H. Peterson, General Partner
Education: BSEE, with distinction, Iowa State University; MBA, University of California at Los Angeles
Background: Investment Officer, Union Venture Corporation; Engineer, Hewlett Packard Company

ENERTEK PARTNERS

601 West Fifth Avenue
Columbus, OH 43201

Telephone: 614-424-7005
Fax: 614-424-4874

Mission: not available

Fund Size: $25 million
Founded: not available
Average Investment: $500,000
Minimum Investment: not available

Investment Criteria: Startup to Second-stage

Industry Group Preference: Biotechnology, Computer Related, Electronics, Energy/Natural Resources, Environmental Protection, High Technology, Software

Portfolio Companies: not available

Officers, Executives and Principals

Paul F. Purcell, President
Education: BA, Siena College; MBA, State University of New York
Background: Vice President Scientific Advances, Rand Capital Corporation; Vice President, Bank of New York
Directorships: Several technology-based companies

ENTERPRISE PARTNERS

5000 Birch Street
Suite 6200
Newport Beach, CA 92660

Telephone: 714-833-3650
Fax: 714-833-3652

Other Office Locations
7979 Ivanhoe Avenue, Suite 550
La Jolla, CA 92037
Phone 619-454-8833

12011 San Vincente Boulevard, Suite 330
Los Angeles, CA 90049
Phone 310-476-3000

Mission: Actively seeking new investments

Fund Size: $200 million
Founded: 1985
Average Investment: $2 million
Minimum Investment: No minimum

Investment Criteria: Seed, Research and Development, Startup, First-stage, Second-stage, Mezzanine, Leveraged Buyout

Industry Group Preference: Biotechnology, Communications, Computer Related, Consumer, Distribution, Electronic Components and Instrumentation, Genetic Engineering, Industrial Products and Equipment, Medical/Health Related

Portfolio Companies: Homedco, TOKOS, On Assignment, Ligand, Regency Health

Officers, Executives and Principals

James H. Berglund, General Partner (La Jolla)

James P. Gauer, General Partner (Los Angeles)

Charles D. Martin, General Partner (Newport Beach)
Background: General Partner, Westar Capital

Andrew E. Senyei, General Partner (Newport Beach)
Background: Founder, President, Molecular Biosystems; Chief Executive Officer, Adeza Biomedical, Inc.; Assistant Professor, Departments of Obstetrics, Gynecology and Pediatrics
Directorships: Molecular Biosystems, Ligand Pharmaceuticals, Regency Health Services, Genetrix, Paidos Healthcare, Sonus Pharmaceuticals, Adeza

Jack W. Reich, Senior Vice President (La Jolla)

ESSEX-WOODLANDS HEALTH VENTURES, L.P.

2170 Buckthorne Place, Suite 170
The Woodlands, TX 77380

Telephone: 713-367-9999
Fax: 713-298-1295

Other Office Locations
190 South LaSalle Street
Suite 2800
Chicago, IL 60603
Phone 312-444-6040, Fax 312-444-6034

Mission: Only after attaining a thorough understanding of the selected market segment will the principals of Essex-Woodlands Health Ventures, L.P. pursue potential investment candidates. Essex-Woodlands will generally assume the role of lead investor in structuring and syndicating a financing and will take a proactive approach to managing their investments and actively participate in the creation, development and growth of each new enterprise.

Fund Size: $50 million
Founded: 1994
Average Investment: $2 million
Minimum Investment: $1 million

Investment Criteria: Seed to Second-stage

Geographic Preference: Central corridor of the United States

Industry Group Preference: Biomedical, Medical/Health

Portfolio Companies: Active Services Corporation, American Holistic Centers, DigiTrace Care Services, Inc., Healthcare Resource Management, Inc., Health Systems Technology, Inc., Hepatix, Inc., MIST, Inc., Protocol Work Systems, Inc., Ring Medical Inc., Sedona Healthcare Group, Inc., Targeted Genetics Corporation, Zonagen, Inc.

Officers, Executives and Principals

James L. Currie, General Partner (Chicago)
Education: BA, Pennsylvania State University
Background: President and Principal Stockholder, Central Scientific, Inc.
Directorships: DigiTrace Care Services, Protocol Work Systems, Zonagen, Inc.

Marc S. Sandroff, General Partner (Chicago)
Education: BA, Washington University; MBA, University of Chicago
Background: Participated in venture capital process of Allstate Insurance Company; direct operating responsibilities as a general partner and/or management principal of several rehabilitation and long term care facilities
Directorships: Active Service Corporation, American Holistic Centers, Health Systems Technology, Protocol Work Systems, Sedona Healthcare

Martin P. Sutter, General Partner (Woodlands)
Education: BS, Louisiana State University; MBA, University of Houston
Background: President, Woodlands Venture Capital Co.; various operations, marketing and finance positions in the health care industry
Directorships: Hepatix, Targeted Genetics Corporation, Ring Medical, Zonagen, Inc.

EUCLID PARTNERS CORPORATION

50 Rockefeller Plaza
Suite 1022
New York, NY 10020

Telephone: 212-489-1770
Fax: 212-757-1686
E-mail: Fred.Wilson@aol.com

Mission: Actively seeking new investments

Fund Size: not available
Founded: 1970
Average Investment: not available
Minimum Investment: $750,000

Investment Criteria: Startup, First-stage, Second-stage, Control-block Purchases

Industry Group Preference: Communications, Computer Related, Genetic Engineering, Medical/Health Related

Portfolio Companies: Grasp Information Corporation, Sys-Tech Solutions, Ascor, Inc., Avail Systems, Inc., Biosite Diagnostics, Inc., Channel Computing, Inc., CrossComm Corporation, Multex Systems, Neomorphics, Inc., Secretech, Inc., Software Developers Co., Symphony Pharmaceuticals, Upgrade Corporation of America, Banyan Systems, Itron, Read-Rite, Telxon, Therion Biologics

Officers, Executives and Principals

A. Bliss McCrum, Jr., Partner
Education: Princeton University; MBA, Wharton
Background: Senior Officer, Director, and Executive Committee Member, Dominick and Dominick
Directorships: Avail Systems, Ascor

Milton J. Pappas, Partner
Education: Case Western Reserve University; Cleveland Marshall Law School; CFA
Background: Vice President, Drexel Harriman Ripley, Cleveland Trust Company, Merrill, Turben and Co., Inc., First of Michigan Corporation
Directorships: Sys-Tech Solutions, The Software Developers Company, Therion Biologics

Stephen K. Reidy, Partner
Education: Middlebury College; MBA, Columbia University; MA, International Affairs, Columbia
Background: Metropolitan Life, U.S. Information Agency (USSR and West Germany)
Directorships: Biosite Diagnostics, Secretech, Symphony Parmaceuticals

Frederick R. Wilson, Partner
Education: MIT; MBA, Wharton
Background: Gibbs and Cox Naval Architects
Directorships: Grasp Information Corporation, Multex Systems, Upgrade Corporation of America

FLUKE CAPITAL MANAGEMENT

11400 Southeast 6th Street, Suite 230
Bellevue, WA 98004

Telephone: 206-453-4590
Fax: 206-453-4675

Mission: not available

Fund Size: not available
Founded: not available
Average Investment: $500,000
Minimum Investment: not available

Investment Criteria: Startup to Leveraged Buyout

Geographic Preference: Pacific Northwest region of the United States

Industry Group Preference: Biotechnology, Communications, Computer Related, Electronics, High Technology, Industrial Products

Portfolio Companies: not available

Officers, Executives and Principals

Dennis P. Weston, Chief Operating Officer
Education: Central Washington University; MBA, University of Washington; CPA

David L. Fluke

John M. Fluke, Jr.

Margaret Hofman

FORWARD VENTURES

10975 Torreyana Road
Suite 230
San Diego, CA 92121

Telephone: 619-546-1848
Fax: 619-452-8799

Mission: not available

Fund Size: $2 million
Founded: not available
Average Investment: $250,000
Minimum Investment: not available

Investment Criteria: Seed to Startup

Geographic Preference: Southern California

Industry Group Preference: Biotechnology, Medical/Health

Portfolio Companies: Actigen, Onyx Pharmaceuticals, Sequana Therapeutics, ARIAD Pharmaceuticals, Cell Therapeutics, InSite Vision, Ixsys, Neocrin, Ooncotech, PRIZM, Somatix Therapy, Visaderm

Officers, Executives and Principals

Dr. Ivor Royston, MD, General Partner
Background: Founder/Investor, Hybritech, IDEC and GeneSys Therapeutics; Scientist, Johns Hopkins, NIH, Stanford, University of California San Diego
Directorships: Actigen, Cytocare, Sequana Therapeutics Inc., Somatix Therapy Corporation, Unisyn Technologies

Standish M. Fleming, General Partner
Education: BA, Amherst; MBA, University of California at Los Angeles
Background: President and Chief Executive Officer, GeneSys Therapeutics; Ventana
Directorships: Actigen

FOUR C VENTURES

237 Park Avenue
Suite 801
New York, NY 10017

Telephone: 212-692-3680
Fax: 212-692-3685

Mission: not available

Fund Size: $115 million
Founded: not available
Average Investment: $1 million
Minimum Investment: not available

Industry Group Preference: Broadcast/Cable/Radio, Communications, Computer Related, High Technology, Information Services, Publishing, Software

Portfolio Companies: Netframe, Object Design, Kendall Square, Wireless Access, EO, Centerline Software

Officers, Executives and Principals

Alexandra M. Giurgiu, Partner
Education: BS, MS, Engineering

Jeanne M. Sullivan, Partner
Education: BS, Marketing; JD, Law

Elserino Piol, Partner

Jiuliano Raviola, Partner

FRANKLIN VENTURE CAPITAL, INC.

237 Second Avenue South
Franklin, TN 37064

Telephone: 615-791-9462
Fax: 615-791-9636

Mission: Healthcare focused funds

Fund Size: $113 million
Founded: 1986
Average Investment: $5,000,000
Minimum Investment: not available

Investment Criteria: Seed to Second-stage

Industry Group Preference: Biotechnology, Healthcare Information Systems, Medical/Health

Portfolio Companies: Active Services Corporation, Arcon HealthCare, Inc., DigiTrace Care Services, Inc., ElderHealth, Inc., Health Systems Technologies, Inc., Healthcare Resource Management, Inc., Long Term Care Group, Inc. MedicaLogic, Inc., Meridian Occupational Healthcare Associates, Inc., Primary Health, Inc. Ring Medical Inc., Symmetry Health Partners

Officers, Executives and Principals

Larry H. Coleman, Ph.D., President
Education: AB, University of North Carolina; Ph.D., Immuno-biochemistry, University of South Dakota
Background: President, HCA Capital Corporation; Manager, Immunology Research and Development, Minnesota Mining and Manufacturing; Director, Research and Development, SmithKline

W. David Swenson, Vice President
Education: BS, Austin Peay University; MBA, Vanderbilt University
Background: Senior Strategic Planning Analyst, Chief Financial Officer, The Center for Health Studies, Hospital Corporation of America

James C. Hoffman, Managing Partner

John T. Booth, Chairman
Education: BA, Amherst; JD, Harvard
Background: Chairman, American Health Capital; Executive Vice President, Director of Blyth Eastman Dillon and Co.

Cornelia Holland, Chief Financial Officer

GATEWAY ASSOCIATES

8000 Maryland Avenue, Suite 1190
St. Louis, MO 63105

Telephone: 314-721-5707
Fax: 314-721-5135

Mission: not available

Fund Size: $53 million
Founded: not available
Average Investment: $1.5 million
Minimum Investment: not available

Investment Criteria: Strong Management

Industry Group Preference: Biotechnology, Communications, Computer Related, Industrial Products, Information Services, Medical/Health, Software

Portfolio Companies: Access America Telemanagement Inc., Applied Technology Genetics Corporation, Biotage, Inc., Bridge Information Systems, Canji Inc., ChemDesigns Corporation, Citation Cable Systems Ltd., Claruss Medical Systems, Inc., Coldar Technology Inc., CompuCom Systems, Inc., Computer Technology Corporation, CytoDiagnostics Inc.

Officers, Executives and Principals

Constantine E. Anagnostopoulos, General Partner
Education: PhD, Organic Chemistry, Harvard University; Graduate of Executive Program in Business Administration, Columbia University
Background: Corporate Vice President, Monsanto Co.; Vice Chairman, Monsanto Corporation Development and Growth Committee; President and Chief Executive Officer, Monsanto Venture Capital

Gregory R. Johnson, General Partner
Education: PhD, Solid State Physics, University of Rochester; BS, MIT
Background: Vice President, Monsanto Venture Capital Co.; Corporate New Ventures and Acquisitions Analyst, Monsanto Europe

John S. McCarthy, General Partner
Education: MBA, St. Louis University; BS, Business Administration, Washington University
Background: Assisted in founding of Gateway; Vice President/Manager, Centerre Bank's Metopolitan Division
Directorships: Novellus System

Richard F. Ford, General Partner
Education: Graduate, Executive Program in Business Administration of Columbia University; BA, Economics, Princeton University
Background: Founder of Gateway; President and Chief Executive Officer, Centerre Bancorporation; Manager, Merrill Lynch, St. Louis
Directorships: St. Louis Regional Commerce and Growth Association, American Bankers Association Commercial Lending Division

GLENWOOD

3000 Sand Hill Road
Building 4, Suite 230
Menlo Park, CA 94025

Telephone: 415-854-8070
Fax: 415-854-4961

Mission: not available

Fund Size: $75 million
Founded: not available
Average Investment: $3 million
Minimum Investment: not available

Investment Criteria: First-stage, Later-stage; revenues at least $10 million

Industry Group Preference: High Technology

Portfolio Companies: Iworks Entertainment, Magellen Systems, Paradigm Technology, Octel Communications, Supertek Computers, Mattson Technology, Aptix, SPEA Software

Officers, Executives and Principals

Dag Tellefsen, Managing Partner
Education: BSCE, Princeton University; MBA, Stanford University
Background: Partner, Continental Capital; OceanRoutes; Raychem; Consultant, McKinsey
Directorships: Arix, Octel Communications, KLA Instruments, several private companies

Jim Timmins, Partner
Education: BA, University of Toronto; MBA, Stanford University
Background: Principal, Hambrecht and Quist; Investment Banker, McKewon and Timmins, Salomon Brothers
Directorships: Iworks Entertainment, Magellan Systems, Paradigm Technology

Lauren Silvernail, Partner
Education: BA, Biophysics, MBA, Stanford University
Background: Co-Founded, Sierra Pacific; Bio-Rad Laboratories; Varian Associates
Directorships: Biological Components, Natural Language, Opus Systems

GLYNN VENTURES

3000 Sand Hill Road
Building Four, Suite 235
Menlo Park, CA 94025

Telephone: 415-854-2215
Fax: 415-854-8083

Mission: not available

Fund Size: $25 million
Founded: 1983
Average Investment: $500,000
Minimum Investment: $250,000

Investment Criteria: Startup, First-stage, Second-stage, Mezzanine, Leveraged Buyout

Industry Group Preference: Communications, Computer Related, Consumer, Electronic Components and Instrumentation, Genetic Engineering, Industrial Products and Equipment, Medical/Health Related

Portfolio Companies: not available

Officers, Executives and Principals

John W. Glynn, Jr., General Partner
Education: BS, Notre Dame; JD, University of Virginia; MBA, Stanford
Background: General Partner, Lamoreaux, Glynn Associates; Special Partner, New Enterprise Associates
Directorships: Molecular Design, The Learning Company

Steve Rosston

Daryl Messinger

GRYPHON VENTURES, L.P.

222 Berkeley Street
Suite 1600
Boston, MA 02116

Telephone: 617-267-9191
Fax: 617-267-4293
E-mail: all@gryphoninc.com

Mission: Actively seeking new investments

Fund Size: $56 million
Founded: 1986
Average Investment: $2 million
Minimum Investment: $1 million

Investment Criteria: Startup, First-stage, Second-stage

Geographic Preference: United States

Industry Group Preference: Communications, Energy/Natural Resources, Fuel Additives, Genetic Engineering, Industrial Products and Equipment, Lubricant Additives, Medical/Health Related, Refinery Chemicals

Portfolio Companies: Energy Biosystems, IGEN, Optex Communications Corporation, Geltech, Hyperion Catalysis International, Inc., Scotgen BioPharmaceuticals, Quantex Corporation

Officers, Executives and Principals

William F. Aikman, Managing General Partner
Education: Brown University; University of Pennsylvania; Harvard University
Background: President, Gryphon Management Company, Inc.; President and Chief Executive Officer, Massachusetts Technology Development Corporation
Directorships: Massachusetts Certified Development Corporation, Geltech, Optex

Edward B. Lurier, General Partner
Background: Vice Chairman, Damon Corporation; Senior Vice President, all of Damon product companies; Board of Trustees, Dana Farber Cancer Center
Directorships: Energy Biosystems, Hyperion, IGEN, Optex, Scotgen Biopharmaceuticals

Andrew J. Atkinson, Vice President, Investment Analysis
Education: Harvard University, honors
Background: Market Strategist and Planner, Dun and Bradstreet Software; Founding Member and Senior Marketing Research Analyst, McCormack and Dodge Corporation; Research and Analysis Group, Management Consultant on shareholder value issues
Directorships: Optex

HALLADOR VENTURE PARTNERS

PO Box 15299
Sacramento, CA 95851

Telephone: 916-920-0191
Fax: 916-920-3018

Mission: not available

Fund Size: $20 million
Founded: not available
Average Investment: $500,000
Minimum Investment: not available

Investment Criteria: Seed to Second-stage

Geographic Preference: California

Industry Group Preference: Biotechnology, Communications, Computer Related, Information Services, Medical/Health, Software

Portfolio Companies: Adams Scientific, Alldata, Analyte, Endgate, Gigatronics, Manzanita Software Systems, Merksamer Jewelers, Pacific Grain Products, Peninsula Engineering Group, Qualimetics, Sysgen, Tech Valley Publishing, Testronics.

Officers, Executives and Principals

Chris L. Branscum, General Partner
Education: Sacramento State; JD, McGeorge School of Law
Background: Partner, Arthur and Young

David C. Hardie, Manager
Education: Cal Poly; MBA, Harvard
Background: Chief Executive Officer, Halador Petroleum Company

HANCOCK VENTURE PARTNERS

One Financial Center, 44th Floor
Boston, MA 02111

Telephone: 617-348-3707
Fax: 617-350-0305

Mission: not available

Fund Size: $1 billion
Founded: not available
Average Investment: $2 million
Minimum Investment: not available

Investment Criteria: Expansion to Buyouts

Industry Group Preference: Biotechnology, Communications, Computer Related, Medical/Health, Software

Portfolio Companies: Advanced Computer Communications, Arch Communications, Ontos, Progress Software, Raxco, Sierra On-Line, Genesis Holding, Applied Microsystems, Credence, Access Technology

Officers, Executives and Principals

D. Brooks Zug, Managing General Partner
Education: BS, Lehigh; MBA, Harvard
Background: Co-Founder, Hancock Venture Partners; Paine Webber Hackson and Curtis; Sun Life of Canada
Directorships: Advisory Committee Member, Advent Funds, Advent Techno-Venture, Europe Capital Partners, Euroventures Germany, Halder Holdings B.V.

Edward W. Kane, Managing General Partner
Education: BS, University of Pennsylvania; MBA, Harvard
Background: Commercial Banking Division, New England Merchants National Bank; Major, U.S. Army Military Intelligence
Directorships: AlCorp, XYlogics, Mutual Risk Management

Frederick C. Maynard, General Partner
Education: Wesleyan; MBA, Dartmouth
Background: Manufacturers Hanover Trust
Directorships: Genesis Holdings Ltd., Kaepa

Kevin S. Delbridge, General Partner
Education: BS, Western New England University; MS, University of Massachusetts
Background: CIGNA Investment Group, Coopers and Lybrand
Directorships: Advisory Boards, Accel Partners III, Arral Pacific Equity Trust II, Asia Pacific Growth Fund, China Vest, Inter Asia Capital, Newtek Ventures II

Laurie J. Thomsen, General Partner
Education: BA, Williams College; MA, Management, Boston University
Background: Loan Officer, U.S. Trust Company, John Hancock Corporate Finance
Directorships: Curaflex Health Services, Pacific Linen; Advisory Boards, Austin Ventures, T. Rowe Price Threshold Fund

Ofer Nemirovsky, General Partner
Education: BS, Electrical Engineering, BS Economics, University of Pennsylvania
Background: Hewlett-Packard
Directorships: Dendrite International, Raxco Software, Traveling Software

Robert M. Wadsworth, General Partner
Education: MBA, with distinction, Harvard; BS, Systems Engineering, Computer Science, University of Virginia
Background: Booz Allen and Hamilton
Directorships: IDE Associates, Minco Acquisition Corporation

HARVEST VENTURES

5339 Prospect Road, #417
San Jose, CA 95129-5033

Telephone: 408-996-3200
Fax: 408-996-1765

Other Office Locations
767 Third Avenue, 7th Floor
New York, NY 10017
Phone 212-838-7776, Fax 212-593-0734

Mission: not available

Fund Size: $100 million
Founded: not available
Average Investment: $1 million
Minimum Investment: not available

Investment Criteria: Startup to Leveraged Buyout

Industry Group Preference: High Technology

Portfolio Companies: Advanced Technology Laboratories, CAE Systems, Comstron Corporation, CSP, Evans and Sutherland Computer Corporation, Ferrofluidics, International Microelectronic Products, Interpore, Micro Linear Corporation, MRW, Optigraphics, Sutter Biomedical, Taylor Medical

Officers, Executives and Principals

Lloyd E. Marvin, Managing General Partner
Background: Marketing, Fairchild Semiconductor; Product Manager, Large Scale Integration; Co-founder, Four Phase Systems; Founder and Vice President, Marketing, Compression Labs
Directorships: Five high-tech companies

Harvey J. Wertheim, Managing General Partner
Background: Director and Vice President, Research and Science Investors; Price Waterhouse; Chairman, Executive Committee, Board of Governors, NASBIC
Directorships: President and Director, Van Rietschoten Capital Corporation, Bohlen Capital, European Development Capital Corporation, Noro Capital Corporation

Harvey P. Mallement, Managing General Partner
Background: Managing Partner, Masco Associates; Assistant to the President, Ward Foods
Directorships: Symbol Technologies, Board of Industrial Ceramics, Wallace and Tiernan

William Randon, General Partner
Education: BA, Law, University of Geneva, Switzerland; MBA, Wharton
Background: President, M&T Capital; Bankers Trust Company

William J. Kane, General Partner
Education: BS, Microbiology, MBA, MIT
Background: Broadvie Associates, Warner Lambert
Directorships: Taylor Medical Inc.

HEALTHCARE INVESTMENT CORPORATION

379 Thornall Street
Edison, NJ 08837

Telephone: 908-906-4600
Fax: 908-906-1450

Mission: not available

Fund Size: $375 million
Founded: not available
Average Investment: $500,000 - $10 million
Minimum Investment: not available

Investment Criteria: Liquidity of at least $100 million after 3-5 years

Industry Group Preference: Biotechnology, Medical/Health

Portfolio Companies: Cytomed Inc., Genetic Therapy, Gynopharma Inc., Lukens Medical Corporation, Magainin Pharmaceuticals Inc., Medigene Inc., Medimmune Inc., Oncologix Inc., Osteotech Inc., Biotransplant Inc., Diacrin Inc., Osteoarthritis Sciences Inc., Pharmagenics Inc., Pharmavene Inc, Permier Allergy Inc., Premier Anesthesia

Officers, Executives and Principals

Wallace H. Steinberg, Chairman of the Board
Education: BS, Pharmacy, MS, Pharmaceutical Chemistry, Rutgers University
Background: Director of Research and Development, Johnson and Johnson; Director, Health Care Division; Vice President, J&J Development Corporation

John W. Littlechild, Vice Chairman
Education: BSC, University of Manchester; MBA, Manchester Business School
Background: Established Advent Venture Capital Co. in the UK; Founded Advent International Corporation in Boston; Manager, Advent

Ronald Shiftan, Vice Chairman
Education: University of Virginia; JD, Columbia
Background: Fifteen years with Bear, Stearns and Co. Inc. serving as a General Partner and headed the firms international corporate finance department

Harold R. Werner, Vice Chairman
Education: BS, MS, Princeton University; MBA, Harvard University
Background: Director, New Ventures, Johnson and Johnson Development Corporation; Senior Vice President, Robert S. First Inc.

James H. Cavanaugh, President
Education: MA, PhD, University of Iowa
Background: President, SmithKline and French Labs pharmaceuticals division and laboratory business; President, Allergan International
Directorships: Chairman of Executive Committee of the Board of Trustees of the National Committee for Quality Health Care 1988

James S. Kuo, Managing Director for Venture Analysis
Education: MD, University of Pennsylvania; MBA, Health Care Management, Wharton
Background: Founding Member, Vice President Medical Venture Capital at The Castle Group Ltd.

HILL, CARMAN, KIRBY AND WASHINGTON

885 Arapahoe
Boulder, CO 80302

Telephone: 303-442-5151
Fax: 303-442-8525

Mission: not available

Fund Size: $118 million
Founded: not available
Average Investment: $500,000 - $1 million
Minimum Investment: not available

Investment Criteria: Seed to Second-stage

Geographic Preference: Western Rocky Mountains region of the United States

Industry Group Preference: Biotechnology, Communications, Electronics, High Technology, Medical/Health, Software

Portfolio Companies: Adept Technology, Aptix Corporation, Aspen Peripherals, AudioLogic, CADIS, Crystal Semiconductor, Cyto Therapeutics, GRID Systems, KaPRES Software, MIPS Computer Systems, Micro Insurance, Radish Communications, Silicon Graphics

Officers, Executives and Principals

Thomas G. Washington, General Partner
Education: BA, Dartmouth; JD, with distinction, University of Michigan
Background: Founding General Partner, Horsley Keogh and Associates; Corporate Lawyer

Carl D. Carman, Partner
Education: BS, University of Kentucky
Background: Founder, The Master Fund; Vice President of Research and Development, NBI; President NBI; Vice President Engineering, Data General; Inforex; IBM

John G. Hill, Partner
Education: BA, MBA, University of Michigan
Background: Founding General Partner, Hill, Carman, Kirby and Washington; District Manager, Storage Technology Corporation; Marketing, IBM

Paul J. Kirby, Partner
Education: BS, honors, Electrical Engineering, Computer Science; MBA, Harvard
Background: Hewlett Packard, Project Manager

HILLMAN MEDICAL VENTURES

Two Walnut Grove Drive, Suite 130
Horsham, PA 19044-2255

Telephone: 215-443-5531
Fax: 215-443-5970

Mission: not available

Fund Size: not available
Founded: not available
Average Investment: $500,000 - $3 million
Minimum Investment: not available

Investment Criteria: not available

Geographic Preference: Eastern United States

Industry Group Preference: Biotechnology, Medical/Health

Portfolio Companies: Biosurface Technology, Cellcor, CorBec Pharmaceuticals, Cytyc, Enzymatics, Fiberoptic Sensor Technology, Genvec, Illumenex, Intra-Sonix, Mediventure, Ohmicron, SpectRX, Triplex Pharmaceuticals, Ultracision

Officers, Executives and Principals

Ronald J. Brenner, PhD, Managing Partner
Education: MS, PhD, Pharmaceutical Chemistry, University of Florida; BS, Pharmacy, University of Cincinnati
Background: President and Chief Executive Officer, Cytogen Corporation, J&J Co.; Group Chairman, Vice President, J&J International; President and Chairman, McNeil Pharmaceuticals
Directorships: Triplex Pharmaceutical Corporation, Enzymatics, Ohmicron, Mediventures, Gen Vec, CorBec Pharmaceutical

Charles G. Hadley, General Partner
Education: Phi Beta Kappa, George Washington University; MBA, JD, Stanford University
Background: Vice President, Cashon Biomedical Development; Vice President Corporate Development, Imatron; Business Development Consultant, Ghana, West Africa
Directorships: Intra-sonix, Ultracision, SpectRX, Fiberoptic Sensor Technology, Illumenex, Delaware Valley Venture Group, START Technology Partnership

Gary W. Cashon, PhD, General Partner
Education: BA, Biology, David Lipscomb College; PhD, Microbiology, Immunology, University of Missouri; Postdoctural work, Baylor
Background: President, Cashon Biomedical Development; Vice President Marketing and Planning, Centocor; Microbiology Systems Division, Becton Dickinson
Directorships: Cellcor, Intra-Sonix, CorBec Pharmaceuticals

Hal S. Broderson, MD, Associate General Partner
Education: Phi Beta Kappa, Indiana University; MD, University of Kentucky; MBA, Wharton; Gloeckner Award
Background: Director of Strategic Analysis and Planning, Smith Kline and French Labs; Co-Founder, Triplex Pharmaceuticals
Directorships: Gen Vec

HMS GROUP
One First Street, Suite 6
Los Altos, CA 94022

Telephone: 415-917-0390
Fax: 415-917-0394

Mission: The founders of HMS have years of experience in investing in and helping to build successful companies in the information industry, and industry relationships to make material contributions to early-stage companies in which they have invested.

Fund Size: $19 million
Founded: 1982
Average Investment: $1.5 million
Minimum Investment: $500,000

Investment Criteria: Seed, Startup, First-stage

Industry Group Preference: Computer Related, Electronics, High Technology, Software

Portfolio Companies: not available

Officers, Executives and Principals

Frank R. Atkinson, General Partner
Education: AB, Stanford; MBA, University of California at Los Angeles
Background: Continental Capital Corporation; Triad Venture Captial Corporation; Consultant, Thompson Clive and Partners;
Directorships: President and founder of the Western Association of Venture Capitalists

R.G. Grey, General Partner
Education: BS, MBA, University of California at Los Angeles; JD, University of San Francisco
Background: Founded Vidar Corporation Telecommunications Consulting firm (Transwitch) and Vanguard Venture Capital

Michael C. Hone, General Partner
Education: BS, JD, University of California
Background: Workout Expert; Faculty, University of San Francisco; Continental Capital Corporation; Founded first HMS Venture Capital Fund

HOOK PARTNERS

13760 Noel Road
Suite 705
Dallas, TX 75240

Telephone: 214-991-5457
Fax: 214-991-5458

Mission: Actively seeking new investments

Fund Size: $25 million
Founded: 1978
Average Investment: $100,000 - $250,000
Minimum Investment: $100,000

Investment Criteria: Seed, Startup

Industry Group Preference: Communications, Computer Related, Consumer, Distribution, Electronic Components and Instrumentation, Medical/Health Related

Portfolio Companies: Vitesse Semiconductor, Harmonic Lightwaves, Power Integrations, NetSolve, Clarify, Adaptive Solutions, TriQuint Semiconductors, Genta, IC Works, Wireless Access, MAXM Systems, VidaMed

Officers, Executives and Principals

David J. Hook, Partner
Background: Has invested in over 30 early-stage high-technology companies

John B. Hook, Partner
Background: Has invested in over 35 early-stage high-technology companies

Albert A. Augustus
Background: Has been in venture capital since 1968; Invested in nine venture capital funds; Monitored Hook Partner portfolio companies

INCO VENTURE CAPITAL MANAGEMENT

One New York Plaza
37th Floor
New York, NY 10004

Telephone: 212-612-5619
Fax: 212-612-5617

Mission: not available

Fund Size: $40 million
Founded: 1974
Average Investment: $500 - $1 million
Minimum Investment: $250,000

Investment Criteria: Second-stage, Mezzanine, Leveraged Buyout, Special Situations

Industry Group Preference: Biotechnology, Communications, Computer Related, Consumer, Distribution, Electronic Components and Instrumentation, Energy/Natural Resources, Genetic Engineering, Medical/ Health Related

Portfolio Companies: Immunogen, Hauston Biotechnology, Liant Software, Tartan, Xenova, Datamedia, ViraChem, TVSM Holdings, Nimbus Medical

Officers, Executives and Principals

Douglas A. Lindgren, President and Managing Principal

INMAN AND BOWMAN

1717 Embarcadero Roads, Suite 2000C
Palo Alto, CA 94303

Telephone: 415-493-8890
Fax: 415-424-8080

Other Office Locations
4 Orinda Way
Building D, Suite 150
Orinda, CA 94563
Phone 510-253-1611, Fax 510-253-9037

Mission: not available

Fund Size: $44 million
Founded: not available
Average Investment: $1 million
Minimum Investment: not available

Investment Criteria: Startup to Leveraged Buyout

Geographic Preference: Rocky Mountains region of the United States

Industry Group Preference: Biotechnology, Communications, Computer Related, Electronics, Energy/Natural Resources, High Technology, Industrial Products, Medical/Health

Portfolio Companies: not available

Officers, Executives and Principals

William B. Elmore, General Partner
D. Kirkwood Bowman, General Partner
Grant M. Inman, General Partner

INSTITUTIONAL VENTURE PARTNERS

3000 Sand Hill Road
Building 2, Suite 290
Menlo Park, CA 94025

Telephone: 415-854-0132
Fax: 415-854-5762

Mission: Lead investor in high technology ventures

Fund Size: $700 million
Founded: 1980
Average Investment: $1 - $4 million
Minimum Investment: not available

Investment Criteria: Seed, Second-stage, Late-stage, Public

Geographic Preference: Western United States and other areas selectively

Industry Group Preference: Biotechnology, Communications, High Technology, Medical/Health, Software

Portfolio Companies: Abaxis, Accordant Health Services, Adaptive Solutions, Agile Networks, Altera, Amati Communications, Applied Digital Access, Applied Medical Resources, Aptix Archive, Argonaut Technologies, Aristacom International, Ascent Logic, Aspect Telecommunications, Ateq, Athena Neurosciences, Atmel, Avalon Ventures, Aviron, Biometric Imaging, Biopsys Medical, Bridge Communications, Cardiac Pathways, Catalyst Ventures, Centillion Networks, Cemax-Icon, Cipher Data Products, Cirrus Logic, Clarify, Cogit, Collabra Software, Collagen, Conductus, Covalent Systems, Crescendo Communications, CV Therapeutics, Diffusion, Dominion Dental Services, Endosonics, Enzytech, eT Communications, Exabyte, Excite, Frequency Technology, FormFactor, GenPharm International, Genta, Glycogen, GolfWeb, GW Communications, HCM Claim Management, Heritage Court, Interconnectix, I.C. Works, IDUN Pharmaceuticals, Imagyn Medical, ImmuLogic Pharmaceutical, Integrated Medical Resources, Juniper Networks, KaPRE Software, Lightspan Partnership, LookingGlass Technologies, LSI Logic, MAXM Systems, Megabios, Menlo Care, Mercury Diagnostics, Metra Biosystems, Microcide Pharmaceuticals, Micropolis, MIPS Computer Systems, MMC Networks, Mpath Interactive, NeoCAD, NeoPath, Netiva, Netlabs, Netlink, NeTpower, Netrix Systems, Objectivity, Onyx Pharmaceuticals, Orquest, Pacific Monolithics, PercuSurge, Pharmacopeia, Platinum Software, Point Medical Polycom, Portable Software Prograft Medical, Quality Semiconductor, Rapid City Communications, Red Pepper Software, River Medical, Seagate Technology, Sequana Therapeutics, Sequent Computer Systems, Silicon Light Machines, Somatix Therapy, StarRidge Networks, Storm Primax, Stratus Computer, SuperMac Technology, Symyx Technologies Synernetics, SynOptics Communications, Teleos Communications, Trade Reporting and Data Exchange, Transmeta, Telcom Semiconductor, Therma-Wave, Tularik, Unify, Vadem, Viewstar, Vivid Semiconductor, Vivus, Wavespan, Wellfleet Communications, Whistle Communications, Whitetree, Wietek

Officers, Executives and Principals

Samuel D. Colella, General Partner
Education: BS, Business and Engineering, University of Pittsburgh; MBA, Stanford University
Background: President, Spectra-Physics; Senior Manager, Technical Products Division, Corning Glass
Directorships: Argonaut, CV Therapeutics, Imagyn, Integrated Medical Resources, IVAC, Pharmacopeia, Vivus

Reid W. Dennis, General Partner
Education: BS, Electrical Engineering, MBA, Stanford University
Background: President, American Express Investment Management Company; Manager, Investment Management Operations, Firemans' Fund Insurance Company
Directorships: Aviron, Cemax-Icon, NeTpower

Mary Jane Elmore, General Partner
Education: BS, Mathematics, Purdue University; MBA, Stanford University
Background: Sales Development, Technical Marketing, Product Management, Intel
Directorships: Clarify, Frequency Technology, Storm-Primax, Unify

Norman A. Fogelsong, General Partner
Education: BS, Industrial Engineering, Stanford University; JD, MBA, Harvard
Background: General Partner, The Mayfield Fund; McKinsey and Co.; Computer Programmer and Systems Analyst, Hewlett-Packard
Directorships: Aristacom, Aspect Telecommunications, I.C. Works, NeTpower, KaPRE Software, Objectivity, PenSoft, Portable Software

Ruth Quindlen, General Partner
Education: BS, Economics, Georgetown University; MBA, The Wharton School at University of Pennsylvania
Background: Managing Director, Alex, Brown and Sons
Directorships: Cogit, Diffusion, LookingGlass Technologies, Mpath Interactive, Netiva

L. James Strand, M.D., General Partner
Education: BA, MA, MD, University of California at San Francisco; MBA, Santa Clara University
Background: President, Advanced Marketing Decisions; Vice President of Medical Affairs and Director of Marketing Planning, Syntex Laboratories; Medical Director and Chairman of Product Assessment Committee, Alza; Chief Executive Officer and Director, DDI Pharmaceuticals; Chief Executive Officer and Director, Laserscope
Directorships: Accordant Health Services, Aviron, Dominion Dental, Heritage Court, Microcide Pharmaceuticals, Point Medical, Prograft

T. Peter Thomas, General Partner
Education: BS, Electrical Engineering, Utah State University; MS, Computer Science, University of Santa Clara
Background: Director of Marketing, OEM Memory Systems Division of Intel Corporation; Engineer, Sylvania EDL and Fairchild Communications
Directorships: Adaptive Solutions, Applied Medical Resources, Ascent Logic, Amtel Corporation, eT Communications, Form Factor, Mediamatics, IC Works, Silicon Light Machines, Telcom Semiconductor, Transmeta, Vadem, Vivid

Geoffery Y. Yang, General Partner
Education: BSE, Information Systems Engineering; BA, Economics, Princeton; MBA, Stanford
Background: Associate, First Venture Partners; System Engineer and Marketing Representative, IBM Corporation; Associate, Goldman Sachs
Directorships: Excite, GolfWeb, GW Communications, MMC Networks, Netlink, StarRidge Networks, Wavespan, Whistle Communications, Whitetree

INTERNATIONAL TECHNOLOGY

237 Park Avenue
Suite 801
New York, NY 10017

Telephone: 212-692-3680
Fax: 212-692-3685

Mission: not available

Fund Size: $41 million
Founded: not available
Average Investment: $500,000
Minimum Investment: not available

Investment Criteria: First-stage, Second-stage

Industry Group Preference: Communications, Computer Related, Electronics, High Technology, Software

Portfolio Companies: not available

Officers, Executives and Principals

Alexandra Glurglu, President
Jeanne M. Sullivan, Vice President
Roclo M. Proano, Manager

INTERSOUTH PARTNERS

1000 Park 40 Plaza, Suite 290
Durham, NC 27713

Telephone: 919-544-6473
Fax: 919-544-6645

Other Office Locations
3001 United Founders Boulevard
Oklahoma City, OK 73112
Phone 405-843-7890, Fax 405-843-8048

Mission: not available

Fund Size: $50 million
Founded: 1985
Average Investment: $1 - $4 million
Minimum Investment: not available

Investment Criteria: Startup to Second-stage

Industry Group Preference: Biotechnology, Computer Related, Energy/Natural Resources, Environmental
  Protection, High Technology, Information Services, Medical/Health, Software

Portfolio Companies: not available

Officers, Executives and Principals

Dennis J. Dougherty, Founder and General Partner
Roy O. Rodwell, Founder and General Partner
Mitch Mumma, General Partner
Greg Main, Partner

JOHNSTON ASSOCIATES

181 Cherry Valley Road
Princeton, NJ 08540

Telephone: 609-924-3131
Fax: 609-683-7524

Mission: not available

Fund Size: $40 million
Founded: 1968
Average Investment: $1 million
Minimum Investment: not available

Investment Criteria: Seed, Leveraged Buyout

Geographic Preference: Northeastern United States

Industry Group Preference: Biotechnology, Medical Devices, Pharmaceuticals

Portfolio Companies: Sepracor, Inc., i-Stat Corporation, SEQ Ltd., A-Company Orthodontics, HemaSure, Inc., BioSepra, Inc., Ecogen, Inc., Environgen, Inc., Versicro, Inc., Cytogen Corporation

Officers, Executives and Principals

Robert F. Johnston, President
Education: BA, Princeton; MBA, New York University
Background: F.S. Smithers and Co., Smith Barney and Co.
Directorships: I-Stat Corporation, Envirogen, Inc., SEQ, Immunicon Corporation

Richard G. Horan, Vice President
Education: AB, Dartmouth; MBA, Amos Tuck School at Dartmouth
Background: Corporate Finance Capital Markets Group, Bank of America; Co-Founder, SEQ Ltd.

Robert B. Stockman, Vice President
Education: AB, Harvard University; MBA, Amos Tuck School at Dartmouth
Background: Investment Analyst, Narragansett Capital Corporation; Accountant, Price Waterhouse

KLEINER PERKINS CAUFIELD AND BYERS

2750 Sand Hill Road
Menlo Park, CA 94025

Telephone: 415-233-2750
Fax: 415-233-0300

Other Office Locations
Four Embarcadero Center
San Francisco, CA, 94111
Phone 415-421-3110, Fax 415-421-3128

Mission: not available

Fund Size: $500 million
Founded: not available
Average Investment: $3 million
Minimum Investment: not available

Investment Criteria: Seed, Startup

Geographic Preference: West Coast of the United States

Industry Group Preference: Biotechnology, Communications, Computer Related, Electronics, High Technology, Information Services, Medical/Health

Portfolio Companies: Arris Pharmaceuticals, Athena Neurosciences, Biosurface Tech, Genetech, Genat, Geron, Blycomed, IDEC, InSite Vision, Onyx, Penederm, America On-line, Kalpana, Shiva, American Superconductor, Aptix, Cadre, Silicon Comiler, AOT Corporation, Cypress Semiconductor, LSI Logic

Officers, Executives and Principals

E. Floyd Kvamme, General Partner
Regis McKenna, General Partner
Bernard Lacroute, Venture Partner
Alexander E. Barkas, Partner
Brook H. Byers, Partner
Doug MacKenzie, Partner
James P. Lally, Partner
Kevin R. Compton, Partner

LANDMARK PARTNERS

920 Hopmeadow Street
P.O. Box 188
Simsbury, CT 06070

Telephone: 860-951-9760
Fax: 860-651-8890

Other Office Locations
660 Madison Avenue, 23rd Floor
New York, NY 10021
Phone 212-754-0411, Fax 212-754-1494

Mission: not available

Fund Size: $300 million
Founded: not available
Average Investment: $1 million
Minimum Investment: not available

Investment Criteria: Seed to Mezzanine

Industry Group Preference: Biotechnology, Communications, Computer Related, Electronics, High Technology, Industrial Products, Medical/Health, Software

Portfolio Companies: not available

Officers, Executives and Principals

Brent R. Nicklas, General Partner
Stanley F. Alfeld, President
John A. Griner, Executive Vice President
Thomas K. Sweeny, Vice President
Timothy L. Haviland, Vice President

LAWRENCE, TYRRELL, ORTALE AND SMITH

3100 West End Avenue, Suite 500
Nashville, TN 37203-1304

Telephone: 615-383-0982
Fax: 615-269-0463

Other Office Locations
Richland Ventures
3100 West End Avenue
Suite 400
Nashville, TN 37203-1304

Mission: not available

Fund Size: $115 million
Founded: not available
Average Investment: $1 million
Minimum Investment: not available

Investment Criteria: not available

Geographic Preference: Eastern, Southern, Southwestern United States

Industry Group Preference: Communications, Computer Related, Educational, Environmental Protection, Medical/Health, Service Industries, Software, Transportation

Portfolio Companies: not available

Officers, Executives and Principals

Jack Tyrrell, General Partner
W. Patrick Ortale III, General Partner
Michael Blackburn, General Partner
John Chadwick, General Partner

LOUISIANA SEED CAPITAL CORPORATION

339 Florida Street
Suite 525, P.O. Box 3435
Baton Rouge, LA 70821

Telephone: 504-383-1508
Fax: 504-383-1513

Mission: not available

Fund Size: $14.3 million
Founded: not available
Average Investment: $500,000
Minimum Investment: not available

Investment Criteria: Seed to Mezzanine

Geographic Preference: Louisiana

Industry Group Preference: Biotechnology, Communications, Consumer Related, Electronics, Energy/Natural Resources, Industrial Products, Medical/Health

Portfolio Companies: not available

Officers, Executives and Principals

Kevin Couhig, President
Greg Naquin, Executive Vice President
Carol Perrin, Assistant Vice President

MARQUETTE VENTURE PARTNERS

520 Lake Cook Road
Suite 450
Deerfield, IL 60015

Telephone: 847-940-1700
Fax: 847-940-1742

Mission: not available

Fund Size: $189 million
Founded: not available
Average Investment: $500,000 - $5 million
Minimum Investment: not available

Investment Criteria: Early to Later-stage

Geographic Preference: Midwestern United States

Industry Group Preference: Biotechnology, Computer Related, High Technology, Information Services, Medical/Health

Portfolio Companies: Advanced Rehabilitation Resources, Afferon, Exogen, Biostar, Cirrus Diagnostics, Collagenex, Genetic Design, Immtech International, Medvest, Oaktree Health Plan, Palindrome Corporation, Power Trends, Republic Telcom Systems, Tro Learning, Wynstar, Bizmart, Naegele Outdoor Advertising, Sports Authority

Officers, Executives and Principals

James E. Daverman, General Partner
Education: University of Michigan; MBA, Wharton
Background: First Chicago Venture Capital; General Partner, Wind Point Partners; Vice President, Asset Management Group, First National Bank of Chicago

John Patience, General Partner
Education: BA, JD; MBA, Wharton
Background: McKinsey and Co.

Lloyd D. Ruth, General Partner
Education: BS, Industrial Engineering, Cornell University; MS, Computer Science, Naval Post Graduate School; MBA, Stanford
Background: Sprout Group of Donaldson, Lufkin and Jenrette, Inc., Progressive Casualty Insur ice Co.

Andrew Morley, Partner
Education: BS, Electrical Engineering, Yale University; MBA, Harvard Business School
Background: Hill Carman Ventures, Ameritech, Digital Communications Associates, Lotus evelopment, IBM

James R. Simons, Partner
Education: BA, Economics and History, MBA, Northwestern
Background: First Boston Corporation, Trammell Crow Company

Keith M. Kerman, M.D., Partner
Education: M.D., Brown University; MBA, Wharton School at University of Pennsy. ania
Background: U.S. Healthcare, Hospital of University of Pennsylvania, Hospital at University of Cincinnati

MASSACHUSETTS TECHNOLOGY DEVELOPMENT FUND

148 State Street
Boston, MA 02109

Telephone: 617-723-4920
Fax: 617-723-5983

Mission: not available

Fund Size: $15 million
Founded: not available
Average Investment: $250,000
Minimum Investment: not available

Investment Criteria: Seed to Second-stage

Geographic Preference: Massachusetts

Industry Group Preference: Biotechnology, Broadcast/Cable/Radio, Communications, Computer Related, Defense, Environmental Protection, High Technology, Industrial Products, Information Services, Medical/Health, Software

Portfolio Companies: Aspen Technology, AudioFile, College Counsel, Component Software, Interleaf, Symbiotics, Display Components, XYlogics, Kronos Inc., AMDEV, Inc., EXOS, ABOVO, Optical MicroSystems, Voicetek, Millitech, Falcon Detection Technologies

Officers, Executives and Principals

John F. Hodgman, President
Robert Crowley, Executive Vice President

MATRIX PARTNERS

One International Place
Suite 3250
Boston, MA 02110

Telephone: 617-890-2244
Fax: 617-890-2288

Other Office Locations
2500 Sand Hill Road, Suite 113
Menlo Park, CA 94025
Phone 415-854-3131, Fax 415-854-3296

Mission: Actively seeking new investments

Fund Size: $195 million
Founded: 1982
Average Investment: $1 million
Minimum Investment: $500,000

Investment Criteria: Startup, First-stage, Second-stage, Mezzanine, Leveraged Buyout

Industry Group Preference: Communications, Computer Related, Electronic Components and Instrumentation, Genetic Engineering, Medical/Health Related

Portfolio Companies: not available

Officers, Executives and Principals

Timothy A. Barrows, General Partner (Boston)
Paul J. Ferri, General Partner (Boston)
Frederick K. Fluegel, General Partner (Menlo Park)
W. Michael Humphreys, General Partner (Boston)
Andrew Marcuvitz, General Partner (Boston)
Joseph D. Rizzi, General Partner (Menlo Park)
Andrew W. Verhalen, General Partner (Menlo Park)

MBW VENTURE CAPITAL

350 Second Street
Los Altos, CA 94022

Telephone: 415-941-2392
Fax: 415-941-2865

Other Office Locations
365 South Street
Morristown, NJ 07960
Phone 201-285-5533, Fax 201-285-5108

Mission: not available

Fund Size: $150 million
Founded: not available
Average Investment: $1 million
Minimum Investment: not available

Investment Criteria: not available

Industry Group Preference: Biotechnology, Communications, High Technology, Medical/Health

Portfolio Companies: Alexon Biomedical, Athena Neuro Sciences, Managed Care Associates, Datawatch Corporation, Intermedia Communications

Officers, Executives and Principals

James R. Weersing, Managing Director
Education: Mechanical Engineering, MBA, Stanford University
Background: Founding Partner of MBW; Founder several health care companies
Directorships: Sensor Medics, Birtcher, Lifescan, Sequoia, Sutter, Elgar Electronics, Applied Technology Labs, Gelman Sciences

Philip E. McCarthy, Managing Director
Education: BS, JD, Cornell University
Background: Co-founded several biotech companies;10 years venture capital experience, buyout experience
Directorships: California Biotechnology, Inc., Immunogen, Inc., Liposome Inc., Plant Genetics, Inc., Oximetrix, Availl, Inc.

Richard M. Goff, General Partner
Education: CPA, MBA, magna cum laude, Alma College
Background: Founding member MBW; Vice President, Chief Financial Officer, Venture Capital Funds, Michigan Investment Fund, Doan Associates
Directorships: Better Entertainment Cable

Lawrence A. Brown, Principal
Education: BA, English Literature, Premedical Science, University of Pennsylvania
Background: Senior Executive, SmithKline Corporation
Directorships: Continental Capital Corporation, Biogrowth, Cemax, Immunodiagnostics

Thomas A. Tisch, Principal
Education: MS, MBA, Stanford University; Post-graduate Biomedical Engineering
Background: President, Mesa Ventures, Inc., Hueristics Inc.; Management and Investment in computer, tele-
 communications, software fields
Directorships: Software publishing company

Judith L. Sosinski, Treasurer, Controller
Education: Engineering Science, Mathematics, Biology, Cleveland State University

MED TECH VENTURES

201 Tabor Road
Morris Plains, NJ 07950

Telephone: 201-540-6212
Fax: 201-540-2119

Mission: Actively seeking new investments

Fund Size: $20 million
Founded: 1983
Average Investment: $500,000 - $10 million
Minimum Investment: $250,000

Investment Criteria: Seed to Initial Public Offering; human therapeutic focus, revenues not required

Industry Group Preference: Biotechnology, Genetic Engineering, Medical/Health

Portfolio Companies: not available

Officers, Executives and Principals

Fred G. Weiss, President
Education: BA, University of Pennsylvania; MBA, University of Chicago
Background: Vice President, Planning, Investment and Development, Warner-Lambert Co.; Vice President, Treasurer, Warner Lambert Co.

Marilyn Hartig, PhD, Vice President

Wendell Wierenga, PhD, Vice President

MEDICAL SCIENCE PARTNERS

20 William Street
Suite 250
Wellesley, MA 02181-4102

Telephone: 617-739-4813
Fax: 617-277-0113

Mission: not available

Fund Size: $36 million
Founded: not available
Average Investment: $250,000
Minimum Investment: not available

Investment Criteria: Seed to Second-stage

Industry Group Preference: Biotechnology, Medical/Health

Portfolio Companies: Ascent Pharmaceuticals, Diatech, Hybridon, Implemed, Light Sciences, Microsurge, Oravax

Officers, Executives and Principals

Dr. André L. Lamotte, Managing General Partner
Education: BS, Ecole Centrale Paris; MSc, ScD, MIT; MBA, Harvard
Background: General Manager, Merieux Institute; Marketing Manager, Sandoz Region III;. Business Development Manager, Sandoz Pharmaceutical Division; Corporate Engineer, Air Products and Chemicals

Joseph F. Lovett, General Partner
Education: BAS, Economics, University of Vermont; MBA, California State Polytechnic University
Background: Senior Vice President, Damon Biotechnology; Vice President, General Manager, two diagnostic businesses with Mallinckrodt; Marketing Manager, CR Bard, Inc.

MEDICUS VENTURE PARTNERS

2180 Sand Hill Road, Suite 400
Menlo Park, CA 94025

Telephone: 415-854-7100
Fax: 415-854-5700

Mission: not available

Fund Size: not available
Founded: not available
Average Investment: $1 million
Minimum Investment: not available

Investment Criteria: Seed to First-stage

Industry Group Preference: Biotechnology, Computer Related, Electronics, High Technology, Medical/ Health, Software

Portfolio Companies: Advanced Surgical Intervention, Inc., Anergen Corporation

Officers, Executives and Principals

Frederick J. Dotzler, General Partner
Education: BS, Industrial Engineering, Iowa State University; MBA, University of Chicago; MA, Economics, University of Louvain, Belgium
Background: General Partner, Crosspoint Venture Partners; Vice President, Marketing and Sales, Merrimack Laboratories; Director of Marketing, Millipore

John M. Reher, General Partner
Education: MA, Management, Northwestern University; BS, Mathematics, Business Economics, Illinois Benedictine College
Background: Director, Genentech; Financial Analyst, Manager, Director, GD Searle

MEDVENTURE ASSOCIATES

4 Orinda Way, Building D, Suite 150
Orinda, CA 94563

Telephone: 510-253-0155
Fax: 510-253-9037

Mission: not available

Fund Size: $12 million
Founded: not available
Average Investment: $500,000
Minimum Investment: not available

Investment Criteria: Seed to First-stage

Geographic Preference: Western United States

Industry Group Preference: Biotechnology, Medical/Health

Portfolio Companies: not available

Officers, Executives and Principals

Annette Campbell-White, Managing General Partner
Henry M. Weinert, Partner
John C. Klock, Partner
Robert L. Green, Partner

MENLO VENTURES

3000 Sand Hill Road, Building #4, Suite 100
Menlo Park, CA 94025

Telephone: 415-854-8540
Fax: 415-854-7059
E-mail: dubose@menlo.ventures.com

Mission: To provide long-term capital and management support to early-stage and emerging growth companies

Fund Size: $710 million
Founded: 1976
Average Investment: $4 million
Minimum Investment: $1 million

Investment Criteria: Seed to Later-stage

Geographic Preference: United States

Industry Group Preference: Biotechnology, Communications, Computer Related, Healthcare Services, Medical Devices, Software

Portfolio Companies: Ascend Communications, Asyst Technologies, Gilead Sciences, UUNet Technologies, InfoSeek, Evolutionary Technologies, HNC Software, Matrix Pharmaceutical, Clarify, Red Brick, EndoVascular Technologies

Officers, Executives and Principals

H. Dubose Montgomery, General Partner
Education: BS, MS, Electrical Engineering, BS, Management Science, MIT; MBA, Harvard
Background: Research, Bell Laboratories

Thomas H. Bredt, General Partner
Education: BS, Science Engineering, University of Michigan; MEE, Electrical Engineering, New York University; Ph.D., Computer Science, Stanford
Background: Senior Vice President and Director, Information Systems Group, Dataquest Inc. Hewlett Packard, Bell Laboratories; Electrical Engineering Faculty, Stanford

Douglas C. Carlisle, General Partner
Education: BS, Electrical Engineering, University of California at Berkeley; JD, MBA, Stanford
Background: Design Engineer, ROLM Corporation

John W. Jarve, General Partner
Education: BS, MS, Electrical Engineering, MIT; MBA, Stanford University
Background: Charles Stark Draper Laboratory at Harvard Medical School, Booz, Allen and Hamilton, Intel Corporation

Michael D. Laufer, M.D., General Partner
Education: BS, Bioengineering, University of Colorado; MD, Stanford University School of Medicine
Background: Medical Director, Emergency Medicine, University of California at San Francisco, Mount Zion Medical Center; Faculty, University of California at San Francisco and Stanford University

Sonja L. Hoel, General Partner
Education: BS, Commerce, University of Virginia; MBA, Harvard University Graduate School of Business
Background: Associate, Edison Venture Fund; Business Development, Symantec Corporation; Investment Analyst, TA Associates

MERRILL, PICKARD, ANDERSON AND EYRE

2480 Sand Hill Road
Suite 200
Menlo Park, CA 94025

Telephone: 415-854-8600
Fax: 415-854-0345

Mission: Committed to investing in early-stage information technology companies

Fund Size: $285 million
Founded: not available
Average Investment: $750,000 - $3.5 million
Minimum Investment: not available

Investment Criteria: Seed to Second-stage

Geographic Preference: United States

Industry Group Preference: Biotechnology, Computer Related, Electronics, High Technology

Portfolio Companies: Applied Digital Access, Aspect Telecommunications, Bridge Communications, Grand Junction Networks, Kalpana, American Online, The Learning Company, ProTools, PureSoftware

Officers, Executives and Principals

Bruce W. Dunlevie, General Partner
Education: BA, History, Rice University; MBA, Stanford
Background: Vice President and General Manager Personal Computer Systems Division, Everex Systems; Investment Banker, Goldman Sachs and Co.
Directorships: WAVC, Chromatic Research, GeoWorks, Kalpana, Rambus

James C. Anderson, General Partner
Education: MBA, Stanford; BSEE, MSEE, Purdue University
Background: Marketing and Management, Hewlett-Packard; Design Engineer, Beckman Instruments; WAVC; National Venture Capital Association
Directorships: Auspex Systems, Kalpana, Network Computing Devices, Network Equipment Technologies

Kathryn C. Gould, General Partner
Education: MBA, University of Chicago; BSc, Physics, University of Toronto
Background: Executive Recruiter; Vice President Marketing, Oracle Corporation; Marketing Engineering, Finance, and Strategic Planning, Data Systems Design, Gould
Directorships: Applied Digital Access, Grand Junction Networks, Primary Access, Rocket Science Games

Steven Merrill, General Partner
Education: MBA, Wharton; BA, Sociology, Stanford
Background: President, Bank of America's Venture Capital Group
Directorships: WAVC, National Venture Capital Association, Red Pepper Software, Maxim Integrated Products

Theodore R. Meyer, Chief Financial Officer
Education: MBA, Stanford, Arjay Miller Scholar; BA, Economics, Stanford
Background: Chief Financial Officer, Priam, Silicon Solutions, Trademark Software; Financial Management, Hewlett-Packard, Price Waterhouse

MK GLOBAL VENTURES
2417 East Bayshore Road, Suite 520
Palo Alto, CA 94303

Telephone: 415-424-0151
Fax: 415-493-2753

Mission: not available

Fund Size: $65 million
Founded: not available
Average Investment: $2 million
Minimum Investment: not available

Investment Criteria: Startup to Later-stage

Industry Group Preference: Communications, Computer Related, High Technology, Information Services, Software

Portfolio Companies: Proxim, Hypermedia Communications, Spinergy, Semitest, Cross Access, Stratege, Lanquest, NetFrame

Officers, Executives and Principals

Michael D. Kaufman, Managing General Partner
Education: MS, Polytechnic University of New York
Background: Oak Investment Partners

Austin Grose, Chief Financial Officer
Education: MBA, Thunderbird
Background: Arthur Anderson and Co.

Greg Lahann, General Partner
Education: BS, San Jose State
Background: Price Waterhouse

Rigdon Currie, General Partner
Education: BS, Georgia Institute of Technology; MBA, Harvard
Background: Xerox

Susan Kaufman, General Partner
Education: MA, New York University
Background: Vice President, Save Warmblod and Associates

MOHR, DAVIDOW VENTURES

3000 Sand Hill Road, Building #1, Suite 240
Menlo Park, CA 94025

Telephone: 415-854-7236
Fax: 415-854-7365

Mission: not available

Fund Size: $147 million
Founded: not available
Average Investment: $500,000
Minimum Investment: not available

Investment Criteria: Seed to Second-stage

Industry Group Preference: Biotechnology, Communications, Computer Related, Electronics, Medical/Health, Service Industries, Software

Portfolio Companies: Actel Corporation, Auspex Systems, Cardia Pathways, Cardiovascular Imaging, CATS Software, ChemTrak Inc., Coactive Computing, Kalpana, Knowledge Adventure, Logic Modeling, Neurobiological Technologies, Power Integrations

Officers, Executives and Principals

Jonathan D. Feiber, General Partner
Education: BA, Computer Science, University of Colorado
Background: Vice President Networking, Sun Microsystems, Inc.; Director, Software Engineering Technologies, Amdahl Corporation

Lawrence G. Mohr, Jr., General Partner
Education: BS, Engineering, Cornell University; MS, Engineering, MBA, Stanford; CPA
Background: Partner, Hambrecht and Quist; Vice President, Bank of America Capital Corporation

Peter A. Roshko, General Partner
Education: BS, Industrial Engineering, Stanford; MBA, Harvard
Background: Consultant, Arthur Anderson and Co.'s Management Information Consulting Group; Consultant, Pittiglio, Rabin, Todd and McGrath

William H. Davidow, General Partner
Education: PhD, Electrical Engineering, Stanford University; AB, MS, summa cum laude, Dartmouth College
Background: Senior Vice President Marketing and Sales and Vice President of Microcomputer Divisions, Intel Corporation

MONTANA SCIENCE AND TECHNOLOGY ALLIANCE

46 North Last Chance Gulch, Suite 2B
Helena, MT 59620

Telephone: 406-444-2778
Fax: 406-444-1585

Mission: Actively seeking new investments

Fund Size: $12.5 million
Founded: 1985
Average Investment: $350,000
Minimum Investment: $100,000

Investment Criteria: Seed, Start-up, First-stage, Second-stage, Mezzanine

Geographic Preference: Montana

Industry Group Preference: Computer Related, Electronics, Technology, Information Services, Medical/Health

Portfolio Companies: Nurture Biotech, Lattice Materials Corporation, TMA/Schmitt, Ultrafem, Gateway Software, Optima, Mycotech, Chromatochem, Positive Systems, Inc., Northern Rockies Venture Fund, Glacier Venture Fund, Keep It Simple Systems

Officers, Executives and Principals

David P. Desch, Senior Investment Manager
Bobbie Dixon, Investment Manager

MONTGOMERY MEDICAL VENTURES

600 Montgomery Street
San Francisco, CA 94111

Telephone: 415-627-2451
Fax: 415-627-2054

Mission: Making few, if any, new investments

Fund Size: $136 million
Founded: 1984
Average Investment: $500,000
Minimum Investment: not available

Investment Criteria: Seed to First-stage

Industry Group Preference: Biotechnology, Medical/Health

Portfolio Companies: not available

Officers, Executives and Principals

Dr. Richard D. Propper, Managing General Partner
Leslie Huang, Chief Financial Officer
Dr. Stephen J. Sogin, General Partner
Jack Olshansky, General Partner
Stephen Weiss, General Partner
Alan Kittner, Limited Partner
Peter Yorke, Limited Partner

MORGAN STANLEY VENTURE PARTNERS

1251 Avenue of the Americas
New York, NY 10020

Telephone: 212-703-6981
Fax: 212-703-7951

Other Office Locations
555 California Street
San Francisco, CA 94104
Phone 415-576-2344, Fax 415-576-2099

Mission: not available

Fund Size: $200 million
Founded: not available
Average Investment: $3 - $10 million
Minimum Investment: not available

Investment Criteria: Second-stage to Leveraged Buyout

Industry Group Preference: Biotechnology, High Technology, Medical/Health

Portfolio Companies: AutoImmune Genetics Institute, Neurex, Archive, Aspect Telecommunications, MAXM Systems, Netlink, Silicon Compiler Systems, Managed Health Network, Nellco, Linear Technology, Cadre Technology, Sequent Computer

Officers, Executives and Principals

Guy L. de Chazal, General Partner
Education: BSME, Manchester, England; MBA, Harvard
Background: Citicorp Venture Capital, McKinsey and Co.

Fredric W. Harman, General Partner (NY)
Education: BSEE, MSEE, Stanford; MBA, Harvard
Background: Huges Communications

Robert J. Loarie, General Partner (CA)
Education: BS, Illinois Institute of Technology; MBA, Harvard
Background: Weiss, Peck and Greer

Andrew C. Cooper, Vice President
Education: BA, BS, Duke

Scott S. Halsted, Vice President
Education: AB, BE, Dartmouth; MM, Northwestern
Background: Intermedics Orthopedics, Hexcel Medical

Virginia M. Turezyn, Vice President
Education: BA, Queens College
Background: Ernst and Whiney

M. Fazle Husain, Associate
Education: BSChE, Brown; MBA, Harvard
Background: Corporate Finance, Morgan Stanley; The Boston Consulting Group

MORGENTHALER VENTURES

700 National City Bank Building
Cleveland, OH 44114

Telephone: 216-621-3070
Fax: 216-621-2817

Other Office Locations
2730 Sand Hill Road, #280
Menlo Park, CA 94025
Phone 415-233-7600, Fax 415-233-7606

Mission: not available

Fund Size: $275 million
Founded: 1968
Average Investment: $3 - $5 million
Minimum Investment: $500,000

Investment Criteria: Startup to Leveraged Buyouts, Special Situations

Geographic Preference: United States

Industry Group Preference: Biotechnology, Communications, Hardware, Healthcare Services and Devices, Industrial Products, Information Technology, Software

Portfolio Companies: American Paper, Chrysalis, Censtor, Cytel, ProAir Services, Endgate, Gliatech, NeT-power, Applied Intelligent Systems, Premisys Communications, Perclose, Quick Logic, Ribozyme, Sequana, Vivo Software, Wastequip, Hypres, Inverness Castings Group, ReGenisys, Vical, Centennial Security Holdings, Informix, Medtronic, CardioThoracic Systems, Intrinsa, Molecular Applications Group

Officers, Executives and Principals

David T. Morgenthaler, Managing Partner
Education: BS, MS, Mechanical Engineering, MIT
Background: President and Chairman, National Venture Capital Association; President, Foseco
Directorships: Ribozyme

John D. Lutsi, General Partner
Education: BS, Youngstown State University; MBA, Loyola College
Background: Senior Vice President, Private Investments, Pitcairn Financial Management Group; Vice President Finance, Raymark Corporation, Carborundum Company
Directorships: American Paper, ProAir

Robert C. Bellas, Jr., General Partner
Education: BS, Engineering, U.S. Naval Academy; MBA, Stanford
Background: General Manager, Electronics Products Division of Gulf Oil; Marketing and Management, Acurex Corporation, EMI Therapy Systems
Directorships: Vical, CardioThoracic Systems, Molecular Applications Group

Robert D. Pavey, General Partner
Education: BS, Physics, William and Mary; MS, Metallurgical Engineering, Columbia; MBA, Harvard
Background: President, National Venture Capital Association; Management, Foseco
Directorships: AISI, Chrysalis, Endgate, Gliatech, Intrinsa

Gary J. Morgenthaler, General Partner
Education: BA, Harvard
Background: Founder, Chief Executive Officer, Ingres Corporation; McKinsey and Co.; Tymshare, Inc.; Stanford University
Directorships: Premisys, NeTpower, Molecular Applications Group

Paul S. Brentlinger, Partner
Education: BA, MBA, University of Michigan
Background: Senior Vice President, Corporate Finance, Vice President Corporate Development, Harris Corporation
Directorships: Hypres, Wastequip, Centennial Security Holdings, Inverness Castings Group

Peter G. Taft, Principal
Education: MBA, Harvard University, BA, Amherst College
Background: Corporate Finance Department, McDonald and Company Securities, Inc.
Directorships: American Paper Group, ProAir

G. Gary Shaffer, Partner
Education: BA, Engineering sciences, Dartmouth College; MBA, Stanford
Background: Consultant, Arthur D. Little, Inc.; Marketing Manager, Spectraphysics

Theodore A. Laufik, Chief Financial Officer and Partner
Education: BBA, MBA, Cleveland State University; CPA
Background: CPA and Chief Financial Officer of a real estate development firm; Touche Ross and Company

NEW YORK LIFE VENTURE CAPITAL

51 Madison Avenue
Suite 207
New York, NY 10010

Telephone: 212-576-4623
Fax: 212-576-8080

Mission: Actively seeking new investments

Fund Size: $511 million
Founded: 1982
Average Investment: $1 million
Minimum Investment: $500,000

Investment Criteria: Early-stage, First-stage; annual sales of $500,000

Geographic Preference: United States

Industry Group Preference: Biotechnology, Communications, Computer Related, Electronics, High Technology, Medical/Health, Software

Portfolio Companies: not available

Officers, Executives and Principals

Paul T. Smith, Senior Vice President
John L. Mattana, Investment Vice President
Philip A. Smith, Investment Vice President
Richard F. Drake, Investment Vice President
Dominique O. Sémon, Assistant Vice President

NEW YORK STATE SCIENCE AND TECH FUND

99 Washington Avenue, Suite 1730
Albany, NY 12210

Telephone: 518-473-9749
Fax: 518-473-6876

Mission: not available

Fund Size: $17 million
Founded: not available
Average Investment: $200,000
Minimum Investment: not available

Investment Criteria: Startup to Second-stage

Geographic Preference: New York

Industry Group Preference: Biotechnology, High Technology, Medical/Health

Portfolio Companies: Advanced Refractory Technologies, Amarel Precision Instruments, Array Analysis, Aspex Inc., Connectivite, Geotech, Hampshire Instruments, Holotek, Infrared Components, Tessera, Music Pen, United Biomedical

Officers, Executives and Principals

John Clannemea, Program Manager

NEWTEK VENTURES

3000 Sand Hill Road, Building #3, Suite 140
Menlo Park, CA 94025

Telephone: 415-854-9744
Fax: 415-854-9749

Other Office Locations
500 Washington Street, Suite 720
San Francisco, CA 94111
Phone 415-986-5711, Fax 415-986-4618

Mission: not available

Fund Size: $50 million
Founded: not available
Average Investment: $500,000
Minimum Investment: not available

Investment Criteria: not available

Geographic Preference: Rocky Mountains, West Coast of the United States

Industry Group Preference: Biotechnology, Communications, Computer Related, Electronics, High Technology, Information Services, Medical/Health, Software

Portfolio Companies: Cadnetix, Sutter Biomedical, Xoma Corporation, Itere, International Power Technology, Prometrix, Cypress Semiconductor, Lukens Corporation, Greyhawk Systems, Care Corporation, Sterile Products, Qume

Officers, Executives and Principals

John E. Hall, General Partner
Education: BS, Accounting, MBA, Finance, San Jose State University
Background: Chief Financial Officer, Vice President, Finance and Administration, Cadnetix, Newtek, Syntex, Intel; Wrote business plan for Apple Computer
Directorships: Basic Measuring Instruments

Peter Wardle, General Partner
Education: Dartmouth
Background: Managing Partner, HF Swift and Co.
Directorships: Quntel, Molectron, FAFCO, SED, Antekna, QC Corporation

ONE LIBERTY VENTURES

One Liberty Square
Boston, MA 02109

Telephone: 617-423-1765
Fax: 617-338-4362

Mission: not available

Fund Size: $100 million
Founded: not available
Average Investment: $500,000
Minimum Investment: not available

Investment Criteria: Seed to Second-stage

Industry Group Preference: Biotechnology, High Technology, Medical/Health

Portfolio Companies: ADRA Systems, Anesta, Computer Technology Corporation, Credence Systems, Cytyc, Elantec, Fusion Systems, IDEXX, Itran, Netlink, Spectra, AudiLogic, Boreas, CellCall

Officers, Executives and Principals

Daniel J. Holland, Managing General Partner
Education: BS, MIT; MBA, Harvard
Background: President, Massachusetts Capital Resource Co., First National Bank of Chicago, Boston; Vice President, American Research and Development; Engineer, TRW; Industrial Liaison Officer, MIT

Edwin Kania, General Partner
Education: AB, Physics, Dartmouth; MBA, Harvard
Background: Investment Officer, First Capital Corporation; General Manager, J. Cunningham; Research Associate, Agribusiness, Harvard Business School

Joseph T. McCullen, Jr., General Partner
Education: BA, Villanova
Background: McCullen Partners; Vice President, New England Life; Special Assistant to the President of US Assistant Secretary; US Navy; Merck and Co.

ONSET VENTURES

2490 Sand Hill Road
Menlo Park, CA 94025-6940

Telephone: 415-327-5470
Fax: 415-327-5488

Other Office Locations
8911 Capital of Texas Highway
Austin, TX 78759
Phone 512-349-2255, Fax 512-349-2258

Mission: Actively seeking new investments

Fund Size: $100 million
Founded: 1984
Average Investment: $500,000 - $3 million
Minimum Investment: not available

Investment Criteria: Seed and Early-stage

Industry Group Preference: Information and Medical Technology

Portfolio Companies: not available

Officers, Executives and Principals

Robert F. Kuhling, Jr., Partner
Education: MBA, Harvard; BA, Economics, Hamilton College
Background: Director of Design Automation Marketing, Sun Microsystems; Vice President and Manager, Electronics Design, Automation Business, GE; Calma

Terry L. Opdendyk, Partner
Education: BS, Michigan State University, Honors College; MS, Computer Science, Stanford University
Background: General Partner, Founder, Onset Venture Partnership; President, Visicorp; Executive, Intel; Manager, Hewlett Packard

Thomas E. Winter, Partner
Education: MS, Industrial Management, BS, Aeronautical Engineering, Georgia Institute of Technology

OREGON RESOURCE AND TECHNOLOGY FUND

4370 N.E. Halsey
Suite 233
Portland, OR 97213

Telephone: 503-282-4462
Fax: 503-282-2976
E-mail: wlembree@admin.ogi.edu

Mission: not available

Fund Size: $13 million
Founded: 1986
Average Investment: $250,000
Minimum Investment: not available

Investment Criteria: Seed to Startup

Geographic Preference: Oregon

Industry Group Preference: Biotechnology, Computer Related, Electronics, Energy/Natural Resources, Environmental Protection, High Technology, Industrial Products, Information Services, Manufacturing/Processing, Medical/Health, Software

Portfolio Companies: Cabana RV, Full Sail Ales, Oregon Dehydration, International Bioclinical, Virtual Corporation, Radisys Corporation, ELD Manufacturing, FEI Co., Anitvirals, Ralin Medical, Pacific, Basin Shelter Company, 3C Semiconductor, Cascade Oncogenics, PrintPaks, Sapient Health Network, Templex Technology

Officers, Executives and Principals

John Beaulieu, President
Education: BA, MA, University of Santa Clara
Background: Marketing and Financing, Ford Motor Co.; General Management Consulting, Arthur Young and Co.; Vice President, American Standard; Senior Vice President, American Bank Stationary; President, Steelcraft Corporation

Wayne Embree
Education: BA, Natural Sciences, MA, Urban and Regional Planning, University of Oregon
Background: Oregon Legislative Assembly; Consultant Marketing and Finance, Arizona Governors Office; Manager of Space Systems and Communication Operations, US Air Force

Doug Moore, Chief Financial Officer
Education: BA, Mathematics, Willamette University; MA, Industrial Administration, Carnegie-Mellon University
Background: Boise Cascade, Evans Products, Dow Chemical

OXFORD BIOSCIENCE PARTNERS II

315 Post Road West
Westport, CT 06880

Telephone: 203-341-3300
Fax: 203-341-3309

Other Office Locations
650 Town Center Drive, Suite 810
Costa Mesa, CA 92626
Phone 714-754-5719, Fax 714-754-6802

45 Milk Street, 9th Floor
Boston, MA 02109
Phone 617-457-5250, Fax 617-482-5931

Mission: Invests in SHO and early stage private financings.

Fund Size: $54 million
Founded: 1992
Average Investment: $500,00 - $3 million
Minimum Investment: not available

Investment Criteria: Return on Investment

Industry Group Preference: Biotechnology, Medical Devices, Medical Sciences

Portfolio Companies: Prizm, Geron, Vivus, OsteoArthritic Sciences, Human Genome Sciences, AVID, Collaborating Clinical Research, Colleciate Healthcare, Exelixis, Materni Care, Microioe, Quadramed, Ribogene, Ring, Senatics, Signal, Sosei, Terrapin, TomTec

Officers, Executives and Principals

Alan G. Walton, PhD, General Partner
Education: PhD, DSc, Nottingham University
Background: General Partner, Oxford Partners; President, University Genetics; Professor at Harvard, Case Western
Directorships: AVID, Collaborating Clinical Research, Exglixis, Human Genome Sciences, Senatics

Cornelius T. Ryan, General Partner (CA)
Education: BA, University of Ottawa; MBA, Wharton
Background: General Partner, Oxford Partners; President, Randolph Computers; Vice President, GTE
Directorships: MateriCare, QuadraMed, Ring

Edmund M. Olivier, General Partner (CT)
Education: BS, Rice University; MBA, Harvard
Background: General Partner, Fairfield Venture Partners; Vice President, Scientific Products Division of Corning Glass; Vice President, Diamond Shamrock
Directorships: Genset, Prizm, Sosgi, Terrapin

Jonathan Fleming, General Partner

PARAGON VENTURE PARTNERS

3000 Sand Hill Road, Building #2, Suite 190
Menlo Park, CA 94025

Telephone: 415-854-8000
Fax: 415-854-7260

Mission: not available

Fund Size: $70 million
Founded: not available
Average Investment: $2 million
Minimum Investment: not available

Investment Criteria: Seed to Second-stage

Industry Group Preference: Biotechnology, Communications, Computer Related, Environmental Protection, High Technology, Medical/Health, Software

Portfolio Companies: SynOptics Communications, Read-Rite Corporation, On Assignment, ReSound Corporation, Credence Systems, ParcPlace Systems, NetLabs Inc., TopoMetrix

Officers, Executives and Principals

John S. Lewis, General Partner
Education: BS, University of California at Berkeley; MBA, Harvard
Background: Vice President, Citicorp Venture Capital; Vice President, Citibank
Directorships: Seattle Silicon Technology, Inc.

Robert F. Kibble, General Partner
Education: MA, Oxford; MBA, University of Virginia
Background: Vice President, Citicorp Venture Capital; Vice President, Citibank/International Branch
Directorships: Doelz Networks

PATHFINDER VENTURE CAPITAL FUNDS

3000 Sand Hill Road, Suite 290, Building One
Menlo Park, CA 94025-7112

Telephone: 415-854-0650
Fax: 415-854-9010

Other Office Locations
7300 Metro Boulevard, Suite 585
Minneapolis, MN 55439-2310
Phone 612-835-8389, Fax 612-835-1121

Mission: not available

Fund Size: $98 million
Founded: not available
Average Investment: $500,000
Minimum Investment: not available

Investment Criteria: Startup to Later-stage

Geographic Preference: Upper Midwestern, Western States

Industry Group Preference: Computer Related, Medical/Health, Software

Portfolio Companies: not available

Officers, Executives and Principals

Barbara L. Santry, Investment Partner
Education: BS, Nursing, Georgetown University; MBA, Stanford
Background: Senior Vice President, Dain Bosworth; Vice President, Alex Brown and Sons; Hospital Strategic
  Planning, American Medical International; Arthur Anderson and Co.

Eugene J. Fischer, Investment Partner
Education: BS, University of Minnesota; MS, University of California at Davis
Background: General Partner, Technology Funding; Vice President, Bank of America's Sunnyvale Corporate
  Banking ZGroup

Andrew J. Greenshields, Investment Partner
Education: BS, University of Minnesota
Background: Co-founder, Pathfinder; Senior Vice President, First Midwest Capital Corporation; Contract
  Negotiation, Aerospace Division of Honeywell
Directorships: Board of Governors of National Association of Small Business Investment Companies

Brian P. Johnson, Investment Partner
Education: BS, University of South Dakota; MBA, University of St. Thomas
Background: Vice President, FBS Venture Capital Company; Mergers and Acquistions, International Multi-
  foods; President, Minnesota Venture Capital Association

Gary A. Stoltz, Investment Partner
Education: Case Institute of Technology, Northwestern University Graduate School of Management
Background: Founder and Officer, DATA 100; Field Management, Control Data

Jack K. Ahrens II, Investment Partner
Education: BS, Indiana University
Background: President, United Capital Corporation of Illinois

PEREGRINE VENTURES

12400 Wilshire Boulevard, Suite 230
Los Angeles, CA 90025

Telephone: 310-458-1441
Fax: 310-394-0771

Other Office Locations
20833 Stevens Creek Boulevard, Suite 102
Cupertino, CA 95104
Phone 310-996-7212, Fax 310-394-0771

Mission: not available

Fund Size: $44 million
Founded: 1981
Average Investment: $1.5 million
Minimum Investment: not available

Investment Criteria: Seed to Leveraged Buyout

Industry Group Preference: Biotechnology, Electronics, Information Services, Medical/Health, Telecommunications

Portfolio Companies: not available

Officers, Executives and Principals

Gene Miller, General Partner
Education: BS, JD, New York University; MBA, Harvard
Background: Principal, Xerox Development Corporation; Vice President, Security Pacific Venture Capital Group

Frank LaHaye, General Partner
Education: BS, Stanford University
Background: Principal, Xerox Development Corporation; Vice President, Teledyne Inc.

PIDC, PENN VENTURE FUND

1500 Market Street #2600 Center Square West
Philadelphia, PA 19102-2143

Telephone: 215-496-8020
Fax: 215-977-9618

Mission: not available

Fund Size: not available
Founded: not available
Average Investment: $200,000
Minimum Investment: not available

Investment Criteria: Seed to First-stage

Geographic Preference: Greater Philadelphia area

Industry Group Preference: Aerospace, Biotechnology, Communications, Computer Related, Electronics, Energy/Natural Resources, Environmental Protection, High Technology, Medical/Health

Portfolio Companies: not available

Officers, Executives and Principals

Ray Devlin

POLY VENTURES

901 Route 110
Farmingdale, NY 11735

Telephone: 516-249-4710
Fax: 516-249-4713

Mission: not available

Fund Size: $53 million
Founded: not available
Average Investment: $500,000
Minimum Investment: not available

Investment Criteria: Seed to First-stage

Industry Group Preference: Biotechnology, Communications, Computer Related, Electronics, Energy/Natural Resources, High Technology, Industrial Products, Medical/Health, Software

Portfolio Companies: not available

Officers, Executives and Principals

Dr. Robert M. Brill, Managing General Partner
Education: BS, Engineering Physics, BA, Physics, Phi Beta Kappa, Lehigh University; PhD, Physics, Brown University
Background: President and Chief Executive Officer, Algorex; Chairman and Chief Executive Officer, Hybrid Systems Corporation; Vice President and General Manager, Harris Corporation; CMOS Semiconductor Division, IBM

Dr. Shelley A. Harrison, Managing General Partner
Education: BS, Electrical Engineering, New York University; MS, PhD, Electrophysics, Polytechnic University
Background: Chairman and Chief Executive Officer, Symbol Technologies; President, Harrison Enterprises; Technical Staff, Bell Telephones; Professor, Electrical Sciences, State University New York Stoneybrook

Herman Fialkov, Managing General Partner
Education: BA, Administrative Engineering, New York University
Background: President, General Transistor Corporation, Geiger and Fialkov L.P., Aleph Null Corporation

Susanne Harrison, Managing General Partner
Education: BA, Hunter College; MA, State University New York, Stoneybrook; MBA, Adelphi University
Background: Symbol Technologies; Vice President, Harrison Enterprises; Vice President, Investment Banking, Steinberg and Lyman

PRINCE VENTURES

10 South Wacker Drive, Suite 2575
Chicago, IL 60606

Telephone: 312-454-1408
Fax: 312-454-9125

Other Office Locations
One Gorham Island
Westport, CT 06880
Phone 203-227-8332, Fax 203-226-5302

Mission: not available

Fund Size: $65 million
Founded: not available
Average Investment: $1 million
Minimum Investment: not available

Investment Criteria: Seed to Leveraged Buyout

Industry Group Preference: Biotechnology, Medical/Health

Portfolio Companies: not available

Officers, Executives and Principals

Angus M. Duthie, General Partner
Gregory F. Zaic, General Partner
James W. Fordyce, General Partner
Mark J. Gabrielson, General Partner

RAYTHEON VENTURES

141 Spring Street
Lexington, MA 02173

Telephone: 617-860-2270
Fax: 617-860-2691

Mission: not available

Fund Size: $25 million
Founded: not available
Average Investment: $500,000
Minimum Investment: not available

Investment Criteria: Startup to Second-stage

Industry Group Preference: Biotechnology, Communications, Computer Related, Electronics, Energy/Natural Resources, High Technology, Industrial Products, Medical/Health, Software

Portfolio Companies: not available

Officers, Executives and Principals

Samuel W. Tishler, Vice President
Daniel E. J. Gaudette, Business Manager

SAFEGUARD SCIENTIFICS

435 Devon Park Drive
800, The Safeguard Building
Wayne, PA 19087

Telephone: 215-293-0600

Mission: not available

Fund Size: $100 million
Founded: not available
Average Investment: $1 million
Minimum Investment: not available

Investment Criteria: Second-stage

Geographic Preference: Eastern United States

Industry Group Preference: Communications, Computer Related, Electronics

Portfolio Companies: not available

Officers, Executives and Principals

Gary J. Anderson, Executive Vice President
Walter W. Buckley, Acquisition Analyst

SANDERLING

2730 Sand Hill Road, Suite 200
Menlo Park, CA 94025

Telephone: 415-854-9855
Fax: 415-854-3648

Mission: not available

Fund Size: $60 million
Founded: not available
Average Investment: $250,000
Minimum Investment: not available

Investment Criteria: Seed to Early-stage

Industry Group Preference: Biotechnology, Medical/Health

Portfolio Companies: not available

Officers, Executives and Principals

Fred A. Middleton, General Partner
Education: BS, Chemistry, MIT; MBA, Harvard
Background: Consultant, McKinsey and Co.; Vice President, Chase Bank, New York; President, Genentech
  Development Corporation; Founded Morgan Stanley Ventures

Robert G. McNeil, PhD, General Partner
Education: PhD, Molecular Biology, Biochemistry, Genetics, University of California at Irvine
Background: Portfolio Manager, Shuman Agnew and Associates; Co-founder, Andron McNeil and Co.;
  Founder, Sanderling Venture Partners

Edward Kanner, Chief Financial Officer

SENMED VENTURES

4445 Lake Forest Drive, Suite 600
Cincinnati, OH 45242

Telephone: 513-563-3240
Fax: 513-563-3261

Mission: Actively seeking new investments and opportunities to initiate start-ups

Fund Size: $50 million
Founded: 1987
Average Investment: $750, 000 - $2 million
Minimum Investment: $750,000

Investment Criteria: Seed to Later-stages

Geographic Preference: United States

Industry Group Preference: Biotechnology, Medical/Health

Portfolio Companies: Arris Pharmaceutical Corporation, Biosite Diagnostics, Inc., Corvita Corporation, Electrochemical Drug Delivery, Focal, Inc., I-Flow Corporation, Luxar Corporation, MitoKor, Neoprobe Corporation, OrthoLogic Corporation, Spectranetics Corporation, Synaptic Pharmaceutical Corporation, Trimeris, Inc., Zynaxis, Inc.

Officers, Executives and Principals

Vincent Paglino, Vice President, Manager
Education: MS, Aerospace Engineering, MBA, Management and Finance
Background: Director, Research and Development and Strategic Marketing, private surgical products company; Director of Corporate Planning, Sencorp, General Electric, United Technologies
Directorships: I-Flow, Neoprobe

Suzette Dutch, Director, Planning and Business Analysis
Education: BS, Case Western Reserve University; MBA, Finance and Decision Science, Wharton
Background: Senior Market Analyst, SmithKline Beckman and French Labs

Clint 'Skip' Dederick, Group Director, Venture Projects
Education: BA, Chemistry and Biology, University of Delaware; MBA, Marketing, University of Virginia
Background: Vice President Marketing and Business Development, Praxis Biologics; Director of Marketing, Seragen, Inc. Biotech Consultant, Eli Lilly and Company
Directorships: OrthoLogic Corporation, Neoprobe Corporation, Secretech, Inc., Electrochemical Drug Delivery, Inc.

John Rice, Ph.D., Director, Medical Technology
Education: BS, Microbiology, MS, Ph.D., Microbiology, Virology, Ohio State University
Background: Manager, Biotech Section, Battelle Memorial Institute; Associate Professor, Microbiology, Ohio State University

Stephen Gailar, Group Director, Venture Projects
Education: BA, Indiana University; MS, Industrial Administration, Purdue University, Krannert School of Business
Background: Chief Executive Officer, The Marlstone Corporation; Vice President, Business Development, Bio-Response, Eli Lilly and Co.

Richard D'Augustine, Group Director, Venture Projects
Education: BSME, RPI: MBA, Seton Hall University
Background: Vice President, Business Development, Ethicon Endo-Surgery (Johnson and Johnson)
Directorships: Enable Medical Corporation

Dennis B. Costello, Group Director, Venture Projects
Education: BS, United States Naval Academy; MBA, Harvard Business School
Background: President and Chief Executive Officer, Clonetics Corporation; Vice President, American Critical Care; Hana Biologics; Regent Hospital Products

SEQUOIA CAPITAL
3000 Sand Hill Road, Building Four
Suite 280
Menlo Park, CA 94025

Telephone: 415-854-3927
Fax: 415-854-2977

Mission: not available

Fund Size: $400 million
Founded: not available
Average Investment: $500,000
Minimum Investment: not available

Investment Criteria: Seed to Mezzanine

Industry Group Preference: Biotechnology, Communications, Computer Related, Electronics, High Technology, Industrial Products, Medical/Health

Portfolio Companies: Atari, Apple, CADO Systems, Altos, Electronic Arts, Quarterdeck, Biotrack, Sierra Semiconductor, Vitesse Semiconductor, Magellan, Biosys, Shaman

Officers, Executives and Principals

Don Valentine, Founder
Background: Founder, National Semiconductor; Senior Sales and Marketing Executive, Fairchild Semiconductor
Directorships: LSI Logic, Electronic Arts, Altos, Pyramid Technology, Biotrack, Valid Logic; Chairman, Cisco Systems, Sierra Semiconductor, Central Point Software, Microchip

Douglas Leone, Partner
Education: Engineering, Cornell and Columbia; MS, Management, MIT
Background: Sun Microsystems, Hewlett-Packard, Prime Computer
Directorships: Arbor Software

Gordon Russell, Partner
Background: Vice President, General Manager, Syntex; Founding Vice President, General Manager, Coherent Medical; Chairman, Palo Alto Medical Foundation
Directorships: Total Pharmaceutical Care, Chemtrak, SnagStat Medical, Endovascular Technology, Biosym

Mark Stevens, Partner
Education: Engineering, University of Southern California; MBA, Harvard
Background: Intel; Test Equipment Engineer, Hughes Aircraft; Marketing Consultant, Electronic Designs
Directorships: TSSI, Aspect Development

Michael Moritz, Partner
Background: Time Warner; Founder, Technologic Partners; Authored books about Apple and Chrysler
Directorships: Global Village Communications, AppSoft

Pierre Lamond, Partner

SEVIN ROSIN FUNDS
13455 Noel Road, Suite 1670
Dallas, TX 75240

Telephone: 214-702-1100
Fax: 214-702-1103

Other Office Locations
550 Lytton Avenue
Suite 200
Palo Alto, CA 94301
Phone 415-326-0550, Fax 415-326-0707

Mission: not available

Fund Size: $300 million
Founded: 1981
Average Investment: $2 million
Minimum Investment: $500,000

Investment Criteria: Early to Startup

Geographic Preference: United States

Industry Group Preference: Biotechnology, Computer Related, Electronics, High Technology, Medical/ Health

Portfolio Companies: Compaq, Lotus, Cyrix, Convex, Cypress, Cyberonics, VTEL, Citrix Systems, Benchmarq Microelectronics, ArQule

Officers, Executives and Principals

John Jaggers, General Partner (Dallas)
Education: BA, MEE, Rice University, MBA, Harvard University
Background: Rotan Mosle

Charles Phipps, General Partner (Dallas)
Education: BSEE, Case; MBA, Harvard University
Background: Texas Instruments

Dennis Gorman, General Partner (Dallas)
Education: BS/MS, Computer Science, MIT; MBA, MIT
Background: Texas Instruments

Jon W. Bayless, General Partner (Dallas)
Education: BSEE, University of Oklahoma; MEE, University of Alabama; Ph.D., Electrical Engineering, Arizona State University
Background: Arthur A. Collins, E-Systems, Motorola

Stephen L Domenik, General Partner (Palo Alto)
Education: BA, Physics, MEE, University of California at Berkeley
Background: Weitek, Cyrix Corporation

Stephen M. Dow, General Partner (Palo Alto)
Education: BA, Economics, MBA, Stanford University
Background: Booz Allen and Hamilton

Jennifer Gill Roberts, General Partner (Palo Alto)
Education: BSEE, MBA, Stanford University; MEE, University of Texas at Austin
Background: Hewlett-Packard, Sun Microsystems

SUTTER HILL VENTURES

755 Page Mill Road, Suite A-200
Palo Alto, CA 94304-1005

Telephone: 415-493-5600
Fax: 415-858-1854

Mission: not available

Fund Size: $100 million
Founded: not available
Average Investment: $100,000 - $5 million
Minimum Investment: not available

Investment Criteria: Seed to Leveraged Buyout

Industry Group Preference: Biotechnology, Computer Related, Educational, High Technology, Medical/ Health

Portfolio Companies: Apollo Computer, Banyan Systems, Celeritek, COR Therapeutics, Diablo Systems, Dionex, Gemini Research, Ingres, Integrated Genetics, Interventional Technologies, LifeScan, Meaurex, Mentor Graphics, Quantum, Qume, Xidex

Officers, Executives and Principals

David L. Anderson, General Partner
Education: BS, Electrical Engineering, MIT; MBA, Harvard
Background: Watkins-Johnson
Directorships: Apollo Computer, Dionex, Cytel

G. Leonard Baker, Jr., General Partner
Education: BA, Mathematics, Yale; MBA, Stanford University
Background: Cummins Engine
Directorships: Lifescan, Weitek, Banyan Systems

Paul M. Wythes, General Partner
Education: BS, Mechanical Engineering, Princeton University; MBA, Stanford University
Background: Honeywell, Beckman Instruments
Directorships: Xidex, Tellabs, Stuart Medical

Tench Coxe, General Partner
Education: BA, Economics, Dartmouth; MBA, Harvard
Background: Digital Communications Associates, Lehman Brothers
Directorships: Edify Corporation, Primary Access Corporation, ArcSys, Inc.

William H. Younger, Jr., General Partner
Education: BS, Electrical Engineering, University of Michigan; MBA, Stanford University
Background: Cummins Engine, Hewlett-Packard
Directorships: Ingres, COR Therapeutics, Interventional Technologies

TECHNOLOGY FUNDING, INC.

2000 Alameda de las Pulgas, Suite 250
San Mateo, CA 94403

Telephone: 415-345-2200
Fax: 415-345-1797

Mission: not available

Fund Size: $300 million
Founded: not available
Average Investment: $1 million
Minimum Investment: not available

Investment Criteria: First Stage to Mezzanine

Industry Group Preference: Biotechnology, Communications, Computer Related, Electronics, Environmental Protection, High Technology, Medical/Health, Software

Portfolio Companies: not available

Officers, Executives and Principals

Charles R. Kokesh, Managing General Partner
Gregory T. George, General Partner
Thomas J. Toy, Partner
Peter Benardoni, General Partner

TECHNOLOGY LEADERS II, L.P.

435 Devon Park Drive
800, The Safeguard Building
Wayne, PA 19087-1945

Telephone: 610-971-1515
Fax: 610-975-9330

Other Office Locations
Boston
Phone 617-338-7171, Fax 617-338-7117

San Francisco
Phone 415-399-4569, Fax 415-576-3362

Mission: Actively seeking new investments

Fund Size: $113 million
Founded: 1994
Average Investment: $2 million
Minimum Investment: $1 million

Investment Criteria: First Stage to Mezzanine

Industry Group Preference: Biotechnology, Information Services, Information Technology, Medical/Health

Portfolio Companies: not available

Officers, Executives and Principals

Robert E. Keith, Jr., Chief Operating Officer
Education: BS, American History, Amherst; JD, Temple University
Background: Managing Director, Radnor Venture Partners; Various executive positions, Fidelity Bank
Directorships: Cambridge Tech Partners, Gandalf Technologies, Wave Technologies International, ACTS, Assessment Systems, Datamatix, Deven Resources, EMAX Solution Partners, Hamilton Lane

Chris Moller, Managing Director
Education: BA, Molecular Biology, Pomona College; PhD, Immunology, University of Pennsylvania School of Medicine
Background: Research Associate, City of Hope Research Institute; Post Doctoral Fellow, Roche Institute of Molecular Biology; Vice President, Radnor Venture

Gary J. Anderson, MD, Managing Director
Education: BS, Wayne State University; MD, University of Michigan; Post Doctoral Training, Internal Medicine, Cardiology, Biophysics, Indiana University
Background: Executive Vice President, Safeguard Scientifics; Professor of Medicine and Physiology, Associate Dean, Hanemann University School of Medicine; President, Biomedical Consulting Associates
Directorships: Micro Decisionware, Myco Pharmaceuticals, Tangram Systems, Laser Communications, Applied Technology Genetics, Datamatix, Technology Leaders, EMAX Solution Partners

Ira M. Lubert, Managing Director
Education: BS, Hotel Management, Pennsylvania State University
Background: Chairman, GF Management; Managing Director, Radnor Venture Partners; Vice President Aquisitions, Safeguard Scientifics; Combined Technologies; ITT; IBM
Directorships: CompuCom Systems, Deven Resources, Telemarketing Concepts, Applied Telematics, Alphatronix, Front Royal

Mark J. DeNino, Managing Director
Education: BS, Finance and Accounting, Boston College; MBA, Harvard
Background: President, CMS Corporate Finance, Inc.
Directorships: HELP Systems, Inc., EMAX Solution Partners, Inc.

TECHNOLOGY VENTURE INVESTORS

2480 Sand Hill Road, Suite 101
Menlo Park, CA 94025

Telephone: 415-854-7472
Fax: 415-854-4187

Mission: not available

Fund Size: $270 million
Founded: not available
Average Investment: $500,000 - $5 million
Minimum Investment: not available

Investment Criteria: First-stage to Leveraged Buyout

Geographic Preference: Western United States

Industry Group Preference: Biotechnology, Communications, Computer Related, Electronics, High Technology

Portfolio Companies: Adaptec, Altera, kArchive, Cadnetix, Cirrus Logic, Compaq, Cygnus Therapeutic, Linear Technology, Microsoft, Nellcor, Office Depot, Sierra Semiconductor, Sun Microsystems, Symantec, Synopsys, VeriFone, Vitalink, Walker Interactive, Zycad

Officers, Executives and Principals

Burton J. McMurtry, General Partner
Education: BA, BSEE, Rice University
Background: President, Palo Alto Investment Co.; General Partner, Institute Venture Partners; President, National Venture Capital Association, WAVC
Directorships: Cadnetix, Nellcor, VeriFone

David F. Marquardt, General Partner
Education: BSME, Columbia University; MSEE, MBA, Stanford
Background: Institutional Venture Associates; President, WAVC; Director, National Venture Capital Association and named "Venture Capitalist of the Year" Dataquest/Venture Magazine, 1987
Directorships: Adaptec, Archive, Microsoft, Sun Microsystems

Mark G. Wilson, General Partner
Education: BSChE, highest honors, University of California at Berkeley; JD, Stanford
Background: Pfizer Inc.; Vice President Administration and Chief Financial Officer, System Industries; Synapse Computer Corporation

Robert C. Kagle, General Partner
Education: Sobey Scholar; Mechanical, Electrical Engineering, General Motors Institute; MBA, Stanford
Background: Manager, Boston Consulting Group; Director, Vice President, WAVC
Directorships: Synopsys, XA Systems, Zycad

THOMPSON CLIVE, INC.

3000 Sand Hill Road
Building One, Suite 185
Menlo Park, CA 94025-7102

Telephone: 415-854-0314
Fax: 415-854-0670
E-mail: vc@internet.net

Other Office Locations

24 Old Bond Street
London W1X3DA
England
Phone 44-171-491-4809, Fax 44-171-493-9172

55, rue la Boetie
75008 Paris
France
Phone 33-1-4413-3606, Fax 33-1-4413-3746

Mission: Actively seeking new investments

Fund Size: $1 - $3 million
Founded: 1977
Average Investment: $1 - $5 million
Minimum Investment: $500,000

Investment Criteria: Startup, First-stage, Second-stage, Mezzanine, Leveraged Buyout, Special Situations

Industry Group Preference: Biotechnology, Communications, Computer Related, Distribution, Electronic Components and Instrumentation, Energy/Natural Resources, Genetic Engineering, High Technology, Industrial Products and Equipment, Medical/Health Related, Software

Portfolio Companies: not available

Officers, Executives and Principals

Peter Ziebelman, Managing Director (Menlo Park)
Education: BSc, Computer Science, Psychology, honors, Yale University; MS, Management, Stanford University; Sloan Fellow
Background: Marketing and Sales, Semiconductor Group of Texas Instruments, Ryan McFarland Corporation

Richard Thompson, Principal (London)

Colin Clive, Principal (London)

Michael Elias, Principal (Menlo Park and Paris)
Education: BA, honors, Biological Anthropology, Harvard University; MSx, Neurobiology, Cambridge University; Marshall Scholarship
Background: Founding Member, Neuroscience Limited

Greg Ennis, Principal (Menlo Park)
Education: AB, Economics, Political Science, Stanford; MBA, University of California at Los Angeles
Background: Citibank, Frankfurt, Germany

Robert E. Patterson, Principal (Menlo Park)

UTAH VENTURES

419 Wakara Way, Suite 206
Salt Lake City, UT 84108

Telephone: 801-583-5922
Fax: 801-583-4105

Mission: not available

Fund Size: $11 million
Founded: not available
Average Investment: $750,000
Minimum Investment: not available

Investment Criteria: Seed to First-stage

Geographic Preference: West Coast, Rocky Mountains region of the United States

Industry Group Preference: Biotechnology, Communications, Computer Related, Electronics, High Technology, Industrial Products, Medical/Health, Software

Portfolio Companies: not available

Officers, Executives and Principals

Allan M. Wolfe, General Partner
James C. Dreyfous, General Partner

VENKOL VENTURES

1100 Summer Street
Stamford, CT 06905

Telephone: 203-969-7400
Fax: 203-961-0120

Mission: not available

Fund Size: not available
Founded: not available
Average Investment: $1 million
Minimum Investment: not available

Investment Criteria: Startup to Leveraged Buyout

Industry Group Preference: Biotechnology, Medical/Health

Portfolio Companies: not available

Officers, Executives and Principals

M.S. Koly, President
Samuel Herschkowitz, Vice President

VENTURE CAPITAL FUND OF NEW ENGLAND

160 Federal Street, 23rd Floor
Boston, MA 02110

Telephone: 617-439-4646
Fax: 617-439-4652

Mission: not available

Fund Size: $80 million
Founded: 1981
Average Investment: $1 million
Minimum Investment: $500,000

Investment Criteria: Startup to Second-stage

Geographic Preference: Northeastern United States

Industry Group Preference: Biotechnology, Broadcast/Cable/Radio, Communications, Computer Related, Electronics, High Technology, Industrial Products, Information Services, Medical/Health, Software

Portfolio Companies: Progress Software, Cytogen, Groundwater Technology, Concord Computing, Individual, Protocare, Mentor Clinical Care, Credence Systems, Spectrian, Steinbrecher, Thermatrix, Western Wireless, Ultracision, U.S. Data, Loudoun Telecommunications, Transcend Therapeutics

Officers, Executives and Principals

Harry J. Healer, General Partner
Education: BSBA, Babson College
Background: Vice President, First Capital Corporation of Boston; Vice President, First Venture Capital Corporation
Directorships: Concord Computing Corporation, Cytogen, Groundwater Technology, Thermatrix, Extraction Systems, Optimax Systems, Progress Software, Preception Technology

Kevin J. Dougherty, General Partner
Education: BA, Williams College
Background: Vice President, Bank of Boston; Vice President, Massachusetts Capital Resource Company
Directorships: Keytek Instruments, Pathway Design, Mentor Clinical Care Prestocare, Commonwealth Care, Occupational Health and Rehabilitation, Individual, Sierra Research and Technology, High Road

Richard A. Farrell, General Partner
Education: BSBA, MBA, Boston University
Background: President, First Capital Corporation of Boston; President, First Venture Capital Corporation
Directorships: Allied Devices Corporation, Auburn International, Cadec Systems, Cape-Island, Dowden Communications

William C. Mills, General Partner
Education: BA, Chemistry, Princeton; MS, Chemistry, MIT; MM, Management, MIT
Background: Partner, Paine Webber Venture Management
Directorships: Cytogen, Spectrian, Ultracision, Transcend Therapeutics, Omnirel

VENTURES MEDICAL

16945 Northchase Drive, Suite 2150
Houston, TX 77060

Telephone: 713-873-5748
Fax: 713-873-5950

Mission: not available

Fund Size: $32 million
Founded: not available
Average Investment: $750,000 to $1.5 million
Minimum Investment: $500,000

Investment Criteria: Seed to Startup

Industry Group Preference: Biotechnology, Medical/Health

Portfolio Companies: not available

Officers, Executives and Principals

Anchie Y. Kuo, General Partner
William T. Mullaney, General Partner

THE VERTICAL GROUP

18 Bank Street
Summit, NJ 07901

Telephone: 908-277-3790
Fax: 908-273-9434

Other Office Locations
4020 Moorpark Avenue
San Jose, CA 95117
Phone 408-261-7780, Fax 408-261-7783

61 Broadway, Suite 918
New York, NY 10006
Phone 212-480-0600, Fax 212-480-0623

Mission: not available

Fund Size: $60 million
Founded: not available
Average Investment: $1 million
Minimum Investment: not available

Investment Criteria: None

Industry Group Preference: Biotechnology, Medical/Health

Portfolio Companies: not available

Officers, Executives and Principals

Richard Emmitt, General Partner
Jack W. Lasersohn, General Partner
John E. Reynolds, General Partner
Stephen Baksa, General Partner

ZERO STAGE CAPITAL

101 Main Street
17th Floor, Kendall Square
Cambridge, MA 02142

Telephone: 617-876-5355
Fax: 617-876-1248

Mission: not available

Fund Size: $40 million
Founded: not available
Average Investment: $750,000
Minimum Investment: not available

Investment Criteria: Early-stage, Proprietary Technology

Geographic Preference: Northeastern United States

Industry Group Preference: High Technology

Portfolio Companies: Perspective Biosystems, Matritech, Mercury Computer, Telebit, Swan Technologies, Ibis Technology, IVS Corporation, ADT Corporation, Aseco Corporation, Broadband Networks, SystemSoft

Officers, Executives and Principals

Paul Kelly, Managing General Partner, President
Education: BS, Harvard; MBA, Northwestern University
Background: Investment Officer, Weiss Technology Development Corporation

Gordon Baty, Managing General Partner
Education: BS, MS, PhD, Finance, MIT
Background:Chief Executive Officer, Wormser Energy Context Corporation

Stanley L. Fung, General Partner
Education: BSEE, University Massachusetts; MBA, MIT
Background: Investment Officer, Avent International

C

Minority/Socially-Useful Funds

ALLIED CAPITAL ADVISORS

1666 K Street Northwest, Suite 901
Washington, DC 20006

Telephone: 202-331-1112
Fax: 202-659-2053

Mission: Committed to investing in strong, growing companies by providing growth financing, buyout and acquisition capital, and financing for recapitalization

Fund Size: $450 million
Founded: 1958
Average Investment: $1.5 million
Minimum Investment: $1 million

Investment Criteria: Second-stage to Leveraged Buyout

Industry Group Preference: Diversified

Portfolio Companies: not available

Officers, Executives and Principals

David Gladstone, Chairman
Education: BA, Government and Economics, University of Virginia; MA, Computer Science and Government, American University; MBA, Harvard
Background: Management Consultant, Price Waterhouse and Co.; Internal Consultant, IT&T
Directorships: NASDAQ, George Washington University, Riggs National Corporation

G. Cabell Williams, President
Education: BS, Rollins College
Directorships: Environmental Enterprises Fund

Brooks H. Browne, Executive Vice President
Education: BA, Political Science, Williams College; MBA, International Business, Harvard

John M. Scheurer, Executive Vice President

William F. Dunbar, Executive Vice President
Education: BA, Davidson College; MBA, Harvard
Background: Venture America
Directorships: Chairman of NASBIC

ARK CAPITAL MANAGEMENT

150 North Wacker Drive, Suite 2650
Chicago, IL 60606-1609

Telephone: 312-541-0330
Fax: 312-541-0335

Mission: Ark is a private equity investment advisor focusing on investment opportunities in middle market companies seeking growth capital ranging from $1 million to $3.5 million. In addition, Ark emphasizes investments in minority-owned businesses fitting its investment criteria.

Fund Size: $24 million
Founded: 1991
Average Investment: not available
Minimum Investment: $1 million

Investment Criteria: Later-stage, Growth, Growth Acquisition

Geographic Preference: United States

Industry Group Preference: Food Services, High Technology,Industrial, Manufacturing, Medical/Health

Portfolio Companies: not available

Officers, Executives and Principals

Michael Y. Granger, Principal
Education: MBA, Amos Tuck School, Dartmouth
Background: Investment Manager, Xerox Venture Capital; Principal, CIGNA Venture Capital

Xcylur R. Stoakley, Principal
Education: MBA, BSEE
Background: Manager of Venture Capital Investments, Ameritech Corporation

CAF INC.

655 15th Street Northwest, Suite 375
Washington, DC 20005

Telephone: 202-388-8543
Fax: 202-895-2799

Mission: not available

Fund Size: not available
Founded: not available
Average Investment: less than 250,000
Minimum Investment: not available

Investment Criteria: Small and minority business development

Industry Group Preference: Retailing, Service Industries

Portfolio Companies: not available

Officers, Executives and Principals

Shelly Metz-Galloway, President

CALVERT SOCIAL VENTURE PARTNERS

7201 Wisconsin Avenue, Suite 310
Bethesda, MD 20814

Telephone: 301-718-4272
Fax: 301-656-4421
E-mail: Calven2000@aol.com

Mission: To be a model institutional investor and innovator in the financial services field. Only invests in those companies which demonstrate clear market and financial potential.

Fund Size: $10 million
Founded: 1989
Average Investment: $250,000
Minimum Investment: $50,000

Investment Criteria: Startup to second-stage

Geographic Preference: District of Columbia, New Jersey to North Carolina

Industry Group Preference: Energy/Natural Resources, Environmental Protection

Portfolio Companies: Advanced Asphalt, AquaPharm, BioBrite, Blackberry, Cardiologic, Katrina, MediJect, MEE Productions, Monitoring Technology, Mycotech, ReGain, Tiregator, Advanced Therapies, Composite Particles, CORE Technologies, Cycloid, Mavis Publications, Ocean Optics, Calypte, University Online

Officers, Executives and Principals

D. Wayne Silby, Principal
Background: Chair, Calvert Group; President, Calvert Social Investment Fund; Co-convener, Social Venture Network

John G. Guffey, Principal
Background: Co-founder, Calvert; Vice-Chair, Calvert Group of Funds; Chair, Calvert Social Investment Foundation

John May, Principal
Background: Managing Partner, E.D., Wilt Investments, L.P.

Michael Tang, Principal
Background: Currently Chief Executive Officer, National Materials, L.P.

CAPITAL CIRCULATION CORPORATION

2035 Lemoine Avenue
Fort Lee, NJ 07024

Telephone: 201-947-8637
Fax: 201-585-1965

Mission: not available

Fund Size: not available
Founded: not available
Average Investment: $150,000
Minimum Investment: not available

Investment Criteria: SSBIC, Expansion

Geographic Preference: Northeastern United States

Industry Group Preference: Diversified

Portfolio Companies: not available

Officers, Executives and Principals

Judy M. Kao, General Manager

CAPITAL DIMENSIONS VENTURE FUND, INC.

Two Appletree Square
Suite 335
Minneapolis, MN 55425-1637

Telephone: 612-854-3007
Fax: 612-854-6657

Mission: Reducing investment activity

Fund Size: $21 million
Founded: 1987
Average Investment: $500,000
Minimum Investment: $250,000

Investment Criteria: First-stage, Second-stage, Mezzanine, Leveraged Buyout

Industry Group Preference: Communications, Computer Related, Energy/Natural Resources, Industrial Products and Equipment

Portfolio Companies: not available

Officers, Executives and Principals

Dean R. Pickerell, President
Thomas F. Hunt, Jr., Vice President
Brenda L. Leonard, Investment Manager

CHICAGO COMMUNITY VENTURES, INC.

25 East Washington Street, #2015
Chicago, IL 60602

Telephone: 312-726-6084
Fax: 312-726-0167

Mission: not available

Fund Size: not available
Founded: not available
Average Investment: $150,000
Minimum Investment: not available

Investment Criteria: SSBIC, Startup to Mezzanine

Geographic Preference: Midwestern United States

Industry Group Preference: Communications, Consumer Related, Industrial Products

Portfolio Companies: not available

Officers, Executives and Principals

Phyllis E. George, President

CITY CENTER MESBIC

8 North Main Street
Dayton, OH 45402

Telephone: 513-461-4614
Fax: 513-222-7035

Mission: not available

Fund Size: not available
Founded: not available
Average Investment: $50,000
Minimum Investment: not available

Investment Criteria: SSBIC, First-stage to Buyouts

Geographic Preference: Ohio

Industry Group Preference: Diversified

Portfolio Companies: not available

Officers, Executives and Principals

Steven J. Budd, President
Steven D. Naas, Financial Analyst
Willia R. Smith, Loan Officer

COMMONS CAPITAL

198 Hummock Pond Road
Nantucket, MA 02554

Telephone: 508-325-4045

Mission: not available

Fund Size: not available
Founded: not available
Average Investment: $200,000
Minimum Investment: not available

Investment Criteria: Seed to Mezzanine

Industry Group Preference: Environmental Protection

Portfolio Companies: not available

Officers, Executives and Principals

Edward Tasch, General Partner

ELK ASSOCIATES FUNDING CORPORATION

747 Third Avenue
Suite 4-C
New York, NY 10017

Telephone: 212-355-2449
Fax: 212-759-3338
E-mail: GaryatElk@aol.com

Mission: Debt financing/secured; some debt with equity features

Fund Size: $30 million
Founded: 1980
Average Investment: $350,000
Minimum Investment: $50,000

Investment Criteria: SSBIC, Expansion, Taxi Medallion Lending

Geographic Preference: Northeastern United States

Industry Group Preference: Diversified

Portfolio Companies: not available

Officers, Executives and Principals

Gary C. Granoff, President
Ellen M. Walker, Vice President
Lee A. Forlenza, Vice President

ENVIRONMENTAL ALLIES

2330 Marinship Way
Suite 300
Sausalito, CA 94965

Telephone: 415-331-5500
Fax: 415-331-1212

Mission: not available

Fund Size: $80 million
Founded: not available
Average Investment: $500,000 - $25 milion
Minimum Investment: not available

Investment Criteria: Seed to Later-stage

Industry Group Preference: Energy/Natural Resources, Environmental Protection, Manufacturing/Processing

Portfolio Companies: Apache Nitrogen Corporation, Bay Area Tank and Marine, Biosyn Technology, Mincon, Mission Trail, Amtrak, National Tire Services, Pace, Cleansoils, Greenfield Environmental, Cyclean, Prins Recycling, Proven Alternatives, Valley Systems, Profco, Purefill, Sanborn, Transphase, Triangle Labs, Awing Leasing, Appliance Control Technology

Officers, Executives and Principals

Roy Schwartz, Director of Equipment Finance

ENVIRONMENTAL PRIVATE EQUITY FUND II, L.P.

233 South Wacker Drive, Suite 9500
Chicago, IL 60606-3103

Telephone: 312-258-1400
Fax: 312-258-0334

Mission: not available

Fund Size: $61 million
Founded: not available
Average Investment: $1 million
Minimum Investment: not available

Investment Criteria: First and Second-stage

Industry Group Preference: Energy/Natural Resources, Environmental Protection

Portfolio Companies: not available

Officers, Executives and Principals

Bret Maxwell, Managing Director
Education: BS, Industrial Engineering; MBA, Northwestern
Background: Arthur Anderson and Co., General Electric

Oliver Nicklin, President
Education: BS, Chemical Engineering, University of Texas; MBA, Harvard
Background: Founder, President, First Analysis; William Blair and Co.

EQUAL OPPORTUNITY FINANCE, INC.
420 South Hurstbourne Parkway, #201
Louisville, KY 40222-8002

Telephone: 502-423-1943
Fax: 502-423-1945

Mission: not available

Fund Size: not available
Founded: not available
Average Investment: $250,000
Minimum Investment: not available

Investment Criteria: SSBIC, Startup to Buyouts

Geographic Preference: Kentucky, Indiana, Ohio, West Virginia

Industry Group Preference: Diversified

Portfolio Companies: not available

Officers, Executives and Principals

Franklin P. Justice, President
David A. Sattich, Vice President

FAR EAST CAPITAL CORPORATION

977 North Broadway
Suite 401
Los Angeles, CA 90012

Telephone: 213-687-1361
Fax: 213-626-7497

Mission: not available

Fund Size: $2.5 million
Founded: 1989
Average Investment: $250,000
Minimum Investment: $100,000

Investment Criteria: SBA, SSBIC

Geographic Preference: California

Industry Group Preference: Diversified

Portfolio Companies: not available

Officers, Executives and Principals

Tom C. Wang, Vice President, Manager

FIRST AMERICAN CAPITAL FUNDING

10840 Warner Avenue, #202
Fountain Valley, CA 92708

Telephone: 714-965-7190
Fax: 714-965-7193

Mission: not available

Fund Size: not available
Founded: not available
Average Investment: $50,000
Minimum Investment: not available

Investment Criteria: SSBIC, Startups

Industry Group Preference: Financial Services

Portfolio Companies: not available

Officers, Executives and Principals

Chuoc Vota, President

FIRST COUNTY CAPITAL, INC.

135-14 Northern Boulevard, 2nd Floor
Flushing, NY 11354

Telephone: 718-461-1778
Fax: 718-461-1835

Mission: Loan and equity financing

Fund Size: not available
Founded: 1989
Average Investment: $100,000
Minimum Investment: not available

Investment Criteria: SSBIC, Startup to Later-stages

Geographic Preference: New York

Industry Group Preference: Biotechnology, Communications, Computer Related, Consumer Related, Medical/Health

Portfolio Companies: not available

Officers, Executives and Principals

Zenia C. Yuan, President
Education: BS
Background: Real estate and finance

Orest Glut, Financial Manager
Education: MBA, New York University
Background: Senior Loaning Officer; 30+ years experience in banking field

FJC GROWTH CAPITAL CORPORATION

200 West Court Square
Suite 750
Huntsville, AL 35801

Telephone: 205-922-2918
Fax: 205-922-2909

Mission: Actively seeking new investments

Fund Size: $1 million
Founded: 1989
Average Investment: $250,000 - $500,000
Minimum Investment: $100,000

Investment Criteria: Second-stage

Industry Group Preference: Consumer Related, Manufacturing/Processing, Real Estate/Construction, Wholesaling/Distribution

Portfolio Companies: not available

Officers, Executives and Principals

Francisco L. Collazo, President
William B. Noojin, Vice President and General Manager

FUTURE VALUE INVESTORS

330 East Kilbourn Avenue
Suite 711
Milwaukee, WI 53202

Telephone: 414-278-7321

Mission: not available

Fund Size: $3.5 million
Founded: not available
Average Investment: $250,000
Minimum Investment: not available

Investment Criteria: SSBIC

Geographic Preference: Wisconsin

Industry Group Preference: Diversified

Portfolio Companies: not available

Officers, Executives and Principals

William P. Beckett, President
Education: Graduate and Undergraduate Degrees, University of Wisconsin, Milwaukee
Background: Economy Development Manager, Wisconsin Power and Light Co.; Executive Director of Minority Business Development, Wisconsin Department

Adrienne Bauman, Investment Advisor

INTERNATIONAL PAPER CAPITAL FORMATION

6400 Poplar Avenue
Memphis, TN 38197

Telephone: 901-763-6217
Fax: 901-763-6076

Mission: not available

Fund Size: not available
Founded: not available
Average Investment: $40,000 - $300,000
Minimum Investment: not available

Investment Criteria: SSBIC, Later-stage, Expansion

Industry Group Preference: Diversified

Portfolio Companies: not available

Officers, Executives and Principals

Mr. Bob Higgins, Vice President and Controller
Pam Taylor, Officer

MARYLAND SMALL BUSINESS DEVELOPMENT FINANCING AU

826 East Baltimore Street
Baltimore, MD 21202

Telephone: 410-333-4270
Fax: 410-333-2552

Mission: not available

Fund Size: not available
Founded: not available
Average Investment: $250,000
Minimum Investment: not available

Investment Criteria: Startup to Acquisitions

Geographic Preference: Maryland

Industry Group Preference: Diversified

Portfolio Companies: not available

Officers, Executives and Principals

Stanley W. Tucker, Executive Director
Randy Croxton, Manager

MEDALLION FUNDING
205 East 42nd Street, Suite 2020
New York, NY 10017

Telephone: 212-682-3300
Fax: 212-983-0351

Mission: not available

Fund Size: $75 million
Founded: not available
Average Investment: $100,000
Minimum Investment: not available

Investment Criteria: SSBIC, Second-stage

Geographic Preference: New York

Industry Group Preference: Broadcast/Cable/Radio, Medical/Health, Service Industries, Transportation

Portfolio Companies: not available

Officers, Executives and Principals

Alvin Murstein, President
Michael Fanger, Vice President

MESBIC VENTURES HOLDING COMPANY

North Central Plaza One, Suite 710
12655 North Central Expressway
Dallas, TX 75243

Telephone: 972-991-1597
Fax: 972-991-1647
E-mail: mesbic@gan.net

Mission: To provide long-term venture capital to well-managed growing businesses owned and managed by mostly African-American and Hispanic-American company builders

Fund Size: $46 million
Founded: 1970
Average Investment: $500,000
Minimum Investment: $500,000

Investment Criteria: Second-stage, Mezzanine, Buyouts

Geographic Preference: Primarily Southwestern United States, must have at least 51% of revenues within the United States

Industry Group Preference: Aerospace, Automobile, Broadcast, Communications, Contract Manufacturing, Electronics, Engineering Services, Food Manufacturers, Proprietary Products, Specialty Industries

Portfolio Companies: El Dorado Communications, Inc., F.A.C.E. Inc., H-R Industries, Inc. McDonald Technologies International, Inc., Radio One, Inc., Simeus Holdings, Inc.

Officers, Executives and Principals

Donald Lawhorne, President
Education: BBA, MBA
Background: College Teacher, Manufacturing Supervisor, 14 years venture capital experience

Thomas Gerron, Executive Vice President and Chief Financial Officer
Education: BBA
Background: Controller, Management Consulting Firm; 16 years venture capital experience; CPA

Divakar R. Kamath, Executive Vice President
Education: BSME, MS, MBA
Background: Senior Executive, Acquisition Fund; 18 years venture capital experience

Oscar Trevino, Jr., Senior Vice President
Education: BBA, MBA, JD
Background: Consumer and asset-based lending experience, five years venture capital experience

Linda Roach, Senior Vice President
Education: BA, MBA
Background: College Teacher, Corporate Lender, one year venture capital experience

NEIGHBORHOOD FUND

1950 East 71st Street
Chicago, IL 60649

Telephone: 312-753-5670
Fax: 312-753-5699

Mission: not available

Fund Size: $2.18 million
Founded: not available
Average Investment: $100,000
Minimum Investment: not available

Investment Criteria: SSBIC

Geographic Preference: Midwestern United States

Industry Group Preference: Diversified

Portfolio Companies: not available

Officers, Executives and Principals

James Fletcher, Chairman
David Shryock, President
Derrick Collins, Assistant Vice President

OPPORTUNITY CAPITAL CORPORATION

2201 Walnut Avenue
Suite 210
Fremont, CA 94558

Telephone: 510-651-4412
Fax: 510-651-0128

Mission: Actively seeking new investments

Fund Size: not available
Founded: 1970
Average Investment: $100,000 - $300,000
Minimum Investment: $500,000

Investment Criteria: Second-stage, Mezzanine, Leveraged Buyout

Industry Group Preference: Communications, Consumer, Electronic Components and Instrumentation, Industrial Products and Equipment, Medical/Health Related

Portfolio Companies: not available

Officers, Executives and Principals

J. Peter Thompson, Managing Partner
Lewis E. Byrd, Portfolio Director

PACIFIC VENTURE CAPITAL, LTD.

222 South Vineyard Street, #PH-1
Honolulu, HI 96813-2445

Telephone: 808-521-6502
Fax: 808-521-6541

Mission: not available

Fund Size: not available
Founded: not available
Average Investment: $150,000
Minimum Investment: not available

Investment Criteria: SSBIC, Startup to Buyouts

Geographic Preference: Hawaii

Industry Group Preference: Diversified

Portfolio Companies: not available

Officers, Executives and Principals

Dexter J. Taniguchi, President

RENAISSANCE CAPITAL CORPORATION

34 Peachtree Street Northwest, #2230
Atlanta, GA 30303

Telephone: 404-658-9061
Fax: 404-658-9064

Mission: not available

Fund Size: not available
Founded: not available
Average Investment: $150,000
Minimum Investment: not available

Investment Criteria: SSBIC, Expansion

Geographic Preference: Southern United States

Industry Group Preference: Diversified

Portfolio Companies: not available

Officers, Executives and Principals

Anita P. Stephens, Business Development

RUTGERS MINORITY INVESTMENT COMPANY

180 University Avenue
Newark, NJ 07102

Telephone: 201-648-5287
Fax: 201-648-1110

Mission: not available

Fund Size: $2.4 million
Founded: not available
Average Investment: $50,000
Minimum Investment: not available

Investment Criteria: SSBIC, Startup to Second-stage

Geographic Preference: Northeastern United States

Industry Group Preference: Diversified

Portfolio Companies: not available

Officers, Executives and Principals

Oscar Figueroa, President
Education: MA, Economics, Pennsylvania State University
Background: Regional Manager, NJ Small Business Development Center
Directorships: Soccer Education Associates

SAN JOAQUIN BUSINESS INVESTMENT GROUP

1900 Mariposa Mall, #100
Fresno, CA 93721

Telephone: 209-233-3580
Fax: 209-233-3709

Mission: not available

Fund Size: not available
Founded: not available
Average Investment: $100,000
Minimum Investment: not available

Investment Criteria: SSBIC

Geographic Preference: California

Industry Group Preference: Biotechnology, Industrial Products, Medical/Health

Portfolio Companies: not available

Officers, Executives and Principals

Eugene Waller, President

TRANSPORTATION CAPITAL

315 Park Avenue South
New York, NY 10010

Telephone: 212-598-3235
Fax: 212-598-3102

Mission: not available

Fund Size: $20 million
Founded: not available
Average Investment: $60,000
Minimum Investment: not available

Investment Criteria: SSBIC

Industry Group Preference: Transportation

Portfolio Companies: Taxi Cab Medallions

Officers, Executives and Principals

Jonathan H. Hirsch
Paul J. Borden

TSG VENTURES, INC.

177 Broad Street
12th Floor
Stamford, CT 06901

Telephone: 203-406-1500
Fax: 203-406-1590

Mission: Actively seeking new investments

Fund Size: not available
Founded: 1971
Average Investment: 1.5 million
Minimum Investment: $250,000

Investment Criteria: Second-stage, Leveraged Buyout

Industry Group Preference: Communications, Computer Related, Consumer, Distribution, Industrial Products and Equipment, Medical/Health Related

Portfolio Companies: not available

Officers, Executives and Principals

Duane E. Hill, President and Chief Executive Officer
Darryl B. Thompson, Senior Vice President
Cleveland A. Christopher, Vice President
Lawrence C. Morse, PhD, Vice President

UNC VENTURES

711 Atlantic Avenue
Boston, MA 02111

Telephone: 617-482-7070
Fax: 617-482-9720

Mission: not available

Fund Size: $30 million
Founded: not available
Average Investment: $100,000 - $2 million
Minimum Investment: not available

Investment Criteria: Minority companies: Startup to Acquisition

Industry Group Preference: Communications, Electronics, High Technology, Information Services, Medical/ Health

Portfolio Companies: Accent Hair Salons Inc., Biogrowth, Cirrus Logic, Cybernetics Systems International Corporation, Granite Broadcasting, Infolink, Ruggles Bedford Associates Inc., Suncoast Communications, The Westpark Limited Partnerships, U.S. Radio L.P., WDG-III San Francisco Medical Center, L.P., WDG Ventures, Ltd., Xinix, Inc.

Officers, Executives and Principals

Edward Dugger III, Managing Partner
Education: AB, cum laude, Harvard College; MA, Public Affairs and Urban Planning, Princeton University
Background: Irwin Management
Directorships: United Way of Massachusetts Bay, Greater Boston YMCA, Museum of Fine Arts Council, Museum of the National Center

Veronic Zizza, Treasurer

VALLEY CAPITAL CORPORATION

100 Martin Luther King Boulevard
Suite 212, Krystal Building
Chattanooga, TN 37402

Telephone: 423-265-1557
Fax: 423-265-1588

Mission: Actively seeking new investments

Fund Size: $2 million
Founded: 1982
Average Investment: $25,000 - $300,00
Minimum Investment: Less than $100,000

Investment Criteria: First-stage to Later-stage

Geographic Preference: Tennessee

Industry Group Preference: Communications, Computer Related, Consumer, Distribution, Electronic Components and Instrumentation, Energy/Natural Resources, Industrial Products and Equipment, Medical/Health Related

Portfolio Companies: not available

Officers, Executives and Principals

Lamar J. Partridge, President
Faye Robinson, Administrative Assistant

VALLEY MANAGEMENT, INC.

100 West Martin Luther King Boulevard
Suite 210, Krystal Building
Chattanooga, TN 37402

Telephone: 423-265-0774
Fax: 423-265-1588

Mission: Actively seeking new investments

Fund Size: $15 million
Founded: 1993
Average Investment: $500,000
Minimum Investment: $100,000

Investment Criteria: First-stage to Later-stage

Geographic Preference: Tennessee, Georgia, Alabama, Mississippi, Kentucky, North Carolina

Industry Group Preference: Communications, Consumer, Distribution, Electronic Components and Instrumentation, Industrial Products and Equipment, Medical/Health Related

Portfolio Companies: not available

Officers, Executives and Principals

Langston J. Walker, President
Lamar J. Partridge, Chief Executive Officer

VENTURE OPPORTUNITIES CORPORATION

150 58th Street
New York, NY 10155

Telephone: 212-832-3737
Fax: 212-223-4912

Mission: not available

Fund Size: not available
Founded: not available
Average Investment: $250,000
Minimum Investment: not available

Investment Criteria: SSBIC, Startup to Leveraged Buyout

Geographic Preference: Northeastern United States

Industry Group Preference: Communications, Computer Related, Electronics, Industrial Products, Medical/ Health

Portfolio Companies: not available

Officers, Executives and Principals

A. Fred March, President
Flora March, Executive Vice President

D

Strategic Partners

ABBOTT LABS

One Abbott Park Road
Abbott Park, IL 60064-3500

Telephone: 847-937-6100
Fax: 847-937-1511

Mission: not available

Fund Size: $6.88 billion
Founded: not available
Average Investment: $2 million
Minimum Investment: not available

Industry Group Preference: Medical/Health Related

Portfolio Companies: North American Biologicals

Officers, Executives and Principals

Richard H. Morehead, Vice President, Corporate Development and Planning

ADOBE SYSTEMS, INC.

345 Park Avenue
San Jose, CA 95110

Telephone: 408-536-6000
Fax: 408-536-6799

Mission: not available

Fund Size: $229 million
Founded: not available
Average Investment: $1 million
Minimum Investment: not available

Industry Group Preference: Computer Related

Portfolio Companies: Electronics for Imaging, Inc. (EFI)

Officers, Executives and Principals

Daniel Putnam, Senior Vice President, New Product Development

AMERICAN TELEPHONE AND TELEGRAPH

32 Avenue of the Americas
New York, NY 10013-2412

Telephone: 908-221-6203
Fax: 908-221-5217

Mission: not available

Fund Size: $63.1 billion
Founded: not available
Average Investment: $25 million
Minimum Investment: not available

Industry Group Preference: Communications

Portfolio Companies: McCaw Cellular Communications, Inc.

Officers, Executives and Principals

Richard Bodman

AMERITECH DEVELOPMENT CORPORATION

10 South Wacker Drive
Chicago, IL 60606

Telephone: 312-609-6000
Fax: 312-207-0615

Mission: not available

Fund Size: $4.9 billion
Founded: not available
Average Investment: $1 million
Minimum Investment: not available

Industry Group Preference: Communications

Portfolio Companies: Triconex

AMGEN, INC.

1840 Dehavilland Drive
Thousand Oaks, CA 91320-1789

Telephone: 805-499-5725
Fax: 805-499-9315

Mission: not available

Fund Size: $682 million
Founded: not available
Average Investment: $15 million
Minimum Investment: not available

Industry Group Preference: Medical/Health Related

Portfolio Companies: Regeneron Pharmaceuticals, Inc.

Officers, Executives and Principals

Bob Attiyeh, Senior Vice President, Finance and Corporate Development

APPLE COMPUTER, INC.
20525 Mariani Avenue
Cupertino, CA 95014

Telephone: 408-996-1010
Fax: 408-974-2483

Mission: not available

Fund Size: $6.3 billion
Founded: not available
Average Investment: $1 million
Minimum Investment: not available

Industry Group Preference: Computer Related

Portfolio Companies: Adobe Systems, Inc.

Officers, Executives and Principals

Michael Spindler

BAUSCH AND LOMB

One Lincoln First Square
Rochester, NY 14601-0054

Telephone: 716-338-6000

Mission: not available

Fund Size: $1.7 billion
Founded: not available
Average Investment: not available
Minimum Investment: not available

Industry Group Preference: Medical/Health Related

Portfolio Companies: not available

Officers, Executives and Principals

Ronald L. Zarrella, Chief Operating Officer

BOISE CASCADE CORPORATION

One Jefferson Square
Boise, ID 83728-0001

Telephone: 208-384-6161
Fax: 208-384-4912

Mission: not available

Fund Size: $4 billion
Founded: not available
Average Investment: $2 million
Minimum Investment: not available

Industry Group Preference: Distribution, Industrial Products and Equipment

Portfolio Companies: BMC West Corporation

Officers, Executives and Principals

George Harad

BRISTOL MEYERS SQUIBB

345 Park Avenue
New York, NY 10154-0037

Telephone: 212-546-4000
Fax: 212-546-4020

Mission: not available

Fund Size: $11.2 billion
Founded: not available
Average Investment: $7.5 million
Minimum Investment: not available

Industry Group Preference: Medical/Health Related

Portfolio Companies: Advanced Magnetics, Inc., Chemtrak Inc.

Officers, Executives and Principals

Richard L. Gelb

BURLINGTON INDUSTRIES, INC.

P.O. Box 21207
Greensboro, NC 27420

Telephone: 919-379-2000
Fax: 919-379-2245

Mission: not available

Fund Size: $535 million
Founded: not available
Average Investment: $8 million
Minimum Investment: not available

Industry Group Preference: Manufacturing/Processing

Portfolio Companies: Galey and Lord, Inc.

Officers, Executives and Principals

Park Davidson, Treasurer

C. R. BARD, INC.
730 Central Avenue
Murray Hill, NJ 07974

Telephone: 908-277-8000
Fax: 908-277-8363

Mission: not available

Fund Size: $876 billion
Founded: not available
Average Investment: $1.5 million
Minimum Investment: not available

Industry Group Preference: Medical/Health Related

Portfolio Companies: Intromed

Officers, Executives and Principals

Robert Ernest, Vice President, Business Development

CENTOCOR, INC.

200 Great Valley Parkway
Malvern, PA 19355

Telephone: 215-651-6000
Fax: 215-889-0895

Mission: not available

Fund Size: $53 million
Founded: not available
Average Investment: $2.5 million
Minimum Investment: not available

Industry Group Preference: Medical/Health Related

Portfolio Companies: Corvas International, Inc.

Officers, Executives and Principals

James Woody

CORNING, INC.

Houghton Park
Corning, NY 14831

Telephone: 607-974-9000
Fax: 607-974-8830

Mission: not available

Fund Size: $3.3 billion
Founded: not available
Average Investment: $2.5 million
Minimum Investment: not available

Industry Group Preference: Diversified

Portfolio Companies: Unilab Corporation

Officers, Executives and Principals

Roger Ackerman, Chief Operating Officer

DEFENSE SOFTWARE AND SYSTEMS (DSS)

200 Route 17
Mahwah, NJ 07430

Telephone: 201-529-2026
Fax: 201-529-3163

Mission: not available

Fund Size: $11.1 billion
Founded: not available
Average Investment: not available
Minimum Investment: not available

Industry Group Preference: Computer Related

Portfolio Companies: Millimeter Wave Technology (MWT)

Officers, Executives and Principals

George Morgenstern, Chief Executive Officer

DIGITAL EQUIPMENT CORPORATION

146 Main Street
Maynard, MA 01754-2571

Telephone: 508-493-5111
Fax: 508-493-2571

Mission: not available

Fund Size: $13.9 billion
Founded: not available
Average Investment: $2 million
Minimum Investment: not available

Industry Group Preference: Computer Related

Portfolio Companies: Ross Systems, Inc., Stratacom, Inc.

Officers, Executives and Principals

John Smith, Senior Vice President, Operations

DOW CHEMICAL COMPANY

2030 Dow Center
Midland, MI 48674

Telephone: 517-636-1000

Mission: not available

Fund Size: $18.8 billion
Founded: not available
Average Investment: $7 million
Minimum Investment: not available

Industry Group Preference: Diversified

Portfolio Companies: Ecogen, Polycon

Officers, Executives and Principals

Fred P. Corson, Vice President of Research and Development

FORD MOTOR COMPANY

The American Road, P.O. Box 1899
Dearborn, MI 48121

Telephone: 313-322-3000
Fax: 313-323-0816

Mission: not available

Fund Size: $2.6 billion
Founded: not available
Average Investment: $100 million+
Minimum Investment: not available

Industry Group Preference: Industrial Products and Equipment

Portfolio Companies: Excel Industries, Inc.

Officers, Executives and Principals

Roger E. Maugh

GENERAL MOTORS CORPORATION

3044 West Grand Boulevard
Detroit, MI 48202-3091

Telephone: 313-556-5000
Fax: 313-974-5168

Mission: not available

Fund Size: $123.1 billion
Founded: not available
Average Investment: $100 million+
Minimum Investment: not available

Industry Group Preference: Industrial Products and Equipment

Portfolio Companies: Valence Technology, Inc., and 4th Dimension Software, Ltd.

Officers, Executives and Principals

Robert O'Connell, Chief Financial Officer

HOECHST, MARION, ROUSSEL, INC.

10236 Marion Park Drive
Kansas City, MO 64137

Telephone: 816-966-4000

Mission: not available

Fund Size: $2.9 billion
Founded: not available
Average Investment: not available
Minimum Investment: not available

Investment Criteria: not available

Industry Group Preference: Medical/Health Related

Portfolio Companies: Immulogic Pharmaceutical Corporation, Gensia Pharmaceuticals, Cortech Inc.

Officers, Executives and Principals

Malcolm Barbour

HORMEL AND COMPANY
Austin, TX 55912

Telephone: 507-437-5611
Fax: 507-437-5117

Mission: not available

Fund Size: $2.7 billion
Founded: not available
Average Investment: not available
Minimum Investment: not available

Industry Group Preference: Consumer

Portfolio Companies: United States Filter Corporation

Officers, Executives and Principals

Forrest Dryden

INTEL CORPORATION

2200 Mission College Boulevard
P.O. Box 58119
Santa Clara, CA 95052-8119

Telephone: 408-765-8080
Fax: 408-765-1399

Mission: not available

Fund Size: $4.8 billion
Founded: not available
Average Investment: not available
Minimum Investment: not available

Industry Group Preference: Computer Related

Portfolio Companies: Microtest, Inc.

Officers, Executives and Principals

Leslie Vadasz, Director of Business Development

JOHNSON AND JOHNSON

One Johnson and Johnson Plaza
New Brunswick, NJ 08933

Telephone: 908-524-0400
Fax: 908-828-4107

Mission: not available

Fund Size: $12.5 billion
Founded: not available
Average Investment: not available
Minimum Investment: not available

Industry Group Preference: Medical/Health Related

Portfolio Companies: Gene Shears Pty. Ltd.

Officers, Executives and Principals

James R. Utaski

LITTON INDUSTRIES, INC.

360 North Crescent Drive
Beverly Hills, CA 90210-4867

Telephone: 310-859-5000
Fax: 310-859-5940

Mission: not available

Fund Size: $5.7 billion
Founded: not available
Average Investment: not available
Minimum Investment: not available

Industry Group Preference: Electronic Components and Instrumentation, Industrial Products and Equipment

Portfolio Companies: Research Frontiers Inc.

Officers, Executives and Principals

Joseph T. Casey

MASCOTECH, INC.

21001 Van Born Road
Taylor, MI 48180

Telephone: 313-274-7405
Fax: 313-374-6136

Mission: not available

Fund Size: $3.1 billion
Founded: not available
Average Investment: not available
Minimum Investment: not available

Industry Group Preference: Consumer

Portfolio Companies: Trimas Corporation

Officers, Executives and Principals

Lee Gardner, President, Chief Operating Officer
Richard A. Manoogian, Chief Executive Officer

MATSUSHITA COMMUNICATIONS INDUSTRIAL, INC.

50 Meadowland Parkway
Secaucus, NJ 07094

Telephone: 201-348-7710
Fax: 201-348-7016

Mission: not available

Fund Size: $56 billion
Founded: not available
Average Investment: not available
Minimum Investment: not available

Industry Group Preference: Electronic Components and Instrumentation

Portfolio Companies: Fleet Call, Creative Technology Ltd.

Officers, Executives and Principals

Akiya Imura

MEDRAD, INC.

1 Medrad Drive
Indianola, PA 15051

Telephone: 800-633-7231

Mission: not available

Fund Size: $57 million
Founded: not available
Average Investment: not available
Minimum Investment: not available

Industry Group Preference: Medical/Health Related

Portfolio Companies: Digivision

Officers, Executives and Principals

Thomas Witmer, Chief Executive Officer

MEDTRONIC, INC.

7000 Central Avenue Northeast
Minneapolis, MN 55432

Telephone: 612-574-4000
Fax: 612-574-4879

Mission: not available

Fund Size: $1.2 billion
Founded: not available
Average Investment: not available
Minimum Investment: not available

Industry Group Preference: Medical/Health Related

Portfolio Companies: Spectranetics

Officers, Executives and Principals

William W. Georg, Chairman and Chief Executive Officer
Arthur D. Collins, Jr., President and Chief Operating Officer
Glenn D. Nelson, M.D., Vice-Chairman
Robert I. Ryan, Chief Financial Officer
Dale Beumer, Vice President, Treasurer - Investor Relations
Christopher J. O'Connell, Director of Investor Relations

MERCK AND COMPANY, INC.

126 East Lincoln Avenue
Rahway, NJ 07065-5039

Telephone: 908-594-4000

Mission: not available

Fund Size: $8.6 billion
Founded: not available
Average Investment: not available
Minimum Investment: not available

Industry Group Preference: Medical/Health Related

Portfolio Companies: Immulogic Pharmaceutical Corporation, ImClone Systems, Inc.

MERRILL LYNCH AND COMPANY, INC.

World Financial Center, North Tower
New York, NY 10281

Telephone: 212-449-1000
Fax: 212-449-0842

Mission: not available

Fund Size: $12.4 billion
Founded: not available
Average Investment: not available
Minimum Investment: not available

Industry Group Preference: not available

Portfolio Companies: IDEXX Laboratories, Inc.

Officers, Executives and Principals

Jerome Kenney, Vice President of Corporate Strategy and Research

MOTOROLA, INC.

1303 East Algonquin Road
Schaumburg, IL 60196

Telephone: 847-576-5000
Fax: 847-576-4768

Mission: not available

Fund Size: $11.3 billion
Founded: not available
Average Investment: not available
Minimum Investment: not available

Industry Group Preference: Computer Related, Electronic Components and Instrumentation

Portfolio Companies: StrataCom, Inc., Network Computing Devices, Inc. (NCD)

Officers, Executives and Principals

Carl Koenemann, Chief Financial Officer

NESTLE U.S.A., INC.

U.S. Corporate Offices
800 North Brank Boulevard
Glendale, CA 91203

Telephone: 818-549-6000
Fax: 818-549-6952

Mission: not available

Fund Size: $8.4 million
Founded: not available
Average Investment: not available
Minimum Investment: not available

Industry Group Preference: Consumer

Portfolio Companies: VISX, Inc.

Officers, Executives and Principals

Joseph Weller, Chairman and Chief Executive Officer

NIPPON STEEL U.S.A., INC.

10 East 50th Street, 29th Floor
New York, NY 10022

Telephone: 212-486-7150
Fax: 212-593-3049

Mission: not available

Fund Size: $19.8 billion
Founded: not available
Average Investment: not available
Minimum Investment: not available

Industry Group Preference: Industrial Products and Equipment

Portfolio Companies: Simtek Corporation

Officers, Executives and Principals

Hiroshi Suetsugu, President and Chief Executive Officer

OMNI INSURANCE COMPANY

1000 Parkwood Circle, Suite 1000
Atlanta, GA 30339

Telephone: 404-952-4500
Fax: 404-933-8285

Mission: not available

Fund Size: not available
Founded: not available
Average Investment: not available
Minimum Investment: not available

Industry Group Preference: Consumer

Portfolio Companies: Dateq Information Network, Inc.

Officers, Executives and Principals

Lowell Sims

PFIZER

235 East 42nd Street
New York, NY 10017-5755

Telephone: 212-573-2323
Fax: 212-573-2641

Mission: not available

Fund Size: $7 billion
Founded: not available
Average Investment: not available
Minimum Investment: not available

Industry Group Preference: Consumer, Medical/Health Related

Portfolio Companies: Opta Food Ingredients, Inc.

Officers, Executives and Principals

Barry Bloom

POLICY MANAGEMENT SYSTEMS CORPORATION

One PMS Center
Blythewood, SC 29016

Telephone: 803-735-4000
Fax: 803-735-6499

Mission: not available

Fund Size: $415 million
Founded: not available
Average Investment: not available
Minimum Investment: not available

Industry Group Preference: Diversified

Portfolio Companies: FAI Insurances Ltd.

Officers, Executives and Principals

Robert L. Gresham

QUALITY FOOD CENTERS, INC.

10166 Northeast 8th Street, P.O. Box 3967
Bellevue, WA 98009

Telephone: 206-455-3761
Fax: 206-462-2214

Mission: not available

Fund Size: $518.2 million
Founded: not available
Average Investment: not available
Minimum Investment: not available

Industry Group Preference: Consumer

Portfolio Companies: not available

Officers, Executives and Principals

Marc Evanger, Chief Financial Officer
Dan Kourkoumelis, President

RALSTON PURINA COMPANY
Checkerboard Square
St. Louis, MO 63164

Telephone: 314-982-1000

Mission: not available

Fund Size: $7.9 billion
Founded: not available
Average Investment: not available
Minimum Investment: not available

Industry Group Preference: Consumer

Portfolio Companies: Eveready Battery Co., Protein Technologies International, Continental Baking, Hostess

Officers, Executives and Principals

James R. Elsesser, Chief Financial Officer

RHONE-POULENC RORER, INC.

500 Arcola Road
Collegeville, PA 19426

Telephone: 215-454-8000
Fax: 215-454-8028

Mission: not available

Fund Size: $3.8 billion
Founded: not available
Average Investment: not available
Minimum Investment: not available

Industry Group Preference: Medical/Health Related

Portfolio Companies: ISIS Pharmaceuticals, The Immune Response Corporation

Officers, Executives and Principals

Gilles D. Brisson

E

Venture Capital Funds
Outside the United States and Canada

Non-US Currencies and Their US Dollar Equivalents as of November 1997

Symbol	Currency	US$ value of 1 unit
£	UK pounds	1.63
A$	Australian dollars	0.700000
Bfr	Belgian francs	0.027345
C$	Canadian dollars	0.718391
Dkr	Danish kronen	0.148036
DM	Deutschmarks	0.5636
Dr.	Greek drachmas	0.003586
Ecu	European [Union] currency units	1.111000
Esc	Portuguese escudos	.005540
Ffr	French francs	0.168308
FM	Finnish markkas	0.188573
G	Dutch guilders	0.500375
L	Italian lire	0.000577
Nkr	Norwegian kronen	0.140321
Pta	Spanish pesetas	0.006683
R	South African rands	0.211305
Sch	Austrian schillings	0.079968
Sfr	Swiss francs	0.683247
SK	Slovak korunas	0.02960
Skr	Swedish kronen	0.131770
W	Korean won	0.001076
Z	Polish zlotys	0.2924

ABBOTT DIAGNOSTICA GmbH

New Product Development
Max-Planck-Ring 2
65205 Delkenheim
Germany

Telephone: 49-6122-581255
Fax: 49-6122-581473

Mission: Actively seeking new investments as a member of the Euroventures network

Fund Size: Ecu5 million
Founded: 1985
Average Investment: not available
Minimum Investment: not available

Investment Criteria: All stages

Geographic Preference: Belgium, Luxembourg, The Netherlands

Industry Group Preference: Biotechnology, Medical/Health Related

Portfolio Companies: not available

Officers, Executives and Principals

Dr. Howard Grey

ABEL VENTURE MANAGERS

43 Meadway
Esher
Surrey
KT10 9HG
United Kingdom

Telephone: 44-1372-470373
Fax: 44-1372-469228
E-mail: 100636.3313@compuserve.com

Mission: Actively seeking new investments

Fund Size: £24 million
Founded: 1990
Average Investment: £500,000
Minimum Investment: £100,000

Investment Criteria: Expansion, Management Buy-in, Management Buy-out, Rescue/Turnaround, Venture Purchase of Quoted Shares, Receiverships, Preflotation Financings

Geographic Preference: United Kingdom

Industry Group Preference: All sectors considered, but specialising in Communications, Computer Related, Electronics

Portfolio Companies: Test Industries plc, BVR, Compact Data Limited, Diomed Limited, Mechadyne International plc, Quadrant Healthcare plc, Ionitermie Limited, PIC European Services Limited

Officers, Executives and Principals

Paul Banner MA, FIA
Philip Corbishley BSc, CEng

ABINGWORTH MANAGEMENT LIMITED

26 St James's Street
London SW1A 1HA
United Kingdom

Telephone: 44-171-839-6745
Fax: 44-171-930-1891

Mission: Actively seeking new investments

Fund Size: £100 million
Founded: 1973
Average Investment: £900,000
Minimum Investment: £500,000

Investment Criteria: All stages

Geographic Preference: United Kingdom, United States

Industry Group Preference: Communications, Computer Related, Consumer Related, Distribution, Electronic Components and Instrumentation, Genetic Engineering, Industrial Products and Equipment, Medical/Health Related

Portfolio Companies: British Biotech plc, Cantab Pharmaceuticals plc, Comino Limited, RM plc, NP Record plc

Officers, Executives and Principals

Marius Gray, Chairman
David Quysner, Chief Executive Officer
Jeryl Andrew, Director
Stephen Bunting, Director
David Leathers, Director
David Morrison, Director

AB M. S. KOBBS SÖNER

Södra Hamngatan 19-21
P. O. Box 11028
40421 Gothenburg
Sweden

Telephone: 46-31-131230
Fax: 46-31-711-3542

Mission: Actively seeking new investments

Fund Size: Skr40 million
Founded: 1809
Average Investment: not available
Minimum Investment: Skr300,000

Investment Criteria: not available

Geographic Preference: Sweden

Industry Group Preference: All sectors considered

Portfolio Companies: not available

Officers, Executives and Principals

Henrik Wingstrand, Managing Director
Petter Wingstrand, Deputy Managing Director

ABN AMRO CAUSEWAY LIMITED

7 Hanover Square
London W1R 9HE
United Kingdom

Telephone: 44-171-495-2525
Fax: 44-171-491-2050

Mission: Actively seeking new investments

Fund Size: not available
Founded: 1983
Average Investment: £4 million
Minimum Investment: £2.5 million

Investment Criteria: Expansion, Management Buy-in, Management Buy-out, Secondary Purchase/Replacement Capital

Geographic Preference: United Kingdom

Industry Group Preference: All sectors considered

Portfolio Companies: Edens Trading Group, Mill House Inns, Novo Group

Officers, Executives and Principals

Lionel Anthony, Chief Executive Officer and Chairman
David Becker Walker, Director
Geoffrey Vero, Director
Patrick Bulmer, Director
Tim Lawrence, Director
Carolyn Maddox, Director

ABN AMRO CORPORATE INVESTMENTS

Foppingadreef 22 (AA 3240)
P. O. Box 283
1000 EA Amersterdam
The Netherlands

Telephone: 31-20-628-0732
Fax: 31-20-628-7822

Other Office Locationss

ABN AMRO Capital (U. S. A.) Inc.
135 South LaSalle Street
Chicago, IL
United States
Phone 312-904-6445, Fax 312-606-8427

ABN AMRO Causeway Limited
7 Hanover Square
London W1R 9HE
United Kingdom
Phone 44-171-495-2525, Fax 44-171-491-2050

ABN AMRO/HG Asia
31st Floor, Edinburgh Tower
15 Queen's Road
Central
Hong Kong
Phone 852-2846-4335, Fax 852-2525-0902

ABN AMRO Germany
Mainzer Landstrasse 65
60329 Frankfurt am Main
Germany
Phone 49-69-2690-0410, Fax 49-69-2690-0419

Mission: Actively seeking new investments in strong, growing companies through its various offices and its two affiliates, NSM Finance SA (83.9% owned by ABN AMRO) and IMI-ABN AMRO (a 50/50 joint venture with the Istituto Mobiliare Italiano)

Fund Size: G1 billion
Founded: not available
Average Investment: G7.5 million
Minimum Investment: G1 million

Investment Criteria: Expansion/Development, Management Buy-out, Management Buy-in, Bridge, Replacement, Mezzanine

Geographic Preference: Europe, North America, Asia

Industry Group Preference: All sectors considered except Financial Institutions and Real Estate

Portfolio Companies: not available

Officers, Executives and Principals

Bob Kramer, Senior Vice President (Amsterdam)
Leo Schenk, Senior Vice President (Amsterdam)
Jan Stolker, Senior Vice President (Amsterdam)
Cor van't Spijker, Senior Vice President (Amsterdam)
Dancker Bijleveld, Senior Vice President (International Venture Capital, Amsterdam)
Joe Rizzi, Senior Vice President (Chicago)
Dennis O'Malley, Senior Vice President (Chicago)
Lionel Anthony, Chief Executive Officer (London)
Marc Staal, Senior Vice President (Hong Kong)
Roel Schoemaker, Vice President (Frankfurt)

ABRUZZO CAPITAL SpA

Via Silvio Pellico 28/1
65123 Pescara
Italy

Telephone: 39-85-421-7674
Fax: 39-85-422-1186

Mission: Actively seeking new investments

Fund Size: Ecu3.5 million
Founded: not available
Average Investment: not available
Minimum Investment: not available

Investment Criteria: Seed, Start-up, Early-stage, Expansion/Development

Geographic Preference: Italy

Industry Group Preference: All sectors considered

Portfolio Companies: not available

Officers, Executives and Principals

Emilio Tenaglia

AB SEGULAH

Styrmansgatan 2
P. O. Box 5483
11484 Stockholm
Sweden

Telephone: 46-8-665-3270
Fax: 46-8-665-3278
E-mail: sachs@algonet.se, urwitz@algonet.se

Mission: Actively seeking new investments

Fund Size: Skr70 million
Founded: not available
Average Investment: not available
Minimum Investment: Skr5 million

Investment Criteria: not available

Geographic Preference: Europe

Industry Group Preference: All sectors considered

Portfolio Companies: not available

Officers, Executives and Principals

Gabriel Urwitz, Managing Director
Daniel Sachs, Investment Manager

ABTRUST FUND MANAGERS LIMITED

10 Queens Terrace
Aberdeen AB10 1QG
United Kingdom

Telephone: 44-1224-631999
Fax: 44-1224-647010

Other Office Locations
6 Fraser Street
Inverness
Phone 44-1463-717214, Fax 44-1463-717211

Mission: To provide above-average long-term capital appreciation, principally by investing development capital in private companies in Scotland

Fund Size: £60 million
Founded: 1986
Average Investment: £1 million
Minimum Investment: £200,000

Investment Criteria: Expansion, Management Buy-in, Management Buy-out, Secondary Purchase/Replacement Capital, Venture Purchase of Quoted Shares

Geographic Preference: United Kingdom (Scotland)

Industry Group Preference: All sectors considered

Portfolio Companies: Anderson Cars Group Limited, Atlantic Power and Gas Holdings Limited, Healthcare Scotland Limited, Grampian Country Food Group Limited

Officers, Executives and Principals

Hugh V. M. Little
Allan Dunn
Robert Beattie

A. C. INVEST AB

Expolaris Center
93178 Skelleftea
Sweden

Telephone: 46-910-17590
Fax: 46-910-776-830

Mission: Actively seeking new investments

Fund Size: Skr35 million
Founded: not available
Average Investment: not available
Minimum Investment: Skr500,000

Investment Criteria: not available

Geographic Preference: Sweden

Industry Group Preference: All sectors considered

Portfolio Companies: not available

Officers, Executives and Principals

Henning Ericsson, Managing Director

ACLAND

20 bis avenue Rapp
75007 Paris
France

Telephone: 33-1-4442-7000
Fax: 33-1-4442-7777

Mission: Actively seeking new investments

Fund Size: Ffr 413 million
Founded: not available
Average Investment: not available
Minimum Investment: Ffr10 million

Investment Criteria: Management Buy-out

Geographic Preference: Europe, France

Industry Group Preference: All sectors considered

Portfolio Companies: Verliac, Mouvex, France Porte, Axson, Loxam, Edrasco

Officers, Executives and Principals

Antoine Chappuis
Jean Plamandon
Laurent Chevalier
Snjiv Gomez

A.C.T. VENTURE CAPITAL LIMITED

Windsor Business Centre
58 Howard Street
Belfast BT1 6PJ
United Kingdom

Telephone: 44-1232-247266
Fax: 44-1232-247372
E-mail: info@actv.ie

Other Office Locations
Jefferson House
Eglinton Road
Donnybrook
Dublin 4
Ireland
Phone 353-1-260-0966, Fax 353-1-260-0538

Mission: Actively seeking new investments

Fund Size: £75 million
Founded: 1994
Average Investment: £2 million
Minimum Investment: £400,000

Investment Criteria: All stages except Start-up

Geographic Preference: Irish Republic, Northern Ireland

Industry Group Preference: All sectors considered

Portfolio Companies: Allegro Ltd., Imari Ltd., Clashfern Holdings Ltd., Fitzpatricks' Enterprises Ltd., MDS Telephone Systems, Connacht Court Group

Officers, Executives and Principals

Niall Carroll
Aidan Byrnes
Walter Hobbs
Owen Murphy

ADC

36 rue de Mont Thabor
75001 Paris
France

Telephone: 33-1-4260-7278
Fax: 33-1-4296-0312

Mission: Actively seeking new investments

Fund Size: Ffr5 million
Founded: not available
Average Investment: not available
Minimum Investment: Ffr50,000

Investment Criteria: Start-up, Early-stage

Geographic Preference: Europe

Industry Group Preference: Communications, Information Technology

Portfolio Companies: SILOGIC, ARTHUS Conseil, Cognitive Système Europe, TELEDIA

Officers, Executives and Principals

Jean-Claude Bertaut

ADINVEST AG

Lavaterstrasse 45
8027 Zürich
Switzerland

Telephone: 41-1-202-2155
Fax: 41-1-202-1942

Mission: Actively seeking new investments

Fund Size: not available
Founded: not available
Average Investment: not available
Minimum Investment: not available

Investment Criteria: Early-stage, Expansion/Development, Management Buy-out, Replacement/Share Purchases, Turnaround

Geographic Preference: None

Industry Group Preference: All sectors considered

Portfolio Companies: not available

Officers, Executives and Principals

Dr. Neil V. Sunderland
Victor Balli

ADVENT INTERNATIONAL plc

123 Buckingham Palace Road
London SW1W 9SL
United Kingdom

Telephone: 44-171-333-0800
Fax: 44-171-333-0801
E-mail: uk.aigpe.com

Mission: not available

Fund Size: £400 million
Founded: not available
Average Investment: £8 million
Minimum Investment: £3 million

Investment Criteria: Bridge Finance, Expansion, Management Buy-in, Management Buy-out, Refinancing Bank Debt, Secondary Purchase/Replacement Capital, Venture Purchase of Quoted Shares

Geographic Preference: United Kingdom, Western Europe, North America, Asia, Central Europe, South America

Industry Group Preference: Chemical and Materials, Communications, Computer Related, Consumer Related, Energy, Environmental, Industrial Products and Services, Media, Medical Related

Portfolio Companies: INSPEC Group (United Kingdom), Colofon BV (Netherlands), Cable Management Ireland (Irish Republic), KabelVision (Germany), BIP Group (United Kingdom)

Officers, Executives and Principals

Dr. John Walker
Massimo Prelz
Will Schmidt
John Singer
Scott Lanphere
Ron Sheldon
Geoffrey Shopland

ADVENT LIMITED

25 Buckingham Gate
London SW1E 6LD
United Kingdom

Telephone: 44-171-630-9811
Fax: 44-171-828-1474/4919
E-mail: info@adventfunds.co.uk

Mission: Actively seeking new investments

Fund Size: £105 million
Founded: 1981
Average Investment: £800,000
Minimum Investment: £250,000

Investment Criteria: Start-up, First-stage, Second-stage, Special Situations

Geographic Preference: North America, Western Europe

Industry Group Preference: Communications, Computer Related, Electronic Components and Instrumentation, Genetic Engineering, Industrial Products and Equipment, Medical/Health Related

Portfolio Companies: Arris Pharmaceuticals Corp, Intercom Data Systems Ltd., Maison Blanc Ltd., Vanguard Medica Ltd., Varicare Ltd.

Officers, Executives and Principals

David Cooksey, Chairman
Colin Amies, General Partner
Jerry Benjamin, General Partner
Alan Speirs, General Partner
Martin Williams, Finance Director

AENEAS INVESTMENT MANAGMENT AND CONSULTING SA

32 Kifissias Avenue
15125 Maroussi
Athens
Greece

Telephone: 30-1-684-7872
Fax: 30-1-684-7473

Mission: Actively seeking new investments as arm of the Commerical Bank of Greece

Fund Size: Ecu5million
Founded: 1994
Average Investment: not avaible
Minimum Investment: Ecu200,000

Investment Criteria: Start-up, Early-stage, Expansion/Development, Management Buy-in, Turnaround, Mezzanine, Bridge

Geographic Preference: Greece, Cyprus

Industry Group Preference: Biotechnology, Communications, Computer Software, Consumer Related, Electronics Related, Medical/Health Related

Portfolio Companies: not available

Officers, Executives and Principals

George Ganetsos
John Giannopoulos
Aristidis Fronistas
Panagiotis Perlikos

AFFÄRSSTRATEGERNA I SVERIGE AB

P. O. Box 10277
10055 Stockholm
Sweden

Telephone: 46-8-662-4030
Fax: 46-8-660-8319
E-mail: cgfridh@astrateg.se; henrik@vencap.se

Mission: Actively seeking new investments

Fund Size: Skr50 million
Founded: 1990
Average Investment: Skr3 million
Minimum Investment: Skr500,000

Investment Criteria: Early-stage

Geographic Preference: Sweden

Industry Group Preference: Health Care, Telecommunications

Portfolio Companies: Artema Medical AB, Artimplant AB, Confidence International AB, Enercom AB, Game Design AB, Optosof AB, Radio Design AB, Samba Sensors AB, Goseber Bruk AB

Officers, Executives and Principals

Claes-Göran Fridh
Henrik Tisell
Ulf Sedig

AGAB AKTIENGESELLSCHAFT FÜR ANLAGEN UND BETEILIGUNGEN

Opernplatz 2
60313 Frankfurt am Main
Germany

Telephone: 49-69-1387-130
Fax: 49-69-1387-1320

Mission: Actively seeking new investments

Fund Size: DM610 million
Founded: not available
Average Investment: not available
Minimum Investment: DM5 million

Investment Criteria: All stages except Start-up

Geographic Preference: none

Industry Group Preference: All sectors considered

Portfolio Companies: not available

Officers, Executives and Principals

Dr. Wilhelm Esselmann
Heinz Brinker

AGRINOVA

100 boulevard du Montparnasse
75682 Paris
France

Telephone: 33-1-43-232234
Fax: 33-1-43-233319

Mission: Actively seeking new investments

Fund Size: Ffr73 million
Founded: not available
Average Investment: not available
Minimum Investment: Ffr2 million

Investment Criteria: Expansion/Development, Leveraged Buy-out

Geographic Preference: Europe

Industry Group Preference: Agriculture/ Forestry/ Fish, Biotechnology, Industrial Products, Medical/Health Related,

Portfolio Companies: Guilloteau, Vals, Genset, Le CEP Français, Solabia

Officers, Executives and Principals

Jean-Marie Voisin, Managing Director

AGRO PARTENAIRES

38 rue du Louvre
75001 Paris
France

Telephone: 33-1-4026-0169
Fax: 33-1-4026-1747

Mission: Actively seeking new investments

Fund Size: Ecu3.5 million
Founded: not available
Average Investment: not available
Minimum Investment: Ecu15,000

Investment Criteria: Start-up, Expansion/Development, Management Buy-in

Geographic Preference: Europe, France

Industry Group Preference: Agriculture/Forestry, Consumer Products/Services,

Portfolio Companies: not available

Officers, Executives and Principals

André Polloni
Anny Daubet

AGU AKTIENGESELLSCHAFT FÜR UNTERNEHMENSBETEILIGUNGEN

Harald Quandt Haus
Am Pilgerrain 17
61325 Bad Homburg
Germany

Telephone: 49-6172-402176
Fax: 49-6172-402178

Mission: Actively seeking new investments

Fund Size: DM83.5 million
Founded: not available
Average Investment: not available
Minimum Investment: DM10 million

Investment Criteria: Management Buy-out, Leveraged Buyout

Geographic Preference: Germany

Industry Group Preference: All sectors considered

Portfolio Companies: not available

Officers, Executives and Principals

Werner Quillman
Thomas H. Retzlaff
Michael Boltz

A. H. SMÅFÖRETAGSINVEST AB

Regeringsgatan 48, 6tr
P. O. Box 7528
10392 Stockholm
Sweden

Telephone: 46-8-242503
Fax: 46-8-791-8270

Mission: Actively seeking new investments in small companies as a joint venture of **Atle AB** and **Handelsban-**
ken

Fund Size: Skr50 million
Founded: 1994
Average Investment: not available
Minimum Investment: Skr500,000

Investment Criteria: All stages

Geographic Preference: Sweden

Industry Group Preference: All sectors considered

Portfolio Companies: not available

Officers, Executives and Principals

Bo Thorson, Managing Director
Gunnar Huss
Curt Källström

AITEC

Av. Duque d' Avila 23-1° Dt.
1000 Lisbon
Portugal

Telephone: 351-1-352-0665
Fax: 351-1-352-6314
E-mail: mdl@avila.inesc.pl

Mission: Actively seeking new investments

Fund Size: not available
Founded: not available
Average Investment: not available
Minimum Investment: not available

Investment Criteria: Seed, Start-up, Early-stage, Expansion/Development

Geographic Preference: Europe, Brazil, Macau

Industry Group Preference: Computer Related, Computer Software, Electronics Related

Portfolio Companies: not available

Officers, Executives and Principals

Manuel Laranja
Manuel Festas

ALLIANCE ENTREPRENDRE

5 rue Masseran
75007 Paris
France

Telephone: 33-1-4449-6850
Fax: 33-1-4449-6855

Mission: Actively seeking new investments

Fund Size: Ffr50 million
Founded: not available
Average Investment: not available
Minimum Investment: Ffr2 million

Investment Criteria: Expansion/Development, Replacement

Geographic Preference: France

Industry Group Preference: All sectors considered

Portfolio Companies: not available

Officers, Executives and Principals

Lionnel Thomas, Managing Director
Henry Peyroux, Deputy Managing Director

ALLIANZ UNTERNEHMENSBETEILIGUNGSGESELLSCHAFT AG

Königinstrasse 28
80802 Munich
Germany

Telephone: 49-89-3800-2223
Fax: 49-89-347521

Mission: Actively seeking new investments

Fund Size: DM46 million
Founded: not available
Average Investment: not available
Minimum Investment: DM5 million

Investment Criteria: Expansion, Management Buy-out, Management Buy-in

Geographic Preference: none

Industry Group Preference: All sectors considered

Portfolio Companies: not available

Officers, Executives and Principals

Dr. Helmut Wimmer
Dr. Anton Wiegers

ALMI FÖRETAGSPARTNER AB

Tegelbacken 4
11152 Stockholm
Sweden

Telephone: 46-8-402-0900
Fax: 46-8-406-0300
E-mail: info@almi.se

Mission: Actively seeking new investments

Fund Size: Skr4.5 billion
Founded: not available
Average Investment: not available
Minimum Investment: not available

Investment Criteria: not available

Geographic Preference: Sweden

Industry Group Preference: All sectors considered

Portfolio Companies: not available

Officers, Executives and Principals

Per A. Smeds

ALPHA ASSOCIÉS

89 rue Taitbout
75009 Paris
France

Telephone: 33-1-4286-3000
Fax: 33-1-4016-764323

Mission: Actively seeking new investments

Fund Size: Ffr955 million
Founded: 1985
Average Investment: not available
Minimum Investment: Ffr10 million

Investment Criteria: Second-stage, Leveraged Buy-out

Geographic Preference: France, Germany

Industry Group Preference: All sectors considered

Portfolio Companies: not available

Officers, Executives and Principals

Alain Blanc-Brude, President
Antoine Issaverdens, General Secretary
Nicolas ver Hulst, Director
Thomas Schlytter Henrichsen, Director
Florence Fesneau, Associate Director
Patricia Desquesnes, Director, External Relations

ALPINVEST HOLDING NV

Gooimeer 3 Postbus 5073
1410 AB Naarden
The Netherlands

Telephone: 31-35-695-2600
Fax: 31-35-694-7525

Mission: Actively seeking new investments

Fund Size: Ecu240 million
Founded: not available
Average Investment: not available
Minimum Investment: Ecu800,000

Investment Criteria: not available

Geographic Preference: Austria, Belgium, France, Germany, United Kingdom, Scandinavia, Switzerland

Industry Group Preference: not available

Portfolio Companies: not available

Officers, Executives and Principals

C. M. Vermeulen
Th. A. Vervoort

ALTA BERKELEY ASSOCIATES
9-10 Savile Row
London W1X 1AF
United Kingdom

Telephone: 44-171-734-4884
Fax: 44-171-734-6711

Other Office Locations
6 rue d'Italie
P. O. Box 326
1211 Geneva 3
Switzerland
Phone 41-22-318-0870, Fax 41-22-318-0919

Mission: Actively seeking new investments

Fund Size: £60 million
Founded: 1982
Average Investment: £1 million
Minimum Investment: £100,000

Investment Criteria: Seed, Research and Development, Startup, First-stage, Second-stage, Leveraged Buy-out, Special Situations

Geographic Preference: Western Europe

Industry Group Preference: Communications, Computer Related, Distribution, Genetic Engineering, Medical/Health Related

Portfolio Companies: not available

Officers, Executives and Principals

Bryan Wood, Partner (Geneva)
David Needham, Partner (London)
Laurie Rostron, Partner (London)
Hugh Smith, Partner (London)
Marie-Louise Murville (London)

A. M. F. PENSION

Luntmakargatan 34
11388 Stockholm
Sweden

Telephone: 46-8-787-4000
Fax: 46-8-104788

Mission: Actively seeking new investments

Fund Size: Skr200 million
Founded: not available
Average Investment: not available
Minimum Investment: not available

Investment Criteria: All stages

Geographic Preference: Sweden

Industry Group Preference: All sectors considered

Portfolio Companies: not available

Officers, Executives and Principals

Jan-Erik Erenius, Managing Director
Tor Marthin, Finance Director
Mats Guldbrand
Tom Jensen
Sten Kottmeier
Elisabeth Svensson

AMP INVESTMENTS AUSTRALIA LIMITED

Level 20, AMP Building
33 Alfred Street
Sydney Cove
New South Wales 2000
Australia

Telephone: 612-9257-5771
Fax: 612-9257-2746

Mission: Actively seeking new investments

Fund Size: A$3.3 billion
Founded: 1993
Average Investment: not available
Minimum Investment: A$500,000

Investment Criteria: Second-stage, Leveraged Buy-out

Geographic Preference: Australia (but other investments not excluded)

Industry Group Preference: Consumer Related

Portfolio Companies: not available

Officers, Executives and Principals

Dr. Peter Cassidy, Head of Private Investments
Marcus Darville, Manager, Business Development Fund
Graham Timms, Manager, Infrastructure Investments

ANTIN GESTION

41 avenue de l'Opéra
75002 Paris
France

Telephone: 33-1-4298-6795
Fax: 33-1-4298-6706

Mission: Actively seeking new investments

Fund Size: Ffr175 million
Founded: not available
Average Investment: not available
Minimum Investment: Ffr5 million

Investment Criteria: Expansion/Development

Geographic Preference: Europe

Industry Group Preference: All sectors considered

Portfolio Companies: Palladium, Jacadi

Officers, Executives and Principals

Jean-Christophe Morandeau

ANVAR

43 rue Caumartin
75436 Paris
France

Telephone: 33-1-4017-8300
Fax: 33-1-4266-0220

Mission: Promoting and financing technological innovation, especially for small and medium-sized companies
  and research and development partnerships

Fund Size: Ecu225 million
Founded: not available
Average Investment: not available
Minimum Investment: not available

Investment Criteria: Seed, Start-up, Early-stage, Expansion/Development, Bridge

Geographic Preference: Europe, United States

Industry Group Preference: Biotechnology, Communications, Computer Related, Electronics Related,
  Energy, Medical/Health Related

Portfolio Companies: not available

Officers, Executives and Principals

Henri Guillaume
Jeane Seyvet
Omar Senhaji
Gérard Hontebeyrie

APAX PARTNERS AND CO. VENTURES LTD.

15 Portland Place
London WIN 3AA
United Kingdom

Telephone: 44-171-872-6300
Fax: 44-171-636-6475

Other Office Locations
45 Avenue Kléber
75784 Paris
France
Phone 33-1-4553-0378, Fax 33-1-4704-2373

Möhlstrasse 22
81675 Munich
Germany
Phone 49-89-9989-090, Fax 49-89-9989-0932

Bahnhofstrasse 17
8702 Zollikon
Switzerland
Phone 41-1-391-5268, Fax 41-1-391-5935

Mission: Actively seeking new investments

Fund Size: £500 million
Founded: not available
Average Investment: £4 million
Minimum Investment: £1 million

Investment Criteria: All stages except Seed

Geographic Preference: United Kingdom, Europe

Industry Group Preference: All sectors considered

Portfolio Companies: Computacenter, Scotia Holdings, Virgin Radio, Quexco, Demon Internet

Officers, Executives and Principals

Ronald Cohen
Adrian Beecroft
Dr. Peter Englander
Clive Sherling
Jon Moulton
John McMonigall

APAX PARTNERS ET CIE.

45 Avenue Kléber
75784 Paris
France

Telephone: 33-1-4553-0378
Fax: 33-1-4704-2373

Mission: Actively seeking new investments

Fund Size: Ffr2.6 billion
Founded: not available
Average Investment: not available
Minimum Investment: Ffr5 million

Investment Criteria: Start-up, Early-stage, Expansion/Development, Leveraged Buy-in, Leveraged Buy-out, Turnaround/Restructuring

Geographic Preference: France, Germany, Spain, Switzerland, United Kingdom, United States

Industry Group Preference: All sectors considered, but especially Information Technology, Media, Medical/ Health Related, Specialised Distribution

Portfolio Companies: Aigle, Coletica, Danel, Effik, HMI Metrologie International, Sephora, Socamel, Xpedite Systems

Officers, Executives and Principals

Maurice Tchenio
Martine Clavel
Patrick de Giovanni
Rudolphe Lambert
Jean-Jacques Lejal
Edgard Misrahi
Claude Rosevegue
Laurent Ganem

APAX PARTNERS UND CO. AG

Möhlstrasse 22
81675 Munich
Germany

Telephone: 49-89-9989-090
Fax: 49-89-9989-0932

Mission: Actively seeking new investments

Fund Size: Ecu50 million
Founded: not available
Average Investment: not available
Minimum Investment: Ecu1.5 million

Investment Criteria: Start-up, Early-stage, Expansion/Development, Management Buy-out, Management Buy-in, Turnaround

Geographic Preference: Austria, Germany, Switzerland

Industry Group Preference: Communications, Consumer Related, Industrial Services, Medical/Health Related, Recycling Related

Portfolio Companies: not available

Officers, Executives and Principals

Dr. Martin Halusa
Dr. Michael Hinderer
Michael Phillips
Dr. Thomas Scheiner

APAX PARTNERS UND CO. AG

Bahnhofstrasse 17
8702 Zollikon
Switzerland

Telephone: 41-1-391-5268
Fax: 41-1-391-5935

Mission: Actively seeking new investments

Fund Size: not available
Founded: not available
Average Investment: not available
Minimum Investment: Sfr3 million

Investment Criteria: Seed, Start-up, Expansion/Development, Management Buy-out, Management Buy-in, Bridge, Early-stage

Geographic Preference: Switzerland, Europe, United States

Industry Group Preference: All sectors considered, but especially Media, Medical/Health Related, Telecommunications

Portfolio Companies: not available

Officers, Executives and Principals

Dr. Martin Halusa
Dr. Michael Hinderer
Max Burger-Calderon
Dr. Ulrich Geilinger
Michael Phillips
Dr. Thomas Scheiner

ARCA IMPRESA GESTIONI SpA

Via della Moscova 3
20121 Milan
Italy

Telephone: 39-2-63-61251
Fax: 39-2-29-006481
E-mail: arcme@iol.it

Mission: Mainly investing in growing companies or industrial restructuring

Fund Size: L80 billion
Founded: 1995
Average Investment: L2-5 billion
Minimum Investment: L1 billion

Investment Criteria: Development Capital, Leveraged Buy-out, Management Buy-out

Geographic Preference: Italy

Industry Group Preference: All sectors considered

Portfolio Companies: not available

Officers, Executives and Principals

Giorgio Cirla, Managing Director
Lorenzo Scaravelli, Director
Enrico Palandri, Senior Officer

ARCA MERCHANT SpA

Via della Moscova 3
20121 Milan
Italy

Telephone: 39-2-6361252
Fax: 39-2-29005411
E-mail: arcme@iol.it

Mission: Acquiring minority or majority shareholdings in, and underwriting convertible bond issues on behalf of, developing companies; supporting, assisting and supplying capital to managers interested in buy-outs or buy-ins; and acquiring shareholdings from those unable to ensure the continuity of a shareholding in a company

Fund Size: L250 billion
Founded: 1987
Average Investment: L2-3 billion
Minimum Investment: L500 million

Investment Criteria: Development Capital, Management Buy-out, Management Buy-in

Geographic Preference: Italy

Industry Group Preference: All sectors considered

Portfolio Companies: not available

Officers, Executives and Principals

Giorgio Cirla, Managing Director
Mauro Gambaro, Director

ARGOS SODITIC FRANCE

14 rue de Bassano
75783 Paris
France

Telephone: 33-1-5367-2050
Fax: 33-1-5367-2055
E-mail: argosfce@micronet.fr

Mission: Actively seeking investments for the Euroknights group of funds in medium-sized companies with revenues between $25 million and $490 million, proven profitability and clearly defined strategic plans

Fund Size: $210 million
Founded: 1989
Average Investment: $7.5 million
Minimum Investment: $2.5 million

Investment Criteria: Management Buy-out and Buy-in, Development Capital

Geographic Preference: Continental Europe

Industry Group Preference: All sectors considered, but especially Construction and Real Estate

Portfolio Companies: Chabert Duval, Molinel, Cébé International SA, Plasticentre SA, IPSOS Holding SA

Officers, Executives and Principals

Gilles Mougenot, Chief Executive Officer
Education: advanced research degree in Business Law, University of Paris; Graduate, French Comparative Law Institute
Background: Partner, Initiative et Finance (France)

Louis Godron, Managing Director
Education: Graduate in Engineering, Ecole Centrale de Paris
Background: Investment Analyst, Initiative et Finance (France)

Dinah Benhamou, Investment Analyst
Education: Graduate, Ecole Supérieure de Commerce de Paris
Background: Auditor, Arthur Andersen

Thierry Butlewski, Investment Analyst
Education: Graduate, Ecole Supérieure de Commerce de Reims; degree in Business Law
Background: Auditor, Arthur Andersen

Catherine Gras, Investment Analyst
Education: Graduate, ESSEC
Background: Auditor, Peat Marwick

ARGOS SODITIC ITALIA Srl

Via Cerva 28
Milan 20122
Italy

Telephone: 39-2-77491
Fax: 39-2-781175

Mission: Actively seeking new investments

Fund Size: Ecu120 million
Founded: 1996
Average Investment: Ecu8 million
Minimum Investment: Ecu3 million

Investment Criteria: Leveraged Buy-out, Special Situations, Control-block Purchases, Development Capital

Geographic Preference: Italy

Industry Group Preference: Communications, Consumer, Distribution, Industrial Products and Equipment, Medical/Health Related

Portfolio Companies: not available

Officers, Executives and Principals

Raymond Totah, Partner and Managing Director
Education: Graduate, Milan Bocconi University
Background: Director, member companies of the Fineurop group

Fabio Galli, Manager
Education: Graduate, Milan Bocconi University

ARGOS SODITIC SA

Rua Silva Carvalho 347
1200 Lisbon
Portugal

Telephone: 351-1-387-0700
Fax: 351-1-387-0768

Mission: Actively seeking new investments

Fund Size: not available
Founded: not available
Average Investment: not available
Minimum Investment: not available

Investment Criteria: Leveraged Buy-out, Special Situations, Control-block Purchases, Development Capital

Geographic Preference: not available

Industry Group Preference: Communications, Consumer, Distribution, Industrial Products and Equipment, Medical/Health Related

Portfolio Companies: not available

Officers, Executives and Principals

Miguel Pais Do Amaral
Francisco Santana Ramos

ARGOS SODITIC SA

114 rue du Rhône
1204 Geneva
Switzerland

Telephone: 41-22-849-6633
Fax: 41-22-849-6627
E-mail: argosch@iprolink.ch

Other Office Locations
14 rue de Bassano
75116 Paris
France
Phone 33-1-5367-2050, Fax 33-1-5367-2055

Via Cerva 28
Milan 20122
Italy
Phone 39-2-77491, Fax 39-2-781175

Rua Silva Carvalho 347
1200 Lisbon
Portugal
Phone 351-1-387-0700, Fax 351-1-387-0768

Mission: Actively seeking new investments

Fund Size: Ecu120 million
Founded: 1989
Average Investment: Ecu6 million
Minimum Investment: Ecu2 million

Investment Criteria: Leveraged Buy-out, Leveraged Buy-in, Special Situations, Control-block Purchases, and
Development Capital

Geographic Preference: France, Italy, Portugal, Switzerland

Industry Group Preference: Communications, Consumer, Distribution, Industrial Products and Equipment,
Medical/Health Related

Portfolio Companies: Ceramic (Portugal), Chabert-Duval (France), Molinel (France), Saludaes (Portugal),
Cébé International SA (France), Plasticentre SA (France), IPSOS Holding SA (France)

Officers, Executives and Principals

Edoardo Bugnone
Guy Semmens

A.S.C. GROUP

24 Raffles Place
17-04 Clifford Centre
Singapore 048621

Telephone: 65-535-8066
Fax: 65-535-6629

Mission: Actively seeking new investments

Fund Size: $150 million
Founded: 1989
Average Investment: $5-$10 million
Minimum Investment: $5 million

Investment Criteria: Start-up, Mezzanine, Special Situations

Geographic Preference: ASEAN countries

Industry Group Preference: Communications, Computer Related, Consumer, Distribution, Electronic Components and Instrumentation, Energy/Natural Resources, Genetic Engineering, Industrial Products and Equipment, Medical/Health Related

Portfolio Companies: not available

Officers, Executives and Principals

Victor Yeo Mong Yang, Executive Director
Lee Cheong Seng, Managing Director
David Chia Tian Sin, Associate Director
John Lim Yew Kong, Senior Manager
Ang Peng Seng, Manager

ASTORG COMPAGNIE D'INVESTISSEMENTS

27 rue de la Ville l'Evêque
75008 Paris
France

Telephone: 33-1-4007-0514
Fax: 33-1-4924-9782

Mission: Actively seeking new investments

Fund Size: Ffr600 million
Founded: not available
Average Investment: not available
Minimum Investment: Ffr15 million

Investment Criteria: Development, Leveraged Buy-out, Leveraged Buy-in

Geographic Preference: France

Industry Group Preference: All sectors considered

Portfolio Companies: CEE, CFPI, Frémaux, GFI Industries, Marc Orian, Prat, Sephora, Stephane Kélian, Superba, Valdermars Publications, Vygon

Officers, Executives and Principals

François Poirier, Managing Director

ATA SECURITIES INC.

Emirhan Cad
145 Atakule 80700
Balmumcu, Istanbul
Turkey

Telephone: 212-227-4819
Fax: 212-227-4868

Mission: Offering security and investment banking services for the Turkish market

Fund Size: not available
Founded: 1991
Average Investment: not available
Minimum Investment: not available

Investment Criteria: Expansion/Development, Turnaround/Restructuring

Geographic Preference: Turkey

Industry Group Preference: Consumer Related

Portfolio Companies: not available

Officers, Executives and Principals

Mehmet Sami

ATCO PARTNER BETEILIGUNGSBERATUNG

Königsallee 30
40212 Düsseldorf
Germany

Telephone: 49-211-865770
Fax: 49-211-323-0851

Mission: Actively seeking new investments

Fund Size: DM100 million
Founded: not available
Average Investment: not available
Minimum Investment: DM5 million

Investment Criteria: Expansion/Development, Management Buy-outs Management Buy-in, Replacement

Geographic Preference: Austria, Germany, Switzerland

Industry Group Preference: Chemical/Materials, Consumer Related, Industrial Products, Manufacturing, Medical/Health Related, Pollution/Recycling Related

Portfolio Companies: not available

Officers, Executives and Principals

Roel Schoemaker
John van Grootel
Dr. Anthony Bunker
Jeroen De Bruyn

ATLAS VENTURE

P. O. Box 5225
Naarderpoort 1
1410 AE Naarden
The Netherlands

Telephone: 31-35-695-4800
Fax: 31-35-695-4888
E-mail: amsterdam@atlasventure.nl

Other Office Locations

32 bis boulevard Haussmann
75009 Paris
France
Phone 33-1-4523-4120, Fax 33-1-4523-4121

Steinstrasse 70
81667 Munich
Germany
Phone 49-89-448-1199, Fax 49-89-447-1411, E-Mail wschauerte@atlasventure.de

Mission: Actively seeking new investments

Fund Size: Ecu200 million
Founded: not available
Average Investment: not available
Minimum Investment: Ecu400,000

Investment Criteria: not available

Geographic Preference: Europe, United States

Industry Group Preference: Biotechnology, Communications, Computer Related, Computer Software, Electronics Related, Medical/Health Related

Portfolio Companies: not available

Officers, Executives and Principals

Michiel de Haan
Jaap van Hellemond
Gerard Montanus
Philippe Schuit
Evert Smid
Rob Zegelaar

ATLAS VENTURE

32 bis boulevard Haussmann
75009 Paris
France

Telephone: 33-1-4523-4120
Fax: 33-1-4523-4121

Mission: Actively seeking new investments as part of the Atlas Venture Group (based in the Netherlands)

Fund Size: Ffr220 million (in France)
Founded: not available
Average Investment: not available
Minimum Investment: Ffr3 million

Investment Criteria: Seed, Start-up, Early-stage

Geographic Preference: Europe, France

Industry Group Preference: Biotechnology, Information Technology, Medical/Health Related, Pharmaceuticals, Telecommunications

Portfolio Companies: not available

Officers, Executives and Principals

Philippe Claude
Joel Besse
Jean-Yves Quentel
Séverine Lapèze

ATLAS VENTURE GmbH

Steinstrasse 70
81667 Munich
Germany

Telephone: 49-89-448-1199
Fax: 49-89-447-1411
E-mail: wschauerte@atlasventure.de

Mission: Actively seeking new investments as part of the Atlas Venture Group (based in the Netherlands)

Fund Size: DM100 million
Founded: 1990
Average Investment: DM3 million
Minimum Investment: DM500,000

Investment Criteria: Seed, Start-up, Early-stage, Expansion/Development

Geographic Preference: Austria, Germany, Switzerland

Industry Group Preference: Biotechnology, Communications, Computer Related, Computer Software, Electronics, Medical/Health Related

Portfolio Companies: Adcon GmbH, Dalim GmbH, Bin Tec GmbH, Genias GmbH, ESP Ltd., Klotz Digital GmbH, Mesacon GmbH, Micronas AG, Morphosys GmbH, SEZ AG, Software Ley GmbH, TomTec Inc., WaveLight GmbH, Micromet GmbH, SHD Datentechnik GmbH, Poet Inc., TransScan Ltd., ETH BV, AET BV

Officers, Executives and Principals

Dr. Werner Schauerte
Dr. Rolf Schneider-Günther
Ing Johannsen

ATLE AB

P. O. Box 7308
10390 Stockholm
Sweden

Telephone: 46-8-24-6210
Fax: 46-8-21-1021

Mission: Actively seeking new investments

Fund Size: Ecu332 million
Founded: not available
Average Investment: not available
Minimum Investment: Ecu50,000

Investment Criteria: Expansion/Development, Management Buy-in, Management Buy-out, Turnaround, Early-stage

Geographic Preference: Europe

Industry Group Preference: All sectors considered

Portfolio Companies: not available

Officers, Executives and Principals

Gunnar Huss

AUXITEX

8 rue du Château Trompette
33000 Bordeaux
France

Telephone: 33-5681-3460
Fax: 33-5681-7104

Mission: Actively seeking new investments

Fund Size: Ffr120 million
Founded: not available
Average Investment: not available
Minimum Investment: Ffr500,000

Investment Criteria: Expansion/Development

Geographic Preference: France (Southwestern region)

Industry Group Preference: All sectors considered

Portfolio Companies: Albadécor, Bec, COM1, Majesté, Marie-Brizard, Yvon Mau, Serma Technologie, Soulé

Officers, Executives and Principals

Bertrand Roux, President
Marie-Cécile Trillaud, Company Secretary

AVENIR ENTREPRISES

23 avenue Franklin Roosevelt
75008 Paris
France

Telephone: 33-1-5383-7430
Fax: 33-1-5383-7457

Mission: Actively seeking new investments

Fund Size: Ffr430 million
Founded: not available
Average Investment: not available
Minimum Investment: Ffr500,000

Investment Criteria: Expansion/Development, Leveraged Buy-out, Leveraged Buy-in

Geographic Preference: France

Industry Group Preference: All sectors except Tourism

Portfolio Companies: Partenaires, Mayet, Staci, SDMS, Pictorial, BEc, Editor Holding, Jacadi, Maxi-Livres, Neuhauser

Officers, Executives and Principals

Daniel Venon, Managing Director
François Chollet
Danièle Jenck
Geneviève Dubarry
Jacques Solleau
François Constantin
Jean-Louis Etchegoyhen

AVENIR TOURISME

23 avenue Franklin Roosevelt
75008 Pariss
France

Telephone: 33-1-5383-7438
Fax: 33-1-5383-7458

Mission: Actively seeking new investments

Fund Size: Ffr115 million
Founded: not available
Average Investment: not available
Minimum Investment: Ffr1 million

Investment Criteria: Expansion/Development, Leveraged Buy-out

Geographic Preference: France

Industry Group Preference: Tourism Related

Portfolio Companies: not available

Officers, Executives and Principals

Serge Mesguich, Managing Director

AXA ASSET MANAGEMENT GESTION

40 rue du Colisée
75008 Paris
France

Telephone: 33-1-4075-5736
Fax: 33-1-4075-5858

Mission: Actively seeking new investments

Fund Size: Ffr500 million
Founded: not available
Average Investment: not available
Minimum Investment: not available

Investment Criteria: All stages

Geographic Preference: France

Industry Group Preference: Industry and Services

Portfolio Companies: not available

Officers, Executives and Principals

Dominique Senequier

AXIS PARTICIPATIONES EMPRESARIALES

C/Prim. 19 - 3°
28004 Madrid
Spain

Telephone: 34-1-523-1654
Fax: 34-1-532 -1933

Mission: Actively seeking new investments

Fund Size: Ecu64.5 million
Founded: not available
Average Investment: not available
Minimum Investment: Ecu323,000

Investment Criteria: Start-up, Early-stage, Expansion/Development

Geographic Preference: Spain

Industry Group Preference: All sectors considered

Portfolio Companies: not available

Officers, Executives and Principals

Ana Martin Acebes, Partner
Joaquin Simon, Partner
Daniel Bilbao, Partner
Emilio Ramos, Partner

BAG AKTIENGESELLSCHAFT FÜR INDUSTRIEBETEILIGUNGEN

Tempowerkring 6
21079 Hamburg
Germany

Telephone: 49-40-7901-2345
Fax: 49-40-7901-2344

Mission: Actively seeking new investments

Fund Size: DM5 million
Founded: not available
Average Investment: not available
Minimum Investment: DM200,000

Investment Criteria: Start-up, Early Stage, Expansion

Geographic Preference: Germany (Northern region)

Industry Group Preference: All sectors considered

Portfolio Companies: not available

Officers, Executives and Principals

Wolfram Birkel

BALKANBANK PLC

18 Vitosha Boulevard
1040 Sofia
Bulgaria

Telephone: 359-2-881221
Fax: 359-2-872305

Mission: Actively seeking new investments

Fund Size: Ecu10 million
Founded: 1987
Average Investment: not available
Minimum Investment: not available

Investment Criteria: Seed, Start-up, Early-stage, Expansion/Development

Geographic Preference: not available

Industry Group Preference: Electronics Related, Consumer Products/Services, Industrial Products, Transportation, Manufacturing, Agriculture/ Forestry

Portfolio Companies: not available

Officers, Executives and Principals

Krassimir Todorov

BANCBOSTON CAPITAL

Bank of Boston House
39 Victoria Street
London SW1H 0ED
United Kingdom

Telephone: 44-171-932-9053
Fax: 44-171-932-9117

Mission: Actively seeking new investments

Fund Size: £100 million
Founded: not available
Average Investment: £3 million
Minimum Investment: £500,000

Investment Criteria: Expansion, Management Buy-in, Management Buy-out, Secondary Purchase/Replacement Capital, Acquisition

Geographic Preference: Europe, United Kingdom, North America

Industry Group Preference: All sectors considered

Portfolio Companies: Fitech, BCE Business Funding, Brewton Group, Games Workshop, National Express

Officers, Executives and Principals

Peter Borgers
Andrew Kellett
Mark Storey
Paul Nelson

BANCBOSTON CAPITAL

Jardine House
1 Connaught Place - Suite 801
Hong Kong

Telephone: 852-2526-4361
Fax: 852-2845-922

Mission: Actively seeking new investments

Fund Size: not available
Founded: not available
Average Investment: not available
Minimum Investment: not available

Investment Criteria: Expansion, Management Buy-in, Management Buy-out, Secondary Purchase/Replacement Capital, Acquisition

Geographic Preference: not available

Industry Group Preference: All sectors considered

Portfolio Companies: Fitech, BCE Business Funding, Brewton Group, Games Workshop, National Express

BANCO MELLO DE INVESTIMENTOS SA

Rua Alexandre Herculano, 50, 5°
1250 Lisbon
Portugal

Telephone: 351-1-312-5147
Fax: 351-1-312-5002

Mission: Providing finance for industrial companies being assisted by existing initiatives for industrial development, including those with potential for growth and operating in sectors offering significant competitive advantages (through its M Development fund) and those introducing new products or new technologies (through its M Innovation fund)

Fund Size: Esc4 billion
Founded: 1997
Average Investment: not available
Minimum Investment: not available

Investment Criteria: Turnaround, Expansion, Management Buy-out, Management Buy-in, Recapitalization

Geographic Preference: Portugal

Industry Group Preference: All sectors considered

Portfolio Companies: not available

Officers, Executives and Principals

Dr. Pedro Manuel Brandao Rodrigues, Executive Director
Education: Graduate in Engineering, University of Lisbon; MSc in Engineering and Management and PhD, University of Birmingham
Background: Group Leader, Product Development, and Manager, Business Development, Alusuisse Lonza AG, Zürich; Managing Director, Promindustria SA, Lisbon; Director, Risfomento - Sociedade de Capital de Risco SA

Maria do Rosario Mayoral Robles Machado Simoes Ventura, Head of Turnaround Banking and Venture Capital Department
Education: Graduate in management, Portuguese Catholic University, Lisbon
Background: Lecturer, Financial Institutions and Banking Operations, University of Lisbon; Director, Sulpedip SA; Head of Projects and Venture Capital Department, Sociedade Financeira Portuguesa; Head of Corporate Finance Department, Banco Mello

Luis Augusto Nesbitt Rebelo da Silva, Manager of Turnaround Banking and Venture Capital Department
Education: Graduate in Organization and Management, Instituto Superior de Economia, Lisbon
Background: Analyst, Foreign Trade Development Department, Portuguese Institute of Foreign Trade, Lisbon; Management Assistant, Unirisco; Senior Executive Manager, F. Turismo - Capital de Risco SA; Project Analyst, Sulpedip SA

Pedro Vicente, Manager of Turnaround Banking and Venture Capital Department
Education: Graduate in Management, Portuguese Catholic University, Lisbon; MBA, New University of Lisbon
Background: Assistant and later Finance Director, Quatrum; Finance Director, Socasa; Account Manager, Corporate Banking Department, Banco Comercial Portugues; Operations Director, Unifina

BANCO PORTUGUES DE INVESTIMENTO SA

rua Tenente Valadim 284
4100 Oporto
Portugal

Telephone: 351-2-60 99 951
Fax: 351-2-60 00 464

Mission: Actively seeking new investents

Fund Size: not available
Founded: not available
Average Investment: not available
Minimum Investment: not available

Investment Criteria: not available

Geographic Preference: Portugal

Industry Group Preference: All sectors considered

Portfolio Companies: not available

Officers, Executives and Principals

Dr. Artur Santos Silva

B. AND S. VENTURES Srl

Via Ippolitio Nievo 33
20145 Milan
Italy

Telephone: 39-2-3361-0230
Fax: 39-2-3361-0199

Mission: Actively seeking new investments

Fund Size: Ecu45 million
Founded: not available
Average Investment: not available
Minimum Investment: Ecu1.5 million

Investment Criteria: Expansion/Development, Management Buy-in, Replacement

Geographic Preference: Italy

Industry Group Preference: All sectors considered

Portfolio Companies: not available

Officers, Executives and Principals

Luciano Balbo
Luigi Sala

BANEXI

12 rue Chauchat
75009 Paris
France

Telephone: 33-1-4014-4077
Fax: 33-1-4014-7999

Mission: Actively seeking new investments

Fund Size: Ffr4.7 billion
Founded: 1969
Average Investment: Ffr10 million
Minimum Investment: Ffr1 million

Investment Criteria: Start-up, Expansion/Development, Management Buy-out, Management Buy-in, Replacement, Bridge

Geographic Preference: Europe, United States

Industry Group Preference: All sectors considered

Portfolio Companies: not available

Officers, Executives and Principals

Franck Boget
Michel Bouissou

BANEXI VENTURES

12 rue Chauchat
75009 Paris
France

Telephone: 33-1-4014-5245
Fax: 33-1-4014-7999

Mission: Actively seeking new investments

Fund Size: Ffr42 million
Founded: not available
Average Investment: not available
Minimum Investment: Ffr500,000

Investment Criteria: All stages

Geographic Preference: France, Europe, United States

Industry Group Preference: All sectors considered

Portfolio Companies: not available

Officers, Executives and Principals

Bernard Maitre, Managing Director
Philippe Méré, Company Secretary
Sophie Pierrin-Lepinard

BANK AUSTRIA T.F.V. HIGH TECH-UNTERNEHMENS BETEILIGUNG GmbH

Wallnerstrasse 8
1010 Vienna
Austria

Telephone: 43-1-532-1960
Fax: 43-1-532-196019
E-mail: tfv@via.at

Mission: Actively seeking new investments

Fund Size: Sch320 million
Founded: not available
Average Investment: $1-$2 million
Minimum Investment: $300,000

Investment Criteria: Seed, Start-up, Early-stage

Geographic Preference: Austria, Germany

Industry Group Preference: Communications, Computer Related, Computer Software, Electronics, Information Technology

Portfolio Companies: Hyperwave

Officers, Executives and Principals

Heinz Rieder, Managing Director
Reinhard Jonke, Managing Director
Günther Eibel, Investment Manager

BANQUE DE VIZILLE

Espance Cordelier
2 rue Président Carnot
69002 Lyons
France

Telephone: 33-4-7256-9100
Fax: 33-4-7277-5855

Mission: Actively seeking new investments

Fund Size: Ffr920 million
Founded: not available
Average Investment: not available
Minimum Investment: Ffr1 million

Investment Criteria: Expansion/Development, Leveraged Buy-out, Management Buy-out, Management Buy-in

Geographic Preference: France (Southeastern region)

Industry Group Preference: All sectors considered

Portfolio Companies: Descour et Cabaud, H.I.T., Groupe Aldes, Groupe Gindre Duchavany

Officers, Executives and Principals

Michel Cotte, Managing Director
Antoine Jarmak, Deputy Managing Director

BANQUE INDOSUEZ ACQUISITION FINANCE

Indosuez House
122 Leadenhall Street
London EC3V 4QH
United Kingdom

Telephone: 44-171-971-4000
Fax: 44-171-628-4724

Other Office Locations
47 rue de Monceau
75008 Paris
France
Phone 33-1-4420-3825, Fax 33-1-4420-3953

Via Brera 21
20121 Milan
Italy
Phone 39-272-303246, Fax 39-272-303201

Wilhelm-Leuschner-Strasse 9-11
60392 Frankfurt am Main
Germany
Phone 49-69-2429-600, Fax 49-69-2429-6029

Regerinsgatan 38
11156 Stockholm
Sweden
Phone 46-879-66900, Fax 46-879-60040

Mission: Supplying debt and equity capital in buy-outs and acquisitions

Fund Size: not available
Founded: 1992
Average Investment: £5-£10 million
Minimum Investment: £3 million

Investment Criteria: Bridge Finance, Expansion, Management Buy-in, Management Buy-out, Refinancing Bank Debt, Secondary Purchase/Replacement Capital, Venture Purchase of Quoted Shares

Geographic Preference: Western Europe

Industry Group Preference: All sectors considered

Portfolio Companies: not available

Officers, Executives and Principals

Mary Clippingdale
Ken Penton
Graham Barker

David Lock
David Lilley
Alex Cooper-Evans
Nick Young
Tom Marsden

BARCLAYS ACQUISITION FINANCE

Barclays Bank plc
54 Lombard Street
London EC3P 3AH
United Kingdom

Telephone: 44-171-699-3186
Fax: 44-171-699-2770

Other Office Locations

Barclays Acquisition Finance Midlands
4th Floor, 15 Colmore Row
Birmingham B3 2BY
Phone 44-121-236-2424, Fax 44-121-236-9305

Barclays Acquisition Finance North West
51 Mosley Street
Manchester M60 2AU
Phone 44-161-200-5250, Fax 44-161-200-5294

Mission: Actively seeking new investments

Fund Size: not available
Founded: not available
Average Investment: not available
Minimum Investment: not available

Investment Criteria: Expansion, Management Buy-in, Management Buy-out, Secondary Purchase/Replacement Capital, Corporate Acquisition

Geographic Preference: United Kingdom

Industry Group Preference: All sectors considered

Portfolio Companies: Field Packaging, United Kenning Rentals, Pilkington's Tiles, Edgbaston Group

Officers, Executives and Principals

Anton Fawcett
Arthur James
Tony Nash
Mark Advani

BARCLAYS CAPITAL DÉVELOPPEMENT

19 avenue de l'Opéra
75001 Paris
France

Telephone: 33-1-5345-1150
Fax: 33-1-5345-1170

Mission: Actively seeking new investments

Fund Size: Ffr150 million
Founded: not available
Average Investment: not available
Minimum Investment: Ffr3 million

Investment Criteria: Expansion/Development, Management Buyout, Management Buy-in

Geographic Preference: France

Industry Group Preference: All sectors

Portfolio Companies: Garconnet, Oréfi, SFEE, Catimini, Auxitec, CGPS

Officers, Executives and Principals

Gonzague de Blignières
Charles Diehl
Olivier Millet
Guillaume Jacquemeau
Cédric Sicard

BARING CAPITAL INVESTORS LTD.

140 Park Lane
London W1Y 3AA
United Kingdom

Telephone: 44-171-408-1282
Fax: 44-171-493-1368

Other Office Locations
148 boulevard Haussmann
75008 Paris
France
Phone 33-1-4359-0366, Fax 33-1-4359-5059

Via Brera 3
20121 Milan
Italy
Phone 39-2-7200-3101, Fax 39-2-876929

Heimhuderstrasse 72
20148 Hamburg 13
Germany
Phone 49-40-449690, Fax 49-40-458364

Mission: Actively seeking new investments

Fund Size: $1 billion
Founded: 1986
Average Investment: not available
Minimum Investment: $10 million

Investment Criteria: Leveraged Buy-out

Geographic Preference: Europe

Industry Group Preference: Diversified

Portfolio Companies: not available

Officers, Executives and Principals

Otto van der Wyck, Executive Director (London)
John Burgess, Executive Director (London)
Michel Guillet, Executive Director (Paris)
Alberto Tazartes, Executive Director (Milan)
Jens Reidel, Executive Director (Hamburg)

BARING CAPITAL PARTNERS

148 boulevard Haussmann
75008 Paris
France

Telephone: 33-1-4359-0366
Fax: 33-1-4359-5059

Mission: Actively seeking new investments

Fund Size: Ffr5 billion
Founded: not available
Average Investment: not available
Minimum Investment: Ffr50 million

Investment Criteria: Leveraged Buy-out

Geographic Preference: Europe

Industry Group Preference: All sectors considered

Portfolio Companies: Allevard, Acova, Serap

Officers, Executives and Principals

Michel Guillet
Patrice Hoppenot
Michel Nespoulos
Raymond Svider

BARING HELLENIC VENTURES SA (BHV)

17 Akademia Street
10671 Athens
Greece

Telephone: 30-1-362-2096
Fax: 30-1-362-7766

Mission: Investing in a diversified portfolio of unquoted investments

Fund Size: Dr864 million
Founded: 1991
Average Investment: not available
Minimum Investment: not available

Investment Criteria: Expansion/Development, Turnaround/Restructuring, Replacement

Geographic Preference: Cyprus, Greece

Industry Group Preference: not available

Portfolio Companies: Goody's SA, Chipita International SA, Endysi SA, Maxim-K. Pertsinides SA, Mark Aalen SA, Epiphania SA, Mangos Studio SA, Data Information Systems SA, Babyland Toys SA, Eurodrip SA, Panagia SA

Officers, Executives and Principals

Angelos Plakopitas, Managing Director
Education: BA in Economic and Business Sciences, University of Athens; MBA, New York University
Background: General Manager, Shelman (wood products company); 14 years experience in corporate banking with Citibank and Hellenic Industrial Development Bank

BARING VENTURE PARTNERS

23 rue Vernet
75008 Paris
France

Telephone: 33-1-4720-4440
Fax: 33-1-4720-4442

Mission: Actively seeking new investments

Fund Size: Ffr1.67 billion
Founded: not available
Average Investment: not available
Minimum Investment: not available

Investment Criteria: All stages

Geographic Preference: Europe, United States

Industry Group Preference: All sectors considered

Portfolio Companies: not available

Officers, Executives and Principals

Pierre-Michel Piccino, Senior Partner
Aleksander Kierski, Partner

BARING VENTURE PARTNERS LTD.

74 Brook Street
London W1Y 1YD
United Kingdom

Telephone: 44-171-290-5000
Fax: 44-171-290-5020

Other Office Locations
P. O. Box 12491
St Louis, MO 63132
United States
Phone 314-993-0007, Fax 314-993-0464

14 boulevard des Tranchees
1206 Geneva
Switzerland
Phone 41-22-346-4855, Fax 41-22-346-4967

Darro 22
28002 Madrid
Spain
Phone 34-1-563-7149, Fax 34-1-563-7089

Friedrichstrasse 2-6
60323 Frankfurt am Main
Germany
Phone 49-69-173919, Fax 49-69-173980

23 rue Vernet
75007 Paris
France
Phone 33-1-4720-4440, Fax 33-1-4720-4442

Mission: Actively seeking new investments

Fund Size: £285 million
Founded: 1984
Average Investment: not available
Minimum Investment: £35,000

Investment Criteria: Seed, Start-up, First-stage, Second-stage, Mezzanine

Geographic Preference: North America, Europe, Latin America, Asia-Pacific

Industry Group Preference: Communications, Computer Related, Consumer, Distribution, Electronic Components and Instrumentation, Energy/Natural Resources, Genetic Engineering, Industrial Products and Equipment, Medical/Health Related

Portfolio Companies: not available

Officers, Executives and Principals

Richard Onians, Managing Partner (London)
Terrence Tehranian, Partner (London)
Pierre-Michel Piccino, Senior Partner (Paris)
Aleksander Kierski, Partner (Paris)
L. Edward Klein, Senior Partner (St Louis)
Jose Angel Sarasa, Senior Partner (Madrid)
Timothy Green, Partner (London)
David Huckfield, Partner (London)
Dirk Kanngiesser, Partner (Frankfurt)

BARING VENTURE PARTNERS SA

Darro 22 - portal A bajo izqda.
28002 Madrid
Spain

Telephone: 34-1-563-7149
Fax: 34-1-563-7089

Mission: Actively seeking new investments

Fund Size: Ecu32,955,776
Founded: not available
Average Investment: not available
Minimum Investment: Ecu75,000

Investment Criteria: Start-up, Expansion/Development

Geographic Preference: not available

Industry Group Preference: Biotechnology, Communications, Consumer Related, Electronics Related, Industrial Products, Medical/Health Related

Portfolio Companies: not available

Officers, Executives and Principals

José Angel Sarasa, Partner
David Baker, Partner
Manuel Marina, Partner
Javier Bernal, Partner
Dolores Monléon, Partner

BARING VENTURE PARTNERS UNTERNEHMENSBERATUNG GmbH

Friedrichstrasse 2-6
60323 Frankfurt am Main
Germany

Telephone: 49-69-173919
Fax: 49-69-173980

Mission: Actively seeking new investments

Fund Size: not available
Founded: not available
Average Investment: not available
Minimum Investment: DM800,000

Investment Criteria: Start-up, Early-stage, Expansion/Development

Geographic Preference: Germany

Industry Group Preference: All sectors considered

Portfolio Companies: not available

Officers, Executives and Principals

Dirk Kanngiesser

BAYERISCHE BETEILIGUNGS GmbH (BAY BG)

Königinstrasse 33
80539 Munich
Germany

Telephone: 49-89-2866-830
Fax: 49-89-2866-8311
E-mail: 101511.2014@compuserve.com

Other Office Locations
B.W.B. Bayerische Wagnisbeteiligungs GmbH
Lena-Christ-Strasse 2
82031 Grünwald
Phone 49-89-641-7848, Fax 49-89-641-7848

Mission: Actively seeking new investments in small and medium-sized enterprises in Bavaria and in seed and start-up situations throughout Germany

Fund Size: DM100 million
Founded: 1994
Average Investment: DM1 million
Minimum Investment: DM100,000

Investment Criteria: Expansion, Management Buy-out, Management Buy-in, Spin-off, Start-up, Turnaround, Going Public

Geographic Preference: Germany (Southern region)

Industry Group Preference: All sectors considered

Portfolio Companies: not available

Officers, Executives and Principals

Hartmut Langhorst
Dr. Klaus Bauer
Günther Henrich
Dr. Wolf Willig

BB KAPITALBETEILIGUNGS GmbH

Fasanenstrasse 7-8
10623 Berlin
Germany

Telephone: 49-30-3159-450
Fax: 49-30-312-1262

Mission: Committed to investing in strong, growing companies

Fund Size: not available
Founded: 1986
Average Investment: not available
Minimum Investment: DM3 million

Investment Criteria: Growth Financing, Management Buy-out, Management Buy-in

Geographic Preference: Germany

Industry Group Preference: All sectors considered

Portfolio Companies: Acerplan Planungs GmbH, Andersen Apparatebau und Umformtechnik GmbH, BB-Leasing GmbH, Berliner Bürgerbräu GmbH, Breitfeld und Schliekert GmbH, BWP-U, Colors Music and Marketing, Colors of Music Publishing, Deutsche BA Luftfahrt GmbH, GCM, GSD, Henke Pressedruck GmbH, Innova Zug GmbH, LPKF CAD/CAM, Ludwig Beck am Rathauseck Textilhaus Feldmeier AG, Marek Lieberberg Konzertagentur GmbH, MERO, Music Plus, svt, TA, Thal GmbH, Willy Vogel AG, others

Officers, Executives and Principals

Eberhard Witt, Managing Director
Education: Diplom Kaufmann
Background: Mannesmann Konzernrevision GmbH; Deutsche Bank AG; Deutsche Beteiligungs GmbH

Udo Hartmann, Managing Director
Education: Graduate in German Law; Master of Laws, University of Illinois
Background: Marquard and Bahls AG; Managing Director, Zementwerk Berlin

BBV DE PROMOCION EMPRESARIAL SA

Pº de la Castellana 81 7a
28046 Madrid
Spain

Telephone: 34-1-374-2266
Fax: 34-1-374-4839

Mission: Actively seeking new investments

Fund Size: not available
Founded: not available
Average Investment: not available
Minimum Investment: Ecu500,000

Investment Criteria: Expansion/Development, Management Buy-out, Management Buy-in, Replacement

Geographic Preference: Spain, Europe

Industry Group Preference: Communications, Computer Related, Consumer Related/Services, Electronics Related, Industrial Products, Medical/Health Related, Services

Portfolio Companies: not available

Officers, Executives and Principals

Enrico Rubio Otano, Partner
Javier Muños Arias, Partner
Paulino Lopez Vélez, Partner
Antonio Peres, Partner

B. C. PARTNERS LIMITED

105 Piccadilly
London W1V 9FN
United Kingdom

Telephone: 44-171-408-1282
Fax: 44-171-493-1368

Mission: Actively seeking new investments

Fund Size: £600 million
Founded: not available
Average Investment: £8.5 million
Minimum Investment: not available

Investment Criteria: Management Buy-in, Management Buy-out

Geographic Preference: Western Europe

Industry Group Preference: All sectors considered

Portfolio Companies: Bricom, Buffetti, Nutreco, MDIS, Brembo

Officers, Executives and Principals

Otto van der Wyck
John Burgess
Simon Palley
Bolaji Odunsi
Ian Riley
Stefano Quadrio Curzio

BEBAG BODENSEE BETEILIGUNGS AG

Dufourpark/Rötelistrasse 16
9000 St Gallen
Switzerland

Telephone: 41-1-286661
Fax: 41-1-281937

Mission: Actively seeking new investments, concentrating on companies with excellent growth potential with competitive position and experienced management

Fund Size: not available
Founded: not available
Average Investment: not available
Minimum Investment: Sfr3 million

Investment Criteria: Expansion/Development, Management Buy-out, Replacement/Share Purchases

Geographic Preference: Switzerland, Europe

Industry Group Preference: All sectors considered

Portfolio Companies: not available

Officers, Executives and Principals

Dr. Walter Meier

BETEILIGUNGSGESELLSCHAFT AACHENER REGION mbH (B. G. A.)

Roermonder Strasse 63
52134 Herzogenrath
Germany

Telephone: 49-2407-51561
Fax: 49-2407-18259

Mission: Actively seeking new investments

Fund Size: DM48 million
Founded: not available
Average Investment: not available
Minimum Investment: DM500,000

Investment Criteria: Expansion, Management Buy-out, Management Buy-in

Geographic Preference: Germany (Aachen region)

Industry Group Preference: Chemicals, Construction Materials, Metals, Services

Portfolio Companies: not available

Officers, Executives and Principals

Jürgen Peters
Heinz Dassen
Dr. Hendrik Junghanns

BETEILIGUNGSGESELLSCHAFT FÜR DIE DEUTSCHE WIRTSCHAFT (BdW)

Gutleutstrasse 85
60329 Frankfurt am Main
Germany

Telephone: 49-69-273-0090
Fax: 49-69-273-009190

Mission: Actively seeking new investments

Fund Size: DM 595 million
Founded: 1969
Average Investment: not available
Minimum Investment: DM 1.4 million

Investment Criteria: Expansion/Development, Management Buy-out, Management Buy-in, Bridge, Spin-off

Geographic Preference: Europe

Industry Group Preference: not available

Portfolio Companies: not available

Officers, Executives and Principals

Hans Damisch, Managing Director
Werner Kathemann, Managing Director
Hans-Konrad von Koester, Managing Director
Dr. Dietrich Weber, Managing Director
Dieter Leonhardt, Director
Armin Schuler, Director

BETEILIGUNGSGESELLSCHAFT FÜR INDUSTRIE, HANDWERK, HANDEL UND VERKEHR mbH

Postfach 760242
22052 Hamburg
Germany

Telephone: 49-40-6117-000
Fax: 49-40-6117-0019

Mission: Actively seeking new investments in small and medium-sized enterprises, especially in support of innovative techniques and/or developing new sectors

Fund Size: DM4.6 million
Founded: not available
Average Investment: not available
Minimum Investment: not available

Investment Criteria: not available

Geographic Preference: Germany (especially Hamburg region)

Industry Group Preference: All sectors considered

Portfolio Companies: not available

Officers, Executives and Principals

Dr. Stefan Papirow
Dieter Braemer

BEV BIENEK ENTERTAINMENT VENTURES

Eckenheimer Landstrasse 449
60435 Frankfurt am Main
Germany

Telephone: 49-69-9542-1256
Fax: 49-69-9542-1222
E-mail: bev.bienek@t-online.de

Mission: Actively seeking new investments

Fund Size: not available
Founded: 1996
Average Investment: Ecu500,000
Minimum Investment: Ecu50,000

Investment Criteria: Start-up, Expansion/Development, Management Buy-out, Management Buy-in, Turn-around/Restructuring, Replacement

Geographic Preference: Europe, North America

Industry Group Preference: Communications, Computer Software, Entertainment

Portfolio Companies: not available

Officers, Executives and Principals

Karsten Bienek

BIDASSOA INVESTISSEMENTS

16 avenue de Friedland
75008 Paris
France

Telephone: 33-1-5377-2000
Fax: 33-1-4561-0504

Mission: Actively seeking new investments

Fund Size: Ffr49 million
Founded: not available
Average Investment: not available
Minimum Investment: Ffr2 million

Investment Criteria: Development

Geographic Preference: France (Southeastern region), Spain (Northern region)

Industry Group Preference: All sectors considered

Portfolio Companies: not available

Officers, Executives and Principals

Jacques Saint Martin
Jean-Philippe Larramendy
Pascal Royer
Pierre Marlange
Janine Monbrard

BIOINDUSTRIA Srl

Via Dalmazia 21/C
72100 Brindisi
Italy

Telephone: 39-831-588040
Fax: 39-831-588050

Mission: Actively seeking new investments

Fund Size: Ecu500,000
Founded: not available
Average Investment: not available
Minimum Investment: Ecu50,000

Investment Criteria: Start-up, Early-stage

Geographic Preference: Italy, Greece, Spain, Portugal

Industry Group Preference: Agriculture/Forestry, Biotechnology, Industrial Products, Medical/Health
 Related, Pollution/Recycling Related

Portfolio Companies: not available

Officers, Executives and Principals

Giorgio Caiulo

BIOTECHNOLOGY INVESTMENTS LTD. (B. I. L.)

c/o Five Arrows House
St Swithin's Lane
London EC4N 8NR
United Kingdom

Telephone: 44-171-280-5000
Fax: 44-171-623-6261

Mission: Actively seeking new investments

Fund Size: Ecu227 million
Founded: not available
Average Investment: not available
Minimum Investment: Ecu420,000

Investment Criteria: Seed, Start-up, Expansion/Development, Early-stage

Geographic Preference: not available

Industry Group Preference: Biotechnology, Medical/Health Related

Portfolio Companies: not available

Officers, Executives and Principals

Jeremy Curnock-Cook
Tanneke Zeeuw

BIRMINGHAM TECHNOLOGY (VENTURE CAPITAL) LTD.

Aston Science Park
Love Lane
Birmingham B7 4BJ
United Kingdom

Telephone: 44-121-359-0981
Fax: 44-121-359-0433
E-mail: 101515.2571@compuserve.com

Mission: Actively seeking new investments

Fund Size: £2 million
Founded: not available
Average Investment: not available
Minimum Investment: £20,000

Investment Criteria: Expansion, Start-up, Early-stage

Geographic Preference: No preference but investee companies should be prepared to relocate to Birmingham

Industry Group Preference: Computer Related, Medical Related

Portfolio Companies: Techsonix Ltd., AD2 Ltd., The Logistics Business Ltd., Aston Molecules Ltd., Cimtel Ltd.

Officers, Executives and Principals

Derek Harris

B. K. K. - KAPITAL MANAGEMENT GmbH

Grolmanstrasse 52
10623 Berlin
Germany

Telephone: 49-30-313-0473
Fax: 49-30-312-6379

Mission: Actively seeking new investments

Fund Size: DM35 million
Founded: not available
Average Investment: not available
Minimum Investment: DM3 million

Investment Criteria: Expansion, Management Buy-out, Management Buy-in

Geographic Preference: Germany

Industry Group Preference: All sectors considered

Portfolio Companies: not available

Officers, Executives and Principals

Dr. Kamal Askar

B. N. P. DÉVELOPPEMENT

20 rue Chauchat
75009 Paris
France

Telephone: 33-1-4014-6463
Fax: 33-1-4014-2968

Mission: Actively seeking new investments

Fund Size: Ffr500 million
Founded: not available
Average Investment: not available
Minimum Investment: Ffr500,000

Investment Criteria: Development

Geographic Preference: France

Industry Group Preference: All sectors considered

Portfolio Companies: not available

Officers, Executives and Principals

Dominique Foissaud, Company Secretary

B. N. U. CAPITAL - SOCIEDADE DE CAPITAL DE RISCO

Rua do Comércio 78
1100 Lisbon
Portugal

Telephone: 351-1-342-8835
Fax: 351-1-342-8995

Mission: Actively seeking new investments

Fund Size: Ecu20 million
Founded: not available
Average Investment: not available
Minimum Investment: Ecu100,000

Investment Criteria: Early-stage, Expansion/Development, Management Buy-out

Geographic Preference: Portugal

Industry Group Preference: Industrial Products, Medical/Health Related

Portfolio Companies: not available

Officers, Executives and Principals

Luis Vilela Pimentel
Francisco Rocio Medens
Francisco Cruz Rosa

BRABANTSE ONTWIKKELINGSMIJ NV (BOM)

Van Stirumlaan 4-E
P. O. Box 3240
5003 De Tilburg
The Netherlands

Telephone: 31-13- 463-4400
Fax: 31-13- 463-4090

Mission: Actively seeking new investments

Fund Size: not available
Founded: not available
Average Investment: not available
Minimum Investment: Ecu100,000

Investment Criteria: Start-up, Early-stage, Expansion/Development, Management Buy-out, Management Buy-in

Geographic Preference: Netherlands

Industry Group Preference: All sectors considered

Portfolio Companies: not available

Officers, Executives and Principals

E. M. Veen

BRITISH LINEN SECURITIES

P. O. Box 49
4 Melville Street
Edinburgh EH3 7NZ
United Kingdom

Telephone: 44-131-453-1919
Fax: 44-131-243-8324

Other Office Locations
8 Frederick Place
London EC2R 8AT
Phone 44-171-601-6840

19-21 Spring Gardens
Manchester M2 1EB
Phone 44-161-832-4444

Mission: Actively seeking new investments in companies with profitable trading records and strong potential for growth

Fund Size: £20 million
Founded: 1978
Average Investment: £1 million
Minimum Investment: £500,000

Investment Criteria: Expansion, Management Buy-in, Management Buy-out, Secondary Purchase/Replacement Capital, Venture Purchase of Quoted Shares

Geographic Preference: United Kingdom

Industry Group Preference: All sectors considered except High-tech, Biotechnology, Construction, Real Estate

Portfolio Companies: Highway Vehicle Leasing plc, Haughton Holdings Limited, Surgicraft Group Limited, Walker Dickson Group Limited

Officers, Executives and Principals

Charles Young, Director
Sheena Nimmo, Manager

BRITISH STEEL (INDUSTRY) LTD.
Bridge House
Bridge Street
Sheffield S3 8NS
United Kingdom

Telephone: 44-114-273-1612
Fax: 44-114-270-1390
E-mail: bsiho@bsi.onyxnet.co.uk

Other Office Locations
Canterbury House
2-6 Sydenham Road
Croydon
Surrey CR9 2LJ
Phone 44-181-686-2311, Fax 44-181-680-8616

Cleveland House
7 Woodlands Road
Middlesbrough
Cleveland TS1 3BH
Phone 44-1642-244633, Fax 44-1642-244446, E-Mail bsinorth@bsi.onyxnet.co.uk

Grovewood Business Centre
Strathclyde Business Park
Bellshill
Lanarkshire ML4 8NQ
Phone 44-1698-854045, Fax 44-1698-845123

Lewis Road
East Moors
Cardiff CF1 5EJ
Phone 44-1222-471122, Fax 44-1222-492622,
E-Mail 101327.1456@compuserve.com

Mission: Strengthening the economic base of steel communities by supporting the growth of new and existing businesses, thus helping to provide better long-term employment prospects for local people

Fund Size: £5 million
Founded: 1975
Average Investment: £50,000
Minimum Investment: £20,000

Investment Criteria: Expansion, Management Buy-in, Management Buy-out, Early-stage, Rescue/Turn-around, Start-up

Geographic Preference: Restricted to the traditional steelmaking areas of England, Scotland and Wales

Industry Group Preference: mainly Manufacturing and Related Services; all sectors considered except Construction, Real Estate, Retail, Agriculture, Financial Services

Portfolio Companies: Pierceton Engineering Ltd., Porter Plant Ltd., Whiteley Read Ltd., Thompson Pettie Tube Products Ltd.

Officers, Executives and Principals

Vernon Smith, Managing Director (Sheffield)
Stuart Williamson, Company Secretary (Sheffield)
Keith Williams, Investment Manager (Sheffield)
Mary Broadhead, Investment Executive (Sheffield)
Nigel Feirn, Investment Executive (Sheffield)
John Northcott, Business Development Manager (Croydon)
Adrian Lewis, Area Manager, Northern England (Middlesbrough)
John Fairlie, Regional Manager, Scotland (Bellshill)
David Hughes, Regional Manager, Wales (Cardiff)
Stuart Green, Area Manager, Yorkshire and Humberside (Sheffield)

BROWN SHIPLEY VENTURE MANAGERS LTD.

Founders Court, Lothbury
London EC2R 7HE
United Kingdom

Telephone: 44-171-606-6555
Fax: 44-171-600-2279

Mission: Actively seeking new investments in established private companies with annual pre-tax profits of at least £750,000

Fund Size: £104 million
Founded: 1987
Average Investment: £2 million
Minimum Investment: £1.5 million

Investment Criteria: Second-stage, Leveraged Buy-out

Geographic Preference: United Kingdom

Industry Group Preference: All sectors considered

Portfolio Companies: Rowco, Noskab, Croxton, Dalehead Foods Holdings, Bounty, Denham, The Home Entertainment Corporation

Officers, Executives and Principals

David Wills, Managing Director
Roy Parker, Director
Richard Kemp, Director
Mark Hallala, Director
Andrew Moye, Director

B. T. CAPITAL PARTNERS

c/o Bankers Trust Company
1 Appold Street
Broadgate
London EC2A 2HE
United Kingdom

Telephone: 44-171-982-2629
Fax: 44-171-982-3318

Mission: Actively seeking new investments as the private equity arm of the Bankers Trust Company

Fund Size: not available
Founded: not available
Average Investment: not available
Minimum Investment: Ecu4 million

Investment Criteria: Expansion/Development, Management Buy-out, Management Buy-in, Replacement

Geographic Preference: not available

Industry Group Preference: All sectors considered

Portfolio Companies: not available

Officers, Executives and Principals

Mark Collinson
Manjit Dale

BTP CAPITAL INVESTISSEMENT

66 avenue des Champs Elysées
75008 Paris
France

Telephone: 33-1-4055-3481
Fax: 33-1-5389-5567

Mission: Actively seeking new investments

Fund Size: Ffr115 million
Founded: not available
Average Investment: not available
Minimum Investment: Ffr1 million

Investment Criteria: Expansion/Development

Geographic Preference: France

Industry Group Preference: not available

Portfolio Companies: not available

Officers, Executives and Principals

Gérard Matheron, Managing Director
Daniel Pele

BUSINESS INNOVATION FUND

Molyneux House
67-69 Bride Street
Dublin 8
Ireland

Telephone: 353-1-4750-3305
Fax: 353-1-475-2044
E-mail: kschutte@homenet.ie

Mission: Actively seeking new investments

Fund Size: Ecu2.1 million
Founded: not available
Average Investment: not available
Minimum Investment: Ecu30,000

Investment Criteria: Seed, Start-up

Geographic Preference: Ireland

Industry Group Preference: All sectors considered

Portfolio Companies: not available

Officers, Executives and Principals

Karl Schütte

BUSINESS LINK DONCASTER

White Rose Way
Doncaster
South Yorkshire DN4 5ND
United Kingdom

Telephone: 44-1302-761000
Fax: 44-1302-739999

Mission: Actively seeking new investments

Fund Size: £800,000
Founded: not available
Average Investment: £75,000
Minimum Investment: £50,000

Investment Criteria: Expansion, Management Buy-in, Management Buy-out, Rescue/Turnaround, Start-up

Geographic Preference: United Kingdom (South Yorkshire)

Industry Group Preference: All sectors considered

Portfolio Companies: not available

Officers, Executives and Principals

Brian Crangle
Bryce Staniland

B. V. BETEILIGUNGS GmbH

Kardinal-Faulhaber-Strasse 1
80333 Munich
Germany

Telephone: 49-89-291-3222
Fax: 49-89-228-5828

Mission: Actively seeking new investments

Fund Size: DM30 million
Founded: not available
Average Investment: not available
Minimum Investment: DM2 million

Investment Criteria: Expansion/Development, Management Buy-out, Management Buy-in

Geographic Preference: Germany, Europe

Industry Group Preference: All sectors considered

Portfolio Companies: not available

Officers, Executives and Principals

Achim Lutterbuck
Gerd-Eike Mellinghoff

B. W. B. BAYERISCHE WAGNISBETEILIGUNGS GmbH

Lena-Christ-Strasse 2
82031 Grünwald
Germany

Telephone: 49-89-641-7848
Fax: 49-89-641-7848

Mission: Actively seeking new investments in small and medium-sized enterprises

Fund Size: DM17 million
Founded: not available
Average Investment: not available
Minimum Investment: DM500,000

Investment Criteria: All stages considered

Geographic Preference: Germany (Bavaria)

Industry Group Preference: All sectors considered

Portfolio Companies: not available

Officers, Executives and Principals

Günther Henrich
Dr. Wolf Rüdiger Willig

BZW PRIVATE EQUITY LIMITED

4th Floor, Pickfords Wharf
Clink Street
London SE1 9DG
United Kingdom

Telephone: 44-171-407-2389
Fax: 44-171-407-3362

Mission: Actively seeking new investments

Fund Size: Open
Founded: 1979
Average Investment: £3 million
Minimum Investment: £1 million

Investment Criteria: Management Buy-in, Management Buy-out

Geographic Preference: United Kingdom, France

Industry Group Preference: All sectors considered except Real Estate

Portfolio Companies: New Look, Rubicon, Leyland Trucks, Vymura, Superbreak

Officers, Executives and Principals

Errol Bishop, Head of Private Equity
Graeme White, Managing Director
Simon Henderson, Investment Executive

CAIRNSFORD ASSOCIATES LIMITED

Upper Kingswell
58-62 Heath Street
London NW3 1EN
United Kingdom

Telephone: 44-171-431-0881
Fax: 44-171-794-7052
E-mail: vs@cainsford.co.uk

Mission: Actively seeking new investments, concentrated on information technology companies and acquisitions for investee companies

Fund Size: £10 million
Founded: 1992
Average Investment: £500,000
Minimum Investment: £150,000

Investment Criteria: Expansion, Management Buy-out, Management Buy-in, Other Early-stage

Geographic Preference: United Kingdom

Industry Group Preference: Communications, Computer Related, Consumer Related, Electronics Related, Industrial Automation, Industrial Products and Services, Manufacturing, Medical Related, Services

Portfolio Companies: Arts Communication and Technology Ltd., Garwood Communications Ltd., Willhire Ltd., Advanced Communications and Information Systems Ltd.

Officers, Executives and Principals

Vincent Robert Smith, Director
Education: BA in Business Studies; Chartered Accountant

Patrick Walker, Director
Education: BA; MBA, Cornell University

CAMBRIDGE RESEARCH AND INNOVATION LIMITED

13 Station Road
Cambridge CB1 2JB
United Kingdom

Telephone: 44-1223-312856
Fax: 44-1223-65704

Mission: Actively seeking new investments with strong intellectual property rights

Fund Size: £2.5 million
Founded: 1987
Average Investment: £100,000 - £150,000
Minimum Investment: £5,000

Investment Criteria: Seed, Research and Development, Start-up

Geographic Preference: United Kingdom (East Anglia, East Midlands)

Industry Group Preference: Communications, Computer Related, Consumer, Electronic Components and Instrumentation, Energy/Natural Resources, Genetic Engineering, Industrial Products and Equipment, Medical/Health Related

Portfolio Companies: Cambridge Display Technology Limited, Cambridge Positioning Systems Limited, Brax Genomics Limited, Net Plus Internet Software Ltd., Boston Biosystems Inc., Advanced Rendering Technologies Ltd., Cambridge Molecular Technologies

Officers, Executives and Principals

Chris Smart, Chief Executive Officer
Duncan Smart, Director
Lucy Block, Investment Manager

CANDOVER INVESTMENTS PLC

20 Old Bailey
London EC4M 7LN
United Kingdom

Telephone: 44-171-489-9848
Fax: 44-171-248-5483

Mission: Actively seeking new investments

Fund Size: £500 million
Founded: not available
Average Investment: not available
Minimum Investment: £500,000

Investment Criteria: Expansion, Management Buy-in, Management Buy-out, Secondary Purchase/Replacement Capital

Geographic Preference: Western Europe

Industry Group Preference: All sectors considered

Portfolio Companies: Jarvis Hotels, Midland Independent Newspapers, Vero Group plc, Stoves plc, Kenwood Appliances

Officers, Executives and Principals

Stephen Curran
Doug Fairservice

CAPITAL FOR COMPANIES

Quayside House
Canal Wharf
Leeds LS11 5PU
United Kingdom

Telephone: 44-113-243-8043
Fax: 44-113-245-1777

Other Office Locations
100 Old Hull Street
Liverpool
L3 9AB
Phone 0131-0227-2030, Fax 0131-227-2444

Mission: Providing equity and preference shares to unquoted companies

Fund Size: £9 million
Founded: 1983
Average Investment: £350,000
Minimum Investment: £200,000

Investment Criteria: Expansion, Management Buy-in, Management Buy-out, Other Early-stage, Other Purchase of Quoted Shares, Refinancing Bank Debt

Geographic Preference: United Kingdom (especially the M62 corridor and Northern England)

Industry Group Preference: Chemical and Materials, Communications, Consumer Related, Electronics Related, Industrial Automation, Industrial Products and Services, Leisure, Manufacturing, Medical Related, Transport

Portfolio Companies: not available

Officers, Executives and Principals

Barry Anysz, Chief Executive
Kenneth Abbot, Director
Andrew Needham, Investment Executive

CAPITAL PRIVÉ

9 rue de Phalsbourg
75854 Paris
France

Telephone: 33-1-4429-2100
Fax: 33-1-4429-2110

Mission: Actively seeking new investments

Fund Size: not available
Founded: 1990
Average Investment: not available
Minimum Investment: $1 million

Investment Criteria: Second-stage, Mezzanine, Leveraged Buy-out, Special Situations, Control-block Purchases

Geographic Preference: not available

Industry Group Preference: Diversified

Portfolio Companies: not available

Officers, Executives and Principals

Jean-Louis de Bernardy, President
Benoit Bassi, Managing Director
Mark Foulds
Philippe Houdouin

CAPMAN CAPITAL MANAGEMENT OY

Aleksanterinkatu 15B
00100 Helsinki
Finland

Telephone: 358-9-6155-800
Fax: 358-9-6155-8300

Mission: Actively seeking new investments

Fund Size: FM700 million
Founded: 1989
Average Investment: FM8 million
Minimum Investment: FM2 million

Investment Criteria: Second-stage, Leveraged Buy-out, Special Situations, Mezzanine

Geographic Preference: Finland, Scandinavia, Central and Eastern Europe

Industry Group Preference: Diversified

Portfolio Companies: not available

Officers, Executives and Principals

Ari Tolppanen, President
Olli Liitola, Director
Peter Buch Lund, Director
Tuomo Raasio, Director
Vesa Vanha-Honko, Director
Heikki Westerlund, Director

CAPRICORN VENTURE PARTNERS NV

Parijsstraat 74
3000 Leuven
Belgium

Telephone: 32-16-293828
Fax: 32-16-293871

Mission: Actively seeking new investments, associated with Baring Ventures Partners Ltd and allied with Altas Investeringroep

Fund Size: Ecu7.5 million
Founded: not available
Average Investment: not available
Minimum Investment: Ecu1 million

Investment Criteria: Seed, Start-up, Early-stage, Expansion/Development

Geographic Preference: Belgium, France, Germany, Netherlands

Industry Group Preference: All sectors considered

Portfolio Companies: not available

Officers, Executives and Principals

Dr. Jos B. Peters, Partner
Richard Onians, Partner

CATALANA D'INICIATIVES C.R. SA

Paseo de Gracia 2, 2-B
08007 Barcelona
Spain

Telephone: 34-3-317-8161
Fax: 34-3-318-9287

Mission: Actively seeking new investments

Fund Size: not available
Founded: not available
Average Investment: not available
Minimum Investment: $1 million

Investment Criteria: Expansion/Development, Management Buy-out, Management Buy-in, Mezzanine, Bridge

Geographic Preference: Spain

Industry Group Preference: All sectors considered

Portfolio Companies: not available

Officers, Executives and Principals

Francesc Raventós, Chief Executive
Background: Economist

Joan Carbonell, General Manager
Background: Economist

Manuel Albanell, General Manager
Background: Engineer

Jordi Dagà, General Manager
Background: Economist

Jose M. Massenella
Background: Economist

CDC-PARTICIPATIONS

Tour Maine Montparnasse
33 avenue de Maine
P. O. Box 173
75755 Paris
France

Telephone: 33-1-4064-2200
Fax: 33-1-4064-2222

Mission: Actively seeking new investments

Fund Size: Ffr10 billion
Founded: not available
Average Investment: not available
Minimum Investment: not available

Investment Criteria: Expansion/Development

Geographic Preference: Europe, France

Industry Group Preference: Communications, Environment, Technology, Tourism

Portfolio Companies: not available

Officers, Executives and Principals

Willy Stricker, President
Michel Dupont, Managing Director

CD TECHNICOM SA

Avenue Destenay 13
4000 Liège
Belgium

Telephone: 32-4-221-9811
Fax: 32-4-221-9999
E-mail: deville@interpec.bc

Mission: Investing in well-managed, high-potential information technology companies

Fund Size: $30 million
Founded: 1988
Average Investment: $500,000
Minimum Investment: $250,000

Investment Criteria: Start-up, Later Stage

Geographic Preference: Belgium, Europe

Industry Group Preference: Communications, Computer Related, Computer Software, Electronics, Industrial Automation

Portfolio Companies: not available

Officers, Executives and Principals

Philippe Deville, Chief Executive Officer
Education: postgraduate degree in Business, Solvay School, Brussels; Graduate degrees in Mathematics, Universities of Washington and Namur
Background: technical and management positions, Tractebel

CENTREWAY DEVELOPMENT CAPITAL LIMITED

Griffin House
9 Coventry Road
Coleshil
Birmingham B46 3BB
United Kingdom

Telephone: 44-1675-466796
Fax: 44-1675-466795
E-mail: futurestart@btinternet.com

Mission: Making commercial venture capital investments of up to £150,000 in businesses that also benefit the community.

Fund Size: £3 million
Founded: 1991
Average Investment: £100,000
Minimum Investment: £50,000

Investment Criteria: Start-up, Early-stage, Expansion, Secondary Purchase/ Replacement Capital, Rescure/ Turnaround, Management Buy-out, Management Buy-in, Refinancing Bank Debt

Geographic Preference: United Kingdom only

Industry Group Preference: All sectors considered

Portfolio Companies: Abingcourt Ltd., BHP Machine Tool Co. Ltd., Oxbury Industries Ltd., Village Foods Ltd.

Officers, Executives and Principals

A. J. Cross, Chairman
K. D. Caley, Managing Director
A. Carvell, Investment Manager

CENTROFINANZIARIA SpA

Via Flaminia 888
00191 Rome
Italy

Telephone: 39-6-333-1708
Fax: 39-6-333-1709

Mission: Actively seeking new investments

Fund Size: Ecu15,703,000
Founded: not available
Average Investment: not available
Minimum Investment: not available

Investment Criteria: Expansion/Development, Early-stage, Management Buy-out, Management Buy-in

Geographic Preference: Italy

Industry Group Preference: All sectors considered

Portfolio Companies: not available

Officers, Executives and Principals

Ettore Quadrani

C. F. J. P. E.
12 rue Chauchat
75009 Paris
France

Telephone: 33-1-4014-9807
Fax: 33-1-4014-9744

Mission: Actively seeking new investments

Fund Size: Ffr1.1 billion
Founded: not available
Average Investment: not available
Minimum Investment: Ffr20 million

Investment Criteria: Development

Geographic Preference: France

Industry Group Preference: All sectors considered

Portfolio Companies: Sofedit, Ciat, Descours et Cabaud, Quadral, CITA/SIDEL

Officers, Executives and Principals

Jean-Louis Delvaux
Marie-Cécile Matar

CHARTERHOUSE DEVELOPMENT CAPITAL LIMITED

85 Watling Street
London EC4M 9BX
United Kingdom

Telephone: 44-171-248-4000
Fax: 44-171-334-5333

Other Office Locations
47 avenue George V
75008 Paris
France
Phone 33-1-4723-5233

Mission: Actively seeking new investments

Fund Size: £2 million
Founded: 1934
Average Investment: not available
Minimum Investment: not available

Investment Criteria: Second-stage, Leveraged Buy-out

Geographic Preference: Western Europe

Industry Group Preference: Diversified

Portfolio Companies: Porterbrook, Celtic Energy, HRC, Miracle Garden Care, UBI

Officers, Executives and Principals

Edward Cox, Chairman (London)
Gordon Bonnyman, Managing Director (London)
Nigel Hamway, Managing Director (London and Paris)
Geoff Arbuthnott, Director (London)
Katherine Hood, Director (London)
Roger Pilgrim, Director (London)
Tom Plant, Financial Director (London)

CHASE CAPITAL PARTNERS

125 London Wall
London EC2Y 5AJ
United Kingdom

Telephone: 44-171-777-3365
Fax: 44-171-777-4731

Mission: Actively seeking new investments as a subsidiary of Chase Manhattan Bank

Fund Size: £2 billion
Founded: not available
Average Investment: £5 million
Minimum Investment: £2 million

Investment Criteria: Expansion, Management Buy-in, Management Buy-out, Rescue/Turnaround, Secondary Purchase/ Replacement Capital, Recapitalisations

Geographic Preference: Asia, North America, Western Europe, Latin America

Industry Group Preference: All sectors considered

Portfolio Companies: Bell Cablemedia plc, De Fenix, Vanguard Medica, La Compagnie Greenfield SA

Officers, Executives and Principals

Ferdinando Grimaldi
Andrew Martin
Jonathan Meggs
Shahan Soghikian
Lindsay Stuart
Tim Walsh

CHASE CAPITAL PARTNERS

150 Beach Road
31-00 Gateway West
Singapore 189720

Telephone: 65-290-1394
Fax: 65-290-1337

Mission: Actively seeking new investments as a subsidiary of Chase Manhattan Bank

Fund Size: $4 billion
Founded: 1984
Average Investment: not available
Minimum Investment: $3 million

Investment Criteria: Leveraged Buy-out, Start-up, First-stage, Second-stage

Geographic Preference: Asia Pacific, including Australasia

Industry Group Preference: Automotive Parts, Chemicals, Electronics, Energy, Healthcare, Media, Retail Distribution, Telecommunications

Portfolio Companies: not available

Officers, Executives and Principals

Ting Yu Seng, General Partner
Education: BSc in Electronic Engineering, University of Birmingham; MSc in Management Science, University of London

Harry F. McKinley, Jr., Managing Director
Education: BA, Brigham Young University; MBA, New York University
Background: Chemical Bank, Bankers Trust Company, Gemini Consulting (formerly The MAC Group)
Directorships: Indocean Fund, Schroder Capital Partners Asia Pacific Fund II, Plantation Timber Products Group, Richina Pacific Limited (formerly Mainzeal Group Limited)

John D. Lewis, Principal
Education: BA, University of Virginia; MA, Johns Hopkins School of Advanced International Studies
Directorships: Member, Investment Committee, The India Private Equity Fund LP; Director, Vista Healthcare Pte. Ltd.

CHASE CAPITAL PARTNERS ITALIA SpA

Via Catena 4
20121 Milan
Italy

Telephone: 39-2-8052171
Fax: 39-2-8052321
E-mail: chasecpi@micronet.it

Mission: Actively seeking new investments as a subsidiary of Chase Manhattan Bank

Fund Size: not available
Founded: not available
Average Investment: not available
Minimum Investment: not available

Investment Criteria: Expansion/Development, Management Buy-out, Management Buy-in, Replacement Capital

Geographic Preference: Italy

Industry Group Preference: All sectors considered

Portfolio Companies: not available

Officers, Executives and Principals

Fabio Lorenzo Sattin, Managing Director
Giovanni Campolo, Director
Maurizio Perroni, Manager
Matteo Carlotti, Manager
Elisabetta Vitali, Analyst
Roberto Tremi, Senior Consultant

CHASE GEMINA ITALIA SpA

Via F. Turati 18
20121 Milan
Italy

Telephone: 39-2-659-0351
Fax: 39-2-655-5925

Mission: Actively seeking new investments

Fund Size: Ecu40 million
Founded: not available
Average Investment: not available
Minimum Investment: Ecu500,000

Investment Criteria: Expansion/Development, Management Buy-out, Management Buy-in, Replacement

Geographic Preference: Italy

Industry Group Preference: All sectors considered

Portfolio Companies: not available

Officers, Executives and Principals

Fabio Lorenzo Sattin
Giovanni Campolo

CICLAD

4 rue Ancelle
92521 Neuilly
France

Telephone: 33-1-4747-0074
Fax: 33-1-4747-7206

Mission: Actively seeking new investments

Fund Size: Ffr350 million
Founded: not available
Average Investment: not available
Minimum Investment: Ffr3 million

Investment Criteria: Leveraged Buy-out, Management Buy-out, Management Buy-in

Geographic Preference: France

Industry Group Preference: All sectors considered

Portfolio Companies: Satelec, VSD, Terres d'Aventure, ITM Mémogarde, Vermed, Siraga, Dalie, Arthus-Bertrand, Mécalectro, Gérard Pasquier, IMV

Officers, Executives and Principals

Lionel Lambert
Thierry Thomann
Jean-François Vaury
Didier Genoud

CINVEN LTD.

Pinners Hall
105-108 Old Broad Street
London EC2N 1EH
United Kingdom

Telephone: 44-171-661-3333
Fax: 44-171-256-2225
E-mail: cinven.co.uk

Mission: Actively seeking new investments

Fund Size: not available
Founded: 1976
Average Investment: £10 million
Minimum Investment: £500,000

Investment Criteria: Start-up, First-stage, Second-stage, Buy-out, Buy-in

Geographic Preference: Western Europe

Industry Group Preference: All sectors considered

Portfolio Companies: Dunlop Slazenger, Amicus Healthcare, Addis, Automotive Products

Officers, Executives and Principals

Robin Hall, Managing Director
John Brown, Deputy Managing Director

CITA

48 avenue Victor Hugo
75116 Paris
France

Telephone: 33-1-4500-2002
Fax: 33-1-4500-0415

Mission: Actively seeking new investments

Fund Size: Ffr400 million
Founded: not available
Average Investment: not available
Minimum Investment: Ffr10 million

Investment Criteria: Development, Restructuring, Leveraged Buy-out, Management Buy-out

Geographic Preference: France

Industry Group Preference: All sectors considered

Portfolio Companies: Genoyer, Sidel, Nobel Plastiques, REP, Sommer Alibert Inc., Axisco, Sofinnova

Officers, Executives and Principals

Henri Biard
Phillippe Queveau

CITIBANK N. A.

P. O. Box 200
Cottons Centre, Hays Lane
London SE1 2QT
United Kingdom

Telephone: 44-171-234-2387
Fax: 44-171-234-2398

Other Office Locations
Citibank Paris
Phone 33-1-4906-1097

Mission: Actively seeking new investments

Fund Size: not available
Founded: not available
Average Investment: not available
Minimum Investment: not available

Investment Criteria: Mezzanine

Geographic Preference: Europe

Industry Group Preference: All sectors considered

Portfolio Companies: Kässbohrer Geländefahrzeug GmgH (Germany), Ferembal (France)

Officers, Executives and Principals

Stephen J. Karper, Managing Director
Robert C. Van Goethem, Director
James J. Maguire, Director
Didier F. Denat, Vice President (France)

CIT SYNERGO AB

Chalmers Teknikpark
41288 Gothenburg
Sweden

Telephone: 46-31-772-4030
Fax: 46-31-82-7035
E-mail: ingrara@cit.chalmers.se

Mission: Actively investing in spin-offs from the Chalmers University of Technology, Gothenburg

Fund Size: Skr5 million
Founded: 1988
Average Investment: Skr500,000
Minimum Investment: Skr100,000

Investment Criteria: not available

Geographic Preference: Sweden (Gothenburg)

Industry Group Preference: not available

Portfolio Companies: not available

Officers, Executives and Principals

Ingvar Andersson

CLOSE INVESTMENT MANAGEMENT LIMITED

36 Great Helen's
London EC3A 6AP
United Kingdom

Telephone: 44-171-426-4000
Fax: 44-171-426-4004

Mission: Actively seeking new investments

Fund Size: £125 million
Founded: not available
Average Investment: £2.5 million
Minimum Investment: £1 million

Investment Criteria: Bridge Finance, Expansion, Management Buy-in, Management Buy-out, Refinancing Bank Debt, Rescue/Turnaround, Secondary Purchase/Replacement Capital, Venture Purchase of Quoted Shares

Geographic Preference: United Kingdom

Industry Group Preference: All sectors considered except Real Estate

Portfolio Companies: Grove Industries, Hamilton Acorn, Seawheel, Link Plastics, Halliard Ltd., Chessington Computer Services

Officers, Executives and Principals

Jonathan Thornton, Chairman
John Snook, Managing Director
R. D. Kent, Director
Nick MacNay, Director
Neil Murphy, Director
P. J. Stone, Director
P. L. Winkworth, Director
Simon Wildig, Partner

CLYDESDALE BANK EQUITY LIMITED

150 Buchanan Street
Glasgow G1 2HL
United Kingdom

Telephone: 44-141-223-3727
Fax: 44-141-223-3724

Mission: Actively seeking new investments

Fund Size: £50 million
Founded: not available
Average Investment: £1.5 million
Minimum Investment: £250,000

Investment Criteria: Expansion, Management Buy-in, Management Buy-out, Secondary Purchase/Replacement Capital, Venture Purchase of Quoted Shares, Development, Acquisition

Geographic Preference: United Kingdom

Industry Group Preference: All sectors considered except Real Estate, Financial Services, Film and Television and very High Tech

Portfolio Companies: McQueen International Ltd., Pierre Victoire Ltd., Worldfresh Organisation Ltd., Ritchie (U. K.) Ltd.

Officers, Executives and Principals

Neil Kennedy
Bill Nixon
Craig Rattray

C. N. B. TECHNOLOGY FINANCE COMPANY LTD.

1st-2nd Floors, 122-1 Jeoksun-dong
Chongro-ku
Seoul
Korea

Telephone: 82-2-736-0190
Fax: 82-2-736-9877

Other Office Locations
375 Choryang-dong
Dong-ku
Pusan
Korea
Phone 82-151-42-8248, Fax 82-151-464-1982

Mission: Actively seeking new investments

Fund Size: not available
Founded: 1985
Average Investment: not available
Minimum Investment: $250,000

Investment Criteria: Start-up, First-stage, Second-stage, Mezzanine

Geographic Preference: not available

Industry Group Preference: Communications, Computer Related, Consumer, Distribution, Electronic Components and Instrumentation, Energy/Natural Resources, Genetic Engineering, Industrial Products and Equipment, Medical/Health Related

Portfolio Companies: not available

Officers, Executives and Principals

Chong Myung Rhee, President
Pil Lae Park, Executive Senior Vice President
Sae Young Kim, Senior Vice President
Sang Pil Shim, Senior Vice President
Chong Kon Kim, General Manager
Hwa Jung Kim, General Manager
Kyung Ki Kim, General Manager

COFINEP

41 rue Libergier
51100 Rheims
France

Telephone: 33-2683-3050
Fax: 33-2683-3554

Mission: Actively seeking new investments

Fund Size: Ffr70 million
Founded: not available
Average Investment: not available
Minimum Investment: Ffr1 million

Investment Criteria: All stages

Geographic Preference: France (Marne, Aisne, Ardennes)

Industry Group Preference: All sectors considered

Portfolio Companies: Malteurop International SA, Sucreries de Berneuil, Cedrepa, Champagne Gardet

Officers, Executives and Principals

Jean-Pierre Huet, Managing Director

COLLER ISNARD LIMITED

74 Brook Street
London W1Y 1YD
United Kingdom

Telephone: 44-171-290-5030
Fax: 44-171-290-5035

Mission: Actively seeking new investments

Fund Size: Ecu75 million
Founded: not available
Average Investment: Ecu1.6 million
Minimum Investment: Ecu300,000

Investment Criteria: All stages

Geographic Preference: Worldwide

Industry Group Preference: All sectors considered

Portfolio Companies: not available

Officers, Executives and Principals

Jeremy Coller, Partner
Arnaud Isnard, Partner

COMMERCIAL CAPITAL SA

32 Kifissias Avenue
15125 Maroussi
Athens
Greece

Telephone: 30-1-684-6116
Fax: 30-1-684-6117

Mission: Actively seeking new investments

Fund Size: Ecu72,426,000
Founded: not available
Average Investment: not available
Minimum Investment: Ecu350,000

Investment Criteria: All stages

Geographic Preference: Greece, Romania, Bulgaria, Russia, Ukraine, Albania

Industry Group Preference: Chemical and Materials, Communications, Computer Software, Consumer
  Related, Medical/Health Related, Services

Portfolio Companies: not available

Officers, Executives and Principals

Aristideis Fronistas
A. Anggelopoulos
A. Doxiades
S .Levis

COMMERZ BETEILIGUNGS GmbH

Neue Mainzer Strasse 32-36
60311 Frankfurt am Main
Germany

Telephone: 49-69-1362-2970
Fax: 49-69-1362-9876

Mission: Actively seeking new investments

Fund Size: DM91 million
Founded: not available
Average Investment: not available
Minimum Investment: DM2 million

Investment Criteria: Expansion/Development, Management Buy-out, Management Buy-in

Geographic Preference: Germany

Industry Group Preference: All sectors considered

Portfolio Companies: not available

Officers, Executives and Principals

Dieter Firmenich
Gerhard Koning
Dr. Gert Schorradt

COMMERZ UNTERNEHMENSBETEILIGUNGS AG

Leisewitzstrasse 37b
30175 Hannover
Germany

Telephone: 49-0511-280-0701
Fax: 49-0511 280-0737
E-mail: hannover.finanz@p-net.de

Mission: Actively seeking new investments in growing companies as a managed fund within the Hannover Finanz Group

Fund Size: DM130 million
Founded: 1986
Average Investment: DM8 million
Minimum Investment: DM2 million

Investment Criteria: Later-stage, Development, Buy-out, Replacement

Geographic Preference: Germany; rest of Europe with syndication partners

Industry Group Preference: Engineering, Financial Services, Logistics, Manufacturing, Media, Services, Telecommunications, Trade

Portfolio Companies: not available

COM NET SpA

Viale Erminio Spalla 41
00142
Rome
Italy

Telephone: 39-6-503-6192
Fax: 39-6-503-7184

Mission: not available

Fund Size: not available
Founded: not available
Average Investment: not available
Minimum Investment: not available

Investment Criteria: not available

Geographic Preference: not available

Industry Group Preference: Communications, Computer Related

Portfolio Companies: Satellite Technology

Officers, Executives and Principals

Andre Scheevo

COMPAGNIE DE FINANCEMENT INDUSTRIEL

40 rue de Chateaudun
75009 Paris
France

Telephone: 33-1-4526-6016
Fax: 33-1-4526-6024

Mission: Actively seeking new investments

Fund Size: Ffr495 million
Founded: not available
Average Investment: not available
Minimum Investment: Ffr5 million

Investment Criteria: Expansion/Development, Management Buy-out, Replacement

Geographic Preference: France

Industry Group Preference: All sectors considered

Portfolio Companies: not available

Officers, Executives and Principals

Dominique Oger, Managing Director
Patrick Lenté, Director
Jean-Louis Ennesser, Partner
Patrick Bertiaux, Partner
Michele Philippe-Serpault, Partner

COMPAGNIE FINANCIÈRE E. DE ROTHSCHILD BANQUE

47 rue du Faubourg St-Honoré
75008 Paris
France

Telephone: 33-1-4017-2453
Fax: 33-1-4017-2391

Mission: Actively seeking new investments

Fund Size: Ffr350 million
Founded: not available
Average Investment: not available
Minimum Investment: Ffr3 million

Investment Criteria: Expansion/Development, Leveraged Buy-out, Replacement

Geographic Preference: France, Europe

Industry Group Preference: All sectors considered

Portfolio Companies: Sofedit, Cider, Kindy

Officers, Executives and Principals

Christian Deblaye
Pierre-Michel Passy

COMPASS INVESTMENT MANAGEMENT LIMITED

17-18 Dover Street
London W1X 4DQ
United Kingdom

Telephone: 44-171-409-0014
Fax: 44-171-629-4623

Mission: Actively seeking new investments

Fund Size: £16 million
Founded: not available
Average Investment: £50,000-£500,000
Minimum Investment: no minimum

Investment Criteria: Bridge Finance, Management Buy-in, Management Buy-out, Early-stage, Secondary Purchase/Replacement Capital, Expansion Finance

Geographic Preference: North America, United Kingdom

Industry Group Preference: All sectors considered

Portfolio Companies: American Mirrex Corporation, Federated Foods Inc., McCall Pattern Co.

Officers, Executives and Principals

Dennis Hallahane
Peter Dale

COPERNICUS CAPITAL MANAGEMENT

u. Krak. Przedmiescie 79, 2nd Floor
00079 Warsaw
Poland

Telephone: 48-22-268580
Fax: 48-22-254462
E-mail: 100710.1515@compuserv.

Mission: Actively seeking new investments

Fund Size: $25 million
Founded: 1994
Average Investment: $2 million
Minimum Investment: $750,000

Investment Criteria: Start-up, Early-stage, Expansion/Development, Bridge, Replacement, Turnaround/
  Restructuring

Geographic Preference: Poland

Industry Group Preference: Communications, Industrial Automation, Industrial Products, Manufacturing,
  Medical/Health Related, Pollution/Recycling

Portfolio Companies: not available

Officers, Executives and Principals

Neil M. Milne, Managing Director
Jeffrey Grady, Partner
Jerzy Strzelecki, Partner
Krzysztof Jakaczynski, Partner
Darek Klonowksi, Partner

COVENT INDUSTRIAL VENTURE CAPITAL INVESTMENT COMPANY LIMITED

Kutvölgyi ut. 23
1125 Budapest XII
Hungary

Telephone: 36-1-155-2493
Fax: 36-1-156-8496

Mission: Actively seeking new investments

Fund Size: Ecu5,376,800
Founded: not available
Average Investment: not available
Minimum Investment: Ecu50,000

Investment Criteria: Seed, Start-up, Early-stage, Expansion/Development, Turnaround, Mezzanine, Bridge

Geographic Preference: Hungary

Industry Group Preference: Biotechnology, Communications, Finance and Insurance, Industrial Automation, Medical/Health Related

Portfolio Companies: not available

Officers, Executives and Principals

Janos Bolyky
László Kalácska

CREDITANSTALT INVESTMENT LIMITED

125 London Wall
London EC2Y 5DD

Telephone: 44-171-600-4250
Fax: 44-171-417-4899

Mission: Actively seeking new investments

Fund Size: not available
Founded: not available
Average Investment: not available
Minimum Investment: not available

Investment Criteria: not available

Geographic Preference: Central and Eastern Europe

Industry Group Preference: not available

Portfolio Companies: not available

Officers, Executives and Principals

James Stewart

CREDIT SUISSE DEPARTEMENT S1

8070 Zürich
Switzerland

Telephone: 41-1-333-5260
Fax: 41-1-333-3899

Mission: Actively seeking new investments, concentrating on well established companies

Fund Size: not available
Founded: not available
Average Investment: not available
Minimum Investment: Sfr3 million

Investment Criteria: Expansion/Development, Management Buy-out, Replacement/Share Purchases, Turn-around

Geographic Preference: Switzerland, Worldwide

Industry Group Preference: All sectors considered

Portfolio Companies: not available

Officers, Executives and Principals

Christian Lubicz
Beat Haemmerli

CROSSROADS MANAGEMENT (U. K.) LIMITED

Regency House
97-107 Hagley Road
Edgbaston
Birmingham B16 8LA
United Kingdom

Telephone: 44-121-456-1771
Fax: 44-121-456-2904
E-mail: jmccuk@aol.com

Mission: Investing exclusively in fixed-life and managed venture funds, and providing consultancy and advisory services to institutional investors

Fund Size: £300 million
Founded: not available
Average Investment: not available
Minimum Investment: not available

Investment Criteria: not available

Geographic Preference: not available

Industry Group Preference: Financial Services

Portfolio Companies: not available

Officers, Executives and Principals

John McCrory
Angela Willetts
Mark Drugan

C. S. K. VENTURE CAPITAL COMPANY, LIMITED

7th Floor, Kenchiku Kaikan
5-26-20 Shiba
Minato-ku
Tokyo 108
Japan

Telephone: 81-3-3457-5588
Fax: 81-3-3457-7070

Mission: Actively seeking new investments

Fund Size: $103 million
Founded: 1991
Average Investment: $1.3 million
Minimum Investment: $300,000

Investment Criteria: Start-up, First-stage, Second-stage, Mezzanine

Geographic Preference: Japan, United States, Israel

Industry Group Preference: Communications, Computer Related, Consumer, Distribution, Electronic Components and Instrumentation, Medical/Health Related

Portfolio Companies: not available

Officers, Executives and Principals

Isao Okawa, Chairman
Masahiro Aozono, President
Nobumasa Tokumaru, Managing Director
Fumio Takahashi, Director

C.V. C. CAPITAL BERATUNGS GmbH

Friedrich-Ebert-Anlage 49
60327 Frankfurt
Germany

Telephone: 49-69-740174
Fax: 49-69-749690

Mission: Actively seeking new investments

Fund Size: not available
Founded: not available
Average Investment: not available
Minimum Investment: Sfr12 million

Investment Criteria: Management Buy-out, Management Buy-in

Geographic Preference: Germany, Switzerland, Austria

Industry Group Preference: All sectors considered

Portfolio Companies: not available

Officers, Executives and Principals

Steven Koltes
Charles Schwarch

C.V.C. CAPITAL PARTNERS

40 rue La Pérouse
75116 Paris
France

Telephone: 33-1-4502-2300
Fax: 33-1-4502-2301

Mission: Actively seeking new investments

Fund Size: Ffr300 million
Founded: not available
Average Investment: not available
Minimum Investment: Ffr20 million

Investment Criteria: Management Buy-out, Leveraged Buy-out

Geographic Preference: France, Europe

Industry Group Preference: All sectors considered

Portfolio Companies: not available

Officers, Executives and Principals

Findlay Black
Philippe Gleize
Frédéric Maire
Bertrand Finet

C. V. C. CAPITAL PARTNERS LIMITED

Hudson House
8-10 Tavistock Street
London WC2E 7PP
United Kingdom

Telephone: 44-171-420-4200
Fax: 44-171-420-4231

Mission: Actively seeking new investments

Fund Size: £800 million
Founded: not available
Average Investment: £10 million
Minimum Investment: £1 million

Investment Criteria: Bridge Finance, Expansion, Management Buy-in, Management Buy-out, Refinancing Bank Debt, Rescue/Turnaround, Secondary Purchase/Replacement Capital

Geographic Preference: Western Europe, Hungary

Industry Group Preference: All sectors considered

Portfolio Companies: Brunner Mond, Sylvania Lighting, Victrex, Hydron, Belhaven

Officers, Executives and Principals

Marc Boughton
Tony Clinch
William Comfort
Jonathan Feuer
Robert Lucas
Donald Mackenzie
Hardy McLain
David Milne
Iain Parham
Michael Smith

CYGNUS VENTURE PARTNERS LIMITED

4-10 Guilford Road
Chertsey, Surrey
KT16 9MM
United Kingdom

Telephone: 44-1932-562563
Fax: 44-1932-563041
E-mail: 101602.120@compuserve.com

Mission: Actively seeking new investments

Fund Size: £30 million
Founded: 1988
Average Investment: £100,000 to £3 million
Minimum Investment: £100,000

Investment Criteria: Start-up, Early-stage, Expansion/Development, Management Buy-out, Management Buy-in, Turnaround/Restructuring

Geographic Preference: United Kingdom, Europe, North America

Industry Group Preference: Biotechnology, Communications, Computer Related, Computer Software, Finance and Insurance, Medical/Health Related, Real Estate

Portfolio Companies: not available

Officers, Executives and Principals

Colin Pearce, Director
Nigel Keen, Director
Bill Birkett, Director

DANISH DEVELOPMENT FINANCE CORPORATION

Gladsaxevej 376
2860 Soborg
Denmark

Telephone: 45-39-66 04 00
Fax: 45-39-66 13 11
E-mail: 101354.3700@compuserv.com

Mission: Actively seeking new investments

Fund Size: Ecu70 million
Founded: not available
Average Investment: not available
Minimum Investment: Ecu30,000

Investment Criteria: Seed, Start-up, Early-stage

Geographic Preference: Denmark, Europe, North America

Industry Group Preference: Biotechnology, Computer Related, Computer Software, Electronics Related, Industrial Automation, Medical/Health Related

Portfolio Companies: not available

Officers, Executives and Principals

Dr. Uffe Bundgaard-Jorgensen, Partner
Kent Hansen, Partner
Frede Morck, Partner
Sten Helde Hemmingsen, Partner
Mogens Olsen, Partner
Linda Sjöström, Partner

DANSK KAPITALANLAEG A/S

P. O. Box 1080
1008 Copenhagen K
Denmark

Telephone: 45-33-157030
Fax: 45-33-937044

Mission: Actively seeking new investments

Fund Size: Ecu110 million
Founded: not available
Average Investment: not available
Minimum Investment: Ecu500,000

Investment Criteria: Start-up, Expansion/Development, Management buy-out, Replacement, Turnaround/ Restructuring

Geographic Preference: Denmark

Industry Group Preference: All sectors considered

Portfolio Companies: not available

Officers, Executives and Principals

Niels Kristian Agner, Partner
Flemming Honoré, Partner
Kjeld Bock, Partner
Jorgen Dyhrfjeld, Partner
Arne J. Gillin, Partner
Peter B. Kristensen, Partner

DCC MANAGEMENT OY

Tykistökatu 4A
20520 Turku
Finland

Telephone: 358-21 637-5756
Fax: 358-21 637-5729

Mission: Actively seeking new investments

Fund Size: FM35 million
Founded: not available
Average Investment: FM1-2 million
Minimum Investment: FM300,000

Investment Criteria: Start-up, Expansion, Management Buy-out

Geographic Preference: Finland

Industry Group Preference: All sectors considered

Portfolio Companies: not available

Officers, Executives and Principals

Juha Mikkola, Managing Director
Education: BSc, MBA

Heikki Tuomaala, Director
Education: MSc in Engineering

DCC plc

DCC House
Brewery Road Stillorgan
Blackrock
County Dublin
Ireland

Telephone: 353-1-283-1011
Fax: 353-1-283-1018

Mission: Actively seeking new investments

Fund Size: not available
Founded: not available
Average Investment: not available
Minimum Investment: Ecu5 million

Investment Criteria: Management Buy-out

Geographic Preference: Europe, North America

Industry Group Preference: Consumer Related, Computer Related, Energy, Medical/Health Related

Portfolio Companies: not available

Officers, Executives and Principals

James Flavin
Morgan Crowe
David Gavagan
Dr. George Young

DEFI GESTION SA

Avenue De Gratta-Paille 1
1000 Lausanne 30
Switzerland

Telephone: 41-21-648-5656
Fax: 41-21-648-5660

Mission: Actively seeking new investments

Fund Size: not available
Founded: not available
Average Investment: not available
Minimum Investment: Sfr1 million

Investment Criteria: Expansion/Development, Management Buy-out, Replacement/Share Purchases

Geographic Preference: Switzerland, France, Italy, Germany

Industry Group Preference: All sectors considered

Portfolio Companies: not available

Officers, Executives and Principals

Fred Stuber
Philipe Rao
Mohammed Diab

DERBYSHIRE ENTERPRISE BOARD LIMITED

95 Sheffield Road
Chesterfield
Derbyshire S41 7JH
United Kingdom

Telephone: 44-1246-207390
Fax: 44-1246-221080

Mission: Actively seeking new investments

Fund Size: £3 million
Founded: not available
Average Investment: £320,000
Minimum Investment: £50,000

Investment Criteria: All stages except Start-up

Geographic Preference: United Kingdom (Derbyshire, East Midlands)

Industry Group Preference: All sectors considered except Real Estate and Retail

Portfolio Companies: Advanced Composites Group, Peter Geeson Ltd., Cobb Slater Ltd., Bespoke Furniture Ltd.

Officers, Executives and Principals

Andrew Street
Gordon Wilding

DEUTSCHE BETEILIGUNGS AG

Emil-von-Behring-Strasse 2
60439 Frankfurt am Main
Germany

Telephone: 49-69-957-8701
Fax: 49-69-957-87-199

Mission: Actively seeking new investments

Fund Size: not available
Founded: 1965
Average Investment: not available
Minimum Investment: not available

Investment Criteria: Leveraged Buy-out

Geographic Preference: Europe, United States, Asia

Industry Group Preference: Diversified

Portfolio Companies: not available

Officers, Executives and Principals

Karl-Heinz Fanselow, Chairman, Board of Management
Roland Jetter, Managing Director
Reinhard Löffler, Managing Director
Heinrich R. Stedler, Assistant Managing Director

D. F. C. LTD.

Grosvenor House
141-143 Drury Lane
London WC2B 5TB
United Kingdom

Telephone: 44-171-836-3424
Fax: 44-171-379-4931

Mission: Actively seeking new investments in medium-sized private companies

Fund Size: Ecu1.8 million
Founded: not available
Average Investment: not available
Minimum Investment: Ecu300,000

Investment Criteria: Expansion/Development, Mezzanine/Bridge

Geographic Preference: Spain, Portugal, France

Industry Group Preference: All sectors considered

Portfolio Companies: not available

Officers, Executives and Principals

Jose Luis Mombru
Michael Jordan
J. Lloveras
Robert Poldermans

DOW EUROPE SA

Bachtobelstrasse 3
8810 Horgen
Switzerland

Telephone: 41-1-728-2039
Fax: 41-1-728-2097

Mission: Actively seeking strategic investments in new chemistry-related businesses

Fund Size: not available
Founded: not available
Average Investment: not available
Minimum Investment: not available

Investment Criteria: Start-up, Early-stage, Expansion/Development

Geographic Preference: Europe

Industry Group Preference: Chemical and Materials, Electronics

Portfolio Companies: not available

Officers, Executives and Principals

Jean-Daniel Dor
Robert Lensch
Claude Fussler
Paul Morris

DUNEDIN CAPITAL PARTNERS LIMITED

Napier House
27 Thistle Street
Edinburgh EH2 1BT
United Kingdom

Telephone: 44-131-225-6699
Fax: 44-131-624-1234
E-mail: dunedin@sol.co.uk

Mission: Actively seeking new investments in order to achieve substantial long-term growth in assets

Fund Size: £65.5 million
Founded: 1973
Average Investment: £2 million
Minimum Investment: £1 million

Investment Criteria: All stages except Seed, especially Development, Management Buy-out, Management Buy-in

Geographic Preference: United Kingdom

Industry Group Preference: All sectors considered except Biotechnology

Portfolio Companies: LDV Limited, Scottish Highland Hotels PLC, Motherwell Bridge Holdings Limited, Latchways Limited, Travel and General Holdings Limited, Cawoods Group Limited, Golden Wonder (Holdings) Limited, Macdonald Hotels plc, John Wood Group PLC, Coal Products (Holdings) Limited

Officers, Executives and Principals

Simon Miller, Chairman
Brian Finlayson, Managing Director
Ross Marshall, Director
Ewan Jeffrey, Director
Helen Bagan, Director

DYNAMUST

100 boulevard Montparnasse
75014 Paris
France

Telephone: 33-1-4323-2920
Fax: 33-1-4323-3413

Mission: Actively seeking new investments

Fund Size: Ffr150 million
Founded: not available
Average Investment: not available
Minimum Investment: Ffr3 million

Investment Criteria: Expansion/Development, Leveraged Buy-out

Geographic Preference: France

Industry Group Preference: Industrial Products and Services

Portfolio Companies: not available

Officers, Executives and Principals

Gilles Gramat, Managing Director
Jean-Michel Solier, Company Secretary

ECI VENTURES

Brettenham House
Lancaster Place
London WC2E 7EN
United Kingdom

Telephone: 44-171-606 1000
Fax: 44-171-240 5050

Mission: Actively seeking new investments

Fund Size: £240 million
Founded: 1976
Average Investment: £2.5 million
Minimum Investment: £750,000

Investment Criteria: Leveraged Buy-out, Special Situations, Control-block Purchases

Geographic Preference: United Kingdom

Industry Group Preference: Communications, Consumer, Distribution, Electronic Components and Instrumentation, Genetic Engineering, Industrial Products and Equipment, Medical/Health Related

Portfolio Companies: Guardian Computer Services, Service Team, MTL, OSI Group, York House

Officers, Executives and Principals

Sir John Banham, Chairman
David Wansbrough, Deputy Chairman
Jonathan Baker, Senior Partner
Stephen Dawson, Senior Partner
Roger Hay, Senior Partner
Paul Jobson, Partner
Ken Landsberg, Partner
Martin Makey, Partner

EGAN AND TALBOT CAPITAL LIMITED

Buckden Wood
Perry Road
Buckden, Huntingdon
Cambridgeshire PE18 9XQ
United Kingdom

Telephone: 44-1480-812218
Fax: 44-1480-812981

Mission: Actively seeking new investments

Fund Size: £2 million
Founded: 1991
Average Investment: £113,000
Minimum Investment: £20,000

Investment Criteria: Expansion, Management Buy-in, Management Buy-out, Other Early-stage, Refinancing Bank Debt, Rescue/Turnaround, Start-up

Geographic Preference: United Kingdom (East Anglia and northern Home Counties)

Industry Group Preference: All sectors considered except Construction, Financial Services, Real Estate

Portfolio Companies: Precept Design Consultants Plc, Christy Trading Company Limited, Hero Systems Limited

Officers, Executives and Principals

Martin Rigby, Managing Director
Education: MA in History, University of Oxford; MBA, Cranfield University
Background: British Army; 3i plc, Cambridge

EIBA BETEILIGUNGS UND FINANZ GmbH

Bleicherweg 30
8021 Zürich
Switzerland

Telephone: 41-1-281-1081
Fax: 41-1-281-1087

Mission: Actively seeking new investments, concentrating on small and medium sized Swiss companies

Fund Size: not available
Founded: not available
Average Investment: not available
Minimum Investment: Sfr1 million

Investment Criteria: Early-stage, Expansion/Development, Management Buy-out, Replacement/Share Purchases

Geographic Preference: Switzerland

Industry Group Preference: All sectors considered

Portfolio Companies: not available

Officers, Executives and Principals

Dr. Martin Mäder

EIKEN CHEMICAL COMPANY LIMITED
5-26-20 Oji
Kita-ku
Tokyo
Japan

Telephone: not available

Mission: not available

Fund Size: $9 billion
Founded: not available
Average Investment: $6.5 million
Minimum Investment: not available

Investment Criteria: not available

Geographic Preference: not available

Industry Group Preference: All sectors considered

Portfolio Companies: Advanced Magnetics

Officers, Executives and Principals

H. Kagawa

EISAI COMPANY

Koishikawa 4
Bunkyo-ku
Tokyo
Japan

Telephone: not available

Mission: not available

Fund Size: $1.6 billion
Founded: not available
Average Investment: $3.5 million
Minimum Investment: not available

Investment Criteria: Pharmaceuticals

Geographic Preference: not available

Industry Group Preference: Medical/Health Related

Portfolio Companies: ISIS

Officers, Executives and Principals

Haruo Naito

ELDERSTREET INVESTMENTS LTD

32 Bedford Row
London WC1R 4HE
United Kingdom

Telephone: 44-171-831-5088
Fax: 44-171-831-5077

Mission: Seeking good management teams in which to invest, either from its higher-risk, higher-reward portfolio or from its lower-risk portfolio, which is run with Kleinwort Benson Development Capital

Fund Size: £10 million
Founded: 1990
Average Investment: £700,000
Minimum Investment: £500,000

Investment Criteria: Expansion, Management Buy-in, Management Buy-out, Refinancing Bank Debt, Secondary Purchase, Replacement Capital

Geographic Preference: United Kingdom

Industry Group Preference: All sectors considered

Portfolio Companies: Elmbridge Holdings Ltd., Select Software Tools PLC, F. G. Chambers and Co Ltd., Weyrad Electronics Ltd., Sage Group PLC, Cedars Village Ltd., I. D. Data Holdings Ltd., Starburst Ltd., Pharmasol Ltd., A. and M. Furniture Hire Ltd., Baldwin and Francis Ltd., Golf Park Developments Ltd., W. Fearnehough Ltd., Thorn Microwave Devices Ltd., Moseley Brothers Ltd., College of Railway Technology Ltd., E. L. S. Ltd., Quality and Safety Services Ltd., Steve Dudman Plant Ltd., VIS Interactive PLC

Officers, Executives and Principals

Michael Jackson, Managing Director
Richard Porter, Finance Director
Chris Kay
Chris Powles
David Taylor
Will Riley

ELECTRA FLEMING ET ASSOCIÉS

31 rue de Lisbonne
75008 Paris
France

Telephone: 33-1-5383-7910
Fax: 33-1-5383-7920

Mission: Actively seeking new investments

Fund Size: Ffr490 million
Founded: not available
Average Investment: not available
Minimum Investment: Ffr25 million

Investment Criteria: Management Buy-out, Management Buy-in, Replacement

Geographic Preference: Belgium, France, Switzerland

Industry Group Preference: All sectors considered

Portfolio Companies: not available

Officers, Executives and Principals

Jean Ducroux
Laurence Albertini
Frédéric Crot
Nicolas Paulmier

ELECTRA FLEMING LIMITED

65 Kingsway
London WC2B 6QT
United Kingdom

Telephone: 44-171-831-6464
Fax: 44-171-404-5388

Other Office Locations
Electra Fleming et Associés
31 rue de Lisbonne
75008 Paris
France
Phone 33-1-5383-7910, Fax 33-1-5383-7920

B. and S. Electra SpA
Via Ippolito Nievo 33
20145 Milan
Italy
Phone 39-2-336-10230, Fax 39-2-336-10199

Electra Fleming Inc.
25th Floor, 70 East 55th Street
New York, NY 10022
United States
Phone 1-212-319-0081, Fax 1-212-319-3069

JF Electra Limited
47th Floor, Jardine House
1 Connaught Place
Central
Hong Kong
Phone 852-2840-6850, Fax 852-2530-5525

Mission: Actively seeking new private equity investments, preferably majority interests in British and Continental European companies with good management and strong market positions, or operating in defensible market niches; also minority positions when providing capital for expansion or refinancing, especially in the United States and Asia

Fund Size: £1.3 billion
Founded: 1935
Average Investment: not available
Minimum Investment: £2 million

Investment Criteria: Second Stage, Mezzanine, Development and Expansion Capital, Management Buy-out and Buy-in

Geographic Preference: United Kingdom, Continental Europe, United States, Asia

Industry Group Preference: All sectors considered

Portfolio Companies: Aegis Group, Amtico, Dolland and Aitchison, Eversholt, Freightliner, Gower, Holt Lloyd, Inspectorate, Invicta Leisure, PHS, Premium Credit, Premoda Group, SLD Holdings, The Stationery Office, TM Group, Transpool, Unipart, Winchester Growers, others

Officers, Executives and Principals

Fred Vinton, Chairman
Education: Graduate in Economics, Harvard University
Background: Senior Vice President, J. P. Morgan; Chief Operating Officer, N. M. Rothschild; Chief Executive, Entreprises Quilmes

Hugh Mumford, Managing Director
Education: Graduate in Natural Science and in Law, University of Cambridge; Chartered Accountant
Background: KPMG

Robert Clarke, Director
Education: Graduate in Economics, Finance and Accountancy, London School of Economics; Chartered Accountant
Background: Price Waterhouse

Nigel McConnell, Director
Education: Graduate in Economics, Queen's University, Belfast; chartered accountant
Background: Director, Prudential Venture Managers

Tim Snyder, Director
Education: Graduate in Business Studies, City of London School of Business; Chartered Accountant
Background: Director, NatWest Ventures

David Symondson, Director
Education: Graduate in Agriculture, University of Reading; Chartered Accountant
Background: KPMG

Jean Ducroux, Managing Director, Electra Fleming et Associés, Paris

Luciano Balbo, Managing Director, B. and S. Electra SpA, Milan

Peter Carnwath, Managing Director, Electra Fleming Inc., New York

John Levack, Director, JF Electra Limited, Hong Kong

Andrew Russell, Director, JF Electra Limited, Hong Kong

ELECTRICITÉ DE FRANCE

1 avenue Charles de Gaulle
92140 Clamart
France

Telephone: 33-1-4765-4321
Fax: 33-1-4765-4004

Mission: Actively seeking new investments

Fund Size: not available
Founded: not available
Average Investment: not available
Minimum Investment: not available

Investment Criteria: not available

Geographic Preference: France

Industry Group Preference: not available

Portfolio Companies: not available

Officers, Executives and Principals

Pierre-Renaud Martin

E. M. V. - EUROPEAN MEDICAL VENTURES

6 rue Ancelle
92200 Neuilly-sur-Seine
France

Telephone: 33-1-4747-6900
Fax: 33-1-4640-7938

Mission: Actively seeking new investments

Fund Size: Ffr95 million
Founded: not available
Average Investment: not available
Minimum Investment: Ffr3 million

Investment Criteria: Start-up, Early-stage

Geographic Preference: Europe, Israel, United States

Industry Group Preference: Biotechnology, Medical/Health Related

Portfolio Companies: Applied Spectral Imagine (Israel), Biovector Therapeutics, Cardiogap, Lynx Therapeu-
tix (United States), Résintel, Oravax (United States), Vanguard (United Kingdom)

Officers, Executives and Principals

Bernard Daugeras

E. M. WARBURG, PINCUS AND COMPANY INTERNATIONAL LIMITED

Almack House
28 King Street
London SW1Y 6QW
United Kingdom

Telephone: 44-171-306-0306
Fax: 44-171-321- 0881
E-mail: 649-4708@mcimail.com

Mission: Actively seeking new investments

Fund Size: £5 billion
Founded: not available
Average Investment: £20 million
Minimum Investment: £5 million

Investment Criteria: Expansion, Management Buy-out, Early-stage, Rescue/Turnaround, Secondary Purchase/Replacement Capital, Venture Purchase of Quoted Shares

Geographic Preference: Europe

Industry Group Preference: All sectors considered

Portfolio Companies: Argent Group plc, Comcast U. K. Cable Partners Ltd., Craegmoor Healthcare Ltd., Channel 5, Cox Insurance

Officers, Executives and Principals

Louis Elson
Michael Hoffman
Edward McKinley
Dominic Shorthouse

ENTERPRISE EQUITY (N. I.) LIMITED

Bullock House
2 Linenhall Street
Belfast BT2 8AA
United Kingdom

Telephone: 44-1232-242500
Fax: 44-1232-242487
E-mail: 100753.3335@compuserve.com

Mission: Actively seeking new investments

Fund Size: £7 million
Founded: 1987
Average Investment: £290,000
Minimum Investment: £50,000

Investment Criteria: Expansion, Management Buy-in, Management Buy-out, Other Early-stage, Start-up

Geographic Preference: Northern Ireland only

Industry Group Preference: All sectors considered

Portfolio Companies: Munster Simms Engineering Ltd., SDC Trailers Ltd., Sherman Cooper Ltd., B.C.O. Technologies (Northern Ireland) Ltd.

Officers, Executives and Principals

Bob McGowan-Smyth, Investment Director
Education: Chartered Accountant
Background: Coopers and Lybrand, Belfast; extensive venture capital experience

ENTERPRISE INVESTORS

ul. Nowy Swiat 6/12
00-400 Warsaw
Poland

Telephone: 48-22-625-1964
Fax: 48-22-625-7933
E-mail: ei@ikp.atm.com.pl

Other Office Locations
375 Park Avenue, Suite 1902
New York, NY 10152
United States
Phone 212-339-8330, Fax 212-339-8359

Mission: Promoting the development of the private sector in Poland by actively seeking new investments in commercially viable small and medium-sized companies with potential for growth, and also by providing loans, technical assistance and training projects, on the basis of their management capabilities and competitive positions, the strength of the market, and partners' willingness to share risk

Fund Size: $351 million
Founded: 1990
Average Investment: $4 million
Minimum Investment: $1 million

Investment Criteria: Start-up, Early-stage, Expansion/Development, Management Buy-out, Management Buy-in

Geographic Preference: Poland

Industry Group Preference: All sectors considered

Portfolio Companies: not available

Officers, Executives and Principals

Robert Faris, President and Chief Executive Officer
Background: Director of Corporate Development, Amoco Chemical Division of Standard Oil of Indiana; President and General Partner, Alan Patricof Associates; investor in small high-technology businesses and adviser to several international investment funds

Barbara Lundberg, Executive Vice President and General Director, Warsaw Office
Background: Exxon; McGraw Hill; Alan Patricof Associates; Vice President, Kidder Peabody

Jacek Siwicki, Executive Vice President
Background: First Deputy Minister of Privatization and Adviser to the Prime Minister; Consultant, International Finance Corporation

Tuomo Hatakka, Executive Vice President
Background: brand management; Consultant/Manager, Bain and Company: Director, CAL

Robert Manz, Vice President
Background: Financial Analyst, Dillon, Read and Co. Inc.

Dariusz Pronczuk, Vice President
Background: Financial Analyst, Multicraft and PDG Partners; Vice President, Hejka Michna Inc.

Michal Rusiecki, Vice President
Background: Project Director, Ministry of Privatization

EPARGNE PARTENAIRES

2 square Pétrarque
75116 Paris
France

Telephone: 33-1-5350-2600
Fax: 33-1-4370-2610

Mission: Actively seeking new investments

Fund Size: Ffr544 million
Founded: not available
Average Investment: not available
Minimum Investment: Ffr10 million

Investment Criteria: Expansion/Development, Management Buy-out

Geographic Preference: Europe

Industry Group Preference: Communications, Consumer Related, Industrial Products, Medical/Health Related, Pollution/Recycling Related, Transportation

Portfolio Companies: André Courrèges SA, SDME/Select Distribution, Everest, Groupe Alma

Officers, Executives and Principals

François Lombard, Partner
Pierre Battini, Partner
Marie Desportes, Partner

EPICEA

33 rue de la Fédération
75752 Paris
France

Telephone: 33-1-4056-1691
Fax: 33-1-4056-1919

Mission: Actively seeking new investments

Fund Size: Ffr200 million
Founded: not available
Average Investment: not available
Minimum Investment: Ffr1 million

Investment Criteria: Start-up, Expansion/Development

Geographic Preference: Europe, France

Industry Group Preference: Biotechnology, Defense/Military Related, Electronics Related, Information Technology

Portfolio Companies: not available

Officers, Executives and Principals

Alain Montret, Managing Director
Pascal Demichel
March Rispal
Serge Bindel

EPTA CONSORS

Via Camperia 9
20123 Milano
Italy

Telephone: 39-2-88271
Fax: 39-2-8645-2918

Mission: Actively seeking new investments

Fund Size: not available
Founded: not available
Average Investment: not available
Minimum Investment: not available

Investment Criteria: All stages

Geographic Preference: Italy

Industry Group Preference: All sectors considered

Portfolio Companies: not available

Officers, Executives and Principals

Giorgio Mosterts
Marco Bolgiani

EQT PARTNERS AB

P. O. Box 16409
Birger Jarlsgatan 14
10327 Stockholm
Sweden

Telephone: 46-8-440-5300
Fax: 46-8-440-5319
E-mail: conni@eqt.se

Mission: Actively seeking new investments in Nordic medium-sized companies as investment adviser to Scandinavian Equity Partners Limited

Fund Size: Skr2.9 billion
Founded: 1994
Average Investment: not available
Minimum Investment: Skr500 million

Investment Criteria: Expansion/Development, Management Buy-out, Management Buy-in

Geographic Preference: Denmark, Finland, Norway, Sweden

Industry Group Preference: not available

Portfolio Companies: Sabroe Refrigeration A/S, Perlos, Orrefors Kosta Boda, Duni AB

Officers, Executives and Principals

Conni Jonsson, Managing Director
Bengt Hellström, Investment Manager
Thomas von Koch, Investment Manager
Jan Ståhlberg, Investment Manager
Bjørn Høi Jensen, Investment Manager
Fredrik Åtting, Investment Manager

EQUITY VENTURES LTD.

Du Pont House
Bristol Business Park
Bristol BS16 1QD
United Kingdom

Telephone: 44-117-931-1318
Fax: 44-117-976-3839
E-mail: equity@ventures.demon.co.uk

Mission: Actively seeking new investments

Fund Size: £5 million
Founded: not available
Average Investment: £100,000
Minimum Investment: £25,000

Investment Criteria: Expansion, Management Buy-out, Management Buy-in

Geographic Preference: England

Industry Group Preference: All sectors considered

Portfolio Companies: Jackson Vending Ltd., Acrohone Ltd.

Officers, Executives and Principals

Robert Lindemann
David Tallboys

ESFIN PARTICIPATIONS

139/141 avenue Charles de Gaulle
92200 Neuilly-sur-Seine
France

Telephone: 33-1-4745-9005
Fax: 33-1-4745-9019

Mission: Actively seeking new investments

Fund Size: Ffr65 million
Founded: not available
Average Investment: not available
Minimum Investment: Ffr500,000

Investment Criteria: Start-up, Early-stage, Expansion/Development, Replacement,

Geographic Preference: France, Central Europe

Industry Group Preference: Consumer Related, Industrial Products and Services, Information Technology

Portfolio Companies: SFEIR, SDC, Géovariances, Intersport, Plein Ciel Diffusion, Dipsys

Officers, Executives and Principals

Bruno d'Hauthuille, Managing Director

ETEBA

12-14 Amalias Avenue
10236 Athens
Greece

Telephone: 30-1-3242651
Fax: 30-1-3296350

Mission: Actively seeking new investments

Fund Size: not available
Founded: not available
Average Investment: not available
Minimum Investment: not available

Investment Criteria: All stages

Geographic Preference: Greece

Industry Group Preference: All sectors considered

Portfolio Companies: not available

Officers, Executives and Principals

V. Vranas
Ch. Stamatopoulos
D.N. Paschaligos

EUROCONTINENTAL (ADVISERS) LTD.

5th Floor, 30 Coleman Street
London EC2R 5AE
United Kingdom

Telephone: 44-171-600-1689
Fax: 44-171-600-1967

Mission: Actively seeking new investments

Fund Size: £25 million
Founded: not available
Average Investment: £1 million
Minimum Investment: £200,000

Investment Criteria: Expansion, Management Buy-in, Management Buy-out, Other Early-stage, Refinancing Bank Debt, Rescue/Turnaround, Secondary Purchase/ Replacement Capital

Geographic Preference: Western Europe

Industry Group Preference: All sectors considered

Portfolio Companies: Contship Italia (Italy), Ilog (France), Ipes Iberica (Spain)

Officers, Executives and Principals

Albert Gabizon
Deyman Eastmond
Joe Mancini

EUROMERCHANT BALKAN FUND (EBF)

17 Akademia Street
10671 Athens
Greece

Telephone: 30-1-362-2096
Fax: 30-1-362-7766

Other Office Locations
Sofia Representative Office
39 Vitosha Blvd, 1st Floor
Sofia
Bulgaria
Phone 359-2-980-1619, Fax 359-2-805-900

Mission: Participating in ventures in which foreign partners provide management expertise, contribute most of the share capital and take into account the fact that EBF has a long-term but finite investment horizon

Fund Size: $27.3 million
Founded: 1995
Average Investment: not available
Minimum Investment: not available

Investment Criteria: Expansion/Development, Turnaround/Restructuring, Replacement

Geographic Preference: Balkan countries

Industry Group Preference: not available

Portfolio Companies: Chipita Bulgaria, Delrom, Romcolor, Neoset

Officers, Executives and Principals

Angelos Plakopitas, Managing Director
Education: BA in Economic and Business Sciences, University of Athens; MBA, New York University
Background: General Manager, Shelman (wood products company); 14 years experience in corporate banking with Citibank and Hellenic Industrial Development Bank

Christos Katsanis, Regional Executive Officer, Balkans
Education: BA in Economics, University of Athens; DESS and DEA in Management and Monetary Economics, Institut d'Administration des Entreprises and Sorbonne
Background: Ionian Bank; County Natwest, London; Xiosbank, Sofia

Mirolub Voutov, General Manager (Sofia)
Education: BSc in Electrical Engineering, Imperial College, London; advanced study, Twente Technical University, The Netherlands; PhD in Electronics, Bulgarian Academy of Science
Background: experience in the United States and Japan as well as with Daewoo and Mitsubishi in Bulgaria; also formerly in charge of UNDP technical assistance to small and medium-sized enterprises in Bulgaria

EUROMEZZANINE GESTION

50 rue Fabert
75007 Paris
France

Telephone: 33-1-4955-7095
Fax: 33-1-4950-4898

Mission: Actively seeking new investments

Fund Size: Ffr590 million
Founded: not available
Average Investment: not available
Minimum Investment: Ffr10 million

Investment Criteria: Management Buy-in, Turnaround/Restructuring, Replacement

Geographic Preference: Europe

Industry Group Preference: All sectors considered

Portfolio Companies: not available

Officers, Executives and Principals

Philippe Lefelle, Managing Director
Christine Panier
Gilles Angely

EUROPAR

135 avenue Wagram
75017 Paris
France

Telephone: 33-1-4622-6713
Fax: 33-1-4622-6712

Mission: Actively seeking new investments

Fund Size: Ffr200 million
Founded: not available
Average Investment: not available
Minimum Investment: Ffr2 million

Investment Criteria: Expansion/Development

Geographic Preference: not available

Industry Group Preference: All sectors considered

Portfolio Companies: Novalliance, MSP, Vétoquinol, Giraud CFCA, Sucreries de Bourbon

Officers, Executives and Principals

Guy Santa Maria

EUROPEAN ACQUISITION CAPITAL LTD.

26 Finsbury Square
London EC2A 1DS
United Kingdom

Telephone: 44-171-382-1700
Fax: 44-171-588-3401

Mission: Actively seeking new investments

Fund Size: £65 million
Founded: 1991
Average Investment: £9 million
Minimum Investment: £4 million

Investment Criteria: Expansion, Management Buy-in, Management Buy-out

Geographic Preference: Western Europe

Industry Group Preference: All sectors considered except Biotechnology and Real Estate

Portfolio Companies: Tom Cobleigh plc, WRM Group Limited, Stalwart Group Limited, Gripperrods Limited, ADS Anker

Officers, Executives and Principals

Bert Wiegman
Cheong Lau
Paul Downes
Bill Robinson
Adam Sack
Robert Mason

EURO SYNERGIES

48 bis rue Fabert
75007 Paris
France

Telephone: 33-1-4955-7070
Fax: 33-1-4556-0014

Mission: Actively seeking new investments

Fund Size: Ffr840 million
Founded: not available
Average Investment: not available
Minimum Investment: Ffr15 million

Investment Criteria: Management Buy-out, Management Buy-in

Geographic Preference: Europe

Industry Group Preference: All sectors considered

Portfolio Companies: SFR/Entrelec, Sofedit, Stampal, Cefat, Wesumat

Officers, Executives and Principals

Christophe Fercocq
Hervé Franc

EUROVENTURES BENELUX

H. Henneaulaan 366
1930 Zaventem
Belgium

Telephone: 32-2-725-1838
Fax: 32-2-721-4435

Other Office Locations
Joh. Vermeerplein 9
1071 DV Amsterdam
The Netherlands
Phone 31-20-664-5500, Fax 31-20-676-8810

Mission: Actively seeking new investments

Fund Size: Bfr3.5 billion
Founded: 1985
Average Investment: Bfr45 million
Minimum Investment: not available

Investment Criteria: Expansion/Development, Management Buy-out, Management buy-in, Bridge

Geographic Preference: Belgium, The Netherlands, Luxembourg

Industry Group Preference: All sectors considered

Portfolio Companies: Applied Medical Research Ltd., Atex Inc., BCG Interim Management International BV, Biora AB, Crown Gear Holding BV, Dams Transinvest NV, Ecke Data Systems International BV, Euroventures Benelux Seed Fund BV, Executive Interim Management AG, Genpharm International Inc., Intech Technology BV, Ion Beam Applications SA, Matrix Integrated Systems Acquisitions Corp., Multimedia NV, Pharma Development NV, Quadrant Healthcare Ltd., Rhein Biotech GmbH

Officers, Executives and Principals

Roger Claes, Partner (Zaventem)
Education: Master's degree in Electronics and Computer Sciences, University of Louvain
Background: Operations Manager, Research and Development Manager, Product Development Engineer, Electronic Components and Systems, GTE Corporation

Martijn Kleijwegt, Partner (Amsterdam)
Education: Master's degree in Economics, University of Amsterdam
Background: Corporate Finance, Philips International

Johan Ulens, Controller (Zaventem)
Education: degree in Business Economics, University of Louvain
Background: Senior Cost Accountant, GTE Sylvania NV; Senior Internal Auditor in Europe, GTE Corporation; Financial Controller, GTE Precision Materials Division; Financial Director, Crane Ferguson Machine Co. SA

Frits van der Have, Partner (Amsterdam)
Education: MBA, School of Management, Delft

Background: Analyst/Portfolio Manager, Kempen and Co.; Management Assistant, Orange Nassau Group; Deputy Manager, Investment Department, ABN Bank

Paul Verdurme, Partner (Zaventem)
Education: Master's degree in Law and Economics, University of Louvain
Background: Manager, Bank Brussel Lambert

Sabinne Vermassen, Legal Counsel (Zaventem)
Education: degree in Law, University of Ghent; postGraduate degree in Management, Vlerick School, Ghent
Background: Associate Attorney, Loeff Claeys Verbeke

EUROVENTURES BV

Julianaplein 10
5211 BC 's-Hertogenbosch
The Netherlands

Telephone: 31-73-613-7800
Fax: 31-73-612-2395

Other Office Locations
Euroventures Benelux
H. Henneaulaan 366
1930 Zaventem
Belgium
Phone 32-2-725-1838, Fax 32-2-721-4435

Euroventures Benelux
Joh. Vermeerplein 9
1071 DV Amsterdam
The Netherlands
Phone 31-20-664-5500, Fax 31-20-676-8810

Euroventures Deutschland GmbH und Co K G
Kölner Strasse 27
50226 Frechen
Germany
Phone 49-2234-955-460, Fax 49-2234-955-4620

Euroventures France
27 rue Ville l'Evêque
75008 Paris
France
Phone 33-1-4007-0518, Fax 33-1-4924-9972

Euroventures Genevest (Suisse) Management SA
16 rue du Grand-Bureau
1227 Carouge
Geneva
Switzerland
Phone 41-22-343-5000, Fax 41-22-343-5005

Euroventures Germany CV
Begijnenhof 35
5611 EK Eindhoven
The Netherlands
Phone 31-40-451735, Fax 31-40-444525

Euroventures Management AB
Birger Jarlsgatan 27
P. O. Box 7210
10388 Stockholm
Sweden
Phone 46-8-247790, Fax 46-8-208997, E-Mail info@euroventures.se

Mission: Managing the Euroventures network of funds

Fund Size: dependent on the various funds in the Euroventures network
Founded: 1984
Average Investment: not available
Minimum Investment: not available

Investment Criteria: dependent on the various funds in the Euroventures network

Geographic Preference: Europe

Industry Group Preference: All sectors considered

Portfolio Companies: not available

Officers, Executives and Principals

Michael J. Geary, Chief Executive Officer
Corne Roest, Chief Executive Officer

EUROVENTURES DEUTSCHLAND GmbH UND CO. K G

Kölner Strasse 27
50226 Frechen
Germany

Telephone: 49-2234-955-460
Fax: 49-2234-955-4620

Mission: Actively seeking new investments as part of the Euroventures network

Fund Size: DM1 million
Founded: not available
Average Investment: not available
Minimum Investment: DM300,000

Investment Criteria: Start-up, Early-stage, Expansion, Management Buy-out, Management Buy-in

Geographic Preference: Germany

Industry Group Preference: All sectors considered

Portfolio Companies: not available

Officers, Executives and Principals

Dr. Klaus Nathusius

EUROVENTURES FRANCE

27 rue de la Ville l'Evêque
75008 Paris
France

Telephone: 33-1-4007-0518
Fax: 33-1-4924-9972

Mission: Actively seeking new investments as part of the Euroventures network

Fund Size: Ffr240 million
Founded: 1986
Average Investment: Ffr8 million
Minimum Investment: Ffr2 million

Investment Criteria: Management Buy-out, Management Buy-in, Development, Mezzanine

Geographic Preference: France

Industry Group Preference: All sectors considered

Portfolio Companies: not available

Officers, Executives and Principals

Daniel Toulemonde
Jacques Mecheri

EUROVENTURES GENEVEST (SUISSE) MANAGEMENT SA

16 rue du Grand-Bureau
1227 Carouge
Geneva
Switzerland

Telephone: 41-22-343-5000
Fax: 41-22-343-5005

Mission: Actively seeking new investments as part of the Euroventures network

Fund Size: not available
Founded: not available
Average Investment: not available
Minimum Investment: Sfr1 million

Investment Criteria: Start-up, Early-stage, Expansion/Development, Bridge, Mezzanine, Turnaround, Management buy-out

Geographic Preference: Europe

Industry Group Preference: All sectors considered

Portfolio Companies: not available

Officers, Executives and Principals

Bruno Senoner
Les Hawrylyshyn

EUROVENTURES GERMANY CV

Begijnenhof 35
5611 EK Eindhoven
The Netherlands

Telephone: 31-40-451735
Fax: 31-40-444525

Mission: Actively seeking new investments as part of the Euroventures network

Fund Size: DM6.7 million
Founded: not available
Average Investment: not available
Minimum Investment: DM500,000

Investment Criteria: Start-up, Early-stage, Expansion, Management Buy-out, Management Buy-in

Geographic Preference: Europe

Industry Group Preference: Industrial Automation, Industrial Products, Manufacturing, Transportation

Portfolio Companies: not available

Officers, Executives and Principals

Eckart Bohm

EUROVENTURES MANAGEMENT AB

Birger Jarlsgatan 27
P. O. Box 7210
10388 Stockholm
Sweden

Telephone: 46-8-247790
Fax: 46-8-208997
E-mail: info@euroventures.se

Mission: Actively seeking new investments as part of the Euroventures network

Fund Size: Skr730 million
Founded: not available
Average Investment: not available
Minimum Investment: Skr1 million

Investment Criteria: Start-up, Expansion/Development, Management Buy-out, Bridge, Early-stage

Geographic Preference: Sweden, Norway, Denmark, Finland

Industry Group Preference: Biotechnology, Communications, Electronics Related, Industrial Products, Medical/Health Related

Portfolio Companies: not available

Officers, Executives and Principals

Per Wahlström, Partner
Thomas Wernhoff, Partner
Lennart Jacobsson, Partner
Kristine Cakste, Partner

EXCEL PARTNERS SA

Claudio Coello 78
28001 Madrid
Spain

Telephone: 34-1-578-3676
Fax: 34-1-431-9303

Mission: Maximising total return to shareholders by achieving above-average returns to investors in two funds (Excel Capital Partners I and II), as a subsidiary of the Rothschild Group

Fund Size: Pta3 billion
Founded: 1992
Average Investment: Pta330 million
Minimum Investment: Pta100 million

Investment Criteria: Early-stage, Expansion/Development, Management Buy-outs, Management Buy-ins

Geographic Preference: Iberian Peninsula and Spanish cross-border operations

Industry Group Preference: All sectors considered

Portfolio Companies: not available

Officers, Executives and Principals

Tara Wright

FACE AUVERGNE-LOIRE

14 avenue Marx Dormoy
63000 Clermont Ferrand
France

Telephone: 33-73-933947
Fax: 33-73-351315

Mission: Actively seeking new investments

Fund Size: not available
Founded: not available
Average Investment: not available
Minimum Investment: Ecu8,000

Investment Criteria: Seed, Start-up

Geographic Preference: France

Industry Group Preference: Biotechnology, Consumer Products/Services, Electronics Related, Industrial Automation, Industrial Products, Medical/Health Related

Portfolio Companies: not available

F. A. I. R. SA

Rue du Vertbois 13B
4000 Liège
Belgium

Telephone: 32-41-216211
Fax: 32-41-235765

Mission: Actively seeking new investments

Fund Size: Ecu1.1 million
Founded: not available
Average Investment: not available
Minimum Investment: Ecu12,000

Investment Criteria: Seed, Start-up

Geographic Preference: Belgium

Industry Group Preference: All sectors considered

Portfolio Companies: not available

Officers, Executives and Principals

Bernard Bolly, Partner

F. B. G. BETEILIGUNGSBERATUNGS GmbH

Neuer Jungfernstieg 20
20353 Hamburg
Germany

Telephone: 49-40-349-6470
Fax: 49-40-358-9581

Mission: Actively seeking new investments

Fund Size: DM100 million
Founded: not available
Average Investment:
Minimum Investment: DM3 million

Investment Criteria: Management Buy-out, Management Buy-in, Late-stage, Growth

Geographic Preference: Germany

Industry Group Preference: All sectors considered

Portfolio Companies: not available

Officers, Executives and Principals

Wolfgang Bensel
Maximilian Drechsel

FIFE ENTERPRISE

Kingdom House
Saltire Centre
Glenrothes
Fife KY6 2AQ
United Kingdom

Telephone: 44-1592-623000
Fax: 44-1592-623149
E-mail: fifeenterprise@scotent.co.uk

Mission: Actively seeking new investments

Fund Size: £1,740,000
Founded: not available
Average Investment: £30,000
Minimum Investment: £5,000

Investment Criteria: Expansion, Management Buy-in, Management Buy-out, Early-stage, Start-up

Geographic Preference: Scotland (Fife only)

Industry Group Preference: Biotechnology, Chemicals and Materials, Computer Related, Electronics Related, Industrial Automation, Industrial Products and Services, Manufacturing, Medical/Health Related, Services

Portfolio Companies: not available

Officers, Executives and Principals

Robert Barr

FINADVANCE

Parc d'Ariane, Bâtiment D
boulevard de la Grande Thumine
13083 Aix-en-Provence
France

Telephone: 33-4220-0600
Fax: 33-4264-0457

Other Office Locations
14 rue de la Corraterie
121 Geneva
Switzerland

Mission: Actively seeking new investments

Fund Size: Ffr75 million
Founded: not available
Average Investment: not available
Minimum Investment: Ffr2 million

Investment Criteria: Leveraged Buy-out, Expansion/Development

Geographic Preference: France (Southeastern region)

Industry Group Preference: All sectors considered

Portfolio Companies: France-Air, Ercem, Bayard, Podis, Canat, Charles Frères

Officers, Executives and Principals

Olivier Gillot
Hervé Legoupil

FINANCES ET COMMUNICATION DÉVELOPPEMENT

4 rue Gaillon
75002 Paris
France

Telephone: 33-1-4526-2280
Fax: 33-1-4526-2150

Mission: Actively seeking new investments

Fund Size: Ffr375 million
Founded: not available
Average Investment: not available
Minimum Investment: Ffr5 million

Investment Criteria: Expansion/Development

Geographic Preference: France

Industry Group Preference: Communitications, Media Related, Multimedia

Portfolio Companies: not available

Officers, Executives and Principals

François Caries, President
Jean-François Moral, Managing Director
Jean-Antoine Breuil

FINANCIAL INVESTMENTS COMPANY TRANSYLVANIA SA

2 Nicolae Iorga Street
2200 Brasov
Romania

Telephone: 40-68-418-312
Fax: 40-68-153-844

Other Office Locations
Apartment 3, 2nd Floor
Hotel Bucuresti
63-68 Calea Victoriei Street
Bucharest
Phone 40-01-311-1583, Fax 40-01-311-1767

1 Dianei Street
Constanta
Phone 40-41-691-172, Fax 40-41-614-695

Unirii Boulevard E1-E2 Bl. Micro II
Buzau
Phone 40-38-426-499, Fax 40-38-426-599

43 Piata Trandafirilor
Targu Mures
Phone 40-65-165-174, Fax 40-65-168-451

Hotel Bulevard
10 Piata Unirii
Sibiu
Phone 40-69-214-650, Fax 40-69-215-010

6 Independentei Boulevard
Focsani
Phone 40-37-626-272, Fax 40-37-626-266

Mission: Actively seeking new investments, participating in established businesses and supporting strong companies with high potential for growth

Fund Size: $139 million
Founded: 1996
Average Investment: $2 - $10 million
Minimum Investment: $50,000

Investment Criteria: Start-up, First-stage, Mezzanine

Geographic Preference: Europe

Industry Group Preference: Chemicals and Materials, Communications, Consumer Related, Construction/ Building Products, Energy, Financial Services, Industrial Products and Equipment, Medical/Health

Portfolio Companies: not available

Officers, Executives and Principals

Mihal Fercala, Chairman and General Manager
Floriean Firu, Deputy General Manager and Director, Strategy and Portfolio Management
Vasile Serbu, Accounting Manager
Lucian Ionescu, Director, Privatization and Brokerage
Aurica Podoreanu, Director, Informatics
Ion Ghita, Human Resources Manager
Gheorghe Marinescu, Foreign Relations Manager

FINANCIÈRE D'AQUITAINE

304 boulevard du Président Wilson
33000 Bordeaux
France

Telephone: 33-5690-4287
Fax: 33-5690-4296

Mission: Actively seeking new investments

Fund Size: Ffr81 million
Founded: not available
Average Investment: not available
Minimum Investment: Ffr300,000

Investment Criteria: Start-up, Early-stage, Expansion/Development

Geographic Preference: France (Aquitaine region)

Industry Group Preference: Industrial Products and Services

Portfolio Companies: Groupe Aqualande, Yvon Mau, Sucal

Officers, Executives and Principals

Didier Mathieu, President

FINANCIÈRE D'INVESTISSEMENT ARO

Rue R. Jules Ampefiloha 725
101 Antananarivo
Madagascar

Telephone: 261-2-34260
Fax: 261-2-22147

Mission: Actively seeking new investments

Fund Size: $2 million
Founded: 1988
Average Investment: $40,000
Minimum Investment: $5,000

Investment Criteria: Start-up, Expansion/Development

Geographic Preference: Madagascar

Industry Group Preference: All sectors considered

Portfolio Companies: not available

Officers, Executives and Principals

Pascal Rakotomavo, Chairman
Patrick Razafindrafito, Chief Executive

FINANCIÈRE GALLIERA

21 rue Mont-Thabor
75001 Paris
France

Telephone: 33-1-4286-0902
Fax: 33-1-4286-0988

Mission: Actively seeking new investments

Fund Size: Ffr95 million
Founded: not available
Average Investment: not available
Minimum Investment: Ffr3 million

Investment Criteria: Expansion/Development

Geographic Preference: France

Industry Group Preference: All sectors considered

Portfolio Companies: Ets Eppe, Limagrain, Laboratoires Dolisos, Groupe Giraud, Otor, Industries des Transports (SPIT), Recoland, Financière de la Mer, Bijoux Altesse, Financière Supergroup

Officers, Executives and Principals

Jean-Claude Labro
Hughes Jacquin
Pierre-Marie Bouré
Daniel Zenaty

FINANCIÈRE SAINT-DOMINIQUE

48 bis rue Fabert
75340 Paris
France

Telephone: 33-1-4955-7000
Fax: 33-1-4955-7085

Mission: Actively seeking new investments

Fund Size: Ffr6800 million
Founded: not available
Average Investment: not available
Minimum Investment: Ffr10 million

Investment Criteria: Early-stage, Expansion/Development, Bridge, Management Buy-out, Replacement, Turnaround/Restructuring

Geographic Preference: Europe

Industry Group Preference: All sectors considered

Portfolio Companies: Générale Routière, Cuir, Rialto, Financière Jet Services, Soloc, Astral, EPC, Malesherbes Industries, Finabio, Lab, Trigano, Pinault Equipement

Officers, Executives and Principals

Denis Mortier
Pierre-Emmanuel Dardel
Dominique Peninon

FINANCIÈRE VECTEUR

9 avenue Newton
78183 Saint Quentin-en-Yvelines
France

Telephone: 33-1-3460-9081
Fax: 33-1-3064-6792

Mission: Actively seeking new investments

Fund Size: Ffr60 million
Founded: not available
Average Investment: not available
Minimum Investment: Ffr1 million

Investment Criteria: Early-stage, Expansion/Development, Leveraged Buy-out

Geographic Preference: Paris

Industry Group Preference: All sectors considered

Portfolio Companies: General Electronique, Ponroy Santé, S.T.O.A.

Officers, Executives and Principals

Christian de Roissy
Jean-Brice Birgourdan
Olivier Martin

FINLOMBARDA SpA

Piazza Belgioioso 2
20121 Milan
Italy

Telephone: 39-2-760441
Fax: 39-2-780819

Mission: Actively seeking new investments

Fund Size: not available
Founded: not available
Average Investment: not available
Minimum Investment: not available

Investment Criteria: Start-up, Early-stage, Expansion/Development, Bridge

Geographic Preference: Italy

Industry Group Preference: Consumer Related, Energy, Industrial Automation, Industrial Products, Manufacturing

Portfolio Companies: not available

Officers, Executives and Principals

Francesco Cattaneo
Mario Cucchi

FINNISH FUND FOR INDUSTRIAL COOPERATION LIMITED (FINNFUND)

P. O. Box 391
Ratakatu 27
00121 Helsinki
Finland

Telephone: 358-0-348-434
Fax: 358-0-3484-3346

Mission: Actively seeking new investments

Fund Size: FM500 million
Founded: not available
Average Investment: not available
Minimum Investment: not available

Investment Criteria: Seed, Start-up, Expansion

Geographic Preference: Developing countries, Central and Eastern Europe

Industry Group Preference: Manufacturing, Services

Portfolio Companies: not available

FINNISH INDUSTRY INVESTMENT LIMITED

P. O. Box 685
Kaivokatu 8
00101 Helsinki
Finland

Telephone: 358-0-2705-2770
Fax: 358-0-622-2277

Mission: Improving the potential of small and medium-sized industrial companies and supporting services, and developing the capital investment market

Fund Size: FM320 million
Founded: 1995
Average Investment: not available
Minimum Investment: not available

Investment Criteria: not available

Geographic Preference: Finland

Industry Group Preference: not available

Portfolio Companies: not available

Officers, Executives and Principals

Juha Marjosola, Managing Director
Education: MSc in Economics

Jaana Ekström, Assistant
Education: Certificate of Commercial College

FINOVELEC

6 rue Ancelle
92200 Neuilly-sur-Seine
France

Telephone: 33-1-4747-6900
Fax: 33-1-4640-7938

Mission: Actively seeking new investments

Fund Size: Ffr300 million
Founded: not available
Average Investment: not available
Minimum Investment: Ffr2 million

Investment Criteria: Start-up, Early-stage

Geographic Preference: Europe, Israel, Japan, North America

Industry Group Preference: Biotechnology, Computer Related, Computer Software, Electronics Related, Energy, Industrial Products, Medical/Health Related

Portfolio Companies: Radvision (Israel), Pixtech, Silmag, Zydacron (United States), Wonderware (United States)

Officers, Executives and Principals

Jean Jacquin, Managing Director
Jacques Chatain

FIRST HUNGARIAN INVESTMENT ADVISORY Rt

P. O. Box 906/82
1386 Budapest
Hungary

Telephone: 36-1-268-1902
Fax: 36-1-268-1648
E-mail: fhia@pronet.hu

Mission: Investing in business opportunities that result from the economic changes taking place in Hungary and investing in equities in order to achieve long-term capital appreciation

Fund Size: $125 million
Founded: 1989
Average Investment: $5.5 million
Minimum Investment: $2.5 million

Investment Criteria: Expansion/Development

Geographic Preference: Hungary

Industry Group Preference: All sectors considered

Portfolio Companies: Biorex Pharmaceutical Research Co. Ltd., Danube Knitwear, Mirelite Frozen Foods, North American Bus Industries, Kábeltel Cable Operatior, Resti Catering, Csabai Canning

Officers, Executives and Principals

Peter Róna, President and Chief Executive Officer
Michael Carter, Managing Director
László Blága, Senior Investment Manager
Csaba Zoltán, Senior Investment Manager
Victória Zombory, Senior Investment Manager
János Kovács, Senior Portfolio Manager
András Bodor, Analyst

FLEMING VENTURES LIMITED

Admiral Hawke House
Green Street
Sunbury-on Thames TW16 6PA
United Kingdom

Telephone: 44-1932-779880
Fax: 44-1932-779880

Mission: Actively seeking new investments

Fund Size: £5.5 million
Founded: not available
Average Investment: not available
Minimum Investment: £500,000

Investment Criteria: Expansion, Early-stage

Geographic Preference: North America, Western Europe

Industry Group Preference: Communications, Computer Related, Other Electronics Related

Portfolio Companies: Gemplus Sca, IS Solutions plc

Officers, Executives and Principals

Peter English
Bernard Fairman

FONDINVEST GESTION

Tour Maine Montparnasse 33
Avenue du Maine
75755 Paris
France

Telephone: 33-1-4064-3300
Fax: 33-1-4064-2226

Mission: Actively seeking new investments as private equity adviser in connection with two venture capital
funds, Fondinvest I and Fondinvest II

Fund Size: Ffr 640 million
Founded: 1994
Average Investment: not available
Minimum Investment: not available

Investment Criteria: Start-up, Early-stage, Expansion/Development, **Management Buy-out**, Management
Buy-in, Replacement

Geographic Preference: Europe, United States

Industry Group Preference: All sectors considered

Portfolio Companies: not available

Officers, Executives and Principals

Charles Soulignac, Chief Executive Officer

FOND RIZIKOVÉHO KAPITÁLU SRO

Konviktská 5
11000 Prague 1
Czech Republic

Telephone: 42-2-2422-94228
Fax: 42-2-264995
E-mail: riskfund@notesnet.cz

Mission: Actively seeking new investments

Fund Size: Ecu3.1 million
Founded: 1995
Average Investment: Ecu100,000
Minimum Investment: Ecu22,000

Investment Criteria: Early-stage

Geographic Preference: Czech Republic

Industry Group Preference: All sectors considered

Portfolio Companies: AB Mobalpa SRO, Staspo SRO, Apolon AS

Officers, Executives and Principals

Michal Nosek MBA, Chief Executive Officer
Radek Lastovicka, Investment Manager
Stanislav Srámek, Investment Analyst

FONDS D'INVESTISSEMENT RTVL

Centre Mercure
445 boulevard Gambetta
59976 Tourcoing
France

Telephone: 33-3-2024-9787
Fax: 33-3-2027-1804
E-mail: rtvl@nordnet.fr

Mission: Investing in new companies to promote economic growth in the region of Nord/Pas-de-Calais

Fund Size: Ffr15 million
Founded: 1991
Average Investment: Ffr150,000-500,000
Minimum Investment: Ffr150,000

Investment Criteria: Seed, Start-up, Early-stage

Geographic Preference: France (Nord/Pas-de-Calais region only)

Industry Group Preference: All sectors considered

Portfolio Companies: not available

Officers, Executives and Principals

Henri Feltz, President of the Supervisory Board
Education: Master's degree in Economics; Chartered Accountant
Background: Financial Chartist, Emile Meeschaert; Finance Manager, Groupe Phildar; Managing Director, Holding Financière de Loury

Eric Grimonprez, Chief Executive Officer
Education: Graduate, ESCP, Paris; Chartered Accountant
Background: Courtaulds Group, Honeywell Bull

Michel Samyn, Financial Manager
Education: Graduate in Accountancy
Background: Assistant Accountant, Phildar-Filature du Sartel; Chief Accountant, Logicil; Financial Manager, Gipel

FONDS PARTENAIRES GESTION

121 boulevard Haussmann
75008 Paris
France

Telephone: 33-1-5383-8000
Fax: 33-1-5383-8020

Mission: Actively seeking new investments

Fund Size: Ffr2.6 billion
Founded: not available
Average Investment: not available
Minimum Investment: Ffr250 million

Investment Criteria: Expansion/Development, Leveraged Buy-out, Leveraged Buy-in

Geographic Preference: Europe

Industry Group Preference: All sectors considered

Portfolio Companies: not available

Officers, Executives and Principals

Eric Licoys, President and Managing Director
Blandine Cassou, Company Secretary

FOREIGN AND COLONIAL VENTURES LTD.

8th Floor, Exchange House
Primrose Street
London EC2A 2NY
United Kingdom

Telephone: 44-171-782-9829
Fax: 44-171-782-9834
E-mail: fcventures@dial.pipex.com

Mission: Actively seeking new investments

Fund Size: £220 million
Founded: 1985
Average Investment: £3 million
Minimum Investment: £1 million

Investment Criteria: All stages, but Later-stage preferred

Geographic Preference: Western Europe

Industry Group Preference: All sectors considered

Portfolio Companies: Codeissue, Computacenter, First Mortgage Securities, Dewhurst Butcher, Stalwart

Officers, Executives and Principals

James Nelson
Rod Richards
Michael Boxford
William Eccles
John Stevens
Cecile Astrup
Stephen Cavell
Perry Chapman
Simon Fitch
Andrew Gray

FÖRETAGS BYGGARNA AB

Norrmalmstorg 14
11146 Stockholm
Sweden

Telephone: 46-8-678-1450
Fax: 46-8-678-1460
E-mail: partners@businessbuilders.se

Mission: Acting as lead investor in early-stage companies with potential for international growth

Fund Size: Skr40 million
Founded: not available
Average Investment: Skr4 million
Minimum Investment: Skr500,000

Investment Criteria: Early-stage

Geographic Preference: Sweden

Industry Group Preference: Healthcare, Information Technology

Portfolio Companies: MiniDoc AB, Cetronic AB, EnerCom AB, MultiSound Technology AB, Companies Venture KB

Officers, Executives and Principals

Lars Lingren, Partner
Martin Genvik, Partner
Per-Henrik Norhagen, Partner

FÖRETAGSKAPITAL AB

Kungsgatan 30, 15 tr
P. O. Box 1301
11183 Stockholm
Sweden

Telephone: 46-8-441-9140
Fax: 46-8-219310
E-mail: info@fkapital.se

Mission: Holding minority investments in small and medium-sized companies, providing know-how and venture capital, and actively seeking new investments, mainly in growth companies

Fund Size: Skr365 million
Founded: 1973
Average Investment: Skr5 million
Minimum Investment: Skr2 million

Investment Criteria: All stages considered, but especially Expansion/Development

Geographic Preference: Sweden

Industry Group Preference: All sectors considered except Real Estate

Portfolio Companies: Array Printers AB, Companies Venture KB, C. E. Johansson AB, Conveytech Holding AB, Facit AB, Håells AB, IVT Industrier AB, Johnson Pump International AB, Klippan Safety AB, Konverta AB, Medical Invest AB, Mentor Gruppen AB, Metorex International OY, Micronic Laser Systems AB, Nazem and Co. LP, Plockmatic International AB, Spectrogon AB, Totebo AB, Traction Development AB, Tolk-TV AB, Weda Poolcleaner AB, Åke Larson Gruppen AB

Officers, Executives and Principals

Hans Dirtoft, Managing Director
Eric Martin, Vice Managing Director
Lief Brundell, Investment Manager
Anders Craft, Investment Manager
Gunnar Gredenman, Investment Manager

FOUR SEASONS VENTURE CAPITAL AB

Sveavägen 17
P. O. Box 1415
11184 Stockholm
Sweden

Telephone: 46-8-145420
Fax: 46-8-216995

Mission: Actively seeking new investments as part of the Advent International network of venture capital companies

Fund Size: Skr324 million
Founded: not available
Average Investment: not available
Minimum Investment: Skr1 million

Investment Criteria: All stages

Geographic Preference: Europe

Industry Group Preference: not available

Portfolio Companies: not available

Officers, Executives and Principals

Lars-Olof Gustavsson
Gösta Oscarsson

FRANCE-ESPAGNE INVESTISSEMENTS

29 rue de Masure
64100 Bayonne
France

Telephone: 33-59-582244
Fax: 33-59-582174

Mission: Actively seeking new investments

Fund Size: not available
Founded: not available
Average Investment: not available
Minimum Investment: Ecu300,000

Investment Criteria: Seed, Start-up, Expansion/Development

Geographic Preference: Euorpe, France, Spain, Portugal

Industry Group Preference: All stages considered

Portfolio Companies: not available

Officers, Executives and Principals

Jacques Lassus

F. R. F. I. - CONSEIL REGIONAL D'ALSACE

35 avenue de la Paix
67070 Strasbourg
France

Telephone: 33-88-156867
Fax: 33-88-156889

Mission: Actively seeking new investments

Fund Size: not available
Founded: not available
Average Investment: not available
Minimum Investment: Ecu10,000

Investment Criteria: Seed, Start-up

Geographic Preference: France

Industry Group Preference: All sectors considered

Portfolio Companies: not available

Officers, Executives and Principals

Jean Lachmann

FRIE IPE CAPITAL I

Av. Júlio Dinis, 9 - 1°
1050 Lisbon
Portugal

Telephone: 351-1-7950022
Fax: 351-1-7950027

Mission: Actively seeking new investments as a fund under management by IPE Capital - Sociedade de Capital de Risco SA

Fund Size: Esc2.5 billion
Founded: 1993
Average Investment: Esc34.6 million
Minimum Investment: Esc22.9 million

Investment Criteria: Seed, Start-up, Mezzanine

Geographic Preference: Europe

Industry Group Preference: Environment, High-tech Industries, Leisure

Portfolio Companies: Faiancas Subril SA, Macem SA, Maconde SA, Molin, SA, V. A. España SA

Officers, Executives and Principals

Francisco Soares, President, IPE Capital
Education: Master's degree, John F. Kennedy School of Government, Harvard University; MSc in Management
Background: Economic Adviser, Ministry of Industry; President, Aitec SA; Director, Ambelis SA; Professor, ISEG (Technical University of Lisbon); Director, IPE SA

Rui Goncalves Soares, Director, IPE Capital
Education: MBA in International Management

Maria Amelia Santos, Director, IPE Capital; Financial Manager, IPE SA
Education: Graduate in Business Administration
Background: Project Manager, Nutrinvest; Activities Manager, Portuguese Government of Macao; Investment and Planning Manager, IPE SA

Carlos Frage Figueiredo, Investment Manager, IPE Capital
Education: Graduate in Business Administration
Background: Business Manager, Sulpedip SA; Project Manager, Paraempresa, Banco Portugues do Atlantico, Fundo de Turismo

Antonio Jorge Pimento da Silva, Portfolio Manager, IPE Capital
Education: Graduate in Business Administration
Background: Analyst, IPE SA, Departamento Central de Planeamento; Consultant, World Bank, Guinea-Bissau; Manager, Instituto de Credito de Angola

FRIE IPE RETEX / PALEP

Av. Júlio Dinis, 9 - 1°
1050 Lisbon
Portugal

Telephone: 351-1-7950022
Fax: 351-1-7950027

Mission: Actively seeking new investments as a fund under management by IPE Capital - Sociedade de Capital de Risco SA

Fund Size: Esc5 billion
Founded: 1994
Average Investment: not available
Minimum Investment: not available

Investment Criteria: Seed, Start-up, Mezzanine

Geographic Preference: Europe

Industry Group Preference: Environment, High-tech Industries, Leisure

Portfolio Companies: not available

Officers, Executives and Principals

Francisco Soares, President, IPE Capital
Education: Master's degree, John F. Kennedy School of Government, Harvard University; MSc in Management
Background: Economic Adviser, Ministry of Industry; President, Aitec SA; Director, Ambelis SA; Professor, ISEG (Technical University of Lisbon); Director, IPE SA

Rui Goncalves Soares, Director, IPE Capital
Education: MBA in International Management

Maria Amelia Santos, Director, IPE Capital; Financial Manager, IPE SA
Education: Graduate in Business Administration
Background: Project Manager, Nutrinvest; Activities Manager, Portuguese Government of Macao; Investment and Planning Manager, IPE SA

Carlos Frage Figueiredo, Investment Manager, IPE Capital
Education: Graduate in Business Administration
Background: Business Manager, Sulpedip SA; Project Manager, Paraempresa, Banco Portugues do Atlantico, Fundo de Turismo

Antonio Jorge Pimento da Silva, Portfolio Manager, IPE Capital
Education: Graduate in Business Administration
Background: Analyst, IPE SA, Departamento Central de Planeamento; Consultant, World Bank, Guinea-Bissau; Manager, Instituto de Credito de Angola

FRIULIA SpA

Via Locchi 19
34123 Trieste
Italy

Telephone: 39-40-3197421
Fax: 39-40-3197400
E-mail: daniela.geatti@friulia.inet.it

Mission: Developing the economy of the Friulia-Venezia Giulia region in northeastern Italy

Fund Size: Ecu230 million
Founded: 1967
Average Investment: Ecu750,000
Minimum Investment: Ecu50,000

Investment Criteria: Expansion/Development, Bridge, Turnaround/Restructuring

Geographic Preference: Italy (Friulia-Venezia Giulia region only)

Industry Group Preference: Chemical and Materials, Industrial Products, Electronics Related

Portfolio Companies: not available

Officers, Executives and Principals

Flavio Pressacco, Chairman
Furio Tomaselli

FSD CAPITAL DÉVELOPPEMENT

48 rue Fabert
75340 Paris
France

Telephone: 33-1- 4955-7045
Fax: 33-1-4950-4980

Mission: Actively seeking new investments

Fund Size: Ffr500 million
Founded: not available
Average Investment: not available
Minimum Investment: Ffr10 million

Investment Criteria: Expansion/Development, Leveraged Buy-out

Geographic Preference: not available

Industry Group Preference: All sectors considered

Portfolio Companies: Atral, Générale Routière, Trigano

Officers, Executives and Principals

Alain Caffi
Hubert Méraud
Pierre Decré
Pascal Stefani

F. TURISMO - CAPITAL DE RISCO SA

R. Duque Pamela, 2 3ºE, 1300
1000 Lisbon
Portugal

Telephone: 351-1-353-3656
Fax: 351-1-314-4008

Mission: Actively seeking new investments

Fund Size: Ecu26,132,586
Founded: not available
Average Investment: not available
Minimum Investment: Ecu300,000

Investment Criteria: Early-stage, Expansion/Development, Replacement, Turnaround/Restructuring

Geographic Preference: Portugal, Mozambique, Angola, Brazil, Spain, United States

Industry Group Preference: Services

Portfolio Companies: not available

Officers, Executives and Principals

José Roquette
Francisco Lopes
Jorge Catarino

FYLKINVEST AB

Regeringsgatan 48
P. O. Box 7490
10392 Stockholm
Sweden

Telephone: 46-8-242506
Fax: 46-8-791-8270

Mission: Actively seeking new investments

Fund Size: Skr42 million
Founded: not available
Average Investment: not available
Minimum Investment: not available

Investment Criteria: All stages

Geographic Preference: Sweden

Industry Group Preference: All sectors considered

Portfolio Companies: not available

Officers, Executives and Principals

Jan-Erik Wiberg

GALILEE INVESTISSEMENTS

55 rue La Boétie
75008 Paris
France

Telephone: 33-1-4413-3501
Fax: 33-1-4413-3746

Mission: Actively seeking new investments

Fund Size: Ffr152 million
Founded: not available
Average Investment: not available
Minimum Investment: Ffr2 million

Investment Criteria: Start-up, Early-stage, Expansion/Development, Management Buy-out, Management Buy-in, Turnaround/Restructuring

Geographic Preference: France

Industry Group Preference: Communications, Computer Related, Computer Software, Electronics Related, Energy, Environment, Medical/Health Related

Portfolio Companies: Sybel, Jouan, Infogrames, Lab, Gea Esker, Emme

Officers, Executives and Principals

Joël Flichy

GARTMORE PRIVATE CAPITAL

Gartmore House
16-18 Monument Street
London EC3R 8AJ
United Kingdom

Telephone: 44-171-782-2000
Fax: 44-171-782-2658

Mission: Actively seeking new investments

Fund Size: £112 million
Founded: not available
Average Investment: not available
Minimum Investment: £300,000

Investment Criteria: Second-stage, Mezzanine, Leveraged Buy-out, Special Situations, Control-block Purchases

Geographic Preference: United Kingdom

Industry Group Preference: Communications, Computer Related, Consumer, Distribution, Electronic Components and Instrumentation

Portfolio Companies: Basys Holdings, Harbury Group, HMC Brauer, Mason Corporate Holdings, The Rope Company

Officers, Executives and Principals

Michael Walton, Director, Venture Capital
Mary Douglas, Director
Jamie Johnson, Director
Donald Maclennan, Director
Brian Phillips, Director

GeBeKa GESELLSCHAFT FÜR BETEILIGUNGEN UND KAPITALVERWALTUNG mbH UND CO.

Plan 5
20095 Hamburg
Germany

Telephone: 49-40-324417
Fax: 49-40-324915

Mission: Actively seeking new investments

Fund Size: DM33 million
Founded: not available
Average Investment: not available
Minimum Investment: DM1 million

Investment Criteria: Management Buy-out, Management Buy-in, Expansion

Geographic Preference: none

Industry Group Preference: All sectors considered

Portfolio Companies: not available

Officers, Executives and Principals

Hellmut Rother
Christoph Baumgärtner

G. E. CAPITAL EQUITY CAPITAL GROUP

Clarges House
6-12 Clarges Street
London W1Y 8DH
United Kingdom

Telephone: 44-171-302-6310
Fax: 44-171-302-6936
E-mail: eroyce@ge.geis.com

Mission: Actively seeking new investments

Fund Size: not available
Founded: not available
Average Investment: £15 million
Minimum Investment: £3 million

Investment Criteria: Expansion, Secondary Purchase/Replacement Capital, Management Buy-out, Management Buy-in, Refinancing Bank Debt, Mezzanine

Geographic Preference: European Union, Eastern Europe, North America, Asia

Industry Group Preference: Communications, Computer Related, Consumer Related, Financial Services, Industrial Products and Services, Medical/Health Related, Electronics Related, Manufacturing, Transport

Portfolio Companies: Dreyers Ice Cream, Polish Cable, Redhook Brewery

Officers, Executives and Principals

Andrew Beaton
Elliot Royce
Bob Shanfield

GEMINI CAPITAL FUND MANAGEMENT LTD.

Maskit Street, P. O. Box 12548
Industrial Zone
Herzliya 46733
Israel

Telephone: 972-9-958-3596
Fax: 972-9-958-4842

Mission: Actively seeking new investments

Fund Size: $27 million
Founded: 1993
Average Investment: $1 million
Minimum Investment: $300,000

Investment Criteria: Seed, Research and Development, Startup, First-stage, Second-stage

Geographic Preference: Israel

Industry Group Preference: Communications, Computer Related, Electronic Components and Instrumentation, Energy/Natural Resources, Genetic Engineering, Industrial Products and Equipment, Medical/Health Related, Software

Portfolio Companies: not available

Officers, Executives and Principals

Dr. A.I. Mlavsky, President
Yossi Sela, Executive Vice President
Tali Aben, Vice President
Gil Sberlo, Comptroller

GENES GmbH VENTURE SERVICES

Kölner Strasse 27
50226 Frechen
Germany

Telephone: 49-2234-955-460
Fax: 49-2234-955-4620

Other Office Locations
Porsestrasse 19
39104
Magdeburg
Germany

Mission: Focusing investment activity on transnational deals and pre-IPO investments by divesting existing funds and setting up new international venture capital funds

Fund Size: not available
Founded: 1978
Average Investment: not available
Minimum Investment: not available

Investment Criteria: Expansion and Development Capital, Management Buy-out and Buy-in, Bridge Financing

Geographic Preference: Europe

Industry Group Preference: Automotive Suppliers, Commercial Space Business, Industrial Products and Equipment, Machine Construction, New Materials, Recycling

Portfolio Companies: IFA Machinenbau GmbH, Mawema Engineering GmbH, POLTE Armaturen GmbH, Polystal Composites GmbH, Intercar Ukraine Ltd.., Bauhütte Naumburg GmbH, Heidemann Werke GmbH, Wille System GmbH, Industriearmaturen POLTE GmbH (MAW)

Officers, Executives and Principals

Dr. Klaus Nathusius, Managing General Partner (Frechen)
Dr. Detlev Geiss, Senior Partner (Frechen)
Joerg Kreisel, Senior Partner (Frechen)
Eckart Bohm, Senior Partner (Frechen)
Werner Staab, Associate (Magdeburg)

GENESE INVESTISSEMENTS

6 rue Ancelle
92200 Neuilly-sur-Seine
France

Telephone: 33-1-4747-6900
Fax: 33-1-4640-7038

Mission: Actively seeking new investments

Fund Size: Ffr12 million
Founded: not available
Average Investment: not available
Minimum Investment: Ffr300,000

Investment Criteria: Seed

Geographic Preference: Europe, North America

Industry Group Preference: Biotechnology, Communications, Computer Related, Electronics Related, Medical/Health Related, Software

Portfolio Companies: Zydacron, Drillflex, Iname, Generix, Microsurge

Officers, Executives and Principals

Jean-Marc Patouillaud, Director

GENEVEST CONSULTING GROUP SA

10 rue du Vieux-Collège
1204 Geneva
Switzerland

Telephone: 41-22-312-3333
Fax: 41-22-312-3366
E-mail: sl@aol.com

Mission: Actively seeking new investments

Fund Size: not available
Founded: 1983
Average Investment: not available
Minimum Investment: $250,000

Investment Criteria: Start-up, First-stage, Second-stage, Mezzanine, Special Situations, Buy-back Venture Capital Investments

Geographic Preference: Belgium, The Netherlands, Scanadinavia, Switzerland, United States

Industry Group Preference: Communications, Computer Related, Electronic Components and Instrumentation, Energy/Natural Resources, Genetic Engineering, Industrial Products and Equipment

Portfolio Companies: not available

Officers, Executives and Principals

Tor Lingjaerde, Chairman
Yngvar Hvistendahl, Director
Sven C. Lingjaerde, Investment Manager

GEPAFIN SpA

Via Mario Angeloni 51
06124 Perugia
Italy

Telephone: 39-75-500-5153
Fax: 39-75-500-5156
E-mail: gepafin@krenet.it

Mission: Actively seeking new investments

Fund Size: not available
Founded: not available
Average Investment: not available
Minimum Investment: not available

Investment Criteria: Seed, Start-up, Early-stage, Expansion/Development, Management Buy-out, Management Buy-in, Turnaround/Restructuring

Geographic Preference: Italy

Industry Group Preference: All sectors considered

Portfolio Companies: not available

Officers, Executives and Principals

Marco Tili

GES GESTION/GAN AVENIR

2 rue Pillet-Will
75009 Paris
France

Telephone: 33-1-4247-5516
Fax: 33-1-4247-5663

Mission: Actively seeking new investments

Fund Size: Ffr1.3 billion
Founded: not available
Average Investment: not available
Minimum Investment: Ffr5 million

Investment Criteria: Early-stage, Expansion/Development, Leveraged Buy-out

Geographic Preference: France

Industry Group Preference: All sectors considered

Portfolio Companies: not available

Officers, Executives and Principals

René Ehrmann
Pierre Michel Deleglise
Bruno Dufraisse
Didier Levy-Rueff

GESTION DE CAPITAL RIESGO DEL PAIS VASCO

Gran Via, 29-2 planta
48009 Bilbao
Spain

Telephone: 34-4-944-790192
Fax: 34-4-944-790050

Mission: Actively seeking new investments

Fund Size: Ecu28 million
Founded: not available
Average Investment: not available
Minimum Investment: Ecu70,000

Investment Criteria: All stages

Geographic Preference: Europe

Industry Group Preference: All sectors considered

Portfolio Companies: not available

Officers, Executives and Principals

José Maria Losada

GILDE INVESTMENT FUNDS

Newtonlaan 91
P. O. Box 85067
3508 AB Utrecht
The Netherlands

Telephone: 31-30-251-0534
Fax: 31-30-254-0004
E-mail: info@gilde.nl

Mission: Actively seeking new investments

Fund Size: Ecu135 million
Founded: not available
Average Investment: not available
Minimum Investment: Ecu100,000

Investment Criteria: Start-up, Early-stage, Expansion/Development, Management Buy-out, Management Buy-in, Replacement

Geographic Preference: Europe, United States

Industry Group Preference: Communications, Computer Related, Computer Software, Electronics Related

Portfolio Companies: not available

Officers, Executives and Principals

Leendert J. van Driel
Diederik Heyning
Toon den Heijer
Frans Van Schaik
Boudewijn Molenaar

G. I. M. V.

Karel Oomsstraat 37
2018 Antwerp
Belgium

Telephone: 32-3-248-2321
Fax: 32-3-238-4193

Mission: Actively seeking new investments

Fund Size: Ecu395 million
Founded: not available
Average Investment: not available
Minimum Investment: Ecu250,000

Investment Criteria: All stages

Geographic Preference: Europe, United States, Asia

Industry Group Preference: All sectors considered

Portfolio Companies: not available

Officers, Executives and Principals

Philip Vermeulen, Partner
D. Boogmans, Partner
G. Van Acker, Partner
Raynier van Outryve d'Ydewalle, Partner
P. Van Beneden, Partner
S. Nicolay, Partner

GIMVINDUS NV
Matenstraat 214
2845 Niel
Belgium

Telephone: 32-3-880-8120
Fax: 32-3-844-7508

Mission: Actively seeking new investments

Fund Size: Ecu772.7 million
Founded: not available
Average Investment: not available
Minimum Investment: Ecu1.3 million

Investment Criteria: Expansion/Development, Management Buy-out, Management Buy-in, Turnaround/
  Restructuring, Bridge

Geographic Preference: Europe

Industry Group Preference: Industrial Products

Portfolio Companies: not available

Officers, Executives and Principals

Roger Malèvé

GLAXO HOLDINGS PLC

Lansdowne House
Berkeley Square
London WIX 6BP
United Kingdom

Telephone: 44-171-493-4060
Fax: 44-171-408-0228

Mission: Actively seeking new investments

Fund Size: $1.41 billion
Founded: not available
Average Investment: $5 million
Minimum Investment: not available

Investment Criteria: not available

Geographic Preference: not available

Industry Group Preference: Medical/Health Related

Portfolio Companies: Gilread, Amylin Pharmaceuticals Inc.

G. L. E. DEVELOPMENT CAPITAL

28 Park Street
London SE1 9EQ
United Kingdom

Telephone: 44-171-403-0300
Fax: 44-171-403-1742
E-mail: gle-dev-cap@geo2.poptel.org.uk

Mission: Specialising in investments in established London-based companies with annual sales of between £1 million and £20 million

Fund Size: £16 million
Founded: not available
Average Investment: £400,000
Minimum Investment: £100,000

Investment Criteria: Expansion, Management Buy-in, Management Buy-out, Secondary Purchase/Replacement Capital, Early Stage, Development, Acquisition

Geographic Preference: United Kingdom (London and Southeastern England)

Industry Group Preference: All sectors considered

Portfolio Companies: Whitecross Group Ltd, Newultra Ltd, Beyond Communications Ltd

Officers, Executives and Principals

Mark Wignall, Managing Director
Jonathan Gregory, Assistant Director
Paul Chapman, Assistant Director

GLOBAL FINANCE

17 Akademia Street
10671 Athens
Greece

Telephone: 30-1-362-2096
Fax: 30-1-362-7766

Mission: Managing venture capital funds (Euromerchant Balkan Fund and Baring Hellenic Ventures SA) and providing financial services

Fund Size: not available
Founded: 1991
Average Investment: not available
Minimum Investment: not available

Investment Criteria: Expansion/Development, Turnaround/Restructuring, Replacement

Geographic Preference: Greece, Balkan countries, Cyprus

Industry Group Preference: not available

Portfolio Companies: Euromerchant Balkan Fund (EBF), Baring Hellenic Ventures SA (BHV)

Officers, Executives and Principals

Angelos Plakopitas, Managing Director
Education: BA in Economic and Business Sciences, University of Athens; MBA, New York University
Background: General Manager, Shelman (wood products company); 14 years experience in corporate banking with Citibank and Hellenic Industrial Development Bank

Ioannis Papaioannou, Investment Manager
Education: MS, Stanford University; MBA, INSEAD
Background: experience in industrial engineering and management, in consulting and in academia, in the United States and Greece

Theodore Klakidis, Investment Associate
Education: MSc in Mathematics, Georgetown University; MPP in International Trade and Finance, Harvard University

GOLDMAN SACHS INTERNATIONAL

Peterborough Court
133 Fleet Street
London EC4A 2BB
United Kingdom

Telephone: 44-171-774-1000
Fax: 44-171-774-4123
E-mail: charlie.bott@gs.com

Mission: Actively seeking new investments

Fund Size: £1 billion
Founded: 1995
Average Investment: £20 million
Minimum Investment: £5 million

Investment Criteria: Expansion, Management Buy-out, Secondary Purchase/Replacement Capital, Development, Acquisition

Geographic Preference: Western Europe, North America, China

Industry Group Preference: All sectors considered

Portfolio Companies: Diamond Cable, GCR Holdings Limited, Stirling Cooke Browne, Pears Portfolio, Alliance Hotelerie, Suez Portfolio

Officers, Executives and Principals

Charlie Bott, Executive Director
Stephen Peel, Executive Director
Muneer Satter, Partner
Ramez Sousou, Executive Director

GOLDMAN SACHS PARIS

2 rue de Thann
75017 Paris
France

Telephone: 33-1-4212-1122
Fax: 33-1-4212-1199

Mission: Actively seeking new investments

Fund Size: Ffr8.7 billion
Founded: not available
Average Investment: not available
Minimum Investment: Ffr75 million

Investment Criteria: Expansion/Development, Leveraged Buy-out, Management Buy-out

Geographic Preference: Europe, North America, Asia

Industry Group Preference: All sectors considered

Portfolio Companies: Bran and Luebbe (Germany), Tarkett (Germany), Diamond Cable (United Kingdom), Stirling Cook (United Kingdom)

Officers, Executives and Principals

Jean De Pourtalès

GRANVILLE PRIVATE EQUITY MANAGERS LIMITED

Mint House
77 Mansell Street
London E1 8AF
United Kingdom

Telephone: 44-171-488-1212
Fax: 44-171-481-3911

Other Office Locations
Cheshire House
18 Booth Street
Manchester M2 4AN
Phone 44-161-236-6600, Fax 44-161-236-6650

39-40a York Place
Leeds LS1 2ED
Phone 44-113-242-4200, Fax 44-113-242-8119

Castle Chambers, Fourth Floor
Castle Street
Liverpool LS1 9SH
Phone 44-151-258-1859, Fax 44-151-258-1860

Cleveland Business Centre
1 Watson Street
Middlesbrough TS1 2RQ
Phone 44-1642-251083, Fax 44-1642-251832

Granville Iberia
Tuset 18, Eighth Floor
08006 Barcelona
Spain
Phone 34-3-237-0633, Fax 34-3-416-1691

41 avenue Montaigne
75008 Paris
France
Phone 33-1-4952-0600, Fax 33-1-4952-0601

Mission: Actively seeking new investments

Fund Size: £92 million
Founded: 1973
Average Investment: £7 million
Minimum Investment: £1 million

Investment Criteria: Expansion, Management Buy-out, Management Buy-in, Investor Buy-out, Leveraged
  Buy-out

Geographic Preference: United Kingdom, Western Europe

Industry Group Preference: All sectors considered, but especially Business Services, Computer Software, Facilities Management, Information Technology Services, Logistics and Distribution, Outsourcing, Security

Portfolio Companies: ARM Group Ltd., Barrett Steel Ltd., Calder Aluminium, Campbell Bewley, Corin, Contract Services, Erin Group Ltd., Fermec Holdings Ltd., Grosvenor Personnel Services, Healthcare Scotland, Ludgate Communications, Matalan, Merlin, Metroline, Principal Hotels, Rite-Vent, World Systems, Valetmatic Holdings Ltd.

Officers, Executives and Principals

Michael Proudlock, Chairman (London)
Mike Fell, Managing Director (London)
Mark Owen, Director (London)
Mark Fuller, Director (Manchester)
David Martin, Director (Leeds)

GREAT WINCHESTER CAPITAL FUND MANAGERS

12 Hans Road
London SW3 1RT
United Kingdom

Telephone: 44-171-584-4277
Fax: 44-171-584-4264

Mission: Actively seeking new investments

Fund Size: £3 million
Founded: not available
Average Investment: £800,000
Minimum Investment: £250,000

Investment Criteria: All stages except Seed

Geographic Preference: United Kingdom

Industry Group Preference: All sectors considered

Portfolio Companies: JPI Group Ltd, Jigsaw Day Nurseries plc, The Terence Chapman Group plc, The Antique Wine Co (GB) Ltd

Officers, Executives and Principals

Anthony Campling

GRESHAM TRUST plc

Barrington House
Gresham Street
London EC2V 7HE
United Kingdom

Telephone: 44-171-606-6474
Fax: 44-171-606-3370

Mission: Specializing in financing mid-sized management buy-out and expansion capital transactions, all investments being structured in line with management's wishes on realisation timing

Fund Size: £150 million
Founded: not available
Average Investment: £2.5 million
Minimum Investment: £1 million

Investment Criteria: Expansion, Management Buy-in, Management Buy-out, Refinancing Bank Debt, Replacement Capital

Geographic Preference: United Kingdom

Industry Group Preference: All sectors considered

Portfolio Companies: Life Style Care PLC, TVI Europe Ltd, Intermotor Holdings Ltd, Belsize Holdings Limited

Officers, Executives and Principals

Trevor Jones, Managing Director
David Ascott, Director
Mike Walker, Director
Peter Brooks, Director
Keku Aga, Director
Paul Thomas, Director
Mike Langford, Director
Ryan Robson, Investment Manager
Iain Kennedy, Investment Executive
Neil Stragg, Investment Executive

GROSVENOR VENTURE MANAGERS LTD.

Regal Court
42-44 High Street
Slough
Berkshire SL1 1EL
United Kingdom

Telephone: 44-1753-811-812
Fax: 44-1753-811-813

Mission: Actively seeking new investments

Fund Size: not available
Founded: 1981
Average Investment: not available
Minimum Investment: $1 million

Investment Criteria: Second-stage, Special Situations

Geographic Preference: not available

Industry Group Preference: Communications, Computer Related, Consumer, Distribution, Electronic Components and Instrumentation, Energy/Natural Resources, Genetic Engineering, Industrial Products and Equipment, Medical/Health Related

Portfolio Companies: not available

Officers, Executives and Principals

Janis Anderson, Managing Director
William Edge, Director
Trevor Bayley, Investment Executive
Julian Carr, Investment Executive
Stephen Edwards, Investment Executive

GROUPE MAAF

143 boulevard Haussman
75008 Paris
France

Telephone: 33-1-4420-8922
Fax: 33-1-4563-8017

Mission: Actively seeking new investments

Fund Size: Ffr90 million
Founded: not available
Average Investment: not available
Minimum Investment: Ffr2 million

Investment Criteria: Early-stage, Expansion/Development

Geographic Preference: Europe

Industry Group Preference: All sectors considered

Portfolio Companies: not available

Officers, Executives and Principals

Jean-Louis Bonnet
David Pastel
Brigitte Sagnes

GROUPEMENT PROMOTION CAPITAL

47 avenue d'Ouchy
P. O. Box 205
1000 Lausanne 13
Switzerland

Telephone: 41-21-617-7291
Fax: 41-21-617-7303

Mission: Actively seeking new investments, specializing in start-ups with preference for new technology

Fund Size: not available
Founded: not available
Average Investment: not available
Minimum Investment: not available

Investment Criteria: Start-up, Early-stage, Replacement Capital

Geographic Preference: Switzerland: Canton of Vaud

Industry Group Preference: Chemical/Materials, Communications, Computer Related, Consumer Related, Electronics, Medical/Health Related

Portfolio Companies: not available

Officers, Executives and Principals

Gérard J. Gogniat, Partner

GUIDANT EUROPE SA

Excelsiorlaan 37
1930 Zaventem
Belgium

Telephone: 32-2-714-1470
Fax: 32-2-714-1414

Mission: Investing in new medical technologies

Fund Size: not available
Founded: not available
Average Investment: not available
Minimum Investment: not available

Investment Criteria: Seed, Start-up, Early-stage

Geographic Preference: Europe

Industry Group Preference: Medical/Health Related

Portfolio Companies: not available

Officers, Executives and Principals

Richard van Oostrom, Partner
Dr. Rolf Sammler

GUINNESS MAHON DEVELOPMENT CAPITAL LIMITED

33 St Mary at Hill
London EC3 3AJ
United Kingdom

Telephone: 44-171-623-6222
Fax: 44-171-623-4313
E-mail: 100743.127@compuserve.com

Mission: Actively seeking new investments

Fund Size: not available
Founded: 1985
Average Investment: £750,000
Minimum Investment: £250,000

Investment Criteria: Expansion, Management Buy-in, Management Buy-out, Rescue/Turnabout, Secondary Purchase/Replacement Capital

Geographic Preference: United Kingdom

Industry Group Preference: not available

Portfolio Companies: Colorsil BV, All Childrens Trading Company Ltd., Britt Allcroft Group Ltd., Sooty International Ltd.

Officers, Executives and Principals

Gordon Power, Managing Director
Malcolm Moss, Director
Simon Turner, Assistant Director
Roger Penlington, Investment Director
Guy Peddy, Investment Executive

GUJARAT STATE FERTILIZERS COMPANY LIMITED (GUJARAT)

T. O. Fertilizernagar
391750 Baroda
Gujarat
India

Telephone: 91-265-72451
Fax: 91-265-72966

Mission: not available

Fund Size: not available
Founded: not available
Average Investment: $1 million
Minimum Investment: not available

Investment Criteria: not available

Geographic Preference: India (State of Gujarat)

Industry Group Preference: Genetic Engineering

Portfolio Companies: Ecogen

Officers, Executives and Principals

Dr. M. H. Mehta

HALDER BETEILIGUNGSBERATUNG GmbH

Untermainanlage 5
60329 Frankfurt am Main
Germany

Telephone: 49-69-242-5330
Fax: 49-69-236-866

Mission: Investing private equity in mature, profitable and well-managed companies with annual sales of between £12 million and £120 million

Fund Size: £60 million
Founded: 1991
Average Investment: £2.3 million
Minimum Investment: £1 million

Investment Criteria: Management Buy-out, Management Buy-in, Expansion/Development, Bridge, Replacement

Geographic Preference: Germany, Belgium, Luxemburg, The Netherlands

Industry Group Preference: Consumer Related, Industrial Products, Manufacturing, Services

Portfolio Companies: 1 and 1 Holding GmbH, DIFI Dierk Filmer GmbH, Helmut Dressel GmbH, Erich Jaeger GmbH, Bernd Steudle GmbH, Wego System AG

Officers, Executives and Principals

Paul De Ridder
Joachim Kramer

HALDER HOLDINGS BV

Lange Voorhout 9
2514 EA The Hague
The Netherlands

Telephone: 31-70-361-8618
Fax: 31-70-361-8616

Other Office Locations
Halder Beteiligungsberatung GmbH
Untermainanlage 5
60329 Frankfurt am Main
Germany
Phone 49-69-242-5330, Fax 49-69-236-866

Halder Invest NV
Mechelsesteenweg 267
2018 Antwerp
Belgium
Phone 32-3-239-3600, Fax 32-3-281-6152

Mission: Investing private equity in mature, profitable and well managed companies with annual sales of between $15 million and $175 million

Fund Size: $175 million
Founded: 1984
Average Investment: $3.5 million
Minimum Investment: $2 million

Investment Criteria: Expansion/Development, Management Buy-out, Management Buy-in, Bridge, Replacement

Geographic Preference: Belgium, Germany, Luxembourg, The Netherlands

Industry Group Preference: Consumer Related, Industrial Products, Manufacturing, Services, Transportation

Portfolio Companies: 1 and 1 Holding GmbH, Altrex Beheer BV, Arma BV, Atlanta-Hoogezand BV, Benefood BV, DIFI Dierk Filmer GmbH, Helmut Dressel GmbH, ETS Lapperre BHAC NV, Fancom Holding BV, HAMACH Beheer BV, Hedavo Holding BV, Erich Jaeger GmbH, Kempen and Co. NV, NV Meppeler Machinefabriek, Olliff and Partners Plc, Papierfabriek Doetinchem BV, Rigida Groep BV, Rutges Holding BV, Schmidt und Link Werkzeugbau GmbH, Bernd Steudle GmbH, Vekoma Holding BV, Wego Systems AG, X-Flow BV

Officers, Executives and Principals

Sam J. Alleman (The Hague)
Paul A. Deiters (The Hague)
Rene Smits (The Hague)
Pieter van der Meijden (The Hague)
Marcel van Wijk (The Hague)
Paul De Ridder (Frankfurt)
Antoine van den Abeele (Antwerp)

HAMBRO EUROPEAN VENTURES

16 place Vendôme
75001 Paris
France

Telephone: 33-1-4260-5717
Fax: 33-1-4286-9019

Other Office Locations
41 Tower Hill
London EC3N 4HA
United Kingdom
Phone 44-171-702-3593, Fax 44-171-338-9264

Mission: Actively seeking new investments

Fund Size: Ffr750 million
Founded: not available
Average Investment: not available
Minimum Investment: Ffr15 million

Investment Criteria: Leveraged Buy-out, Leveraged Buy-in, Management Buy-out, Expansion/Development, Turnaround

Geographic Preference: Europe

Industry Group Preference: Consumer Related, Engineering, Leisure

Portfolio Companies: not available

Officers, Executives and Principals

James Weir

HAMBRO EUROPEAN VENTURES LIMITED

41 Tower Hill
London EC3N 4HA
United Kingdom

Telephone: 44-171-702-3593
Fax: 44-171-338-9264

Other Office Locations
16 place Vendôme
75001 Paris
France
Phone 33-1-4260-5717, Fax 33-1-4286-9019

Mission: Actively seeking new investments

Fund Size: £100 million
Founded: not available
Average Investment: £3 million
Minimum Investment: £1 million

Investment Criteria: Expansion, Management Buy-in, Management Buy-out, Refinancing Bank Debt, Rescue/Turnaround, Secondary Purchase/Replacement Capital, Venture Purchase of Quoted Shares

Geographic Preference: Western Europe

Industry Group Preference: All sectors considered except Real Estate

Portfolio Companies: Foster Menswear, Thorn Security, Franklin Hotels, Catalana de Polimers, Glass's Information Services

Officers, Executives and Principals

Julian Brock
Jeremy Hand
Graham Lee
Marc Philippe
William Sporborg
Peter Taylor
Edmund Truell
Jamie Weir

HAMBRO-GRANTHAM MANAGEMENT LTD.

2 Bligh Street, Level 8
Sydney
New South Wales 2000
Australia

Telephone: 61-2-221-4311
Fax: 61-2-221-7094

Mission: Actively seeking new investments

Fund Size: not available
Founded: 1984
Average Investment: not available
Minimum Investment: $500,000

Investment Criteria: Second-stage, Mezzanine

Geographic Preference: not available

Industry Group Preference: Communications, Computer Related, Consumer, Distribution, Energy/Natural Resources, Genetic Engineering, Industrial Products and Equipment

Portfolio Companies: not available

Officers, Executives and Principals

John Grant, Executive Chairman
Richard Gregson, Managing Director
Peter Johnson, Director
Peter Wallace, Director
Malcolm Dunnell, Investment Manager
Rajeev Dhawan, Investment Analyst
Robert Thomson, Investment Analyst

HAMBROS ADVANCED TECHNOLOGY TRUST

20-21 Tooks Court
Cursitor Street
London EC4V 1LB
United Kingdom

Telephone: 44-171-242-9900
Fax: 44-171-405-2863

Mission: Actively seeking new investments

Fund Size: not available
Founded: 1992
Average Investment: £400,000
Minimum Investment: £250,000

Investment Criteria: Expansion, Early-stage

Geographic Preference: United Kingdom

Industry Group Preference: not available

Portfolio Companies: Surface Active Limited, Recognition Systems Limited, Amber Logic Limited, AFA Systems International Limited

HANNOVER FINANZ GmbH

Leisewitzstrasse 37b
30175 Hanover
Germany

Telephone: 49-511-280-0701
Fax: 49-511-280-0737
E-mail: hannover.finanz@p-net.de

Mission: Actively seeking new investments in growing companies, both for its own account and on behalf of three funds under its management (Commerz Unternehmensbeteiligungs AG, Provinzial Beteiligungs GmbH, and WeHaCo Kapitalbeteiligungs GmbH)

Fund Size: DM450 million
Founded: 1979
Average Investment: DM8 million
Minimum Investment: DM2 million

Investment Criteria: Later-stage, Development, Buy-out, Pre-IPO, Replacement

Geographic Preference: Germany; rest of Europe with syndication partners

Industry Group Preference: Engineering, Financial Services, Logistics, Manufacturing, Media, Services, Telecommunications, Trade

Portfolio Companies: AIXTRON Semiconductor Technologie, Alt United Garment Service, AWECO Kunststofftechnik Gerätebau, Biologische Analysensystem, BAG Med., BIG, Peter Butz, Commerz Unternehmensbeteiligung, De Maekelboerger Neubrandenburger Back- und Konditoreiwaren, Display Design und Instore Marketing, Dittmers Korrosionsschutz, Grundstücksverwertungsgesellschaft Berndshof, H. Schneider, Hannover Finanz Vermögens-Verwaltung, Wandel und Goltermann Management Holding, HL Leasing, Hanseatische Verlags-Beteiligung, Eduard Hengstenberg, HKW Römerbrücke ZWO, Hübner Elektromeschinen, IFCO, itp Finanzservice, Dr. Jodlbauer Food Consulting, KAPPA Messtechnik, Luther und Maelzer, Management und Marketing Dennig, Markant Südwest Handel, Mecoswiss Mechanische Componenten, MobilCom Holding, MS "Katharina S" Reederei Siemer, Oettinger Bier Brauhaus Oettingen, o. m. t. Oberflächen- und Materialtechnologie, PRISMA Holding, Quicktest, Dirk Rossmann, Rossman Ost Drogeriemärkte, Schoeller Plast Industries, technotrans, VEMAG Maschinenbau, Willy Vogel, WIV Westdeutsche Industrieinstandhaltung-Verwaltung, Wortmann und Filz

Officers, Executives and Principals

Albrecht Hertz-Eichenrode, BA, Lic. es. sc. pol.
Joachim Simmross, Dipl.-Kfm.
Andreas Schober, Dipl.-Ing., MSEE
Claus von Loeper, Dipl.-Kfm., MBA
Herbert-Ernst Finke, Dipl.-Kfm.
Johannes Voss, Dipl.-Ing.
Jörg-Friedrich Bätjer, Dipl.-Volkswirt
Arvid Lenze, Legal Counsel
Thomas Winkler, Dipl.-Betriebswirt

HELLENIC BUSINESS DEVELOPMENT AND INVESTMENT COMPANY SA

64 Kifissias Avenue
15125 Maroussi
Athens
Greece

Telephone: 30-1-689-8770
Fax: 30-1-689-8777

Mission: Actively seeking new investments

Fund Size: Ecu26.7 million
Founded: not available
Average Investment: not available
Minimum Investment: Ecu72,000

Investment Criteria: Seed, Start-up, Early-stage, Expansion/Development

Geographic Preference: Greece

Industry Group Preference: Computer Software, Consumer Related, Electronics Related, Industrial Automation, Industrial Products, Medical/Health Related

Portfolio Companies: not available

Officers, Executives and Principals

Elizabeth Kitsou

HIGHLAND OPPORTUNITY LIMITED

Economic Development Service
Highland Council
Glenurquhart Road
Inverness IV3 5NX
United Kingdom

Telephone: 44-1463-702000
Fax: 44-1463-710848

Mission: Actively seeking new investments

Fund Size: Ecu2 million
Founded: not available
Average Investment: not available
Minimum Investment: Ecu1,500

Investment Criteria: Seed, Start-up, Expansion/Development, Turnaround

Geographic Preference: United Kingdom

Industry Group Preference: Consumer Products and Services, Electronics Related, Industrial Products, Manufacturing, Services, Transport

Portfolio Companies: not available

Officers, Executives and Principals

Hugh Black

HODGSON MARTIN LTD.

36 George Street
Edinburgh EH2 2LE
United Kingdom

Telephone: 44-131-226-7644
Fax: 44-131-226-7647

Mission: Actively seeking new investments

Fund Size: not available
Founded: 1980
Average Investment: not available
Minimum Investment: $500,000

Investment Criteria: Expansion, Management Buy-in, Management Buy-out, Secondary Purchase/Replacement Capital

Geographic Preference: Europe, North America

Industry Group Preference: Construction, Consumer Related, Environmental, Financial Services, Leisure

Portfolio Companies: KDM International PLC, Wharfside Hotels PLC, Cheval Investment Management Ltd., Lombard International Assurance SA, Scottish Academic Press Ltd.

Officers, Executives and Principals

Allan F. Hodgson, Managing Director
Martin A. Greig, Director
George D. Gwilt, Director
Dr. Thomas L. Johnston, Director
Yvonne Savage, Director
David D. Stevenson, Director
Elizabeth Hatfield, Legal and Compliance
Derek Sword, Investment Assistant

HOEGH INVEST A/S

Parkveier 55
P. O. Box 2416-Solli
0201 Oslo
Norway

Telephone: 47-22-122-800
Fax: 47-22-552-276

Mission: Investing own funds in high-growth technology companies

Fund Size: not available
Founded: not available
Average Investment: not available
Minimum Investment: not available

Investment Criteria: not available

Geographic Preference: United States

Industry Group Preference: Electronics, Life Sciences, Software

Portfolio Companies: not available

Officers, Executives and Principals

Ove Hoegh, Partner
Carl Preben Hoegh, Partner

HOLLAND VENTURE BEHEERMIJ BV

Haaksbergweg 55
1101 BR Amsterdam
The Netherlands

Telephone: 31-20-697-6841
Fax: 31-20-697-3326
E-mail: adventure@hventure.nl

Mission: Actively seeking new investments with special interest in information technology

Fund Size: £150 million
Founded: not available
Average Investment: not available
Minimum Investment: Ecu130,000

Investment Criteria: Start-up, Early-stage, Expansion/Development, Management Buy-out, Management Buy-in, Bridge

Geographic Preference: Europe

Industry Group Preference: Communications, Computer Related, Computer Software, Consumer Related, Electronics, Industrial Products, Information Technology

Portfolio Companies: not available

Officers, Executives and Principals

Dr. E. R. Deves, Director
Dr. A .A. Nagtegaal, Director

HORIZONTE VENTURE MANAGEMENT GmbH

Bauermarkt 6
1010 Vienna
Austria

Telephone: 43-1-533-5601
Fax: 43-1-533-56014
E-mail: horizont@ping.at

Other Office Locations
Teslova 30
1000 Ljubljana
Slovakia
Phone 386-61-126-1440, Fax 386-61-125-9446, E-mail: hvm@cunct.si

Mission: Actively seeking investments in small and medium-sized enterprises which have the potential to achieve internationally important market positions

Fund Size: Sch370 million
Founded: 1985
Average Investment: Sch12 million
Minimum Investment: Sch2 million

Investment Criteria: Start-up, Early Stage Financing, Expansion/Development, Management buy-out, Replacement

Geographic Preference: Austria, Slovenia

Industry Group Preference: Biotechnology, Communications, Computer Related, Computer Software, Electronics Related, Medical/Health Related

Portfolio Companies: not available

Officers, Executives and Principals

Dr. Franz R. Krejs, Managing Director
Dr. Alfred Matzka, Managing Director
Maartin Prohazka, Partner

HSBC PRIVATE EQUITY

Vintner's Place
68 Upper Thames Street
London EC4V 3BJ
United Kingdom

Telephone: 44-171-336-9955
Fax: 44-171-336-9961

Mission: Investing a mixture of captive and external funds as the European private equity arm of the HSBC Group

Fund Size: £750 million
Founded: 1968
Average Investment: £10 million
Minimum Investment: £750,000

Investment Criteria: All stages

Geographic Preference: Western Europe

Industry Group Preference: All sectors considered

Portfolio Companies: Sterling Organics, Forbuoys, Innovex, Schaffner, Bryan Contract Hire

Officers, Executives and Principals

Ian Forrest, Partner
Chris Masterson, Partner
Richard Connell, Partner
Phil Goodwin, Partner
Rober Heath, Partner
Vince O'Brien, Partner
Alex Shinder, Partner

HUNGARIAN AMERICAN ENTERPRISE FUND

Rákóczi út 1-3
Budapest 1088
Hungary

Telephone: 36-1-266-7175
Fax: 36-1-266-7086
E-mail: 102445.2435@compuserve.com

Mission: Actively seeking new investments

Fund Size: Ecu23 million
Founded: not available
Average Investment: not available
Minimum Investment: Ecu400,000

Investment Criteria: Expansion/Development, Replacement

Geographic Preference: Hungary

Industry Group Preference: Computer Related, Computer Software, Consumer Related, Industrial Products, Manufacturing, Medical/Health Related

Portfolio Companies: not available

Officers, Executives and Principals

Charles A. Huebner

I C C VENTURE CAPITAL

72-74 Harcourt Street
Dublin 2
Ireland

Telephone: 353-1-475-5700
Fax: 353-1-475-0437

Mission: Actively seeking new investments, concentrating on private Irish companies

Fund Size: Ecu25 million
Founded: not available
Average Investment: not available
Minimum Investment: Ecu250,000

Investment Criteria: Expansion/Development, Management Buy-in, Management Buy-out, Replacement, Bridge

Geographic Preference: Ireland

Industry Group Preference: All sectors except Real Estate

Portfolio Companies: not available

Officers, Executives and Principals

David Fassbender
Prisca Grady
Tom Kirwan
Edward McDaid
John Tracey

ICVEN SA

Tour Pascal La Défense 7 Sud
92075 Paris
France

Telephone: 33-1-4767-6353
Fax: 33-1-4767-6500

Mission: Actively seeking new investments as the corporate venture arm of IBM Europe

Fund Size: not available
Founded: not available
Average Investment: not available
Minimum Investment: not available

Investment Criteria: All stages

Geographic Preference: Europe

Industry Group Preference: Communications, Computer Related, Consumer Related/Services, Electronics
 Software

Portfolio Companies: not available

Officers, Executives and Principals

Gary Bullard
Heiner Sussner
Andrew Knox

I D I

4 rue Ancelle
92521 Neuilly
France

Telephone: 33-1-4747-7117
Fax: 33-1-4747-7206

Mission: Actively seeking new investments

Fund Size: Ffr990 million
Founded: not available
Average Investment: not available
Minimum Investment: Ffr5 million

Investment Criteria: Early-stage, Expansion/Development, Leveraged Buy-out, Leveraged Buy-in

Geographic Preference: France

Industry Group Preference: All sectors considered

Portfolio Companies: Armor, Pip (Holding of CNIM), GPS, ECO-ARC, Orveillan, IMV, Extrapole, Pixtech
Silmag

Officers, Executives and Principals

Christian Langlois-Meurinne, President
François Marmissolle, Managing Director
Georges Ramain, Associate Director
Anne Challamel, Associate Director

IDIA (INSTITUT DE DÉVELOPPEMENT DES INDUSTRIES AGRICOLES ET ALIMENTAIRES)

35 avenue Franklin Roosevelt
75008 Paris
France

Telephone: 33-1- 4359-9141
Fax: 33-1-4289-9002
E-mail: 100655.2755@compuserv.com

Mission: Actively seeking new investments

Fund Size: Ffr1565 million
Founded: not available
Average Investment: not available
Minimum Investment: not available

Investment Criteria: All stages

Geographic Preference: France, Europe

Industry Group Preference: Agriculture/ Forestry/Fisheries, Biotechnology

Portfolio Companies: not available

Officers, Executives and Principals

Guy Nebot, Managing Director
Alan Berlière
Gérard Demorgny
Jean-Claude Noël
Jacques Mony
Paul Charrin
Gilles Colinet
Frank Boniszyn

I. D. J. LTD.
Suite 33, 140 Park Lane
London W1Y 3AA
United Kingdom

Telephone: 44-171-499-0355
Fax: 44-171-495-1149

Mission: Actively seeking new investments

Fund Size: not available
Founded: not available
Average Investment: not available
Minimum Investment: £500,000

Investment Criteria: All stages

Geographic Preference: North America, United Kingdom

Industry Group Preference: All sectors considered

Portfolio Companies: Standard Platforms plc, CSMA Limited, Fabris Lane International Limited, Dicom
  Group plc

Officers, Executives and Principals

David Comer
Christopher Horspool
Paul Hudson
John Incledon
John Yates
Paul Winson

IDP INDUSTRIAL DEVELOPMENT PARTNERS GmbH

Limburgerstrasse 9
61462 Königstein/Taunus
Germany

Telephone: 49-6174- 4017
Fax: 49-6174-4010

Other Office Locations
IDP Investment AG, Zug
Chalet Alamut
3378 Schönried
Switzerland
Phone 41-30-44422, Fax 41-30-44425

IDP Investments Inc.
211 Congress Street
Boston, MA 02110
United States
Phone 617-482-6200, Fax 617-482-6201

8571 S.E. 82nd Street
Mercer Island, WA 98040
United States
Phone/Fax 206-236-2035

Mission: Actively seeking new investments

Fund Size: DM31.3 million
Founded: not available
Average Investment: not available
Minimum Investment: DM500,000

Investment Criteria: Expansion/Development, Management Buy-out, Management Buy-in, Bridge, Replacement

Geographic Preference: Germany, Switzerland, North America

Industry Group Preference: Communications, Consumer Related, Electronics Related, Industrial Products, Services

Portfolio Companies: not available

Officers, Executives and Principals

Thomas Fissler
Dr. Peter Hengel (Switzerland)
Robert H. Reilly (Boston)
Herb G. Holley (Mercer Island)

ILE-DE-FRANCE

Parc des Erable, Bâtiment 3
66 route de Sartrouville
78230 Le Pecq
France

Telephone: 33-1-3015-6400
Fax: 33-1-3015-6409

Mission: Actively seeking new investments

Fund Size: Ffr60 million
Founded: not available
Average Investment: not available
Minimum Investment: Ffr100,000

Investment Criteria: Start-up, Early-stage, Expansion/Development

Geographic Preference: France (Ile-de-France region)

Industry Group Preference: Industry and Services

Portfolio Companies: not available

Officers, Executives and Principals

Pascal Gauthier
Bertrand Penicaud

I. M. INNOVATIONS MÄKLARNA AB

Narvavägen 32
P. O. Box 10090
10055 Stockholm
Sweden

Telephone: 46-8-660-5200
Fax: 46-8-660-5201

Mission: Assisting growth companies in the commercial exploitation of innovations and in the expansion of entrepreneurially based operations, by giving active support and raising venture capital

Fund Size: not available
Founded: 1994
Average Investment: Skr8 million
Minimum Investment: Skr3 million

Investment Criteria: Start-up, Expansion, Mezzanine

Geographic Preference: Sweden (primarily), other Scandinavian countries

Industry Group Preference: All sectors considered

Portfolio Companies: not available

Officers, Executives and Principals

Johan af Klint MBA, Managing Director
Rolf Tedestedt MBA, Venture Capitalist
Erland Roos MBA, Venture Capitalist
Anders Grånäs MBA, Analyst

INDEKON OY
P. O. Box 293
Snellmaninkatu 10
53101 Lappeenranta
Finland

Telephone: 358-53-415-2420
Fax: 358-53-415-2508

Mission: Actively seeking new investments

Fund Size: FM40.8 million
Founded: not available
Average Investment: FM1 million
Minimum Investment: FM100,000

Investment Criteria: Start-up, Expansion, Management Buy-out, Turnaround

Geographic Preference: Finland

Industry Group Preference: All sectors considered

Portfolio Companies: not available

Officers, Executives and Principals

Veli-Matti Kimanen, Managing Director
Education: LLM, MBA (Exec.)

Katriina Lindroos, Financial Manager
Education: MSc in Economics

INDIANOVA (SOCIÉTÉ FINANCIÈRE D'INNOVATION POUR LES INDUSTRIES AGRICOLES ET ALIMENTAIRES)

35 avenue Franklin Roosevelt
75008 Paris
France

Telephone: 33-1-4359-9141
Fax: 33-1-4289-8002

Mission: Actively seeking new investments

Fund Size: Ffr158 million
Founded: not available
Average Investment: not available
Minimum Investment: Ffr200,000

Investment Criteria: All stages

Geographic Preference: France, Worldwide

Industry Group Preference: Agriculture, Biotechnology, Food Processing

Portfolio Companies: not available

Officers, Executives and Principals

Guy Nebot, Managing Director
Jean-Claude Noël
Paul Charrin
Gilles Colinet

INDUSTRIAL DEVELOPMENT BOARD FOR NORTHERN IRELAND

Corporate Finance Division
IDB House
64 Chichester Street
Belfast BT1 4JX
United Kingdom

Telephone: 44-1232-233233
Fax: 44-1232-545000

Mission: Using government funds to help promote industrial development in Northern Ireland

Fund Size: not available
Founded: not available
Average Investment: not available
Minimum Investment: not available

Investment Criteria: Expansion, Management Buy-in, Management Buy-out, Early-stage, Rescue/Turn-around, Seed, Start-up

Geographic Preference: Northern Ireland

Industry Group Preference: Manufacturing and Tradeable Services only

Portfolio Companies: not available

Officers, Executives and Principals

Charles Harding

INDUSTRIAL DEVELOPMENT FUND

Kalkofnsvegi 1
150 Reykjavik
Iceland

Telephone: 354-569-9990
Fax: 354-562-9992
E-mail: idf@ismennt.is

Mission: Actively seeking foreign investments in Iceland and overseas as a state-owned fund

Fund Size: not available
Founded: not available
Average Investment: not available
Minimum Investment: not available

Investment Criteria: All stages

Geographic Preference: Iceland

Industry Group Preference: All sectors considered

Portfolio Companies: not available

Officers, Executives and Principals

Thorvardur Alfonsson

INDUSTRIAL TECHNOLOGY SECURITIES LIMITED

Westminster House
South Park
Gerrards Cross
Buckinghamshire SL9 BHH
United Kingdom

Telephone: 44-1753-885524
Fax: 44-1753-882359
E-mail: jan@indtech.demon.co.uk

Mission: Actively seeking new investments

Fund Size: not available
Founded: not available
Average Investment: £250,000
Minimum Investment: £150,000

Investment Criteria: Expansion, Management Buy-out, Management Buy-in, Seed, Start-up

Geographic Preference: United Kingdom

Industry Group Preference: Biotechnology, Communications, Computer Related, Electronics Related, Energy, Environmental, Industrial Automation, Medical

Portfolio Companies: not available

Officers, Executives and Principals

Jan Berglund
Michael Cohen

INDUSTRIEBANK LIOF NV

Boschstraat 76
P. O. Box 1310
6201 BH Maastricht
The Netherlands

Telephone: 31-43-3220-280
Fax: 31-43-3280-280

Mission: Actively seeking new investments

Fund Size: Ecu38,000
Founded: not available
Average Investment: not available
Minimum Investment: Ecu40,000

Investment Criteria: Start-up, Early-stage, Expansion/Development, Management Buy-out, Management Buy-in

Geographic Preference: The Netherlands

Industry Group Preference: Communications, Consumer Related, Electronics Related, Industrial Automation, Industrial Products, Medical/Health Related, Pollution/Recycling Related

Portfolio Companies: not available

Officers, Executives and Principals

H. F. H. Joosten
F. H. J. Koelman

INDUSTRIE-BETEILIGUNGS GmbH (IBG)

Bockenheimer Landstrasse 10
60323 Frankfurt am Main
Germany

Telephone: 49-69-718-4038
Fax: 49-69-718-2812

Mission: Actively seeking new investments

Fund Size: DM215.1 million
Founded: not available
Average Investment: not available
Minimum Investment: DM5 million

Investment Criteria: Growth, Management Buy-out, Leveraged Buy-out

Geographic Preference: Germany, other German-speaking countries

Industry Group Preference: All sectors considered

Portfolio Companies: not available

Officers, Executives and Principals

Ulrich Fischer
Dr. Klaus Weigel

INDUSTRIFONDEN

Vasagatan 11
P. O. Box 1163
11191 Stockholm
Sweden

Telephone: 46-8-144345
Fax: 46-8-796-7552

Mission: Actively seeking new investments

Fund Size: Skr 2.6 billion
Founded: not available
Average Investment: not available
Minimum Investment: Skr1 million

Investment Criteria: All stages

Geographic Preference: Sweden

Industry Group Preference: All sectors considered

Portfolio Companies: not available

Officers, Executives and Principals

Lars Öjefors, Managing Director
Sten K. Johansson

INDUSTRI KAPITAL SVENSKA AB

Birger Jarlsgatan 2
11434 Stockholm
Sweden

Telephone: 46-8-678-9500
Fax: 46-8-678-0336
E-mail: stockholm@industrikapital.se

Other Office Locations
Industri Kapital AS
Klingenberggaten 7B
0111 Oslo
Norway
Phone 47-22-839055, Fax 47-22-839058

Industri Kapital (Deutschland) GmbH
Alter Wall 34-36
20457 Hamburg
Germany
Phone 49-40-369-8850, Fax 49-40-369-88530

Industri Kapital Limited
Brettenham House
5 Lancaster Place
London WC2E 7EN
United Kingdom
Phone 44-171-304-4300, Fax 44-171-304-4320

Mission: Initiating, structuring and financing management buy-outs of medium-sized and large companies in Scandinavia and elsewhere in northern Europe

Fund Size: Skr4 billion
Founded: 1989
Average Investment: not available
Minimum Investment: Skr40-50 million

Investment Criteria: Management buy-out

Geographic Preference: Sweden, Norway, Denmark, Iceland, Finland, Germany, Belgium, The Netherlands, Luxembourg, France, Austria, Switzerland

Industry Group Preference: All sectors considered

Portfolio Companies: Nobia AB, Addum AB, Amas BV, Ellos Gruppen AB, Lithells AB, Guldfynd Holding AB, Crisplant Industries A/S, Hjem Is Europa A/S, Oxford Aviation AB, AB Nyge Aero Norden, AB Idesta

Officers, Executives and Principals

Björn Saven, Chairman and Chief Executive (Stockholm)
Kim Wahl, Director (Oslo)

Harald Mix, Director (Stockholm)

Christian Lorenzen, Director (Hamburg)

Detlef Dinsel, Director (Hamburg)

Anne Holm Rannaleet, Finance Director (Stockholm)

Gustav Öhman, Director (London)

Michael Rosenlew, Director (Stockholm)

Mads Ryum Larsen, Associate Director (London)

John Blydenstein, Associate (London)

Erik Larsson, Associate (London)

Thomas Ramsay, Associate (Stockholm)

Hans Vanoorbeek, Associate (London)

Stefan Linder, Associate (Stockholm)

Peter Welge, Associate (Hamburg)

INITIATIVE ET FINANCE INVESTISSEMENT

16 rue Chauveau Lagarde
75008 Paris
France

Telephone: 33-1-4266-2700
Fax: 33-1-4266-3033

Mission: Actively seeking new investments

Fund Size: Ffr502 million
Founded: not available
Average Investment: not available
Minimum Investment: Ffr1 million

Investment Criteria: Leveraged Buy-out, Leveraged Buy-in

Geographic Preference: France, Europe

Industry Group Preference: All sectors considered

Portfolio Companies: GSI, Biopat, Erard Lab, CS Laboratoires, Jet Services, Edap, Rousso

Officers, Executives and Principals

Gérard Lesauvage

INNOINVEST PIEMONTE SpA

Via Curtatone 5
10131 Torino
Italy

Telephone: 39-11-660-4041
Fax: 39-11-660- 3333

Mission: Actively seeking new investments

Fund Size: Ecu650,000
Founded: not available
Average Investment: not available
Minimum Investment: not available

Investment Criteria: Seed

Geographic Preference: Italy

Industry Group Preference: All sectors considered

Portfolio Companies: not available

Officers, Executives and Principals

Emanuele Pillitteri

INNOLION

57 rue Saint Roch
75001 Paris
France

Telephone: 33-1-4455-3955
Fax: 33-1-4461-5143

Mission: Actively seeking new investments

Fund Size: Ffr750 million
Founded: not available
Average Investment: not available
Minimum Investment: Ffr500,000

Investment Criteria: All stages

Geographic Preference: France, United States

Industry Group Preference: Biotechnology, Communications, Computer Related, Computer Software, Electronics Related, Medical/Health Related

Portfolio Companies: GemPlus, Pixtech, Chorus, Silmag, US Robotics, Flamel, Biocryst, Créative Bio Molécules

Officers, Executives and Principals

Pierre-Gabriel Vallée

INNOVACOM

23 rue Royale
75008 Paris
France

Telephone: 33-1-4494-1500
Fax: 33-1-4494-1515

Mission: Actively seeking new investments

Fund Size: Ffr380 million
Founded: not available
Average Investment: not available
Minimum Investment: Ffr1 million

Investment Criteria: Start-up, Early-stage, Expansion/Development

Geographic Preference: Canada, France, Germany, United States

Industry Group Preference: Communications, Computer Related, Computer Software, Electronics Related. Information Technology

Portfolio Companies: Business Objects, Arche Communications

Officers, Executives and Principals

Denis Champenois, Managing Director
Jérôme Lecoeur, Partner
Jean-Claude Leveque, Partner
Jacques Meheut, Partner
François Scolan, Partner

INNOVATIONSAGENTUR GmbH

Taborstrasse 10
1020 Vienna
Austria

Telephone: 43-1-216-5293
Fax: 43-1-216-529399
E-mail: innov innovation.co.at

Mission: Promoting the creation of new technology companies

Fund Size: Sch112 million
Founded: 1989
Average Investment: Sch4 million
Minimum Investment: not available

Investment Criteria: Seed, Start-up

Geographic Preference: Austria

Industry Group Preference: Biotechnology, Computer Related, Electronics Related, Medical/Health Related

Portfolio Companies: not available

Officers, Executives and Principals

Helmut G. Dorn, Executive Director
Education: Graduate in Economics, University of Vienna, London School of Economics, Johns Hopkins University in Bologna
Background: Executive Director, Bürges Förderungsbank GmbH

INNOVATIONSKAPITAL I GÖTEBORG AB

P. O. Box 5419
40229 Gothenburg
Sweden

Telephone: 46-31-357558
Fax: 46-31-778-5838
E-mail: staffan@innova kap.se

Mission: Actively seeking new investments

Fund Size: Skr55 million
Founded: 1994
Average Investment: Skr3 million
Minimum Investment: Skr500,000

Investment Criteria: Start-up, Early-stage

Geographic Preference: Sweden

Industry Group Preference: Biotechnology, Computer Related, Computer Software, Electronics Related, Medical/Health Related

Portfolio Companies: Radians Innova, Formex, Pileo Electronics, Samba Sensors, Ivee Development

Officers, Executives and Principals

Staffan Ingeborn, Managing Director
Ulf Corne, Investment Manager

INNOVATRON SMART CARD VENTURES NV

137 boulevard de Séastopol
75002 Paris
France

Telephone: 33-1-4013-3900
Fax: 33-1-4013-3909

Mission: Actively seeking new investments

Fund Size: Ecu10 million
Founded: not available
Average Investment: not available
Minimum Investment: Ecu1.5 million

Investment Criteria: Seed, Start-up, Bridge

Geographic Preference: not available

Industry Group Preference: Communications, Computer Related, Consumer Related, Electronics Related,
  Transportation

Portfolio Companies: not available

Officers, Executives and Principals

Jean Moulin
Guy Grymberg
Roland Moreno

INNOVENTURE EQUITY PARTNERS AG

Gerbergasse 5
8023 Zürich
Switzerland

Telephone: 41-1-211-4171
Fax: 41-1-211-4230

Mission: Actively seeking new investments

Fund Size: not available
Founded: not available
Average Investment: not available
Minimum Investment: Sfr1 million

Investment Criteria: Early-stage, Expansion/Development, Management Buy-out, Replacement/Share Purchases, Turnaround

Geographic Preference: Switzerland, Europe, United States

Industry Group Preference: All sectors considered

Portfolio Companies: not available

Officers, Executives and Principals

Dr. Robert Nussbaum
Hans Wyss
Dr. Hans-Peter Koller

INSTITUT LORRAIN DE PARTICIPATION

24 rue du Pablais
P. O. Box 332
57007 Metz
France

Telephone: 33-8775-9350
Fax: 33-8775-9351

Mission: Actively seeking new investments

Fund Size: Ffr160 million
Founded: not available
Average Investment: not available
Minimum Investment: Ffr200,000

Investment Criteria: All stages

Geographic Preference: France (Lorraine)

Industry Group Preference: All sectors

Portfolio Companies: not available

Officers, Executives and Principals

Claude Coulais

INSTITUTO NACIONAL DE INDUSTRIA - GRUPO SODI

Gr. Empres. de Desarrollo
Pl. Maques de Salamanca 8
28071 Madrid
Spain

Telephone: 34-1-396-1339
Fax: 34-1-575-5641

Mission: Actively seeking new investments

Fund Size: Ecu110 million
Founded: not available
Average Investment: not available
Minimum Investment: Ecu160,000

Investment Criteria: Start-up, Early-stage, Expansion/Development

Geographic Preference: Spain

Industry Group Preference: All sectors considered

Portfolio Companies: not available

Officers, Executives and Principals

Enrique Centelles Echeverria
J.R. Puertas
P. Nalda Condado

INTER-RISCO - SOCIEDADE DE CAPITAL DE RISCO

Av. da Boavista 1180-6B
P. O. Box 1429
4107 Oporto
Portugal

Telephone: 351-2-600-1168
Fax: 351-2-600-1976

Mission: Actively seeking new investments

Fund Size: Ecu12.8 million
Founded: not available
Average Investment: not available
Minimum Investment: Ecu500,000

Investment Criteria: Expansion/Development, Management Buy-out, Management Buy-in, Replacement

Geographic Preference: Portugal

Industry Group Preference: All sectors considered

Portfolio Companies: not available

Officers, Executives and Principals

José Luis Alvares Ribeiro
Artur Santos Silva
Mario Pereira Pinto

INTERCAPITAL INVESTMENTS BV

Northbuilding, Jupiterstraat 248
2132 HK Hoofddorp
The Netherlands

Telephone: 31-23-564-1554
Fax: 31-23-564-0684

Mission: Actively seeking new investments

Fund Size: Ecu40 million
Founded: not available
Average Investment: not available
Minimum Investment: Ecu500,000

Investment Criteria: Early-stage, Expansion/Development, Management Buy-out, Management Buy-in, Turnaround/Restructuring, Bridge

Geographic Preference: Europe

Industry Group Preference: Communications, Computer Related, Electronics Related, Industrial Products, Pollution/Recycling Related, Services

Portfolio Companies: not available

Officers, Executives and Principals

A. H. H. M. Huijgers, Partner
P. A. Schröder, Partner

INTERMEDIATE CAPITAL GROUP PLC

62-63 Threadneedle Street
London EC2R 8HE
United Kingdom

Telephone: 44-171-628-9898
Fax: 44-171-628-2268

Other Office Locations
133 boulevard Haussman
750 Paris
France
Phone 33-1-4495-8686, Fax 33-1-4495-8687

Mission: Actively seeking new investments, with the aim of becoming the leading provider of flexible mezzanine capital in Europe

Fund Size: £400 million
Founded: 1989
Average Investment: £8 million
Minimum Investment: £2 million

Investment Criteria: Bridge, Expansion, Management Buy-in, Management Buy-out, Refinancing Bank Debt, Secondary Purchase/Replacement Capital, Mezzanine

Geographic Preference: Western Europe

Industry Group Preference: All sectors considered except Real Estate

Portfolio Companies: not available

Officers, Executives and Principals

Tom Attwood, Managing Director
Tom Bartlam, Managing Director
Jean-Loup de Gersigny, Managing Director
Andrew Jackson, Managing Director
Paul Piper, Investment Director
Martin Conder, Assistant Director
Simon Morrell, Assistant Director
Andrew Phillips, Assistant Director
Christopher Stacey, Manager
Denis Viet-Jabcobson, Manager
Marcus Wood, Manager

INVESTMENT AB BURE

Massans Gatan 8
P. O. Box 5419
40229 Gothenburg
Sweden

Telephone: 46-31-357635
Fax: 46-31-778-5838

Mission: Actively seeking new investments

Fund Size: Ecu365 million
Founded: not available
Average Investment: not available
Minimum Investment: Ecu500,000

Investment Criteria: Expansion/Development, Early-stage, Replacement, Turnaround/Restructuring

Geographic Preference: Europe

Industry Group Preference: Communications, Computer Related, Medical/Health Related, Services

Portfolio Companies: not available

Officers, Executives and Principals

Ulf Ivarsson

I. P. B. M. (INSTITUT DE PARTICIPATION DU BOIS ET DU MEUBLE)

35 avenue Franklin Roosevelt
75008 Paris
France

Telephone: 33-1-4289-1370
Fax: 33-1-4289-5890

Mission: Actively seeking new investments

Fund Size: Ffr256 million
Founded: not available
Average Investment: not available
Minimum Investment: not available

Investment Criteria: All stages

Geographic Preference: France

Industry Group Preference: Forestry Related

Portfolio Companies: not available

Officers, Executives and Principals

Guy Nebot, Managing Director
André Mairey, Deputy Managing Director
Gilles Colinet
Paul Charrin

I. P. O. (INSTITUT DE PARTICIPATIONS DE L'OUEST)

32 avenue Camus
44000 Nantes
France

Telephone: 33-4035-7531
Fax: 33-4035-2737

Mission: Actively seeking new investments

Fund Size: Ffr650 million
Founded: not available
Average Investment: not available
Minimum Investment: Ffr500,000

Investment Criteria: Start-up, Early-stage, Expansion/Development

Geographic Preference: France

Industry Group Preference: All sectors considered

Portfolio Companies: not available

Officers, Executives and Principals

Philippe Giffard, President
Alain Beriou, Managing Director
François Rouault de la Vigne, Director
Thierry Pastre, Director
Hughes des Garets, Director

I. R. D. I. MIDI-PYRÉNÉES

10 place Alphonse Jourdain
31000
France

Telephone: 33-6121-9900
Fax: 33-6121-9600

Mission: Actively seeking new investments

Fund Size: Ffr362 million
Founded: not available
Average Investment: not available
Minimum Investment: Ffr200,000

Investment Criteria: Early-stage, Expansion/Development

Geographic Preference: France (Midi-Pyrenees Region)

Industry Group Preference: Industry, Services

Portfolio Companies: not available

Officers, Executives and Principals

Bernard Lagorsse, Managing Director
Renaud Du Lac, Investments Manager
François Cavalie, Investments Manager
Bruno De Cambiaire

IRITECH SpA

Piazza della Libertà 20
00192 Rome
Italy

Telephone: 39-6-324-23412
Fax: 39-6-324-2347

Mission: Actively seeking new investments

Fund Size: Ecu25 million
Founded: not available
Average Investment: not available
Minimum Investment: Ecu100,000

Investment Criteria: Seed, Start-up, Early-stage

Geographic Preference: Europe, North America

Industry Group Preference: Energy, Electronics, Pollution and Recycling Related

Portfolio Companies: not available

Officers, Executives and Principals

Alesandro De Dominicis
Giancarlo Tammi

ISEP

Bruul 81
2800 Mechelen
Belgium

Telephone: 32-15-202662
Fax: 32-15- 203709

Mission: Providing venture capital for small and medium-sized enterprises

Fund Size: $20 million
Founded: 1983
Average Investment: $2 million
Minimum Investment: $300,000

Investment Criteria: Early-stage, Expansion/Development, Management buy-out, Bridge, Turnaround / Restructuring

Geographic Preference: Europe

Industry Group Preference: All sectors considered

Portfolio Companies: Aliplast, Theuma, Xeikon

Officers, Executives and Principals

F. Van Overbeke

IVORY AND SIME BARONSMEAD plc

Clerkenwell House
67 Clerkenwell Road
London EC1R 5BH
United Kingdom

Telephone: 44-171-242-4900
Fax: 44-171-242-2048
E-mail: 100043.3035@compuserve.com

Mission: Actively seeking new investments

Fund Size: £160 million
Founded: not available
Average Investment: £2 million
Minimum Investment: £500,000

Investment Criteria: Expansion, Management Buy-in, Management Buy-out, Secondary Purchase/Replacement Capital, Other Early Stage, Turnaround

Geographic Preference: United Kingdom, North America

Industry Group Preference: All sectors considered

Portfolio Companies: FI Group plc, Oasis Stores plc, Stoplock Holdings Ltd, Ridley Quiney and Co Ltd, Ionica

Officers, Executives and Principals

Graham Barnes
Wol Kolade
Lindsay Whitelaw

IVORY AND SIME DEVELOPMENT CAPITAL

1 Charlotte Square
Edinburgh EH2 4DZ
United Kingdom

Telephone: 44-131-225-1357
Fax: 44-131-225-2375

Other Office Locations
1 Angel Court, 14th Floor
Throgmorton Street
London EC2R 7AE
United Kingdom
Phone 44-171-600-6655, Fax 44-171-600-4371

Mission: Actively seeking new investments

Fund Size: not available
Founded: 1985
Average Investment: not available
Minimum Investment: $750,000

Investment Criteria: Second-stage, Special Situations, Refinancing of Small Quotes, Final Round (Pre-listing)

Geographic Preference: not available

Industry Group Preference: Communications, Computer Related, Consumer, Distribution, Electronic Components and Insturmentation, Energy/Natural Resources, Genetic Engineering, Industrial Products and Equipment, Medical/Health Related

Portfolio Companies: not available

Officers, Executives and Principals

Mark Tyndall, Director (London and Edinburgh)
Andrew Steel, Director (Edinburgh)
Richard Muir-Simpson, Senior Investment Manager (Edinburgh)
Lindsay Whitelaw, Investment Manager (Edinburgh)

JAFCO INVESTMENT (U. K.) LIMITED

Nomura House
1 St Martin's-le-Grand
London EC1A 4NP
United Kingdom

Telephone: 44-171-489-8066
Fax: 44-171-248-5070
E-mail: jasonlov@dircon.uk.co

Mission: Actively seeking new investments

Fund Size: £66 million
Founded: 1973
Average Investment: £750,000
Minimum Investment: £200,000

Investment Criteria: All stages

Geographic Preference: Western Europe

Industry Group Preference: Electronics, Healthcare, Information Technology, Life Sciences, Medical Related

Portfolio Companies: not available

Officers, Executives and Principals

Dr. Jason Loveridge
Yasuo Horikoshi
Nobuo Fukuda

JOHNSON AND JOHNSON DEVELOPMENT CORPORATION

Runnymede Malthouse
Runnymede Road
Egham TW20 9BD
United Kingdom

Telephone: 44-1784-497005
Fax: 44-1784-497001

Mission: Actively seeking new investments

Fund Size: not available
Founded: not available
Average Investment: not available
Minimum Investment: not available

Investment Criteria: Seed, Start-up, Other Early Stage

Geographic Preference: Europe, United States

Industry Group Preference: Biotechnology, Medical/Health Related

Portfolio Companies: not available

Officers, Executives and Principals

Dr. Peter Scott

J. P. B. GESTION

36 rue de Mont Thabor
75001 Paris
France

Telephone: 33-1-4260-7278
Fax: 33-1-4296-0312

Mission: Actively seeking new investments

Fund Size: Ffr25 million
Founded: not available
Average Investment: not available
Minimum Investment: not available

Investment Criteria: All stages

Geographic Preference: France

Industry Group Preference: All sectors considered

Portfolio Companies: Jouan, ITI, Bodet, Aplix, Cerep, Malbec, MDA

Officers, Executives and Principals

Jean-Paul Boulan

J. P. MORGAN CAPITAL CORPORATION

60 Victoria Embankment
London EC4Y 0JP
United Kingdom

Telephone: 44-171-325-4899
Fax: 44-171-325-8258

Mission: Actively seeking new investments

Fund Size: not available
Founded: not available
Average Investment: not available
Minimum Investment: Ecu10 million

Investment Criteria: Expansion/Development, Management Buy-out, Management Buy-in

Geographic Preference: Europe, North America

Industry Group Preference: All sectors considered

Portfolio Companies: not available

Officers, Executives and Principals

Philippe M. Costeletos, Partner
Brian T. Murphy, Partner

KAPITALBETEILIGUNGSGESELLSCHAFT FÜR DIE MITTELSTÄNDISCHE WIRTSCHAFT BAYERNS mbH

Königinstrasse 33
80539 Munich
Germany

Telephone: 49-89-2866-840
Fax: 49-89-2866-8444

Mission: Actively seeking new investments in medium-sized companies

Fund Size: DM347 million
Founded: not available
Average Investment: not available
Minimum Investment: DM100,000

Investment Criteria: not available

Geographic Preference: Germany (Bavaria)

Industry Group Preference: All sectors considered

Portfolio Companies: not available

Officers, Executives and Principals

Hartmut Langhorst
Robert Ruf

KAPITALBETEILIGUNGSGESELLSCHAFT FÜR DIE MITTELSTÄNDISCHE WIRTSCHAFT IN NORDRHEIN-WESTFALEN mbH

Hellerbergstrasse 12
41460 Neuss
Germany

Telephone: 49-2131-1070
Fax: 49-2131-107222

Mission: Actively seeking new investments

Fund Size: DM5.9 million
Founded: not available
Average Investment: not available
Minimum Investment: DM100,000

Investment Criteria: Early-stage, Expansion

Geographic Preference: Germany (North Rhine-Westphalia)

Industry Group Preference: Crafts, Manufacturing, Trade

Portfolio Companies: not available

Officers, Executives and Principals

Hans-Herbert Strombeck

KARSLKOGA INVEST AB

69180 Karlskoga
Sweden

Telephone: 46-586-82950
Fax: 46-586-55343

Mission: Actively seeking new investments

Fund Size: Skr90 million
Founded: not available
Average Investment: not available
Minimum Investment: not available

Investment Criteria: All stages

Geographic Preference: Sweden

Industry Group Preference: All sectors considered

Portfolio Companies: not available

Officers, Executives and Principals

Olle Johansson, Managing Director
Ruben Alverblad

KBL FOUNDER SA

43 Boulevard Royal
2955 Luxembourg
Luxembourg

Telephone: 352-4797-2280
Fax: 352-4797-2822

Mission: Actively seeking new investments

Fund Size: Ecu17 million
Founded: not available
Average Investment: not available
Minimum Investment: Ecu50,000

Investment Criteria: Start-up, Expansion/Development

Geographic Preference: Europe, Germany

Industry Group Preference: Biotechnology, Communications, Computer Related, Computer Software, Electronics Related, Energy, Medical/Health Related

Portfolio Companies: not available

Officers, Executives and Principals

E. Bonnie
J. Weynandt

KELLOCK LIMITED

Abbey Gardens
4 Abbey Street
Reading RG1 3BA
United Kingdom

Telephone: 44-1734-585511
Fax: 44-1734-502480

Mission: Providing cashflow finance to a variety of companies

Fund Size: not available
Founded: not available
Average Investment: £250,000-£2 million
Minimum Investment: £50,000

Investment Criteria: Expansion, Refinancing Bank Debt, Rescue/Turnaround, Seed, Start-up

Geographic Preference: United Kingdom

Industry Group Preference: Computer Related, Distribution, Electronics Related, Industrial Products and Services, Manufacturing, Printing

Portfolio Companies: not available

Officers, Executives and Principals

Russell Warner
Robert Whittaker
Richard Ingoldby
Philip Murray
Sean Butler
Ben Allen

KERA LIMITED

P. O. Box 1127
Haapaniemenkatu 40
70111 Kuopio
Finland

Telephone: 358-20-46011
Fax: 358-20-460-3240

Mission: Actively seeking new investments

Fund Size: not available
Founded: not available
Average Investment: not available
Minimum Investment: not available

Investment Criteria: Start-up, Early-stage, Expansion/Development

Geographic Preference: Finland

Industry Group Preference: Communications, Computer Related, Computer Software, Electronics Related, Industrial Products

Portfolio Companies: not available

Officers, Executives and Principals

Leo Houtsonen, Partner
Jukka Suokas

KK RESEARCH AG/ KK TRUST AG

Grobenstrasse 32
6301 Zug
Switzerland

Telephone: 41-1-251-9020
Fax: 41-1-251-7669

Mission: Actively seeking new investments

Fund Size: not available
Founded: not available
Average Investment: not available
Minimum Investment: not available

Investment Criteria: Expansion/Development, Management Buy-out, Replacement/Share Purchases

Geographic Preference: Switzerland

Industry Group Preference: All sectors considered

Portfolio Companies: not available

Officers, Executives and Principals

Helga Kern
Günter R. Käser

K. L. B. INVESTMENT COMPANY, LIMITED

15-15 Yoido-dong
Youngdeungpo-ku
Seoul 150-010
Korea

Telephone: 82-2-783-2925
Fax: 82-2-783-2069

Mission: Actively seeking new investments

Fund Size: not available
Founded: 1990
Average Investment: not available
Minimum Investment: $100,000

Investment Criteria: Second-stage, Mezzanine

Geographic Preference: not available

Industry Group Preference: Communications, Computer Related, Consumer, Distribution, Electronic Components and Instrumentation, Energy/Natural Resources, Genetic Engineering, Industrial Products and Equipment, Medical/Health Related

Portfolio Companies: not available

Officers, Executives and Principals

Chang-Ki Min, President and Chief Executive Officer
Young-Keun Kang, Vice President and Director
B.S. Cho, Senior Investment Officer
J.S. Jung, Senior Investment Officer
T.E. Park, Senior Investment Officer

KLEINWORT BENSON DEVELOPMENT CAPITAL LIMITED

10 Fenchurch Street
London EC3M 3LB
United Kingdom

Telephone: 44-171-956-6600
Fax: 44-171-626-8616
E-mail: kbdc@kben.co.uk

Mission: Actively seeking new investments

Fund Size: £150 million
Founded: 1980
Average Investment: £3 million - £7 million
Minimum Investment: £400,000

Investment Criteria: Expansion, Management Buy-in, Management Buy-out, Refinancing Bank Debt, Rescue/Turnaround, Secondary Purchase/Replacement Capital

Geographic Preference: United Kingdom, Western Europe

Industry Group Preference: All sectors considered

Portfolio Companies: Discovery Inns, Kennedys Garden Centres, London and Henley, Cintex

Officers, Executives and Principals

Barry Dean, Managing Director
Background: venture capitalist since 1976; director of companies in engineering, information technology, healthcare, marketing, design, retail

Ian Grant
Background: considerable experience as a deal maker and company director in consumer goods, leisure, services, real estate

Richard Green
Background: Chartered Accountant and Corporate Financier; company director and deal maker in leisure, consumer goods, engineering, manufacturing

Emyr Hughes
Background: venture capitalist for more than 20 years; company director and deal maker, especially for privatizations and employee buy-outs, in retail, manufacturing, distribution

Andrew Hartley
Background: 3i plc; extensive experience in computers, communications, electronics, manufacturing, transportation

Jane Bloor
Background: Kleinwort Benson, Chicago; company director in retail and engineering

Philip Conboy
Background: Kleinwort Benson Corporate Finance; deal maker in engineering, manufacturing, real estate

Patricia Toner
Background: Coopers and Lybrand

Sebastian McKinlay
Education: BSc, London School of Economics

KLEINWORT BENSON MEZZANINE CAPITAL

20 Fenchurch Street
London EC3P 3DB
United Kingdom

Telephone: 44-171-956-5139
Fax: 44-171-626-3933

Mission: Actively seeking new investments

Fund Size: £200 million
Founded: not available
Average Investment: £7 million
Minimum Investment: £2 million

Investment Criteria: Bridge, Expansion, Management Buy-in, Management Buy-out, Refinancing Bank Debt, Secondary Purchase/Replacement Capital

Geographic Preference: Western Europe

Industry Group Preference: All sectors considered

Portfolio Companies: Glass's Guide, MediMedia International, Scotia Pharmaceuticals, Quadramatic, Franklin Hotels

Officers, Executives and Principals

Erik Linnes, Partner
Martin Stringfellow, Partner
Simon Wakefield, Partner
Christopher Howe, Partner
Richard Collins, Partner
Kevin Murphy, Partner

KONSORTIUM AG UNTERNEHMENSBETEILIGUNGSGESELLSCHAFT STUTTGART

Haussmannstrasse 32
70188 Stuttgart
Germany

Telephone: 49-711-242388
Fax: 49-711-2360514

Mission: Actively seeking new investments

Fund Size: DM17 million
Founded: not available
Average Investment: not available
Minimum Investment: DM500,000

Investment Criteria: All stages

Geographic Preference: Germany (Southern region)

Industry Group Preference: All sectors considered

Portfolio Companies: not available

Officers, Executives and Principals

Heinz Schmolke
Frank Lamprecht

KOREA DEVELOPMENT INVESTMENT FINANCE CORPORATION (KDIFC)

4th Floor, Handock B/D
735, Yeoksam-dong
Kangnam-ku
Seoul 135-081
Korea

Telephone: 82-2-538-2411/5
Fax: 82-2-538-1583
E-mail: ygyun@tggroup.trigem.co.kr

Mission: Seeking to become one of the best venture capital companies in Asia by specializing in investments in telecommunications

Fund Size: W62,600 million
Founded: 1982
Average Investment: W700 million
Minimum Investment: W300 million

Investment Criteria: Early-stage, Mezzanine, Late-stage

Geographic Preference: Korea, Southeast Asia, United States

Industry Group Preference: Computer Software, Electronic Components and Instrumentation, Telecommunications

Portfolio Companies: Shinsung ENG Co., Ltd., Hi-tron Systems Inc., Sam Woo Co., Ltd., Joowha Ind. Co., Ltd., Naray Mobile Telecommunication Co., Ltd., Telson Electronics Co., Ltd., Dooin Electronics Co., Ltd., Dongmyoung Electric Co., Ltd., Clean Creative Co., Ltd., I-Net Technologies, Inc., Solvit Co., Ltd., Cybertek Holdings Co., Ltd., Ko-tech Co., Ltd., Hanscom Co., Ltd., others

Officers, Executives and Principals

Yeo-Gyeong Yun, President and Chief Executive Officer
Education: BSc in Economics, Utah State University; MS in Industrial Economics, Purdue University
Background: Northern Illinois Gas Co.; Korea Institute of Science and Technology; Korea Technology Advancement Corporation (K-TAC)
Directorship: Vice Chairman (Vice President), Korea Institute of Science and Technology

Duck-Bong Park, Executive Vice President
Education: Graduate in Business Administration, Pusan National University
Background: Dongkuk Steel Mill Co., Ltd.; Chin Yang

Sung-Shin Kwak, Executive Vice President
Education: BS in Business Administration and MBA, Seoul National University; MBA, Harvard University
Background: Korea Exchange Bank; accounting manager, Kukje Corporation; member, Korea Institute of Certified Public Accountants

Hyun-Suk Chai, Senior Manager, Venture Capital Division
Education: BS and MS in Electronics, Korea University
Background: Oriental Precision Co.; Samsung Electronics

Young-Il Kim, Senior Manager, Financing Division
Education: BS in Business Administration and MBA, Seoul National University
Background: San Tong and Co., Certified Public Accountants; Daeyoo Securities; member, Korea Institute of
  Certified Public Accountants

Byung-Ryul Lim, Senior Manager, Mergers and Acquisitions Division
Education: Graduate, Yonsei University
Background: Korea Chamber of Commerce and Industry

Seung-Chul Lee, Senior Manager, Planning and Administration Division
Education: BS in Business Administration and MBA, Seoul National University
Background: Sam Il Accounting Firm; Shin Young Securities; member, Korea Institute of Certified Public
  Accountants

KOREA TECHNOLOGY FINANCE CORPORATION

43 Insa-dong
Jongro-ku
Seoul 110-290
Korea

Telephone: 82-2-739-5411
Fax: 82-2-739-7266

Other Office Locations
44-1, 2-ga, Jungang-dong
Jung-ku
Pusan 600-012
Phone 82-51-245-1375, Fax 82-51-242-5459

83, 2-ga, Seomun-ro
Jung-ku
Taegu 700-252
Phone 82-53-254-4418, Fax 82-53-254-4420

133, 5-ga, Keumnam-ro
Dong-ku
Kwangju 501-025
Phone 82-62-226-5410, Fax 82-62-228-5402

Mission: Actively seeking new investments

Fund Size: not available
Founded: 1984
Average Investment: not available
Minimum Investment: $500,000

Investment Criteria: Research and Development, Mezzanine

Geographic Preference: not available

Industry Group Preference: Communications, Computer Related, Consumer, Electronic Components and Instrumentation, Energy/Natural Resources, Genetic Engineering, Industrial Products and Equipment, Medical/Health Related

Portfolio Companies: not available

Officers, Executives and Principals

Yong Sang Song, President and Chief Executive Officer
Shin Kyu Choi, Senior Vice President

KREDITANSTALT FÜR WIEDERAUFBAU (KFW)

Palmengartenstrasse 5-9
60325 Frankfurt am Main
Germany

Telephone: 49-69-74310
Fax: 49-69-7431-2944

Other Office Locations
Charlottenstrasse 33/33a
10117 Berlin
Telephone 49-30-202-640, Fax 49-30-202-64188

Mission: Actively seeking new investments

Fund Size: DM1.13 billion
Founded: not available
Average Investment: not available
Minimum Investment: not available

Investment Criteria: All stages

Geographic Preference: Germany, Central and Eastern Europe

Industry Group Preference: All sectors considered

Portfolio Companies: not available

Officers, Executives and Principals

Rudolf Klein
Dr. Heinrich Harries
Hans W. Reich
Dr. Manfred Schüler
Dr. Gert Vogt
Dr. Friedrich Voss

KUBOTA CORPORATION

1-2-47 Shikitsu-higashi
Naniwa-ku
Osaka 556
Japan

Telephone: 81-6-648-2111
Fax: 81-6-648-3862

Mission: not available

Fund Size: $6.8 billion
Founded: not available
Average Investment: not available
Minimum Investment: not available

Investment Criteria: not available

Geographic Preference: not available

Industry Group Preference: Agricultural Equipment, Cement Roofing, Iron Piping

Portfolio Companies: Mycogen

Officers, Executives and Principals

Shigekazu Mino, President

LA FINANCIÈRE DE BRIENNE

2 place Rio de Janeiro
75362 Paris
France

Telephone: 33-1-4495-2961
Fax: 33-1-4495-2969

Mission: Actively seeking new investments, specializing in aeronautics and defense industries

Fund Size: Ffr100 million
Founded: 1993
Average Investment: not available
Minimum Investment: Ffr3 million

Investment Criteria: Early-stage, Expansion/Development

Geographic Preference: France

Industry Group Preference: Aeronautics, Computer Related, Computer Software, Electronics Related, Industrial Products

Portfolio Companies: not available

Officers, Executives and Principals

Thierry Letailleur

LANCASHIRE ENTERPRISES plc

Enterprise House
17 Ribblesdale Place
Winckley Square
Preston
Lancashire PR1 3NA
United Kingdom

Telephone: 44-1772-203020
Fax: 44-1772-880697

Mission: Actively seeking new investments

Fund Size: £15 million
Founded: not available
Average Investment: £150,000
Minimum Investment: £2,000

Investment Criteria: Expansion, Management Buy-in, Management Buy-out, Early-stage, Refinancing Bank Debt, Secondary Purchase/Replacement Capital, Seed, Start-up

Geographic Preference: United Kingdom (Northwestern England)

Industry Group Preference: All sectors considered

Portfolio Companies: Crown Eyeglass plc, Mass Transfer International Ltd, Result 2000 plc, TBS Cygma plc, Computer Collection Systems Ltd

Officers, Executives and Principals

David Hall
Douglas Stellman
Jack Sutcliffe
Eric Tung
Mark Shields
Gordon Harter
Deborah Heyes

LARPENT NEWTON AND COMPANY LIMITED

4th Floor, 24-26 Baltic Street West
London EC1Y 0UL
United Kingdom

Telephone: 44-171-251-9111
Fax: 44-171-251-2609

Mission: Actively seeking new investments in industries which are innovative, produce internationally trade-able goods and/or services, and operate in growing and/or changing markets

Fund Size: £70 million
Founded: not available
Average Investment: not available
Minimum Investment: £250,000

Investment Criteria: Expansion, Early-stage, Start-up

Geographic Preference: United Kingdom (within 2 hours' drive of London)

Industry Group Preference: not available

Portfolio Companies: Biotal Ltd, Surrey Medical Imaging Systems Ltd, TLS PLC, Bensons Crisps PLC

Officers, Executives and Principals

Charles Breese
David Smart

LAS AMERICAS ADMINISTRADORO DE FONDOS DE INVERSION

Miraflores No. 249, 6th Floor
Santiago
Chile

Telephone: 56-2-633-7812
Fax: 56-2-639-3748

Mission: Actively seeking new investments

Fund Size: $45 million
Founded: 1992
Average Investment: $5 million
Minimum Investment: $1 million

Investment Criteria: Seed, Start-up, Special Situations

Geographic Preference: Latin America, especially Chile

Industry Group Preference: Communications, Computer Related, Consumer, Distribution, Electronic Components and Instrumentation, Energy/Natural Resources, Genetic Engineering, Industrial Products and Equipment, Medical/Health Related

Portfolio Companies: Infraestructura 2000, EFO SA, Camino de la Madera, Concesionaria Chucumata

Officers, Executives and Principals

Carlos Alberto Délano Abbott, President
Horacio Peña Novoa, General Manager
Hector Mauricio Avila, Venture Manager

LAZARD VENTURES

21 Moorfields
London EC2P 2HT
United Kingdom

Telephone: 44-171-588-2721
Fax: 44-171-638-2141

Mission: Actively seeking new investments

Fund Size: not available
Founded: 1969
Average Investment: not available
Minimum Investment: $500,000

Investment Criteria: Expansion, Management Buy-in, Management Buy-out, Secondary Purchase/Replacement Capital

Geographic Preference: United Kingdom

Industry Group Preference: All sectors considered

Portfolio Companies: UIG, Parkwood Holdings, Futurestar, Rollers (UK)

Officers, Executives and Principals

Tom Glucklich, Chief Executive Officer
Charles Cox, Director
Mark Hawkesworth, Director

LBB SEED CAPITAL FUND GmbH BERLIN

Bundesallee 184/185
10717 Berlin
Germany

Telephone: 49-30-853-1029
Fax: 49-30-854-4617

Mission: Actively seeking new investments

Fund Size: Ecu5 million
Founded: 1990
Average Investment: Ecu200,000
Minimum Investment: Ecu100,000

Investment Criteria: Seed, Start-up, Early-stage

Geographic Preference: Germany

Industry Group Preference: Communications, Computer Related, Computer Software, Electronics Related, Industrial Automation, Medical/Health Related

Portfolio Companies: not available

Officers, Executives and Principals

Roger Bendisch, General Manager
Wolfgang Radszuweit, General Manager

LBO FRANCE

1 rue François 1 er
75008 Paris
France

Telephone: 33-1-4235-0021
Fax: 33-1-4561-0064

Mission: Actively seeking new investments

Fund Size: not available
Founded: not available
Average Investment: not available
Minimum Investment: Negotiable

Investment Criteria: Leveraged Buy-out

Geographic Preference: Europe

Industry Group Preference: All sectors considered

Portfolio Companies: not available

Officers, Executives and Principals

Elisabeth Amsellem
Gilles Cahen-Salvador
Jean-Daniel Camus
Robert Daussun
Daniel Janin
Guy Van der Mensbrugghe

LEBON DÉVELOPPEMENT

14 rue de Prony
75017 Paris
France

Telephone: 33-1-4429-9823
Fax: 33-1-4622-8686

Mission: Actively seeking new investments

Fund Size: Ffr240 million
Founded: not available
Average Investment: not available
Minimum Investment: Ffr5 million

Investment Criteria: Leveraged Buy-out, Leveraged Buy-in

Geographic Preference: France

Industry Group Preference: Industrial Products and Services

Portfolio Companies: not available

Officers, Executives and Principals

Jean-Yves Latombe, Managing Director

LEGAL AND GENERAL VENTURES LIMITED
Temple Court
11 Queen Victoria Street
London EC4N 8EL
United Kingdom

Telephone: 44-171-489-1888
Fax: 44-171-528-6444

Other Office Locations
Legal and General Ventures SA
28 boulevard Malesherbes
75008 Paris
France
Phone 33-1-4312-9110, Fax 33-1-4312-9111

LGV-Candover GmbH
Kaiserstrasse 10
60311 Frankfurt am Main
Germany
Phone 49-69-2998-770, Fax 49-69-2998-7777

Mission: Actively seeking new investments

Fund Size: £325 million
Founded: 1988
Average Investment: not available
Minimum Investment: £1 million

Investment Criteria: Expansion, Management Buy-in, Management Buy-out, Secondary Purchase/Replacement Capital. Infrastructure Project Financing

Geographic Preference: Western Europe

Industry Group Preference: All sectors considered

Portfolio Companies: Coal Products Holding Ltd, IPT Ltd, Golden Wonder, Hay Hall Group Ltd, Tally GmbH

Officers, Executives and Principals

Charles Peal, Chief Executive
Roger Charlesworth, Marketing Director
Eric Cooper, Managing Director
Adrian Johnson, Managing Director
Ian Taylor, Managing Director
Ron Bell, Finance Director

LF EUROPE (LFE)

Preuscamp 12
7822 Meslin
Belgium

Telephone: 32-68-250-230
Fax: 32-68-552-602

Mission: Making equity investments, entering into joint ventures, and providing management and financial services as the European investment arm of Li and Fung Limited of Hong Kong, focusing on European companies with strong management teams, established distribution channels, products that would lend themselves to overseas manufacturing, potential to grow beyond sales of $2 million, and capacity to realize high growth and profitability by sourcing products from East Asia

Fund Size: not available
Founded: not available
Average Investment: $1 million
Minimum Investment: $200,000

Investment Criteria: First-stage, Second-stage

Geographic Preference: Europe

Industry Group Preference: Apparel, Fashion Accessories, Giftware, Houseware, Promotional Items, Shoes and Bags, Sporting Goods, Toys

Portfolio Companies: not available

Officers, Executives and Principals

Dr. Victor Fung, Chairman, Li and Fung Limited
Education: BS and MS, Massachusetts Institute of Technology; PhD, Harvard University
Background: Assistant Professor, Harvard Business School; Planning Officer, Citibank, New York
Directorships: Chairman, Prudential Asia and Transtech Inc.

William Fung, Group Managing Director, Li and Fung Limited
Education: BA, Princeton University; MBA, Harvard Business School
Directorships: Member, Hong Kong Trade Development Council and Textile Advisory Board

Philippe Ullens, Managing Partner, LFE
Education: Graduate in Management, University of Louvain; MBA, Harvard Business School
Background: Head of the Fencing Division, Bekaert; Manager, Boston Consulting Group, Paris
Directorships: Director of several small and medium-sized Belgian companies

Paolo Pellizzari, Managing Partner, LFE
Education: Graduate in Civil Engineering, University of Louvain; MBA, INSEAD, France
Background: Kiel, New Hampshire; Consultant, Boston Consulting Group, Paris; Chief Executive Officer, Neuhaus, Belgium
Directorships: Chief Executive Officer, Inducolor, Belgium

L. I. C. A. DEVELOPMENT CAPITAL LIMITED

102 Jermyn Street
London SW1Y 6EE
United Kingdom

Telephone: 44-171-839-7707
Fax: 44-171-839-4363

Mission: Actively seeking new investments

Fund Size: £20 million
Founded: 1991
Average Investment: £1 million
Minimum Investment: £350,000

Investment Criteria: Expansion, Management Buy-in, Management Buy-out, Refinancing Bank Debt, Rescue/Turnaround

Geographic Preference: United Kingdom

Industry Group Preference: Automotive, Chemical and Materials, Communications, Consumer Related, Electronics Related, Environmental, Industrial Automation, Industrial Products and Services, Leisure, Manufacturing, Media, Publishing, Transport

Portfolio Companies: LICA-Carden Limited, B.S.T. Batteries Limited, Double-Axial Wave-Drive Limited, Parkwood Engineering, Planet Ice

Officers, Executives and Principals

Stephen Hill
John Salkeld

LIGUR SEED CAPITAL

c/o Filse SpA
Via Peschiera 16
16122 Genoa
Italy

Telephone: 39-10-8318-891
Fax: 39-10-814919

Mission: Actively seeking new investments

Fund Size: not available
Founded: not available
Average Investment: not available
Minimum Investment: Ecu14,000

Investment Criteria: Seed, Start-up

Geographic Preference: Europe

Industry Group Preference: All sectors considered

Portfolio Companies: not available

Officers, Executives and Principals

Marco Bernocchi
Guido Testa

LIMBURGSE PARTICIPATIE-MAATSCHAPPIJ

Guffenslaan 9
P.O Box 2
3500 Hasselt
Belgium

Telephone: 32-11-222177
Fax: 32-11-221921

Mission: Actively seeking new investments

Fund Size: Ecu126 million
Founded: not available
Average Investment: not available
Minimum Investment: Ecu7.5 million

Investment Criteria: Seed, Start-up, Early-stage, Expansion/Development, Management buy-out, Management Buy-in, Bridge

Geographic Preference: Belgium

Industry Group Preference: All sectors considered

Portfolio Companies: not available

Officers, Executives and Principals

Bernard Martens, Partner
Guido Quanten, Partner

LLOYDS DEVELOPMENT CAPITAL LIMITED

50 Grosvenor Street
London W1X 9FH
United Kingdom

Telephone: 44-171-499-1500
Fax: 44-171-647-2000

Other Office Locations
60 Church Street
Birminghan
Phone 44-1210-200-1787, Fax 44-121-236-5269

6/7 Park Row
Leeds
Phone 44-113-244-1001, Fax 44-113-242-1822

Mission: Actively seeking new investments

Fund Size: £150 million
Founded: 1981
Average Investment: £1-£3 million
Minimum Investment: £500,000

Investment Criteria: All stages except Seed, Start-up, Early Stage, Purchase of Quoted Shares

Geographic Preference: United Kingdom

Industry Group Preference: All sectors considered except Real Estate

Portfolio Companies: Deltron Electronics Ltd, JBA Holdings plc, Silk Industries Ltd, Page Aerospace Ltd, PMI Ltd

Officers, Executives and Principals

M. W. Joseph, Managing Director
P. Sellers
C. John
S. Veale
D. Eales
J. Dillon
N. Bacon
S. Rhodes
A. Ball
P. Lane
B. Dale

LMBO FINANCE

4 rue de la Paix
75002 Paris
France

Telephone: 33-1-4703-6868
Fax: 33-1-4703-6869

Mission: Actively seeking new investments

Fund Size: Ffr105 million
Founded: not available
Average Investment: not available
Minimum Investment: Ffr1 million

Investment Criteria: Management Buy-out, Leveraged Buy-out

Geographic Preference: France

Industry Group Preference: All sectors considered

Portfolio Companies: AEES, Bertin, Distillerie du Périgord, Domaine de Chastelet, Frameto, Média Cosmos, Rhodia, SFIS, Gaillard Rondino, Stabi, Testas, Télémagazine, Patrimoine Management Technologies

Officers, Executives and Principals

Gérard Favarel
Thierry Blondel
Annie Riss
Jean-Claude Sirop
Jacques Vachelard
Anne Vuillet

LONDON VENTURES (FUND MANAGERS) LIMITED

14 Grosvenor Crescent
London SW1X 7EE
United Kingdom

Telephone: 44-171-316-1010
Fax: 44-171-316-1001

Mission: Actively seeking new investments

Fund Size: £1.4 million
Founded: not available
Average Investment: £73,000
Minimum Investment: £5,000

Investment Criteria: Expansion, Management Buy-in, Management Buy-out, Early Stage, Seed, Start-up

Geographic Preference: United Kingdom (Greater London only)

Industry Group Preference: Communications, Computer Related, Consumer Related, Environmental, Industrial Automation, Industrial Products and Services, Leisure, Manufacturing, Media, Medical Related, Services

Portfolio Companies: SMi Ltd, Metro Publishing Limited, Douglas Plating Limited, Soro Products Limited

Officers, Executives and Principals

James Orman
Leo Dunne

LOTHIAN ENTERPRISE LIMITED

21 Ainslie Place
Edinburgh EH3 6AJ
United Kingdom

Telephone: 44-131-220-2100
Fax: 44-131-225-2658

Mission: Providing investment for local companies, in order to develop the economy of the region, as the venture capital arm of Lothian Regional Council

Fund Size: £4.6 million
Founded: not available
Average Investment: £150,000
Minimum Investment: £10,000

Investment Criteria: Expansion, Management Buy-in, Management Buy-out, Early Stage, Seed, Start-up

Geographic Preference: Scotland (Lothian region)

Industry Group Preference: All sectors considered except Real Estate and Retail

Portfolio Companies: The Edinburgh Press Ltd, Ascada Ltd, Charles Kelly Ltd, Watershed Systems Ltd

Officers, Executives and Principals

Kathy Greenwood
Dallas Milne
Jeremy Hayward

LOXKO VENTURE MANAGERS LIMITED

Alton House
174-177 High Holborn
London WC1V 7AA
United Kingdom

Telephone: 44-171-240-5024
Fax: 44-171-379-8030

Mission: Actively seeking new investments

Fund Size: £2 million
Founded: not available
Average Investment: £210,000
Minimum Investment: Open

Investment Criteria: All stages

Geographic Preference: Western Europe

Industry Group Preference: Chemical and Materials, Construction, Energy, Environmental, Financial Services, Industrial Automation, Industrial Products and Services, Manufacturing, Medical Related, Services, Transport

Portfolio Companies: Transintech Ltd

Officers, Executives and Principals

Reg Clark

MALMÖHUS INVEST AB (MIAB)

Studentgatan 6
21138 Malmö
Sweden

Telephone: 46-40-73680
Fax: 46-40-611-1843

Other Office Locations
Mässansgata 8
41251 Gothenburg
Phone 46-31-874450, Fax 46-31-812455

Mission: Working as an active partner in small and medium-sized high-technology companies with development potential

Fund Size: Skr150 million
Founded: 1979
Average Investment: Skr2 - 5 million
Minimum Investment: Skr500,000

Investment Criteria: Seed

Geographic Preference: Sweden (Southern region)

Industry Group Preference: High Technology, Medical/Health Related

Portfolio Companies: Agrovision AB, Barrkeryds Maskin AB, BioSys AB, Envifront AB, FAS Machinery International AB, Frigadon AB, Glimek AB, Heatex AB, Jetline AB, Lamitec Tools AB, Mecatron AB, Metimur AB, Neos Robotics AB, Ni-Me- Hydrid AB, OMC Systems AB, Opsis AB, Pascal Medical AB, Prisonex AB, Reologica Instruments AB, Safir Software AB, SPT Plasmateknik AB, Time Space Radio AB, Wilnor AB, Xena Audio AB

Officers, Executives and Principals

Håkan Nelson, Executive Director (Malmö)
Education: Bachelor of Economics, University of Lund
Background: PK-Banken; Regional Development Fund

Nils Homann, Investment Manager (Malmö)
Education: MBA, University of Gothenburg
Background: Regional Development Fund; PK-Banken; Göta-Banken; Finansskandic; Industrikredit

Henrik Ljung, Controller and Investment Manager (Malmö)
Education: MBA, University of Lund; CPA
Background: KPMG Bohlins; Höganäs AB

Anna Christerson, Company Lawyer and Investment Manager (Malmö)
Education: MBA, LLM, Universities of Lund, Copenhagen, Rovaniemi
Background: Maloney and Burch, Washington DC; Trelleborg Industries AB; District Courts

Susanne Surhammar, Company Secretary (Malmö)
Education: Secretarial school; fluent in English
Background: Axel-Johnsson LAB System AB; Nyman Schultz AB; Brankato AB

Carl-Axel Edwardsson, Investment Manager (Gothenburg)
Education: Bachelor of Economics, University of Lund
Background: Hogia, Regional Development Fund

MARCEAU INVESTISSEMENTS

10-12 avenue de Messine
75008 Paris
France

Telephone: 33-1-4074-2525
Fax: 33-1-4074-2500

Mission: Actively seeking new investments

Fund Size: Ffr2 billion
Founded: not available
Average Investment: not available
Minimum Investment: Ffr30 million

Investment Criteria: Turnaround/Restructuring

Geographic Preference: Europe

Industry Group Preference: All sectors considered

Portfolio Companies: not available

Officers, Executives and Principals

Isabelle Poix-Daude

MARCH INVESTMENT FUNDS

Telegraphic House
Waterfront Quay
Salford Quays
Manchester M5 2XW
United Kingdom

Telephone: 44-161-872-3676
Fax: 44-161-848-0181
E-mail: richardm@jsb.co.uk

Mission: Actively seeking new investments

Fund Size: £4 million
Founded: not available
Average Investment: £800,000
Minimum Investment: £100,000

Investment Criteria: Expansion, Management Buy-in, Management Buy-out, Refinancing Bank Debt, Rescue/Turnaround, Secondary Purchase/Replacement Capital

Geographic Preference: United Kingdom (Northwestern England)

Industry Group Preference: All sectors considered

Portfolio Companies: A1 Security and Electrical Ltd., James North Footwear Ltd., Bulldog Tools Ltd., JSB Computer Systems Ltd., Woodland Pottery Holdings Ltd.

Officers, Executives and Principals

Richard Marshall
Tony Allen

MATKAILUNKEHITYS NORDIA OY

P. O. Box 255
Vuorikatu 18
00101 Helsinki
Finland

Telephone: 358-20460-3508
Fax: 358-20460-3505
E-mail: pasi.koppinen@nordia.fi

Other Office Locations
Sepönkatu 4
40100 Jyväskylä
Phone 358-20460-2260, Fax 358-20460-2297, E-Mail tuula.paananen@nordia.fi

Mission: Actively seeking new investments as a subsidiary of Kera Oy

Fund Size: FM62 million
Founded: 1989
Average Investment: FM2.4 million
Minimum Investment: FM1 million

Investment Criteria: Turnaround

Geographic Preference: Finland

Industry Group Preference: Tourism

Portfolio Companies: Bomba-Lomat Oy, Kittilän Kehitysyhtiö Oy, Kolin Hissi Oy, Kuusamon Tropiikki Oy, Lomakeskus Saimaanranta Oy, Olostunturi Oy, Saariselän Tunturihotellit Oy, Tunturikiinteistöt Oy, Ylläs-Ski Oy Finland

Officers, Executives and Principals

Ritva Korhonen, MSc (Econ), Managing Director
Tuula Paananen, Director
Pasi Koppinen, Assistant
Esko Tikka (Regional Manager, Kera Oy), Director
Eero Ahola (Vice President, Finnair), Director
Kalle J. Korhonen (Head of Division, Ministry of Trade and Industry), Director
Yrjö Pekka Kurki (Managing Director, Lappland Travel), Director
Pauli Lievonen (Head of Development, Kera Oy), Director
Pirjo-Riitta Vatanen (Director General, MEK), Director
Kari Österlund (Managing Director, Hasse Travel), Director
Veikko Niminen, LLM (Tietolaki Oy), Company Secretary

MAXUS CAPITAL AB

Linnégatan 6
11447 Stockholm
Sweden

Telephone: 46-8-667-2330
Fax: 46-8-661-2124
E-mail: magnus.wahlbaeck@maxcap.se

Mission: Actively seeking new investments

Fund Size: not available
Founded: not available
Average Investment: not available
Minimum Investment: Skr2 million

Investment Criteria: Management Buy-out, Expansion/Development

Geographic Preference: Denmark, Finland, Iceland, Norway, Sweden

Industry Group Preference: All sectors considered

Portfolio Companies: not available

Officers, Executives and Principals

Magnus Wahlbäck, Managing Director
Knut Gangstad, Deputy Managing Director

MB CORPORATE FINANCE LTD

P. O. Box 165
Fabianinkatu 23
00131 Helsinki
Finland

Telephone: 358-9-131-011
Fax: 358-9-1310-1310

Mission: Actively seeking new investments

Fund Size: FM86 million
Founded: not available
Average Investment: not available
Minimum Investment: FM3 million

Investment Criteria: Expansion, Buy-out, Bridge

Geographic Preference: Nordic countries, European Union

Industry Group Preference: All sectors considered

Portfolio Companies: not available

Officers, Executives and Principals

Juhani Suomela, MSc (Econ), Managing Director
Pekka Hietaniemi, MSc (Eng), MSc (Econ), General Manager
Matti Mertsola, MSc (Eng), General Manager
Kari Rytkönen, LLM, General Manager
Pekka Sunila, MSc (Eng), MSc (Econ), General Manager

MEDICAL VENTURE MANAGEMENT

Holmensgate 4, P. O. Box 1387 Vika
0114 Oslo
Norway

Telephone: 47-2-283-8607
Fax: 47-2-283-5766

Mission: Actively seeking new investments

Fund Size: not available
Founded: 1989
Average Investment: not available
Minimum Investment: not available

Investment Criteria: Seed, Startup, First-stage, Second-stage, Mezzanine

Geographic Preference: not available

Industry Group Preference: Distribution, Genetic Engineering, Medical/Health Related

Portfolio Companies: not available

Officers, Executives and Principals

Fredrik C. Schreuder, Managing Partner
Erik Amble, Partner

MEDIOCREDITO LOMBARDO SpA

Via Broletto 20
20121 Milan
Italy

Telephone: 39-2-88701
Fax: 39-2-878275

Mission: Actively seeking new investments

Fund Size: not available
Founded: not available
Average Investment: not available
Minimum Investment: not available

Investment Criteria: Expansion/Development, Management Buy-out, Management Buy-in, Bridge, Turn-around/Restructuring

Geographic Preference: Italy

Industry Group Preference: All sectors considered

Portfolio Companies: not available

Officers, Executives and Principals

Pierluigi Novello
Carlo Pietrantoni
Angelo Ghisalberti
Paolo Grandi
Luca Rossi

MEES PIERSON INVESTERINGSMAATSCHAPPIJ BV

Rokin 55
1012 KK Amsterdam
The Netherlands

Telephone: 31-20-521-1188
Fax: 31-20-521-1962

Mission: Actively seeking new investments

Fund Size: Ecu642 million
Founded: not available
Average Investment: not available
Minimum Investment: Ecu400,000

Investment Criteria: Expansion/Development, Management Buy-out, Management Buy-in, Bridge

Geographic Preference: Netherlands, Germany

Industry Group Preference: All sectors considered

Portfolio Companies: not available

Officers, Executives and Principals

M.W. Dekker
J.Keyzer

MERCAPITAL SA

Fortuny 6
28010 Madrid
Spain

Telephone: 34-1-557-8000
Fax: 34-1-308-6878
E-mail: meurita@mercapital.com

Mission: Actively seeking new investments

Fund Size: Ecu290 million
Founded: not available
Average Investment: not available
Minimum Investment: Ecu5 million

Investment Criteria: Expansion/Development, Management Buy-out, Management Buy-in, Replacement, Bridge

Geographic Preference: Spain

Industry Group Preference: All sectors considered

Portfolio Companies: not available

Officers, Executives and Principals

Javier Loizaga

MERCURY ASSET MANAGEMENT PLC

Private Equity Division
33 King William Street
London EC4R 9AS
United Kingdom

Telephone: 44-171-280-2800
Fax: 44-171-203-5833

Mission: Actively seeking new investments in emerging growth companies with successful, cohesive and talented management teams and good market positions

Fund Size: £600 million
Founded: 1985
Average Investment: not available
Minimum Investment: £2 million

Investment Criteria: Expansion, Management Buy-in, Management Buy-out, Refinancing Bank Debt, Rescue/Turnaround, Secondary Purchase/Replacement Capital

Geographic Preference: United Kingdom, Irish Republic

Industry Group Preference: All sectors considered, but especially Electronics, Healthcare, Leisure, Media, Pharmaceuticals, Support Services, Telecommunications

Portfolio Companies: Vero, Belfast International Airport, British Aluminium, Southalls, Priory Hospitals, Parc, BTG, Allegro, NTL, Pleroma, Britt Allcroft, Two Way TV, Luminar, Club 18-30, Thad, Vega, DVR

Officers, Executives and Principals

Ian Armitage, Managing Director
Education: Graduate, University of Oxford
Background: 3i plc

Frances Jacob, Director
Education: Graduate in Engineering
Background: Production Engineer; 3i plc

Linda Wilding ACA, Director
Background: Research Biochemist, Science Research Council; Corporate Finance, Ernst and Young

Barclay Douglas CA, Director
Education: Graduate in Law, University of Aberdeen
Background: Chartered Accountant, Arthur Andersen; Murray Johnstone; Finance Director, Sock Shop

Lindsay Dibden ACA, Director
Education: Graduate in Aeronautical Engineering, Imperial College, London
Background: Corporate Finance, Coopers and Lybrand

Jeremy Sharman, Director
Education: Graduate in Mathematics, University of Oxford
Background: LEK Partnership; Corporate Finance, S. G. Warburg and Company

Nick Turner ACA, Director
Education: Graduate in Economics, University of Cambridge
Background: Touche Ross

MERIFIN CAPITAL GROUP

Avenue Lloyd George 6
P. O. Box 8
1000 Brussels
Belgium

Telephone: 32-2-646-2580
Fax: 32-2-646-3036

Mission: Actively seeking new investments as a private international investment group

Fund Size: not available
Founded: not available
Average Investment: not available
Minimum Investment: Ecu200,000

Investment Criteria: Early-stage, Expansion/Development, Management buyout, Management buy-in, Turn-around/Restructuring

Geographic Preference: Europe, North America

Industry Group Preference: All sectors considered

Portfolio Companies: not available

Officers, Executives and Principals

Coen N. Teulings, Partner
J.M. Vandendaelen, Partner

MERITA CAPITAL OY PROFITA FUND I

Aleksanterinkatu 36A
00020 Merita
Finland

Telephone: 358-9-1654-2788
Fax: 358-9-625-878

Mission: Actively seeking new investments in growth companies as a venture capital fund managed by Merita Capital Oy, a subsidiary of Merita Bank

Fund Size: FM120 million
Founded: 1996
Average Investment: FM3 million
Minimum Investment: FM1 million

Investment Criteria: Start-up, Expansion, Buy-out, Turnaround

Geographic Preference: Finland

Industry Group Preference: All sectors considered

Portfolio Companies: not available

Officers, Executives and Principals

Jouko Helomaa, LLM, Managing Director, Merita Capital Oy
Torleif Söderlund, MSc (Econ), Director, Investments
Jaakko Kaikkonen, LLM, Director, Investments

METRA CORPORATION

P. O. Box 230
John Stenberginranta 2
00101 Helsinki
Finland

Telephone: 358-070-951
Fax: 358-0739-295

Mission: Actively seeking new investments

Fund Size: not available
Founded: not available
Average Investment: FM1-5 million
Minimum Investment: Negotiable

Investment Criteria: Start-up, Manangement Buy-out

Geographic Preference: Nordic countries, European Union

Industry Group Preference: All sectors considered

Portfolio Companies: not available

MEZZANINE MANAGEMENT LIMITED

Mansfield House
1 Southampton Street
London WC2R 0LR
United Kingdom

Telephone: 44-171-836-4406
Fax: 44-171-240-8320

Mission: Actively seeking new investments

Fund Size: £500 million
Founded: not available
Average Investment: not available
Minimum Investment: £3 million

Investment Criteria: All stages except Start-up

Geographic Preference: Western Europe, North America

Industry Group Preference: Chemical and Materials, Communications, Consumer Related, Energy, Industrial Automation, Industrial Products and Services, Leisure, Manufacturing, Media, Medical/Health Related, Services, Transport

Portfolio Companies: Core Labs, IRO, TLC Beatrice, Lhysa, Morel

Officers, Executives and Principals

Rory Brooks
George Davidson
Benjamin Edwards
Nathalie Faure Beaulieu
Angus Penman
James Read

MIDINVEST OY

Ylistönmäentie 31
40500 Jyväskylä
Finland

Telephone: 358-14-4451-100
Fax: 358-14-4451-120
E-mail: jtk@jsp.fi

Mission: Actively seeking new investments

Fund Size: FM11.3 million
Founded: 1994
Average Investment: FM150,000
Minimum Investment: FM100,000

Investment Criteria: Start-up, Expansion, Management Buy-out

Geographic Preference: Finland (Central region)

Industry Group Preference: All sectors considered

Portfolio Companies: not available

Officers, Executives and Principals

Visa Virtanen, Lic. Econ., Managing Director

MIDLAND ENTERPRISE FUND FOR THE SOUTH EAST

The Cadmus Organisation Ltd.
Suite G, Kings Business Centre
Reeds Lane, Sayers Common
Hassocks
West Sussex BN6 9LS
United Kingdom

Telephone: 44-1273-835455
Fax: 44-1273-835466

Mission: Actively seeking new investments (up to a maximum of £150,000) in growth companies with experienced management teams

Fund Size: £775,000
Founded: 1993
Average Investment: £80,000
Minimum Investment: £25,000

Investment Criteria: Expansion, Management Buy-in, Management Buy-out, Start-up

Geographic Preference: United Kingdom (Hampshire, Sussex, Surrey, Kent, Isle of Wight)

Industry Group Preference: All sectors considered

Portfolio Companies: Chesswood Group Ltd., Best Odds Ltd., HS One Design Ltd., Rolac Industries Ltd.

Officers, Executives and Principals

Howard Matthews, Director
Education: Graduate in Economics and Commerce, University of Southampton
Background: 3i plc
Directorships: The Halo Company (Sussex) Ltd., Aspects Beauty Company Ltd.

MIDLAND GROWTH CAPITAL

Midland Bank plc
10 Lower Thames Street
London EC3R 6AE
United Kingdom

Telephone: 44-171-260-7935
Fax: 44-171-260-6767

Mission: Investing in British companies which are at least three years old and which offer potential for growth

Fund Size: £25 million
Founded: 1992
Average Investment: £450,000
Minimum Investment: £150,000

Investment Criteria: Expansion, Management Buy-in, Management Buy-out, Refinancing Bank Debt, Rescue/Turnaround, Secondary Purchase/Replacement

Geographic Preference: United Kingdom

Industry Group Preference: All sectors considered

Portfolio Companies: Cardinal Broach Company Ltd., Lady in Leisure Ltd., The Reward Group Ltd., Skip Units Ltd., Connaught Group Ltd.

Officers, Executives and Principals

Robert Henry
Caroline Owens
John Brandon
John Collins
John Slatter
Gerry Jennings
Chris Buckle

MIDLANDS VENTURE FUND MANAGERS LIMITED

The Square
Beeston
Nottingham NG9 2JG
United Kingdom

Telephone: 44-115-967-8400
Fax: 44-115-967-8687

Mission: Actively seeking new investments as managing company for the Midland Enterprise Fund for the West Midlands and the Midland Enterprise Fund for the East Midlands

Fund Size: £2.5 million
Founded: not available
Average Investment: £75,000
Minimum Investment: £20,000

Investment Criteria: Expansion, Management Buy-in, Management Buy-out, Early-stage, Refinancing Bank Debt, Rescue/Turnaround, Start-up

Geographic Preference: United Kingdom (East and West Midlands only)

Industry Group Preference: All sectors considered except Real Estate

Portfolio Companies: Yeowart (Garages) Ltd., Fastpack Ltd., P and B Packaging Ltd., Advance Ferrite Ltd., Slottseal Ltd.

Officers, Executives and Principals

John O'Neill

MISTRAL INVESTISSEMENTS

Immeuble "Le Stratège" Bureau Club du Millénaire
34000 Montpellier
France

Telephone: 33-67-697415
Fax: 33-67-697469

Mission: Actively seeking new investments

Fund Size: Ecu900,000
Founded: not available
Average Investment: not available
Minimum Investment: Ecu30,000

Investment Criteria: Seed, Start-up, Early-stage

Geographic Preference: Europe

Industry Group Preference: Agriculture/Forestry, Biotechnology, Communications, Electronics Related, Medical/Health Related

Portfolio Companies: not available

Officers, Executives and Principals

Philippe Dubois

MITSUI AND COMPANY LIMITED

1-2-1 Otemachi
Chiyoda-ku
Tokyo 100
Japan

Mission: not available

Fund Size: $134 billion
Founded: not available
Average Investment: not available
Minimum Investment: not available

Investment Criteria: not available

Geographic Preference: Japan

Industry Group Preference: Computer Related, Global On-line Data Transmissions, Network Information Services

Portfolio Companies: Metricom

Officers, Executives and Principals

Naohiko Kumagai, President

MITTELSTÄNDISCHE BETEILIGUNGSGESELLSCHAFT BADEN-WÜRTTEMBERG GmbH (MBG)

Werastrasse 15
70182 Stuttgart
Germany

Telephone: 49-711-16456
Fax: 49-711-1645-777
E-mail:

Mission: Promoting small and medium-sized enterprises as well as young entrepreneurs

Fund Size: DM265 million
Founded: 1971
Average Investment: DM400,000
Minimum Investment: DM40,000

Investment Criteria: not available

Geographic Preference: Germany (Baden-Württemberg)

Industry Group Preference: All sectors considered

Portfolio Companies: not available

Officers, Executives and Principals

Heinz Haller, Manager
Hartmut Hübler, Manager

MITTELSTÄNDISCHE BETEILIGUNGSGESELLSCHAFT BERLIN-BRANDENBURG GmbH

Steinstrasse 104-106
14480 Potsdam
Germany

Telephone: 49-331-649-630
Fax: 49-331-649-6321

Mission: Promoting small and medium-sized enterprises

Fund Size: DM35.6 million
Founded: not available
Average Investment: not available
Minimum Investment: DM100,000

Investment Criteria: All stages

Geographic Preference: Germany (Berlin and Brandenburg)

Industry Group Preference: All sectors considered

Portfolio Companies: not available

Officers, Executives and Principals

Rainer Langmaack
Waltraud Wolf

MITTELSTÄNDISCHE BETEILIGUNGSGESELLSCHAFT HESSEN GmbH

Abraham-Lincoln-Strasse 38-42
65189 Wiesbaden
Germany

Telephone: 49-611-774-276
Fax: 49-611-774-296

Mission: Promoting innovation by small and medium-sized enterprises

Fund Size: DM40 million
Founded: not available
Average Investment: not available
Minimum Investment: DM250,000

Investment Criteria: All stages

Geographic Preference: Germany (Hesse)

Industry Group Preference: All sectors considered

Portfolio Companies: not available

Officers, Executives and Principals

Karlheinz Zahn
Geralt Goder

MITTELSTÄNDISCHE BETEILIGUNGSGESELLSCHAFT MECKLENBURG-VORPOMMERN mbH (MBMV)

Am Grünen Tal 19
19063 Schwerin
Germany

Telephone: 49-385-34040
Fax: 49-385-377138

Mission: Promoting small and medium-sized enterprises

Fund Size: DM38.2 million
Founded: not available
Average Investment: not available
Minimum Investment: DM100,000

Investment Criteria: All stages

Geographic Preference: Germany (Mecklenburg-Western Pomerania)

Industry Group Preference: All sectors considered

Portfolio Companies: not available

Officers, Executives and Principals

Uwe Schmeichel
Wolfgang Strutz

MITTELSTÄNDISCHE BETEILIGUNGSGESELLSCHAFT NIEDERSACHSEN mbH

Schiffgraben 33
30175 Hanover
Germany

Telephone: 49-511-337-050
Fax: 49-511-337-0555

Mission: Promoting small and medium-sized enterprises and encouraging restructuring and rationalization

Fund Size: DM9.4 million
Founded: not available
Average Investment: not available
Minimum Investment: not available

Investment Criteria: All stages

Geographic Preference: Germany (Lower Saxony)

Industry Group Preference: All sectors considered

Portfolio Companies: not available

Officers, Executives and Principals

Bettina Schmidt
Werner Wippo

MITTELSTÄNDISCHE BETEILIGUNGSGESELLSCHAFT RHEINLAND-PFALZ mbH

Theodor-Römheld-Strasse 22
55130 Mainz
Germany

Telephone: 49-6131-9850
Fax: 49-6131-985-499

Mission: Promoting small and medium-sized enterprises

Fund Size: DM25.6 million
Founded: not available
Average Investment: not available
Minimum Investment: DM100,000

Investment Criteria: All stages

Geographic Preference: Germany (Rhineland-Palatinate)

Industry Group Preference: Crafts, Manufacturing, Trade

Portfolio Companies: not available

Officers, Executives and Principals

Rüdiger Bucher
Hans-Joachim Metternich

MITTELSTÄNDISCHE BETEILIGUNGSGESELLSCHAFT SACHSEN mbH

Anton-Graff-Strasse 20
01309 Dresden
Germany

Telephone: 49-351-44090
Fax: 49-351-4409-450

Mission: Promoting small and medium-sized enterprises as well as young entrepreneurs

Fund Size: DM158 million
Founded: not available
Average Investment: not available
Minimum Investment: DM100,000

Investment Criteria: Expansion/Development, Start-up, Buy-out, Buy-in

Geographic Preference: Germany (Saxony)

Industry Group Preference: All sectors considered

Portfolio Companies: not available

Officers, Executives and Principals

Wolfgang Hanke
Eva Köhler

MITTELSTÄNDISCHE BETEILIGUNGSGESELLSCHAFT SACHSEN-ANHALT mbH

Grosse Diesdorfer Strasse 228
39108 Magdeburg
Germany

Telephone: 49-391-737-520
Fax: 49-391-737-5215

Mission: Promoting small and medium-sized enterprises

Fund Size: DM56 million
Founded: not available
Average Investment: not available
Minimum Investment: DM50,000

Investment Criteria: All stages

Geographic Preference: Germany (Saxony-Anhalt)

Industry Group Preference: All sectors considered

Portfolio Companies: not available

Officers, Executives and Principals

Gerhard Arnold
Dieter Oehne

MITTELSTÄNDISCHE BETEILIGUNGSGESELLSCHAFT THÜRINGEN mbH

Europaplatz 5
99091 Erfurt
Germany

Telephone: 49-361-7447-230
Fax: 49-361-7447-231

Mission: Promoting small and medium-sized enterprises

Fund Size: DM61.5 million
Founded: not available
Average Investment: not available
Minimum Investment: DM200,000

Investment Criteria: All stages

Geographic Preference: Germany (Thuringia)

Industry Group Preference: All sectors considered

Portfolio Companies: not available

Officers, Executives and Principals

Franz Gerstner
Dr. Ursula Gabler

MONTAGU PRIVATE EQUITY LTD.

10 Lower Thames Street
London EC6R 3AE
United Kingdom

Telephone: 44-171-260-9840
Fax: 44-171-220-7312

Mission: Actively seeking new investments

Fund Size: not available
Founded: 1968
Average Investment: not available
Minimum Investment: $1 million

Investment Criteria: Leveraged Buy-out, Special Situations

Geographic Preference: Europe

Industry Group Preference: All sectors considered

Portfolio Companies: not available

Officers, Executives and Principals

Ian Forrest, Managing Director
David Castles, Director
Roger Heath, Director
Chris Masterson, Director
Vince O'Brien, Director
Phil Goodwin, Director
Richard Connell, Director

MORGAN GRENFELL DEVELOPMENT CAPITAL LTD.

23 Great Winchester Street
London EC2P 2AX
United Kingdom

Telephone: 44-171-545-8000
Fax: 44-171-545-5282

Other Office Locations
35 St Andrew's Square
Edinburgh EH2 2AD
Phone 44-131-557-8600, Fax 44-131-557-8306

Mission: Actively seeking new investments

Fund Size: not available
Founded: 1989
Average Investment: not available
Minimum Investment: not available

Investment Criteria: Expansion, Management Buy-in, Management Buy-out, Refinancing Bank Debt, Secondary Purchase/Replacement Capital

Geographic Preference: Western Europe

Industry Group Preference: not available

Portfolio Companies: The Sweater Shop, Beni Food Group, Taunton Cider, British School of Motoring, NI Intressenter

Officers, Executives and Principals

Robert Smith, Chairman and Chief Executive Officer (London)
Norman Murray, Deputy Chief Executive Officer (Edinburgh)

MORGAN GRENFELL INVESTISSEMENT

11-13 avenue de Friedland
75008 Paris
France

Telephone: 33-1-5383-7710
Fax: 33-1-5383-7714

Mission: Actively seeking new investments

Fund Size: Ffr516 million
Founded: not available
Average Investment: not available
Minimum Investment: Ffr40 million

Investment Criteria: All stages

Geographic Preference: France

Industry Group Preference: All sectors considered

Portfolio Companies: not available

Officers, Executives and Principals

Emmanuel Harlé, Managing Director

MSELE NEDVENTURES LIMITED

c/o P. O. Box 1163
Saxonwold 2132
Republic of South Africa

Telephone: 27-11-484-1507
Fax: 27-11-642-0691

Mission: Actively seeking new investments

Fund Size: not available
Founded: not available
Average Investment: not available
Minimum Investment: not availabe

Investment Criteria: All stages

Geographic Preference: South Africa

Industry Group Preference: All sectors considered

Portfolio Companies: not available

Officers, Executives and Principals

Pierre Smit

MTI MANAGERS LIMITED

Langley Place
99 Langley Road
Watford
Hertfordshire WD1 3PE
United Kingdom

Telephone: 44-1923-250244
Fax: 44-1923-247783
E-mail: 100447.357!@compuserve.com

Mission: Actively seeking new investments

Fund Size: £24 million
Founded: not available
Average Investment: not available
Minimum Investment: £250,000

Investment Criteria: Start-up, Early-stage, Expansion, Management Buy-in, Management Buy-out, Rescue/ Turnaround

Geographic Preference: United Kingdom

Industry Group Preference: Biotechnology, Chemical and Materials, Communications, Computer Related, Electronics Related, Industrial Automation, Industrial Products and Services, Manufacturing, Medical Related

Portfolio Companies: Intelligent Environments Group plc, Dynamic Logic Limited, Cardcast PLC, Scimat Limited, Intelligence Quotient International Ltd

Officers, Executives and Principals

Paul Castle
Richard Ford
Ernie Richardson

M. U. K. KAPITALBETEILIGUNGS GmbH

Richmodstrasse 13-15
50667 Cologne
Germany

Telephone: 49-221-9257-960
Fax: 49-221-9257-966

Mission: Actively seeking new investments

Fund Size: DM30.6 million
Founded: not available
Average Investment: not available
Minimum Investment: DM1 million

Investment Criteria: All stages

Geographic Preference: Germany (Cologne, Bonn, Leverkusen, Siegburg)

Industry Group Preference: All sectors considered

Portfolio Companies: not available

Officers, Executives and Principals

Dieter Malchus
Friedrich Schake

MURRAY AVENIR

23 avenue Franklin Roosevelt
75008 Paris
France

Telephone: 33-1-5383-7443
Fax: 33-1-5383-7459

Mission: Actively seeking new investments

Fund Size: Ffr96 million
Founded: not available
Average Investment: not available
Minimum Investment: Ffr4 million

Investment Criteria: Management Buy-out, Management Buy-in

Geographic Preference: France

Industry Group Preference: All sectors considered except High Technology

Portfolio Companies: Adage, Bretagne-Agro, Macspe TBI Holding

Officers, Executives and Principals

Neil MacLeod
Jean-Paul Vaillant

MURRAY JOHNSTONE PRIVATE EQUITY LIMITED

7 West Nile Street
Glasgow G1 2PX
United Kingdom

Telephone: 44-141-226-3131
Fax: 44-141-248-5636

Mission: Actively seeking new investments

Fund Size: £300 million
Founded: not available
Average Investment: not available
Minimum Investment: £500,000

Investment Criteria: Bridge, Expansion, Management Buy-in, Management Buy-out, Refinancing Bank Debt, Rescue/Turnaround, Secondary Purchase/Replacement Capital

Geographic Preference: Western Europe

Industry Group Preference: All sectors considered

Portfolio Companies: Greater Manchester Buses North Ltd, Xyratex Ltd, New World Domestic Appliances Ltd, Mercury Taverns Ltd, Ferranti Technologies Ltd

Officers, Executives and Principals

Jonathan Diggines
David MacLellan
Iain Tulloch

NASH, SELLS AND PARTNERS LIMITED

25 Buckingham Gate
London SW13 6LD
United Kingdom

Telephone: 44-171-828-6944
Fax: 44-171-828-9958

Mission: Actively seeking new investments

Fund Size: £100 million
Founded: not available
Average Investment: not available
Minimum Investment: £1 million

Investment Criteria: All stages considered, but especially Later-stage

Geographic Preference: United Kingdom

Industry Group Preference: Chemicals, Environment, Food, Healthcare, Infrastructure, Leisure, Transportation

Portfolio Companies: ISL Leisure, Linden, Care UK, Westerleigh Group

Officers, Executives and Principals

Kevin Grassby
James Heath

NATIONAL INVESTMENT FUND VICTORIA SA
ul. Dluga 5
00263 Warsaw
Poland

Telephone: 48-22-635-6344
Fax: 48-22-635-6314

Mission: Maximising the value of net assets per share by taking an active management approach to investments in companies under the Mass Privatization Program, as well as unquoted high-growth companies, as a specialist private equity fund under management by Polskie Towarzystwo Pryvatyzacyjne - Kleinwort Benson (PTP-KB)

Fund Size: Z330 million
Founded: 1995
Average Investment: Z5 million
Minimum Investment: not available

Investment Criteria: Management Buy-out, Management Buy-in, Development, Replacement

Geographic Preference: Poland

Industry Group Preference: Consumer Related, Distribution, Food Processing, Light Industry, Services

Portfolio Companies: ERG, HAFT, Intermoda, ZPO Modena, Polmozbyt Rzeszow, Weltom, Okregowe PZZ, Byd-Meat, Canoe-Meat, Transgor, PRDM w Bielsku- Bialej, Kablobeton, PBPW, PRDM w Kedzierzynie-Kozla, Mostostal, Remur, Mera- Pnefal, KFAP, Polam-Naklo, Tofama, Spomasz, Byfuch, Spomasz, Kalskor, Metalchem-Koscian, PZL Debica, ZWSE-Wroclaw, Elbud, ZWSE-Krakow, Biowet, Centrostal, Niwka, Ostrowies

Officers, Executives and Principals

Dr. Jerzy Drygalski, Chairman of the Management Board, PTP-KB and Victoria
Education: MSc and PhD, Lodz University
Background: Professor, Lodz University; Founder and Director, Passa Consulting Group; Chairman, Liquidation Committee for the State Press Conglomerate; Under- Secretary and Secretary, Ministry of Privatization; Director, BMF Capital and BMF SA (Consultancy)

Marek Gorski, Senior Investment Director, PTP-KB, and Deputy Chairman, Victoria
Education: Master's degree in Foreign Trade, Gdansk University
Background: Marketing Specialist, Elpax Co.; Director of Information, Ministry of Privatization; President, Polish Agency for Foreign Investment

Janusz Heath, Deputy Chairman and Managing Director, PTP-KB, and Authorized Representative, Victoria
Education: MBA, Aston University; Diploma in Marketing, Chartered Institute of Marketing
Background: British Army; varied commercial experience; Aitken Hume International Plc; United Kingdom Executive Director, Development Capital Corporation Limited; Chief Executive, BTS Group PLC; Chief Executive, Waverley Cameron PLC

Iain Haggis, Director, PTP-KB, and Authorized Representative, Victoria
Education: Graduate in Business Studies, Plymouth Polytechnic
Background: Assistant Finance Manager, Reuters; Financial Controller, Halifax Property Services; Finance Director, GVG GmbH

NATWEST MARKETS ACQUISITION FINANCE

135 Bishopsgate
London EC2M 3UR
United Kingdom

Telephone: 44-171-375-5000
Fax: 44-171-375-5464

Mission: Actively seeking new investments

Fund Size: £2 billion
Founded: not available
Average Investment: not available
Minimum Investment: £1 million

Investment Criteria: Bridge, Expansion, Management Buy-in, Management Buy-out, Other Purchase of Quoted Shares, Refinancing Bank Debt, Rescue/Turnaround, Secondary Purchase/Replacement Capital, Venture Purchase of Quoted Shares

Geographic Preference: North America, Western Europe

Industry Group Preference: All sectors considered

Portfolio Companies: TM Group, The Sweater Shop, British Fuels Ltd, Dunlop Slazenger Group Ltd, Farnell Electronics plc

Officers, Executives and Principals

Graham Randell
Chris Allflatt
Nick Petrusic
Piers Harmer
John Foy
Stuart Sweeney
Peter Gray

NATWEST MARKETS MEZZANINE FINANCE

Fenchurch Exchange
8 Fenchurch Place
London EC3M 4TE
United Kingdom

Telephone: 44-171-374-3000
Fax: 44-171-374-3572

Mission: Actively seeking new investments

Fund Size: not available
Founded: not available
Average Investment: not available
Minimum Investment: £2 million

Investment Criteria: Management Buy-in, Management Buy-out, Acquisition, Expansion, Replacement Capital

Geographic Preference: Western Europe

Industry Group Preference: All sectors considered

Portfolio Companies: Flying Colours Leisure Group, Harris Chemical Europe, CAL Group, Blue Boar, Pilkington Tiles

Officers, Executives and Principals

Barrie Moore
Tina Sharp
John Sealy
Tim Lasham

NATWEST VENTURES LIMITED

Fenchurch Exchange
8 Fenchurch Place
London EC3M 4TE
United Kingdom

Telephone: 44-171-374-4444
Fax: 44-171-374-3580
E-mail: enquiries@nwmvent.nwmarkets.com

Other Office Locations
Wellesley House
37 Waterloo Street
Birmingham B2 5TJ
Phone 44-121-236-1641, Fax 44-121-236-2089

33-35 Queen Square
Bristol BS1 4LU
Phone 44-117-927-3731, Fax 44-117-929-1627

Kintore House
74-77 Queen Street
Edinburgh EH2 4NS
Phone 44-131-243-4589, Fax 44-131-243-4588

Lion House
41 York Place
Leeds LS1 2ED
Phone 44-113-244-3444, Fax 44-113-243-9848

Clarence House
Clarence Street
Manchester M2 4DW
Phone 44-161-832-8827, Fax 44-161-832-3158

Berliner Allee 42
40212 Düsseldorf
Germany
Phone 49-211-139080, Fax 49-211-1390855

Edificio Torre Europa
Paseo de la Castellana
95-Planta 19
28046 Madrid
Spain

Via Brera n. 3
21021 Milan
Italy
Phone 39-2-806951, Fax 39-2-864-52424

9 rue Phalsbourg
75017 Paris
France
Phone 33-1-44292100, Fax 33-1-44292110

Calle Luis Vives 6
46003 Valencia
Spain
Phone 34-6-392-4166, Fax 34-6-392-5541

6600 Peachtree Dunwoody Road
300 Embassy Row, Suite 630
Atlanta, GA 30328
United States
Phone 1-770-399-5633, Fax 1-770-393-4825

NatWest Pioneer Fund
Radford House
Radford Boulevard
Nottingham NG7 5QG
Phone 44-115-979-0818, Fax 44-942-4278

Mission: Supplying private equity across a broad range of sectors as part of the NatWest Group

Fund Size: £1 billion
Founded: 1969
Average Investment: £7 million
Minimum Investment: £1 million

Investment Criteria: Management Buy-in, Management Buy-out, Institutional Buy- out, Development Capital, Existing Share Purchase

Geographic Preference: Western Europe

Industry Group Preference: All sectors considered

Portfolio Companies: Bodegas Campo Burgo, El Rancho, Mercury Taverns, Porter Lancastrian, Rusts of Cromer, Wimpy Restaurants Group, Abbot Barton Group, Barcom, DBS Nationwide, Expocolour, Gibbons Refractories, Groupe Soloc, Industrias Y Fundiciones Iglesias, John Barker Group, Magnus, Morris Homes, PKL Group (UK), Pelham Homes, Peterhouse Group, Robison and Davidson, Rodgers Plant Hire, Thomas Steelwork, Trevi Holdings, Victor Homes, Charco 99, France Portes, Hill Leigh Group, Wade Building Services, Chemical Express, Chemical Manufacturing and Refining, HRP Refrigerants, Solrec, Sterling Technology, Victrex, Abec Group, Alperton Ford and Alperton Truck, Artcraft, Charringtons Fuels, Financière Orefi, Graphics Arts Equipment, Groupe OMB, Ireland Alloys, KRCS Group, King Ford, Linn Motor Group, London Graphic Centre, MG Duff, Mentec International, Pacific and European Tmber Agency, Pentagon, Pinault Equipment, Productos Quimicos Sevillanos, Qudis, Straker, The Motorhouse of Cannocks Car Supermarket, WW Group, Erin, Cornwall Light and Power, Albacom, Celsa Eichhoff, Cramwell, Crompton Lighting, Electron Technologies, Groupe Coreci, Intelligent Environments, Joyce-Loebl, Keltek, Metrum Information Storage, Pelcombe Group, Plasmon, Radiodetection, Soule, Technolog, Torin, Wexford Electronix, Zincocelere, Aerospace Composite Technologies, Aljio SL, Camlaw, Centrepiece Engineering, Clare Equipment, Cortworth, Cubra Castings, Eaton- Willians Group, Edgemond Group, 4D Rubber Co, G. Cussons, Gencel Group, Halco Group, Horwich Castings, I. Holland, ITP, International Process Technologies, Lafon, Motherwell

Bridge, PADAC, Players Group, Presswork (Metals), Ratcliff Group, SES Group, Silicone Altimex, Simpson Industries, Stackright, Staffs Silent Gear, TT Pumos, Toolex Alpha, Tubex, UFFO, Vic-Tree (Birmingham), W. Fearnehough, Eurobrake, Lab Radio, SJ Clark (Cables), Summit Accessories, Tricom Automotive, Beck Food Group, Beni Food Group, Golden Wonder, Grampian Country Food Group, Holding Fromagere, JJ Barker, Lacasa, Lyons Seafood Group, Marr Foods, Nudespa, Pascoe's Group, The Tetley Group, Wirral Foods, Witwood Food Products, Corin, Finagest, Goldsborough Healthcare, Hydron, Keep Able, Medic-Aid, Aynsley Group, Celmac, Cloverleaf Group, Jean Pierre Stremler and Associates, LMS International, Levington Horticulture, Metwell, Millbrook Furnishing Industries, Moorfield, Poole Pottery, Quest Consumer Products, Tutbury Crystal, Alan Turner Group, Personal Assurance, Crown Leisure, Festive Holidays, Flying Colours, Heights of Abraham (Matlock, Bath), Lyric Hotels, National Leisure Catering, Principal Hotels (Europe), Strathmore Hotels, Wookey Hole Caves, Brann, CTP Logistics, Caledonian Publishing, Dragon Rouge, Fletcher Newspapers, LLP, John Wood Group, Presidio Oil Company, AMG Industries, Bolton Brady Repair and Service, Phipps Faire, Recra Enviromental, CAL Group, CCA Group, Clarke Rubicon, Cobrhi, Colorgraphic, Guyot Graphco, Hartcliffe, John Cleland, Merlin Flexible Packaging, Peerless, Pillans and Wilson, Signs and Labels, Viscose Closures, Ward Packaging, Whitehead and Wood, Wallis Laboratory, Hallamshire Investments, Hamptons Group, Vico Properties, Anglian Fast Food, Hugh Fay, Petty Wood, Everythings a £1, Focus Retail Group, Harveys, Heal's (1990), Histoire D'or, MSSR, New Look, Oceanhaven, The Factory Shop, The Tulchan Group, United News Shops Holdings, ATR Group, Brewton, Ego Computers, Gearhouse Group, Goresline, Hauser Holding, Hay Group, Interactive Media Services, KS Group, Lascom, Lewis Electric Group, Melville Exhibition Services, Network Si Group, Safig, Stortext, Technology Services International, Zergo, Bonneterie, D'Armor, Comer International, Eveden, Fargeot, Frank Theak, Henri-Lloyd (International), Industrias Mutra, J. Rosenthal and Sons, John Partridge, Lee Cooper Group, Masons of Leek, Pepe Group, Bell Freight Transport Group, Bristow Helicopter Group, British Car Rental (BCR), British World Aviation, Colirail, United Carriers Group

Officers, Executives and Principals

David Shaw, Chief Executive

NEDERLANDSE PARTICIPATIE MAATSCHAPPIJ NV

Breitnerstraat 1
P. O. Box 7224
1007 JE Amsterdam
The Netherlands

Telephone: 31-20-5705555
Fax: 31-20-6710855

Mission: Providing finance for an unlimited period of time, in the form of equity or convertible loans without mortgage or other security

Fund Size: Ecu920 million
Founded: 1948
Average Investment: Ecu4,850,000
Minimum Investment: Ecu460,000

Investment Criteria: Expansion/Development, Management Buy-out, Management Buy-in, Bridge, Replacement Turnaround/Restructuring

Geographic Preference: Netherlands, Belgium, Germany

Industry Group Preference: All sectors considered except Real Estate

Portfolio Companies: Aestron Design International BV, Arianne Beheer BV, Beleggingsmaatschappij De Ark Ninkerk BV, Athlone Groep NV, Atlanta Hoogezand BV, Gemeenschappelijk Bezit Auping BV, AXXICON Group BV, Bastion Hotels Europe BV, BCC Holding Amstelveen BV, Beagle Investments BV, Beton Son BV, B and G Beheer BV, Boekhandels Groep Nederland BV, De Boer Holding BV, Bolding Pak Beheer BV, Bosch and Keuning NV, Firma Bosman Holding BV, B.P.F. Beheer BV, Bruynzeel Zaandam BV, Business Consulting Services BV, Central Industry Group BV, Curtec Holding BV, Decostone Holding BV, Dehnert and Jansen BV, Delft Instruments NV, Diamond Tools Group BV, Drentea Kantoormeubelen BV, Drie Aircraft Holding BV, Driessen Aircraft Holding BV, Eekels Pompen BV, Electron Beheer BV, Emba Techniek Groep NV, Joh. Enschedé BV, Farrington Data Processing Holland BV, Zeepfabriek De Nieuwe Fenix BV, Fugro NV, Gestel Holding BV, Geveke NV, Geveke Industrial BV, G.G. Groep BV, Gimeg Holding BV, Glas-Heinz BV, BV Goedhart, Keol-en Luchttechnische Appraten, Jan van Gool BV, Verenigde Bedrijven Groeneveld BV, Beheer Maatschappij Grote Voort BV, Handelsveem Beheer BV, Harvest Holding BV, HAS Nederland BV, Koninklijke Hausemann and Hötte NV, Holland Chemical International BV, Helpman Holding BV, Helvoet Holding NV, HIT Groep BV, HVC Beheer BV, Hyva Holding BV, Koninklijke IBC BV, ID Systems Automatiseringsgroep BV, Iduna NV, Jansen Post and Cocx BV, Verenigde Bedrijven Janssen and De Jong BV, Keesing Beheer BV, L. Konings Beheer BV, H. Koopmans Beheer BV, Koopmans Koninklijke Meelfabrieken BV, Holding Kramers en Ruys BV, Koninklikje Textiel Veredelingsindustrie v/h G.J.ten Cate and Zonen NV, Kuiken NV, Van Kuyk Holding BV, Koninklijke Landré and Glinderman NV, Van Lanschot's Beleggings-Compangnie BV, Lips United BV, Lorry Finance BV, Koninklijke Frans Maas Groep NV, Macintosh NV, Manotherm Holding BV, Merrem and la Porte Beheer BV, Mervo Holding BV, Louis Nagel BV, NBM- Amstelland NV, Neroc BV, Netagco Holding BV, Nimox NV, Van Oord Groep NV, Oranjewoud Beheer BV, Pentagoes Beheer BV, Perfecta International Holding BV, Petroplus International BV, PMB Beheer BV, Holding Poeth Tegelen BV, Polynorm NV, Postijon Beheer NV, Prolion BV, Partners in Technologie- Overdracht (PTO) BV, RAM Mobile Data (Netherlands)BV, RMI (Holland) Beheer BV, Roberts Beheer BV, Rood Testhouse International NV, Roveco Sport Beheer BV, Beheer Maatschappij Rijnhaave BV SAMAS-GROEP NV, Koninklijke Schouten Group NV, Schreiner Luctvaart Groep BV, Sparta Rijwielen -en Motorenfabriek BV, Spijker Holding BV, Stadler and Sauerbier Holding BV, Stronghold Paper Group BV, Swets and

Zeitlinger Holding NV, Tel Holding BV, Thijssen Holding BV, Tramedico Holding BV, Upper Ten Tobacco Holding BV, Vanderlande Industries BV, VEGE Holding BV, Vegro Beheer BV, P. Vermeer Verenigde Bedrijven BV, Vicoma Holding Hoogvliet BV, Visbeen Holding BV, Meubelfabrieken 'Vroomshoop' Beheer BV, De Weger Architecten -en Ingenieursbureau BV, Wiener Holding BV, Wijnne and Barends' Cargadoors -en Agentuurkantoren BV, X-tal Electronics BV, Dambach-Werke GmbH, Goetz and Müller GmbH and Co., Chemunex SA, NV Henschel Engineering SA

Officers, Executives and Principals

J.D. Hooglandt, Chairman
A.G. Jacobs, Vice Chairman
Prof. M.J.L. Jonkart, Company Secretary
A.A. Anbeek van der Meijden, Supervisory Board
L.D. de Bièvre, Supervisory Board
H.J. Hielkema, Supervisory Board
J.H.Holsboer, Supervisory Board
J.G. ten Hoonte, Supervisory Board
J.M.Overmeer, Supervisory Board
G.A. Reudink, Supervisory Board
M.W. Dekker, General Manager
J. Keyzer, Manager
R. Brama, Investment Manager
J.W.G. Corne, Investment Manager
C. van Keeken, Investment Manager
C. Koerts, Investment Manager
O.R. Servaas, Investment Manager
R.H. van der Wurf, Investment Manager

NESBIC GROEP BV

Savannahweg 17
P. O. Box 8530
3503 RM Utrecht
The Netherlands

Telephone: 31-30-241-0202
Fax: 31-30-241-4833

Mission: Actively seeking new investments

Fund Size: Ecu250 million
Founded: not available
Average Investment: not available
Minimum Investment: Ecu200,000

Investment Criteria: Seed, Expansion/Development, Management Buy-out, Management Buy-in

Geographic Preference: Europe

Industry Group Preference: Agriculture/Forestry/Fish, Chemical/Materials Communications, Computer Software, Consumer Related, Energy

Portfolio Companies: not available

Officers, Executives and Principals

Ellard J. Blaauboer
Menno Reinders
Madeleine van Ginkel
Arnaud Diemont
Jaap Leemhuis
Leo van Doorne

NIPPON ENTERPRISE DEVELOPMENT CORPORATION

JBP Oval 3F
5-52-2 Jingumae
Shibuya-ku
Tokyo 150
Japan

Telephone: 81-3-3797-9559
Fax: 81-3-3797-9589
E-mail: ned-co@magical.egg.or.jp

Other Office Locations
540 Cowper Street, Suite 200
Palo Alto, CA 94301
United States
Phone 415-854-8760, Fax 415-462-9379, E-Mail aminakuchi@aol.com

c/o LTCB Asia Limited
Level 9, 1 Pacific Place
88 Queensway
Hong Kong
Phone 852-2520-0909, Fax 952-2865-6756, E-Mail motosimo@hkstar.com

Mission: Actively seeking new investments and providing a full range of financial and advisory services to emerging growth companies by creating alliances with Japanese companies

Fund Size: $500 million
Founded: 1972
Average Investment: $1 million
Minimum Investment: not specified

Investment Criteria: First-stage, Second-stage, Mezzanine

Geographic Preference: Japan, United States (West Coast), East and Southeast Asia

Industry Group Preference: Biotechnology, Communications, Computer Related, Electronic Components and Instrumentation, Genetic Engineering, Medical/Health Related, Retailing

Portfolio Companies: not available

Officers, Executives and Principals

Shogo Nakajima, President
Toshiyuki Furukawa, Managing Director
Yuji Ito, General Manager
Makoto Hikichi, Assistant General Manager
Jun Hosoya, Manager
Yumiko Muroi, Manager
Akira Minakuchi, Representative (United States)
Moto Shimoyamada, Representative (Hong Kong)

NITZANIM MANAGEMENT AND DEVELOPMENT

Kibbutz Ga'ash 60951
Israel

Telephone: 972-9-508154
Fax: 972-9-508118
E-mail: 100274.3670@compuserve.com

Mission: Actively seeking new investments

Fund Size: not available
Founded: 1993
Average Investment: $1 million
Minimum Investment: $100,000

Investment Criteria: Seed, Research and Development, Start-up, First-stage, Second-stage

Geographic Preference: not available

Industry Group Preference: Communications, Computer Related, Electronic Components and Instrumentation, Medical/Health Related

Portfolio Companies: not available

Officers, Executives and Principals

Matty Karp, President
Yair Safray, Vice President

N. M. ROTHSCHILD AND SONS LIMITED

New Court, St Swithin's Lane
London EC4P 4DU
United Kingdom

Telephone: 44-171-280-5000
Fax: 44-171-280-5400

Other Office Locations
Leeds (John King), Phone 113-243-4347
Manchester (Philip Yeates), Phone 161-827-3800

Mission: Actively seeking new investments

Fund Size: Open
Founded: not available
Average Investment: not available
Minimum Investment: Open

Investment Criteria: All stages

Geographic Preference: United Kingdom

Industry Group Preference: not available

Portfolio Companies: not available

Officers, Executives and Principals

Paul Tuckwell
David Chantler
Christopher Coleman
Alison Goold
Debra Lewis
Alistair Dick
Ter-Lee Maxwell

NOPTOR OY

P. O. Box 20
Keilaniemi
02151 Espoo
Finland

Telephone: 358-0-450-4787
Fax: 358-0-450-4848

Mission: Actively seeking new investments

Fund Size: FM70 million
Founded: not available
Average Investment: not available
Minimum Investment: FM250,000

Investment Criteria: Seed, Start-up, Expansion

Geographic Preference: Europe, North America

Industry Group Preference: Chemicals, Energy, Environment Technology

Portfolio Companies: not available

Officers, Executives and Principals

Kari Lampinen, President
Education: M.Sc. Economics

NORDDEUTSCHE INNOVATIONS- UND BETEILIGUNGS GmbH (NIB)

Michaelisstrasse 22
20459 Hamburg
Germany

Telephone: 49-40-351301
Fax: 49-40-343264

Mission: Actively seeking new investments

Fund Size:DM41 million
Founded: not available
Average Investment: not available
Minimum Investment: DM1 million

Investment Criteria: Expansion/Development

Geographic Preference: none

Industry Group Preference: Construction, Medical/Health Related, Services, Trade

Portfolio Companies: not available

Officers, Executives and Principals

Goetz von Hardenberg
Martin Lauer
Axel Sanders

NORDDEUTSCHE KAPITALBETEILIGUNGSGESELLSCHAFT mbH (NORD KB)

Osterstrasse 44
30159 Hanover
Germany

Telephone: 49-511-361-2490
Fax: 49-511-361-4602

Mission: Actively seeking new investments

Fund Size: DM246 million
Founded: not available
Average Investment: not available
Minimum Investment: DM1.5 million

Investment Criteria: not available

Geographic Preference: none

Industry Group Preference: All sectors considered

Portfolio Companies: not available

Officers, Executives and Principals

Günter Körner
Gerd Kastrup
Matthias Kues

NORD HOLDING GmbH

Osterstrasse 44
30159 Hanover
Germany

Telephone: 49-511-361-2490
Fax: 49-511-361-4602

Mission: Actively seeking new investments

Fund Size: DM38 million
Founded: not available
Average Investment: not available
Minimum Investment: DM3 million

Investment Criteria: not available

Geographic Preference: none

Industry Group Preference: All sectors considered

Portfolio Companies: not available

Officers, Executives and Principals

Günter Körner
Matthias Kues
Gerd Kastrup

NORDIC CAPITAL

Stureplan 4
11435 Stockholm
Sweden

Telephone: 46-8-440-5050
Fax: 46-8-611-7998

Mission: Actively seeking new investments

Fund Size: Skr1.5 billion
Founded: not available
Average Investment: not available
Minimum Investment: not available

Investment Criteria: All stages

Geographic Preference: Europe

Industry Group Preference: All sectors considered

Portfolio Companies: not available

Officers, Executives and Principals

Robert Andreen, Managing Director
Morgan Olofsson, Director
Lars Förberg, Investment Manager
Ulf Rosberg, Investment Manager
Fredrik Strömholm, Investment Manager

NORPEDIP

Av. Dr. Antunes Guimaraes 103
4100 Oporto
Portugal

Telephone: 351-2-610-2087
Fax: 351-2-610-2089

Mission: Actively seeking new investments

Fund Size: Ecu81.9 million
Founded: not available
Average Investment: not available
Minimum Investment: not available

Investment Criteria: Seed, Start-up, Expansion/Development, Management Buy-out, Management Buy-in

Geographic Preference: France, United Kingdom, Spain

Industry Group Preference: Biotechnology, Chemical/Materials, Communications, Computer Related, Electronics Related, Energy

Portfolio Companies: not available

Officers, Executives and Principals

José Antonio Barros
Rogerio Barros Ferreira
Hierpo Lopes

NORSK HYDRO A.S.

Bygdoy Alle 2
0257 Oslo 2
Norway

Telephone: 47-2-432-100
Fax: 47-2-432-574

Mission: not available

Fund Size: not available
Founded: not available
Average Investment: not available
Minimum Investment: not available

Investment Criteria: not available

Geographic Preference: not available

Industry Group Preference: Natural Resources Processing

Portfolio Companies: not available

Officers, Executives and Principals

Egil Mykelbust

NORSK VEKST A/S

Haakon VIIsgatan 2
P. O. Box 1223 Vika
0110 Oslo
Norway

Telephone: 47-22-010400
Fax: 47-22-010404

Mission: Actively seeking new investments in small and medium-sized enterprises

Fund Size: Nkr 600 million
Founded: not available
Average Investment: not available
Minimum Investment: not available

Investment Criteria: All stages

Geographic Preference: Norway, Sweden

Industry Group Preference: All sectors considered

Portfolio Companies: not available

Officers, Executives and Principals

Trond Bjoernoey
Lars Grinde
Jarle Gundersen

NORTH-EAST HUNGARIAN REGIONAL DEVELOPMENT CO. LTD.
c/o MBFB
1365 Budapest 5 Pf. 678
Hungary

Telephone: 36-1-1530222
Fax: 36-1-1110074

Other Office Locations
4400 Nyiregyhaza,
Szaravas V. 1-3
Hungary
Phone 36-42-42-645, Fax 36-42-420641

Mission: Providing small and medium-sized enterprises with venture capital in the northeastern region of Hungary

Fund Size: Ecu5 million
Founded: 1994
Average Investment: Ecu130,000
Minimum Investment: Ecu50,000

Investment Criteria: Expansion/Development

Geographic Preference: Northeastern Hungary

Industry Group Preference: Agriculture and Forestry, Consumer Related, Industrial Products, Manufacturing, Services

Portfolio Companies: not available

Officers, Executives and Principals

L. Csillag, Managing Director
Laszlo Csoknyai, Managing Director

NORTHERN ENTERPRISE (MANAGER) LIMITED

6th Floor, Cale Cross House
156 Pilgrim Street
Newcastle Upon Tyne NE1 6SU
United Kingdom

Telephone: 44-191-233-1892
Fax: 44-191-233-1891

Mission: Actively seeking new investments

Fund Size: £3 million
Founded: not available
Average Investment: £52,300
Minimum Investment: £5,000

Investment Criteria: Expansion, Management Buy-in, Management Buy-out, Early-stage, Refinancing Bank Debt, Rescue/Turnaround, Secondary Purchase/Replacement Capital, Seed, Start-up

Geographic Preference: United Kingdom (Cleveland, County Durham, Northumberland, Tyneside, Wearside)

Industry Group Preference: Biotechnology, Chemical and Materials, Communications, Computer Related, Consumer Related, Electronics Related Energy, Environmental, Industrial Automation, Industrial Products and Services, Leisure, Manufacturing, Services, Transport

Portfolio Companies: Christine Nugent Business Travel Ltd, Pipe Equipment Specialists Ltd, Non-Linear Dynamics Ltd, F. J. Reeve (Northern) Ltd, Thermal Detection Ltd

Officers, Executives and Principals

Barrie Hensby

NORTHERN IRELAND INNOVATION PROGRAMME INVESTMENTS LIMITED

Chamber of Commerce House
22 Great Victoria Street
Belfast BT2 7BJ
Northern Ireland

Telephone: 44-1232-241619
Fax: 44-1232-439899

Mission: Actively seeking new investments

Fund Size: £2 million
Founded: not available
Average Investment: £40,000
Minimum Investment: £20,000

Investment Criteria: Seed, Start-up, Other Early-stage

Geographic Preference: Northern Ireland

Industry Group Preference: Biotechnology, Chemical and Materials, Communications, Computer Related, Electronics Related, Energy, Industrial Automation, Industrial Products and Services, Manufacturing, Medical Related, Services, Transport

Portfolio Companies: not available

Officers, Executives and Principals

John Stringer

NORTHERN VENTURE MANAGERS LIMITED

Northumberland House
Princess Square
Newcastle Upon Tyne NE1 8ER
United Kingdom

Telephone: 44-191-232-7068
Fax: 44-191-232-4070

Mission: Actively seeking new investments

Fund Size: £35 million
Founded: not available
Average Investment: £600,000
Minimum Investment: £200,000

Investment Criteria: All stages except Seed

Geographic Preference: Europe

Industry Group Preference: All sectors considered

Portfolio Companies: Deep-Sea World, Lambert Smith Hampton, McKinnon and Clarke, Royston Engineering Group, Manby Park Electronics

Officers, Executives and Principals

Alastair Conn, Partner
Michael Denny, Partner
Tim Levett, Partner
Robert Dickinson, Partner
Nathaniel Hone, Partner

NOVARE KAPITAL AB

10332 Stockholm
Sweden

Telephone: 46-8-614-2130
Fax: 46-8-614-2198

Mission: Providing minority investments in technology-based growth companies

Fund Size: Skr 100 million
Founded: 1995
Average Investment: not available
Minimum Investment: not available

Investment Criteria: Early-stage

Geographic Preference: Sweden

Industry Group Preference: not available

Portfolio Companies: not available

Officers, Executives and Principals

Börje Ekholm, Managing Director
Swante Welander, Investment Manager
Erik Davidsson, Investment Manager

NOVI-NORTH JUTLAND SCIENCE PARK

Niels Jernes Vej 10
P. O. Box 8330
9220 Aalborg
Denmark

Telephone: 45-98-158533
Fax: 45-98-158550

Mission: Actively seeking new investments

Fund Size: not available
Founded: not available
Average Investment: not available
Minimum Investment: not available

Investment Criteria: Seed, Start-up, Expansion/Development

Geographic Preference: not available

Industry Group Preference: Communications, Computer Related, Computer Software, Electronics Related

Portfolio Companies: not available

Officers, Executives and Principals

Lauge Slitting

NPE INVESTMENT ADVISERS A/S

Stockholmsgrade 41
2100 Copenhagen OE
Denmark

Telephone: 45-35-260212
Fax: 45-35-260214

Mission: Actively seeking new investments

Fund Size: Ecu21.5 million
Founded: not available
Average Investment: not available
Minimum Investment: Ecu1 million

Investment Criteria: Expansion/Development, Bridge, Replacement, Management Buy-out, Management buy-in

Geographic Preference: Denmark, Norway, Sweden, Finland

Industry Group Preference: All sectors considered

Portfolio Companies: not available

Officers, Executives and Principals

Leif Jensen, Partner
S. Sylvet Jensen, Partner

NSM FINANCE SA

3 avenue Hoche
75008 Paris
France

Telephone: 33-1-4766-6609
Fax: 33-1-4888-5348

Mission: Actively seeking new investments in strong, profitable and growing medium- sized companies with turnovers between Ffr100 million and Ffr1 billion, as part of the ABN AMRO Group

Fund Size: Ffr550 million
Founded: 1990
Average Investment: Ffr30 million
Minimum Investment: Ffr15 million

Investment Criteria: Expansion/Development, Management Buy-out, Management Buy-in, Replacement Capital, Leveraged Buy-out

Geographic Preference: France

Industry Group Preference: All sectors considered except Financial Institutions and Real Estate

Portfolio Companies: AXIOHM, CIRE, Darfeuille, JEC, ORTEC, Topinfo, AMD, IMV, OTOR, Poclain Hydraulics, Steiner, AFE, Descours et Cabaud, Plasthom, Hyparlo, La Flachere, OTRA, Satelec, Tipiak

Officers, Executives and Principals

Hervé Claquin, Chief Executive Officer
Nicolas Dourassoff, Managing Director

NUTEK (NÄRINGS- OCH TEKNIKUTVECKLINGSVERKET)
Liljeholmsvägen 32
11786 Stockholm
Sweden

Telephone: 46-8-681-9100
Fax: 46-8-196826
E-mail: thomas.ronstrom@nutek.se

Mission: Actively seeking new investments

Fund Size: not available
Founded: not available
Average Investment: not available
Minimum Investment: not available

Investment Criteria: Seed

Geographic Preference: Sweden

Industry Group Preference: Manufacturing

Portfolio Companies: not available

Officers, Executives and Principals

Birgitta Erngren
Tomas Järnmark

OKO VENTURE CAPITAL OY

P. O. Box 362
Arkadiankatu 23
00101 Helsinki
Finland

Telephone: 358-0-4041
Fax: 358-0-404-2815

Mission: Actively seeking new investments as part of Okobank

Fund Size: FM16.3 million
Founded: not available
Average Investment: FM1.5-5 million
Minimum Investment: FM1 million

Investment Criteria: Expansion, Management Buy-out, Restructuring

Geographic Preference: Scandinavia, Europe

Industry Group Preference: All sectors considered

Portfolio Companies: not available

Officers, Executives and Principals

Arto Naukkarinen, President
Education: MSc in Engineering; BSc in Economics; MBA

Erkki Vesola, Investment Manager
Education: MSc in Economics

ÖKOLOGIK AG

Innovationszentrum
Am Weichselgarten 7
91058 Erlangen
Germany

Telephone: 49-9131-691-380
Fax: 49-9131-691-382

Mission: Actively seeking new investments in enterprises producing goods or services relevant to protecting and improving the natural environment

Fund Size: not available
Founded: not available
Average Investment: not available
Minimum Investment: DM50,000

Investment Criteria: Start-up, Growth

Geographic Preference: Germany

Industry Group Preference: All sectors considered

Portfolio Companies: not available

Officers, Executives and Principals

Harald Schuderer

ONO PHARMACEUTICALS COMPANY LIMITED

2-1-5 Dosomachi
Chuo-ku
Osaka 541
Japan

Telephone: 81-6-222-5551
Fax: 81-6-222-5706

Mission: not available

Fund Size: not available
Founded: not available
Average Investment: not available
Minimum Investment: not available

Investment Criteria: not available

Geographic Preference: not available

Industry Group Preference: Medical/Health Related

Portfolio Companies: Telios Pharmaceuticals Inc.

Officers, Executives and Principals

Kazuo Sano

ORFIMAR

59 avenue Marceau
75116 Paris
France

Telephone: 33-1-4723-0020
Fax: 33-1-4720-3978

Mission: Actively seeking new investments

Fund Size: Ffr300 million
Founded: not available
Average Investment: not available
Minimum Investment: not available

Investment Criteria: All Stages

Geographic Preference: France

Industry Group Preference: All sectors considered

Portfolio Companies: not available

Officers, Executives and Principals

Sébastien Picciotto
Jean-Paul Vannier

OSNABRÜCKER BETEILIGUNGS- UND CONSULT GmbH

Wittekindstrasse 17-18
49074 Osnabrück
Germany

Telephone: 49-541-312-3050
Fax: 49-541-312-3099

Mission: Actively seeking new investments

Fund Size: not available
Founded: not available
Average Investment: not available
Minimum Investment: DM500,000

Investment Criteria: All stages

Geographic Preference: Germany (Osnabrück region)

Industry Group Preference: All sectors considered

Portfolio Companies: not available

Officers, Executives and Principals

Werner Viere

PALLAS FINANCE

61 rue de Monceau
75008 Paris
France

Telephone: 33-1-4074-2230
Fax: 33-1-428-92588

Mission: Actively seeking new investments as part of a joint venture with Electra Fleming Limited

Fund Size: Ecu100 million
Founded: not available
Average Investment: not available
Minimum Investment: Ecu4.5 million

Investment Criteria: Expansion/Development, Management Buy-out, Management Buy-in

Geographic Preference: Europe, North America

Industry Group Preference: Communications, Computer Related, Consumer Products/Services, Electronics Related, Software Related

Portfolio Companies: not available

Officers, Executives and Principals

Robert Lattès
Jean Ducroux
Laurence Albertini
Nicolas Paulmier

PANTHEON VENTURES LIMITED

43-44 Albermarle Street
London W1X 3FE
United Kingdom

Telephone: 44-171-493-5685
Fax: 44-171-629-0844

Mission: Investing internationally in both new and existing holdings (secondary interests) in private equity funds on behalf of major institutional investors

Fund Size: £500 million
Founded: not available
Average Investment: £5 million
Minimum Investment: £200,000

Investment Criteria: All stages

Geographic Preference: Worldwide

Industry Group Preference: All sectors considered

Portfolio Companies: not available

Officers, Executives and Principals

Carol Kennedy, Partner
Rhoddy Swire, Partner
R.A. Bowley, Partner

PARCOM VENTURES BV

Euclideslaan 67
P. O. Box 85415
3508 AK Utrecht
The Netherlands

Telephone: 31-30- 256-3100
Fax: 31-30-254-3598
E-mail: parcom@worldaccess.nl

Mission: Actively seeking new investments

Fund Size: Ecu218.2 million
Founded: not available
Average Investment: not available
Minimum Investment: Ecu200,000

Investment Criteria: Expansion/Development, Management Buy-out, Management Buy-in, Turnaround/ Restructuring

Geographic Preference: Europe

Industry Group Preference: Consumer Related, Industrial Products, Manufacturing

Portfolio Companies: not available

Officers, Executives and Principals

Aris Wateler
Roeland Brokking

PARIBAS AFFAIRES INDUSTRIELLES

3 rue d'Antin
75002 Paris
France

Telephone: 33-1-4298-1332
Fax: 33-1-4298-7379

Mission: Actively seeking new investments

Fund Size: Ecu7 billion
Founded: not available
Average Investment: not available
Minimum Investment: Ecu4 million

Investment Criteria: Expansion/Development, Management Buy-out, Management Buy-in, Replacement, Bridge

Geographic Preference: Europe, United States, Southeast Asia

Industry Group Preference: All sectors considered

Portfolio Companies: not available

Officers, Executives and Principals

Michel Paris
Hervé Couffin
André-Joël Motte
Dominique Megret

PARIBAS INVESTISEMENT DÉVELOPPEMENT

41 avenue de l'Opéra
75002 Paris
France

Telephone: 33-1-4298-1234
Fax: 33-1-4298-7650

Mission: Actively seeking new investments

Fund Size: Ffr756 million
Founded: not available
Average Investment: not available
Minimum Investment: Ffr3 million

Investment Criteria: Expansion/Development

Geographic Preference: Europe

Industry Group Preference: All sectors considered

Portfolio Companies: MGI Coutier, Securidev, Cartier Industrie, Camaieu, Gemplus, Cegid

Officers, Executives and Principals

Philippe Latorre
Lise Nobre
Philippe Duei
Bertrand Guigon
Michel Paris
Philippe Taranto

PARNIB HOLDING NV

Burg. Van Karnebeeklaan 8
2585 BB Den Haag
The Netherlands

Telephone: 31-70-302-2800
Fax: 31-70-345-2598

Other Office Locations
Parnib Belgie NV
Corner Building
Uitbreidingstraat 18
2600 Antwerpen
Belgium
Phone 32-3-286-9140, Fax 32-3-286-9150

Mission: Actively seeking new investments

Fund Size: G700 million
Founded: 1982
Average Investment: not available
Minimum Investment: G2-15 million

Investment Criteria: Expansion/Development, Management Buy-out, Management Buy-in, Bridge, Replacement

Geographic Preference: Belgium, Netherlands, Germany, Denmark, France

Industry Group Preference: All sectors considered

Portfolio Companies: not available

Officers, Executives and Principals

Emile J. van der Burg
Emile J. Bakker
Jacob P. van der Zwan

PARTECH INTERNATIONAL

4 rue Ancelle
92521 Neuilly
France

Telephone: 33-1-4747-4444
Fax: 33-1-4747-9905

Mission: Actively seeking new investments

Fund Size: Ffr165 million
Founded: not available
Average Investment: not available
Minimum Investment: Ffr500,000

Investment Criteria: Seed, Start-up, Early-stage, Development

Geographic Preference: Europe, United States, Japan

Industry Group Preference: Biotechnology, Communications, Computer Related, Computer Software, Electronics Related, Medical/Health Related

Portfolio Companies: Apsylog, Business Objects, Biovector Therapeutics, Pixtech, Silmang

Officers, Executives and Principals

Michel Jauguey, Managing Director
Anne-Isabelle de la Bourdonnaye

PARTICIPEX

1 rue Esquermoise
Grand Place
P. O. Box 112
59027 Lille
France

Telephone: 33-2021-9380
Fax: 33-2021-9389

Mission: Actively seeking new investments

Fund Size: Ffr320 million
Founded: not available
Average Investment: not available
Minimum Investment: Ffr1 million

Investment Criteria: Expansion/Development, Replacement

Geographic Preference: France, Belgium

Industry Group Preference: All sectors considered

Portfolio Companies: not available

Officers, Executives and Principals

Claude Bouin, Managing Director
Xavier Mahieux
Henri-Luis Delloye

PARVALIND GÉRANCE

48 rue Fabert
75340 Paris
France

Telephone: 33-1-4955-7000
Fax: 33-1-4956-1404

Mission: Actively seeking new investments

Fund Size: Ffr570 million
Founded: not available
Average Investment: not available
Minimum Investment: Ffr20 million

Investment Criteria: Expansion/Development

Geographic Preference: Europe

Industry Group Preference: All sectors considered

Portfolio Companies: Sopal, Kermad, Carpentras and Donarier Entrelec, Sparflex

Officers, Executives and Principals

Jean de Severac, Managing Director
Marc-Oliver Bosshardt, Director
Patrice Chastenet de Gery, Director
Yves Roucaud, Director
Patrick Bergot
Thierry Degroote

PBG INVESTMENT FUND LIMITED

ul. Sienkiewicza 85-87
90-057 Lodz
Poland

Telephone: 48-42-363734
Fax: 48-42-362232

Mission: Actively seeking new investments

Fund Size: Ecu4.75 million
Founded: not available
Average Investment: not available
Minimum Investment: Ecu500,000

Investment Criteria: Expansion/Development, Turnaround/Restructuring

Geographic Preference: Poland

Industry Group Preference: All sectors considered

Portfolio Companies: not available

Officers, Executives and Principals

Jerzy Jozkowiak

PECHEL INDUSTRIES

55 rue La Boétie
75008 Paris
France

Telephone: 33-1-4413-3800
Fax: 33-1-4413-3720

Mission: Actively seeking new investments

Fund Size: Ffr500 million
Founded: not available
Average Investment: not available
Minimum Investment: not available

Investment Criteria: All stages

Geographic Preference: Europe, France, Asia

Industry Group Preference: Consumer Related, Media

Portfolio Companies: not available

Officers, Executives and Principals

Edouard Silvy, President
Yves Alexandre, Managing Director
Thibaut de Chassey, Director

PHENIX DÉVELOPPEMENT GESTION ET CIE

6 avenue Kléber
75116 Paris
France

Telephone: 33-1-4417-2419
Fax: 33-1-4417-2246

Mission: Actively seeking new investments

Fund Size: Ffr350 million
Founded: not available
Average Investment: not available
Minimum Investment: Ffr3 million

Investment Criteria: Expansion/Development, Leveraged Buy-out

Geographic Preference: France

Industry Group Preference: All sectors considered

Portfolio Companies: Bijoux Altesse, Cafétérias Eric, Kindy Otor Emballage, Sergent Major, Secap

Officers, Executives and Principals

Régis Mitjavile
Frédéric Colin
Danielle Abou

PHILDREW VENTURES

Triton Court
14 Finsbury Square
London EC2 1PD
United Kingdom

Telephone: 44-171-628-6366
Fax: 44-171-638-2817

Mission: Actively seeking new investments

Fund Size: £410 million
Founded: not available
Average Investment: £5 million
Minimum Investment: £1 million

Investment Criteria: Expansion, Management Buy-in, Management Buy-out, Early-stage, Rescue/Turn-around, Secondary Purchase/Replacement Capital, Start-up

Geographic Preference: United Kingdom

Industry Group Preference: Chemical and Materials, Construction, Consumer Related, Environmental, Industrial Products and Services, Manufacturing, Services, Transport

Portfolio Companies: Ultra Electronics, Flying Colours Leisure Group, Locum Group, Tuffnells, Seafood Company

Officers, Executives and Principals

Simon Freethy
Henry Gregson
Tim Hart
Ian Hawkins
Ron Hobbs
Robert Jenkins
Frank Neale
Ruth Storm
Chris Tennant

PHILIPS MEDICAL SYSTEMS NEDERLAND BV

Groenewoudseweg 1
5621 BA Eindhoven
The Netherlands

Telephone: 31-40-279-1111
Fax: 31-40-785-486

Mission: not available

Fund Size: not available
Founded: not available
Average Investment: not available
Minimum Investment: not available

Investment Criteria: not available

Geographic Preference: not available

Industry Group Preference: Electronic Components and Instrumentation

Portfolio Companies: ISG Technologies Inc. (ISG)

Officers, Executives and Principals

H. Van Bree, Chairman

PHOENIX FUND MANAGERS LIMITED

1 Laurence Pountney Hill
London EC4R 0EU
United Kingdom

Telephone: 44-171-638-3818
Fax: 44-171-638-3487
E-mail: 101643.240@compuserv.com

Mission: Actively seeking new investments

Fund Size: not available
Founded: 1991
Average Investment: not available
Minimum Investment: not available

Investment Criteria: Second-stage, Mezzanine, Leveraged Buy-out, Special Situations, Management Buy-in, Expansion, Refinancing Bank Debt, Rescue/Turnaround

Geographic Preference: Western Europe

Industry Group Preference: All sectors considered

Portfolio Companies: The Orion Publishing Group, Wates Leisure, MRG Medical Holdings, SilverPlatter, Wentworth Research

Officers, Executives and Principals

Martin Smith, Chairman
Education: Theoretical Physics, University of Oxford; MA, MBA Economics, Stanford University
Background: McKinsey and Co.; Citicorp International Bank; Chairman, Bankers Trust

David Gregson, Managing Director
Education: Mathematics and Physics, University of Cambridge; MBA, Manchester Business School
Background: 12 years in investing in unquoted equities; Globe Investment Trust

P. Hugh Lenon, Director
Education: Economics and Law, University of Stirling; Chartered Accountant
Background: Investment Manager, Globe Investment Trust; Corporate Finance, Touche Ross

Alastair Muirhead, Partner
Education: St John's College, University of Oxford
Background: Chartered Accountant, Price Waterhouse; Saudi International Bank; Managing Director, Charterhouse Bank Limited

James Thomas, Manager
Education: Law, University of Manchester University
Background: S.G. Warburg and Co. Banking Team and Corporate Finance

PICARDIE INVESTISSEMENT

67 Mail Albert 1er
8005 Amiens
France

Telephone: 33-2291-7020
Fax: 33-2291-6670

Mission: Actively seeking new investments

Fund Size: Ffr105 million
Founded: not available
Average Investment: not available
Minimum Investment: Ffr800,000

Investment Criteria: Early-stage, Expansion/Development

Geographic Preference: France (Picardy)

Industry Group Preference: All sectors considered

Portfolio Companies: Le Creuset, Kindy, Unither

Officers, Executives and Principals

Jean-Pierre Dumas, President
Gil Forteguerre, Director
Philippe Pruvot

PIKESPO INVEST OY LTD

P. O. Box 172
Kehräsaari
33201 Tampere
Finland

Telephone: 358-03-271-4100
Fax: 358-03-271-4104

Mission: Investing in industrial companies and engaging in equity financing with a minority share

Fund Size: FM 25.5 million
Founded: 1985
Average Investment: FM 700,000
Minimum Investment: FM 200,000

Investment Criteria: Start-up, Expansion, Management buy-out

Geographic Preference: Finland

Industry Group Preference: Manufacturing

Portfolio Companies: not available

Officers, Executives and Principals

Hannu Partala, Managing Director
Education: BSc in Economics

Eero Stenholm, Development Manager
Education: MSc in Administration

PIONEER INVESTMENT POLAND

Intraco Stawki 2
00-193 Warsaw
Poland

Telephone: 48-22-635-9908
Fax: 48-22-635-6976

Mission: Actively seeking new investments

Fund Size: $60 million
Founded: 1995
Average Investment: $2.5 million
Minimum Investment: $1 million

Investment Criteria: Expansion/Development, Management Buy-out, Management Buy-in, Bridge

Geographic Preference: Poland

Industry Group Preference: Agriculture/Forestry/Fish, Communications, Computer Related, Consumer Related, Construction/Building Products and Services, Wood Products

Portfolio Companies: not available

Officers, Executives and Principals

David N. Hartford, Executive Vice President

PIPER INVESTMENT MANAGEMENT LIMITED

Eardley House
182-184 Campden Hill Road
London W8 7AS
United Kingdom

Telephone: 44-171-727-3866
Fax: 44-171-727-8969

Mission: Actively seeeking new investments

Fund Size: £7 million
Founded: not available
Average Investment: £700,000
Minimum Investment: £250,000

Investment Criteria: Expansion, Management Buy-in, Management Buy-out, Early- stage, Refinancing Bank Debt, Rescue/Turnaround, Secondary Purchase/ Replacement Capital, Start-up

Geographic Preference: United Kingdom

Industry Group Preference: Consumer Related, Leisure

Portfolio Companies: Pied a terre (Holdings) Ltd, Sofa Workshop Ltd, Pitcher and Piano Ltd, Cranks Retail Ltd

Officers, Executives and Principals

Christopher Curry
Crispin Tweddell

PKPF (POVAZSKY A KYSUCKY PODNIKATEL'SKY FOND A. S.)

Horny Val. 15/17
010 01 Zilina
Slovakia

Telephone: 42-89-624039
Fax: 42-89-624065

Mission: Contributing to the economic development of the Zilina and Trencin regions, as a PHARE (European Union) regional investment company pilot project, by financially supporting small and medium-sized enterprises and reinforcing the equity of such companies for a period of around five years

Fund Size: SK200 million
Founded: 1994
Average Investment: SK15 million
Minimum Investment: SK5 million

Investment Criteria: Start-up, Early-stage, Expansion/Development, Management Buy-out, Bridge

Geographic Preference: Slovakia (Zilina and Trencin regions)

Industry Group Preference: Manufacturing, Services, Tourism

Portfolio Companies: not available

Officers, Executives and Principals

Werner De Block, Chief Executive Officer
Jozef Klucka, Investment Manager
Eva Kovácová, Investment Manager
Bubica Sokoliková, Investment Manager
Silvia Bǝhmová, Office Manager

POLAND PARTNERS MANAGEMENT COMPANY

ul. Podwale 13
00-950 Warsaw
Poland

Telephone: 48-22-635-7690
Fax: 48-22-317920
E-mail: 104316.517@compuserv.com

Other Office Locations
700 13th Street NW
Washington, DC 20036
USA
Phone 1-202-737-7000, Fax 1-202-737-7604

Mission: Actively seeking equity or equity like investments in private or privatizing businesses

Fund Size: $63 million
Founded: 1994
Average Investment: $4 million
Minimum Investment: $2 million

Investment Criteria: Seed, Start-up, Early-stage, Expansion/Development, Bridge

Geographic Preference: Poland only

Industry Group Preference: Building Supplies/Materials, Consumer Related, Finance/Insurance, Food Processing

Portfolio Companies: Office Depot, Town and City, Euronet, Mediplast, Boss'a, Phoenix Privatisation Partners, Polska Telewizja Kablowa

Officers, Executives and Principals

Steven J. Buckley, President
Steven T. Arfield, Vice President
Robert Conn, Vice President
Anna Lesiak, Investment Director
Leszek Piaskowski, Investment Director

PRELUDE TECHNOLOGY INVESTMENTS LIMITED

Sycamore Studios
New Road
Over
Cambridge CB4 5PJ
United Kingdom

Telephone: 44-1954-288090
Fax: 44-1954-288099
E-mail: prelude@dial.pipex.com

Mission: Actively seeking new investments in early-stage businesses that use proprietary technology to generate competitive advantage and offer potential for rapid growth

Fund Size: £25 million
Founded: 1985
Average Investment: £1 million
Minimum Investment: £250,000

Investment Criteria: Seed, Start-up, First-stage

Geographic Preference: United Kingdom

Industry Group Preference: Biotechnology, Communications, Computer Related, Electronic Components and Instrumentation, Industrial Products and Equipment, Medical/Health Related

Portfolio Companies: Quadrant Healthcare plc, Xaar Ltd, Peptide Therapeutics Group plc, Vocalis Ltd, Core Technologies Limited

Officers, Executives and Principals

Dr. Robert Hook, Managing Director
Andrew Allars, Director

PRIVATE EQUITY INVESTMENT MANAGERS (PTY) LTD

24 Napier Road
Richmond
Johannesburg 2000
South Africa

Telephone: 27-11-482-4504
Fax: 27-11-482-3107

Mission: Actively seeking new investments

Fund Size: R10 million
Founded: 1994
Average Investment: R2.5 million
Minimum Investment: R500,000

Investment Criteria: Second-stage, Special Situations

Geographic Preference: Republic of South Africa: Gauteng

Industry Group Preference: Communications, Computer Related, Consumer, Distribution, Electronic Components and Instrumentation

Portfolio Companies: not available

Officers, Executives and Principals

A.P. Du Preez, Chairman
G.C. Swanepoel, Managing Director
J.G. Steyn, Director

PROCORDIA

Frosundaviks alle 15
17197 Stockholm
Sweden

Telephone: 46-8-624-5000
Fax: 46-8-655-8010

Mission: not available

Fund Size: $38.4 billion
Founded: not available
Average Investment: not available
Minimum Investment: not available

Investment Criteria: not available

Geographic Preference: not available

Industry Group Preference: Consumer, Food, Medical/Health Related

Portfolio Companies: Luther Medical Products Inc.

Officers, Executives and Principals

Soren Gyll, Chief Executive Officer

PROCURITAS PARTNERS KB

Skeppsbron 20
11130 Stockholm
Sweden

Telephone: 46-8-244300
Fax: 46-8-244303
E-mail: procuritas@procuritas.se

Mission: Actively seeking new investments

Fund Size: Skr260 million
Founded: 1986
Average Investment: not available
Minimum Investment: not available

Investment Criteria: Management Buy-out

Geographic Preference: Sweden, Denmark, Norway

Industry Group Preference: All sectors considered

Portfolio Companies: not available

Officers, Executives and Principals

Mikael Ahlström, Funding Manager
Hans Karlander, Managing Partner

PROGRAMA SEED CAPITAL / SCCR

Passeig de Gràcia, 2, 2n B
08007 Barcelona
Spain

Telephone: 34-3-317-8161
Fax: 34-3-318-9287

Mission: Actively seeking new investments

Fund Size: not available
Founded: not available
Average Investment: not available
Minimum Investment: Ecu50,000

Investment Criteria: Seed

Geographic Preference: Europe, Spain, France, Italy, Switzerland

Industry Group Preference: All sectors considered

Portfolio Companies: not available

Officers, Executives and Principals

Anna Xicoy

PROMINDÚSTRIA - SOCIEDADE DE INVESTIMENTO SA
Av. João XXI 63
Piso 2 Edificio CGD Apartado 1795
1017 Lisbon
Portugal

Telephone: 351-1-790-5463
Fax: 351-1-790-5481

Mission: Investing in new and expanding companies, managing investment funds through finance consultancy services and credit operations

Fund Size: not available
Founded: 1987
Average Investment: Esc136,500
Minimum Investment: not available

Investment Criteria: Start-up, Expansion/Development, Management Buy-out

Geographic Preference: Portugal, Spain

Industry Group Preference: All sectors considered

Portfolio Companies: Net SA, Matrena SA, Prominser Lda, IAF Lda, Telgecom SA, Imotron SA, Pardal Monteiro Mármores SA, Technivest SA, EIA SA, Contactel, Emparque SA, Ambelis SA, Esence SA, EID SA, Quinta Nova SA, Map SA, IPT SA, Fibope SA, Macem SA, Maconde SA

Officers, Executives and Principals

Rui Gomes do Amaral, Executive Director
José Eduardo Ferreira Rodrigues, Executive Director
Jorge Ferreira Braga, Management
José Pedro Guimarães, Management
Leonor Balão, Technical Staff
Alexandra Faustino, Technical Staff

PROVINZIAL BETEILIGUNGS GmbH

Leisewitzstrasse 37b
30175 Hanover
Germany

Telephone: 49-511-280-0701
Fax: 49-511-280-0737
E-mail: hannover.finanz@p-net.de

Mission: Actively seeking new investments in growing companies as a managed fund within the Hannover Finanz Group

Fund Size: DM100 million
Founded: 1988
Average Investment: DM8 million
Minimum Investment: DM2 million

Investment Criteria: Later-stage, Development, Buy-out, Pre-IPO, Replacement

Geographic Preference: Germany; rest of Europe with syndication partners

Industry Group Preference: Engineering, Financial Services, Logistics, Manufacturing, Media, Services, Telecommunications, Trade

Portfolio Companies: not available

PROXIFI

320 rue St Honoré
75001 Paris
France

Telephone: 33-1-395-30452
Fax: 33-1-395-22433

Mission: Actively seeking new investments

Fund Size: not available
Founded: not available
Average Investment: not available
Minimum Investment: Ecu7,000

Investment Criteria: Start-up, Early-stage, Management Buy-out, Management Buy-in

Geographic Preference: France

Industry Group Preference: All sectors considered

Portfolio Companies: not available

Officers, Executives and Principals

Pascal Gauthier
Paul Douriez
B. de Villaines

PRUDENTIAL VENTURE MANAGERS LIMITED

1 Waterhouse Square, Holborn Bars
London EC1N 2ST
United Kingdom

Telephone: 44-171-831-7747
Fax: 44-171-831-9528

Mission: Specializing in unquoted equity investments as an arm of Prudential Corporation plc

Fund Size: £500 million
Founded: 1986
Average Investment: not available
Minimum Investment: £2 million

Investment Criteria: Management Buy-in, Management Buy-out, Expansion, Institutional Purchase, Secondary Purchase/Replacement Capital

Geographic Preference: United Kingdom, Western Europe

Industry Group Preference: All sectors considered

Portfolio Companies: Birthdays Group, Levington Group, Quexco, Saint Martins, The Tetley Group

Officers, Executives and Principals

Jonathan Morgan, Managing Director
Kay Ashton, Director
Martin Clarke, Director
Gus Guest, Director
Neil MacDougall, Director
Alistair Mackintosh, Director
Andrew Smith, Director
Matthew Turner, Director

QUADRIGA CAPITAL MANAGEMENT GmbH

Hamburger Allee 2-10
60486 Frankfurt am Main
Germany

Telephone: 49-69-7950-0025
Fax: 49-69-7950-0060
E-mail: quandriga@capital.f.eunet.d

Mission: Actively seeking new investments

Fund Size: Ecu100 million
Founded: not available
Average Investment: not available
Minimum Investment: Ecu7.5 million

Investment Criteria: Management Buy-out, Management Buy-in

Geographic Preference: Austria, Belgium, Denmark, Germany, Switzerland

Industry Group Preference: All sectors considered

Portfolio Companies: not available

Officers, Executives and Principals

Dr. Andreas Fendel
Max W. Römer
Christoph Weise

QUESTER CAPITAL MANAGEMENT LTD.

2 Queen Anne's Gate Buildings
Dartmouth Street
London SW1H 9BP
United Kingdom

Telephone: 44-171-222-5472
Fax: 44-171-222-5250

Mission: Actively seeking new investments

Fund Size: not available
Founded: 1984
Average Investment: not available
Minimum Investment: $100,000

Investment Criteria: Bridge Finance, Expansion, Management Buy-in, Management Buy-out, Refinancing Bank Debt, Rescue/Turnaround, Secondary Purchase/Replacement Capital, Start-up, Venture Purchase of Quoted Shares

Geographic Preference: Western Europe

Industry Group Preference: All sectors considered

Portfolio Companies: Aethos Communications Systems Ltd, Biotrace International PLC, Active Imaging plc, Epic MultiMedia Group plc, Sauflon Pharmaceuticals Ltd

Officers, Executives and Principals

Andrew Holmes, Managing Director
Simon Acland, Director
John Spooner, Director

RAGGIO DI SOLE BIOTECHNOLOGIE SpA

Via Delle Antille 29
00040 Pomezia (Rome)
Italy

Telephone: 39-6-910-7494
Fax: 39-6-910-7497

Mission: Actively seeking new investments

Fund Size: not available
Founded: not available
Average Investment: not available
Minimum Investment: Ecu150,000

Investment Criteria: Start-up, Early-stage

Geographic Preference: Europe

Industry Group Preference: Biotechnology

Portfolio Companies: not available

Officers, Executives and Principals

G. Battista Cozzone

R. B. S. KAPITALBETEILIGUNGSGESELLSCHAFT RHEINISCH-BERGISCHER SPARKASSEN mbH

Sternstrasse 58
40479 Düsseldorf
Germany

Telephone: 49-211-952-910
Fax: 49-211-952- 9191

Mission: Actively seeking new investments

Fund Size: not available
Founded: not available
Average Investment: not available
Minimum Investment: DM500,000

Investment Criteria: All stages

Geographic Preference: Germany (North Rhine-Westphalia)

Industry Group Preference: All sectors considered

Portfolio Companies: not available

Officers, Executives and Principals

Jochen Walter

REFIT GmbH UND CO. KG

Riesengebirgstrasse 52
93057 Regensburg
Germany

Telephone: 49-941-64289
Fax: 49-941-68912

Mission: Actively seeking new investments in technology-based enterprises

Fund Size: Ecu2,400,000
Founded: 1989
Average Investment: not available
Minimum Investment: Ecu10,000

Investment Criteria: Seed, Start-up, Early-stage

Geographic Preference: Germany (Upper Palatinate, Lower Bavaria, Upper Franconia)

Industry Group Preference: not available

Portfolio Companies: Bodeneffektfahrzeuge GmbH, Condiam Diamantwerkzeuge GmbH, KASI faserverstärkte Metalle GmbH, METATRAIN GmbH, Robotersystem Yberle GmbH, Schuster medizinische Systeme GmbH, Spherics Mess- und Analysetechnik GmbH, Ulrich Daxer - Ideen fürs Pferd GmbH

Officers, Executives and Principals

Dr. Thomas Brennauer, Chairman of the Supervisory Board
Michael Dusch, Managing Director

REGIONALE BETEILIGUNGSGESELLSCHAFT DER KREISSPARKASSE HANNOVER mbH

Breite Strasse 6-8
30159 Hanover
Germany

Telephone: 49-511-321811
Fax: 49-511-321897

Mission: Actively seeking new investments

Fund Size: DM50 million
Founded: not available
Average Investment: not available
Minimum Investment: DM500,000

Investment Criteria: All stages

Geographic Preference: Germany (Hanover region)

Industry Group Preference: All sectors considered

Portfolio Companies: not available

Officers, Executives and Principals

Friedrich Hesse
Dieter Pflugrad

R. E. L. CONSEILS / R. E. L. PARTENAIRES

148 boulevard Hausssmann
75008 Paris
France

Telephone: 33-1-5383-8620
Fax: 33-1-5383-0632

Mission: Actively seeking new investments

Fund Size: Ffr407 million
Founded: not available
Average Investment: not available
Minimum Investment: Ffr5 million

Investment Criteria: Leveraged Buy-out, Management Buy-out, Management Buy-in

Geographic Preference: France, Europe

Industry Group Preference: All sectors considered

Portfolio Companies: Editions Nuit et Jour, Furnotel, RS Isolsec, EM Technologies, Mecaseat

Officers, Executives and Principals

Philippe Fessart
Emmanuel Le Grand
Laurent Allégot
Michel Horps

RENAISSANCE PARTNERS

ul. Lowicka 44
02-551 Warsaw
Poland

Telephone: 48-22-480773
Fax: 48-39-122416

Mission: Actively seeking new investments

Fund Size: Ecu31 million
Founded: not available
Average Investment: not available
Minimum Investment: not available

Investment Criteria: All stages

Geographic Preference: Central and Eastern Europe

Industry Group Preference: All sectors considered

Portfolio Companies: not available

Officers, Executives and Principals

Jacek S. Witak
Alois J. Strnad
Kornel Spiro
Peter G. Stark

RISFOMENTO - SOCIEDADE DE CAPITAL DE RISCO SA

Av. Júlio Dinis, 735 - 2°
4050 Oporto
Portugal

Telephone: 351-2-600-6717
Fax: 351-2-600-6751

Mission: Actively seeking new investments, as part of the Banco de Fomento e Exterior Group

Fund Size: Ecu53.4 million
Founded: not available
Average Investment: not available
Minimum Investment: not available

Investment Criteria: Expansion/Development, Management Buy-out, Management Buy-in, Replacement

Geographic Preference: Portugal

Industry Group Preference: Biotechnology, Communications, Computer Related, Energy, Industrial Products, Medical/Health Related

Portfolio Companies: not available

Officers, Executives and Principals

Dr. Ana Maria Fernandes

ROLOFINANCE - ROLO BANCA 1473 SpA

Via Zamboni 20
40126 Bologna
Italy

Telephone: 39-51-6407-229
Fax: 39-51-6407-279

Other Office Locations
Passaggio Centrale 2 (Ang.Orefici)
20123 Milan
Phone 39-2-8875-412, Fax 39-2-8875-334

Mission: Actively seeking new investments in strong growth companies by providing financing, buy-out and acquisition capital

Fund Size: L70 billion
Founded: 1994
Average Investment: L5-7 billion
Minimum Investment: L3 billion

Investment Criteria: Expansion/Development, Bridge

Geographic Preference: Italy

Industry Group Preference: All sectors considered except Finance and Real Estate

Portfolio Companies: Protti SpA (Cornaredo-Milan)

Officers, Executives and Principals

Alberto Franceschini, Principal
Education: Graduate in Economics; Chartered Accountant
Background: Reconta Touche Ross; La Compagnia Finanziaria; Fineurop

Walter Comelli, Executive (Bologna)
Education: Graduate in Economics; MBA, University of California Los Angeles
Background: IBM Italia; Volvo Italia; Price Waterhouse Management Consultants

Eleonora Di Lauro, Executive (Milan)
Education: Graduate in Economics; Chartered Accountant
Background: ENI; Finanziaria ICCRI-Bruxelles Lambert

Stefano Albonetti, Officer (Bologna)
Education: Graduate in Law; MBA, University of Bologna
Background: Credito Romagnolo

Daniela Ingrosso, Officer (Milan)
Education: degree in Economics; Chartered Accountant
Background: Banca Commerciale Italiana

Santo Borsellino, Officer (Bologna)
Education: Graduate in Economics

ROTHSCHILD AUSTRALIA CAPITAL INVESTORS LIMITED

1 Collins Street
Melbourne
Victoria 3000
Australia

Telephone: 61-3-9254-4900
Fax: 61-3-9254-4940

Other Office Locations
1 O'Connell Street, 16th Floor
Sydney
New South Wales 2000
Phone 61-2-9323-2000, Fax 61-2-9323-2323

Mission: Actively seeking new investments

Fund Size: A$90.2 million
Founded: 1992
Average Investment: A$7 million
Minimum Investment: A$5 million

Investment Criteria: Second-stage, Mezzanine, Leveraged Buy-out, Special Situations

Geographic Preference: Australia, New Zealand

Industry Group Preference: Manufacturing/Processing

Portfolio Companies: not available

Officers, Executives and Principals

Peter Chapman, Chief Executive
Graeme Monkhouse, Associate Director
Peter Wiggs, Associate Director
Spencer Young, Associate Director

ROTHSCHILD BIOSCIENCE UNIT

Rothschild Asset Management Ltd
Five Arrows House
St Swithin's Lane
London EC4N 8NR
United Kingdom

Telephone: 44-171-280-5000
Fax: 44-171-623-6261

Mission: Actively seeking new investments as manager of Biotechnology Investments Ltd. and International Biotechnology Trust

Fund Size: £285 million
Founded: not available
Average Investment: £1 -3.5 million
Minimum Investment: £100,000

Investment Criteria: Bridge, Expansion, Early-stage, Purchase of Quoted Shares, Secondary Purchase/ Replacement Capital, Seed, Start-up, Venture Purchase of Quoted Shares

Geographic Preference: Worldwide

Industry Group Preference: Biotechnology, Medical/Health Related

Portfolio Companies: Biocompatibles International plc, Capteur Sensors and Analysers, Therexsys Ltd, Southern Cross Biotech Pty, Biotrin International Ltd

Officers, Executives and Principals

Jeremy Cumock Cook
Véronique Bouchet
John Hermann
Alan Jeffers
Shirley Lanning
Bruce McHarrie
Geoffrey Vernon
Nicole Vitullo
Edward Wawrzynczak
Tanneke Zeeuw

ROTHSCHILD VENTURES ASIA PTE. LTD.

20 Cecil Street
The Exchange 09-00
Singapore 049705

Telephone: 65-535-8311
Fax: 65-538-1935

Mission: Actively seeking new investments

Fund Size: not available
Founded: 1990
Average Investment: not available
Minimum Investment: $100,000

Investment Criteria: Seed, Startup, First-stage, Second-stage, Mezzanine, Leveraged Buy-out, Special Situations

Geographic Preference: not available

Industry Group Preference: Communications, Computer Related, Consumer, Distribution, Electronic Components and Instrumentation, Energy/Natural Resources, Genetic Engineering, Industrial Products and Equipment, Medical/Health Related

Portfolio Companies: not available

Officers, Executives and Principals

Keen-Whye Lee, Managing Director
Mark T. Geh, Executive Director
Sek Onn Boey, Executive Director
Kong Hooi Lee, Manager

ROYAL BANK DEVELOPMENT CAPITAL LTD

26 St Andrew Square
Edinburgh EH2 1AF
United Kingdom

Telephone: 44-131-556-2555
Fax: 44-131-557-2900

Mission: Actively seeking new investments as a part of the Royal Bank of Scotland Group

Fund Size: not available
Founded: not available
Average Investment: £2 million
Minimum Investment: £500,000

Investment Criteria: Expansion, Management Buy-in, Management Buy-out, Refinancing Bank Debt, Secondary Purchase/Replacement Capital

Geographic Preference: United Kingdom

Industry Group Preference: All sectors considered

Portfolio Companies: Saville and Holdsworth, Macdonald Hotels, Dynamic Leisure, The Benfield Group Limited

Officers, Executives and Principals

Douglas Kearney
Hamish Mackenzie
Joe McGrane
Brian Scouler

ROYAL BANK OF SCOTLAND (ACQUISITION FINANCE)

138-142 Waterhouse Square
London EC1N 2TH
United Kingdom

Telephone: 44-171-427 8304
Fax: 44-171-427 9930

Other Office Locations
Birmingham (Robert Freer), Phone 121-212-1166
Edinburgh (Bill Troup), Phone 131-523-4936
Glasgow (David Sneddon), Phone 141-249-1725
Leeds (Tim Murphy), Phone 113-244-3966
Manchester (Sandy Nellies), Phone 161-242-3359
Nottingham (Martin Block), Phone 115-947-6521
Reading (Adam Eifion-Jones), Phone 1734-594890

Mission: Actively seeking new investments

Fund Size: not available
Founded: not available
Average Investment: not available
Minimum Investment: not available

Investment Criteria: not available

Geographic Preference: Europe

Industry Group Preference: All sectors considered

Portfolio Companies: not available

Officers, Executives and Principals

Leith Robertson
Ian Hazelton
Nigel Smith

SAARLÄNDISCHE KAPITALBETEILIGUNGS GmbH

Johannisstrasse 2
66111 Saarbrücken
Germany

Telephone: 49-681-30330
Fax: 49-681-3033-100

Mission: Actively seeking new investments

Fund Size: not available
Founded: not available
Average Investment: not available
Minimum Investment: not available

Investment Criteria: All stages

Geographic Preference: Germany (Saarland)

Industry Group Preference: All sectors considered

Portfolio Companies: not available

Officers, Executives and Principals

Achim Kies
Gerhard Koch
Jürgen Müsch

SAAR-LOR-LUX

c/o Région de Lorraine
Place Gabr. Hocquard B. P. 1004
57036 Metz
France

Telephone: 33-87-33-6183
Fax: 33-87-33-6071

Other Office Locations
7 Rue du Saint Esprit
1475 Luxembourg
Phone 46-19-7198

Mission: Actively seeking new investments

Fund Size: not available
Founded: not available
Average Investment: not available
Minimum Investment: not available

Investment Criteria: Seed, Start-up

Geographic Preference: France (Lorraine), Germany (Saarland), Luxembourg

Industry Group Preference: All sectors considered

Portfolio Companies: not available

Officers, Executives and Principals

Lucien Bechtold
Regis Brun

SADEPO OY

Pohjoisrantakatu 11
28100 Pori
Finland

Telephone: 358-39-633-3442
Fax: 358-39-633-2130

Mission: Actively seeking new investments

Fund Size: FM2.5 million
Founded: not available
Average Investment: FM150,000-1.5 million
Minimum Investment: not available

Investment Criteria: Start-up, Expansion, Management Buy-out

Geographic Preference: Finland (Satakunta region)

Industry Group Preference: All sectors considered

Portfolio Companies: not available

Officers, Executives and Principals

Arja Pöysti, Managing Director
Education: Certificate of Commerical College

SAINT PETERSBURG REGIONAL VENTURE FUND MANAGEMENT

10 Bolshoi Pr. VO.
199034 St Petersburg
Russia

Telephone: 7-812-325-8474
Fax: 7-812-325-8477

Other Office Locations
Regional Venture Fund Management GmbH und Co. KG.
Hamburger Allee 2-10
60486 Frankfurt
Germany
Phone 49-69-795-000-24, Fax 49-69-795-000-60

Mission: Actively seeking investments as part of the initiative by G-7 and EU governments to support newly
privatized companies in Russia

Fund Size: Ecu38 million
Founded: not available
Average Investment: not available
Minimum Investment: Ecu230,000

Investment Criteria: All stages

Geographic Preference: Russia

Industry Group Preference: All sectors considered

Portfolio Companies: not available

Officers, Executives and Principals

Wolfgang Engler
Christophe Weise

SAMBRINVEST SA

17 Boulevard de l'Yser
P. O. Box 1
6000 Charleroi
Belgium

Telephone: 32-71-330224
Fax: 32-71-317742

Mission: Actively seeking new investments as manager of Fonds de Capital D'Amorcage and Fond de Capital Risque Objectif 1

Fund Size: Ecu52.5 million
Founded: not available
Average Investment: not available
Minimum Investment: not available

Investment Criteria: Seed, Start-up, Early-stage, Expansion/Development, Management buy-out , Management Buy-in

Geographic Preference: Belgium

Industry Group Preference: Biotechnology, Computer Related, Computer Software, Industrial Automation, Pollution/Recycling Related

Portfolio Companies: not available

Officers, Executives and Principals

Roger Baisir, Partner
Guy Preaux, Partner
Denis Tillier, Partner
Claude Dewolf, Partner

SAMENAR SA

53 Cours Pierre Puget
13006 Marseilles
France

Telephone: 33-91-817402
Fax: 33-91-817746

Mission: Actively seeking new investments

Fund Size: Ecu5.3 million
Founded: not available
Average Investment: not available
Minimum Investment: Ecu20,000

Investment Criteria: Start-up, Early-stage, Expansion/Development

Geographic Preference: France

Industry Group Preference: Biotechnology, Consumer Products/Services, Electronics Related, Industrial Products

Portfolio Companies: not available

Officers, Executives and Principals

Jean-Claude Noë

SAVON TEKNIA OY

P. O. Box 1750
Savilahdentie 6
70211 Kuopio
Finland

Telephone: 358-71-240-202
Fax: 358-71-240-241

Mission: Actively seeking new investments

Fund Size: FM32 million
Founded: not available
Average Investment: FM 500,000-1.5 milion
Minimum Investment: FM200,000

Investment Criteria: Seed, Start-up, Expansion, Management Buy-out

Geographic Preference: Finland (Eastern region)

Industry Group Preference: Environmental Technology, Health Care, Other Industries

Portfolio Companies: not available

Officers, Executives and Principals

Jorma Pylkkänen, Managing Director
Education: MSc in Economics

Matti Lappalainen, Director
Education: BSc

SBC EQUITY PARTNERS AG

Swiss Bank Center
8010 Zürich
Switzerland

Telephone: 41-1-239-8508
Fax: 41-1-239-8511

Mission: Actively seeking new investments, concentrating on well established medium-sized companies

Fund Size: not available
Founded: not available
Average Investment: not available
Minimum Investment: Sfr5 million

Investment Criteria: Expansion/Development, Management Buy-out, Replacement/Share Purchases

Geographic Preference: Switzerland, Western Europe

Industry Group Preference: All sectors considered

Portfolio Companies: not available

Officers, Executives and Principals

Bernard Steck
Dr. Alexander Krebs

S. B. G. SPARKASSEN-BETEILIGUNGS GmbH UND CO. KG

Friedrichstrasse 103
40217 Düsseldorf
Germany

Telephone: 49-211-826-3066
Fax: 49-211-826-6168

Mission: Actively seeking new investments

Fund Size: not available
Founded: not available
Average Investment: not available
Minimum Investment: DM300,000

Investment Criteria: not available

Geographic Preference: Germany (North Rhine-Westphalia)

Industry Group Preference: All sectors considered

Portfolio Companies: not available

Officers, Executives and Principals

Joachim Voss
Karlheinz Müller
Jürgen Germies

S. C. GELSOR SA

Splaiul Uniril 6 Bl. B3
Et. 2, Sector 4
Bucharest
Romania

Telephone: 40-1-330-6560
Fax: 40-01-330-5915

Mission: Actively seeking new investments

Fund Size: Ecu3.5 million
Founded: 1993
Average Investment: not available
Minimum Investment: Ecu150,000

Investment Criteria: Expansion/Development, Turnaround/Restructuring

Geographic Preference: Europe

Industry Group Preference: All sectors considered

Portfolio Companies: not available

Officers, Executives and Principals

Marian Petrescu, General Manager
Sorin Ovidiu Vintu, Partner

SCHLESWIG-HOLSTEINISCHE KAPITAL-BETEILIGUNGS GmbH

Martensdamm 6
24103 Kiel
Germany

Telephone: 49-431-900-1060
Fax: 49-431-900-1032

Mission: Actively seeking new investments

Fund Size: not available
Founded: not available
Average Investment: not available
Minimum Investment: DM500,000

Investment Criteria: All stages

Geographic Preference: Germany (Schleswig-Holstein)

Industry Group Preference: All sectors considered

Portfolio Companies: not available

Officers, Executives and Principals

Hans-Dieter Grube
Werner Schnolow

SCHRODER ASSOCIATI Srl

Corso Europa 12
20122 Milan
Italy

Telephone: 39-2-7600-4740
Fax: 39-2-7600-4706

Mission: Promoting management buy-ins and buy-outs in Italy

Fund Size: L200 billion
Founded: not available
Average Investment: L8 billion
Minimum Investment: not available

Investment Criteria: Management Buy-in, Management Buy-out

Geographic Preference: Italy

Industry Group Preference: not available

Portfolio Companies: not available

Officers, Executives and Principals

Paolo Colonna, Managing Director
Donato Dall'ava, Partner
Gianluca Andema, Partner

SCHRODER PARTENAIRES

41 avenue George V
75008 Paris
France

Telephone: 33-1-4073-8500
Fax: 33-1-4070-1108

Other Office Locations
20 Southampton Street
London WC2E 7QG
United Kingdom
Phone 44-171-632-1000, Fax 44-171-240-5072

Mission: Actively seeking new investments

Fund Size: Ffr950 million
Founded: not available
Average Investment: not available
Minimum Investment: Ffr15 million

Investment Criteria: Leveraged Buy-out, Expansion/Development

Geographic Preference: France

Industry Group Preference: All sectors considered

Portfolio Companies: Kindy, Cidelcem, Cirrus, Cottes, Data Controle

Officers, Executives and Principals

Gérart Tardy
Vincent Debré
Bernard Giroud
Hervé Marion
Christophe Bonnet
Peter Baines
Michel Jolivet
Jean-Berbard Meurisse
Annette Liétard

SCHRODER VENTURES

20 Southampton Street
London WC2E 7QG
United Kingdom

Telephone: 44-171-632-1000
Fax: 44-171-240-5072

Other Office Locations
41 avenue George V
75008 Paris
France
Phone 33-1-4073-8500, Fax 33-1-4070-1108

Mission: Actively seeking new investments

Fund Size: £765 million
Founded: not available
Average Investment: £5 million
Minimum Investment: £500,000

Investment Criteria: Expansion, Management Buy-in, Management Buy-out, Early-stage, Rescue/Turn-around, Secondary Purchase/Replacement Capital, Start-up, Seed

Geographic Preference: Europe

Industry Group Preference: All sectors considered

Portfolio Companies: Parker Pen, Boulton and Paul Ltd, Roxboro, Mitel, Chiroscience Group plc

Officers, Executives and Principals

Peter Smitham, Partner
Damon Buffini
Carl Parker

SCL CORPORATE FINANCE SA

Avenue de Mon-Repos 24
1005 Lausanne
Switzerland

Telephone: 41-21-311-6272
Fax: 41-1-311-6277

Mission: Actively seeking new investments

Fund Size: not available
Founded: not available
Average Investment: not available
Minimum Investment: Sfr5 million

Investment Criteria: Expansion/Development, Replacement/Share Purchases, Turnaround

Geographic Preference: Switzerland, East Asia

Industry Group Preference: All sectors considered

Portfolio Companies: not available

Officers, Executives and Principals

Bernard Cuendet
Marc Henon

SCOTTISH ENTERPRISE

120 Bothwell Street
Glasgow G2 7JP
United Kingdom

Telephone: 44-141-248 2700
Fax: 44-141-204 3648
E-mail: brian.kerr@scotent.co.uk

Mission: Actively seeking new investments

Fund Size: £23 million
Founded: not available
Average Investment: £350,000
Minimum Investment: £50,000

Investment Criteria: Expansion, Early-stage, Management Buy-in, Management Buy-out, Rescue/Turn-around, Start-up

Geographic Preference: Scotland

Industry Group Preference: Biotechnology, Computer Related, Electronics Related, Energy, Industrial Products and Services, Manufacturing, Medical/Health Related, Services

Portfolio Companies: Award plc, Quadstone Ltd, Well Equip Ltd

Officers, Executives and Principals

Brian Kerr
Calum Paterson

SDR SODERE - FINANCIÈRE LABOURDONNAIS

26 rue Labourdonnais
97400 St-Denis
Réunion

Telephone: 262-904141
Fax: 262-200507

Mission: Actively seeking new investments

Fund Size: Ffr48 million
Founded: not available
Average Investment: not available
Minimum Investment: Ffr50,000

Investment Criteria: Start-up, Early-stage, Expanion/Development

Geographic Preference: Indian Ocean Region

Industry Group Preference: All sectors considered

Portfolio Companies: Sucreries de Bourbon, Canal Plus Réunion, Air Austral

Officers, Executives and Principals

Albert Trimaille, Managing Director
Isabelle Poulet, Investment Manager

S-E-BANKEN FÖRETAGSINVEST

Hamngatan 24
10640 Stockholm
Sweden

Telephone: 46-8-763-7900
Fax: 46-8-763-7909
E-mail: josu@sebanken.se

Mission: Actively seeking new investments as the venture capital arm of Skandinaviska Enskilda Banken

Fund Size: Skr200 million
Founded: not available
Average Investment: not available
Minimum Investment: Skr2 million

Investment Criteria: All stages

Geographic Preference: Sweden

Industry Group Preference: All sectors considered

Portfolio Companies: not available

Officers, Executives and Principals

Jan Sundberg
Fredrick Johansson
Ethel Tjernström

SED VENTURES
62 rue La Boétie
75008 Paris
France

Telephone: 33-1-4289-8397
Fax: 33-1-4289-8452

Mission: Actively seeking new investments

Fund Size: Ffr150 million
Founded: not available
Average Investment: not available
Minimum Investment: Ffr1 million

Investment Criteria: Start-Up, Early Stage, Expanion/ Development

Geographic Preference: France, United Kingdom, United States

Industry Group Preference: Agriculture Related, Biotechnology, Environment, Medical/Health Related

Portfolio Companies: Applied Graphic Solutions

Officers, Executives and Principals

Clive Anthony Davies, President and Managing Director (United Kingdom)
Ellen Ann Strain, Managing Director
Reginald Auguste-Dormeuil

SEED CAPITAL BRANDENBURG GmbH

Im Technologiepark 1
15236 Frankfurt an der Oder
Germany

Telephone: 49-335-557-1690
Fax: 49-335-557-1699

Mission: Actively seeking new investments

Fund Size: DM5 million
Founded: not available
Average Investment: not available
Minimum Investment: DM100,000

Investment Criteria: Seed, Start-up, Early-stage

Geographic Preference: Germany only

Industry Group Preference: All sectors considered

Portfolio Companies: not available

Officers, Executives and Principals

Dr. Michael Gross

SEED CAPITAL COMPANY LIMITED

Nevädzova 5
82101 Bratislava
Slovakia

Telephone: 42-7-23-7472
Fax: 42-7-52-22434
E-mail: agency@nadsme.sanet.sk

Mission: Developing small and medium-sized private companies and providing equity and special loan financing to young, growing companies

Fund Size: Ecu3 million
Founded: 1994
Average Investment: Ecu75,000
Minimum Investment: Ecu5,000

Investment Criteria: Seed, Start-up

Geographic Preference: Slovakia

Industry Group Preference: Biotechnology, Chemical/Materials, Consumer Related, Healthcare, Industrial Products, Manufacturing, Pollution/Recycling

Portfolio Companies: JMI, ALK, EKOBAT, Agro-Diesel, Pilex Atelier, Jakama

Officers, Executives and Principals

Bystrik Berthoty
Education: Graduate in Engineering; postgraduate diploma in Corporate Finance
Background: executive manager and financial management consultant

SEED CAPITAL FUND KEMPEN

c/o G. I. M.V. Karel Oomstraat 37
2018 Antwerp
Belgium

Telephone: 32-3-248-2321
Fax: 32-3-238-4193

Mission: Supporting the economic development of the Kempen region

Fund Size: Ecu2.3 million
Founded: not available
Average Investment: not available
Minimum Investment: Ecu50,000

Investment Criteria: Seed, Start-up, Early-stage

Geographic Preference: Belgium (Kempen region)

Industry Group Preference: Biotechnology, Communications, Electronics Related, Energy, Industrial Products, Medical/Health Related

Portfolio Companies: not available

Officers, Executives and Principals

Philip Vermeulen, Partner
Dirk Boogmans, Partner
Luc Peeters, Partner

SEED CAPITAL INVESTMENTS BV

Bernadottelaan 15
P. O. Box 8323
3503 RH Utrecht
The Netherlands

Telephone: 31-30-294-1456
Fax: 31-30-294-1526

Mission: Actively seeking new investments

Fund Size: Ecu1 million
Founded: not available
Average Investment: not available
Minimum Investment: Ecu20,000

Investment Criteria: Seed

Geographic Preference: Netherlands

Industry Group Preference: Agriculture, Biotechnology, Chemical/Materials, Consumer Related, Electronics Related, Energy, Industrial Automation, Industrial Products, Medical/Health Related, Pollution/Recycling, Transportation

Portfolio Companies: not available

Officers, Executives and Principals

Dr. Willem J. van Oort

SEED CAPITAL LIMITED

The Magdalen Centre
The Oxford Science Park
Oxford OX4 4GA
United Kingdom

Telephone: 44-1865-784466
Fax: 44-1865-784412
E-mail: 106063.311@compuserve

Mission: Actively seeking new investments in early-stage technology companies in and around Oxford

Fund Size: £2 million
Founded: 1983
Average Investment: £150,000
Minimum Investment: £30,000

Investment Criteria: Seed

Geographic Preference: England (mainly Oxford)

Industry Group Preference: Communications, Computer Related, Consumer, Electronic Components and Instrumentation, Energy/Natural Resources, Genetic Engineering, Industrial Products and Equipment, Medical/Health Related

Portfolio Companies: PSI Atomisers, Dextra Laboratories, Integral Vision, Cytocell, Prodat Systems PLC

Officers, Executives and Principals

Lucius Cary, Managing Director

SEED INVEST SARDEGNA Srl

c/o BIC Sardegna
Via Maddalena 14
09124 Cagliari
Italy

Telephone: 39-70-663534
Fax: 39-70-659273

Mission: Actively seeking new investments

Fund Size: not available
Founded: not available
Average Investment: not available
Minimum Investment: not available

Investment Criteria: Seed, Start-up, Early-stage

Geographic Preference: Italy

Industry Group Preference: All sectors considered

Portfolio Companies: not available

Officers, Executives and Principals

Guiseppe Pennisi

SEVILLA SEED CAPITAL FUND

Av de la Constitucion 24
Cabildo - Casa A- 1° Pta
41001 Sevilla
Spain

Telephone: 34-5-462-6811
Fax: 34-5-462-7901

Mission: Actively seeking new investments

Fund Size: Ecu1.8 million
Founded: not available
Average Investment: not available
Minimum Investment: Ecu20,000

Investment Criteria: Seed, Start-up, Early-stage

Geographic Preference: Spain, Portugal, Morocco

Industry Group Preference: Biotechnology, Communications, Consumer Products, Electronics Related, Industrial Products, Manufacturing, Services

Portfolio Companies: not available

Officers, Executives and Principals

Angeles de la Torre, Partner

S. F. I. R.
Rua Rosa Araùjo 29
1250 Lisbon
Portugal

Telephone: 351-1-352-3560
Fax: 351-1-352-3572

Mission: Actively seeking new investments

Fund Size: Ecu8.5 million
Founded: not available
Average Investment: not available
Minimum Investment: Ecu500,000

Investment Criteria: Expansion/Development, Turnaround/Restructuring

Geographic Preference: Portugal

Industry Group Preference: All sectors considered

Portfolio Companies: not available

Officers, Executives and Principals

Nuno Manuel De Brito
José Maria Ricciardi
Rogério Carlos Fernandes da Silva
Dr. Carlos Manuel Calvario
Dr. Rafael Branco Valverde

S. F. M. ET ASSOCIÉS SA

Spitalgasse 27
3001 Bern
Switzerland

Telephone: 41-31-328-4444
Fax: 41-31-328-4445

Mission: Actively seeking new investments

Fund Size: not available
Founded: not available
Average Investment: not available
Minimum Investment: Sfr500,000

Investment Criteria: Expansion/Development, Replacement/Share Purchases, Turnaround

Geographic Preference: Switzerland, France, Italy, Spain

Industry Group Preference: All sectors considered

Portfolio Companies: not available

Officers, Executives and Principals

Hanspeter Studer
Victoria Doebbel
Beat Siegrist

S. G. CAPITAL DÉVELOPPEMENT

Tour Société Générale
Cours Valmy
92987 Paris
France

Telephone: 33-1-4213-6595
Fax: 33-1-4213-7779

Mission: Actively seeking new investments

Fund Size: Ffr1.16 billion
Founded: not available
Average Investment: not available
Minimum Investment: Ffr5 million

Investment Criteria: Early-stage, Expansion/Development, Management Buy-out, Management Buy-in

Geographic Preference: France, Europe, United States

Industry Group Preference: All sectors considered

Portfolio Companies: not available

Officers, Executives and Principals

Gérard Rubat-Ciagnus

SHANNON DEVELOPMENT COMPANY

Park House
National Technology Park
Castleroy
Limerick
Ireland

Telephone: 353-6133-6555
Fax: 353-6133-6545
E-mail: prendergaste@shannon-dev.ie

Mission: Actively seeking new investments

Fund Size: Ecu24.9 million
Founded: not available
Average Investment: not available
Minimum Investment: Ecu20,000

Investment Criteria: Seed, Start-up, Management Buy-in, Management Buy-out, Expansion/Development, Early Stage

Geographic Preference: Ireland

Industry Group Preference: Biotechnology, Communications, Computer Related, Computer Software, Electronics Related, Medical/Health Related

Portfolio Companies: not available

Officers, Executives and Principals

Eoghan Prendergast
J. Dillon
D. Beary
M. Moore
E.O'Grady

SHIRAT ENTERPRISES

Eliahu House
2 Ibn Givrol Street
Tel Aviv 64077
Israel

Telephone: 972-3-696-8224
Fax: 972-3-695-3847

Mission: Actively seeking new investments

Fund Size: Ecu20 million
Founded: not available
Average Investment: not available
Minimum Investment: not available

Investment Criteria: Seed, Start-up, Early-stage, Bridge, Expansion/Development,

Geographic Preference: not available

Industry Group Preference: Communications, Computer Related, Consumer Related, Electronics Related, Energy, Medical/Health Related

Portfolio Companies: not available

Officers, Executives and Principals

Eliezer Manor

SIEGERLANDFONDS EINS BETEILIGUNGSPARTNER DER MITTELSTÄNDISCHEN WIRTSCHAFT GmbH UND CO.

Weidenauer Strasse 167
57076 Siegen
Germany

Telephone: 49-271-706-282
Fax: 49-271-706-285

Mission: Actively seeking new investments

Fund Size: DM5.6 billion
Founded: not available
Average Investment: not available
Minimum Investment: DM200,000

Investment Criteria: All stages

Geographic Preference: Germany (North Rhine-Westphalia)

Industry Group Preference: All sectors considered

Portfolio Companies: not available

Officers, Executives and Principals

Peter Töpfler
Marion Bangard

SINGER AND FRIEDLANDER DEVELOPMENT CAPITAL LIMITED

31 Park Square
Leeds LS1 2PF
United Kingdom

Telephone: 44-113-243-5000
Fax: 44-113-245-9822

Mission: Assisting proven management teams to complete transactions, with the objective of supporting, rather than directing, the future growth of their businesses

Fund Size: not available
Founded: 1993
Average Investment: £1 million
Minimum Investment: £500,000

Investment Criteria: Expansion, Management Buy-in, Management Buy-out, Refinancing Bank Debt, Rescue/Turnaround, Secondary Purchase/Replacement Capital

Geographic Preference: United Kingdom

Industry Group Preference: All sectors considered except Real Estate Speculation

Portfolio Companies: TRS Cabinet Company Limited, London United Busways 1994 Limited

Officers, Executives and Principals

George Shiels, CA, Managing Director
Mark Winderbank, ACA, Director

SIPAREX Group

139 rue Vendôme
69006 Lyons
France

Telephone: 33-04-7283-2323
Fax: 33-04-7283-2300
E-mail: Siparex@Siparex.com

Other Office Locations
114 rue La Boétie
75008 Paris
Phone 33-01-5393-0220, Fax 33-01-5393-0230

Mission: Actively seeking new investments

Fund Size: not available
Founded: 1977
Average Investment: Ffr3-30 million
Minimum Investment: Ffr3-30 million

Investment Criteria: Expansion/Development, Management Buy-out, Bridge, Later-s tage, Leveraged Buy-out

Geographic Preference: Europe, North America

Industry Group Preference: All sectors considered

Portfolio Companies: not available

Officers, Executives and Principals

Dominique Nouvellet, Managing Director
René Maury, Deputy General Manager
Denis Rodarie, Company Secretary

SITRA

Uudenmaankatu 16B
P. O. Box 329
00121 Helsinki
Finland

Telephone: 358-9-618-991
Fax: 358-9-645-072
E-mail: sitra@sitra.fi

Mission: Providing private equity financing for technology companies

Fund Size: FM1.1 billion
Founded: 1967
Average Investment: not available
Minimum Investment: FM500,000

Investment Criteria: Seed, Start-up, Early-stage, Expansion/Development, Management Buy-out

Geographic Preference: Finland, Europe, United States, Russia, Baltic countries

Industry Group Preference: Biotechnology, Chemicals and Materials, Communications, Computer Related, Consumer Related, Electronics Related, Industrial Automation, Industrial Products and Services, Medical/Health Related, Transportation

Portfolio Companies: Bio-Orbit Oy, Bioka Oy, Interferm Oy, Microbial Oy, DIARC Technology Oy, Oy Fluid-Bag AB, Optatech Oy, Rauma Materials Technology Inc., Aplicom Oy, Sysmen Oy, Vista Communication Instruments Oy, Design Power Inc., DeskArtes Oy, Kielikone Oy, Solid Information Systems Oy, ViSolutions Inc., Aalto Filtration Oy, Auramatrix IFO Oy, Oy Go Distance AB Ltd., Oy Hope Finlandia Ltd., Oy Mytek Ltd., Skywings Ltd., Tapvei Oy, CCM Instruments AB, Mapvision Ltd., RollTest Oy, David Holding Oy, E and D Design Oy, Erikkilä Nostotekniikkaa Oy, Finnsonic Oy, Grafisystems Oy, High Speed Technology Oy Ltd., Ion Blast Oy, JOT Invest Oy, LVC-Group Oy, Megatrex Oy, Mega-Epox Oy, Neorem Magnets Oy, Polarmatic Oy, Roctex Oy AB, TR-Tech. Int. Oy, Unicraft Oy, Abmin Technologies Oy, Cellomeda Oy, Clids Oy, Diomed Ltd., FibroGen Inc., Fimet Oy, Fluilogic Systems Oy, Instmel Oy, KONE Instruments Oy, Labmaster Oy, MAP Medical Technologies Oy, Neuromag Oy, Pharming BV, Shanghai Fimet Medical Instrument Corporation, Benemec Oy, Mega Electronics Ltd., Metorex International Oy, Micronas Semiconductor Holding AG, Okmetic Oy, Optonex Oy, Rados Technology Oy, Modulaire Oy, Sampower Oy

Officers, Executives and Principals

Matts Anderson, President
Education: MSc in Economics
Background: Vice President, Finnfund Limited

Jukka Aaltonen, Director, Information Technology
Education: MSc in Engineering
Background: Systems Manager, Imatran Voima; Research and Development Engineer, Valmet Automation; Technical Attaché, Finnish Consulate, United States; Project Manager, Dativo

Aaro Cantell, Director, International Fund Investments
Education: MSc in Engineering
Background: Fiskars Oy AB; Fibox Oy AB; planning and marketing consultant

Tapani Haikola, Director, Advanced Manufacturing and Materials Technology
Education: MSc in Engineering
Background: Project Manager, Wärtsilä Diesel; Section Manager, Technical Research Center of Finland

Antti Hannula, Director, Information Technology
Education: LLM; MBA
Background: Newspaper Reporter, Turun Sanomat; Economics Correspondent, Kauppalehti; Account and Contract Manager, Oracle Finland; Lawyer, Central Federation for Small Industries

Jukka Häyrynen, Director, Seed Finance
Education: MSc in Engineering
Background: Manager, Customer Services, Technical Research Center of Finland

Pasi Jänkälä, Business Controller
Education: MSc in Economics
Background: active in the venture capital field since the early 1990s

Dr. Kalevi Kurkijärvi, Director, Biotechnology
Education: PhD in Biochemistry
Background: Research Scientist, Finnish Academy of Science and Turku University; Vice President, Wallac

Olli Lindblad, Director of Finance and Legal Counsel
Education: LLM; MSc in Economics
Background: President, Skop Finance Limited

Jari Mieskonen, Director, Technology Transfer and Seed Financing
Education: MSc in Engineering
Background: Researcher, International Institute for Applied Systems Analysis and Technical Research Center of Finland; Project Manager, Finntech

Seppo Mäkinen, Director, Biotechnology
Education: MSc in Physical Chemistry
Background: Chemist, State Institute of Agricultural Chemistry; Scientist, Jyväskylä University; Application Specialist, Millipore

Anu Nokso-Koivisto, Director, Corporate Finance
Education: MSc in Engineering
Background: Assistant Director and Deputy Managing Director, Industrialization Fund of Finland

Dr. Timo Petäjä, Director, Biotechnology
Education: PhD in Chemistry
Background: Research and Development Manager, Oulu Limited; managerial positions, Alko Limited

Matti Turunen, Director, Advanced Manufacturing and Materials Technology
Education: MSc in Engineering
Background: Senior Research Engineer, Jones and Laughlin Steel Corporation and Mefos; Managing Director, Uddeholm; Sales Director, Ovako; Partner, Tradenet Group

SKANDIA INVESTMENT AB

Sveavägen 38
10350 Stockholm
Sweden

Telephone: 46-8-788-1030
Fax: 46-8-203566

Mission: Actively seeking new investments

Fund Size: Skr410 million
Founded: not available
Average Investment: not available
Minimum Investment: Skr5 million

Investment Criteria: All stages

Geographic Preference: Sweden, Denmark, Finland, Iceland, Norway

Industry Group Preference: All sectors considered

Portfolio Companies: not available

Officers, Executives and Principals

Christer Dajlström, Managing Director
Magnus Hardmeier, Investment Manager
Henrik Westfeldt, Investment Manager
Mikael Selin, Financial Analyst and Controller

SLOTTSBACKEN VENTURE CAPITAL

Slottsbacken 8
11130 Stockholm
Sweden

Telephone: 46-8-456-8880
Fax: 46-8-456-8898
E-mail: info@acr.se

Mission: Identifying, evaluating, developing, financing and cooperating with emerging growth companies which have demonstrated market acceptance in the telecommunications, computer and media industries

Fund Size: Skr200 million
Founded: 1996
Average Investment: Skr10 million
Minimum Investment: Skr1 million

Investment Criteria: Start-up, Early-stage, Expansion

Geographic Preference: not available

Industry Group Preference: Computer Related, Media, Telecommunications

Portfolio Companies: BolagsFakta AB, Protect Data AB, Ventana Corp (United States)

Officers, Executives and Principals

Claes Ander, Partner
Background: active as a communications and marketing executive for over 20 years, with ABB Fläkt, Atlas Copco, Inter Innovation and other companies; also active as a business development consultant

Håkan Claesson, Partner
Background: senior management positions, Texaco Sweden and Inter Innovation; Managing Director, De la Rue Inter Innovation; also active as a business development consultant

Dr. Leif Rylander, Partner
Education: PhD, School of Business, Stockholm University
Background: 30 years as a manager in Swedish high-tech companies; President and Chief Executive Officer of Inter Innovation for five years

SLOVAK AMERICAN ENTERPRISE FUND

Radlinského 27
P. O. Box 66
810 05 Bratislava
Slovakia

Telephone: 42-7-326-544
Fax: 42-7-362-530

Mission: Actively seeking new investments, specializing in development of Slovak small and medium-sized companies

Fund Size: Ecu50 million
Founded: not available
Average Investment: not available
Minimum Investment: Ecu266,000

Investment Criteria: Expansion/Development, Management Buy-out, Management Buy-in, Turnaround/ Restructuring

Geographic Preference: Slovakia

Industry Group Preference: All sectors considered

Portfolio Companies: not available

Officers, Executives and Principals

Leighton Klevana

SND (NORWEGIAN INDUSTRIAL AND REGIONAL DEVELOPMENT FUND)

P. O. Box 448
Sentrum Akergaten 13
0104 Oslo
Norway

Telephone: 47-22-002500
Fax: 47-22-423222

Mission: Actively seeking new investments

Fund Size: Ecu288,069,696
Founded: not available
Average Investment: not available
Minimum Investment: not available

Investment Criteria: Start-up, Early-stage, Expansion/Development, Management Buy-out, Management Buy-in, Turnaround/Restructuring

Geographic Preference: Norway

Industry Group Preference: Communications, Computer Related, Computer Software, Construction, Electronics Related, Industrial Products, Manufacturing, Medical/Health Related, Pollution/Recycling, Services

Portfolio Companies: not available

Officers, Executives and Principals

Willy E. Wiik
Thor Svegaarden
Bjorn Henrik Rassmussen

S. N. V. B. PARTICIPATIONS

4 place André Maginot
54000 Nancy
France

Telephone: 33- 8334-5563
Fax: 33-8334-5325

Mission: Actively seeking new investments

Fund Size: Ffr200 million
Founded: not available
Average Investment: not available
Minimum Investment: Ffr1 million

Investment Criteria: Expansion/Development, Leveraged Buy-out

Geographic Preference: France (Regions of Ile-de-France, Champagne, Ardennes, Lorraine)

Industry Group Preference: All sectors considered

Portfolio Companies: ELM Leblanc, Maximo, Dolisos, Descours et Cabaud, Champagne Vranken

Officers, Executives and Principals

Henri-Jaron, Managing Director

SOCADIF

26 quai de la Rapée
75012 Paris
France

Telephone: 33-1-4473-2638
Fax: 33-1-4473-1523

Mission: Actively seeking new investments

Fund Size: Ffr90 million
Founded: not available
Average Investment: not available
Minimum Investment: Ffr2 million

Investment Criteria: All stages

Geographic Preference: France

Industry Group Preference: All sectors considered

Portfolio Companies: not available

Officers, Executives and Principals

Patrick Grumelart
Patrick Lemaire

SOCIEDAD REGIONAL DE PROMOCION DEL PRINCIPADO DE ASTURIAS SA (SRP)

Parque Tecnologico de Asturias
33420 Llanera
Spain

Telephone: 34-8-526-0068
Fax: 34-8-526-4455

Mission: Actively seeking new investments

Fund Size: Pta3 billion
Founded: 1984
Average Investment: not available
Minimum Investment: not available

Investment Criteria: All stages

Geographic Preference: Spain (Asturias)

Industry Group Preference: All sectors considered

Portfolio Companies: not available

Officers, Executives and Principals

José de Jove Sela

SOCIÉTÉ CENTRALE POUR L'INDUSTRIE

9 avenue Hoche
75008 Paris
France

Telephone: 33-1-4289-3010
Fax: 33-1-4989-4785

Mission: Actively seeking new investments

Fund Size: Ffr800 million
Founded: not available
Average Investment: not available
Minimum Investment: Ffr2 million

Investment Criteria: Expansion/Development

Geographic Preference: France

Industry Group Preference: All sectors considered

Portfolio Companies: Mecatherm, Stedim, Jet multimedia, Instrason, G. Cartier industrie, Groupe Decan, Systar, Laflachère

Officers, Executives and Principals

Gérard Pluvinet, Managing Director
Aimable Paillart
Henry Huyghues-Despointes
François Barbier
Jérôme Bourgoin
Xavier Thimbault

SÖDERHAMN INVEST AB

Skolhusgatan 11
P. O. Box 141
82623 Söderhamn
Sweden

Telephone: 46-270-10312
Fax: 46-270-19675
E-mail: jiri.formanek@soderhamn-invest.se

Mission: Actively seeking new investments

Fund Size: not available
Founded: not available
Average Investment: not available
Minimum Investment: Skr200,000

Investment Criteria: All stages

Geographic Preference: Sweden

Industry Group Preference: All sectors considered

Portfolio Companies: not available

Officers, Executives and Principals

Jiri Formanek, Managing Director

SOFINETI

48 bis rue Fabert
75340 Paris
France

Telephone: 33-1-4955-7045
Fax: 33-1-4550-4980

Mission: Actively seeking new investments

Fund Size: Ffr130 million
Founded: not available
Average Investment: not available
Minimum Investment: Ffr2 million

Investment Criteria: Expansion/Development

Geographic Preference: France

Industry Group Preference: Communications, Computer Related, Electronics, Software Related

Portfolio Companies: CKD, Dutch Industries, Gelt

Officers, Executives and Principals

Pierre-Emmanuel Dardel
Alain Caffi
Pierre Geerolf

SOFININDEX

5 rue Scribe
75009 Paris
France

Telephone: 33-1-4494-8600
Fax: 33-1-4265-0695

Mission: Actively seeking new investments

Fund Size: Ffr494 million
Founded: not available
Average Investment: not available
Minimum Investment: Ffr2 million

Investment Criteria: Expansion/Development

Geographic Preference: France, Worldwide

Industry Group Preference: All industrial sectors considered

Portfolio Companies: not available

Officers, Executives and Principals

Christiane Massa

SOFINNOVA SA

51 rue Saint Georges
75009 Paris
France

Telephone: 33-1-44-53-53-00
Fax: 33-1-45-26-78-90

Other Office Locations
Sofinnova Inc.
1 Market Plaza, Suite 2630
San Francisco, CA 94105
United States
Phone 415-597-5757, Fax 415-597-5750

Mission: Actively seeking new investments

Fund Size: $220 million
Founded: 1972
Average Investment: $2 million
Minimum Investment: $500,000

Investment Criteria: Startup to Second-stage

Geographic Preference: United States (West Coast), France

Industry Group Preference: Biotechnology, Electronics, High Technology, Medical/Health Care

Portfolio Companies: Resound, Neuron Data, Silmag, Internet, Oravax, CV Therapeutics, Terrapin, Ray Dream, Metlabs, Centrum, Network Peripherals, Premisys, Genset, Auravision

Officers, Executives and Principals

Jean-Barnard Schmidt, President, Sofinnova SA
Education: MBA, Columbia University
Background: General Partner, Burr Egan, Deleage and Co.

Alain Azan, President, Sofinnova Inc.
Education: Insead

Dr. Alix Marduel MD, Vice President, Sofinnova Inc.
Education: MD, Paris University
Background: ICI - Pharma.

SOFIPA SpA

Via Paisello 39
00198 Rome
Italy

Telephone: 39-6-855-0300
Fax: 39-6-853-02559

Mission: Actively seeking new investments

Fund Size: Ecu148 million
Founded: 1995
Average Investment: not available
Minimum Investment: Ecu500,000

Investment Criteria: Expansion/Development, Management Buy-out, Management Buy-in, Replacement, Bridge, Turnaround/Restructuring

Geographic Preference: Italy, Europe

Industry Group Preference: All sectors considered

Portfolio Companies: not available

Officers, Executives and Principals

Francesco Panfilo
Enrico De Cecco
Giovanni Ciochetta

SOFIREM

4 rue des Grandes-Terres
P.O. 220
92503 Rueil-Malmaison
France

Telephone: 33-1-4752-3820
Fax: 33-1-4749-6493

Mission: Actively seeking new investments as the agency for the French National Coal Board

Fund Size: not available
Founded: not available
Average Investment: not available
Minimum Investment: Ecu50,000

Investment Criteria: Seed, Start-up, Early-stage, Expansion/Development

Geographic Preference: France

Industry Group Preference: Chemical/Materials, Consumer Related, Industrial Automation, Industrial Products/Equipment/Machinery, Manufacturing

Portfolio Companies: not available

Officers, Executives and Principals

Albert Suissa
Jean-François Rocchi

SOGINNOVE

Tour Société Générale
17 cours Valmy
92972 Paris
France

Telephone: 33-1-4213-7925
Fax: 33-1-4213-7779

Mission: Actively seeking new investments

Fund Size: Ffr132 million
Founded: not available
Average Investment: not available
Minimum Investment: Ffr1.5 million

Investment Criteria: Expansion/Development

Geographic Preference: France

Industry Group Preference: All industrial sectors considered

Portfolio Companies: not available

Officers, Executives and Principals

Gérard Rubat-Ciagnus

SoPaF (SOCIETA PARTECIPAZIONI FINANZIARIE SpA)

Largo Richini 6
20122 Milan
Italy

Telephone: 39-2-58-3741
Fax: 39-2-58-304126

Other Office Locations
SoPaF International SA
2 Boulevard Royal
2953 Luxembourg

SoPaF Investments SA
Via S. Gottardo 10
6900 Lugano
Switzerland
Phone 41-91-923-4702, Fax 41-91-923-4775

Mission: Acquiring medium-sized unquoted Italian industrial companies with revenues of between L100 billion and L1,000 billion, and minority participations in medium- sized and large companies with larger revenues, both directly, as a merchant bank, and indirectly, through the venture capital fund IEP (founded in 1994)

Fund Size: L350 billion
Founded: 1976
Average Investment: L20 billion
Minimum Investment: L5 billion

Investment Criteria: Expansion/Development, Management Buy-out, Management Buy-in

Geographic Preference: Italy

Industry Group Preference: Manufacturing

Portfolio Companies: Argel, Superga, K-Way, Eider, Sadi, Castelgarden, Genset, Cifa, Sesi Dabb, Redaelli Tecna, Om Lesmo, SGAT, Coeclerici, Air Europe, Marangoni, Colmark, Italiana Occhiali, Euticals, Conchiglia, Techosp.

Officers, Executives and Principals

Jody Vender, Chief Executive Officer
Giuseppe Daveri, Chief Executive Officer
Alberto Azario, Managing Director
Francesco de Giglio, Vice President
Edoardo Lanzavecchia, Vice President
Carlo Mammola, Vice President

SoPaF INTERNATIONAL SA

2 Boulevard Royal
2953 Luxembourg

Telephone: 41-91-923-4702
Fax: 41-91-923-4775

Other Office Locations
SoPaF Investments SA
Via S. Gottardo 10
6900 Lugano
Switzerland
Phone 41-91-923-4702, Fax 41-91-923-4775

Mission: Acquiring minority participations in private companies outside Italy

Fund Size: L80 billion
Founded: 1991
Average Investment: $3 million
Minimum Investment: $1 million

Investment Criteria: Expansion/Development, Management Buy-out

Geographic Preference: Developed Countries, Emerging Markets

Industry Group Preference: All sectors considered

Portfolio Companies: Walker Financial (United States), Nutreco Holding (The Netherlands), Maloney Steel Craft (Canada), Financière GSR (France), Eurodrip (Greece), Norte (Argentina), Automotive Products (United Kingdom), Cathay Investment Fund (China), others

Officers, Executives and Principals

Jody Vender, Chairman, SoPaF International, and Chief Executive Officer, SoPaF (Milan)
Giuseppe Daveri, Director, SoPaF International, and Chief Executive Officer, SoPaF (Milan)
Alberto Azario, Director, SoPaF International, and Managing Director, SoPaF (Milan)
Paolo Sassetti, Director, SoPaF International and SoPaF Investments
Paolo Agrifoglio, Senior Manager, SoPaF International and SoPaF Investments
Paolo Lenzi, Analyst, SoPaF International and SoPaF Investments

SOPROMEC

1 rue du Vieux Colombier
75006 Paris
France

Telephone: 33-1-4354-3400
Fax: 33-1-4354-4140

Mission: Actively seeking new investments

Fund Size: Ffr104 million
Founded: not available
Average Investment: not available
Minimum Investment: Ffr50,000

Investment Criteria: All stages

Geographic Preference: Europe, France

Industry Group Preference: Industry and Services

Portfolio Companies: not available

Officers, Executives and Principals

Jacques Lesueur
Erik Pouilly

SORIDEC

ZAC d'Alco
254 rue Michel Teule
34080 Montpellier
France

Telephone: 33-67-618080
Fax: 33-67-417021

Mission: Actively seeking new investments

Fund Size: Ecu11 million
Founded: not available
Average Investment: not available
Minimum Investment: Ecu15,000

Investment Criteria: Seed, Start-up, Early-stage, Expansion/Development, Management Buy-out, Management Buy-in, Turnaround

Geographic Preference: France

Industry Group Preference: Biotechnology, Electronics Related, Industrial Automation, Industrial Products, Manufacturing, Medical/Health Related

Portfolio Companies: not available

Officers, Executives and Principals

Marc Delatte
Bernard Olivier

SOSET SA

R. José Pedro da Silva 11 R/C
2900 Setubal
Portugal

Telephone: 351-65-39881
Fax: 351-65-20161

Mission: Actively seeking new investments

Fund Size: not available
Founded: not available
Average Investment: not available
Minimum Investment: Ecu500,000

Investment Criteria: Early-stage, Expansion/Development, Management Buy-out

Geographic Preference: Portugal

Industry Group Preference: All sectors considered

Portfolio Companies: not available

Officers, Executives and Principals

Dr. Antonio Palhinhas Afonso

SOUTH WEST INVESTMENT GROUP LIMITED

Trevint House
Strangways Villas
Truro
Cornwall TR1 2PA
United Kingdom

Telephone: 44-1872-223883
Fax: 44-1872-42470

Mission: Actively seeking new investments

Fund Size: not available
Founded: not available
Average Investment: £75,000
Minimum Investment: £25,000

Investment Criteria: All stages

Geographic Preference: United Kingdom (Cornwall and Devon)

Industry Group Preference: All sectors considered

Portfolio Companies: Solent Aerospace Ltd

Officers, Executives and Principals

John Berry

SOUTH WEST SCOTLAND INVESTMENT FUND LIMITED

118 English Street
Dumfries DG1 2DE
United Kingdom

Telephone: 44-1387-260070
Fax: 44-1387-260029
E-mail: donald.mackinnon@dumgal.gov.uk

Mission: Actively seeking new investments

Fund Size: £1 million
Founded: not available
Average Investment: £90,000
Minimum Investment: £50,000

Investment Criteria: Start-up, Expansion, Early-stage

Geographic Preference: Scotland (Dumfries and Galloway only)

Industry Group Preference: All sectors considered

Portfolio Companies: Pet and Garden Manufacturing Ltd

Officers, Executives and Principals

Donald MacKinnon

SPARKASSEN-BETEILIGUNGSGESELLSCHAFT LUDWIGSHAFEN AM RHEIN mbH

P. O. Box 211209
67012 Ludwigshafen/Rhein
Germany

Telephone: 49-621-5992-433
Fax: 49-621-5992-443

Mission: Actively seeking new investments

Fund Size: not available
Founded: not available
Average Investment: not available
Minimum Investment: DM150,000

Investment Criteria: All stages

Geographic Preference: Germany (Ludwigshafen and Mannheim region)

Industry Group Preference: All sectors considered

Portfolio Companies: not available

Officers, Executives and Principals

Gerhard Alles
Walter Röper

S. P. E. F.
11 rue Leblanc
75513 Paris
France

Telephone: 33-1-4039-6085
Fax: 33-1-4039-6066

Other Office Locations
1 rue de la République
69001 Lyons
Phone 7827-3565

2 boulevard de Strasbourg
3100 Toulouse
Phone 6162-3700

Espace Corbin
10 rue Victor Poirel
5400 Nancy
Phone 8337-1717

Mission: Actively seeking new investments

Fund Size: Ffr1,400 million
Founded: not available
Average Investment: not available
Minimum Investment: Ffr1.5 million

Investment Criteria: Expansion/Development, Management Buy-out, Management Buy-in

Geographic Preference: France

Industry Group Preference: Chemical/Materials, Communications, Consumer Related, Industrial Automation, Pollution/Recycling Related

Portfolio Companies: Intersport, Cana, Mecachrome, Feu Vert, Poclain Hydraulics, Krys, Pomme de Pain, Mougeot, Sleever, Sederma, Le Bourget

Officers, Executives and Principals

March Wauthoz
Daniel Foin
Jérôme Covo
Xavier Thauron

SPI SpA

Via Maurizio Bufalini 8
00161 Rome
Italy

Telephone: 39-6-854541
Fax: 39-6-8545-4375

Mission: Actively seeking new investments

Fund Size: Ecu127 million
Founded: not available
Average Investment: not available
Minimum Investment: Ecu100,000

Investment Criteria: Seed, Start-up, Early-stage, Expansion/Development

Geographic Preference: Italy, France, Spain

Industry Group Preference: Biotechnology, Computer Related, Computer Software, Finance/Insurance/Real Estate, Industrial Automation, Medical/Health Related

Portfolio Companies: not available

Officers, Executives and Principals

Romualdo Volpi

SPINNO-SEED OY

Tekniikantie 12
02150 Espoo
Finland

Telephone: 358-0-4354-3101
Fax: 358-0-451-4600

Mission: Actively seeking new investments

Fund Size: FM2.43 million
Founded: not available
Average Investment: FM200,000
Minimum Investment: FM50,000

Investment Criteria: Seed, Start-up

Geographic Preference: Finland (Uusimaa region)

Industry Group Preference: All sectors considered

Portfolio Companies: not available

Officers, Executives and Principals

Ilona Rantakallio, Managing Director
Education: MSc in Engineering; MBA

SPITTA SCHWEDELER GmbH UND CO.

Gerokstrasse 1
70188 Stuttgart
Germany

Telephone: 49-711-239-730
Fax: 49-711-239-7311
E-mail: 100105.1165@compuserv.com

Mission: Serving the interests of environmentally conscious investors, and small and medium-sized enterprises, which care about both profits and social purposes

Fund Size: not available
Founded: 1996
Average Investment: DM1 million
Minimum Investment: DM250,000

Investment Criteria: Seed, Start-up, Early-stage, Expansion/Development, Turnaround/Restructuring

Geographic Preference: Europe, North America

Industry Group Preference: Energy, Medical/Health Related, Pollution/Recycling

Portfolio Companies: Broncho-Air Medizintechnik AG (Germany), Es Reco de Randa SA (Spain), GEPA-Beteiligungs AG (Germany), Genesis Biofuels (United Kingdom), Demeter Biotechnologies Ltd. (United States)

Officers, Executives and Principals

Erasmus Spitta, Managing Director
Education: Graduate in Agriculture; Graduate in Economics, Hamburg University
Background: Co-Founder, Bockemühl und Spitta (management consultancy)

Alexander Schwedeler, Managing Director
Background: Deutsche Bank; Hewlett-Packard; Project Manager, Bockemühl und Spitta

S. P. R. - SOCIEDADE PORTUGUESA CAPITAL DE RISCO SA

Rua D. Manuel II 296-10
4000 Oporto
Portugal

Telephone: 351-2-606-7165
Fax: 351-2-609-7165

Mission: Actively seeking new investments

Fund Size: Ecu19.5 million
Founded: not available
Average Investment: not available
Minimum Investment: Ecu100,000

Investment Criteria: Expansion/Development

Geographic Preference: Portugal

Industry Group Preference: All sectors considered

Portfolio Companies: not available

Officers, Executives and Principals

A. Ferreira de Castro
Dr. Antonio Almeida

S. R. I. B. SA (G. I. M. B.)

32 rue de Stassart
1050 Brussels
Belgium

Telephone: 32-2-548-2211
Fax: 32-2-511-9074

Mission: Supporting the economic development of the Brussels Region by providing risk capital

Fund Size: Ecu75 million
Founded: 1984
Average Investment: Ecu750,000
Minimum Investment: Ecu115,000

Investment Criteria: Seed, Start-up, Early-stage, Expansion/Development, Management buy-out, Bridge

Geographic Preference: Belgium (Brussels Region)

Industry Group Preference: Biotechnology, Communications, Industrial Automation, Industrial Products, Manufacturing, Transportation

Portfolio Companies: not available

Officers, Executives and Principals

Serge Vilain, President
Julien van der Burght, Vice President
Eddy van der Gelder, General Manager
Etienne Noel, Assistant General Manager

S. R. I. W. SA

13 avenue Destenay
4000 Liège
Belgium

Telephone: 32-41-219-811
Fax: 32-41-219-999

Mission: Actively seeking new investments

Fund Size: Ecu598.6 million
Founded: not available
Average Investment: not available
Minimum Investment: Ecu150,000

Investment Criteria: All stages

Geographic Preference: Belgium

Industry Group Preference: Biotechnology, Electronics Related, Finance, Insurance Businesses, Industrial Products, Industrial Automation, Manufacturing

Portfolio Companies: not available

Officers, Executives and Principals

Jean-Claude Dehovre, Partner
Bernard Marchand, Partner
Louis Tordeurs, Partner
Jean Sequaris, Partner

STALLMANN VENTURE CAPITAL GmbH

Im Hesterkamp 5
45768 Marl-Polsum
Germany

Telephone: 49-2365-97800
Fax: 49-2365-72867

Mission: Actively seeking new investments

Fund Size: not available
Founded: not available
Average Investment: not available
Minimum Investment: DM250,000

Investment Criteria: All stages

Geographic Preference: Germany (North Rhine-Westphalia)

Industry Group Preference: Biotechnology, Computer Software, Electronics Related, Laser Technology

Portfolio Companies: not available

Officers, Executives and Principals

F. Michael Stallman

STAR VENTURES MANAGEMENT

Possartstrasse 9
81679 Munich
Germany

Telephone: 49-89-419-4300
Fax: 49-89-419-43030
E-mail: 100563.341@compuserv.com

Other Office Locations
Druyanov Business Center
11 Galgalei Haplada Street
Hertelia Pituach 46105
Israel

Mission: Actively seeking new investments

Fund Size: $150 million
Founded: 1992
Average Investment: $1.5 million
Minimum Investment: $500,000

Investment Criteria: Start-up, Early-stage, Expansion/Development

Geographic Preference: Europe, Israel, North America

Industry Group Preference: Communications, Computer Related, Computer Software, Electronics Related

Portfolio Companies: not available

Officers, Executives and Principals

Dr. Meir Barel, Managing Director

START FUND OF KERA OY

P. O. Box 247
Vuorikatu 18
00101 Helsinki
Finland

Telephone: 358-0-20-460-3450
Fax: 358-0-20-460-3451

Mission: Actively seeking new investments

Fund Size: FM185.5 million
Founded: not available
Average Investment: FM1-5 million
Minimum Investment: FM500,000

Investment Criteria: Seed, Start-up,Expansion,Management Buy-outs,

Geographic Preference: Finland

Industry Group Preference: Communications, Computer Related, Computer Software, Electronics Related, Forest Products Related, Industrial Products, Manufacturing, Medical/Health Related

Portfolio Companies: not available

Officers, Executives and Principals

Erkki Kariola, Managing Director
Education: MSc in Engineering; BSc in Economics

Ulla Niemelä, Legal Advisor
Education: LLM

START INVEST AB
Maskingatan 5
P. O. Box 8794
40276 Gothenburg
Sweden

Telephone: 46-31-779-7900
Fax: 46-31-779-0685

Mission: Actively seeking new investments in small and medium-sized enterprises

Fund Size: Skr40 million
Founded: not available
Average Investment: not available
Minimum Investment: Skr500,000

Investment Criteria: All stages

Geographic Preference: Sweden (Gothenburg area)

Industry Group Preference: All sectors considered

Portfolio Companies: not available

Officers, Executives and Principals

Åke Johansson, Managing Director
Veronica Kronhamm

STARTFONDS ZUID NEDERLAND BV

Van Limburg Stirumlaan 4E
P. O. Box 454
5000 AL Tilburg
The Netherlands

Telephone: 31-13-463-5400
Fax: 31-13 467-6664

Mission: Actively seeking new investments

Fund Size: Ecu800,000
Founded: not available
Average Investment: not available
Minimum Investment: Ecu25,000

Investment Criteria: Seed, Start-up

Geographic Preference: Netherlands

Industry Group Preference: Biotechnology, Chemical/Materials, Computer Related, Industrial Automation, Industrial Products, Medical/Health Related

Portfolio Companies: not available

Officers, Executives and Principals

G.W. A. van Overbeek de Meyer

STAUFERKREIS KAPITALBETEILIGUNGS GmbH

Marktstrasse 2
73033 Göppingen
Germany

Telephone: 49-7161-603-760
Fax: 49-7161-603-759

Mission: Actively seeking new investments in small and medium-sized companies

Fund Size: not available
Founded: not available
Average Investment: not available
Minimum Investment: DM300,000

Investment Criteria: All stages

Geographic Preference: Germany (Göppingen district in Baden-Württemberg)

Industry Group Preference: All sectors considered

Portfolio Companies: not available

Officers, Executives and Principals

Rainer Auwärter

STICHTING SHELL PENSIOENFONDS

P.O Box 65
2501 CB Den Haag
The Netherlands

Telephone: 31-70-319-9336
Fax: 31-70-319-9247

Mission: Actively seeking new investments

Fund Size: not available
Founded: not available
Average Investment: not available
Minimum Investment: not available

Investment Criteria: Expansion/Development, Management Buy-out, Turnaround/Restructuring

Geographic Preference: North America

Industry Group Preference: All sectors considered

Portfolio Companies: not available

Officers, Executives and Principals

M.J. Jansen

SUBG AG UNTERNEHMENSBETEILIGUNGSGESELLSCHAFT DER WIRTSCHAFTSREGION AACHEN

Markt 45-47
52062 Aachen
Germany

Telephone: 49-241-470-560
Fax: 49-241-470-5620

Mission: Actively seeking new investments

Fund Size: DM33 million
Founded: not available
Average Investment: not available
Minimum Investment: DM1 million

Investment Criteria: All stages

Geographic Preference: Germany (Aachen region)

Industry Group Preference: All sectors considered

Portfolio Companies: not available

Officers, Executives and Principals

Heinrich Eickhaus
Horst Gier

SÜD K. B. GmbH

Postfach 106049
70049 Stuttgart
Germany

Telephone: 49-711-127-7067
Fax: 49-711-127-3040

Mission: Actively seeking new investments

Fund Size: DM55 million
Founded: not available
Average Investment: not available
Minimum Investment: DM500,000

Investment Criteria: All stages

Geographic Preference: Germany (Baden-Württemberg)

Industry Group Preference: All sectors considered

Portfolio Companies: not available

Officers, Executives and Principals

Wigand Reetz
Werner Epp

SUEZ FINANCE CONSEIL

27 rue de la Ville l'Evêque
75008 Paris
France

Telephone: 33-1-4007-0513
Fax: 33-1-4924-9972

Mission: Actively seeking new investments

Fund Size: Ffr400 million
Founded: not available
Average Investment: not available
Minimum Investment: Ffr10 million

Investment Criteria: Expansion/Development, Leveraged Buy-out

Geographic Preference: Europe

Industry Group Preference: All sectors considered

Portfolio Companies: not available

Officers, Executives and Principals

Jacques Mecheri
Michel Rowan
Philippe Sevin
Daniel Toulemonde
Philippe Renié

SUEZ FINANZBERATUNG GmbH

Oberliederbacher Weg 25
65843 Sulzbach/Ts.
Germany

Telephone: 49-6196-750091
Fax: 49-6196-74243

Mission: Actively seeking new investments as a subsidiary of Compagnie de Suez, Paris

Fund Size: DM71 million
Founded: 1987
Average Investment: DM10 million
Minimum Investment: DM8 million

Investment Criteria: Expansion, Management Buy-out, Management Buy-in

Geographic Preference: Germany, Austria, Switzerland

Industry Group Preference: All sectors considered

Portfolio Companies: not available

Officers, Executives and Principals

Peter Todtenhaupt, Managing Director

SUEZ VENTURES

1 rue d'Astorg
75008 Paris
France

Telephone: 33-1-4007-0515
Fax: 33-1-4924-9261

Mission: Actively seeking new investments

Fund Size: Ffr195 million
Founded: not available
Average Investment: not available
Minimum Investment: Ffr2 million

Investment Criteria: Early-stage, Expansion/Development

Geographic Preference: Europe, France

Industry Group Preference: Industrial Products and Services, Information Technology, Medical/Health Related

Portfolio Companies: Reltek Com, Kortex, Groupe Decan, Sebia, Sederma

Officers, Executives and Principals

Christian Cleiftie
Dominique Agrech
Roland Cohen
Dominique Rigolet

SULPEDIP SA

Av. de Berna 24-7° Dto.
1000 Lisbon
Portugal

Telephone: 351-1-793-7773
Fax: 351-1-7967-284

Mission: Actively seeking new investments

Fund Size: Ecu30.7million
Founded: not available
Average Investment: not available
Minimum Investment: Ecu100,000

Investment Criteria: All stages

Geographic Preference: Portugal

Industry Group Preference: Biotechnology, Computer Related, Computer Software, Electronics Related, Energy, Industrial Automation

Portfolio Companies: not available

Officers, Executives and Principals

Beiräo Belo

SWEDFUND INTERNATIONAL AB

Sveavägen 24-26
P. O. Box 3286
10365 Stockholm
Sweden

Telephone: 46-8-725-9400
Fax: 46-8-203093
E-mail: swedfund@algonet.se

Mission: Providing risk capital and know-how, on a commercial basis and working together with Swedish industry, for long-term investments in difficult environments

Fund Size: Skr600 million
Founded: 1979
Average Investment: not available
Minimum Investment: Skr1.5 million

Investment Criteria: not available

Geographic Preference: Africa, Asia, Latin America, Central Europe, Eastern Europe

Industry Group Preference: not available

Portfolio Companies: not available

Officers, Executives and Principals

Olle Arefalk, Managing Director
Jan-Erik Fihhmyr, Deputy Managing Director

SYNERFI SA

288 boulevard du Souverain
1160 Brussels
Belgium

Telephone: 32-3-675-5757
Fax: 32-3-675-5800

Mission: Actively seeking new investments

Fund Size: Ecu13.5 million
Founded: not available
Average Investment: not available
Minimum Investment: Ecu125,000

Investment Criteria: Expansion/Development, Management Buy-out, Management Buy-in, Turnaround/ Restructuring, Replacement, Bridge

Geographic Preference: Belgium, Luxemburg, France

Industry Group Preference: All sectors considered

Portfolio Companies: not available

Officers, Executives and Principals

Dr. Pierre L. Robin, Partner
Hugues Bultot, Partner
Natalie Solé, Partner

TATRA RAIFFEISEN CAPITAL

Vajanského nabr. 5
P. O. Box 9
810 06 Bratislava
Slovakia

Telephone: 42-7-271-220
Fax: 42-7-271-222

Mission: Actively seeking new investments

Fund Size: Ecu11.4 million
Founded: not available
Average Investment: not available
Minimum Investment: Ecu200,000

Investment Criteria: All stages

Geographic Preference: Slovakia

Industry Group Preference: Chemical/Materials, Construction/Building Products, Energy, Finance/Insurance/Real Estate, Industrial Products, Transportation

Portfolio Companies: not available

Officers, Executives and Principals

Dusan Adamec

TAY EURO FUND

Enterprise House
45 North Lindsay Street
Dundee DD1 1HT
United Kingdom

Telephone: 44-1382-223100
Fax: 44-1382-201319
E-mail: john.g.gardner@scotent.co.uk

Mission: Actively seeking new investments

Fund Size: Ecu600,000
Founded: not available
Average Investment: not available
Minimum Investment: Ecu30,000

Investment Criteria: Seed, Start-up, Early-stage

Geographic Preference: Scotland

Industry Group Preference: Biotechnology, Computer Related, Computer Software, Electronics Related, Industrial Products, Manufacturing

Portfolio Companies: not available

Officers, Executives and Principals

Graham H. McKee, Partner
John Gardner

TBG (TECHNOLOGIE-BETEILIGUNGS-GmbH DER DEUTSCHEN AUSGLEICHSBANK)

Ludwig-Erhard-Platz 1-3
53179 Bonn
Germany

Telephone: 49-228-831-2549
Fax: 49-228-831-2493
E-mail: densing@tbgbonn.bn.eunet.de

Mission: Actively seeking new investments as a subsidiary of Deutsche Ausgleichsbank

Fund Size: DM320 million
Founded: 1989
Average Investment: DM1.2 million
Minimum Investment: DM100,000

Investment Criteria: Seed, Start-up, Early-stage, Expansion/Development, Management Buy-out, Management Buy-in

Geographic Preference: Germany

Industry Group Preference: All sectors considered

Portfolio Companies: not available

Officers, Executives and Principals

Hansgeorg Rasch, Managing Director
J.-Wolfgang Posselt, Managing Director
Ernst Mayer, Deputy Managing Director

TCR EUROPE

280 boulevard Saint-Germain
75341 Paris
France

Telephone: 33-1-4705-7154
Fax: 33-1-4705-7173

Mission: Actively seeking new investments

Fund Size: Ffr200 million
Founded: not available
Average Investment: not available
Minimum Investment: Ffr15 million

Investment Criteria: Early-stage, Expansion/Development

Geographic Preference: France, Italy, Spain

Industry Group Preference: All sectors considered

Portfolio Companies: Polygone

Officers, Executives and Principals

Jean-François Borde
Vivian de Mesquita
Marco de Alfaro
Christian Deorleac

TECHNOLOGIE-FONDS GmbH UND CO. BETEILIGUNGEN KG

Im Hesterkamp 5
45768 Marl-Polsum
Germany

Telephone: 49-2365-97800
Fax: 49-2365-72867

Mission: Actively seeking new investments

Fund Size: not available
Founded: not available
Average Investment: not available
Minimum Investment: DM500,000

Investment Criteria: Start-up, Early-stage

Geographic Preference: Germany

Industry Group Preference: All sectors considered

Portfolio Companies: not available

Officers, Executives and Principals

Jürgen Leschke
F. M. Stallman

TECHNOLOGIEHOLDING VC GmbH

Gernerstrasse 7
80638 Munich
Germany

Telephone: 49-8915-70020
Fax: 49-8915-700299
E-mail: strascheg@technologieholding.de

Other Office Locations
Kaiser-Friedrich-Promenade 59
61348 Bad Homburg
Phone 49-6175-67650, Fax 49-6175-676519

Nikolaistrasse 55
04109 Leipzig
Phone 49-341-2188652, Fax 49-341-2188653

Mission: Actively seeking new investments

Fund Size: DM120 million
Founded: 1988
Average Investment: DM1.5 million
Minimum Investment: DM500,000

Investment Criteria: Seed, Startup, First-stage, Second-stage, Early-stage, Expansion/Development

Geographic Preference: Germany, Austria, Switzerland, France

Industry Group Preference: Chemical Materials, Communications, Computer Related, Distribution, Electronic Components and Instrumentation, Industrial Products and Equipment

Portfolio Companies: GLI, Com-M-Tex, Schweers Intec, NetManSys, Condata, CAE, POET, Speed, 3V Multimedia, diamond, DTM DataTeleMark, Mobis, INOVIT, Adcon, commIT, GSSB, Electronic Forms, Netconsult, BinTech, Alaska, ATS, XXL, CPU, Micronas, Scanlab, VS Sensoric, HL Planar, Enertron, Heges, Astec, Iras, CodeKey, Wilo, WaveLight, SEZ, Plasmos, LAS, Compur, Stracon, ACTech, Alphaform, WS+S

Officers, Executives and Principals

Falk F. Strascheg, Managing Director
Education: Graduate in Electronic Engineering
Background: Divisional Manager, NCR; Managing Director, Laser Associates (Germany); Founder and Chairman, Laser-Optronic; Head of European Operations, Coherent Inc.; Joint Managing Director, Heidelberg Instruments

Dr. Gert Köhler, Managing Director
Education: Master's degrees in Mathematics, Physics and Business Administration, Universities of Tübingen, Stuttgart and Grenoble; doctorate, University of Grenoble
Background: Operations Research, DGRST (France); Inter-Unternehmnesberatung; Project Manager, McKinsey and Co. (Germany); Managing Director, GFI

TECHNOLOGY DEVELOPMENT CENTRE FINLAND (TEKES)

P. O. Box 69
Malminkatu 34
00101 Helsinki
Finland

Telephone: 358-0-693-691
Fax: 358-0-694-9196

Mission: Actively seeking new investments as a government agency

Fund Size: FM400 million
Founded: not available
Average Investment: FM500,000-3 million
Minimum Investment: Negotiable

Investment Criteria: Seed, Start-up, Expansion, Management Buy-out

Geographic Preference: Finland

Industry Group Preference: Manufacturing

Portfolio Companies: not available

TECHNOSTART GmbH

Industriestrasse 2
760565 Stuttgart
Germany

Telephone: 49-711-784-6343
Fax: 49-711-784-6344

Mission: Actively seeking new investments

Fund Size: Ecu3.4 million
Founded: not available
Average Investment: not available
Minimum Investment: Ecu100,000

Investment Criteria: Seed, Start-up, Early-stage, Expansion/Development

Geographic Preference: Europe

Industry Group Preference: Biotechnology, Chemical/Materials, Communications, Industrial Automation, Inudustrial Products, Pollution/Recycling Related

Portfolio Companies: not available

Officers, Executives and Principals

Maximillian Garbas
Dr. Wolfgang Ruhrmann
Michael Mayer

TEKNIA VENTURE INVEST LIMITED

P. O. Box 1750
70211 Kuopio
Finland

Telephone: 358-71-240200
Fax: 358-71-240241

Mission: Actively seeking new investments

Fund Size: Ecu5.6 million
Founded: not available
Average Investment: not available
Minimum Investment: Ecu50,000

Investment Criteria: Seed, Start-up, Early-stage, Expansion/Development, Management Buy-out

Geographic Preference: Europe, Finland, Russia

Industry Group Preference: Biotechnology, Industrial Products, Manufacturing, Medical/Health Related, Pollution/Recycling, Software

Portfolio Companies: not available

Officers, Executives and Principals

Matti Lappalainen, Partner
Jorma Pylkkänen

TEKNO ADVISORS OY

Isokatu 32B
90100 Oulu
Finland

Telephone: 358-81-815-5200
Fax: 358-81-815-5201

Mission: Actively seeking new investments

Fund Size: FM100 million
Founded: not available
Average Investment: FM2.5 million
Minimum Investment: FM1 million

Investment Criteria: Start-up, Expansion, Management Buy-out, Turnaround

Geographic Preference: Finland (Northern region)

Industry Group Preference: Biotechnology, Computer Related, Electronics, Mechanical Engineering, Tele-communications, Wood Processing

Portfolio Companies: not available

Officers, Executives and Principals

Jorma Terentjeff, Managing Director
Education: MSc in Engineering

Seppo Kaikkonen, Director
Education: BSc in Engineering; MBA

Jukka Koponen, Director
Education: LLM, Legal Counsel

Vesa-Pekka Kursu, Director
Education: MSc in Engineering

TEKNOINVEST MANAGEMENT

Grev Wedels plass 5
0151 Oslo
Norway

Telephone: 47-2282-5870
Fax: 47-2282-5871
E-mail: teknoinvest@telepost.no

Mission: Actively seeking new investments

Fund Size: $20 million
Founded: 1984
Average Investment: not available
Minimum Investment: $100,000

Investment Criteria: Seed, Start-up, First-stage, Second-stage

Geographic Preference: Norway, Sweden, United States

Industry Group Preference: Biotechnology, Communications, Computer Related, Electronic Components and Instrumentation, Medical/Health Related

Portfolio Companies: not available

Officers, Executives and Principals

Bjørn Bjorå, Managing Director
Steinar Engelsen, Director

TENEO GRUPO DE EMPRESAS DE DESARROLLO (I. N. I.)

Pl. Marq. de Salamanca 8
28071 Madrid
Spain

Telephone: 34-1-396-1339
Fax: 34-1-396-1034

Mission: Actively seeking new investments

Fund Size: Ecu75 million
Founded: not available
Average Investment: not available
Minimum Investment: Ecu170,000

Investment Criteria: Expansion/Development, Management Buy-out

Geographic Preference: Spain

Industry Group Preference: All sectors considered

Portfolio Companies: not available

Officers, Executives and Principals

Enrique Centelles Echeverria, Partner
Juan R. Puertas, Partner

TERTIAIRE DÉVELOPPEMENT

12 rue Tronchet
75008 Paris
France

Telephone: 33-1-4266-9077
Fax: 33-1-4266-5022

Mission: Actively seeking new investments

Fund Size: Ffr45 million
Founded: not available
Average Investment: not available
Minimum Investment: Ffr1 million

Investment Criteria: Expansion/Development

Geographic Preference: France, Israel

Industry Group Preference: All sectors considered

Portfolio Companies: Otor, BDDP

Officers, Executives and Principals

Hervé Debache, President

THOMPSON CLIVE AND PARTNERS LIMITED

24 Old Bond Street
London W1X 4JD
United Kingdom

Telephone: 44-171-491-4809
Fax: 44-171-493-9172
E-mail: tc-london@dial.pipex.com

Other Office Locations
Thompson Clive Europe
55 rue La Boétie
75008 Paris
France
Phone 33-1-4413-3606, Fax 33-1-4413-3746

Thompson Clive Inc.
Building 1, Suite 185
3000 Sand Hill Road
Menlo Park, CA 94025
United States
Phone 415-854-0314, Fax 415-864-0670

Mission: Actively seeking new investments

Fund Size: £100 million
Founded: 1977
Average Investment: £2 million
Minimum Investment: £750,000

Investment Criteria: Expansion, Management Buy-in, Management Buy-out, Other Early-stage, Rescue/ Turnaround, Secondary Purchase/Replacement Capital, Venture Purchase of Quoted Shares

Geographic Preference: North America, Western Europe

Industry Group Preference: Information Technology, Life Sciences

Portfolio Companies: Isotron plc, Medicom International Limited, Phonic Ear Holdings Inc, Terence Chapman Associates Ltd, Sifam Limited

Officers, Executives and Principals

Richard Thompson
Colin Clive
Robin Meyer
Nat Hone
Charles Fitzherbert

THOMPSON CLIVE EUROPE

55 rue la Boetie
75008 Paris
France

Telephone: 33-4413-3606
Fax: 33-1-4413-3746
E-mail: 72147.3402@compuserve.com

Mission: Actively seeking new investments

Fund Size: not available
Founded: 1977
Average Investment: not available
Minimum Investment: not available

Investment Criteria: Start-up, First-stage, Second-stage, Mezzanine, Leveraged Buy-out, Special Situations

Geographic Preference: not available

Industry Group Preference: Biotechnology, Communications, Computer Related, Distribution, Electronic Components and Instrumentation, High Technology, Industrial Products and Equipment, Medical/Health Related, Software

Portfolio Companies: not available

Officers, Executives and Principals

Michael Elias

THOMSON-C. S. F. VENTURES

173 boulevard Haussmann
75415 Paris
France

Telephone: 33-1-5377-8420
Fax: 33-1-5377-8733
E-mail: 101707.1412@compuserve.com

Other Office Locations
c/o Cetia, Inc.
Suite 201, 45 Cabot Street
Santa Clara, CA 95051-6637
United States
Phone 408-247-3064, Fax 408-247-5132

Mission: Actively seeking new investments

Fund Size: $60 million
Founded: 1986
Average Investment: not available
Minimum Investment: $500,000

Investment Criteria: Start-up, First-stage, Second-stage, Mezzanine

Geographic Preference: Europe, North America, Asia

Industry Group Preference: Communications, Computer Related, Computer Software, Consumer Related, Electronic Components and Instrumentation, Electronics Related

Portfolio Companies: not available

Officers, Executives and Principals

Jean-Michel Barbier, Managing Director
Nicolas Barsalou
Francoise Lohézic

3i DEUTSCHLAND GESELLSCHAFT FÜR INDUSTRIEBETEILIGUNGEN mbH

Bockenheimer Landstrasse 55
60325 Frankfurt am Main
Germany

Telephone: 49-69-7100-000
Fax: 49-69-7100-39

Other Office Locations
Burggrafenstrasse 5
40545 Düsseldorf
Phone 49-211-954-440, Fax 49-211-954-4449

Mission: Actively seeking new investments and advising 3i Eurofund I (founded in 1993) on investments in Germany

Fund Size: not available
Founded: 1986
Average Investment: DM4-5 million
Minimum Investment: DM1.5 million

Investment Criteria: Management Buy-out, Management Buy-in, Development

Geographic Preference: Germany, Austria, Switzerland (German-speaking cantons)

Industry Group Preference: All sectors considered except Financial Services

Portfolio Companies: Woma Apparatebau, AS-Creation, Siegener Verzinkerei, Schlott Tiefdruck, ACI AG, others

Officers, Executives and Principals

Andrew Richards, Managing Director
Ulrich Eilers, Manager, Düsseldorf
Thomas Geller, Manager, Hamburg region
Andreas Kochhäuser, Manager, Stuttgart region
Thomas Rubahn, Manager, Munich region and Austria
Steffen Lehmann, Manager, Frankfurt region and Switzerland
Harald Rönn, Manager, Frankfurt region and Switzerland
Peter Cullom, Manager, Finance and Special Projects
Claudia Bischoff, Manager, Marketing and Public Relations

3i FRANCE

141 avenue Charles de Gaulle
92521 Neuilly
France

Telephone: 33-1-4715-1100
Fax: 33-1-4745-3124

Mission: Actively seeking new investments

Fund Size: Ffr1.5 billion
Founded: not available
Average Investment: not available
Minimum Investment: Ffr5 million

Investment Criteria: Expansion/Development, Mangement Buy-out, Management Buy-in, Leveraged Mangement Buy-out

Geographic Preference: Europe

Industry Group Preference: All sectors considered

Portfolio Companies: not available

Officers, Executives and Principals

Frédéric de Broglie, Managing Director
Clément Cordier, Associate Director
Bertrand Fesneau, Associate Director
Paul Traynor, Associate Director
Guy Zarzavatdjian, Associate Director
François Le Corno, Company Secretary
Florence Jouffroy, Public Relations

3i GROUP PLC

91 Waterloo Road
London SE1 8XP
United Kingdom

Telephone: 44-171-928-3131
Fax: 44-171-928-0058

Other Office Locations
Aberdeen (Keith Mair), Phone 44-1224-638666
Birmingham (Paul Traynor), Phone 44-121-200-3131
Bristol (David Williams), Phone 44-117-927-7412
Cambridge (Jim Martin), Phone 44-1223-420031
Cardiff (Chris Graham), Phone 44-1222-394541
Edinburgh (Mike Pacitti), Phone 44-131-459-3131
Glasgow (Willie Watt), Phone 44-141-248-4456
Leeds (Jonathan Russell), Phone 44-113-243-0511
Leicester (Mike Piper), Phone 44-116-255-5110
Liverpool (Ian Lobley), Phone 44-151-236-2944
London (Richard Campin, Tim Harrison, David Hunter, Alastair Morrison, Patrick Sheehan, Tom Sweet-Escott,
  Ian Nolan, Nigel Guy, Jonathan Taylor, Patrick Dunne), Phone 44-171-928-3131
Maidstone (Sue Hunter), Phone 44-1622-685680
Manchester (Stephen Ross), Phone 44-161-839-3131
Newcastle (Antony Ross), Phone 44-191-222-1966
Nottingham (Mike Prentis), Phone 44-115-941-2766
Reading (Jane Crawford), Phone 44-118-958-4344
Southampton (Clive Moody), Phone 44-1703-632044
Watford (Alan MacKay), Phone 44-1923-233232

3i Deutschland Gesellschaft für Industriebeteiligungen mbH
Bockenheimer Landstrasse 55
60325 Frankfurt am Main
Germany
Phone 49-69-7100-000, Fax 49-69-7100-39

3i France
141 avenue Charles de Gaulle
92521 Neuilly
France
Phone 33-1-4715-1100, Fax 33-1-4745-3124

3i - Investors in Industry SpA
Via Gaetano Negri 8
20123 Milan
Italy
Phone 39-2-720-03210

Mission: 3i is the United Kingdom's leading specialist provider of investment capital to unquoted businesses;
  since 1945 it has invested more than £8 billion in more than 12,000 businesses. 3i takes a long-term view of its
  investments, whether equity or loan capital; they are characterized by their minority shareholdings, leaving
  managements in control of their businesses.

Fund Size: not available

Founded: 1945 by the Bank of England and the British clearing banks; listed on the London Stock Exchange since 1994

Minimum Investment: £100,000

Investment Criteria: Start-up, Growth Capital, Management Buy-in, Management Buy-out

Geographic Preference: United Kingdom, France, Germany, Japan, Italy, Spain

Industry Group Preference: All sectors considered

Portfolio Companies: 3,300 companies

Officers, Executives and Principals

Sir George Russell, Chairman
John Melbourn, Deputy Chairman
Ewen Macpherson, Chief Executive
Brian Larcombe, Executive Director
Lord Camoys, Non-Executive Director
John Gardiner, Non-Executive Director
William Govett, Non-Executive Director
Ralph Quartano, Non-Executive Director
Tony Brierley, Company Secretary
Dr. Richard Summers, Executive Director

THROUNARFELAG ISLANDS PLC

Sudurlandsbraut 22
00108 Reykjavik
Iceland

Telephone: 354-568-8266
Fax: 354-568-0191

Mission: Actively seeking new investments, specializing in high-technology industries

Fund Size: not available
Founded: not available
Average Investment: not available
Minimum Investment: not available

Investment Criteria: Expansion/Development, Management Buy-out, Management Buy-in, Turnaround/ Restructuring, Replacement, Bridge

Geographic Preference: Iceland, Europe

Industry Group Preference: Biotechnology, Communications, Computer Related, Computer Software, Electronics Related, Industrial Products, Information Technology, Medical/Health Related, Transportation

Portfolio Companies: not available

Officers, Executives and Principals

H. Jakobsson
S.E. Jonsdottir

THÜRINGER INDUSTRIEBETEILIGUNGENS GmbH UND CO. KG

Breite Gasse 4/5
99084 Erfurt
Germany

Telephone: 49-361-5678-276
Fax: 49-361-5678-271

Mission: Actively seeking new investments

Fund Size: DM67 million
Founded: not available
Average Investment: not available
Minimum Investment: DM2 million

Investment Criteria: not available

Geographic Preference: Germany (Thuringia)

Industry Group Preference: All sectors considered

Portfolio Companies: not available

Officers, Executives and Principals

Dr. Gerhard Hoffmann-Becking

TIANGUIS LIMITED

5 Edwardes Place
London W8 6LR
United Kingdom

Telephone: 44-171-603-7788
Fax: 44-171-603-7667
E-mail: 100622.3455@compuserve.com

Mission: Actively seeking new investments

Fund Size: not available
Founded: not available
Average Investment: not available
Minimum Investment: Ecu100,000

Investment Criteria: Start-up, Early-stage, Management Buy-in, Management Buy-out, Turnaround/Restructuring

Geographic Preference: Europe, North America, Australia, Southeast Asia

Industry Group Preference: Agricultural, Chemical and Materials, Computer Software, Fisheries, Forestry, Industrial Products, Pollution and Recycling Related

Portfolio Companies: not available

Officers, Executives and Principals

Stephen R. Smith

TOKYO SMALL AND MEDIUM BUSINESS INVESTMENTS AND CONSULTATION COMPANY

15-6 Nihonbashi Kabuto-cho
Chuo-ku
Tokyo 103
Japan

Telephone: 81-3-3668-1811
Fax: 81-3-3668-8635

Other Office Locations
12th Floor, 2-3-10 Hon-cho
Aoba-ku, Sendai-shi 980
Phone 81-22-213-7966, Fax 81-22-213-7997

Mission: Actively seeking new investments

Fund Size: not available
Founded: 1963
Average Investment: not available
Minimum Investment: $100,000

Investment Criteria: Startup, First-stage, Second-stage, Mezzanine

Geographic Preference: not available

Industry Group Preference: Communications, Computer Related, Consumer, Distribution, Electronic Components and Instrumentation, Industrial Products and Equipment, Medical/Health Related

Portfolio Companies: not available

Officers, Executives and Principals

Toshihiko Yano, President
Kanzo Ichiki, Executive Vice President
Morio Kawamura, Senior Managing Director
Yoshiaki Takagi, Managing Director
Yoshimitsu Hanawa, Director

TRANSATLANTIC CAPITAL LTD

17 Devonshire Street
London W1N 2EY
United Kingdom

Telephone: 44-171-436-1216
Fax: 44-171-436-1226

Mission: Actively seeking new investments

Fund Size: £9 million
Founded: not available
Average Investment: not available
Minimum Investment: £25,000

Investment Criteria: Start-up, Early-stage, Development, Expansion

Geographic Preference: North America, Western Europe

Industry Group Preference: Biotechnology, Environmental, Medical Related

Portfolio Companies: Alliance Medical Ltd, Ethical Pharmaceuticals Ltd, Cardinal Medical Ltd, Micromed Ltd

Officers, Executives and Principals

Gordon Dean
Fred Offer

TRANSPAC CAPITAL PTE. LTD.

6 Shenton Way
20-09 DBS Building Tower Two
Singapore

Telephone: 65-224-1211
Fax: 65-225-5538

Other Office Locations
1 Pacific Place, 33rd Floor
88 Queensway
Hong Kong
Phone 852-525-2661, Fax 852-877-6612

51
Room 408, 2004 Nanjing Xilu
Shanghai 200040
China
Phone 86-21-248-3040, Fax 86-21-248-4607

Hotel Landmark Canton, Room 817
Qiaoguang Lu, Guangzhou
Guangdong 510115
China
Phone 86-20-335-5988, Fax 86-20-333-5988

Secondary Tower Block, Sixth Floor
Wisma MCIS, Jalan Barat
46200 Petaling Jaya
Selangor
Malaysia
Phone 60-3-756-0560, Fax 60-3-755-4205

Wisma Rajawali, 14th Floor
Jalan Jenderal Sudirman 34
Jakarta 10220
Indonesia
Phone 62-21-570-0669, Fax 62-21-573-4684

Maneeya Centre Building, Eighth Floor
518/5 Ploenchit Road
Bangkok 10330
Thailand
Phone 66-2-652-0791, Fax 66-2-652-0793

Mission: Actively seeking new investments

Fund Size: not available
Founded: 1989
Average Investment: not available
Minimum Investment: $500,000

Investment Criteria: First-stage, Mezzanine

Geographic Preference: not available

Industry Group Preference: All sectors considered

Portfolio Companies: not available

Officers, Executives and Principals

Dr. Christopher Leong, President (Singapore and Hong Kong)
Mr. Wong Lin Hong, Senior Vice President (Singapore)
Mr. Koo Pak Ching, Senior Vice President (Malaysia)

TRIGON CAPITAL PRAHA

Francouzska 16
12000 Prague 2
Czech Republic

Telephone: 42-2-2424-6052
Fax: 42-2-254980

Mission: Actively seeking new investments

Fund Size: Ecu1.75 million
Founded: not available
Average Investment: not available
Minimum Investment: not available

Investment Criteria: Early-stage, Expansion/Development, Management Buy-out, Management Buy-in

Geographic Preference: not available

Industry Group Preference: not available

Portfolio Companies: not available

Officers, Executives and Principals

Henry Kolowrat, Partner
Joakim Helenius, Partner

TRYGG HANSA

Fleminggatan 18
10626 Stockholm
Sweden

Telephone: 46-8-693-1000
Fax: 46-8-652-7450
E-mail: th.remaev@trygghansa.se

Mission: Actively seeking new investments

Fund Size: Skr40 million
Founded: not available
Average Investment: not available
Minimum Investment: not available

Investment Criteria: All stages

Geographic Preference: Sweden

Industry Group Preference: All sectors considered

Portfolio Companies: not available

Officers, Executives and Principals

Lars Thunell, Managing Director
Lars Lundqvist, Finance Director
William af Sandberg
Eva Reman

TUAB

Regeringsgatan 48
P. O. Box 7519
10392 Stockholm
Sweden

Telephone: 46-8-242507
Fax: 46-8-791-8270

Mission: Actively seeking new investments

Fund Size: Skr40 million
Founded: not available
Average Investment: not available
Minimum Investment: not available

Investment Criteria: All stages

Geographic Preference: Sweden

Industry Group Preference: Biotechnology, Electronics Related, Materials

Portfolio Companies: not available

Officers, Executives and Principals

Willy Heyman, Managing Director
Jan Lundblad, Deputy Managing Director

TUFTON CAPITAL LTD

Little Tufton House
3 Dean Trench Street
London SW1P 3HB
United Kingdom

Telephone: 44-171-340 2877
Fax: 44-171-222 0312
E-mail: 101640.3155@compuserve.com

Mission: Actively seeking new investments as a leading British recovery fund

Fund Size: £10 million
Founded: 1994
Average Investment: £1-3 million
Minimum Investment: £500,000

Investment Criteria: Expansion, Management Buy-in, Refinancing Bank Debt, Rescue/Turnaround, Secondary Purchase/Replacement Capital

Geographic Preference: United Kingdom, France, Scandinavia

Industry Group Preference: Consumer Related, Energy, Industrial Products and Services, Leisure, Media, Other Manufacturing, Transport

Portfolio Companies: Bradley Holdings Limited, Quiligotti plc, Deanes Holdings plc, Phoenix Timber Group plc

Officers, Executives and Principals

Dr. Lars Ahrell, Chairman
Jeremy Brassington, Managing Director
John Greig, Corporate Finance Director
Billy Corry, Financial Analyst

TVM TECHNO VENTURE MANAGEMENT GmbH

Dennigerstrasse 15
81679 Munich
Germany

Telephone: 49-89-9989-920
Fax: 49-89-9989-9255

Other Office Locations
TVM Techno Management
Limited Partnership
101 Arch Street
Boston, MA 02110
Phone 617-345-9320, Fax 617-345-9377

Mission: Actively seeking new investments

Fund Size: DM350 million
Founded: not available
Average Investment: not available
Minimum Investment: DM1 million

Investment Criteria: Start-up, Early-stage, Expansion/Development

Geographic Preference: Germany, Western Europe, United States

Industry Group Preference: Biotechnology, Communications, Computer Related, Computer Software, Electronics Related, Medical/Health Related

Portfolio Companies: not available

Officers, Executives and Principals

Waldemar Jantz
Peter Kaleschke

ULSTER DEVELOPMENT CAPITAL LTD.

1 Arthur Street
Belfast
Northern Ireland

Telephone: 44-1232-246765
Fax: 44-1232-232982

Mission: Actively seeking new investments

Fund Size: not available
Founded: 1985
Average Investment: £200,000
Minimum Investment: £50,000

Investment Criteria: Second-stage, Mezzanine, Leveraged Buy-out

Geographic Preference: Northern Ireland

Industry Group Preference: Consumer, Distribution, Industrial Products and Equipment, Medical/Health Related

Portfolio Companies: Nectar Holdings Ltd, Munster Simms Engineering Ltd,

Officers, Executives and Principals

Tom McStraw, Investment Manager

UPM GROEP

Galileïlaan 35
3584 BC Utrecht
The Netherlands

Telephone: 31-30-251-4288
Fax: 31-30-252-1254

Mission: Actively seeking new investments

Fund Size: Ecu40 million
Founded: not available
Average Investment: not available
Minimum Investment: Ecu500,000

Investment Criteria: Expansion/Development, Management Buy-out, Management Buy-in

Geographic Preference: Netherlands, United Kingdom, Belgium, Germany

Industry Group Preference: Communications, Consumer Related, Medical/Health Related

Portfolio Companies: not available

Officers, Executives and Principals

H. Bujak
H. N. van Middendorp

UNION BANK OF SWITZERLAND

Bahnhofstrasse 45
8021 Zürich
Switzerland

Telephone: 41-1-234-2011
Fax: 41-1-234-2023

Mission: Investing on a very selected basis

Fund Size: not available
Founded: not available
Average Investment: not available
Minimum Investment: not available

Investment Criteria: Expansion/Development, Management Buy-out, Management Buy-in, Replacement, Bridge

Geographic Preference: Switzerland, Europe, United States, Asia

Industry Group Preference: All sectors considered

Portfolio Companies: not available

Officers, Executives and Principals

Robert Kahn
Dr. H.C. Tanner
Markus Zehnder

UNION D'ÉTUDES ET D'INVESTISSEMENTS

100 boulevard du Montparnasse
75014 Paris
France

Telephone: 33-1-4323-2121
Fax: 33-1-4323-3319

Mission: Actively seeking new investments

Fund Size: Ffr5 billion
Founded: not available
Average Investment: not available
Minimum Investment: Ffr15 million

Investment Criteria: Expansion/Development, Management Buy-out, Management Buy-in

Geographic Preference: Europe, United States

Industry Group Preference: Biotechnology, Consumer Related, Electronics Related, Industrial Automation, Industrial Products, Medical/Health Related

Portfolio Companies: not available

Officers, Executives and Principals

Gilles Gramat
Jacques Lechalupé

UNION EUROPÉENNE DE CIC FINANCE

4 rue Gaillon
75002 Paris
France

Telephone: 33-1-4266-7149
Fax: 33-1-4266-7871

Mission: Actively seeking new investments

Fund Size: Ffr1.2 billion
Founded: not available
Average Investment: not available
Minimum Investment: Ffr 5 million

Investment Criteria: Expansion/Development, Management Buy-out, Leveraged Buy-out

Geographic Preference: Europe, France, Asia

Industry Group Preference: Communications, Consumer Related, Industrial Products, Medical/Health Related, Pharmaceuticals

Portfolio Companies: Nature et Découvertes, Groupe de Presee Michel Hommell, I Ile-de-France Pharmaceutique, Sucreries de Berneuil et Regnault

Officers, Executives and Principals

Sidney Cabessa, President
Carl Arnou
François Messager

VAEKSTFONDEN

Tagensvej 137
2200 Copenhagen
Denmark

Telephone: 45-35-868635
Fax: 45-35-868636
E-mail: vf@vaekstfonden.dk

Mission: Actively seeking new investments

Fund Size: Dkr2 billion
Founded: 1992
Average Investment: Dkr1.8 million
Minimum Investment: Dkr100,000

Investment Criteria: Start-up, Early-stage, Expansion/Development

Geographic Preference: not available

Industry Group Preference: Biotechnology, Communications, Computer Related, Industrial Products, Medical/Health Related, Pollution/Recycling Related

Portfolio Companies: not available

Officers, Executives and Principals

Bent Kiemer

VALORA UNTERNEHMENSBETEILIGUNG AG

Brückenstrasse 8
36391 Sinntal-Mottgers
Germany

Telephone: 49-6664-552
Fax: 49-6664-7420

Mission: Actively seeking new investments, mainly in new, unlisted companies

Fund Size: DM7.75 billion
Founded: not available
Average Investment: not available
Minimum Investment: DM100,000

Investment Criteria: All stages

Geographic Preference: Germany (Baden-Württemberg, Hesse, Thuringia)

Industry Group Preference: Industry, Real Estate

Portfolio Companies: not available

Officers, Executives and Principals

Ulrich Drumm
Thomas H. Frank

VAR ACTION - CCI DU VAR

Relais de la Bourse
Boulevard Leclerc
83097 Toulon
France

Telephone: 33-94-228029
Fax: 33-94-228090

Mission: Actively seeking new investments

Fund Size: not available
Founded: not available
Average Investment: not available
Minimum Investment: Ecu75,000

Investment Criteria: Start-up, Early-stage, Expansion/Development

Geographic Preference: France

Industry Group Preference: All sectors considered

Portfolio Companies: not available

Officers, Executives and Principals

Jean Bottasso
Michelle Sallerin

VAUBAN FINANCE

12 rue Tronchet
75008 Paris
France

Telephone: 33-1-4924-0707
Fax: 33-1-4924-0808

Mission: Actively seeking new investments

Fund Size: Ffr165 million
Founded: not available
Average Investment: not available
Minimum Investment: Ffr500,000

Investment Criteria: Early-stage, Expansion/Development

Geographic Preference: France

Industry Group Preference: All sectors considered

Portfolio Companies: not available

Officers, Executives and Principals

Robert Mazaud
Benoît Pastour
Damien Béaré

V. C. M. VENTURE CAPITAL MANAGEMENT

Moosstrasse 7/B
82319 Starnberg, Bavaria
Germany

Telephone: 49-815-72324
Fax: 49-8151-3028

Mission: Actively seeking new investments

Fund Size: not available
Founded: 1991
Average Investment: not available
Minimum Investment: $100,000

Investment Criteria: Second-stage, Mezzanine, Special Situations

Geographic Preference: not available

Industry Group Preference: All sectors considered

Portfolio Companies: not available

Officers, Executives and Principals

Dr. Hellmut Kirchner, Managing Director
Thomas Schwartz, Managing Director
Stefan Herzog, Managing Director

VENCAP INTERNATIONAL FUND MANAGERS LTD

King Charles House
Park End Street
Oxford OX1 1JD
United Kingdom

Telephone: 44-1865-295285
Fax: 44-1865-792232
E-mail: 100335.2536@compuserve.com

Mission: Actively seeking new investments

Fund Size: £113 million
Founded: not available
Average Investment: not available
Minimum Investment: not available

Investment Criteria: All stages

Geographic Preference: Worldwide

Industry Group Preference: All sectors considered

Portfolio Companies: not available

Officers, Executives and Principals

Michael Ashall
Jenny Fenton

VENTURE FUND ROTTERDAM BV

Veerkade 7
P. O. Box 23341
3001 KH Rotterdam
The Netherlands

Telephone: 31-10-414-3444
Fax: 31-10-433-2879

Mission: Investing in strong, growing companies (not starters) with excellent management or in search of excellent management support

Fund Size: Ecu30 million
Founded: 1982
Average Investment: not available
Minimum Investment: Ecu500,000

Investment Criteria: Expansion/Development, Management Buy-outs, Turnaround, Mezzanine, Bridge

Geographic Preference: Belgium, The Netherlands, Luxembourg

Industry Group Preference: All sectors considered

Portfolio Companies: not available

Officers, Executives and Principals

R.F. de Vicq, Partner
A.F. Poort, Partner
Th.A. Philippa

VERITAS VENTURE CAPITAL MANAGEMENT LTD.

P. O. Box 2074
Herzlia Pituach, 46120
Israel

Telephone: 972-9-561621
Fax: 972-9-561619

Mission: Actively seeking new investments

Fund Size: not available
Founded: 1990
Average Investment: not available
Minimum Investment: $100,000

Investment Criteria: Seed, Research and Development, Start-up, First-stage, Second-stage, Mezzanine

Geographic Preference: not available

Industry Group Preference: Genetic Engineering, Medical/Health Related

Portfolio Companies: not available

Officers, Executives and Principals

Yadin Kaufmann, Managing Director
Giedeon Tolkowski, Managing Director

VLAAMSE INVESTERINGSVENNOOTSCHAP NV

Bollebergen 2a
9052 Zwijnaarde
Belgium

Telephone: 32-9-221-3364
Fax: 32-9-221-3469
E-mail: viv@innet.be

Mission: Investing in, and providing management support to, independent growing companies generating substantial value added

Fund Size: Bfr2.5 billion
Founded: 1981
Average Investment: Bfr40 million
Minimum Investment: Bfr10 million

Investment Criteria: Expansion/Development, Management Buy-out, Management Buy-in, Replacement, Bridge

Geographic Preference: Belgium (within 400 kilometers of Ghent)

Industry Group Preference: All sectors considered

Portfolio Companies: not available

Officers, Executives and Principals

J. Smets, Managing Director
Luc de Clippele, Secretary-General
Francis Ampe, Manager, Participations
Frank Claeys, Manager, Financing
Philip Vercruyssen, Senior Investment Manager

VUOTEKNO OY
Laivanrakentajantie 2
00980 Helsinki
Finland

Telephone: 358-0-317-033
Fax: 358-0-318-739

Mission: Actively seeking new investments

Fund Size: FM16 million
Founded: not available
Average Investment: FM500,000-1.5 million
Minimum Investment: FM300,000

Investment Criteria: Start-up, Expansion, Management Buy-out, Turnaround

Geographic Preference: Finland

Industry Group Preference: Building Materials, Industrial Products, Services

Portfolio Companies: not available

Officers, Executives and Principals

Pekka Viukari, Managing Director
Education: M.Sc. in Engineering

WAFA TRUST
416 rue Mostafa El Maani
Casablanca
Morocco

Telephone: 212-2-208646
Fax: 212-2-209489

Mission: Actively seeking new investments

Fund Size: not available
Founded: not available
Average Investment: not available
Minimum Investment: not available

Investment Criteria: All stages

Geographic Preference: Morocco

Industry Group Preference: All sectors considered

Portfolio Companies: not available

Officers, Executives and Principals

Fath-Allah Berrada

W. B. FINANCE ET PARTENAIRES

30 cours Albert 1er
75008 Paris
France

Telephone: 33-1-4561-5580
Fax: 33-1-4561-9794

Mission: Actively seeking new investments

Fund Size: Ffr400 million
Founded: not available
Average Investment: not available
Minimum Investment: Ffr15 million

Investment Criteria: Leveraged Buy-out, Special Situations

Geographic Preference: France

Industry Group Preference: All sectors considered

Portfolio Companies: not available

Officers, Executives and Principals

Walter Butler

WeHaCo KAPITALBETEILIGUNGS GmbH

Leisewitzstrasse 37b
30175 Hannover
Germany

Telephone: 49-511-280-0701
Fax: 49-511-280-0737
E-mail: hannover.finanz@p-net.de

Mission: Actively seeking new investments in growing companies as a managed fund within the Hannover Finanz Group

Fund Size: DM100 million
Founded: 1990
Average Investment: DM8 million
Minimum Investment: DM2 million

Investment Criteria: Later-stage, Development, Buy-out, Pre-IPO, Replacement

Geographic Preference: Germany; rest of Europe with syndication partners

Industry Group Preference: Engineering, Financial Services, Logistics, Manufacturing, Media, Services, Telecommunications, Trade

Portfolio Companies: not available

WESTDEUTSCHE GENOSSENSCHAFTS-BETEILIGUNGS GmbH

Sentmaringer Weg 1
48151 Munster
Germany

Telephone: 49-251-706-4721
Fax: 49-251-706-4726

Mission: Actively seeking new investments

Fund Size: DM104.4 million
Founded: not available
Average Investment: not available
Minimum Investment: DM1 million

Investment Criteria: Expansion/Development, Early-stage, Late-stage, Management Buy-out, Management Buy-in

Geographic Preference: Germany

Industry Group Preference: All sectors considered

Portfolio Companies: not available

Officers, Executives and Principals

Bernhard Wingenfeld
Klaus-Dieter Sommer

WESTDEUTSCHE KAPITALBETEILIGUNGS GmbH

Friedrichstrasse 103
40217 Düsseldorf
Germany

Telephone: 49-211-826-3066
Fax: 49-211-826-6168

Mission: Actively seeking new investments

Fund Size: DM60 million
Founded: not available
Average Investment: not available
Minimum Investment: DM2 million

Investment Criteria: Expansion/Development, Management Buy-out, Management Buy-in

Geographic Preference: Germany (North Rhine-Westphalia)

Industry Group Preference: All sectors considered

Portfolio Companies: not available

Officers, Executives and Principals

Joachim Voss
Karlheinz Müller
Jürgen Germies

WESTDEUTSCHE UNTERNEHMENS-BETEILIGUNGS-AG

Friedrichstrasse 103
40217 Düsseldorf
Germany

Telephone: 49-211-826-3066
Fax: 49-211-826-6168

Mission: Actively seeking new investments

Fund Size: not available
Founded: not available
Average Investment: not available
Minimum Investment: DM2 million

Investment Criteria: Expansion/Development, Management Buy-out, Management Buy-in

Geographic Preference: Germany (North Rhine-Westphalia)

Industry Group Preference: All sectors considered

Portfolio Companies: not available

Officers, Executives and Principals

Joachim Voss
Karlheinz Müller
Jürgen Germies

WESTERN N. I. S. ENTERPRISE FUND

4 Muzeyny Provulok, 3rd Floor
252001 Kiev
Ukraine

Telephone: 380-44-291-0280
Fax: 380-44-291-0289

Other Office Locations
15 West 39th Street, 11th Floor
New York, NY 10018
United States
Phone 212-556-9320, Fax 212-556-9321

169 Stefan cel Mare
TIS Business Center
2004 Chisinau
Moldova
Phone 373-2-625-220, Fax 373-2-625-853

Mission: Investing in small and medium-sized enterprises operating in what are expected to be the fastest growing sectors in Ukraine, Moldova and Belarus; providing them with capital and the necessary management tools to evolve from entrepreneurial ventures into professionally managed companies; arranging for experienced western executives to work with local management in order to prepare and position them for growth; and seeking to achieve long-term appreciation with a modest current return on its capital, which was initially provided by the United States government.

Fund Size: $150 million
Founded: 1994
Average Investment: $2.3 million
Minimum Investment: $500,000

Investment Criteria: Start-up, Early-stage, Expansion/Development, Management Buy-in

Geographic Preference: Ukraine, Moldova, Belarus

Industry Group Preference: Agriculture/Forestry/Fisheries, Communications, Construction Materials, Consumer Services, Food Services/Products, Furniture Manufacturing, Hotel, Industrial Equipment, Management Information Systems, Pharmaceuticals

Portfolio Companies: not available

Officers, Executives and Principals

Glenn H. Hutchins, Chairman of the Board
Scott A. Carlson, President and Chief Executive Officer
Harold J. Schroeder, Chief Investment Officer
Mindy Luxenberg-Grant, Controller
Natalie A. Jaresko, Country Manager, Ukraine
Gregory Berenstein, Country Manager, Moldova
Vladimir Gontcharenok, Country Representative, Belarus

WEST MIDLANDS ENTERPRISE BOARD LTD.

Wellington House
31-34 Waterloo Street
Birmingham B2 5TJ
United Kingdom

Telephone: 44-121-236 8855
Fax: 44-121-233 3942
E-mail: wmeb@dial.pipex.com

Mission: Actively seeking new investments

Fund Size: not available
Founded: 1982
Average Investment: not available
Minimum Investment: $250,000

Investment Criteria: Leveraged Buy-out

Geographic Preference: United Kingdom (West and East Midlands, Oxfordshire)

Industry Group Preference: Consumer, Distribution, Electronic Components and Instrumentation, Genetic Engineering, Industrial Products and Equipment

Portfolio Companies: Middleton Maintenance Group Holdings Limited

Officers, Executives and Principals

P.G. Collings, Chief Executive
I.M. Booth, Venture Capital Manager
R. Swainbank, Finance Director
T.R. Hazell, Executive

YORKSHIRE ENTERPRISE LIMITED

St Martin's House
210-212 Chapeltown Road
Leeds LS7 4HZ
United Kingdom

Telephone: 44-113-237-4774
Fax: 44-113-237-4922

Mission: Actively seeking new investments

Fund Size: £10.1 million
Founded: not available
Average Investment: £175,000
Minimum Investment: £30,000

Investment Criteria: Expansion, Management Buy-in, Management Buy-out, Early-stage, Refinancing Bank Debt, Rescue/Turnaround, Start-up, Secondary Purchase/Replacement Capital

Geographic Preference: United Kingdom (Yorkshire and Humberside only)

Industry Group Preference: Chemical and Materials, Computer Related, Consumer Related, Electronics Related, Industrial Automation, Industrial Products and Services, Leisure, Manufacturing

Portfolio Companies: COE, The Laser Cutting Company, Noel Village (Steel Founder), Sheppee International, United Cutlers

Officers, Executives and Principals

John Cook
Donald Law
Nigel Barraclough

YORKSHIRE FUND MANAGERS LTD.

St Paul's House
Park Square
Leeds LS1 2PJ
United Kingdom

Telephone: 44-113-244-2585
Fax: 44-113-244-1425

Mission: Actively seeking new investments

Fund Size: not available
Founded: 1989
Average Investment: not available
Minimum Investment: $250,000

Investment Criteria: Startup, Second-stage, Leveraged Buy-out, Special Situations

Geographic Preference: United Kingdom

Industry Group Preference: Computer Related, Distribution, Electronic Components and Instrumentation, Industrial Products and Equipment

Portfolio Companies: ICM plc, RFS (E) Limited, Wots in Store, Freshney

Officers, Executives and Principals

Philip Cammerman, Managing Director
Richard King, Investment Director
David Gee, Investment Executive
Joanna Smith, Investment Assistant

YORKSHIRE VENTURE CAPITAL LTD.

Don Valley House
Savile Street East
Sheffield S4 7UQ
United Kingdom

Telephone: 44-114-272-2272
Fax: 44-114- 272-5718

Mission: Actively seeking new investments

Fund Size: not available
Founded: 1989
Average Investment: not available
Minimum Investment: $250,000

Investment Criteria: Second-stage, Leveraged Buy-out

Geographic Preference: United Kingdom

Industry Group Preference: Communications, Computer Related, Consumer, Distribution, Electronic Components and Instrumentation, Energy/Natural Resources, Genetic Engineering, Industrial Products and Equipment, Medical/Health Related

Portfolio Companies: Image Systems Europe Ltd, 3T Productions Ltd, Multimedia Investments plc

Officers, Executives and Principals

Paul Gilmartin, Managing Director
Jeremy Mobbs, Director

ZERNIKE SEED FUND BV

Zernike Park 4
9747 AN Groningen
The Netherlands

Telephone: 31-50-745745
Fax: 31-50-634556

Mission: Actively seeking investments

Fund Size: Ecu8 million
Founded: not available
Average Investment: not available
Minimum Investment: Ecu25,000

Investment Criteria: Seed, Start-up, Early-stage

Geographic Preference: Netherlands, Germany, Belgium

Industry Group Preference: Agriculture/Forestry, Biotechnology, Computer Related, Industrial Automation, Industrial Products, Medical/Health Related

Portfolio Companies: not available

Officers, Executives and Principals

Lex de Lange

ZÜRCHER KANTONALBANK

8010 Zürich
Switzerland

Telephone: 41-1-220-3006
Fax: 41-1-211-6697

Mission: Actively seeking new investments

Fund Size: not available
Founded: not available
Average Investment: not available
Minimum Investment: not available

Investment Criteria: Expansion/Development, Management Buy-out

Geographic Preference: Switzerland

Industry Group Preference: All sectors considered

Portfolio Companies: not available

Officers, Executives and Principals

Martin Scholl
Stefan Marthaler

ZURMONT MANAGEMENT AG

Genferstrasse 8
8027 Zürich
Switzerland

Telephone: 41-1-206-7399
Fax: 41-1-201-5139

Mission: Actively seeking new investments, concentrating on well-established companies

Fund Size: not available
Founded: not available
Average Investment: not available
Minimum Investment: Sfr1 million

Investment Criteria: Expansion/Development, Management Buy-out, Replacement/Share Purchases

Geographic Preference: Switzerland, Central Europe

Industry Group Preference: All sectors considered

Portfolio Companies: not available

Officers, Executives and Principals

Guido Patroncini
Johannes Fehr

INDICES

INDEX OF COMPANY NAMES

INDEX OF EXECUTIVE NAMES

Berman, Thomas D., Partner; BRINSON PARTNERS, INC., 138, 139

Bernal, Javier, Partner; BARING VENTURE PARTNERS SA, 1154

Bernand, Christophe, Vice President; BROADMARK CAPITAL CORPORATION, 141

Berner, H.S., Treasurer; R. C. BERNER AND COMPANY, 652

Berner, Robert C., President; R. C. BERNER AND COMPANY, 652

Bernocchi, Marco; LIGUR SEED CAPITAL, 1428

Bernstein, Alan, Vice President; DRESNER CAPITAL RESOURCES, INC., 251

Berrada, Fath-Allah; WAFA TRUST, 1683

Berry, Arthur W., Managing Director; PECKS MANAGEMENT PARTNERS, LTD., 605

Berry, John; SOUTH WEST INVESTMENT GROUP LIMITED, 1611

Berry, William M., Jr., Executive Vice President; ALLIANCE FINANCIAL OF HOUSTON, 62

Bertaut, Jean-Claude; ADC, 1088

Berterretche, Jackie, Chief Financial Officer; HAMBRECHT AND QUIST GROUP, 344

Berthoty, Bystrik; SEED CAPITAL COMPANY LIMITED, 1575

Bertiaux, Patrick, Partner; COMPAGNIE DE FINANCEMENT INDUSTRIEL, 1216

Berylson, John G., President; GCC INVESTMENTS, INC., 317

Besse, Joel; ATLAS VENTURE, 1125

Beste, Frederick J., III; NEPA VENTURE FUNDS, 536

Bettino, Lawrence A., Investment Manager; DILLON READ VENTURE CAPITAL, 241

Betts, Christopher, Partner; SIGNAL CAPITAL CORPORATION, 707

Beumer, Dale, Vice President, Treasurer - Investor Relations; MEDTRONIC, INC., 1061

Bianchi, Annette, General Partner; WEISS, PECK AND GREER VENTURE PARTNERS, 833

Biard, Henri; CITA, 1204

Bichara, Axel, Partner; ATLAS VENTURE, 879

Bienek, Karsten; BEV BIENEK ENTERTAINMENT VENTURES, 1164

Bijleveld, Dancker, Senior Vice President; ABN AMRO CORPORATE INVESTMENTS, 1081

Bilbao, Daniel, Partner; AXIS PARTICIPATIONES EMPRESARIALES, 1132

Bill, Lawrence W., Vice President; R AND D FUNDING CORPORATION, 651

Bindel, Serge; EPICEA, 1256

Binkley, Nick, Partner; FORREST BINKLEY AND BROWN, 301

Bird, Walter M., III, General Partner; CLAFLIN CAPITAL MANAGEMENT, INC., 199

Birgourdan, Jean-Brice; FINANCIÈRE VECTEUR, 1290

Birkel, Wolfram; BAG AKTIENGESELLSCHAFT FÜR INDUSTRIEBETEILIGUNGEN, 1133

Birkett, Bill, Director; CYGNUS VENTURE PARTNERS LIMITED, 1228

Birmingham, Kathleen F., Associate; MASSACHUSETTS TECHNOLOGY DEVELOPMENT CORPORATION (MTDC), 465

Birnbaum, Stevan A., General Partner; OXFORD VENTURE CORPORATION, 586

Birnberg, Jeffrey, President; TAPPAN ZEE CAPITAL CORPORATION, 754

Biro, Timothy G., Partner; BRANTLEY VENTURE PARTNERS, 884

Bischoff, Claudia, Manager, Marketing and Public Relations; 3i DEUTSCHLAND GESELLSCHAFT FÜR INDUSTRIE-BETEILIGUNGEN mbH, 1652

Bishop, Errol, Head of Private Equity; BZW PRIVATE EQUITY LIMITED, 1183

Bishop, Sally, Research Associate; VENTURE GROWTH ASSOCIATES, 815

Bisulca, Michael S., Partner; JOHNSEN SECURITIES, 409

Bixby, Will K., Senior Vice President; BANC ONE CAPITAL PARTNERS CORPORATION, 101

Bixler, Edward M., President; THE BENEFIT CAPITAL COMPANIES INC., 121

Bjoernoey, Trond; NORSK VEKST A/S, 1495

Bjorå, Bjørn, Managing Director; TEKNOINVEST MANAGEMENT, 1646

Blaauboer, Ellard J.; NESBIC GROEP BV, 1484

Black, Findlay; C.V.C. CAPITAL PARTNERS, 1226

Black, Hugh; HIGHLAND OPPORTUNITY LIMITED, 1350

Black, Philip, General Partner; WEISS, PECK AND GREER VENTURE PARTNERS, 833

Black, Richard, Vice President; HELIX INVESTMENTS, LTD., 355

Blackburn, Michael W., Associate; RICHLAND VENTURES, 666

Blackburn, Michael, General Partner; LAWRENCE, TYRRELL, ORTALE AND SMITH, 939

Blackburn, Thomas C., Vice President; KANSAS VENTURE CAPITAL, INC., 415

Blaeser, John A., General Partner; E G AND G VENTURE PARTNERS, 907

Comfort, William; C. V. C. CAPITAL PARTNERS LIMITED, 1227

Compton, Kevin R., Partner; KLEINER PERKINS CAUFIELD AND BYERS, 937

Compton, Robert A., General Partner; CID EQUITY PARTNERS, 193

Conboy, Philip; KLEINWORT BENSON DEVELOPMENT CAPITAL LIMITED, 1409

Condado, P. Nalda; INSTITUTO NACIONAL DE INDUSTRIA - GRUPO SODI, 1384

Conder, Martin, Assistant Director; INTERMEDIATE CAPITAL GROUP PLC, 1387

Congleton, William H., Chairman; PALMER PARTNERS, L.P., 591

Conley, Frances M., Founder; ROANOKE CAPITAL, LTD., 670

Conley, Gerald R., Principal; ROANOKE CAPITAL, LTD., 670

Conn, Alastair, Partner; NORTHERN VENTURE MANAGERS LIMITED, 1499

Conn, Robert, Vice President; POLAND PARTNERS MANAGEMENT COMPANY, 1530

Connaughay, Barbara, Business Analyst; EMERALD VENTURE GROUP, 261

Connell, Richard, Partner; HSBC PRIVATE EQUITY, 1355; Director; MONTAGU PRIVATE EQUITY LTD., 1467

Connelly, Michael J., President; LEPERCQ CAPITAL MANAGEMENT, 436

Conner, Douglas P., Principal; CARDINAL VENTURES, L.L.C., 163

Connolly, John, Vice President; MDS HEALTH VENTURES CAPITAL CORPORATION, 479

Connors, Kevin G., Partner; DSV PARTNERS, 254, 906

Conroy, James A., Vice President and Limited Partner; OLYMPUS PARTNERS, 572

Constantin, François; AVENIR ENTREPRISES, 1129

Constine, David, General Partner; CORPORATE VENTURE PARTNERS, L.P., 222, 898

Conte, Jean-Pierre L., Vice President; THE NTC GROUP, 566

Cook, Errol M., Managing Director; WARBURG, PINCUS VENTURES, 830

Cook, James C., Partner; FIRST UNION CAPITAL PARTNERS, 293

Cook, Jeremy Cumock; ROTHSCHILD BIOSCIENCE UNIT, 1551

Cook, John; YORKSHIRE ENTERPRISE LIMITED, 1691

Cook, Orval, Senior Vice President; ALPHA CAPITAL PARTNERS, 64

Cook, Robert L., Jr., Vice President; BANC ONE VENTURE CORPORATION, 102

Cooke, Anne, Analyst; FIDELITY CAPITAL, 281

Cooksey, David, Chairman; ADVENT LIMITED, 1091

Coonrad, Richard, General Partner; THE FOOD FUND, L. P., 299

Cooper, Andrew C., Vice President; MORGAN STANLEY VENTURE PARTNERS, 514, 957

Cooper, Eric, Managing Director; LEGAL AND GENERAL VENTURES LIMITED, 1425

Cooper, Jeffrey M., Principal; NEW VENTURE RESOURCES, 543

Cooper, Julia, Treasurer; ARTHUR P. GOULD AND COMPANY, 84

Cooper, Kendall J., Partner, Chief Financial Officer; DOMINION VENTURES, INC., 245

Cooper, Peter, Analyst; DEALMAKER CAPITAL CORPORATION, 237

Cooper-Evans, Alex; BANQUE INDOSUEZ ACQUISITION FINANCE, 1145

Coppedge, Roy F., III, Director; BOSTON VENTURES MANAGEMENT, INC., 134

Corbishley, Philip, BSc, CEng; ABEL VENTURE MANAGERS, 1076

Cordier, Clément, Associate Director; 3i FRANCE, 1653

Corely, Leslie M., President; LM CAPITAL CORPORATION, 445

Corley, Ricardo, Vice President; LM CAPITAL CORPORATION, 445

Corn, Murray, Vice President; STAMFORD FINANCIAL, 734

Corne, J.W.G., Investment Manager; NEDERLANDSE PARTICIPATIE MAATSCHAPPIJ NV, 1483

Corne, Ulf, Investment Manager; INNOVATIONSKAPITAL I GÖTEBORG AB, 1380

Cornett, Walter G., III; CERULEAN FUND/WGC ENTERPRISES, INC., 179; President; WGC ENTERPRISES, 843

Cornwall, G. Rick, Assistant Vice President; FEDERAL BUSINESS DEVELOPMENT BANK, 279

Corry, Billy, Financial Analyst; TUFTON CAPITAL LTD, 1666

Corry, Reed A., Executive Vice President; BROADMARK CAPITAL CORPORATION, 141

Corson, Fred P., Vice President of Research and Development; DOW CHEMICAL COMPANY, 1050

Costeletos, Philippe M., Partner; J. P. MORGAN CAPITAL CORPORATION, 1399

Costello, Dennis B., Group Director, Venture Projects; SENMED VENTURES, 979

Cote, Joseph G., Co-President; PROSPECT STREET INVESTMENT MANAGEMENT COMPANY, INC., 642

Cotte, Michel, Managing Director; BANQUE DE VIZILLE, 1143

Couffin, Hervé; PARIBAS AFFAIRES INDUSTRIELLES, 1513

Couhig, Kevin H., President and Chief Executive Officer; SOURCE CAPITAL CORPORATION, 714

de Giovanni, Patrick; APAX PARTNERS ET CIE., 1111

de Haan, Michiel, General Partner; ATLAS VENTURE, 879, 1124

de Koning, Joep M.J.; THE BATAVIA GROUP, LTD., 111

de la Bourdonnaye, Anne-Isabelle; PARTECH INTERNATIONAL, 1516

de la Torre, Angeles, Partner; SEVILLA SEED CAPITAL FUND, 1580

de la Vigne, François Rouault, Director; I. P. O. (INSTITUT DE PARTICIPATIONS DE L'OUEST), 1390

de Lange, Lex; ZERNIKE SEED FUND BV, 1694

De Leeuw, David E., Managing Partner; McCOWN De LEEUW AND COMPANY, 476

de Lopez, Zulma Vilella; NORTH AMERICA INVESTMENT CORPORATION, 549

de Mesquita, Vivan; THREE CITIES RESEARCH, INC., 771

de Mesquita, Vivian; TCR EUROPE, 1639

de Nicola, Anthony J., General Partner; WELSH, CARSON, ANDERSON AND STOWE, 835

De Pourtalès, Jean; GOLDMAN SACHS PARIS, 1331

De Ridder, Paul; HALDER BETEILIGUNGSBERATUNG GmbH, 1342; HALDER HOLDINGS BV, 1343

de Roissy, Christian; FINANCIÈRE VECTEUR, 1290

de Severac, Jean, Managing Director; PARVALIND GÉRANCE, 1518

de Vicq, R.F., Partner; VENTURE FUND ROTTERDAM BV, 1679

de Villaines, B.; PROXIFI, 1538

de Vogel, Willem F.P.; THREE CITIES RESEARCH, INC., 771

De Vries, Robert J.; DE VRIES AND COMPANY, INC., 236

Dean, Barry, Managing Director; KLEINWORT BENSON DEVELOPMENT CAPITAL LIMITED, 1408

Dean, Gordon; TRANSATLANTIC CAPITAL LTD, 1660

Dean, John C., President and Chief Executive Officer; SILICON VALLEY BANK, 709

DeAngelis, Kenneth P., General Partner; AUSTIN VENTURES, 92

Dearen, Dan L., Senior Associate; VENTANA MANAGEMENT, 803

Deas, Ian G., Chief Financial Officer; PANTHEON VENTURES, INC., 595

Debache, Hervé, President; TERTIAIRE DÉVELOPPEMENT, 1648

Deblaye, Christian; COMPAGNIE FINANCIÈRE E. DE ROTHSCHILD BANQUE, 1217

Debré, Vincent; SCHRODER PARTENAIRES, 1567

Decker, Michael, General Partner; WINGATE PARTNERS, INC., 851

Decré, Pierre; FSD CAPITAL DÉVELOPPEMENT, 1310

Dederick, Clint 'Skip', Group Director, Venture Projects; SENMED VENTURES, 978

Deery, Craig, Managing Director; BANCBOSTON CAPITAL / BANCBOSTON VENTURES, 103

Degroote, Thierry; PARVALIND GÉRANCE, 1518

Dehovre, Jean-Claude, Partner; S. R. I. W. SA, 1620

Deiters, Paul A.; HALDER HOLDINGS BV, 1343

Dekker, M.W.; MEES PIERSON INVESTERINGSMAATSCHAPPIJ BV, 1444; General Manager; NEDERLANDSE PARTICI-PATIE MAATSCHAPPIJ NV, 1483

Del Presto, Peter V., Senior Vice President and Principal; PNC EQUITY MANAGEMENT CORPORATION, 631

Delatte, Marc; SORIDEC, 1609

Delbridge, Kevin S., General Partner; HANCOCK VENTURE PARTNERS, 922

Deleage, Jean, Founder; BURR, EGAN, DELEAGE AND COMPANY, 144

Deleglise, Pierre Michel; GES GESTION/GAN AVENIR, 1322

Delimitros, Tom H., General Partner; AMT VENTURE PARTNERS, LTD., 74

DeLitto, Thomas M., President and Director; PERMAL CAPITAL MANAGEMENT, 611

Delloye, Henri-Luis; PARTICIPEX, 1517

Delvaux, Jean-Louis; C. F. J. P. E., 1196

DelVesco, Arthur, General Partner; WINDPOINT PARTNERS, 849

Demchick, Barbara S., Controller; INNOVEST GROUP, INC., 382

Demer, Ron, Vice President; PHOENIX GROWTH CAPITAL CORPORATION, 617

Demichel, Pascal; EPICEA, 1256

Demmler, L. Frank, Vice President; PITTSBURGH SEED FUND PARTNERS, 626

Demorgny, Gérard; IDIA (INSTITUT DE DÉVELOPPEMENT DES INDUSTRIES AGRICOLES ET ALIMENTAIRES), 1360

Dempsey, Neal, General Partner; BAY PARTNERS, 115

DeMuth, Donald F., General Partner; DEMUTH, FOLGER AND WETHERILL, 238

den Heijer, Toon; GILDE INVESTMENT FUNDS, 1324

Diulie, Joe D., General Partner; NEST VENTURE PARTNERS, 537

Dixon, Bobbie, Investment Manager; MONTANA SCIENCE AND TECHNOLOGY ALLIANCE, 955

Dixon, Donald R., Partner; TRIDENT CAPITAL, INC., 775

do Amaral, Rui Gomes, Executive Director; PROMINDÚSTRIA - SOCIEDADE DE INVESTIMENTO SA, 1536

Dobbin, William J., General Partner; CAPFORM PARTNERS, 152

Dobi, Eric, Associate; THE JORDAN, EDMISTON GROUP, INC., 411

Doebbel, Victoria; S. F. M. ET ASSOCIÉS SA, 1582

Doherty, J.B., Managing General Partner; TDH, 756

Dolan, A. Barr, Partner; CHARTER VENTURE CAPITAL, 182

Dolbec, Michael D., Associate; GREYLOCK MANAGEMENT CORPORATION, 337

Domenik, Stephen L, General Partner; SEVIN ROSIN FUNDS, 981

Donaghy, James W., President; HOLDING CAPITAL GROUP, INC., 367

Donnelly, James F., General Partner; CULLINANE AND DONNELLY VENTURE, 900

Donnelly, Patrick K., President; VIRGINIA CAPITAL, L.P. 821

Donnini, David A., Principal; GOLDER, THOMA, CRESSEY, RAUNER, INC., 330

Donoghue, Michael F., Managing Director; CORESTATES ENTERPRISE FUND, 218

Donovan, David, Vice President and Partner; SOMMERSET CAPITAL CORPORATION, 711

Dooley, Kevin C., Senior Vice President and Legal Counsel; CHURCHILL CAPITAL, INC., 188, 190

Doomany, George, Managing Director; BANKERS TRUST CAPITAL CORPORATION, 109

Dor, Jean-Daniel; DOW EUROPE SA, 1237

Dorman, Nancy L., Administrative General Partner; NEW ENTERPRISE ASSOCIATES, 540

Dorn, Helmut G., Executive Director; INNOVATIONSAGENTUR GmbH, 1379

Dorrington, Keith J., Senior Vice President; MDS HEALTH VENTURES CAPITAL CORPORATION, 479

Dotzler, Frederick J., General Partner; MEDICUS VENTURE PARTNERS, 948

Doubleday, Gloria W., Vice President; COMMONWEALTH BIOVENTURES, 893

Dougery, John R., Partner; DOUGERY AND WILDER, 247, 904

Dougherty, Craig, Principal; NORTH AMERICAN BUSINESS DEVELOPMENT COMPANIES, L.L.C., 550

Dougherty, Dennis J., Founder and General Partner; INTERSOUTH PARTNERS, 935

Dougherty, Kevin J., General Partner; VENTURE CAPITAL FUND OF NEW ENGLAND, 809, 992

Douglas, Barclay, CA, Director; MERCURY ASSET MANAGEMENT PLC, 1446

Douglas, J. Derek, Vice President; VENTURES WEST MANAGEMENT, INC., 818

Douglas, Mary, Director; GARTMORE PRIVATE CAPITAL, 1314

Douglas, Neal M., General Partner; AT&T VENTURES, 88

Douglass, David L., General Partner; DELPHI BIOVENTURES, L.P., 902

Douglass, Sam P., Chairman; EQUUS CAPITAL CORPORATION, 269

Dourassoff, Nicolas, Managing Director; NSM FINANCE SA, 1503

Douriez, Paul; PROXIFI, 1538

Dovey, Brian H., General Partner; DOMAIN ASSOCIATES, 244, 903

Dow, Stephen M., General Partner; SEVIN ROSIN FUNDS, 982

Dowd, Christopher P., Associate; NATIONAL CITY CAPITAL, 524

Downer, Charles W.; DOWNER AND COMPANY, 248

Downer, John A., Vice President; PRUDENTIAL EQUITY INVESTORS, INC., 645

Downes, Paul; EUROPEAN ACQUISITION CAPITAL LTD., 1266

Doxiades, A.; COMMERCIAL CAPITAL SA, 1212

Drake, Peter F., Ph.D., Partner; VECTOR FUND MANAGEMENT, L.P., 795

Drake, Richard F., Investment Vice President; NEW YORK LIFE VENTURE CAPITAL, 961

Draper, Colin J., Managing Partner; AMERICAN ACQUISITION PARTNERS, 68

Draper, Timothy C., Managing Director; DRAPER FISHER ASSOCIATES, 249

Drazan, Jeffrey M., General Partner; SIERRA VENTURES, 704

Dreben, Jeffrey, Vice President; CANADIAN VENTURE FOUNDERS CORPORATION, 151

Drechsel, Maximilian; F. B. G. BETEILIGUNGSBERATUNGS GmbH, 1280

Dresner, Steven M., President; DRESNER CAPITAL RESOURCES, INC., 251

Dreyfous, James C., General Partner; UTAH VENTURES, 990

Drugan, Mark; CROSSROADS MANAGEMENT (U. K.) LIMITED, 1223

Drumm, Ulrich; VALORA UNTERNEHMENSBETEILIGUNG AG, 1674

Drury, W. Roger, Senior Vice President, Finance; HUMANA VENTURE CAPITAL, 373

Hall, Stephen M., Partner; TRIDENT CAPITAL, INC., 775

Hallahane, Dennis; COMPASS INVESTMENT MANAGEMENT LIMITED, 1218

Hallala, Mark, Director; BROWN SHIPLEY VENTURE MANAGERS LTD., 1176

Haller, Heinz, Manager; MITTELSTÄNDISCHE BETEILIGUNGSGESELLSCHAFT BADEN-WÜRTTEMBERG GmbH (MBG), 1458

Halper, Adrienne, Managing Director; BANKERS TRUST CAPITAL CORPORATION, 109

Halperin, Philip W., Principal; WESTON PRESIDIO CAPITAL, 842

Halpern, John D., Partner; HALPERN, DENNY AND COMPANY, 342

Halprin, Stephen E., General Partner; OSCCO VENTURES, 583; General Partner; OSCCO VENTURES, III, 584

Halsted, Scott S., Vice President; MORGAN STANLEY VENTURE PARTNERS, 514, 957

Halstedt, Steven C., General Partner; THE CENTENNIAL FUNDS, 174

Halter, Pieter, General Partner; SOUTHERN CALIFORNIA VENTURES, 716

Halusa, Dr. Martin; APAX PARTNERS UND CO. AG, 1112, 1113

Hambrecht, William R., Co-Chief Executive Officer; HAMBRECHT AND QUIST GROUP, 344

Hambro, Alexander R., General Partner; HAMBRO INTERNATIONAL EQUITY PARTNERS, 345

Hamilton, Charles A., Managing Director; ROBERTSON STEPHENS AND COMPANY, L.P., 671

Hamilton, Jeffrey T., General Partner; WESTFORD TECHNOLOGY VENTURES, L.P., 841

Hamilton, S.L.R., Associate Director; JOHNSON AND JOHNSON DEVELOPMENT CORPORATION, 410

Hammner, Patrick F., Vice President; CAPITAL SOUTHWEST CORPORATION, 160

Hamren, Jeff, General Partner; CROWN ADVISORS, 226

Hamway, Nigel, Managing Director; CHARTERHOUSE DEVELOPMENT CAPITAL LIMITED, 1197

Hanawa, Yoshimitsu, Director; TOKYO SMALL AND MEDIUM BUSINESS INVESTMENTS AND CONSULTATION COMPANY, 1659

Hance, Carol W., Managing Director; STRATEGIC ADVISORY GROUP, INC., 744

Hance, Pierce W., Managing Director; STRATEGIC ADVISORY GROUP, INC., 744

Hand, Brian, Managing Director; FIRST ANALYSIS CORPORATION, 284

Hand, Jeremy; HAMBRO EUROPEAN VENTURES LIMITED, 1345

Hanevold, Mary Kay, Investment Analyst; MESIROW PRIVATE EQUITY, 497

Hanfenest, Brian, Associate; MORGAN KEEGAN MERCHANT BANKING FUND II, L.P., 513

Hanke, Wolfgang; MITTELSTÄNDISCHE BETEILIGUNGSGESELLSCHAFT SACHSEN mbH, 1464

Hanks, Robert J., Principal; NEW ENGLAND PARTNERS, 539

Hannula, Antti, Director, Information Technology; SITRA, 1590

Hansen, Kent, Partner; DANISH DEVELOPMENT FINANCE CORPORATION, 1229

Haque, Promod, Investment Manager; NORWEST VENTURE CAPITAL, 563

Hara, George, Venture Partner; ACCEL PARTNERS, 53, 867

Harad, George; BOISE CASCADE CORPORATION, 1042

Hardie, David C., Manager; HALLADOR VENTURE PARTNERS, 921

Harding, Charles; INDUSTRIAL DEVELOPMENT BOARD FOR NORTHERN IRELAND, 1367

Hardmeier, Magnus, Investment Manager; SKANDIA INVESTMENT AB, 1591

Hardymon, G. Felda; BESSEMER VENTURE PARTNERS, 125

Harlé, Emmanuel, Managing Director; MORGAN GRENFELL INVESTISSEMENT, 1469

Harman, Fredric W., General Partner; OAK INVESTMENT PARTNERS, 569; General Partner; MORGAN STANLEY VENTURE PARTNERS, 957

Harmer, Piers; NATWEST MARKETS ACQUISITION FINANCE, 1477

Harnett, Anthony J., Chairman; NATURAL VENTURE PARTNERS, INC., 529

Harper, I.N. Rendall, General Partner; KEYSTONE MINORITY CAPITAL FUND, L.P., 420

Harpster, Tyee; NIPPON ENTERPRISE DEVELOPMENT CORPORATION, 546

Harries, Dr. Heinrich; KREDITANSTALT FÜR WIEDERAUFBAU (KFW), 1415

Harrington, John K., Vice President; NELSON CAPITAL CORPORATION, 535

Harris, Derek; BIRMINGHAM TECHNOLOGY (VENTURE CAPITAL) LTD., 1168

Harris, Hayden H., Partner; ENTERPRISE DEVELOPMENT FUND, 263

Harris, Kathy, Vice President; SIRROM CAPITAL, 710

Harris, Stephen W.; TDH, 756

Harrison, Dr. Shelley A., Managing General Partner; POLY VENTURES, 973

Harrison, Eric S., Associate; INNOCAL, L.P., 380

Harrison, John C., Vice President; SIRROM CAPITAL, 710

Heerskink, Ewout, Vice President; ONEX CORPORATION, 575

Heflin, William T., Vice President; ARETE VENTURES, 80

Hegele, W. Chris, General Partner; KITTY HAWK CAPITAL, 424

Hegi, Frederick B., Jr., General Partner; WINGATE PARTNERS, INC., 851

Heidrich, A. Grant III, General Partner; MAYFIELD FUND, 473

Helenius, Joakim, Partner; TRIGON CAPITAL PRAHA, 1663

Helle, Daniel G., Managing Partner; CONTINENTAL ILLINOIS VENTURE CORPORATION, 214

Heller, Ron, Director; FROST CAPITAL PARTNERS, INC., 311

Hellman, F. Warren; HELLMAN AND FRIEDMAN, 357

Hellman, Robert B., Partner; McCOWN De LEEUW AND COMPANY, 476

Hellström, Bengt, Investment Manager; EQT PARTNERS AB, 1258

Helman, William W., Partner; GREYLOCK MANAGEMENT CORPORATION, 337

Helomaa, Jouko, LLM, Managing Director, Merita Capital Oy; MERITA CAPITAL OY PROFITA FUND I, 1449

Hemmer, Vincent H., Associate; GOLDER, THOMA, CRESSEY, RAUNER, INC., 330

Hemmingsen, Sten Helde, Partner; DANISH DEVELOPMENT FINANCE CORPORATION, 1229

Henagan, Barbara M., Senior Managing Director; BRADFORD VENTURES, LTD., 136

Hendershott, Philip L., Chairman; ALTAIR VENTURES, INC., 67

Henderson, Robert P., Partner; GREYLOCK MANAGEMENT CORPORATION, 337

Henderson, Simon, Investment Executive; BZW PRIVATE EQUITY LIMITED, 1183

Hendrick, John T., General Partner; AVALON VENTURES, 880

Hendrickson, Sara M., President; SHAD RUN INVESTMENTS, INC., 698

Hendrie, Gardner C., Partner; SIGMA PARTNERS, 706

Hengel, Dr. Peter; IDP INDUSTRIAL DEVELOPMENT PARTNERS GmbH, 1362

Henkens, Jos C., General Partner; ADVANCED TECHNOLOGY VENTURES, 58, 868

Hennessy, Daniel J., Principal; CODE, HENNESSY AND SIMMONS, LP, CODE, HENNESSY AND SIMMONS II, LP, 204

Henon, Marc; SCL CORPORATE FINANCE SA, 1569

Henrich, Günther; BAYERISCHE BETEILIGUNGS GmbH (BAY BG), 1156; B. W. B. BAYERISCHE WAGNISBETEILI-
GUNGS GmbH, 1182

Henrichsen, Thomas Schlytter, Director; ALPHA ASSOCIÉS, 1103

Henri-Jaron, Managing Director; S. N. V. B. PARTICIPATIONS, 1595

Henry, Albert J., Chairman; HENRY AND COMPANY, 358

Henry, Jeanne Larkin, Partner, Chief Financial Officer, United States; ATLAS VENTURE, 879

Henry, Robert; MIDLAND GROWTH CAPITAL, 1454

Hensby, Barrie; NORTHERN ENTERPRISE (MANAGER) LIMITED, 1497

Hensler, D. Jack, Managing Principal; FRY CONSULTANTS, INC., 313

Henson, Paul, President; KANSAS CITY EQUITY PARTNERS, 414

Herbert, Edward C., Partner; DAVIS GROUP, 233

Herbert, G. Arthur, Principal; CEO ADVISORS, 177

Hereford, John M., Associate; UNIROCK MANAGEMENT CORPORATION, 790

Hermann, John; ROTHSCHILD BIOSCIENCE UNIT, 1551

Herndeen, Paul S., Vice President; PRUDENTIAL EQUITY INVESTORS, INC., 646

Hernon, Martin J., Partner; BOSTON CAPITAL VENTURES, 131

Herrera, Gilbert A., Principal; G.A. HERRERA AND COMPANY, 315

Herring, Steve, Senior Consultant; STAMFORD FINANCIAL, 735

Herrman, Rick, Partner; THE CATALYST GROUP, INC., 171, 172

Herschkowitz, Samuel, Vice President; VENKOL VENTURES, 991

Hertz-Eichenrode, Albrecht, BA, Lic. es. sc. pol.; HANNOVER FINANZ GmbH, 1348

Herzog, Stefan, Managing Director; V. C. M. VENTURE CAPITAL MANAGEMENT, 1677

Hesse, Friedrich; REGIONALE BETEILIGUNGSGESELLSCHAFT DER KREISSPARKASSE HANNOVER mbH, 1545

Heyes, Deborah; LANCASHIRE ENTERPRISES plc, 1418

Heyman, Willy, Managing Director; TUAB, 1665

Heyning, Diederik; GILDE INVESTMENT FUNDS, 1324

Hiatt, Thomas A., General Partner; MIDDLEWEST VENTURES, 501

Hichens, Donald, General Partner; LIBERTY ENVIRONMENTAL PARTNERS, 441

Hickey, Janet A., General Partner; SPROUT GROUP, 729

Hickman, John H., III, Chairman; BUFFALO CAPITAL CORPORATION, 143

Loveridge, Dr. Jason; JAFCO INVESTMENT (U. K.) LIMITED, 1396

Lovett, Joseph F., General Partner; MEDICAL SCIENCE PARTNERS, 947

Low, Dr. Paul, Senior Advisor; WEISS, PECK AND GREER VENTURE PARTNERS, 833

Low, Frank H., Senior Vice President; HARVEST PARTNERS, INC., 351

Lowe, C.L., President; LOWE FINANCIAL GROUP, INC., 448

Lowenstein, Paul J., Chairman and Chief Executive Officer; CANADIAN CORPORATION FUNDING, LTD., 150

Lubar, David J., President; LUBAR AND COMPANY, 451

Lubash, Barbara, Venture Partner; CROSSPOINT VENTURE PARTNERS, 225

Lubert, Ira M., Managing Director; RADNOR VENTURE PARTNERS, L.P., 653; Managing Director; TECHNOLOGY LEADERS II, L.P., 986

Lubicz, Christian; CREDIT SUISSE DEPARTEMENT S1, 1222

Lubin, Richard K., Managing Director; BERKSHIRE PARTNERS, LLC, 124

Lucas, Robert; C. V. C. CAPITAL PARTNERS LIMITED, 1227

Lue, Keith, Vice President; HELIX INVESTMENTS, LTD., 355

Luikart, James L., Vice President; CITICORP VENTURE CAPITAL, LTD., 198

Lum, Charles, Acting Director; INNOVATION ONTARIO CORPORATION, 381

Lund, Peter Buch, Director; CAPMAN CAPITAL MANAGEMENT OY, 1189

Lund, Stephen, Investment Manager; WORKING VENTURES CANADIAN FUND, INC., 857

Lundberg, Barbara J., Executive Vice President; ENTERPRISE INVESTORS, 264

Lundberg, Barbara, Executive Vice President and General Director, Warsaw Office; ENTERPRISE INVESTORS, 1253

Lundberg, Dave, Associate; CHARTER VENTURE CAPITAL, 182

Lundblad, Jan, Deputy Managing Director; TUAB, 1665

Lundqvist, Lars, Finance Director; TRYGG HANSA, 1664

Lundstrom, Albert C., Principal; THE O'RENICK COMPANIES, INC., 580

Lunn, Randall R., Managing Partner; TVM TECHNO VENTURE MANAGEMENT, 781

Lurier, Edward B., General Partner; GRYPHON VENTURES, L.P., 341, 920

Lutsi, John D., General Partner; MORGENTHALER VENTURES, 515, 959

Lutterbuck, Achim; B. V. BETEILIGUNGS GmbH, 1181

Luxenberg-Grant, Mindy, Controller; WESTERN N. I. S. ENTERPRISE FUND, 1689

Lynch, Christopher W., Partner; PIONEER CAPITAL CORPORATION, 623

Lynch, Samuel E., Manager; BLUE CHIP VENTURE COMPANY, 127

Lyons, Paul A., Jr., Principal; HANIFEN IMHOFF CAPITAL PARTNERS LLP 348

Lytell, Michael, President; FIRST PRINCETON CAPITAL, 290

M'Quade, Noreen, Office Manager; GCC INVESTMENTS, INC., 317

MacDonald, F.M., Investment Manager; ROYAL BANK CAPITAL CORPORATION, 677

MacDonald, William I., Senior Vice President; LEASING TECHNOLOGIES INTERNATIONAL, INC., 433

MacDougall, Neil, Director; PRUDENTIAL VENTURE MANAGERS LIMITED, 1539

Macey, M. William, Partner; STERLING VENTURES, LTD., 740

MacFarlane, Ian, Chairman; FRY CONSULTANTS, INC., 313

Machens, G. Michael, General Partner; PHILLIPS-SMITH SPECIALTY RETAIL GROUP, 616

Macinnes, Michael M., Vice President; FLORIDA CAPITAL VENTURES, LTD., 297

Mackenzie, Donald; C. V. C. CAPITAL PARTNERS LIMITED, 1227

MacKenzie, Doug, Partner; KLEINER PERKINS CAUFIELD AND BYERS, 937

Mackenzie, Hamish; ROYAL BANK DEVELOPMENT CAPITAL LTD, 1553

MacKinnon, Donald; SOUTH WEST SCOTLAND INVESTMENT FUND LIMITED, 1612

Mackintosh, Alistair, Director; PRUDENTIAL VENTURE MANAGERS LIMITED, 1539

Maclean, Richard T.; BLUE RIDGE INVESTORS, LTD., 128

MacLellan, David; MURRAY JOHNSTONE PRIVATE EQUITY LIMITED, 1474

Maclennan, Donald, Director; GARTMORE PRIVATE CAPITAL, 1314

MacLeod, Neil; MURRAY AVENIR, 1473

MacNaughton, Angus A., President; GENSTAR INVESTMENT CORPORATION, 324

MacNay, Nick, Director; CLOSE INVESTMENT MANAGEMENT LIMITED, 1207

Macpherson, Ewen, Chief Executive; 3i GROUP PLC, 1655

Macrae, G. Kenneth, General Partner; KEYSTONE VENTURE CAPITAL MANAGEMENT COMPANY, 421

Maczkov, Nicholas A., Managing Principal; FRY CONSULTANTS, INC., 314

Maddox, Carolyn, Director; ABN AMRO CAUSEWAY LIMITED, 1079

Mix, Harald, Director; INDUSTRI KAPITAL SVENSKA AB, 1374

Mlavsky, Dr. A.I., President; GEMINI CAPITAL FUND MANAGEMENT LTD., 1317

Moazzami, Reza, Associate; SHAW VENTURE PARTNERS, 702

Mobbs, Jeremy, Director; YORKSHIRE VENTURE CAPITAL LTD., 1693

Mocarski, Thadeus J., Partner; FLEET EQUITY PARTNERS, 296

Mochary, Matthew N., Associate; SPECTRUM EQUITY INVESTORS, L.P., 723

Mohan, Ravi, Associate; BATTERY VENTURES, 882

Mohr, Lawrence G., Jr., General Partner; MOHR, DAVIDOW VENTURES, 954

Molenaar, Boudewijn; GILDE INVESTMENT FUNDS, 1324

Moller, Chris, Managing Director; TECHNOLOGY LEADERS II, L.P., 985

Moller, Christopher, PhD, Managing Director; RADNOR VENTURE PARTNERS, L.P., 653

Mombru, Jose Luis; D. F. C. LTD., 1236

Momsen, Robert R., Partner; INTERWEST PARTNERS, 390

Monbrard, Janine; BIDASSOA INVESTISSEMENTS, 1165

Moncreif, L. Ray, President and Chief Executive Officer; MOUNTAIN VENTURES, INC., 517

Monkhouse, Graeme, Associate Director; ROTHSCHILD AUSTRALIA CAPITAL INVESTORS LIMITED, 1550

Monléon, Dolores, Partner; BARING VENTURE PARTNERS SA, 1154

Monosson, Adolf F., President; BOSTON FINANCIAL AND EQUITY CORPORATION, 133

Monosson, Deborah J., Vice President; BOSTON FINANCIAL AND EQUITY CORPORATION, 133

Montano, Albert J., Chairman; VENTANA FINANCIAL RESOURCES, INC., 802

Montanus, Gerard, General Partner; ATLAS VENTURE, 879, 1124

Montgomery, H. Dubose, General Partner; MENLO VENTURES, 492, 950

Montgomery, Laura, Vice President; NEWBURY, PIRET AND COMPANY, INC., 545

Monticelli, Stephen P., Managing Director; BACCHARIS CAPITAL, INC., 97

Montret, Alain, Managing Director; EPICEA, 1256

Mony, Jacques; IDIA (INSTITUT DE DÉVELOPPEMENT DES INDUSTRIES AGRICOLES ET ALIMENTAIRES), 1360

Moore, Barrie; NATWEST MARKETS MEZZANINE FINANCE, 1478

Moore, C.R., Analyst; MOORE AND ASSOCIATES, 512

Moore, Daniel E., General Partner; VENTURA AMERICA, 806

Moore, Doug, Chief Financial Officer; CASCADIA PACIFIC MANAGEMENT, LLC, 169; Chief Financial Officer; OREGON RESOURCE AND TECHNOLOGY FUND, 966

Moore, Douglas W., Vice President; TRILWOOD INVESTMENTS, LTD., 776

Moore, George B., Vice President; HOAK COMMUNICATIONS PARTNERS, L.P., 366

Moore, Guerry L., Managing Director; MOORE AND ASSOCIATES, 512

Moore, Jeffrey G., President; MATRIX CAPITAL MARKETS GROUP, INC., 469

Moore, M.; SHANNON DEVELOPMENT COMPANY, 1584

Moorhead, Rodman, III, Senior Managing Director; WARBURG, PINCUS VENTURES, 830

Moragne, John H., Partner; TRIDENT CAPITAL, INC., 775

Moral, Jean-François, Managing Director; FINANCES ET COMMUNICATION DÉVELOPPEMENT, 1283

Morandeau, Jean-Christophe; ANTIN GESTION, 1108

Morby, Jacqueline C., Senior General Partner; TA ASSOCIATES, 752

Morck, Frede, Partner; DANISH DEVELOPMENT FINANCE CORPORATION, 1229

More, Ginger M.; OAK INVESTMENT PARTNERS, 570

Moreda, Manuel A.; NORTH AMERICA INVESTMENT CORPORATION, 549

Morehead, Richard H., Vice President, Corporate Development and Planning; ABBOTT LABS, 1035

Moreno, Roland; INNOVATRON SMART CARD VENTURES NV, 1381

Morgan, Jonathan, Managing Director; PRUDENTIAL VENTURE MANAGERS LIMITED, 1539

Morgenstern, George, Chief Executive Officer; DEFENSE SOFTWARE AND SYSTEMS (DSS), 1048

Morgenthaler, David T., Managing Partner; MORGENTHALER VENTURES, 515, 959

Morgenthaler, Gary J., General Partner; MORGENTHALER VENTURES, 516, 960

Morinaga, Mitsuo, Managing Principal; FRY CONSULTANTS, INC., 314

Moritz, Michael, Partner; SEQUOIA CAPITAL, 980

Morley, Andrew, Partner; MARQUETTE VENTURE PARTNERS, 941

Morrell, Simon, Assistant Director; INTERMEDIATE CAPITAL GROUP PLC, 1387

Morris, Ian, Vice President and Chief Financial Officer; VENCAP, INC., 799

Morris, Paul; DOW EUROPE SA, 1237

O'Grady, E.; SHANNON DEVELOPMENT COMPANY, 1584

O'Grady, Standish, Principal; HAMBRECHT AND QUIST GROUP, 344

O'Malley, Dennis, Senior Vice President; ABN AMRO CORPORATE INVESTMENTS, 1081

O'Malley, Michael E.A., Principal; MDT ADVISORS, INC., 481

O'Neill, James J., Senior Vice President; ROTHSCHILD VENTURES, INC., 676

O'Neill, John; MIDLANDS VENTURE FUND MANAGERS LIMITED, 1455

Oakford, Scott I., Managing Director; HAMILTON ROBINSON AND COMPANY, INC., 347

Oberholtzer, William J., Vice President; ALPHA CAPITAL PARTNERS, 64

Ocko, Matt, Vice President; HELIX INVESTMENTS, LTD., 355

Odunsi, Bolaji; B. C. PARTNERS LIMITED, 1159

Oehne, Dieter; MITTELSTÄNDISCHE BETEILIGUNGSGESELLSCHAFT SACHSEN-ANHALT mbH, 1465

Oei, T.P., Vice President; JOHNSON AND JOHNSON DEVELOPMENT CORPORATION, 410

Oesterle, William S., General Partner; CID EQUITY PARTNERS, 193

Offer, Fred; TRANSATLANTIC CAPITAL LTD, 1660

Oger, Dominique, Managing Director; COMPAGNIE DE FINANCEMENT INDUSTRIEL, 1216

Öhman, Gustav, Director; INDUSTRI KAPITAL SVENSKA AB, 1374

Öjefors, Lars, Managing Director; INDUSTRIFONDEN, 1372

Okawa, Isao, Chairman; C. S. K. VENTURE CAPITAL COMPANY, LIMITED, 1224

Oken, Glenn, Partner; FCP INVESTORS, 278

Olivier, Bernard; SORIDEC, 1609

Olivier, Edmund M., General Partner; OXFORD BIOSCIENCE PARTNERS II, 967

Olivier, Serge, Regional Director; GESTION CAPIDEM, INC., 326

Olofsson, Morgan, Director; NORDIC CAPITAL, 1492

Olsen, Mogens, Partner; DANISH DEVELOPMENT FINANCE CORPORATION, 1229

Olshansky, Jack, General Partner; MONTGOMERY MEDICAL VENTURES, 511, 956

Olson, Nancy S., General Partner; ST. PAUL VENTURE CAPITAL, 732

Omohundro, Richard E., Jr., Co-President; PROSPECT STREET INVESTMENT MANAGEMENT COMPANY, INC., 642

Onians, Richard, Managing Partner; BARING VENTURE PARTNERS LTD., 1153; Partner; CAPRICORN VENTURE PARTNERS NV, 1190

Opdendyk, Terry L., Partner; ONSET VENTURES, 577, 965

Orlando, Jim, Investment Manager; BCE VENTURES, INC., 117

Orloff, Roger B., President; THE ACQUISITION SEARCH CORPORATION, 54

Orman, James; LONDON VENTURES (FUND MANAGERS) LIMITED, 1432

Oronsky, Arnold L., Partner; INTERWEST PARTNERS, 391

Orr, Larry, Senior Associate; TRINITY VENTURES, 777

Orr, R. Wilson, III, Vice President; SSM CORPORATION, 731

Orsak, Michael Colby; JAFCO AMERICA VENTURES, INC., 405

Ortale, W. Patrick, III, General Partner; LAWRENCE, TYRRELL, ORTALE AND SMITH, 939

Ortale, W. Patrick, Partner; RICHLAND VENTURES, 666

Osborn, William C., Partner; VENTURE INVESTMENT MANAGEMENT COMPANY, LLC, 816

Oscarsson, Gösta; FOUR SEASONS VENTURE CAPITAL AB, 1304

Österlund, Kari (Managing Director, Hasse Travel), Director; MATKAILUNKEHITYS NORDIA OY, 1439

Otano, Enrico Rubio, Partner; BBV DE PROMOCION EMPRESARIAL SA, 1158

Overbeck, Glenda, Associate; HOUSTON VENTURE PARTNERS, 371

Overbeke, F. Van; ISEP, 1393

Overmeer, J.M., Supervisory Board; NEDERLANDSE PARTICIPATIE MAATSCHAPPIJ NV, 1483

Owen, Mark, Director; GRANVILLE PRIVATE EQUITY MANAGERS LIMITED, 1333

Owens, Caroline; MIDLAND GROWTH CAPITAL, 1454

Owens, Nancy P., Vice President and Chief Financial Officer; THE NORTH CAROLINA ENTERPRISE FUND, 554

Oyster, Jeffery, Partner; ZS FUND L.P., 861

Ozechov, Ygal I., General Partner; NEWBURY VENTURES, 544

Paananen, Tuula, Director; MATKAILUNKEHITYS NORDIA OY, 1439

Paauwe, Theresia, Secretary; CIRCLE VENTURES, INC. 195

Page, Jennifer H., Senior Associate; CID EQUITY PARTNERS, 193

Paglino, Vincent, Vice President, Manager; SENMED VENTURES, 978

Pahl, Milt, President and Chief Executive Officer; NATIVE VENTURE CAPITAL COMPANY, LTD., 528

Paillart, Aimable; SOCIÉTÉ CENTRALE POUR L'INDUSTRIE, 1598

Paine, F. Ward, General Partner; OSCCO VENTURES, 583; General Partner; OSCCO VENTURES, III, 584

Painter, J. Scott, Principal; CHANEN, PAINTER AND COMPANY, LTD., 180

Paladino, Albert E., Managing Partner; ADVANCED TECHNOLOGY VENTURES, 58, 868

Palandri, Enrico, Senior Officer; ARCA IMPRESA GESTIONI SpA, 1114

Palley, Simon; B. C. PARTNERS LIMITED, 1159

Palmer, Charles L., President; NORTH AMERICAN BUSINESS DEVELOPMENT COMPANIES, L.L.C., 550

Palms, Dr. Peter J., IV, President; PALMS AND COMPANY, INC., 594

Pandef, Ludmil, President; AXA CAPITAL CORPORATION, 95

Panem, Sandra, Ph.D., President; VECTOR FUND MANAGEMENT, L.P., 795

Panfilo, Francesco; SOFIPA SpA, 1603

Panier, Christine; EUROMEZZANINE GESTION, 1264

Papageorgiou, Gus, Investment Manager; BCE VENTURES, INC., 117

Papaioannou, Ioannis, Investment Manager; GLOBAL FINANCE, 1329

Papantonis, Nicholas, Partner; ASPEN VENTURES, 877

Papirow, Dr. Stefan; BETEILIGUNGSGESELLSCHAFT FÜR INDUSTRIE, HANDWERK, HANDEL UND VERKEHR mbH, 1163

Pappajohn, John, President; PAPPAJOHN CAPITAL RESOURCES, 596

Pappas, Milton J., Partner; EUCLID PARTNERS CORPORATION, 272, 912

Parham, Iain; C. V. C. CAPITAL PARTNERS LIMITED, 1227

Paris, Michel; PARIBAS AFFAIRES INDUSTRIELLES, 1513; PARIBAS INVESTISEMENT DÉVELOPPEMENT, 1514

Paris, Robert W., Chairman/President; BANCORP HAWAII, SBIC, 104

Parizeau, Ernest C., General Partner; NORWEST VENTURE CAPITAL, 563

Park, David, Partner; PAUL CAPITAL PARTNERS, 603

Park, Duck-Bong, Executive Vice President; KOREA DEVELOPMENT INVESTMENT FINANCE CORPORATION (KDIFC), 1412

Park, Pil Lae, Executive Senior Vice President; C. N. B. TECHNOLOGY FINANCE COMPANY LTD., 1209

Park, T.E., Senior Investment Officer; K. L. B. INVESTMENT COMPANY, LIMITED, 1407

Parker, Carl; SCHRODER VENTURES, 1568

Parker, David J., Principal; AMPERSAND VENTURES, 873

Parker, Marshall D., Vice President; KANSAS VENTURE CAPITAL, INC., 415

Parker, Peggy, Regional Port Manager; COMDISCO VENTURE GROUP, 891

Parker, Peter D., General Partner; AMPERSAND VENTURES, 873

Parker, Roy, Director; BROWN SHIPLEY VENTURE MANAGERS LTD., 1176

Parlier, Elmer, Vice President, Investments; MOUNTAIN VENTURES, INC., 517

Parr, Jeff, Managing Director; CLAIRVEST GROUP, INC., 200

Parsons, Donald H., Jr., General Partner; THE CENTENNIAL FUNDS, 174

Parsons, James A., General Partner; RFE INVESTMENT PARTNERS, 663

Partala, Hannu, Managing Director; PIKESPO INVEST OY LTD, 1526

Partridge, Lamar J., President; VALLEY CAPITAL CORPORATION, 792, 1030; Chief Executive Officer; VALLEY MANAGE-MENT, INC., 1031

Paschaligos, D.N.; ETEBA, 1261

Pasquesi, John; HELLMAN AND FRIEDMAN, 357

Passy, Pierre-Michel; COMPAGNIE FINANCIÈRE E. DE ROTHSCHILD BANQUE, 1217

Pastel, David; GROUPE MAAF, 1337

Pastour, Benoît; VAUBAN FINANCE, 1676

Pastre, Thierry, Director; I. P. O. (INSTITUT DE PARTICIPATIONS DE L'OUEST), 1390

Paterson, Calum; SCOTTISH ENTERPRISE, 1570

Paterson, Richard D., Executive Vice President; GENSTAR INVESTMENT CORPORATION, 324

Patience, John, General Partner; MARQUETTE VENTURE PARTNERS, 941

Patko, Andra, President; HFT CORPORATION, 361

Patouillaud, Jean-Marc, Director; GENESE INVESTISSEMENTS, 1319

Patricof, Alan J., Chairman; PATRICOF AND COMPANY VENTURES, INC., 601

Patroncini, Guido; ZURMONT MANAGEMENT AG, 1696

Patterson, Arthur C., General Partner; ACCEL PARTNERS, 52, 866

Patterson, J., Investment Manager, Small Business Funds; ROYAL BANK CAPITAL CORPORATION, 677

Poole, Walker, Senior Vice President; NATIONSBANK LEVERAGED CAPITAL GROUP, 527

Poort, A.F., Partner; VENTURE FUND ROTTERDAM BV, 1679

Porter, Richard, Finance Director; ELDERSTREET INVESTMENTS LTD, 1245

Porter, Thomas S., Partner; ENTERPRISE DEVELOPMENT FUND, 263

Posselt, J.-Wolfgang, Managing Director; TBG (TECHNOLOGIE-BETEILIGUNGS-GmbH DER DEUTSCHEN AUS-GLEICHSBANK), 1638

Potters, Heather, Vice President; ENTERPRISE INVESTORS, 264

Potuin, Gustave, Regional Vice President; ROYNAT, INC., 679

Pouilly, Erik; SOPROMEC, 1608

Poulet, Isabelle, Investment Manager; SDR SODERE - FINANCIÈRE LABOURDONNAIS, 1571

Pouschine, John L., Senior Vice President; ELECTRA INC., 259

Powell, David, Senior Associate; BROADMARK CAPITAL CORPORATION, 141

Power, Gordon, Managing Director; GUINNESS MAHON DEVELOPMENT CAPITAL LIMITED, 1340

Powles, Chris; ELDERSTREET INVESTMENTS LTD, 1245

Pöysti, Arja, Managing Director; SADEPO OY, 1557

Prakash, Gautam A.; BESSEMER VENTURE PARTNERS, 125

Pratt, Gordon G., Senior Vice President; CONNING AND COMPANY, 212

Preaux, Guy, Partner; SAMBRINVEST SA, 1559

Prelz, Massimo; ADVENT INTERNATIONAL plc, 1090

Prendergast, Eoghan; SHANNON DEVELOPMENT COMPANY, 1584

Prendergast, John, Director, Operations; THE CASTLE GROUP, LTD., 170

Pressacco, Flavio, Chairman; FRIULIA SpA, 1309

Prior, John J., Jr., Managing Director; NEEDHAM AND COMPANY, INC., 533

Prizzi, Jack, Special Limited Partner; HARVEST PARTNERS, INC., 351

Proano, Roclo M., Manager; INTERNATIONAL TECHNOLOGY, 934

Prohazka, Maartin, Partner; HORIZONTE VENTURE MANAGEMENT GmbH, 1354

Pronczuk, Dariusz, Vice President; ENTERPRISE INVESTORS, 264, 1254

Propper, Dr. Richard D., Managing General Partner; MONTGOMERY MEDICAL VENTURES, 956

Prosswimmer, R. Alan, Managing Director; THE BENEFIT CAPITAL COMPANIES INC., 121

Prothro, C. Vincent, Managing General Partner; SOUTHWEST ENTERPRISE ASSOCIATES, L.P., 718

Proudlock, Michael, Chairman; GRANVILLE PRIVATE EQUITY MANAGERS LIMITED, 1333

Pruett, Michelle, Senior Business Analyst; EMERALD VENTURE GROUP, 261

Pruvot, Philippe; PICARDIE INVESTISSEMENT, 1525

Puddington, John C., President; TRILWOOD INVESTMENTS, LTD., 776

Puertas, J.R.; INSTITUTO NACIONAL DE INDUSTRIA - GRUPO SODI, 1384

Puertas, Juan R., Partner; TENEO GRUPO DE EMPRESAS DE DESARROLLO (I. N. I.), 1647

Purcell, C.W., Secretary; LUBRIZOL CORPORATION, 452

Purcell, Paul F., President; BATTELLE VENTURE PARTNERS (aka SCIENTIFIC ADVANCES, INC.), 112; President; SCIENTIFIC ADVANCES, 694; President; ENERTEK PARTNERS, 909

Puricelli, Stephen M., General Partner; CORPORATE VENTURE PARTNERS, L.P., 222, 898

Purkayastha, Dev, General Partner; IDANTA PARTNERS LTD., 375

Pusey, Gregory, President; LIVINGSTON CAPITAL, LTD., 444

Putnam, Daniel, Senior Vice President, New Product Development; ADOBE SYSTEMS, INC., 1036

Pylkkänen, Jorma, Managing Director; SAVON TEKNIA OY, 1561; TEKNIA VENTURE INVEST LIMITED, 1644

Quadrani, Ettore; CENTROFINANZIARIA SpA, 1195

Quagliaroli, John A., President; FOWLER, ANTHONY AND COMPANY, 304

Quanten, Guido, Partner; LIMBURGSE PARTICIPATIE-MAATSCHAPPIJ, 1429

Quartano, Ralph, Non-Executive Director; 3i GROUP PLC, 1655

Quattlebaum, Richard, Senior Partner; REALTY FUNDING GROUP INTERNATIONAL, 657

Queally, Paul, General Partner; WELSH, CARSON, ANDERSON AND STOWE, 835

Quentel, Jean-Yves; ATLAS VENTURE, 1125

Queveau, Phillippe; CITA, 1204

Quillman, Werner; AGU AKTIENGESELLSCHAFT FÜR UNTERNEHMENSBETEILIGUNGEN, 1097

Quindlen, Ruth, General Partner; INSTITUTIONAL VENTURE PARTNERS, 933

Quinn, Maureen P., Assistant Vice President; CORESTATES ENTERPRISE FUND, 218

Quy, Roger J., PhD, General Partner; TECHNOLOGY PARTNERS, 760

Stubbs, Keith, Manager, Business Development; J.B. POINDEXTER AND COMPANY, INC., 398

Stuber, Fred; DEFI GESTION SA, 1233

Stuchin, Miles, Chairman and Chief Exeutive Officer; FIRST CHARTER PARTNERS, INC., 287

Studer, Hanspeter; S. F. M. ET ASSOCIÉS SA, 1582

Stutz, Rolf S., General Partner; CLAFLIN CAPITAL MANAGEMENT, INC., 199

Styles, Daniel G., General Partner; SUN VALLEY VENTURES, 749

Styles, Katherine, Associate; ARTHUR ROCK AND COMPANY, 876

Suetsugu, Hiroshi, President and Chief Executive Officer; NIPPON STEEL U.S.A., INC., 1066

Suguta, Y.; KOBE STEEL USA, 425

Suhler, John S., General Partner; V S AND A COMMUNICATIONS PARTNERS, L.P., 825

Suissa, Albert; SOFIREM, 1604

Sullivan, J. Roger, Jr., Special Partner; GROTECH CAPITAL GROUP, 339

Sullivan, Jeanne M., Partner; FOUR C VENTURES, 915; Vice President; INTERNATIONAL TECHNOLOGY, 934

Summers, Dr. Richard, Executive Director; 3i GROUP PLC, 1655

Sumner, Preston, Director; STEPHENSON MERCHANT BANKING, INC., 737

Sun, Anthony, General Partner; VENROCK ASSOCIATES, 801

Sundberg, Jan; S-E-BANKEN FÖRETAGSINVEST, 1572

Sunderland, Dr. Neil V.; ADINVEST AG, 1089

Sunila, Pekka, MSc (Eng), MSc (Econ), General Manager; MB CORPORATE FINANCE LTD, 1441

Suokas, Jukka; KERA LIMITED, 1405

Suomela, Juhani, MSc (Econ), Managing Director; MB CORPORATE FINANCE LTD, 1441

Surhammar, Susanne, Company Secretary; MALMÖHUS INVEST AB (MIAB), 1436

Sussman, Robert A., Vice President; HOAK COMMUNICATIONS PARTNERS, L.P., 366

Sussner, Heiner; ICVEN SA, 1358

Sutcliffe, Jack; LANCASHIRE ENTERPRISES plc, 1418

Sutherland, Donald J., President; QUINCY PARTNERS, 650

Sutherland, Ivan E., Special Partner; ADVANCED TECHNOLOGY VENTURES, 868

Sutherland, William R., Special Partner; ADVANCED TECHNOLOGY VENTURES, 58, 868

Sutter, Martin P., General Partner; ESSEX-WOODLANDS HEALTH VENTURES, L.P., 271, 911

Sutter, William P., Jr., Managing Director and Executive Vice President; MESIROW PRIVATE EQUITY, 497

Svegaarden, Thor; SND (NORWEGIAN INDUSTRIAL AND REGIONAL DEVELOPMENT FUND), 1594

Svensson, Elisabeth; A. M. F. PENSION, 1106

Svider, Raymond; BARING CAPITAL PARTNERS, 1149

Swain, Stephen J., Associate Director; ALIMANSKY CAPITAL GROUP, INC., 60

Swainbank, R., Finance Director; WEST MIDLANDS ENTERPRISE BOARD LTD., 1690

Swanepoel, G.C., Managing Director; PRIVATE EQUITY INVESTMENT MANAGERS (PTY) LTD, 1532

Swartz, James P., General Partner; ACCEL PARTNERS, 53, 867

Sweatman, Michael, President; GREEN MOUNTAIN CAPITAL, L.P., 335

Sweeney, Brian M., President; SWEENEY & COMPANY, INC., 751

Sweeney, Gail C., Managing Principal; SOVEREIGN FINANCIAL SERVICES, 721

Sweeney, Paul W., Partner; HORIZON CAPITAL PARTNERS, L.P., 369

Sweeney, Stuart; NATWEST MARKETS ACQUISITION FINANCE, 1477

Sweeny, Thomas K., Vice President; LANDMARK PARTNERS, 938

Swenson, Ronald W., President; WESTERN TECHNOLOGY INVESTMENT, 839

Swenson, W. David, Vice President; FRANKLIN VENTURE CAPITAL, INC., 916

Swire, Rhoddy, Partner; PANTHEON VENTURES LIMITED, 1511

Sword, Derek, Investment Assistant; HODGSON MARTIN LTD., 1351

Sword, William, Jr., Managing Director; CAPITAL CITIES CAPITAL, INC., 153

Symondson, David, Director; ELECTRA FLEMING LIMITED, 1248

Szustak, William, Chief Financial Officer; TECH VENTURES, INC., 758

Taft, Peter G., Principal; MORGENTHALER VENTURES, 516, 960

Takagi, Yoshiaki, Managing Director; TOKYO SMALL AND MEDIUM BUSINESS INVESTMENTS AND CONSULTATION COMPANY, 1659

Takahashi, Fumio, Director; C. S. K. VENTURE CAPITAL COMPANY, LIMITED, 1224

Tallboys, David; EQUITY VENTURES LTD., 1259

Tammi, Giancarlo; IRITECH SpA, 1392

Tang, Michael, Principal; CALVERT SOCIAL VENTURE PARTNERS, 1002

Taniguchi, Dexter J., President; PACIFIC VENTURE CAPITAL, LTD., 1023

Tanimoto, Tadashi, Engagement Manager; AZCA, INC., 96

Tankersley, G. Jackson, Jr., General Partner; THE CENTENNIAL FUNDS, 174

Tanner, Dr. H.C.; UNION BANK OF SWITZERLAND, 1670

Taranto, Philippe; PARIBAS INVESTISEMENT DÉVELOPPEMENT, 1514

Tardif, Pierre, President; GESTION CAPIDEM, INC., 326

Tardy, Gérart; SCHRODER PARTENAIRES, 1567

Tarr, Jake D., Jr., Vice President; ARETE VENTURES, 80

Tasch, Edward, General Partner; COMMONS CAPITAL, 1007

Taylor, Craig C., General Partner; ASSET MANAGEMENT ASSOCIATES, INC., 87

Taylor, David; ELDERSTREET INVESTMENTS LTD, 1245

Taylor, Gregory D., Treasurer; LUBRIZOL CORPORATION, 452

Taylor, Hugh, Managing Director; NEWBURY, PIRET AND COMPANY, INC., 545

Taylor, Ian, Managing Director; LEGAL AND GENERAL VENTURES LIMITED, 1425

Taylor, John, Managing Director; AMERICAN STRATEGIC INVESTMENTS, L.P., 71

Taylor, Mary, Associate; THE JORDAN, EDMISTON GROUP, INC., 411

Taylor, Pam, Officer; INTERNATIONAL PAPER CAPITAL FORMATION, 1017

Taylor, Peter; HAMBRO EUROPEAN VENTURES LIMITED, 1345

Taylor, Robert E., Jr., Vice President; WINGATE PARTNERS, INC., 851

Taylor, William C., Vice President; PRINCETON AMERICAN FINANCIAL SERVICES CORPORATION, 638

Taylor, William H., II, General Partner; TAYLOR AND TURNER, 755

Tazartes, Alberto, Executive Director; BARING CAPITAL INVESTORS LTD., 1148

Tchenio, Maurice; APAX PARTNERS ET CIE., 1111

Teal, Robert G., General Partner; CAPFORM PARTNERS, 152

Tedestedt, Rolf, MBA, Venture Capitalist; I. M. INNOVATIONS MÄKLARNA AB, 1364

Teeger, John L., President; FOUNDERS EQUITY, INC., 303

Tehranian, Terrence, Partner; BARING VENTURE PARTNERS LTD., 1153

Tellefsen, Dag, Managing Partner; GLENWOOD, 918

ten Hoonte, J.G., Supervisory Board; NEDERLANDSE PARTICIPATIE MAATSCHAPPIJ NV, 1483

Tenaglia, Emilio; ABRUZZO CAPITAL SpA, 1082

Tenbroek, James P., Associate; GOLDER, THOMA, CRESSEY, RAUNER, INC., 330

Tennant, Chris; PHILDREW VENTURES, 1522

Tennant, David R., Managing Principal; FRY CONSULTANTS, INC., 313

Tepner, Harvey L., Managing Director; LOEB PARTNERS CORPORATION, 446

Terentjeff, Jorma, Managing Director; TEKNO ADVISORS OY, 1645

Tessler, Daniel; TESSLER AND CLOHERTY, INC., 763

Testa, Guido; LIGUR SEED CAPITAL, 1428

Teulings, Coen N., Partner; MERIFIN CAPITAL GROUP, 1448

Thacher, Lynn D., Secretary and Treasurer; THACHER FINANCIAL GROUP, INC., 765

Thacher, William W., President; THACHER FINANCIAL GROUP, INC., 765

Thauron, Xavier; S. P. E. F., 1614

Thimbault, Xavier; SOCIÉTÉ CENTRALE POUR L'INDUSTRIE, 1598

Thom, Benjamin A.; ADS CAPITAL CORPORATION, 56

Thom, Lambert, Vice President; BANGERT DAWES READE DAVIS AND THOM, 106

Thoma, Carl D., Principal; GOLDER, THOMA, CRESSEY, RAUNER, INC., 329

Thomann, Thierry; CICLAD, 1202

Thomas, James, Manager; PHOENIX FUND MANAGERS LIMITED, 1524

Thomas, Lionnel, Managing Director; ALLIANCE ENTREPRENDRE, 1100

Thomas, Paul, Director; GRESHAM TRUST plc, 1335

Thomas, T. Peter, General Partner; INSTITUTIONAL VENTURE PARTNERS, 933

Thomas, William R., President and Chairman of the Board; CAPITAL SOUTHWEST CORPORATION, 160

Thompson, Darryl B., Senior Vice President; TSG VENTURES, INC., 779, 1028

Thompson, J. Peter, Managing Partner; OPPORTUNITY CAPITAL, 579; Managing Partner; OPPORTUNITY CAPITAL CORPORATION, 1022

Thompson, M.L.D., Partner; DAVIS GROUP, 233

Veil, Joseph A., Vice President, Investments; THE NORTH CAROLINA ENTERPRISE FUND, 554

Vélez, Paulino Lopez, Partner; BBV DE PROMOCION EMPRESARIAL SA, 1158

Vender, Jody, Chief Executive Officer; SoPaF (SOCIETA PARTECIPAZIONI FINANZIARIE SpA), 1606; Chairman, SoPaF International, and Chief Executive Officer, SoPaF; SoPaF INTERNATIONAL SA, 1607

Venegar, Richard, Director; LEVMARK CAPITAL CORPORATION, 437

Venon, Daniel, Managing Director; AVENIR ENTREPRISES, 1129

Ventura, Maria do Rosario Mayoral Robles Machado Simoes, Head of Turnaround Banking and Venture Capital Department; BANCO MELLO DE INVESTIMENTOS SA, 1137

ver Hulst, Nicolas, Director; ALPHA ASSOCIÉS, 1103

Vercruyssen, Philip, Senior Investment Manager; VLAAMSE INVESTERINGSVENNOOTSCHAP NV, 1681

Verdurme, Paul, Partner; EUROVENTURES BENELUX, 1269

Verhalen, Andrew W., General Partner; MATRIX PARTNERS, 470, 943

Verma, Deborah C., Treasurer; J.G. FOGG AND COMPANY, INC., 402

Vermassen, Sabinne, Legal Counsel; EUROVENTURES BENELUX, 1269

Vermeulen, C. M.; ALPINVEST HOLDING NV, 1104

Vermeulen, Philip, Partner; G. I. M. V., 1325; Partner; SEED CAPITAL FUND KEMPEN, 1576

Vernallis, Mark, General Partner; KEYSTONE MINORITY CAPITAL FUND, L.P., 420

Vernon, Geoffrey; ROTHSCHILD BIOSCIENCE UNIT, 1551

Vero, Geoffrey, Director; ABN AMRO CAUSEWAY LIMITED, 1079

Veronis, John J., General Partner; V S AND A COMMUNICATIONS PARTNERS, L.P., 825

Vervoort, Th. A.; ALPINVEST HOLDING NV, 1104

Vesely, Jon S., Managing Director; CODE, HENNESSY AND SIMMONS, LP, CODE, HENNESSY AND SIMMONS II, LP, 204

Vesola, Erkki, Investment Manager; OKO VENTURE CAPITAL OY, 1505

Vicente, Pedro, Manager of Turnaround Banking and Venture Capital Department; BANCO MELLO DE INVESTIMENTOS SA, 1137

Viere, Werner; OSNABRÜCKER BETEILIGUNGS- UND CONSULT GmbH, 1509

Viet-Jabcobson, Denis, Manager; INTERMEDIATE CAPITAL GROUP PLC, 1387

Vignola, Leonard, Managing Director; BEACON PARTNERS, INC., 119

Vilain, Serge, President; S. R. I. B. SA (G. I. M. B.), 1619

Vilella, Fiori; NORTH AMERICA INVESTMENT CORPORATION, 549

Villanueva, Daniel D., Managing Director; BASTION CAPITAL CORPORATION, 110

Villanueva, James, Vice President; BASTION CAPITAL CORPORATION, 110

Vines, Richard A., Partner; GEOCAPITAL PARTNERS, 325

Vinton, Fred, Chairman; ELECTRA FLEMING LIMITED, 1248

Vintu, Sorin Ovidiu, Partner; S. C. GELSOR SA, 1564

Virtanen, Visa, Lic. Econ., Managing Director; MIDINVEST OY, 1452

Visser, Mark P., Analyst; BEHRMAN CAPITAL, 120

Vitale, Jody B., Partner; VITALE HOLDINGS, INC., 823

Vitale, Joseph, Partner; VITALE HOLDINGS, INC., 823

Vitali, Elisabetta, Analyst; CHASE CAPITAL PARTNERS ITALIA SpA, 1200

Vitullo, Nicole; ROTHSCHILD BIOSCIENCE UNIT, 1551

Viukari, Pekka, Managing Director; VUOTEKNO OY, 1682

Vogel, Dale J., General Partner; U. S. VENTURE PARTNERS, 784

Vogt, Dr. Gert; KREDITANSTALT FÜR WIEDERAUFBAU (KFW), 1415

Voisin, Jean-Marie, Managing Director; AGRINOVA, 1095

Volpel, John, Director of Investment Evaluation; TECH VENTURES, INC., 758

Volpi, Romualdo; SPI SpA, 1615

von Bauer, Eric E., President and Chief Executive Officer; THE CAPITAL STRATEGY MANAGEMENT COMPANY, 161

von der Goltz, H.J., General Partner; BOSTON CAPITAL VENTURES, 131

von Hardenberg, Goetz; NORDDEUTSCHE INNOVATIONS- UND BETEILIGUNGS GmbH (NIB), 1489

von Koch, Thomas, Investment Manager; EQT PARTNERS AB, 1258

von Koester, Hans-Konrad, Managing Director; BETEILIGUNGSGESELLSCHAFT FÜR DIE DEUTSCHE WIRTSCHAFT (BdW), 1162

Von Lehman, Joseph C., Jr.; RIVER CITIES CAPITAL FUND, 669

von Loeper, Claus, Dipl.-Kfm., MBA; HANNOVER FINANZ GmbH, 1348

Young, Robert A., Investment Manager; DILLON READ VENTURE CAPITAL, 242

Young, Spencer, Associate Director; ROTHSCHILD AUSTRALIA CAPITAL INVESTORS LIMITED, 1550

Younger, William H., Jr., General Partner; SUTTER HILL VENTURES, 983

Yuan, Zenia C., President; FIRST COUNTY CAPITAL, INC. 1014

Yun, Yeo-Gyeong, President and Chief Executive Officer; KOREA DEVELOPMENT INVESTMENT FINANCE CORPORA-
    TION (KDIFC), 1412

Zachem, Tyler T., Principal; McCOWN De LEEUW AND COMPANY, 477

Zackuson, David, General Partner; STONEBRIDGE PARTNERS, 743

Zahn, Karlheinz; MITTELSTÄNDISCHE BETEILIGUNGSGESELLSCHAFT HESSEN GmbH, 1460

Zahren, Bernard J., President; ZAHREN FINANCIAL CORPORATION, 860

Zaic, Gregory F., General Partner; PRINCE VENTURES, 974

Zak, Michael J., General Partner; CHARLES RIVER VENTURES, 181

Zamlynski, Marian M., Operations Manager and Vice President; IEG VENTURE MANAGEMENT, INC., 376

Zand, H. Herman, Treasurer; VENCON MANAGEMENT, INC., 800

Zarrella, Ronald L., Chief Operating Officer; BAUSCH AND LOMB, 1041

Zarzavatdjian, Guy, Associate Director; 3i FRANCE, 1653

Zebro, David M., Executive Vice President; STRATEGIC INVESTMENTS AND HOLDINGS, INC., 745

Zeeuw, Tanneke; BIOTECHNOLOGY INVESTMENTS LTD. (B. I. L.), 1167; ROTHSCHILD BIOSCIENCE UNIT, 1551

Zegelaar, Rob, Partner; ATLAS VENTURE, 879, 1124

Zehnder, Markus; UNION BANK OF SWITZERLAND, 1670

Zeisler, John E., Partner; INTERWEST PARTNERS, 391

Zemel, Leon, Financial Analyst; THE PLATINUM GROUP, INC., 629

Zenaty, Daniel; FINANCIÈRE GALLIERA, 1288

Zentner, Gary J., President; PNC EQUITY MANAGEMENT CORPORATION, 631

Zhang, Frederick Keming, General Partner; CLAFLIN CAPITAL MANAGEMENT, INC., 199

Zicarelli, Robert F., Managing General Partner; NORWEST VENTURE CAPITAL, 562

Ziebelman, Peter, Managing Director; THOMPSON CLIVE, INC., 767, 988

Zielinski, James, Managing Director; BANKERS TRUST CAPITAL CORPORATION, 109; Managing Director; THE JORDAN,
    EDMISTON GROUP, INC., 411

Zietz, Nora, Partner; NEW ENTERPRISE ASSOCIATES, 541

Zigman, Paul C., Partner; AMPERSAND VENTURES, 873

Zimbone, Rick, Senior Vice President; BOSTON ENERGY TECHNOLOGY GROUP, 132

Zimmerman, Mark, Vice President; LINC CAPITAL PARTNERS, INC., 442

Zimmerman, Martin, Chairman; LINC CAPITAL PARTNERS, INC., 442

Ziolkowski, Andrew M., Managing Director; SAE VENTURES, 685

Zizza, Veronic, Treasurer; UNC VENTURES, 1029

Zizza, Veronica, Treasurer; UNC VENTURES, 786

Znaimer, Sam, Vice President; VENTURES WEST MANAGEMENT, INC., 818

Zoltán, Csaba, Senior Investment Manager; FIRST HUNGARIAN INVESTMENT ADVISORY Rt, 1295

Zombory, Victória, Senior Investment Manager; FIRST HUNGARIAN INVESTMENT ADVISORY Rt, 1295

Zuckerman, Arthur S., Administrative General Partner; SPROUT GROUP, 729

Zuckerman, Steven A., Partner; McCOWN De LEEUW AND COMPANY, 477

Zug, D. Brooks, Managing General Partner; HANCOCK VENTURE PARTNERS, 922

GEOGRAPHIC INDEX

Finland

CAPMAN CAPITAL MANAGEMENT OY, 1189
DCC MANAGEMENT OY, 1231
FINNISH FUND FOR INDUSTRIAL COOPERATION
   LIMITED (FINNFUND), 1292
FINNISH INDUSTRY INVESTMENT LIMITED, 1293
INDEKON OY, 1365
KERA LIMITED, 1405
MATKAILUNKEHITYS NORDIA OY, 1439
MB CORPORATE FINANCE LTD, 1441
MERITA CAPITAL OY PROFITA FUND I, 1449
METRA CORPORATION, 1450
MIDINVEST OY, 1452
NOPTOR OY, 1488
OKO VENTURE CAPITAL OY, 1505
PIKESPO INVEST OY LTD, 1526
SADEPO OY, 1557
SAVON TEKNIA OY, 1561
SITRA, 1589
SPINNO-SEED OY, 1616
START FUND OF KERA OY, 1623
TECHNOLOGY DEVELOPMENT CENTRE FINLAND
   (TEKES), 1642
TEKNIA VENTURE INVEST LIMITED, 1644
TEKNO ADVISORS OY, 1645
VUOTEKNO OY, 1682

France

ACLAND, 1086
ADC, 1088
AGRINOVA, 1095
AGRO PARTENAIRES, 1096
ALLIANCE ENTREPRENDRE, 1100
ALPHA ASSOCIÉS, 1103
ANTIN GESTION, 1108
ANVAR, 1109
APAX PARTNERS AND CO. VENTURES LTD., 1110
APAX PARTNERS ET CIE., 1111
ARGOS SODITIC FRANCE, 1116
ARGOS SODITIC SA, 1119
ASTORG COMPAGNIE D'INVESTISSEMENTS, 1121
ATLAS VENTURE, 878, 1125
AUXITEX, 1128
AVENIR ENTREPRISES, 1129
AVENIR TOURISME, 1130
AXA ASSET MANAGEMENT GESTION, 1131
B. N. P. DÉVELOPPEMENT, 1170
BANEXI, 1140
BANEXI CORPORATION, 105
BANEXI VENTURES, 1141
BANQUE DE VIZILLE, 1143
BANQUE INDOSUEZ ACQUISITION FINANCE, 1144
BARCLAYS CAPITAL DÉVELOPPEMENT, 1147
BARING CAPITAL INVESTORS LTD., 1148
BARING CAPITAL PARTNERS, 1149
BARING VENTURE PARTNERS, 1151
BARING VENTURE PARTNERS LTD., 1152

BIDASSOA INVESTISSEMENTS, 1165
BROADMARK CAPITAL CORPORATION, 141
BTP CAPITAL INVESTISSEMENT, 1178
C. F. J. P. E., 1196
C.V.C. CAPITAL PARTNERS, 1226
CAPITAL PRIVÉ, 1188
CDC-PARTICIPATIONS, 1192
CHARTERHOUSE DEVELOPMENT CAPITAL LIM-
   ITED, 1197
CICLAD, 1202
CITA, 1204
CITIBANK N. A., 1205
COFINEP, 1210
COMPAGNIE DE FINANCEMENT INDUSTRIEL, 1216
COMPAGNIE FINANCIÈRE E. DE ROTHSCHILD
   BANQUE, 1217
DOWNER AND COMPANY, 248
DYNAMUST, 1239
E. M. V. - EUROPEAN MEDICAL VENTURES, 1250
ELECTRA FLEMING ET ASSOCIÉS, 1246
ELECTRA FLEMING LIMITED, 1247
ELECTRICITÉ DE FRANCE, 1249
EPARGNE PARTENAIRES, 1255
EPICEA, 1256
ESFIN PARTICIPATIONS, 1260
EURO SYNERGIES, 1267
EUROMEZZANINE GESTION, 1264
EUROPAR, 1265
EUROVENTURES BV, 1270
EUROVENTURES FRANCE, 1273
F. R. F. I. - CONSEIL REGIONAL D'ALSACE, 1306
FACE AUVERGNE-LOIRE, 1278
FINADVANCE, 1282
FINANCES ET COMMUNICATION DÉVELOPPE-
   MENT, 1283
FINANCIÈRE D'AQUITAINE, 1286
FINANCIÈRE GALLIERA, 1288
FINANCIÈRE SAINT-DOMINIQUE, 1289
FINANCIÈRE VECTEUR, 1290
FINOVELEC, 1294
FONDINVEST GESTION, 1297
FONDS D'INVESTISSEMENT RTVL, 1299
FONDS PARTENAIRES GESTION, 1300
FRANCE-ESPAGNE INVESTISSEMENTS, 1305
FSD CAPITAL DÉVELOPPEMENT, 1310
GALILEE INVESTISSEMENTS, 1313
GENESE INVESTISSEMENTS, 1319
GES GESTION/GAN AVENIR, 1322
GOLDMAN SACHS PARIS, 1331
GRANVILLE PRIVATE EQUITY MANAGERS LIM-
   ITED, 1332
GROUPE MAAF, 1337
HAMBRECHT AND QUIST GROUP, 343
HAMBRO EUROPEAN VENTURES, 1344
HAMBRO EUROPEAN VENTURES LIMITED, 1345
I D I, 1359

Germany

Kazakhstan
PALMS AND COMPANY, INC., 593

Luxembourg
INCORPORATED INVESTORS, 379
KBL FOUNDER SA, 1403
SAAR-LOR-LUX, 1556
SoPaF (SOCIETA PARTECIPAZIONI FINANZIARIE
SpA), 1606
SoPaF INTERNATIONAL SA, 1607

Madagascar
FINANCIÈRE D'INVESTISSEMENT ARO, 1287

Malaysia
HAMBRECHT AND QUIST GROUP, 343
TRANSPAC CAPITAL PTE. LTD., 1661

Moldova
WESTERN N. I. S. ENTERPRISE FUND, 1689

Morocco
WAFA TRUST, 1683

The Netherlands
ABN AMRO CORPORATE INVESTMENTS, 1080
ALPINVEST HOLDING NV, 1104
ATLAS VENTURE, 878, 1124
BRABANTSE ONTWIKKELINGSMIJ NV (BOM), 1172
ELECTRA FLEMING LIMITED, 1247
EUROVENTURES BENELUX, 1268
EUROVENTURES BV, 1270
EUROVENTURES GERMANY CV, 1275
GILDE INVESTMENT FUNDS, 1324
HALDER HOLDINGS BV, 1343
HOLLAND VENTURE BEHEERMIJ BV, 1353
INDUSTRIEBANK LIOF NV, 1370
INTERCAPITAL INVESTMENTS BV, 1386
MEES PIERSON INVESTERINGSMAATSCHAPPIJ BV,
1444
NEDERLANDSE PARTICIPATIE MAATSCHAPPIJ NV,
1482
NESBIC GROEP BV, 1484
PARCOM VENTURES BV, 1512
PARNIB HOLDING NV, 1515
PHILIPS MEDICAL SYSTEMS NEDERLAND BV, 1523
SEED CAPITAL INVESTMENTS BV, 1577
STARTFONDS ZUID NEDERLAND BV, 1625
STICHTING SHELL PENSIOENFONDS, 1627
UPM GROEP, 1669
VENTURE FUND ROTTERDAM BV, 1679
ZERNIKE SEED FUND BV, 1694

Norway
HOEGH INVEST A/S, 1352
INDUSTRI KAPITAL SVENSKA AB, 1373
MEDICAL VENTURE MANAGEMENT, 1442
NORSK HYDRO A.S., 1494

NORSK VEKST A/S, 1495
SND (NORWEGIAN INDUSTRIAL AND REGIONAL
DEVELOPMENT FUND), 1594
TEKNOINVEST MANAGEMENT, 1646

The Philippines
HAMBRECHT AND QUIST GROUP, 343

Poland
COPERNICUS CAPITAL MANAGEMENT, 1219
ENTERPRISE INVESTORS, 264, 1253
NATIONAL INVESTMENT FUND VICTORIA SA, 1476
PBG INVESTMENT FUND LIMITED, 1519
PIONEER INVESTMENT POLAND, 1527
POLAND PARTNERS MANAGEMENT COMPANY,
1530
RENAISSANCE PARTNERS, 1547
SCHOONER CAPITAL INTERNATIONAL, L.P., 692

Portugal
AITEC, 1099
ARGOS SODITIC SA, 1118, 1119
B. N. U. CAPITAL - SOCIEDADE DE CAPITAL DE
RISCO, 1171
BANCO MELLO DE INVESTIMENTOS SA, 1137
BANCO PORTUGUES DE INVESTIMENTO SA, 1138
F. TURISMO - CAPITAL DE RISCO SA, 1311
FRIE IPE CAPITAL I, 1307
FRIE IPE RETEX / PALEP, 1308
INTER-RISCO - SOCIEDADE DE CAPITAL DE RISCO,
1385
NORPEDIP, 1493
PROMINDÚSTRIA - SOCIEDADE DE INVESTI-
MENTO SA, 1536
RISFOMENTO - SOCIEDADE DE CAPITAL DE RISCO
SA, 1548
S. F. I. R., 1581
S. P. R. - SOCIEDADE PORTUGUESA CAPITAL DE
RISCO SA, 1618
SOSET SA, 1610
SULPEDIP SA, 1633

Reunion
SDR SODERE - FINANCIÈRE LABOURDONNAIS,
1571

Romania
FINANCIAL INVESTMENTS COMPANY TRANSYL-
VANIA SA, 1284
S. C. GELSOR SA, 1564

Russia
PALMS AND COMPANY, INC., 593
SAINT PETERSBURG REGIONAL VENTURE FUND
MANAGEMENT, 1558

Singapore
A.S.C. GROUP, 1120

CATEGORY INDEX

WESTERLY PARTNERS, 838
WESTERN N. I. S. ENTERPRISE FUND, 1689
WESTFINANCE CORPORATION, 840
WESTFORD TECHNOLOGY VENTURES, L.P., 841
WESTON PRESIDIO CAPITAL, 842
WILLIAM A.M. BURDEN AND COMPANY, 845
WILLIAM BLAIR VENTURE PARTNERS, 846
WILLIAM E. SIMON AND SONS, INC., 847
WINDPOINT PARTNERS, 849
WINTHROP VENTURES, 852
WORKING VENTURES CANADIAN FUND, INC., 856
WORLDWIDE FINANCIAL SERVICES, 858
XEROX TECHNOLOGY VENTURES, 859
YORKSHIRE VENTURE CAPITAL LTD., 1693
ZS FUND L.P., 861

Composites
TECH VENTURES, INC., 758

Computer Related
ABEL VETURE MANAGERS
ABINGWORTH MANAGEMENT LIMITED, 1077
ABS VENTURES LP, 865
ACCEL PARTNERS, 52, 866
ACQUISITION SEARCH CORPORATION, THE, 54
ADLER AND COMPANY, 55
ADOBE SYSTEMS, INC., 1036
ADS CAPITAL CORPORATION, 56
ADVANCED TECHNOLOGY VENTURES, 58, 868
ADVENT INTERNATIONAL plc, 1090
ADVENT LIMITED, 1091 1091
AENEAS INVESTMENT MANAGMENT AND CON-
  SULTING SA, 1092
AITEC, 1099
ALAN I. GOLDMAN AND ASSOCIATES, 59
ALIMANSKY CAPITAL GROUP, INC., 60
ALLIANCE BUSINESS INVESTMENT COMPANY,
  6161
ALLSOP VENTURE PARTNERS, 870
ALPHA PARTNERS, 65
ALTA BERKELEY ASSOCIATES, 1105
AMERICAN RESEARCH AND DEVELOPMENT, 70
AMERICAN STRATEGIC INVESTMENTS, L.P., 7171
AMPERSAND VENTURES, 873
ANTARES CAPITAL CORPORATION, 76
ANTHEM CAPITAL, L.P., 77
ANVAR, 1109
ARETE VENTURES, 80
ARTHUR P. GOULD AND COMPANY, 84
ARTHUR ROCK AND COMPANY, 876
ASIA PACIFIC FUNDING GROUP INTERNATIONAL,
  85
ASPEN VENTURES, 877
ASSET MANAGEMENT ASSOCIATES, INC., 87
AT&T VENTURES, 88
ATLANTIC CAPITAL, 89
ATLANTIC COASTAL VENTURES, L.P., 90

ATLAS VENTURE, 878, 1124, 1125
ATLAS VENTURE GmbH, 1126
AUSTIN VENTURES, 92
AVALON VENTURES, 880
AVERY BUSINESS DEVELOPMENT SERVICES, 94
AXA CAPITAL CORPORATION, 95
BACHOW AND ASSOCIATES, INC., 98
BANCBOSTON CAPITAL / BANCBOSTON VEN-
  TURES, 103
BANEXI CORPORATION, 105
BANGERT DAWES READE DAVIS AND THOM, 106
BANK AUSTRIA T.F.V. HIGH TECH-UNTERNEH-
  MENS BETEILIGUNG GmbH, 1142
BANKERS TRUST CAPITAL CORPORATION, 109
BARING VENTURE PARTNERS LTD., 1152
BATTERSON VENTURE PARTNERS, 113
BAXTER ASSOCIATES, INC., 114
BAY PARTNERS, 115
BBV DE PROMOCION EMPRESARIAL SA, 1158
BEACON PARTNERS, INC., 119
BENEFIT CAPITAL COMPANIES INC., THE, 121
BERENSON MINELLA VENTURES, 122
BERKELEY INTERNATIONAL CAPITAL CORPORA-
  TION, 123
BESSEMER VENTURE PARTNERS, 125
BIRMINGHAM TECHNOLOGY (VENTURE CAPITAL)
  LTD., 1168
BLUE CHIP VENTURE COMPANY, 127
BLUE RIDGE INVESTORS, LTD., 128
BOSTON FINANCIAL AND EQUITY CORPORATION,
  133
BRANTLEY VENTURE PARTNERS, 884
BROADMARK CAPITAL CORPORATION, 141
BRUCE F. GLASPELL AND ASSOCIATES, 142
BUFFALO CAPITAL CORPORATION, 143
BURR, EGAN, DELEAGE AND COMPANY, 144
C.S.K. VENTURE CAPITAL COMPANY, LIMITED,
  1224
CABLE AND HOWSE VENTURES, 146, 886
CAIRNSFORD ASSOCIATES LIMITED, 1184
CAMBRIDGE RESEARCH AND INNOVATION LIM-
  ITED, 1185
CAMPBELL VENTURES, 148
CAPFORM PARTNERS, 152
CAPITAL DIMENSIONS VENTURE FUND, INC., 154,
  1004
CAPITAL FOR BUSINESS, INC., 887
CAPITAL RESOURCE PARTNERS, 158
CAPITAL SERVICES AND RESOURCES, INC., 159
CAPITAL STRATEGY MANAGEMENT COMPANY,
  THE, 161
CAPITAL TECHNOLOGIES, INC., 162
CARILLON CAPITAL, INC., 165
CARL MARKS AND COMPANY, INC., 166
CARNEGIE VENTURE RESOURCES, INC., 167
CASCADIA PACIFIC MANAGEMENT, LLC, 169

Consumer

Convergent Technologies

Crafts

Drugs

Educational

Edutainment

Electric and Gas Utility Related

Electronic Components and Instrumentation

Electronic Displays

Electronics

Energy / Natural Resources

COMMERZ UNTERNEHMENSBETEILIGUNGS AG, 1214
CONSUMER VENTURE PARTNERS, 213
CORESTATES ENTERPRISE FUND, 218
CROSSPOINT VENTURE PARTNERS, 224
CROSSROADS MANAGEMENT (U. K.) LIMITED, 1223
CYGNUS VENTURE PARTNERS LIMITED, 1228
DEUCALION VENTURE PARTNERS, 239
DILLON READ VENTURE CAPITAL, 241
DRYSDALE ENTERPRISES, 253
FINANCIAL INVESTMENTS COMPANY TRANSYL-
    VANIA SA, 1284
FIRST AMERICAN CAPITAL FUNDING, 1013
FIRST ANALYSIS CORPORATION, 284
G. E. CAPITAL EQUITY CAPITAL GROUP, 1316
GOLDER, THOMA, CRESSEY, RAUNER, INC., 329
HANNOVER FINANZ GmbH, 1348
HODGSON MARTIN LTD., 1351
LOXKO VENTURE MANAGERS LIMITED, 1434
MERIDIAN VENTURE PARTNERS, 495
NORTH CAROLINA ENTERPRISE FUND, THE, 554
NORTHWOOD VENTURES, 561
POLAND PARTNERS MANAGEMENT COMPANY,
    1530
PRIVATE CAPITAL CORPORATION, 639
PROVINZIAL BETEILIGUNGS GmbH, 1537
ROSEWOOD CAPITAL, 675
S. R. I. W. SA, 1620
SCHOONER CAPITAL INTERNATIONAL, L.P., 692
SIERRA VENTURES, 704
SOUTH ATLANTIC VENTURE FUND, 715
SPI SpA, 1615
TA ASSOCIATES, 752
TATRA RAIFFEISEN CAPITAL, 1636
VENTURE CAPITAL FUND OF NEW ENGLAND, 809,
    992
WeHaCo KAPITALBETEILIGUNGS GmbH, 1685

Fisheries
AGRINOVA, 1095
IDIA (INSTITUT DE DÉVELOPPEMENT DES INDUS-
    TRIES AGRICOLES ET ALIMENTAIRES), 1360
NESBIC GROEP BV, 1484
PIONEER INVESTMENT POLAND, 1527
TIANGUIS LIMITED, 1658
WESTERN N. I. S. ENTERPRISE FUND, 1689

Food / Beverage Manufacturing
BANC ONE VENTURE CORPORATION, 102
MESBIC VENTURES HOLDING COMPANY, 496, 1020
PROCORDIA, 1533
SCHOONER CAPITAL INTERNATIONAL, L.P., 692

Food Processing
NATIONAL INVESTMENT FUND VICTORIA SA, 1476
PFINGSTEN PARTNERS, L.P., 613

POLAND PARTNERS MANAGEMENT COMPANY,
    1530
PROCORDIA, 1533
STRATEGIC INVESTMENTS AND HOLDINGS, INC.,
    745

Food Products / Packaging and Manufacturing
CIT GROUP / EQUITY INVESTMENTS / THE CIT
    GROUP / VENTURE CAPITAL INC., THE, 196
KEY EQUITY CAPITAL CORPORATION, 419
PALMS AND COMPANY, INC., 593
PROCORDIA, 1533
WESTERN N. I. S. ENTERPRISE FUND, 1689

Food Services
ALLIANCE BUSINESS INVESTMENT COMPANY, 61
ARK CAPITAL MANAGEMENT, 82, 1000
ASIA PACIFIC FUNDING GROUP INTERNATIONAL,
    85
CLAIRVEST GROUP, INC., 200
COPLEY VENTURE PARTNERS, 216
DRYSDALE ENTERPRISES, 253
ELECTRA INC., 259
FOWLER, ANTHONY AND COMPANY, 304
GROTECH CAPITAL GROUP, 339
KEY EQUITY CAPITAL CORPORATION, 419
NASH, SELLS AND PARTNERS LIMITED, 1475
NATWEST USA CAPITAL CORPORATION, 530
PALM BEACH CAPITAL CORPORATION, 590
POINT VENTURE PARTNERS, 632
PRIVATE CAPITAL CORPORATION, 639
PROCORDIA, 1533
ROSEWOOD CAPITAL, 675
SOUTH ATLANTIC VENTURE FUND, 715
VISTA GROUP, 822
WESTERN N. I. S. ENTERPRISE FUND, 1689

Forestry
AGRINOVA, 1095
AGRO PARTENAIRES, 1096
BALKANBANK PLC, 1134
BIOINDUSTRIA Srl, 1166
I. P. B. M. (INSTITUT DE PARTICIPATION DU BOIS ET
    DU MEUBLE), 1389
IDIA (INSTITUT DE DÉVELOPPEMENT DES INDUS-
    TRIES AGRICOLES ET ALIMENTAIRES), 1360
MISTRAL INVESTISSEMENTS, 1456
NESBIC GROEP BV, 1484
NORTH-EAST HUNGARIAN REGIONAL DEVELOP-
    MENT CO. LTD., 1496
PIONEER INVESTMENT POLAND, 1527
START FUND OF KERA OY, 1623
TIANGUIS LIMITED, 1658
WESTERN N. I. S. ENTERPRISE FUND, 1689
ZERNIKE SEED FUND BV, 1694

Fuel Additives
GRYPHON VENTURES, L.P., 341, 920

Horticulture

Hotels

Housewares

Imaging

Industrial Automation

Industrial Products

Industrial Products / Equipment

COMMERZ UNTERNEHMENSBETEILIGUNGS AG, 1214

COMMUNICATIONS EQUITY ASSOCIATES, INC., 210

FINANCES ET COMMUNICATION DÉVELOPPE-MENT, 1283

HANNOVER FINANZ GmbH, 1348

HOAK COMMUNICATIONS PARTNERS, L.P., 366

L. I. C. A. DEVELOPMENT CAPITAL LIMITED, 1427

LONDON VENTURES (FUND MANAGERS) LIMITED, 1432

MERCURY ASSET MANAGEMENT PLC, 1446

MEZZANINE MANAGEMENT LIMITED, 1451

PECHEL INDUSTRIES, 1520

POMONA CAPITAL, 635

PROVINZIAL BETEILIGUNGS GmbH, 1537

RIVER CAPITAL, 668

SLOTTSBACKEN VENTURE CAPITAL, 1592

SPECTRUM EQUITY INVESTORS, L.P., 723

TUFTON CAPITAL LTD, 1666

WeHaCo KAPITALBETEILIGUNGS GmbH, 1685

Media and Communications Technology
BANCBOSTON CAPITAL / BANCBOSTON VEN-TURES, 103

Medical Devices
CROSSPOINT VENTURE PARTNERS, 224

JOHNSTON ASSOCIATES, 936

MENLO VENTURES, 492, 950

MORGENTHALER VENTURES, 515, 959

OXFORD BIOSCIENCE PARTNERS II, 967

PETERSON-SPENCER-FANSLER COMPANY, 612

POLARIS VENTURE PARTNERS, 633

SPROUT GROUP, 728

U.S. MEDICAL RESOURCES CORPORATION, 782

VECTOR FUND MANAGEMENT, L.P., 795

WEISS, PECK AND GREER VENTURE PARTNERS, 833

Medical / Health Related
ABBOTT DIAGNOSTICA GmbH, 1075

ABERLYN CAPITAL MANAGEMENT COMPANY, INC., 51

ABINGWORTH MANAGEMENT LIMITED, 1077

ABS VENTURES LP, 865

ACCEL PARTNERS, 52, 866

ACQUISITION SEARCH CORPORATION, THE, 54

ADLER AND COMPANY, 5555

ADS CAPITAL CORPORATION, 56

ADVANCED TECHNOLOGY VENTURES, 58, 86858, 868

ADVENT INTERNATIONAL plc, 1090, 1090

ADVENT LIMITED, 1091

AENEAS INVESTMENT MANAGMENT AND CON-SULTING SA, 1092

AFFÄRSSTRATEGERNA I SVERIGE AB, 1093

AGRINOVA, 1095, 1095

ALAFI CAPITAL, 869

ALAN I. GOLDMAN AND ASSOCIATES, 59

ALIMANSKY CAPITAL GROUP, INC., 60

ALLIANCE BUSINESS INVESTMENT COMPANY, 61

ALLSOP VENTURE PARTNERS, 870

ALPHA PARTNERS, 65

ALTA BERKELEY ASSOCIATES, 1105

AMERICAN ACQUISITION PARTNERS, 68

AMERICAN RESEARCH AND DEVELOPMENT, 70

AMERICAN STRATEGIC INVESTMENTS, L.P., 7171

AMPERSAND VENTURES, 873873

ANTARES CAPITAL CORPORATION, 76

ANVAR, 1109

APAX PARTNERS ET CIE., 1111

APAX PARTNERS UND CO. AG, 1112, 1113

ARCH VENTURE PARTNERS, 79

ARGENTUM GROUP, THE, 81

ARGOS SODITIC ITALIA Srl, 1117

ARGOS SODITIC SA, 1118, 1119

ARK CAPITAL MANAGEMENT, 82, 1000

ARTESIAN CAPITAL, 83

ARTHUR P. GOULD AND COMPANY, 84

ARTHUR ROCK AND COMPANY, 876

ASIA PACIFIC FUNDING GROUP INTERNATIONAL, 85

ASPEN VENTURE PARTNERS, L.P., 86

ASPEN VENTURES, 877

ASSET MANAGEMENT ASSOCIATES, INC., 87

AT&T VENTURES, 88

ATCO PARTNER BETEILIGUNGSBERATUNG, 1123

ATLANTIC CAPITAL, 89

ATLANTIC MEDICAL CAPITAL, L.P., 91

ATLAS VENTURE, 878, 1124, 1125

ATLAS VENTURE GmbH, 1126

AUSTIN VENTURES, 92

AVALON VENTURES, 880

AVERY BUSINESS DEVELOPMENT SERVICES, 94

AXA CAPITAL CORPORATION, 95

B. N. U. CAPITAL - SOCIEDADE DE CAPITAL DE RISCO, 1171

BAILEY AND COMPANY, INC., 99

BANC ONE CAPITAL PARTNERS CORPORATION, 101

BANCBOSTON CAPITAL / BANCBOSTON VEN-TURES, 103

BANGERT DAWES READE DAVIS AND THOM, 106

BANKERS TRUST CAPITAL CORPORATION, 109

BARING VENTURE PARTNERS LTD., 1152

BARING VENTURE PARTNERS SA, 1154

BARING VENTURE PARTNERS UNTERNEHMENS-BERATUNG GmbH, 1155

BATAVIA GROUP, LTD., THE, 111

BATTERSON VENTURE PARTNERS, 113

BAXTER ASSOCIATES, INC., 114

BAXTER INTERNATIONAL, 883

BBV DE PROMOCION EMPRESARIAL SA, 1158

BCI ADVISORS, INC., 118

Medical Instruments

Medical Research

Medical Sciences

Medical Supplies

Medical Technology

Metals